THE CAMPAIGN IN ITALY
1943-45

OFFICIAL HISTORY OF THE INDIAN ARMED FORCES
IN THE SECOND WORLD WAR
1939-45

THE CAMPAIGN IN ITALY
1943-45

The Naval & Military Press Ltd

Published by

The Naval & Military Press Ltd
Unit 5 Riverside, Brambleside
Bellbrook Industrial Estate
Uckfield, East Sussex
TN22 1QQ England

Tel: +44 (0)1825 749494

www.naval-military-press.com
www.nmarchive.com

In reprinting in facsimile from the original, any imperfections are inevitably reproduced and the quality may fall short of modern type and cartographic standards.

ERRATA

Page 220 line 14 for 19th Indian Division *read* 10th Indian Division
Page 468 line 11 for Roncofreddo *read* Roncofredo
Page 469 line 27 for Roncoforedo *read* Roncofredo
Page 469 line 23 for M. Gattons *read* M. Gattona
Page 241 to 257 for page heading PURSUIT IN RIPA *read* PURSUIT TO RIPA
Page 662 below page map heading for April 1944 *read* April 1945
Page 669 below page map heading for April 1944 *read* April 1945
Page 672 below page map heading for April 1944 *read* April 1945
Page xiv line 5 for Piano di Castello *read* Pian di Castello
Page xiv line 8 for 1-15 September *read* 12-15 September

TO ALL WHO SERVED

ADVISORY COMMITTEE

Chairman
SECRETARY, MINISTRY OF DEFENCE, INDIA

Members

DR TARA CHAND
DR S. N. SEN
PROF K. A. NILAKANTA SASTRI
PROF MOHAMMAD HABIB
DR R. C. MAJUMDAR
GENERAL K. S. THIMAYYA
LIEUT-GENERAL SIR DUDLEY RUSSELL
LIEUT-GENERAL S. P. P. THORAT
MILITARY ADVISER TO THE HIGH COMMISSIONER
    FOR PAKISTAN IN INDIA

Secretary
DR BISHESHWAR PRASAD

CAMPAIGNS IN THE WESTERN THEATRE

- NORTH AFRICAN CAMPAIGN 1940-43
- CAMPAIGN IN WESTERN ASIA
- CAMPAIGN IN ITALY 1943-45
- OPERATIONS IN EAST AFRICA AND GREECE

PREFACE

I have great pleasure in presenting the tenth volume in the series "The Official History of the Indian Armed Forces in World War II". It has been prepared by the Combined Inter-Services Historical Section, an organisation set up by the Government of India after the end of the Second World War and continued after the partition of India as a joint venture of the two Dominions, India and Pakistan, to produce an official history of the part played by the armed forces of pre-partition India in the war of 1939-45. This history was to be an objective record of military operations and organisational activities of the armed forces of India at the time. It was planned to publish this history in about twenty-five volumes including the volumes relating to the medical aspects of the war. The volumes of general history have been divided into three series, campaigns in the eastern theatre, campaigns in the western theatre and general war administration and organisation.

Two volumes in the series relating to the campaigns in the western theatre, *The North African Campaign* and *The Campaign in Western Asia*, have already been published. The present volume, the third in the series, describes the campaigns in Italy, where the Allied armies including the Indian divisions were assigned the task of driving Italy out of the war, containing the German forces and driving up the peninsula to strike at the under-belly of the Nazi homeland, and thereby draw the German armies away from Russia and cooperate with the Allied invasion to be mounted on the western coast of France. The terrain of Italy did not favour an attack from the south and was admirably suited for defence. The Allied armies were committed to a long and costly offensive in the peninsula of Italy which came to an end only in the spring of 1945 after the German forces had been driven back with severe losses in a series of battles. The Indian forces, though limited to a strength of three divisions only, distinguished themselves for high courage and tenacity in the battles of the Sangro, Cassino, the Liri valley, the Gothic Line, the Senio and several other engagements, and co-operated with the British, Canadian and American forces to bring victory to the United Nations.

The draft of the earlier part of the narrative was prepared by Lt.-Col. Cocksedge and the rest by Dr. Dharm Pal. The whole has subsequently been revised in the light of vetters' comments and edited by the chief editor. The account is based mainly on official despatches and war diaries of the Indian units taking part in the war. The published histories of the American, Canadian and British armies have also been of considerable help in getting a correct picture of the operations.

The narrative has been read by Lieut.-General Sir Dudley Russell, KBE, CB, DSO, MC and Lieut.-General S. P. P. Thorat, DSO, General Officer Commanding-in-Chief, H.Q., Eastern Command, both members of the Advisory Committee, to whom I am personally obliged. General Russell was General Officer Commanding the 8th Indian Division in the Italian Campaign and his comments have been particularly valuable. I am also grateful to Brigadier H. B. Latham of the Cabinet Historical Section, London, for his valuable suggestions. Lt.-General Sir Francis Tuker was kind enough to read and comment on a portion of the narrative. I am also indebted to Pakistan Historical Section, General Staff Branch, and Office of the Chief of Military History, Washington, D.C. for their useful comments. The book has been seen through the press by Mr. P. N. Khera to whom I express my thanks. The maps and charts have been prepared by Mr. T. D. Sharma, the cartographer.

In conclusion, I thank the Ministries of Defence, India and Pakistan, for their ungrudging support and encouragement.

The Government of India have placed the documents at our disposal, but for the statements and views expressed in this volume, I accept full responsibility.

BISHESHWAR PRASAD

New Delhi
November 1960

CONTENTS

		Page
INTRODUCTION		xix

CHAPTER

I.	THE GLITTERING PRIZE OF NAPLES	1
II.	OUTPOSTS OF THE WINTER LINE	13
III.	THE BATTLE OF THE SANGRO	34
IV.	CAPTURE OF VILLA GRANDE	56
V.	CASSINO (THE FEBRUARY ATTACK)	86
VI.	CASSINO (OPERATION 'DICKENS')	117
VII.	PLANS FOR THE SPRING OFFENSIVE	144
VIII.	THE ASSAULT OF THE GUSTAV LINE	159
IX.	THE BATTLE OF THE LIRI VALLEY	184
X.	THE STATIC ADRIATIC FRONT	209
XI.	THE ADVANCE TO THE ARNO	230
XII.	ADVANCE TO CITTA DI CASTELLO	259
XIII.	ADVANCE WEST OF THE TIBER	283
XIV.	THE ADVANCE TO FLORENCE	300
XV.	ADVANCE TO THE ANGHIARI LATERAL ROAD	325
XVI.	OPERATION VANDAL	342
XVII.	THE BREAKING OF THE GOTHIC LINE (CAPTURE OF TAVOLETO)	359
XVIII.	THE THRUST TOWARDS M. S. COLOMBA	381
XIX.	ADVANCE TO THE RIVER MARECCHIA	398
XX.	ATTACK ON M. CALVANA	410
XXI.	CAPTURE OF FEMMINA MORTA	427
XXII.	CAPTURE OF M. DELLA MODINA	439
XXIII.	THE BATTLE OF THE RIVERS (ADVANCE TO THE RIVER FUIMICINO)	449
XXIV.	ADVANCE TO THE RIVER SAVIO	468
XXV.	ADVANCE TO THE RIVER RONCO	491
XXVI.	ATTACK ON M. PIANOERENO	506
XXVII.	ADVANCE TO THE RIVER LAMONE	528
XXVIII.	ADVANCE TO THE RIVER SENIO	544
XXIX.	THRUST TOWARDS VENA DEL GESSO	560
XXX.	DEFENCE OF MONTE GRANDE	582
XXXI.	THE SENIO DEFENCE LINE	593
XXXII.	THE PLAN	605
XXXIII.	THE ASSAULT ACROSS THE SENIO AND SANTERNO	619
XXXIV.	ADVANCE TO THE RIVER RENO	642
XXXV.	ADVANCE TO THE RIVER ADIGE	660
APPENDICES		679
BIBLIOGRAPHY		693
INDEX		694

APPENDICES

1. ORDER OF BATTLE—8TH INDIAN DIVISION (September 1943)
2. ORDER OF BATTLE—4TH INDIAN DIVISION (January 1944)
3. ORDER OF BATTLE—4TH INDIAN DIVISION (February 1944)
4. ORDER OF BATTLE—10TH INDIAN DIVISION (March 1944)
5. SHORT SUMMARY OF GERMAN ORDER OF BATTLE (June 1944)
6. SHORT GERMAN ORDER OF BATTLE (September 1944)
7. DIVISIONAL AND BRIGADE COMMANDERS

MAPS

Map of Italy	facing chapter	1
Crossing of the Biferno & the Trigno (October-November '42)	facing page	17
8 Indian Division's Advance to the River Sangro (6-19 November 1943)	facing page	27
The crossing of the Sangro by V Corps—(27-30 November 1943)	facing page	35
2nd New Zealand Division's thrust towards Orgogna (2-3 December 1943)	page	57
Cassino area	facing page	87
Monte Cassino and Cassino town	page	104
The Liri Valley Offensive (May 1944)	facing page	145
Dispositions of Rival Forces (11 May 1944)	page	147
Operation Honker (11-16 May 1944)	facing page	153
8 Indian Division's advance to Guarcino (1-4 June 1944)	facing page	201
The Ortona—Orsogna Sector	facing page	209
Rome area	page	232
17 Indian Infantry Brigade's attack on the Ripa ridge (18-19 June 1944)	page	248
4 Indian Division's advance (8-12 June 1944)	page	255
Advance in the Tiber Valley (30 June-22 July 1944)	page	260
10 Indian Division's advance to Citta di Castello (6-22 July 1944)	page	268
10 Indian Infantry Brigade's attack on Trestina (9-12 July 1944)	page	285
4 Indian Division's advance (9-17 July 1944)	page	288
21 Indian Infantry Brigade's advance to Montespertoli (23-27 July 1944)	page	304
Empoli area	page	308
21 Indian Infantry Brigade's advance to the river Arno (27 July-4 August 1944)	page	310
Advance towards Bibbiena	page	326
Anghiari area	page	328
M. Castiglione area	page	336
Subbiano area	page	345
Alpe di Catenaia area	page	352
Allied and German Dispositions (25 August 1944)	facing page	361
4 Indian Division's advance to S. Marino (25 August-20 September 1944)	facing page	363

4 Indian Division's advance to Urbino (25-28 August 1944)	page 365
4 Indian Division's advance to Tavoleto—S. Giovanni (29 August—6 September 1944)	page 369
Piano di Castello—Coriano area	page 382
4 Indian Division's advance to M.S. Colomba	page 384
43 Indian Infantry Brigade's advance to river Marano (1-15 September 1944)	page 404
Fifth Army breaks through the Gothic Line (13-22 September 1944)	facing page 409
8 Indian Division's advance to M. Calvana (1-3 September 1944)	page 420
8 Indian Division's advance to Femmina Morta (12-18 September 1944)	page 429
Bibbiena area	facing page 439
11 Indian Infantry Brigade's attack on the Montebello-Scorticata ridge (22-23 September 1944)	page 453
43 Indian Infantry Brigade's bridge-head on the river Marecchia (23-24 September 1944) . . .	page 455
S. Martino Sogliano area	page 465
M. Farneto area	page 470
20 Indian Infantry Brigade's attack on M. Cavallo (21-23 October 1944)	facing page 491
10 Indian Infantry Division's bridge-heads on the river Ronco (23-30 October 1944)	facing page 499
Marradi area	facing page 513
M. Cavallara area	page 516
M. Pianoereno area	facing page 519
21 Indian Infantry Brigade's attack on M. Pianoereno and M. Romano (17-22 October 1944)	page 522
Dispositions of 10 Indian Infantry Brigade (20 November 1944)	facing page 531
10 Indian Division's advance to the river Lamone (24 November—2 December 1944)	facing page 533
V Corps plan for the December Offensive . . .	facing page 543
Pideura—Olmatello area (10 Indian Division's advance, 14-15 December 1944)	page 549
10 Indian Division's advance to the river Senio (10-20 December 1944)	page 554
Faenza area (43 Indian Infantry Brigade's advance, 17-20 December 1944)	page 557
17 Indian Infantry Brigade's advance to M.S. Bartolo (3-14 November 1944)	page 563

Dispositions of 8 Indian Division in the Serchio Valley . . . . *page* 576
Dispositions of 10 Indian Division in S. Clemente area (February 1945) . . . . *page* 588
Monte Grande area (dispositions of 25 Indian Infantry Brigade, March 1945) . . . . . . *page* 590
43 Indian Infantry Brigade's attack on Senio river defences (February—March 1945) . . . . *page* 598
Allied and German dispositions (9 April 1945) . . *page* 606
V Corps dispositions (9 April 1945) . . . . . . *page* 609
Dispositions of 8 Indian Division (7-9 April 1945) *page* 614
8 Indian Division's advance to Scolo Tratturo (9-10 April 1945) . . . . *facing page* 615
Medicina area . . . . *facing page* 641
43 Indian Infantry Brigade's advance to Medicina *page* 645
10 Indian Division's advance to the river Idice (17-21 April 1945) . . . . *facing page* 647
25 Indian Infantry Brigade's advance to the river Reno (21-23 April 1945) . . . . *facing page* 657
8 Indian Division's advance to the river Po (21-25 April 1945) . . . . *page* 662
8 Indian Division's bridge-head over the river Po (25-26 April 1945) . . . . *page* 669
17 Indian Infantry Brigade's advance to Vescovana (26-28 April 1945) . . . . *page* 672

ILLUSTRATIONS

General Dwight David Eisenhower (Supreme Allied Commander, Mediterranean Forces, 1943)	facing page	6
General Sir Henry Maitland Wilson (Supreme Allied Commander, Mediterranean Forces, 1943-44)	,, ,,	7
General Sir Harold Alexander (Commander 15th Army Group, 1943)	,, ,,	12
General Viscount Bernard Montgomery (Commander Eighth Army, July 1942—Dec. 1943)	,, ,,	12
General Sir Oliver Leese (Commander Eighth Army, 1944)	,, ,,	13
Troops of 1/5 Essex Regt. take a shot at a German Mk. IV tank with a PIAT mortar	,, ,,	13
Indian soldiers examine one of the many Mk. IV German tanks knocked out near Mozzagrogna	,, ,,	38
Lieut.-General Sir Charles Allfrey (Commander V Corps)	,, ,,	39
Major-General Sir Francis Tuker (Commander 4th Indian Division, Jan. 1942—Feb. 1944)	,, ,,	39
Sikhs advancing under cover of smoke for breaking the Gustav Line	,, ,,	162
Lieut.-General Sir M. C. Dempsey (Commander XIII Corps)	,, ,,	162
Lieut.-General W. Mark Clark (Commander, American Fifth Army)	,, ,,	163
Major-General Sir Dudley Russell (Commander 8th Indian Division, January 1943)	,, ,,	163
Naik Yeshwant Ghadge, V.C. (3/5 Mahratta)	,, ,,	272
Sepoy Kamal Ram, V.C. (3/8 Punjab)	,, ,,	272
Sappers and Miners improving Jeep tracks to enable troops to advance to San Domino and Monte Gorgacce	,, ,,	273
Sepoy Ali Haider V.C. (6/13 F.F. Rif.)	,, ,,	273
Major-General Denys W. Reid (Commander 10th Indian Division, Feb. 1944—Dec. 1946)	,, ,,	374
Major-General W. L. Lloyd (Commander 10th Indian Division, July 1943—Jan. 1944)	,, ,,	374
Fall of San Marino	,, ,,	375
Madras Sappers and Miners have laid a road in Italy	,, ,,	375

Major-General A. W. W. Holworthy (Commander 4th Indian Division, March 1944—Jan. 1945)	„ „	412
A patrol leader of the 18th Garhwal Rifles gives instructions before setting out	„ „	412
Armoured cars of the Central India Horse set off on patrol from their HQ in the middle of an Italian village	„ „	413
Panoramic view of Cassino	„ „	413
Jaipur Infantry operating in Lugo	„ „	524
Smoke rising as Tavoleto is shelled	„ „	524
Rifleman Thaman Gurung, V.C. (1/5 R.G.R.) . . .	„ „	525
Rifleman Sher Bahadur Thapa, V.C. (1/9 G.R.) . . .	„ „	525
Armoured Cars of the 6th Duke of Connaught's Own Lancers north of Moro river chasing the enemy	„ „	564
Allied tank moving to Pietrolunga, prior to its capture	„ „	564
Sepoy Namdeo Jadhao, V.C. (1/5 Mahratta)	„ „	565
Ropeway over the river Ronco built by Indian Sappers and Miners carries men and stores	„ „	565

ABBREVIATIONS

A & SH	Argyll and Sutherland Highlanders.
A Tk Regt	Anti-Tank Regiment.
DD Tanks	Dupleix Drive Tanks.
DIV	Division.
DLI	Durham Light Infantry.
FOO	Forward Observation Officer.
GR	Gurkha Rifles.
HQ	Headquarters.
LSTs	Landing Ships, Tanks.
MAAF	Mediterranean Allied Air Forces.
MG	Machine Gun.
NCO	Non-Commissioned Officer.
PIAT	Projector Infantry Anti-Tank.
Pt	Point.
RA	Royal Artillery.
RAF	Royal Air Force.
RIASC	Royal Indian Army Service Corps.

INTRODUCTION

Italy jumped into the Second World War when the fortunes of the anti-Axis Powers were at a low ebb. Hitler's armies had thrown Poland out of the arena, and in the west had overrun Holland, Belgium and northern France. The British Expeditionary Force, operating in France to stem the tide of Nazi sweep towards the shores of the Atlantic, had with difficulty extricated itself and crossed the English Channel, with depleted strength and shorn off of its equipment. Mussolini found that time auspicious for his plunge into the war which had become hot enough, for he did not want to be left out when his victorious Axis partner would distribute the spoils on the defeat of the Western Powers. By all calculations then, the end of the war was not distant, and the only outcome of it could be the defeat and humiliation of the United Kingdom after the abject surrender of France. Italian appetite for colonies in Africa and the Adriatic lands in the Balkan Peninsula was now whetted, and Mussolini was keen to get the benefit of annexing them by his participation in the war as the partner of his Nazi ally, the Fuehrer of Germany.

Italy's ambition in the Arab lands of northern and eastern Africa and in the empire of Ethiopia was an inheritance from the nineteenth century, which had, however, remained unrealised. Mussolini exploited the international situation in the mid-thirties to direct his arms against Ethiopia, which at once brought a chorus of opposition from the pacific Western Powers. The League of Nations, weakened and disintegrating, imposed sanctions against the aggressor, but failed to prevent the incorporation of the only free African state into the empire of Italy. Mussolini had been longing to extend his foothold by dominating the entire Mediterranean coast and the Red Sea and Indian Ocean littoral. This was bound to bring him into conflict with the two colonial empires of Great Britain and France. Hence he sought the friendship of Germany, which he secured by the agreement of 1936 establishing the "vertical line between Rome and Berlin", which, according to Mussolini, was "not a partition but rather an Axis round which all European states animated by the will to collaboration and peace can also collaborate." This Axis was further strengthened by Japan's pact with Germany, and a new balance of power was established between the highly militarised states of Germany, Italy and Japan, on the one side, and England, France, Russia and the United States, loosely united by the bonds of vague friendliness, on the other. However, till 1940, Italy did not indicate her hand, and beyond the invasion of Albania, did not use the involvement of France and the United Kingdom in the war to launch on any further aggression. Even when Hitler had annexed Austria, Czecho-Slovakia and Poland, Mussolini had remained content with merely expanding his armed strength without striking a blow elsewhere. He had even entered into trade agreements with France and Britain. But this forbearance was neither to his liking nor in his interest; and when Hitler wooed him before striking at France, Mussolini met him at Brenner Pass on 18 March 1940 "in cordial colloquy", which paved the path for his eventual entry into the war. Hitler's triumphs must have tempted him to share in them and relinquish his attitude of "inglorious, irrevocable isolation", which he had pursued so long. His remark that, "It is humiliating to remain with our hands folded while others write history," sums up his position aptly; and the swing from passivity to active participation in the war was to be a quick one.

After this meeting Italian attitude became pronouncedly more and more hostile towards Great Britain and France, and the country was being briskly prepared "for the inevitability of war". Mussolini was in no mood to accept the French offer of concession in respect of his claims to Tunis, Jibuti and the Suez Canal. He proclaimed his resolve to adhere to the pact with Germany, and when France was reeling under the Nazi blow, he communicated his decision to go to war to his military chiefs on 28 May 1940, but it was not till 10 June, that actual hostilities were initiated by him.

On the continent of Europe, Mussolini failed to obtain any large slices of territory; and he was even deprived of any gains on the southern coast of France. His adventure beyond the Adriatic did not go well for him, rather it resulted in revolts in the Balkans which Hitler was forced to fight. But Africa promised a better field for Italy's ambitions, and African victories would certainly open the way for ultimate subjugation of Egypt, Syria and the Arab states of the Middle East. His army was poised against Egypt in the Western Desert, and he had a reckonable force in east Africa. But the British command in the Middle East, though numerically weak initially, took up the challenge and within two years had thrown Italy out of the list in Africa, both in the north and the east, and practically destroyed her military potential. The vast lines of Italian prisoners of war were a glaring mark of the lack of enthusiasm of people in the war and the extreme demoralisation which was the inevitable result of dictatorship. Italian empire in Eritrea and Ethiopia soon vanished and the whole of east Africa was held by the Commonwealth forces. In North Africa, the German General Rommel, with his Afrika Korps, had assumed leadership and was using the Italian troops more as gun fodder than independent, powerful legions out for world conquest, a role which the Duce had initially assigned to them. Even Rommel's advance was halted at El Alamein, the German armies were rolled back and retreated into Libya where they were saved from complete destruction by a timely downpour of rain which delayed the fast mounting chase by the British Eighth Army, moving rapidly on the heels of the retreating German and Italian forces.

Churchill rightly called the Battle of Alamein "the turning point in British military fortunes during the whole war". He wrote "Up to Alamein we survived. After Alamein we conquered". This was exactly so, for the Eighth Army moved on undaunted through Libya into Tunisia, and the British First Army had landed into Algeria and the American forces had made Morocco their base. The Axis forces were caught up between the two steam rollers from the east and the west, and it was clear at the opening of the year 1943 that Rommel's offensive in North Africa had petered out and the Mediterranean coast was once again safe for the British navy. The defeat of German and Italian forces in North Africa was marked by a simultaneous check to Hitler's Russian adventure at Stalingrad, which soon led to the retreat of Nazi forces from Russia as well. These victories of the Allied arms paved the way for final victory, and in January 1943, President Roosevelt and Prime Minister Churchill met at Casablanca to plan out the successive stages of the eventual defeat and disaster of Germany and her allies. It was no longer a conference for defence to devise the means of staving off defeat and destruction of democracy, but the two leaders met in an atmosphere of hope and jubilation, sketching out the steps to destroy Nazism and Fascism, and to offer help to the Russians by opening fresh fronts to engage the German armies and thus relieve pressure on the Soviet forces.

Stalin had been pressing hard for an invasion of France along the Atlantic coast which alone, he thought, could divert German hordes from their adventure in Russia. The problem of the Second Front, to be opened by an amphibious invasion from the shores of Great Britain, had engaged the attention of Anglo-American planners and military leaders; but the staggering logistics of the venture had retarded its early execution. The United States was keen about it, but the American opinion could not give it priority over the defeat of Japan in the Pacific, where American interests were primary and of immense importance. The British Government was now less concerned with the German presence in France and the Low Countries for the Battle of Britain had ended, and the Anglo-American air forces had gained superiority in the skies and were battering and smashing the German industrial potential which alone could sustain Hitler's offensives. Moreover, to Churchill and his Cabinet the security of North Africa, preponderance in the Middle East and the complete safety of the Mediterranean sea route were more dominant interests than relieving pressure on Stalin by engaging in a difficult and expensive expedition of uncertain value. To Churchill, therefore, knocking Italy out of the war seemed to be the logical sequence to victory in Africa; and this point he pressed on his American colleague at Casablanca.

The most striking decision of the Casablanca Conference was to declare the aim of the United Nations as the "unconditional surrender of Germany and Japan" before the war could end. Strategy for the year was defined and the main lines of offensive action in the different theatres of war were laid down. The primary purpose of planning was to fight Germany and defeat her within 1943; and this object was to be achieved by mounting an invasion through France. Both western and southern coasts of France were considered, though the major weight was to be placed on the former. But even the most optimistic calculations could not envisage assault on the Normandy coast before the middle of 1944. Russian situation, however, could not admit of inactivity till then; hence action was contemplated in the Mediterranean region. The Chiefs of Staff report entitled 'The Conduct of the War in 1943', while emphasising that "operations in the European theatre will be conducted with the object of defeating Germany in 1943 with the maximum forces," outlined the direction of the main offensive in the Mediterranean. There, the chief aim was "the occupation of Sicily, with the object of (*i*) making the Mediterranean line of communications more secure, (*ii*) diverting German pressure from the Russian front, and (*iii*) intensifying the pressure on Italy". It was ostensibly a limited object and reflected the divergent views of the two partners. But it was clear, judging from the results contemplated, that Sicily must be a mere jumping-off ground for the eventual invasion of the mainland of Italy; and that Sicily was at best a mere compromise. To relieve pressure from Russia or to enlist Turkey as an active ally, it was essential that the opening secured by the capture of Sicily must lead to the occupation of Italy and exploiting the success there to strike at the underbelly of Germany. The target date for the landing on Sicily was fixed as the 'favourable June moon'.

There was a subsequent conference (the Trident Conference) in Washington in May 1943, which, as Churchill cabled to Stalin, was "to settle further exploitation in Europe after Sicily." At Casablanca the outlines of a strategy had been sketched which, as emphasised above, had no other object than the ultimate invasion of Italy to knock her out of the war. At Washington, this purpose was made explicit. In his opening speech, Winston Churchill painted in lurid colours the advantages that might accrue to the United Nations by the collapse of Italy, which was inevitable. The first was the "chill of loneliness over the German people" which it would cause and thereby "be the beginning of their doom". The second would be to bring Turkey, "who had always measured herself with Italy in the Mediterranean" on the side of the United Nations, and thereby obtain "permission to use bases in her territory from which to bomb Ploesti and clear the Aegean". The third "effect of the elimination of Italy would be felt in the Balkans, where patrols of various nationalities were with difficulty held in check by large Axis forces, which included twenty-five or more Italian divisions". If these were withdrawn Germany would be forced to give up the Balkans, or divert forces from the Russian front. Lastly, it would lead to the elimination of the Italian Fleet which would release a large British naval force for use elsewhere. Thus Churchill pleaded that Italian invasion would relieve pressure from Russia even without opening the so-called Second Front; and also would provide effective employment to a large British and American force then engaged in North Africa, in the interval between the defeat of Sicily and the opening of the Second Front on the Atlantic.

Churchill's estimate was that there were nearly thirty divisions, British, American and French, in the Mediterranean area, comprising the "finest and most experienced divisions and the main part of their army", and these would remain idle after Sicily, if no further action was taken against Italy. This position, according to him, "could not be justified to the British nation or to our Russian allies. We hold it our duty to engage the enemy as continuously and intensely as possible, and to draw off as many hostile divisions as possible from the front of our Russian allies." It was clear that Italy could not long or successfully resist such strong pressure, and under the impact of a determined invasion of the mainland, the morale of the people would crack and Mussolini's supremacy might come to an end. In that event, Hitler would have to throw in his forces into Italy to prevent the Allied advance through that peninsula and across the Alps into Germany. Hence the prime object of Italian venture was to compel or induce Italy to quit the war. The taking of Sicily was the "indispensable preliminary, and the invasion of the mainland of Italy and the capture of Rome" were "the evident steps". The Prime Minister of the United Kingdom further emphasised the gains which might accrue from the defeat of Italy and wrote: "Should Italy be made to quit the war the following practical advantages would be gained by us. The Germans would be forced to provide troops to occupy the Riviera, to maintain a new front along the Po or on the Brenner, and above all to fill the void in the Balkans caused by the demobilisation and withdrawal of Italian divisions. Up to the present the guerillas etc. have only been nourished by parachute packets dropped from less than a dozen aeroplanes. The occupation of the southern parts of Italy, . . would give us access to the Adriatic and the power to send shiploads of munitions to Adriatic ports, and also agents and possibly small Commando bands . . the aiding of the patriot bands in Yugoslavia and the fomenting of revolt in Greece and Albania are measures of high importance, all of which, together with our main operations, will influence the action of Turkey. In this way the utmost aid in our power will be given to Russia and also to "Bolero"." These were mighty arguments and at Washington and again at Quebec both the "Trident" and the "Quadrant" Conferences agreed to the expansion of Mediterranean campaign in Sicily by including Italy within its orbit. At Quebec the Chiefs of Staff proposed to prosecute future operations in the Mediterranean region in three phases; first, to drive Italy out of the war and establish airfields near Rome; second, "to seize Sardinia and Corsica and then press hard against the Germans in the north of the peninsula to stop their joining in the fight against "Overlord"."

Winston Churchill's perseverance and emphatic advocacy of the advantages of invasion of Italy had the necessary response in Washington and Moscow; and the decision was in favour of stepping up from Sicily into the toe of Italy. This was the logical step to the long and arduous campaigns in North Africa, "the natural fruition of our whole series of victories from Alamein onwards". To Stalin it seemed merely as a minor relief from German pressure to be adopted as an interim measure till 'Overlord' was launched against the western coast of France. To President Roosevelt and his military advisers, it was only an interlude which would satisfy his British ally and provide engagement for British forces. The political situation in Italy had made it imperative that some such step must be adopted to end the Fascist regime and enable the Italian people to turn against their German ally.

The invasion of Sicily began on 10 July and the United States Seventh Army and the British Eighth Army completed the conquest of that island in thirty-five days; the first Allied units crossed the Strait of Messina on 17 August. This bridgehead was expanded by the crossing over of two divisions of the Eighth Army within the next fortnight. In the Sicilian fight, the Indian troops were not called in any strength, while the Canadian, British and American forces drove the Italian and German divisions in front of them. Meanwhile, Mussolini had fallen, he was shorn of all powers by his King and made a prisoner. Badoglio formed the new government, and signed an armistice with the Allies. The plan to occupy the airports outside Rome could not materialise because the German forces were prompt to capture them and hold Rome as well. The King and Badoglio with their government were moved to Bari in south Italy where they established their government. The people of Italy welcomed the exit of their fatherland from the war and Italian army and navy surrendered to the United Nations. But the fight was taken up by the Germans who now despatched their divisions into Italy to hold the northward drive of the British and United States Armies.

The Italian campaign was a stubborn fight against the German forces holding the strategic lines and defending every river crossing and all passes and roads crossing the Apennines. The Eighth Army, which included three Indian divisions, had to defeat all obstructions imposed by the Germans and battle against cold, snow and rain which made passage across the mountainous country or river valleys an arduous task. But step by step, with their American allies to their left, on the western coast, the Commonwealth force broke the German lines, one after the other, and made for its northern objective. Sangro, Volturno, Garigliani and Cassino are names which conjure up memories of a grim fight in which Indian troops distinguished themselves and had a very necessary and important training in mountain warfare. The discomfiture of the Germans in Italy paved the way for their ultimate defeat and the destruction of Hitler and his Nazi regime. This campaign made 'Overlord' possible and made it easy for the Anglo-American armies to overrun France and Western Germany. Stalin had the necessary respite; the Balkan revolts were facilitated and the end of war was brought nearer.

BISHESHWAR PRASAD

CHAPTER I

The Glittering Prize of Naples

The Pattern of European Politics

Italy, which had been the torch bearer of European civilization in the days of the Roman Empire, had fallen on evil days and at the beginning of the nineteenth century was a mere 'geographical expression' without any national unity or political cohesion. But already powerful forces were at work, which were to rid the country of foreign influence and to weld the discordant elements into a unified national state. The fiery idealism of Mazzini, the practical statesmanship of Cavour, the heroic exploits of Garibaldi and the robust patriotism of the rulers of Savoy achieved the immense task of creating the unified independent national state of Italy. This task was accomplished by 1870 and Italy was now in a position to play its role in the comity of European nations. At about the same time another national state, more powerful than that of Italy, came into existence. Bismarck's policy of 'blood and iron' resulted in the creation of a strong and powerful Germany, whose restless ambition and the desire for 'Lebensraum' affected the balance of power in Europe and occasioned the outbreak of two World Wars. The Dual Alliance made in 1879 between Germany and the ramshackle empire of Austria-Hungary was a historic event since Germany was able to consolidate its position in the very heart of Europe. Angered by the seizure of Tunis by France, Italy swung over to the side of the Central Powers and thus in 1882 the Dual Alliance was converted into the Triple Alliance.

The Central Powers occupied an area of great strategic importance. Both France and Russia—powerful neighbours of the Central Powers—felt threatened by the emergence of the strong centre. Chafing at the humiliating defeat suffered at the hands of Prussia at Sedan in 1870 and the loss of the two rich provinces of Alsace and Lorraine, France cherished hopes of revenge and the cry of 'Revanche' was a potent force in French politics. At the same time there was fierce rivalry between Russia and Austria-Hungary for a dominant role in the Balkans. Thus France and Russia were drawn by self-interest into an alliance in 1894. England, whose self-complacency was rudely disturbed by the upsetting of the balance of power in Europe by the overwhelming power of the Central Powers became the ally of France in 1904 and Russia in 1907, thus forming the Triple Entente (1907) as a counterpoise to the Triple Alliance. Europe was now divided into two armed camps and the way was prepared for the outbreak of the First World War in 1914. The pattern of European politics had been set in a mould with which we are all familiar—Germany bestriding Central Europe like a colossus (with Italy tagged on as an appendix) and the Allies (Russia, France and England) ranged in opposition to her vaulting ambition.

The task facing Italy before the outbreak of the First World War was twofold— to set its house in order and to carve out an empire in Africa. While the Italian statesmen devoted their time and attention to the improvement of the finances and the administration they also followed energetically the policy of acquiring colonies. Though late in the field, as compared with the other European rivals, Italy had the satisfaction of acquiring colonies in Africa. Before the outbreak of the First World War in 1914, Italy had annexed important colonies—Eritrea, Italian Somaliland and Libya.

Into the Vortex of War

Although Italy had become an ally of the Central Powers she could not afford to antagonise Great Britain. The long straggling coast is Italy's Achilles heel, for it is vulnerable to attack by an enemy possessing a powerful navy. Hence she maintained amicable relations with England, and after 1900 her attitude towards the Triple Entente was a source of weakness to the central alliance. When the war came in 1914, Italy deserted the Triple Alliance, declared her neutrality and later joined the Allied Powers on 23 May 1915 when the latter held out to her the promise of giving her control over the Adriatic and Aegean Seas and an extension of her African empire. But the Versailles Treaty of 1919 came as a rude shock to Italy since her national aspirations were not satisfied. Although Italy acquired some former Austrian territory, her imperialistic ambitions in Dalmatia, Albania, the Near East, and Africa remained unfulfilled. Smarting under this national humiliation and chafing at the worsening economic conditions in the country, the Italians welcomed the advent to power in 1922 of Mussolini, who satisfied the national craving for glory by establishing a strong and powerful government, which would not be trifled with easily by the Great Powers. He soon made his power felt. He established a protectorate over Albania in 1926 and almost converted the Adriatic Sea into an Italian lake. In 1935 he rounded off the Italian African empire by the conquest of Abyssinia. In 1937 took place the historic event known as the Rome-Berlin Axis by which Italy and Germany became Allies. With the advent to power of Hitler in 1933 a new Germany had been born like a phoenix, out of the ashes of the old Germany, which had perished during World War I. Hitler had galvanised Germany into action, he added to the territory and resources of Germany by regarding the treaty of Versailles merely as a scrap of paper. Germany was growing from strength to strength and Mussolini instinctively turned for friendship and alliance to Hitler, who like him was fast tending towards dictatorship and an aggressive foreign policy. Once more the European politics were beginning to be woven into the familiar pattern—a strong powerful Germany (occupying an area of great strategic importance) with Italy as an ally. The stage was set for World War II.

At the outbreak of World War II on 3 September 1939, Italy remained aloof and did not jump into the fray. But when the tide of victory rolled on in favour of Germany, and France lay bleeding to death (10 June 1940), Mussolini stood in shining armour by the side of Hitler, his powerful ally. The die had been cast; Italy had joined the worldwide struggle as the ally of Germany. Mussolini's ambition was to flash like a Lancelot through the lists. Fate, however, had decreed otherwise, and his ambition of re-capturing the glory of the Roman Empire turned out to be a mere mirage.

The North African Campaign

When Italy joined the war the Axis forces were triumphant in Europe. The time was ripe for Mussolini to reap the harvest—a large army of about 215,000 in Libya was poised for attack on Egypt; another large army of about 200,000 in Italian East Africa (Eritrea, Italian Somaliland and Abyssinia) was ready to invade the Sudan, Kenya and British Somaliland. The Italian forces showed some enterprise in the beginning; British Somaliland was overrun; Kassala and Gallabat in the Sudan were occupied; the Italian forces took up positions on its frontier, southwards of Bardia, for the invasion of Egypt. This marked the farthest limit of Italian advance. The initiative soon passed to the other side; on 9 December 1940, General Wavell, Commander-in-Chief of the Middle East Forces, launched a powerful attack which led to the defeat of the Italian forces and their disastrous retreat to El Agheila on 7 February 1941. But now a formidable opponent appeared on the scene, General Rommel at the head of his well trained *Afrika Korps*. On 31 March 1941, he attacked the Allied forces and drove them into Egypt by 13 April 1941. The only redeeming feature of this disastrous Allied retreat was that Tobruk held out and constituted a big nuisance to the Axis forces advancing into Egypt. On 18 November 1941, General Auchinleck, the new Commander-in-Chief of the Middle East Forces, seized the initiative and attacked the Axis forces, which reeled under the powerful blows and were driven back to El Agheila at the end of December 1941. General Rommel, however, lost no time in reorganising his forces and in launching a counter-offensive on 21 January 1942 and pushing back the Allied forces to the El Gazala positions on 7 February 1942.

The spring offensive began with the Axis attack on the Allied El Gazala defensive positions on 26 May 1942. After stubborn defence the Allied forces were pushed back to the El Alamein line by 30 June 1942. General Rommel's attack on the Alam el Halfa ridge (31 August—6 September 1942) failed and the El Alamein line held firm. Then General Montgommery, Commander of the Eighth Army, made a fresh powerful attack on 23 October 1942 and by 4 November 1942 had inflicted a crushing defeat on the Axis forces, which were soon on the run. The Eighth Army took up the chase westwards, while a British-American force having landed in North-West Africa under General Eisenhower began to drive eastwards. The Axis forces were trapped in Tunisia and forced to surrender on 13 May 1943. Of the quarter of a million Axis soldiers remaining in North Africa hardly seven hundred managed to escape. The remainder, with more than a thousand guns and several hundred tanks, laid down their arms. Meanwhile the Italian forces in Eritrea, Somaliland and Abyssinia too had been defeated, though they had offered stiff resistance, especially in the defence of Keren. Every vestige of Axis influence had been removed from Africa and the way was prepared for the Allied offensive against Italy or elsewhere.

War on the Russian Front

Meanwhile on the vast Russian front the German and the Russian forces were locked in a titanic struggle. On 22 June 1941, the Nazi forces surged forward for an attack on Russia and in a short time made deep inroads into Russian territory. Russian resistance however stiffened and Moscow and Leningrad remained surprisingly defiant. Then in winter the Rusians launched back a counter-offensive and made some gains. But the German line held firm. Then in the summer of 1942 the Axis forces made a powerful thrust towards the Caucasus. By 25 August they had advanced as far as Mozdok, one hundred miles from the Caspian Sea. They failed to capture Stalingrad and thereafter the Axis advance in the Caucasus came to a halt. The Nazi momentum petered out, and in winter the German forces were on the retreat under pressure of the Russian counter-offensives. The Russian morale was raised considerably when on 2 February 1943 the last remnants of twenty-two Axis beleaguered divisions before Stalingrad laid down their arms. This marked a turn in the fortunes of war. The Nazi forces suffered continuous reverses in the summer of 1943 on the Soviet land.

The Grand Strategy

The Allied grand strategy was considerably influenced by the momentous drama then being staged on the plains of Russia. It was imperative that Axis pressure on the Soviet forces should be eased by diverting the German forces to the other fronts. The Americans were keen on the build-up of the Allied forces for the invasion of France so as to engage as large a number of Axis divisions as possible. Due to shipping shortage and other reasons it was not possible to undertake this gigantic task immediately. Nevertheless the United States did not wish to divert the resources on any other venture which might delay this vital task. The British view was that the success in North Africa should be fully exploited by knocking Italy out of the war, thus compelling Germany to undertake the defence of the Italian peninsula as well as to replace the Italian troops, who were garrisoning the Balkans. These rival views clashed at the Casablanca Conference held in mid-January 1943. President Roosevelt and Mr. Churchill together with their Chiefs of Staff reviewed the main events of the war and made plans for future operations. A compromise was made between the rival views. Plans were to be prepared for the cross-Channel invasion in 1944. The immediate objective, however, after clearing Axis forces from North Africa was the capture of the island of Sicily to serve "as a base for operations against southern Europe and to open the Mediterranean to the shipping of the United Nations." Accordingly the Combined Chiefs of Staff issued a directive to General Dwight D. Eisenhower (who was appointed Supreme Commander with General Sir Harold Alexander as his deputy) to plan for the operation (which was given the code-name of 'Husky') for the assault and capture of Sicily.

While General Eisenhower and his planning staff were busy in making a plan for operation 'Husky', President Roosevelt and Mr. Churchill and their Chiefs of Staff met in a conference in Washington in May 1943 to decide the vital question as to when the next blow should be struck after the capture of Sicily. At this conference (known as the 'Trident' Conference) there was again a fundamental difference of views between the British and the American Chiefs of Staff. The old familiar arguments reappeared but with greater vehemence. The British Chiefs of Staff presented their case with great skill. They were emphatically of the view that the knocking of Italy out of the war was an essential preliminary operation to the main cross-Channel operation. They emphasised "that the Russian Army was the only land force that could produce decisive results in 1943. The efforts of our armies should therefore be directed towards diverting the Germans from the Russian front in order to enable the Russian armies to inflict decisive defeat upon them......... If we were going to knock out Italy we ought to do so immediately after Sicily and with all the means at our disposal.........If capturing Sicily proved to be easy we ought to go directly into Italy."[1] The

[1] Arthur Bryant: *The Turn of the Tide, 1939-1943*, (1957), pp. 634-5.

British Chiefs of Staff elaborated their arguments still further: "A hard struggle between the Russians and the Germans was imminent, and we should do all in our power to help the former and disperse the latter......... The Germans were faced with operations in Russia, with possible trouble in the Balkans, and with dangers in Italy, France and Norway. Their forces were already widely stretched, and they could not further reduce them either in Russia or in France......... If Italy were knocked out of the war Germany would have to replace the twenty-six Italian divisions in the Balkans. They would also have to reinforce the Brenner Pass, along the Riviera, and on the Spanish and Italian frontiers. This dispersal was just what we needed for a cross-Channel operation, and we should do everything in our power to increase it. The defences on the coast of France would present no difficulty unless they were held by determined men and the Germans had mobile reserves with which to counter-attack."[2]

The Americans, who had set their heart on a full-scale assault across the English Channel in the spring of 1944, were alarmed at these British proposals, for they strongly felt that it would not be possible to draw off an appreciable number of German forces from the Russian front unless large-scale offensive operations were undertaken in Italy, but this would so dissipate Allied resources as to prevent the build-up of the forces for the assault across the Channel. Hence they proposed that after the capture of Sicily only "limited offensive operations" should be undertaken in the Mediterranean area. Their main demand, in fact, was that the strength of the Allied forces engaged in the Mediterranean theatre of war should be restricted so as not to prejudice the success of the main operation for the assault across the Channel.

The 'Trident' Conference arrived at a compromise between these two conflicting views. The British agreed on the target date and the size of the forces for the assault across the Channel. On the other hand, the Americans gave up their opposition to further operations in the Mediterranean, provided that these were strictly limited in scope.[3] Accordingly on 26 May 1943, the Combined Chiefs of Staff informed General Eisenhower, Commander of the Allied forces in the Mediterranean, of their decision that the major attack on Europe would be made from the United Kingdom, probably in the early summer of 1944. He was therefore instructed to plan such operations "in exploitation of the conquest of Sicily as would be best calculated to eliminate Italy from the war and to contain the maximum number of German divisions."[4]

[2] *Ibid*, p. 635.
[3] Lt.-Col. G. W. L. Nicholson: *The Canadians in Italy, 1943-1945* (Official History of the Canadian Army in the Second World War), Vol. II, p. 183.
[4] Alexander's Despatch: *The Allied Armies in Italy from 3rd September 1943 to 12th December 1944*, p. 2880.

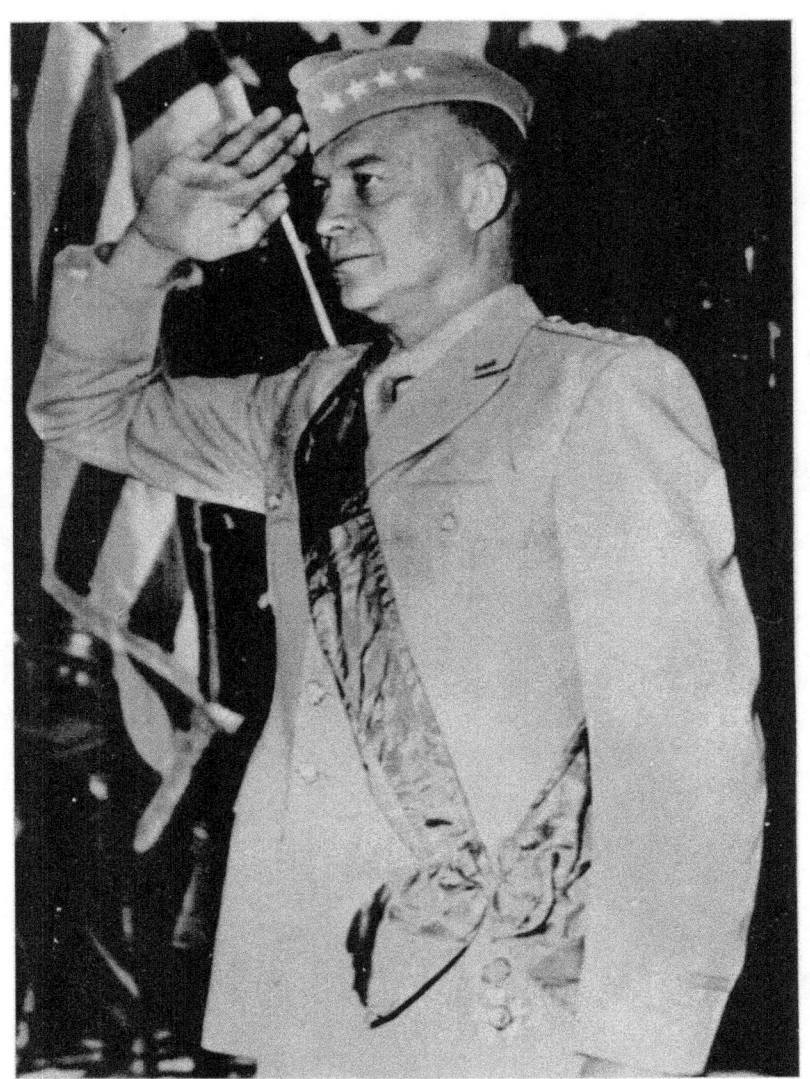

General Dwight David Eisenhower
(Supreme Allied Commander, Mediterranean Forces, 1943)

General Sir Henry Maitland Wilson
(Supreme Allied Commander, Mediterranean Forces, 1943-44)

Conquest of Sicily

Before dawn on 10 July 1943, within two months of the collapse of the Axis forces in Tunisia, Allied troops landed in Sicily to carry out operation 'Husky'. The interval between the surrender in North Africa and the invasion of Sicily had been fully utilised for the preparation for this assault, which began, as early as January 1943. Immediately on the receipt in North Africa of orders to plan operation 'Husky', a planning staff was set up and heavy air raids were directed on Axis bases along the Italian mainland and in Sicily. Moreover, as a preliminary to 'Husky', some Italian island bases in the central Mediterranean, had been occupied by the Allied troops—Pantellaria on 11 June and Lampedusa on 13 June 1943. Only the Sicilian operation had been delayed owing to the shortage of shipping and of landing craft. However the assault was planned and the south-east corner of the island was selected for landing by two task forces, the Eastern and Western.

General Eisenhower's assault force in the Mediterranean was styled the 15th Army Group which was placed under the command of General Sir Harold Alexander and comprised the American Seventh Army under General Patton and the British Eighth Army under General Montgomery. On 19 May 1943, General Alexander issued instructions for the assault on Sicily. The Eighth Army, the landing element of the Eastern Task Force, was to attack the south-eastern Sicilian beaches between Syracuse and Pozzallo, just west of the southern tip of the island. The Seventh Army, in the Western Task Force, was to attack the southern Sicilian beaches between Cape Scaramia and Licata.

General Montgomery's plan was to employ two corps for the assault—the XIII Corps on the right and the XXX Corps on the left. The XIII Corps (commanded by Lieut.-General Miles C. Dempsey) was to assault in the northern half of the Gulf of Noto ; the 5th Division was to capture Cassibile and push on north to Syracuse while the 50th Division was to capture Avola and protect the corps' left flank. A brigade of the 1st Airborne Division was to be landed in gliders west of Syracuse and Commando troops were to land south of the port to carry out the operation for the capture of Syracuse. After a successful completion of the assault phase of the operations the XIII Corps was to push on north to capture Catania.

The XXX Corps (commanded by Lieut.-General Sir Oliver Leese) was to carry out the initial task of capturing the town Pachino and its airfield, the 51st Division was to capture the town while the 1st Canadian Division was to seize the airfield. The landings of the independent 231st Infantry Brigade on the beaches on the right of the 51st Division were to provide right flank protection to the XXX Corps. A Special Service Brigade of two Royal Marine Commandos was to land on the Canadians' left. After securing Pachino the XXX Corps was to seize the line of the road from Noto to Ispica and then to secure the high ground in the area Pozzallo—Ragusa.

The Axis forces in Sicily consisted of two German divisions—the *15th Panzer Grenadier Division*[5] and the *Hermann Goering Panzer Division* (reinforced later by elements of the *1st Parachute Division* and the *29th Panzer Grenadier Division*), and nine Italian divisions—four field and five coastal divisions. The Italians were weak in equipment and in fighting quality and were spread out round the entire coastline. Their morale was at the lowest ebb. By the beginning of July, however, five German divisions were concentrated in south Italy, one in Sardinia and a regimental group in Corsica.[6]

On the afternoon of 9 July 1943, the assault convoys began to arrive in the rendezvous area south and west of Malta, they then sailed to the north, each convoy towards its own assigned beach. Early in the morning of 10 July the seaborne troops went ashore, as planned, in spite of a heavy swell. Complete tactical surprise was achieved. The Italian resistance was rarely more than nominal and only in Gela, in the American sector, was there any real attempt made to oppose the landings. There, the second German counter-attack with tanks broke through the American front. However, by the second day, the American troops had established themselves and were pushing inland. That evening, Syracuse was captured. Thereafter, though occasionally checked, by 25 July the Allied troops had pushed the Axis forces back into the north-east of the island and the fighting developed into a German rearguard action to cover the evacuation of their troops from Sicily across the Straits of Messina. By 17 August, the whole of Sicily was in Allied occupation.

Among the beach organisations, which had fed the divisions with all their requirements across the beaches after the initial landings, were two Indian infantry battalions—the 3rd Battalion 10th Baluch Regiment and the 3rd Royal Battalion 12th Frontier Force Regiment. The latter was with the 5th and 50th Divisions, while the former served with the 50th Division and the 231st Brigade. These two Indian battalions at the landings in Sicily had little fighting role and were employed on other duties.

The conquest of Sicily yielded rich results, political as well as strategic, for the Allied lines of communication through the Mediterranean were made safe, the Fascist regime in Italy had collapsed (with the resignation of Mussolini on 25 July) and a bridge into the continent was secured. The stage was set for the invasion of the

---

[5] It was not a real *Panzer Division* and had only one tank battalion; it was renamed *Panzer Grenadier Division* after the Sicilian campaign.
[6] Alexander's Despatch: *The Conquest of Sicily, from 10th July 1943 to 17th August 1943.*

Italian mainland. The Allied conquest of Sicily was a creditable achievement. It was the result of "an amphibious assault planned and executed on an unprecedented scale, and a subsequent advance of the ground forces over extremely difficult country against a clever and stubborn foe who took full advantage of the defensive possibilities afforded by the rugged topography".[7] It would be, however, unfair not to pay tribute to the high fighting qualities of the German soldier and the strategical and tactical skill displayed by Field-Marshal Kesselring. His plan was for the nine Italian divisions, mostly strung along the coast, to check the initial advance of the Allied troops and for the two German divisions (the *15th Panzer Grenadier Division* and the *Hermann Goering Panzer Division*) deployed inland to launch the counter-attacks. The plan failed for the Italians had no heart in the business, and consequently there was little opposition to the landing of the Allied troops on the beaches of Sicily. Field-Marshal Kesselring met the deteriorating situation with skill and confidence. He strengthened the two German divisions by elements of the *1st Parachute Division* and the *29th Panzer Grenadier Division*. Thus reinforced, the German troops made skilful use of the terrain to check the Allied advance. Though Field-Marshal Kesselring failed to stem the tide of Allied success he managed to get breathing time (of 38 days) to organise his forces for the defence of Italy. "Although caught off balance by the invasion and the failure of their Italian allies to offer effective resistance, Kesselring's troops had acquitted themselves well. With somewhat less than four divisions, little air strength and practically no naval support, the Germans had for five and a half weeks opposed an Allied force of more than twelve divisions enjoying absolute superiority in the air and on the sea. The enemy's withdrawal from the island, with much of his heavy equipment, had been made in his own time, and had been so skilfully conducted that neither the Allies' pursuing armies had been able to hasten its progress nor their air forces seriously interrupt its execution. From every aspect the German evacuation of Sicily must be numbered among the successful retreats in the history of warfare."[8] At the same time full credit must be given to the Allied soldiers of General Palton's U.S. Seventh Army and General Montgomery's Eighth Army for having defeated such skilful antagonists in the short period of 38 days in that difficult terrain.

German Forces in South Italy

The conquest of Sicily had important political consequences. It was one of the contributory factors which led to the fall of Mussolini on 25 July. The new government headed by Marshal Badoglio was

---

[7] Nicholson: *The Canadians in Italy, 1943-1945, op. cit.,* Vol. II, p. 175.
[8] *Ibid.*

friendly to the Allies. Shortly afterwards, on 8 September 1943, Italy signed the Armistice and thus one of the Axis partners was knocked out of the ring. At the same time, the occupation of this island marked the consummation of the North African strategy, which was designed to open the Mediterranean to the Allied shipping and to provide a base for attacks on southern Europe. But a decision had been taken by the Allied leaders at Washington at the 'Trident' Conference in May 1943, to launch the main attack against Germany in the north-west Europe in the spring of 1944. Thus the Italian Campaign was converted into a subordinate enterprise and its main role came to be one of contributing to the success of the main Allied attack in north-west Europe by tying down some German forces in Italy. In short, the campaign in Italy was a great holding attack "for its main object was the diversion of German strength to a theatre as far removed as possible from the vital point, the Channel coast".[9] Nevertheless the unexpectedly quick victory in Sicily had convinced the U.S. Chiefs of Staff that the time for bolder action in Italy had come. Both General Eisenhower and the Combined Chiefs of Staff recommended operations on the mainland. The earlier conservative plans were therefore scrapped and a direct assault on Naples was decided upon.

The German forces in Italy were well deployed to meet the Allied threat of the invasion of Italy. On 3 September 1943, when the Allied invasion of Italy took place the German forces in South Italy, consisting of eight divisions, were commanded by Field-Marshal Kesselring. These divisions were organised under Headquarters *Tenth Army* (Colonel-General von Vietinghoff) into two corps—the *XIV Panzer Corps* in the north and *LXXVI Panzer Corps* in the south, the *XI Flieger Corps* (Air Corps) being directly under Kesselring. The *XIV Panzer Corps* consisted of the *16th Panzer Division*, *Hermann Goering Panzer Division* and the *15th Panzer Grenadier Division*. The *LXXVI Panzer Corps* consisted of the *29th Panzer Grenadier Division*, the *26th Panzer Division* and the *1st Parachute Division*. The *XI Flieger Corps* comprised the *3rd Panzer Grenadier Division* and the *2nd Parachute Division*. Two divisions (the *29th Panzer Grenadier Division* and the *26th Panzer Division*) were in Calabria and one division (the *1st Parachute Division*) was in area Altamura (in Apulia) to meet the threat of the Allied invasion of Italy's 'toe' and 'heel'. Three divisions (the *16th Panzer Division*, the *15th Panzer Grenadier Division* and *Hermann Goering Panzer Division*) were in the Naples area, where the threat of Allied attack was the greatest. Two divisions (the *3rd Panzer Grenadier Division* and the *2nd Parachute Division*) were in the area of Rome to meet the

[9] Alexander's Despatch: *The Allied Armies in Italy, from 3rd September 1943 to 12th December 1944.*

Allied threat to that city. The dispositions of the German forces in south Italy were intended to cover the vital points which were likely to be attacked by the Allies—Calabria, Naples and Rome. In addition there were German forces in north Italy to act as a reserve or to meet any Allied threat in the Genoa—Spezia area. Army Group 'B' in north Italy consisted of four corps commanded by Field-Marshal Rommel.

General Alexander's Plan

General Alexander's plan was to make a double attack, one directed against Calabria and the other against the Gulf of Salerno, south of Naples. The XIII Corps of the Eighth Army (commanded by Lieut-General M. C. Dempsey) consisting of the 1st Canadian Division and the 5th British Division, was to attack across the Strait of Messina and secure the 'toe' of Italy. D Day for this operation (Baytown) was to be 3 September 1943. The main attack (Avalanche) was to be made a few days later by the American Fifth Army (commanded by Lieut-General Mark Clark) consisting of the VI U.S. Corps and the X British Corps. The Fifth Army was to make an assault in the Gulf of Salerno area and capture Naples. In addition to these two operations, General Alexander had also made plans for a third operation (Slapstick) wherein the 1st Airborne Division was to seize Taranto—a port of importance in the build-up of the Eighth Army. The 78th Division and a little later the 8th Indian Division were to reinforce the 1st Airborne Division. The V Corps (commanded by Lieut-General Charles Allfrey) was to have under command these three divisions and its initial role was to "secure a base in the 'heel' of Italy covering the parts of Taranto and Brindisi, and if possible Bari". In short General Alexander's plan was for the American Fifth Army to land on the shores of the Gulf of Salerno and capture Naples; the XIII Corps (of the Eighth Army) to secure Italy's 'toe' and the V Corps to secure the 'heel'.

Capture of Naples and Foggia

On 3 September 1943, the XIII Corps of the Eighth Army launched an assault across the Strait of Messina. There was hardly any opposition. The 5th Division swung up the west coast while the 1st Canadian Division secured Reggio di Calabria and pushed on to Catanzaro, which was captured on 10 September. Field-Marshal Kesselring, however, seemed to have divined the Allied intentions of striking the main blow in the Gulf of Salerno area. He refused to be drawn into a battle in Italy's 'toe' or 'heel' but prepared for the grim struggle which was to be waged for the city of Naples. Hence the German rearguards were content to delay the advance of the XIII Corps by mines and demolitions. On 9 September the

Fifth Army assaulted the beaches of Salerno. For several days the tide of battle ebbed and flowed. German divisions were rushed to Salerno and it was only with great difficulty that the Fifth Army succeeded in repelling the fierce German counter-attacks, which gained in intensity between 12 and 14 September. Such was the severity of the struggle that for long the issue of the battle hung in the balance. But at last on 15 September the edge of the German attacks was blunted. To relieve pressure on the Fifth Army it was imperative that the XIII Corps of the Eighth Army should move forward so as to threaten the south flank of the German forces at Salerno. This Corps pushed north to join up with the Fifth Army's right and to capture Potenza, an important road centre about 55 miles east of Salerno. By 15 September the forward troops of the XIII Corps had gained the Castrovillari—Scalea line and on the next day linked up with the Fifth Army patrols, west of Vallo. This threat to the left flank of the German forces at Salerno eased the pressure on the Fifth Army enabling it to regain the initiative. The Fifth Army then prepared to secure the line Avellino—Castellamane in order to attack and capture Naples. German opposition was overcome and the Allied troops entered Naples on 1 October. The XIII Corps secured Potenza on 20 September and then halted its advance in order to improve the supply and administrative situation.

Meanwhile good progress had been made in the 'heel' of Italy. The 1st Airborne Division had captured Taranto without opposition on 9 September and had then fanned out to secure Brindisi and Bari. The possession of Bari, the best harbour on the east coast, was of great importance since it enabled the Allies to use it as a base of supplies for operations to the north. The 78th British Division was landed at Bari and the V Corps was then in a position with its two divisions—the 1st Airborne Division and the 78th British Division —to push on from Bari area to secure Foggia, which was captured on 27 September. It marked a useful gain, as the possession of the group of airfields in the plain of Foggia enabled the Allied Strategic Air Force to strike at important centres of Axis war production. By 1 October 1943, the first phase of the Italian campaign came to an end. The Fifth Army had secured its objective, Naples, and the Eighth Army had secured Potenza and Foggia.

General Sir Harold Alexander
(Commander 15th Army Group, 1943)

General Viscount Bernard Montgomery
(Commander Eighth Army, July 1942—Dec. 1943)

General Sir Oliver Leese
(Commander Eighth Army, 1944)

Troops of 1/5 Essex take a shot at a German MK. IV tank with a PIAT mortar

CHAPTER II

Outposts of the Winter Line

German Dispositions (1 October 1943)

After twenty-two days of hard fighting the Fifth Army had secured the port of Naples, so necessary for its advance up the Tyrrhenian coast, and the Eighth Army had captured the important Foggia airfields. The Allied forces were now ready to push on towards Rome, a position of vital strategic importance. "Whoever holds Rome", said Mr. Churchill, "holds the title deeds of Italy."

Field-Marshal Kesselring, too, was alive to the importance of retaining the possession of Rome, and for that purpose exhibited his supreme skill in deploying his forces to prevent the Allied progress towards Rome. The two corps of the *Tenth Army* stood athwart the Allied line of advance up the west coast and the Adriatic coast. On the Adriatic coast the *LXXVI Panzer Corps* had three divisions—the *1st Parachute Division* on the coast, the *29th Panzer Grenadier Division* inland and the *16th Panzer Division* in the Termoli area. On the west coast the *XIV Panzer Corps* had four divisions—the *Hermann Goering Panzer Division* on the coast responsible as far east as Nola and the *26th Panzer Division* extending to Benevento, beyond which was the sector of the *29th Panzer Grenadier Division* of the *LXXVI Panzer Corps*. The other two divisions, the *3rd* and *15th Panzer Grenadier Divisions*, were concentrated behind the Volturno river. The *XI Flieger Corps* with the *2nd Parachute Division* was in the Rome area.

So far the German strategy had been to withdraw by gradual stages to a strong defensive line on the northern Apennines (known as the Gothic Line), but soon after there was a change in Hitler's policy, who decided to put a stop to further withdrawal and to hold a strong defensive line as far south as possible in Italy. This line was known as the 'Winter Line'. "It was based on the east coast on the River Sangro and on the west on the Garigliano backed by the Aurunci Mountains on the coast and the strong Cassino position rising to the *massif* of Monte Cairo; the centre of the Peninsula, the rugged mountains of the Abruzzi, where bears roamed in the fastnesses of the National Park, was considered too difficult to admit of manoeuvre by large forces. On this line the Italian peninsula is at its narrowest, only eighty-five miles from sea to sea. Delaying positions could be held in front of it in order to gain time for the weather to deteriorate still further and allow artificial defences to be constructed to add to the natural strength of the position."[1] To give depth to this line Kesselring decided to offer resistance from strong defensive positions behind the Volturno river on the west coast and the rivers Biferno and Trigno on the Adriatic coast (the outposts of the Winter Line).

The Crossing of the R. Volturno

At the beginning of October 1943, the Fifth and the Eighth Armies stood poised for an attack on the outposts of the Winter Line viz., on the German defence line behind the rivers Volturno, Biferno and Trigno. The X and VI Corps of the Fifth Army closed up to the river Volturno by the end of the first week in October. The assault across the river was delayed by miserable weather. The attack was however launched on the night of 12 October. On the left the X Corps attacked with three divisions—the 46th Division on the left was directed against Cancello and the 7th Armoured Division in the centre was directed against Grazzanise while the 56th Division on the right crossed the Volturno in the Capua area. On the right, the VI Corps attacked in the mountainous area east of Capua. The Germans offered strong resistance but by 25 October both the Corps were able to force a crossing and consolidate their bridge-heads.

Capture of Termoli

While the Fifth Army was crossing the Volturno the Eighth Army (V and XIII Corps) tried to secure the line Termoli—Campobasso—Vinchiaturo. General Montgomery selected the XIII Corps for this task. This corps was to attack with two divisions—the 78th Division to operate along the coast and the 1st Canadian Division to advance from the plain of Foggia into the mountain mass to the north and the west. At the same time the V Corps was to assume command of the remaining formations (the 1st Airborne Division, the 5th Division and the 8th Indian Division) and carry out the threefold task of organising the administrative build-up, securing the army lines of communication and protecting the left flank of the XIII Corps.

The 78th Division, with the 4th Armoured Brigade and the Special Service Brigade under command, began an attack along Route 16 with the object of crossing the river Biferno and capturing Termoli. Armour and infantry carried out a frontal assault while the Special Service Brigade delivered a most successful hook by sea on 3 October. After stiff fighting, in which fortunes varied, Termoli was captured on 7 October, the river crossing secured and pursuit pushed

---

[1] Alexander's Despatch: *The Allied Armies in Italy from 3rd September 1943 to 12th December 1944.*

on to another river obstacle, the Trigno. The German commander switched his *16th Panzer Division* from the river Volturno (on the Fifth Army's front) to the Adriatic coast and committed it piecemeal against the Eighth Army.

While the 78th Division was engaged in a desperate struggle to drive out the Germans from Termoli, the 1st Canadian Division was advancing up Route 17 against stiffening opposition. The XIII Corps was strengthened by the 5th Division, which came under command on 9 October. On 11 October this division began to operate on the right of the 1st Canadian Division. Both these divisions made fairly good progress. The 5th Division captured Casacalenda (on Route 87) on 13 October while the 1st Canadian Division captured Campobasso on 14 October and Vinchiaturo on 15 October. Thus by 15 October, the XIII Corps had carried out the task allotted to it. But the advance of the Eighth Army was soon halted to enable the necessary administrative build-up.

After the capture of Termoli the Eighth Army regrouped. As operations on the coast road (Route 16) were becoming more divorced from those on the mountain Route 17, on account of the nature of the terrain and the divergence of the axes, General Montgomery decided to regroup the Eighth Army so that two corps (instead of one) should be in the line—one using Route 16 and the other Route 17. While the XIII Corps (1st Canadian Division and the 5th Division) continued to use Route 17, the V Corps (the 78th Division and 8th Indian Division) was brought forward into the line to use Route 16. The objective of the Eighth Army was Route 86, between Vasto and Isernia. Route 86, one of the main roads from central Italy, ran parallel to the river Trigno, fifteen miles beyond the Biferno. On 11 October 1943, the V Corps took over command of the right sector of the coast and Route 16; the XIII Corps continued moving along Route 17. The V Corps had initially one division—the 78th Division—in the line. But a week later the 8th Indian Division too came into the line and assumed command of the Larino sector at midnight 19/20 October 1943.

The 8th Indian Division in the Line

The 8th Indian Division, which was to play an important part in the attack on the Winter Line, had landed at Taranto on 19 September 1943.[2] It had seen service in West Asia and North Africa and during the summer of 1943 had undergone intensive training for combined operations and mountain warfare. It was thus well equipped to play its part in the Allied operations in Italy.

---

[2] The Divisional Commander with a small staff had preceded the Division to Taranto to arrange for its arrival there.

The 8th Indian Division was commanded by Major-General Dudley Russell, C.B.E, D.S.O, M.C, and comprised:

17th Indian Infantry Brigade
    1st Battalion Royal Fusiliers
    1st Battalion 12th Frontier Force Regiment
    1st Battalion 5th Royal Gurkha Rifles

19th Indian Infantry Brigade
    1st Battalion 5th Essex Regiment
    3rd Battalion 8th Punjab Regiment
    6th Battalion 13th Royal Frontier Force Rifles

21st Indian Infantry Brigade
    5th Battalion Royal West Kent Regiment
    1st Battalion 5th Mahratta Light Infantry
    3rd Battalion 15th Punjab Regiment.[3]

Artillery
    3, 52 and 53 Field Regiments RA
    4 Mahratta A Tk Regt. IA
    26 Lt AA Regt. RA
Engineers and other ancillary units.

The 8th Indian Division was posted to the V Corps whose Commander, Lieut.-General C. W. Allfrey, C.B., D.S.O., M.C., had under his command the 4th Indian Division in his Corps during the last phases of the operations in Tunisia, and had a high opinion of Indian formations. The divisional headquarters opened at Ururi, at midnight 19/20 October 1943, when the 8th Indian Division assumed command of the Larino sector. Two brigades—the 19th and the 21st, were in reserve while the forward line was held by the 17th Indian Infantry Brigade, which relieved the 11th Infantry Brigade of the 78th Division at Larino on Route 87, and four miles southeast of a crossing over the Biferno. The 78th Division, directed on Vasto, remained on the right of the 17th Indian Infantry Brigade The 5th Division was on its left. Beyond them, with headquarters at Campobasso and preparing to cross the river Biferno south-west of that town, was the 1st Canadian Division.

Topography

The country over which the fighting was then going on consisted mainly of the eastern Apennine foothills, rising in places to two thousand feet. Numerous water-courses ran from south-west to north-east into the Adriatic Sea at right angles to the Eighth Army's

[3] See Appendix I.

line of advance, and cut the hills into a series of steep-sided, irregular ridges of high ground. Up the Adriatic coast, as far as the plains of the Po valley, the ridges continued in heart-breaking monotony. Vision was generally limited from one ridge to the next. Occasionally, from some high pinnacle, one might catch a glimpse of the ridges beyond.

Roads, more often than not, followed the crests of the ridges, at right angles to the Eighth Army's line of advance, and were few and seldom of good quality. The road allotted to the 8th Indian Division was, at best, a second class road. Rains, just beginning, had softened its surface, which had never been intended for the traffic which now rolled along it. All bridges had been systematically destroyed by the Germans in their withdrawal and the hilly nature of the country frequently made diversions impossible. Mines and booby traps had been freely used to help in delaying the advance. The sappers and their Bailey bridging equipment were to prove their worth in many a difficult situation.

Advance to the Trigno

The V Corps advanced, with the 78th Division on the right and the 8th Indian Division on the left, to establish bridge heads over the river Trigno. The 78th Division, after securing Montecilfone, established a bridge-head over the river Trigno, on the axis of Route 16, during night 23/24 October. After driving out the Germans across the river in its sector during the next night, the British division prepared to launch attacks on the main German position on the San Salvo ridge, a dominant feature overlooking the west bank. The first attack on San Salvo during night 27/28 October did not succeed; thereupon the main attack was launched on 3 November 1943.

Meanwhile the 8th Indian Division, too, had made progress so as to launch the main attack on 2 November on the strong German position at the village of Tufillo, on the west bank of the Trigno. Before launching the main attack on Tufillo, the first task of the 8th Indian Division was to close up to the river Trigno and seize the road crossing of the river between Montefalcone and Palmoli. The 17th Indian Infantry Brigade led the initial advance of the 8th Indian Division from Larino to the river Trigno. On 20 October 1943, the gunners fired their first shots for the Indian division in Italy. During the night of 20/21 October the 1st Royal Fusiliers, less two companies, crossed the Biferno and secured the high ground of the Serra del Larco, one mile beyond the river.[4] Artillery fire harassed the 1st Royal Fusiliers, who had a brief fire fight with a German standing patrol, five hundred yards west of the river, but the Germans took

---

[4] 17th Ind. Inf. Bde O.I. No. 1, dated 20 October 1943.

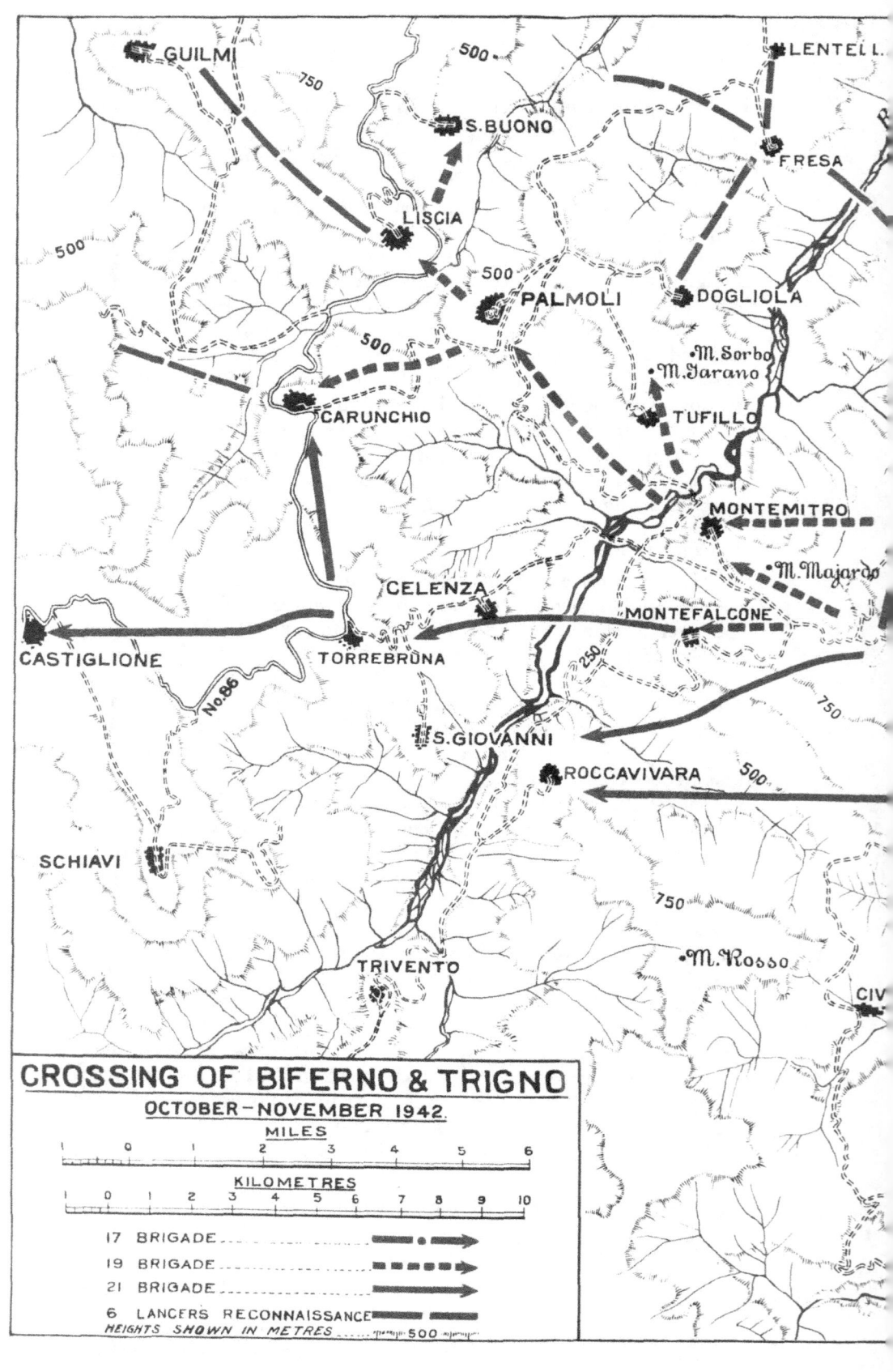

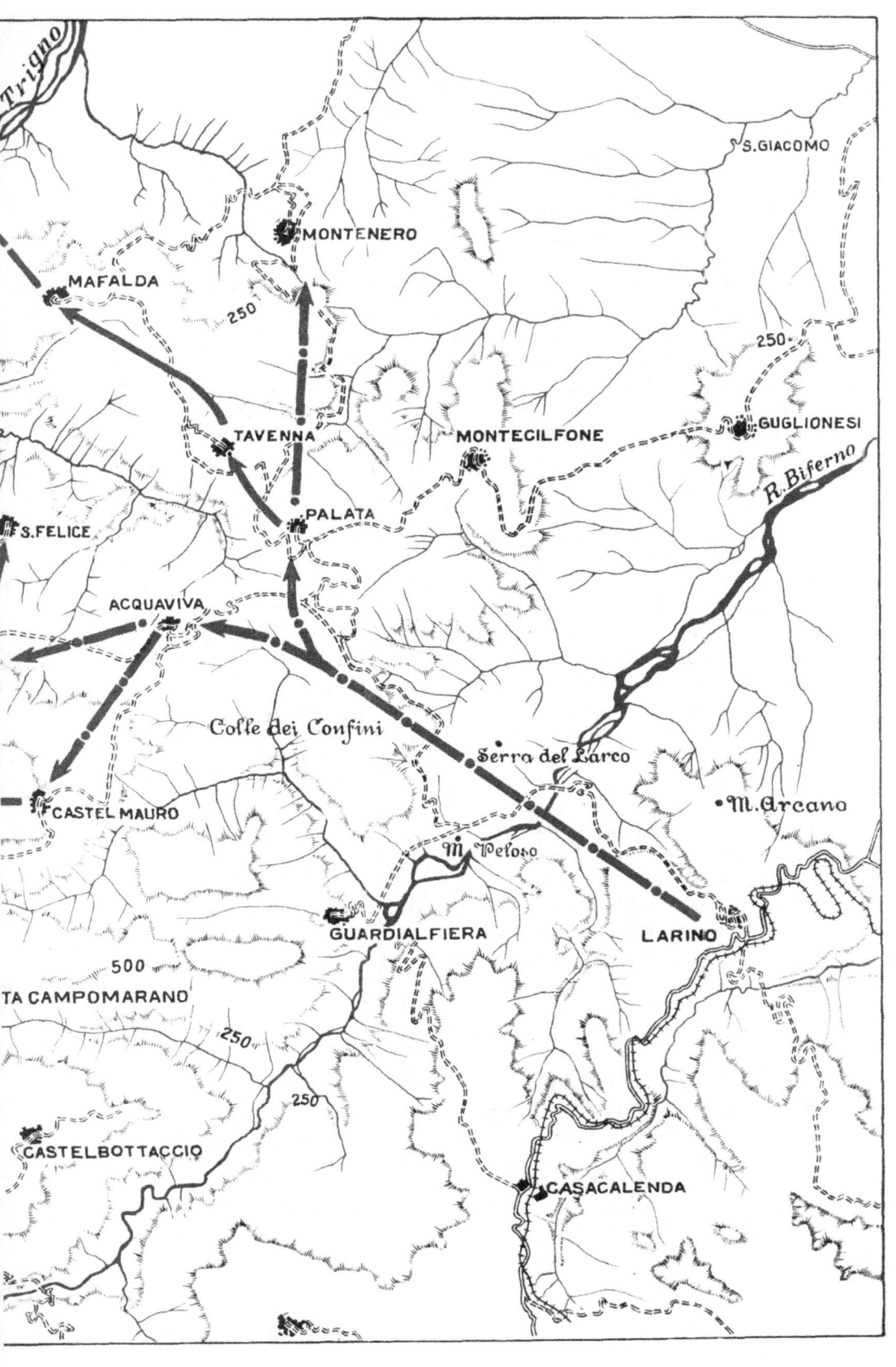

no other steps to oppose the advance and sappers were able to construct a Bailey bridge on the site of the one which had been blown. Patrols reconnoitred forward to locate the Germans and to report on the going. There were some skirmishes with German patrols but nothing serious developed. A Squadron 6th Lancers reached Colle del Confini, three miles west of the Biferno on 22 October 1943.

Early on 23 October, two battalions of the 17th Indian Infantry Brigade, headed by the 6th Lancers, moved in a north-westerly direction through the positions gained by the 1st Royal Fusiliers. The 1/12 Frontier Force Regiment, on the right, relieved A Squadron 6th Lancers at Colle del Confini and then, pushing on, met a German rearguard covering Palata, which patrols had never succeeded in entering. The 1/12 Frontier Force Regiment, supported by the machine guns of the Mahratta Light Infantry, had their first action, a brief affair but a successful one. Palata was occupied without further trouble at 0600 hours on 24 October 1943. The 1/5 Royal Gurkha Rifles on the left, after assembling at M. Peloso, attained its objective Acquaviva by 0700 hours on 24 October 1943, without opposition, though the road had been badly cratered.

On the northern flank, patrols of the 6th Lancers maintained contact with the 78th Division, which by this time had occupied Montenero and Montecilfone and had made a crossing over the river Trigno near Route 16. On the southern flank, patrols linked up with the 5th Canadian Reconnaissance Regiment. The next day, 26 October 1943, the link was strengthened when the 1/5 Royal Gurkha Rifles captured Castelmauro, three miles south-west of Acquaviva.

The 19th Indian Infantry Brigade made the next move towards the river Trigno when, on the afternoon of 25 October, it took over the lead from the 17th Indian Infantry Brigade, which returned for reorganisation and rest. The 19th Indian Infantry Brigade also employed two battalions forward. In the north, 1/5 Essex went up and down the hill to Montemitro. Opposition, still from the parachutists, gradually increased, particularly around S. Felice. But by 27 October, Montemitro had been taken. To the south, 3/8 Punjab also had to overcome resistance from parachutists before occupying M. Majardo on 26 October and Montefalcone at 0745 hours the next day.

The occupation of Montemitro and Montefalcone gave the division a firm grip on the east bank of the Trigno and provided a screen behind which preparations for the crossing were to proceed. The villages in the area were tight clusters of strongly built houses, conspicuously placed on or near the tops of the higher peaks among the hills. All motorable roads (which were few) passed through or close by them. From them, excellent observation was obtainable over the approaches from every direction.

The River Trigno

Fifteen miles inland from the Adriatic, the 8th Indian Division's axis of advance crossed the river Trigno by a stone bridge, approximately one hundred yards in length. German rearguards had destroyed this bridge, when the leading companies of the division were already in Montemitro and Montefalcone. Much hard labour was required before vehicles were able to cross. In the area of the bridge, the river ran between steep, almost precipitous, hills which rose to fifteen hundred feet above the river bed. Where the main features jutted out towards the river, they frequently ended in a cliff-face at the edge of the river, which itself was one hundred yards wide. Its main stream, which generally followed the northern side of a boulder-stream bed, was one hundred feet across and not more than two feet deep, unless in flood. After the rain, it became a torrent swift enough to sweep a man off his feet.

The villages on the peaks were connected by tracks following the crest of the high ridges between them. Outside the villages, numerous isolated stone houses broke into the pattern of the hill-sides. Between the rocky main features the hill-sides were cultivated in a patchwork system and dotted with thick clumps of shrub and bramble.

Recent rains had made the going heavy. Diversions at blown bridges and craters became impassable and bridges had to be built. The arrival of two Indian Mule Companies, the 13th and 34th, helped in solving the problem of supply.

The 19th Indian Infantry Brigade had been ordered to carry out the crossing of the Trigno. While this brigade was occupied with its preparations, the 21st Indian Infantry Brigade moved up on both the flanks. On the right, 5th Battalion Royal West Kent Regiment and A Squadron 6th Lancers, supported by the 111th Army Field Regiment, Royal Artillery, went to Mafalda. On 30 October, the 17th Indian Infantry Brigade sent two companies of the 1st Royal Fusiliers to relieve the 8th Battalion Argyll and Sutherland Highlanders in Montenero. In the south, the 1st Battalion 5th Mahratta Light Infantry and a squadron of the 6th Lancers patrolled from Castelmauro to Roccavivara, which was finally occupied on 31 October 1943. The next day, 3/15 Punjab relieved 3/8 Punjab in Montefalcone.

German Positions

The main objectives of the attack were Tufillo, and the two-thousand-foot peak beyond it, M. Farano, which was ideally sited for defence, on a narrow ridge and on a false crest above the road. It was held by a German battalion of high morale (*3rd Parachute Regiment*[5]) which had been pulled back due westwards, and now stood astride the 8th Indian Division's line of advance. All the hill-top villages, Fresa, Dogliola, Tufillo, Celenza, appeared to be bases for one or two companies, with approximately four guns apiece. From these villages, sections with automatic weapons were sent out to posts overlooking the river. Approaches to and the crossings over the river were littered with anti-tank and anti-personnel mines. Only two artillery batteries had been located, one south-east of Palmoli, the other west of Celenza. Tracked vehicles had been heard but tanks were not available in the area in any numbers.

M. Farano was known to be defended, but information concerning Mount Sorbo to the north-east was vague. From Tufillo in daylight the Germans could see all movement on the ridge forward of Montemitro and their mortars and artillery claimed a steady toll of those troops of the 8th Indian Division who attempted to move there by day. Nevertheless officers of the 6/13 Royal Frontier Force Rifles did carry out a daylight reconnaissance of the river. They spent the morning crawling down on their bellies and the afternoon crawling back again. Unfortunately, the reconnaissance was not entirely a success because they did not find the crossing places, for which they had been searching. Officer patrols had selected crossing places but information concerning them was not complete.

For three days before the attack was due to go in, heavy rain hampered all preparations. Tracks became quagmires on which vehicles slithered and stuck for hours when trying to reach the forward battalions. Some tanks, which had managed to get forward before the rains now had to be supplied by pack transport. West of Acquaviva, the road had been blown in five places. Even jeeps could not navigate the diversions. At Montefalcone the hill-side had been dynamited. To by-pass this, a track was bulldozed straight down the hillside from the river bank. While engaged in that work, the bulldozer stuck in full view of the Germans and could not be recovered until after dark. However, by the last day of the month, all bridges east of the Trigno were complete and the 19th Indian Infantry Brigade stood poised, if wet, ready to launch its attack at 0355 hours on 2 November 1943.

V Corps Plan to Cross the River Trigno

The Commander of the V Corps planned to seize the Trigno bridge-heads and to attack the Vasto-Montazzoli ridge with two

---

[5] 1 Parachute Regiment appeared to have been taken out of the battle and was thought to be preparing positions in the area of Guardiagrele, at the upper reaches of the river Sangro, along which the Germans intended to hold their winter positions (known as the Abruzzi line).

divisions—the 78th Division on the right and the 8th Indian Division on the left. The 78th Division was to attack the San Salvo ridge (a very strong natural position) dominating the west bank of the Trigno. Then it was to advance to secure the town of Vasto, with the high ground immediately beyond, and Monteodorisio, five miles inland, with the ground covering the crossing over the river Sinello. After securing these objectives the 78th Division was to close up to the river Sangro. The 8th Indian Division was to cross the river Trigno and attack the strong position at Tufillo. It was to capture series of high points and cut the Vasto-Isernia lateral road at Carunchio. Then it was to push on to the north-west and south-west and capture Gissi, Montazzoli and Castiglione. The 8th Indian Division was to assault and capture these objectives with two brigades, reserving the third brigade for the role of exploiting the success of the 78th Division, which was to lead the main attack of the V Corps. The role of the third Indian brigade was to pass through San Salvo and capture Gissi.

19th Indian Infantry Brigade Plan

Major-General Russell defined the purpose of the forthcoming operation as advance across the river Trigno with a view to securing the road Palmoli—Carunchio—Torrebruna. The 19th Indian Infantry Brigade was selected for the main task of capturing Tufillo; the 21st Indian Infantry Brigade was to cross the river Trigno opposite Celenza in order to make an advance on Torrebruna and to protect the left flank of the division. The 17th Indian Infantry Brigade, in reserve at Palata, was to be ready to move through San Salvo to Gissi.

Brigadier T. S. Dobree, D.S.O., M.C., Commander of the 19th Indian Infantry Brigade planned to accomplish his task in two phases:[6]

> Phase I—To capture the spur running south-east from Tufillo to the river.
>
> Phase II—To extend the bridge-head southwards from Tufillo across the road (Red Route).

In Phase I, 6/13 Royal Frontier Force Rifles, with one Mahratta Machine Gun platoon, was to advance, cross the right bank of the river immediately north-east of the bridge, ninety-five minutes after Phase I had opened. Their objective was accurately defined as H 513680—H 505655—H 510654, that is continuing the bridge-head of 6/13 Royal Frontier Force Rifles across the road and river Monrola (which flows into the Trigno from the north-west) and back to the Trigno, 1½ miles south-west of the bridge. The inter-battalion boundary ran from the bridge (inclusive to 1/5 Essex) along the lower western slopes of the Tufillo spur to the track, half a mile west of

---

[6] 9th Ind. Inf. Bde O.O. No. 4, dated 31 October 1943; and O.O. No. 5, dated 1 November 1943.

Tufillo. Since this was considered to be the more vulnerable flank, 1/5 Essex was to be aided by:

    C Squadron 6th Lancers
    B Squadron 50th Royal Tanks
    15th Anti-Tank Battery (less 17-pounder troop) i.e. six 6-pounder guns, towed by carriers from 3/8 Punjab
    C Company (less two platoons) 5th Mahratta Light Infantry (Medium Machine Gun).

Four Field Regiments were also in support by means of concentrations. 3/8 Punjab was held in reserve in the area Montemitro, to be prepared to assist 6/13 Royal Frontier Force Rifles and to exploit along the road towards Palmoli on D Day plus 1.

Aircraft were to bomb Dogliola, Celenza and Palmoli at first light.

H Hour was to be 0355 hours on 1 November 1943.[7]

For this operation the 19th Indian Infantry Brigade had under command:

    One Squadron 6th Lancers
    Two companies, 5th Mahratta Light Infantry (Medium Machine Gun)
    Advance Section Brigade Workshop Company
    One Company, 33rd Field Ambulance
    One Section, 8th Indian Division Provost Company

The following were in support:[8]

    One Squadron, 50th Battalion Royal Tank Regiment
    8th Indian Division Artillery
    111 Field Regiment
    8th Indian Division Engineers.

The Trigno Bridge-head

At 0355 hours on 2 November, the 19th Indian Infantry Brigade attacked. Moves forward from the cover of Montemitro had begun at 2300 hours on 1 November 1943. There was many a muttered curse as men tripped and fell, with their full load of equipment, and had to be fished out of the gorse bushes or brambles. Apart from these minor mishaps, there was no serious delay. To the minute, the leading troops slipped into the waters of the Trigno. As they crossed, the barrage by the supporting artillery burst ahead of them. The division's first major battle had begun.

Kittyhawks of the Desert Air Force had already made repeated low-level attacks, with the German gun positions as their particular targets. The artillery programme was to last for two hours, by which

---

[7] Later it was changed to 0355 hours on 2 November. See War Diary 19 Ind Inf Bde, 31-10-1943.
[8] 8 Ind Div O.O. No. 3, dated 28 October 1943.

time the first objectives were expected to be taken. Unfortunately, the infantry scrambling up the hill was unable to keep pace with the barrage, which moved one hundred yards in five minutes, and much of the advantage to be derived from the barrage was lost.

6/13 Royal Frontier Force Rifles failed to strike its selected crossing places but plunged through where it was (H 534665). Its advance up the spur to Tufillo was led by one company, the spur being too narrow for more to be employed. B Company by-passed all opposition and secured its objective, the top of the steepest part of the spur. C Company then passed through to capture Tufillo. By 0800 hours, they had reached the village. Resistance was very determined. The outskirts of the village were mined and booby trapped. Many houses contained snipers. German grenades and mortar bombs formed a thick curtain of fire across the approaches. Exposed as these were, C Company could not retain the hold which it had gained. Hence it withdrew two hundred yards to the crest of the spur and clung to that position, in spite of savage counter-attacks. D Company moving up to a minor feature on the right flank, also encountered tough opposition and came under withering fire. It was ultimately halted three hundred yards from its objective, Pt. 317.

1/5 Essex did not cross the river until 0600 hours. Thereby it lost the advantages of the night and the mist which, to a certain extent, had aided 6/13 Royal Frontier Force Rifles. It seemed certain that the Essex was observed crossing the river, for it was subjected to fierce artillery and mortar fire on the river bed. Later, as it climbed the hill to its objectives, the leading companies were subjected to a murderous fire from German machine guns located on their flanks and rear, particularly along the sides of the road. The convex nature of the hill-side made it impossible for the Essex to gain advantage against those German posts. Their heavy losses, including their commanding officer, caused some confusion in the Essex. Despite this, they pressed on. The right forward company reached its objective, a spur (H 518673) running southwards from the Tufillo feature, and approximately one mile north-west of the bridge, but was then driven back. The left forward companies were caught again by machine gun fire from the direction of Celenza and were unable to move. Mounting casualties made the position of the Essex untenable. It was therefore withdrawn to the river bank and, ultimately, by 0900 hours to its original forming-up place in the low ground west of Montemitro, leaving only scattered posts on the left bank.

On the right, 6/13 Royal Frontier Force Rifles was warned that Allied aircraft would bomb Tufillo during the morning. At 1030 hours, the aircraft arrived and bombed the village most effectively.

Some bombs fell among the men of the Frontier Force Rifles but caused no damage. Afterwards it was learned that this was a raid made in error which had been intended for another target.

In Tufillo, the German paratroopers continued to hold out. C Company 6/13 Royal Frontier Force Rifles, having now lost the initiative, could make no further progress. Throughout the day, in a steady drizzle of rain, B and C Companies maintained their positions under continual fire from German artillery and mortars, the major part of which appeared to be situated between Tufillo and Celenza. D Company, on its minor feature completely exposed to the Germans, holding M. Farano and Tufillo, had a high percentage of casualties. German paratroopers, making good use of the natural cover provided, assembled close to D Company, and, at 1700 hours, launched a strong counter-attack. Artillery support failed to halt the attack, and then the company commander asked his forward observation officer to shorten the range. This he continued to do, until the shells fell on the Germans. The latter faltered and withdrew.

The many casualties of both the battalions had to be brought back over difficult ground, part of which was under German observation. No vehicles could be employed forward of Montemitro. Mules and men were, therefore, employed. Stretcher bearers were heroic. They were steadfast under fire and untiring. Some of the mule drivers took a hand in the battle. They tied up their mules in a comparatively safe spot, unslung their rifles and opened fire on the Germans.

That afternoon, when it was realised that the Germans were in much greater strength than anticipated, preparations were made to reinforce the two battalions already committed west of the river. The 5th Battalion Royal West Kent Regiment (less one company) moved up immediately south of M. Majardo while one company remained in Mafalda. 3/15 Punjab from Montefalcone patrolled across the river but suffered five casualties. 3/8 Punjab moved down the hill towards the river in preparation for an attack that night. 1/5 Mahratta Light Infantry was ordered to concentrate at Acquaviva by 3 November.

That night, 2/3 November, 6/13 Royal Frontier Force Rifles, aided by one company 3/8 Punjab, resumed its attack. A and B Companies moved round through D Company and attacked Tufillo from the east. C Company remained south of the village at the top of the spur. The 3/8 Punjab Company attacked farther to the right up a subsidiary spur. Thick shrubbery and the dark night caused confusion and made inter-communication difficult. There had been so many casualties in 6/13 Royal Frontier Force Rifles that companies were very weak. German tracer bullets set fire to a haystack and the attackers were silhouetted against its light. When the Germans saw how weak the attackers were they put in a strong counter-attack and forced the forward companies back to the line held by D Company.

The remainder of that day saw a repetition of the first attack. The Germans were in possession of good observation over all the positions occupied by the troops of the 8th Indian Division, west of the Trigno, and took full advantage of it. Between 1600 and 1700 hours, German infantry attacked 6/13 Royal Frontier Force Rifles from the direction of M. Farano and the German Air Force, represented by two ME 109s put in a belated appearance. Aided by artillery defensive fire, the Indian battalion beat off the attack without losing ground, though a few more casualties were sustained.

The following night, 3/4 November, 3/8 Punjab crossed the river to deliver the assault with the Frontier Force Rifles. The Punjabis were to attack M. Sorbo while 6/13 Royal Frontier Force Rifles went for M. Farano. At 2200 hours, the first phase began, 3/8 Punjab advanced silently for one hour until approximately level with the forward companies of 6/13 Royal Frontier Force Rifles. Then for phase II, an artillery barrage opened, which was to aid the Punjabis to the summit. Their left forward company suffered some casualties from the barrage and was somewhat disorganised. The right forward company swung away to the north in order to avoid the barrage. This company proceeded to lose touch with battalion headquarters. The battalion commander thereupon moved his two reserve companies up to the left forward company and sent his adjutant to recall the stray company. After several adventures, the adjutant found the lost company and directed it back into the reserve. On the way, this company knocked out two German machine gun posts and captured five prisoners.

Both battalions advanced to within three hundred yards of their objective. 6/13 Royal Frontier Force Rifles met strong opposition again, had considerable casualties, and was halted in an exposed position and eventually withdrew to a place, one thousand yards east of Tufillo. 3/8 Punjab was halted short of the German defence line by a high proportion of automatic weapons and accurate mortar fire. In accordance with the normal practice of the Germans any position lost was immediately and strongly counter-attacked. All positions were held by *3rd Parachute Regiment*.

At dawn, the battalions reorganised and dug in still short of their objectives. German defensive fire had taken a toll of the mule trains carrying forward their supporting weapons and replenishments of ammunition. Each battalion had a company of Mahratta machine guns. The shelling caused serious losses and left the forward troops short of ammunition. Nevertheless, both held their positions.

Reconnaissance patrols on the night of 4/5 November reported that a number of positions previously held by the Germans were unoccupied. 6/13 Royal Frontier Force Rifles had also heard sounds of German movement in Tufillo. At dawn the parachutists had withdrawn to rejoin their battered *16th Panzer Division*, which had been compelled to retire before the 78th Division.

The 8th Indian Division was thus able to carry out a general advance. 3/8 Punjab occupied M. Farano, 6/13 Royal Frontier Force Rifles Tufillo, and the Essex Palmoli, this last close on the heels of a large body of retreating Germans. 3/15 Punjab, which had been probing the defences around Celenza, entered the village after overcoming slight opposition. Patrols from the 6th Lancers entered Dogliola and Fresa.

Between 1 and 4 November 1943, the Germans had overlooked all the forward positions of the 19th Indian Infantry Brigade and had made full use of their 105-mm self-propelled guns. The weather had not been favourable for operations, any movement of vehicles off the tracks being extremely difficult. German positions were found, on inspection, to be very cleverly camouflaged and well-sited. The mortars were concealed on reverse slopes in pits 10 feet deep. Little use was made of anti-personnel mines or booby traps near their positions but all roads and tracks to them were mined.

The main concern of the 8th Indian Division during the operations immediately preceding and following the crossing of the river Trigno was the problem of vehicle movement. The route through Montefalcone was so bad that most vehicles had to use the bulldozed track, which by-passed the village. The Bailey bridge (Jhelum) across the Trigno, completed at 1200 hours on 8 November, had steep and difficult approaches on which considerable engineer work had to be done to make the tracks on both sides passable. The road diversion in Montefalcone was constructed up a long flight of steps, which were levelled off with wood and concrete. Its gradient was so steep that most vehicles had to be towed up with a winch. The crews of the winch lorries worked day and night. It was a remarkable effort and enabled the supply columns to carry on during the difficult period, before the division could be supplied along the coast road.

On 6 November 1943, reconnaissance disclosed many serious demolitions on the road from Palmoli to Liscia, San Buono, and Gissi. Diversions, which were made to by-pass these demolitions, rapidly became quagmires, with the result that the advance of the 19th and 21st Indian Infantry Brigades was considerably delayed. On 7 November at 1030 hours, a patrol from 1/5 Essex entered Carunchio and was relieved later by 1/5 Mahratta Light Infantry. The same day, 3/15 Punjab occupied Torrebruna with one company. The 19th Indian Infantry Brigade was then ordered to concentrate at Palmoli with one battalion (6/13 Royal Frontier Force Rifles) at Liscia, whilst the 21st Indian Infantry Brigade and the 6th Lancers patrolled towards Guilmi, S Michele and Castiglione Messer Marino. The casualties suffered by the 19th Indian Infantry Brigade in securing the Trigno bridge-head were rather heavy. 6/13 Royal Frontier Force Rifles had 38 killed, 209 wounded and 14 missing. 1/5 Essex had 139 wounded.

Left Flank Protection of the 8th Indian Division

The 21st Indian Infantry Brigade, based on Carunchio, was protecting the left flank of the 8th Indian Division. Battalions from this brigade, with the co-operation of the 6th Lancers, patrolled deep to the south and west discovering German positions and their strength. One Lancer patrol went eight miles from its base, the last four in German held territory, to Rossello. The German platoon in the village having no fear of attack, so far behind their own forward defences, had omitted to take any precautions. As the Lancers rushed the village, two Germans in shirt-sleeves came out of a building. One was killed and the other surrendered. The shot raised the alarm, firing began in all directions and, before the patrol could withdraw with its prisoner, a motor-cycle combination roared out of the village, a machine gun on it firing into the house where the Lancers had gone to ground. A non-commissioned officer[9] covered the withdrawal of the remainder of the patrol which returned without any casualties.

Advance to Gissi

Meanwhile the 17th Indian Infantry Brigade, which had passed under the command of the 78th Division on 2/3 November, was exploiting the success of the British division. This division had secured San Salvo after stiff opposition on 3 November and by 5 November had captured Vasto, Cupello and Montedorisio. The 17th Indian Infantry Brigade exploited this success by attacking from the north-east through Cupello to Furci, along Route 86. The brigade had moved, through Petacciato, to San Salvo on 4 November. Twenty miles in bright moonlight had taken ten hours; many vehicles had stuck in the sand. The 78th Division captured Cupello on 5 November; and the 17th Indian Brigade with the 50th Royal Tanks (less one Squadron), A Squadron 56th Reconnaissance Regiment, 166th Field Regiment Royal Artillery and 52nd Field Regiment Royal Artillery under command, was consequently ordered to be in Cupello by dawn of 6 November. From Cupello at 0800 hours on 6 November the 17th Indian Brigade moved on foot and in mechanical transport southwards along Route 86. 1/5 Royal Gurkha Rifles, supported by tanks, formed the advanced guard. At about 1100

---

[9] Daffadar Gurdev Singh.

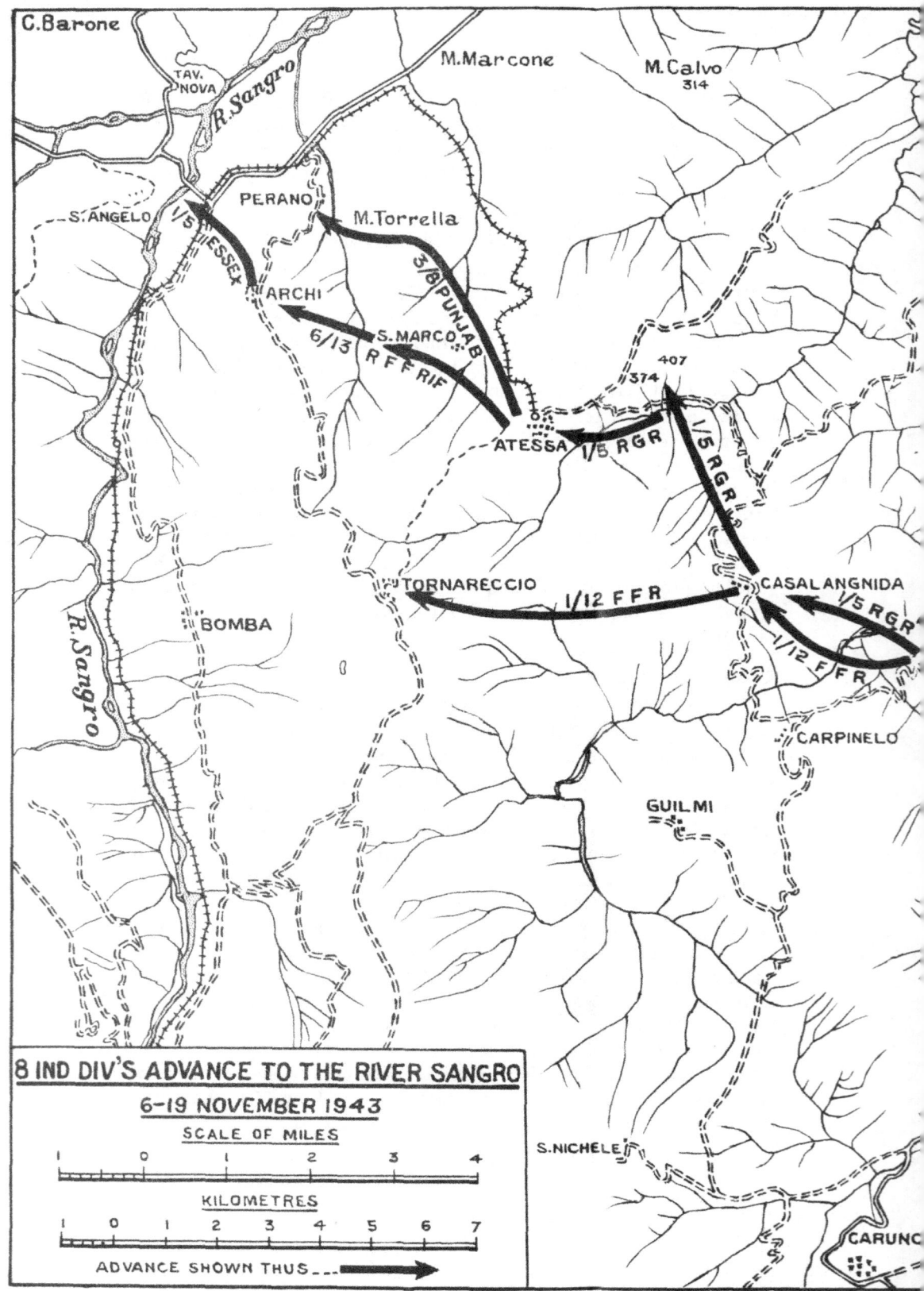

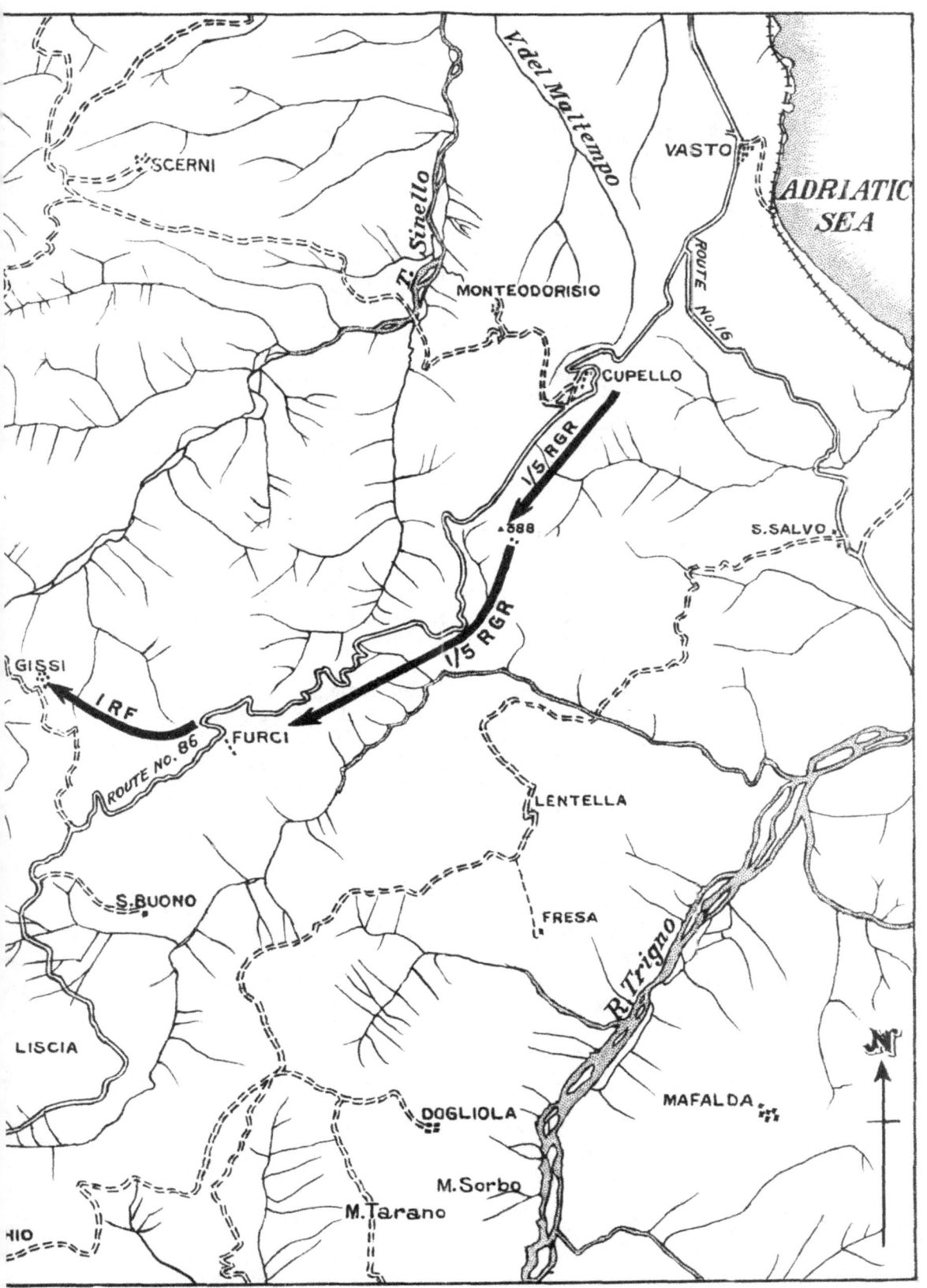

hours, the Gurkhas encountered hostile mortar and machine gun fire at Pt. 388; opposition was, however, light, and was easily overcome. The Gurkhas secured Furci at 1600 hours. The brigade spent the night 6/7 at Furci.

On 7 November, the weather again changed for the worse and more rain fell. 1st Royal Fusiliers, however, advanced from Furci and occupied Gissi without opposition. Patrols southwards during the day contacted the 19th Indian Infantry Brigade at S. Buono, and the 6th Lancers at Lentella. At 1700 hours on 7 November the 17th Indian Infantry Brigade passed from the 78th Division back to the 8th Indian Division, taking the 166th (Newfoundland) Army Field Regiment, Royal Artillery with it. This Newfoundland unit had supported the 4th Indian Division in the final attack for Tunis and it was to serve with all the Indian divisions during the Italian Campaign. On this occasion, it spent two months with the 8th Indian Division.

Capture of Atessa

Meanwhile the 78th Division had pushed on the pursuit and by 8 November driven the Germans across the river Sangro, their sector extending from the coast to Paglieta. In the sector of the 8th Indian Division, however, the German rearguards offered resistance and it was not till 19 November that they were driven across the river Sangro.

The 17th Indian Infantry Brigade, continuing towards the river Sangro on 8 November, crossed the torrent Sinello on a two-battalion front (6,000 yards) and bridge-heads were established by 0900 hours, with 1/5 Royal Gurkha Rifles on the right about Pt. 385, and 1/12 Frontier Force Regiment about Pt. 650. Casalanguida on the west bank of the river Sinello continued to hold out. In the afternoon 1/12 Frontier Force Regiment attacked the village behind an artillery barrage. Their forward observation officer and his gunners were untiring in overcoming difficulties. When their carrier became bogged they marched, carrying all their heavy equipment, in an effort to keep up with the infantry. One company reached the outskirts of the village but was forced to withdraw by a German counter-attack with tanks. During the night, however, the Germans pulled out and by 1130 hours on 9 November, 1/12 Frontier Force Regiment occupied the village. From Casalanguida patrols went out to probe into German defences; 1st Royal Fusiliers—halfway to Scerni; 1/5 Royal Gurkha Rifles—to Atessa; and 1/12 Frontier Force Regiment—to Tornareccio.

Serious demolitions on the road continued to slow down the 17th Indian Infantry Brigade's advance. 1st Royal Fusiliers had captured the bridge over the torrent Sinello intact. This bridge had been prepared for demolition, but the attack by the Royal Fusiliers had been so sudden that the Germans had left without firing their charges. German engineer patrols, which returned that night to blow the bridge, were either killed or captured.

The Gurkhas now took over the lead and on 12 November gained the ridge, Pt. 407—Pt. 374, in the low lying ground west of the river Osento and north-east of Atessa. The battalion was subjected to severe shelling, in which the commanding officer received a serious arm wound. But it was mainly due to this officer's determination to close with the Germans and the excellent support provided by the battery commander, who was also wounded, that the battalion was able to establish itself on the hill. The weather then broke and in a few hours it was impossible to get any sort of vehicle forward to the battalion.

The next objective for the Gurkhas was Atessa, situated on a hill, rising sheer from the river and held by the *11th Battalion, 76th Panzer Grenadier Regiment.* The attack has been vividly described by Major Morland-Hughes, the officiating battalion commander, who some months later was killed in action. It is quoted below.

"D Company was committed to looking after vehicles, still bogged all over the place. I left a platoon to look after battalion headquarters, put A Company on a feature two thousand yards east of the town, which it dominated to form a base for operations and, immediately darkness fell, started to infiltrate towards the place with C Company and two platoons of B. We made a silent attack but took over gunner FOO with us. He was a grand chap, like all our gunners, and ready for any sort of a party.

"About half way along the ridge towards the town we dropped one platoon of B Company and told them to dig in. It was a good thing they did as they were heavily shelled later, but got no casualties. This platoon made a very useful half-way house later on for runners and mules sent up with much needed ammunition.

"We managed to creep quite close to the enemy's first position without being discovered. Then everything seemed to open up at once and we went straight in with the bayonet.

"By 2100 hours we had captured every post we could find east of the town and were digging in hard, knowing full well what was coming. It came about five minutes later. Our FOO tried to get the guns on to a bit of counter-battery but, as so often happens in a crisis all forms of communication failed. Wireless broke down, signaller wounded, lamp damaged and so on. We got a Bren Gun right forward and shot up the mortar flashes. It seemed to do some good but mostly, I think, it kept us amused.

"Then the first counter-attack came in. They asked for it and they got it. We had one platoon well down where it could fire across our front and it caught the attack in the flank. Our ammunition situation was getting serious, however, and I issued orders for the strictest fire control to be exercised. More mortar and shell fire came down and, as communications were still out of order, I asked the FOO to make his way with an escort of four chaps to A Company, where a telephone down to main battalion headquarters had been installed. It could not have been a pleasant journey for him. There were numerous parties of enemy about and any amount of stuff coming down on the ridge.

"The next counter-attack came in about midnight and was the most serious. It was apparently led by a German officer wearing an Iron Cross as we found his body less than fifty yards from our key position on the next morning. The Germans were covered by their quick-firing machine guns. The main weight fell on 15 Platoon of C Company, which was the key to our whole position. If it had succeeded, the best we could have done would have been to fight our way back down the ridge with C Company headquarters and 14 Platoon. I do not think we could have extracted 13 Platoon or the B Company platoon.

"The situation was saved by a surprise counter-charge put in by L/Naik Bhagtabahadur Thapa (later awarded the Indian Distinguished Service Medal), of 15 Platoon, and his section. Being almost out of ammunition, he let the enemy get to within twenty yards of his post and then drawing his kukri, fell on them. The enemy fled in disorder and Bhagtabahadur, having with some difficulty prevented his men from going after them, re-formed and captured one of the covering machine guns. This last feat was due almost entirely to the personal courage of a youngster who distinguished himself throughout the night. His name is Rifleman Okel Gurung (later awarded both the Indian Order of Merit and the Military Medal and killed in the final battle of the campaign).

"The failure of the big counter-attack together with the shelling of his gun positions which now began, seemed to break the enemy's heart. Shortly after we heard the noise of mechanical transport vehicles leaving the town. We were much cheered by the arrival of our own shells as we knew our FOO must have made his journey safely. I thought it typical of our gunners that he should come all the way back to us again 'just to see the party through to the end'; as he put it. Our patrols now began to push in close to the town and we entered it in daylight the next day at 0900 hours on 13 November 1943."

Capture of Archi

While the Germans were being pushed back to the Sangro, General Montgomery had made an outline plan for breaking through the river Sangro position and pushing on to secure the road from Pescara to Avezzano before the weather became worse and the Germans could reinforce the Winter Line. Of the three possible routes he preferred the coastal road to Pescara, as it afforded better opportunities for air and naval bombardment. He therefore decided to concentrate the 2nd New Zealand Division (under his direct command) in the area between Furci and Gissi in order to relieve the 8th Indian Division (less the 19th Indian Infantry Brigade), which was to sidestep to the right. Thus the V Corps was to be concentrated in the coastal sector for the main drive in the coastal area.

At 1000 hours on 14 November, the 2nd New Zealand Division assumed responsibility for its sector between the V Corps and the XIII Corps. On the right was the V Corps with the 78th Division extending its line from the coast to the area of M. Calvo and the 8th Indian Division, less the 19th Indian Infantry Brigade, in the area Scerni. On the left the 1st Canadian Division (XIII Corps) was pushing on towards Sant Angelo and Castel di Sangro on the Sangro. To cover the deployment and to conceal the arrival of the New Zealanders, the 19th Indian Infantry Brigade (which took over from the 17th Indian Infantry Brigade in area Atessa) was to be used as a screen in the advance to the Sangro.

The 19th Indian Infantry Brigade, with the 19th New Zealand Armoured Regiment, began its advance from Atessa on 15 November. 3/8 Punjab was on the right and 6/13 Royal Frontier Force Rifles on the left. The weather was again at its worst, delaying bridging operations over the torrent Osento at Atessa. Battalions were supplied entirely by mule and by jeeps where it was possible to move them. 3/8 Punjab advanced along the second class road north from Atessa for five miles to M. Marcone, and M. Torrello. There the battalions' line of advance was changed to the west towards the large village of Perano, where German troops were known to be in position. During the night of 16/17 November, 6/13 Royal Frontier Force Rifles on the south flank captured S. Marco, a small village on a narrow ridge, one mile and a half west of the road followed by 3/8 Punjab. The following afternoon, the Punjabis, supported by a squadron of the 19th New Zealand Armoured Regiment, attacked Perano. Artillery of the New Zealand Division, with whom all communications were by telephone, provided a barrage. Surprise achieved in the speed of the attack and in the unexpected direction of it ensured success. Three tanks were knocked out by German anti-tank guns concealed in the valley between the battalion and its objective but casualties were light. German infantry on the slopes below Perano withdrew towards the Sangro, leaving the Punjabis in possession of the village at nightfall.

One mile and a half to the south, Archi towered above Perano. The old-fashioned stone houses of Perano, huddling over its narrow white streets, on its pointed mound above the river valley, presented to the Germans at Archi a picture like that of a sand model. Mortar fire made Perano an uncomfortable spot. In their consolidation, the Punjabis advanced to a hill feature midway between Perano and Archi.

6/13 Royal Frontier Force Rifles meanwhile had a strenuous time. Marching from Carpinelo at 0600 hours on 15 November, the battalion moved through Atessa to reach S. Marco by 2300 hours on 16 November. A German rearguard was encountered there but was driven out with little difficulty north-west to Archi. The commanding officer at once ordered a follow up to the next ridge which was secured by 0300 hours on 17 November. A German counter-attack soon afterwards was beaten off. The track from this ridge to Archi had been blown in several places. The battalion's equipment was therefore carried entirely on mules. By now, the men were so tired and wet that a halt for the day was necessary.

However, all were not to rest. A patrol to Archi was out the whole of the following night (17/18 November), reconnoitring the ridge south of the village. There the patrol struck booby traps and trip flares and was compelled to withdraw. Before dawn on 18 November a carrier patrol was sent through 3/8 Punjab to the north side of Archi. The patrol met no opposition; so a company was sent forward to secure the village. Unfortunately, the company did not follow the route taken earlier by the carrier patrol. Instead, it went straight towards Archi by the line of the track. When within fifty yards of the village, on a steep bare slope the company came under small arms fire from the cemetry and from buildings in the village. Among the casualties inflicted by the fire was the company commander killed. The officer in charge of the carrier patrol thereupon moved across to assume command of the company, which throughout that day continued to hold the positions it had gained. After dark, a second company moved round the right, through 3/8 Punjab and dug in north of Archi, preparatory to an attack on the village. At first light next morning, 19 November, this company entered Archi without opposition.

Before leaving S. Marco, 6/13 Royal Frontier Force Rifles was relieved by two companies of the Essex in the village. The remainder of the Essex moved forward on 18 November to relieve 3/8 Punjab on the hill feature between Perano and Archi. When Archi had been captured, the Essex was able to send patrols to the Sangro on the same day. Confronted by a fast and swollen river, these patrols failed to cross. Heavy rain continued to fall and kept the river in its swollen state. Several postponements of the attempt to cross the river were necessary but opportunity was taken to build up reserves of supplies and ammunition in preparation for the crossing of the river. The stage was now set for the crossing of the Sangro, a formidable task in view of the strong German defences.

The 8th Indian Division had done so well. It had inflicted a clear defeat on the best German formation, over a country ideally suited for defence. The weather, which was entirely against movement, was severe for men accustomed to tropical climates. Yet they proved that they could live and fight in it as well as anybody. Before the division now was the line of elaborate defences on which the German Command intended to stand for the winter. It promised to be the toughest task yet undertaken by the 8th Indian Division.

CHAPTER III

The Battle of the Sangro

The Situation in mid-November

By mid-November 1943 the Eighth Army had closed up to the river Sangro. In the V Corps sector, the 78th Division had extended its line from the coast to Monte Calvo; the two brigades of the 8th Indian Division (the 17th and 21st) were concentrated in the area Scerni-Paglieta. The 19th Indian Infantry Brigade, screening the deployment of the 2nd New Zealand Division (under direct command of the Eighth Army) was in the Archi area. The XIII Corps, on the left, storming through the southern Apennines, had reached the headwaters of the Sangro at Castel di Sangro, thirty-three miles in a straight line north-west of Campobasso. The Canadian patrols were active in that area and at Agnone, where contact was established with the New Zealanders. Thus the Eighth Army had closed up to the Winter Line.

Meanwhile the Fifth Army too had moved up to the Winter Line, which consisted of two defensive lines—the 'Bernhardt Line' based on Monte Camino, Monte Maggiore and the hills on the north side of the Mignano defile (from above Venafro to above Isernia) and the 'Gustav Line' based on the high ground behind the Garigliano and Rapido, with the key fortress of Cassino. Forward of this Winter Line was a delaying line based on the ridge of mountains from Monte Massico on the sea coast, through Monte Santa Croce to the Matese mountains. The task of beating the German opposition on this delaying line was entrusted to the X Corps. The attack was launched on 28 October 1943, and by 4 November the Germans had been pushed back form their commanding positions on Monte Massico and Monte Santa Croce. Thus the X Corps reached the lower Garigliano. The Germans pulled back behind the river. In the north, the VI Corps threw the Germans back to the Bernhardt Line. From 5 to 12 November, the Fifth Army made a serious effort to capture the Monte Camino massif and Monte Lungo (in the mouth of the Mignano Gap) but the German line held firm. Thus the situation in mid-November was that while the Eighth Army had closed up to the Sangro the Fifth Army had moved up to the Garigliano but had failed to break into the Bernhardt Line.

General Alexander's Plan for Breaking the Winter Line

On 8 November 1943, General Alexander had finalised his plan for breaking through this formidable barrier. As the Fifth Army had been comparatively more exhausted by bitter fighting, he selected the Eighth Army to lead the attack. The operations were to be carried out in three phases. In the first phase, the Eighth Army was to cross the Sangro and Pescara rivers, secure the high ground north of Pescara and swing south-west along the great lateral road running across the peninsula from Pescara through Avezzano to Rome, and thus threaten the flank of the German forces defending Rome. In the second phase, the Fifth Army was to attack up the valleys of the Liri and Sacco to reach Frosinone. In the third phase, a seaborne and airborne operation was to be made south of Rome directed on the Alban Hills.

The Winter Line

The strongest defensive line of the Germans, at this time, ran from east to west across the waist of Italy, starting on the Adriatic coast at the mouth of the Sangro river and running south-west along the valley of the Sangro to the southern slopes of seven-thousand-feet high M. Groce. From here, the line followed the precipitous hills of the north side of the Volturno valley, cut across the Mignano gap south-east of Venafro to M. Camino, then ran down to the sea on the Tyrrhenian coast. Known as the Gustav Line, this already formidable natural obstacle had been turned into a very strongly fortified defensive system by the Germans. When they withdrew there was no question of their falling back on hastily prepared defences. Whilst German rearguards had been fighting the delaying actions of October and November, fresh formations had been moved down from northern Italy and, aided by conscripted Italian labour, had been hard at work with explosives, mines, concrete and wire.

In the Eighth Army sector, the Sangro river, fed by the innumerable water courses which drain the Maiella mountains, was as much as three hundred yards across in its lower reaches; though the wet channel was normally only about one hundred feet wide and eighteen inches deep. After heavy rain, however, the river became a torrent, filling the entire channel, and the depth was five feet or more. It was this malignant river, rising to flood and fury at various critical stages of the operation, which frustrated the original plan and magnified every difficulty in preparing and executing the assault.

South of the Sangro, the ground was flat for some three hundred yards; then rose rather abruptly to a ridge 600-800 feet in height, which ran more or less parallel to the river. On the north side, about eight hundred yards beyond the river bank, there was well-defined escarpment covered with stunted trees and broken by gullies. From the escarpment, the ground rose gradually for another

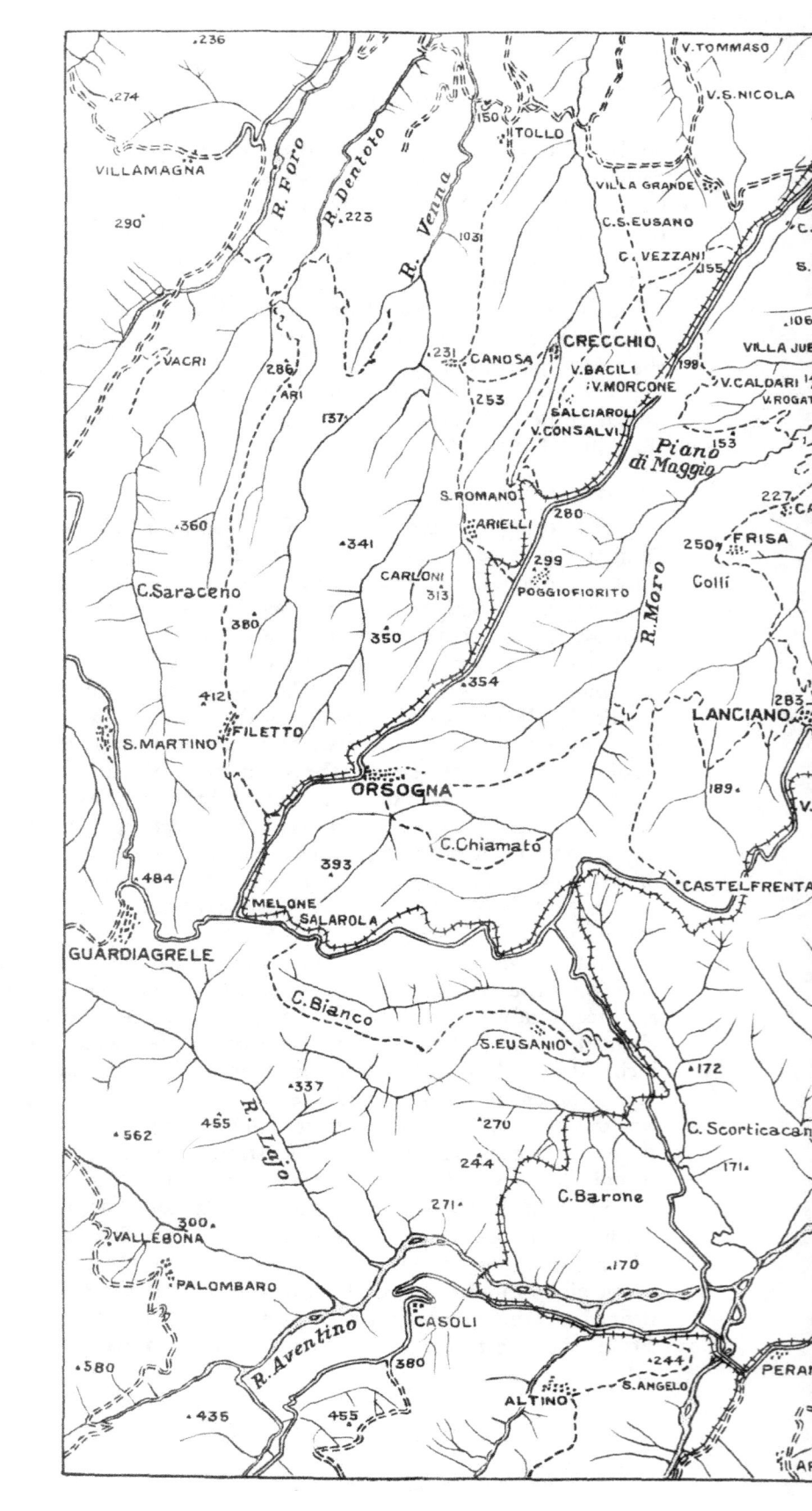

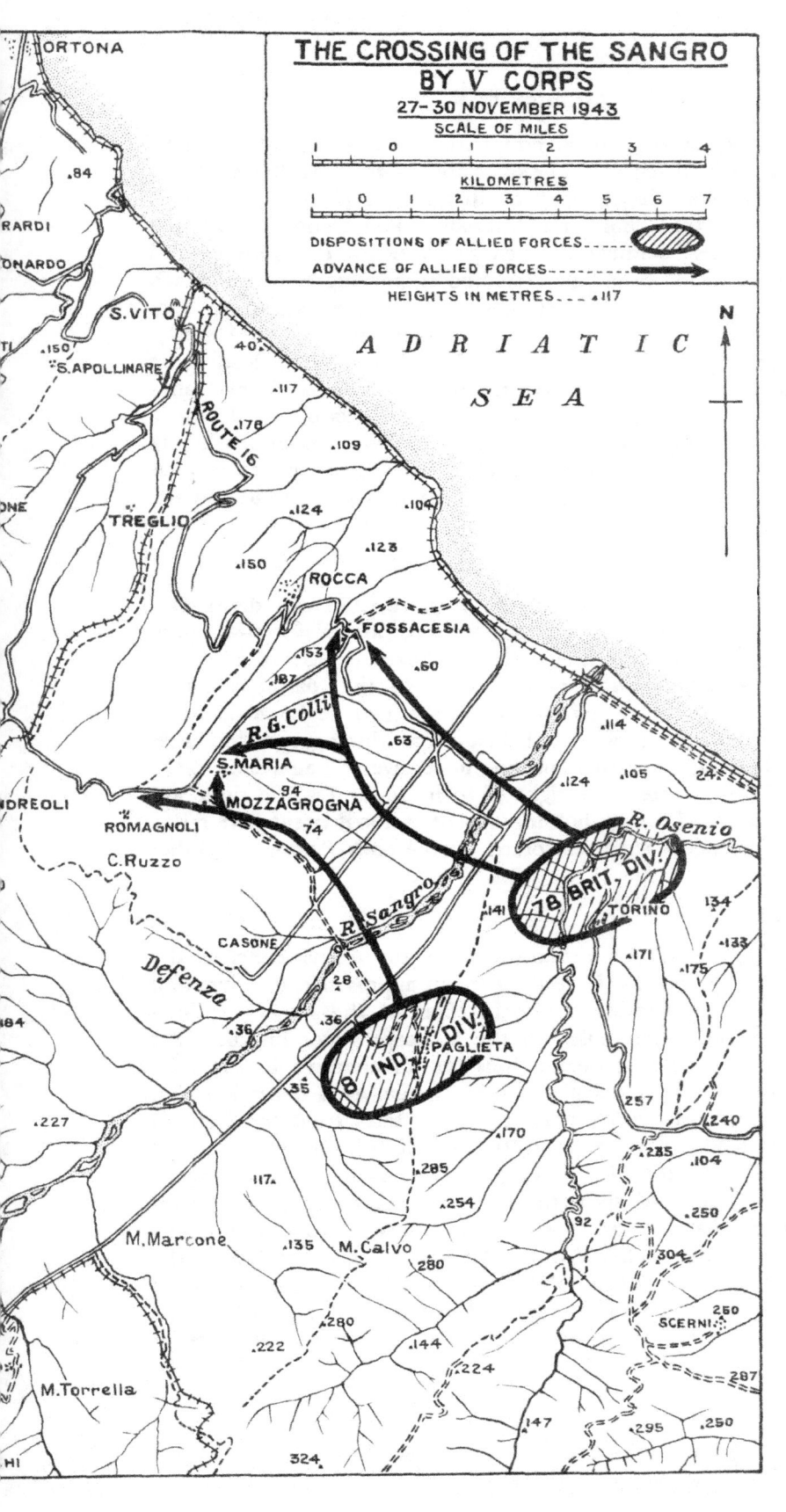

thousand yards, ending in a humpy ridge on which the Germans had built their defences. These positions—the left flank of the Gustav Line—were based on the villages of Fossacesia, S. Maria, Mozzagrogna, Romagnoli and Andreoli. The Germans had dug deep—sometimes as much as twenty feet below the ground—and built a series of machine gun nests and connecting trenches, which were proof against the heaviest shelling. The houses had all been converted into section posts and in the village streets were cleverly-cited machine gun posts. On the roads and road verges leading up to the defences from the river, thousands of anti-tank and anti-personnel mines had been laid to make the banks of the Sangro a veritable death trap for the hostile patrols. From positions in the villages, the Germans had excellent observation of the river valley, as well as of all the roads, which the Eighth Army might use on the southern approaches to the river.

The German Forces

The Sangro bridge-head was held by two German divisions—the *65th Infantry Division* and the *1st Parachute Division*—supported by the *16th Panzer Division* (later relieved by the *26th Panzer Division*). The *65th Infantry Division* held the coastal sector—a front of nearly twelve miles—with only two regiments. *145th Infantry Regiment*, on the coast, held as far as Mozzagrogna inclusive, with two battalions forward and one in reserve at Lanciano. *146th Infantry Regiment* held the right of their front. On the right was the *1st Parachute Division* holding a front of about twenty-five miles. Later the defenders were reinforced by the *90th Panzer Grenadier Division*.

Preparations

The Eighth Army's preparations for the offensive across the Sangro began as soon as the leading troops approached the river and consisted of concentrating the main effort of the Army within a narrow front of fifteen miles, in the V Corps sector on the right flank, whilst simulating preparations for an offensive in the XIII Corps sector, on the left flank. On 10 November, a deception plan was made to conceal three very important facts from the German High Command. They were: (*i*) that the 78th Division's front had been narrowed, (*ii*) that the 8th Indian Division—less the 19th Indian Infantry Brigade—had been relieved and concentrated in the Scerni area, and (*iii*) that the 2nd New Zealand Division had arrived in the line as part of the Eighth Army. To achieve these intentions, the following steps were taken: the 78th Division continued to patrol across the whole length of its original divisional front; the 8th Indian Division was given strict orders that no Indian troops were to expose themselves in the coastal sector. To conceal the presence of the 2nd New Zealand Division, the 19th Indian Infantry Brigade was put under command of Lt.-General Bernard Freyberg with the role of leading the advance of the New Zealanders to the Sangro. New gun areas along that part of the river chosen for the assault were occupied by night and carefully hidden from inquisitive German reconnaissance pilots. To build up the false picture in the XIII Corps sector, on the left flank of the Eighth Army, extensive patrolling was carried out in the Castel di Sangro—Alfedena—Roccaraso sector. Dummy guns were set up in the gun lines. False dumps were established. A duplicate Tactical Headquarters Army was organised with pseudo wireless communications. The most important features of the faked wireless picture were the timings given to lead the Germans to deduce that the attack was not due to be launched until two days after the time for which it had actually been planned.

The original plan of the V Corps, which had to be modified later, for the assault on the Gustav Line consisted of three phases. The first phase was the establishment of a bridge-head across the Sangro in the right, coastal sector by the 78th Division. In the second phase the 8th Indian Division was to break into the main German defensive positions and, in the third, fresh troops of the 78th Division were to exploit through the 8th Indian Division to the Pescara line, nearly twenty-five miles north. Simultaneously, the 2nd New Zealand Division was to strike across the river having as its objective Chieti, then swing south-west down Route 5 to threaten the lines of communication of the German Army in the Avezzano area.

Between the dates 9 to 15 November, active patrolling was carried out by the 78th Division, and its patrols completely dominated the area west of the river between the Sangro and the escarpment. However, on 15 November, heavy rain fell and the river became impassable. The Germans took advantage of this to sow extra minefields west of the river and to strengthen their defences. On more than one occasion, some of the British infantry attempting to cross the river were swept away and drowned. During the active patrolling phase, it had been established from prisoners of war and deserters that, as had been earlier suspected, it was the *65th Infantry Division* which was holding the Sangro Line opposite the V Corps. This division had been there about a month and consisted of only two infantry regiments instead of the normal three; it had not been in action before. The German plan of defence appeared to be to hold the high ground with their main force, whilst maintaining a strong outpost line along the escarpment.

However by this time, the weather had taken a definite turn

for the worse and remained consistently bad for some days. Allied with the Germans was the bitter cold, the stinging rain and a slimy, thick coating of mud on the roads and tracks, which bogged down the heavier vehicles and sent some of the lighter ones careering in long, uncontrollable skids across the tracks to and up in a ditch. In the gun lines, 25-pounders had to be winched and manhandled into position by their muddy, rain-soaked crews, whilst the infantry lived under conditions just as bad as those of the last war. It was in this setting that, on 19 November, Headquarters 8th Indian Division moved by night to Paglieta along a road crammed with the marching troops, mules and vehicles of the 17th and the 21st Indian Infantry Brigades. The division, less the 19th Indian Infantry Brigade, was concentrated in the Paglieta area with its headquarters established in a large farm-house, originally the local Fascist Headquarters.

78th Brigade's Bridge-head

At 0415 hours on 20 November, troops of the 78th Division attacked across the swollen waters of the Sangro and, by first light, succeeded in establishing a bridge-head. Rain poured down the whole day and the following night. Attempts to put bridges across the river failed, chiefly because the approaches to the river were, by that time, in such a chaotic state—nothing better than a sea of mud—that vehicles were unable to get down to the bridging sites with stores for the engineers. The weather had broken completely. Two important developments then became apparent. With the river whipped into such a treacherous condition, bridges would have to be erected before the 8th Indian Division could cross and move forward to the attack; therefore, the attack by the Indian division must be postponed. This meant that the brigade of the 78th Division which had crossed and had established the bridge-head would be isolated for a much longer period than was intended and would have to be reinforced if the bridge-head was to be maintained. The commander of the British division decided that two brigades were necessary to hold the ground on the west bank, and, during the night of 21/22 November, another infantry brigade and the 2nd Battalion Kings Royal Rifle Corps of the 4th Armoured Brigade crossed the Sangro. The river had risen, with the current reaching five knots, but the second brigade managed to get across and, after a stiff fight all the next day, was firmly on its objective by nightfall.

Sappers worked all night on a big bridging programme. The 8th Indian Division was given the task of building a hundred-foot bridge, one thousand yards upstream of the main road. The 7th Indian Field Company carried out this job. At the same time, the

Indian soldiers examine one of the many MK. IV German tanks knocked out near Mozzagrogna

Lieut.-General Sir Charles Allfrey
(Commander V Corps)

Major-General Sir Francis Tuker
(Commander 4th Indian Division,
January 1942—February 1944)

engineers of the 78th Division built a bridge, between the main road and the sea, whilst the V Corps sappers started work on a third bridge, five hundred yards downstream the Paglieta bridge, which had been destroyed. The 8th Indian Division finished off its bridge in the first hour of daylight under cover of a smoke screen laid by the gunners and, at 0730 hours, the bridge was ready to take tanks.[1] The Indian sappers were justly proud of their achievement. Mines sown on both banks of the river and a soft, boggy approach were two of the difficulties with which they had to contend. An immense quantity of material, ranging from army track to faggots and railway sleepers, was put down and sucked up greedily by the deep mud on the approaches to the bridge. In places, the mud seemed to have no firm bottom whatsoever and tons of material had to be used before there was a hard surface.

With the rise of the river, further fording was almost impossible, but on 22 November some tanks of the 3rd City of London Yeomanry found a shallow crossing and moved across singly to lie up under the escarpment. During that night, the first two anti-tank guns crossed the Sangro. The infantry in the bridge-head heaved a sigh of relief that at last they had something to counter the German tank attack if it came.

By 23 November, there was every reason for the Germans to brace themselves for a heavy blow. It was a fine day at last and there were at least six British battalions across the river. German outposts on the approaches of Mozzagrogna had been driven in and considerable casualties had been inflicted. Tanks and anti-tank guns were west of the river. Fighter-bombers gave the Germans their first experience of concentrated air attacks with more than two hundred sorties. Men of the 8th Indian Division on the Paglieta ridge had a grand view of the bombing. They watched the flights of "planes go over", the anti-aircraft fire shoot up to meet them, and the tongues of flame leap from the target areas. Clouds of dust drifted lazily into the sky and mixed with smoke from fires started by the bombing. Bad weather, however, hampered operations and it was not till 27 November that the 8th Indian Division led the main attack on the German defences. While the 8th Indian Division carried out preparations for the main assault the battle had opened elsewhere. The 19th Indian Infantry Brigade (under the command of the 2nd New Zealand Division) established a bridgehead at Il Calvario, eight miles inland from Mozzargrogna. We shall, therefore, at first, describe the operations of the 19th Indian Infantry Brigade and the 2nd New Zealand Division's thrust towards Castelfrentano.

---

[1] War Diary No. 7 Field Company, Sappers & Miners.

The 19th Indian Infantry Brigade's Bridge-head

By 19 November, the 19th Indian Infantry Brigade, screening the advance of the 2nd New Zealand Division, had closed up to the Sangro by driving out the Germans from their stronghold at Archi and patrolling down to the river bank. General Freyberg's plan was to cross the river Sangro in the three mile sector immediately below its confluence with the torrent Aventino, with the 6th New Zealand Infantry Brigade, having the 19th New Zealand Armoured Regiment under command. This reach of the river was, however, completely overlooked and dominated by the hills between the rivers Sangro and Aventino above the confluence. It was therefore essential that the left flank should be secured and neutralised. Hence the 19th Indian Infantry Brigade was assigned the role of capturing S. Angelo, Il Calvario and Altino on this high ground between the rivers.

Brigadier Dobree issued instructions for clearing the Germans from the Altino ridge, as a preliminary to the attack by the 6th New Zealand Infantry Brigade. In the first phase, 3/8 Punjab, attacking silently and crossing the river Sangro at 0300 hours on 23 November, was to capture Il Calvario. The actual crossing place was in a straight line between Archi and Il Calvario. 3/8 Punjab was to exploit to Altino. In the second phase, 1/5 Essex, supported by the New Zealand Division Artillery and the 3rd Field Regiment, was to cross the Sangro at 0500 hours, two hours after 3/8 Punjab, a quarter of a mile south-west of the Perano bridge over the Sangro and two miles due west of Perano.[2] Objective for 1/5 Essex was S. Angelo. The valley of the Aventino was the responsibility of the 6th New Zealand Brigade, north of the 19th Indian Infantry Brigade. 6/13 Royal Frontier Force Rifles was to remain in reserve in the Archi area with the task of protecting the left flank of the brigade, south of Archi. A small brigade headquarters was to be established on the roadside half way between Perano and Archi, while the main headquarters stayed in the northern outskirts of Perano.[3]

According to this plan, Phase I began at 0300 hours on 23 November, with C Company of 3/8 Punjab leading the attack west of the river which was in spate. It was a silent advance with the wooded hill feature of Il Calvario as its objective. C Company reached the far bank without incident and was followed by the rest of the battalion. The men clambered out of the river, wet and shivering with cold, and began to climb to their objective. A bridge-head, which later proved of great value, was established on a thickly wooded mound on the northern bank of the river.

---

[2] 19 Ind. Inf. Bde. O.O. No. 9, dated 21 November 1943.
[3] Ibid.

Only a hundred yards short of the objective, cross fire from German machine guns and tanks whistled around the men of the leading platoons. But the machine gun positions had been spotted; a Naik[4] and six men wormed their way towards the German gunners. When they had crawled to within a few yards of the unsuspecting Germans, the Naik told his Bren gunner to cover one team of German gunners and led his remaining men in a fierce charge on the second gun. The Germans decided that discretion was the better part of valour and one gun team surrendered, whilst the other abandoned its post and fled. As the Naik proudly collected his captives, the other companies pressed home the attack. The tanks were dealt with by the New Zealand gunners in support of the attack; they sent some well placed shells crashing around the tanks, which withdrew.

Meanwhile, 1/5 Essex had also crossed the river and by 0630 hours, when it was established on the far bank of the river, it launched an attack on S. Angelo, a village one mile north-east of the objective of 3/8 Punjab. The assault was on a three-company front with two groups of houses to the right and north-east of the village and the village itself as the objectives. The leading sections encountered steep cliffs and were able to find only one path running up the spur towards S. Angelo. All the companies, one behind the other, advanced up this axis and eventually were in a position to put in their attack. Unfortunately, they had fallen behind the artillery programme.

They were met by a withering hail of fire from German machine guns. One company—although most of the men of one platoon had been killed or wounded during the hazardous approach up the spur —reached the outskirts of the village. They fought fiercely for a group of houses and, having gained them, prepared for the German counter-attack. The Germans threw in a counter-attack, but as they advanced, a Bren gunner, who held one of the houses single-handed, opened up on them from a window, killing two of the Germans and wounding others. The rest then fled.

At first light, both 1/5 Essex, clinging grimly to the outskirts of S. Angelo, and 3/8 Punjab on the left at Il Calvario were in a perilous position. Throughout the day, the two battalions were exposed to murderous machine gun, artillery and mortar fire from both flanks. The Punjab unit was particularly exposed to it as owing to the ground being rocky only one company had been able to dig in. The other companies lay out in the open and received a merciless battering. To make matters worse, during the night the river had risen to four feet and it was impossible to get tanks or anti-tank guns across to support the hard-pressed battalions. Even mules were

[4] A non-commissioned officer.

swept off their feet and carried down the river with their precious loads of ammunition and medical supplies. The crossing places were under heavy fire and the only stores which did reach the forward troops were carried on the backs of Indian carrier parties, who struggled back and forth across the Sangro and earned the undying gratitude of their comrades. Repeated attempts were made to carry the wounded back across the river, but when several had been drowned, it was given up as a bad job.

During the day (23 November 1943), cut off and on the German side of a fast flowing river, the two battalions were heavily counter-attacked. It was quite obvious from the fury of the attacks that the Germans realised the importance of pushing the British and Indian infantry back across the river. They loosened the grip of the right forward company of the Essex on the group of houses north-east of S. Angelo and forced it to retire. On the left, 3/8 Punjab met and smashed no fewer than three counter-attacks. One company had three commanders wounded one after the other during the day. Finally, Jemadar Sumere Ram took over the command of the twelve remaining weary men of the company and reorganised them. In the late afternoon, he and his men repulsed the fourth German counter-attack. The position of the battalion was so precarious that towards evening, the commanding officer of 3/8 Punjab was ordered to withdraw to his initial bridge-head and to contact the Essex on his right. Having issued his orders for the withdrawal, he went off to confer with the Essex, whom he believed to be in S. Angelo, and was taken prisoner.

With the reserve company of 3/8 Punjab on the initial bridge-head, the forward companies began their withdrawal from the Il Calvario feature covered by C Company. The other companies had all their commanders either killed or wounded and the withdrawal was carried out by junior Viceroy's Commissioned Officers. In the darkness and the confusion many men lost their way and only a small force arrived at the rendezvous. The Adjutant then assumed command of the battalion and reorganised the remaining men. A doctor crossed the river to tend the wounded, who had waited so patiently on the river banks throughout the day. Supplies were forded over to the battalion. In the morning on 24 November, the picture became brighter when most of the men, who had lost themselves during the withdrawal, turned up.

Captain Girdhari Singh was convinced that the Germans had taken a beating the day before and would not return to Il Calvario or counter-attack again. He asked permission from brigade headquarters to reoccupy Calvario and having received permission, climbed the hill again that morning with thirty-five men, passing the bodies of their comrades who had fallen the day before. The

Germans had had enough. The 3/8 Punjab then established itself firmly on Il Calvario and on 25 November occupied the village of Altino also, which was one mile to the west, and had been evacuated by the Germans.

The Essex, at the same time, worked its way forward through the outskirts of S. Angelo, where it had seen such fierce fighting and, by 1030 hours on 24 November, into the village itself, from which the Germans had gone.

It had been a particularly fierce engagement for the two infantry battalions of the 19th Indian Infantry Brigade, but their dogged resistance in breaking up the German counter-attacks had been rewarded by the withdrawal of the badly mauled German force and the establishment of a bridge-head across the Sangro for the 2nd New Zealand Division.

2nd New Zealand Division's Thrust towards Castelfrentano

By 27 November the Eighth Army stood poised for the main assault on the German defences. The 17th Indian Infantry Brigade of the 8th Indian Division began its attack at 2130 hours on 27 November; the 2nd New Zealand Division attacked a little later. To make the story complete we shall first describe the operations of the 2nd New Zealand Division. The plan was for two brigades of the 2nd New Zealand Division (the 5th and 6th) to attack northwards over the Sangro towards Castelfrentano, whilst the 19th Indian Infantry Brigade on the left flank provided a diversion at the bridge over the river Aventino, a thousand yards from its junction with the Sangro. The attack by the 2nd New Zealand Division was successful and by 2 December it had secured Castelfrentano three miles south-west of Lanciano. A deep penetration had been made into the German main position and the way was prepared for an advance towards the formidable position on the heights of the Orsogna—Guardiagrele ridge.

The role of the 19th Indian Infantry Brigade was to provide left flank protection of the 2nd New Zealand Division. In the early hours of 28 November, while the 2nd New Zealand Division attacked northwards over the Sangro, 1/5 Essex with mortars and light machine guns provided a diversion at the bridge over the torrent Aventino, a thousand yards from its junction with the Sangro, and 3/8 Punjab patrolled towards Casoli and Reccascalegna. During the afternoon of 29 November, the 2nd New Zealand Division secured its western flank north of the Sangro by capturing C. Barone. The 19th Indian Infantry Brigade, less 1/5 Essex, was thereupon permitted to move back and concentrate 3/8 Punjab at Atessa and 6/13 Royal Frontier Force Rifles at S. Marco. 1/5 Essex patrolled to Casoli during the night of 29/30 November and reported that the town had been evacuated by the Germans, and then it concentrated at Atessa on 30 November. Having accomplished its task of establishing a bridge-head and providing left flank protection for the 2nd New Zealand Division the 19th Indian Infantry Brigade rejoined the 8th Indian Division.

The 8th Indian Division's Bridge-head

The story now reverts to the operations of the 8th Indian Division. In the coastal sector, the weather had played a trump card for the Germans. After 22 November it had rained unceasingly in the mountains to the south-west and on 23 November the river was in flood. By the evening the centre bridge was washed away and, by nightfall, no bridge could be used. The engineers had to divert their resources from the bridges to the approaches and even so were unable to work on the immediate approaches to the bridges, since the broad bed of the river, across which tracks were made to the bridges themselves, was now almost entirely covered by water. However, during the night of 22/23 November, the bridge-head on the far side of the deep and fast flowing river had been further enlarged by the 36th Brigade of the 78th Division. Three battalions held the line of the road, one mile west of the Sangro between Route 16 and the road from the Sangro to Mozzagrogna, 2nd King's Royal Rifles Corps of the 4th Armoured Brigade occupied the area of C. Casone. Here the troops were in a critical position. They were severely handicapped by the lack of supporting weapons and, when daylight came, it was impossible to give them any air support as the aircraft were bogged down on the landing grounds. They badly needed ammunition for their few tanks, anti-tank guns and machine guns.

A decision was made to ferry the much needed ammunition and supplies by sea to the beach, south of Fossacesia station. Ammunition was transported by road from the Vasto area to the beach south of the Sangro, where two Dukw companies were harbouring. The Dukws worked unceasingly for the next forty-eight hours and ferried across some two thousand tons of ammunition. A heavy swell was running most of the time, which unfortunately sank one Dukw at sea with a load of ammunition for the machine gunners but the crew was saved and sufficient ammunition was shipped to the bridge-head to keep the machine guns firing. It was a remarkable achievement on the part of the Dukw crews, who worked unceasingly and without sleep.

On 23 November 1943, V Corps Operation Order No. 4 was published with a new plan. The pace of the build-up having been considerably slowed down by the weather, a course involving less exploitation was substituted. The 8th Indian Division was to capture Mozzagrogna, San Maria and the Colli feature in that order. The

78th Division was still to roll up the line to the sea, but was given the more limited objective of exploiting to the R. Moro whilst the 8th Indian Division established a firm hold in the Lanciano area, some five miles north of the Sangro. General Montgomery had, however, again been compelled to modify his plan in order to make it independent of tanks and of weather. He instructed the V Corps to reorganise the bridge-head on a two-divisional basis, bringing the 8th Indian Division up on the left of the 78th Division, and to plan the capture of the Sangro ridge by a series of very limited operations each supported by the whole Corps artillery. The plan was to launch the attack before dawn on 26 November to capture the German localities half-way up the ridge towards San Maria. Two days later a further attack was to be delivered against San Maria and Mozzagrogna and, subsequently, the 78th Division was to operate from S. Maria in a north-easterly direction towards Fossacesia in order to clear the ridge.[5]

On 24 November, another Corps Operation Order was issued changing the method of operation once again. An attack in four phases was ordered with target dates for each phase. In the first phase, one battalion of the 8th Indian Division was to capture the spur one thousand yards south-east of Mozzagrogna on 26 November. In the second phase, one brigade, less one battalion, of the 8th Indian Division was to take Mozzagrogna and San Maria on 28 November. In the third phase, one brigade of the 78th Division was to capture the Colli feature on 29 or 30 November. In the fourth phase, the same brigade of the 78th Division was to capture Fossacesia as soon as possible after the third phase. The task for the 78th Division was to exploit to the R. Moro on the coast-road axis.

Between the publication of these Operation Orders and during the night of 23/24 November, the river began to subside. It was heart-breaking for the engineers when they were able to examine their bridges and wire ferries. The right-hand bridge had been damaged by the flood water and all the wire ferries had been swept away by the furious pace of the river. The two upstream bridges were intact but their approaches were still flooded to a depth of two feet.

When daylight came, the airfields began to dry and the 78th Division, in the bridge-head, and the 8th Indian Division, on the east bank, having waited in the rain and mud patiently for the order to move, had the satisfaction of seeing the first planes wing down on the German positions just after 1100 hours. That night, 24/25 November, the first unit of the 8th Indian Division crossed the river. Patrols from the 17th Indian Infantry Brigade had been out towards Mozzagrogna during the previous two nights. Men of the 3rd

[5] Montgomery: *El Alamein to the River Sangro*, p. 120.

Battalion 15th Punjab Regiment relieved 2nd Battalion Lancashire Fusiliers of the 78th Division in the gully below Mozzagrogna. The next day was fairly quiet for the troops in the bridge-head but the Germans were pounded from the air by the fighter-bombers and medium bombers of the Royal Air Force. After dusk, one company of the 1st Battalion 12th Frontier Force Regiment crossed the river to reinforce 3/15 Punjab, who had advanced their position to the top of the escarpment, south of the Mozzagrogna road, and a company of the 1st Battalion 5th Mahratta Light Infantry strengthened the battalion of the King's Royal Rifles Corps of the 4th Armoured Brigade, which was still in position around C. Casone to the left of 3/15 Punjab. The 21st Indian Infantry Brigade held from the ravine to C. Casone, the western flank of the 78th Division's bridge-head. Phase 1 of the Corps plan had been carried out successfully when the spur, one thousand yards south-east of Mozzagrogna, was taken by 1/12 Frontier Force Regiment during the night of 25/26 November.

Next night more men of the 17th and the 21st Indian Infantry Brigades crossed the river, together with mules carrying their equipment and supplies, and 1/12 Frontier Force Regiment relieved 3/15 Punjab astride the road. In the ten hours of darkness vehicles, guns, tanks and carriers of both the divisions rumbled across the bridges. Next day it was decided to disregard secrecy and to get the tanks across in daylight. The Germans shelled the bridges fiercely but could not stem the flow of vehicles and tanks, although the shelling of the centre, 'Harry' bridge, was becoming very accurate. That bridge was frequently hidden by the smoke and dust of exploding salvoes. During a lull in the firing just after a tank had crossed and waddled up the far bank, the bridge sagged in the middle and subsided gracefully into the river. However, more than a hundred tanks, anti-tank guns and other supporting arms had by this time crossed the river.

Meanwhile the Royal Air Force had battered the Germans, who were packing everything they had into the line. A company of *1/145 Regiment* was moved forward to reinforce *11/145 Regiment* in Mozzagrogna on 20 November and, four days later, *10 Company of 146th Regiment* was also moved into the village. A small battle group of tanks and flame-throwers of the *26th Panzer Division* was observed moving to Lanciano to give punch to the counter-attacking force. The nebelwerfers under command of the *65th Infantry Division* were being used with considerable effect on the Allied forward troops. One company of the Bengal Sappers of the 8th Indian Division (the 66th Company) lived in a brick factory in full view of the Germans and within a few hundred yards of the river. From the factory, working parties went out each morning to carry on the vital work of bridging, mine-lifting and road construction. A nebelwerfer Observation Post officer, captured later, told his interrogators how he had daily observed the activities of the Indian sappers. Fortunately, they were beyond the range of his mortars and the German artillery had been so starved of ammunition that continuous and full-scale fire had been impossible.

After dark on 27 November, the 5th Battalion Royal West Kent Regiment relieved 1/12 Frontier Force Regiment astride the nullah junction and 1/5 Mahratta Light Infantry relieved 2nd King's Royal Rifle Corps at C. Casone, with patrols on La Defenza ridge.

With the 17th and the 21st Indian Infantry Brigades concentrated in front of Mozzagrogna, the congestion was acute. Wide dispersion was impossible, owing to the rain sodden nature of the ground and the extensive German minefields. Vehicles were mainly parked on the edge of the road, nose to tail, or, in the case of the 17th Indian Infantry Brigade, had to be crammed into a small valley. The standing patrol of Spitfires circling overhead prevented anything more serious than tip and run raids on a small scale, although one attack on the 21st Indian Infantry Brigade Headquarters caused casualties and damage.

The First Attack on Mozzagrogna

The eventual plan for attack was that the 17th Indian Infantry Brigade would capture Mozzagrogna and S. Maria, one thousand yards to the north.[6] The 21st Indian Infantry Brigade was then to advance on the left of the former to seize Romagnoli and the high ground about Andreoli. Later, the 21st Indian Infantry Brigade was to push on the Lanciano whilst a brigade of the 78th Division on the right would take the Colli feature in preparation for the advance of the remainder of the British division and the 4th Armoured Brigade towards Pescara.

The 6th Lancers, with one anti-tank battery and 5th Royal Mahratta (less two companies) were to protect the left flank of the 8th Indian Division and to maintain contact with the 2nd New Zealand Division. The 8th Indian Division artillery (less the 3rd Field Regiment) 111th Field Regiment, 166th Field Regiment and Corps artillery were to support the attacks with a series of timed concentrations (eight Field Regiments and thirty-two medium guns). The maintenance of the division depended on a plan for building up and maintaining three days reserves of rations and ammunition north of the Sangro and upon transporting by mules the maximum supplies across the river on the first day.

It was raining when at 2130 hours on 27 November, the 1st Battalion 5th Royal Gurkha Rifles, advanced on Mozzagrogna from

[6] 8 Ind. Div. O.O. No. 8, dated 24 November 1943.

the south-east. Shells from the Field Regiments of the 8th Indian Division crashed down on the German defences. The German troops withdrew into their subterranean refuges and when the barrage had passed over, came out to rake the forward slopes with machine gun fire as the Gurkhas slithered and slipped in their scramble up to the German positions. At about midnight two companies of 1/5 Royal Gurkha Rifles pierced the German defence line and broke into the village, but the Germans fought back fiercely from well-sited positions and the battle developed into a hand-to-hand fighting. Each house was a German strong-point. No sooner had the Gurkhas stormed one house than they found that the Germans had escaped through a hole in the wall and had turned the house next door into another strong-point. The village became a bedlam of exploding mines, clattering machine guns and the war cries of the Gurkhas. At the head of every alley, machine guns were sited; every corner hid some surprise; but the Gurkhas fought on until the leading troops of A Company reached the far end of the village.

All houses, except a large one at the south-west corner of the village—a building with an Oriental looking rooftop—appeared to be held by the Germans. This lone house was taken over by the battalion headquarters of the Gurkhas and it was difficult to understand why the Germans had not made use of it in their defence plan. It commanded a wonderful view of the valley but, on the other hand, it presented an obvious and easy target for the artillery. After the Gurkhas had entered the house, fighting around it became continuous. Later, when the village had been cleared, fifteen Germans dead, killed either by bayonet or kukri, were found near this house.

Meanwhile, the 1st Battalion Royal Fusiliers was in position, its companies strung out along the road leading from the river to the village. They were waiting for the order to move forward and attack S. Maria and had planned to move through the Gurkhas towards the north edge of Mozzagrogna, before turning north-east along the ridge to secure S. Maria. They were having a most unpleasant time. Both the road and the verges were heavily mined and the German shell fire caused panic among the mules with the Fusiliers. The animals were very difficult to control and their weight, as they moved about, detonated box mines, which had been liberally sown just below the road metalling. The British battalion had numerous casualties. In one case, an extensive German minefield had been laid across the road about half-way up the ridge. At that point, there was a giant crater and the area of the crater was heavily mortared by the Germans. Some men of the Fusiliers, diving into the ditches to avoid the mortaring, were blown up on anti-personnel mines strewn in the ditches. In many cases, it was impossible to move the bodies of men and mules from the road on to the verges for fear of setting off more mines.

The Fusiliers waited under heavy shell fire until the brigade commander decided that, as the village had not been taken, it was impossible for them to move up to their start line for the attack on S. Maria. Since the Gurkhas were having a tough time in Mozzagrogna two companies of the Fusiliers were ordered to enter the village and help them. As they arrived they surprised the crew of a German mortar crawling along a wall to man their weapon.

The headquarters of the Gurkha battalion moved into the church in the main square with a few men of the Fusiliers, who stood guard at the door with sticky bombs in case German tanks attempted to break in. Wounded, carried into the church, were tended by the medical officer. A party of the Royal Fusiliers was besieged in a group of buildings on the opposite side of the square by German tanks and snipers. Grim struggle continued from house to house and from cellar to cellar. Soon the lower half of the village was occupied by the Gurkhas. Yet despite the valiant efforts of the Indian engineers to bridge the giant crater on the road and to clear the mines so that the tanks and supporting arms might get into Mozzagrogna, as dawn approached much still remained to be done before tanks could pass. Whilst the battle had been raging through the night, the bulldozer crew had been fighting against time to clear the roads and the chug-chug of their engines from time to time rose above the battle of machine gun fire and the crack of bursting grenades from the village. The 13th Mule Company of the RIASC did a fine job of work getting supporting arms and ammunition through to the forward troops.

On 28 November, at 0815 hours, the brigade commander ordered the two battered battalions to withdraw from the village to positions east of Mozzagrogna. Casualties had been heavy and communications amounted to little more than runners. Some of the troops received the order to withdraw and others did not. In the confusion, the Fusiliers and the Gurkhas argued as to who should be the last to leave the village. Eventually, the Fusiliers covered the withdrawal of the Gurkhas, but many Gurkhas stayed on and played a grim game of hide and seek with the Germans. Fighting continued in Mozzagrogna until the afternoon when the last Gurkhas, a hundred strong, returned to the lines, bringing their wounded with them.

The Gurkhas and the Fusiliers had been withdrawn one thousand yards east of their objective to the area of the spur (C376008) to rest and reorganise; 1/12 Frontier Force Regiment moved out of reserve and, advancing under cover of a barrage, secured a position on the spur above the two battalions at 1145 hours.

The Second Attack on Mozzagrogna

On 28 November, Major-General Russell ordered the 17th Indian Infantry Brigade to renew the attack on Mozzagrogna that night, and to clear the cratered road south of the village so that tanks of the 50th Battalion Royal Tank Regiment could enter Mozzagrogna in support of the infantry the following morning. The 21st Indian Infantry Brigade was given a task for 29 November, to demonstrate north-west from the road junction (375973) near Casone, on the northern lateral road through the Sangro valley.

On the right of the 8th Indian Division, the 78th Division was ordered to attack the R. Li Colli feature frontally on the morning of 29 November and afterwards to seize S. Maria. The 4th Armoured Brigade, less the 50th Battalion Royal Tank Regiment, was then to attack towards Fossacesia, astride the road S. Maria—Fossacesia, and to mop up east of the town towards the coast.

At 2100 hours on 28 November, 1/12 Frontier Force Regiment, supported by all the Corps artillery moved forward for the second attack on Mozzagrogna. The 1st Battalion Royal Fusiliers was given the responsibility of covering the Indian sappers at work on the crater south of the village. 1/12 Frontier Force Regiment entered the battered village and after clearing the Germans out of a large white house, set about clearing the village. The Germans had evidently had enough the night before, but their resistance was most determined, calling for action house by house—soon Mozzagrogna was a ruin. There was hardly a building left standing and the wrecked church in the square showed black scars where tongues of flame from the flame-throwing tanks had licked the walls. Houses, which had escaped the bombing and shelling, bore the mark of small arms fire and grenade splinters. The bodies of the Gurkhas, the Fusiliers and the Germans lay in the street and alleyways, where they had fallen in the bitter fighting of the night before. Occasionally, a shattering roar shook the village as a booby trap or mine exploded. Below Mozzagrogna, the Indian Sappers worked frantically all night, under intense mortar and shell fire, to clear the cratered road which had proved such an obstacle to the success of the first attack. They lifted hundreds of mines and with bull-dozers filled in the craters. In the village, a platoon of the Dogras was fired on from a house. The Dogras charged the house, broke into it and twenty-one Germans, led by an officer, surrendered without firing another shot. Then the infantry heard the roar of tank-engines above the chugging of the bull-dozers. The engineers had won through, and tanks and supporting arms moved into Mozzagrogna, but not before four of the tanks had been blown up on mines.

It was just getting light as one of the tanks rumbled through the village to the far side. The tank commander had been given the exact location of three German tanks, which had opened fire the night before on a party of the Indian infantry protecting the Sappers at work. Sure enough, the three tanks were there, facing the wrong way. It seemed almost too good to be true; without hesitation the elated gunner despatched the three tanks in almost as many seconds. In all, one hundred prisoners were captured from the *65th Infantry Division.*

The German defence of Mozzagrogna had collapsed. During the morning of 29 November, as the tired but triumphant infantry of the 17th Indian Infantry Brigade was clearing up the battered village, they received a special message of congratulations from General Montgomery. Headquarters of the brigade was established on a stretch of road below Mozzagrogna, the forward positions of the brigade being some three hundred yards west of the village.

To the Gurkhas was given the opportunity of reoccupying the ground they had vacated the day before. Positions, once taken, were held despite German counter-attacks and brisk shelling. Three Gurkhas, who had been taken prisoner on the night of the first attack, killed their guard and rejoined the battalion. A Subedar, who had remained in the village after the withdrawal, told how he and his men had driven off attack after attack made by the German flame-throwers. Finally, their ammunition exhausted, they had sallied forth with kukri and bayonet and put the Germans to flight.

During the day the Mozzagrogna area was frequently shelled by German artillery and mortars but the Germans could not break the brigade's hold on the village. In the 21st Indian Infantry Brigade, 1st Battalion 5th Mahratta Light Infantry patrolled well forward of the left flank of the 17th Indian Brigade but had nothing to report.

North of the 8th Indian Division, the 78th Division attacked the Colli feature frontally, according to plan, on the morning of 29 November and by nightfall had cleared the ridge. The next problem was how to get forward the tanks of the 4th Armoured Brigade so that on the morning of 30 November the tanks and the 78th Division could clear S. Maria and the ridge between Colli and Fossacesia. The only solution was for the 8th Indian Division to attack and secure the road junction, north-west of Mozzagrogna, where the road branched off to S. Maria. Between the junction and S. Maria the road had to be cleared of the Germans, still holding out at the road junction and round a large monastery north of S. Maria.

Orders were given on 29 November for the 17th Indian Infantry Brigade to consolidate in the Mozzagrogna area and to capture the road junction that night. The 21st Indian Infantry Brigade was given the task of patrolling towards Lanciano, a large town about four thousand yards ahead of the foremost positions of the 17th Indian Infantry Brigade, in preparation for the attack by the 8th

Indian Division in that direction. The 19th Indian Infantry Brigade, having completed its task with the New Zealanders, was ordered to take over from the 21st Indian Infantry Brigade by midnight 29 November. The 6th Lancers were directed to cover the left flank of the 21st Indian Infantry Brigade's positions.

That night the attack by the 8th Indian Division was a complete success, in spite of considerable opposition from German patrols. 1/5 Gurkha pushed forward and secured the vital road junction; 1/12 Frontier Force Regiment attacked and established itself in the large monastery near S. Maria, linking up with the troops of the 78th Division. The Indian Sappers again wrestled with the problem of putting the road in shape below the village of Mozzagrogna so that the 44th Battalion Royal Tank Regiment of the 4th Armoured Brigade could pass through. They strengthened the 80-feet Bailey bridge, that had been thrown over the enormous crater and cleared the road through the village and beyond the road junction to S. Maria. As dawn broke on the morning of 30 November, tanks of the 44th Battalion Royal Tank Regiment advanced up the road through the war-scarred village of Mozzagrogna.

The Germans fully realised the gravity of the situation and at 1030 hours they launched their final counter-attack against the 17th Indian Infantry Brigade bridge-head with infantry and self-propelled guns. In fifty minutes, they were given a severe mauling by the Allied artillery, tanks and planes which sent them reeling back north of Imbaro. Tanks of the 4th Armoured Brigade swung right at the road junction, joined up with the 78th Division and attacked towards Fossacesia. By noon the village was captured and, four hours later, the combined force of tanks and infantry had reached the sea.

The Situation on 30 November

By 30 November 1943, the V Corps was firmly established across the river Sangro. It had been a tough fight and a bloody battle for all concerned but, only three weeks after reaching the river, the Corps had smashed through the line the Germans had intended to hold during the winter months. The 2nd New Zealand Division on the left flank of the V Corps was extending its bridge-head and patrolling forward to Castelfrentano, which it captured on 2 December 1943. For the success of this operation the 19th Indian Infantry Brigade had made no mean contribution. The Indian brigade had helped to conceal the presence of the New Zealand division and had put in a determined attack, which secured the flank of the latter, when it made an assault north of the Sangro. On 29/30 November, with the knowledge of a job well done, the 19th Indian Infantry Brigade had returned to the 8th Indian Division. In the central sector of the corps front, the 8th Indian Division had broken through the German defences and was ready to follow up. The 78th Division, on the right coastal sector, also had a firm footing across the river and had rolled up the German line by breaking through to the sea in the Fossacesia area.

So far as the Germans were concerned, there was no doubt about the fact that they had been hard hit in the battle of the Sangro. At least a thousand Germans had been taken prisoner and many more had been killed. The *65th Infantry Division*, which had borne the brunt of the attack, had been almost decimated.

Over on the west side of Italy, fighting had flared up in the Fifth Army sector and the German High Command was in difficulties there. Nevertheless, the Germans held on doggedly to the defence of the Gustav Line and reacted boldly and swiftly; fresh troops were also rushed into southern Italy. The *90th Panzer Grenadier Division* was hurrying fast to replace the *65th Infantry Division*.

Though the Germans were in a bad way, the Allied forces were no better off. The V Corps was in no position to follow up the successful crossing of the river obstacle with an advance in strength. Very bad weather made movement extremely difficult and compelled the air forces to remain grounded on their air-fields; so no use could be made of the air superiority. In addition, the troops of the Eighth Army were tired out and needed rest; also there was no reserve division to exploit the gains. The 78th Division had suffered heavy casualties and needed rest. Nevertheless, in spite of these difficulties, the Eighth Army Commander ordered an advance beyond the river Sangro.

Capture of Romagnoli

When the 19th Indian Infantry Brigade returned to the 8th Indian Division, it enabled a reserve once more to be formed in the division and the role of the 21st Indian Infantry Brigade to be changed from a feint to a real thrust against the German defences. The 5th Battalion Queens Own Royal West Kent Regiment—the British unit of the 21st Indian Infantry Brigade—was ordered to secure Romagnoli by way of the southern outskirts of Mozzagrogna; the 1st Battalion 5th Mahratta Light Infantry was directed to capture the Redicoppe feature, one and a quarter mile south-west of Romagnoli, on the same ridge and on the road leading to Andreoli and Lanciano from the south, all of which were still held by the Germans.

With the 17th Indian Infantry Brigade firm in the Mozzagrogna area, the two battalions of the 21st Indian Infantry Brigade already in position to the south-east, patrols of the Lancers on La Defenza hill and the New Zealanders beyond them advancing on Castelfrentano from the south-east, the 5th Royal West Kent Regiment, moved through Mozzagrogna to attack Romagnoli at about 1330 hours on 30 November. The launching of the attack had been postponed three times, owing to the difficulty in getting the battalion forward.

Smaller than Mozzagrogna in size but similar in character, Romagnoli stood on the crest of a highly cultivated ridge, little more than a mile west of Mozzagrogna. A track from Mozzagrogna to Romagnoli, which ran along the top of the ridge, was chosen as the axis of advance, which was on a two-company front with D Company, on the right, moving across country, and A Company, on the left, moving up the line of the track. B and C Companies followed A Company along the track. Open fields with hedgerows, in which were occasional trees, covered the area. The German positions were on the eastern outskirts of Romagnoli and, before the attack went in, the men of the 5th Royal West Kent Regiment were bombed and strafed by the Allied aircraft and by a heavy, but sharp, ten minute artillery concentration. When the 5th Royal West Kent Regiment moved forward, came under brisk machine gun fire from the right flank and from the village itself. D Company suffered heavily, its commander and another officer were killed and fifty men, or two-thirds of the company, became casualties. A Company also had a tough time; its commander was killed and a number of men killed or wounded.[7]

At this stage the commander of B Company, moving up in reserve, took command of the rapidly deteriorating situation. The survivors of A Company were amalgamated with B Company to form four platoons, and a new plan of attack was adopted. The German positions were located in well dug trenches concealed in hedges outside the village. These were pin-pointed. All the available Bren guns and 2-inch and 3-inch mortars in the battalion were collected and concentrated fire was directed on the German posts. Some twenty Bren guns, four 3-inch and six 2-inch mortars were employed. The Brens opened up and raked the German defenders with fire, whilst bomb after bomb from the mortars crashed down on them. With the barrage of fire B Company attacked and carried out a highly successful pincer movement, breaking into the village, which came into its possession by the evening. The 5th Royal West Kent Regiment consolidated its hard won positions.

The Germans then sent a strong fighting patrol, supported by fire from their mortars, in an effort to drive back the 5th Royal West Kent Regiment or to do them as much damage as possible. Three times the Germans assaulted and three times the defensive fire from the divisional artillery and air action smashed the attacks and sent

[7] Casualties were: Killed 3 Officers and 17 Other Ranks, wounded 33 Other Ranks.

the Germans back to cover. Romagnoli remained in the hands of the 5th Royal West Kent Regiment.

Attack on Redicoppe

Meanwhile, at 1330 hours on 30 November, the 1st Battalion 5th Mahratta Light Infantry had attacked the Redicoppe feature with two troops of the 50th Battalion Royal Tank Regiment in support. The Germans had deep dug-outs, their machine guns were well sited, trees had been cut down to provide a good field of fire and the entire position was a tough nut to crack. With the tanks the Mahrattas fought their way forward into the German posts against heavy machine gun fire. Many acts of courage and bravery distinguished the fight. One Naik saw his platoon commander hit by a burst of fire, and rushed straight at the machine gun and lobbed a hand grenade amongst the crew. He then seized the muzzle of the gun and snatched it out of the hands of the terrified German. The Mahrattas suffered many casualties; the battalion commander was also killed. But by 1550 hours the objective was gained. As the afternoon closed into evening, the Mahrattas found themselves desperately short of ammunition, when a strong German counter-attack struck the left forward company. The tanks were then asked to help with their machine gun fire. However, the position was untenable; as darkness fell, the Mahrattas were forced to withdraw below the crest and to dig in astride the Roman road and track junction.

On 1 December, 3/15 Punjab (21st Indian Infantry Brigade) moved up to the C. Ruzzo to provide closer support to the Mahrattas, who were thus able to continue the operations against Redicoppe begun the previous day. But soon after it was found that the Germans had pulled back from Redicoppe and Andreoli under cover of darkness. The two places were occupied. Headquarters of the 21st Indian Infantry Brigade moved from Casone area to a position south-east of Romagnoli and the 5th Royal West Kent Regiment and the Mahrattas consolidated their gains in the Romagnoli and Andreoli sector. The 3/15 Punjab remained in reserve.

It now became apparent from patrol and interrogation reports, that the Germans were withdrawing their battered forces as quickly as possible to the Moro valley, where nature offered yet another strong defensive line. Their withdrawal tactics were much the same as before. Small mobile detachments of infantry, with self-propelled guns, stayed behind to hinder the Allied advance and to cover their own engineers at work on demolitions.

CHAPTER IV

Capture of Villa Grande

When the Eighth Army had established bridge-heads over the Sangro the Army Commander felt the necessity of strengthening the assault formations. The 78th Division, which had suffered ten thousand casualties since landing in Sicily six months previously, needed relief. The Army Commander, therefore, switched over the 1st Canadian Infantry Division from the mountain sector (XIII Corps) to the Adriatic coast. On 2 December at 1600 hours the command of the sector held by the 78th Division passed to the 1st Canadian Division. The 4th Armoured Brigade, which had been operating with the 78th Division, came under command of the Canadians, and the 38th (Irish) Brigade of the 78th Division also remained with them. Two brigades, 1st and 2nd of the 1st Canadian Division, concentrated behind a screen provided by the 4th Armoured Brigade and the 38th (Irish) Brigade, then in contact with the Germans in the area of S. Vito and Treglio. On the left of the Canadians the 8th Indian Division had secured Romagnoli and Andreoli and was pushing on towards Lanciano. South of the 8th Indian Division, the New Zealanders had pushed forward and, by 2 December, captured Castelfrenteno, three miles south-west of Lanciano and on the road to Guardiagrele.

Two main thrusts were now to be developed, by the Canadians towards Ortona and by the New Zealanders towards Orsogna. On the night of 2/3 December the 25th Battalion of the 6th New Zealand Brigade opened the attack towards Orsogna. They penetrated into Orsogna soon after first light but were pushed back by a fierce counter-attack. It was clear that the Germans were determined to hold Orsogna at all costs. The Canadians too encountered difficulties. Although the 38th (Irish) Brigade captured S. Vito on 3 December and reached the line of the river Moro the weather conditions were so bad that the Bailey bridges over the Sangro were washed away. The result was that the Canadian division's build-up and the assault across the Moro were delayed. As the *90th Panzer Grenadier Division* appeared to be holding the Moro in considerable strength, the 2nd Canadian Brigade moved up to positions overlooking the river on the left of the 38th (Irish) Brigade. By the evening of 5 December the 38th (Irish) Brigade, which was exhausted, pulled out of the line and the 1st Canadian Brigade took over the right sector of the division's front.

CAPTURE OF VILLA GRANDE

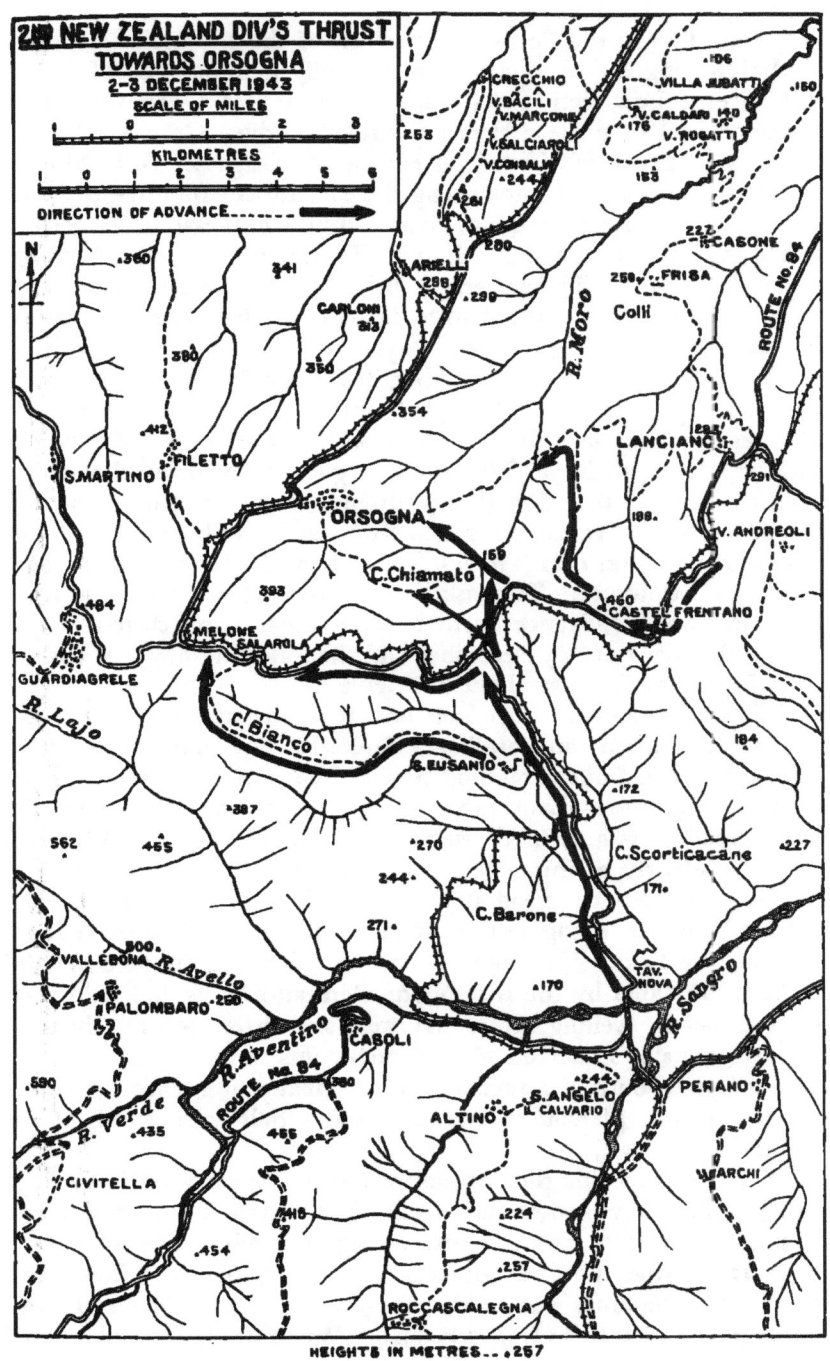

Capture of Lanciano

According to the Corps plan the role of the 8th Indian Division in the crossing of the river Moro was only a minor one of reconnaissance in the direction of Frisa. The initial tasks were to capture Lanciano and to make a thrust towards Treglio. On 2 December, Major-General Russell issued instructions to Brigadier B. S. Mould, D.S.O., O.B.E., M.C., commanding the 21st Indian Infantry Brigade, to capture the road junction, half a mile south-east of Lanciano, where the road from S. Vito through Treglio met the road Mozzagrogna—Lanciano. Thereafter, the brigade was to thrust northwards as far as possible along the road to Triglio in order to clear a passage for the Corps armour early next day.

At 2200 hours on 2 December, Brigadier Mould ordered 3/15 Punjab to pass through the 1/5 Mahratta Light Infantry and to advance on the town of Lanciano within the limits of artillery support. The 5th Royal West Kent Regiment was given the second task of helping the 38th (Irish) Brigade and the 4th Armoured Brigade, whose advance towards S. Vito was being held up by vigorous German action near Treglio, from where the Germans were able to shoot up Route 16. The task allotted to the 5th Royal West Kent Regiment was to advance north towards Treglio and clear the area during the night of 2/3 December and the following day. 1/5 Mahratta Light Infantry was held in reserve.

The 3/15 Punjab moved off and reached the line of the road and nullah, which ran parallel to Route 84, one mile south-east of Lanciano, on a front extending half a mile north and south of the road Mozzagrogna—Lanciano. By 0530 hours on 3 December, the road junction was secured without opposition. But the Germans reacted violently to this advance on Lanciano. Their artillery and mortars pounded the road junction and bridge. During the day, repeated dive bombing attacks were made on the forward Punjab positions by Fokke-Wulf fighter-bombers. But the Punjabis refused to be intimidated by the fury of the German attacks and held their ground; when evening came, they were still sitting securely in their positions outside Lanciano while detachments were sent to cut Route 84 north and south of Lanciano—one company to a place, two miles north, and one platoon to area, one and a half miles south of the town.

On the other line the advance of the 5th Royal West Kent Regiment on Treglio was more successful. The battalion moved off across country without its tank support, having been relieved in Romagnoli by 1/12 Frontier Force Regiment. At 0500 hours on 3 December, one of its companies was on the Treglio road, three thousand yards north of the objective of 3/15 Punjab. When the latter had secured the road junction south-east of Lanciano, tanks of the 14th Canadian

Armoured Regiment of the 1st Canadian Tank Brigade were able to move forward to support the 5th Royal West Kent Regiment. Thereafter the advance of this battalion with the support of the Canadian tanks became more rapid and the Germans were forced to leave Treglio, thereby opening the way to S. Vito for the 38th (Irish) Brigade. The latter attacked and captured S. Vito on 3 December and on the next day reached the line of the river Moro.

On the previous day, 2 December, C Squadron, 6th Lancers had worked up round the left flank of the 8th Indian Division and reached the road which ran south-west from Lanciano to Castelfrentano. Armoured cars turned north and raced up the road towards Lanciano until the leading car drove round the last corner into the town to come face to face with a German tank. The Lancer crew was quick off the mark and fired two rounds from the 37-millimeter gun before the Germans sent a shot crashing into the armoured car, which was set on fire.

During the night, 2/3 December, the Lancer and 3/15 Punjab patrols penetrated into Lanciano and reported the town clear. Next morning, 3 December, D Company of 3/15 Punjab entered the town and was greeted by the delighted inhabitants with a rousing reception. It was the largest town which the 8th Indian Division had captured since entering on the Italian campaign and 3/15 Punjab and the Lancers were justly proud of their achievement. Soon after midday, Commander 21st Indian Infantry Brigade established his headquarters in the town. Lanciano was to provide good warm billets during the winter months and an excellent base for operations farther north.

Capture of Frisa

Having accomplished its initial double task of capturing Lanciano and making a thrust towards Treglio, the 8th Indian Division prepared to carry out its second task, viz., of advancing towards Frisa. The capture of Lanciano on 3 December opened up a number of routes which could be used for the pursuit of the Germans. A and C Squadrons of the 6th Lancers swung right from Lanciano along the two roads leading north-east to S. Vito. A demolished bridge, some five miles short of S. Vito, held up A Squadron. On the other hand, C Squadron was halted just east of Treglio ; B Squadron went north for Frisa and was stopped by brisk small arms and mortar fire when it reached the bridge over the torrent Foldrino, about half way between Lanciano and Frisa. The bridge having been blown, the squadron commander, decided to push on over a diversion and the Lancers advanced to Frisa where they captured an astonished German observation post. They were then heavily fired on from the village of Casone, one mile to the north-east, by four German machine guns. Carriers raced forward towards the village and, at the same time, a Jemadar[1] (Viceroy's Commissioned Officer) who was commanding the two leading troops sent off his Daffadar (a non-commissioned officer) with seven men to outflank the machine guns. By very clever use of ground and cover the Lancers closed right up to the German posts; one machine gun was captured in hand-to-hand fighting and the other posts were soon put out of action.

Meanwhile headquarters of the 21st Indian Infantry Brigade was established in Lanciano and the town was converted into a firm base for future operations. The 5th Royal West Kent Regiment was astride the S. Vito roads, 1/5 Mahratta Light Infantry was on the Frisa road, while 3/15 Punjab guarded the approaches to Lanciano from the west and south. The Mahratta foot-patrols pushed north towards Frisa and the Punjab patrols went some miles east. Guided by a Lancer patrol, one troop of tanks of the 14th Canadian Armoured Regiment, which had taken over from the 50th Battalion Royal Tank Regiment, had worked round from Andreoli to the road Lanciano—Castelfrentano and eventually came into Lanciano from the south. Mopping up continued for the remainder of the day, the Lancers distinguishing themselves by capturing 25 prisoners of war. The Germans had certainly left Lanciano in a hurry. A considerable number of bridges and culverts in and around the town had been prepared for demolition but had not been blown. Divisional engineers were soon hard at work removing the charges.

Waves of German light bombers came over to bomb the forward positions held by the 21st Indian Infantry Brigade but lost one or two aircraft in each raid; the Light Anti-Aircraft Regiment with the 8th Indian Division taking a toll of German planes. To supplement the Bofors fire, the infantry fired everything it had at the attacking planes and the German raids were of very short duration.

On 4 December, a strong mobile column of Canadian tanks, Lancers' armoured cars and a company of the 5th Royal West Kent Regiment moved up the road from Lanciano to Frisa to cover the building of a Bailey bridge over the torrent Foldrino, where B Squadron of the Lancers had been held up. The torrent was successfully bridged and the force then continued its reconnaissance of the Frisa-Casone ridge, which was found to be only lightly held by machine guns and mortars. Meanwhile, the combined rifle troops of the Lancers were covering another bridging party of divisional engineers, at the demolition on the S. Vito road, which had held up A Squadron of the Lancers. When the bridge was built, the road, which was in the Canadian sector, was handed over to the Canadian division.

At first light on 5 December, a mobile column[2] of the 21st Indian

---

[1] Jemadar Hazura Singh, Daffadar Kirpal Singh and Daffadar Khair Singh.
[2] Consisting of one Squadron 14th Canadian Armoured Regiment, one Squadron 6th Lancers two companies 5th Royal West Kent Regiment and one detachment sappers.

Infantry Brigade moved forward and occupied the Frisa—Casone ridge against slight opposition, then pushed on to the destroyed bridge over the Moro (at C 317087), one mile north of Casone. Behind the mobile column, the rest of the 21st Indian Infantry Brigade moved up from Lanciano to the ridge and line of the road from Casone through Frisa to Colli, a front of some two miles. The brigade headquarters was established in Frisa and patrols contacted the Canadians on the right and the New Zealanders on the left.

Thus, in the first few days of December, the Eighth Army was following up the retreating Germans, who yielded ground reluctantly and only under pressure. In the central sector, the 8th Indian Division thrust forward with a narrow, winding, third-class road for its axis, a road barely two-way in many places. The 6th Lancers and the 21st Indian Infantry Brigade led. The 19th Indian Infantry Brigade still recuperating from the Sangro crossing, was concentrated in reserve around Andreoli. The 17th Indian Infantry Brigade, in the area S. Maria—Mozzagrogna, was reorganising and re-fitting.

The country through which advance was now made was much more broken than before by streams flowing between steep ravines, vineyards on their sides alternated by olive groves, enclosed by low stone walls. The cultivators lived in small, strongly built, scattered stone cottages, which were converted into strong-points and used by both sides at different periods. They afforded welcome protection against shellfire and inclement weather. The weather also hindered movement and aggravated the supply problem for the 8th Indian Division. All operations had to be conducted on a mule pack basis, "mule head" being established in the neighbourhood of Frisa and Casone. Divisional RIASC Units were pooled and the Divisional Maintenance Area was reorganised. The Divisional Troops Transport Company RIASC became responsible for all transport demands. Each of the three Brigade Transport Companies specialised in handling one of the three main commodities—ammunition, petrol, food. Periodic changes were made to avoid monotony and, at the same time, to widen the individual's field of experience.

Change in the Role of the 8th Indian Division

Circumstances brought about a change in the role of the 8th Indian Division. According to the original Corps plan, the role of the 8th Indian Division in the crossing of the river Moro was only a minor one of reconnaissance in the direction of Frisa. There had been no suggestion that the 8th Indian Division would have to cross the river. But as the days went by, with resistance stiffening considerably in front of the Canadians and the New Zealanders, it became apparent that the role of the 8th Indian Division would have to be changed. The New Zealanders, on the left, had been firmly checked in their advance on Orsogna on 3 December. On 7 December the New Zealanders put in their first large-scale attack against Orsogna with two brigades supported by a heavy artillery barrage. Some troops of each brigade reached their objective. Men of the 24th Battalion fought their way into the main square of Orsogna. However, their tanks could not get in, the Germans counter-attacked strongly, and it was decided to withdraw the New Zealanders and attack at a later date, when better weather conditions and air support would be available. In the north, the Canadians were probing across the river Moro and also encountering stiff opposition. On 6 December, however, they did manage to establish two bridge-heads across the river. One was in the vicinity of the coast road at the mouth of the Moro, the other in the area of Villa Rogatti, a village just forward and on the right flank of the 8th Indian Division. Rogatti was the more successful of the two Canadian bridge-heads, especially as nearly a complete squadron of the 44th Battalion Royal Tank Regiment had been able to get to the west bank.[3]

On the morning of 7 December the corps commander decided to exploit the situation around Villa Rogatti. He, therefore, ordered Major-General Russell to take over the left flank sector of the 1st Canadian Division, a task he accomplished by sending the 21st Indian Infantry Brigade to relieve the 2nd Canadian Infantry Brigade in the Villa Rogatti area. The 17th Indian Infantry Brigade moved into the Frisa area. The new role of the 8th Indian Division was to carry out a 'demonstration' to draw the German reserves away from the Canadian and New Zealand sectors. It was also to develop a thrust to cut the Ortona—Orsogna lateral road. The main attack was to be made by the Canadians. The 2nd Canadian Brigade moved into the area of S. Apollinare in order to launch the main attack through San Leonardo and on to the lateral road.

The Crossing of the River Moro

The crossing of the river Moro presented serious difficulties. This river meanders through a valley about three quarters of a mile wide between steep banks, which constituted a serious obstacle to the attacking infantry. At its widest the river was no more than fourteen feet across and was easily fordable at most places. On the eastern side of the valley, the Frisa ridge suddenly drops away almost sheer in an escarpment which, from the German point of view was a great wall of rock broken here and there by clumps of trees. The track along its crest from Frisa through S. Apollinare to Route 16 later became a valuable supply route for the 8th Indian Division. From the edge of the escarpment northwards there was a fine view

---

[3] This tank battalion had been in support of the 78th Division and came under command of the 1st Canadian Division when the British formation was relieved.

of the Moro battlefield. The only road which crossed the river in the divisional area ran through Frisa and the village of Casone and then wound steeply down to where the road bridge had been blown. The bridge was built many feet above the water line between steep banks and so was much wider than the river itself. On the far side of the river, the road zig-zagged just as steeply up to the Piano di Maggio feature before going west and north to V. Caldari. One thousand yards north of V. Caldari it joined the lateral road Ortona—Orsogna.

On the west flank of the Moro valley the hills were held by the *90th Panzer Grenadier Division* from the sea to V. Caldari. Their neighbour in the south was *67th Panzer Grenadier Regiment* of the *26th Panzer Division*. From the Adriatic to Route 16 inclusive was held by *361st Grenadier Regiment*. From Route 16 to V. Caldari, on the 8th Indian Division's front, was held by *200th Grenadier Regiment*. *II Battalion* of this regiment occupied Ruatti and V. Caldari. *III Battalion* was reported by prisoners to be employed in coastal defence duties in the vicinity of Ortona. *I Battalion* was resting in central reserve.

It had been mentioned earlier that the 8th Indian Division was ordered to carry out a 'demonstration' to draw the German reserve away from the Canadian and New Zealand sectors. Major-General Russell decided that, if the Germans were to be deceived, a bridge would have to be constructed over the river Moro. By this means it was hoped to convince the Germans that an attack by the division was impending. The construction of the bridge was a difficult task but it was accomplished and the bridge was called the 'Impossible Bridge'.[4]

On the night of 7/8 December, in accordance with the corps plan, the 5th Royal West Kent Regiment crossed the river one mile north-east of the blown bridge, and took over the defence of Ruatti from the Princess Patricia's Canadian Light Infantry. B Company of 1/5 Mahratta Light Infantry, with a small force of the Lancers, also crossed the river (at C 317087) in the vicinity of the blown bridge, to cover the first sapper reconnaissance for 'Impossible Bridge'. The crossing of the Moro and the occupation of positions was unopposed but, soon afterwards, the British and Indian troops were subjected to particularly fierce German infantry attacks supported by tanks. Three companies of the *90th Panzer Grenadier Division* attacked the

---

[4] "A reconnaissance of the Moro banks revealed a point at which a right-angled bend in the road made it an impossible site from which to launch a bridge from the south bank. But, argued Lieut.-Colonel C. M. MacLachlan, O.B.E., commander of the Divisional sappers, if it is impossible to build a bridge from the near bank, why not build it backwards from the enemy's bank? Thereafter, if the Germans discover it, they will be certain that we needed this crossing badly. If they do not discover it, we might surprise them by using it. Thus originated the project which became famous as 'Impossible Bridge'." *The Tiger Triumphs*, p. 24.

5th Royal West Kent Regiment, while another company of Grenadiers attacked the Mahratta Light Infantry.

The 5th Royal West Kent Regiment settled down to a three hour slogging match with the Germans. Tanks of the 44th Battalion Royal Tank Regiment, which remained in the area after the take over from the Canadians, gave the infantry valuable support. There was also a platoon of machine guns with the 5th Royal West Kent Regiment; and infantry, tanks, and machine guns gave the Germans punch for punch. Eventually the Germans withdrew, leaving eleven of their dead and five prisoners from *II Battalion 200th Grenadier Regiment*.

Things were not going quite so well with B Company of 1/5 Mahratta Light Infantry. The first attack, which the Germans launched at 0130 hours after heavy artillery concentrations was broken up by the artillery defensive fire and the German commander was compelled to make another plan. At 0400 hours, he sent some tanks and one or two machine guns to attract attention in the direction of the road, then put his main attack in from the company's rear. The feint drew the Mahratta company commander away from his headquarters at a critical time and the Germans broke into the company positions. After fierce hand-to-hand fighting, the Mahrattas were forced back over the river, leaving their dead and a number of prisoners in German hands. As soon as the situation was known, the artillery defensive fire was called for to cover their withdrawal. Shells whined over the river and burst among the Germans just as they were loading their prisoners into transport. German escort and Mahratta prisoners ran for cover but taking different directions. In the confusion, many of the prisoners escaped, crossed the river and made their way back to the battalion.

Meanwhile the Canadians were getting ready for their main attack on S. Leonardo, which was to be the main Canadian bridge-head over the Moro. The attack was made in the afternoon of 8 December. The Canadians were unable to reach S. Leonardo, which was about one thousand yards beyond the river, but they were able to complete work on their crossing place by dawn on 9 December. A second attack was put in and by 1000 hours the Canadians had captured S. Leonardo. Fierce German counter-attacks failed to throw out the Canadians from their bridge-heads—at S. Leonardo end on the coast. Thus the Canadian bridge-heads held above the Moro. As for the New Zealanders, operating on the left flank of the 8th Indian Division, they remained in their positions, north-east of Orsogna, where they had consolidated after the failure of their second attack on 7 December.

Meanwhile, the 8th Indian Division, in fulfilment of its role to distract the German attention from the main Canadian attack to secure S. Leonardo bridge-head, had ordered the Mahratta Light Infantry, in the afternoon of 8 December, to make a 'demonstration' across the Moro, whilst the Canadian attack went in near the coast to capture S. Leonardo. One platoon C Company, which was given the job, carried it out exceptionally well. It had to cross the river, attack the ridge, left of the site chosen for 'Impossible Bridge', and then withdraw behind the cover of an artillery barrage and smoke-screen. A creeping artillery barrage was laid on to advance from the escarpment west of the river to V. Caldari. At 1430 hours, the platoon crossed the river behind the barrage and fired approximately two thousand rounds of small arms ammunition and a number of grenades at the German positions. A mortar smoke-screen was laid a few hundred yards to the flank of the platoon, whilst long-range machine gun fire was put through the smoke-screen in short bursts to simulate Bren gun fire. The Germans were taken in completely by this "Chinese Cracker" attack; it drew heavy shell fire on Ruatti and mortar fire on the smoke-screen, which might otherwise have been employed against the Canadians. Particularly noticeable was the amount of metal which the Germans put down in and behind the mortar smoke-screen. Their job well done, the Mahratta patrol withdrew, without suffering any casualties. General Allfrey, the V Corps Commander, and the Canadian General Officer Commanding congratulated the Indian battalion on its success.

During this period, German shelling became gradually heavier; the Frisa—Casone ridge was notoriously unhealthy. Tip and run air raids were also more frequent, Lanciano being badly battered by them. Divisional gun areas received frequent German artillery concentrations; the Divisional Rear Headquarters, which had established itself in front of the main headquarters was also shelled.

The 'Impossible Bridge'

With a stalemate on the front of the 2nd New Zealand Division and the Canadians making only slow progress on the right flank, the time had come for the 8th Indian Division to lend a hand. It was decided that the 21st Indian Infantry Brigade would cross the river Moro and attack the Caldari feature to attract German units away from the Canadian and New Zealand sectors. The principal obstacle to a full-scale attack across the Moro was the difficulty of getting either tanks or anti-tank guns over the stream to support the infantry. The crossing used by the 44th Battalion Royal Tank Regiment had become impassable. So far as the 'Impossible Bridge' was concerned, the narrowness of the approaches to the bridge, the lack of parking space for vehicles and the constant shelling and heavy fire from mortars and machine guns made its construction a hazardous operation.

But the risk had to be accepted and 3/15 Punjab was ordered to form three strong independent fighting patrols. They were to cross the river at night and cover the bridge site while the engineer lorries, with the bridging stores, came down and unloaded in the dark. These patrols had orders to prevent German patrols from interfering with the vital work on the bridge site, but, if they were attacked by a strong force or by tanks, they were to withdraw after giving the sappers as much warning as possible. On the night of 8/9 December, the three patrols crossed the Moro and the sappers of the 69th Indian Field Company set to work. They carried the bridging material across the river by hand, swept the approaches for mines, cut steps into the banks and prepared everything for construction to start the next day. During daylight on 9 December, Impossible Bridge was built backwards from the far side of the river, with the site still protected by the three patrols. By day, 17-pounders of the 4th Mahratta Anti-Tank Regiment, a squadron of the 50th Battalion Royal Tank Regiment and all available medium machine guns covered 3/15 Punjab from the east bank of the Moro. This tank battalion had again joined the division to release the 14th Canadian Armoured Regiment for the Canadian sector.

The completion of the bridge by 1830 hours on 9 December made it possible for a battalion to attack across the Moro and, at 2155 hours on 9 December, the remainder of 3/15 Punjab, with its supporting arms, crossed the river over Impossible Bridge. The battalion attacked houses on the crest of the ridge, which were German strong-points and observation posts. This move clashed with a German attack on the 5th Royal West Kent Regiment in Ruatti and towards the bridge site and for a time the situation remained confused whilst hard fighting took place. The houses were eventually captured by a bayonet charge, in which 3/15 Punjab was ably assisted by Mahratta machine gunners, who, when not required to man their machine guns, fixed bayonets and charged with 3/15 Punjab.

Whilst the attack went in, the engineers were busy strengthening and improving the bridge which, by 0730 hours on 10 December, was ready for the first tanks to cross. The Germans were considerably shaken when they saw three tanks of the 50th Battalion Royal Tank Regiment climbing from the river bed, where they thought no diversion was possible. Altogether, fourteen tanks crossed over to help 3/15 Punjab to consolidate. During the mopping up period the tanks gave valuable close support to the infantry. In this engagement Havildar Badlu Ram of 3/15 Punjab lived up to his reputation for dare-devilry. His speciality was stalking Germans with a tommy-gun. When his ammunition ran out, Badlu Ram came back to the leading tank of the 50th Battalion Royal Tank Regiment and the crew obligingly handed him fresh tommy-gun magazines. This fine non-commissioned officer was awarded the Order of Merit but did not live to know it. He was killed later in the fighting at Consalvi.

Probably the units, which were most enthusiastic about the opening of Impossible Bridge, were the 5th Royal West Kent Regiment, the squadron of the 44th Battalion Royal Tank Regiment, the machine gun platoon in Villa Rogatti and the Mule Corps. Since taking over the village from the Canadians, the small force had been maintained solely by a nightly mule caravan, which had to move along a most precarious route before reaching the village. With the bridge open, mine-sweeping was started and motor transport was able to move up the road on the far bank towards Villa Rogatti.

The Fight for the "Gully"

The consolidation of the 1st Canadian Division's Moro bridgeheads marked the end of the first phase of the battle for Ortona. The second phase of the battle lasted till 19 December when the Canadians succeeded in driving out the Germans from their strong defensive positions across a "gully", carrying a tiny watercourse across the front just south of the lateral road from Ortona to Orsogna. In this phase of the battle the Canadians broke out of S. Leonardo on 10 December to attack the cross-roads two miles south of Ortona, on the Ortona—Orsogna lateral. Weather was against them but they made good progress until they came to the main German positions outside Ortona, where the latter had fortified a deep re-entrant (the "gully") running parallel to, and just short of, the lateral road Ortona—Orsogna. This re-entrant caused the road from S. Leonardo to swing sharply inland and make a hairpin bend where it crossed the bottom of the "gully". German trenches manned by troops of the *1st Parachute Division*, who had been brought up to reinforce the battered *90th Panzer Grenadier Division*, were on the Canadian side of the "gully", where Canadian gunners could not see their target area and where mud, machine gun fire and mines halted the tanks and infantry. On 11 December the Canadians attacked the "gully" but without success. The situation looked gloomy but, during the day a Canadian tank officer taught the Germans a sharp lesson. He was on reconnaissance in the area of the lateral road, almost due west of S. Leonardo and on the extreme left of the Canadians, when he discovered a German tank leaguer of five or six tanks with the crews asleep. He reported the location and a mixed force of tanks and Canadian infantry set out to deal with the unsuspecting Panzer Grenadiers. The Germans were completely taken by surprise, all their tanks being destroyed and a battalion headquarters, *III Battalion 361st Regiment*, captured. This engagement had an important result as the area dominated a small sector of the lateral road and the destruction of the German tanks gave the Canadians a valuable footing on the road for later operations.

On the night of 11/12 December, when a battalion of the 3rd Canadian Brigade attacked towards Casa Berardi, on the lateral road in unceasing rain, fierce fire from the "gully" held it up. The battalion was counter-attacked several times on 12 and 13 December by a mixed force of tanks, infantry and engineers and suffered such heavy casualties that it had to be withdrawn. Another battalion of the 3rd Canadian Brigade attacked on 13 December, but it could also register no impression. In five hours' fighting, the battalion was very badly mauled by the German defenders of the "gully".

Several frontal attacks on the "gully" had failed; a new plan was therefore necessary. Hence it was decided to attack north-east up the lateral road from the area, which the Canadians dominated, consequent on the destruction of the tank leaguer, so as to outflank the "gully". The Royal 22nd Regiment of the 3rd Canadian Brigade attacked at 0730 hours on 14 December. The Germans put up a fierce fight but, by the evening, C. Berardi was captured, thereby making the "gully" uncomfortable for the Germans. Next day, however, the Canadians on the road were attacked by German infantry with some tanks. There was a bloody engagement with heavy casualties on both sides. Later in the day, another frontal attack was put in against the "gully", but it failed too; and a forty-eight hours pause was ordered for the Canadian division. At 0800 hours on 18 December, the German positions were subjected to the fire of thirteen artillery regiments. Under cover of this devastating fire the Canadians surged forward for the attack and after a keenly contested engagement compelled the Germans to pull out of the "gully" on 19 December. The fight for the "gully" was over and the Canadians had secured the cross-roads preparatory to the attack on Ortona.

Extending the Bridge-head

To ease the German pressure on the Canadians (in their stubborn fight for the "gully") the 8th Indian Division was ordered to make a thrust towards the Ortona—Orsogna lateral road. By the morning of 10 December, the 21st Indian Infantry Brigade had a firm footing across the Moro. The 5th Royal West Kent Regiment remained on the right of the brigade front, in Ruatti; 3/15 Punjab on the left, astride the road from "Impossible Bridge" to V. Caldari, on the Piano di Maggio plateau.

Reports from various sources gave the impression that the

Germans were pulling out of V. Caldari. But this was not true. The 21st Indian Infantry Brigade was heavily mortared during the day and 3/15 Punjab had considerable trouble from German snipers west of its positions. However, the snipers were easily dealt with by the Indians, who, attacking with tank and artillery support, killed fourteen and captured many more on 10 December and the following day, for the loss of twelve other ranks killed or wounded.

On the right flank, the Canadians had attacked S. Leonardo for the second time and, after heavy fighting the 2nd Canadian Brigade had taken the town by 1000 hours on 9 December. Their next task was to break out of S. Leonardo on 10 December and continue their advance on Ortona. In order to maintain pressure and help the Canadian thrust, the 21st Indian Infantry Brigade was ordered to attack in the direction of Consalvi, a village a little more than two miles due west along the Piano di Maggio from the 3/15 Punjab positions.

On 10 December, patrols from the 21st Indian Infantry Brigade worked their way towards Consalvi to reconnoitre for the attack, but this plan was never put into effect as the Germans heavily reinforced V. Caldari that night and formed up for a counter-attack on the brigade's bridge-head. But concentrated shelling by the Allied guns upset the German preparations and no counter-attack developed, although there was fighting in the houses on the outskirts of V. Caldari. Rain and storm in the night of 10/11 December gave a warning that the advance might be considerably slowed down. At this stage, the plan was changed. The 21st Indian Infantry Brigade was ordered to enlarge its hold on the Piano di Maggio so that the 17th Indian Infantry Brigade could cross the Moro, pass through the 21st Indian Infantry Brigade and carry on the advance along the axis of the V. Caldari road to the Ortona—Orsogna lateral.

The enlarging began during the night of 11/12 December when one company of 1/5 Mahratta Light Infantry crossed the river Moro, moved through 3/15 Punjab and, supported by artillery, attacked German positions west of that battalion. The 5th Royal West Kent Regiment and 3/15 Punjab helped the Mahratta with a heavy concentration of mortar and machine gun fire on V. Caldari, which diverted the attention of the Germans. By 2200 hours the Mahratta company had gained, without much difficulty, its objective, the line of the track running from the cross tracks, twelve hundred yards south-west of V. Caldari to the river Moro, one mile south-west of Impossible Bridge, and held fast. Twenty-two hours later, at 2000 hours on 12 December, the remainder of the Mahratta battalion advanced through 3/15 Punjab, supported by tanks of the 50th Battalion Royal Tank Regiment and machine guns. Its objective was a German position eight hundred yards short of the lateral road and south-east of Consalvi, on a spur which ran down to the cross tracks mentioned above. Soon after passing through 3/15 Punjab, the leading men of 1/5 Mahratta Light Infantry heard the sound of lorry engines coming from the direction of V. Caldari; it was German B Echelon transport bringing up supplies for their forward troops. The Mahrattas, who by now were some distance in front of the forward positions, lay in wait on the V. Caldari road and two German lorries drove into the trap. After a few minutes of panic, during which most of the twenty Germans from the two lorries tried to dive under the culvert, the disgruntled and badly frightened Germans were herded together by the Mahrattas and marched away. Some Germans went short of rations and ammunition that night, for the occupants of the two lorries had all been cooks and B Echelon men with rations. The prisoners considered the Mahratta ambush most unfriendly; one of them complained bitterly that it was not fair to capture B Echelon troops.

But there was still more work to be done; the battalion moved forward for an attack to its start line, which had been gained by a Mahratta company the previous night. Corps and divisional artillery fired heavy concentrations. The 50th Royal Tank Regiment was in close support. As in the case of the company attack, the brigade commander ordered the 5th Royal West Kent Regiment and 3/15 Punjab to stage a diversion; the Germans apparently had not learned a lesson the night before and, for the second time, they were completely hoodwinked. Indian and British patrols went forward to draw fire; all the 2-inch and 3-inch mortars opened up on V. Caldari and the machine guns fired off belt after belt of ammunition into the village. The Germans retaliated and, for a while, it was most unpleasant for the 5th Royal West Kent Regiment and 3/15 Punjab.

However, the Mahratta Light Infantry met a startled enemy and caught him on the wrong foot. The last lap up the slopes to its objective was covered by the two leading companies at the double, shouting the war cry of 'Shivaji Maharaj Ki Jai'. Fifty-four Germans of *II Battalion 200th Grenadier Regiment* were taken prisoners. Some of their positions were trenches and dug-outs in front of houses; the occupants of one dug-out on the extreme left of the objective resisted stubbornly. Tanks were so hampered by the close country that they were unable to see their targets. The commander of one of the Mahratta companies, made a quick plan to deal with the strong-point. He contacted the tank commander and arranged that when the Mahrattas located the German position they would fire tracer into it. The tank commander agreed to fire at the place where the tracer disappeared. As soon as the Germans spotted the men crawling forward, they opened fire; thereupon the Mahrattas replied with a burst of tracer. A tank of the 50th Battalion Royal Tank Regiment sent a round of high explosives into the strong-point, causing a tree to crash down on the dug-out, where it killed a German sniper in his weapon pit. The other occupants of the dug-out scrambled out and ran towards a large white house. This was exactly what the tanks had been waiting for. They sent armour piercing and high explosive shells tearing into the house; artillery concentrations were also called for. Within a few minutes at 2330 hours, all resistance had ceased, the Mahrattas consolidated on the objective and prepared for a German counter-attack. The Germans must have been seriously disorganised by the Mahratta success and by the feint attack against V. Caldari, for the usual immediate counter-attack did not materialise.

However, at 1700 hours on 13 December, a counter-attack did come in; it was fierce and energetic. First came the rumble of German tanks as they moved along the lateral road; then infantry opened fire from the same direction. By clever use of ground the Germans closed right up to the Mahratta forward position, where there was bitter fighting, with the German tanks moving up and down the road shooting into the Mahratta positions, but keeping out of view of the tanks of the 50th Battalion Royal Tank Regiment and anti-tank guns, which had worked as far forward as the muddy ground would let them. The fighting went on all night, a noisy night for everybody, with the Germans heavily mortaring the Mahratta infantry. Bursting grenades and the shouting as the battle rose to a crescendo made their approach to the lateral road a memorable operation. The Mahrattas held firmly to the captured positions but were unable, owing to the casualties and disorganisation caused by the German counter-attack during the night, to put in, as planned, another attack by one company to take Pt. 239, the crest of high ground on the lateral road, due east of Consalvi. At 0500 hours, on 14 December the Germans attacked with seven tanks and ninety Panzer Grenadiers, but again the Mahrattas sent them reeling back. It was the final German attempt. During the day, the battalion reorganised and sent patrols forward to the lateral road. A large white house, which dominated the Mahratta left flank, was cleared with the help of the tanks.

Since crossing the Moro and taking over from the Canadians in Villa Rogatti on 7 December, the 5th Royal West Kent Regiment had been given very little rest by the Germans. Although Villa Rogatti did not directly cover the site of the 'Impossible Bridge', the village was the key to the establishment of the bridge-head and was a thorn in the German side. On four successive nights after the 5th Royal West Kent Regiment had moved in, the Germans launched determined counter-attacks. All the attacks were beaten off but the battalion suffered many casualties from the nightly shelling and mortaring. Villa Rogatti remained in a state of siege, but the success of the bridgehead was largely due to the way in which the battalion held on to the battered village. The Germans were always expecting a large-scale attack from the village, hence their frequent counter-attacks, which were an expensive failure and drew troops away from the area captured by 3/15 Punjab and 1/5 Mahratta Light Infantry.

The Advance to the Ortona—Orsogna Lateral Road

Whilst the 21st Indian Infantry Brigade was extending the Moro bridge-head, the 17th Indian Infantry Brigade, commanded by Brigadier J. Scott-Elliott, crossed the river Moro to carry out the next phase of the plan, an advance through V. Caldari, to the lateral road on the night of 13/14 December. It was intended to be a two battalion attack with V. Caldari as the objective of the 1st Battalion Royal Fusiliers and Pt. 198, on the lateral road, the objective of the 1st Battalion 5th Royal Gurkha Rifles. V. Caldari was situated to the right of the road running from the 'Impossible Bridge' to the lateral road and about eight hundred yards short of the lateral road itself. Pt. 198 was a pimple on the rising ground of the lateral road, about six hundred yards south of the junction where the Caldari road joined the lateral road.

After taking over Frisa from the 21st Indian Infantry Brigade, the 17th Indian Infantry Brigade had sent nightly patrols down to the river front due west from Frisa and below the left flank of the 21st Indian Infantry Brigade. Early in the evening of 13 December the 1st Royal Fusiliers and 1/5 Royal Gurkha Rifles moved up to the Piano di Maggio and assembled behind the screen provided by 1/5 Mahratta Light Infantry.

The brigade attacked at 2300 hours on 13 December, with the 1st Royal Fusiliers making for V. Caldari and 1/5 Gurkha Rifles in reserve until V. Caldari was clear. German defensive fire was heavy and accurate; artillery, mortar and machine gun fire caused many casualties among the Fusiliers, who were held up in front of the cemetery and so lost the effect of the artillery barrage moving ahead of them. Yet by 0530 hours, after a night of fierce fighting, the Fusiliers reported the village to be clear of the Germans, forty of them having paid with their lives for the defence of V. Caldari.

The Gurkhas then came into the picture, fighting their way forward against considerable opposition, which stiffened as they approached the road. However, with Mozzagrogna still fresh in their memories, they battled on and, by 0710 hours on 14 December, reached Pt. 198, where they defied every German attempt to push them back. At this time, this Gurkha battalion held the most forward position of all the troops of the Eighth Army and was meeting with particularly fierce resistance from the Germans. In the afternoon at 1440 hours a strong German force with two self-propelled guns attacked Pt. 198; the Gurkhas held fast, refusing to give ground and the counter-attack was broken up by defensive fire. In this engagement, one Havildar[5] distinguished himself by knocking out one of the attacking tanks with a PIAT. When the counter-attack had been smashed, the Gurkhas consolidated on Pt. 198 but their strength had been reduced to two and a half companies.

The next night, 14/15 December, while the Fusiliers and the Gurkhas consolidated their hard won gains, the 1/12 Frontier Force Regiment, having been relieved in Frisa by 6/13 FF Rif. came up between the Gurkhas and 1/5 Mahratta Light Infantry and extended the flank of the 17th Indian Infantry Brigade, by attacking at 0430 hours with artillery support and securing positions astride the lateral road, eight hundred yards south of Pt. 198. Two companies, D and A, to the right and left respectively, had just begun to mop up in their areas when they heard the rumble of German tanks on the lateral road from the direction of Orsogna. These two forward companies, on the line of the road and railway just north of the road, had no tanks to support them. For a while, the forward elements were cut off from the road but eventually they managed to get back after one of the German tanks had been disabled. The two companies then withdrew some two hundred yards from the road, and the third company (B Company) moved up on their left flank to the White House (C 290093). In the early hours of 16 December, the three companies were given the job of knocking out the German tanks. With seven tanks of the 50th Battalion Royal Tank Regiment supporting them, they rushed a group of houses, where the German tanks had been located. But they found only two disabled tanks, for the rest of the German force had retreated in the night. The 8th Indian Division was then slowly but surely extending its positions on the lateral road in a grip which the Germans could not break.

To make the position more secure, Major-General Russell ordered the 21st Indian Infantry Brigade to capture the villages of Salciaroli and Consalvi, both situated one thousand yards west of the road Ortona—Orsogna, due west of the Mahratta positions on the Piano di Maggio, and half a mile and one mile respectively south of the Frontier Force battalion's positions on the road. Both villages lay amidst thick olive groves where visibility was sometimes restricted to one hundred yards. Every house was defended and required a carefully planned assault to destroy its occupants. Deep mud made most tracks impassable, even to jeeps, so mules were largely employed.

On 15 December, 1/5 Essex of the 19th Indian Infantry Brigade

[5] Gopi Pershad Gurung.

relieved the 5th Battalion Royal West Kent Regiment in Villa Rogatti, the latter being required to secure a stretch of the lateral road south of the 1/12 Frontier Force Regiment position. The 5th Royal West Kent Regiment passed through the other two battalions of the 21st Indian Infantry Brigade to attack Pt. 239, on the lateral road at dawn on 16 December. One squadron of the City of London Yeomanry and Corps and divisional artillery were in support of the battalion. The 5th Royal West Kent Regiment put in a most spirited attack although heavy going slowed down the squadron of tanks. The Germans were caught off their guard, and yielded thirty-six prisoners of war besides four of their tanks being destroyed. As the afternoon drew into evening, the battalion consolidated its position on the lateral road. Patrols pushed out towards the village of Consalvi and contacted the Germans whilst some other patrols got into touch with the 1/12 Frontier Force Regiment on the right flank.

On the night of 16/17 December, 3/15 Punjab moved forward from its area astride the Caldari road, through 1/5 Mahratta Light Infantry, to occupy new positions in the area of the road and track junction (C 277075) and Pt. 264, three quarters of a mile south of Consalvi commanding the lateral road, left of the 5th Royal West Kent Regiment position. This objective was reached unopposed.

By 17 December, the 8th Indian Division was able to report the lateral road well and truly cut. On the right of the divisional front was the 17th Indian Infantry Brigade, with 1/5 Royal Gurkha Rifles around Pt. 198, 1/12 Frontier Force Regiment to the left, and 1st Royal Fusiliers back in the V. Caldari area. Jubatti on the right flank, half a mile north-east of Caldari and between the Indian and Canadian divisions, had been occupied by the Germans up to the night of 16/17 December. Patrols from 1/5 Essex had later found the village vacated and patrols from 1/5 Royal Gurkha Rifles had closed the gap by contacting the Canadians on the lateral road (C 300114), twelve hundred yards north-west of Villa Jubatti. South of the 17th Indian Infantry Brigade was the 21st Indian Infantry Brigade, also with two battalions on the road; the 5th Royal West Kent Regiment south of 1/12 Frontier Force Regiment around Pt. 239 and 3/15 Punjab to the left of the former about Pt. 264; 1/5 Mahratta Light Infantry was still short of the road on the Piano di Maggio feature. The 19th Indian Infantry Brigade remained in reserve.

The forward battalions of both the 17th and 21st Indian Infantry Brigades had tanks in close support and anti-tank guns well up. Patrols went forward from the road, over the railway line, towards the villages of Crecchio, Salciaroli and Consalvi, where the Germans waited for the next move by the 8th Indian Division. Constant harrying by fighting patrols and possibly the threat presented by the advance on their flank (their direct line of withdrawal being intersected by three deep ravines through which ran tributaries of the river Arielli) persuaded the Germans to move out of those villages. Salciaroli was occupied on 18 December by the 5th Royal West Kent Regiment and Consalvi on the 19th by 3/15 Punjab.

Attack on Orsogna

Meanwhile the 2nd New Zealand Division had been hammering at the strong German positions in Orsogna, on the left flank of the 8th Indian Division. The New Zealand Division had taken up position to the north-east of Orsogna, waiting for better weather conditions before attacking the town. For nearly a week, only patrol activities were in evidence. Then on 14/15 December, the New Zealanders put in their third attack; this time it was decided to outflank the town of Orsogna from the north-east. At 0100 hours on 15 December, the 5th New Zealand Brigade attacked, its objective being the lateral road north-east of Orsogna. The 6th New Zealand Brigade put in a diversionary attack against Orsogna. All that night and the next day, they fought to get on to the road, whilst the diversionary attack on Orsogna drew much of German opposition. During the day tanks moved up to help the New Zealand forces, and, on the night of 15/16 December, the infantry attacked again. Determined fighting continued through the second night into the next day, 16 December; by last light, the tired but triumphant infantry of the 5th New Zealand Brigade was astride the lateral road and the tanks were moving south-west towards Orsogna, having secured one hundred prisoners of war and five anti-tank guns.

In order to assist the 8th Indian Division, the 5th New Zealand Brigade then turned north, striking towards Arielli, a town on the left flank of the Indian division, nearly two miles south-west of Consalvi, while the 6th New Zealand Brigade continued fighting for Orsogna, where the Germans were resisting bitterly. It had become apparent that a swift break-through by the New Zealanders on the left of the V Corps front was not possible.

Reorganisation

By this time, the line-up of formations on both sides had undergone certain alterations. As has been indicated earlier, the Germans had brought their reinforced *1st Parachute Division* from the Maiella mountain sector back into the battle on the coast. The *90th Panzer Grenadier Division* was side-stepped southwards from the coast and the *65th Infantry Division* came in again to help the *26th Panzer Division* around Orsogna—Guardiagrele. On 21 December 1943, the *1st Parachute Division* was holding from Ortona to Villa Grande. West of the river Arielli and north of Crecchio was the

90th Panzer Grenadier Division with three battalions, one from each regiment, forward. To their south, from Le Piano to Orsogna were the *26th Panzer Division* and the *65th Infantry Division*. The *334th Infantry Division* was reported to be moving down from Genoa.

In the Eighth Army, two corps were operating between the sea and the Maiella mountains. Any offensive in the mountain sector (where the XIII Corps had a holding role) was out of the question. It was the coastal sector which was of vital importance. General Montgomery therefore decided to regroup his divisions so as to strengthen his right flank. He ordered the Headquarters XIII Corps with the 5th Division to move across to the coastal sector, leaving the 78th Division to hold the mountain flank directly under army command. It was his intention to continue the drive northwards on a two-corps front—on the right the V Corps, with the 1st Canadian and the 8th Indian Divisions; on the left, the XIII Corps with the 2nd New Zealand and the 5th British Divisions. He ordered the V Corps to swing the 8th Indian Division up towards Tollo on the left flank of the Canadian division so that the 5th British Division might be brought into the line between the 8th Indian Division and the 2nd New Zealand Division. His plan was for the Canadians to launch attacks for the capture of Ortona and for the 8th Indian Division to push along the inland route through Villa Grande and Tollo to outflank Ortona from the west.

Capture of Ortona

The third phase of the battle for Ortona began immediately after the conclusion of the second phase on 19 November. On 20 December the Canadians moved up the lateral road from the crossroads towards Ortona. They reached the outskirts of the town. That night, heavy explosions shook Ortona as German engineers carried out demolitions, which turned the town into an ideal battle area for house-to-house fighting and set the stage for eight days of fierce close quarter struggle in which no mercy was shown or expected.

Perched on a ledge above the Adriatic, Ortona was a town of ten thousand people, with a port invaluable to the Eighth Army if captured intact. The Germans had other ideas. Troops of the *1st Parachute Division* were entrusted with the defence of the town, a comparatively simple matter. There was only one approach to the town, from the south-west. To the west, was a steep ravine, whilst east of the town was the Adriatic and Ortona fort. General Heidrich, ruthless but resolute and brave, organised the defence and his paratroopers were every bit as tough as he. It was to be the Canadians' first experience in street fighting on a large scale. Before the battle was eventually won on 28 December, the town had become a shambles of tumbled masonry and rubble, which was the grave of Canadians, Germans and Italians alike.

Thrust towards Villa Grande

While the Canadians launched attacks on Ortona the 8th Indian Division made a thrust towards Villa Grande. On 17 December, the 19th Indian Infantry Brigade took up the advance north from the lateral road with the town of Tollo as its objective, which was about two and half miles north-west from the forward positions of the division. The 6th Lancers raced ahead of the forward troops. But before reaching Tollo, it was necessary for the division to cross the river Arielli, which flows to the Adriatic coast where it enters the sea, about three miles north-west of Ortona. In the coastal sector the road and railway, running from Ortona to Orsogna, formed the main line of communication, and from this second class highway radiated numerous minor roads leading to the different villages, viz. Villa Grande, Tollo, C. Vezzani, Crecchoi, and Arielli. Of these Villa Grande became the scene of bitter fighting. Its church and high tower stood at the cross-roads in the heart of the village, and its narrow, cobbled streets scarcely allowed two vehicles to pass. The eastern and southern approaches to the village passed through continuous olive groves. Its western edge was flanked by a deep and narrow gully. To the north, the ground climbed gradually to the open fields and pasture land on the plateau of the Piano di Moregine, from where there was an excellent view over Villa Grande. The other village, C Vezzani, together with Eusano, was simply a large cluster of poor farm tenements and cattle sheds. It was situated on the east bank of the Arielli at a point where the sides of the gully fell away steeply. Any hostile force crossing the river from the west could not be seen until it was almost inside the western fringe of the village. Around Crecchio and Arielli, olive groves and vineyards restricted visibility to a few hundred yards. Farmsteads, small clusters of grey stone, two-storied cottages dotted the landscape and could easily be converted into strong-points.

At 1100 hours on 17 December, the 6/13 Royal Frontier Force Rifles, with tanks of the 50th Battalion Royal Tank Regiment and armoured cars of the 6th Lancers, advanced north from the lateral road. The brigade commander had planned to move on two routes. The first, 'Item' route, ran from the Ortona—Orsogna lateral at Pt. 198 in 1/5 Royal Gurkha Rifles area ; thence it ran slightly west of north, along the east bank of the river Arielli to join the road from C. Berardi (on the lateral in the Canadian sector) to Tollo, one and a half miles to its south-east. The second, 'How' route, took off from Item route one mile north of the latter's junction with the lateral and zig-zagged along the west bank of a gully to Villa Grande, on the road from C. Berardi to Tollo. This situation of Villa Grande made it an important position to fight for.

6/13 Royal Frontier Force Rifles patrolled from the lateral east of Item track while 1/5 Essex infiltrated between Item route and the river Arielli in the direction of C. Vezzani. A patrol from 6/13 Royal Frontier Force Rifles surprised a small German party in farm buildings at the junction of How and Item tracks (C 287118) and captured one anti-tank gun and a lorry. When the British tanks arrived to make that area safe, 1/5 Essex crossed over to advance along How track towards Villa Grande. Meanwhile, C Squadron 6th Lancers continued the move towards C. Vezzani. On Item route, the advance was held up by the narrowness of the track.

German tanks were most active though cautious during this phase of operations, their favourite tactics being to lie up behind houses, only coming out into the open to deal with an infantry threat. However, the 50th Battalion Royal Tank Regiment and the infantry anti-tank gunners were a match for the Germans. They knocked out or captured twelve tanks, many half-tracked vehicles and self-propelled guns. Movement was extremely slow in the close country whilst the weather was so bad that two German tanks and a self-propelled gun were found abandoned, where they had sunk deep into the mud. The Germans were not in the habit of abandoning any equipment but the thick mud had beaten them on this occasion.

As the 19th Indian Infantry Brigade advanced slowly towards Villa Grande, clearing and improving How and Item routes, the 17th and the 21st Indian Infantry Brigades consolidated and mopped up in the area of the lateral road. Wreckage was everywhere; burnt-out and crippled tanks, shattered anti-tank guns and half-tracked vehicles showed how bitter had been the fighting for the lateral road. The Germans had paid dearly for their obstinate defence. During this mopping up period, the 5th Division came into the line between the New Zealanders and the 8th Indian Division, under the command of the XIII Corps.

The First Attack on Villa Grande

While the 19th Indian Infantry Brigade was advancing towards Villa Grande the Germans were making feverish preparations for its defence. General Heidrich had no intention of surrendering the village of Villa Grande without a fight. *1st Battalion 3rd Parachute Regiment* held the village; and as the 19th Indian Infantry Brigade advanced from the lateral road, the Germans put the finishing touches to their preparations. The defences were formidable. Dugouts had been excavated below the ground floors of houses, which commanded possible approaches to the village, and the floors themselves had been strengthened with wooden beams and piles of earth. Anti-tank guns, sited in houses or at the end of village lanes, covered all tank approaches.

The plan for the 19th Indian Infantry Brigade was to take Villa Grande on 22 December, then cut the road running west from the village towards Tollo. The 21st Indian Infantry Brigade was to be ready to pass through the 19th Indian Infantry Brigade after the capture of Villa Grande and exploit to the line of the Arielli river. Brigadier Dobree planned to attack Villa Grande from the south with one battalion supported by all divisional and corps artillery. A diversionary attack was to be staged towards C. Vezzani by a small force of tanks, one squadron 6th Lancers and one company 3/8 Punjab moving along Item track.[6]

On the night of 21/22 December, a bitterly cold night, 1/5 Essex with C Squadron of the 50th Battalion Royal Tank Regiment in support, moved to a start line south of Villa Grande. The men froze as they waited for the barrage to start, whilst the gunners back in the gun lines stamped their feet and tried to get some warmth into their benumbed hands. Just before dawn the fury of a heavy artillery barrage broke on Villa Grande. Flashes from hundreds of guns stabbed the darkness of the night; it seemed that all the artillery in the world was firing shells into the village. The Essex waited tensely in the intense cold for the order to attack; German paratroopers sought refuge in their dugouts until the rain of shells should cease. When the guns stopped, the Essex men attacked at 0600 hours on 22 December. The leading company broke into some houses on the southern edge of the village. The Germans fought with determination to break the Essex hold; but the British Infantry grimly held on to its gains. Then the order was given to advance into the village. As the men moved forward, the Essex ran into murderous machine gun and mortar fire, which cut through the leading troops like a knife. Those men, who did succeed in getting a footing in the village, fought a fierce hand-to-hand battle with the paratroopers. There was the clap of bursting grenades, the quick clatter of German machine guns and the shouts in English and German as the battle moved to a climax. Villa Grande was too tough a nut to crack that day. The Essex withdrew to the houses they had captured on the southern edge of the village whilst the paratroopers re-organised and waited for the next attack.

The Essex in Villa Grande were meeting such stiff resistance that leverage from the flank became necessary. The 21st Indian Infantry Brigade was ordered to advance up Item track, secure the village of

[6] 19 Ind. Inf. Bde. O.O. No. 11, dated 21 December 1943.

Vezzani, and push forward to the junction of Item track and the road Villa Grande—Tollo. One battalion of the brigade was to attack, whilst the rest of the brigade was to advance to the Tollo road either up Item track, or through Villa Grande, if the village had been cleared. This move would not only help the Candian division but would also put the 21st Indian Infantry Brigade in a good position overlooking the Arielli river.

The Second Attack on Villa Grande

At 0530 hours on 23 December, 1/5 Essex put in its second attack on Villa Grande. Advancing on the same axis as for the previous attack, the infantry and tanks went forward to renew their fighting with the paratroopers. For the second time, the battalion was held up in the southern outskirts of the village by German machine gun fire. The Essex fought on stubbornly and managed to establish a hold on the first houses; the British tanks sent high explosive and armour piercing shells into the German strong-points. Then, at 1200 hours, when it seemed that the Germans were wavering, the Essex, with their tank support, prepared to extend their footing in the village. As the battle weary force advanced, German shells struck the attackers; a prelude to a fierce German counter-attack. Parachutists sallied forth from their dugouts, to be met with a hail of fire and, after a fierce fight, they were forced back to their shelters.

The 1/5 Essex had won the second round of the battle for Villa Grande and held the southern outskirts of the village, despite repeated German attempts to dislodge them during the day. Villa Grande became the scene of tough house-to-house fighting. So it went on all day as in Ortona, with sections of the Essex sometimes separated from the paratroopers in the next house by only a thin wall. Slowly but surely, the Essex extended their hold on Villa Grande and, for the rest of the day, machine guns and tommy-guns chattered an accompaniment to the din of battle. By nightfall their hold on the village was secure. That night, a darkness so thick that men could hardly see their hands in front of their faces, put a stop to further operations.

The column providing the diversion against C. Vezzani, when 1/5 Essex first attacked Villa Grande on 22 December, had met little opposition though the village was heavily mined and booby trapped. The squadron of the 6th Lancers remained to occupy the village. The 21st Indian Infantry Brigade then began its part in the battle. On the morning of 23 December, the 3/15 Punjab from Casone, supported by B Squadron 50th Battalion Royal Tank Regiment, advanced up Item track and took over C. Vezzani. By 1500 hours, in the afternoon, 3/15 Punjab had consolidated and exploited along Item track to the group of houses known as Eusano, about twelve hundred yards short of the Tollo road. That was as far as this battalion was able to go. Item track north of C. Vezzani ran along a crest in full view of German positions on the west bank of the river Arielli. It was suicidal to try a further advance until Villa Grande and the country between Villa Grande and Vezzani had been cleared and a different approach made available. However, patrols did go out and located Germans outposts in some houses on Item track, about five hundred yards short of the Tollo road.

During the night and early next morning, 3/15 Punjab was frequently shelled and, at 0600 hours on 24 December, a company of Germans formed up in the river bed west of C. Vezzani and counter-attacked the Punjab battalion. The counter-attack was beaten off but not before the Germans had penetrated into one company position at C. Vezzani. D Company 1/5 Mahratta Light Infantry at the time in the area half a mile north of Villa Caldari, was placed under the command of 3/15 Punjab the next day. The defence of the C. Vezzani—Eusano area was a difficult problem. Houses in the area had been so battered by shell and mortar fire that they provided no cover and, as had been seen that morning, the Germans had a perfect covered approach in the Arielli river bed. Since it represented a serious threat to their line of communication from Tollo to Villa Grande, the Germans were impelled to pay considerable attention to the 3/15 Punjab salient. Artillery and nebelwerfer fire made it a most unpleasant spot. The 3/15 Punjab however continued to hold C. Vezzani.

The Third Attack on Villa Grande

There was no lull in the fighting in Villa Grande on Christmas eve. While 3/15 Punjab on Item track was dealing with the German counter-attack at C. Vezzani, the Essex and the paratroopers came out into the ring for the third round of the battle for Villa Grande. Heavy fighting swept the village all day and the Essex had to battle furiously for every yard of its advance. German resistance was particularly stubborn in the area of the village church, where it was suspected the paratroopers had an observation post, until a shell from a six pounder anti-tank gun hit the tower fair and square. The tower was not completely destroyed, but the German observation post was most reluctant to resume occupation of the battered church. An outflanking move by the Essex carrier platoon during the day achieved some success and gained a hold on houses on the east side of the village.

When Christmas day came, the battle still raged in the village. It seemed that the Essex were battering their heads against a stone wall by trying to take the village from the south. To reinforce this battalion, C Company of 3/8 Punjab was placed under its command to be used in increasing the pressure from the east.

Christmas morning was heralded by salvoes of shells in the Villa Grande area. Then, in the afternoon at 1530 hours C Company of 3/8 Punjab joined the fray. With tanks of the 50th Battalion Royal Tank Regiment in support, it attacked the village from the east. The tanks floundered through the thick mud, giving covering fire to the infantry from a flank as the men advanced towards Villa Grande. Machine gun fire from a group of houses on the main road, three hundred yards short of the village, greeted the invaders and showed that the German paratroops had not been caught off their guard by the direction of this new attack. These houses had been repeatedly cleared by the patrols of 1/5 Essex but, on each occasion, the Germans had reoccupied them as soon as the patrols had withdrawn. Any further advance by C Company of 3/8 Punjab towards the village was impossible until the houses had been cleared. Consequently, this company swung round and launched the attack. With tommy-guns blazing they charged the German positions whilst the tanks continued to give covering fire. The paratroopers fought back but the charge was made with such vehemence that the attackers were hurled into the German positions, where grenades and tommy-guns, used at close quarters, forced the latter to surrender.

After having cleared the houses, C Company of 3/8 Punjab continued the advance towards the village. Only a short distance had been covered when it was held up by cross-fire from the village. Little cover existed on the flat ground for the advancing infantry; the only solution was to move forward behind a smoke-screen. No 2-inch mortars were available to lay smoke as the crew had been wounded during the advance and the mortars had not yet been brought forward by other men in the platoon. Three German machine guns with tracer had been captured during the attack and the company commander ordered his men to open fire with the tracer on three widely separated haystacks. Within a few minutes the three stacks were alight, sending clouds of smoke billowing into the air. Aided by this, the company charged into Villa Grande, made for the two nearest houses and challenged the Germans to throw them out. Paratroopers fired on the houses from three directions, but the fire was returned through the windows. Continued pressure by 1/5 Essex and 3/8 Punjab helped to extend the hold on the village as far as the cross-roads opposite the church which gave them the major part of the village. But the Germans still held out to the north of the village square, though they were considerably shaken by the break-through.

On the Christmas day, General Montgomery sent the following message to the 8th Indian Division:

"I send herewith as a Xmas present to 8th Indian Division, 100,000 cigarettes and a large number of Sunday papers from England. I would like to congratulate your Division on very fine performance since it has been in Eighth Army. You have done everything that was demanded of you and most of it under very unpleasant conditions of weather, mud and so on. Please tell all your officers and men how very pleased I am with what they have done. A happy Xmas to you all."

On the two following days, 26 and 27 December, fighting continued and aided by tanks, an effort was made to drive out the last Germans. This effort failed in the face of heavy machine gun fire. The commander of the 8th Indian Division then ordered the 21st Indian Infantry Brigade to capture the high ground north of Villa Grande, which overlooked the junction of the roads to Ortona and Tollo. This road junction was of great importance for here the road Villa Grande—Tollo met the only lateral route which the German transport might use between Villa Grande and Ortona. Its capture would compel the Germans in Villa Grande to withdraw or surrender.

The 5th Battalion Royal West Kent Regiment was given the job of capturing this high ground and it moved to the area on the road, due east of Villa Grande, on the night of 27/28 December. A Company 1/5 Mahratta Light Infantry was sent to meet the 5th Royal West Kent Regiment on its way to the start line and to cover its left flank attack by dealing with the paratroopers still in Villa Grande. Fortunately, at 0230 hours on 28 December, the Germans acted on plan 'Ortona' and pulled out of Ortona, Villa Grande and the spur north of Villa Grande. A fighting patrol from 1/5 Mahratta Light Infantry penetrated the village and discovered that it had been evacuated by the German paratroopers, except for a few stragglers.

The Eighth Army's Offensive Halted

Although the V Corps (the 1st Canadian and 8th Indian Divisions) secured its objectives—Ortona and Villa Grande—the XIII Corps (2nd New Zealand Division and the 5th British Division) failed to break through the German defences at Orsogna. On 23 December a fierce attack was made, a brigade of the 5th Division captured Arielli but the 5th New Zealand Brigade failed to break through the German defences. Orsogna remained unconquered.

Before the end of the year the Eighth Army's offensive on the Adriatic coast was halted by the severity of the winter. Minor advances were made by the Canadians and the Indians before the end of the year. On 31 December the Canadians captured the villages of S. Nicola and S. Tommaso, just west of Ortona. Pt. 59, overlooking the sea about two miles above Ortona, was captured on 4 January 1944. Thus in the first week of January 1944, when the offensive was halted, the Canadians held a long front running from the sea at Pt. 59 along a small stream called the Riccio (inclusive S. Nicola and S. Tommaso), to Villa Grande, north-west of C. Berardi.

Exploitation from Villa Grande

On the left of the Canadians, the 8th Indian Division, too, made small gains by the end of the year. From Villa Grande, the 21st Indian Infantry Brigade exploited north and north-west. At 2100 hours on 28 December 1943, working to a timed artillery programme arranged with the divisional gunners, 1/5 Mahratta Light Infantry passed in a westerly direction through the 5th Royal West Kent Regiment (still in position north of Villa Grande) to seize the high ground half a mile north-west of the junction of the Tollo and Ortona roads. The Mahrattas encountered no small arms opposition but heavy shelling caused delays and some confusion. Leaders had to concentrate to keep direction in a black night over most difficult country. However, at 0400 hours, their objective was reached and the battalion re-organised and dug in. A crater in the road, a quarter of a mile north-west of the road junction, caused considerable delay to the tanks supporting the Mahratta Light Infantry. The battalion was frequently shelled and mortared but fortunately there was no counter-attack.

Foot patrols from B Squadron, 6th Lancers probed northwards, on the right flank through S. Nicola towards S. Tommaso, which was still held by a German rearguard, about one company strong. The final stage of the exploitation was for 1/5 Mahratta Light Infantry to advance to the cross-roads on the crest overlooking the Arielli valley, after dusk on 31 December. The 5th Royal West Kent Regiment came forward to release the Mahrattas for this undertaking. There was to be no artillery support. As a night operation in normal circumstances it would have been comparatively simple; but the weather broke up the battalion attack as effectively as a complete division of Germans might have done it. A blinding blizzard swept over the divisional front into the faces of the advancing troops, making any sort of controlled movement impossible. Visibility was nil, men floundered about in the snow storm until touch between neighbouring companies was lost. The cold was so severe that the unfortunate Mahrattas in the open could barely stand. There was nothing for it but to call off the attack and the battalion withdrew to Villa Grande.

By 2 January 1944, the 21st Indian Infantry Brigade was sitting on the high ground astride the Tollo road, north-west of Villa Grande, with the intention to push on along the road towards Tollo. But the patrols reported the area to be water-logged, as well as being dominated by German positions on the Tollo ridge across the river Arielli. The brigade commander having decided that any further advance was out of the question called a halt.

That day, a fighting patrol from the 5th Royal West Kent Regiment attempted to seize a group of farm buildings, called the Silo, on a spur overlooking a ravine, one mile north-west of Villa Grande. They went out by daylight over rather open ground and were repelled by well-directed machine gun fire, losing some men including the officer in charge. That night, 2/3 January, 1/5 Royal Gurkha Rifles relieved the 5th Royal West Kent Regiment north-west of Villa Grande and sent a company to the Silo area, which was occupied without opposition.

Twenty-four hours later, 1/5 Royal Gurkha Rifles put in a battalion attack to capture some farm houses standing on the track from S. Tommaso to Tollo where the track crossed the northern end of the Pian di Moregine. By 0500 hours on 4 January 1944, this battalion, despite determined German resistance, was finally established on its objective.

On 5 January 1944, the 14th Canadian Armoured Regiment replaced the 50th Royal Tank Regiment and Headquarters 1st Royal Fusiliers moved to S. Nicola. Under cover of darkness, the 1st Royal Fusiliers established two companies in the area of the track and stream crossing, eight hundred yards west of S. Nicola, and thereby closed the gap between the Canadians and the Gurkhas. This marked the most northerly advance of the 8th Indian Division on the Adriatic sector during the winter of 1943/44. Fierce German resistance, coupled with the bad weather conditions, seemed as though it would impose a halt on the Eighth Army; such was indeed the case. The early days of the new year marked the limit of the Army's advance before the renewal of the offensive in the spring. Since the Eighth Army had landed at Reggio in September 1943, the Germans had been pushed back six hundred and fifty miles, with the 8th Indian Division taking its full share in the pushing.

It was a fitting moment for General Montgomery to bring to an end his highly successful leadership of the Eighth Army. He handed over to General Sir Oliver Leese and left for England where planning for the invasion of France had to be finalised.

CHAPTER V

Cassino

THE FEBRUARY ATTACK

The Tunis Conference (25 December 1943)

General Alexander's plan of November 1943 for the capture of Rome had envisaged the operations to be carried out in three phases. In the first phase, the Eighth Army was to break through the Winter Line on the Adriatic coast, advance to the great lateral road which ran across the peninsula from Pescara through Avezzano to Rome, establish a bridge-head across the Pescara river and thus threaten the flank of the German forces engaged in the defence of Rome. In the second phase, the Fifth Army was to drive up the Liri and Sacco valleys to capture Frosinone and thus approach Rome from the south. In the third phase, there was to be an amphibious operation south of Rome directed on the Alban Hills (this operation was given the code name of 'Shingle'). The third phase of the operations was to be dependent on the progress of the first two. But this plan could not be implemented. The first phase of the battle for Rome began when the Eighth Army launched the attack across the river Sangro on 26 November 1943. By the end of December the Eighth Army's advance came to a halt, twenty-five miles from its objective, Pescara. The first phase of the battle for Rome therefore miscarried. The second phase began on 1 December 1943 when the Fifth Army launched the attack. This operation also did not come up to the expectations, for by 10 December "although the Monte Camino feature had been taken, progress into the Liri Valley was slow, and it still required a break-through of the Mignano Defile before the way to Cassino would be clear."[1] Thus the first, as well as the second phase of the battle for Rome had miscarried. Consequently the third phase of the operations, dependent on the success of the first two phases, had to be temporarily abandoned.

Due to the stubborn resistance offered by the Germans on the eighty-mile front, stretching from the Adriatic Sea to the Tyrrhenian Sea, neither the Eighth nor the Fifth Army was able to break through the Gustav Line. To consider the over-all strategy to be followed, a conference was held on 25 December 1943 at Tunis between Mr. Churchill and the principal Commanders-in-Chief in the Medi-

---

[1] *Report by the Supreme Allied Commander Mediterranean to the Combined Chiefs of Staff on the Italian Campaign, 8th January 1944 to 10th May 1944*, p. 5.

terranean Theatre. After listening to General Eisenhower's appreciation of the military situation, Mr. Churchill declared firmly "that it would be folly to allow the campaign in Italy to drag on and to face the supreme operations against Europe in the spring with the task in Italy half finished."[2] There was general agreement on this principle but the main problem was how to break the stalemate on the Italian front. The only way to avoid a further long and arduous mountain campaign was to carry out an amphibious attack so as to threaten the German communications. But if the amphibious attack was to achieve its main object of drawing off the reserves from the main Liri front, thus enabling the II U.S. Corps to break through the Gustav Line, it was essential that the initial landing should be carried out by a force not less than two assault divisions. The crux of the problem, however, was the shortage of LSTs (Landing-Ship, Tanks). It was imperative to retain the 56 LSTs, due to return to the United Kingdom on 15 January 1944 (for the invasion of France) until 5 February to enable the Anzio landing to take place on 25 January 1944. But would the Combined Chiefs of Staff agree to this proposal, which was likely to interfere with the main operation 'Overlord' for the invasion of France? In a telegram to President Roosevelt, on 25 December 1943, Mr. Churchill forcefully represented the urgency of agreeing to this proposal. "Having kept these fifty-six LSTs in the Mediterranean so long, it would seem irrational to remove them for the very week when they can render decisive service. What, also, could be more dangerous than to let the Italian battle stagnate and fester on for another three months? We cannot afford to go forward leaving a vast half-finished job behind us. It therefore seemed to those present that every effort should be made to bring off Anzio on a two-division basis around January 20, and orders have been issued to General Alexander to prepare accordingly. If this opportunity is not grasped we must expect the ruin of the Mediterranean campaign of 1944."[3] The Combined Chiefs of Staff agreed to the proposal and thus the Tunis Conference registered a triumph for Mr. Churchill's policy of expanding operation 'Shingle' in size and scope. The original 'Shingle' plan had envisaged an amphibious landing of one division. According to the revised plan the initial landing force was to consist of not less than two assault divisions. Not only was the size of the assaulting force increased but the scope of the operation was also widened. According to the original plan the amphibious flanking attack was to be made to assist the main Fifth Army when it had reached a line north of Frosinone. But according to the revised plan a much larger operation was to be carried out regardless of the position of the Fifth Army on the south.

[2] *Ibid*, p. 6.
[3] Churchill: *Closing the Ring*, p. 387.

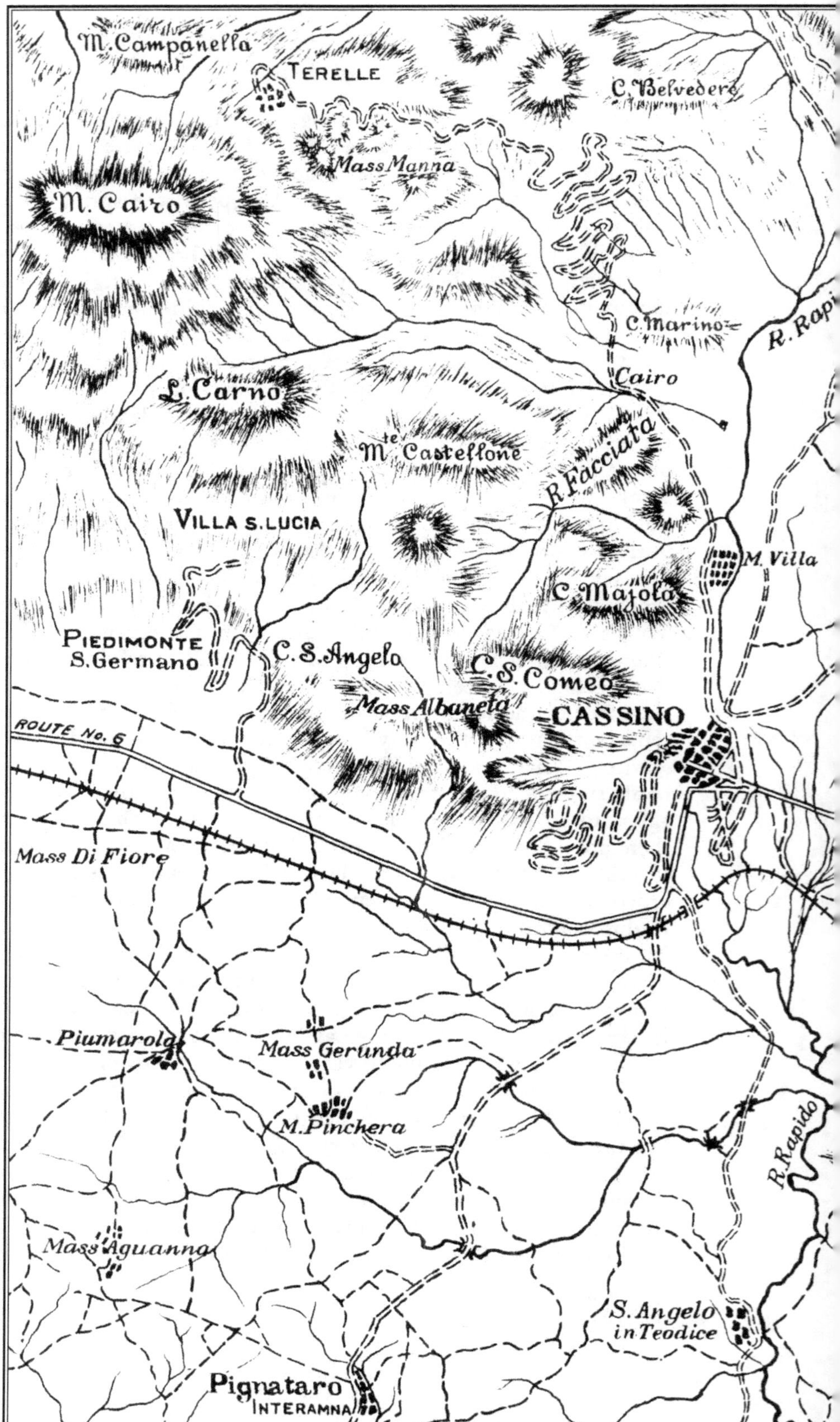
M. Campanella
TERELLE
C. Belvedere
Mass Manna
M. Cairo
C. Marino
Cairo
L. Carno
Mte Castellone
R. Facciata
VILLA S. LUCIA
M. Villa
C. Majola
PIEDIMONTE
S. Germano
C. S. Angelo
C. S. Comeo
Mass Albaneta
CASSINO
ROUTE No. 6
Mass Di Fiore
Piumarola
Mass Gerunda
M. Pinchera
R. Rapido
Mass Aguanna
S. Angelo
in Teodice
Pignataro
INTERAMNA

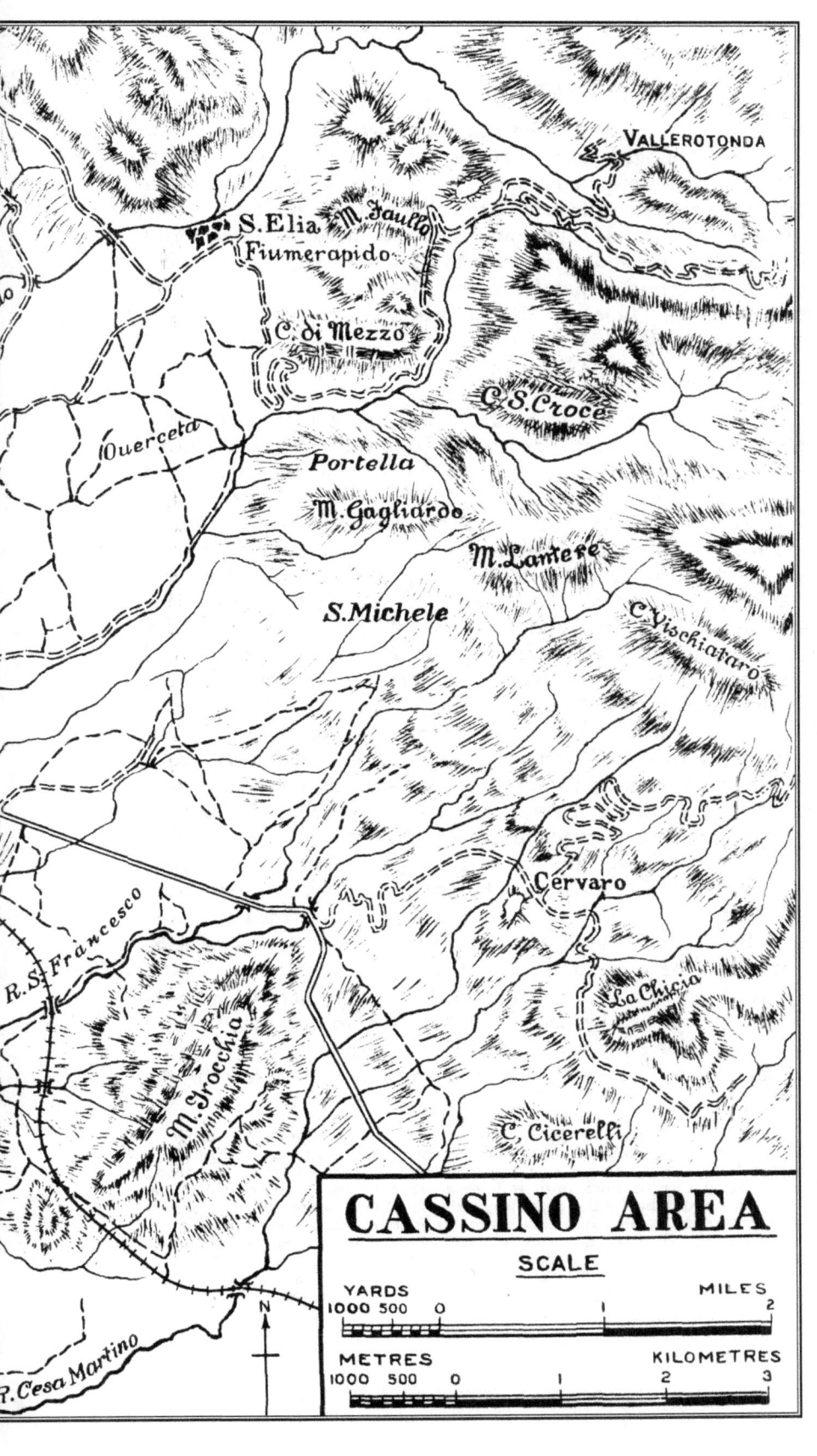

Thus the Tunis decision marked the emergence of a revised plan for the operation 'Shingle', with its conception of an amphibious operation as a major project and not a mere supplement to the Fifth Army's main attack. The core of the plan was that the Fifth Army was to make a powerful thrust towards Cassino and Frosinone shortly prior to the assault landing in order to draw the maximum number of German reserves to that front, and then to break through the formidable Gustav Line and link up with the amphibious landing force.

The Gustav Line

The Fifth Army was to be the spear-head of the Allied attack on the Gustav Line, which barred the way to Rome. The Gustav Line was based on the high ground behind the Garigliano and Rapido, with its key fortress being Monte Cassino. The Ortona—Maiella sector was the eastern flank of the well prepared defence line to which the Germans had withdrawn during the autumn of 1943. In front of the Fifth Army, the defences followed generally the valley of the R. Garigliano,[4] and were known as the Gustav Line. This position across Italy, from Ortona to the Minturno, was an impressive, natural, defence line where the peninsula is at its narrowest and where roads are few. The mountains stretch from shore to shore in an almost continuous barrier. The Liri valley provided the path taken by the main highway, Route 6, from Naples to Rome. The only other road to Rome from Naples, Route 7, followed the coast, but it had been seriously damaged by the Germans and, to a certain extent, by the bombing of the Allied air forces. Between Routes 6 and 7 lay the Aurunci mountains over which there were no roads. The Fifth Army facing the Gustav Line had therefore two possible approaches to the Rome plain. The first was by sea and the second up the Liri valley. We are more particularly concerned with the latter, where the battle line faced west not north, as might be assumed from the geographical lie of Italy.

With the stretch of the hills on its flanks and a narrow entrance, the Liri valley was easily defended. M. Cairo massif, rising to five thousand feet above the valley, and sprawling some ten miles northwards and westwards in the angle formed by the valleys of the

---

[4] The river Garigliano undergoes throughout its length a confusing change of names. In the Matese mountains and some twenty miles north-east of Cassino, a stream, the Rapido, has its source. From that point it flows first west then south, within a mile of Cassino town until it joins another stream, the Gari, which has come only two and a half miles from its origin on Monte Cassino. Over the next five miles, where the combined stream winds considerably, maps disagree. For our purpose it will be called the Gari. At the end of those five miles, the Gari meets a bigger stream, the Liri, which flows in from the west. The result of their union follows a southerly course and bears the name Garigliano. Two miles from the Gulf of Gaeta, the river is joined by the Ausente from the north.

Rapido and the Liri was the northern bulwark to the Liri valley position. M. Cairo was dwarfed by the mighty, snow-covered Matese mountains to the north-east, but from the Rapido valley and the hills on its east, this feature was imposing enough to awe the bravest soul. Wherever one might be, one was harassed by the feeling that eyes on M. Cairo were watching every move. More often than not, the summit was hidden in cloud, but that did not entirely overcome this dread. To a superficial inspection, the hills looked bare and smooth, with no natural cover for assaulting troops. Closer inspection, however, showed that many ridges and heights were contained, though often absorbed, in the main feature; there was a shrub, frequently a thick shrub; rocks on the hill-side were big enough to provide ample cover and to impose a terrible obstacle against movement. The difficulties presented by the rocks, the shrub and the steepness of the hill-sides need emphasis. Houses were few. Ravines, down which, after rains, swollen torrents rushed, were narrow and usually enclosed by the sides of sheer cliff.

At the extreme south-easterly corner of this mass, above Route 6, the railway and the rivers, stood the ancient Benedictine Monastery of Cassino. The great dome on which it stood, though only some fifteen hundred feet high, and therefore small in comparison with M. Cairo, towered above the valleys to the east and south. A more detailed description of the Monastery will be given later.

During the four months gained by the fighting withdrawal from southern Italy, the Germans had considerably strengthened the Gustav Line defences. They had paid particular attention to the centre of the line, which had been strongly fortified by defensive works. On the north the mountains acted as a good barrier. Here the defences were improved by the siting of mortars and machine guns on the reverse slopes and the covering of the forward slopes with automatic weapons in well camouflaged emplacements. The natural avenues of approach were mined, and every trail was swept by machine guns. Further to the south, there was a strong defence line stretching from the village of Cairo to S. Ambrogio. The Germans displayed great art and ingenuity in fortifying this line. Cassino was protected by diverting the water of the Rapido to the flat ground east of the river, converting it into a quagmire, in which the armour would be bogged down. The approaches to the river were thoroughly mined. The west bank was extensively wired. There were extensive minefields between the river and the mountains. To the west of the river emplacements were blasted and dug into the steep barren slopes, thus providing concrete and steel fortifications, which were strong enough not to be shattered even by the direct hits of artillery shells. There were concealed communication trenches leading to machine gun emplacements. Fields of fire were cleared and so interlocked as to command all approaches from the east. A large number of observation posts on the mountains, and it is thought even in the Abbey of Monte Cassino, gave the Germans a perfect view of the approaches to the Rapido. Further, Cassino was strongly fortified. The approaches to the town were guarded by self-propelled guns and tanks while there were a large number of machine gun emplacements in the buildings. Posts of strategic importance were garrisoned by snipers and well-armed troops. A large number of machine gun emplacements on the slopes of the hills behind the town afforded it good protection. The roads leading south from Cairo and S. Elia, as well as Route 6 were mined and covered by artillery, mortar and nebelwerfer fire. Cassino was in fact the key of the Gustav Line. The Rapido Line, south to the river Liri, was also strongly fortified, though it lacked the overwhelming advantages of Cassino.[5]

As the area around Cassino was the key to the portion of the Gustav Line lying north of the Liri river it is necessary to give a brief description of its defences. Four miles to the north-west of Cassino towered the massive M. Cairo, whose peaks were covered with snow. The vital area of defence was half of the district, which extended over two miles to the west and three miles to the north of Cassino. This area, which was held in strength by the Germans, guarded Cassino and the northern entrance to the Liri valley. M. Castellone and S. Angelo Hill were the western limits of the Cassino defences. The area south of Majola Hill (near the centre of the district) was of great strategic importance and was held in overwhelming strength by the Germans. Monastery Hill (Pt. 516) and the surrounding hills, dominated the town. Pt. 593, about one-half mile to the north-west, served as the outer bastion of Monastery Hill. In its turn Pt. 593 was protected by S. Angelo and Majola Hills. The ridge which ran north-east to Cassino, had three important points, terminating in Castle Hill (Pt. 193) on the western outskirts of the town. Another key point was the Hangman's Hill (Pt. 435), three-fourths of the way up the south-western slopes of the Monastery Hill.[6] In view of these strong defences the Germans were confident that the Gustav Line would effectively check the Allied advance. Their hopes were not unfounded.

Closing up to the Gustav Line

By the middle of January 1944, the Fifth Army closed up to the Gustav Line and prepared to launch attacks on its formidable defences. On the left the X Corps stretched from the coast near the mouth of the Garigliano river to a short distance above the junction

---

[5] *Fifth Army History*, part IV, "Cassino and Anzio," pp. 7-8.
[6] *Ibid*, pp. 87-8.

of the Liri and Gari rivers. In the centre the II U.S. Corps was aligned along the Rapido river north to the vicinity of S. Elia. On the right was the French Expeditionary Corps guarding the north flank of the Fifth Army.

The German forces were being regrouped to meet the Allied attack. The *94th Infantry Division* held a front of about twelve miles from the coast along the lower Garigliano. Next was the *15th Panzer Grenadier Division* covering a front of eight miles, nearly as far as Route 6, just south of Cassino. Then there was the *44th Infantry Division* guarding the front as far as the village of Cairo. Next came the *5th Mountain Division* stretching for about eleven miles north-east from Cairo. As the Allied attack developed, two additional divisions strengthened the Gustav Line—the *71st Infantry Division* in the sector of the *44th Infantry Division* and the *90th Panzer Grenadier Division* in the sector of the Garigliano river line.

General Alexander's Plan

General Alexander had prepared a plan by which a frontal attack on the Gustav Line was to be co-ordinated by an outflanking amphibious landing at Anzio to cut the German lines of communication.[7] The plan, as finalised by 12 January, envisaged a three-pronged attack on the Gustav Line: the French Expeditionary Corps to seize the high ground north of Cassino on 12 January, the II U.S. Corps to capture Monte Trocchio on the 15th and reach the Rapido river, and the X Corps to cross the lower Garigliano in the Minturno area on the 17th and attack northwards up the Ausente river valley towards S. Giorgio. Then, with its left and right flanks thus protected, the II U.S. Corps was to force the Rapido in the area of S. Angelo on 20 January and exploit rapidly, supported by armour, westwards and north-westwards. Two days later the VI U.S. Corps was to land at Anzio and threaten the rear of the German forces.

The January Offensive

The preliminary operations were completed by 15 January—the French Expeditionary Corps captured Monte Santa Croce and the II U.S. Corps secured Monte Trocchio, the last hill before the Rapido. The Fifth Army was thus poised for an attack on the Gustav Line. Opening the offensive, the X Corps crossed the river Garigliano towards the Aurunci mountains. To its east, the II U.S. Corps made a frontal drive across the Rapido on 20 January, while the French Expeditionary Corps, on the right, went through the mountains to try to turn the Rapido defences from the north. Two days later, the VI U.S. Corps landed at Anzio with the object of cutting the road from Cassino to Rome.

[7] Alexander's Despatch, *op. cit.*

The X Corps gained initial success. The *94th Infantry Division* was powerless to stem the Allied advance. Field-Marshal Kesselring acted with energy. Three divisions were switched on to the defence of this front—the *90th Panzer Grenadier Division* brought from the Eighth Army front, the *29th Panzer Grenadier Division* brought from the Rome area and the *Hermann Goering Panzer Division*, which had been earmarked for the defence of France. These three divisions launched powerful counter-attacks and frustrated the attempt of the X Corps to envelop the southern flank of the Gustav Line.

The attack by the II U.S. Corps across the Rapido also failed. The attack was thwarted by murderous fire from the Cassino spur on the right flank, a feature which commanded the whole of the entrance to the Liri valley. In order to outflank that feature, the II U.S. Corps moved farther north to co-operate more closely with the French Expeditionary Corps in the mountains. Another American crossing of the Rapido was made north of Cassino in spite of fierce opposition. Their objectives were M. Castellone and M. Albaneta, both slightly higher than Monte Cassino and to the north of it. After six days of severe fighting, the Americans and the French secured the hills overlooking the village of Cairo. This was the situation on 29 January, when in the night, the II U.S. Corps opened the new offensive with the object of capturing, by a pincer movement, Cassino and the spur above it. From the north, one force moving along the west bank of the Rapido, was to attack the town. A second force farther north, was to capture the summit of M. Majola, on which they already had a footing, and M. Castellone, following up with an attack south-eastwards to Monastery Hill, or Monte Cassino, which completely dominated the town. Repeated gallant attempts to take the town failed, and the result of two weeks' fighting was the occupation of only a few houses in the outskirts of the town.

The force in the hills achieved considerable success against determined opposition. On 2 February, much of M. Castellone was held by the Americans. Four days later, they had fought to within 300 yards of Monastery Hill despite withering fire from the Germans. For nearly another week, the II U.S. Corps pressed its attacks but Cassino continued to hold out. Ten weeks of almost uninterrupted figfting had taken a heavy toll of lives in the II U.S. Corps. The survivors were greatly exhausted by battle and foul weather. When the last attack failed on 11 February, command of the sector passed to the New Zealand Corps and the first phase of the battle of Cassino came to an end. The task of capturing Cassino was entrusted to the New Zealand Corps.

Neither the X Corps nor the II U.S. Corps was able to make

any headway against strong German opposition. The issue of the battle was, however, being decided at Anzio, where the VI U.S. Corps landed on 22 January without encountering much opposition. Field-Marshal Kesselring had not expected an attack at Anzio and, therefore only elements of the *90th Panzer Grenadier Division* were guarding this area. He, however, reacted with vigour to the challenge. He rightly divined that the impetus of the attack of the X Corps had died down and therefore he withdrew some troops from the lower Garigliano front. He also withdrew troops from the stagnant Adriatic front. At the same time he rushed troops to Anzio from north Italy. By 30 January 1944, when the Allied build-up was complete at Anzio for launching the major attack, Field-Marshal Kesselring had managed to assemble elements of eight divisions south of Rome. When the VI U.S. Corps launched a vigorous offensive on 30 January it was unable to break through the strong German defences. Then the Germans counter-attacked on 3 February. Although the attacks were repulsed it was clear that unless reinforcements arrived it would not be possible for the Allies to overcome German resistance.

The New Zealand Corps

Taking stock of the situation at the end of January 1944, General Alexander found that Field-Marshal Kesselring had succeeded in sealing off the Anzio bridge-head and had repulsed the attacks of the X Corps across the Garigliano and of the II U.S. Corps across the Rapido. The attempt to envelop the Gustav Line defences from the right by increasing the pressure of the II U.S. Corps and the French Expeditionary Corps in the hills above Cassino in order to capture it also encountered stiff opposition. Hence, General Alexander came to the conclusion that it would be necessary to strengthen the 2nd New Zealand Division if it was to have a reasonable chance of success in its task of exploitation. Accordingly he instructed Lieut.-General Sir Oliver Leese, the commander of the Eighth Army, to despatch the 4th Indian Division (operating on the static Adriatic sector) to the Cassino front to form part of a temporary New Zealand corps under Lieut.-General Freyberg. At 1000 hours on 3 February 1944, the New Zealand corps, initially comprising the 2nd New Zealand Division and the 4th Indian Division, came into being and passed under the command of the Fifth Army.

At this time hopes ran high of the success of an enveloping movement in the hills north of Cassino. General Clark felt the necessity of strengthening the American troops in their enveloping attack on Monte Cassino from the north. He therefore instructed General Freyberg to detail a brigade to relieve the 36th U.S. Division, holding the line of the Rapido, in order to enable the latter to take part in the enveloping attack on Cassino from the north. The 5th New Zealand Brigade relieved the 36th U.S. Division and at 0900 hours on 6 February the New Zealand corps took over from the U.S. corps command of the Rapido line south of Cassino, with Route 6 forming the boundary with the II U.S. Corps.

Lieut.-General Freyberg's first plan of operations made on 4 February 1944 represented a continuation of the American plan. The Americans were to make an enveloping attack in the hills north of Cassino so as to avoid a frontal assault on the formidable defences of Cassino. The role of the 2nd New Zealand Division was to establish a bridge-head across the Rapido when a decision had been reached in the mountains north of Cassino. The 4th Indian Division was not to be committed immediately and its future role was to be dependent on the outcome of the American attack. In spite of strenuous efforts the American troops failed to break through the German defences. The last attack made on 11 February met with no better results. As the thrust of the 2nd New Zealand Division was to be dependent on the success of the American attack this part of the operation could not be carried out.

4th Indian Division in the Line

The 4th Indian Division, which now prepared to take part in the battle of Cassino, was a veteran formation, which had taken a prominent part in the operations in North and East Africa. The division had arrived at Taranto from Egypt on 8 December 1943, and on 17 January 1944 had moved forward to the static Orsogna sector on the Adriatic coast, where it remained only for two weeks. Handing over the Orsogna sector to the 5th Canadian Armoured Division, the 4th Indian Division prepared to take part in the battle of Cassino.

The 4th Indian Division, commanded by Major-General F. I. S. Tuker, C.B., D.S.O., O.B.E., consisted of:

7th Indian Infantry Brigade:
    1st Battalion Royal Sussex Regiment
    4th Battalion 16th Punjab Regiment
    1st Battalion 2nd King Edward VII's Own Gurkha Rifles.

5th Indian Infantry Brigade:
    1st Battalion 4th Essex Regiment
    1st Battalion 9th Gurkha Rifles
    1st Battalion 6th Rajputana Rifles.

11th Indian Infantry Brigade:
    2nd Queen's Own Cameron Highlanders
    4th Battalion 6th Rajputana Rifles
    2nd Battalion 7th Gurkha Rifles.

Artillery:
  1, 11 and 31 Field Regiments RA
  149 A Tk Regt. RA
  57 Lt. AA Regt. RA.
Engineers and other ancillary units.[8]

The 7th Indian Infantry Brigade was the first to move into the line. It concentrated on the lower, eastern slopes of M. Castellone near Cairo village at midnight on 11 February. This brigade had been selected to lead the attack and, as a preliminary to that operation, it was to take over from the American troops on the front of its advance in the night of 12/13 February. At the time, the II U.S. Corps had four infantry regiments forward in the region of Monte Cassino, one infantry regiment on M. Castellone and one in the northern outskirts of Cassino town.

The New Zealand Corps Plan

General Alexander was reluctant to commit his exploiting force but when by 8 February it became evident that the American attack would not succeed he warned the New Zealand corps to be prepared to take over the American sector in case the final attack on 11 February also failed. Keeping this contingency in mind Lieut.-General Freyberg drew up a plan of operations on 9 February. This plan differed fundamentally from the first plan of 4 February. According to the first plan Cassino was to be turned by an enveloping attack in the hills to its north by the American troops and then the New Zealand division was to establish a bridge-head across the Rapido. As has been mentioned, it was not possible to implement the plan for the American enveloping attacks had failed. General Freyberg was now convinced that the clearing of Monte Cassino was essential to a drive down the Liri valley. A frontal attack now took the place of the enveloping attack. The strong German pressure on the Anzio bridge-head was having its repercussions. As long as the Anzio bridge-head was in danger, the demand for a vigorous offensive on the Cassino front (to draw off German troops from the Anzio bridge-head) was irresistible. Although disappointed at the slow progress of the Allied forces in Italy, Mr. Churchill found some consolation in the thought that the Allied offensive in Italy was compelling the Germans to fight in South Italy, 'far from other battlefields'. He believed that it was necessary to continually engage the Germans for "even a battle of attrition is better than standing by and watching the Russians fight".[9] It was indeed to be a battle of attrition for the Germans

[8] Appendix II and Appendix III.
[9] Churchill: *Closing the Ring;* p. 431.

had succeeded in sealing off the Anzio bridge-head and were in a strong position to repel the frontal attacks on Cassino. The Allied forces were to wear themselves out in fruitless frontal attacks on Cassino.

The corps plan in its detail was as follows:—

(i) The 4th Indian Division, operating from the Castellone feature, was to attack and capture the Monastery Hill and the high feature (Pt. 593), exploiting south so as to cut Route 6 and capture Cassino from the west.

(ii) The 2nd New Zealand Division was to assist with fire on Cassino and Route 6 from the east side of the river Rapido, and was to be prepared to cross the river Rapido to assist the 4th Indian Division in capturing Cassino.

(iii) After the capture of Cassino, exploitation towards Pignataro and construction of crossings over the river Rapido on Route 6 were to be done by the United States Task Force[10] 'B'.

To complete the New Zealand corps, the 78th Division was placed under its command on 8 February. This third division, consisting of the 11th and 36th Infantry Brigades and the 38th (Irish) Infantry Brigade, was to be used for exploitation only, unless operations by the Germans compelled its employment in a defensive role.

The 7th Indian Infantry Brigade in the Line

The 7th Indian Infantry Brigade encountered many difficulties in carrying out the relief. In the early morning of 12 February, the Germans having launched one strong, unsuccessful counter-attack against the American regiment holding M. Castellone, began to infiltrate from the direction of Terelle. By first light, they had taken up position on the Manna feature, two miles from and two thousand five hundred feet above the concentration area of the 7th Indian Infantry Brigade near Cairo village. An attack by the units of the 34th U.S. Division, however, drove them off Manna, but such a threat compelled the 7th Indian Infantry Brigade to deploy two battalions in reserve positions. This delayed the relief until the following night, and in the interval the brigade suffered a number of casualties from German artillery and mortar fire.

At nightfall on 13 February, the Indian brigade moved forward to relieve the American forces. The climb was a long one over a rough mountain trail, and it was rendered more arduous by the recent spell of bad weather. German artillery and mortar fire fell on the route throughout its length, causing casualties among the troops moving up. All the positions held by the U.S. corps were

---

[10] New Zealand Corps O.I. No. 4, dated 9 February 1944.

on open hill-sides, exposed to German fire, and the more forward positions were close to the Germans and overlooked by them. Movement by daylight was a hazardous venture. Hence, it was not until the early hours of 15 February that the 7th Indian Infantry Brigade took command of the sector with 1 Royal Sussex astride Pt. 593, 4/16 Punjab on the left (in area Majola), holding the ridge about one thousand yards north of the Monastery, and 1/2 Gurkha Rifles in reserve. The divisional headquarters was set up at Cervaro, five miles east of Cassino, across the Rapido valley. The 5th Indian Infantry Brigade was at Portella and the 11th Indian Infantry Brigade at S. Michele, three and a half and two and a half miles, respectively, north-west of Cervaro.

The divisional artillery, to which had been added the guns of the Newfoundland Field Regiment, was deployed east and south of M. Trocchio, five thousand to six thousand yards south-east of Cassino. It was a prominent, isolated feature three thousand five hundred yards long, running from the north-east to south-west between Route 6 and the railway. It was conspicuous for its one thousand five hundred-foot peak which, surmounted by an ancient castle, offered a blank, cliff face towards Monte Cassino, and provided an air target for the Germans, who employed their aircraft offensively for the first time since the arrival of the division in Italy. Their tip and run raids caused little damage, and the 57th Light Anti-Aircraft Regiment succeeded in destroying seven German aircraft.

On the right of the 7th Indian Infantry Brigade was the 36th U.S. Division. The boundary between them ran north-east to south-west along the valley, approximately one thousand yards north-west of Pt. 593. On its left was the remainder of the 34th U.S. Division and beyond it, along the R. Gari, lay the X Corps. The opposition was provided by the *44th Infantry Division*, holding Pt. 193 (Castle Hill), Pt. 165, Pt. 445, Pt. 450, Pt. 569, Pt. 593, Pt. 468 and Pt. 575. On the right, the front turned north towards M. Castellone. On the left, it cut through Cassino town, north of Route 6.

On taking over the positions round Pt. 593, the 7th Indian Infantry Brigade discovered that the situation was less favourable and less secure than the number of American regiments holding the position indicated. In crossing the Rapido, capturing Cairo village and M. Castellone, repeated attacks and counter-attacks and continual exposure to mortar and artillery fire, in shallow "foxholes" scraped on the surface of the rock, whittled away the numbers of the Americans until every regiment had lost eighty percent of its normal strength. The survivors were utterly exhausted, as much by exposure to the frost and snow as by German offensive actions. Moreover, the Germans were found to be still firmly ensconced among the ruins of an old fort on the summit of Pt. 593. No troops could stay on the forward slopes of the ridge because they came under fire either from Pt. 575, twelve hundred yards to the west, or from positions to the east on Monte Cassino. The 7th Indian Infantry Brigade had, therefore, to take Pt. 593 before beginning its attack on the Monastery.

Major-General Tuker's Opposition to Frontal Attacks on Cassino

Major-General Tuker had approved of the original plan of 4 February for an enveloping attack on Cassino. He had clearly told Lieut.-General Freyberg that nothing would induce him to attack the Monte Cassino feature (which included both the Monastery and Pt. 593) directly unless "the garrison was reduced to helpless lunacy by sheer unending pounding for days and nights by air and artillery".[11] In fact he strongly advocated an attack to turn the Monastery Hill and to isolate it. Major-General Tuker, however, fell ill on 4 February and the officiating command of the 4th Indian Division devolved on Brigadier H. W. Dimoline. "At a time when, as never in its history, Fourth Indian Division needed a commander of sufficiently wide experience and standing to insist on the acceptance of his findings, it was bereft of its leader."[12]

Realising the urgency of the situation due to the imminence of strong German counter-attacks on the Anzio bridge-head, Lieut.-General Freyberg had modified the original plan of 4 February for he was hopeful of achieving some success by frontal attacks on Monte Cassino from the positions secured by the American troops. Major-General Tuker was considerably perturbed when he learnt that the original plan for an enveloping attack had been modified and that the operation had been broadened into a direct attack on Cassino. He therefore took the earliest opportunity to express his strong disapproval of the corps plan of 9 February 1944. On 12 February he addressed the following communication to the New Zealand Corps:—

"1. I have today seen the officiating Comd 4 Ind Div and the Bde Comds at 4 Div H.Q. and there discussed the present situation in the "Monastery" area of CASSINO in the light of our latest recces and recent activities of the 2 American Corps.

2. From NZ Intelligence Summary No. 17 of 6 Feb para 3(c) it is apparent that the enemy are in concrete and steel emplacements on the "Monastery" Hill.

From a wide experience of attacks in mountain areas I

---

[11] Letter from Lieut.-General Sir Francis Tuker to Dr. Bisheshwar Prasad (Director, Historical Section, Ministry of Defence, Government of India, New Delhi) dated 20 October 1957.
[12] Lieut.-Colonel G. R. Stevens, O.B.E.: *Fourth Indian Division*, p. 279.

know that infantry cannot 'jump' strong defences of this sort in the mountains. These defences have to be "softened up" either by being cut off on *all* sides and starved out or else by continuous and heavy bombardment over a period of days. Even with the latter preparation, success will only be achieved in my opinion if a thorough and prolonged air bombardment is undertaken with really heavy bombs a good deal larger than "Kittybomber" missiles.

3. We have complete air superiority in this theatre of war but the "softening" of the Monastery hill has not been started.

An attack cannot be undertaken till this "softening" process is complete. This has always been the view that I have voiced and it is now confirmed by what I later hear.

Already, three attacks have been put in and have failed—at some considerable cost, I am told. Another attack without *air* "softening" will only lead to a similar result. The Monastery feature is a far more formidable feature than TAKROUNA and resembles the higher parts of GARCI which were rightly deemed inaccessible to infantry attack once the first initial surprise had gone. At GARCI the enemy was in field defences and not in concrete emplacements.

4. If proper air "softening" is not possible then the alternative remains:—
   i.e. to turn the Monastery Hill and to isolate it.

This course I regard to be possible as the enemy is, I believe, still only in field defences in the mountain areas to the West and S.W. of MONTE CASTELLONI. Using MONTE CASTELLONI and the area now held by the American 2 Corps as a firm base, and making it a firm base, we can attack in fast short jabs to the West and S.W. of CASTELLONI and cut no. 6 road West of the Monastery Hill. With this, and an attack of CASSINO to keep that place quiet, the river can, I feel, be crossed lower down and that the crossing joined up with the cutting from the North of No. 6 road, thus isolating MONASTERY HILL.

5. To go direct for the MONASTERY HILL now without softening it properly is only to hit one's head straight against the hardest part of the whole enemy position and to risk the failure of the whole operation."[13]

[13] Main HQ 4 Ind. Div. to Main New Zealand Corps, No. 433/G, dated 12 February 1944, Appendix B1, War Diary 4 Ind. Div.

Later the same day, after studying the literature about the Monastery acquired in Naples, he addressed the following communication to General Freyberg:—

"1. After considerable trouble and investigating many bookshops in NAPLES, I have at last found a book, dated 1879, which gives certain details of the construction of the MONTE CASSINO Monastery.

2. The Monastery was converted into a fortress in the 19th Century. The Main Gate has massive timber branches in a low archway consisting of large stone blocks 9 to 10 metres long. This Gate is *the only* means of entrance to the Monastery.

3. The walls are about 15 ft high, or more where there are Monk's cells against the walls. The walls are of solid masonry and at least 10 ft thick at the base.

4. Since the place was constructed as a fortress as late as the 19th Century it stands to reason that the walls will be suitably pierced for loopholes and will be battlemounted.

5. MONTE CASSINO is therefore a modern fortress and must be dealt with by modern means. No practicable means available within the capacity of field engineers can possibly cope with this place.

It can only be directly dealt with by applying "blockbuster" bombs from the air, hoping thereby to render the garrison incapable of resistance. The 1,000-lb bomb would be next to useless to effect this.

6. Whether the Monastery is now occupied by a German Garrison or not, it is certain that it will be held as a keep by the lost remnants of the Garrison of the position. It is therefore also essential that the building should be so demolished as to prevent its effective occupation at that time.

7. I would ask that you would give me definite information *at once* as to how this fortress will be dealt with as the means are not within the capacity of this Division.

8. I would point out that it has only been by investigation on the part of this Div, with no help whatsoever from "I" sources outside, that we have got any idea as to what this fortress comprises although the fortress has been a thorn in our side for many weeks.

When a formation is called upon to reduce such a place, it should be apparent that the place is reducible by the means at the disposal of that Div or that the means are ready for it, without having to go to the bookstalls of

NAPLES to find out what should have been fully considered many weeks ago."[14]

Thus Major-General Tuker made a forceful plea for either 'softening' the Monastery Hill by a thorough air bombardment (preliminary to the frontal assault on Monte Cassino) or turning and isolating the hill. Nevertheless, his forceful arguments failed to dissuade Lieut.-General Freyberg from launching frontal attacks on Monte Cassino but, perhaps as a result of this protest, there was a change in the attitude towards the bombing of the Monastery, as a preliminary to attack.

Two questions crop up at this stage, firstly whether the bombing of the Monastery was justifiable, and secondly whether Lieut.-General Freyberg acted wisely in ignoring Major-General Tuker's plea for turning and isolating the Monstery Hill. As regards the bombing of the Monastery the Germans stoutly maintained that they respected the neutrality of the abbey; the Allies on the other hand suspected that the Germans were using the Monastery as an observation post. The argument in favour of the bombing has been forcefully advanced as: "Even if the Germans were certainly known to have observed the neutrality of the monastery, they made it impossible for the Allied troops to do likewise. The hill crowned by the monastery happened to be the commanding feature of the battlefield. The Germans had every right to defend it, and they would have neglected to do so only at the almost certain risk of opening to the Allies the road to Rome. But once the enemy had decided to include Montecassino in his defensive system the building on its summit inevitably became a legitimate target, for though the mountain might have been defended it could not have been captured, without attention to its summit. No one now doubts—and the Allies well knew at the time—that military activity was going on in the immediate vicinity of the abbey. Was this activity to claim immunity? If not, the bombing of targets on that steep declivity would have been equivalent in practical effect to bombing the monastery itself. It is the nature of war not to be a game played to the whistle between white lines."[15]

As regards the second question (whether General Freyberg acted wisely in ignoring Major-General Tuker's views) it may be admitted that Major-General Tuker was trying to anticipate the plan of the spring offensive of 1944 by which San Angelo bridge-head was secured and Monte Cassino completely turned. Lieut.-General Freyberg, however, felt that due to the force of circumstances, it was

---

[14] Main HQ 4 Ind. Div. to Main New Zealand Corps, No. 433/1/G dated 12 February 1944. Appendix 'Q1' to War Diary 4 Ind. Div.
[15] N. C. Phillips: *Italy* (volume I)—*The Sangro to Cassino* (Official History of New Zealand in the Second World War 1939-45), p. 216.

not possible for him to adopt the plan of turning the Monastery Hill. "His freedom was narrowly bounded, now as later, by earlier political, strategic and even tactical decisions. There was the political decision not to relax pressure on the enemy throughout the winter. This entailed a strategic decision as to the means of breaching the German Winter Line—a left hook by 10 Corps, a right hook by the French Expeditionary Corps and a punch down the centre by 2 Corps. This last thrust, directed at the heart of the enemy defences at the mouth of the Liri valley and at Cassino, was the one in which Clark chose to persist. Both the politics and the strategy might have been questioned, but their tactical consequences had to be accepted, and it was these that Freyberg inherited. A perspective view shows that the New Zealand Corps took up a battle already half fought, or more than half fought, by American troops who had shown admirable tenacity and won palpable success. The pith of one German criticism of the bombing of the abbey indeed is that it did not occur until the fighting in the first battle of Cassino was already subsiding.

"Freyberg cannot be blamed for not doing in February what Alexander did in May. The great May offensive was launched on a front of several miles by two armies, with no clear idea where the break would come but only a determination to exploit success. Freyberg, on the other hand, in command of a single corps in the depth of winter, had to make the best use of his resources to force a passage through a selected point in the enemy defences rather than wait for a success to turn up and then reinforce it. He could not bring the Allied superiority in men and machines to bear in a process of attrition. In deciding to attack Monastery Hill, the lynchpin of the defensive system, he was maintaining the momentum of an American drive which had brought our troops within a few hundred yards of the monastery walls: the next step, the seizure of Monte Cassino was all but predestined. He was in fact exploiting a turning movement, but it was the town and not the abbey of Cassino that he hoped to turn. The plan finally adopted was that one which survived the critical scrutiny of several plans. And when after its failure Freyberg had to rethink the problem, he could still see no means of avoiding the need to capture Monastery Hill; what he did vary was the direction from which it was attacked. In the circumstances of early February, his plan offered the best hope of success."[16]

The Divisional Plan

According to the instructions issued on 9 February 1944, by the corps commander, the role of the 4th Indian Division was to attack and capture the Monastery Hill and Pt. 593, exploit south to cut

[16] *Ibid*, pp. 217-18.

Route 6 and capture Cassino from the west. In implementation of this plan the commander of the 4th Indian Division issued the following detailed instructions on 11 February:

(a) The 7th Indian Infantry Brigade was to move forward from Cairo area to a forming up area to be selected by it on M. Comeo. The role of this brigade was threefold:
 (i) to attack and capture the Monastery Hill and hill feature Pt. 593,
 (ii) to exploit to the southern slopes of the Monastery Hill to control Route 6 by small arms fire,
 (iii) to exploit eastwards to join up with the 2nd New Zealand Division south of Cassino.

(b) The 5th Indian Infantry Brigade was to step forward behind the 7th Indian Infantry Brigade into the Cairo area. It was to have one battalion immediately available for the support of the 7th Indian Infantry Brigade, if required. It was also to be prepared to:—
 (i) take over from the 7th Indian Infantry Brigade on the Monastery Hill and hill feature Pt. 593 in order to release the latter for its exploitation roles,
 (ii) form a firm base on M. Castellone,
 (iii) pass through the 7th Indian Infantry Brigade to carry out one or both of the (first two mentioned) exploitation roles assigned to the 7th Indian Infantry Brigade.

(c) The following artillery was to render support throughout the operation:—
 (i) The New Zealand Corps artillery (144 field guns and 32 medium guns) with, on call, the II U.S. Corps artillery (72 105-mm's, 24 155-mm's, 48 8"-howitzers).
 (ii) The 31st Field Regiment was to be in close support of the 7th Indian Infantry Brigade. The 1st Field Regiment was to be in close support of the 5th Indian Infantry Brigade.

(d) The attack was to take place on the night of 13/14 February.[17]

The operations were originally planned to begin on the night of 12/13 February. But delays caused in the relief compelled several postponements, which enabled the 2nd New Zealand Division and the air forces to tide over the bad weather and play their part in rendering support to the 7th Indian Infantry Brigade.

Monte Cassino or Monastery Hill

Before proceeding to describe the operations carried on by the 4th Indian Division, we may review the nature of its objective. On

[17] 4 Ind. Div. O.I. No. 3, 11 February 1944.

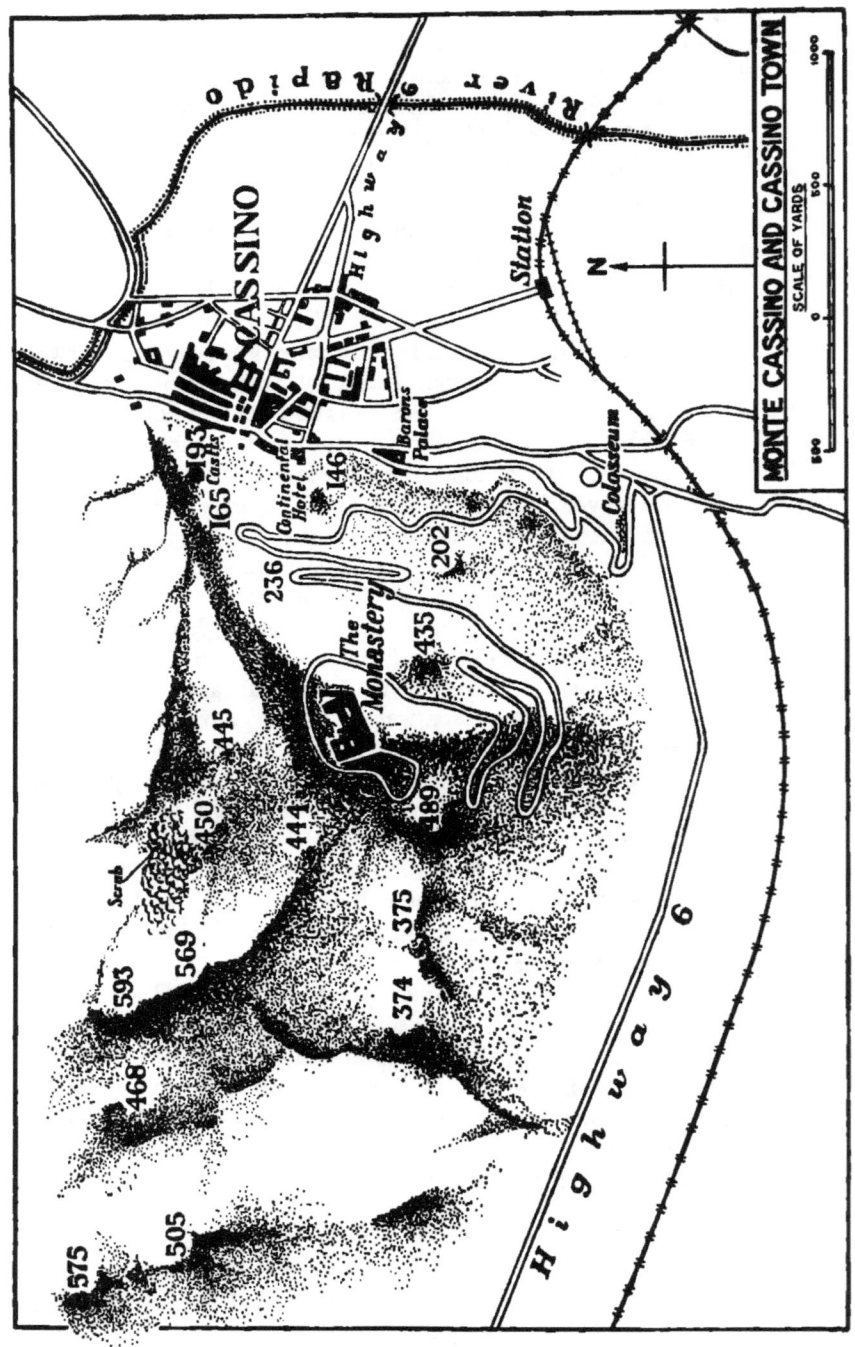

the right, west-end, was Pt. 593. This feature formed the southern peak of a rocky ridge, one thousand one hundred yards long, narrow on top and steep-sided down to the ravines on its east and west flanks. The northern end of this ridge was called "Snake's Head", from its representation on the map. Shrub, of a thorny type, hindered rather than concealed movement. Digging was almost impossible. Both sides built one and two-man sangars, such as were common on the North-West Frontier of India. A footpath ran along the crest of the ridge, but it was covered throughout its length by fire from the peak, Pt. 593, an abrupt rise of one hundred and fifty feet above the ridge. The sides of Pt. 593, were covered with large, white boulders, which provided excellent cover for the defenders. The ridge between Pt. 593 and the Monastery was undulating with two prominent dips. Here, too, the surface was rocky, but not to the same extent as on Pt. 593. The whole of the ridge was in view from both ends. A cart track followed the crest of the ridge.

Monte Cassino (or Monastery Hill) was a fortress of great strength. Methods of attacking it had been studied at the Italian Staff College as a regular exercise. Without any artificial works, the position was generally considered to be impregnable. But it had been fortified by pill-boxes of steel and concrete and emplacements drilled and blasted in the rock to make it one of the principal bastions of the German defences. The Monastery, which lay at the extreme (easterly) end of the feature, commanded the approaches from all directions and dominated the town of Cassino, the greater part of the Rapido valley, and the entire eastern end of the Liri valley. It had been converted into a fortress with an imposing gate of massive timber, which was the only entrance. The walls were fifteen feet high, ten feet thick at their base, and were loopholed. They rose sheer above the face of a cliff. They were unscaleable and thick enough to withstand any weapons which the infantry might bring against them. Heavy calibre bombs were needed to breach such walls.

The Bombing of the Monastery

At 0830 hours on 15 February, heavy and medium bombers carried out a bombardment to breach the walls of the Monastery. Waves of bombers, comprising one hundred and forty-two heavy and eighty-seven medium bombers, dropped three hundred and eighty tons of bombs and sixty-six tons of incendiaries. Weather conditions had enabled this attack to be carried out on 15 February, instead of on the 16th as originally planned. The bombers were all remarkably accurate in their bombing, though not so in their timing. And owing to lack of co-ordination between the commanders of the ground and the air forces, the forward troops on the ground could not have timely information to adjust their positions to conform with the bomb safety line. Consequently about twelve bombs from the first group of heavy bombers fell amongst the forward troops of the 7th Indian Infantry Brigade and inflicted twenty-four casualties.. These forward troops were in close contact with the Germans and could adjust their positions at night or under cover of smoke.[18] The operation was successful. The Monastery buildings were wrecked but the breaches in the walls did not reach down to the ground level.

During the bombing a conference was summoned by the commander 4th Indian Division at Headquarters 7th Indian Infantry Brigade, when it was decided that the attack on the Monastery could not be made on 15 February, as 4/6 Rajputana Rifles and 1/9 Gurkha Rifles, which were needed by the 7th Indian Infantry Brigade for the attack, were still on the far side of the Rapido valley, the Rajputana Rifles at Portella and the Gurkha at S. Michele. The maintenance route, which the battalions would have to follow from Cairo village was a long one, under constant fire and very congested. Hence the arrangement was that Pt. 593 would be attacked in the night of February 15/16, as originally arranged, and the main attack on the Monastery would be launched the following night.

Failure of the Attempt to Capture Pt. 593

Beginning the operation, 1 Royal Sussex set out after dark on 15 February to rush Pt. 593. The battalion had moved into the line two nights before, but had not been able to carry out detailed reconnaissance of the German positions, or of the ground between them, largely because, by day, movement was quite impossible without incurring losses. Consequently, no appreciation was possible of the strength of the position and only one company was used against it. Heavy machine gun and mortar fire caught the company in its forming-up area. To add to its difficulties, when only seventy yards beyond its startline, the company encountered an impassable line of rocks, which had not been marked on their maps. Intense fire at close range lashed the company mercilessly. After several unsuccessful attempts to find a way round the obstacle, the Sussex men withdrew, having suffered twenty casualties.[19]

A cloudy sky the following day made possible the use of only fighter-bombers for the continuation of the bombing of the Monastery. And in the night, the entire 1 Royal Sussex was employed against Pt. 593, though the narrowness of the ridge and the nature of the surface on the objective allowed of only a one-company frontage.

[18] Appendix 'L-2' to 4 Ind. Div. War Diary, February 1944.
[19] War Diary 7 Ind. Inf. Bde.

By 2220 hours, the forward company, having found a way round the previous night's obstacle, had gained a footing on the sides of Pt. 593. The German positions proved to be unexpectedly strong. They were firmly established among the ruins of an old fort on the summit, from the shelter of which they overlooked the attacking forces. Small arms weapons being of little use in such a position, grenades were used. But by the time a second company could arrive at Pt. 593, the first company had exhausted its supply of grenades and had suffered heavy casualties. Several German posts were captured, but those on the summit still held out. When the attackers had lost seven officers and sixty-three other ranks, this second attempt to capture Pt. 593 was also abandoned.[20] Soon afterwards, two companies of 4/6 Rajputana Rifles moved up to reinforce the Royal Sussex astride Pt. 593.

7th Indian Infantry Brigade's Plan

These operations provide an example of the necessity for striking a balance between operational demands and administrative possibilities. Two failures to take Pt. 593 indicated that the commander must now employ the greatest possible strength permitted by the difficulties of maintenance and by the nature of the ground. The limitations imposed by both these factors on the scope and method of attack were unusually severe. All the German strong-points in the area were mutually supporting at close ranges. To overcome such a defence system, two methods might be employed—to attack all strong-points simultaneously, or to destroy each strong-point in succession, beginning from one of the flanks. The commander of the 4th Indian Division had originally favoured the second method, beginning at Pt. 575 and then rolling up the defences in succession from west to east. This would have required a larger force than was available or than could be maintained over so difficult and exposed a route as the division's maintenance track. Compelled to modify this mode of operation, the commander elected to begin his rolling up from Pt. 593. Almost two brigades would be required for the task; the difficulties of assembling, deploying and supplying such a force in an area so dominated by the hostile force, must be faced.

As already mentioned, an augmented brigade had been selected for the task, and the following additional troops were placed under the command of the 7th Indian Infantry Brigade:

    4/6 Rajputana Rifles
    1/9 Gurkha Rifles
    Two companies 2nd Camerons
    Two companies 2/7 Gurkha Rifles

[20] *Ibid.*

Browning Troop 170 Light Anti-aircraft Battery
Tactical Headquarters 149 Anti-Tank Battery
513 Anti-Tank (motor) Battery.
B and C Companies Machine Gun Rajputana Rifles.
Two Advance Dressing Stations 17 Field Ambulance 12th Field Company was in support of the 7th Indian Infantry Brigade.

Brigadier O. de T. Lovett, D.S.O., commander of the 7th Indian Infantry Brigade, made the following plan of operation:

(i) At 2359 hours on 17 February, 4/6 Rajputana Rifles, with under command 1 Royal Sussex, two companies 2nd Cameron and C Company MG Rajputana Rifles was to advance astride ridge Pt. 593—Pt. 444 as far as including Pt. 444, retaining Pt. 593 as a firm base.

(ii) At 0200 hours on 18 February, 1/9 Gurkha Rifles on the right and 1/2 Gurkha Rifles on the left were to pass through the positions held by 4/16 Punjab and attack the Monastery, then both the battalions were to exploit down the hill-side and dominate Route 6 with small arms fire. 1/9 Gurkha was to contact the New Zealanders.

(iii) 4/16 Punjab was to hold the existing positions east of Pt. 593, until 1/9 Gurkha Rifles and 1/2 Gurkha Rifles passed through, then it was to come into the brigade reserve and be prepared to move forward to the Monastery Hill.

(iv) The 5th Indian Infantry Brigade (1/4 Essex and 1/6 Rajputana Rifles) was to concentrate near Portella, prepared to exploit success on Monte Cassino by attacking the Cassino town from the north.[21]

In implementation of the brigade plan, commander of 4/6 Rajputana Rifles issued the following instructions:

(i) the attack was to be made on a two-company front—B on the right and C on the left. They were to be followed by the Battalion Headquarters, D Company and A Company in succession,

(ii) the first stage was to be the capture of Pt. 593 as far as Pt. 569 and thence to Pt. 476,

(iii) the second stage was to capture Pt. 444. Owing to artillery concentration on Pt. 444 arrival at that point was not to be before 0200 hours.[22]

Thus the role of 4/6 Rajputana Rifles was to capture Pt. 593 and then to advance along the ridge to Pt. 444 in the rear of the Monastery. Two hours after the launching of the attack by 4/6

---

[21] 7 Ind Inf. Bde. O.I. No. 32, 17 February 1944.
[22] Verbal orders given by O.C. 4/6 Raj Rif for the attack on Pt. 593, Appendix 'B', War Diary 4/6 Raj Rif.

Rajputana Rifles, 1/2 and 1/9 Gurkha were to pierce through the German defences on the left and storm the Monastery. To implement this plan, commander of 1/2 Gurkha Rifles issued the following instructions:—

(i) The battalion was to move from area Majola to the forming up place in wadi in rear of Pt. 450—Pt. 445. C, the leading company, was to be followed by B Company, Battalion Headquarters, A Company and D Company. Then without delay B and C Companies, which were to lead the attack, were to fan out and move up the slope and cross the crest at 0215 hours. They were to move as fast and silently as possible, cross the fields, move down into the main wadi and climb up the wooded slope to the objectives. B Company's objective was the northwest corner and north face excluding the north-east corner of the Monastery. C Company's objective was the north-east corner of the Monastery and the road.

(ii) A Company was to cross the crest just in the rear of C Company, turn half left and capture Pt. 445.

(iii) D Company was to follow in the rear of B and C Companies to the wooded slope; then pass through C Company and clear the south-east corner of the Monastery.

(iv) All the Companies were to hold firmly to the ground gained. Then A Company was to be moved up and a plan made for exploitation on to Pt. 435 with A and B Companies, possibly in conjunction with 1/9 Gurkha Rifles.[23]

Commander 1/9 Gurkha Rifles issued the following instructions:

(i) A Company, followed by C Company, Battalion Headquarters, B Company, D Company and the Regimental Aid Post were to march in the order of battle straight for their objectives. The battalion objectives were the west wall of the Monastery and down to Pt. 453.

(ii) The objectives of the various companies were defined as below: A Company to secure from wooded area to road leading up to the Monastery, C Company to go through A Company across the road and up to the Monastery's garden wall, B Company with its left flank on the Monastery to Pt. 453, D Company to be in reserve, with the probable task of capturing the spur running south of the Monastery.[24]

---

[23] Notes for orders for attack on Monastery, Appendix D 2, War Diary 1/2 G.R.
[24] War Diary 1/2 G.R., 17 February.

2nd New Zealand Division's Plan

Now that the 4th Indian Division contemplated launching a full-scale attack, the 2nd New Zealand Division was to begin operations south of the Cassino town the same night. Thus the 5th New Zealand Brigade was to cross the river Rapido south of Cassino, at 2130 hours on 17 February, with the object of thrusting westwards and northwards to link up with the 4th Indian Division. The main object of the operation was to secure the Cassino railway station and the ground immediately to its north and south so as to hold the Germans in Cassino town at bay while armour and supporting infantry pushed along the railway embankment across the Rapido and drove forward into the Liri valley. In outline the plan was for the 28th Battalion to cross the Rapido with two companies and capture Cassino railway station so that the engineers might be able to bridge the river to enable armour to cross. Then, supported by the tanks, the rest of the battalion was to attack Cassino from the south and link up with the 4th Indian Division. At the same time the 23rd Battalion was to pass through to enlarge the 28th Battalion's bridge-head. The plan suffered from a serious defect for the assault was to be launched on a narrow front entailing the deployment of only two companies for the initial assault. The widening of the front by a simultaneous river crossing farther south (in area S. Angelo) would have drawn off German forces from the main narrow front south of Cassino. But this proposal was not accepted for three weighty reasons. Both sides of the Rapido were thickly mined and the Germans were dug in on the far bank; therefore a river crossing would have encountered stiff opposition. The limited resources of engineers and bridging equipment were a serious handicap for undertaking the southern crossing. Moreover, if the attack failed, the assaulting force would be isolated west of the river. Therefore in spite of its obvious limitations of assaulting on a narrow front the plan for a crossing of the Rapido south of Cassino was accepted.

Failure to Capture Pt. 593

Monte Cassino was bombed for the third time on 17 February. The sky was still overcast and again only fighter-bombers could be employed. Five groups of Kittyhawks and Mustangs bombed the place between 1600 hours and 1700 hours with a high degree of accuracy. The weight of bombs dropped this day and the day before was however only twenty-three and a half tons.[25]

The close proximity of the foremost troops to the German positions made direct artillery support impossible. Therefore heavy

---

[25] The bombing of Monte Cassino and the Monastery feature; Appendix L 2, War Diary 4 Ind Div.

concentrations were arranged, with the aid of the artillery of the 34th and 36th U.S. Divisions and two medium regiments, on possible German forming-up areas. The French artillery and other medium regiments were given counter-battery tasks.

Dispositions for the launching of the attack were completed on the night of 17/18 February and the battalions, which were to lead the attack, moved up the rough track. The Germans however were on the alert and swept the track with a harassing fire inflicting casualties. Thus only 20 mules out of a total of 200 accompanying 4/6 Rajputana Rifles reached the forward zone. In spite of this initial set-back the attack was launched at the scheduled time. At 2359 hours on 17 February, 4/6 Rajputana Rifles opened the attack on a two-company front, with B Company on the right and C Company on the left. They fought their way through intense machine gun, grenade and mortar fire. By 0045 hours on 18 February the attack was held up by determined German opposition. The companies were pinned by machine gun fire and grenades. They suffered heavy casualties in close fighting with the Germans, who were well dug in, behind thick walls and sangars, with a deep ditch astride the hill, which was enfiladed with machine guns and within grenade range. In spite of fierce opposition the two companies edged their way forward to within a hundred yards of the objective. This forward position was reached by 0140 hours. The Germans launched a counter-attack to drive off the Indian troops but the latter repelled the attack and did not yield an inch of ground. The situation was however not encouraging for the Indian troops were subjected to withering fire. As the two leading companies failed to make further progress the commanding officer decided to launch an attack with A Company on the left of D Company.[25] But probably he was not sanguine of success and decided merely to probe into German defences. He contented himself with launching the attack with one platoon only, keeping the bulk of his company in reserve. The platoon launched the attack at 0430 hours. The attack proved to be a mere demonstration and did not yield any results. The heroic efforts of 4/6 Rajputana Rifles to storm their way through the German defences ended in failure. From the summit and their well dug-in positions the Germans seemed to scoff at the futile attempts of the Indian troops to capture the objective. The situation was tantalising for only a hundred yards of no man's land separated the rival forces. But this area was of deadly peril, swept as it was by withering fire. Thus all the frantic efforts of 4/6 Rajputana Rifles to capture the vital Pt. 593 ended in failure. How heroic their effort was, can be realised from the fact that some of

[26] War Diary 7 Ind. Inf. Bde.

the riflemen and the officers did succeed in piercing the German defences.[27]

The Death Trap

While 4/6 Rajputana Rifles was busy hammering at the German positions on Pt. 593, 1/2 Gurkha Rifles moved forward on the left with two companies up, to begin the attack on the Monastery. The approach march had started at 0045 hours from Majola area with C Company leading, followed by B Company, Battalion Headquarters, A Company and D Company. As the headquarters group was moving south-west, one mortar bomb landed on the path wounding the signal officer, the officer commanding porter company, the brigade signaller, four riflemen, two NCOs including the Signal Havildar. The signal set was also knocked down. The headquarters was thus disorganised. However, by 0300 hours, B and C Companies, which were to lead the attack, and some of the headquarters group arrived just on the north slopes of Pt. 450, after being engaged by spandaus coming down the nulla. At 0400 hours when A and D Companies and most of the headquarters group had arrived, B and C Companies deployed for the attack, their left flank resting on Pt. 450.

Their advance was beset with difficulties from the beginning. Beyond the crest, which formed their start line, aerial reconnaissance had revealed a belt of shrub, like that found on many of the neighbouring hills, which normally interfered with movement very little. The shrub that the two leading companies now entered, was of an entirely different character, being chest high and thickly covered with thorns. As soon as the Gurkhas entered this thicket, a few yards beyond the position of 4/16 Punjab, they were met by a devastating hail of bullets and grenades from German emplacements, so close that they were within a grenade's throw of the start line and yet completely hidden in the darkness. The German defences were based on machine gun posts, fifty yards apart. Between these were weapon pits, each containing one man with a pistol and a large number of grenades. Owing to their proximity to the Gurkha positions, these posts were not softened up by the artillery fire. The shrub was dense and a formidable obstacle at the best of times. The German fire, as proved throughout the attack, was a model of accuracy. Both the companies were met by devastating cross-fire from mutually supporting spandaus on the Pt. 450—Pt. 445 spur, and from posts on the forward slopes of the Monastery,

---

[27] When Cassino was finally captured the bodies of Major Markham-Lee, Jemadar Maru Ram (who was posthumously awarded the Indian Order of Merit) and a number of riflemen were found inside the fort which crowned the summit of Pt. 593. See Stevens: *Fourth Indian Division*, p. 288.

and in enfilade from the right flank from high ground Pt. 593 and
Pt. 569. In addition, the Germans flung a continual stream of
grenades from their posts, which took a heavy toll of life among
the Gurkhas. Within fifteen minutes the two leading companies
were reduced to a platoon each. Yet the sturdy Gurkhas fought
with grim determination against tremendous odds, and some of the
men of C Company succeeded in crossing the death trap and in
reaching the nulla in front of the objective. While the gallant
Gurkhas of C Company gained the meagre shelter of the shallow
nulla, B Company was pulled back to the cover of shrub and trees
and dug in. A Company was then pushed forward between Pt. 450
and Pt. 445 and reached the nulla in front of the Monastery with
the remainder of C Company. Thus reinforced, the Gurkhas from
their shelter in the nulla tried to edge their way forward to the
Monastery. But their gallant effort did not succeed. For one hour
they tried to force their way through the German defences but without any success. By 0500 hours, B Company had come up and was
consolidating around Pt. 450 and to the north-west with the battalion headquarters only twenty yards in the rear on the reverse slope.
As no headway was made against the German defences, the Gurkhas
were recalled from the forward positions to the reverse slope of
Pt. 445. They had made a heroic effort to break through the
German defences. Most of the men in the leading companies had
been struck down within a few minutes of the launching of the
attack. The survivors, many of them already wounded, fought on.
They closed with the Germans, wiped out some of their posts and
desisted only when all but a handful of both the leading companies
had been killed or wounded and they had received an order to withdraw and dig defensive positions.

Failure to Capture Pt. 444

While 4/6 Rajputana Rifles and 1/2 Gurkha Rifles were hammering at the German positions, 1/9 Gurkha Rifles was also at grips
with the tenacious defenders. At 0215 hours, 1/9 Gurkha Rifles
from jump-off positions in the sector of 4/16 Punjab deployed with
A Company in the lead. From the top of the ridge—known as
'Snake's Head'—A Company swept forward towards Pt. 444. As the
Gurkhas passed through a small orchard they were subjected to a
heavy converging fire from Pt. 593 and Pt. 450. They swung to the
left until they reached the right of 1/2 Gurkha Rifles and then
attacked up the ridge to Pt. 450. At 0235 hours, B Company came
up and as Pt. 569 was obviously held by the Germans, they advanced
and attacked the eastern slopes of the ridge up to Pt. 593. At 0310
hours, one platoon of C Company followed B Company and was
soon in the thick of the fighting. At 0400 hours the rest of C

Company arrived and was sent forward to fill in the gap between A and B Companies. At 0440 hours, D Company came up and as A Company had suffered heavy casualties it was sent forward to reinforce them. But the gallant Gurkhas strove in vain to smash the German defences. Not much progress was made except by B Company and a platoon of C Company, who got over the ridge and moved down the reverse slopes, where they came under withering fire from Pt. 569 and suffered heavy casualties.[28]

The Situation at Dawn

In the faint glimmer of the dawn it was observed that the situation was none too pleasant. Except in the centre, where the two forward companies of 1/9 Gurkha Rifles had made a dent in the German defence line, not much progress had been made on either flank. B, C and D Companies of 4/6 Rajputana Rifles were astride Pt. 593, having failed in the attempt to capture the crest. A platoon of A Company was on the left flank and the remainder was in reserve. The forward platoon was however withdrawn to a position in the rear of the battalion headquarters in reserve. B and C Companies of the Royal Sussex were sent back in order to thin out on the hill. By 0700 hours on 18 February reorganisation was completed and 4/6 Rajputana Rifles established contact with D Company 4/16 Punjab, who was occupying a position on its left flank.[29]

1/9 Gurkha Rifles and 1/2 Gurkha Rifles were also pinned down in front of their objectives. By 0500 hours on 18 February, it was clear that the Germans still held the reverse slope of the ridge from Pt. 569 to Pt. 445, and in the dense jungle on the ridge the companies of 1/9 Gurkha Rifles had stuck, as had the companies of 1/2 Gurkha Rifles on their left flank. At 0630 hours, reorganisation took place. C and D Companies of 1/9 Gurkha Rifles in contact with 1/2 Gurkha Rifles on the left and the Royal Sussex on the right, held the crest of the ridge while A and B Companies were withdrawn slightly behind D and C Companies respectively. Throughout the operation the battalion headquarters was established on the Snake's Head feature.[30]

At dawn the position on the 1/2 Gurkha Rifles' front had been stabilised as follows: A Company, with about twenty men of C Company from Pt. 445 with one company 4/16 Punjab on their left; D Company on A Company's right with B Company (24 men) on their right linking with some platoons of 1/9 Gurkha Rifles.[31]

[28] War Diary 1/9 G.R.
[29] War Diary 4/6 Raj. Rif.
[30] War Diary 1/9 G.R.
[31] *Ibid.*

The attack on the Monastery had failed. With the recall of the two forward companies of 1/9 Gurkha Rifles the 7th Indian Infantry Brigade was practically occupying its original jump-off positions. The heroic effort had failed. The Monastery stood as defiant as ever.

The casualties sustained by the Indian troops in this formidable task of attacking the strong German defences were fairly heavy. The casualties of 4/6 Rajputana Rifles amounted to 196 of all ranks.[32] The casualties of 1/2 Gurkha Rifles were 149—11 officers (4 killed or missing and 7 wounded) and 138 other ranks (34 killed or missing and 104 wounded[33]). The casualties of 1/9 Gurkha Rifles were 94— 1 officer and 34 other ranks wounded, 1 officer and 52 other ranks missing and 6 other ranks killed.[34]

Failure of the New Zealanders to Establish a Bridge-head

While the Indian troops were hammering at the strong German defensive positions, the 2nd New Zealand Division, with an American armoured force under command, was engaged in the equally difficult operation of establishing a bridge-head across the Rapido. Under cover of an extremely heavy artillery bombardment two companies of the 28th Maori Battalion led the assault at 2100 hours on 17 February. They advanced along the general line of the railway embankment, under intense mortar and machine gun fire, through an area thickly sown with anti-personnel mines. The Maoris encountered thick belts of wire in front of Cassino railway station. After fierce fighting the station was captured before dawn. The Germans however held one vital strong-point nearby—a rocky outcrop, which later became well-known as the Hummocks. From this commanding position the German machine guns, mortars and rifles poured down a withering fire. Unfortunately when dawn came herculean efforts by the New Zealand sappers had failed to bridge the river, so the Maoris were in the unhappy position of being without the support of tanks and anti-tank guns. Throughout the morning the two companies of Maoris holding the railway station area were heavily mortared. At 1600 hours, a strong infantry attack supported by tanks developed. After stubborn resistance the forward companies were obliged to withdraw over the Rapido.[35] Thus the New Zealanders too failed to break through the strong German defences.

Reorganisation

Both the attacks on the German defences by the Indians and the

[32] War Diary 4/6 Raj. Rif.
[33] War Diary 1/2 G.R.
[34] War Diary 7 Ind. Inf. Bde.
[35] *Roads to Rome* (the Second New Zealand Division in action), p. 29.

New Zealanders had failed. The commander of the 4th Indian Division decided that a renewal of the attack on the Monastery stood little chance of success and would only result in further heavy casualties. The capture of Pt. 575 was essential before any further move was made. In the meantime, he must secure his front by reorganising with two brigades forward. General Freyberg agreed with this decision.

The 7th Indian Infantry Brigade was holding Pt. 593 (4/6 Rajputana Rifles and 1 Royal Sussex) and Pt. 450 (1/2 Gurkha Rifles who had been withdrawn together with 1/9 Gurkha Rifles from Pt. 444, which was untenable). The left flank of 1/2 Gurkha Rifles was in contact with 4/16 Punjab at Pt. 474, still in its original firm base.[36] The 7th Indian Infantry Brigade's front was now defined as including Pt. 593 ridge south-eastwards to exclusive Pt. 450. The 5th Indian Infantry Brigade was to take over Pt. 450 and continue the line down to but excluding Pt. 193, where the Germans were still installed. After one night's rest for reorganisation and reconnaissance, 1/2 and 1/9 Gurkha Rifles returned to relieve 4/6 Rajputana Rifles (on Snake's Head and the ridge south from it to Pt. 593) and 4/16 Punjab (just north of the line Pt. 445) respectively in the night of 1/20 February, and the command of the divisional left sector passed to the 5th Indian Infantry Brigade at 2359 hours on 19 February.[37]

2 Camerons and the 149th Anti-Tank Regiment Royal Artillery were ordered to provide porters and stretcher bearers for the 5th Indian Infantry Brigade, while 2/7 Gurkha Rifles and the 57th Light Anti-Aircraft Regiment Royal Artillery performed a similar task for the 7th Indian Infantry Brigade.

With the reorganisation thus completed the 4th Indian Division prepared to take part in another operation for the capture of Cassino. The attempt to capture Cassino had ended in failure. Two veteran divisions had smashed themselves against the sternest of defences. The 4th Indian Division had adopted the course which took advantage of earlier successes. Great courage and endurance, the highest standard of training and experience in mountain warfare, weighty fire support, all had proved to be inadequate. The 4th Indian Division was, substantially, where it had been when first taking over from the Americans. A pause was necessary. With it the planning for a new attack began.

---

[36] War Diary 4 Ind. Div. dated 18 February.
[37] War Diary 4 Ind. Div. dated 19 February.

CHAPTER VI

Cassino

OPERATION 'DICKENS'

Priority for the Campaign in Italy

By 18 February 1944, the direct attack by the New Zealand Corps on Cassino had failed. At the same time the fierce German counter-attacks on the Anzio bridge-head were being repelled. It was on 16 February that the Germans launched a major offensive to drive the Allied forces into the sea at Anzio. The attack was launched by a strong force of over four divisions, supported by 450 guns. It was a particularly vicious attack and for two days the issue of the battle hung in the balance. Luckily the Allied forces not only weathered the storm and repelled the attacks but they also counter-attacked the German assaulting forces in flank, inflicting considerable casualties on them. The battle of Anzio was won, for though the Germans made another fierce counter-attack at the end of February it was held without much difficulty. Thus the situation on 19 February was that whereas the New Zealand Corps failed to break the main front at Cassino the Germans failed to drive the Allied into the sea at Anzio.

General Sir Henry Maitland Wilson who had succeeded General Eisenhower as Supreme Allied Commander Mediterranean Theatre (SACMED) studied the New Zealand Corps front in the company of General Alexander. Later, he addressed to General Wilson a communication outlining his plan for the spring offensive. He stressed the importance of forcing the Germans "to commit the maximum number of divisions to operations in Italy at the time 'Overlord' is launched." To achieve this object he planned a major offensive up the Liri valley to link up with the Allied forces at the Anzio bridgehead. To ensure succcess it was necessary to attain local superiority of three to one in infantry. It was essential therefore to reinforce his existing twenty-one divisions by seven and a half divisions by mid-April. The regrouping of the forces also became necessary—only a single corps on the Adriatic coast, the Eighth Army transferred to the Cassino front and the Fifth Army deployed on the lower Garigliano and the Anzio bridge-head.

General Wilson not only approved the plan but also placed his views before the British Chiefs of Staff. He pleaded for the granting of priority to the campaign in Italy and the cancellation of the operation 'Anvil' (an invasion of southern France in support of 'Overlord'). He was strongly opposed to withdrawing troops from Italy until Rome had been captured. The British Chiefs of Staff had already sent a telegram on 4 February 1944 to the American Chiefs of Staff questioning the wisdom of undertaking the operation 'Anvil' in view of the deadlock on the Cassino front and Anzio bridge-head. The Americans, however, were keen on undertaking the operation 'Anvil'. The American Chiefs of Staff had in reply proposed a conference between General Eisenhower and the British Chiefs of Staff to decide the issue. General Wilson's weighty opinion now turned the scales in favour of the British point of view. The British Chiefs of Staff telegraphed to Washington and the American Chiefs of Staff assented to the British proposal. On 26 February General Wilson received a new directive giving the campaign in Italy priority over all other Mediterranean operations until further orders.

Operation 'Dickens'

There was no prospect of an early break-out of the Allied forces from the Anzio bridge-head to link up with the forces operating on the Cassino front until the latter was broken. The problem of Cassino seemed to defy solution. General Freyberg realised the futility of executing the New Zealand Corps plan of a double thrust on the Monastery and the Cassino railway station. The direct attack on Cassino had failed—would it be possible to turn the strong German defences at Monte Cassino and to make attacks on the flanks? Earlier attempts to outflank Monastery Hill from the north had ended in failure for the terrain favoured the defenders—"deep ravines, rocky escarpments, and knife-edges" limited the deployment of infantry to small parties, who could only be maintained by porters and to a limited extent by mules. Monastery Hill was in fact cut off completely from the north by a steep and deep ravine, which was difficult to cross. A wider turning movement was also not possible on account of the chief obstacle—M. Cairo, a precipitous peak covered with snow. To outflank Monte Cassino from the south by an attack across the river Rapido was not easy due to the flooding of the ground east of the river and strong dug-in positions of the Germans on the far bank.[1] The crossing of the river Rapido farther south, in S. Angelo area, bristled with the same difficulties. Thus General Freyberg reluctantly came to the conclusion that outflanking of Monte Cassino was not possible at that time and the only alternative was to launch another direct attack on Cassino. The difficulties of launching a direct attack on Cassino were almost insuperable. Monte Cassino was a strong fortress. The superb observation which

[1] Churchill: *Closing the Ring*, p. 449.

it afforded to the Germans enabled them to concentrate defensive fire quickly and effectively against attacks from any direction. The rocky ground, furrowed by deep, narrow gullies and swept by fire made it impossible to deploy the large forces, which might win a quick decisive success. The alternative was a series of limited attacks against each position in turn. However, the troops employed in this latter way, on capturing any one position, would be exposed to enfilade fire from other positions. Moreover, a slow, delibrate advance of this nature would reveal the successive objectives to the Germans and give them the opportunity of reinforcing and positioning their troops to meet it. The only way to overcome this difficulty was to launch a direct attack on Cassino, preceded by a heavy air and artillery attack to stun the defenders. General Freyberg put his faith in the weight of metal. He had high hopes that once Cassino had been pulverised by a heavy air and artillery attack it would be possible for the infantry, supported by tanks, to achieve success.

Cassino town, then, was to be the chief objective of the attack. The attack on the town from the east would have encountered much opposition from carefully prepared German positions. The attack from the north offered better prospects of success. General Freyberg decided to attack from the north of Cassino, in the outskirts of which Allied troops had a footing. The town and the roads leading into it from the north were overlooked from the Monastery, but it was thought that, even when destroyed, the houses of Cassino would provide some cover. The key to the northern part of the town was Castle Hill (Pt. 193). German supply vehicles were using the steep, winding tracks up to the Monastery from the southern end of the town. At various parts in its climb up the face of Monastery Hill, that road passed close to Points 193, 165, 202 and 435 in that order. Castle Hill was, therefore, the first and essential objective. The only approach to Castle Hill was through the town, since the northern face and shoulder of the hill fell away almost vertically and contained caves and dug-outs in which machine guns had been installed.

Lieut.-General Freyberg issued instructions on 21 February 1944. The corps plan of attack envisaged, firstly, a three-and-a-half hour air bombing programme on the town and Monastery. Immediately afterwards, the 6th New Zealand Infantry Brigade and the 19th New Zealand Armoured Regiment, assisted by fire from the 5th New Zealand and 7th Indian Infantry Brigades, were to capture Castle Hill and the part of the town north of Route 6. One battalion of the 5th Indian Infantry Brigade was to relieve the New Zealanders on Castle Hill, as soon as practicable after its capture. Thereafter, the 6th New Zealand Brigade was to advance to a second objective, south of the town, while the 5th Indian Infantry Brigade exploited southwards from Castle Hill along the eastern slopes of Monastery Hill to capture Hangman's Hill (Pt. 435) and, finally, the Monastery. Such in outline was the New Zealand Corps plan. The code-word for the operation was 'Dickens'.

The operation was to be carried out in the following three phases:—

Phase I—Preliminary Operations

(a) The 2nd New Zealand Division was to relieve the 91st United States Reconnaissance Battalion and the 133rd United States Infantry Regiment and deploy troops for the attack on Cassino.

(b) The 4th Indian Division was to attack and capture Pt. 445, and hold the existing positions firmly and construct positions along the general line Pt. 450—Pt. 455 eastwards to the divisional boundary, sited to cover by fire the western outskirts of Cassino and the northern and eastern slopes of Monte Cassino. This was to be done by the 7th Indian Infantry Brigade, which was to assume the command of the complete sector.

Phase II—Air Attack

This phase of the operation was to consist of air attack on Cassino by 12 groups of heavy bombers (360 aircraft—900 tons bombs) and 7 groups of medium bombers (280 aircraft—250 tons bombs). Fighter bombers might also be available for direct support, particularly during Phase III. Phase II was to take about 3½ to 4 hours. Before Phase II, all troops were to be withdrawn behind bomb safety line and were to re-occupy the positions on conclusion.

Phase III—Attack on Cassino

(a) The 2nd New Zealand Division was to capture Cassino and Pt. 193, and exploit to the south to open up Route 6, and to the east and south-east to clear the Germans between R. Rapido and R. Gari so that construction of crossing over R. Rapido could be effected. The outline plan of the 6th New Zealand Infantry Brigade (which was to launch the attack) was for one armoured reigment to lead, followed by two infantry battalions. The start line was to be the northern outskirts of Cassino and the objective Route 6 and exploitation to the Cassino railway station. An armoured regiment was to be in Cervaro area.

(b) During night D/D+1 the 5th New Zealand Brigade and the New Zealand Corps Engineers were to open up Route 6 from the east, and if the Cassino railway station had been secured, to open up a vehicle route along the railway line. United States Combat Groups were positioned ready to go through on either or both these routes.

(c) The role of the 4th Indian Division in this phase of the operation was to be as follows:—

(i) The 7th Indian Infantry Brigade was to assist with fire the attack of the 2nd New Zealand Division by neutralising German guns and preventing German movement on the northern and eastern slopes of Monte Cassino.

(ii) The 5th Indian Infantry Brigade was to take over Pt. 193 after its capture by the 2nd New Zealand Division.[2]

Artillery support for the operation was to be provided by the artillery of the X Corps, the New Zealand Corps and a large number of American Field Artillery Battalions, a total of six hundred and ten pieces of all calibre.

Divisional Plan

In implementation of the corps plan the commander of the 4th Indian Division issued instructions on 22 February for the reorganisation of the forward brigades. Thoughout the operation the 7th Indian Infantry Brigade was to hold securely the existing divisional sectors.

Phase I

This phase of the operation was to be carried out by the 7th Indian Infantry Brigade with 2/7 Gurkha Rifles and Camerons under command. The latter was to relieve 1/6 Rajputana Rifles on 23 February and the former was to relieve 1/9 Gurkha Rifles in the night 23/24 February. On relief 1/6 Rajputana Rifles and 1/9 Gurkha Rifles were to concentrate in the 5th Indian Infantry Brigade's assembly area (Villa—Cairo). On completion of relief of 1/9 Gurkha Rifles by 2/7 Gurkha Rifles, the 7th Indian Infantry Brigade was to take over the 5th Indian Infantry Brigade's existing sector and be responsible for the whole divisional sector. The 7th Indian Infantry Brigade was to prepare and occupy by first light on 24 February the positions on the spurs along

---

[2] New Zealand Corps O.I., 21 February 1944, and 5 Ind. Inf. Bde. O.O. No. 1, 24 February 1944.

the general line Pt. 450—Pt. 445 eastwards to the divisional boundary.

Phase II

The 7th Indian Infantry Brigade was to withdraw troops behind the bomb safety line before the commencement of the air attack on Cassino.

Phase III

The 7th Indian Infantry Brigade was to give every possible assistance to the 2nd New Zealand Division by fire on to German positions throughout its sector. The 5th Indian Infantry Brigade was to assemble in Villa—Cairo area and maintain close liaison with the 6th New Zealand Brigade and take over from that brigade Pt. 193 with one battalion. The 5th Indian Infantry Brigade was to mop up German posts in the vicinity of Pt. 193 and exploit southwards along the eastern slopes of Monte Cassino and capture Pt. 435.[3]

The Brigade Plan

The role of the 2nd New Zealand Division in the operation Dickens was to capture Cassino town, Castle Hill, and the railway station. The role of the 4th Indian Division was twofold—the 7th Indian Infantry Brigade to assist with fire the attack of the 2nd New Zealand Division and the 5th Indian Infantry Brigade to take over from the New Zealanders on Castle Hill and move forward to attack and capture Pt. 435. In implementation of the divisional plan Brigadier D.R.E.R. Bateman, D.S.O., O.B.E., commander of the 5th Indian Infantry Brigade issued detailed instructions on 24 February. The operation was to be carried out in four phases:

(a) *Phase I*

(i) 1/4 Essex was to take over Pt. 193 from the 6th New Zealand Infantry Brigade and establish a firm base, including this feature and the north entrance to Cassino.

(ii) On completion of relief, 1/4 Essex was to secure Pt. 165 and include this in its position.

(iii) 1/6 Rajputana Rifles was to move into position ready to pass through 1/4 Essex for Phase II.

(b) *Phase II*

(i) 1/6 Rajputana Rifles was to pass through 1/4 Essex and secure the first bound, road-bend (850212), and establish position (approximately one company).

[3] 4 Ind. Div. O.I. No. 4, 22 February 1944.

(ii) Then 1/6 Rajputana Rifles was to move south on axis of road and secure the second bound (area 851207) and establish position (approximately one company).
  (iii) One squadron of tanks was to move into position for Phase III.

(c) *Phase III*
  (i) 1/6 Rajputana Rifles supported by tanks was to advance and secure the next bound, Pt. 202.
  (ii) Thereafter the task of 1/6 Rajputana Rifles was to secure firmly the position established and to exploit to Pt. 435.
  (iii) 1/9 Gurkha Rifles was to move into position to carry out Phase IV.

(d) *Phase IV.*
  (i) 1/9 Gurkha Rifles was to pass through 1/6 Rajputana Rifles and capture Pt. 435.
  (ii) On completion of Phase IV, 1/4 Essex was to be prepared to exploit west from Pt. 435 to maintain touch with the right flank of the advance along Route 6 and/or to enter and mop up area of the Monastery.

The following troops were under command of the 5th Indian Infantry Brigade for the operation Dickens:—

A Company Machine Gun Rajputana Rifles
4th Field Company
11th Brigade Porter Company
Advance Dressing Station 26th Indian Field Ambulance
1401st Indian Pioneer Company.

The following troops were in support:—

Corps artillery (360 guns) with the 2nd New Zealand Division
1st Field Regiment in close support
4.2-inch Mortar Group (24 mortars) also on call 7th Indian Brigade for DF tasks
One Squadron New Zealand tanks available in close support.

The operation 'Dickens' was to commence on 24 February but due to bad weather, it was postponed till 15 March. Accordingly a slight modification was made in the plan. In the operational instructions issued on 3 March by the commander of the 5th Indian Infantry Brigade, an additional phase—Phase V—was added.

Having been relieved on Pt. 193 and the outskirts of Cassino by 4/6 Rajputana Rifles, 1/4 Essex, supported by C Squadron 20th New Zealand Armoured Regiment less one troop, was to advance and secure the Monastery feature. The following additional troops were under command of the 5th Indian Infantry Brigade[4]:—

C Squadron 20th New Zealand Armoured Regiment
4/6 Rajputana Rifles

The Maintenance Route

While the operational plans were being finalised the divisional sappers were busy in improving the tracks for the maintenance of the Indian troops. The maintenance route for the 7th Indian Infantry Brigade crossed the Rapido valley from Portella to Villa in full view of the German troops on Monte Cassino and M. Cairo. The sappers were employed form 16 February in making mule and jeep tracks for maintenance. By the end of February two jeep tracks called the Cavendish road (from 845241 to 839231) and the Roorkee road (from track junction 852234 to the 7th Indian Infantry Brigade Headquarters 846218) had been constructed.[5] On 1 March work began on widening the Cavendish road, one mile long, to enable the tanks to use it. This work was completed on 11 March. The supply head was in the bowl under the shelter of Snake's Head and was named 'Madras Circus'. The maintenance route in the valley northwest of Snake's Head was harassed a good deal by German artillery and appropriately received a name with a strong flavour of the wild west—'Dead Man's Gulch'. In similar strain, the depression north of the Pt. 450—Pt. 450 ridge became the 'Death Valley'.

Plan for Diversionary Operation

With the completion of the task of widening the Cavendish road to make it passable to tanks the commander of the 4th Indian Division planned a diversionary operation. At Massa Albaneta, between Pts. 593 and 575, the ground was comparatively open and suitable for the employment of tanks. Advantage was therefore to be taken of this and tanks were to be sent to cause confusion in the rear of the German positions by raiding them near Pt. 593, and the west of it. This offensive action, it was hoped, would assist the 5th Indian Infantry Brigade in its attack on the Monastery. Accordingly the commander of the 4th Indian Division issued instructions on 11 March for the diversionary operation. The 7th Indian Infantry Brigade was to be prepared to exploit the success of operation 'Dickens' by directing the 7th Indian Brigade Reconnaissance

---

[4] 5 Ind. Inf. Bde. O.I. No. 2, 3 March 1944.
[5] Report on construction of Tank Road, Appendix K, War Diary H.Q. R.E. 4 Ind. Div., and H.Q. R.E. 4 Ind. Div. O.O. dated 1 March 1944.

Squadron, with under command D Company 760th United States Tank Battalion (17 Stuart tanks) to advance on axis Cavendish road—Albaneta house (832216) to area Albaneta, Pt. 593, feature (835215) and to exploit south-westwards towards Monte Cassino.[6]

Reorganisation

While the plans were being finalised reorganisation was taking place to enable the 4th Indian Division to play its part in the operation 'Dickens'. As already described, after the failure of the 7th Indian Infantry Brigade to capture the Monastery its front was defined as including Pt. 593 ridge south-eastwards to exclusive Pt. 450. The 5th Indian Infantry Brigade took over Pt. 450 and held the line down to, but excluding, Pt. 193. In the night of 19/20 February, 1/2 and 1/9 Gurkha Rifles relieved 4/6 Rajputana Rifles (on Snake's Head and the ridge south from it to Pt. 593) and 4/16 Punjab (just north of the line Pt. 450—Pt. 445) respectively. The command of the left divisional sector passed to the 5th Indian Infantry Brigade at 2359 hours on 19 February.

1/9 Gurkha Rifles carried out the preliminary operation for the capture of Pt. 445. Under cover of an artillery barrage two platoons of C Company moved forward at 0330 hours on 23 February to attack and capture a house (on Pt. 445) which was known to be a machine gun post. They came under heavy machine gun fire and had to withdraw. It was obvious that the Germans held the forward positions in strength.[7] Therefore, the preliminary operation for the capture of Pt. 445 was cancelled. Preparations however continued. The 5th Indian Infantry Brigade was withdrawn to the Villa area to prepare for the main operation. To make this withdrawal possible, 2/7 Gurkha Rifles and 2 Camerons were placed under command of the 7th Indian Infantry Brigade. The 2 Cameron relieved 1/6 Rajputana Rifles while 2/7 Gurkha Rifles relieved 1/9 Gurkha Rifles on the night of 24/25 February. Then at 0250 hours on 25 February, the 7th Indian Infantry Brigade assumed command of the whole divisional front. Thereafter, the 4th Indian Division held the 5th Indian Infantry Brigade ready to send it into the attack, when the main operation commenced.

On 3/4 March the Camerons relieved the Royal Sussex near Pt. 593. The position there had stabilised in some places only forty yards from the Germans, who overlooked them all. The 7th Indian Infantry Brigade, in consequence, was holding positions which afforded little cover against weather and could not be materially improved because they were so closely observed by the Germans.

[6] Main 4 Ind. Div. to Rear 4 Ind. Div. 11 March 1943, Appendix I, War Diary 4 Ind. Div.
[7] War Diary 1/9 G.R.

Casualties in the brigade, on the front and on the supply line, during the four weeks it remained there, amounted to nearly sixty a day. Constant rain and snow, with frost every night, added to the hardships but the men bore these trying conditions with great fortitude.

The Rival Forces

To implement the new plan of operations, the New Zealand Corps stood poised for an attack on Cassino. It had lined up so that, on its right, it was in touch with the 3rd Algerian Division, and facing south towards Monte Cassino was the 7th Indian Infantry Brigade, with one battalion of the 11th Indian Infantry Brigade in the line and another acting as porters. Next came one battalion of the 6th New Zealand Brigade in the northern outskirts of Cassino town. To its left and facing west along the Rapido, was the 5th New Zealand Brigade with two infantry battalions, a machine gun battalion and New Zealand Division Cavalry Regiment up. Beyond them, and continuing the line opposite S. Angelo, was the 11th British Infantry Brigade of the 78th Division.

Major-General F. I. S. Tuker, C.B., D.S.O., O.B.E., who had led the 4th Indian Division through adversity and triumph since January 1942, had been compelled by sickness to hand over command to his energetic Artillery Commander, Brigadier K. Dimoline, C.B.E., D.S.O., before operations began on 15 February. On 9 March, Major-General A. Galloway, C.B.E., D.S.O., M.C., of the 1st Armoured Division assumed temporary command of this Indian division.[8]

Pitted against the New Zealand Corps were the best German troops in Italy, the *1st Parachute Division*. The *15th Panzer Grenadier Division*, which had borne the brunt of the Allied attacks in January and February, was relieved by the paratroopers towards the end of February. The men of the parachute division were known as the "Green Devils" of Cassino, and received much high praise from their Commander-in-Chief, who had issued in January an order that the position must be held at all cost, since even a defensive victory would be of political value. The paratroopers did not belie the trust reposed in them by the Fuehrer. In the defence of Cassino they displayed a valour and a heroism which elicited praise even from their enemies.

The *1st Parachute Division* consisted of three regiments (*1st Parachute Regiment*, *3rd Parachute Regiment* and *4th Parachute Regiment*) and ancillary troops.[9] This division held in strength Cassino and the surrounding hills to M. Cairo. *3rd Parachute Regiment* was in Cassino ; *4th Parachute Regiment* in the hills north and west of slope

---

[8] For Order of Battle 4 Ind. Div. see Appendix II.
[9] Analysis of enemy strength, Appendix A to 4 Ind. Div. Intelligence Summary No. 46, 10 March 1944.

of M. Cairo. 3rd *Parachute Regiment* was deployed in and around Cassino with the 1st *Battalion* on the Monastery Hill, Castle Hill, and Pt. 236, and the 2nd *Battalion*, with three companies of the 3rd *Battalion* attached in Cassino.[10]

Operation 'Bradman'

The New Zealand Corps, composed of the 2nd New Zealand Division, the 4th Indian Division, the 78th Division and Combat Command 'B' 1st United States Armoured Division, was deployed on the Cassino front ready to commence the operation 'Dickens' which was planned to involve the maximum combined effort of the Allied Air Forces and all available ground forces. Phase I—the deployment of the troops for the attack on Cassino had already been completed. Phase II—the air bombardment of Cassino—began on 15 March 1944. This phase of the operation had been given the code name 'Bradman'.

The German intercept service must have been very puzzled on 14 March, assuming that the service was intercepting, by a typical English message which was sent out that day, 'Bradman will be batting to-morrow'. At 0830 hours on 15 March, the air attack on Cassino began; it lasted until midday. Three hundred and thirty-eight heavy bombers and one hundred and seventy-six medium bombers took part. 1,100 tons of bombs were dropped on the town. While the attack on Cassino was in progress more than three hundred fighter bombers attacked targets in the immediate vicinity while two hundred and eighty fighters gave cover protection. The terrific bombardment reduced the town to a heap of rubble.

At 1200 hours the bombing ceased and the artillery programme opened. Six hundred and ten pieces of artillery from the X British Corps, the II U.S. Corps and the New Zealand Corps were employed. Eighty-eight guns laid down a creeping barrage under cover of which the 2nd New Zealand Division advanced to the attack on Cassino while the 78th Division held the line west to the X British Corps boundary. The remaining artillery was given the task of neutralising German defence positions in addition to counter-battery work. The artillery programme lasted until 1600 hours during which time 1,200 tons of shells were fired into the town.[11]

The tremendous weight of bombs and artillery fire on 15 March, however, failed to destroy altogether the German defences in Cassino and on the Monastery Hill. The German troops did not suffer heavy casualties, sheltered as they were by cellars, steel and concrete pill-boxes, caves, and tunnels. Though many ammunition dumps were

[10] 4 Ind. Div. Intelligence Summary No. 50, 15 March 1944.
[11] *Report by the Supreme Allied Command Mediterranean to the Combined Chiefs of Staff on the Italian Campaign* (8 January 1944 to 10 May 1944).

blown up and possibly protected weapons destroyed, the heavy weapons and artillery did not suffer serious damage. The heavy bombing and shelling in fact did not lower the morale of the German soldiers, who emerged out of their cellars, dazed but undaunted, to offer dogged resistance to the Allied advance.[12] They fought with a grim tenacity which evoked admiration. General Alexander was so much impressed by the high morale of the paratroopers that he could not help paying them a noble tribute. "The tenacity of these German paratroopers is quite remarkable, considering that they were subjected to the whole Mediterranean Air Force plus the better part of 800 guns under greatest concentration of fire-power which has ever been put down and lasting for six hours. I doubt if there are any other troops in the world who could have stood up to it and then gone on fighting with the ferocity they have."[13]

The Attack on Cassino by the New Zealanders

Behind a creeping barrage the 6th New Zealand Brigade led the assault at 1200 hours on 15 March. The leading battalion—the 25th Battalion—entered Cassino, then turned to the west and captured Castle (P. 193) after confused fighting at 1630 hours. The second battalion—the 26th Battalion—following close on the heels of the leading battalion advanced to within one hundred and fifty yards of Route 6 by 1700 hours. Further progress was however checked. Rubble blocked the narrow streets and provided cover for the Germans, who emerged from their shelters little shaken by the bombing. In other places, the huge craters became filled with rainwater, which made them an efficient anti-tank obstacle. Deprived of their tank support, their wireless sets rendered almost completely useless by the effect of the rain, the New Zealanders were compelled to crawl over the debris in a continuous battle with snipers and machine gun posts, a laboriously slow progress. Nevertheless, after fierce house-to-house fighting, the New Zealanders succeeded in penetrating into a greater part of the town before the close of the day.[14]

The two chief German strong-points were astride Route 6, one round the Continental Hotel and the other about four hundred yards to the east. The third battalion—the 24th New Zealand Battalion —moved up in support of the second battalion but not much progress was made. Heavy rainfall throughout the night impeded the operations. The slowing up of the advance enabled the Germans to develop new strong-points and reinforce others. The operations for the capture of the railway station had therefore to be delayed.

---

[12] *Fifth Army History*, Part V, "The Drive to Rome", pp. 179-180.
[13] General Alexander's telegram to Prime Minister dated 20 March 1944. Churchill: *Closing the Ring*, pp. 449-450.
[14] *Roads to Rome*, op. cit., p. 29.

1/4 Essex Takes Over from the New Zealanders

Rainfall impeded the progress of the 5th Indian Infantry Brigade also when, in the wake of the 6th New Zealand Brigade, it entered Cassino and then moved forward to take over from the 25th New Zealand Battalion. Heavy rainfall, a pitch dark night and the German defensive fire hampered its movement. Nevertheless by 2230 hours on 15 March, 1/4 Essex, the leading battalion, had relieved the 25th New Zealand Battalion. The two leading companies of 1/4 Essex were established at the Castle and Pt. 175 (across the ravines behind the Castle) respectively, the third company was on the outskirts of Cassino and the fourth company held a reserve position on the road along the hill-side to the north. One company of 1/4 Essex moved forward to seize the lower hair-pin bend at Pt. 165, on the hill-side 300 yards above the Castle. This objective was secured by 0245 hours on 16 March. These dispositions (i.e. Pt. 165, Pt. 175 and Castle) enabled 1/4 Essex to establish its grip on the bottle-neck through which the 4th Indian Division was to enter the battle.

Failure of Attack on Pt. 236

Moving behind 1/4 Essex, 1/6 Rajputana Rifles ran into trouble. Only two companies (A and B) had reached the Castle. The remainder ceased to exist as a fighting entity when shelling inflicted heavy casualties on them. A direct hit on battalion headquarters killed almost all the officers. The company officers were killed or wounded. At 0245 hours on 16 March, A Company advanced from the Castle to secure Pt. 236, at the second hair-pin bend. Much hung upon the capture of this position. Except for the Monastery, it was the last position to give direct observation of the roads leading into the town from the north. Moreover, it dominated the whole hill-side and flanked the 5th Indian Infantry Brigade's route of advance towards Pt. 435. By 0335 hours, A Company had edged its way forward to within 150 yards of the objective when it was subjected to withering small arms and shell fire and compelled to withdraw. At 0540 hours both A and B Companies of 1/6 Rajputana Rifles were located in area Pt. 165 with C Company 1/4 Essex. At 0830 hours the two forward companies of 1/6 Rajputana Rifles attacked again under cover of smoke, but this move also failed in the face of heavy fire. Both the companies were placed under command 1/4 Essex at 1000 hours on 16 March. Considerable German small arms fire directed against any movement led to the decision not to attack again by daylight.

Capture of Hangman's Hill

Meanwhile, 1/9 Gurkha Rifles had scored a notable success. Following in the wake of 1/6 Rajputana Rifles, it arrived on the outskirts of Cassino at 0100 hours on 16 March. This battalion was pinned down by fire on the slopes of the western outskirts of the town. C and D Companies however managed to reach the Castle. These two advanced companies therefore were committed to the attack. Their objective was the Hangman's Hill (Pt. 435).[15] D Company was subjected to severe spandau fire, losing 15 men within a minute. Further progress was thus checked. C Company also lost touch with the battalion, but went on unsupported, picking its way through several strongly held positions. Ultimately, the company captured the Hangman's Hill, the battalion's objective, with only an hour or two of darkness to spare. This success was not known to the battalion or brigade until some hours later.

Reinforcements for the Isolated Company

Thus the 5th Indian Infantry Brigade had secured substantial success. The day (16 March) was spent by 1/4 Essex, two companies of 1/6 Rajputana Rifles and a company of 1/9 Gurkha Rifles in consolidating their forward positions. From its positions on the bare slopes of Monastery Hill, the 5th Indian Infantry Brigade could do little to assist the New Zealanders in the southern part of the town. Still faced with the task not completed on the previous night, the Indian brigade was ordered to capture, during the night of 16/17 March, the hill-side from hair-pin bend (Pt. 236) to Hangman's Hill (Pt. 435) and thereby to threaten the flank and rear of the Germans in the town. The brigadier directed the two companies of 1/6 Rajputana Rifles (under command 1/4 Essex) from Pt. 165 to the hair-pin bend (Pt. 236) in a renewed attack, to be put in at dusk, at 1900 hours on 16 March. After dark at 2300 hours, 1/9 Gurkha Rifles less C Company, with the remainder of 1/6 Rajputana Rifles, was to advance to Hangman's Hill through Pt. 202, which 1/6 Rajputana Rifles was to hold.

A and B Companies of 1/6 Rajputana Rifles captured the hair-pin bend at 2100 hours on 16 March, but a German strong-point on Pt. 236 itself, above the bend, continued to hold out. In a strong counter-attack delivered at 0430 hours on 17 March, the Germans regained the bend and forced the two companies of 1/6 Rajputana Rifles back to Pt. 165. While 1/6 Rajputana Rifles failed to maintain its hold on the hair-pin bend, 1/9 Gurkha Rifles was more fortunate for unobtrusively it secured Hangman's Hill, arriving there just in time to reinforce its fourth company which, already on Hangman's Hill, was being strongly counter-attacked. The counter-attack was repulsed and the position consolidated.

[15] On the summit of the feature, Pt. 435, stood the concrete stanchion of an aerial ropeway, which climbed the face of M. Cassino to the Monastery. The gibbet-like appearance of this stanchion, as seen from the plains below, gave Pt. 435 its name of 'Hangman's Hill'.

Maintenance Problem

With the Germans still on the hair-pin bend and Pt. 202, the 5th Indian Infantry Brigade was faced with an acute maintenance problem. The supply route to the Castle ran over the open slopes at the foot of Monastery Hill, which were under direct German observation by day and subjected to mortar fire by night. Until the end, the route was kept open, though at some cost in casualties. Hangman's Hill lay nearly a thousand yards further on, across the steep and rough hill-side. Supply parties crossing this stretch of thousand yards, in which were several German posts, braved a fire-swept hill-side and the constant risk of meeting German patrols.

Early in the morning of 17 March, when 1/4 Essex had been on Castle Hill for just over twenty-four hours and 1/9 Gurkha Rifles had just reached Hangman's Hill, the commander of the 5th Indian Infantry Brigade ordered his fourth battalion, 4/6 Rajputana Rifles, to act as porters and to co-ordinate the arrangements for supplying the battalions. Certain sappers and pioneers were also available.

The 4th Field Company, Indian Engineers, was to supply 1/4 Essex, and an Indian Pioneer Company, with a strong escort of 4/6 Rajputana Rifles, was to supply 1/9 Gurkha Rifles by way of the Castle Hill.

B and C platoons of the 4th Field Company, Indian Engineers, left headquarters in Cassino at 1730 hours on 17 March with 50 Garhwali porters to carry food, water and ammunition to the Castle. They reached the Castle at 2115 hours and left that place for Cassino at 2345 hours. The despatch of a supply train to Hangman's Hill presented difficulties. The plan was for the Indian Pioneer Company to supply 100 porters to the rendezvous at the 5th Indian Infantry Brigade Headquarters at 1800 hours on 17 March. Twelve mules were to be collected from the 17th Mule Company. 4/6 Rajputana Rifles was to supply protection party for the porters and also to assist in the porterage duties by carrying extra ammunition, etc. The party was to proceed by the route via Pt. 193, left of Pt. 202 to Pt. 435. A and D Companies 4/6 Rajputana Rifles were detached to carry out these duties. The column moved off at 1900 hours but suffered 19 casualties from shelling on cross-roads (856236). However, it reached Pt. 193 at 2210 hours without further mishap. At 2220 hours the party left Pt. 193 for Pt. 165. The Germans were meanwhile on the alert and swept the hill-side with fire. At 0145 hours on 18 March the Brigade Headquarters informed that due to heavy bombardment the porters were seized with panic and refused to carry out their duties. At that time the bulk of protection and porter personnel were with 1/4 Essex companies on Pt. 165. On receipt of this information the two companies of 4/6 Rajputana Rifles were ordered to fight their way through to Hangman's Hill as it was imperative that the supplies should reach 1/9 Gurkha Rifles. Accordingly at 0410 hours on 18 March, A and D Companies of 4/6 Rajputana Rifles started on their perilous journey, carrying as much ammunition and supplies as possible. It was a hazarduous venture but the column wended its way without attracting much notice and at 0630 hours on 18 March had the satisfaction of delivering the precious supplies to 1/9 Gurkha Rifles. This important task was accomplished without serious casualties—only 8 men were reported to be missing.[16] As it was not possible to return during the day the two companies of 4/6 Rajputana Rifles remained on Hangman's Hill. While the supply train was on its way to Hangman's Hill, the Germans raided Pt. 165 at 0355 hours on 18 March but were driven back.

Capture of Pt. 202

Meanwhile the New Zealanders too had gained some success. Although on 16 March no substantial gains were made, on 17 March the 6th New Zealand Infantry Brigade resumed its attack on the town of Cassino. After fierce fighting during the day the railway station and a knoll known as the Hummocks were captured and securely held. Elsewhere progress was slow and expensive. Almost every building or stump of a building contained a sniper's or a machine gunner's post, and each post was supported by fire from several others and by heavy mortar and machine gun fire, which the Germans were able to direct with great accuracy by reason of their intimate knowledge of the town, and the splendid observation they had on Monastery Hill. The New Zealand Brigade's task for the night of 17/18 March was to prepare routes forward for tanks; at the same time one company of the 24th New Zealand Battalion was to move by way of Castle Hill and Pt. 165 to secure Pt. 202, below Hangman's Hill. Thereafter this company was to attack from the rear the Continental Hotel, the garrison of which was still holding out. The plan to attack the Continental Hotel from the rear was decided on because it could not be reached from the north or from the east. At dawn (18 March) the company secured Pt. 202. Attempts however to push forward to the hotel were checked by intense fire from Pt. 146, between Pt. 202 and its objective.

The Germans too were not sitting idle. Under cover of darkness on the night of 17/18 March, they reinforced their troops in the ruined houses below the Castle. Principal among these houses was a conspicuous, twin-towered building. The exact method by which reinforcement was achieved was not known. The Germans might have used a tunnel leading from the Monastery or, more likely, they might have crept down the ravine north of the Castle.

[16] War Diary 4/6 Raj. Rif.

From this vantage point—the ruined houses below the Castle—they were able to harass the troops in the Castle a good deal. The 25th New Zealand Brigade tried, without success, to turn them out. In the evening of 18 March, the New Zealand tanks moved to shoot up these buildings. Unfortunately the angle of fire caused the 'Overs' to hit the Castle, causing casualties to 1/4 Essex. This pocket of German resistance added considerably to the difficulties of the 5th Indian Infantry Brigade, because the ground for the deployment of troops on Monastery Hill was now limited to a route, through the Castle itself. The Castle had only one gate, and that was well registered by German weapons, so the Indian troops had to move out to attack in single file.

Attacks and Counter-attacks (19 March)

As movement on the hill-side was impossible by day, the operations of the 5th Indian Infantry Brigade were confined mostly to hours of darkness. Nevertheless, attempts to probe into German defences continued. At 1600 hours on 18 March, B Company 1/4 Essex advanced to drive out the Germans from Pt. 236 but was pinned down by heavy fire. At 1900 hours when this company was still unable to move forward, D Company, which had been relieved on Pt. 165 by a company of 4/6 Rajputana Rifles at 1815 hours, formed up for the attack in support of B Company. But no progress was made due to heavy fire.

Meanwhile efforts continued to be made to supply the isolated troops at Hangman's Hill. 4/6 Rajputana Rifles had done all that was humanly possible, but they could carry only a limited quantity of supplies, over and above their arms and equipment. Arrangements were therefore made to supply Hangman's Hill by air. At 1550 hours, on 18 March, containers were dropped from forty-eight aircraft on the positions occupied by 1/9 Gurkha Rifles. The ground was not good for the operation. Many of the containers, though on the whole accurately dropped, bounced down the steep, rocky slope out of range. The amount received by the Gurkhas was however enough to allow them to take part in an attack on the Monastery.

The New Zealand Corps had made important gains—Hangman's Hill could serve as a stepping stone for an attack on the Monastery; with the capture of the railway station and Pt. 202 the German opposition could be liquidated. Accordingly General Freyberg ordered a vigorous offensive on 19 March with the double object of storming the Monastery and clearing Cassino town. Meanwhile the Germans too realised that the climax of the battle was about to be reached. They were not content to remain on the defensive but launched vigorous counter-attacks on 19 March. Thus the operations of 19 March marked the real trial of strength between the rival forces.

The forward troops of the 4th Indian Division were regrouped to enable a large force to be concentrated at Hangman's Hill for an attack on the Monastery. The plan was that the Machine Gun Battalion, Rajputana Rifles, would act as porters and thus relieve 4/6 Rajputana Rifles of this duty. The latter would then relieve 1/4 Essex on Castle Hill so that the Essex might move forward to join 1/9 Gurkha Rifles on Hangman's Hill. The remaining elements of 1/6 Rajputana Rifles were to be formed into a composite company and placed under the command of 4/6 Rajputana Rifles, to bring that battalion nearer its fighting strength. These reliefs were to be completed by 0200 hours on 19 March. At 0600 hours on 19 March, 1/9 Gurkha Rifles and 1/4 Essex were to assault the Monastery. At the same time the 7th Indian Infantry Brigade was to carry out its diversionary operation. The tanks of the 7th Brigade Reconnaissance Squadron were to debouch from Madras Circus at 0600 hours on 19 March and mop up any German positions on Pt. 445. At the same time, the 24th New Zealand Battalion was to assist the advance by launching strong attacks on the Continental Hotel.

In the night of 18/19 March, a company of the Machine Gun Battalion, Rajputana Rifles, took supplies to Hangman's Hill and returned without incident. A and D Companies 4/6 Rajputana Rifles made their way to the Castle with the wounded Gurkhas. They then went again to Hangman's Hill with supplies. Meanwhile, the remainder of 4/6 Rajputana Rifles were busy in carrying out the relief of 1/4 Essex, which was completed by 0300 hours on 19 March. Before 1/4 Essex could move forward to attack the Monastery the Germans launched a powerful counter-attack at 0530 hours. At that time B and D Companies 1/4 Essex were forward of Pt. 165 getting ready to push on to Hangman's Hill; one platoon 4/6 Rajputana Rifles was at Pt. 165, one platoon composite company 1/6 Rajputana Rifles (under command 4/6 Rajputana Rifles) was at Pt. 175. The garrison of the Castle consisted of A and C Companies 1/4 Essex, one company less a platoon of 4/6 Rajputana Rifles, the composite company, less a platoon of 1/6 Rajputana Rifles, some Sappers and Miners details, together with the artillery observation group of the 1st Field Regiment, Royal Artillery. The whole garrison did not exceed 150 rifles.

The German attack was launched by *1st Battalion Parachute Regiment*. Relieved at Pt. 706 on the night of 17/18 March this battalion moved to the Monastery. Artillery fire, particularly at Alabaneta (Pt. 468) held up its progress for sometime but it arrived in the Monastery without further mishap. In the night of 18/19 March, the battalion moved down the hill through its own forward defended locatities in the direction of Pt. 236 and Pt. 165. A platoon of 4/6 Rajputana Rifles was overwhelmed, and then the Germans surged forward for the attack on Pt. 193,[17] which was delivered from three sides. Boldly the Germans led the attack, hurling grenades over the walls into the courtyard, while snipers on the hill-side took toll of the defender. But if the assault was made with energy the defence too was conducted vigorously. From behind the loopholes of the battlements machine guns swept the approaches with fire. The struggle continued for twenty minutes and then the German paratroopers withdrew to reorganise for the second attack. At 0700 hours a second attack developed—as fierce and vehement as the first —but it was also beaten back. After a short interval the third attack was launched. The defenders were reduced to terrible straits for there were left only three officers and 60 men fit to carry on the defence. At 0900 hours the Germans carried out another attack on the Castle, this time from the east, that strong-point of houses below the hill. To check this onslaught British mortars and medium machine guns fired heavy concentrations close to the western wall. The New Zealand tanks covered the southern wall. Again the German attack was held but this assault and the fact that German machine guns covered the gateway to the Castle showed that the attack was as vigorous as the defence was valiant. At 1200 hours, A Company 2/7 Gurkha Rifles reached the Castle. This welcome reinforcement encouraged the defenders to meet further attacks with confidence. During the afternoon some Germans succeeded in breaching a wall, which collapsed, burying two officers and twenty men of the Essex. When the Germans tried to rush through this gap they were subjected to a withering fire and compelled to retire. With the repulse of this attack the defenders heaved a sigh of relief. The terrible ordeal was over. The fierce German onslaught was checked with firmness and courage.

Meanwhile the two forward companies, B and D, of 1/4 Essex, ordered to continue to Hangman's Hill and take part in the attack on the Monastery, had pressed forward against stiffening opposition. Only 75 survivors managed to reach Hangman's Hill at 1015 hours. It had been planned to launch the asault on the Monastery at 1400 hours but it was evident that the attack could not come so long as the Germans seriously threatened the Castle and the communications with the base. Therefore, before launching the attack on the Monastery it was of vital importance to strengthen the garrison at the Castle and to avert the serious threat to the communications. Hence the two Essex companies were sent back in the evening to reinforce the garrison of the Castle. On the way they again met

[17] Summary of information No. 55 dated 20 March; War Diary 4 Ind. Div.

trouble. Eventually some fought their way through and reached the Castle at 2200 hours while others returned to Hangman's Hill.

Often, during the Cassino operations, smoke was employed in large quantities to neutralise the German observation posts on Monastery Hill. On this day particularly generous use was made of artillery smoke, though not entirely with success. The officer commanding the battery in support of 1/9 Gurkha Rifles was on Hangman's Hill. His report makes no bones about those smoke shells.

"The smoke nuisance now became acute . and continued throughout the afternoon with such accuracy that the C.O.'s (1/9 Gurkha Rifles) sangar received three direct hits with the shell itself . . Attempts by the B.C. (Battery Commander) urged on by the C.O., to move it became . . fruitless and relations in all directions assumed an atmosphere of strain. The galling aspect of the whole business was that the smoke placed there screened nothing from nobody."

The same officer reported how they, on Hangman's Hill, admired the calm voice of his opposite number in the Castle as he passed information and called for fire through his wireless set.

A muster of the troops on Hangman's Hill showed that they were much too weak in numbers to carry out the attack on the Monastery with any hope of success. Inevitably, therefore, the attack was postponed. News had been received of the allotment to the 4th Indian Division of one battalion from the 78th Division, 6th Battalion Queen's Own Royal West Kent Regiment, and it was the turn of the new comers to be employed on this task.

Meanwhile the 7th Indian Infantry Brigade's diversionary operation had begun and had made excellent progress. The force consisted of the 7th Brigade Reconnaissance Squadron strengthened by 19 Shermans and 21 light tanks from D Company 760th United States Tank Battalion and from B Squadron, 20th New Zealand Armoured Regiment. The force was formed into two columns, one with 3 Shermans and 21 light tanks and the other with 16 Shermans. The columns moved off from Madras Circus, at the head of brigade's supply route, at 0600 hours on 19 March. At 0900 hours the heavy column passed through the advanced guard, engaged the Germans at Albaneta, succeeded in neutralising their positions on Pt. 593 and Pt. 575, and began to move along a track leading to the Monastery. The effect produced on the Germans by this success was revealed in a somewhat agitated wireless message, reporting to headquarters that tanks had broken through their main line and that an infantry attack was probable.

At 1020 hours, on receiving news of this encouraging progress, the commanders of the New Zealand Corps and of the 4th Indian

Division agreed that, if the tanks could approach sufficiently close to the Monastery to give support, the troops on Hangman's Hill would attack the Monastery. Otherwise, no attempt would be made to attack the Monastery until the supply situation was secure and Cassino cleared of the Germans.

Shortly after that, at about midday, the tanks came to a halt. The track was so narrow and the ground on both sides so rough and steep, that the tanks were obliged to move in single file. The going was too rough for the Shermans. Moreover, the track was mined. The commander of the 7th Indian Infantry Brigade reported that considerable engineer work was needed before the tanks could reach the Monastery. This work was impossible because the track was under heavy fire, from mortars and machine guns. He was told by his divisional commander to exhaust every possibility of getting on. If still unsuccessful, the force would withdraw to Madras Circus before dark and prepare to renew the attack next day. In the hope that light tanks would be able to negotiate the rough ground better, the light column was sent forward. The heavy column was withdrawn. The light column was successful to some extent. Unfortunately, the 7th Indian Infantry Brigade had few reserves available to tackle the positions as strong and as extensive as those on Monte Cassino. Finally, at 1730 hours, the order was given for the force to withdraw. Every effort had been unavailing. Nearly a dozen tanks had been damaged or knocked out and one had struck a mine and blocked the track.[18]

Meanwhile the 2nd New Zealand Division was engaged in clearing Cassino town. The 6th New Zealand Infantry Brigade launched the attack at 0300 hours on 19 March but failed to capture the Continental Hotel, the chief centre of German resistance.

The Castle Bottleneck

The operations of 19 March proved to be indecisive. The efforts of the New Zealand Corps were not crowned with success, German forces still held out in Cassino town, the assault on the Monastery could not be made and the diversionary operation (by the 7th Indian Infantry Brigade) had not been successful. On the other hand the Germans had almost succeeded in blocking the bottleneck. The persistent and fierce attacks made to capture the Castle showed that they were alive to the necessity of threatening the vital British line of communication. It was evident that the isolated troops of the 4th Indian Division at Hangman's Hill and Pt. 202 were not capable of launching the attack on the Monastery. That project had perforce to be given up. It was of more vital importance to secure the Castle

---

[18] OP 7 Ind. Inf. Bde. Tk. Hook, dated 19 March 1944, Appendix 'T', War Diary 4 Ind. Div.

as a firm base and to remove the threat to the communications. Consequently it was decided that the troops at the Castle, wearied by the long struggle, should be relieved by the 6th Royal West Kent Regiment borrowed from the 78th Division. 1/4 Essex, who had suffered heavy casualties, was to be withdrawn not only from the Castle but also from Pt. 435. Pt. 175 was also to be formed into a firm base so as to give support by fire to the troops on Pt. 193. There was already one platoon of 1/6 Rajputana Rifles on this feature. A composite company of 4/6 Rajputana Rifles consisting of the mortar platoon, and all porter personnel of B and C Companies (approximately 75 other ranks) had moved out from the Castle at 0755 on 19 March to strengthen this vital outpost. One company of 4/6 Rajputana Rifles and A Company of 2/7 Gurkha Rifles moved out of the Castle (which was taken over by the 6th Royal West Kent Regiment) to strengthen the garrison of Pt. 175. Thereafter the tide of the battle was to ebb and flow round these two vital points—the Castle and Pt. 175.

Reliefs were harassed throughout the night of 19/20 March by heavy mortar and artillery fire. Divisional artillery, itself heavily shelled, replied magnificently. Reliefs were completed by 0425 hours on 20 March. The 6th Royal West Kent Regiment became responsible for the defence of Pt. 193. 4/6 Rajputana Rifles was responsible for the defence of Pt. 175 and the prevention of infiltration along the wadis from west to south of this feature, and along the road out of Cassino to the north. The company of 2/7 Gurkha Rifles remained under command of 4/6 Rajputana Rifles in a counter-attack role in the area Pt. 175.

By the first light on 20 March, it was confirmed that the Germans had again reinforced their garrison. Henceforth, the battle became a test of endurance. The Germans committed their last reserves on 21 March. The exhaustion experienced by them was probably greater. Their morale was declining. The main task for the New Zealand Corps became the closing of the German supply route from west and south.

The 5th Indian Infantry Brigade was ordered to recapture Pt. 165 and the hair-pin bend, in order to prevent further infiltration through those points or down the ravine north of Castle Hill. German reinforcements down this ravine were reported, by a prisoner, to pass under the cover of Pt. 445, which had figured in the February fighting. The 7th Indian Infantry Brigade was, therefore, instructed to secure Pt. 445. Thus the object for the night of 20/21 March was for a company of the 6th Royal West Kent Regiment to attack Pt. 165 and Pt. 236, with one company 2/7 Gurkha Rifles (7th Indian Infantry Brigade) at the same time raiding Pt. 445. Brigadier Lovett however expressed doubts about the success of the raid on Pt. 445. He was of the view that it would be an expensive operation. Moreover, Pt. 445 did not control the wadi—troops could therefore move along the bottom of the wadi or along the road on the north face of the Monastery. He was, however, told by the divisional commander to implement the plan of a two-pronged attack—one directed against Pt. 165 and Pt. 236 and the other against Pt. 445. Zero hour for the attack by the 6th Royal West Kent Regiment was 2300 hours and that by 2/7 Gurkha Rifles 2200 hours. The attack by the 6th Royal West Kent Regiment was however postponed to 2400 hours due to difficult going. Similarly the attack by 2/7 Gurkha Rifles was postponed to 2230 hours.

Both attacks to secure these objectives went in on the night of 20/21 March. At 0045 hours on 21 March the company of the 6th Royal West Kent Regiment reached the Yellow House (85252130), an intermediate objective in its advance to Pt. 165, when a tremendous explosion in the area inflicted casualties and caused some confusion. Remanants of the company returned to the start line, where they were reassembled by 0235 hours. By the time they were reorganised and were ready to set out again, at 0330 hours, German machine guns, trained on the Castle gate, made another advance impossible.

The attack by C Company 2/7 Gurkha Rifles on Pt. 445 also did not make much progress. The company advanced to attack a house (held by the Germans) on the slope in front of the Monastery but came under heavy machine gun and mortar fire. Grenades too were hurled down on the Gurkhas leading the attack. Thrice did the valiant Gurkhas try to capture the house but everytime the attack was beaten back. Thereupon they abandoned the attempt after a struggle lasting two hours, having suffered 18 casualties—1 killed, 14 wounded and 3 missing.[19]

Meanwhile a strong German counter-attack (estimated strength one company) had developed against Pt. 175. After harassing artillery and mortar fire the Germans launched the attack at 2300 hours on 20 March. The brunt of the struggle was borne by the composite company 4/6 Rajputana Rifles, A company 2/7 Gurkha Rifles being held in a counter-attack role. After a fierce struggle, which lasted for thirty minutes, the attack was repulsed. Then again the Germans surged forward for the attack at 0130 hours on 21 March. This attack was also beaten back. For the third time the Germans hammered at the strong positions at 0210 hours. This attack too was repulsed by 0330 hours. Although intermittent rifle and machine gun fire continued until dawn no further German counter-attack developed against Pt. 175. The total casualties of the

---

[19] War Diary 2/7 G.R.

composite company 4/6 Rajputana Rifles on Pt. 175 were 32 killed, wounded and missing.[20]

Although the German attacks on Pt. 175 were repulsed they tried to infiltrate between Pt. 165 and the Castle. Such a move had dangerous possibilities. The loss of Pt. 175, overlooking as it did the road from Villa to Cassino, which was the 5th Indian Infantry Brigade's main supply route, would have been disastrous. The brigade was accordingly instructed, as a matter of great urgency, to organise Pt. 175 and Castle Hill into strong-points. Each feature must be capable of protecting itself and providing direct support to the other. Each must be closely linked with the 7th Indian Infantry Brigade's positions, to the right, so that there might be no more infiltration. Mines and wire were sent up. The garrison was reinforced by the reserve machine guns of the 6th Royal West Kent Regiment. By the time the brigade was relieved, a strong defensive system had been constructed.

The final German attack on Castle Hill took place at first light on 22 March. The assaulting party consisted of 36 Germans, mainly belonging to *1 Company 1st Parachute Regiment*. They advanced from the Monastery due north to the bottom of the wadi and from there they climbed to attack the Castle. But they were caught by heavy defensive fire. The attack failed. 27 Germans were taken prisoners and the rest lost their lives from artillery fire.[21] Thereafter, the Germans passed to the defensive in this sector, enabling the 4th Indian Division to concentrate all its fire on hair-pin bend and Pt. 165, from which the Germans had troubled the New Zealanders in the town below.

Withdrawal of Troops from Hangman's Hill

While the tide of battle had ebbed and flowed round the Castle, maintenance difficulties had been experienced in supplying the isolated troops on Hangman's Hill. As already described, 4/6 Rajputana Rifles had been successful in carrying supplies to Hangman's Hill on 18 March. Supplies had been also dropped from the aircraft on Hangman's Hill. As 4/6 Rajputana Rifles was required to relieve 1/4 Essex on Castle Hill so that the latter might take part in an attack on the Monastery, the Medium Machine Gun Battalion Rajputana Rifles was ordered to act as porters. On the night of 18/19 March a company of this battalion carried supplies to Hangman's Hill and returned without incident. Stiffening German opposition however prevented the supplies reaching Hangman's Hill later. Therefore, from 19 March until the withdrawal of the troops from Hangman's Hill, they had to be supplied by air. The

---

[20] War Diary 4/6 Raj. Rif.
[21] 4 Ind. Div. Intelligence Summary No. 57, dated 22 March 1944.

isolated C Company of the 24th New Zealand Infantry Battalion on Pt. 202 was also supplied by air. These supplies enabled the isolated troops on Hangman's Hill and Pt. 202 to maintain their hold over these vital posts.

It was decided on 23 March to abandon any further attacks on Cassino. It became imperative then to withdraw 1/9 Gurkha Rifles and other troops from Hangman's Hill. How to get the orders for the withdrawal through to 1/9 Gurkha Rifles from the brigade presented a tricky problem. Communication by wireless was unreliable, owing to screening and atmospherics. To put those instructions into a message which might be passed with any degree of certainty as to its being received and, if received, understood was impracticable. Telephone cables could not be maintained unbroken. A written message sent by a runner was out of the question. The risk of its falling into German hands was too great. The problem was solved, but the solution emphasised the extreme seriousness of the situation. Three officers volunteered their service from within the brigade, and they were given detailed instructions for communication to the officer commanding 1/9 Gurkha Rifles. These instructions each of the three volunteers committed to memory. When they set out, at half hourly intervals on the night of 23/24 March they carried nothing in writing.

At 0340 hours on 24 March, one of them walked into the Battalion Headquarters 1/9 Gurkha Rifles with the brigadier's instructions. After describing the situation and the various courses left open to the Army Command, the messenger detailed the action to be taken by those on Hangman's Hill in the event of the withdrawal being ordered. The decision to withdraw would be communicated to them by one of three methods—(*i*) by the wirelessed code-word "Roche"; (*ii*) by a series of three green and three red Verey lights, fired from Castle Hill and M. Trocchio, across the Rapido valley; (*iii*) by a Bofors light anti-aircraft gun firing bursts of six rounds along Route 6, south of Hangman's Hill.

After receipt of any of these signals, all would withdraw under cover of darkness to Cassino, using any route thought fit by the commanding officer. The withdrawal would be covered by diversions in the form of artillery concentrations on Monastery Hill and by a Royal West Kent raid from Castle Hill. The New Zealanders in Cassino would help to the best of their ability. To carry it further, misleading messages about supplies of rations and ammunition for future days would continue to be passed. This was confirmed by the second volunteer officer, at 0515 hours. The third volunteer, however, did not get through.

The code-word "Roche" was received at 1200 hours on 24 March, and that night, at 2015 hours the withdrawal from Hangman's Hill began. Because of its casualties, the battalion could not take all the equipment then on the hill, so some was, of necessity, destroyed. The order of withdrawal was D Company, A Company, C Company, B Company, Battalion Headquarters 1/9 Gurkha Rifles, plus the gunner observation post personnel, Essex personnel and the New Zealand Company, which was on Pt. 202. Companies, one behind the other, moved through Pt. 202, then sharp left to the Castle, a route selected by the officer commanding in consultation with the two officers, who had made the trip the night before. At 2300 hours the leading company passed through Castle Hill and headed for the town, having met no opposition on the way. North of Cassino, a column of sixteen jeeps ferried the survivors to Portella, where hot tea and food awaited them. So ended a remarkable feat of arms.

That same night, the New Zealand company on Pt. 202 came back. The diversion by the 6th Royal West Kent Regiment and heavy artillery concentrations on Pt. 165, hair-pin bend and the Monastery aided the successful accomplishment of this delicate operation.[22]

Having failed to break through the strong German defensive positions at Cassino, the New Zealand Corps was disbanded at 1200 hours on 26 March. The 4th Indian Division then came under the command of the XIII Corps and moved to Venafro, thirty miles east of Cassino.

The Assessment

The mighty efforts to capture Cassino had ended in failure; Cassino was as defiant as ever. The tenacity with which the Germans held their ground, the stubborn valour with which they fought the battle, and the supreme confidence with which they carried on the struggle, have earned for them high praise. In spite of superiority in air, artillery, infantry and armour the Allies failed to break through the German defences. But when every tribute has been paid to the gallant foe, full meed of praise is reserved for the Allied troops, who spared no efforts to storm the strong German defences. The total of 2106 casualties (287 killed, 1582 wounded and 237 missing) sustained by the three divisions of the New Zealand Corps during the period 15 to 26 March 1944 testify to the fierce struggle that was waged round Cassino. The 4th Indian Division suffered 1079 casualties (132 killed, 792 wounded and 155 missing).

In six weeks of bitter fighting around Cassino the 4th Indian Division suffered over four thousand casualties in officers and men. The 7th Indian Infantry Brigade had been in its positions opposite Monte Cassino for six weeks, suffering a constant drain of casualties. The 5th Indian Infantry Brigade had been continuously in action

[22] War Diary 4 Ind. Div.

for eight days. The 4th Indian Division had no reserves untouched when it was decided on 23 March 1944 to abandon the attack on Cassino. The 4th Indian Division had indeed played a notable part in the famous battles of Cassino.

Among the many acts of gallantry of the Indian troops one calls for particular mention. On 24 February 1944 Subedar Subramanyan, Queen Victoria's Own Madras Sappers and Miners, earned the George Cross by giving his life for his comrades in "an act of unsurpassed bravery". With a British officer and five sappers, he was clearing a path through a minefield, near Mignano, in order to extricate another officer. As the party worked, one of the sappers trod on a shrapnel mine. In the four seconds which elapsed before the mine jumped and detonated, the Subedar made his decision and threw himself on the grenade. When it exploded, the grenade caused such severe injuries that the Subedar died within a few minutes. The sappers in the party received minor injuries but the remainder escaped unhurt.

In what high regard the troops of the 4th Indian Division were held by its commander, Major-General Tuker, is clear from the following words with which he addressed them from the hospital:

"The Division has made the whole of my life worth living. It has shown me what my old battalion showed me, but on a huge scale in varied colours—courage, daring, utter devotion, utter endurance until death. May God bless them in all their supreme nobility and selflessness."

A little later Major-General Tuker sent them the following soul-stirring farewell message:

"You have built a brotherhood in arms such as has seldom been equalled in our long history.

"Your great battles are carved deep on the tablets of this war. I have never known you to falter. I have only seen your courage, your tenacity and the skill and fierceness of your attack, that has won you victories, which has astonished the rest of the Army."

High tribute but well deserved indeed!

CHAPTER VII

Plans For the Spring Offensive

General Alexander's Plan

The Fifth Army had worn itself out in fruitless, costly frontal attacks on Cassino. The only alternative was to by-pass this formidable position by launching the main attack up the Liri valley. At the same time it was necessary to break through the strong German forces, which were drawn like an iron ring round the Anzio bridgehead. This bridge-head, south of Rome, had been held only at great cost to the Allied strength. Although it constituted an invaluable potential threat, the Anzio landing had not induced the Germans to fall back from their winter positions. It was clear that an all-out effort would have to be made to effect the junction of the main Allied forces (driving up the Liri valley) with the troops in the Anzio bridgehead, preparatory to driving the German forces north of Rome. The possibility of an Allied advance northward up the east coast of Italy was ruled out on account of its numerous rivers and many natural barriers. The Liri valley decidedly offered an easier route to Rome; and it was in this valley that General Alexander decided to launch his main attack.

General Alexander's plan was to launch simultaneous attack with the Eighth Army and the Fifth Army in the sector extending from Cassino to the sea. He made the Fifth Army responsible for the sea flank, including Anzio and the Aurunci mountains south of the Liri, and brought the weight of the Eighth Army into an attack up the Liri valley. The Eighth Army was to launch the assault in the Liri valley and advance along Route 6, while the Fifth Army was to seize the Ausonia defile and push forward generally parallel with the Eighth Army but keeping south of the Liri and its tributary, the Sacco. At a suitable time, the forces at Anzio were to emerge from their bridge-head, cut Route 6 in the Valmontone area, twenty-five miles from Rome, and prevent the supply and withdrawal of the German forces, which opposed the Fifth and the Eighth Armies.[1]

The Eighth Army Plan

To implement General Alexander's plan, Lieut.-General Leese, commander of the Eighth Army, planned to attack with the II Polish Corps on the right and the XIII Corps on the left. The role of the II Polish Corps (operating north of Cassino) was to outflank

[1] Headquarters Allied Armies in Italy O.O. No. 1, dated 5 May 1944.

Monte Cassino Abbey, cut Route 6, then capture the Monastery and later move on Piedimonte and the high ground in the Roccasecca area, north-west of Piedimonte. This thrust was designed to assist the XIII Corps (the spear-head of the Eighth Army's attack), which was to force a crossing of the Gari and advance up the Liri valley. The X Corps, covering a wide front in the mountains (on the right of the II Polish Corps) was to demonstrate on the extreme right flank, with the object of making the Germans believe that an attack was to be launched in that direction, and thus divert the German attention from the main attack by the II Polish Corps and the XIII Corps. The I Canadian Corps, in the Eighth Army reserve, was to be held in readiness either to assist or to pass through the XIII Corps as the situation warranted.

So far as the artillery preparations were concerned, one thousand and sixty guns of all types were deployed on the Eighth Army front. The nature of the ground governed their siting and thus approximately three hundred of these guns were in the Polish sector, the remainder being placed behind the XIII Corps. The corps artillery plan was to open with a forty-minute counter-battery programme by all the medium and heavy artillery; during the same period, the field and heavy anti-aircraft guns were to undertake counter-mortar tasks and concentrations on the forward positions of the Germans. Once the assault boats were launched across the Gari, the attack was to be supported by a slow barrage with lifts of one hundred yards every six minutes. This barrage was to be fired by seventeen field regiments and four and a half medium regiments.

In the matter of air support, at this time[2] the Mediterranean Allied Air Forces (MAAF) had 3960 combat planes to support the ground campaign. As against this figure the Germans could muster 700, of which only 320 were in a position to affect the battle tactically. Thus complete supremacy was obtained by the Allied Air Forces over the *Luftwaffe* in Italy. While the ground stalemate continued through the Spring, this great advantage in the air had been exploited by a nearly non-stop offensive against the supply lines of the Germans with the express intention of so weakening them logistically that they could not withstand the eventual Allied ground attack. From 24 March onwards, all through rail-tracks to Rome and the front were continuously cut by two lines of interdiction across Italy, one on the general line Cecina-Ancona and the other roughly San Stefano—San Benedetto. Simultaneously, a complex programme of attacks against ports, shipping, mechanical transport and northern Italian railyards contributed to the attrition of German supplies.

From 25 March the main air effort was switched to the reduction of German air strength in Italy by attacks on airfields and air-

[2] Air Ministry Report "Operation Diadem".

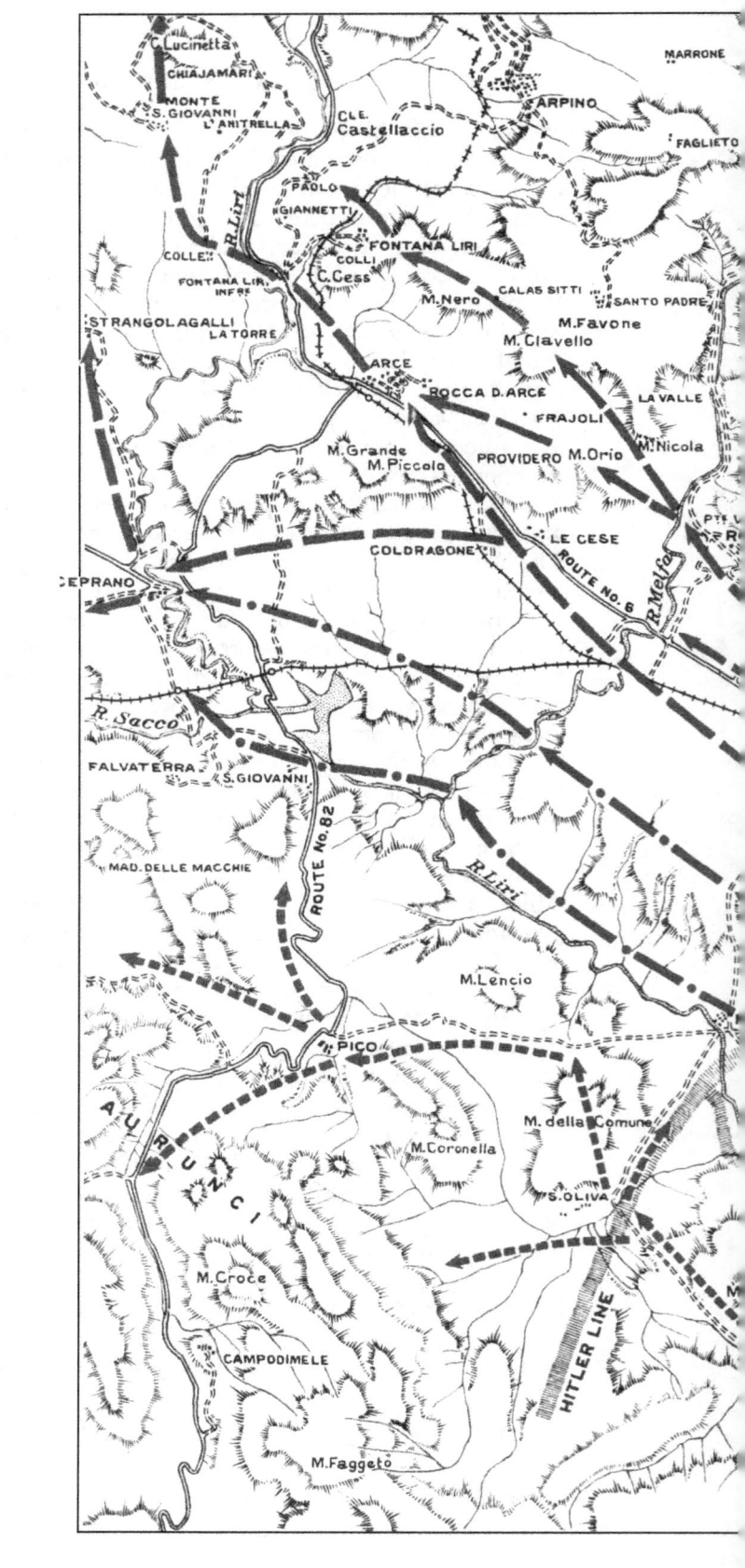

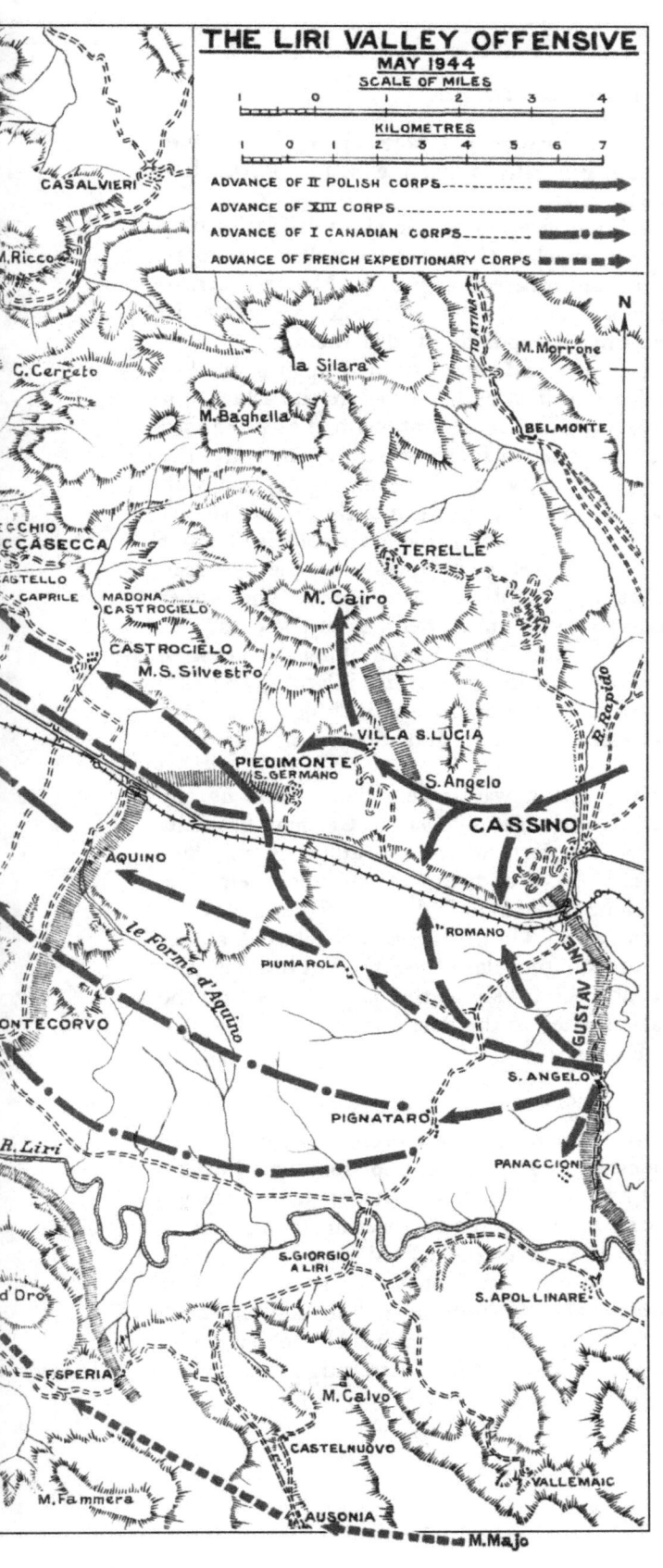

craft concentrations. Both tactical and strategical air forces were used in the phase, tactical generally appearing south of the line Rimini-Pisa, strategic north of it.

There was to be no intensification of air effort in Liri valley prior to the opening of the attack. A fighter controller was to be installed in a specially prepared observation post on Monte Trocchio so that when the battle was under way he could allot aircraft from a "Cabrank" as the assaulting divisions demanded them.

The selection of D Day and H Hour depended upon a number of factors. Planning had begun in March but before the attack was launched considerable regrouping and preparations had to be carried out, which could not be completed before late April. In Italy, the month of May was one of the best periods for campaigning, both on the ground and in the air. It was the spring month, neither so wet as to impede movement, nor so dry as to introduce problems of water supply or unending dust. The average temperature generally rises seven degrees above that for April to 64 degrees. The upper range is 75 to 85 degrees, the minimum 45 degrees on the coast and 32 degrees in the mountains. Rainfall decreases along the coast to an average of 2.42 inches but remains substantial inland. The Liri valley averages rather more than four inches and is subject to sudden thunder-storms which may produce floods and sticky soil. Visibility is generally excellent.[3]

The exact date for the attack was largely determined by the choice of a night attack to open the offensive. German positions were so well known and so well fortified that an attack in the dark appeared to offer the best chances of breaking through their foremost defences. At the same time moonlight would be useful for the exploitation of the first gains. On the day finally selected, sunset was at 2012 hours and the moon, four days from the last quarter, rose at 2331 hours. The selection of 11 May as the date for opening the offensive was doubtless also related to the date selected for the Allied landings in North-West Europe.

Rival Forces

General Alexander was convinced that a decisive victory would not be won except by concentrating vastly superior forces at the vital point of attack. He was firmly of the view that "to have a reasonable chance of effective penetration against defences in Italian terrain, it is necessary for the side that takes the offensive to have a local superiority of at least three to one in infantry." It speaks volumes of his ability as a strategist that he did succeed in concentrating vastly superior forces for the Liri valley offensive. He achieved this object by cleverly playing on Field-Marshal Kesselring's fears of an

[3] *Fifth Army History*, part V, "The Drive to Rome", p. 23.

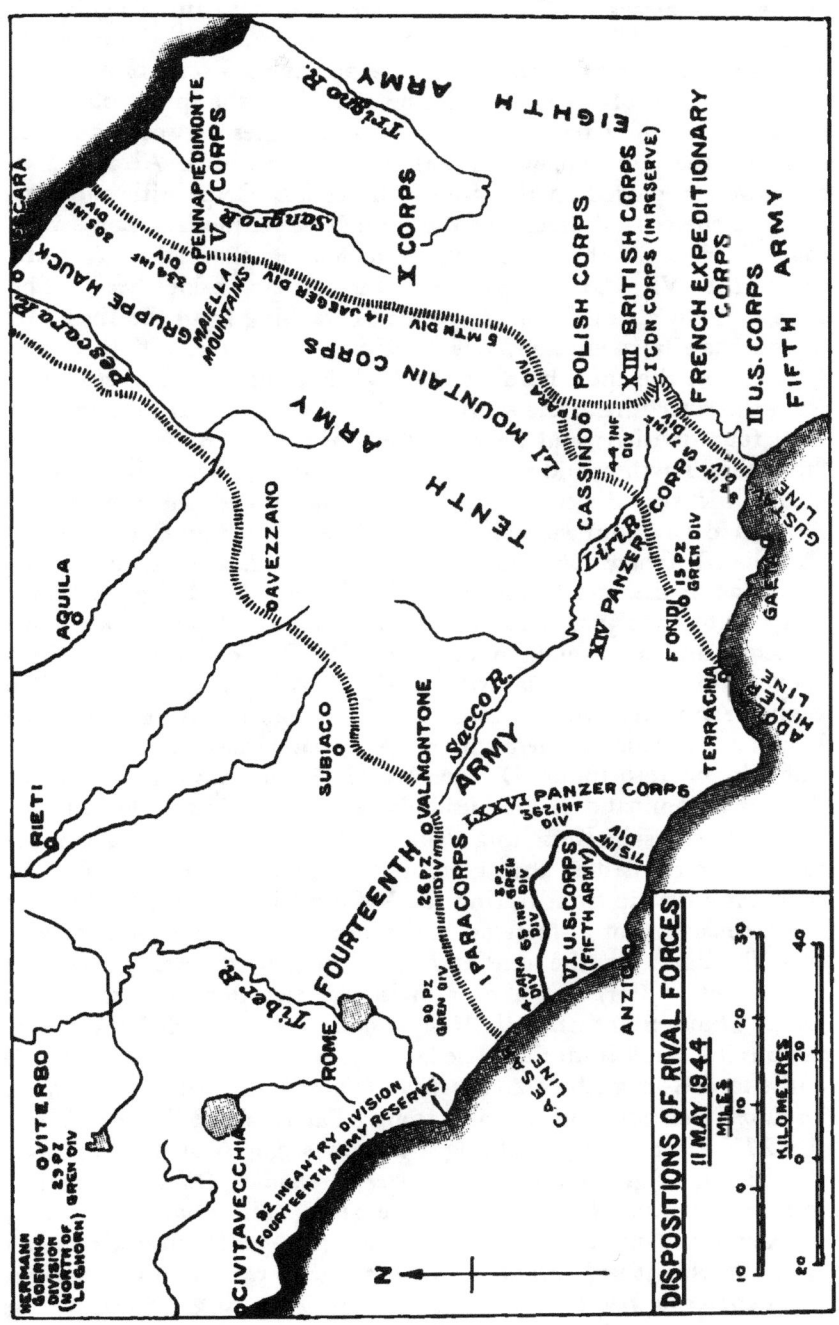

amphibious attack in Civitavecchia area and by camouflaging the build-up of the Allied forces at the focal point of attack. The success of these measures of deception can be appreciated only if we study the dispositions of the rival forces on the eve of the spring offensive. At that time the narrow front of about 16 miles between the river Liri and the Tyrrhenian Sea was held by the Fifth Army. Two corps were deployed on this front—the II U.S. Corps with two divisions on the coastal flank and the French Expeditionary Corps with four divisions in the mountainous region on the right. A third corps—the VI U.S. Corps—held the Anzio bridge-head. The Eighth Army's long front of 55 miles, extending from the river Liri to the Maiella mountains, was held by three corps. Of these the XIII Corps, the spear-head of the Eighth Army's attack, stretched from the river Liri to the southern edge of Cassino. It held the line with four divisions and an armoured brigade. Two divisions (the 8th Indian Division and the 4th British Division) were in the forward area while two divisions (the 78th Division and the 6th British Armoured Division) were in reserve. The I Canadian Corps (the 1st Canadian Infantry Division and the 5th Canadian Armoured Division) was in the rear behind the XIII Corps. The II Polish Corps, to its right, was just north of Cassino. It was deployed with two divisions and an armoured brigade. The X Corps held the hills above Atina and thus guarded the Eighth Army's right flank. The Eighth Army reserve consisted of the 6th South African Armoured Division. Further to the right on the Adriatic coast was the V Corps (the 4th and 10th Indian Divisions), an independent formation under the direct command of the Headquarters, Allied Armies in Italy.

Field-Marshal Kesselring deployed his forces in such a manner as to meet the Allied threat on all vital points of attack. On the stagnant Adriatic front (facing the V Corps) he organised a holding force, consisting of a small 'ad hoc' command ('*Gruppe Hauck*') with two divisions. In the centre, facing the Eighth Army, was the *LI Mountain Corps* with four divisions; two divisions (the *114th Jaeger Division* and the *5th Mountain Division*) guarded the mountainous left flank from the Maiella to the northern slopes of M. Cairo and two divisions (the *1st Parachute Division* and the *44th Infantry Division*) defended the Cassino front. Facing the Fifth Army was the *XIV Panzer Corps* holding a narrow sector (from Terracina to the Liri river) with the *15th Panzer Grenadier Division* and two infantry divisions (the *94th* and the *71st*). The *Fourteenth Army* at Anzio had in the line five divisions (the *3rd Panzer Grenadier Division*, the *362nd Infantry Division*, the *715th Infantry Division*, the *65th Infantry Division* and the *4th Parachute Division*). As regards the mobile reserves they were grouped around the Anzio bridge-head or strung out along the western coast. Of the three

Panzer Grenadier Divisions, one (the *15th*) was in the Fondi area to guard the Tenth Army's flank against amphibious attack, the second (the *90th*) in area on the northern flank of the Anzio bridge-head and the Tiber, and the third (the *29th*) in Viterbo area, guarding Civitavecchia. The fourth *Panzer Grenadier Division—the 3rd—* was in the line on the Anzio sector but it was practically of not much use on account of the heavy losses it had sustained. Of the two armoured divisions, one (the *26th Panzer Division*) was in reserve on the Anzio sector and the second (the *Hermann Goering Division*) was north of Leghorn, having been earmarked for France.

If we study carefully the German dispositions we shall notice two striking features. Firstly, along the vital line of defence (i.e. the line of the Garigliano from Cassino to the sea) there were only four German divisions to oppose more than thirteen Allied divisions. In short General Alexander had by clever moves succeeded in gaining overwhelming superiority in numbers at the vital point of attack. Secondly, the mobile reserves were grouped round the Anzio bridge-head or strung out along the western coast so that they were too far away to influence the course of battle. This was largely due to the apprehensions felt by Field-Marshal Kesselring about an Allied amphibious landing at Civitavecchia. Nothing contributed so much to these apprehensions as the Allied Cover Plan, whose aim was to deceive Field-Marshal Kesselring as to the build-up of the Allied forces on the main Liri front, and the strong possibility of an amphibious attack at Civitavecchia north of Rome. The I Canadian Corps with its two divisions and the 36th U.S. Division were assigned the task of inducing Field-Marshal Kesselring to believe that a sea-borne landing would take place at Civitavecchia. For this purpose they were to adopt all the means of deception. At the same time measures of 'concealment and camouflage on a very large scale' were to be adopted to prevent Field-Marshal Kesselring from guessing accurately the build-up of the Allied forces on the main Liri front. These measures were entirely successful. The fate of the German commander who was called upon to meet the Allied attack with vastly inferior forces (four divisions against thirteen) and with his mobile reserves far away from the vital point of attack can be imagined rather than described. General Alexander completely outwitted and outmanoeuvred Field-Marshal Kesselring.

The Gustav Line

It was fortunate that General Alexander succeeded in outwitting Field-Marshal Kesselring and in gaining superiority of forces at the vital point of attack. But for this brilliant strategy it is doubtful whether General Alexander would have clinched the issue and won a resounding victory. For the task facing him was undoubtedly very strenuous, particularly as Field-Mrashal Kesselring had made two strong defensive lines, known as the Gustav Line and the Hitler Line, to bar the advance of the Allied troops to Rome. How formidable the task was of forcing an entry through this gateway to Rome will be clear to us only if we appreciate the strength and weakness of the Liri valley defensive positions.

The Liri valley was a well defined depression, from four to seven miles in width, running from south-east to north-west and flanked by roughly parallel mountain ranges. To the north were the steep slopes of M. Cairo, terminating abruptly at Monte Cassino. To the south, were the forbidding limestone masses of the Aurunci range. The river Gari cut across the eastern mouth of the Liri valley from north to south, with river Liri running along the southern edge of the valley to meet the Gari at the south-east corner. The neck of land enclosed by these two rivers, shortly before their confluence, about six miles south of Cassino, was called the 'Liri Appendix'. From this 'Appendix', the valley ran north-west, parallel to Route 6, for about twenty miles until reaching Arce, a town on Route 6, where this highway to Rome turned sharp left to run across the valley until it reached the town of Ceprano. At this time of the year the rich alluvial soil had begun to yield abundant, tall crops, their profusion all the greater as they were untended. Dotted among the rolling corn-fields were occasional groves of fig and walnut trees. Along the banks of the streams were thin lines of trees of various types.

In the Liri valley the Germans had built two lines of defences. The Gustav Line which crossed Italy and had been intended to be the Winter Line, had in fact been held across the Liri valley, despite two major assaults by the American forces. From M. Cairo, the line descended to Monte Cassino and thence ran along the west bank of the river Rapido (river Gari)[4] to S. Ambrogio, S. Andrea and up into the hills again to M. Majo—M. Faito, around which the British 46th and the 56th Divisions had been fighting in February 1944. The last stretch to the coast ran through Castelforte, south-westwards along the foothills to M. Scauri. The strongest part of the line was from Cassino, along the river Gari to its junction with the river Liri. The Gari itself was a good tank obstacle from forty to sixty feet wide, seven to eight deep and flowing fast between flat, exposed banks. Behind it was a network of wire, concrete defences and earth-works, with shelters deep enough to protect their occupants from air or artillery bombardment. In the siting of the defences, every mound and undulation was used. S. Angelo was converted into a fortress bristling with automatic weapons. The escarpment

---

[4] Most maps call it R. Rapido north of S. Angelo and R. Gari south thereof.

just south of the village was a warren of deep dug-outs and trenches. Minefields littered the water meadows on the banks of the Gari. This part of the Gustav Line was about four thousand yards from front to rear. The Fuehrer had sent a personal message ordering that the Line would be held at all costs.

The 'Hitler Line'

Eight miles west of the Gari was a second defensive position, originally named by the Germans the 'Hitler Line' and later, when its inadequacy was realised, the 'Dora Line'. These defences branched off the Gustav Line on M. Cairo and ran through V.S. Lucia, circled Piedimonte, Aquino and Pontecorvo on the east, went along the river Liri where it runs southwards and into the foothills of the Aurunci Mountains at S. Oliva. In these mountains the defences were not continued in any strength because, apparently, the mountains were considered to be a sufficient natural barrier.

Information from a prisoner indicated that the Germans had begun to build defences on the line south from the junction of the river Liri and Forma Quesa—M. D'Oro—M. Fammera (via Esperia) —Spigon—thence westwards to M.S. Angelo—M. Mola—Formia. From Esperia this line presented a cliff face to the east of south.[5]

Across the Liri valley the 'Hitler Line' was well defined with almost continuous wire defences, behind which were stretches of anti-tank ditches and minor defences such as machine gun and anti-tank gun positions. On the fringe of the 'Hitler Line' proper were numerous, semi-mobile, armoured pill-boxes each manned by two men with a light machine gun. Then came an intricate system of reinforced concrete gun emplacements and weapon pits, all linked by tunnels and communication trenches. The anti-tank nodal points consisted of nine Panther turrets on well-built concrete bases with living quarters below the ground. Whilst the turret guns had all round traverse, two or three mobile anti-tank guns were echeloned back on the flanks. Each of these localities may be likened to the head of a spear, with the turret guns corresponding to the point and the mobile guns to the shoulders. When the 'Hitler Line' was attacked these guns took heavy toll of the Allied armour. Deep shelters with concrete roofs, five feet thick and covered by a twenty foot layer of earth, provided good protection against air or artillery bombardment.

The 'Hitler Line' was built over a period of five months during the winter and was never quite completed. When the spring crops came, the Germans, for all their thoroughness, neglected to clear their fields of fire. Thus many of the strong emplacements were almost blind when the final assault was launched. Nevertheless, and

[5] 8 Ind. Div. Intelligence Summary No. 100, dated 6 May 1944.

although in depth it nowhere exceeded a thousand yards, the 'Hitler Line' presented a formidable obstacle. It was the quality and the inadequate numbers of the troops, who were to man it, which proved its greatest weakness.

The Liri valley was a reasonably good tank country, the principal natural obstacle beyond the Gari being the Forme d'Aquino, a straggling stream, which ran from Aquino south-east across the valley until it joined the Liri and varied in width from ten to thirty yards. In places it was merely a marsh and the banks sloped steeply on each side. Defences were built in considerable depth, designed primarily to counter any crossing of the Gari river and penetration of the Gustav Line. The whole of the intervening country between the Gari and the Hitler Line was dotted with strong-points. As previously mentioned, an anti-tank ditch stretched, with some gaps, from north of Route 6 across the valley to the Liri. This ditch had been made by blowing a series of craters; in some cases, where these had become filled with water, they formed complete obstacles but in others the soil was sufficiently firm and dry to permit tanks to cross. Behind this ditch, extensive anti-tank minefields had been sited, covered, in front and rear, by belts of wire twenty feet wide.

From the mountains north and south of the valley the Germans had excellent observation over the whole valley. For the Allies, M. Trocchio provided the best observation. On a clear day, an observer there could see along Route 6 as far as Aquino and along the Liri as far as Pontecorvo.

It appeared at the time that the Germans relied on the anti-tank obstacle offered by the river Gari and placed emphasis on mortars, machine guns and field and medium artillery rather than anti-tank weapons.

XIII Corps Plan

As the XIII Corps formed the spearhead of the Eighth Army attack it is necessary to describe its plan for the Liri valley offensive. Lieut.-General S. C. Kirkman, C.B.E., M.C., Commander XIII Corps, planned to launch an attack across the Gari with two divisions, the British 4th Division on the right and the 8th Indian Division on the left.[6] The front of the XIII Corps was nearly seven miles in length, following the east bank of the Gari from Cassino down to the "Liri Appendix". The operations were to be carried out in three phases. In the first phase the British 4th Division was to establish a bridge-head between exclusive the Cassino railway station and exclusive S. Angelo while the 8th Indian Division was to secure a bridge-head at, and south of S. Angelo. In the second phase the British 4th Division was to enlarge the bridge-head up to and inclu-

[6] XIII Corps O.O. No. 17 (Operation 'Honker'), dated 30 April 1944.

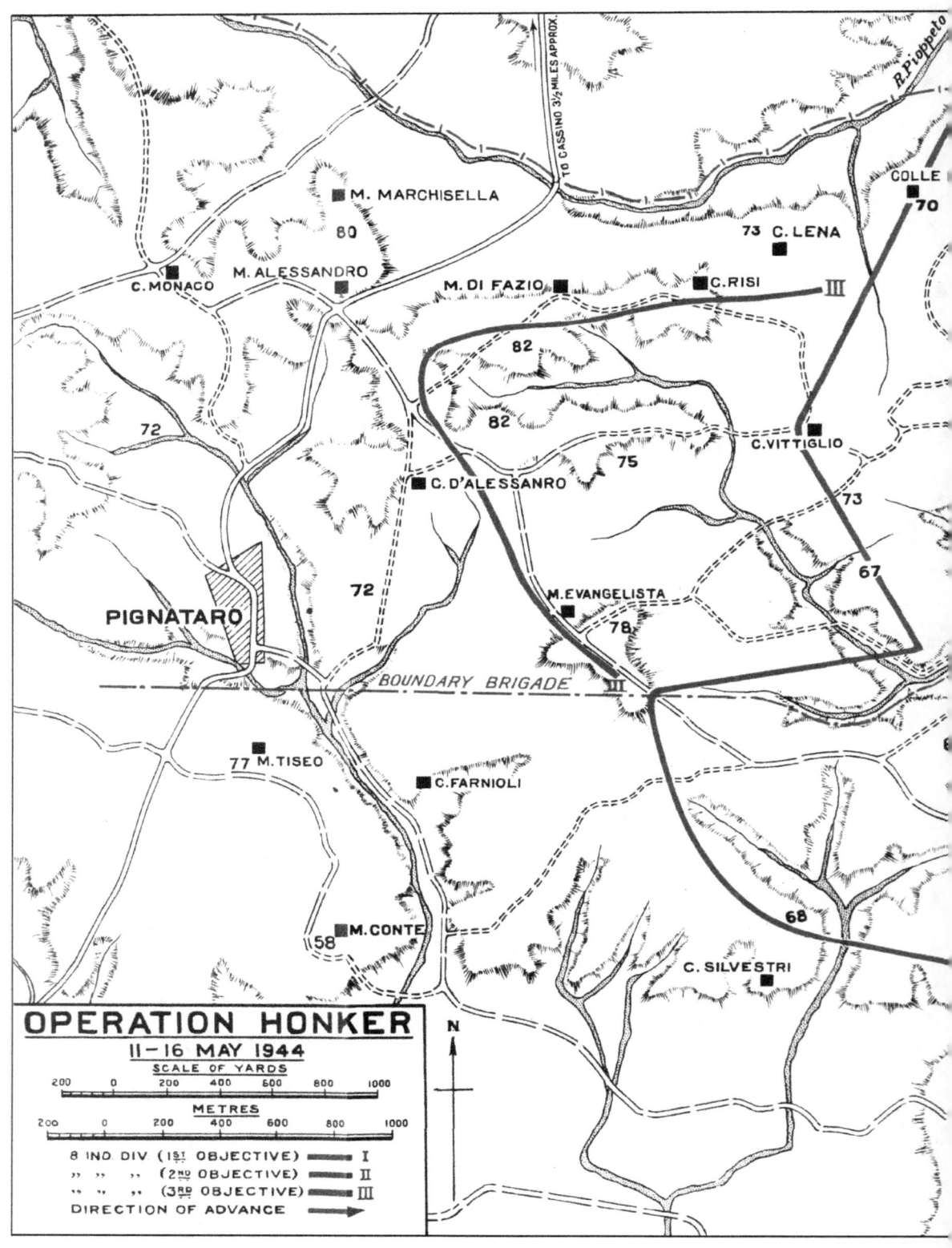

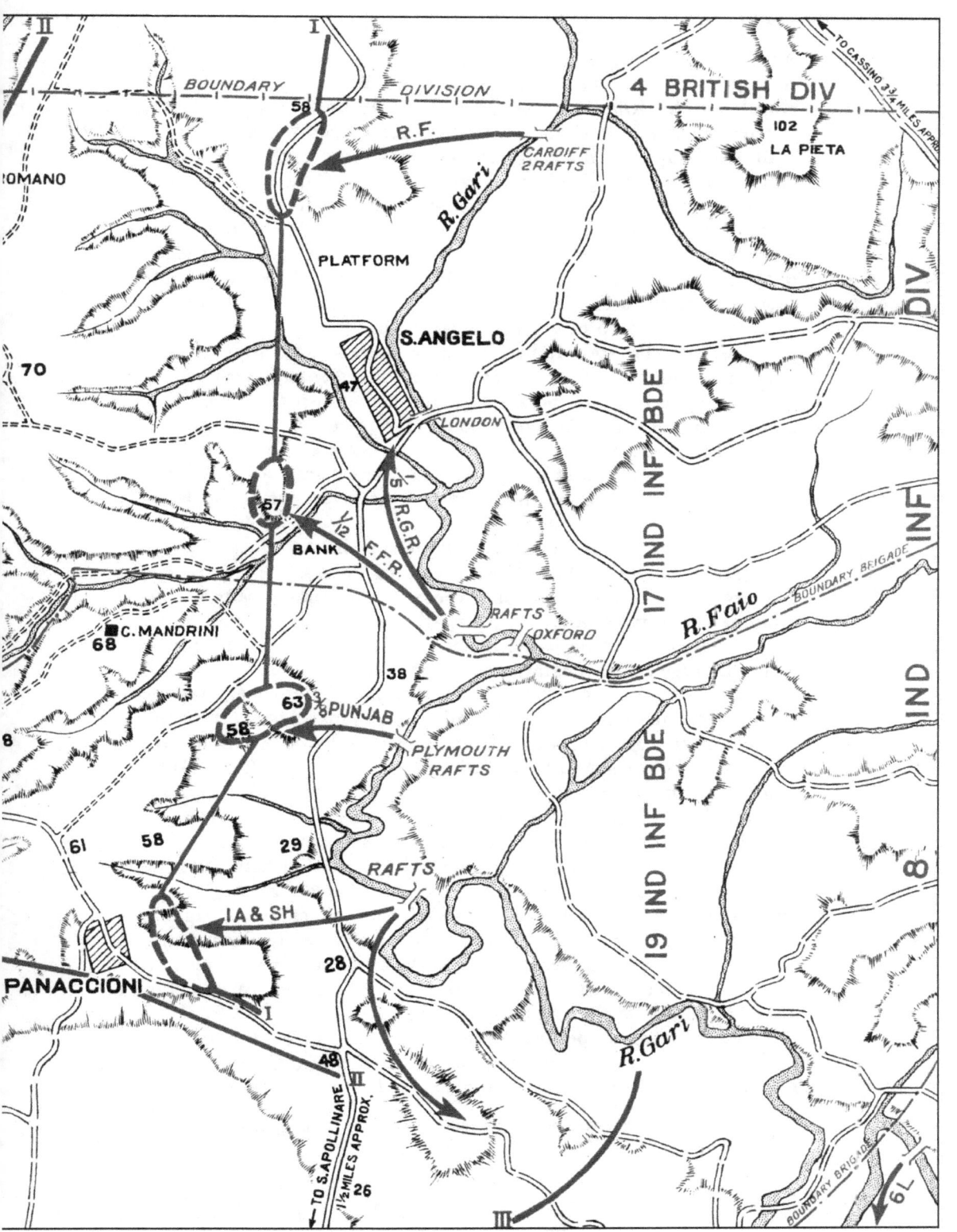

junction, 1000 yards south of S. Angelo, then move north-west to the high ground about Pt. 57, 1/2 mile south-west of S. Angelo. 1/5 Royal Gurkha Rifles, in reserve, was to capture S. Angelo, when ordered to do so. The 19th Indian Infantry Brigade was to attack with 3/8 Punjab on the right and 1st Argyll and Sutherland Highlanders on the left. The former was to cross the Gari, three hundred yards south of the Faio junction, then move west to the line of the track S. Angelo—Panaccioni on the ridge between Pt. 63 and Pt. 58. The latter was to cross the Gari at the light loop in the Gari, thence quarter of a mile east of Panaccioni, to the line of track and spur, south-east of Panaccioni. 6/13 Frontier Force Rifles in reserve was to follow 3/8 Punjab to assist in mopping up.

South of the 19th Indian Infantry Brigade, opposite the Liri Appendix, the 6th Lancers was to contain as many Germans as possible in the Liri Appendix. It was to accomplish this by putting a squadron across the Gari, one thousand yards north of its junction with the Liri. At the same time, the 6th Lancers was to demonstrate and simulate an assault about five hundred yards north of the junction. The squadron which crossed the river was to be withdrawn again by first light.

A heavy weight of artillery fire was to support the attack. Forty-five minutes before the first troops attempted to cross the river, corps artillery was to crash down in a concentrated counter-battery programme for forty minutes.[10] Thereafter, a proportion remained on counter-battery tasks while the majority switched to assist the attack with a barrage and a programme of timed concentrations on selected targets, among them being the Liri Appendix. The barrage was to move at one hundred yards in six minutes. Guns of the 26th Light Anti-Aircraft Regiment were to fire tracer over the heads of the infantry to help them maintain direction. The Corps Light Anti-Aircraft Regiment was given the task of operating smoke canisters to cover the crossing places over the Gari by day.

During the early stages of the attack it was planned that by day the main air support would be directed against German batteries and mortars in the Liri valley and the Atina area. By night, aircraft would harass the German lines of communication. In addition, fighter-bombers would carry out vigorous armed reconnaissance missions, both in and behind the battle area, in order to restrict German movement. Several of their headquarters were selected for special attention on the first day of the battle.

To achieve more speedy and more direct support a static forward air control post known as "Rover David" was established on M. Trocchio. From there, fighter-bombers circling the battle area were

---

[10] All timings were based on the minute at which the leading assault pushed off from the east bank of the Gari. This was called W Hour.

to be briefed for opportunity targets, thus reducing to a minimum the time lag betweeen the origination of a request for aid and its actual fulfilment. The control was to co-operate closely with artillery observation posts, spotter aircraft and all tactical reconnaissance aircraft.

In Phase II, the establishment of a firm bridge-head, the 17th Indian Infantry Brigade was to secure the ridge of high ground,[11] one mile west of S. Angelo. The 19th Indian Infantry Brigade was to reorganise on a similar[12] ridge circling Panaccioni on the west, at a distance of approximately one thousand yards. Artillery was to aid this advance by a barrage and, thereafter, to support the troops holding the ridges by defensive fire tasks designed to smash up German counter-attacks.

Phase III, the extension to the S. Angelo 'Horseshoe', was to be achieved by exploitation of patrols from the ground already captured. Tanks were to be available to assist infantry patrols in this exploitation.[13]

The Liri Appendix was to be liquidated by the 19th Indian Infantry Brigade and its tanks as early as possible. When that had been accomplished, the 6th Lancers would take over the protection of the southern flank of the 8th Indian Division.

For a river crossing operation of this nature, engineers took the place occupied by naval personnel in a seaborne operation. Not surprisingly, therefore, the allotment of engineers to the 8th Indian Division was an unusually large one. There were, in all, five field companies,[14] one pioneer company, one field park company, one Bailey Bridge Platoon (Royal Army Service Corps), One General Transport Company (Royal Army Service Corps) (carrying the bridging), two assault sections, one raft section and two tipper sections. The tasks allotted to them were the construction of Bailey bridges and Class 5 Rafts, the clearance of mines west of the Gari up to, but excluding, the lateral road through S. Angelo, and maintenance of roads and tracks up to, but excluding, the main lateral on the east bank of the Gari.[15]

---

[11] Colle Romano—C. Vittiglio—spur G 845148.
[12] West of road junction Pt. 66—Pt. 68—Panaccioni—X roads Pt. 48.
[13] Ground inside the Horseshoe consisted of ridges and folds, thickly covered with trees and shrub.
[14] Including the three of the division.
[15] Initially, there were to be four Bailey bridges in the 8th Division Sector of the Gari.
    (a) Cardiff—at G 866165, opposite La Pieta in the area of the 1st Royal Fusiliers.
    (b) London—immediately south of S. Angelo on the site of the destroyed bridge. Not to be constructed until the night of D plus 1/2 by which time it was hoped that S. Angelo would be taken.
    (c) Oxford—at G 866147, alongside the junction of the Faio with the Gari, in the area of 1/12 Frontier Force Regiment.
    (d) Plymouth—G 862143, seven hundred yards south-west of Oxford.

To aid it in the attack, the 8th Indian Division had under command:—
- 1st Canadian Armoured Brigade (Shermans)
- 11th Canadian Army Field Regiment (SP)
- 152nd Field Regiment
- 165th Army Field Regiment (less one battery)
- Detachment 3rd Survey Regiment
- B Flight 657th Air Observation Post Squadron
- 1208th Indian Pioneer Company
- 201st Guards Brigade Signal Section
- Detachment 1 Kensington (78th Division)—two Medium Machine Gun platoons and six 4.2-inch mortar platoons.

In support were:—
- XII Tactical Air Command
- Two field companies, Corps Troops Royal Engineers and a total of:—
- Eight Field regiments
- Two medium regiments (1st Canadian and 51st British Medium Regiments)
- Three Heavy anti-aircraft troops, (two of 97th and one of 57th Heavy Anti-aircraft Regiments) (18 guns) in ground role.
- Two self-propelled field regiments
- Two heavy batteries (107th and 121st of 32nd Heavy Regiment)
- One Light Anti-Aircraft battery (less one troop) in ground role.[16]

The 8th Indian Division Prepares for Battle

Early in April 1944, the 8th Indian Division was relieved by the 4th Indian Division in the Orsogna sector on the Adriatic coast to enable it to prepare for the Battle of Cassino II. The 21st Indian Infantry Brigade took over the front between Cassino railway station and La Pieta from the 2nd Independent Parachute Brigade at 0155 hours on 16 April, coming under the command of the 6th Armoured Division.[17] A little later the 17th and 19th Indian Infantry Brigades

---

[16] This includes units under command.

[17] The sector was held with the 5th Royal West Kent around the railway station, 3/15 Punjab in the middle and 1/5 Mahratta Light Infantry on the left. The task assigned to the 21st Indian Infantry Brigade was to prevent German reconnaissance east of the river Gari and to maintain absolute superiority by night over the water meadows skirting the Gari. At the railway station, owing to the proximity of the Germans and their ability to overlook the whole area from Monastery Hill, the troops were unable to make the slightest move by day. After dark, their field of vision was extremely limited. These factors, together with the almost incessant sound of bursting shells and mortars, made it possible for German patrols to get very close quarters before their presence was detected. Unless the garrison was extremely alert, it was in considerable danger of being overrun before the alarm was given.

Points in the railway and throughout the length of the river banks were accurately registered by the German artillery and mortars and hostile shelling was

moved to a training area along the Volturno river, twenty miles south of Cassino. Two regiments of the 1st Canadian Armoured Brigade were allotted to the two brigades—the 11th (Ontario) Armoured Regiment to the 17th Indian Infantry Brigade and the 14th (Calgary) Armoured Regiment to the 19th Indian Infantry Brigade. Combined training followed in river crossings, the handling of assault craft, bridgement, and co-operation of infantry and armour in battle. At the beginning of May dress-rehearsals ensued. Thereafter, the 17th Indian Infantry Brigade took up its positions in the sector in which it was to attack. On 6 May, the 19th Indian Infantry Brigade took up positions on the left of the 17th Indian Infantry Brigade. South of the 19th Indian Infantry Brigade the 6th Lancers still faced the German positions in the Liri Appendix, with two squadrons up on a front of fifteen hundred yards. The 21st Indian Infantry Brigade, having been relieved on 3/4 May in the sector of Cassino railway station, was brought into divisional reserve. Divisional artillery gradually moved into very restricted gun areas between M. Porchio and M. Trocchio. The 8th Indian Division was thus ready to take part in operation 'Honker'.

Concealment and Deception

For several weeks prior to the attack, Allied forces had been engaged in a vast deception scheme, the object of which was to persuade the Germans that the coming full-scale offensive would be launched in another part of Italy and on a date later than the one actually selected. The intensive training could not be concealed but it was essential to conceal the time and place of the attack. To achieve the first, all brigades were instructed to prepare and issue relief and training programmes as far ahead as 21 May and these programmes were made known to all troops. Concealment of place involved concentrating and maintaining, unknown to the Germans, the large forces required for the assault in a relatively confined space, the area east of M. Trocchio not visible to German observation posts.

Units moving to the forward zone from the training areas left

---

frequent. This shelling, however, varied considerably according to what was happening in the German forward areas. Their patrols, in strength from three to twelve men, frequently crossed the river by night. But the outposts of the 21st Indian Infantry Brigade were also well placed and alert and therefore the hostile patrols seldom succeeded in penetrating to any depth.

For intelligence security reasons, the 21st Indian Infantry Brigade's patrols were not often permitted to cross the Gari. Their activities were usually limited to protective patrolling and covering the sapper working parties who, every night, were busy lifting mines. Many of these mines had been hastily sown by the Americans to cover their withdrawal from S. Angelo earlier in the year and few records of their location existed.

The 21st Indian Infantry Brigade remained in this sector until relieved on 3/4 May by the 28th Infantry Brigade, 4th British Infantry Division. The 21st Indian Infantry Brigade then went to reorganise and rest at Dragoni on the river Volturno, where the other brigades of the 8th Indian Division had been training.

behind sufficient transport to represent continued occupation; assembly areas were not marked with formation signs until the last possible moment; dummies took the place of tanks moving forward for the final concentration; troops assembled forward at night; guns taking up positions, which had not previously been occupied, remained silent until the opening of the attack; every tree along that stretch of Route 6 hid dumps of patrol, ammunition, food or equipment. Sappers constructing tracks in the forward areas strewed them with brushwood before dawn.

The early morning mist helped to hinder observation by the German observation posts, but, leaving nothing to chance, smokescreen was employed to blind all visibility from the observation posts on Monastery Hill. On one day, shortly before the attack, as many as two thousand seven hundred smoke shells were used for this purpose. All the camouflage officers in the Eighth Army and No. 1 Camouflage Company (Palestinian) were put to work arranging and supervising camouflage on a large scale. The results of all these measures and the care shown by everybody were that a considerable degree of tactical surprise was achieved. Despite the enormous number of troops involved and the vast weight of material that was gradually passed forward, there was no noticeable increase in German shelling in this sector until the moment that the assault began. Later, interrogation of German prisoners showed that they had no conception of the strength which the Allies had built up. However, one drawback in these intensive measures for security and surprise was that infantry was not permitted to assume aggressive patrolling west of the Gari and thereby it lacked the opportunity of knowing the ground well. The stage was thus set for an assault on the Gustav Line preliminary to a move against Rome by the Fifth and Eighth Armies.

CHAPTER VIII

The Assault of the Gustav Line

The Attack Opens

D Day for the attack on the Gustav Line was 11 May 1944. After a day of broiling sunshine, the evening was fine, with a waning moon due to rise at about 2300 hours. Thick mist in the valleys had been forecast. The assaulting infantry of the 8th Indian Division, who had waited patiently through the day in the river valley, hidden from the view of the German observation posts on M. Cassino by the hedges, trees and thick vegetation, began to stir in that otherwise breathless interval which precedes a big battle. Then, as the moon rose,[1] six hundred and fifty guns opened up on the XIII Corps front, shattering the lull in the Liri valley. This tremendous artillery concentration pounded German gun and mortar sites behind their infantry positions. The divisional machine gun unit, 5th Royal Battalion Mahratta Light Infantry, using the newly acquired 4.2-inch mortars, sent bombs over the river on the German positions nearer the stream. machine guns and 4.2-inch mortars of the detachment[2] from 1 Kensingtons (78th Division) joined the artillery in neutralising the Liri Appendix.

With the gun flashes erupting behind them, turning night into twilight, and the curtain of shells over their heads, the leading companies of the assaulting infantry battalions moved down to the river bank. During this time the German guns did not return fire but the water meadows with their many dykes made the task of carrying the assault boats down to the Gari a difficult one. At 2345 hours,[3] how-

---

[1] The planned timings were:—
    (a) W minus 3 hours; Silent preparations start i.e. assembly of assaulting troops in their concentration areas.
    (b) W minus 45 mins; Counter-battery and counter-mortar programme starts; assault troops move from concentration to forming up areas.
    (c) W minus 5 mins; (i) Counter-battery ends. (ii) barrage and concentrations begin.
    (d) W; 'Shove off' (from east bank to Gari).
    (e) W plus 54 mins; Arrive on first objective.
    (f) W plus 2 hours 20 minutes; Leave first objective.
    (g) W plus 3 hours 32 minutes; 17th Brigade arrives on Second objective.
    (h) W plus 3 hours 50 minutes; (i) Fire on S. Angelo & 'Platform' ceases. (ii) 1/5 Royal Gurkha Rifles attack S. Angelo.
    (j) W plus 4 hours 14 minutes; 19th Brigade arrives on second objective.
    (k) W plus 4 hours 45 minutes; pre-arranged artillery programme ends.
    (W was the time at which the first flight of assault boats left the near bank of the river).
[2] Two platoon medium machine guns and six platoons 4.2-inch mortars.
[3] Zero hour for the Fifth Army was 2300 hours; for II Polcorps it was 0100 hours 12 May.

ever, the first assault boats were launched[4] and the men of the 17th and the 19th Indian Infantry Brigades started to cross. Five minutes earlier, the guns had changed from counter-battery to concentrations on the nearer targets and to the barrage, which advanced from the river at one hundred yards every six minutes.

A cold, damp mist lay over the valley. To thicken the mist and the clouds of dust and smoke rising from the artillery concentrations, the Germans ignited smoke canisters. By 2330 hours visibility was no more than two feet. Beach master parties and squads laying white tape near the river bank experienced great difficulty in keeping direction. Assaulting troops fell into the many ditches which intersected the low-lying meadows.

The 17th Indian Infantry Brigade Attacks

On the right of the 8th Indian Division, north of S. Angelo, 1st Royal Fusiliers, of the 17th Indian Infantry Brigade, suffered a few casualties when actually crossing the river. Over the river, numerous dykes and the thick cloud of smoke, dust and mist caused some confusion. In single file, each man holding the bayonet scabbard of the man in front, the Fusiliers made for their objective through the German defensive fire, which by now had started raking the ground between the river and S. Angelo. German machine gunners, who had gone to ground when the fury of the artillery bombardment broke on their positions, came out of their dug-outs and sent heavy, intermittent streams of fire into the pitch black smoke-screen to rake the meadows where the British infantry was struggling forward. German mortars opened up and bombs crashed down on the crossing places; the noise of battle was tremendous.

By 0100 hours, all the Fusiliers were across the river, but the artificial fog, together with the strong German defensive fire, had caused confusion. They found themselves hemmed in between two German positions, the 'Platform' in front of them and the village of S. Angelo on their left. It was impossible for the battalion to advance through the curtain of fire, which would not be lifted until S. Angelo had been cleared. At 0200 hours, with twenty-five per cent of their assaulting companies missing, the Fusiliers dug in about five hundred yards forward of the river in the ditches of the meadows.

On the left, 1/12 Frontier Force Regiment having crossed by 0140 hours the river on a two-company front, fourteen hundred yards downstream from S. Angelo, was engaged in fierce fighting at

---

[4] Each forward battalion had sixteen assault boats and an immediate reserve of four. Brigade had a further reserve of ten on wheels in the forward Vehicle Transit area. Each forward battalion also had 32 duckboards to assist in crossing dykes. The 17th Brigade had three Class II rafts, including one in reserve.

the 'Bank'. Its success in getting across was attributed to the fact that reliance was placed on ropes for pulling the boats across and not on paddles. While forming up on the west bank, 1/12 Frontier Force Regiment was subjected to machine gun and mortar fire from both flanks. This fire and the fog made the forming up a difficult operation but, by 0200 hours, its companies were ready to advance towards the 'Bank'. They were by now, unfortunately, considerably behind their own artillery programme.

The Germans had erected a number of trip wires which, when cut or pulled, actuated smoke canisters. These, in turn, gave the cue for German machine gunners to open fire on fixed lines. As the men advanced, the smoke grew thicker until visibility was nil. Some stumbled blindly on while others fell, killed or wounded by machine gun fire. A Company, closely followed by D Company, reached the road below the 'Bank' only to find wire and mines stretching out towards them from the German positions. Stick grenades, thrown from the trenches on the 'Bank', showered on the companies. Halted in their frontal assault, the two companies moved round to the left (south) of 'Bank' and, with bayonets and grenades, put in a flanking assault which reached the top of the feature. Progress was slow, but the men of the Frontier Force Regiment made the best use of their opportunity to get to close quarters with the Germans in dug-outs, caves and quarries. After a series of sharp hand-to-hand encounters, the positions on the 'Bank' were partially cleared.

On the left, C Company had succeeded in reaching the lateral road south of the 'Bank', but only after some desperate encounters were the opposing German positions cleared, both sides suffering casualties. At 0700 hours this company moved two hundred yards farther south to prevent German interference with the construction of Oxford Bridge.

The battalion commander, who was uncertain of the location of one of his companies, instructed the company commander by wireless to fire verey lights. Thick fog snuffed out the lights as soon as they were fired, so that the colonel told the company commander to get his men to shout and show their position. This proved successful and the colonel knew where the company was located.

It was well that reserves were available for, at first light, it was revealed that the Germans were in occupation of the parts of the escarpment within a few yards of the 1/12 Frontier Force Regiment. The battalion did not yet have a secure hold when the Germans opened a withering fire, with machine gunners also shooting from San Angelo on the flank. Casualties were heavy. The reserve company, B, was called up and, making clever use of the folds in the grounds, crept forward and scuppered the German garrison of the remaining dug-outs. Battalion headquarters moved close up under the escarpment to get away from the intense artillery fire, which the Germans now poured into the bridge-head. After very hard and bitter fighting, the hold of the Frontier Force Regiment became secure and contact was made with 3/8 Punjab, to the south, at 0845 hours.

So far as the 17th Indian Infantry Brigade was concerned, the artificial fog had prevented the two assaulting battalions from advancing beyond San Angelo and securing the bridge-head. The third battalion of the brigade, 1/5 Royal Gurkha Rifles, which was to deal with S. Angelo, had suffered a similar handicap. German fire became very heavy indeed when the XIII Corps artillery concentrations eased up and consequently the Gurkhas had more casualties than the assault battalions had sustained when they moved forward to the east bank of the river. At 0100 hours, the Gurkhas were ordered to take over the boats and cross the river into the Frontier Force Regiment's area. D Company proceeded to the river bank to find only four serviceable boats.—twelve boats had been sunk by shell or mortar fire, whilst others had been swept away by the swift current. These four boats were moved from bank to bank by ropes attached on either side. Hauling parties pulled the boats, whilst communications were maintained by shouting from one side of the river to the other. Between 0215 and 0600 hours, the Gurkhas were ferried across the river. Two companies were despatched to the start line for the attack on S. Angelo. The rest of the battalion lined the west bank of the river where the men had crossed.

At first light on 12 May the situation in the 17th Indian Infantry Brigade sector was that the Fusiliers were held up on the right flank, five hundred yards west of the river, the Frontier Force Regiment was hanging grimly on to that part of the 'Bank' which it had captured, whilst the Gurkhas were across the river east of 1/12 Frontier Force Regiment, waiting their chance to attack S. Angelo.

The 19th Indian Infantry Brigade Attacks

We may now proceed to examine the position of the 19th Indian Infantry Brigade, which was operating to the south of the 17th Indian Infantry Brigade. At the very start it met strong opposition. The German initial reaction was to bomb heavily the east bank with their mortars and to put down a thick smoke screen. This was done by a special apparatus on the west bank and by phosphorus smoke shells. Their object appeared to be to create confusion among the assaulting troops and, in this, they were partially successful.[5] Smoke considerably slowed down the crossing of the river and

---

[5] One effect was the disappearance of comparatively large numbers of men which made casualties in the early stages appear heavier than they actually were. When these men reappeared later, many of them established in forward positions, the picture looked brighter.

Sikhs advancing under cover of smoke for breaking the Gustav Line

Lieut.-General Sir M. C. Dempsey
(Commander XIII Corps)

Lieut.-General W. Mark Clark
(Commander American Fifth Army)

Major-General Sir Dudley Russell
(Commander 8th Indian Division, January 1943)

caused the infantry to lose much of the benefit of the artillery barrage. Confusion, arising from loss of contact between sub-units, prevented an immediate assault on the German river line defences. Eastward loops in the river were isolated by several lines of wire obstacles, two to two and half feet above the ground. But there was no continuous minefield and the troops behind the weir were not in numbers. . On the south flank, pill-boxes were encountered. The artillery fire had had little visible effect on them.

3/8 Punjab, on the right, had been given the task of securing the line of the lateral road, about three hundred yards west of the river and slightly beyond an escarpment, then pushing on to capture Pt. 63. This point was located in the San Angelo 'Horseshoe', being about three hundred yards beyond the lateral road. Having completed this operation with A and B, the two forward companies, it was the intention to bring D Company to level up with the other two, and then for all the three to advance. By this time, it was hoped that the Canadian tanks would have arrived, enabling C Company to push through to the outskirts of Pignataro.

3/8 Punjab came under heavy fire when the men reached the bank of the river; German artillery and mortar fire crashed down on the boat launching area. All communications between the forming up place and the river crossings were broken by this fire. The German infantry, from their posts near the river, brought fairly accurate small arms fire to bear on the crossing places and caused some forty casualties. Undeterred, the men of A and B Companies managed to get through the mist towards the far bank. A Company managed to get across but all their boats were swept away on the return journey by the swiftly flowing current, and one platoon landed in B Company's area. B Company had more or less the same experience, except that those boats, which were not carried away by the current, were holed and sunk by shell and machine gun fire; only one boat remained serviceable. This boat was secured by ropes fore and aft and hauling parties pulled the boat backwards and forwards across the river until the remaining troops of B Company, together with some attached personnel, were across.

With the aid of this one boat and two rafts, the rest of the battalion was across the river at 0630 hours, but by now it was very much behind the schedule. Though dawn was breaking visibility was still bad, thanks to the German smoke screen, and the Germans were able only to continue firing on fixed lines into the thick smoke.[6] Meanwhile, A Company on the right, less one platoon which had been swept downstream, had collected on the west bank and was

[6] There was no doubt that the artificial fog caused great confusion to the attacking infantry of the 8th Indian Division during the night, but, when daylight came, the smoke became their ally, helping them to reorganise in the bridge-head.

advancing, stumbling through the smoke towards its objective Pt. 63. The company had not gone very far when it ran into a thick belt of heavily mined wire obstacles. The mines killed and wounded several and the sound of the exploding mines brought down heavy and accurate small arms fire on the rest of the company. Those who had not been blown up fell victim to the German fire. However fifteen survivors pushed on towards the objective. Soon six of these men became casualties before reaching the lateral road, the other nine men however pushed on. But only thirty yards beyond they had to halt and to dig in for the night. They killed several Germans who attacked them during the night. When daylight came, only three fighting men had survived. With their ammunition running short and no signs of the other companies or the Canadian tanks this gallant party was forced to surrender.

B Company of 3/8 Punjab, having crossed the river, found itself without the company commander. He, with several men, had crossed in the first flight but his boat was carried downstream by the current. When he eventually landed he set off into the mist to find his company. Unfortunately, he moved away into the fog and darkness too quickly for the men who had crossed with him, was unable to find his company—which by this time had landed some distance away—and soon found himself, a lone British officer, in the German held territory. B Company when assembled, moved to carry out the orders. By good fortune, it avoided the strong German positions along the road on the inter-brigade boundary and at midday had moved two to three hundred yards north-east of Pt. 63.

When the rest of the battalion was across the Gari, at 0630 hours, D Company advanced on the right towards the escarpment, opposite the Faio Junction. It reached to within a few yards of the objective, then charged the German positions in line abreast. It was a gallant but futile charge, which was halted by a wire obstacle and the combined fire of four German machine guns. The gallant officer,[7] who led the charge, was killed and one complete platoon was wiped out. This platoon crashed through almost into the German positions; they lay where they had fallen, a few yards in front of the muzzles of the German machine guns. A second attack launched by the company captured the ridge. By that time there were only some thirty men who were not wounded.

C Company, which had advanced on the left of D Company, struck the German held ridge three hundred yards farther south, and was pinned down by machine gun fire.

During this phase, the rest of 3/8 Punjab was so closed up under

[7] Major Sujan Singh.

the German positions⁸ that their hand grenades came rolling down the slopes and burst among the Punjab soldiers. A nineteen year old Sepoy, Kamal Ram, of Karauli State, new to the battalion and fighting his first action, attacked two German machine gun posts single handed. He shot or bayoneted the German garrison, capturing both the posts. He then assisted his Havildar in taking a third post. Sepoy Kamal Ram was later awarded the Victoria Cross.

South of 3/8 Punjab, the 1st Argyll & Sutherland Highlanders were pinned down by German fire as soon as they crossed the river. Their misfortunes started very early, even before they had reached the river bed. They suffered many casualties as they were carrying their boats down to the Gari behind the barrage because, unfortunately, their route to the river was through a German defensive fire task. They were unable to call even for artillery support as their Forward Observation Officer's group with the Argylls had suffered casualties from German shelling. Moreover, the area of the assault had been the scene of an unsuccessful American attempt to cross the Gari some time previously. When the Americans had withdrawn, they had heavily mined the east bank of the river to counter any swift German follow up. Although the reserve battalion of the 19th Indian Infantry Brigade had been engaged for some days before the battle in picking up most of these mines, some still remained to explode and kill many men of this battalion as they moved down to the river.

One company and two platoons of the Argyll crossed the river straight into a German defensive fire task. Their boats were riddled with bullets. A raft which had been hastily assembled also suffered the same fate. The rest of the battalion was unable to get across, and the few who did succeed in crossing the river through the thick fog were checked by fire almost as soon as they had landed on the far bank, where they came upon very strongly wired German defences, with two machine guns on the road firing directly at them. Although one platoon of D Company managed to reach the road, the thick fog as well as the din of battle resulted in its missing the German posts and advancing across the road. In the two forward companies, one company commander was killed and the other wounded. However, this small force retained a precarious hold, pinned down by fire in a narrow triangle of soggy, waterlogged ground, about two hundred yards short of the German positions. By holding up as the men did, they protected the left flank of the 3/8 Punjab, with whom they were trying to establish contact at Pt. 29.

German counter-attacks against the 19th Indian Infantry Brigade

---

⁸ Battalion Headquarters was then forward against the face of the German held ridge between D and C Companies, i.e. at G 861146.

at any place were not by more than a platoon but the valley between the 17th and the 19th Indian Infantry Brigades greatly assisted their harassing tactics. Crossing places at the Gari were consistently shelled by concentration of German guns, and at other places too it was heavy.

The 'demonstration' opposite the Liri Appendix by the 6th Lancers was most successful. The river was not crossed but German fire plans which were captured after the battle were found to include as targets the dummy post which the regiment had constructed in their area. When the main attack went in, the Lancers banged pieces of old iron to make it seem as though a bridge was being built in this area. The Germans reacted violently and fire, which would otherwise have been directed against other sectors of the front, fell in the Lancers' position.

The River Gari Bridged

While the infantry was making heroic efforts to cross the river Gari and had met with stern opposition, steps were taken to throw four bridges across the river to enable the tanks to move in support of infantry attack. As soon as the first batch of infantry had crossed the river Gari, bridging operations were taken up, and it was hoped that at least one would be ready for use by 0400 hours on 12 May. But in the north, behind the 1st Royal Fusiliers, work on Cardiff bridge was delayed by the bad visibility and by difficult approaches; and the bridge-head there was too shallow to give adequate protection to the engineers who were, in consequence, subjected to a withering fire. Despite heroic efforts by the Indian sappers, at first light it was decided to abandon work on Cardiff bridge for the time being, and to concentrate on getting the other two bridges, Oxford and Plymouth over the river.[*] The 66th and 69th Field Companies, Sappers and Miners, Indian Engineers, worked hard to construct these two bridges. "By half-past eight on the morning of 12 May, the gallant efforts of hard-working Indian sappers had completed the first of these—"Oxford" Bridge, a mile south of Sant' Angelo. Within another hour the river had been spanned a second time, by what must be considered a triumph of mechanical improvisation. A thousand yards downstream from "Oxford" Bridge, on a site code-

---

[*] The Plymouth Bridge was the first bridge ever carried on tanks—an idea which was conceived in the 8th Indian Division Headquarters A Mess one evening after dinner and which was later taken up and improved. Major-General Dudley Russell, his C.R.E., G.S.O.I. and Commander of a Canadian Tank Regiment were chatting across the table after dinner when the Mess Havildar brought in cigarettes and tobacco rations. As they were talking about bridges they made a bridge out of packets of cigarettes stuck into one another and two tobacco tins. One of them then turned the tins on their sides and Major-General Russell said, "couldn't we build a bridge under cover and roll it forward?" Some one else said, "Why not on tanks?" Thus originated the idea of a bridge being carried on tanks.

named "Plymouth", Canadian mechanics and Indian engineers had succeeded in launching across the 50-foot river a Bailey bridge, borne on the back of one Sherman tank and thrust into position by a second in the rear. Over these bridges rumbled troops of Canadian tanks, camouflaged with green boughs as though decked for a May Day festival. No other tanks crossed the Gari that day on the Army front, for no other bridges were completed."[10]

Until the bridges were ready the 1st Canadian Armoured Brigade could do no more than support the infantry by fire from the east bank. Shortly after midnight, however, the leading squadrons of the 11th and the 14th Canadian Armoured Regiments had moved up to their forward assembly areas, approximately one thousand yards from their crossing places. Routes forward to Oxford and Plymouth Bridges were swept and taped by the Reconnaissance Troops and the squadrons moved forward again at 0730 hours. At the same time, a second squadron and the headquarters of each regiment moved into the forward assembly areas.

B Squadron, 11th Canadian Armoured Regiment, was over Oxford Bridge by 0900 hours. C Squadron, 11th Canadian Armoured Regiment, was to have crossed by Cardiff Bridge and to have assisted the 1st Royal Fusiliers. But, as work on that bridge was temporarily suspended, C Squadron was ordered to follow B Squadron over Oxford Bridge, to push north through S. Angelo and up the west bank of the Gari to assist the 1st Royal Fusiliers who were having a bad time. Unfortunately, the ground west of Oxford Bridge was marshy and both B and C Squadrons had half their tanks bogged before they could reach the lateral road.

In view of this development, C Squadron was ordered to halt until its tanks had been recovered. B Squadron, when it had recovered its tanks, was ordered to remain in the area and give covering fire to 1/12 Frontier Force Regiment and to the Light Aid Detachment and dismounted personnel engaged in digging out C Squadron's tanks.

Delay in the opening of the experimental Plymouth Bridge led to the first tanks of the 14th Canadian Armoured Regiment (C Squadron) being ordered also to cross by Oxford Bridge with the object of moving southwards along the west bank to join 3/8 Punjab. But this squadron also ran into serious difficulties with soggy ground and mines. In consequence, only four of its sixteen tanks reached the lateral road. This at once engaged the German positions on the high ground west of 3/8 Punjab. Very heavy German fire and the dispersion of the infantry made it impossible

---

[10] Colonel C.P. Stacey: *The Canadian Army 1939-1945*, p. 135.

for the tanks to join up with the infantry, so the tanks pushed on alone to Pt. 63, inflicting considerable casualties on the Germans. By 1400 hours the tanks had reached the road junction three hundred yards north-west of Panaccioni.[11]

As the C Squadron moved off to cross by Oxford Bridge, German pressure on the bridge-head of the 19th Indian Infantry Brigade made the situation there critical. A Squadron of the 14th Canadian Armoured Regiment was therefore rushed forward to Plymouth Bridge and arrived soon after that bridge was in place. Only four tanks had crossed when a shell hit the bridge and rendered it temporarily unserviceable.[12] The remainder of A Squadron was then sent to join up with its four tanks, which crossed by Plymouth, and contact 1st Argyll and Sutherland Highlanders, whom the squadron was to support. It worked its way south but failed to contact the Argyll. A Squadron then pushed westwards to the high ground just east of Panaccioni and made contact with C Squadron north-west of that village. Here they remained shooting up German positions and transport moving west out of Pignataro. B Squadron 14th Canadian Armoured Regiment crosed by Oxford Bridge during the afternoon and with two companies of 6/13 Royal Frontier Force Rifles established a firm base on the lateral road in the area of Pt. 63.

The First Day West of the Gari

The British 4th Division, operating on the right of the 8th Indian Division, encountered stiff opposition. On 12 May at 0600 hours, this division was clinging precariously to a very shallow bridge-head to the north of the 8th Indian Division. On its right the 10th Brigade had seized Pt. 37 (G 861188) and Pt. 36 (G 865184) and had reached the lateral road Cassino—Sant' Angelo. The 28th Brigade, on the left and under heavy fire, was just short of the lateral road in the area G 8617. Their engineers had been unable to construct a bridge. Many of their assault boats had been either swept away by the current or had capsized during the crossing. Altogether their situation gave cause for some anxiety. South of the Liri the French Expeditionary Corps (Fifth Army) met fierce resistance but, by 0730 hours, they had captured M. Faito.

However, in the middle a considerable part of infantry of the 8th Indian Division had covered the vital three hundred yards of cornfield between the river banks and the escarpment, and before 1000 hours two bridges spanned the river, enabling the Canadian tanks to cross the Gari and take a hand in the battle. But, S. Angelo was still a thorn in the side of the 8th Indian Division, constituting

---

[11] Operations of 1st Canadian Armoured Brigade.
[12] Nicholson: *The Canadians in Italy 1943-45*, p. 403.

a threat to the bridge-head. Until the village was cleared there could be no further advance beyond the bridge-head.

When the artificial fog cleared from the Liri valley that morning the German garrison of S. Angelo opened heavy fire on the positions occupied by the 17th Indian Infantry Brigade. The Fusiliers in the water-logged ditches between the river and road north of S. Angelo endured this heavy fire all day from German snipers and machine-gunners. Lying out there in the open, this battalion was an easy target. German artillery and mortars joined in the sniping; machine gun and shell fire continued until the evening mist drew a welcome curtain over the positions of the Fusiliers.

1/12 Frontier Force Regiment on the "Bank" also came under heavy fire from S. Angelo, as well as from German positions to the north-west and west. Mopping up continued all day to the accompaniment of the crash of German shells bursting on the "Bank" and the clatter of their machine guns. The Canadian squadron (B Squadron 11th Canadian Armoured Regiment) which had crossed early in the morning, joined the 1/12 Frontier Force Regiment and by 1200 hours the German positions on the "Bank" were finally cleared. By last light, only the posts in and around S. Angelo remained in German hands and 1/12 Frontier Force Regiment had consolidated its position on the "Bank".

The planned attack on Sant' Angelo by 1/5 Royal Gurkha Rifles had been held up the night before by fog and smoke. Having crossed the river, this battalion found itself hopelessly mixed up with the men of 1/12 Frontier Force Regiment. An advance on S. Angelo by two companies of approximately one platoon strength each at 0515 hours had been repulsed by the German garrison. All morning and most of the afternoon of 12 May, the Gurkhas were shelled, sniped and mortared as they waited for the word to attack. Every calibre of gun was employed by the Germans to shell the 17th Indian Infantry Brigade area, which contained exits from the only intact Bailey bridge on the whole front.

However, after several postponements, at 1740 hours D Company of 1/5 Royal Gurkha Rifles, with Canadian tanks in support, formed up south of S. Angelo under cover of the Frontier Force Regiment positions and, preceded by a short but heavy artillery concentration, put in the second attack against the village. The German garrison of S. Angelo was of the same calibre as the paratroopers in Villa Grande. As the Gurkha company moved forward, it came under heavy fire from a fortified white house on the right flank, which was cleared only after fierce fighting. It then pushed on towards the village but again came under heavy fire, this time from Sant' Angelo itself and from a spur which ran from the village almost to the edge of the river. The company attacked the spur, through the defensive fire of seven German machine guns. After covering the last gap at the double, the leading men charged into the strong-point, killing or taking prisoner the whole German garrison. In spite of this success, however, the situation was precarious. All the Canadian tanks were bogged down, whilst the Gurkha company had suffered thirty-eight casualties since the start of the attack, and the men now occupied such exposed positions that any movement brought down German fire upon them. It was decided, therefore, to postpone the attack on Sant' Angelo, the company commander being told to consolidate the ground won. The remainder of the battalion was in the vicinity of the "Bank". Valuable information had been gained about German dispositions in the Sant' Angelo area and it was planned to put in a strong attack, supported by a considerable artillery programme, the next day.

South of the 17th Indian Infantry Brigade, on the right flank of the 19th Indian Infantry Brigade, when the tanks arrived, 3/8 Punjab was able to improve its position slightly. Under cover of the fire support provided by the four tanks of C Squadron 14th Canadian Armoured Regiment, the Battalion Headquarters attacked the centre of the escarpment and C Company its left. Persistence brought its reward. The escarpment was cleared and some thirty prisoners captured. At 0830 hours, two platoons of the 6/13 Frontier Force Rifles swept across Oxford Bridge, attacked and captured Pt. 38 and, by midday, returned to the east bank. Still aided by the tanks 3/8 Punjab reorganised. C Company moved across to the right front and took up position north-east of Pt. 63. B Company dug in between Pt. 63 and Pt. 58. The other two, A and D Companies, were disposed along the escarpment.[13] In a group of houses near Pt. 63, B Company found the commander of A Company and his small party, who had been captured the night before. Hedges and thick crops enabled them to get close to their objective unobserved.

South of 3/8 Punjab, the unfortunate 1st Argyll and Sutherland Highlanders lay out in the open all day, pinned down near the river edge due west of Panaccioni, by fire from the dominating German positions on the Panaccioni ridge.[14] When A Squadron 14th Canadian Armoured Regiment crossed into the 19th Indian Infantry Brigade sector there were hopes of relief but these were dashed by an unfortunate accident. The tank carrying the wireless set, which was turned to the Argyll's net, hit a mine and that set was put out of action. Another attempt by the infantry to attract attention to their position was neutralised by German fire. It was thus impos-

[13] Between G 862148 and G 861145.
[14] 1st Argyll and Sutherland Highlanders' positions were in loop of river between G 858137 and Pt. 28.

sible to enlist the aid of the Canadian tanks. That night, at 0310 hours on 13 May, the battalion, its strength now approximately two hundred all ranks, was ordered to withdraw to the east bank of the Gari to reorganise while 3/8 Punjab carried out protective patrolling from these positions, which now formed a semi-circle of five hundred yards radius centred on Oxford Bridge.

During the afternoon of 12 May, two companies of 6/13 Royal Frontier Force Rifles had been sent across Oxford Bridge with B Squadron 14th Canadian Armoured Regiment and had established a firm base on the lateral road four hundred yards east of Pt. 63.[15] Towards last light, the tanks rallied back to the positions of 6/13 Frontier Force Rifles and remained there for the night, prepared to support 3/8 Punjab and 1/12 Frontier Force Regiment in the event of counter-attack. The situation was now fairly hopeful. Although S. Angelo was still in German hands and neither 1st Royal Fusiliers on the right nor 1st Argyll & Sutherland Highlanders on the left had succeeded in reaching the line of the first objective, there were approximately two infantry brigades and five squadrons of tanks west of the Gari. All German counter-attacks during the day, though only in platoon strength, had been repulsed and the Indian division was in a reasonable position to withstand the full-scale counter-attack which, it appeared certain, the Germans would launch on the night of 12/13 May. The British 4th Division in the north was strengthening its hold. The French in the south were on M. Faito and their armour was approaching S. Andrea from the south-east.

A full-scale Allied air attack had opened at daybreak. Unfortunately, the weather degenerated during the afternoon with the result that many attacks were cancelled. Nevertheless, the Mediterranean Allied Air Forces flew a total of 2,491 sorties and dropped 2,672 tons of bombs. Among these sorties were the first of the planned attacks on the headquarters of Field Marshal Kesselring and of the German *X Corps*. Both objectives were well hit. Some of the confusion and lack of control behind the German front was considered to be attributable to these attacks. German gun areas at Atina, seven miles north of M. Cairo, at Caccino, at Pontecorvo and at S. Giorgio were attacked, with considerable success by more than two hundred fighter bombers and light bombers.[16]

Identifications secured during the day confirmed the German layout along the Gari, from north to south, *1/115 Panzer Grenadier Regiment* and *the Bode Group (II Battalion and I Battalion 576 Panzer Grenadier Regiment)*. *II/576 Regiment* had borne the brunt of the attack and had put up a stiff opposition to the 8th Indian Divi-

---
[15] Operations of 1st Canadian Armoured Brigade.
[16] Air Ministry Report and *Mediterranean Review*.

sion in its attempts to enlarge its bridge-head. Its losses, in killed and wounded, had been heavy, and some fifty prisoners had been taken by the 8th Indian Division. Because of these losses it was thought at the Headquarters 8th Indian Division that the Germans would attempt to reinforce the battalion. *I Battalion* had not escaped unscathed but most of its losses were in its left forward company, No. 3. Its troops in the Appendix were in danger of being cut off but Colonel Bode was prepared to risk this because of their nuisance value.

That no major counter-attack had been launched during the day was attributed to the German unwillingness to commit their reserves at too early a stage. No counter-attack occurred during the night and, apart from some haphazard shelling of the brigade areas, all was quiet. There seemed no doubt that the Germans were considerably disorganised by heavy losses. Another indication of disorganisation was that batches of prisoners taken in the same area sometimes contained men of several different units.

S. Angelo Captured

S. Angelo was by now just a heap of rubble. But, although the upper structure of most buildings had been smashed by the artillery bombardment, the cellars still remained intact. And in these lurked many machine gun nests, whose occupants were still full of fight, having already beaten off two attacks by the Gurkhas. Sant' Angelo was the keystone to the position of the Gustave Line. With it the Germans could check the 8th Indian Division's advance, the most serious Allied threat in the area at this time. Without it, they must pull back from the Gari.

At midday on 13 May, the final attack was launched again by 1/5 Royal Gurkha Rifles. Ahead of them, S. Angelo was given a sharp, five minute pounding by seven field regiments. All the forward troops of the 17th Indian Infantry Brigade, who would have been in danger from the bombardment, had previously been withdrawn to a safe distance. As soon as the shelling ceased, two companies of 1/5 Royal Gurkha Rifles, C on the right and B on the left, aided by two troops of tanks from B Squadron 11th Canadian Armoured Regiment, attacked Sant' Angelo along the axis of the lateral road. Unfortunately, a blown bridge on the lateral road three hundred yards south of the village halted the tanks. A "Scissors" Bridge was sent forward by Headquarters 1st Canadian Armoured Brigade but was not in position until 1800 hours. Five tanks from the previous day's attack were still bogged in the morass alongside the road but, in spite of that, one troop made another attempt to get through the low ground south of the road. Of the troop, one tank (commanded by a non-commissioned officer) did get through, reached

S. Angelo soon after the leading infantry and helped in clearing up the town. Two hours later, a second tank arrived.[17]

A blanket of white smoke and dust over Sant' Angelo enabled the Gurkhas to establish a firm hold on the outskirts within fifteen minutes. Thirty minutes later the officer commanding B Company was wounded. Then, for nearly three hours in the fierce afternoon heat, there was a grim close quarter battle amid the ruins. One by one, isolated parties of Germans, holding out in deep cellars and improvised strong-points, were destroyed or captured. Those Germans, who tried to escape to a flank, were shot down by one of the two Canadian tanks. Those who did escape withdrew north-west from the village. Eventually, towards 1500 hours on 13 May all resistance in S. Angelo had ceased.

There still remained, however, a small German garrison on the "Platform", two hundred yards north-east of the village and dominating the ground gained by 1st Royal Fusiliers. An advance by two platoons against this warren of machine gun posts and infantry trenches began at 1730 hours the same day, the two Canadian tanks again supporting the Gurkhas. But, as the attack went in, a number of white flags were seen to wave and the whole garrison of thirty-seven Germans surrendered.

This marked the completion of the task of 1/5 Gurkha Rifles. They had killed or captured over a hundred Germans. Their own losses were heavy, forty-one killed and one hundred and twenty-nine wounded. But this success was mainly responsible for loosening the German hold on the Gari defences. Success was made possible by the hard fighting of the infantry, the dogged persistence of the Canadians operating their tanks over difficult country and the excellent fire support from the artillery.

At 1630 hours, units of the British 4th Division, north of the 1st Royal Fusiliers, had attacked and overrun some of the German machine gun posts, which had been holding up the Fusiliers. As soon as the Scissors Bridge was in position on the lateral road (1800 hours), C Squadron 11th Canadian Armoured Regiment moved up through S. Angelo, contacted the 1st Royal Fusiliers and helped it up to the line of its first objective, the lateral road. After some fighting, mainly against German infantry, this area was cleared. At 2010 hours, they pushed on together, against little opposition, reached the line of the second objective and by 2200 hours, consolidated in the area of C. Romano.

At the brigade conference, held at 2200 hours the previous day, the Officer Commanding 1/12 Frontier Force Regiment had been ordered to advance, as originally planned, as soon as 1/5 Royal

---

[17] Operations 1st Canadian Armoured Brigade.

Gurkha Rifles had cleared S. Angelo. This move began at approximately 1500 hours from the "Bank" with two companies forward. D Company, on the right, followed the line of the road from the north end of the "Bank" along the ridge to C. Vittiglio. C. Company, on the left, maintaining contact with 3/8 Punjab, advanced due west from its positions some two hundred yards south of the "Bank". Both companies encountered stiff opposition before reaching their objectives and each, needed the assistance of a company from reserve and of tanks before being able to continue. In the valley eight hundred yards west of Sant' Angelo, the battalion captured the headquarters of *II Battalion 576th Regiment,* which had been responsible for the defence of S. Angelo.

By the last part of the night, 1/12 Frontier Force Regiment and B Squadron had reached a line four hundred yards short of the second objective, C Vittiglio—Pt. 67—the spur five hundred yards to the south. The Germans were not strong in anti-tank weapons there, hence few anti-tank mines were encountered. It seems that they had never expected tanks to cross the Gari, but the tanks played havoc with the German infantry strong-points.

At 2400 hours, 1/5 Royal Gurkha Rifles closed up to the forward battalions and occupied positions around Pt. 70.

Panaccioni Captured

On 13 May, the same day on which 1/5 Royal Gurkha Rifles had captured S. Angelo, the 19th Indian Infantry Brigade's task was to push out westwards along the southern arc of the 'Horseshoe'. A secure base had been established by 3/8 Punjab and two companies of 6/13 Royal Frontier Force Rifles in the triangle, Pt. 63—Pt. 58—Pt. 38, where Brigade Tactical Headquarters was then established. 6/13 Royal Frontier Force Rifles was to extend this base by capturing the ridge running from Pt. 58 to Pt. 29. Thereafter, the battalion was to capture (*a*) Pt. 68 (C Mandrini), (*b*) road junction at Pt. 61, and (*c*) Panaccioni. On the successful completion of these tasks 1st Argyll & Sutherland Highlanders was to clear the Appendix.

The Officer Commanding 6/13 Royal Frontier Force Rifles decided to carry out the operation as follows:—

   (*a*) B Company and two troops of tanks to capture Pt. 68.
   (*b*) A Company and two troops of tanks to capture Pt. 61.
   (*c*) D Company to capture the ridge Pt. 58—Pt. 29.
   (*d*) C Company and one troop of tanks to capture Panaccioni.

On 13 May, at 0800 hours, as the morning mist cleared slightly, the Germans began to shell and mortar Oxford and Plymouth bridges. But smoke canisters quickly concealed the bridges again and preparations were not interrupted. At 0945 hours, after sharp artillery concentrations on all objectives, B, A and D Companies of 6/13 Royal Frontier Force Rifles advanced simultaneously through 3/8 Punjab towards their objectives. C Company followed behind A Company. Battalion Headquarters was established on Pt. 63 in a German dug-out. This first advance by 6/13 Royal Frontier Force Rifles went through very close country, intersected by leafy lanes and sunken roads, ideal for the concealment of anti-tank guns. The Germans had used them to hide tanks and self-propelled guns. Here the training carried out on the Volturno paid a good dividend. Infantry spotted the Germans, indicated their positions to the tanks by means of tracer bullets and the tanks engaged the guns with armour piercing shells. In this way, several German armoured vehicles and anti-tank guns were destroyed. Numerous machine-gun posts were also knocked out.

B Company encountered intense mortaring and shelling, but by 1300 hours it had reached its objective, Pt. 68. A German counter-attack was promptly launched against B Company but it was halted and thrown back. D Company 3/8 Punjab was then sent forward from reserve to reinforce B Company 6/13 Royal Frontier Force Rifles, which was reported to be only twenty-five strong. At 1600 hours the companies had completed mopping up and were securely established on Pt. 68. By this time, A and D Companies also had secured their objectives. A company and its tanks, in their advance to Pt. 61, accounted for four German Mk. III tanks and two self-propelled guns. D Company knocked out two German tanks. A Company's objective, from which the Canadian tanks had pulled back the previous evening, had been reoccupied by the Germans with infantry and a strong anti-tank defence. There was fierce fighting for an hour before the Germans were compelled to withdraw from Pt. 61.

The next attack, by C Company against Panaccioni, began at 1730 hours after a ten minute concentration on the village by three field regiments. The German resistance in and around Panaccioni was very stubborn but they suffered heavy casualties, and by 1900 hours on 19 May, the village with forty prisoners had been captured.[18] Owing to the lateness of the hour, the advance into the Liri Appendix was not attempted that evening. Instead, the brigade and its tanks consolidated for the night. 6/13 Royal Frontier Force Rifles was holding an arc with four companies up (including D Company 3/8 Punjab, which was under command). Two companies were around C Mandrini, A Company at Pt. 61 and C Company in Panaccioni. D Company was lying back on the ridge south of Pt. 63 between Pt. 58 and Pt. 29. Tanks were divided between the forward

---

[18] In all, 6/13 F.F. Rif. took approximately eighty prisoners during the day.

companies—B Company six ; A Company ten and C Company five. 3/8 Punjab was tight around Pt. 63, with the amalgamated A and C Companies north of it and B Company to the south. Battalion Headquarters and the medium machine guns of the carrier platoon held the ridge along the road. 1st Argyll and Sutherland Highlanders was still in its area, one and a half miles east of the Gari. Brigade Tactical Headquarters moved during the night to alongside Headquarters 6/13 Royal Frontier Force Rifles at the east end of Pt. 63 feature. The bridge-head of the 8th Indian Division had thus developed into an arc, based on the stream junction immediately south of S. Angelo, about one mile deep and two miles wide.

Early in the afternoon, there had been reports that six German tanks were approaching the left flank of the brigade from Panaccioni and German infantry was seen forming up for a counter-attack in the valley of the stream, three hundred yards north-west of G. Mandrini. These were effectively dispersed by the fire of three regiments and by the appearance of the Canadian tanks. The Germans appeared to be shy of committing their tanks in close support of their infantry.

Their artillery had been busy throughout the day against the bridge areas. Smoke continued to screen the areas from German operations on Monte Cassino and they had no other positions from which direct observation was possible. Consequently, their fire was not very accurate. Nevertheless, at 1100 hours, Plymouth bridge received a direct hit, which made it necessary to close the bridge for three hours until the damage was repaired, and unit transport columns suffered a steady loss in vehicles and personnel. Oxford Bridge, fortunately, remained in use and traffic crossed over to the bridge-head in a continuous stream. Sneak raids by German fighter-bombers caused little damage, though the Luftwaffe was more conspicuous than it had been on the 12th.

Tactical Air Force maintained their offensive with some 1,400 sorties. In the battle area, medium bombers blasted German communications at the western end of the Liri valley, while fighter-bombers concentrated on gun and mortar positions nearer the Gari.

In its summary of the situation, the 8th Indian Division intelligence staff pointed out that, on 13 May, the division had reaped the reward of its hard struggle on the 12th. Attacks then had worn down the Germans, had compelled them to employ their local reserves and had thrown their troops into a state of confusion. The reserve companies (*1 and 5*) *of 576th Regiment* were first of all brought up and thrown in piecemeal. The *III Battalion 115th Panzer Grenadier Regiment*, which was in reserve farther back, had sent three companies forward to stem the advance of the British 4th and the 8th Indian Divisions. But the Germans were so weakened by the struggle on the 12th that these reinforcements were of little use.

Advance From the Bridge-head

On 13 May, the British 4th Division had made a most successful push westwards and had gained positions within one thousand yards of the road Cassino—Pignataro, four thousand yards north-east of Pignataro, and had taken three hundred and forty-five prisoners. The French Expeditionary Corps (Fifth Army) south of the Liri had captured S. Ambrogio, S. Andrea and M. Majo.

At this stage, Commander XIII Corps decided to commit his reserve division, the 78th Division, through the bridge-head gained by the 8th Indian Division with the object of pushing north-west between the British 4th Division and the 8th Indian Division to cut Route 6 and isolate Cassino and the Monastery. This was one of the tasks originally allotted to the British 4th Division. Forward movement to carry out this plan began during the night of 13/14 May, the night on which the 21st Indian Infantry Brigade, the reserve brigade of the 8th Indian Division, also began to move forward.

The 21st Indian Infantry Brigade had 13th Battery (4th Mahratta Anti-Tank Regiment) and D Company 5th Royal Mahratta (machine gun) under command. The 165th Jeep Artillery Regiment was in support. At 0200 hours on 14 May, 3/15 Punjab, A Squadron 6th Lancers and C Squadron 12th Canadian Armoured Regiment crossed the Gari by Oxford Bridge into the 19th Indian Infantry Brigade's bridge-head and moved to an assembly area in the valley, one hundred yards south-west of Pt. 63, between 3/8 Punjab and the reserve company of 6/13 Royal Frontier Force Rifles. Their task was to push through the 19th Indian Infantry Brigade in three bounds in the direction of C. D' Alessandro and cut the road Cassino—Pignataro. The attack passed through the Royal Frontier Force Rifles at 0525 hours but did not go particularly well at first. The ground was hilly and rough, cut by ravines and contained a lot of scrub and other cover. There were no roads except the occasional sunken wagon roads and these were worse than useless as they provided the Germans with excellent defensive positions. Besides, it was foggy during the early part of the day (though later it was fine and sunny) and it was extremely difficult for the tanks to maintain contact with the infantry. They had also to contend with large areas of boggy ground and a most determined opposition, now well equipped with anti-tank weapons. Infantry and tanks fought hard all day but without making much headway. On three occasions, tanks reached the first objective, Pt. 66, but the infantry was unable to get up to them due to the severity and accuracy of German machine gun and mortar fire. Often, too, the tanks would by-pass machine gun and rifle positions in the close country. But these would then open up on the infantry and hold up its progress.

Although this first attack failed to make progress,[19] it did nevertheless inflict severe casualties on the Germans and when, at 1510 hours, 5th Royal West Kent and B Squadron 12th Canadian Armoured Regiment took over from 3/15 Punjab, the Germans were so exhausted that the second force had little difficulty in crashing through to Pt. 66. By 2100 hours, 5th Royal West Kent had consolidated on this feature and had pushed its forward positions another five hundred yards to the north-west to the region of Mass Evangelista, by nightfall on 14 May. Two German 75-mm anti-tank guns had been destroyed and a considerable number of Germans killed or captured by 5th Royal West Kent and their tanks.

Meanwhile, further north, the 17th Indian Infantry Brigade had not been idle. At 0840 hours on 14 May, 1/12 Frontier Force Regiment with B Squadron 11th Canadian Armoured Regiment, had moved up to occupy C. Vittiglio, near which it had spent the previous night. 1st Royal Fusiliers was firmly established on Colle Romano and C. Lena, with two troops of tanks of D Squadron 11th Canadian Armoured Regiment in mutual support. 1/5 Royal Gurkha Rifles was in reserve around Pt. 70. At about 1000 hours, German anti-tank guns opened fire on 1/12 Frontier Force Regiment at C. Vittiglio from a ridge five hundred yards to the south-west. Artillery fire was brought against the guns but they could not be silenced. At 1030 hours, one tank was hit, and some fifty German infantry men were seen forming up five hundred yards west of the line C. Lena—C. Vittiglio. A few minutes later, B and C Squadrons each had a tank knocked out and divisional artillery fire fell short of the forming up place of the Germans, who then attacked in considerable strength. For a while there was confusion. The forward infantry with some tanks withdrew slightly to organise a counter-attack. Fire from the Canadian tanks and from the supporting artillery disorganised the German attack. Immediately, both 1st Royal Fusiliers and 1/12 Frontier Force Regiment with their tanks, launched counter-attacks, which swept the Germans off the high ground. By midday, the forward posts had been re-established. By 1700 hours, the line of the second objective, Colle Romano—C. Vittiglio was securely held, patrols were out to the west and all was quiet. German losses in this abortive attack were eight anti-tank guns, one self-propelled gun and one Mk IV tank.

In the 19th Indian Infantry Brigade sector on 14 May, 3/8 Punjab and 6/13 Royal Frontier Force Rifles held to the positions they had captured the previous day around Panaccioni. But 1st

---

[19] It reached the area of Pt. 68.

Argyll and Sutherland Highlanders re-crossed the Gari at 0500 hours, assembled under cover of the Panaccioni ridge, astride the lateral road and immediately north of the cross-roads on the ridge and at 0900 hours, with A Squadron 14th Canadian Armoured Regiment, advanced south-eastwards from the Panaccioni ridge into the Liri Appendix. They met only scattered resistance, though some machine gun posts did put up a determined resistance. There was no anti-tank defence. By 1520 hours, 1st Argyll and Sutherland Highlanders reported that the Appendix had been cleared of the Germans. It was discovered later that the main body of the Germans had pulled out of the Appendix at 0300 hours on 13 May. Then 1st Argyll and Sutherland Highlanders and their tanks took over the left flank protection of the 8th Indian Division.

The Fourth Day

On 15 May, Major-General Russell ordered the 17th Indian Infantry Brigade to hold fast on the right and patrol to the limit of the 'Horseshoe', the 21st Indian Infantry Brigade to continue its thrust towards the road Cassino—Pignataro, the 19th Indian Infantry Brigade to push towards Pignataro south of the 21st Indian Infantry Brigade and the 6th Lancers to protect the southern flank. Consequently, 1/5 Mahratta Light Infantry of the 21st Indian Infantry Brigade, supported by A Squadron 12th Canadian Armoured Regiment, passed through the 5th Royal West Kent between Pt. 66 and M. Evangelista at 0800 hours and maintained touch with the slowly retreating hostile force. The Mahrattas established a firm base with one company in the triangle of roads, north-west of C. D' Alessandro. A second company and one troop of tanks was then sent north-west along the track to seize the cross-roads, one thousand yards north of Pignataro. Just as this advance was about to begin a sudden burst of German shelling caused a number of casualties among the Mahrattas. But undaunted, this company reached the cross-roads, where a party of fifty Germans abandoned the post and sought shelter in Pignataro. Towards noon, German machine guns firing from the direction of M. Fazio checked the leading troops for a while but an advance by 1/12 Frontier Force Regiment eliminated that opposition also.

From the cross-roads, two companies, each with a troop of tanks, advanced westwards at 1600 hours to the next objectives, M. Marchisella and the spur, five hundred yards farther west. Both overlooked two important road crossings at the river Pioppeto. On their approach to the objectives they were subjected to heavy shelling and mortaring. A Squadron 12th Canadian Armoured Regiment, which gave magnificent support throughout, at this stage lost three tanks by being knocked out by anti-tank guns. But all this failed to halt the attack and, by 2000 hours the Mahrattas were astride the cross-roads at C. Monaco, eight hundred yards west of the road Cassino-Pignataro and fifteen hundred yards north-west of Pignataro. That night, two companies of 5th Royal West Kent moved into the gap between the Mahrattas and Pignataro.[20]

North of the Mahrattas, 1/12 Frontier Force Regiment, joined by A Squadron 11th Canadian Armoured Regiment, also pushed westwards from the east of the Gari at 1000 hours with the object of securing the right flank of the 21st Indian Infantry Brigade. Two strong-points, eight hundred yards east of M. Alessandro, had been holding up the advance of the 1st Royal Fusiliers. As a first task, 1/12 Frontier Force Regiment was ordered to clear these obstacles. Thereafter, the battalion was to secure the line M. Fazio —Pt. 82. All went as planned. Everywhere the Germans left in some haste after offering only moderate opposition, and by 1150 hours all objectives had been seized. A Company was on the right in the strong-points, B Company and a troop of tanks at M. Fazio and C Company at Pt. 82. During the day, the battalion area was heavily shelled and mortared by the Germans but 1/12 Frontier Force Regiment sustained very few casualties. To its rear was concentrated the 1st Royal Fusiliers around C. Vittiglio and, on its left, 1/5 Royal Gurkha Rifles had moved up to the vicinity of C. D' Alessandro. When reorganising, the Mahrattas and 1/12 Frontier Force Regiment joined up and consolidated their positions from river Pioppeto, the divisional boundary, down to the cross-roads at C'Monaco.

In the 19th Indian Infantry Brigade area 1st Argyll and Sutherland Highlanders advanced westwards from Panaccioni while 6/13 Royal Frontier Force Rifles and B Squadron 14th Canadian Armoured Regiment thrust along the inter-brigade boundary on a two company front, from north of Panaccioni towards Pignataro. 3/8 Punjab moved up into the positions vacated by 6/13 Royal Frontier Force Rifles.

Progress by 1st Argyll and Sutherland Highlanders was steady throughout the day until late in the afternoon, when in the area of C. Farnioli, the battalion was pinned down by heavy machine gun fire, two of its tanks were knocked out and a third was bogged. It was thereupon decided to dig in along the ridge overlooking the ravine, which ran south-east from Pignataro to the meadows on the north bank of the Liri. To the south of 1st Argyll and Sutherland Highlanders, C Squadron 6th Lancers had been scouting forward midway between the battalion position and the Liri and met only slight opposition. However, south of Pignataro, the squadron made

[20] The remainder of the 5th Royal West Kent was still at Mass Evangelista. 3/15 Punjab was between that place and C. D'Alessandro.

contact with a German position near M. Conte at 1330 hours. There followed a sharp fire fight as a result of which the right forward troop lost its commander who was killed, three men were wounded and it was compelled to abandon its carriers. Thereafter, the squadron took up position on the river valley road, around Pt. 29, until it moved back for the night to a harbour at C. Silvestri.

Pignataro Captured

Soon after midday, 6/13 Royal Frontier Force Rifles had secured the ridge of high ground, eight hundred yards east of Pignataro. From there, one of the leading companies, D Company, advanced at 1400 hours to secure the next ridge only four hundred yards from the town. Aided by tanks, at 1430 hours, it captured this ridge also, which provided excellent observation over the approaches into the town and out of it and into the deep valley between the ridge and the town.

After a reconnaissance from D Company's position, the battalion commander decided that a frontal attack on the town by daylight would entail heavy casualties. He, therefore, ordered an attack to be put in at dusk. At 1930 hours, the second of his leading companies (C) was moved up to the north of D Company on the ridge four hundred yards from the town. Half an hour later, B and A Companies formed up behind and between C and D Companies. At 2045 hours, under cover of a heavy concentration of shells, which began at 1900 hours from artillery and tanks, and hidden by a smoke-screen begun at 2000 hours, B Company, followed by A Company, moved down into the valley east of the town. At the same time, D Company distracted the attention of the Germans by opening fire from the south.

B Company's task was to capture some German positions on the northern outskirts and then to advance southwards into the town. A Company was to pass north of B Company and attack the town from the west i.e. the rear. When B Company had captured the positions in the north, C Company was to attack from the east. A small battalion headquarters joined D Company. Fierce fighting ensued north of the town, but A Company's attack from the west compelled the Germans to withdraw as quickly as they could, but not before they had suffered heavy casualties. By 2300 hours, the town had been completely cleared and thirty-four prisoners captured. 6/13 Royal Frontier Force Rifles thereupon consolidated its positions in and around Pignataro. The Germans launched one counter-attack, at 0200 hours on 16 May from the north-west, but it was beaten off by artillery fire. Otherwise, the night remained quiet.

The night of 15/16 May passed uneventfully. There were no counter-attacks, and German shelling was light, though there was a fairly heavy air attack in the Liri valley and along Route 6 east of Cassino. 16 May was also a quiet day, which was devoted largely to preparations for the relief of the 8th Indian Division by the 1st Canadian Infantry Division, which took place that night and the following day.

From the R. Pioppeto through Pignataro, to the Liri, the 8th Indian Division now had a firm front. German activity was scattered and unco-ordinated. Prisoners continued to flow in, in a steady stream. 1/12 Frontier Force Regiment, holding the 17th Indian Infantry Brigade's front on the right, reinforced its positions and mopped up a few stragglers and snipers. 1/5 Mahratta, of the 21st Indian Infantry Brigade, in the middle, patrolled northwards and southwards to cover the gaps between itself and the other two brigades while being continuously shelled by the Germans. Its relief by the Canadians was carried out under cover of darkness that night. In the 19th Indian Infantry Brigade area, 6/13 Royal Frontier Force Rifles continued to mop up in and around Pignataro, and in its turn was subjected to German shelling. At 1430 hours, after relief by a Canadian unit, the battalion began its move eastwards across the Gari.

1st Argyll and Sutherland Highlanders patrolled across the ravine to the line M. Tiseo—Pt. 58 and failed to contact the Germans. Units of the 1st Canadian Infantry Brigade passed through during the afternoon, and by last light, were two thousand yards west of Pignataro. Two miles south-west of Pignataro, in the Maze of road junctions on the north bank of the Liri, a German strong-point was overrun.

A Splendid Achievement

Having accomplished its task of seizing the Sant' Angelo 'Horseshoe' the 8th Indian Division pulled out of the line surrendering the command of its sector at 2300 hours on 16 May to the 1st Canadian Infantry Division, which with other formations of the XIII Corps, pursued the Germans to the Hitler Line and broke through it.

With the capture of Pignataro, the task of the 8th Indian Division was accomplished; in five days of fierce fighting, the Gustav Line had been broken. While smashing the line, the division had captured six hundred Germans, killed and buried four hundred and, with the Canadian tanks, accounted for seven tanks, sixteen anti-tanks guns, five self-propelled guns and a large quantity of material. In the process the Germans had been thrown into confusion and were unable to offer co-ordinated resistance or put in any large-scale counter-attack.

The first and, for a while, the only bridges over the Gari had been those of the 8th Indian Division. By that means a precarious hold had been converted into a firm footing and ultimately a thrust which cracked the German Gari defence. The achievement of the 8th Indian Division is highlighted by the inability of the II Polish Corps to break through the strong German defences north of Cassino and by the precarious bridge-head secured by the British 4th Division in the early stages of the attack. It was the initial success gained by the 8th Indian Division in seizing and holding a firm bridge-head at S. Angelo which paved the way for the final victory. The 8th Indian Division emerged out of the battle with added glory and prestige.

CHAPTER IX

The Battle of the Liri Valley

Capture of Cassino

When on 16 May the I Canadian Corps moved up on the left of the XIII Corps and took over the 8th Indian Division's front, the Eighth Army had made substantial gains, for in the XIII Corps sector the 8th Indian Division had secured the Sant' Angelo 'Horseshoe', the British 4th Division had enlarged the Gari bridge-head and, along with the 78th Division, was making thrusts to cut off Route 6. The attack by the II Polish Corps had been, however, a failure. They had gained a foothold on the 'Phantom Ridge' north of Cassino but were subjected to heavy artillery fire and compelled to withdraw on 12 May. It was imperative to capture Cassino and at the same time to close up speedily to the Hitler Line. Consequently while the I Canadian Corps continued the westward advance, the XIII Corps shifted its weight to the right in order to concert with the II Polish Corps in an attack on Cassino. The II Polish Corps and the XIII Corps launched their concerted attack in the morning of 17 May. At 0700 hours on 17 May, the British 4th and the 78th Divisions of the XIII Corps wheeled northwards to cut Route 6, and the II Polish Corps attacked southwards to meet them. During the afternoon, the British 4th Division cut Route 6 two miles west of Cassino and the Polish Corps captured the 'Phantom Ridge' and the commanding Colle S'Angelo ridge in the mountains west of the Monastery. The 78th Division met stern opposition from the parachutists at Piumarola and was checked there until 2000 hours on 17 May. The following morning both Cassino and the Monastery were captured by the British 4th Division and the Poles respectively. Soon after midday, the 78th Division and the Poles made contact on Route 6 at Pt. 58 (G823203). Meanwhile the I Canadian Corps was maintaining a steady advance westwards towards the Hitler Line.

Advance to the Hitler Line

By the evening of 17 May the Eighth Army had broken through the Gustav Line, overcoming the stubborn resistance of the Germans at Cassino—the sheet-anchor of the German defence line. The Eighth Army was now poised for an attack on the Hitler Line. Meanwhile the Fifth Army too had made good progress. It had made the initial attack with two corps—the II U.S. Corps in the coastal sector and the French Expeditionary Corps to the right in the mountainous sector on the southern flank of the Eighth Army. Later the third corps—the VI U.S. Corps in the Anzio bridge-head joined in the attack. In the coastal sector, the II U.S. Corps advanced along Route 7 capturing Santa Maria Infante on 14 May after stiff opposition. This was followed by the capture of Spigno and Castellonorato on 15 May. By 17 May, the II U.S. Corps had captured Formia and was moving fast to capture Itri and Gaeta and thus to cut the road Itri-Pico. The French Expeditionary Corps, on the right, made its way through the precipitous Aurunci mountains. The French captured Monte Majo, the key to the whole Gustav Line in their sector on 13 May. They then cleared the whole west bank of the river Garigliano by capturing Sant Ambrogio and Sant Apollinare. On 14 May the French captured Ausonia and cleared the country to the north between it and the Liri. They exploited their success by capturing Esperia and making a thrust towards M. Della Comune, some four miles south-east of Pico. Thus both the II U.S. Corps and the French Expeditionary Corps were ready to cut the Itri-Pico road.

Aattack on the Hitler Line

The Allied forces had closed up to the Hitler Line. General Alexander ordered the Eighth Army on 18 May "to use the utmost energy to break through the Adolf Hitler Line in the Liri Valley before the Germans had time to settle down in it." General Leese selected the I Canadian Corps to strike the main blow north of Pontecorvo ; the XIII Corps was to maintain pressure at Aquino and to be ready to push on the chase, along with the Canadians, after the breach of the Hitler Line. The II Polish Corps was to press on to Piedimonte S. Germano to turn the Hitler Line from the north. After capturing this strong defensive position the II Polish Corps was to be pulled out of the line for rest and reorganisation. The French Expeditionary Corps of the Fifth Army was to capture Pico and then strike north towards Ceprano to come in behind the Germans facing the Eighth Army.

On the German side, the *90th Panzer Grenadier Division*, facing the Canadians, had to bear the brunt of the attack, while the *1st Parachute Division*, facing the XIII Corps and the II Polish Corps, had a comparatively easier task. Some initial advantage was gained in the XIII Corps sector for the 78th Division captured the Aquino airfield by 1800 hours on 18 May. The Germans, however, continued to hold Aquino in strength. Attempts were made the following day by both the 78th Division and the I Canadian Corps to break through the Hitler Line but without success. It was then realised that the Germans had manned the defences with their main forces. Thereupon the I Canadian Corps was ordered to prepare a deliberate assault on the Hitler Line. For three days the artillery continued to batter the Hitler Line. Then, at 0600 hours on 23 May, the 1st Canadian Infantry Division, supported by approximately eight hundred guns, launched the attack on the Hitler Line between Pontecorvo and Aquino. By daylight on 24 May the Germans were driven out of Pontecorvo. The II Polish Corps, too, captured Piedimonte in the morning of 25 May. By that time the Germans had pulled out of the Line; the Hitler Line was breached and the stage was set for exploitation by the I Canadian Corps and the XIII British Corps.

Meanwhile the Fifth Army had been also making good progress. The French captured Pico on 22 May and were soon pushing on north-west as well as north to Ceprano. The II U.S. Corps captured Fondi on 20 May and Terracina on 23 May; then it advanced to link up with the VI U.S. Corps. The latter in the Anzio bridge-head launched the attack on 23 May and captured Cisterna on 25 May. On the same day the II U.S. Corps linked up with the VI U.S. Corps.

The Role of the 8th Indian Division in the Attack on the Hitler Line

It would be of interest to learn about the part played by the 8th Indian Division in the attack on the Hitler Line. The Eighth Army attacked the Hitler Line with two corps—the 1st Canadian Corps and the II Polish Corps. The XIII Corps had a holding role; while the 78th Division was to maintain pressure on Aquino, the 8th Indian Division was to protect its right flank and at the same time to demonstrate so as to distract the attention of the Germans from the attack by the II Polish Corps on Piedimonte. We shall, therefore, briefly describe the part (though not very significant) played by the 8th Indian Division in the attack on the Hitler Line. On 19 May, the 8th Indian Division took over the sector from Km 135 (G 830200) to the eastern edge of the Aquino airfield. The 21st Indian Infantry Brigade was in the line with 3/15 Punjab in position 500 yards west of the road to Villa San Lucia and 700 yards north of Route 6, and the 5th Royal West Kent Regiment south of 3/15 Punjab in the vicinity of Route 6. 1/5 Mahratta Light Infantry was in reserve. The 19th Indian Infantry Brigade bivouacked in area Romano—in the rear of the 21st Indian Infantry Brigade. The 17th Indian Infantry Brigade remained in its rest area.

The new situation of the division was not a pleasant one. In the hills to the north, the Germans still held Piedimonte and M. Cairo, which gave them an excellent view over its area. In Piedimonte, there were paratroopers who were determined to hold out as long as possible. From their hilltops they could deny to the XIII Corps a free use of Route 6 and could shell troops moving in the Liri valley. When the 8th Indian Division returned to the scene, the Poles had been checked north and north-east of Piedimonte, the hinge position of the Adolf Hitler Line, on a conical hill from which the ground rose in a series of ridges and spurs to the towering peak of M. Cairo. These ridges and spurs were held in strength by the Germans.

On 20 May, the 8th Indian Division re-organised to make a thrust towards Piedimonte, which was originally to be captured by the Poles. 6/13 Royal Frontier Force Rifles (19th Indian Infantry Brigade) took over the positions held by 3/15 Punjab (21st Indian Infantry Brigade) on the road to S. Lucia. The latter was established in new positions south of Piedimonte railway station (G 791210). At the same time, 1/5 Mahratta carried out a relief of the units of the 12th Infantry Brigade (British 4th Division) south of the railway line and immediately west of Piedimonte railway station.

1/5 Mahratta was ordered to protect the southern flank of the 5th Royal West Kent Regiment while the latter was engaged in offensive operations towards Piedimonte. The object of these operations was to assist the Poles in capturing Piedimonte and to provide an infantry screen for their tanks, which were sent to shell the village from the south. 5th Royal West Kent Regiment was detailed to capture two strong-points, 800 yards south of Piedimonte, astride the road leading to Piedimonte from Route 6 and the railway station. 3/15 Punjab was to assist by protecting its start line, which it did with two strong fighting patrols. It was believed at the time that the village was only lightly held. The first indication that this presumption was wrong was when the battalion order group, then on reconnaissance about one mile from the village outskirts, was subjected to intense small arms and artillery fire. The British unit's attack was to be in the nature of a demonstration-in-force while the main attack was to be launched by the Poles from the hills, with the assistance of tanks in the valley shelling the German positions. These tanks therefore provided support for the 5th Royal West Kent Regiment also.

At 1500 hours on 20 May, D Company, 5th Royal West Kent Regiment followed by C and B Companies, advanced towards the cross-tracks, some eight hundred yards south of Piedimonte. Only a short distance had been covered when D Company was subjected to intense small arms fire from the houses in front and the hills on the right flank. Ahead of the attacking infantry, the ground between them and their objective consisted of open cornfields, swept by German fire. Casualties were inevitable but, by trickling forward in platoons, they were kept to a minimum. Stretcher bearers worked most gallantly under machine gun fire to get the casualties collected and their wounds dressed. By 1720 hours, 5th Royal West Kent Regiment had captured the strong-point (G 790216), west of the road near Pt. 126. Before last light, the battalion's final objective, 500 yards west of Pt. 126, had been secured against stiff opposition by the *132nd Regiment, 44th Infantry Division*, which had been brought in from the north of M. Cairo and placed under the command of the *1st Parachute Division*. The leading companies then dug in along a sunken track, only two hundred yards from the German positions, on the lower slopes of the Piedimonte hill.

A mixed battle group of Poles, called 'Bob Group', had been expected to take Piedimonte that night. But before this the *1st Parachute Division* had reinforced the garrison there and, at dawn, the Poles had no more than a footing on the Piedimonte feature.

On 21 May, the whole day, the 5th Royal West Kent Regiment was subjected to very heavy shelling and mortaring. But the main target was the Polish tanks behind the battalion which drew much of this fire. In the night the Poles attacked again, but once again they failed to clear the village. Mines and the terraced slopes prevented the tanks from following up the infantry. In all, for five successive nights, until the Poles did capture Piedimonte on the morning of 25 May, the 5th Royal West Kent Regiment and, indeed, the entire 8th Indian Division were subjected to intense German fire. During those days, 1/5 Mahratta, from positions between the Piedimonte railway station and the track eight hundred yards to the west, patrolled regularly along Route 6 and around Aquino airfield. Every day until the morning of 25 May, patrols reported that the Germans held the eastern edge of the airfield and often further eastward along the railway line. 3/15 Punjab remained in brigade reserve, in positions covering one thousand yards of front, south of the railway and immediately east of Piedimonte station.

The Eighth Army Plan for the Pursuit

After the breach of the Hitler Line, General Leese planned to pursue the beaten German forces with the XIII Corps on the right and the I Canadian Corps on the left. The pursuit was to be carried out in three stages. In the first, the two corps were to secure the line Arce—Ceprano. In the second stage, the 1 Canadian Corps was to push on along the secondary roads south of Route 6 from Ceprano to Ceccano, and in the third along Route 6 to link up with the VI U.S. Corps near Valmontone. The role of the XIII Corps in the second and third stages was to be determined by the strength of German opposition on Route 6, it being of vital importance to clear this route.

The Crossing of the Melfa

The Eighth Army took up the pursuit of the beaten German forces with the XIII Corps directed on Arce and the I Canadian

Corps on Ceprano, as the first objective was the line Arce—Ceprano. The Canadians were able to accomplish this task speedily—the 5th Canadian Armoured Division secured a precarious bridge-head over the Melfa by the evening of 24 May and held it firmly by midday on 25 May. They established another bridge-head near the junction of the Melfa and the Liri. Then the pursuit was continued and Ceprano was occupied on 27 May. Canadians then swept forward like an irresistible tide towards Frosinone.

The XIII Corps made comparatively slower progress. As the 8th Indian Division formed part of this corps its operations will be described in greater detail. The initial advance of the XIII Corps was made with three divisions—the 8th Indian Division on the right, the 78th Division in the middle and the 6th Armoured Division on the left. At dawn on 25 May, the 6th Armoured Division advanced south of Aquino and in the afternoon crossed the Melfa about five hundred yards south of Route 6, but was compelled to withdraw due to heavy fire. The Germans, however, withdrew and next morning the 6th Armoured Division pushed on in their pursuit. The 78th Division advanced from Aquino along Route 6 in the morning of 25 May and by evening reached Roccasecca station and the Melfa. On its right, the 8th Indian Division entered Castrocielo on 25 May and Roccasecca early on the 26th. It then pushed on to the Melfa and discovered a useful ford at Ponte Vecchio, and downstream from it a German bridge intact. From the Melfa the XIII Corps continued the advance to Arce with the 6th Armoured Division on the left and the 8th Indian Division on the right. The 78th Division remained west of the R. Melfa around Roccasecca railway station.

The Role of the 8th Indian Division in the Crossing of the Melfa

Before proceeding further with the account of the operations beyond the R. Melfa it is necessary to describe the role played by the 8th Indian Division in the operation for the crossing of the Melfa. The first task of the 8th Indian Division was to capture Castrocielo and Roccasecca and then to send a mobile column to the north along the side road to Casalvieri in order to prevent any German advance on to the flank and if possible to block the escape of any German troops remaining in Atina. While this mobile column made a thrust towards Cassalvieri the rest of the 8th Indian Division was to cross the Melfa and carry on the pursuit of the German forces.

Major-General Russell selected the 19th Indian Infantry Brigade for this task. Before this brigade was launched on its task of capturing Castrocielo and Roccasecca, the 21st Indian Infantry Brigade had made some gains. At 1100 hours on 25 May, 3/15 Punjab moved through 1/5 Mahratta at Piedimonte railway station and advanced northwards into the hills to secure the line of the spur, one mile north-west of Piedimonte (G 781234—G 771241). German small arms fire caused a slight check, when the battalion was at the foot of the hills, one mile west of Piedimonte. It was only a parting gesture and, by 1430 hours, 3/15 Punjab was established on the spur with patrols pushing towards M. S. Silvestro.

The 19th Indian Infantry Brigade was already on the move in pursuit of the retreating Germans. 6/13 Royal Frontier Force Rifles, with C Squadron 18th New Zealand Armoured Regiment, one platoon 69th Field Company and one machine gun platoon 5th Royal Mahratta Light Infantry led off along Route 6 past the starting point, K135, at 1225 hours on 25 May. Behind them moved 1st Argyll and Sutherland Highlanders, with A Squadron 18th New Zealand Armoured Regiment, one troop 15th Anti-Tank Battery (17 pounder) and one platoon 69th Field Company. 3/8 Punjab remained in reserve for the time being but was earmarked for the task of mopping up west of Castrocielo as far as the track running south-west from Caprile to Route 6.

At about 1300 hours, 6/13 Royal Frontier Force Rifles turned off Route 6 at the junction of the Piedimonte road with the highway and advanced north-westwards along the foot of the spur up which 3/15 Punjab had been sent. 6/13 Royal Frontier Force Rifles had been ordered to clear the foothills south-west and west of M. S. Silvestro, to reconnoitre Castrocielo from the east and, if there was no German resistance, to occupy the village.

1st Argyll and Sutherland Highlanders continued westwards on Route 6. Its orders were to advance along the main road as far as the road junction at Aquino railway station, to protect the right flank of the 78th Division from there to the next road to Castrocielo, one mile to the north-west, and to be prepared to attack Castrocielo if 6/13 Royal Frontier Force Rifles reported the village occupied.

By 1530 hours, both battalions had reached the line of the road from Castrocielo to the Aquino railway station, without opposition; 6/13 Royal Frontier Force Rifles being at the right angle bend and 1st Argyll and Sutherland Highlanders at the junction with Route 6. While 1st Argyll and Sutherland Highlanders remained in the area of the road junction, 6/13 Royal Frontier Force Rifles pushed on towards Castrocielo. C Company entered the town at 1830 hours on 25 May and was immediately followed by D Company. From the village, C Company despatched two platoons to seize Madonna Castrocielo, Pt. 727, a craggy peak, fourteen hundred yards to the north and nearly two thousand feet higher. As the platoons climbed the steep, terraced slopes, German machine guns suddenly opened a hail of fire on them. Large boulders provided excellent shelter for Germans against small arms fire. The New Zealand squadron of tanks was, therefore, asked to create a smoke-screen. This it was able to do very quickly and added high explosive shells to make the Germans keep their heads down. Aided by the smoke-screen, the platoons pushed on, and by 2030 hours had reached the summit. Burning grass, ignited by the smoke shells, helped in driving the Germans from their shelters. As they moved out, most of them were shot down. Altogether nineteen dead were collected. Three Germans were taken prisoner. The remainder fled towards Roccasecca.

In the night of 25/26 May, the 19th Indian Infantry Brigade consolidated its positions with 6/13 Royal Frontier Force Rifles in Castrocielo (two platoons on Pt. 727), and the 1st Argyll and Sutherland Highlanders about one mile to the west. A squadron 6th Lancers, which had relieved the 56th Reconnaissance Regiment north of Route 6, was established one and a half mile west of Castrocielo. 3/8 Punjab was in reserve.

Patrols from 1st Argyll and Sutherland Highlanders reported at 0515 hours on 26 May that Castello had been evacuated by the Germans. 1st Argyll and Sutherland Highlanders was thereupon ordered to occupy it and seize Roccasecca, supported by A Squadron 6th Lancers. 3/8 Punjab was ordered to continue mopping up along the north flank of Route 6 and to be prepared to send one company with A Squadron 6th Lancers up the Melfa gorge towards Casalvieri. 6/13 Royal Frontier Force Rifles was to remain at Castrocielo until relieved.

1st Argyll and Sutherland Highlanders secured Castello by 0845 hours on 26 May and at 1000 hours was in Roccasecca, which was found to be heavily booby-trapped. A Squadron 6th Lancers passed west of Roccasecca, heading for the cemetery half a mile north-west of the village. The Lancers then pushed on northwards until they were halted at 1030 hours by the German small arms fire from S. Trinita. West of Roccasecca, 1st Argyll and Sutherland Highlanders sent patrols to cover an engineer reconnaissance of the crossings over the Melfa. The engineer reconnaissance parties found a ford (G 713284), negotiable by all kinds of vehicles along-side the Ponte Vecchio. But they were extremely surprised and gratified to find a serviceable class 30 bridge of German construction at the crossing south-west of Roccasecca.[1] No immediate action appears to have been taken to derive advantage from these crossings, presumably because the 8th Indian Division had completed the tasks given by the XIII Corps and also because the Germans were mustering around Santo Padre in some strength.

A column, consisting of a company of 3/8 Punjab, A Squadron of

---

[1] Called thereafter "German Bridge".

6th Lancers and a troop of tanks, was sent up the Melfa gorge towards Casalvieri. In the Melfa gorge, adequate blocks had been created by the Germans when retreating. Near the Ponte la Valle, the column overcame a German rearguard of parachutists, killing approximately fifteen and taking fourteen prisoners without loss. By 1630 hours, the column reached the Ponte la Valle which, having been destroyed, presented the Lancers with a gap 210 feet wide. Thereupon the column returned to Roccasecca. Reconnaissance aircraft confirmed that all bridges between Ponte la Valle and Casalvieri had been destroyed.

Outflanking the Providero Defile

In the morning of 26 May, the 6th Armoured Division advanced from the Melfa but was checked by stiff opposition at the Providero defile, a couple of miles south-east of Arce. Under cover of darkness on 26 May, the 6th Armoured Division moved reinforcements forward to the Providero defile, and by 0400 hours on 27 May had established some infantry on the forward slopes of M. Orio—M. Piccolo. During the night the Germans had re-occupied the crests of these steep and thickly wooded hills and of M. Grande. Another attempt by the 6th Armoured Division to burst through the defile was frustrated by heavy fire from both flanks. The rocky, terraced nature of the hillsides prevented manoeuvre by tanks.

To by-pass German resistance in the Providero defile the Commander of the XIII Corps issued orders on 26 May to the 8th Indian Division to carry out a flanking movement directed on Rocca d'Arce. At the same time the 78th Division was ordered to take advantage of the Canadian success, pass through Ceprano after its capture and continue the pursuit along Route 6 to Frosinone. One brigade of the 78th Division struck across country through Coldragone and, by nightfall on 27 May, was a mile east of Ceprano, having met no opposition en route. However, owing to the rough nature of the country, the poor condition of the tracks, the complexity of the move and the dangers of congestion, the rest of the 78th Division stayed at the Melfa for the time being.

Major-General Russell issued orders to brigade commanders in the evening of 26 May. As the ford and German bridge at the Melfa were inadequate, a Bailey bridge was to be constructed alongside the Ponte Vecchio (G 712283), beginning at 0500 hours on 27 May. The 19th Indian Infantry Brigade would cover the construction of the bridge. When the bridge was ready, the 17th Indian Infantry Brigade would pass over the Melfa and advance to capture Frajoli while the 19th Indian Infantry Brigade protected its northern flank. The 21st Indian Infantry Brigade was to be ready to follow the 17th Indian Infantry Brigade.

3/8 Punjab and A Squadron 6th Lancers were detailed by the 19th Indian Infantry Brigade to cover the building of the Bailey bridge. The Lancers reconnoitred westwards from the bridge until they were held up by demolitions and machine gun fire at the southern end of the gorge leading to Frajoli. 3/8 Punjab pushed forward during the day and before dark was holding the crest of M. Nicola, with one company on Pts. 621 and 613, and a second company held Pt. 615. The immediate protection of the bridge was allotted to a third company stationed on the ridge, one thousand yards west of the bridge. The fourth company was one thousand yards south-west of the bridge. The 17th Indian Infantry Brigade was now ready to pass through the positions of 3/8 Punjab to secure the three objectives—M. Clavello, Frajoli and M. Orio.

The 17th Indian Infantry Brigade was called forward in the early hours of 27 May from its concentration area west of M. Trocchio, and by 1000 hours was assembled between Caprile and Route 6. At 1400 hours, 1/12 Frontier Force Regiment on the right and 1st Royal Fusiliers on the left advanced on foot from their forward assembly areas. Both were to cross the Melfa at 1500 hours. The brigade plan was for 1/12 Frontier Force Regiment, on the right, to secure M. Clavello and for the 1st Royal Fusiliers, on the left, to capture M. Orio. Then 1/5 Royal Gurkha Rifles was to capture Frajoli.

1/12 Frontier Force Regiment used the Bailey bridge at the Ponte Vecchio and, by 1540 hours on 27 May, the whole battalion and the supporting tanks (C Squadron 18th New Zealand Armoured Regiment) had crossed to the west bank. The task for 1/12 Frontier Force Regiment was to capture, firstly, the high ground around C. Gerardi and, secondly, M. Clavello. It was hoped that the direction of advance of 1/12 Frontier Force Regiment would deceive the Germans as to the intentions of the 17th Indian Infantry Brigade. From Santo Padre a road ran northwards through Arpino and Sora, outflanking Route 6 and its northward branch, Route 82. The advance of 1/12 Frontier Force Regiment to M. Clavello might persuade the Germans that Santo Padre was the objective and not Arce.

The slopes of M. Nicola, across which the battalion advanced, were so steep and rocky that the New Zealand tanks were unable to keep with the two leading companies, although these were only moving slowly. Fortunately, there was no opposition from the Germans and by 1730 hours the forward companies had gained their first objective, C. Gerardi. For an hour the battalion halted to consolidate and await news of 1st Royal Fusiliers on the left. At 1830 hours, the two leading companies advanced from C. Gerardi and, at 2100 hours, were established on M. Clavello, again without opposition. Battalion headquarters was opened on the lower, southern slopes of M. Clavello while the tanks took up positin in the valley betwen the two objectives.

1st Royal Fusiliers on the left, with A Squadron 18th New Zealand Armoured Regiment, crossed by the German bridge, one mile south of Ponte Vecchio, and advanced along a straight line for the crest of M. Orio. The 1st Royal Fusiliers met only scattered resistance. While 1/12 Frontier Force Regiment was reorganising at C. Gerardi, 1st Royal Fusiliers had reached the crest of M. Orio. Two companies remained there. The rest of the battalion was assembled in the valley, south-east of M. Orio.

1/5 Royal Gurkha Rifles now prepared to carry out the next phase of the operations—capture of Frajoli. They crossed the Melfa by the Ponte Vecchio at 1730 hours. They had under command C Squadron 18th New Zealand Armoured Regiment. Situated as it was on a saddle between M. Clavello and M. Orio, astride the track from Roccasecca to Arce, Frajoli was of considerable tactical value so long as M. Clavello and M. Orio were held. As 1/5 Royal Gurkha Rifles launched attack, the 17th Indian Infantry Brigade held the second of those hills but not the first. The loss of M. Orio robbed the Germans of their observation over the valley between M. Nicola and M. Orio. 1/5 Royal Gurkha Rifles thus expected to get within six hundred yards of Frajoli, before being spotted by the Germans.

The Gurkhas advanced rapidly to Pt. 210, in the valley leading to Frajoli and one mile distant from the village. There, at 1830 hours, the commanding officer issued his orders and the battalion formed up. Only two companies, A and B, and one troop of tanks were to be employed. Half an hour later the attack began. A Company and the tanks led. B Company, with an artillery forward observation officer, followed. News concerning 1/12 Frontier Force Regiment and 1st Royal Fusiliers on the flanks was somewhat vague but the commanding officer decided that, since all sounds of firing had died away, the Germans had been pushed off the heights.

About half a mile beyond their starting point, at 1910 hours, the two leading platoons came under fire from German machine guns concealed in scrub, which covered the hill-side east of the village. A quick outflanking move to the north overcame this opposition and seven Germans were captured. Some others were seen making off for the shelter of the village, but were driven to ground by fire from the tanks. Another encircling move and a brisk firefight produced eight more prisoners for the Gurkhas.

These incidents had served to slow up the advance by imposing more caution on the attackers. Consequently, it was not until 2030 hours that the infantry and tanks succeeded in making contact with the German positions at Frajoli. Then German machine guns brought down a heavy curtain of fire from the village and from the slopes of the hills, north and south of the village. Failing light made accurate fire difficult, a fact which adversely affected the New Zealand tanks as well as the German machine gunners. Divisional artillery, therefore, joined in while the tanks shot up obvious targets like houses so long as those were visible over the gun sights.

The attack on Frajoli by the Gurkhas passed south of the village. From the leading company one platoon struck at the Germans on the northern slopes of M. Orio while a second went through the gap and attacked Frajoli from the west. At 2100 hours, the attack on the village being well under way, the second company sent a platoon, aided by tanks, to deal with German posts on the hill-sides north of the village. By 2130 hours all German resistance in and around Frajoli had ceased. The two companies and the troops of tanks then consolidated their position, circling the village on the west.

From Frajoli, 1/5 Royal Gurkha Rifles sent a fighting patrol towards Rocca d'Arce, an isolated pinnacles of grey rock outcrops completely overshadowing Arce itself from the east and the stretch of Route 6 north of the Providero defile. But these patrols were caught by fierce German artillery fire, lost twenty-one men in killed and wounded and were compelled to return.[2]

With the 8th Indian Division now securely established on its right flank, the 6th Armoured Division, which had withdrawn its forward battalions to the vicinity of Le Cese, attacked M. Piccolo and M. Grande again during the night of 27/28 May. The crests of both the hills were gained before first light but fierce fighting, in which the Germans lost heavily, raged over the hilltops throughout the 28th. In the morning, patrols of the 17th Indian Infantry Brigade went north and west from the positions gained the previous day. 1/12 Frontier Force Regiment was ordered to patrol to M. Favone (a peak at the southern end of the S. Padre ridge where the ridge bends westwards), Calassitti, and M. Nero across the valley from M. Clavello, and a mile and a quarter north of Arce. Those patrols of M. Favone and Calassitti, if unopposed, were to be followed up by a company each. At 0830 hours on 28 May, two companies moved off, A towards M. Favone and B to Calassitti.

On M. Favone approximately one company from *1st Parachute Regiment (1st Parachute Division)* had dug a series of slit trenches on almost inaccessible ledges. By 1000 hours, A Company was heavily engaged by these parachutists. The New Zealand tanks were sent to aid the company but the rocky nature of the steep hill-side

[2] From eye-witness account, Log 8 Ind. Div. of 28 May. War Diary 1/5 G.R. does not mention this incident.

considerably hampered their movement. Superhuman efforts brought them only three quarters of the way up the hill. From there the tanks fired high explosive shells into the trees above the German positions and thus achieved an air-burst effect. On one occasion, the company of Sikhs caught some Germans in the open, inflicted a number of casualties with the bayonet and took seven prisoners.

At this stage, 1045 hours, C Company was sent to reinforce A Company. Yet, despite this reinforcement, the Germans remained in possession of the summit of the hill and it was not until 0750 hours the following day, 29 May, that C Company, with a troop of tanks, could finally gain and hold the summit.[3] B Company encountered opposition at 0915 hours on 28 May, on a small ridge four hundred yards west of M. Fregone, before attaining its objective. 1/5 Royal Gurkha Rifles and 1st Royal Fusiliers were engaged on local patrolling and mopping up their respective areas. That night, while the Germans were still contesting M. Favone, Gurkha patrols were out towards Arce and preparations for an attack on Rocca d'Arce went ahead.

However, advances by the I Canadian Corps on the flank and the more distant pressure of the Allied forces from the Anzio bridgehead threatened the German line of withdrawal. They had, in any case, successfully covered the move of the garrison from Atina and could now afford to surrender the junction of Route 6 and 82 at Arce. Under cover of darkness, during the night of 28/29 May, the *1st Parachute Division* was thus withdrawn from the front of the XIII Corps. One Company of 1/5 Royal Gurkha Rifles occupied Rocca d'Arce at 0815 hours on 29 May. The rest of the battalion entered Arce itself at 1115 hours, close on the heels of 2 Lothians (an armoured regiment of the 6th Armoured Division).

Crossing the River Liri

When the Germans withdrew from Rocca D'Arce and Arce itself, their stubborn defensive battle in the Liri valley came to an end. For one month there was to be little more than rearguard actions. Routes running northwards were few. Large stretches ran through narrow valleys closely hemmed in by steep, rocky mountain sides. Villages, perched on peaks above the road, provided excellent strongpoints for delaying action. The destruction of the numerous bridges also helped the Germans considerably.

The weather was improving rapidly. By day, the sun made all ranks grateful that they had recently cast their battle dress for summer uniform. However, in the mountain valleys there were

---

[3] Casualties were 1/12 F.F.R.—five wounded, German, eleven killed and thirteen prisoners. (Log 8 Ind. Div. 1150 hours 29 May).

sudden heavy showers of rain, which quickly soaked through all clothing and caused the temperature to fall. Nights were definitely chilly, particularly in those valleys through which ran streams of snow water.

Ahead of the 8th Indian Division, the *1st Parachute Division* covered the German retreat with small parties of infantry and a few anti-tank and self-propelled guns. Every road and track was cratered and mined. Bridges were destroyed as soon as the last Germans were across. Although suffering from strain and exhaustion caused covered the German retreat with small parties of infantry and a few good. Their withdrawal was carefully planned and co-ordinated. They were well led and still highly disciplined.

The XIII Corps plan for continuing the advance was for the 8th Indian Division to carry out the pursuit to Altari by way of Route 82 and Veroli,[4] and for the 78th Division to advance to Frosinone by way of Strangolagalli and Ripi. The 6th Armoured Division was to pass through Arce, construct a class 30 bridge over the Liri and then protect the right flank of the 8th Indian Division along Route 28, after which the armoured division was to form the corps reserve. The 78th Division faced difficult country and occasional rearguards, but, by the evening of 31 May, had reached Frosinone and contacted the Canadians there.

In the 8th Indian Division sector the 21st Indian Infantry Brigade took over the lead to secure the line Fontana Liri—L'Anitrella. Handing over its responsibilities around M. Silvestro-Castrocielo to the 19th Indian Infantry Brigade, the 21st Indian Infantry Brigade crossed the Melfa over the German Bridge at 1000 hours on 28 May and spent the night of 28/29 May at the eastern foot of M. Orio, with 1/5 Mahratta in area M. Nero. On 29 May, 1/5 Mahratta, leading the advance of the 21st Indian Infantry Brigade, continued its thrust westwards to the objective Fontana Liri, first capturing the long hill ("Sausage"—G 655352 to G 648345), fifteen hundred yards east of and overlooking Fontana Liri. The advance took the Maharattas across hills, which were "a pleasing mixture of tall wheat crops, vine yards, thick scrub, deep wadis, little gurgling streams and steep rocky gradients."[5] The New Zealand tanks by great perseverance managed to keep up with the infantry and to continue the track later used by supply trains.[6] These tanks were especially adept at flattening the terrace edges though they themselves occasionally slid down the hill-side in an alarming

---

[4] A captured marked map indicated that this was the route allotted to the *1st Parachute Division* (8 Ind. Div. Intelligence Summary No. III dated 30 May 1944).
[5] Newspaper cutting attached to War Diary 1 Mahratta dated 29-5-44.
[6] The New Zealanders were prepared to go anywhere and undertake any task. They took their tanks to seemingly impossible places, up steep mountain sides strewn with boulders and down again.

manner. "Sausage" was reached by 1300 hours without considerable delay, the only opposition being desultory artillery fire. Then 3/15 Punjab advanced at 1730 hours from the western outskirts of Arce to secure Colli (the southern end of "Sausage"), C. Cese (Pt. 430) and Fontana Liri but not to pass west of the railway line, since the 6th Armoured Division patrols were to work along Route 82. By 1900 hours, all these objectives had been captured without encountering the Germans. Fontana Liri had been plentifully mined and booby-trapped.

The 6th Armoured Division, having led the advance along Route 6 to the Liri, was ordered by the XIII Corps to construct crossings for the 8th Indian Division. German artillery made daylight reconnaissance along the river banks difficult. Nevertheless, on the night of 29/30 May, 10th Battalion Rifle Brigade gained a small bridge-head in the vicinity of Fontana Liri Inferiore. Construction of a bridge there (G 625337) was immediately begun and, by dawn, was completed.

Major-General Russell's orders for the crossing of the Liri were issued that evening. The 21st Indian Infantry Brigade was to secure the high ground between Fontana Liri and the river in order to cover an advance on Monte S. Giovanni by the 19th Indian Infantry Brigade. This brigade's tasks were to secure a bridge-head in the area of Colli, two miles west of Fontana Liri, crossing the Liri due west of Arce, and to cover the repair or construction of bridges over the Liri and its tributary east of Fontana Liri Inferiore. The 17th Indian Infantry Brigade was to continue to protect the northern flank of the division until relieved by the 1st Guards Brigade (later changed to the 61st Infantry Brigade).

3/15 Punjab (less two companies) advanced from Pt. 430 (a hill feature 1500 yards north of Fontana Liri) at 0415 hours on 30 May, and crossed the eastward tributary of the Liri. By 0600 hours, A Company had secured Giannetti without any opposition. D Company moved to the north-west of A Company, and three quarters of an hour later, captured Pt. 305. The Punjabis completed the first part of their allotted task by occupying S. Paolo at 0745 hours. From this position of advantage patrols were sent down the river to look for possible tank-crossings. The 21st Indian Infantry Brigade had thus secured the high ground between Fontana Liri and the river in order to cover an advance by the 19th Indian Infantry Brigade to Monte S. Giovanni.

The two battalions of the 19th Indian Infantry Brigade, 1st Argyll and Sutherland Highlanders on the right and 3/8 Punjab on the left, advanced to cross the Liri at 0600 hours on 30 May. 1st Argyll and Sutherland Highlanders crossed in the vicinity of La Torre, due south of Fontana Liri Inferiore. The first troops across used a pole resting on the two banks of the river. Later, a class 5 raft was brought forward to help in transporting carriers and anti-tank guns. Patrols probed northwards to Colli and its cemetery without contacting the Germans. By 1300 hours, the whole battalion, less headquarters, was across the river and holding positions surrounding Fontana Liri Inferiore.

The leading companies of 3/8 Punjab experienced considerable difficulty at the river but eventually, at about midday, they found a crossing over a weir[7] (presumably the dams at G 618321), which one company of 1st Argyll and Sutherland Highlanders had used. These companies advanced up the ridge south of Colli and were disposed within fiive hundred yards of that hamlet.[8]

It had been planned to construct three Bailey bridges over the Liri on the front of the 8th Indian Division, namely,

(a) Barnes Bridge, class 12 at L'Anitrella.
(b) Putney Bridge, class 40 in the middle of Fontana Liri Inferiore.
(c) Hammersmith bridge 2½ miles west of Arce.

Hammersmith bridge was opened in the evening of 30 May and was immediately put into use, though bad exits on the north bank considerably hampered traffic and caused some congestion. The approaches to Putney bridge were thickly mined and called for hard work by bulldozers. Work on Barnes bridge could not begin until the troops had been put across to protect the sappers.

The duty of forming the initial bridge-head for Barnes bridge was given to 3/15 Punjab, at the time on the high ground west of Giannetti. Later, 5th Royal West Kent Regiment was to take over and enlarge the bridge-head. One Punjabi company was despatched from Giannetti at 1915 hours on 30 May. Ahead of this company, the battalion's pioneer platoon had just lifted some two hundred mines on the track running from S. Paolo to the bridge site. A small German rearguard opposed the crossing with small arms and mortar fire, but the locality had fortunately been registered as a defensive fire task and was twice engaged by the divisional artillery. Thereafter, all opposition faded, and on 31 May, by 0100 hours, the company reported that L'Anitrella had been evacuated by the Germans.

Two bridges, one approach and one main, were required at Barnes and these, together with the tracks on them, took twenty-four hours to prepare. But unable to wait, 5th Royal West Kent

---

[7] War Diary 3/8 Punjab.
[8] War Diary 3/8 Punjab appears to have been written from memory. It is inaccurate as regards dates and is consequently unreliable.

Regiment crossed during the morning, accompanied by 9 Squad on 18th New Zealand Armoured Regiment. By the evening this battalion was in area M. Chiajamari. 1/5 Mahratta held the northern flank east of the Liri, having occupied C. Castellaccio. The following day, on 1 June, the 21st Indian Infantry Brigade concentrated around Chiajamari to provide flank protection to the 19th Indian Infantry Brigade.

Capture of Monte S. Giovanni

Meanwhile the 19th Indian Infantry Brigade was pushing on to Monte S. Giovanni. The 1st Argyll and Sutherland Highlanders, with B Squadron 18th New Zealand Armoured Regiment and detachments of machine gunners, 4.2-inch mortars and sappers, advanced from Fontana Liri Inferiore soon after first light on 31 May. Its orders were to secure Monte S. Giovanni, and C. Lucinetta. B Squadron 6th Lancers, a troop of tanks and a detachment of sappers protected the battalion's eastern flank. However by 1000 hours, this flank protection force had passed through Chiajamari, was moving along the road at the northern foot of Cle Lucinetta and was subjected to fire from German artillery. At the same time, 1st Argyll and Sutherland Highlanders was clearing Monte S. Giovanni. Two hours later, a company which had been sent to the crest of C. Lucinetta was astride it, but then it came under fire from German guns.

3/8 Punjab, with C Squadron 18th New Zealand Regiment, followed 1st Argyll and Sutherland Highlanders towards Monte S. Giovanni, then diverged eastwards to circle C. Lucinetta behind B Squadron 6th Lancers. The Punjabis were to cut the road at Casamari and then to form a bridge-head over the torrent Amaseno. When 1st Argyll and Sutherland Highlanders were firmly established on their objectives, 3/8 Punjab replaced the reconnaissance squadron north of the Cle Lucinetta and, at approximately 1430 hours, pressed forward to the road junction at the north-west end of the hill (at G 596399), where the Germans had deployed in some strength. The impact occasioned heavy fighting, and with the withdrawal of B Squadron 6th Lancers, 3/8 Punjab was practically left alone to clear the road junction of the Germans. At 2100 hours, the leading companies were still two hundred yards short of the road junction. The New Zealand tanks were in action against German machine gun posts. Artillery concentrations were called for several times. German fire from artillery, mortars and machine guns was persistent. Then, in the early hours of 1 June, the Germans attacked the forward companies. This attack was beaten back. However, it was no more than a delaying attack for, that night, the Germans withdrew again.

Capture of Veroli

On 1 June 6/13 Royal Frontier Force Rifles took over the lead in the advance towards Veroli. At 0345 hours with B Squadron 6th Lancers and one squadron 18th New Zealand Armoured Regiment under command, it set off from their assembly area east of Monte S. Giovanni, through that village and the valley south-west of Cle Luncinetta and headed for Casamari. Contact having already been broken off by the Germans, there were no incidents. By 0900 hours, the column was in Casamari. From a hilltop there it was possible to see German vehicles climbing the hill at Veroli, four miles to the north-west in a straight line and nine miles by road. Veroli stood on a high spur, which jutted southward from the M. Ernic. On its eastern flank, the spur fell steeply to the valley of the torrent Ondola. South of the town there was a steep cliff. By virtue of its elevated position and difficult approaches, the town was easily convertible into a strong fortress, requiring only a small garrison to impose delay on the Allied columns.

Some delay was caused by the two bridges over the R. Amaseno having been destroyed but, fortunately, the river bed was dry and sappers were able to make a diversion, over which armoured vehicles of the 6th Lancers could pass. B Squadron took up the chase while 6/13 Royal Frontier Force Rifles assembled at Casamari. 6/13 Royal Frontier Force Rifles marched out of Casamari at 1215 hours with D company as advance guard. B Squadron 6th Lancers was pushing on ahead towards Veroli. At about 1400 hours, one troop of B Squadron, 6th Lancers, advanced along the main road and entered Veroli from the north. The armoured cars had just crossed the western one of the two bridges when they came under German fire from the cemetery (at G 519444), one thousand yards north of Veroli. The third vehicle was knocked out by an anti-tank gun, blocked the road and thereby prevented the withdrawal of the other two cars. They were in turn hit and halted by the German gun. Thereupon the men abandoned their cars in the face of a hostile infantry advance, withdrew to the vicinity of the bridges and called for artillery fire on the German positions.

At this time, 6/13 Royal Frontier Force Rifles, advancing on Veroli from the east, was about three thousand yards from the town and had called for artillery fire on the outskirts. From this point, the battalion swung southwards, and at 1600 hours, launched a two-company attack from the south-west. However, the Germans held their fire until the companies were climbing the steep slopes of the southern cliffside. Then they put down a concentration of machine gun and mortar fire, which was so intense that it brought the two companies to a halt. For a while the situation was both confused and uncomfortable. To advance was impossible. The Germans

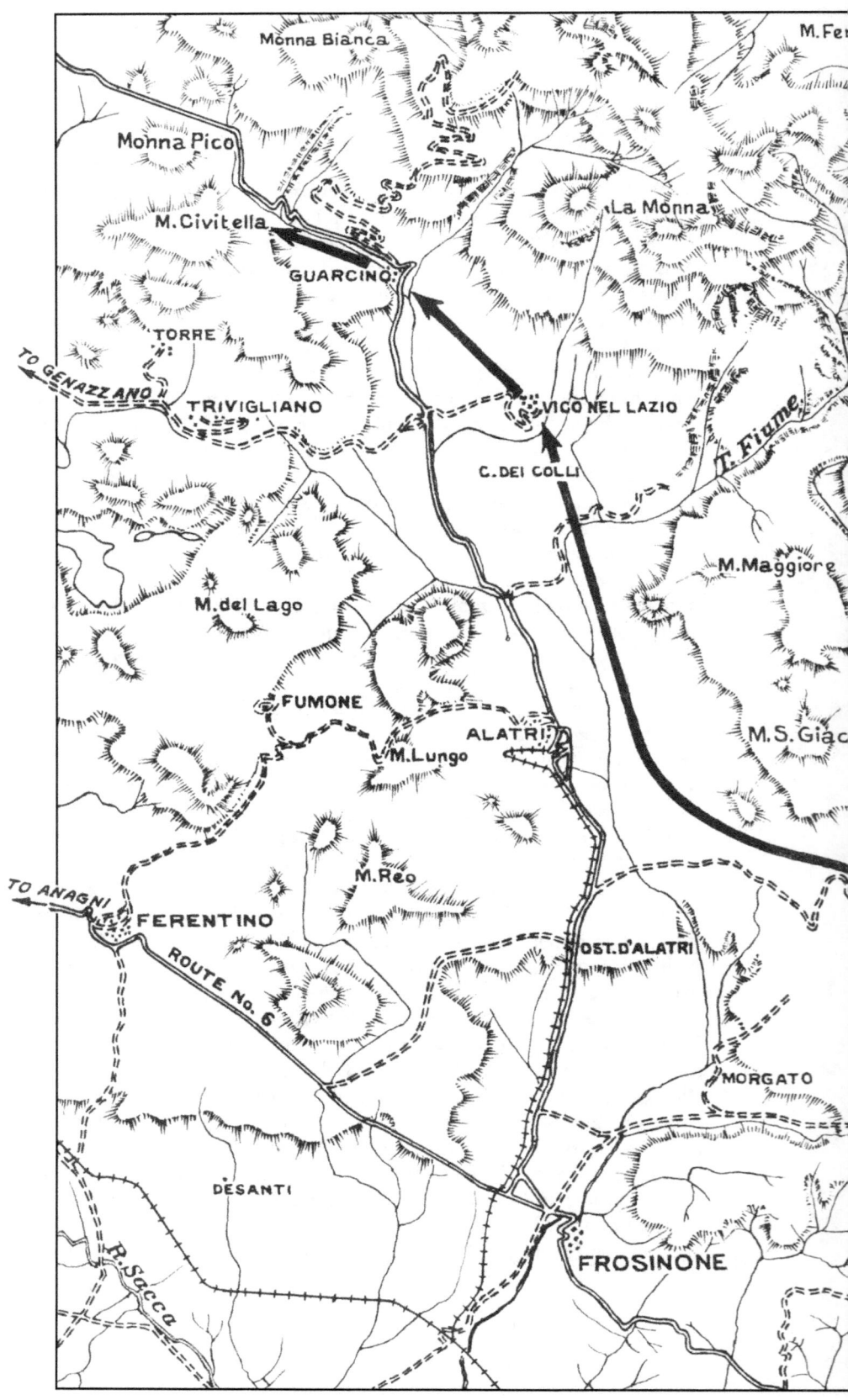

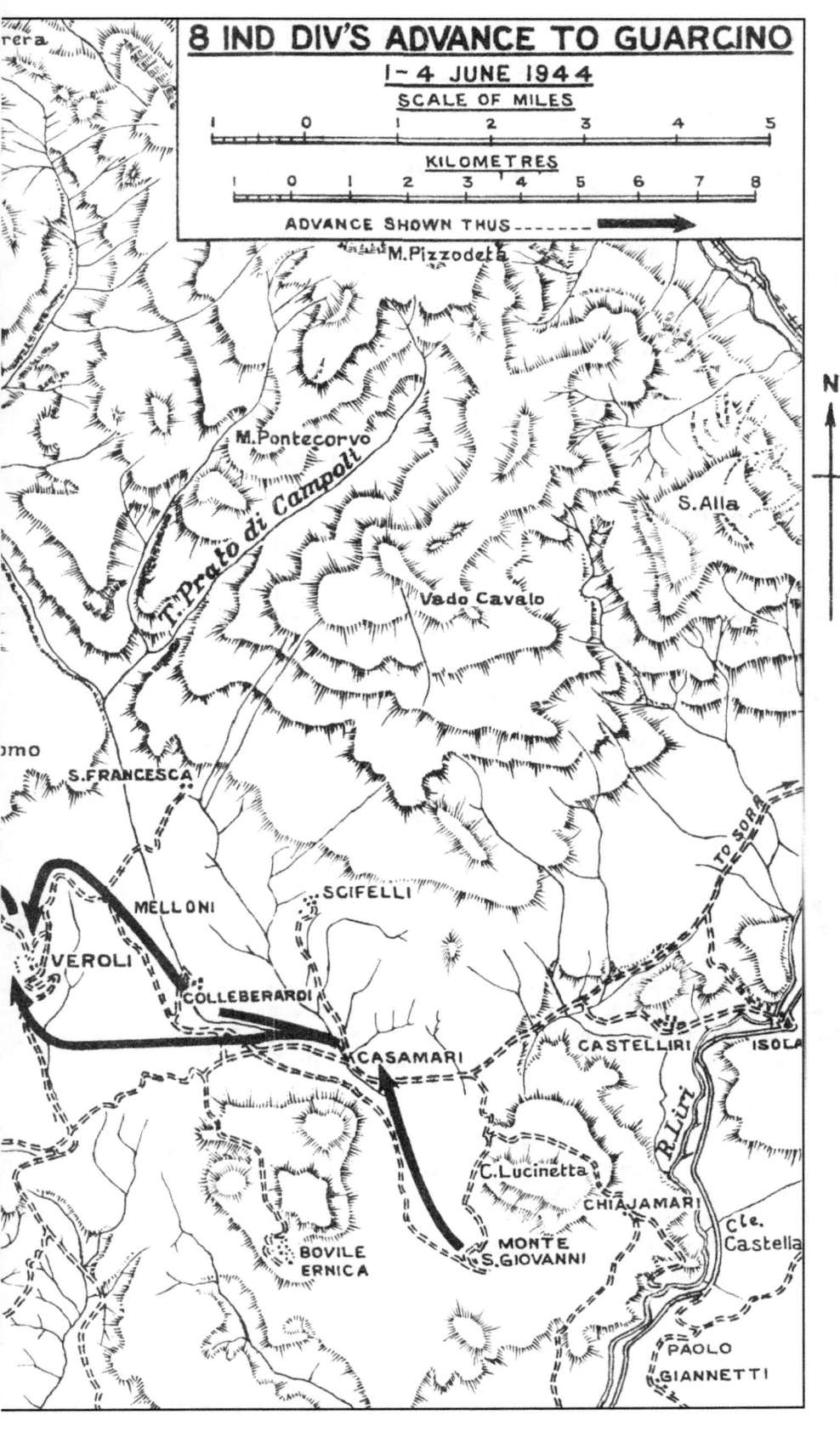

were alert and every move by 6/13 Royal Frontier Force Rifles could be observed by them. It was decided, therefore, to recall the two companies and to wait for darkness. Artillery, 4.2-inch mortars and the squadron of tanks provided concentration of high explosives and a smoke-screen, under cover of which the withdrawal was accomplished without many casualties. 6/13 Royal Frontier Force Rifles then assumed positions for the night, approximately one thousand yards south of Veroli. During this engagement a Royal Air Force fighter on reconnaissance gave most welcome support by unloading the bombs on the western outskirts of Veroli with good effect.

Behind the 6/13 Royal Frontier Force Rifles considerable movement had taken place during the day. When the strength of the German opposition in Veroli was realised, 3/8 Punjab was ordered up to the line of the road on the ridge, two thousand yards east of Veroli, in order to assist 6/13 Royal Frontier Force Rifles and to take over from B Squadron 6th Lancers. 1st Argyll and Sutherland Highlanders was to move to a reserve position at Colleberardi, another thousand yards to the east. But before these orders could be fully executed, B Squadron 6th Lancers, still at the two bridges, was attacked by a strong company of infantry, who advanced through the thick country north of the road. One company from each of 1st Argyll and Suterland Higherlanders and 3/8 Punjab rushed up to meet this threat. The Lancers were then withdrawan behind the two battalions. The Argyll company was placed under the command of 3/8 Punjab and formed a block at the road junction (at G 528443), two thousand yards north-east of Veroli. The Punjabi company took up a supporting position at Melloni, half a mile south of the road junction. Under cover of darkness on 1/2 June, however, the Germans vacated Veroli; a patrol from 6/13 Royal Frontier Force Rifles, which entered from the south-west at 0200 hours, found only one wounded German there. The whole of 6/13 Royal Frontier Force Rifles then advanced into the town, where the battalion received a great welcome from the people. At the same time, an Argyll patrol, approaching from the north, found the two bridges intact and was promptly reinforced by the two companies. In a house near the cemetery, they recovered the officer of the 6th Lancers, who had been wounded and missing the previous day.

The Advance to Vico nel Lazio

The 17th Indian Infantry Brigade now prepared to pass through the 19th Indian Infantry Brigade and to advance towards Alatri. It had been assumed by the XIII Corps that the Germans would take their next stand on a line covering Alatri, Fumone—Ferentino on Route 6. It was on this route that the Allied advance took place. This highway was now the axis for the I Canadian Corps. The XIII

Corps had also to depend on Route 6 to some extent, so both the corps were considerably hampered by traffic congestion on their inadequate lines of communication. The main objective for the XIII Corps became Alatri, towards which the 8th Indian and 78th Divisions were to continue their converging drives. Because of the traffic congestion, the 78th Division was to make its main thrust with one brigade through Veroli. The 8th Indian Division thus found itself compelled to move across country parallel with the road. Thus the Indian division moved across country parallel with the main road to secure Vico nel Lazio, about four miles north of Alatri, while the 78th Division struck at Alatri itself.

A huge crater in Veroli imposed a two-hour delay on the progress of the 17th Indian Infantry Brigade and the poor tracks across country afterwards made movement slow. On occasions, tracks had to be repaired or made. As the 7th Field Company had insufficient men for the task, 1/12 Frontier Force Regiment and 1/5 Royal Gurkha Rifles were called upon to provide working parties while A Squadron 6th Lancers, one squadron 18th New Zealand Armoured Regiment and 1st Royal Fusiliers covered the brigade's advance. This brigade met with no opposition until late in the afternoon, when it came up against the torrent Cosa and its tributary east of Alatri, where German artillery was active. The river lay in a deep gully quite difficult for wheeled vehicles to negotiate and, although a few of the supporting New Zealand tanks[9] managed to cross, they had to be pulled back before nightfall.

Meanwhile, the 78th Division had moved rapidly along the road meeting only slight opposition, and had captured Alatri and M. Lungo and sent patrols forward to Fumone. The 17th Indian Infantry Brigade, however, continued its advance the next morning on 3 June with 1st Royal Fusiliers in the lead, whose next objective was Vico nel Lazio and the road from there to the cross-roads, two thousand yards west of the village. The road junction, two thousand yards north of Alatri, was to be an intermediate bound. Behind 1st Royal Fusiliers, the rest of the brigade was again to be employed on making tracks as the country was bad. A Squadron 6th Lancers found the going too bad for its vehicles and, at 1000 hours, reverted to regimental command. The New Zealand tanks also encountered similar difficulties but beyond the intermediate bound they struck to the road and considerably improved the speed of advance with the result that, by 1545 hours, 1st Royal Fusiliers and its tanks were in Vico nel Lazio, where a battalion of the 61st Infantry Brigade, 6th Armoured Division, had preceded them. The 6th Armoured Division passed through the 78th Division (which was withdrawn into

---

[9] 18 New Zealand Armoured Regiment, less one squadron, was in support of the 17 Ind. Inf. Bde.

reserve) at Alatri at dawn on 3 June and advanced on the axis Alatri—Trivigliano—Genazzano. The 8th Indian Division, on the right, was directed on Guarcino. The 1st Royal Fusiliers advanced further one thousand yards to the north in order to cover operations by the 6th Armoured Division towards Fiuggi and to form a firm base for operations against Guarcino the following day.

Capture of Guarcino

In addition to providing flank protection for the 6th Armoured Division, the 17th Indian Infantry Brigade was required to form a firm base, from which the 21st Indian Infantry Brigade could continue the advance of the 8th Indian Division the following day (4 June). A Squadron 6th Lancers passed from the 17th to the 21st Indian Infantry Brigade. With effect from 4 June, the Sherman tanks of the 18th New Zealand Armoured Regiment were replaced by those of the 12th Canadian Armoured Regiment (Three Rivers Regiment) of the 1st Canadian Armoured Brigade, which had been with the 8th Indian Division for the attack at the river Gari. The following day, the whole of the 1st Canadian Armoured Brigade (at Aquino) was placed under the command of the 8th Indian Division. One squadron of the 12th Canadian Armoured Regiment was allotted to the 19th Indian Infantry Brigade for a special task. The remainder of the Regiment was to support the 21st Indian Infantry Brigade.

For the attack on Guarcino, Brigadier Mould selected 1/5 Mahratta. The other battalions of the brigade, 5th Royal West Kent Regiment and 3/15 Punjab, were to operate on the flanks of the Mahrattas. Times have not been recorded in detail but all appear to have set off from the brigade concentration area, south-west of the cross-roads, at about the same time i.e., 1330 hours on 4 June. One company of 5th Royal West Kent Regiment made for the Hill (G 440550), one thousand yards east of Guarcino and completely dominating the approaches to the town from east and south. While this company completed its task without opposition the rest of the battalion was in the brigade reserve south-west of the cross-roads.

3/15 Punjab struck north-westwards at 1330 hours, on a two-company front, having M. Civitella as its objective. The steep, broken nature of the country, which hampered the march of laden mules accompanying the battalion, and a break in the weather made progress rather slow. Bad weather combined with the hills to interfere considerably in wireless transmission. Slight opposition was encountered late in the afternoon in the vicinity of Pt. 952 and again at Pt. 1131, the crest of M. Civitella. Infantry tactics enabled the battalion to overcome the opposition, but not until 2030 hours were the two leading companies in position on the crest of M. Civitella.

A third company was despatched northwards down the spur from Pt. 1131 with orders to patrol as far as the line of the cross-roads (G 3861) and Pt. 1155. But the patrols encountered no opposition in the early hours of 5 June.

Meanwhile at Guarcino, 1/5 Mahratta had fought a small-scale but highly successful engagement. Guarcino was a fairly large village, lying in a bowl amidst mountain ridges at the junction of the two mountain streams. Its three approaches, from north-east, south and north-west, were along the narrow, precipitous valleys of those streams. The road from Alatri entered at the south of the village across two bridges in a defile. In the village, it zigzagged to gain height above the river bed and then turned sharp left at the foot of a mountain side to follow the valley of the torrent Macerosa towards Subiaco. From the northern outskirts of the village, facing the road from the south like a huge wall, rose the steep, bare slopes of an offshoot of the six-thousand-foot M. Pozzotello, Guarcino itself being at two thousand feet. Most of the mountain sides in the area were bare and rocky with occasional clumps of shrub, particularly in the gulleys or as fences bordering the scattered patches of cultivation.

Guarcino was reported to be held by one hundred men of Alpine troops. Three hundred of them had been reported in the mountains east of the 17th Indian Infantry Brigade and Alatri on 2 June and had probably provided the detachment for Guarcino. The Germans had been unusually careless in selecting the positions to be occupied by their rearguard. These were on the slopes of the mountain immediately north of and above the village, slopes with only the sparse cover provided by an olive grove and one lone white house. Perhaps the rearguard was expected to delay the 8th Indian Division's advance for the hours of daylight and then slip away under cover of darkness in accordance with the text-book conception of a rearguard action. From the German point of view, the positions were bad because the only cover available was small and obvious—the lone white house appeared to be their headquarters. Any movement by day was visible against the bare, grey hill-side. Despite the summer heat the Germans were still wearing their dark green winter uniform which, at a distance, in sunlight was as bad as black for camouflage purposes.

The officer commanding 1/5 Mahratta decided to carry out the attack in three phases, beginning at 1430 hours on 4 June:

  Phase I—to capture the spur (G 4259), running down to the road, seven hundred yards south-west of Guarcino,
  Phase II—to capture the crest of that spur, Pt. 870 (G 415555), one mile slightly north of west from Guarcino, and
  Phase III—to capture Guarcino.

Phase I was successfully accomplished by C Company. Y Company, aided by a troop of tanks and a machine gun platoon, their weapons carried on mules, then passed through C Company and despite difficult going was quickly on its objective. From this ridge the forward companies had an excellent view over the village and its surrounding hills. It was then that the German positions were visible. As soon as the battalion's observation posts and supporting weapons were established, the German rearguard became almost a suicide squad. No German on the hillside could move from his shelter without being seen and any movement was the target for all infantry weapons, the 4.2-inch mortars and the tanks. All of these combined to saturate their positions with fire.

A troop of tanks moved into the defile and brought both its 75-mm guns and its Besa machine guns into action. The platoon of 4.2-inch mortars had not such a target for many a day. To this the Germans replied with machine gun and rifle fire. They appeared to have no artillery or mortars.

In the middle of the firefight, Y Company, on its hilltop, saw a party of some thirty Germans, with mules, marching away from Guarcino. Unfortunately, the artillery wireless set with the company was not functioning properly and the company's weapons had insufficient range.

At 1600 hours, the officer commanding 1/5 Mahratta despatched his third and fourth companies to clear the village and the slopes beyond. A Company was allotted the eastern half and D Company the western half of the village. Dirty grey clouds had been collecting overhead since late morning and, just as the two companies were setting off, there was a torrential rain storm, which reduced visibility to practically nil. Though uncomfortable, the rain helped to screen the advance into the village. In order to impede any efforts by the Germans to derive advantage from the storm, mortars, tanks and machine guns opened a steady fire on their escape routes. There was little opposition among the houses. On the hill-side, fighting patrols collected prisoners. But such of them as had escaped being captured or killed slipped away in the dusk and contact with them was lost. Hard work by divisional sappers provided a diversion at the blown bridges, passable to jeeps, carriers and 15-Cwt trucks, which began to trickle forward to join the Mahrattas at 2100 hours. Space in the village being very restricted and the one main street having been effectively blocked by a demolished house, all vehicles spent the night parked head to tail in that street. The night was dark and the German aircraft had, presumably, already received their briefing, for they devoted their attention to the roads south and east of Guarcino. While the 8th Indian Division secured Guarcino, the 6th British

Armoured Division pushed on to Genazzano, and at nightfall on 4 June, the leading tanks were within two miles of it.

As the Fifth Army moved in closer to Rome, the Germans facing the Eighth Army were left no choice but to retreat northwards by the roads leading to Route 5. Headquarters Eighth Army accordingly decided to turn the I Canadian Corps north from Anagni towards Piglio and to send the XIII Corps along the Genazzano road to cut off the stragglers. It has already been indicated that this task was allotted to the 6th Armoured Division. The role of the 8th Indian Division was that of right flank protection. From Vico, the division had a road for its own use and its own right flank was largely protected by the massive M. Simbruini which, in places, rose to more than six thousand feet and which, between Veroli and Route 5, was not crossed by any tracks.

Capture of Rome

While the XIII Corps was making thrusts towards Guarcino and Genazzano, the I Canadian Corps was pushing along the axis Route 6, after the capture of Frosinone on 31 May. The 6th South African Armoured Division was under the command of the I Canadian Corps in this final phase of the operation. On 4 June when the Canadians had reached the Anagni area and were pushing towards Piglio the I Canadian Corps was withdrawn into Army reserve.

Meanwhile the Fifth Army had been making good progress. Units of the Fifth Army from the Anzio bridge-head captured Valmontone on 2 June and the next day they joined hands with the French Expeditionary Corps. Having cleared the whole area of the Alban hills the Americans pushed on to Rome, which they entered in the morning of 4 June.

The capture of Rome on 4 June 1944 marked the end of an important phase of the Italian campaign. Rome—the coveted prize —had been captured at last. Aware of the advantages of retaining their hold over Rome the Germans had made desperate efforts to stem the Allied advance to its south. Stubborn resistance at the Biferno, Trigno, Sangro and the Moro, had considerably slowed down the Eighth Army's advance. After the capture of Ortona the Eighth Army's advance had come to a halt. The Fifth Army too had been held up before the Gustav Line and Cassino was as defiant as ever. Field-Marshal Kesselring had succeeded in checking the Allied advance south of Rome. In the Spring offensive of 1944, however, he failed to prevent the Allies from breaking through the Gustav and Hitler Lines and capturing Rome. From Rome the pursuit swept on but luckily for Field-Marshal Kesselring the Allied offensive was weakened by the withdrawal of several divisions from

Italy for the invasion of southern France. This respite enabled him to retire to the Gothic Line after checking Allied advance on a series of defensive lines of lesser importance, such as the Trasimene Line, the Arezzo Line and the Olga Line.

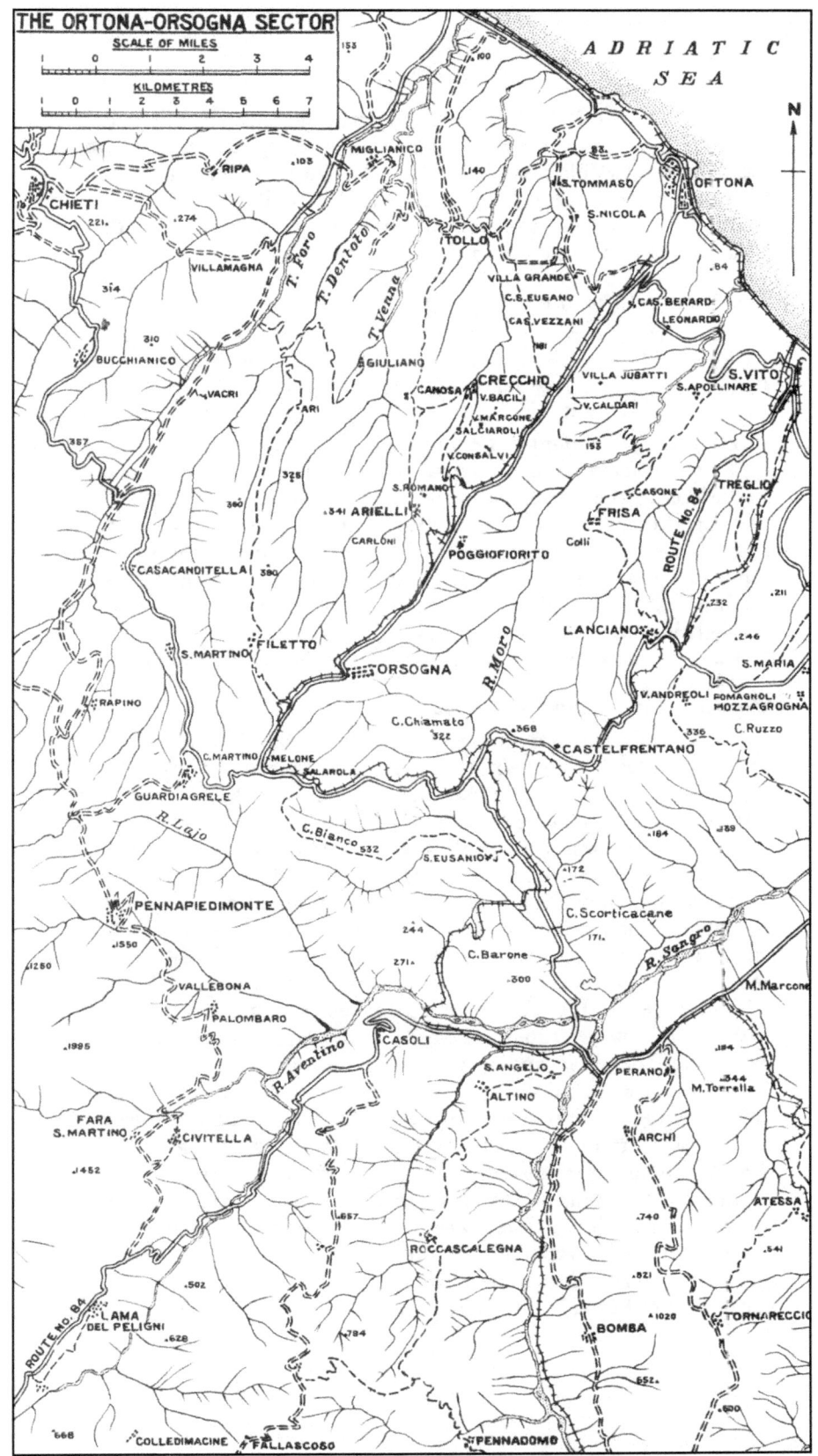

with two Corps—the V Corps on the right and the XIII Corps on the left. In the V Corps the Canadians on the right held the coastal sector as far as Villa Grande and the 8th Indian Division on the left held the sector between Villa Grande and Arielli. In the XIII Corps sector the 4th Indian Division, on the right held the Orsogna sector while the 78th Division held the left sector.

Reorganisation of the German Forces

The German forces on the Adriatic coast were also reorganised. At the beginning of January 1944 the line was held by the *1st Parachute Division* on the coast, the *26th Panzer Division* between Canosa and Arielli, two airborne units opposite the Fontegrande ridge, the *65th Infantry Division* (then being relieved by the *334 Infantry Division*) from Orsogna to Guardiagrele and two Mountain Battalions in the Maiella fronthills. When the Fifth Army's offensive opened in mid-January, the Germans moved their Adriatic reserve, the *90th Panzer Grenadier Division*, across to the west coast, replacing it by the *29th Panzer Grenadier Division*, which had been resting near Venice after being badly mauled on the west coast. As the fighting on the west coast gained in momentum more and more German formations were pulled out of the Adriatic sector.

The 4th Indian Division in the Line

Two Indian formations were in line on the Adriatic coast—the 8th Indian Division in Villa Grande area (in the V Corps) and the 4th Indian Division in Orsogna area (in the XIII Corps). The operations were confined to raids and counter-raids. As the 4th Indian Division was soon afterwards pulled out of the line we shall at first describe briefly the activities of this formation.

Orsogna, twelve miles south-west of Ortona and seven miles west of Lanciano as the crow flies, was ideally suited for defence. It stood on a narrow, commanding ridge which divided the R. Moro and its maze of tributaries from a similar maze forming the R. Arielli. The average width of the ridge-top between Ortona and Orsogna was little more than a thousand yards. At places, where erosion had eaten into the ridge and water courses descended in opposite directions, the crest was no more than a few yards wide. From Orsogna to Guardiagrele, four miles in a straight line to the south-west, the ridge was no more than a knife-edge, wide enough to carry the road which ran along the crest throughout its length from Ortona to Guardiagrele. This white, dusty metalled road, barely of sufficient width for vehicles to pass, was an important supply route for both sides. The ridge was highly cultivated and vineyards and orchards provided a screen for the movement of infantry—an asset which the patrols on either side put to good use in their frequent raids. Three miles south-west of Orsogna, near Guardiagrele station at C. Martino, about the same height at Orsogna, the lateral met the road from Lanciano and formed the cross with Route 84. The road junction at C. Martino was important since the German main supply route and line of withdrawal ran through it.

The south-east face of the Ortona—Orsogna ridge was very steep; for three miles on each side of Orsogna it was almost a vertical cliff. Between this ridge and the next to the south-east, on which Lanciano stood, there was a series of bare, minor ridges all open, and on a clear day in full view from Orsogna. As a New Zealand observer recorded, "Orsogna was the dominant feature of the soldier's landscape. Like a fortress it squatted on its ridge as though on the edge of a sheer cliff. Whenever men moved on the exposed roads and tracks, Orsogna seemed to be watching. With the black rain clouds behind it, as they so frequently were, it was a towering ever present menace." The 4th Indian Division appreciated this situation: "The enemy has first class, direct observation over the whole of the Divisional sector, including the back areas, both from comparatively low features like Orsogna and Guardiagrele and also from the high Maiella and can see everything we do. Particular attention will (therefore) be paid to camouflage, concealment, traffic control and the selection of forming up areas.²"

Orsogna itself had been converted into a fortress, in which every house was a strong-point. The boundary was wired and liberally sown with mine-fields. The garrison had in reserve a counter-attack force of tanks and self-propelled guns. Part of the town, including the very prominent church, stood on a spur jutting out eastwards from the main ridge. A wall, of large stone blocks, buttressed the two miles of the lateral road from the north-east. A mile or so north-east of the town, in the cliffside and south of the lateral roads, were a number of caves.

The 4th Indian Division's position was divided into three brigade sectors. Sector A was from exclusive Crecchio to inclusive Arielli. Sector B, in close contact with the Germans stubbornly defending Orsogna, was from exclusive Arielli, along the lateral road, to within approximately one thousand yards of Orsogna. This brigade had a detachment across the valley on the spur running north-east from the town. The third sector, E, was south of Orsogna, covering the road from Castelfrentano and the R. Sangro to Guardiagrele. Two battalions held this road. One, near Salarola continually patrolled forward to C. Martino. The other was in the area of the road junction at C. Castelnuovo giving depth to the brigade position and covering the gun areas. A position to the

² 4 Ind. Div. O.I. No. I of 1944.

south, on the Bianco track, was held by the third battalion. This brigade was separated from the other two by Orsogna and the valley of the R. Moro.

Sector A was held by the 2nd Independent Parachute Brigade, which passed from the 2nd New Zealand Division to the 8th Indian Division; B Sector was held by the 7th Indian Infantry Brigade; E Sector was held by the 5th Indian Infantry Brigade. Headquarters of the 7th Indian Infantry Brigade was at Spaccareli, on the Roman Road two miles, in a straight line, west of Lanciano. The brigade was deployed with 4/16 Punjab on the right on the Fontegrande ridge; the 1st Royal Sussex in the middle astride the lateral and one mile north-east of Orsogna; 1/2 Gurkha Rifles, on the left, on the spur north-east from Orsogna, between the lateral road to Ortona, and the Roman Road to Lanciano. D Company 1/2 Gurkha Rifles was detached three-quarters of a mile to the south-east, across the valley on the Roman Road. To strengthen this isolated company, D Company 1/6 Rajputana Rifles (5th Indian Infantry Brigade) was placed under the command of 1/2 Gurkha Rifles and took up position south of the Roman Road. In the 5th Indian Infantry Brigade sector, 1/4 Essex was at Salarola and Bianco village on the roads leading to Guardiagrele from Castelfrentano and the Sangro respectively. The remainder of the brigade was on the Rue Mancianese, two miles south of Lanciano, while Brigade Headquarters was in Castelfrentano. The Divisional Headquarters was originally in Lanciano on the next lateral road to the east but on 23 January it moved to Castelfrentano. Rear Headquarters opened at Taverna Nova, on the north bank of the R. Sangro where the 19th Indian Infantry Brigade had helped the New Zealanders across. Thus, for the first time, the 4th and the 8th Indian Divisions were fighting side by side.

The task of the 4th Indian Division was "to hold and improve its present positions and to prepare for future operations." The units which came under the command of the 4th Indian Division included the 111th Army Field Regiment Royal Artillery, the 573rd Pack Transport Company and the 2nd Canadian Armoured Regiment. The 4th Indian Division was opposed by the *334th Infantry Division,* the two airborne battalions and *IV Battalion 98th Mountain Regiment.*

The 4th Indian Division was fated to stay in the Adriatic sector only two weeks. During that time, in spite of reliefs, its battalions set about harassing the Germans. Units arriving in a sector for the first time made it their business to learn about the ground in front of them and about the Germans opposing them, as soon as possible. But there could be no short cuts in this. Daylight reconnaissance and close, restricted patrolling were adopted as a preliminary to more ambitious operations. On 1 February 1944 and at midday, the 4th Indian Division handed over command of the Orsogna sector to the 5th Canadian Armoured Division and set off on its switch across the mountains under better weather conditions. There were many sudden switches of this nature in this division's career.

Further Reorganisation of the Eighth Army

There was nothing of importance to mark the activities of the 4th Indian Division during the short period while it was in the Orsogna sector. On the other hand from early January 1944 until the middle of April 1944, the men of the 8th Indian Division lived and fought under atrocious weather conditions, as they grappled with the tough German defenders of the Winter Line. It was a period of weeks of hard work with no advances to show for it. We shall briefly describe the chief features of the patrolling activities of the 8th Indian Division on the Adriatic coast. In January 1944 the 8th Indian Division operated in the Villa Grande sector. Two brigades and their supporting arms were normally disposed to hold the forward sectors. A third brigade was located in the area Villa Rogatti—Caldari—Villa Jubatti with a counter-attack role. The fourth brigade rested and refitted in and around Lanciano.

Reorganisation of the Eighth Army was carried out on 1 February as troops had to be transferred to the Fifth Army. Therefore the I Canadian Corps relieved the V Corps in the coastal area. The Canadian Corps had under command the 1st Canadian Division on the right and the 8th Indian Division on the left. Simultaneously in the XIII Corps the 4th Indian Division was relieved in the Orsogna sector by the 5th Canadian Armoured Division. Further reorganisation took place on 9 February when the 5th Canadian Armoured Division took over the Villa Grande sector to enable the Canadian Corps to have under command the two Canadian divisions—the 1st Infantry Division and the 5th Armoured Division. The XIII Corps was also reorganised; the 78th Division went into reserve and the 8th Indian Division assumed responsibility for the Orsogna and Casoli sectors.[3]

The Eighth Army, reduced in size, was unable to carry out its task of preventing the Germans for moving formations across to the Fifth Army front. Towards the end of January the *26th Panzer Division* was pulled out and its place was filled by two regiments, *577th* and *578th* of the *305th Infantry Division*, which had been in the Central Italian sector, and one regiment, *146th*, of the *65th Infantry Division*, which had been left behind, when the inter-divisional relief took place and the *65th Infantry Division* moved to

---

[3] 8 Ind. Div. O.O. No. 12, dated 12 February 1944.

Genoa. Later, the *1st Parachute Division* was also to move across from the Adriatic to Cassino.

The 8th Indian Division's Sector

The 8th Indian Division held a wide front of twenty miles with three brigades in the line and the fourth in reserve. On the right was the 2nd Independent Parachute Brigade under command in the Consalvi—Arielli area. In the middle was the 19th Indian Infantry Brigade facing Orsogna. The left sector was held by the 21st Indian Infantry Brigade. The left flank of the latter was guarded by the 6th Lancers and the Italian guerillas.[4] The 17th Indian Infantry Brigade, in reserve, was responsible for the 'Taverna stronghold' based on C. Taverna, Castelfrentano and Lanciano. Headquarters 8th Indian Division opened at Castelfrentano but, on 14 February 1944, it moved to an area, midway between Lanciano and Castelfrentano. We shall not describe the inter-brigade reliefs which frequently took place but shall confine our attention to a description of the raids and counter-raids.

The terrain in the new divisional sector varied considerably from sector to sector. About two miles north-west of Consalvi and due north of Arielli was Canosa. South of it, the country was a series of flat topped ridges between deep ravines running from the Maiella towards the sea and visibility was restricted by the olive trees which covered the country side. The towns of Orsogna and Guardiagrele overlooked most of the divisional northern sector, restricting movement by day in the forward areas. On the left flank of the 8th Indian Division, in the area of Casoli—which lay seven miles due south of Orsogna as the crow flies—the country was broken and the foothills were dominated by the imposing massif of the Maiella mountains.

Raids and Counter-raids

During the night of 11/12 February, 3/8 Punjab raided German held houses on the western edge of the Fontegrande: the latter were caught napping and thrown into a considerable state of confusion. After a 'miniature Brook's benefit' they withdrew, leaving seven dead and equipment, including one machine gun. On 18 February, a patrol of the Mahratta from the 21st Indian Infantry Brigade caught a party of ten Germans off their guard in the tiny village of Vallebona, which nestled under the Maiella mountains and forced them to surrender.

At 0450 hours on 23 February 1944, the right forward positions of the Essex in Fontegrande area suffered a raid, and nine men of

---

[4] 8 Ind. Div. O.O. No. 12, dated 12 February 1944.

Z Company were taken prisoners. During the day, the Germans attacked a platoon of the 1st Royal Fusiliers which had just been established half a mile north-east of Arielli at C. Romano. At 0325 hours the next morning, the Germans put in another raid, this time against 3/8 Punjab one mile north-east of Orsogna, but gained no success.

During the night of 24/25 February, the Germans again attacked the Essex and 3/8 Punjab. Approximately seventy men advanced on an Essex platoon on Fontegrande while another force engaged B Company of 3/8 Punjab on the road, one thousand yards north-east of Orsogna. Both attacks were broken up by artillery defensive fire.

During the early days of March 1944 preparations were on foot for switching the Eighth Army's centre of action to the south as a preliminary to the launching of a new Allied offensive in the Liri Valley, south of Cassino. On 2 March, the 8th Indian Division passed from the command of the XIII Corps to that of the Eighth Army and, two days later, Headquarters XIII Corps moved out of the Eighth Army. On 7 March, 1944, the 8th Indian Division passed again under the command of V Corps, which also included the 3rd Carpathian Division.

At 0545 hours on 3 March a German patrol of twenty men raided the village of Fallascoso (about nine miles south of Casoli), which had been converted into a strong-point, on which the 6th Lancers based their harassing patrols. Before reaching the village the German patrol divided into four parties. Men of the 6th Lancers fought a highly successful engagement, which lasted well into the morning.

During the night of 5/6 March in a snowstorm, the Germans put in an attack against 3/15 Punjab, on the road and railway, a mile and a half from Orsogna. But they were beaten back. They gave another example of their intrepidity on the night of 8/9 March when a patrol raided a platoon of 3/15 Punjab, then holding a position in caves on the road side, one thousand yards north-east of Orsogna. The following night they attacked the Mahrattas holding the ridge west of Fontegrande.

The attack was beaten off with casualties to the Germans. In the evening of 11 March, a German patrol of platoon strength attempted to rush a Mahratta position on the same ridge, but was again beaten off. Again at 2000 hours on 12 March, the Germans attacked the Mahrattas, closing in on one company from three different sides, but it was beaten off with loss to both sides.

On the southern mountain flank, the 6th Lancers was continuously employed in patrolling and ambushes, which yielded a steady dividend of German casualties and prisoners. This game of hide and seek, attack and counter-attack went on in the mud and snow for the rest of the month.

In the first week of April 1944 the 8th Indian Division was disposed with the 21st Indian Infantry Brigade in the Arielli (A) Sector, the 19th Indian Infantry Brigade in the Orsogna (B) sector, Dawnay Force on the western and southern flanks, in C and D sectors and the 17th Indian Infantry Brigade in the Castelfrentano (E) sector. The 4th Indian Division now began to arrive from Western Italy with advance parties to relieve the 8th Indian Division. The 4th Indian Division assumed command of the sector from midnight of 9–10 April. The 8th Indian Division moved back to the Larino area, where the division had first assembled to begin its fighting in Italy. Although they had been continuously fighting since assembling at Larino six months earlier, the men were in great heart and ready for whatever task the summer offensive held for them.

The 4th Indian Division in the Line

When the 4th Indian Division took over the Orsogna sector on 10 April 1944, the 1st Canadian Infantry Division held the Ortona sector, but it was relieved by the 10th Indian Division on 22 April. On the left of the 4th Indian Division in the mountainous sector was the 3rd Carpathian Division (Polish) which had relieved the British 5th Division. From, but excluding, Crecchio the forward positions of the 4th Indian Division ran in a semicircle facing, but excluding Arielli, Orsogna, Guardiagrele, Pennapiedimonte, Lama, Fallascoso. This front was divided into five brigade sectors as follows:—

> A Sector—V. Consalvi—Arielli.
> B Sector—exclusive Arielli to inclusive Orsogna.
> E Sector—exclusive Orsogna to exclusive Guardiagrele and stretching back to Lanciano—Castelfrentano.
> C Sector—inclusive Guardiagrele to exclusive Palombaro and back to S. Eusanio and Casoli.
> D Sector—inclusive Palombaro to the division's left flank at Bomba.

Its three brigades were employed by the 4th Indian Division to hold sectors A, B and E while D Force[5] held the left flank sectors C and D. The initial deployment of the troops of the 4th Indian Division underwent a change on 19 April 1944. On that day the 11th Indian Infantry Brigade took over A sector with two forward

---

[5] D Force commanded by Colonel D. Dawnay, second in command of the 23rd Armoured Brigade consisted of the 9th Manchester, 11th Kings Royal Rifle Corps and Central India Horse.

battalions, 2/7 Gurkha Rifles on the right and 2nd Cameron on the left, and 3/12 Royal Frontier Force Regiment in reserve. The 5th Indian Infantry Brigade took over B sector with two forward battalions—1/6 Rajputana Rifles on the right and 1/4 Essex on the left, and 1/9 Gurkha Rifles in reserve. The 7th Indian Infantry Brigade took over E sector with 1st Sussex in the forward area and two battalions—4/16 Punjab and 1/2 Gurkha Rifles occupying rear positions.

Patrol Activity

Patrol clashes continued to be almost a daily occurrence. During the night of 21/22 April a German platoon attacked positions held by 1/6 Rajputana Rifles on Fontegrande, a mile and a half south of Arielli village. A German attack on 23 April against the positions held by the Essex astride the lateral road north of Orsogna achieved some success. At 0600 hours on 23 April, German troops attacked in the area of the caves, in the cliffside, east of the road, half a mile north-east of Orsogna. Communications were simultaneously cut and no information could be obtained as to the situation. Movement by day was almost impossible. Consequently, it was not until after dark the following evening in 23 April, that patrols could get forward to re-establish contact. They found that one platoon, No. 15, had been overrun and all its members killed or captured. The second platoon was intact. Immediate steps were taken to re-organise the whole company in new positions

Thereafter, for several days, German activity was confined almost entirely to the northern part of the 4th Indian Division's front. Two German platoons which attacked the positions held by 2/7 Gurkha Rifles at the road junction, Pt. 261, three hundred yards north of Crecchio, at 0500 hours on 25 April, were driven off by small arms and mortar fire. The following evening, a German company was seen forming up for attack in that area and was dispersed by artillery and mortar fire.

Patrols from the 4th Indian Division were bringing in a steady supply of prisoners. On the northern flank, at 0130 hours on 1 May, a company of 2/7 Gurkha Rifles raided three groups of German-held houses below and east of the road from Crecchio to Le Piano. The company advanced silently with one platoon directed against each group of houses. Fifteen minutes were allowed on the objectives. Thereafter, the withdrawal was covered by artillery fire. Only the left hand platoon met opposition. It was engaged in a brisk exchange of grenades and small arms fire.

In the early hours of 2 May, two German companies launched an attack against 1/9 Gurkha Rifles (5th Indian Infantry Brigade) who had relieved 1/4 Essex in VI Battalion area, north of Orsogna between 27 and 29 April. The Gurkha left hand forward company, one mile north of Orsogna, bore the brunt of the attack which was launched from the south-west at 0530 hours under cover of artillery, high explosive and smoke shells. When their attack was driven off the Germans dug in, on an east to west line, on a three hundred yards of the Gurkha forward posts. Their proximity to the Gurkhas and poor visibility made it impossible for the divisional artillery to engage the Germans with safety. At the same time, the German positions in and around Orsogna so dominated the ground held by 1/9 Gurkha Rifles that reinforcement by day was impossible. Nevertheless, preparations were made for counter-attack which the Brigade Commander planned to launch after darkness on 2 May, using the Gurkha Reserve Company. On moving forward at 2315 hours, this company found that the Germans had vacated their newly dug positions and in only one place were they to be found. These Germans, seven or eight in number, were put to flight by firing PIAT bombs into the house which they were occupying.

At this stage (5/8 May) there occurred another inter-brigade relief—the 7th Indian Infantry Brigade took over A sector, the 11th Indian Infantry Brigade B sector and the 5th Indian Infantry Brigade E sector. At 0545 hours on 14 May, the Germans raided B sector. In this sector, which had been heavily shelled for several days, 2/7 Gurkha Rifles and 3/12 Royal Frontier Force Regiment were occupying the forward positions, along the road between Arielli and Orsogna. 2/7 Gurkha Rifles faced north-westwards across the river valley. 3/12 Royal Frontier Force Regiment faced up to Orsogna astride the road and one thousand yards from the town, and had its right forward company on a neck of land, overlooking three valleys west of the road. Observation over the valleys was required in order to give early warning of any German attempts to move along them. But that made the company's positions dangerously isolated. The watercourses which the Indian troops might see by day became excellent cover and guides for German movement by night. Furthermore, they led into the company's positions from three different sides. It was through these valleys that the Germans moved at night before attacking in the early morning. A sharp artillery concentration inflicted heavy casualties on the Indian troops. Attacking in three waves with mortar, machine gun and artillery support, the Germans swept into the position and by 0720 hours overran the two forward platoons and company headquarters. As soon as the situation clarified, a counter-attack was put in. One company of the 3/12 Royal Frontier Force Regiment, supported by two troops of tanks of the 40th Royal Tank Regiment, 23rd Armoured Brigade (shermans), advanced at 0935 hours. Divisional artillery put down a heavy concentration on the positions taken by the Germans. The counter-attack seemed to be going well. Several positions had been retaken when the German artillery defensive fire crashed down on the infantry, inflicting considerable casualties and halting them. German machine guns joined in and compelled the company to withdraw.

At 1220 hours, a company from 2nd Cameron moved forward to fill the gap created by the loss of the forward platoons. At 1815 hours, a company from 1/9 Gurkha moved up to Pt. 302, on the Colle Pascuccio to protect the left flank of 3/12 Royal Frontier Force Regiment. At 2000 hours the same day, in fading light, 2nd Cameron attacked in two waves of one company each to expel, with little trouble, all the Germans in the 3/12 Royal Frontier Force Regiment's area. 2/7 Gurkha Rifles and tanks stood by to assist, should the Germans attempt to return to the attack.[6]

An attempt by the 11th Indian Infantry Brigade to advance its front towards Orsogna during the night of 25/26 May resulted in casualties. Two platoons from 3/12 Royal Frontier Force Regiment, assisted by a platoon of 2nd Cameron, were employed against the ridge over which the track led due north from Orsogna. The right forward platoon walked on a minefield covered by concentrated crossfire from German machine guns. Twenty-four men were killed or wounded. The attack was then halted, and the platoons were recalled.

At the end of the month, however an Italian formation, the Utili Division, took over the positions around Orsogna from the 4th Indian Division, which moved into the 10th Indian Division's coastal sector.

The Ortona Salient

The 10th Indian Division in the Line

Having described the operations in the Orsogna sector, we will now take up the activities of the 10th Indian Division in the Ortona sector. Under the command of Major-General D. W. Reid, C.B.E., D.S.O., M.C., the division had arrived in Italy on 28 March 1944 and had remained at Taranto until called forward in mid-April. At 0900 hours on 22 April 1944, command of the Ortona sector passed from the 1st Canadian Infantry Division to the 10th Indian Division.[7]

---

[6] Two companies 2nd Cameron remained in V area under command of 3/12 F.F.R. On 18 May, 1/6 Rajputana Rifles relieved 2nd Cameron in Area VI and that night 2nd Cameron relieved 3/12 F.F.R. in Area V. On 20 May, 4/6 Raj. Rif. returned to the division, and occupied Area X in the 5 Ind. Inf. Bde's sector.

[7] On 7 March 1944 the Canadian Corps sector had reverted to V Corps. The 5th Canadian Armoured Division was withdrawn but the 1st Canadian Infantry Division remained in the Ortona Salient.

The 10th Indian Division consisted of:—
10th Indian Infantry Brigade
    4th Battalion 10th Baluch Regiment
    1st Battalion 2nd Punjab Regiment
    2nd Battalion 4th PWO Gurkha Rifles
20th Indian Infantry Brigade
    3rd Battalion 5th Mahratta Light Infantry
    2nd Battalion 3rd QAO Gurkha Rifles
    8th Battalion Manchester Regiment
25th Indian Infantry Brigade
    3rd Battalion 1st Punjab Regiment
    3rd Battalion 18 Royal Garhwal Rifles
    1st Battalion King's Own Royal Regiment.[8]

Troops coming under command or in support of the 19th Indian Division were:—

    40th Royal Tank Regiment (less one squadron)
    561st Air Observation Post Squadron
    21st Canadian Meteorological Section
    150th Battery, 93rd Anti-Tank Regiment
    5th Field Company Indian Engineers (less one platoon)
    6th Indian Pack Transport Company
    8th Indian Pack Transport Company
    49th Mobile Bath Unit.

There were other Corps and Army troops in the 10th Indian Division area including the 2nd Anti-Aircraft Brigade, the 50th Royal Tank Regiment (less one Squadron) and the 17th Medium Regiment Royal Artillery.

The sector was so extensive that all the three brigades were employed in the line. The forward defended localities ran generally along the east bank of the river Ricci, rather more than half way from Ortona to the R. Arielli, as far as the road Villa Grande—Tollo, thence the line ran along the east bank of the Arielli to the east of Crecchio, where it jointed up with the positions held by the 4th Indian Division which included I. Salciaroli.[9]

The 10th Indian Infantry Brigade, arriving first, relieved the 1st Canadian Infantry Brigade on 21 April in the right, Ortona sector, which extended from the coast down to, inclusive, V. S. Nicola and S. Tommaso, a front of four thousand yards. The Brigade held this position with two battalions up and one in reserve. 4/10 Baluch on the right and 1/2 Punjab on the left held the forward positions while 2/4 Gurkha Rifles was in reserve around Ortona. The 20th Indian Infantry Brigade was the next to arrive and relieve the 3rd Canadian

---
[8] Appendix IV.
[9] 10 Ind. Div. O.O. No. 3, dated 12 May 1944.

Infantry Brigade in the centre, Villa Grande sector, in the nights of 21/22 and 22/23 April. This sector, also four thousand yards, stretched across the Piano di Moregine down to, but excluding, C. S. Eusano and was held with two battalions up and one in reserve. 3/5 Mahratta Light Infantry on the right and 8th Manchester on the left held the forward positions while 2/3 Gurkha Rifles was in reserve around Villa Grande.

The 25th Indian Infantry Brigade, last to arrive, took over from the 2nd Canadian Infantry Brigade during the night of 23/24 April in the left, Crecchio sector, a front of another four thousand yards. This brigade employed two battalions and one company forward with one battalion (less one company) in reserve astride the road Ortona—Orsogna, due north of V. Caldari and one mile and a half south-east of C. Vezzani. 3/18 Royal Garhwal Rifles on the right and 1st King's Own on the left occupied the forward positions while 3/1 Punjab was in reserve. Each brigade had in support one field regiment, one anti-tank troop and one machine gun company. The 10th and the 20th Indian Infantry Brigades each had one heavy mortar platoon while the 25th Indian Infantry Brigade had two. Similarly, the 10th Indian Infantry Brigade had two troops of the 40th Royal Tank Regiment, the 20th Indian Infantry Brigade had a squadron less the two troops and the 25th Indian Infantry Brigade had a full squadron.

Main Headquarters 10th Indian Division opened on the main coast road (Route 16), one mile north of S. Vito. Rear Headquarters was a mile nearer to Ortona on the same road. Defensive positions throughout the sector had usually been based on the houses which dotted the countryside, a habit which pin-pointed positions for the German artillery and their raiding parties. As will be seen, the 10th Indian Division soon discovered the danger involved in it and thereafter ordered that houses should be avoided as far as possible. Where houses were occupied, slit trenches were dug near the house for all its inhabitants. A portion of the garrison manned its slit trenches every night.

The German Forces

The German positions on the coastal sector lay on the west bank of the Ricci, across the valley from the 10th Indian Division, as far south as the Tollo road and thence followed the line of the R. Arielli down to inclusive Crecchio but exclusive Arielli. The *305th Infantry Division* held the sector opposite the 10th Indian Division. *578 Regiment* in the north held the line as far as Tollo with two battalions. From there to excluding Crecchio was held by *577 Regiment* also with two battalions forward. *576 Regiment* and the *Bode Group* were in reserve. The *334th Infantry Division* overlapped to the extent of having one company with *755 Regiment* in the Crecchio area opposing the battalion on the extreme left of the 10th Indian Division's front.

Plans for Counter-Attack

Forward planning to anticipate hostile moves produced detailed schemes which catered both for attack by the Germans or their withdrawal. Brigades had their counter-attack schemes which employed the reserve battalion (or portions of it) with tanks and artillery support to recover important points should these be lost to the Germans.

The divisional scheme (code name Alaska) was defensive in nature and catered for the protection of important centres of communications, or nodal points, behind the forward defended localities. Ortona and five road junctions were selected as nodal points. Three of these junctions were on the main lateral between Ortona and the division's left boundary, at

> (*a*) the junction of the lateral with Route 16 (code name Pincher Creek)
> (*b*) the cross roads formed with the main lateral by the road from the R. Moro and S. Leonardo to Villa Grande and Tollo (code name St. Polycarp)
> (*c*) the junction of the road from "Impossible Bridge" over the R. Moro and the main lateral (code name Ticonderoga).

Two were on the road S. Vito—Frisa, which ran along the south bank of the R. Moro, at:

> (*a*) S. Apollinare (code name Mohawk)
> (*b*) the Junction of this road and that to 'Impossible Bridge' (code name Iroquois).

The code name for the defence of Ortona was Moosejaw. If it became known that the Germans were preparing a large-scale attack these nodal points were to be manned as follows:—

> (*a*) Ortona by not less than one rifle company, with anti-tank guns, as detailed by the 10th Indian Infantry Brigade.
> (*b*) Pincher Creek, St. Polycarp and Ticonderoga, the three on the main lateral, each by one field company and one battery of the 13th Anti-Tank Regiment.
> (*c*) Mohawk and Iroquois on the south bank of the R. Moro, by Corps troops under the command of the 10th Indian Division.[10]

---

[10] 10 Ind. Div. O.I. No. 1, dated 2 May 1944.

In the event of a German withdrawal, pursuit by the 10th Indian Division was to be carried out in three phases. For Phase I, all three brigades were to advance—the 10th Indian Infantry Brigade on the coastal road to establish a bridge-head on the R.Foro; the 20th Indian Infantry Brigade to seize Tollo and then to advance to the R. Foro on its own front and on that of the 25th; the 25th Indian Infantry Brigade to the road Tollo—Canosa, thereafter to concentrate at Ortona. Phase II was the concentration of a force for pursuit beyond the R. Foro to consist of the units of the 7th Armoured Brigade, the 25th Indian Infantry Brigade, artillery, sappers and machine gunners. The 20th Indian Infantry Brigade was eventually to be relieved by the 4th Indian Division and also to be concentrated for the pursuit. Phase III was the advance beyond the R. Foro.[11]

First Moves

The 10th Indian Division had very little time to settle in, for on 21 April, the area of the 10th Indian Infantry Briagde, including Ortona, was shelled as the brigade was moving in and some casualties were suffered. Its reaction was quick and fire was directed on a group of houses across the Ricci, held by the Germans. The 4/10 Baluch Regiment discovered some movement there in the morning and called for artillery action. But the Germans replied by hitting at S. Tommaso with mortar bombs and air burst shells at intervals throughout the day. Immediately after dark, the 10th Indian Infantry Brigade put out three standing patrols to observe the roads from the crossing over the Ricci, two miles west of Ortona. At approximately 2300 hours the patrol nearest the bridge over the river heard sounds of German movement on the west bank of the river. A quarter of an hour later, came reports that the latter had occupied the spur between the two streams, half a mile north of the bridge and were moving southwards towards it. There the standing patrol watched the German patrol (approximately one platoon) launch an attack on an empty house. Subsequently it turned eastwards and, moving parallel to and one hundred yards north of, the road to Ortona, split up into three parties, and at 2345 hours attacked a company headquarters of 4/10 Baluch and an artillery observation post a quarter of a mile east of the 'S' bend in the road. At the same time the third party attacked the standing patrol at the 'S' bend. These attacks were beaten off; but twice again before 0500 hours, they attacked the company's position.

At dusk, on 25 April, the troops of the 10th Indian Infantry Brigade fired on a party of Germans forming up near the junction of

[11] 10 Ind. Div. O.I. No. 2, dated 11 May 1944.

several streams, half a mile north-west of V.S. Tommaso. But under cover of darkness, they slipped southwards, along the ravine leading to Villa Grande. Soon after midnight, they launched an attack with two platoons on the right forward company of 3/5 Mahratta Light Infantry. They struck the rear of the forward positions and in the first flush had penetrated a little. But after a period of confused fighting the situation was restored.

Again, at 2015 hours on the evening of 26 April, a German patrol attacked the Mahratta positions on the Piano di Moregine and the exchange of fire lasted until 2115 hours, when the former had withdrawn. Three hours later, after several alarms, a German platoon attacked the company of 1/2 Punjab, two and a half miles north-east of the Mahrattas and overlooking the Route 16 crossing at the Ricci, two and a half miles north-west of Ortona. The 10th Indian Infantry Brigade prepared to put its counter-attack scheme into operation but no counter-attack was required.

Down in the sector of the 25th Indian Infantry Brigade the Germans had been probing for three nights into the positions of 3/18 Royal Garhwal Rifles around C. S. Eusano—C. Vezzani. But on 26 April they turned their attention to the positions held by a company of 1st Kings Own, about one mile south of C. Vezzani on the track leading to Crecchio, and by another company at V. Bacili. At 2000 hours, after a preliminary concentration of mortar and machine gun fire, which lasted about twenty minutes, German fighting patrols began their attacks. That against the right forward company captured a house held by a rifle section and a gunner observation post, after forcing the occupants to withdraw. However, by midnight, the 1st Kings Own Royal Regiment had counter-attacked and recaptured the house. The southern attack was beaten off after a short exchange of fire. For the next few days in the last week of April, the only activity in the area held by the 10th Indian Division was inter-battalion relief within the brigades.

German Raids

The month of May opened with offensive operations by the Germans. At 0100 hours on 1 May a fighting patrol engaged a Mahratta outpost on the track from S. Nicola to Tollo and one mile west of S. Nicola. The outpost beat off the attack but suffered slight casualties. Shortly before dawn, the Germans heavily shelled and mortared the area of the 8th Manchester. At 0510 hours, a German platoon attacked an outpost located in a group of buildings just east of the road, eight hundred yards north of C. S. Eusano. A white verey light suddenly illuminated the area and small arms fire was opened on the piquet from all sides at a range of fifty yards. Several mortar bombs scored direct hits on the piquet. For ten minutes the fire lasted; then the attackers rushed at the piquet. One of these small parties reached the ruins of the buildings but was eventually driven off by rifle fire. As they withdrew, the piquet was again subjected to heavy mortar fire, which continued until 0605 hours causing heavy loss.

Under cover of darkness on 1/2 May, 3/18 Royal Garhwal Rifles sent a fighting patrol to attack a German post in the Arielli valley, half a mile west of C. S. Eusano. While forming up for their attack the Garhwalis were themselves counter-attacked and forced to withdraw. The two bren gunners, who covered their withdrawal, were lost and two other men were wounded.

Again during the night of 3/4 May, the Germans attacked positions held by 2/4 Gurkha Rifles. This attack was well planned and well performed. At about 2130 hours, a small party approaching the left flank of 2/4 Gurkha Rifles was detected and driven off by small arms fire but left one of their number dead behind them. However, a second small party, which succeeded in infiltrating round the right flank cut all telephone lines leading to the Silo positions. The object of these two parties appears to have been to create diversions and to provide covering fire for the main body.

At 2345 hours on 3 May, machine guns and sub-machine guns opened up from the area of the small ravine, which ran down to the sea from Route 16, a mile and a half north-west of Ortona; these weapons fired long bursts into the rear of the Gurkha centre company. At the same time the Germans, estimated to be a strong platoon, were seen forming up near the crossing of Route 16 over the Ricci. At 0105 hours, on 4 May, under cover of an artillery barrage, they advanced against the Gurkhas, sweeping over any patrols and outposts in their way, and circled round to a track junction in the middle of Macchia, six hundred yards south of Route 16 where the centre company had occupied positions overlooking the Ricci valley. One small German party penetrated another five hundred yards to the south-west before being halted. At 0215 hours, having evacuated its casualties, this party withdrew north-westwards under cover of machine gun fire.

Two miles south-west of 2/4 Gurkha Rifles the Germans attacked 2/3 Gurkha Rifles holding the Piano di Moregine. The right forward company was heavily mortared. A Gurkha patrol moving out to lay an ambush in the area of the stream on the western edge of Piano di Moregine was caught in this fire and suffered some loss. Shortly afterwards considerable hostile movement was heard on that company's front. Artillery defensive fire was brought down and was believed to have caused many German casualties. Despite this, the latter closed in on positions two thousand yards west of S. Nicola.

The Gurkhas met the attack with kukri and grenade and eventually threw them back.

South of the 20th Indian Infantry Brigade on the southern flank of the 25th Indian Infantry Brigade, 3/1 Punjab checked a raid. At 0530 hours on 5 May a platoon of Germans was seen moving eastwards from Crecchio. This party was promptly shelled. An hour and a half later, under cover of the morning mist, a party of approximately twenty Germans attacked a post on the track form C. Vezzani to V. Bacili. They were however driven off but not until they had demolished a building.

During the night of 7/8 May, German patrols, supported by flanking machine gun fire from the ravine on the west edge of the Piano di Moregine, approached the positions held by 2/3 Gurkha Rifles, and an exchange of fire ensued causing losses to both sides. Two nights later, at 0425 hours on 10 May, a strong German platoon, supported by artillery and mortars and machine guns firing from the track, five hundred yards north of C.S. Eusano, infiltrated through the Mahratta positions on the line of the track. They reached positions, four hundred yards east of the track, before being halted by the small arms fire which caused the patrol to withdraw without making any effective attack. At the same time, the Mahratta positions astride the road Villa Grande—Tollo were subjected to shelling and patrol activity, perhaps as a diversion.

At the same time (i.e. during the night of 9/10 May) a fighting patrol of 4/10 Baluch, consisting of Lieut. J. A. Peace, Jemadar Sattara Khan and thirty-nine other ranks attacked a house occupied by the Germans and located Germans in an area called Graveyard. There was fierce hand-to-hand fighting with the Germans entrenched around the house. After overcoming opposition the patrol returned to the base. Fourteen Germans were killed and two taken prisoner. The casualties of the patrol were 1 killed and 2 wounded. Jemadar Sattara Khan, who fought gallantly in overcoming determined opposition and killing 6 Germans was awarded the Military Cross.

For the next week, while a major Allied offensive was launched in Western Italy, the Germans on the Adriatic coast showed little activity. There was, however, a marked tendency on their part to react to any patrols with constant firing of Verey lights and opening of fire at any movement, a sign of nervousness as to the Allied intentions on the east coast. The considerable German movements noticed in the Crecchio area by day light on 11 and 12 May and in the coastal sector were mainly local reliefs in progress.

Patrols from the 10th Indian Division were out night and day looking for indications as to the German reactions to the Allied offensive. For several days there were reports of explosions behind the German lines but no definite indications that these were demolitions or that they were preparing to withdraw.

Probing into German Positions

For the next few days, patrols were busy probing the German positions and intentions. On the night of 19/20 May, a platoon of 1/2 Punjab was involved in a clash in the coastal sector. Its objective was a German outpost comprising a group of houses across the river. At 0130 hours on 20 May, as the raid went in with tommy-guns blazing, divisional artillery provided fire support on previously located machine gun positions. At one German post, a section commander Naik Dausanda Singh was riddled by bullets in the thigh and cheek. Some minutes later, a grenade laid the flesh of his back open to his ribs. Nevertheless, the Naik fought on and, with his section, annihilated the Germans holding the position before turning to wipe out the garrison of a second post. Elsewhere, the rest of the platoon had caused similar destruction and had taken one prisoner. Having completed its task, the patrol, including the wounded, walked the two miles back to headquarters, re-entering the forward defended localities of 2/4 Gurkha Rifles at 0400 hours.

The prisoner provided the rather startling identification of *I battalion, 993 Grenadier Regiment, 278th Infantry Division*, which had recently been formed in northern Italy from the elements of divisions destroyed in Russia and from very young recruits of the 1926 class. This battalion was, according to the prisoner, the first to arrive from Trieste in relief of the *305th Infantry Division* which had begun in the early hours of 19 May. The *994th Grenadier Regiment* of the *278th Infantry Division* was reported to be engaged on coastal defence duties at Pesaro.

The *278th Infantry Division* was probably considered to be insufficiently experienced to be committed to a major battle at this stage. Patrol reports indicated that, by the morning of 20 May, the *278th Infantry Division* had probably taken over the front from the sea down to and including the Tollo road.

On 22 May at 1145 hours, in the 20th Indian Infantry Brigade sector, a Mahratta sniper reported German movement near the road Villa Grande—Tollo, where it ran parallel to the Arielli, a mile and a quarter west of Villa Grande. There was at that point a post, which was known to be periodically occupied by the Germans, and only three-hundred yards from the Mahratta outpost positions. A fighting patrol of two sections was immediately sent to attack the post, under cover of mortar fire. By crawling through the undergrowth, the Mahrattas managed to get within fifty yards of the post before being discovered. From there, they charged the post while the German machine gun went into action. In the hand-to-hand fighting which followed, the patrol inflicted some losses on the Germans. It withdrew under cover of fire from the supporting mortars, taking one prisoner.

A patrol from 3/18 Royal Garhwal Rifles raided the Germans at 0250 hours on 23 May on the extreme southern flank of the 10th Indian Division. Its objective was a group of houses on the ridge between the two branches of the Arielli, one thousand yards south of Crecchio, a position known to be strongly held by the Germans. Complete surprise was achieved. A machine gun post was overrun, the gunner killed, his weapon captured and the remainder of the section put to flight. Within three minutes, however, the Garhwali patrol was counter-attacked from both the flanks and compelled to withdraw.

Operation 'Kishan'

A very successful raid was carried out by one company of 2/3 Gurkha Rifles. The raid, known as Operation 'Kishan', was directed against German positions in the area of Lone House, on the road between the Ricci and the Arielli, due west of S. Nicola. Its object was to secure an identification and to inflict casualties. Considerable reconnaissance of the area had previously been carried out by patrols of the 10th Indian Division. Two platoons assaulted, while the third provided covering fire from the flanks, two bren groups on the right and three on the left. The objective was indicated by fire from Bofors anti-aircraft guns, and the fire plan for artillery and mortars was divided into three phases:—

> Phase I—Concentrations (*a*) on the area astride the road junction on the east bank of the Arielli, one mile east of Tollo. (*b*) On positions—twelve-hundred yards north of the objective with the intention of declaring the enemy. During this phase the Gurkha company advanced to its forming up place, six-hundred yards from its objective.
> Phase II—Two concentrations on the objective, to pin down and destroy the garrison while the attacking troops advanced to the objective.
> Phase III—'Stonks' and 'Murder'[12] on neighbouring positions while the attackers mopped up and withdrew.

Fire support was provided by:—
(*a*) The 68th Field Regiment plus three batteries (the 97th and 154th Field Regiments)
(*b*) 'W' Company 1st Northumberland Fusiliers (Medium Machine Gun)

[12] 'Murder'—is a pin point concentration of all available guns.

(c) One troop (Shermans) 'B' Squadron, 6th Royal Tank Regiment
(d) Half a troop (Bofors 40-m.m.) 118th Light Anti-Aircraft Battery
(e) Twelve 3-inch mortars
(f) 262 Battery (3.7-inch guns), 84th Heavy Anti-Aircraft Regiment
(g) 13 Platoon (4.2-inch mortars) 1st Northumberland Fusiliers
(h) Two 4.2-inch mortars of 100 Anti-Tank Battery

} for counter-mortar tasks

The whole operation, carried out according to a timed programme, was a success with no hitches in the fire plan. The deception plan caused the German fire to be scattered and ineffective. Thirty-five minutes were allowed for the approach (one thousand yards) and assault including a maximum of ten minutes on the objective. The attack went home and caused losses to the German garrison. Identification of the prisoners confirmed that *II Battalion 993rd Grenadier Regiment, 278th Infantry Division* was holding that part of the line. One of the prisoners revealed that the Gurkhas had anticipated, by little more than an hour, a German raid against their own positions on the Piano di Moregine. The German raid was inevitably and indefinitely postponed.

4th Indian Division Takes up the Chase

The 10th Indian Division's stay on the Adratic Coast was coming to an end; the 4th Indian Division was moving up to the coast to take its place. On 3 June 1944, at midday the 4th Indian Division took over the front held by the 10th Indian Division. With the capture of Rome by the Allied forces on 4 June 1944 the German troops pulled out of the defensive positions all along the front. The stage was thus set for the pursuit of German forces on all fronts in Italy, including the pursuit by the 4th Indian Division and other Allied forces up the Adriatic coast.

THE ADVANCE TO THE ARNO

CHAPTER XI

Pursuit to Ripa

Italy—A Secondary Theatre of Warfare

The capture of Rome on 4 June 1944 marked the end of an important phase of the campaign in Italy. The fiercely contested battles of Cassino had excited the awe and admiration of foes and friends alike. The heroic efforts of the Allies to storm the strong Cassino defences and the stubborn valour of the Germans had invested the campaign in Italy with a certain amount of glamour. But with the capture of Rome the campaign was shorn of its glory for the Allied invasion of France was to steal the limelight. Two days after the capture of Rome the Allied forces invaded north-west France and the claims of operation 'Anvil' (for the invasion of southern France) could no longer be ignored. Of course General Alexander strove hard to retain for the Italian campaign the overriding priority in Mediterranean operations which it had been given in February 1944. In an appreciation written on 7 June 1944 he earnestly pleaded that his forces should not be weakened by the withdrawal of troops for operation 'Anvil' so that he might carry the offensive into the Po valley, which would serve as a springboard for the attack on France or Austria. He was confident of success for he had superb faith in his two highly organised and skilful armies. He passionately declared: "Neither the Apennines nor even the Alps should prove a serious obstacle to their enthusiasm and skill."[1]

General Alexander's passionate plea for achieving decisive results by striking at the heart of Germany from the base in the Po valley was not accepted for the Americans were keen on operation 'Anvil'. On 17 June General Marshal told General Wilson that General Eisenhower strongly favoured operation 'Anvil' to clear additional French ports so that Allied forces might be deployed in France 'more rapidly and on a broader front'. There were between 40 and 50 divisions in the United States 'which could not be introduced into France as rapidly as desired or maintained there through the ports of Northwest France or by staging through the United Kingdom.'[2] This argument clinched the issue for although General

---

[1] Alexander's Despatch, *op. cit.*
[2] *Report by the Supreme Allied Commander Mediterranean to the Combined Chiefs of Staff on the Operations in Southern France, August 1944.*

Wilson supported General Alexander's plan and was opposed to the shifting of the main effort from Italy to Southern France, the combined Chiefs of Staff upheld General Eisenhower's point of view. On 14 June General Wilson was informed of this decision. On 2 July he received a directive from the Combined Chiefs of Staff that the assault would be made on 15 August. The operation was to be given overriding priority over the battle in Italy to the extent of a build-up of ten divisions in the south of France. This decision was a bitter disappointment to General Alexander for the Italian campaign was now to be robbed of its glory and Italy was to be reduced to a secondary theatre of warfare. The impact of the over-all strategy on the campaign in Italy was great. General Alexander was to declare later: "Whatever value the invasion of Southern France may have had as a contribution to operations in North-western Europe its effect on the Italian campaign was disastrous. The Allied armies in full pursuit of a beaten enemy were called off from the chase, Kesselring was given a breathing space to reorganise his scattered forces and I was left with insufficient strength to break through the barrier of the Apennines."[3]

Pursuit North of Rome (4-9 June)

The Allied plan for the pursuit north of Rome envisaged two main lines of advance, along the west coast for the Fifth Army and astride the river Tiber for the Eighth Army. Immediate objectives were the port of Civitavecchia for the former and the area Rieti—Terni for the latter. The task assigned to the Eighth Army was so designed as to disrupt the German plans for forming a new continuous front across Italy in that region. The Fifth Army attained its objective on 7 June and, on 12 June, the first Allied ship berthed in the port.

On 4 June 1944, when Rome was captured, the Eighth Army was deployed with the X Corps on the right, the XIII Corps in the centre and the I Canadian Corps on the left. The X Corps with the 2nd New Zealand Division was leading up the Sora-Avezzano road. The XIII Corps was leading the advance with the 8th Indian Division on the Alatri-Guarcino road, and the 6th Armoured Division on the Alatri-Fiuggi road. The I Canadian Corps with the 6th South African Armoured Division was moving forward on the Anagni-Paliano road. General Leese, Commander of the Eighth Army, decided to pull the Canadian Corps out of the line and to employ the X and XIII Corps in pursuit of the beaten German forces north of Rome. On 4 June, the I Canadian Corps passed into the Army reserve but the 6th South African Armoured Division was transferred

---

[3] Alexander's Despatch, *op. cit.*

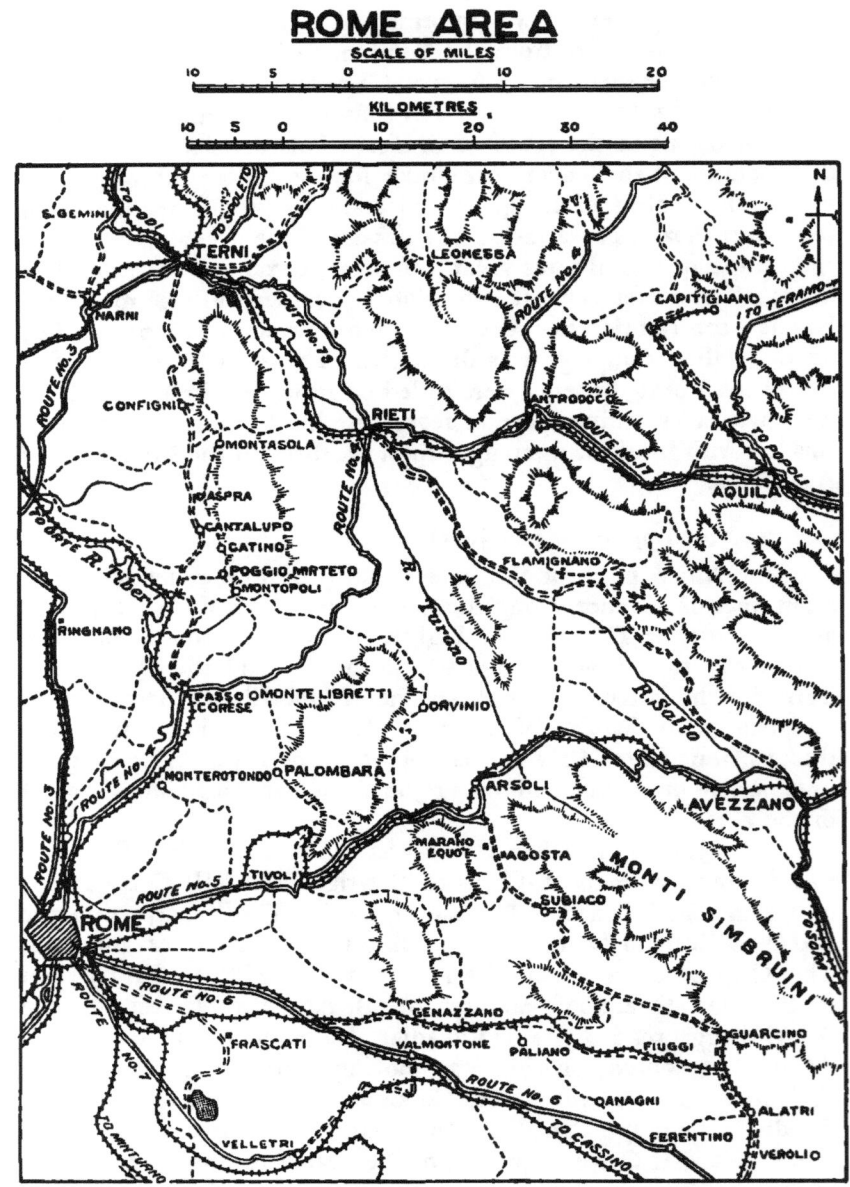

from the Canadian to the XIII Corps, which thus had two armoured divisions. The following day, the 8th Indian Division was transferred from the XIII to the X Corps and, on 6 June, the 10th Indian Division was also posted to the X Corps from the V Corps in the Adriatic sector.

The XIII Corps drove up the Tiber valley towards Terni, 50 miles north-east of Rome. The 6th South African Armoured Division and the 6th British Armoured Division advanced along Routes 3 and 4 (along each bank of the Tiber) while the British 4th Division pushed on along the minor road Tivoli-Palombara to protect the right flank of the XIII Corps. The X Corps, with only the 8th Indian Division in the forward area, advanced by way of Alatri-Subiaco-Arsoli-Orvino to Rieti, the main corps objective. The 8th Indian Division made rapid progress, capturing Guarcino on 4 June, Subiaco on the 6th and Arsoli on the 9th. We shall briefly describe the progress of the 8th Indian Division during this short period (4-9 June) before the Allied forces were reorganised on 9 June for a rapid pursuit of the retreating German forces.

8th Indian Division's Advance to Arsoli

The 21st Indian Infantry Brigade, leading the advance of the 8th Indian Division, had captured Guarcino on 4 June 1944. The 19th Indian Infantry Brigade was now assigned the task of pushing on in pursuit of the Germans towards Arsoli. The pursuit could not be taken up immediately due to the demolitions of the road carried out by the Germans. The 66th Field Company, Indian Engineers, worked throughout the night of 4/5 June to bridge the gap blown by the Germans in the defile south of Guarcino. Early on 5 June this bridge, a triple single Bailey, one hundred and ten feet long, was completed. Just beyond the northern outskirts of Guarcino, fifty yards of the road had been destroyed by blowing up the hillside. There sappers had to blast a new track out of solid rock. Until this was done, vehicles could not pass to the next demolished bridge, a mile and a half beyond Guarcino. This bridge was, in its turn, completed by 2230 hours on 5 June.

The 19th Indian Infantry Brigade was now ready to push on in pursuit of the Germans. On 6 June, a column consisting of C Squadron 6th Lancers, one company 6/13 Royal Frontier Force Rifles and tanks of the 12th Canadian Armoured Regiment pushed ahead across the open table-land before entering the narrow valley through which ran the road to Subiaco. This column encountered no opposition until it approached the outskirts of Subiaco when, in the neighbourhood of the bridge over the torrent Aniene, it came under long range artillery fire, which knocked out one armoured car. Up to this point, progress had been much impeded by extensive demolitions at hairpin bends and on cliff sides. Numerous mines in the gravel road added to the obstacles.

The last stretch of the road before the Aniene was littered with the charred wrecks of more than one hundred German vehicles destroyed by Allied air attacks. At the Aniene, where there was a sheer drop of some two hundred feet from the road to the river bed and a gap of one hundred and twenty feet, the bridge had been completely destroyed. Two bull-dozers trying to make a diversion were blown up on mines. All the divisional sappers and most of the Mahratta anti-tank gunners were employed on road repairs but so much damage had been done north of Affile that bridging equipment could not be taken forward to the Aniene until late in the afternoon of the following day, 7 June. Nevertheless, 6/13 Royal Frontier Force Rifles pushed ahead, with mules, and occupied Subiaco without opposition in the evening of 6 June.

Then 3/8 Punjab set out on foot towards Agosta at dawn on 7 June. They marched across country from Affile to the road junction, two miles south of Agosta. Patrols, working ahead of the battalion, were engaged by German mortar and machine gun fire, and estimated the German strength in Agosta at about sixty men. Since the road through Subiaco was not yet open, it was decided not to press the Germans by launching an infantry assault on Agosta. Throughout the day, divisional artillery shelled the German positions and that night the Germans withdrew. At first light on 8 June patrols from 3/8 Punjab occupied Agosta.

At approximately 1400 hours on 8 June three moves were initiated by the commander of the 19th Indian Infantry Brigade to capture Arsoli, to clear Route 5 as far as Tivoli and to secure Rocca di Botte, three miles south-east of Arsoli. One company of 6/13 Royal Frontier Force Rifles climbed the hill from Agosta to Cervara, then turned northwards to Rocca di Botte. There the company surprised a party of thirty Germans, killed four of them, took three prisoners and then withdrew. The following morning the Germans had fled from the village.

The 1st Battalion Argyll and Sutherland Highlanders, advancing northwards along the road from Agosta with a troop of B Squadron 6th Lancers covering their advance, was within one thousand yards of Arsoli when checked at approximately 1700 hours by German mortar and small arms fire. The battalion deployed and waited for darkness before attacking the town. When, at 2300 hours, the attack was launched, it was unopposed, the Germans having withdrawn after destroying eighty yards of the road south of Arsoli.

The 6/13th Royal Frontier Force Rifles moved, with one company on foot as advanced guard and the remainder (less the company sent to Rocca di Botte) riding on tanks, until German shelling compelled them to dismount and deploy. At 1700 hours the troops of the 6th Lancers with the 6/13 Royal Frontier Force Rifles drove into Roviano unopposed. Meanwhile a mobile column of the 19th Indian Infantry Brigade was engaged in clearing Route 5. Before darkness fell, this column had driven west to within four miles of Vicovaro. The following morning (9 June), while patrols scoured the countryside, another mobile column from the 19th Indian Infantry Brigade entered Tivoli, thus opening up Route 5 between there and Roviano.

Regrouping of the Eighth Army

The Eighth Army regrouped on 9 June as a result of the directive issued by General Alexander on 7 June. Faced with stiff opposition to the east of the Tiber, General Alexander issued orders to both the Armies by which he hoped to derive advantage from the favourable situation west of the Tiber. The Eighth Army was ordered to advance with all possible speed direct on the general area Florence—Bibbiena—Arezzo and the Fifth Army to the area Pisa—Lucca—Pistoia. In accordance with these instructions Lieut.-General Leese carried out the reorganisation of the Eighth Army. The Tiber now became the boundary between the X and the XIII Corps. The former had now under command the 8th Indian Division and the 6th British Armoured Division, with the 10th Indian Division in reserve. The latter had under command the 78th Division and the 6th South African Armoured Division, with the British 4th Division in reserve. Lieut.-General Leese changed the direction of the XIII Corps thrust from striking due north across the Tiber at Terni and Narni to advancing north-westwards on Arezzo. The task for the X Corps was now to capture Terni and the two highways, which led from there to Perugia.

The German Defensive Line

After the loss of Rome on 4 June 1944, Field-Marshal Kesselring planned to pull back his forces to the strong defensive line in northern Apennines (known as the Gothic Line) after delaying the Allied advance on defensive lines of lesser importance, such as the Trasimene Line and the Arezzo Line. From Rome northwards for more than a hundred miles the country was little suited to the German purpose of blocking the Allied advance. The Italian peninsula broadened rapidly north of Rome until, on the latitude of Lake Trasimene, it reached a width of one hundred and fifty miles, a distance equal to that of the Gustav Line and of the Anzio perimeter together. At the Gustav Line, the Apennines occupied nearly two-thirds of the width of the peninsula. East of Lake Trasimene the Apennines were reduced to a narrow range close to the Adriatic coast. The few mountains west of the Apennines could be turned from both flanks as there were several good roads from the south to the north. North of Lake Trasimene, the peninsula narrowed again and the country became generally more mountainous. Farther north still, beyond the R. Arno, the northern Apennines formed a solid barrier spanning the country from coast to coast and blocking all approaches to the plain of Lombardy. The few roads leading north threaded their way up deep valleys and climbed high, winding passes before reaching the plains. The sole gap in the barrier was a narrow corridor of foothills along the east coast between Pesaro and Rimini. Even there the succession of ridges was suitable for defence in depth. This barriers of the northern Apennines had been chosen by the Germans for their next defensive line.

Advance to the Trasimene Line

Field-Marshal Kesselring showed considerable skill in reorganising his forces and forming a fairly coherent defence line across Italy, known as the Trasimene Line. On the east coast it followed the river Chienti; west of the Apennines, it was based on the high ground north of Perugia, Lake Trasimene, Chiusi; from the latter place it ran along the river Astrone to the Orcia and the upper Ombrone. The Allied advance, which had been fairly rapid after the fall of Rome on 4 June 1944, was halted by 20 June by stiffening German resistance on the Trasimene Line.

After the reorganisation of the Allied forces on 9 June the pursuit of the retreating German forces continued vigorously. The American Fifth Army was employing two corps—the IV Corps on the sea coast and the French Expeditionary Corps up Route 2. The former captured Grosseto on 15 June but its advance was held up by stiff resistance at the river Ombrone by 20 June. The latter captured the strong position of Radicofani (the highest point on the road from Rome to Florence) on 18 June and pushed on to the river Orcia (a tributary of the Ombrone) by 20 June. The Eighth Army employed two corps—the XIII and the X. The former advancing from Viterbo captured Orvieto on 14 June and by 20 June was held up by stiffening German position. The Germans were firm in Chiusi and established in good positions between there and Lake Trasimene. The X Corps operated with two divisions—the 6th British Armoured Division on the axis Narni—Todi—Perugia and the 8th Indian Division (which took over from the British 4th Division on Route 4 east of Passo Corese) on the axis Terni—Foligno—Bastia. By 20 June the former had captured Perugia while the latter had secured Bastia and had pushed on to Ripa. On the Adriatic coast the V Corps too had been making progress. Pescara and Chieti were occupied on 10 June. The V Corps continued its advance until on 17 June it was relieved by the Polish Corps. The latter captured S. Benedetto and Grottammare on 20 June. Thus by 20 June the Allied progress had been rapid, but now they came up against stiffening opposition. The battle of the Trasimene Line was about to begin. It is now necessary here to pause and to narrate briefly the advance of the 8th Indian Division to Ripa.

8th Indian Division's Advance to Terni

From Arsoli the 8th Indian Division was switched on to a new sector to speed up the pursuit of the Germans. On 10 June, it assumed command of the British 4th Division's sector in the area Passo Corese. The 17th Indian Infantry Brigade relieved a brigade of the British 4th Division around M. Libretti and prepared to advance to Montopoli. But its progress was slowed down by demolitions which were numerous in that area. Every road and track had to be carefully swept for Teller and box mines. The latter, because of the absence of metal in their make-up, were particularly difficult to locate. On 11 June, the 7th Field Company suffered twenty casualties when one of its scout cars was blown up by a mine on a road, which had already been swept. To the sappers' tasks of building bridges, filling in craters and sweeping for mines, the rain now added that of repairing diversions damaged by flood water. In spite of these handicaps the chase swept on. A patrol of the 6th Lancers entered Montopoli at 1145 hours on 12 June. Following on their heels 1/5 Royal Gurkha Rifles occupied Montopoli in the afternoon. It was now realised that to continue the development of the road northwards through Montopoli and Catino would not only be a slow process but would also consume engineer and labour resources. Hence it would be reasonable to abandon that route in favour of the parallel track, two miles to the west, from Poggio Mirteto railway station, through Cantalupo to Configni. The 61st Infantry Brigade of the 6th British Armoured Division, advancing astride this parallel route, had already occupied Cantalupo on 11 June. The 21st Indian Infantry Brigade, therefore, moved forward to Cantalupo area to advance up this parallel route to Terni, an important road junction, while the 17th Indian Infantry Brigade protected the division's right flank by blocking all tracks leading in from Rieti and the east. The 19th Indian Infantry Brigade was in reserve at M. Libretti.

On 12 June, the 21st Indian Infantry Brigade concentrated in area Cantalupo, and the next day two of its battalions advanced north by the two roads leading from the town. The 5th Royal West Kent Regiment on the right secured Montasola, while 1/5 Mahratta on the left reached Configni without opposition. The two roads allotted to the 21st Indian Infantry Brigade having now become one, the Brigade Commander decided to take up the pursuit with his reserve battalion, 3/15 Punjab, on 14 June. Ahead of 3/15 Punjab were B Squadron 6th Lancers, with a detachment of sappers, and B Squadron 142nd Royal Armoured Corps. In spite of demolitions, craters and mines a steady progress was made. At 0615 hours, a particularly large crater within a mile of Terni compelled the battalion to leave its vehicles and continue on foot. By 0630 hours, the first Punjab patrols, and by 0700 hours the whole battalion had entered Terni. Contact was quickly established with the 24th Guards Brigade at the southern outskirts of the town. Thereafter the day was spent in collecting German stragglers in Terni.

Advance to Foligno

Now that Terni was secured, the 66th Field Company (Indian Engineers) and engineers from the 25th Army Tank Brigade set about the task of bridging the Nera at Terni. By excellent cooperation the British and Indian engineers succeeded in building the bridge so rapidly that they had completed it before the evening, some hours ahead of the time forecast. Meanwhile the 12th Lancers operating on the eastern flank of the 8th Indian Division along Route 4 was encountering numerous demolitions on the way. Since its task was purely protective, the patrols were in no great haste and entered Rieti unopposed at 1340 hours on 13 June.

The bridging of the Nera having been completed the 19th Indian Infantry Brigade swept forward from Terni to Foligno along Route 79. A Squadron 6th Lancers, followed by the 1st Argyll and Sutherland Highlanders led the advance. There were demolitions on the route but all were by-passed and progress was quite rapid. At 0930 hours on 15 June, the Lancers rode into Acquasparta, and collected five German stragglers. The bridge over the torrent Naia, two and a half miles north of Acquasparta, was partly destroyed by Allied bombing but a diversion suitable for all traffic was found close by. The Lancers pressed forward and, at 1230 hours, reached another bridge, a mile and a half south of Massa Martana, just in time to prevent its destruction by a party of German engineers. Again the Lancers put to flight the German demolition party of some thirty men, armed fortunately only with small arms, before the three bridges immediately north of the village could be destroyed. However, in spite of their being so hustled, the Germans managed to set fire to two ammunition dumps on the roadside, three miles north of Massa Martana and thereby checked the 19th Indian Infantry Brigade's advance for nearly three hours. North of Massa Martana, A Squadron 6th Lancers followed both the roads. Towards evening, the troop on the westerly road moved across to rejoin the Squadron near the burning ammunition dumps.

On 16 June at 0545 hours, the advance by the 19th Indian

Infantry Brigade began again with A Squadron 6th Lancers and 6/13 Royal Frontier Force Rifles in the lead. Two destroyed bridges were bypassed after only slight delay and in spite of light German shelling. Then this advanced guard trickled down the long rolling hill road towards Bevagna. At midday, they put to flight German engineers who were engaged in destroying the three bridges over the torrent Teverone, south of Bevagna. One bridge to the south-west of the village, was already down. A second to the west of the village, was partially destroyed but was passable to light vehicles only. But the third, a wooden one south-east of the village and in flames, was passable to all traffic after the Lancers had extinguished the fire.

While the 19th Indian Infantry Brigade was pushing ahead along the main divisional axis, squadrons of the 6th and 12th Lancers were reconnoitring to the east and the west. A Squadron of the 12th Lancers had secured Montefalco and then gone on towards Bevagna. This advance on the right flank enabled the 19th Indian Infantry Brigade to launch the attack on Foligno, which was believed to be held by a few German troops. Preparatory to the attack, C Squadron 6th Lancers moved up on the right flank of the 19th Indian Infantry Brigade to the bridge over the Teverone, two miles south-east of Bevagna, which the 12th Lancers had captured intact. C Squadron was reinforced by a company from 6/13 Royal Frontier Force Rifles and a troop of the 142nd Royal Armoured Corps, which had moved up through Montefalco. This column advanced direct on Foligno. On its left flank the remainder of 6/13 Royal Frontier Force Rifles, with A Squadron of the 6th Lancers and the remainder of the Squadron of the 142nd Royal Armoured Corps, moved towards Foligno from Bevagna. A Squadron of the 12th Lancers also advanced on Foligno from the south. Thus three columns converged on Foligno on 16 June, which was captured without opposition. The town was, in fact, a collecting point for all units before they were despatched northwards in the correct directions. Their miscellaneous nature made cohesion extremely difficult and the advance by the 8th Indian Division from all points of the compass completed the confusion. Those defences which had been organised faced south along Route 3. The western and northern entrances were unguarded. As a consequence none of the 8th Indian Division's columns experienced difficulty in entering Foligno, where the afternoon was spent in rounding up prisoners. 250 Germans were captured. Armoured cars scoured the surrounding country to make this important road junction secure. The 12th Lancers seized a bridge in the north-east outskirts of the town but reported all roads to the north-east and north impassable owing to demolitions. A German rearguard continued to hold out just north of Foligno, astride Route 3 and for two days shelled the town.

A Squadron 6th Lancers accompanied B Company 6/13 Royal Frontier Force Rifles towards Spello. When some two miles north-west of Foligno, this column was halted by a German anti-tank gun, until an infantry platoon had managed to get behind it. The German crew then abandoned the gun and took to their heels. Entry into Spello was effected by 1730 hours with only slight opposition. The Lancers spread out north and west of the town, and, at 1930 hours, intercepted a German convoy apparently hurrying with reinforcements to Foligno. Two vehicles were knocked out and the occupants ran in all directions in confusion. Thereafter the infantry company took up position astride the road a short distance to the north-west of Spello and, at 2230 hours, intercepted more German reinforcements.

Capture of Bastia

On 17 June, the 19th Indian Infantry Brigade turned north-westwards from the Foligno area along the valley below Assisi towards the Tiber, leaving 6/13 Royal Frontier Force Rifles and the 12th Lancers to deal with the thirty or forty Germans who, with machine guns and self-propelled guns, were still holding out a short distance north-east of Foligno. All hostile fire during the night had come from the north-east, none from the north-west.

3/8 Punjab, headed by a troop of A Squadron 6th Lancers and of 142nd Royal Armoured Corps, moved up from Bevagna at 0500 hours on 17 June and took over the advance, with Route 75 as its axis. After passing through Santa Maria Degli Angeli at 0800 hours, the 6th Lancers armoured cars raced ahead to secure the crossing at Bastia, over the R. Chiascio, a tributary of the Tiber. They had been ordered to make all efforts to capture at least one bridge intact. They were, however, too late. The road bridge had been destroyed and the railway bridge was blown as the Lancers came within sight of it. Less than a quarter of a mile from Bastia, a German anti-tank gun knocked out two of the leading armoured cars and a jeep, carrying three officers, received a direct hit.

At this stage, the infantry was called in. 3/8 Punjab debussed near Santa Maria Degli Angeli, and sent its leading company, B, to advance on Bastia from the south-east and A Company from the north-east, under cover of fire from the divisional artillery. Strong German resistance was encountered in Bastia and Santa Maria Degli Angeli was accurately shelled by German guns, but by 1500 hours B Company, aided by tanks, had captured Bastia. A Company reached the road bridge over the Chiascio, and then came under accurate, close range fire from German infantry holding Bastiola on the west bank. To deal with this opposition, the Commanding Officer lined up his tanks and anti-tank guns at point blank range and tried to blast the Germans out of Bastiola while his reserve rifle companies (C and D) prepared to cross the river. A sudden downpour of rain, which began at 1600 hours, hampered preparations. Nevertheless, an hour later, after a sharp artillery bombardment of the German positions, D Company, followed by C Company, crossed the river in the vicinity of the road bridge and together, at nightfall, they established a bridgehead on the western bank around Bastiola. A and B Companies, the troop of tanks and artillery assisted from the east bank, the infantry at times using their PIATS to good effect against German positions on the west bank. Under cover of darkness on 17/18 June, another company was across the river and sappers began to work on a Bailey bridge alongside the road bridge. By first light the next day, 3/8 Punjab had advanced its positions two miles to the Perugia airfield. Behind 3/8 Punjab, 1st Argyll and Sutherland Highlanders had also moved up from Bevagna with the object of occupying Assisi. Although the town itself was not defended, machine gun posts below Assisi covered the roads leading up the side of the hill on which the town stood. In pouring rain, a company deployed through the vine-yards and olive groves. This threat was sufficient to make the Germans withdraw. Assisi was then occupied without further trouble. The people of Assisi were so jubilant that they quite overwhelmed the Argylls and prevented their adopting tactical positions. As a consequence when, later, the Germans shelled the town quite heavily six casualties were sustained. From Assisi, one company reconnoitred to the bridge over the Chiascio at Petrignano. On finding it blown, the company was recalled and the whole battalion concentrated two miles south-west of Assisi.

The Ripa Ridge

With the 6th British Armoured Division closing in on Perugia from the south and the 8th Indian Division from the east (both barely six miles from the city), the X Corps had all but fulfilled the task, which the Army Commander had assigned to it on 7 June. The 6th British Armoured Division was now instructed, after securing Perugia, to strike north-westwards along Route 75 and the northern shores of Lake Trasimene. The Indian division was told to block the northern exits from Perugia east of the Tiber, and then to advance northwards up the Tiber valley, where the river would be the boundary between the two divisions.[4]

Major-General Russell now ordered the 17th Indian Infantry Brigade to lead the advance, and secure the high ground east and north-east of Perugia while the 19th Indian Infantry Brigade was to

[4] X Corps O.I. No. 41, 17 June 1944.

secure its left flank as far north as the general line Petrignano—S. Egidio. The latter was also instructed to clear the area immediately north and north-east of Foligno and to protect the divisional right flank forward of Assisi. The 21st Indian Infantry Brigade was to be in reserve. The 6th Lancers (less one squadron under the command of the 17th Indian Infantry Brigade) was to operate on the left flank, maintaining touch with the 6th British Armoured Division. The 12th Lancers was to operate on the right flank, carrying out deep reconnaissance from Foligno along Route 3 towards Fabriano, and the Adriatic coast around Ancona.

Having moved forward from Fara, the 17th Indian Infantry Brigade assembled south of Assisi on 17 June and prepared to lead the advance the next day. It may be recalled that 3/8 Punjab had spent the night of 17/18 June expanding its bridge-head west of the river Chiascio. By 0700 hours on 18 June, patrols from B Squadron 6th Lancers and 3/8 Punjab were established on the arc of a circle running through Petrignano—the airfield—Ospedalicchio, and Tactical Headquarters 17th Indian Infantry Brigade had opened in the vicinity of Bastiola.

Progress with the Bailey bridge over the Chiascio, alongside the destroyed bridge which carried Route 75, had been slower than expected. However, and in spite of the flooded state of the river, the 17th Indian Infantry Brigade was able to cross by the ford, south of the bridge. The effect of the rain on diversions the previous day and a shortage of troop carrying vehicles had considerably hampered the forward concentration of the 17th Indian Infantry Brigade.

When 1st Royal Fusiliers crossed the Chiascio at 0900 hours on 18 June, in the van of the 17th Indian Infantry Brigade, the battalion was still without one company which had not yet arrived from Fara. Across the river, 1st Royal Fusiliers turned north along the river road and headed for Ripa, via Petrignano. This task had originally been allotted to 1/5 Royal Gurkha Rifles but the Gurkhas had been delayed in starting from Fara by the non-arrival of their transport company vehicles. They had then lost a further eleven hours on the way owing to heavy rain. It was 0615 hours on 18 June when the battalion eventually arrived in its assembly area south of Assisi.

A thick curtain of rain was still falling as the 1st Royal Fusiliers deployed west of the river. Ahead of it, barring the path northwards, was a ridge, one thousand feet higher than the surrounding country and stretching for five miles from the river Chiascio on the east to the river Tiber on the west. South of the ridge, the wide stretch of cultivated land and airfield was almost completely devoid of cover. On the crest of the ridge and evenly dividing its length were two strongly built villages, Ripa and Civitella d' Arno. Its strength and its location made the ridge a key feature for further operations. The task of 1st Royal Fusiliers was to secure Ripa and of 1/5 Royal Gurkha Rifles to capture Civitella d' Arno.

The 1st Royal Fusiliers reached Petrignano by 1000 hours, without incident, but north of the village the battalion was subjected to shelling. For this reason the advance became much slower. At approximately 1300 hours, one company entered Torchiagina, and soon afterwards the German infantry was reported to be holding the line of the track, a front of nearly one mile, midway between Torchiagina and Ripa. Two companies were detailed to attack these German positions with full artillery support at 1530 hours.

One company, on the right, attacked almost due north. By 1645 hours it had reached the bend in the road at Casanova, two thousand yards east of Ripa. There it was pinned down by German mortar and machine gun fire from the north-west and was unable to move forward or backward. On its left, the second company attacked due west from Torchiagina. Little opposition was encountered until the track half-way to Ripa was crossed. Then the company came under concentrated machine gun fire. In battalion headquarters, where the commanding officer had already been wounded by shell fire, news was received that all the officers and a number of other ranks had become casualties, the company commander being killed. Command of the company was assumed by the officer commanding anti-tank platoon. A third company and two tanks were put into the attack on the left of this company at 1730 hours. Continued pressure carried the two companies forward to the cross tracks, only five hundred yards south of Ripa. There again they were halted by mortar and machine gun fire.

This advance on the left had, however, helped the company on the right which, at 1920 hours, advanced towards the road junction, one thousand yards north-east of Ripa. Unfortunately, opposition again stiffened. German shelling and mortaring became intense. Eventually, the company was compelled to withdraw to the road bend at Casanova.

Meanwhile 1/5 Royal Gurkha Rifles was hammering at the strong German position at Civitella d' Arno. Crossing the Chiascio by the Bailey bridge the Gurkhas concentrated in area S. Egidio. At 1715 hours they advanced from this forming up place to attack Civitella d' Arno, from whose prominent tower there was a commanding view over the country to the north and south. A Company was directed on Civitella d' Arno itself while B Company made for the road and ridge running south-west from the village. Each company was supported by one troop of tanks of the North Irish Horse, who had replaced the 142nd Royal Armoured Corps. The weather continued bad and German shelling was intense. Nevertheless, by 1900 hours, B Company was on the road south-west of Civitella d' Arno after brushing aside slight opposition. But A Company met stiffer resistance. Its tanks were hampered by mines and poor visibility. Germans, lying up in the cemetery at the crossroads with bazookas, knocked out two of the tanks, and the North Irish Horse had suffered ten casualties. To offset these losses, the Gurkhas captured intact a 75-mm Anti-Tank Gun. At 2110 hours, A and B Companies were astride the crossroads and C Company had been sent forward to positions astride the road, one thousand yards to the south-east. D Company remained with the Battalion Headquarters at S. Egidio. During the night, A Company extended its gains and, by 0400 hours on 19 June, was in Civitella d' Arno, which stood four hundred yards north of the crossroads. This advance by the Gurkhas may seem slow, but it appears to have been too quick for the Germans because in several places, where they had prepared holes for their mines, the mines had not been laid. While the 1st Royal Fusiliers and 1/5 Royal Gurkha Rifles were launching attacks on Ripa and Civitella d' Arno, B Squadron 6th Lancers was employed in reconnoitring tracks towards Ripa between the two battalions and was frequently and heavily shelled.

After dark on 18 June, patrols from 1st Royal Fusiliers and 1/5 Royal Gurkha Rifles felt their way towards Ripa but were repulsed by a firmly established German force. Both battalions were heavily shelled at intervals throughout the night and when daylight came there was little improvement in their position. 1st Royal Fusiliers and B Squadron 6th Lancers continued their activity around Ripa but with no success.

1/5 Royal Gurkha Rifles, on the other hand, was still pushing ahead. C Company moved forward at 0715 hours on 19 June from the south of Civitella d' Arno through the two forward companies and descended the hillside in a westerly direction to occupy a group of houses, fifteen hundred yards west of Civitella d' Arno. Three quarters of an hour later, A Company moved north from the village down the slopes and up again to Palazzo, on the next ridge, fifteen hundred yards north of Civitella d' Arno. There was a marked increase in the German shelling and mortaring but prisoners stated that the suddenness and speed of these advances had prevented the Germans from occupying new positions.

At 1015 hours on 19 June, as Ripa was still holding out against 1st Royal Fusiliers and B Squadron 6th Lancers, the Gurkhas were ordered to attack it from the west. D Company came up from the reserve for this task. Tanks, which had been reconnoitring along the road towards Ripa, had already lost three of their number, having been knocked out by an anti-tank gun hidden in Ripa. D Company was preceded by a fierce artillery concentration and accompanied by

B Squadron 6th Lancers and tanks of the North Irish Horse when it jumped off at 1100 hours. Surrounding Ripa and blocking all approaches to it, the Germans had prepared adequate defensive positions. From their trenches on a clear day, they had an excellent view over the approaches from the east, south and west. The troops in Ripa were, however, by now badly shaken and in the face of this new threat withdrew northwards. Then D Company reached Ripa at 1140 hours without suffering a single casualty. Thus both Ripa and Civitella d' Arno were secured. At 1200 hours, however, a German counter-attack developed against C Company, fifteen hundred yards west of Civitella d' Arno. A German company crossed the Tibet from the west in full view of C Company, who opened a powerful fire with light machine guns, medium machine guns and artillery, inflicting casualties on the attackers, ten of whom were made prisonners.

In the reorganisation which followed the capture of Ripa, 1st Royal Fusiliers became responsible for the saddle from the road junction (W 801954) to Ripa inclusive, a distance of one mile in a straight line. D Company of 1/5 Royal Gurkha Rifles was withdrawn from Ripa to strengthen the battalion positions around Civitella d' Arno. Although the Ripa ridge had been secured the 17th Indian Infantry Brigade was up against considerable opposition from strong German positions between the Tiber and the Chiascio, the three chief positions being Pianello on the right, Belvedere in the middle and Bosco on the left. By 20 June, in fact, German resistance had stiffened all along the wide Allied front. The battle of the Trasimene Line was about to commence.

The Trasimene Line

Only within two weeks after the fall of Rome on 4 June 1944, Field-Marshal Kesselring had succeeded in reorganising his forces and forming a fairly coherent defence line across Italy, known as the Trasimene Line. Stiff German resistance on this line held up the Allied progress till the end of the month, and this was in keeping with Field-Marshal Kesselring's purpose to withdraw, under cover of delaying actions, to a strong defence line in the high Apennines, the Rimini-Pisa line or more popularly known as the Gothic Line.

As a result of this reorganisation, *Army Group 'C'* had its headquarters at Monsumano, south-west of Pistoia and comprised the *Tenth* and *Fourteenth Armies* (whose boundary line followed the axis Orvieto—Montepulciano) and *Armeegruppe von Zangen*. The *Army Group* had nineteen divisions in the line and six in reserve. Of the two corps of the *Tenth Army*, the *LI Mountain Corps* held the sector from the Adriatic coast to Foligno with four divisions in the line, and the *LXXVI Panzer Corps* extended as far as Lake

Chiusi with its seven divisions in the line. Of the two corps of the *Fourteenth Army*, the *I Parachute Corps* held the sector Montepulciano—Montalcino with four divisions while the *XIV Panzer Corps* was on the west coast with another four divisions in the line. One division was in Corps reserve and three divisions were re-forming in Army Group reserve. *Armeegruppe von Zangen* had under command the *LXXV Corps* (holding the Tuscan and Ligurian coast with two divisions) and *Adriatic Coast Command* (guarding north-east Italy and Slovenia with one division).[5]

On 20 June 1944, when the Allied forces in Italy closed up to the Trasimene Line, they comprised the American Fifth Army, the British Eighth Army and two corps under Headquarters Allied Armies in Italy, viz., the II Polish Corps and the British V Corps. On the west coast, the American Fifth Army had advanced on a front of about fifty miles, with the IV Corps on the left and the French Expeditionary Corps on the right. To the right of the Fifth Army, the Eighth Army had advanced on a broad front with two corps on either side of the Tiber (the XIII Corps had reached the southern shores of Lake Trasimene and the X Corps had secured Perugia and Ripa). The II Polish Corps (which had taken over from the V Corps on the Adriatic coast on 18 June) was under the command of Headquarters Allied Armies in Italy. The Polish Corps had advanced north of Teramo and on 20 June had captured S. Benedetto and Grottammare. The V Corps was in reserve.

Taking advantage of the hilly and generally thickly cultivated country, the Germans offered stiff resistance on the Trasimene Line from 20 to 30 June. At the end of June the line was breached although mopping up operations continued still about 3 July. The Fifth Army made considerable progress; the IV Corps on the left captured Cecina on 2 July while the French Expeditionary Corps on the right secured Siena on 3 July. The Eighth Army, however, encountered extremely stiff opposition. The XIII Corps, forming the spearhead of the Eighth Army's attack, advanced up the Route 71, while the X Corps maintained pressure east of Lake Trasimene. The Germans had prepared a series of defences in depth between Lake Trasimene and Lake Chiusi. Three German divisions (the *334th Infantry Division, 1st Parachute Division,* and *Hermann Goering Division*) and part of a fourth division barred the way of the XIII Corps and offered stubborn resistance to its advance. The XIII Corps, however, launched vigorous attacks and after fierce opposition broke through the strong German defences, clearing Montepulciano and the northern shore of Lake Trasimene.

While the XIII Corps played the leading role in the attack on

---

[5] Order of Battle of German Forces in Italy on 20 June 1944.

the Trasimene Line, the X Corps had the secondary role of maintaining pressure on the Germans on its wide front of about twenty miles. Three German divisions held this front which stretched from the east shore of Lake Trasimene, through M. Passiano, across the river Tiber three miles north-east of Perugia, and thence to the bend in the river Chiascio at Pianello. The *15th Panzer Grenadier Division* held the western sector as far east as M. Rentella, the *94th Infantry Division* was in the centre to the west bank of the Tiber and the *44th Infantry Division* guarded the eastern sector to the river Chiascio. The last was also responsible for a stretch of mountain country, south-west to the mountain massif north of Assisi, where the *5th Mountain Division* was concentrated.

At the same time the X Corps led the attack on the German positions with two divisions in the line—the 6th British Armoured Division on the left and the 8th Indian Division on the right. The former was responsible for the sector between the Tiber and Route 71 (which was inter-corps boundary inclusive to the XIII Corps) and had the double task of exploiting north-west from Perugia to cut Route 71 at the north-western corner of Lake Trasimene, and advancing north to secure the high ground at M. Tezio to protect the left flank of the 8th Indian Division. The task of the 8th Indian Division was to secure the ring of hills, east of the Tiber, where the Germans had taken up strong defensive positions. The 12th Lancers, operating under command of the 8th Indian Division on its right flank, had the task of blocking the roads leading to the Tiber valley from the east and north-east as the advance progressed.

8th Indian Division's Exploitation on the Ripa Ridge

The story now reverts to the activities of the 8th Indian Division. This division did not play a very important part in the battle of the Trasimene Line. It was the XIII Corps, the spearhead of the Eighth Army attack, which had the major role. The role of the X Corps, to which this division belonged, was a lesser one of maintaining pressure on the German forces and keeping level with the advance of the XIII Corps. Consequently the 8th Indian Division consolidated its position on the Ripa ridge preparatory to an advance northwards along the Tiber valley to Umbertide. After the 17th Indian Infantry Brigade had secured Ripa and Civitella d'Arno on 18-19 June, it came up against stiffening opposition from three strong German positions between the Tiber and Chiascio (i.e. Pianello on the right, Belvedere in the centre and Bosco on the left). The 17th Indian Infantry Brigade reorganised preparatory to an attack on these strong positions. On 19 June, 1/5 Royal Gurkha Rifles (from area Civitella d'Arno) probed into German defences at Bosco. At 1245 hours on 19 June, C Company passed through A Company's

17 IND INF BDE'S ATTACK ON RIPA RIDGE
18-19 JUNE 1944

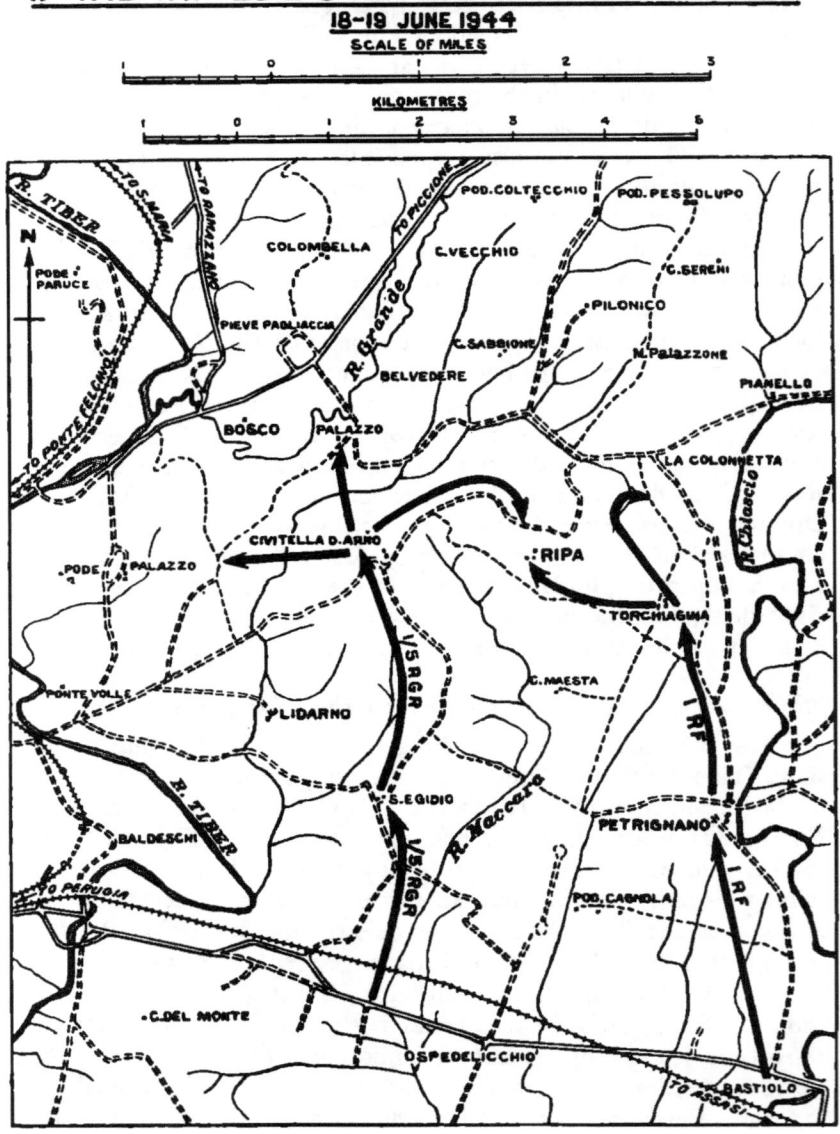

position at Palazzo in order to cross the river Grande. An hour later, B Company moved northwards from the road, west of Civitella d'Arno, to another crossing over the river Grande at Bosco, one mile west of A and C Companies. At 1430 hours, A Company advanced to the river from Palazzo in an attempt to capture Pieve Pagliaccia. All these three attempts to cross the river Grande failed. All bridges over the river had been destroyed. The Germans had registered the river line and were consequently able to check the advance of the Gurkhas by heavy and sustained fire at the river crossings. The forward companies were therefore withdrawan by the evening to Civitella d'Arno.

On the Gurkhas' western flank, the gap which had been created by the movements of B and C Companies towards the river Grande had been filled by the arrival of 1/12 Frontier Force Regiment. This battalion, having concentrated during the morning on 19 June at S. Egidio, advanced from there at 1630 hours to clear the area north-west of S. Egidio as far as the line Bosco-Ponte Valle. Before dark, the two forward companies had reached a line running from the road junction two miles south-west of Civitella d'Arno, southwards to the easterly loop in the Tiber. The advance of these two companies had been slowed up by German shelling and mines and by a German strong point in Ponte Valle. Bosco, nearly three miles to the north-east was still in German hands. Simultaneously on the eastern flank of the 17th Indian Infantry Brigade, 1st Royal Fusiliers had reorganised with the battalion (less one company) in and around Ripa, and one company had secured the road junction at La Colonetta, one mile north-east of Ripa.

Efforts were directed during the day (20 June) towards softening up the German resistance by an artillery pounding of their positions on the general line Pianello—Bosco. Infantry battalions were to be prepared to take immediate advantage of any German withdrawals caused by this fire. Under cover of the fire, 1st Royal Fusiliers occupied Pianello, and was then relieved on the eastern flank by 6/13 Royal Frontier Force Rifles (19th Indian Infantry Brigade) and concentrated five hundred yards north-west of Ripa. 1/5 Royal Gurkha Rifles remained in area Palazzo while 1/12 Frontier Force Regiment moved to a new area between Ripa and Civitella d' Arno. The task for 1/12 Frontier Force Regiment was to take advantage of the pounding by the divisional artillery and to advance to Columbella. An intermediate objective was the ridge of high ground on which stood Belvedere, running north and south along the east bank of the river Grande. 1st Royal Fusiliers was to be prepared to pass through 1/12 Frontier Force Regiment, and 1/5 Royal Gurkha Rifles was to assist 1/12 Frontier Force Regiment by every possible means. The country consisted of open, rolling agricultural land, with fields of ripe standing corn. Lines of trees along the banks of the numerous streams provided almost the only cover, to which the depths of the banks added some further protection. German mortars paid considerable attention to such streams.

1/12 Frontier Force Regiment's attack, beginning at 1915 hours with artillery and tank support,[6] must have been clearly observed by the Germans for they shelled the leading companies furiously. The German positions were not accurately known but they were estimated to contain a number of machine gun and mortar posts. One company, B, led the attack in order to secure first the ridge between the two streams, eight hundred yards south-east of Belvedere. Within the hour, this had been achieved but B Company commander then reported that his eastern flank was being threatened. Two more companies were immediately sent forward, A Company to exploit eastwards along the road in the direction of the front now held by 6/13 Royal Frontier Force Rifles, D Company to advance northwards, along the ridge just captured by B Company, to the line of the east-west track through C. Sabbione. B Company continued the attack to the north-west and, by 2145 hours, had captured Belvedere. But there the battalion was ordered to consolidate, its flanks being exposed to attack from east and west.

The following morning (21 June), while 1/12 Frontier Force Regiment and its tanks were busily engaged in liquidating German machine gun posts on Belvedere ridge, two companies from 1st Royal Fusiliers moved up to relieve 1/12 Frontier Force Regiment of its responsibilities on the line of the road, one mile north of Ripa. Throughout the next day, the Fusiliers endured almost continuous shelling. Meanwhile, in the 17th Indian Infantry Brigade's easterly sector, good progress had been made. 6/13 Royal Frontier Force Rifles had companies widely deployed—one in Pianello, the second on Pt. 437 (M. Palazzone), the third at the road junction, one thousand yards north of Ripa, and the fourth with Battalion Headquarters in Ripa. The hill running north from Pt. 437 was a broad, open feature covered with ripened corn, which showed up clearly for miles around any movement by troops through the corn. A patrol to the higher crest, Pt. 450, at midday found it unoccupied but was heavily shelled. Another patrol to the same area that evening found the Germans occupying the crest in some length.

Throughout the day (21 June), the four battalions between Pianello and the Tiber, endured particularly heavy fire from German artillery, mortars and machine guns. Moreover a strong German counter-attack developed at 1000 hours against B Company 1/12 Frontier Force Regiment at Belvedere. This attack was preceded by

---

[6] Two troops North Irish Horse.

furious mortaring. However, artillery, tanks and small arms fire combined to inflict so many casualties on the Germans that the attack wavered, halted and then receded. There were good reasons for assuming that the Germans across that whole of the 8th Indian Division's front had sustained quite considerable casualties. But they still had the advantage of observation, particularly from M. Croce, west of the Tiber, south of which the 6th British Armoured Division had, for the present, been halted.

There was little change in the situation on 22 June. German shelling continued but with slightly less ferocity. The two flanking units were most actively engaged. At midday, 6/13 Royal Frontier Force Rifles reported that its sub-unit on Pt. 437 (a platoon of D Company) had been compelled to fall back two hundred yards from the crest, when shells from their supporting medium guns fell on their positions. The Germans saw these shells falling on Pt. 437, assumed that the height was no longer occupied and sent one of their patrols to hold it. The Frontier Force platoon promptly counter-attacked and reoccupied the position.

On the western flank, the day's activities reached a climax in the evening. The company of 1/5 Royal Gurkha Rifles in the bridge-head at Bosco was subjected to a sharp burst of shelling from a heavy gun and its forward platoon was compelled to withdraw. Shortly afterwards, some thirty Germans attacked the company in the rear, having apparently filtered across the river Grande farther to the west. For a time, the Germans had the advantage of surprise. When a platoon was sent across from another company, the Gurkhas counter-attacked, regained all lost ground and expanded their bridge-head. A second platoon from the same company, D, was sent up to help in the reorganisation.

For the next three days (23-25 June) the 8th Indian Division strengthened the positions gained, while awaiting the capture of the dominating M. Croce by the 6th British Armoured Division west of the Tiber. Behind the 17th Indian Infantry Brigade, the remainder of the 8th Indian Division was closing up for further attacks. On 24 June, the 21st Indian Infantry Brigade moved up on the left of the 17th Indian Infantry Brigade. The 5th Royal West Kent Regiment relieved 1/5 Royal Gurkha Rifles in area Palazzo that night. The other battalions of the 21st Indian Infantry Brigade bivouacked one mile south-west of Civitella d'Arno, while 1/5 Royal Gurkha Rifles concentrated at Torchiagina.

The 12th Lancers was still patrolling north-east from Foligno and making little progress against the *5th Mountain Division*. In those mountainous areas the armoured cars, being confined to the roads, were at a disadvantage. Occasionally, vehicles were knocked out by German guns or mines, but their task was an essential one and enabled the 8th Indian Division to concentrate its infantry against the more vital Tiber valley positions held by the Germans. On the division's western flank, the 6th Lancers was responsible for maintaining contact across the Tiber with the 6th British Armoured Division. The 25th Army Tank Brigade having now been ordered out of the battle to rest and refit, on 24 June the North Irish Horse was replaced in support of the 8th Indian Division by the 3rd Kings Own Hussars, of the 9th Armoured Brigade.

The next attack by the 8th Indian Division was planned to be a two-brigade affair.[7] In the first instance, the 17th Indian Infantry Brigade on the right, and the 21st Indian Infantry Brigade on the left, were to advance north-west to the line of high ground Piccione—Colombella. Thereafter, the 21st Indian Infantry Brigade was to continue another four miles to the north-west and occupy the high ground between Morleschio and Civitella. The 6th British Armoured Division, west of the Tiber, was to advance at the same time to M. Tezio, six miles north of Perugia, in order to protect the 8th Indian Division's left flank. But the 8th Indian Division could not carry out this attack until the 6th British Armoured Division had cleared the Germans from the crest of the dominating M. Croce, in the eastward loop of the Tiber, four miles north-east of Perugia. But before the Armoured Division could capture M. Croce, the 8th Indian Division was ordered to stand fast and to prepare to be relieved by another formation, the 10th Indian Division.

The disappointment caused by this cancellation of the attack was lessened somewhat when Major-General Russell decided to carry out a part of the plan in order to make the task of the 10th Indian Division easier. He ordered that the 3rd Hussars, with full artillery support, would carry out a raid in force along the line of the road from Ripa to Piccione. In the 17th Indian Infantry Brigade, 1st Royal Fusiliers and 1/5 Royal Gurkha Rifles were to be prepared to support the tanks and to take advantage of any success achieved. In the 21st Indian Infantry Brigade, west of the 17th Indian Infantry Brigade, the 5th Royal West Kent Regiment was to be prepared to complete the task originally allotted to 1/12 Frontier Force Regiment, i.e., to occupy Colombella via Pieve Pagliaccia.

The 3rd Hussars accordingly advanced through the 17th Indian Infantry Brigade, at 1000 hours on 26 June, with two squadrons up. An elaborate, but flexible, artillery programme, employing divisional artillery,[8] 3rd Medium Regiment Royal Artillery and one battery 1st Royal Horse Artillery (self-propelled) had been prepared with so many registered targets that supporting fire could be provided

---

[7] 8 Ind. Div. O.O. No. 21, 24 June 1944.

[8] One Regiment had to be prepared to support the 19 Ind. Inf. Bde. east of Pianello.

immediately on receipt of the call from the 3rd Hussars. C Squadron 3rd Hussars, on the right, kept to the high ground running north from Pt. 437, while A Squadron moved in the lower ground to the west, astride the road. The operation was an outstanding success. The Germans were completely surprised and disorganised. They were prepared to deal with an infantry attack but appeared to be unable to withstand an armoured assault in such strength. As C Squadron approached Pt. 450, German infantry deserted their slit trenches and ran off in all directions under concentrated machine gun fire from the tanks. By midday, C Squadron was half a mile north of Pt. 450.

Along the road, A Squadron met considerable opposition from German positions on the line, Pt. 450—Palazzetta. But here, too, the Germans eventually broke and ran across conveniently open country. At 1400 hours, A Squadron had reached Pod Coltecchio, and during the afternoon the troop of B Squadron, with 1/12 Frontier Force Regiment at Belvedere, reported parties of Germans withdrawing westwards across the river Grande in the vicinity of C. Vecchio. On the road south of Piccione, tank crew spotted and engaged a column of German transport, mules and guns, which was just pulling out in great disorder.

After the tanks had run riot, 1st Royal Fusiliers and 1/5 Royal Gurkha Rifles advanced at 1600 hours. By 2115 hours they had pushed forward two miles against slight opposition. 1st Royal Fusiliers was on the spur running down to the road from Pod Passolupo, and 1/5 Royal Gurkha Rifles was deployed along the ridge through Pod Coltecchio. One company of 1/12 Frontier Force Regiment moved up on the west flank of the Gurkha Rifles to clear a wood still held by the Germans just north of C. Vecchio. Two attempts during the night failed, but a third attack with tanks, at dawn on 27 June, finally routed the Germans. This company then took up positions at the head of the valley, midway between Pod Coltecchio and C. Vecchio.

The attack by the 21st Indian Infantry Brigade on Colombella did not meet with a similar success. The German garrison there was least touched by the events happening east of the river Grande and refused to yield ground. One company of the 5th Royal West Kent Regiment advanced under cover of darkness on 26 June and occupied Pieve Pagliaccia without opposition. But when this company continued its advance further through the woods to Colombella, on its ridge top, the Germans put down a concentration of mortar and machine gun fire. Contact was made with their positions on the south-west edge of the village at 0400 hours. For an hour or so, bitter fighting ensued. At 0530 hours on 27 June, the company, having suffered a number of casualties, was withdrawn to Pieve

Pagliaccia, and Colombella was then subjected to a heavy bombardment by the divisional artillery. Meanwhile the 19th Indian Infantry Brigade (less 6/13 Royal Frontier Force Rifles) was engaged in clearing up the hill area between Assisi and Pianello.

The relief of the 8th Indian Division by the 10th Indian Division was carried out between 28 and 30 June. Command of the sector passed to the 10th Indian Division at midnight 29/30 June. Headquarters 8th Indian Division moved to Carpello, a mile and a half south-east of Foligno. On 30 June, the 12th Lancer's area of responsibility was extended westward to the R. Chiascio and the 19th Indian Infantry Brigade concentrated two miles south-east of Assisi. The 8th Indian Division was thus free, for the present, of all operational commitments. Excluding the very short rest after the crossing of the river Gari, the division had been continuously in contact with the Germans since October 1943.

These few weeks of pursuit through central Italy had begun and ended with tough fighting. In between had been skirmishes of various proportions. Country and climate, despite the season of the year, had combined occasionally to handicap the pursuers. To that a skilled and desperate enemy had added the obstacles presented by broken bridges, demolished buildings and collapsed hillsides, the value of which the mountainous nature of the country served to accentuate. None the less, the pursuit had never flagged. If the road were blocked, the diversion left its vehicles and advanced on foot. Seldom was contact with the Germans lost. All arms conbined skilfully and energetically to harass the Germans and to allow them no respite. Only when the pursuit reached the Tiber valley, between Assisi and Perugia, was the 8th Indian Division finally checked. The last exploit of the division before its relief indicate that the advance was about to begin again.

The 17th Indian Infantry Brigade, which had borne the brunt of the fighting for the Ripa ridge, had suffered three hundred and thirty casualties, including twenty officers.[9] These figures are about three-fifths of the brigade's losses at the river Gari and were largely due to the great activity of German mortars and artillery. The German infantry, with orders to hold out to the last, had fought most stubbornly. Their losses in men and material had been considerable.

Advance up the Adriatic Coast

Having described the role of the Indian formations of the Eighth Army in the pursuit north of Rome, we may now give a brief account of the advance up the Adriatic coast of the 4th Indian Division in the V Corps sector. On 3 June 1944, at midday, the 4th

---

[9] Report by the 17 Ind. Inf. Bde.

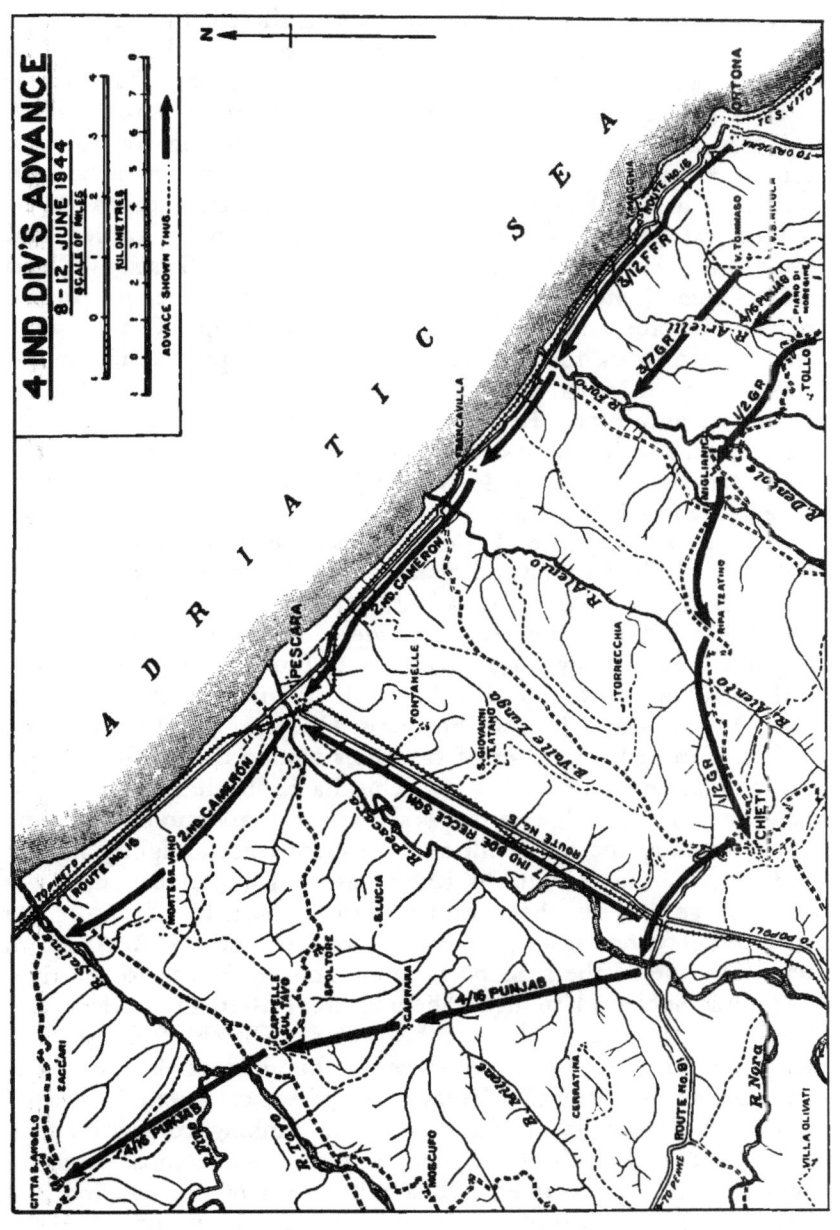

Indian Division took over the front held by the 10th Indian Division. The division had two brigades in the forward line, the 5th Indian Infantry Brigade in the Crecchio sector and the 7th Indian Infantry Brigade in the Villa Grande sector. The troops of the 4th Indian Division probed into German defences. At last, on 7 June (three days after the Allied forces had entered Rome) came the news which had been awaited for so long—the German forces on the Adriatic front were withdrawing. The V Corps plan was to secure the road Pescara—Chieti, including the two places. The advance was to be mounted along two routes, the coast road, Route 16 (called Red Route) and the inland road through Tollo—Ripa Teatina—Chieti (called Blue Route). Blue Route was allotted to the 7th Indian Infantry Brigade and the Italian Bersaglieri Group. Other Italian units were to work forward west of Blue Route, protecting the left flank of the 4th Indian Division. The 11th Indian Infantry Brigade was to advance along Red Route. One battalion was to use the inland tracks while the coast road became the brigade's axis. The 5th Indian Infantry Brigade was to be ready to follow the 11th Indian Infantry Brigade along Route 16.

The pursuit began on 8 June. Considerable progress was made by the 7th Indian Infantry Brigade along the road Villa Grande—Tollo. Both the forward battalions, 4/16 Punjab on the right and 1/2 Gurkha Rifles on the left, were ordered to advance abreast to the Miglianico ridge. By 1030 hours on 8 June, a company of 1/2 Gurkha Rifles had occupied Tollo, a village in no better condition than Ortona when the war had passed beyond it. Widely sown minefields caused a number of casualties among the leading troops. 4/16 Punjab, on the right of 1/2 Gurkha Rifles, had first to cross the valley and the ridge on the west flank of the Piano di Moregine before reaching the R. Arielli and therefore lagged slightly behind the Gurkhas. As 1/2 Gurkha Rifles entered Tollo, 4/16 Punjab was on the ridge between the stream and the R. Arielli, a front of one mile. At 1200 hours, as 4/16 Punjab was crossing the R. Arielli to secure the line of the road north from Tollo to Route 16 the river valley was subjected to light shelling from German artillery and mortars. At that time the spearhead of 1/2 Gurkha Rifles moving along the road west from Tollo was one hundred yards east of the crossing over the torrent La Veena, having been considerably delayed by mines and craters on the road. The flanking companies had, however, outpaced this platoon on the road. One company was on the west bank of the river, half a mile north of the crossing and another half a mile south of it. By nightfall of 8 June, the two battalions were firmly established on the line of the road north and south through Tollo, 1/2 Gurkha Rifles having been recalled to this line.

By the morning of 9 June, a diversion had been made in the vicinity of the Tollo bridge over the Arielli, the bridge having been completely demolished by the Germans, and battalion anti-tank guns and carriers had been taken across. Gurkha patrols, which had entered Miglianico without contacting the Germans, were reinforced to one company strength. By 0830 hours, 1/2 Gurkha Rifles, still advancing along the line of the Blue Route starting from Tollo at 0600 hours, had completely occupied Miglianico. Its two forward companies were pushing on to Ripa Teatina, a village on a very prominent ridge, two and a half miles west of the next river, the Foro. At 1500 hours on 9 June as the two forward companies crossed the R. Foro, their patrols contacted German rearguards in heavily mined and wired positions on the high ground overlooking the river from the west. A platoon of D Company, on the right, rushed the German posts and killed eight of the occupants. In meeting the German counter-attack, which was delivered almost immediately, the Gurkhas killed two more, all without loss to themselves. By 1615 hours the German rearguard was in full flight. Subsequently, however, 1/2 Gurkha Rifles found entry into Ripa Teatina blocked by a large crater on the narrow ridge, only a few hundred yards north-east of the village. Consequently, it was not until dusk that evening, that the first troops entered Ripa Teatina. There was to be no rest. Patrols were probing towards the next river, the Alento, and over it in the direction of Chieti, where partisans were busy taking their revenge on the retreating Germans. One Gurkha patrol pushed across country to enter Chieti at 2200 hours on 9 June.

Neither the 7th nor the 11th Indian Infantry Brigade could rest because the race for Pescara was entering its last lap. Eight o'clock on the morning of 10 June found the Gurkhas already in Chieti, where they had delirious welcome from the population. They immediately pushed on with tanks to the R. Pescara. Their crossing of the river caught the Germans unawares. A Squadron 8th Battalion Royal Tank Regiment, in support of the Gurkhas, shot up a party walking along the river bank, wounded one and took four prisoners. The 7th Indian Infantry Brigade sent ahead the Brigade Reconnaissance Squadron and a detachment of sappers. This squadron found the bridges over the river Pescara all blown up but entered the town, from the west, at 1530 hours. On the way in, a Sherman tank destroyed two German 105-mm guns in concrete emplacements. Pescara was completely deserted and had been thoroughly looted. Its harbour contained numerous sea mines.

Meanwhile the leading troops of the 11th Indian Infantry Brigade were also converging on Pescara. Extensive minefields and damage on the roads and tracks had considerably slowed down its advance. 2/7 Gurkha Rifles used the inland track while 3/12 Royal Frontier Force Regiment advanced along the coast road. The former reached the R. Foro without encountering opposition and then was placed in brigade reserve. Along the coastal road 3/12 Royal Frontier Force Regiment occupied Francavilla and its forward detachments were on the river Alento when 2nd Cameron took over the lead. The Cameron patrol entered Pescara at 1730 hours on 10 June, two hours after the 7th Indian Brigade Reconnaissance Squadron had entered it.

4/16 Punjab now took over the lead in the 7th Indian Infantry Brigade. As Route 81 was found to be cratered the axis of advance was changed to the minor road running north-west from Route 81 crossing over the R. Pescara. At 1630 hours, the leading troops were in Caprara, six miles north-west of Chieti and were receiving a tumultuous welcome. Patrols of armour and infantry immediately pushed on to the next big village, Cappelle sul Tavo. As the first armoured vehicles reached the village, at 2000 hours, the Germans continued their demolitions, indicating that contact with them had been re-established. Infantry closed in on the village and had a short exchange of fire with the German party covering the demolitions. By 2115 hours on 11 June, this party had been driven back and one prisoner captured. On 12 June, 4/16 Punjab continued its advance northwards and at 1115 hours its leading elements were in Citta S. Angelo.

Meanwhile the 11th Indian Infantry Brigade had been advancing along the coastal road. 2nd Cameron took the lead. Before nightfall on 12 June, the battalion was deployed along the east bank of the R. Saline, from the road junction at the Montesilvano station which had been shelled by the Germans throughout the afternoon down to Montesilvano itself. German shelling of the Cameron area continued well into the night, causing a total of six casualties. While this advance was being made orders had been received at Divisional Headquarters on 12 June to consolidate on its present line in preparation for a relief by the 3rd Carpathian Division, the relief to be completed by 15 June. The 1st Carpathian Brigade moved into the 7th Indian Infantry Brigade sector on the night of 13/14 June and the 2nd Carpathian Brigade took over from the 11th Indian Infantry Brigade the following night, command of the divisional sector passing to the 3rd Carpathian Division at 0400 hours on 15 June 1944. The 5th Indian Brigade had already moved to Campobasso, in which area the rest of the month of June was devoted to training for mountain warfare.

CHAPTER XII

Advance to Citta di Castello

Regrouping of the Eighth Army

After the breach of the Trasimene Line, capture of Arezzo and Florence had become the next objectives owing to their importance as administrative and operational bases, respectively, for the attack on the Gothic Line, on the axis the Florence—Bologna Highway, and the road running through Firenzuola to Imola. The Fifth Army was considerably weakened by the transfer of several divisions for the invasion of southern France. Consequently the Eighth Army had become the spearhead of the Allied attack forward, and the XIII Corps was commissioned to occupy Arezzo, an important road centre. Naturally the Corps had to be strengthened to achieve this purpose, and that involved a regrouping of the Eighth Army. Moreover, the 6th British Armoured and the 8th Indian Divisions in the X Corps and the 78th Division in the XIII Corps required rest. Hence Lieutenant-General Leese decided to regroup the Eighth Army. The 10th Indian Division was to relieve the 8th Indian Division and the 6th British Armoured Division and thus take over the X Corps front. The depleted X Corps was to be strengthened later, when further reinforcements arrived. The 6th British Armoured Division was to be transferred to the XIII Corps. The task of the strengthened XIII Corps was to advance up Route 71 to capture Arezzo while the depleted X Corps had the subsidiary role of maintaining pressure astride the road Umbertide—Citta di Castello.

The Arezzo Line

Thrown back from the Trasimene Line at the end of June, the Germans fell back on a new defence line, which ran from Rosignano, on the west coast, to Volterra, from where it swung across the Val di Chiana to the mountainous regoin of Arezzo; on the east coast it was based on the key points, Filottrano and Osimo. By 5 July they had taken up positions on this line, which though broken on the flanks, held firm in the centre. By 9 July the Fifth Army had captured its objectives, Rosignano and Volterra. On the east coast, too, the II Polish Corps was successful in breaking through the general line Filottrano—Osimo by 10 July. In the centre, however, the Eighth Army failed to make much headway against strong

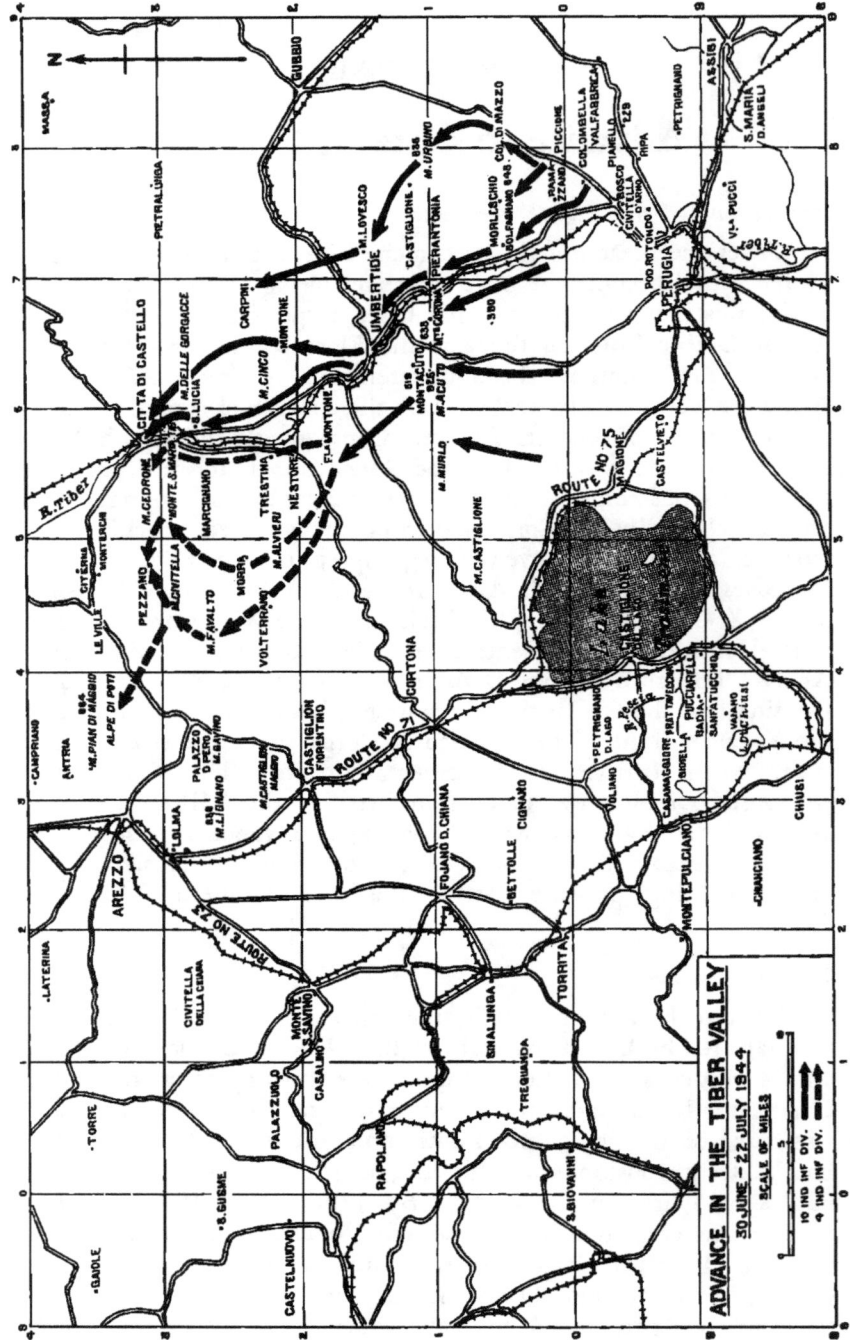

resistance. Four German divisions of the first quality, which had defended the Trasimene Line, now offered prolonged resistance to the advance of the XIII Corps towards Arezzo and it was not till 16 July that this important road centre was captured. The X Corps continued to maintain pressure astride the Tiber valley road through Umbertide and Citta di Castello. The initial advance was made by the 10th Indian Division, which secured Umbertide on 6 July and broke the German defence line based on Montone—Carpini on 7 July. Then the depleted X Corps was strengthened by the 4th Indian Division, which took over the 10th Indian Division's sector west of the Tiber on 8 July. The X Corps continued the advance towards Citta di Castello with the 10th Indian Division to the east and the 4th Indian Division to the west of the Tiber. The former made two thrusts towards Citta di Castello—one directed through M. Delle Gorgacce and the other through S. Lucia. M. Delle Gorgacce and S. Lucia were secured by 14 July but it was not till 22 July that Citta di Castello was captured. Meanwhile, west of the Tiber the 4th Indian Division had made three important thrusts —one directed on Monte S. Maria and M. Cedrone (which guarded Citta di Castello west of the Tiber), the second directed on Monterchi (to cut the lateral road from Citta di Castello to Arezzo) and the third directed on M. Favalto and Alpe di Poti (to threaten Arezzo from the east). M. Favalto and Monte S. Maria were secured by 13 July. Then a thrust was developed towards Alpe di Poti, thus threatening Arezzo from the east. This town, however, was captured by the XIII Corps on 16 July before this thrust could develop. Subsequently, the capture of Alpe di Poti on 17 July loosened the German hold on Pezzano, which barred the advance towards Monterchi. Simultaneously, the capture of M. Cedrone further weakened the German defence of Citta di Castello, which was secured by the 10th Indian Division on 22 July.

The 10th Indian Division in the Line

It is now necessary to describe in detail the progress of the Indian formations—the 10th Indian Division and the 4th Indian Division—towards Citta di Castello. The 10th Indian Division took over the X Corps front from the Pianello bridge over R. Chiascio to Lake Trasimene between 28 June and 2 July 1944. The sector from the Pianello bridge to excluding the river Tiber was taken over on 29 June by the 20th and 25th Indian Infantry Brigades. On 30 June/2 July the 10th Indian Infantry Brigade took over a long front extending for about ten miles west of the Tiber. The right flank of the Corps was covered by the 12th Lancers, and the left by the King's Dragoon Guards. The 10th Indian Division thus covered the X

Corps sector between the II Polish Corps on the Adriatic and the XIII Corps west of Lake Trasimene.[1]

The main advance of the 10th Indian Division was up the Tiber valley and astride the river until Citta di Castello was reached. From there the advance continued northwards but west of the Tiber on the high ground between this river and the Arno. Ahead of the division was an imposing array of mountains. Through the middle of this towering backbone of Italy flowed the river Tiber, south-eastwards from its source in the Alpe di Serra, sixty miles to the north. The Tiber valley was closely restricted to an average width of one mile by the foothills of the mountains, which dropped abruptly to the river level. On the eastern bank, the descent to the valley was less abrupt and the lateral valleys between the hills were wider than on the western bank. Away from the rivers, however, the lateral valleys developed into deep ravines.

Throughout the greater part of this stretch of the river, two roads, one on each bank, traversed the valley, up which ran a railway, more often on the eastern bank as far as Sansepolcro before turning west and south-west through Anghiari to Arezzo. The Tiber valley was studded with market towns and villages. The towns were based on old forts and were situated almost at river level. The villages, often clustered round their church with its prominent tower, were generally situated on the ridges and peaks above the valley.

The terrain was favourable to the Germans. To the east of the river Tiber, from Ripa immediately northwards, the hills were large and easy to move over. There were no definite ridges, but rather separate hill features, which were not over-steep. Further north, however, the hills and country became broken and knife-edged with steep and precipitous valleys running generally east and west, and very deep ravines cutting across the lower hills. West of the Tiber and running northwards were a series of long, high hogbacks, culminating in the pyramidical and bare feature of M. Acuto. From here onwards the terrain was quite different. Although a main hogback ridge continued north as far as M. Cedrone near Monte S. Maria, the hills west of this ran laterally across the line of advance and several valleys had to be crossed. From M. Cedrone due north the ground gradually dropped away until rising steeply to the Monte

---

[1] Under command of the 10 Ind. Div. were the following:—
    3rd King's Own Hussars
    1st King's Dragoon Guards
    A Battery 1st Royal Horse Artillery
    6th Army Jeep Platoon
    2 Pack Transport Company
    26 Indian Pack Transport Company.

In support of the Division were the following:—
    3rd Medium Regiment
    One Flight 654 OP Squadron.

Montazzo feature. West of M. Cedrone, however, the hills rose to about 3544 feet at M. Favalto.[2]

The Germans were withdrawing on the X Corps front on the axis Umbertide—Citta di Castello—Sansepolcro, with the *114th Jaeger Division* to the east and the *44th Infantry Division* to the west of the Tiber. The flanks of these formations were protected, on the east by the *5th Mountain Division*, which, although weak, was adequate to close the gap between the *44th Infantry Division* and the *15th Panzer Grenadier Division* which was moving on the axis Castiglione—Arezzo.[3] The German resistance became more determined on the high ground west of the Tiber, for they were more sensitive to any threat to Route 71 than to the Allied progress east of the river. Moreover, east of the Tiber, their communications were inadequate save for one main road running on the bank of the stream. The ground here was more easily defendable by small bodies of troops, as, unless a frontal attack was made, long and very arduous flanking movements by an attacking force had to be made over difficult and broken country. This was in fact exactly the method followed by the 10th Indian Division in overcoming German resistance in the eastern sector of the Tiber.

Although the ground throughout was suitable for defence, the Germans relied mainly on key features for offering stubborn resistance to the advance of the 10th Indian Division. In no case did they pull back until forced to do so and in no case did they withdraw long distances. Their rough lay-backs were:

(i) M. Tezio—Morleschio.
(ii) M. Murlo—M. Acuto—river Assino—M. Lovesco—Pt. 863 (cover the town of Umbertide).
(iii) M. Bastiola—Montone—M. Cucco—Carpini.

Difficult country (which the Germans stoutly defended) lay between this last lay-back and the positions covering Citta di Castello, this town being defended from the high ground Monte S. Maria—Cedrone—Uppiano—Pt. 407—Goffara, just north of the stream Sovara.[4]

Capture of Umbertide

When patrol activity on 29 June found no reaction on the part of the Germans, the 20th and 25th Indian Infantry Brigades, to the east of the Tiber, pushed northwards along the road Perugia—Umbertide—Citta di Castello on 30 June. Rapid progress was made and the 20th Indian Infantry Brigade reached Piccione and the high ground immediately to its north. 2/3 Gurkha exploited from the

[2] 10 Ind. Div.—Narrative of Operations,
[3] X Corps O.I. No. 43, 7 July 1944.
[4] 10 Ind. Div. Narrative of Operations.

area road junction one mile north of Ripa to Pt. 346 near Ramazzano. 4/10 Baluch in area Pianella scuppered a German post, about one mile north-east of Pianello. The 8th Manchester advancing from Pilonico met some opposition and they were heavily shelled in and around Piccione; so too were 3/5 Mahratta, who were moving up in brigade reserve behind the 8th Manchester. Observation posts in the hills, east of the Tiber valley, gave the Germans a perfect view of the country, over which the advance had taken place.

Nearer the Tiber, the 25th Indian Brigade made steady progress. 1st Battalion King's Own Royal Regiment and a squadron of the 3rd Hussars occupied Colombella at 1000 hours on 30 June. 3/1 Punjab moved forward behind the 1st King's Own Royal Regiment and passed through to occupy Ramazzano feature before last light.[5]

On 1 July the Germans broke contact on the 10th Indian Division front. On 2 July began the first of those outflanking moves through the mountains by which the 10th Indian Division was so often to deceive and defeat the Germans. This outflanking movement developed from Piccione. Covered by armoured reconnaissance patrols, which probed north-eastwards along the road to M. Moutolcino, 3/5 Mahratta climbed the hills immediately north of Piccione, held by the 8th Manchester, and headed for the prominent Col di Mazzo. There the battalion, instead of following up the armoured patrols, suddenly turned to the north-west and dived down into the tree covered depths of the chasm, through which flowed the torrent Ventia. At 1830 hours the Mahrattas reached M. Folone. On their left, 2/3 Gurkha moving over undulating ground of open farmsteads took Morleschio at 2240 hours on 2 July, and patrolled towards Montacutello. Near the Tiber, 3/1 Punjab pushing forward from Ramazzano during the night occupied Civitella at 0430 hours and Solfagnano at 2030 hours on 2 July without any opposition.

Under cover of darkness, 3/5 Mahratta advanced from M. Folone during the night of 2/3 July along the road, which ran in a horseshoe form along the top of the ridge, through M. Fiore to M. Urbino, a long, bald, rocky feature. There, the leading platoon, crossing the top of the feature, came across a German party, in the process of organising its positions. After a short struggle, the German post was destroyed by the first light on 3 July.

By the evening on 3 July, the forward elements of the 1st King's Own pushing forward of Solfagnano were just south of Pierantonio, but the attack on it and the hills to the north did not succeed.

To the west of the Tiber, too, the advance of the 10th Indian Infantry Brigade had come to a halt. The Germans did not make a stand at M. Tezzio, but made good use of the terrain and offered

[5] 25 Ind. Inf. Bde.—Review of operations since 29 June; War Diary 25 Ind. Inf. Bde. July 1944.

determined resistance from a naturally strong defensive position based on Monte Acuto and the adjoining height of M. Corona, which dominated the main road up the Tiber valley. In the night of 2/3 July, the 10th Indian Infantry Brigade was launched on a long range attack on M. Corona, M. Acuto and M. Murlo, which were the objectives of 3/18 Garhwal, 4/10 Baluch and 2/4 Gurkha respectively.

M. Murlo was held by about 70 Germans armed with light machine guns and supported by a self-propelled gun. In the attack on M. Murlo, 2/4 Gurkha was supported by a squadron of 3rd Hussars and one medium machine gun platoon of 1st Royal Northumberland Fusiliers. The 154th Field Regiment supported the attack. B Company of 2/4 Gurkha advanced from Castel Rigone at 0935 hours on 3 July and captured Pt. 818 (M. Murlo) at 1035 hours against spasmodic opposition. At 1120 hours C Company moved up to the left of Pt. 818 to support B Company then being heavily mortared. A German self-propelled gun was also firing. At 1330 hours a German counter-attack developed but it was held back and later the positions thus gained were consolidated.

Intelligence reports suggested that M. Acuto, a broad bald feature, was held by one German company. 4/10 Baluch concentrated just south of the village Pantano at 2100 hours on 2 July for the attack on M. Acuto. The Commander 4/10 Baluch made a plan by which B Company was to pass through Pantano and establish a firm base on feature near C. S. Martino by 2300 hours on 2 July; A Company was to advance on the right and capture M. Acuto by 0400 hours on 3 July; and D Company was to strike west and occupy Pt. 734 by 0500 hours on 3 July. Intelligence reports had stressed that only small parties of Germans were occupying M. Acuto and the surrounding features. B Company however encountered very stiff opposition on the feature near C. S. Martino. It was obvious that the German strength had been underestimated. Thereupon C Company, then in reserve, was also sent up to the support. A Company moved to the right for the attack on M. Acuto and after a stiff fight at the foot of the hill drove the Germans up the hill. One platoon remained at the foot of the hill to serve as a supply base for the remainder of the company while two platoons fought their way to the top at 0830 hours. The Germans counter-attacked the platoon at the foot of the hill but the attack was repulsed. Then the Germans infiltrated around the slopes of the hill, thus threatening to cut off the two platoons on the top. The situation of these platoons became untenable and therefore commander 4/10 Baluch ordered the officer commanding A Company at 0915 hours to extricate his force. The order was carried out and A Company eventually arrived back in a reserve position at Pantano at 1515 hours. D Company however succeeded in gaining the ground near Pt. 734, although it was shelled and mortared. A German counter-attack forming up near M. Acuto was broken up by 1500 hours by the 1st Medium Regiment and the 1st Field Regiment. The attempt of the Baluch to capture M. Acuto was a costly failure, for they suffered 32 casualties.

The attack on M. Corona by 3/18 Garhwal was also not successful. At 1400 hours on 3 July, a fighting patrol of A Company advancing from Pt. 590 to Pt. 506 was checked by German fire. The patrol was pinned down in spite of the fact that artillery fire was directed on German positions. It was only at 2310 hours that the patrol could be extricated.

The advance continued slowly east of the Tiber but it was held up on the 10th Indian Infantry Brigade front by the stubbornness of German resistance. They clung tenaciously to their commanding positions at M. Acuto and M. Corona. However, they had soon to retire from these positions when the town of Cortona fell to the XIII Corps on 3 July. The Germans on the heights overlooking the Tiber valley from the west had lost their escape routes to the northwest. There remained to them only the road running north in the Tiber valley. Moreover Pierantonio had also been occupied by the 1st King's Own on 4 July. With their defensive position covering Umbertide being thus penetrated, the Germans withdrew without further ado and fell back on line M. Bastiola—Montone—M. Cucco—Carpini.

Capture of Umbertide

After the capture of Pierantonio on 4 July, a fighting patrol of the 1st King's Own occupied the approaches to Umbertide on 5 July at 0420 hours. These consisted of a sprawling factory town of yellow and grey-walled houses with red roofs, encircling an ancient fort of massive construction. Umbertide was occupied by 3/1 Punjab before last light on 5 July and during the night patrols probing forward established contact with the Germans at Montone—a village, 4 to 5 miles further north.

Meanwhile the 12th Lancers was carrying on aggressive patrolling on the right flank of the 10th Indian Division. Two mobile columns operated in the mountains, one directed from Matelica on Fabriano and the other from Scritto on the country town of Gubbio, a picturesque collection of brightly coloured houses. Gubbio stood at the narrow entrance to the only route through the hills in this area. The gorge was narrow and its walls steep so that a small force could hold the pass indefinitely. The Germans were not pressed hard at Gubbio and they held that gateway for about a month against the patrols of the 12th Lancers.

Capture of Montone

After the breach of the defensive position covering Umbertide on 4 July, the Germans fell back on the next delaying position, M. Bastiola—Montone—M. Cucco—Carpini. They did not offer resistance at M. Bastiola but concentrated their efforts on Montone, the bastion of the new defensive position. The village of Montone, standing in a cluster of buildings on a peak above the valley, was an almost ideal defensive position. Its hill was the southernmost of a whole series of peaks, most of them two thousand feet high, stretching for miles to the north-east. At Montone, the ridge divided to contain a sharp eastward loop of the Tiber. Approaches to the village from south and west climbed narrow fairly open spurs, the greater part of which was in view from Montone. That stretch of the road from the south, which was hidden under the western flank of the spur, was accurately registered by the German mortars. On the east, the village overlooked a very steep hillside. The road climbing this face twisted and turned in great loops, dominated by the Germans from north and west.

Intelligence reports suggested that *I Battalion, 741 Regiment (the 114th Jaegar Division)* was responsible for the defence of Montone, M. Cucco and Carpini, with 2 Company in the Carpini area, 3 Company at Montone and 1 Company sandwiched in between.[6] 4 Company had two platoons of four heavy machine guns, and one platoon of two heavy machine guns, the latter being in support of 3 Company at Montone.[7]

The 25th Indian Infantry Brigade was given the task of capturing Montone. 3/1 Punjab was to make a frontal attack on it, while a company of the 1st King's Own was to secure M. Cucco and attack Montone from the rear. At the same time the 8th Manchester (the 20th Indian Infantry Brigade) was to advance from Castiglione and capture Carpini, a German position on the left flank of the main German position at Montone.

3/1 Punjab went into the lead for the attack on 5/6 July. The following troops were under command:

    B Squadron 3rd Hussars
    One platoon medium machine guns 1st Royal Northumberland Fusiliers
    One platoon 4.2-inch Mortars 1st Royal Northumberland Fusiliers
    One troop Anti-Tank guns.

In support were:
    97th Field Regiment
    3rd Medium Regiment.

[6] 10 Ind. Div. Intelligence Summary No. 37, dated 6/7 July 1944.
[7] Appendix 'B' to 10 Ind. Div. Intelligence Summary No. 38.

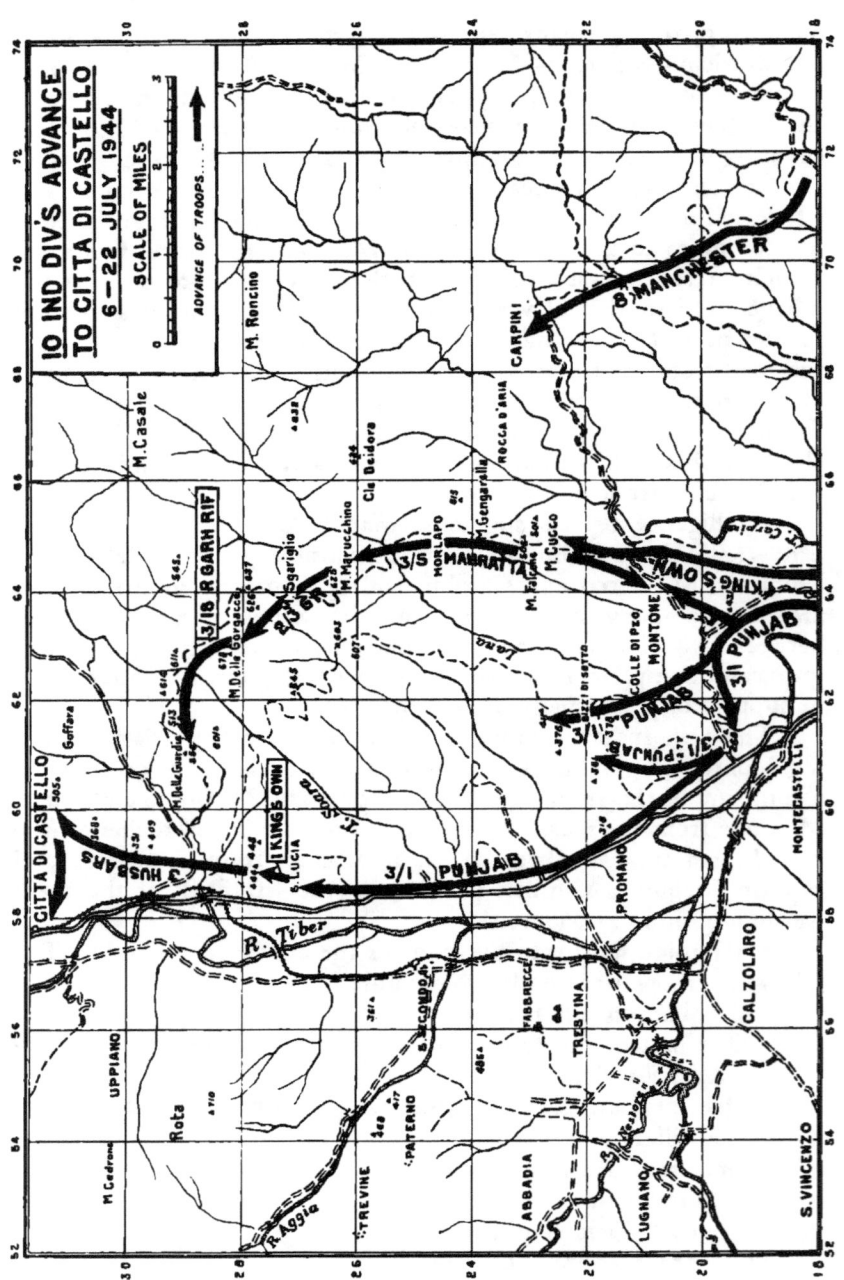

Commander 3/1 Punjab made the following plan of operations:
  (i) D Company less one platoon was to patrol to road junction south Montone.
  (ii) B Company was to advance to this road junction and capture high ground to the north-west.
  (iii) A Company was to proceed west to establish position at road junction south-west of Montone.
  (iv) C Company was to be in reserve.

On 5 July at 2000 hours a fighting patrol of D Company less one platoon moved up from Umbertide. As the men advanced to road junction south of Montone, five or six machine guns opened up and pinned them down. The patrol extricated itself with great difficulty, suffering some casualties; for their estimate was that a large number of Germans were astride the road. At 0520 hours on 6 July, B Company preceded by a squadron of 3rd Hussars advanced up road Umbertide—road junction south of Montone. They were halted at blown bridges until tanks got across. Heavy shelling and mortaring, followed by intense machine gun fire, halted the advance about 1500 yards from the road junction. Tanks were subjected to extremely heavy mortar and artillery fire. On arrival in the area of the road junction, B Company was 'stonked' twice within ten minutes causing several casualties. At 1000 hours, C Company advanced from Umbertide to the help of B Company. The situation did not improve, for all movement in the area of the road junction was halted by heavy artillery and mortar fire. At 1400 hours, A and D Companies were called up and the Commander 3/1 Punjab changed his plan of operations, intending to put B Company on the road junction south of Montone, A Company on the road junction south-west of Montone, D Company in between, and C Company to attack Montone. The attempt to get over the open hillside failed. Any depression in the side of the hill was hit again and again by salvoes of shells. From one of these salvoes the officer commanding the battalion received a fatal wound. The 3/1 Punjab suffered heavy casualties and could not make much progress. The situation at 1715 hours was that B Company was desperately struggling to overcome German resistance at the road junction south of Montone, A Company was still far from its objective, the road junction south-west of Montone and had advanced only to Pt. 268; D Company was in between; and C Company was astride the road at Pt. 431. The battalion positions were subjected to heavy mortar fire continuously until dark. During the night the Germans sent only occasional salvoes.

However, the garrison of Montone fell victim to a daring move which, aided by masterly navigation across miles of rough country in darkness, put the attacking force across the German line of withdrawal. A Company of the 1st King's Own carried out, during the night of 6/7 July, an arduous twelve-mile approach march east of Montone. They crossed ranges of high hills, as well as deep ravines, forded the torrent Carpina, climbed without opposition the dominating M. Cucco, a broad bare mountain, one mile north of Montone, at 0430 hours on 7 July and pushed south to Montone. At 0715 hours the leading troops entered the village but their progress was held up by German machine gun fire from the centre of the village. After several hours of fierce fighting in bullet-swept streets the village was finally cleared at 1420 hours.

Meanwhile the 8th Manchester (the 20th Indian Infantry Brigade) had also captured Carpini, and took over from 3/5 Mahratta at Castiglione. M. Lovesco was reached against light opposition and patrols went forward to R. Assino in the evening of 5 July. Without encountering any opposition, the 8th Manchester occupied on 6 July the line north-east and south-west of Pt. 708, and continued their advance to road Montone—Carpini. Nearing the end of their trek across the mountains from Castiglione, they descended out of the blackness of the night, and put to flight the garrison after a short but brisk fight, in the night of 6/7 July.

The Germans did not defend M. Bastiola, which originally formed part of the Montone defence line. Consequently the 10th Indian Infantry Brigade occupied it without opposition, and from there a gradual edging forward to the R. Nestore took place. It was while holding this line that the 10th Indian Infantry Brigade came under the command of the 4th Indian Division on 8 July, which was called up to strengthen the depleted X Corps.

Capture of M. Delle Gorgacce

By 7 July 1944 the German defensive line based on M. Bastiola—Montone—M. Cucco—Carpini had been breached. Difficult country, which the Germans stoutly defended, lay between this line and the defensive line based on Fraccano—Citta di Castello—Col di Fabri. The 4th Indian Division was now called up to strengthen the depleted X Corps and assume command of the 10th Indian Division's sector west of the Tiber. The X Corps now advanced up the Tiber valley with the 10th Indian Division to the east of the river and the 4th Indian Division to the west. To avoid confusion we shall first describe the advance of the 10th Indian Division to Citta di Castello and then give an account of the progress of the 4th Indian Division west of the Tiber.

In its advance to Citta di Castello the 10th Indian Division made two thrusts—one through M. Delle Gorgacce and the other through S. Lucia. As M. Delle Gorgacce was the chief German defensive position we shall first describe the main thrust of the 10th Indian

Division to this place. After the capture of Montone on 7 July by the 25th Indian Infantry Brigade, the 20th Indian Infantry Brigade took the lead in the advance towards M. Delle Gorgacce. The brigade plan was as follows:

(i) 3/5 Mahratta was to pass through the 1st King's Own at M. Cucco to M. Falcone and then advance through M. Marucchino to M. Delle Gorgacce.

(ii) The 8th Manchester in area road Montone—Carpini was to protect the right flank by carrying out active patrolling and mopping up.

(iii) On the left 2/3 Gurkha was to send fighting patrols to raid German positions, Colle di Pozzo and Promano.

The following troops were under command and in support of the brigade:[8]

> A Squadron 3rd King's Own Hussars
> A Squadron Skinner's Horse
> 96th Field Regiment and a portion of Army Group Royal Artillery
> 10th Field Company.

At 0200 hours on 8 July, 3/5 Mahratta, with one platoon W Company 1st Battalion the Royal Northumberland Fusiliers under command, passed through the 1st King's Own at M. Cucco in time to meet a German force advancing to retake the latter. The German counter-attack was made by part of *II Battalion, 741 Jaeger Regiment,* which was previously in reserve.[9] A keenly contested struggle took place at the features Pt. 501—Pt. 506, a narrow base neck of land with cliffs on both sides. Beyond, the Germans had broken hill features covered with shrub to conceal their movements. So narrow was the ridge leading from M. Cucco to the features Pts. 501-506 that only a platoon of C Company could be employed. For a while, there was pandemonium. Two-inch mortars, grenades, Bren guns, rifles, spandaus and shouting all joined in. Then the Germans opened up with their defensive fire to add to the din. Luckily, most of their shells fell on the track over which the Mahrattas had already passed. The gunner officer with the battalion did some excellent shooting by moonlight. His target had not been previously registered but, after a couple of ranging rounds, he brought down a very effective concentration on the southern slopes of the feature Pt. 501—Pt. 506. The leading Mahratta platoon worked forward in the cover of the hillside, until it was able to rush in with the bayonet. To the turmoil were then added battle cries

---

[8] 20 Ind. Inf. Bde. O.O. No. 4, 6 July 1944.
[9] 10 Ind. Div. Intelligence Summary No. 38, 8 July 1944.

from the Mahrattas and screams from the Germans, who took to their heels in all directions.[10]

After this success, a patrol from C Company went across the wadi at 0700 hours on 8 July to deal with German machine guns on M. Falcone, a green, open, pudding-basin-shaped feature. This was accomplished with the help of machine gunners of the Royal Northumberland Fusiliers. Meanwhile A Company had filtered over the ridge and down the wooded forward slopes of the feature Pts. 501—506, with M. Gengarella as its objective. During the advance of A Company, machine guns engaged known German positions and the three-inch mortars continued to register, keeping about a hundred yards ahead of the leading troops, as they climbed up M. Gengarella. Complete surprise was achieved. Some Germans were caught in their trenches, or hiding under the bushes. Others fled away down the north slopes. B Company then continued its advance to Morlapo, which was occupied without opposition.. At Morlapo, a halt was called and the position consolidated. A detachment of one platoon was established at Pt. 613.

In the morning of 9 July, the Mahrattas continued their advance to the crest of Monte Marucchino, A Company directed on Pt. 607 and D Company on Pt. 625. The advance was slow due to steep hillsides covered with bushes. British guns opened up on the German positions; that was the signal for sections of Germans to spew forth from half a dozen farm houses on the forward slopes. The shooting of the British guns was extremely accurate and both companies met little opposition until they approached the thickly wooded crest. There bursts of machine gun fire greeted them. By about 1800 hours both companies were held up near their objectives by heavy machine gun fire.

2/3 Gurkha now took up the advance. It relieved A and D Companies of 3/5 Mahratta on the reverse slopes of Pt. 625 and Pt. 607 at 2330 hours on 9 July. The Gurkhas were to advance from M. Marucchino to objective M. Delle Gorgacce by stepping up process, keeping always a firm base. They were to have artillery support from the 68th Field Regiment. A medium regiment from Army Group Royal Artillery was also available. They were to have a platoon of medium machine guns under command from 10 July. Their maintenance was to be partly by jeep and partly by mule. Engineers were to improve the track and make a jeep head during the night of 9/10 July.[11] At 0400 hours on 10 July the Gurkhas continued to move forward towards the tops of features Pt. 625 and Pt. 607 under heavy mortar and machine gun fire. The left hand

---

[10] Account of action of 3/5 Mahratta north of Montone (8-15 July); War Diary 3/5 Mahratta.
[11] 20 Ind. Inf. Bde. O.I. No. 1, 9 July 1944.

Naik Yeshwant Ghadge, V.C.
(3/5 Mahratta)

Sepoy Kamal Ram, V.C.
(3/8 Punjab)

Sappers and Miners improving Jeep tracks to enable troops to advance to San Domino and Monte Gorgacce

Sepoy Ali Haider, V.C.
(6/13 F. F. Rif.)

company (A) was held up but the right hand company (D) advanced round the east flank of M. Marucchino and reached the summit of feature Pt. 625 by 0720 hours. By 1000 hours A Company too had secured and consolidated Pt. 607. The Gurkhas now held firm M. Marucchino and prepared to attack M. Delle Gorgacce.

Meanwhile German counter-attacks had developed against the Mahratta positions. In the morning of 9 July, a German patrol engaged their forward post at Pt. 613. But it retired after an exchange of machine gun fire. In the afternoon the attack was renewed. As the German pressure increased, C Company was moved up in support at 2200 hours. At 0200 hours on 10 July a small fighting patrol of C Company to Pt. 624 came under machine gun fire and a shower of grenades, and suffered casualties. At 0430 hours just as the patrol had returned, the Germans, estimated to be 1½ companies, advanced from Pt. 624 and attacked Pt. 613. The attack was held but the Germans closed in and tried to outflank the position. A well-organised counter-attack by a reserve platoon however drove them back to Pt. 624. C Company then hastily re-organised and advanced at 0630 hours to attack Pt. 624. The company commander had no weapons other than those in the company but he was determined to recover the lost ground. The company advanced to close quarters before coming under cross fire from six machine guns. The company commander and six non-commissioned officers were killed. Naik Yashwant Ghadge, the only man of his section unhurt, charged on and rushed the machine gun post. He threw a grenade which knocked out the machine gun and shot one of the gun crew with his Tommy gun. Having no time to charge his magazine, he grasped his gun by the barrel, and beat to death the surviving man of the gun crew. Unfortunately, he was shot in the chest by German snipers and died at the post, which he had captured single-handed. A posthumous Victoria Cross was the reward of this supreme act of gallantry.

The second-in-command withdrew the company to Pt. 613. Soon the mortar officer arrived with two detachments of 3-inch mortars. He re-organised the company in its position on Pt. 613 in time to beat off another German counter-attack at 0730 hours. Later in the afternoon, however, the Germans pulled farther back from Pt. 624 along the ridge. 3/5 Mahratta then advanced its front through Pt. 624 to Pt. 632.

The 20th Indian Infantry Brigade now prepared to launch an attack on M. Delle Gorgacce, the most important of the mountains covering Citta di Castello on the east. The brigade plan was as follows:

 (i) 2/3 Gurkha from M. Marucchino was to patrol to and attack M. Sgariglio and M. Della Gorgacce.

(ii) 3/5 Mahratta was to protect the right flank by local patrolling and watch for hostile movement from the direction of M. Roncino towards M. Cucco.

(iii) The 8th Manchester, in co-operation with B Squadron Skinner's Horse was to patrol the road Montone—Garpini and on to Pietralunga.

The left flank of the 20th Indian Infantry Brigade was protected by the 25th Indian Infantry Brigade, which was advancing east of the Tiber towards S. Lucia

The following troops were under command of the 20th Indian Infantry Brigade:

One Medium machine gun company, 1st Royal Northumberland Fusiliers

Two heavy mortar platoons 1st Royal Northumberland Fusiliers

One battery 13th Anti-Tank Regiment

One platoon 61st Field Company, I.E.

And in support were:

Detachment Skinner's Horse

68th Field Regiment

107th Battery 32nd Heavy Regiment.

2/3 Gurkha had strengthened and extended its grip on M. Marucchino and was patrolling towards the next objective, the massive M. Delle Gorgacce, from which wide stretches of the Tiber valley and the hills flanking it on the east were clearly visible. The slopes of these hills and the valleys between the ridges were heavily forested. Tracks through them were few. The obvious route to M. Delle Gorgacce from M. Marucchino was the track running first north, then north-west. The German defences faced south and south-east astride the track.

2/3 Gurkha was ordered on 13 July to attack and capture M. Delle Gorgacce by first light on 14 July. The method which the battalion commander employed was a diversionary attack by B Company from the right onto the Sgariglio feature during the day while the main attack was to go in during the hours of darkness from the left. In order to gain surprise the main attack was to be silent but previously arranged targets had been given to the gunners so that support might be immediately called for when required. The plan was as follows:

(i) B Company was to make a feint attack during the day on 13 July along the track M. Marucchino on to the M. Sgariglio feature.

(ii) C Company was to attack and seize Pt. 645, a feature on the left, by last light on 13 July, so as to protect the left flank of the battalion.

(iii) As soon as C Company was in position, A and D Companies were to move up and assault Pt. 678 from the left at first light on 14 July.[12]

B Company's feint attack in the afternoon of 13 July on M. Sgariglio feature completely deceived the Germans, who brought their defensive fire on to them. As a result of heavy mortaring and shelling, the company commander and the forward observation officer were seriously wounded. By 1545 hours, however, B Company occupied Pt. 626 in the face of opposition and exploited to Pt. 637. On the left, C Company was in position at Pt. 645 at last light. The main attack by A and D Companies developed at first light on 14 July. Instead of moving along the track the companies selected a more difficult and longer route, down into the ravine to the west, through thick scrub, then up the almost vertical sides of M. Delle Gorgacce's western area. At dawn both the companies reached Pt. 678, with D Company on the right and A on the left. The Germans were about 200 yards ahead in strength in front of A Company. Commander A Company decided to attack with medium machine guns, which had been brought up on mules. D Company was to remain in position on the right as a firm base and to support by fire. A Company's attack was successful, 4 Germans were taken prisoners and the rest scattered. Meanwhile forward elements of D Company had contacted the Germans, who were in a strong position in a house on a ridge, about 200 yards ahead across the valley. One platoon was sent to deal with this German position under covering fire from 2-inch mortars and light machine guns. As the platoon advanced, 20 to 30 Germans were seen to evacuate the house and were shot up. The artillery was also asked for one of pre-arranged targets and 5 rounds of gun-fire came down from the divisional guns right on the target area. Then the platoon rushed the house. A German counter-attack followed immediately afterwards but it was held.

The success of the attack by 2/3 Gurkha on M. Delle Gorgacce was due in a large measure to deception and surprise. The Germans expected an attack to develop from the Sgariglio feature. One company's feint attack on this feature during the afternoon of 13 July confirmed their appreciation. The main attack from the left therefore came unexpectedly.[13]

Further to the east on 13 July, an armoured car and carrier patrol from Skinner's Horse clashed with the Germans in Pietralunga. The strength of the opposition, however, indicated reinforcements and the German intention not to surrender Pietra-

---

[12] Battle of M. Delle Gorgacce, 13/14 July; Appendix J-5; War Diary 2/3 G.R.
[13] 20 Ind. Inf. Bde. Command's notes on operations 28 June to 14 July; Appendix "J-2"; War Diary 20 Ind. Inf. Bde.

lunga easily. The reason was the danger which the loss of this place would represent to their lateral road from the Adriatic coastal sector over the mountains through Acqualangna and Citta di Castello to their line of communication, Route 3 at Cagli and more immediately, to their garrison still holding out at Gubbio.

The Advance to S. Lucia

We have described the advance of the 20th Indian Infantry Brigade from M. Cucco to M. Delle Gorgacce. We shall now narrate the progress of the 25th Indian Infantry Brigade east of the Tiber towards S. Lucia. 3/1 Punjab took the lead in attack on Colle di Pozzo ridge, on the east bank of the Tiber, two miles west of Montone. Small parties of Germans from *741 Jaeger Regiment* held the line Bizzi di Sotto—Pt. 378—Colle di Pozzo—Pt. 277, and also the line Pt. 411—Pt. 376—Pt. 361—Pt. 316. 3/1 Punjab had to attack the ridge and for this purpose had under command one medium machine gun platoon and one heavy mortar platoon of 1st Royal Northumberland Fusiliers and in support one squadron less two troops of 3rd Hussars.[14] Numerous watercourses north of the ridge provided excellent cover for German mortars and artillery. There was little on the 3/1 Punjab side which might provide shelter from German observation posts on the higher slopes. The Colle di Pozzo ridge was surmounted by a fortress-like church and several strongly built houses. There were open fields on the slopes of the ridges, though occasional vineyards provided a measure of concealment. Darkness however helped to overcome some of these disadvantages.

After the 1st King's Own Royal Regiment had occupied Montone on 7 July, the battalion area of 3/1 Punjab was adjusted from right track road junction to the left track road junction, with C Company left, A Company centre, D Company right and B company at Pt. 431 and astride the road. The commander of 3/1 Punjab made the following plan for the attack on the Colle di Pozzo ridge:

Phase I—A Company was to capture Pt. 378 and Colle di Pozzo. B Company advancing behind A Company was to leave one platoon at Pt. 378 for consolidation and the remainder was to advance to the right and capture Bizzi di Sotto.

Phase II—D Company was to move through B Company and patrol to Pt. 376.

Phase III—C Company was to move to the left of D Company to Pt. 361 and consolidate as far as Pt. 316.

By 0345 hours on 10 July, A Company had captured the objec-

[14] Information and Intentions dated 10 July; Appendix "D-3"; War Diary 25 Ind. Inf. Bde.

tive Colle di Pozzo and Pt. 378 against light opposition. At 0430 hours, B Company reached its objective, Bizzi di Sotto. So far there had been negligible opposition. The Germans, however, heavily mortared B Company's positions at Bizzi di Sotto, as well as the road near Colle di Pozzo. One mortar detachment received a direct hit, suffering heavy casualties. After consolidating the gains the Punjabis resumed the advance at 1930 hours. The Battalion Commander, expecting strong opposition, modified his original plan. He brought forward D Company into the centre position between A and B Companies, so that the attack on Pt. 411 might be made by three companies. At 1930 hours, 3/1 Punjab supported by tanks and artillery commenced the attack on the ridge from Pt. 411, then south-west to Pt. 316. A, B and D Companies moved forward on the right to Pt. 411 which they took against opposition. C, the left hand company, however, encountered fierce opposition and although it secured its objective Pt. 316, a strong German counter-attack developed forcing it to withdraw. At 0800 hours on 11 July, however, the company recaptured Pt. 316. Despite considerable opposition 3/1 Punjab made enough headway and by the evening of 11 July established itself along the line of the road from Pt. 378 to the road junction, thus making firm on the Colle di Pozzo ridge. At 1630 hours on 12 July, patrols were sent to S. Lucia area who found it clear of Germans.

Capture of Citta di Castello

By 14 July 1944, the 10th Indian Division had made considerable progress—the 20th Indian Infantry Brigade on the right had secured M. Delle Gorgacce while on the left the 25th Indian Infantry Brigade had secured S. Lucia. The Divisional Commander then ordered the 25th Indian Infantry Brigade to break through the remaining German defensive positions covering Citta di Castello. German resistance, however, stiffened considerably. They continued to resist bitterly and showed no inclination of yielding any ground, except in the face of strong co-ordinated attacks. *741 Jaeger Regiment (the 114th Jaeger Division)*, whose sector extended from the Tiber to Pietralunga, offered stubborn resistance to the advance of the 10th Indian Division to Citta di Castello. *III Battalion* of this regiment was responsible for the ground immediately east of the river, flanked by *II Battalion*. The depleted *I Battalion* provided patrols and was in reserve.[15] The Germans were well entrenched on the high ground to the east overlooking S. Lucia and cliff-sided ridge running east to M. Delle Gorgacce.

On 14 July the 1st King's Own Royal Regiment probed into

[15] 10 Ind. Div. Intelligence Summary No. 43, 13 July 1944.

the German defences beyond S. Lucia and at 0245 hours one of its companies attacked the left flank of the ridge, viz. Pt. 444, but had to withdraw in face of strong opposition. At 2200 hours, the 1st King's Own Royal Regiment sent five patrols, who encountered small arms and mortar fire. From their reports it was clear that the ridge near S. Lucia was a major obstacle. After these preliminary operations had yielded information about German dispositions, the Commander of the 25th Indian Infantry Brigade made a plan to attack and capture Pt. 556—Pt. 601—ridge Pt. 448 to Pt. 444 by first light on 16 July and exploit and capture feature Pt. 424—Pt. 391. The attack was to be made during the night of 15/16 July. On the left the 1st King's Own was to secure objectives Pt. 448 and Pt. 444, while on the right 3/18 Garhwal was to capture Pt. 601 and Pt. 556. After securing these objectives the battalions were to exploit further on orders from the Brigade Headquarters, 3/18 Garhwal up to Pt. 424 and the 1st King's Own Royal Regiment up to feature Pt. 409—Pt. 391.[16]

In the early hours on 16 July the 1st King's own Royal Regiment advanced from the high ground east of S. Lucia, with 3/18 Garhwal on the right protecting its flank in the hills below M. Delle Gorgacce. In front of the 1st King's Own was cliff-sided ravine presenting a serious problem to infantry at any time. The British troops climbed up this ravine, undeterred by the whining of bullets from German machine guns, passing fortunately over their heads. Objectives were the two highest points on the long, open ridge ahead of them, Pt. 448 and Pt. 444. In the depth and darkness of the ravine, path finding was an extremely difficult matter, yet by 0640 hours the men were firmly established on their objectives, after overcoming strong opposition. During the advance they were subjected to heavy shelling, mortaring and machine gun fire. Consequently one company was disorganised and scattered but the company commander managed to collect and re-form his men and resume the advance.

While the 1st King's Own Royal Regiment had thus secured the ridge near S. Lucia, 3/18 Garhwal on the right met considerable opposition on its front. The battalion arrived at the forming-up place very late at 0300 hours on 16 July, losing much precious time in consequence. It failed to make much progress owing to being subjected to heavy shell and mortar fire. By 0855 hours, however, it was established on Pt. 611 but encountered heavy fire once again when the men started moving forward to capture Pt. 614, and failed to capture it. The 3/18 Garhwal was forced to withdraw to area Pt. 678 owing to severe losses.

[16] 25 Ind. Inf. Bde. O.O. No. 2, 15 July 1944.

At 0105 hours on 17 July, after the artillery had fired an intensive concentration for three minutes on Pt. 614, 3/18 Garhwal renewed the attack on German positions. In spite of stiff opposition, they advanced and pushed the Germans out of their commanding positions. At 0130 hours, D Company captured Pt. 611 and A Company then pushed on and secured Pt. 614 one hour later. The advance was further continued and at 0800 hours B Company captured Pt. 512 and then exploited towards Pt. 556. At 0845 hours C Company captured Pt. 601. German opposition was broken; some of them being taken prisoners. The stage was now set for the attack on Citta di Castello.

Since 28 June 1944, the 10th Indian Division had been acting as the right flank guard to the X Corps and had been advancing along the narrow Tiber valley. On 17 July the division lay a few miles to the south of Citta di Castello. The Tiber valley, never broad anywhere, in these parts narrowed into a bottleneck less than half a mile in width, through which ran the road that entered Citta di Castello. Westwards, the hills rose steeply to the Cedrone feature, three miles from the river, and a thousand-feet higher than the bottom of the valley. Eastwards lay the features Pts. 391 and 409, part of a long east-west ridge whose summit was Pt. 368, 600 feet above the river bed. To the north, hidden and guarded by the Cedrone and Pt. 368 features, lay Citta di Castello and the broad flat plain, which ran northwards to Sanespolcro, eight miles away.[17]

By 18 July 1944, the 10th Indian Infantry Brigade of the 4th Indian Division was in occupation of M. Cedrone, Uppiano and M. Arnato, the high ground overlooking Citta di Castello from the west and the 25th Indian Infantry Brigade had occupied features Pts. 444, 448 and M. Delle Guardie east of the Tiber. Thus Pt. 391 and Pt. 368 were the only remaining defensive positions guarding Citta di Castello, but they were the most easily defended positions of all.

On either side of the Tiber, occupying the high ground, was the *114th Jaeger Division*. To the west lay the *44th Infantry Division* and to the east the *5th Mountain Division*. The *114th Jaeger Division*, reduced to about 800 men, had already begun to decrease its front, handing over some of the commitments to the divisions on the flanks. The troops were tired and the morale was low.

At 2030 hours on 19 July the 1st King's Own Royal Regiment laid on a deception plan to induce the Germans to fire. Smoke was put down on German forward positions by artillery and tanks of the 3rd Hussars engaged the Germans from hull-down positions. Thinking that an attack was being made, the Germans disclosed their fire plan. This disclosure was of great value to the 25th Indian Infantry

[17] Battle Account—3rd Hussars 20-23 July; Appx. 'A' to 10 Ind. Div. Narrative of Operations.

Brigade, which was faced with a tough proposition in breaking through the last barrier before Citta di Castello, i.e. the high ground north of the small river Soara. As the ground across the river appeared to be suitable for tanks, the Brigade Commander decided to give the 3rd Hussars a clear run with artillery at call. The troops placed at the disposal of the commanding officer 3rd Hussars by the Divisional Commander were:

> 3rd Hussars Regimental Group (including Chestnut Troop, 1st Royal Horse Artillery, Sapper Section 1st Field Troop, 3rd Field Squadron Royal Engineers).
> One squadron Royal Wiltshire Yeomanry.

These troops were supported by the divisional artillery co-ordinated by Officer Commanding 1st Royal Horse Artillery and the Divisional Sappers. In the event of success the 1st King's Own was to follow up and occupy the ground captured, the objective being a 'V' shaped hill, with the point of the 'V' north-east on Pt. 505 and the arms stretching south-west, i.e. Pts. 391 and 409.

From the start the greatest initial difficulty was the ground. Most careful reconnaissance was carried out by sapper, tank and infantry patrols. Aerial photographs were also of considerable help. Special provision was made against the ground from the administrative side since it was clear that nothing but tracked vehicles could climb on to Pt. 391 and Pt. 409. Two Honeys per squadron were allotted for carriage of ammunition and the remaining two (at regimental headquarters) were converted into medical vehicles for the Medical Officer. In addition, dumps of ammunition were made for the half squadron supporting the operation from Pt. 444 and Pt. 448. Two days' rations were issued to all personnel. At 1930 hours on 20 July, the Commanding Officer 3rd Hussars issued orders for the attack on the German positions.

During the night of 20/21 July, 1st and 2nd Troops 'A' Squadron with two ammunition lorries climbed the hill on to Pt. 444 and Pt. 448. An ammunition dump was established by each troop. Their role was to support the attack by the remainder of A Squadron on Pt. 391.

At 2230 hours a party of sappers and infantry, about 80 strong, accompanied by the Intelligence Officer 3rd Hussars set out from S. Lucia for the ford at the stream Soara (east and north-east from R 580285). This party ran into a German defensive fire task and was very heavily stonked for about half an hour. The majority of the men remained under cover while a few sappers, the sapper officer and the Intelligence Officer pushed on and reached the ford at about 0030 hours on 21 July without incident. The sappers filled in the ditch blocking the ford and by 0300 hours the ford was ready.

At first light the rest of A Squadron and Squadron Headquarters were formed up north of S. Lucia waiting to advance. Meanwhile the Squadron Leader with observation posts from the Chestnut Troop, Medium and Field Regiments, took up their positions on Pt. 444, whence they could observe the whole battle. B Squadron was in reserve.

Thus at 0500 hours when all necessary preliminary steps for the attack had been taken, the ford secured and two troops in position at Pt. 444 and Pt. 448 to support the attack, the 3rd Troop followed by the 4th Troop and Headquarters A Squadron advanced from area north of S. Lucia for the attack on Pt. 391. The 3rd Troop reached the ford at 0545 hours, crossed it, climbed on to the road at R 596289 and turned eastwards to reconnoitre a route up the hillside. Meanwhile the valley was under spasmodic but heavy shell fire. It remained so till late in the afternoon. To achieve the maximum surprise the officer commanding A Squadron gave the order that no one was to fire until the 3rd Troop had gained the top of the hill. For two hours the 3rd Troop repeatedly tried to find a way up the hill. Its efforts were not successful as the tanks were unable to negotiate steep gradients. At 0800 hours, however, a way up the hill was found much further east and the tanks waited in a narrow gully near the top for the 4th Troop and Squadron Headquarters to catch up. Supported by the 3rd Troop, the 4th Troop and Squadron Headquarters passed through the defile and moved left towards the top of Pt. 391 under cover of fire from artillery and tanks on Pt. 444 and Pt. 448. They destroyed and overran a building that was giving trouble and took up positions on the south-east end of Pt. 391, covering Pt. 505.

At 0930 hours the officer commanding the 3rd Hussars ordered B Squadron to advance and pass through A Squadron and capture Pt. 409 and Pt. 505. Led by the 2nd Troop, the squadron moved across the ford at Soara under extremely heavy shell fire. Meanwhile, the 3rd Troop A Squadron had gone on ahead to reconnoitre forward towards Pt. 505, seeking a route for B Squadron. At about 1100 hours, the 2nd Troop B Squadron climbed the hill from the ford and followed the route already taken by the reconnaissance party when a German anti-tank gun opened up from Pt. 368 and knocked out the leading tanks. The troop leader of the 2nd Troop in an attempt to put down smoke to cover the knocked out tanks was killed together with his gunner. The German anti-tank gun was spotted within five minutes of opening up. A quick concentration destroyed the gun and its crew. Tanks and artillery wrought havoc amongst the completely bewildered German infantry, who ran from dugouts to the wood and back again. At 1400 hours heavy German fire was still coming from Pt. 368 which had to be silenced before it might be safe to climb Pt. 505. The 3rd and the 4th Troops B Squadron supported by the Chestnut Troop and tanks on Pt. 444 and Pt. 448, moved westwards shooting up German infantry. Pt. 391 and Pt. 409 were cleared. Then the 1st Troop B Squadron advanced towards Pt. 505 covered by the rest of the squadron. At about 1800 hours Pt. 505, the dominating feature and the final objective was secured. Thus fell the last defensive position guarding Citta di Castello. At 0930 hours on 22 July, C Squadron and sappers entered the town, which was littered with mines and booby-traps. So severely had *741 Jaeger Regiment* suffered that it fell back north-east into the hills and to the line of torrent Selci, which joined the Tiber.

The operation is illustrative of what armour can do when given a free run and average chance of ground movement. Foot reconnaissance by armour for river crossing, gallant and determined mine clearing by the sappers and most determined efforts by troop and squadron leaders to get their armour up the formidable slopes, were the main features of the operation. The action also emphasised the importance of armour having its own artillery.[16]

---

[16] 10 Ind. Div. Narrative of Operations.

CHAPTER XIII

Advance West of the Tiber

The 4th Indian Division in the Line

Having described the advance of the 10th Indian Division to Citta di Castello we may now give an account of the progress of the 4th Indian Division west of the Tiber. This division assumed command of the 10th Indian Division's sector west of the Tiber on 8 July 1944. The following units came under command:

    10th Indian Infantry Brigade Group
    A Squadron Skinner's Horse
    9th Armoured Brigade (less the 3rd Hussars)
    165th Field Regiment (less one battery).

The role of the 4th Indian Division was threefold—to advance through Trestina to M. Cedrone in order to threaten Citta di Castello from the west; to advance through Monte S. Maria towards Monterchi with a view to cut the lateral route from Citta di Castello to Arezzo; to make a thrust towards Alpe di Poti through M. Favalto so as to threaten Arezzo from the east. Facing the 4th Indian Division was the *44th Infantry Division,* which held from the Tiber westwards a front of about twelve miles. It consisted of *131, 312, 134 Grenadier Regiments* and *44 Reconnaissance Battalion. 132 Grenadier Regiment* stretched from the Tiber to about 52 Easting, with *131 Grenadier Regiment* on its immediate right flank.

The country ahead of the 4th Indian Division consisted of an endless series of ridges, indented by numerous streams and ravines. Their crests ran from east to west in a succession of dips and peaks rising to their highest, more than three thousand feet, approximately half way between the river Tiber and the road leading from Lake Trasimene to Arezzo. The ridges were generally well wooded with occasional patches of fields, wherein the already harvested corn still stood in its stooks to provide good cover for the German booby-traps. Strong medieval villas, situated on high isolated peaks, dominated the surrounding countryside. These hamlets were almost invariably the prize of a bitter struggle. Besides, large mansions, farm houses and peasant homesteads dotted the hillsides.

Routes northwards were restricted to two second-class roads, one on each bank of the Tiber. There were many footpaths and cart-tracks but these invariably required improvement before even a jeep could pass. Generally they were blocked by felled trees. Often they were accurately registered by German artillery and mortars and frequently covered by machine guns.

Attack on Trestina Feature

In this ground, initially, the 4th Indian Division took up the running with two brigades, the 7th and the 10th Indian Infantry Brigades. The former made a double thrust, one directed against Monte S. Maria and the second against M. Favalto. The latter made a thrust towards M. Cedrone through Trestina. We shall first describe the advance of the 10th Indian Infantry Brigade towards M. Cedrone.

West of the Tiber, the German forward positions ran from Trestina along the line of the R. Nestore. The 10th Indian Infantry Brigade was directed on to the high ground north of Trestina. The valley of the Nestore, near its junction with the Tiber, was broad, open, flat and completely dominated by the high ground to the north. It had been thickly mined and was prepared as a defensive line in continuation of that based on Montone. *II Battalion 132 Grenadier Regiment* was defending the Trestina feature. Three of its companies, supported by a fourth company, held the strongpoints, the two Houses at R. 561225 and the Church at R 560227. The latter was situated at the highest part of the ridge and dominated the countryside. The reserve was provided by *I Battalion* in the rear of *II Battalion*. *III Battalion* guarded the right flank of *II Battalion*.[1]

The 10th Indian Infantry Brigade, then concentrated south of river Nestore, was assigned the task of capturing the above mentioned strong points of the Trestina feature. The plan was to make a double thrust—on the left 2/4 Gurkha was to capture church area by first light on 10 July and then occupy the area between ring contour (R 567239) and Pt. 485; on the right the 1st Durham Light Infantry was to occupy Trestina feature at 0500 hours on 10 July and mop up the area between that feature and the river Tiber. 4/10 Baluch was in reserve on M. Bastiola, with one company forward at Pt. 330.

The Commander of 2/4 Gurkha made the following plan of operations:—

    (i) 2/4 Gurkha was to advance from the area S. Vincenzo in the following order of march: B Company, C Company, A Company, Tactical Headquarters, Regimental Aid Post and D Company. B and C Companies were to advance along the track through Pt. 330 held by a company of 4/10 Baluch, while Tactical Headquarters, A and D Companies were to go along the main road and turn in

---

[1] 4 Ind. Div. Intelligence Summary No. 113, 11 July 1944.

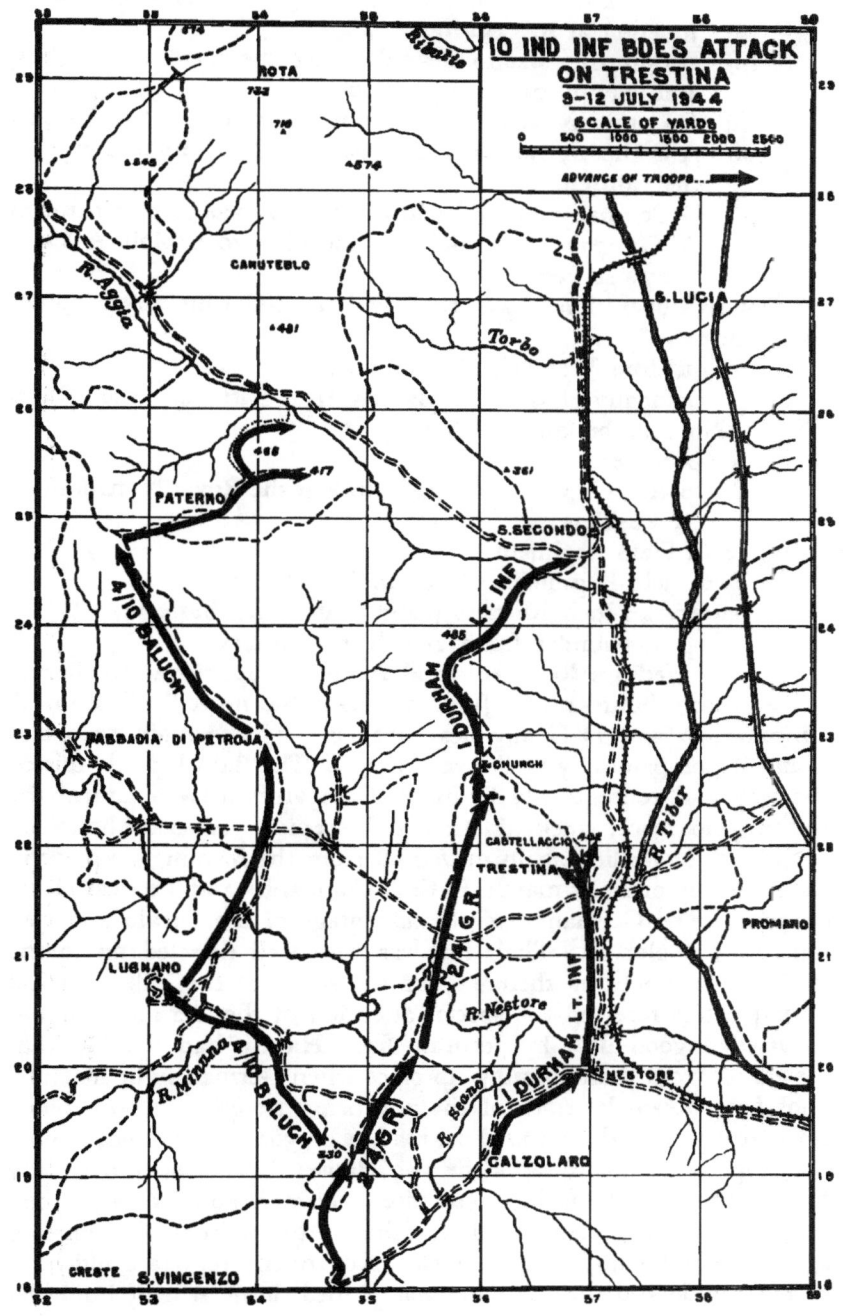

on track (R 555187). The forming up place was the track junction at R. 554201.

(ii) B Company was to clear the start line (road at R 557211) and take up covering position.
(iii) C Company was to advance and capture the two Houses.
(vi) A Company was to pass through C Company and capture the Church.
(v) D Company was to be in reserve. It was to pass through A Company the following morning to exploit A Company's success.

For this operation 2/4 Gurkha had the following troops under command:

B Squadron Warwickshire Yeomanry
Y Company less one platoon 1st Battalion the Royal Northumberland Fusiliers.

In support were:

One platoon Y Company 1st Battalion the Royal Northumberland Fusiliers
154th Field Regiment
Two Field Regiments of 4th Indian Division
Battery 4.2-inch Mortars (82nd Anto-Tank Battery)
Troop 17-pounder (44th Anti-Tank Battery)
One Medium Regiment (2nd Army Group, Royal Artillery).[2]

At 2030 hours on 9 July, 2/4 Gurkha moved off from S. Vincenza, A and D Companies advancing by the main road and C and B Companies by track over Pt. 330. The Baluch guide missed the way and consequently C and B Companies arrived late at the forming up place, track junction at R 554201. At 0005 hours on 10 July, the battalion again moved off from the forming up place in the following order of march, B, C, A Companies and Tactical Headquarters. The Germans had the advantage of the terrain and well did they exploit it. Their fire was very well directed on to the Indian troops fighting their way up the slopes of the hill. Tactical Headquarters received the special attention of the Germans; it was harassed a good deal by accurate fire. Hardly had the Gurkhas moved off from their forming up place when German light machine guns fired down the track of the advancing troops. At 0030 hours B Company cleared the start line, road at R 556212, and at 0040 hours C Company moved towards the two Houses, but it was pursued by heavy mortar and machine gun fire. German position were then subjected to heavy concentration of fire. At 0130 hours C Company again moved forward to the attack. Not much progress could however be made and the company was pinned down at 0205 hours by

[2] 10 Ind. Inf. Bde. O.O. No. 3, 9 July 1944.

heavy fire. Meanwhile, A Company had wheeled to the right of the track, climbed a steep rock, and made a successful attack on the German garrison at the two Houses. The company then pushed towards the Church and at 0415 hours arrived at about 300 yards from the objective. The attack was put in and the Church was captured at 0430 hours. Meanwhile C Company too had pushed on to the two Houses and moved forward to link up with A Company. The Germans searched the area occupied by the Gurkhas with mortar and light machine gun fire.

The Durham too made progress. Advancing from Calzolaro the men entered Nestore at 0455 hours, occupied Trestina station at 1030 hours and pushed on towards Castellaccio which was captured at 1200 hours. At 1545 hours the German reserve battalion, *I Battalion 132 Grenadier Regiment,* made a vain bid to recapture the strategic position of the Church (which commanded the countryside); this counter-attack was however dispersed by artillery and small arms fire. Another counter-attack that followed at 1615 hours was also beaten off. Similiarly a German counter-attack, which developed at 1545 hours against the position of the Durham at Castellaccio, was repulsed. The latter exploited Pt. 402 at 1645 hours. Thus after fierce fighting the Germans were driven from the commanding positions on the high ground north of the Nestore.

After this success, the Durham passed through 2/4 Gurkha to exploit northwards. They occupied Pt. 485 by 0520 hours on 11 July, and a further period of patrolling followed. By 0600 hours on 13 July, their patrols were 300 yards south of Secondo without making contact with the Germans. 4/10 Baluch, after occupying Paterno on the night of 11/12 July patrolled to Pt. 468 and Pt. 417. The way was now prepared for the attack on M. Cedrone, a strong German defensive position, guarding the approaches to Citta di Castello.

Advance to M. Favalto and Monte S. Maria

While the 10th Indian Infantry Brigade captured the Trestina feature and advanced towards M. Cedrone, the 7th Indian Infantry Brigade made a double thrust, one directed against Monte S. Maria and the other against M. Favalto. By the morning of 9 July, both forward battalions of the 7th Indian Infantry Brigade, 1/2 Gurkha and 2/11 Sikh, supported by tanks of the Warwickshire Yeomanry, had advanced to the high ground about M. Alvieri, overlooking the river Nestore. There the battalions separated, 1/2 Gurkha going northwards and 2/11 Sikh almost due west. At 1038 hours the Gurkha battalion surprised a German observation post in the vicinity of Ghironzo, which stood on a seventeen-hundred-foot high peak in a bend of the river Nestore, about a mile north of M. Alvieri. The

288 CAMPAIGN IN ITALY

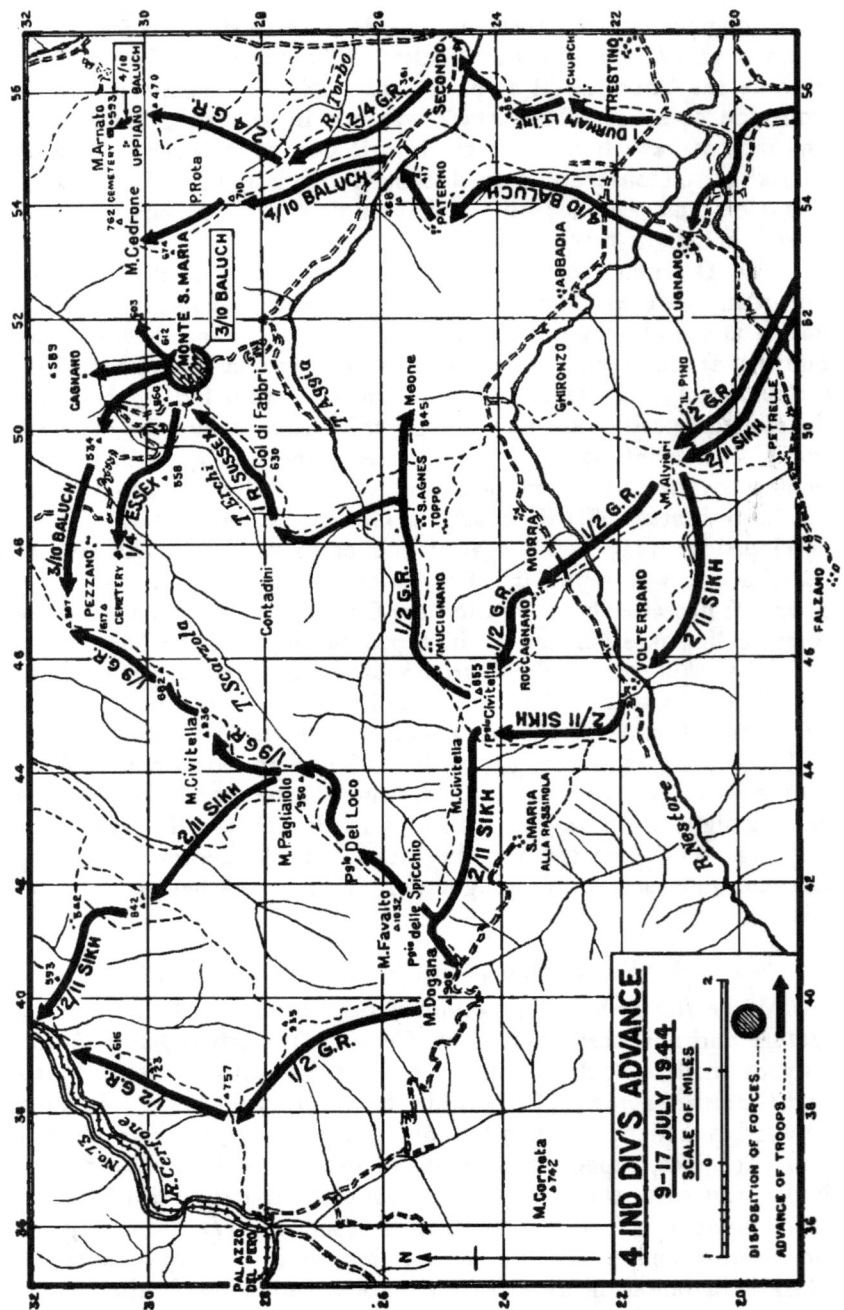

Gurkhas, though only a section in strength, attacked and killed six of the eight Germans garrisoning the post. Meanwhile 2/11 Sikh followed the crest of the ridge west of M. Alvieri. Patrols entered Volterrano, in the early hours of 10 July, without any opposition. The 7th Indian Infantry Brigade was now spread over a front of approximately four miles. Ahead of its two battalions was some tough cross-country climbing. The one confronting 2/11 Sikh was the higher and worse. Since the battalion must keep moving, its weapons, ammunition and supplies were put on mule back. From Volterrano, 2/11 Sikh moved up a narrow, steep and wooded spur to Poggio Civitella, where it arrived in the evening of 10 July. After consolidating its positions on Poggio Civitella, the Sikh battalion turned westwards to the three-thousand-five-hundred-foot high M. Civitella, a mile away. C and D Companies moved forward for attack. By 0730 hours on 11 July they were firmly established there, though they were subjected to slight shelling.

Meanwhile, on 10 July, patrols from 1/2 Gurkha had found Morra unoccupied, but Meone and Mucignano held by small parties of Germans. To clear these pockets of German resistance the Gurkha battalion advanced during the night of 10/11 July from M. Alvieri across the Nestore through Roccagnano to Pt. 855 in the following order of march: A, B, D Companies, Battalion Headquarters and C Company. As the leading company came to the top of the feature Pt. 855 at first light on 11 July, the Sikhs at Poggio Civitella opened fire under the impression that these were enemy troops. A Company immediately charged and killed three Sikhs before the fracas could be stopped. After this unpleasant incident, 1/2 Gurkha formed up with B Company on the left, and A and D Companies on the right for the attack on Mucignano. The plan was for B Company to capture Mucignano village but to allow time for A and D Companies to by-pass the village to the south before they started. The companies moved off, leaving Battalion Headquarters and C Company as firm base on Poggio Civitella. The Germans had pulled out at mid-night and the Gurkhas pushed on through Mucignano to Toppo and S. Agnes. They were firmly established in Meone. Battalion headquarters moved to Toppo and preparations were made for the attack on the German positions on the ridge Contadini—Col di Fabbri, preparatory to the advance on Monte S. Maria.

After establishing a firm base at Toppo, 1/2 Gurkha sent two fighting patrols from C and D Companies, in the afternoon of 11 July, to probe into German positions. The patrols descended the northern slopes from Toppo towards the torrent Aggia. Beyond this torrent was the long Contadini—Col di Fabbri ridge stretching to the northeast and rising steadily towards Monte S. Maria. The Germans had taken up positions on this ridge for the protection of Monte S. Maria. The steep hillsides north and south of the river were very close and afforded the Germans excellent opportunities of shelling the Gurkha troops as they advanced to attack the ridge. Nevertheless, a patrol from C Company attacked the German positions in the wadi and on the forward slopes of the ridge. The patrol killed six Germans and extricated itself after suffering two casualties. To the east, D Company's patrol engaged the Germans in an exchange of fire. The officer of the Royal Artillery Observation Post at S. Agnes helped the patrol considerably by shooting up the Germans attempting to run up the ridge. The Gurkha opened fire from S. Agnes. A brisk exchange of fire ensued.

A and D Companies then advanced to the support of the fighting patrols, A directed on Contadini and D on Col di Fabbri. As these patrols advanced up the ridge they suffered heavy casualties in men and mules from German shell fire. Fortunately the tanks of Warwickshire Yeomanry, which had come up to S. Agnes, directed their fire on German positions and dealt with this menace. At 1830 hours when C Company was despatched in support of A Company, the Germans heavily mortared the forward slopes of the ridge. At 2115 hours A Company managed to reach the top of the hill but was met by spandau fire. The Gurkhas then charged the Germans and pursued them for over a thousand yards. During this action, C Company while advancing to the support of A Company, was mortared by the Germans, suffering 11 casualties. Although A Company was successful in driving the Germans from a part of the ridge, D Company failed to make any progress. There was heavy concentration of mortars on its positions. During the hours of darkness main Battalion Headquarters and B Company moved up and gained some ground. At 0600 hours on 12 July, 1/2 Gurkha was in possession of 1500 yards of the ridge. A Company was on the left with C echeloned half left and behind it. D Company was in the centre. Battalion Headquarters was below D Company and B Company was on the right. The Germans heavily mortared the Gurkha positions throughout the day. A platoon from D Company probing into German positions on the ridge to Col di Fabbri was spandaued and withdrew. Loss of their hold on this ridge so close to their line of withdrawal through Monte S. Maria was a serious event for the Germans. They must have been both surprised and alarmed, in spite of the altertness of their troops on the spot, by the speed and determination of the Gurkha threat across the torrent Aggia. Since 2/11 Sikhs was still on the south bank of the torrent and four miles away, the Gurkha thrust was an isolated, if bold, move. However, the Gurkha companies held grimly to the ridge, in spite of heavy mortaring of their positions.

Early in the morning of 12 July, 2/11 Sikh on the western flank pushed on from M. Civitella through Poggio delle Spicchio and Poggio del Loco towards M. Pagliaiolo. A Company's attack on this feature met with stiff resistance. The advance was encountered by accurate and intense artillery, mortar and machine gun fire. A Sikh soldier displayed great heroism. When his section commander fell severely wounded, he at once took over command. Leading his section with calmness he silenced a German machine gun post, killed two Germans and continued the advance. Although severely wounded he went on to clear two more German posts. He fell dead but by his dauntless bravery he had helped his section to reach the crest of the hill. By last light the Sikh battalion was firmly established on M. Pagliaiolo and M. Favalto. This was to be the limit of the Sikh effort for the time being. 1st Battalion 9th Gurkha Rifles (the 5th Indian Infantry Brigade), which had concentrated in area S. Vincenzo, three miles south-west of the junction of the Nestore with the Tiber, was already on its way to pass through.

On the right, 1st Battalion Royal Sussex Regiment, was also moving forward from Morra, in the Nestore valley to pass through 1/2 Gurkha and capture Monte S. Maria, a delightful walled village of great strategic importance, since it commanded the ground as far as the Tiber. Assuming that the difficulties of the ground would slow down the advance of the 7th Indian Infantry Brigade, the Germans had nearly no troops in this sector. *134 Grenadier Regiment*, the reserve regiment of the *44th Infantry Division*, was hurried to the Monte S. Maria ridge to save the situation.[5] After putting up a stiff fight at the Col di Fabbri ridge, the Germans retired to Monte S. Maria to take up its defence. In the late afternoon of 12 July, the Royal Sussex passed through 1/2 Gurkha, north of Col di Fabbri, and advanced along the crest of the ridge to Monte S. Maria, which was situated on an isolated pinnacle high above the rest of the ridge. To the north and the south there was an abrupt drop to the river valleys. Approaches from the east and the west were along an exposed and unusually narrow ridge. A road climbed to the southern face of the hill, in a series of sharp and complicated bends to cross the ridge about half-a-mile west of the village. From this point, a track ran eastwards to enter the village by the one gate in the walls surrounding it. By last light the Royal Sussex had reached the area R. 503287. The advance was continued but the Royal Sussex was considerably harassed by German artillery and mortar fire. Water courses offered little cover as German mortars registered them accurately. Divisional and corps artillery supported the attack, supplying smoke cover in the more exposed positions. Concentrations of high explosive shells were fired to silence the German

[5] 10 Ind. Div. Intelligence Summary No. 43, 13 July 1944.

artillery and mortars. Tanks co-operating with the infantry were, however, delayed by minefields and craters on the track and became targets for vicious salvoes of artillery and mortar shells. The white smoke of the artillery screen combined with the clouds of brown dust from shell-shattered buildings to obscure the village from the view for several minute at a time. Through the smoke, the occasional stream of tracer bullets, like water from a hose, could be seen. The rapid pattering of the German spandau machine guns was answered by the tattoo of the Bren guns. By 2200 hours the 1st Royal Sussex was within one mile of the village, but there, for a while it halted, for the German observation posts were numerous and the ridge leading to the village was exposed to German fire. The Germans however withdrew under cover of darkness and Monte S. Maria was occupied by 0545 hours on 13 July.

Meanwhile 1/9 Gurkha from the 5th Indian Infantry Brigade had been advancing on the left. It passed through 2/11 Sikh on M. Pagliaiola at 2230 hours on 12 July, the objective being M. Civitella, two miles to the north. A German platoon held the feature but it could not stop the Gurkhas who, by 0700 hours on 13 July, were in possession of M. Civitella.

Attack on M. Cedrone

Thus by 13 July, the 4th Indian Division had made substantial progress. Monte S. Maria, M. Favalto and the Trestina feature had been captured and it was now possible to develop thrusts towards M. Cedrone, Monterchi and Alpe di Poti. We shall first describe the stirring events connected with the capture of M. Cedrone, where the Germans held a strong defensive position whose importance lay in its command of the Tiber valley, east towards Citta di Castello and north towards San Sepolcro. The commanding position of the feature gave the Germans a great advantage over the attacking force. *132 Grenadier Regiment (the 44th Infantry Division)* was guarding this important feature, with *I Battalion* north of Monte S. Maria, *III Battalion* on M. Cedrone and *II Battalion* near the Tiber.[6]

The 10th Indian Infantry Brigade, after capturing the Trestina feature on 10 July 1944, had been advancing towards M. Cedrone. In the morning of 13 July, 4/10 Baluch, the leading battalion of the brigade, concentrated south of M. Cedrone for the attack on this feature. At 1100 hours, C Company while advancing on the feature, Pt. 710, was pinned down by mortar and small arms fire. The rest of the battalion was also heavily mortared and shelled. At 1630 hours the Germans made a counter-attack on C Company but it was

[6] 4 Ind. Div. Intelligence Summaries No. 116 and No. 117, dated 14 and 15 July 1944.

beaten back after hand-to-hand and grenade fighting. The advance was then resumed in the night of 13/14 July against stiff opposition and in the face of heavy mortar fire. However, by 0700 hours on 14 July, C Company had obtained only a footing on the spur south-west from M. Cedrone around Pt. 674. At 1130 hours, D Company (and one platoon of B Company) supported by the 3rd Field Regiment, the 1st Field Regiment, 1st battery 105-mm (self-propelled) and one troop tanks, advanced from Pt. 674 to attack M. Cedrone. On the way, the Baluch were caught in the German defensive fire and sustained considerable casualties. A strong German counter-attack by one company developing from the west of M. Cedrone, forced the Baluch to withdraw to the original position on Pt. 674. Durez Khan, a Naik, displayed great heroism in this attack on M. Cedrone. He led his section through violent German machine gun and mortar fire. Undaunted by the fierce German counter-attack he calmly directed the fire of his section until all his men had suffered injuries. He then fired the light machine gun himself. When his ammunition was exhausted, he took a tommy gun from a dead man and charged the Germans, firing as he advanced. This courageous spirit carried him towards his objective and, in the circumstances, certain death. When M. Cedrone was finally captured on 17 July his body was found far in advance of the other dead of the company.[7] His reckless bravery earned for him the posthumous award of the Indian Order of Merit.

While the main attack on M. Cedrone was made by 4/10 Baluch from the south, 3/10 Baluch of the 5th Indian Infantry Brigade also attacked the feature from the south-west. At 1030 hours on 14 July two of its companies advanced from Monte S. Maria to Pt. 612 to create a diversion for an attack by 4/10 Baluch on M. Cedrone. One company was established at Pt. 603 and another at Pt. 612 in the afternoon, in spite of heavy mortar fire. As the attack by 4/10 Baluch on M. Cedrone did not succeed, the two companies of 3/10 Baluch were withdrawn.

M. Cedrone was proving a ticklish problem. Its position gave good protection to the German mortar positions in the numerous valleys north of the hill, from which they could engage targets on the 10th Indian Infantry Brigade front. It was imperative, therefore, to launch a vigorous attack. 4/10 Baluch having failed to capture M. Cedrone, a fresh battalion (1st Durham Light Infantry) was called forward for the task of liquidating German opposition. On 15 July at 0100 hours the Durham relieved 4/10 Baluch south of M. Cedrone and probed into German defences before launching the attack on 16 July. The brigade plan was for the Durham to launch

[7] Posthumous award for Baluch Naik—the *Diagonals* 24 February 1945; War Diary 10 Ind. Div. Jan.-Mar. 1945.

the attack on M. Cedrone at 2200 hours on 16 July and for 2/4 Gurkha to attack, half an hour earlier, the German defensive positions at Uppiano and M. Arnato, the latter being a mile to the northeast of M. Cedrone. In support of the brigade were:[8]

    C Squadron Royal Wiltshire Yeomanry
    2nd Army Group Royal Artillery
    Y Company 1st Royal Northumberland Fusiliers
    Three troops 4.2-inch mortars
    Three Field Regiments
    Battery self-propelled guns.

The Durham advanced at 2230 hours on 16 July but the men were somewhat surprised by the feebleness of German resistance. A two-hour concentration of artillery had preceded the attack but an additional reason for the lack of resistance was that a relief was taking place on M. Cedrone.[9] The Durham occupied the smmit of the feature, without the relieving German companies on the slopes being aware of that. The unusual activity at the summit however aroused their suspicions and a section was sent to investigate. This section was surprised by the Durham. At 0450 hours on 17 July the German relieving companies launched a counter-attack on the Durham position at the summit. For nearly an hour the Germans hammered at the Durham position until they finally withdrew, exhausted, before a bayonet attack. Another German counter-attack by two companies developed at 2040 hours. After a fierce struggle the Germans were driven away at 2130 hours. This was followed by still another counter-attack at 2200 hours. The attack was held. Thus after a fierce struggle, 1 Durham succeeded in retaining possession of this strategic feature.

On the right, an equally fierce struggle was taking place for the possession of Uppiano, which was held by *6 Company 721 Jaeger Regiment*. 2/4 Gurkha was up against considerable opposition. From the area of the White House (R 548275), south of Pt. 710 (where this battalion had concentrated on 15 July) its patrols had been probing into German positions. At 2145 hours on 15 July, a strong fighting patrol composed of D Company had been sent to find out the strength of the German forces on Pt. 470, but had been caught in the German defensive fire and had suffered casualties. Another reconnaissance patrol, with a covering platoon, had been sent to its support at 2245 hours but had been subjected to light machine gun and mortar fire. Both the patrols had been able to extricate themselves with difficulty. It was obvious that only by a

---

[8] 10 Ind. Inf. Bde. O. O. No. 4, 16 July 1944.
[9] II and III Battalions of *721 Jaegar Regiment* (the *114th Jaegar Division*) had moved from their positions east of the Tiber and were in the process of relieving *134 Grenadier Regiment*.

vigorous attack would the Germans be driven off this feature. A vigorous three pronged attack was launched on 16 July—D Company advanced at 2130 hours from the area of the White House for the attack on Pt. 470; B Company crossed the start line at 0300 hours on 17 July to capture Cemetery Hill (R 555305). D Company was subjected to mortar and light machine gun fire from Pt. 470 while it crossed the nulla and climbed the spur, which ran to M. Arnato from the south-east. By 0300 hours on 17 July, however, it had succeeded in securing this important feature. But B Company failed to reach its objective, the Cemetery, and was pinned down by light machine gun fire. A fire plan was arranged in support of A and B Companies. Thick foliage hampered operations to a large extent. The companies had little idea of the actual positions, with the result that both A and B Companies walked into the fire plan, which had to be stopped. The Germans however had had enough of the fight and fled. By 0535 hours on 17 July, B Company secured Cemetery, A Company moved on to Pt. 593 and secured Uppiano by 0720 hours. In the morning no less than four German assaults were put in to recapture Uppiano and Pt. 470. All were beaten off. A more serious affair developed, however, late at night. At 2030 hours the Germans heavily shelled and mortared company positions. Ten minutes later a strong German counter-attack developed on the Gurkha companies on Pt. 470, Uppiano and Cemetery. Fierce fighting took place. A and D Companies on Uppiano and Pt. 470 respectively held the attack but B Company at Cemetery was pressed hard. By 2400 hours, however, the situation was brought under control. The German attack was beaten back and the Gurkhas were firmly established on the Uppiano feature.

Soon after this, 4/10 Baluch passed through 2/4 Gurkha and by 0255 hours on 18 July had occupied M. Arnato. Twenty Germans withdrew without offering any resistance. At 0440 hours however they counter-attacked but were driven back by the Baluch. With the capture of M. Arnato, the 10th Indian Infantry Brigade had completed its task of occupying the high ground, overlooking Citta di Castello from the west.

Thrust towards Monterchi

While the 10th Indian Infantry Brigade advanced for the attack on M. Cedrone, the 5th Indian Infantry Brigade made a thrust towards Monterchi. By the afternoon of 13 July this brigade had concentrated south of Monte S. Maria and was ready to pass through the 7th Indian Infantry Brigade to capture Pezzano, which was to provide a suitable base for operations against Monterchi. The plan was for the 3/10 Baluch to capture Cagnano and clear opposition east of the Monterchi road, while 1/4 Essex was to capture Pezzano and overcome resistance west of the road. 1/9 Gurkha was to assist 1/4 Essex by attacking Pezzano from M. Civitella.

At 2000 hours on 13 July, two companies of 1/4 Essex crossed the ridge west of Monte S. Maria and trickled down to establish a strong position on the high ground astride the Erchi stream, where the road took so many curious loops before crossing it. By 2350 hours, Pt. 558 and Pt. 560 were secured. This was an excellent move, which caused great annoyance to the Germans. For their part, they made movement a difficult business by promptly shelling any signs of activity. Movement was therefore largely confined to the hours of darkness. By the evening of 14 July the Scarzola stream was crossed and the advance continued to the area 478301. But strong defences and heavy machine gun and mortar fire prevented the seizure of Pezzano, on the next ridge to the north-west.

To help 1/4 Essex, B and C Companies of 1/9 Gurkha advanced down the spur from M. Civitella towards the village at 2030 hours on 14 July. By 1100 hours on 15 July both the companies were established on Pt. 682. There they consolidated for a further attack at 0100 hours on 16 July. B Company captured Pt. 617, within a mile of Pezzano, but encountered light machine gun, small arms and grenade fire when trying to clear the forward slopes. The Germans were very sensitive to movement in this direction. If developed, the advance would pass round the flank and get behind those German units resisting 1/4 Essex, and 4/10 Baluch still farther east at M. Cedrone. Hence the Gurkhas were subjected to a hail of mortar fire. In the valleys north of Pezzano, the Germans had assembled batteries of mortars to support their counter-attack. Without adequate shelter, 1/9 Gurkha lost heavily in the bombardment. Allied artillery was not able to get at the German mortars in their deep and narrow valleys. The Germans (estimated strength one company) emerged from the shelter of the nulla (R 467307) and launched four counter-attacks on B Company. Thereupon D Company was sent forward to support and to take ammunition, as B Company's supply was exhausted. D Company arrived just in time to beat off the fifth counter-attack, which was also partially dispersed by artillery fire. As the Gurkha battalion had suffered heavy casualties, both the companies were withdrawn to Pt. 682 by 0415 hours. Meanwhile, C Company's attack on Pt. 507 had been halted by heavy mortar fire and the company had been forced to return to Pt. 682. Thus the attempt to capture Pezzano had ended in failure.

Meanwhile, 3/10 Baluch was directed against Cagnano. At 2130 hours on 14 July, it moved across the Erchi on to Cagnano and Pt. 589, with only two companies C and D. Little time had been available for reconnaissance with the result that early in their advance the Baluch companies found themselves in a very difficult country intersected by numerous watercourses, which completely upset their attempts at keeping direction in the dark. The companies were forced to withdraw to Monte S. Maria on account of stiff German resistance. At 2030 hours on 15 July, however, C and D Companies raided Pt. 534 but the Germans pulled out before contact was made. The Baluch secured Cagnano without opposition.

After this success at M. Cedrone further to the east early on 17 July, the German commander withdrew his forces from Pezzano. Consequently when A and B Companies of 3/10 Baluch raided Pezzano at 0100 hours on 17 July they found that the Germans had evacuated it. The way was prepared for the attack on Monterchi.

Advance to Alpe di Poti

While the 10th Indian Infantry Brigade was hammering at the strong German position at M. Cedrone, and the 5th Indian Infantry Brigade was making a thrust towards Pezzano and Monterchi, the 7th Indian Infantry Brigade was making preparations for the assault on Alpe di Poti, which dominated the east and north-east of Arezzo. The attack on Alpe di Poti could not be launched until a jeep track was made through the mountains to connect the road at Volterrano with the road running from below M. Favalto to Palazzo del Pero. The attack did not come about till 17 July. But by that time Arezzo had fallen. Though the attack on Alpe di Poti failed in its original object of helping the XIII Corps to capture Arezzo, it indirectly helped to ease the situation. For after the capture of Arezzo on 16 July by the XIII Corps, the Germans gave up the attempt to defend Alpe di Poti. The capture of Arezzo by XIII Corps thus helped the 4th Indian Division to secure easily Alpe di Poti.

Great difficulty was encountered in making the jeep track across the mountains. There was paucity of roads running from south to north. The 10th Indian Infantry Brigade was moving along the badly damaged road on the west bank of the Tiber. The 5th Indian Infantry Brigade had assumed responsibility for the secondary road from Monte S. Maria to Monterchi and its junction with Route 73. West of this road was the rugged mass of mountains which ought to have separated, very effectively, the 4th Indian Division from its neighbours. Roads and tracks, running east or west, came to a dead end against this obstacle. Route 73, the one road making a complete link between the Tiber and Arezzo valleys, was held by the Germans and was of considerable value to them for the supply and reinforcement of their forces. The most vulnerable and at the same time the most important part of Route 73 on this stretch was at Palazzo del Pero, ten miles south-east of Arezzo. There the road was at its most southerly point and feeder tracks came in from south and south-west.

The track which was about to be constructed was meant to link up this strategic village with the road at Volterrano.

With the occupation of M. Civitella, M. Favalto and M. Pagliaiolo, stretches of Route 73 from Sansepolcro to Arezzo were brought under observation. Observation posts on those heights were able to call up fighter bombers and medium artillery to strafe German transport using Route 73. Indian troops on the features above were like gods sitting in judgement.

On 12 July, under cover of the protection provided by 2/11 Sikh and seizure of M. Pagliaiolo, M. Favalto, and M. Civitella, a preliminary survey of a possible route forward was carried out. From Volternano, north-west to S. Maria alla Rassinola, then west, crossing numerous ravines, to M. Dognana, over and to the Cerfone valley, the track would have to follow a boulder-strewn valley, traverse deep clefts, climb steep hillsides and burst through thick woods. Ten days' work was the estimate arrived at after this preliminary survey. Two days were spent in moving forward and assembling the labour and equipment to be employed on the task. On 14 July work on the track began. It was a strange medley of nationalities working on it. Dismounted detachments of men from Central India Horse, providing close protection, held the heights above them. The Bombay and Madras Sappers provided the backbone. Canadian Sappers were the technicians, whose knowledge of explosives was used in removing two and three-ton boulders. British Sappers drove the bulldozers. Italian labour companies lent their help in removing debris, trees and soil. The track known as Jacob's Ladder was opened to jeeps on 15 July. At 1800 hours on that day a patrol of Central India Horse moved into Palazzo del Pero and met an armoured car patrol from the New Zealand Divisional Cavalry Regiment (XIII Corps), which had entered the town from the west. From this time, Allied patrols became very active along Route 73 and by their activities undoubtedly forced the Germans to withdraw from the Tiber valley, earlier than had been their intention.

The next objective of the 7th Indian Infantry Brigade was the impressive mass of Alpe di Poti, north of Route 73 between the Tiber valley and Arezzo. The fall of Arezzo on 16 July made the German position at Alpe di Poti untenable, as they were denied acccess to the roads leading to it, all of which started from the region of Arezzo.

1/2 Gurkha, having been switched across from the right flank to M. Dogana on 16 July, advanced and before 0630 hours next morning occupied Pt. 935, two miles north of M. Dogana and the same distance east of Palazzo del Pero. From there the Gurkhas pushed on to the river Cerfone through Pt. 757, Pt. 723 and Pt. 616, without making contact with the Germans. One company was supporting the reconnaissance squadron of the Central India Horse along the track to Palazzo del Pero, from where it pushed on to Route 73.

In the night of 16/17 July, the Central India Horse took the place of 2/11 Sikh on M. Pagliaiolo and M. Favalto, in order to release that battalion for the attack on Alpe di Poti. By 1600 hours on 17 July, forward elements of 2/11 Sikh secured without opposition Pt. 842 and then pushed on to the river Cerfone, through Pt. 542 and Pt. 593.

In the night of 17/18 July, the 7th Indian Infantry Brigade crossed Route 73 and advanced towards the summit of the Alpe di Poti. 1/2 Gurkha, on the left, advanced from the road, which took off about R 375305, in order to occupy positions facing north and west, with the right of the poistion at Pt. 974—thence Pt. 876—Pt. 869, thence south along 35 Easting. 2/11 Sikh, on the right, advanced from road, which took off about 389315, in order to occupy positions facing north and east, with the right of the position at Pt. 720—Pt. 706, thence Pt. 756, Pt. 854, Pt. 831, and Pt. 966. By 0300 hours on 18 July, the Gurkhas were on their objectives, the Germans apparently having decided not to hold the mountain. Nine hours later, 2/11 Sikh also, assisted by a squadron of tanks from the Royal Wiltshire Yeomanry, secured its objectives, though it had been delayed by heavy mortaring.

By 18 July 1944, the 4th Indian Division had carried out the tasks assigned to it, M. Cedrone (guarding the approaches to Citta di Castello) had been secured; Pezzano, which was to serve as a base for operations against Monterchi had been captured; and Alpe di Poti (whose capture was originally intended to threaten the German force at Arezzo) was secured. East of the Tiber, the advance of the 10th Indian Division had been delayed and it was not till 22 July that Citta di Castello was captured. But already by 16 July, the XIII Corps (the spearhead of the Eighth Army attack) had captured Arezzo, the main objective of the Eighth Army. The Eighth Army now regrouped for the main advance to the Arno.

CHAPTER XIV

The Advance to Florence

The Regrouping of the Eighth Army

With the capture of Arezzo on 16 July 1944 the Eighth Army had secured an administrative base and now prepared to capture Florence, which was to serve as an operational base for the attack on the Gothic Line. Consequently the weight of the Eighth Army's attack had to be shifted to the left so that the XIII Corps, the main striking force, should drive down the valley of the middle Arno to Florence and the X Corps should advance north to secure Bibbiena. Therefore the Eighth Army regrouped between 17 and 22 July 1944. The left boundary of the X Corps was extended so as to include the Arezzo area. Another reason for the regrouping of the Eighth Army was that the role of the Fifth Army was modified considerably. It had been advancing to the river Arno with the IV U.S. Corps on the left and the French Expeditionary Corps on the right. On 22/23 July the Fifth Army had pushed on to the Arno and held a thirty-five mile front along the river, extending from the sea to Empoli, about twenty miles west of Florence. But now the Fifth Army was to be weakened considerably for the French Expeditionary Corps was pulled out of the line as it was needed for operation 'Anvil'. Denuded of troops for the invasion of southern France, the Fifth Army now temporarily went on the defensive along the Arno front, leaving it to the Eighth Army to lead the main Allied attack on Florence.

The Pursuit to the Arno

While the Fifth Army went on the defensive on the Arno from 23 July, the Eighth Army encountered fierce opposition in its advance to Florence and Bibbiena, the objectives of the XIII and X Corps respectively. As the XIII Corps was the main striking force of the Eighth Army we shall first describe its advance to the Arno. The advance of the XIII Corps on Florence began on a front of three divisions. The main thrust was made on the right, where the 6th British Armoured Division drove down the Arno valley, east of the river. In the centre, the British 4th Division advanced astride Route 69, between the Arno and the Monti di Chianti ridge. On the left, the 6th South African Armoured Division advanced west of Monti di Chianti, through Radda and Greve. The advance continued against stiffening opposition. A new situation arose when on 22 July the XIII Corps took over the sector (astride Route 2) from the French

Expeditionary Corps, the 2nd New Zealand Division taking over the right sector and the 8th Indian Division the left one. This extension of the Corps frontage enabled General Kirkman, the Commander of the XIII Corps, to shift the weight of the attack to the left, particularly as the advance had come to a virtual halt on the east flank, east of Route 69. General Kirkman therefore decided to make the main thrust with the 2nd New Zealand Division and the 6th South African Armoured Division in order to secure crossings over the Arno at the west of Florence. The former was to make a thrust north from Castellina in Chianti, across Route 2 at S. Casciano, and north over the Arno at Signa, five miles west of Florence, while the latter was to advance astride the general line Radda—Greve—Impruneta. The three other divisions were assigned the role of the protection of the flanks—the 8th Indian Division and the 6th British Armoured Division of the left and right flanks of the corps and the British 4th Division of the right flank of the striking force. All these three divisions were to follow up the Germans, as opportuniy offered.

By 25 July, the XIII Corps had closed up to the Olga Line, which extended from Mercatale through S. Casciano (ten miles south of Florence) to Montespertoli. At that time the 6th South African Armoured Division was held up south of Mercatale and the 2nd New Zealand Division south of S. Casciano. The 2nd New Zealand Division captured S. Casciano on 27 July after a spirited attack and pushed on the advance until it was halted on 29 July by stiffening resistance. By that time the 6th South African Armoured Division had also been checked on the defensive line from Strada in Chianti to Impruneta. Meanwhile the flanking divisions had been also advancing. The 8th Indian Division, operating on the left of the corps, had reached the Arno east of Empoli. The British 4th Division, guarding the right flank of the 6th South African Armoured Division, cleared the Germans from M. Scalari after stubborn resistance. The stage was now set for the advance to Florence. Four and a half German divisions, concentrated on a front, stretching from Figline on the upper Arno to Montelupo west of Florence, barred the way to the city. On 30 July the 2nd New Zealand Division led the attack, west of Route 2, on strong German positions based on the ridge of Pian dei Cerri. After a fierce struggle the New Zealanders captured the crest of La Poggiona on 2 August, thereby ousting the Germans from the ridge. After a stiff rearguard action on the River Ema, the Germans were across the Arno on 3 August. They blew up all the bridges except Ponte Vecchio. The 6th South African Armoured Division, after capturing Strada and Impruneta, reached the southern outskirts of Florence; the British 4th Division closed up to the Arno south-east of Florence; the 8th Indian Division captured Castiglioni on 1 August and established a bridge-head over the Pesa, about ten miles west of Florence. On 4 August, when the Allies had reached the southern outskirts of Florence, the plan for the Eighth Army's attack on the Gothic Line was fundamentally changed. Instead of launching the attack on the Gothic Line from Florence, the main operational base, the Eighth Army was ordered to attack on a narrow front on the Adriatic coast. This meant a radical regrouping of the Eighth Army. While the Allied forces in Italy regrouped for the attack on the Gothic Line, no serious attempt was made to force a crossing of the Arno in the neighbourhood of Florence. The British 4th Division however utilised the time in liquidating German opposition in the loop of the river opposite Pontassieve. The hill and the monastery at Incontro, the key of the German defence line, were captured on 8 August, and by 10 August German resistance collapsed in the rest of the Arno loop. From Pontassieve to its boundary at Fucecchio the Eighth Army stood on the line of the Arno and its advance through Central Italy was brought to a successful conclusion.

The Role of the 8th Indian Division

Having described the advance of the XIII Corps to the Arno, it is now necessary to give an account of the role of the 8th Indian Division in these operations. The main striking force was provided by the 2nd New Zealand Division and the 6th South African Armoured Division and the role of the 8th Indian Division was to provide left flank protection and to follow up the Germans as opportunity offered. On 22 July, the 8th Indian Division took over the left sector of the French Expeditionary Corps, holding a front north of Poggibonsi, extending from just south of Barberino on Route 2 across to Certaldo and Castelfiorentino. Two brigades were in the line, the 21st Indian Infantry Brigade in area Barberino and the 19th Indian Infantry Brigade in area Certaldo.

Major-General Russell planned to advance on a two brigade front, with the 21st Indian Infantry Brigade on the right and the 19th Indian Infantry Brigade on the left. The former was to advance from area Barberino through Montespertoli to Montelupo, while the latter was to advance from area Certaldo through Castelfiorentino towards the Arno. The 17th Indian Infantry Brigade, in reserve, was to be prepared to advance on either axis with a view to passing through either of the forward brigades. The 8th Indian Division had the following troops under command:
    1st Canadian Armoured Brigade
    98th Field Regiment (self-propelled)
    315th Battery (self-propelled) 105th Anti-Tank Regiment
    1st Army Group, Royal Artillery with under command:

58th Medium Regiment
70th Medium Regiment
5th Heavy Regiment
5th Survey Regiment less one Battery
125th Meteorological Section, R.A.F.
6th Indian Mule Company
One Indian Pioneer Battalion.

The following additional troops were in support:[1]
B Flight 655 Air Observation Post Squadron.

Two German divisions held positions facing the 8th Indian Division—the *4th Parachute Division* and the *29th Panzer Grenadier Division*. Of the former, *12 Parachute Regiment* was astride Route 2, *11 Parachute Regiment* in Barberino—Tavarnelle area, and *10 Parachute Regiment* in area M. Novella. Of the latter, *15 Panzer Grenadier Regiment* flanked *10 Parachute Regiment* (in area M. Novella) on the west, while *71 Panzer Grenadier Regiment* operated north-east of Castelfiorentino.

The Germans were holding Barberino with probably two companies of infantry. Extending north-west from Barberino as far as the river Elsa, there were a number of pockets of resistance, notably at Mugnano, Montebello and the area north-east of Castelfiorentino.

Capture of Montespertoli

On 23 July, the 19th and 21st Indian Infantry Brigades set off in the race for the Arno. The German forces were retreating towards the river, the retreat being covered by rearguards. The initial advance did not encounter any opposition though it was slightly delayed by mines, demolitions and long-range shelling. Opposition however stiffened near Montespertoli, the western extremity of the German defensive line, known as the Olga Line. We shall first describe the progress of the 8th Indian Division to Montespertoli and then give an account of its advance up to the Arno.

The 21st Indian Infantry Brigade had two battalions in the line—1/5 Mahratta Light Infantry in the hills overlooking Route 2, one thousand yards south of Barberino, and the 5th Battalion Queen's Own Royal West Kent Regiment[2] about four thousand yards east of Certaldo. The brigade plan was for 1/5 Mahratta and the 5th Royal West Kent Regiment to converge on the cross-roads north of Fiano, the former advancing by road Barberino—Marcialla and the latter moving up road via S. Lazzaro. Then 3/5 Punjab was to pass through and advance on Montespertoli by the road Pode il Monte and La Torre and 1/5 Mahratta was to move along the road via S. Pietro and converge on Montespertoli.

[1] 8 Ind. Div. O. O. No. 24, dated 18 July; and O. O. No. 25, dated 21 July 1944.
[2] It was temporarily under command of the 19 Ind. Inf. Bde.

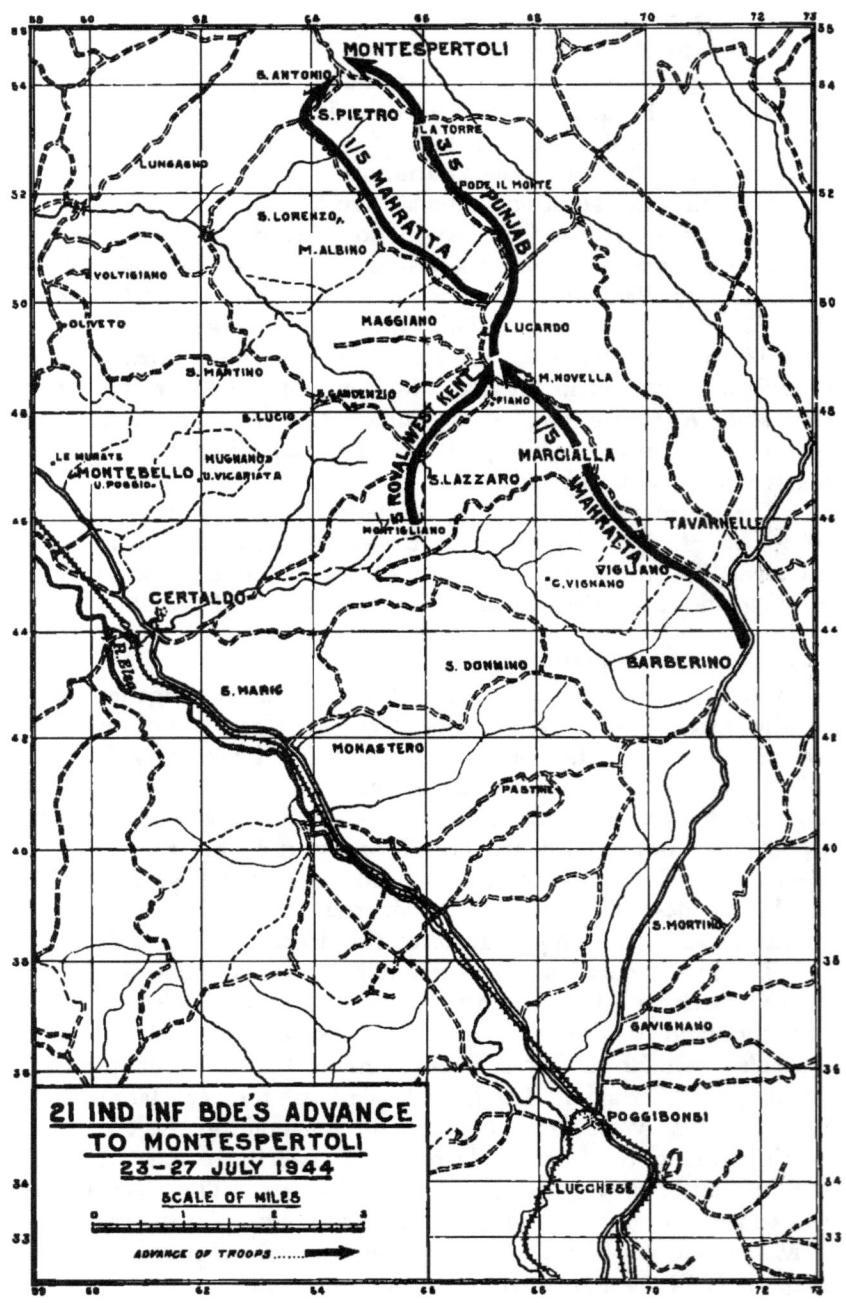

In the night of 22/23 July, the Mahratta patrols to Barberino had reported indications of a German withdrawal. At 0900 hours on 23 July, the 52nd Field Regiment and 4.2-inch mortars of the 5th Royal Mahratta Machine Gun Battalion brought down a heavy concentration on Barberino and the feature situated to the right of the village. C and D Companies then advanced with objectives Barberino and the feature on the right of the village, with one troop of tanks in support of each company. By 0930 hours both the companies were well on their objectives without meeting any opposition. Battalion Headquarters with the two remaining companies then moved into the village. The road skirting the edge of the village had been completely demolished. Teller mines placed at regular intervals under the flagstones of the main street had made it quite impassable. Until the road was repaired, the transport was held up for several hours. However the battalion pioneers set to work in right earnest and within an hour cleared the mines, thus enabling C and A Companies to push forward the advance. They moved north from Barberino for a mile, then swung north-west from the main road and thrust up a secondary road towards Montespertoli. This road and its verges were thick with mines, which the Germans had sown when they withdrew, and culverts were prepared for demolition with time charge. On one occasion, a commander of the pioneer platoon removed one of these charges from a culvert only a few minutes before it was due to explode. The pioneers worked hard, lifting mines, clearing the verges, removing the charges from culverts so that the impatient infantry could push on and contact the retreating Germans. All the way along the road there were freshly cut notches on the trunks of the tall trees, lining the road in and avenue. The notches had been cut by the German Sappers to take a stick of dynamite which, when exploded, would have sent the trees tumbling down to block the road. However, the speed of the German withdrawal was so great that they were not able to carry out this part of their plan. By 1900 hours, the Mahratta had gained contact with the Germans, eight-hundred yards short of the village of Marcialla. Spandau fire came from the village and the tank and self-propelled gun fire from the right flank. There was only a brief halt for, that night, the Germans vacated Marcialla and at 0900 hours on 24 July A Company moved into the village, while C Company went through to form a start line for the advance of Y and D Companies beyond Marcialla.

At 1430 hours Y and D Companies pushed forward to S. M. Novella and captured a Castle about a mile north of Marcialla, although the road leading to the village was completely under observation, and the Germans shelled any movement on it. After the occupation of S. M. Novella, the German shelled the village for ten minutes causing six casualties. The advance was resumed and at nightfall the Mahratta, with the supporting squadron the 14th Canadian Armoured Regiment, gained a mile and a half to the north-west of Marcialla, with companies established on the high ground, south-east of Lucardo.

On the left flank of the 21st Indian Infantry Brigade the 5th Royal West Kent Regiment had begun its advance at about 1745 hours on 23 July, from area Montigliano across very broken country, but it managed to keep pace with the Mahratta on the right. Twenty-four hours later, the British troops were level with the Indians in the village of Fiano, a mile south of Lucardo. 3/15 Punjab, then in reserve about a hundred yards south-east of Marcialla, moved through the Mahratta positions during the night of 24/25 July and, by 0400 hours on 25 July, had occupied Lucardo unopposed. From this village, two roads ran north-west to Montespertoli; 3/15 Punjab pushed up the right hand road while 1/5 Mahratta took the left hand route. In the thick mist, which enveloped the hills until 0930 hours on 25 July, both the Mahratta and the Punjab had patrol clashes with German rearguards. Later, when visibility improved, C Company 1/5 Mahratta attacked M. Albino, where its approach provoked resistance from four or five machine guns. The tanks and artillery engaged this very prominent target before C Company charged forward with fixed bayonets. The Germans, however, had retired in great haste during a lull in the action. The 3/15 Punjab, supported by Canadian tanks, in the meantime, had worked forward up another spur towards Pode il Monte, a small conical shaped feature, capped by a cyprus grove, surrounding an old country mansion. They reached this place in the early evening and took shelter against heavy bursts of shelling. They were following the Germans closely. Earlier in the day, Canadian tanks and artillery observers had seen two German platoons withdrawing towards Montespertoli and had engaged them effectively.[3]

On 26 July D and A Companies of the Mahratta pushed forward to area S. Lorenzo, with the object of capturing the tiny hamlet of S. Pietro, about a mile south-west of Montespertoli. All the tracks in the area of S. Lorenzo were thick with mines and, in spite of the efforts of the pioneer platoon in clearing them, a Sherman tank had its tracks blown off. The bridge north of S. Lorenzo had been blown and there was a very remote chance of getting a diversion made, as the road was completely under observation and any effort on the part of the pioneer platoon even to sweep the road was greeted by spandau fire from S. Antonio. As information about German dispositions was very meagre, Commander A Company decided to send

---

[3] A report on the operations of the 8 Ind. Div. between 1 February—31 July 1944, File 7802.

a patrol to area S. Pietro and then follow up the patrol with the company. The patrol worked up to S. Pietro and having got so far without any opposition did not expect to find any Germans in the vicinity. The platoon commander however was surprised on entering the Church to find a German section getting ready to pull out. An exchange of fire took place but the Germans managed to get away. Then A Company took up positions in the area of the church. This area was very heavily "stonked" by the German mortars in Montespertoli, who apparently had an observation post, with excellent observation of every move the men of the Mahratta company made. After a while, the Mahratta company commander noticed that the mortars always fired on the clanging of the church bell. One bell was the signal for mortar bombs to crash down in the square in front of the church; two clangs brought down mortar fire in the garden behind the church, whilst three clangs of the bell was the signal for fire on a wadi adjacent to the church. After a particularly heavy mortar stonk, the company commander decided to stop the rot. He collected all the Italian civilians and locked them up in the cellar underneath the church. The weird changing of the bell stopped and with it the mortar fire lost most of its accuracy. The enemy agent was never found, but might have been one of those Italians locked up under the church. The Mahratta company suffered eight casualties. Meanwhile by the evening of 26 July, 3/15 Punjab, working forward from Pode il Monte through La Torre, was halted at Pode Rucco, about a mile to the south of Montespertoli, having suffered 23 casualties from shelling, whilst the Mahratta held on grimly to San Pietro under artillery and mortar fire.

The New Zealanders, on the right of the 8th Indian Division, put in a strong attack during the night of 26/27 July, resulting in the capture of S. Casciano, thus forcing the Germans to withdraw on the 8th Indian Division's front. Actually, the Germans had pulled out of their positions in Montespertoli at dusk on 26 July and were helped on their way in the half light by Bren gun and mortar fire from the Mahratta and the Punjab Battalions, and machine gun fire from the Canadian tanks. If they had waited for darkness to cloak their movements they could probably have withdrawn without casualties, but as it was they must have had a considerable number of casualties. The 3/15 Punjab entered Montespertoli without opposition at 0900 hours on 7 July. The village was very heavily mined and the road cut by three huge craters. A bull-dozer soon made these passable.

While the 21st Indian Infantry Brigade advancing from the area Barberino secured Montespertoli, the 19th Indian Infantry Brigade on the left captured the high ground from Gigliola to Cambiano. At 1730 hours on 22 July, a company of 6/13 Royal

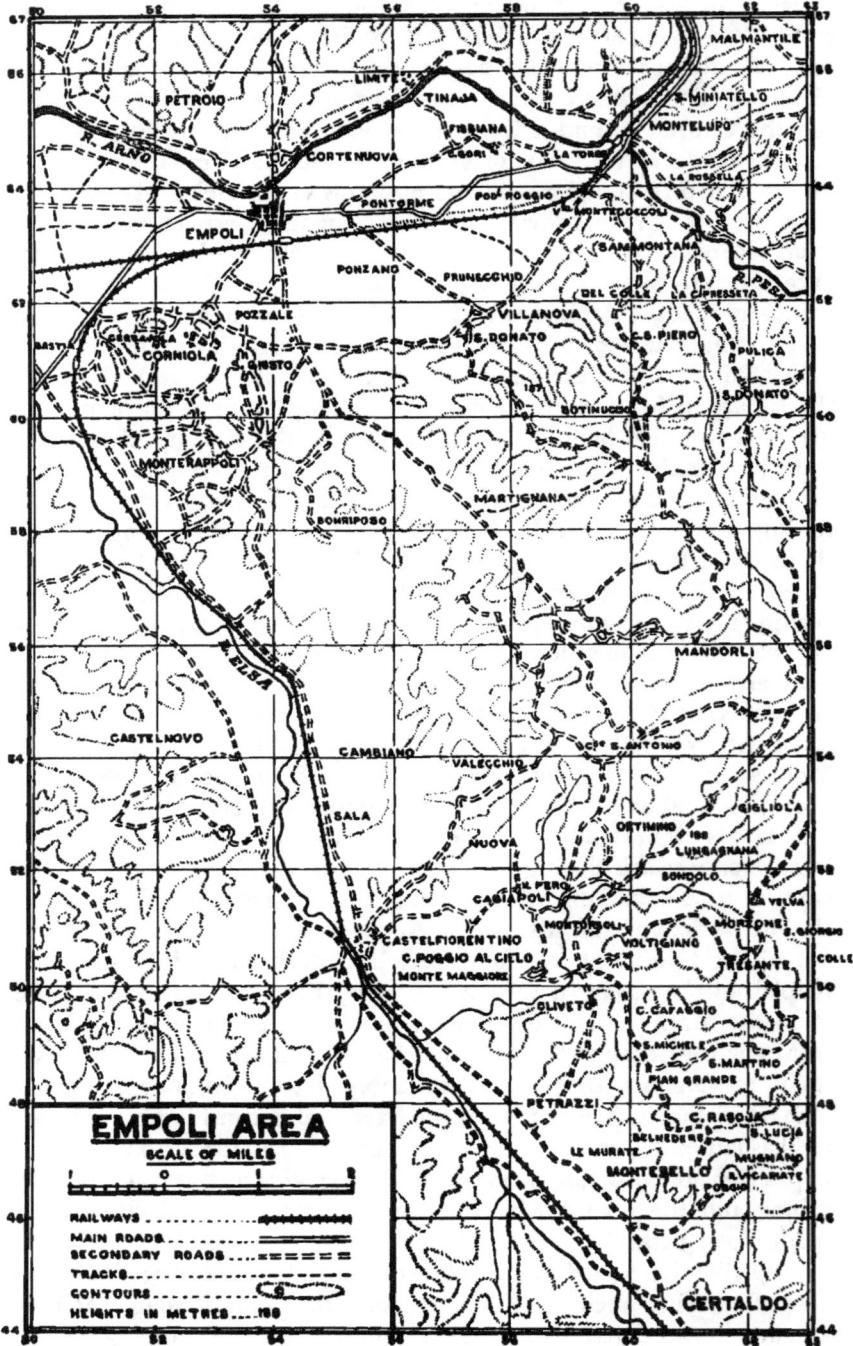

Frontier Force Rifles, with two troops of the 14th Canadian Armoured Regiment in support, led the advance from Certaldo and secured Montebello without opposition at 1830 hours. The next day some progress was made and by last light the forward companies were located at Montebello and Mugnano. The Germans had pulled back and were withdrawing mainly north-east towards Montespertoli. While withdrawing they had carried out a very thorough demolition and mining programme. That considerably slowed down the advance of the 21st Indian Infantry Brigade. By 26 July, however, 6/13 Royal Frontier Force Rifles had secured Lungagnana and Ortimino and was ready to capture the objective—the defence line based on S. Antonio and Gigliola. The company directed on S. Antonio was unable to enter the village owing to opposition from infantry supported by Tiger tanks. Similarly the company directed towards Gigliola met with opposition. As the company reached the summit of this hill, Pt. 189, two German medium machine guns and tanks opened fire. The Germans were driven away after a stiff fight. Later the company suffered 6 casualties due to German shelling. By 2000 hours the battalion was well secured in its position, the objective Gigliola—S. Antonio was captured and the stage was now set for a rapid advance to the Arno.

To the left, the 1st Argyll and Sutherland Highlanders too secured its objective Cambiano—Valecchio without much difficulty. On 23 July this battalion advanced from the area Certaldo and occupied Petrazzi and M. Maggiore, preparatory to the capture of Montorsoli and the advance on axis roads leading north-east and north-west from Castelfiorentino. Montorsoli was occupied without opposition on 24 July, Cambiano on the next day and Valecchio at 0300 hours on 26 July. Thus by the early morning of 27 July both the Argyll and 6/13 Royal Frontier Force Rifles had secured the high ground from Gigliola to Cambiano.

The 3/8 Punjab had been released from duties to prepare for a ceremonial parade at Siena. There, on the morning of 26 July, a representative assembly drawn from all units of the division, saw His Majesty the King of England present the ribbon of the Victoria Cross to Sepoy Kamal Ram for his heroism at the breaching of the Gustav Line. This eighteen-year old soldier won the first Indian Army Victoria Cross in Italy.

Advance towards R. Pesa

After overcoming German opposition at Montespertoli the 8th Indian Division made a double thrust—one to the Arno in the Empoli area and the other to the river Pesa. The latter thrust was intended to divert the German attention from the main attack by the 2nd New Zealand Division on the ridge Pian dei Cerri, the main

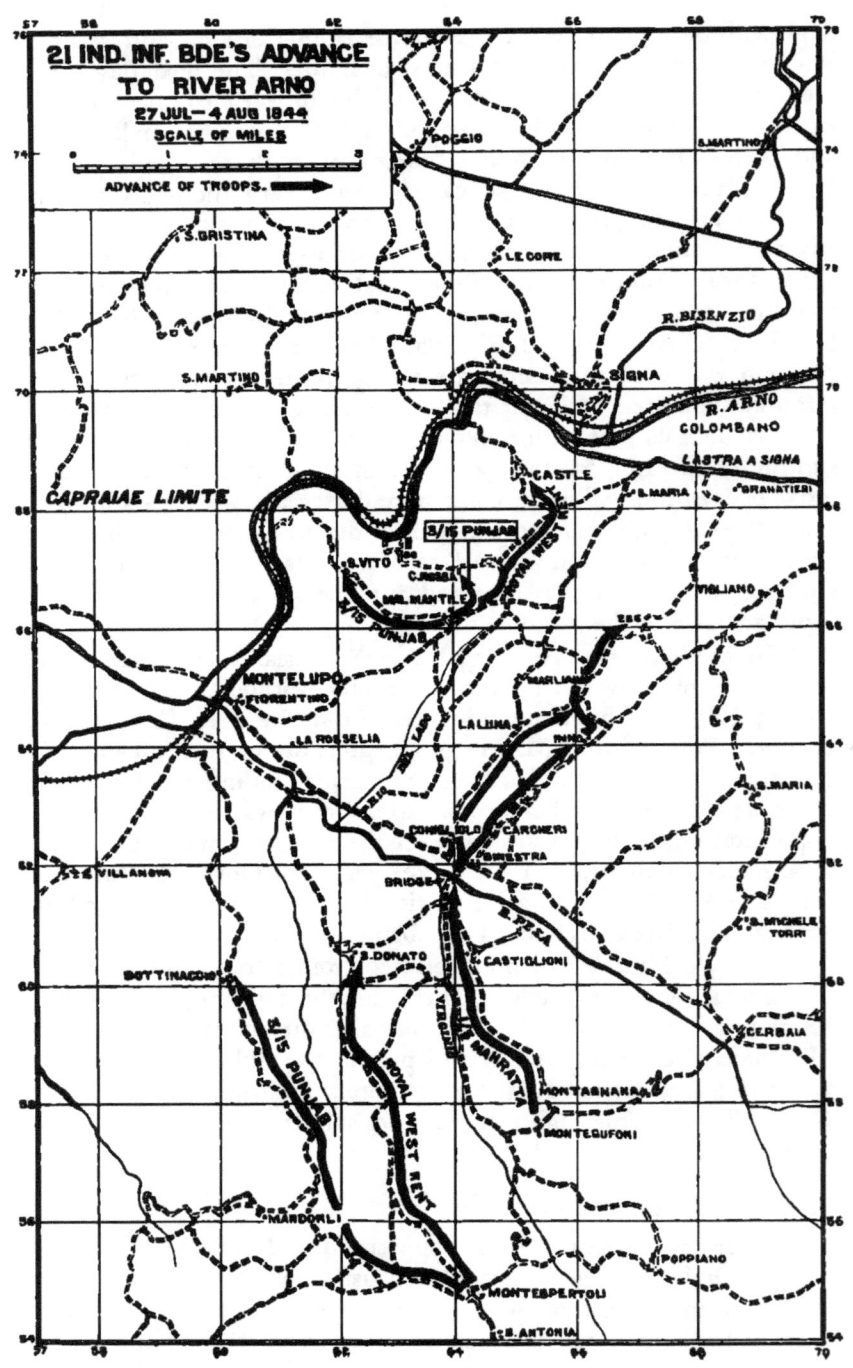

defensive position blocking the road to Florence. We shall first describe the thrust to R. Pesa.

After the capture of Montespertoli early on 27 July the 21st Indian Infantry Brigade advanced towards R. Pesa. The infantry units from 3/15 Punjab scrambled aboard the tanks of their supporting squadron, the 12th Canadian Armoured Regiment, and advanced from Montespertoli towards Bottinaccio, a German outpost, which they occupied at 1835 hours on 27 July. The absence of shell or mortar fire seemed to indicate that the main German force was busy making good its withdrawal beyond the river Pesa.

The 5th Royal West Kent Regiment also had a successful day. Advancing from Fiano area at 0630 hours on 27 July the battalion passed through Montespertoli, mounted on tanks of the 12th Canadian Armoured Regiment, to carry on the pursuit towards the Arno. It completed a rapid advance some four miles along the ridge above a stream, the Virginio, and, at 1900 hours, reached the area of S. Donato, where the ridge dropped down into the valley of the Pesa. Here a few German stragglers were captured and battalion headquarters established near the church. This brought the British battalion within two and a half miles of Montelupo and the Arno, and it was at this point that German resistance stiffened. During the night the battalion area was shelled causing 16 casualties.

1/5 Mahratta came up hard on the heels of the British troops. Advancing from S. Pietro at 2030 hours on 27 July this battalion concentrated south-west of S. Donato and pushed forward patrols to reconnoitre crossing places on the Pesa. The river ran in a north westerly direction to Montelupo and the Arno. The Mahratta found the north bank of the river to the east of Montelupo strongly held by the Germans.

On 28 and 29 July the 21st Indian Infantry Brigade confined its activities to patrolling. On 30 July, 1/5 Mahratta moved over to the Montegufoni area. The 21st Indian Infantry Brigade was now ready to establish a bridge-head over the river Pesa and to demonstrate so as to distract the attention of the Germans from the main attack by the 2nd New Zealand Division on the ridge Pian dei Cerri.

By 1 August, the main German force had been driven back across the Pesa by the swift Allied advance, but a few German posts remained with orders to report Allied progress. The strongest of these pockets on the front of the 21st Indian Infantry Brigade was entrenched among the trees and around the tiny church of Castiglioni, a village just south of the river, on the right of the 8th Indian Division's front. The road from Castiglioni ran down to the Pesa, crossing the river by a bridge, which the Germans had demolished, and joining a lateral road, running parallel to the river, a few yards beyond the bridge. From this lateral, numerous roads ran in northeasterly direction to Florence. The Germans had sufficient time before their withdrawal to lay anti-personnel and anti-tank mines along the roads and tracks, and to destroy bridges and culverts. Such forces as were left behind were supported by three or four self-propelled guns, as the Indian drivers who travelled too fast along those dusty tracks soon found to their cost.

Speed being a vital factor, the 21st Indian Infantry Brigade made ready to establish a bridge-head over the Pesa river. At that time of the year, the stream was almost dry and only about five feet wide. Examination of air photographs, together with information from the local peasants, revealed suitable crossing places for the infantry, transport, tanks and mules. North of the river, a series of parallel spurs, thickly wooded and intersected by steep "gullys", ran down to the Pesa. From these ridges, the Germans had excellent observation of the approach of the Indian troops and good cover for daytime movement. Up the back of the spurs, running in a general northeasterly direction, were three minor roads, along which the brigade was to advance. In such country German Sappers had little trouble in making effective demolitions to delay the advance. The bridge over the Pesa was of course blown. Some eight hundred yards further south, another bridge was destroyed. On the roads, numerous culverts were torn open causing craters which had to be filled in and a large diversion made before the road could be traversed.

Facing the 21st Indian Infantry Brigade was *29 Panzer Grenadier Regiment (the 3rd Panzer Grenadier Division)* with *II Battalion* from the river Arno to the left line of the stream Rio del Lago, *I Battalion* to its south-east and *III Battalion* between road S. Martino-Limite and the R. Arno.[4] *8 Panzer Grenadier Regiment (the 3rd Panzer Grenadier Division)* however moved over from the Empoli area during the night of 30/31 July to relieve the Panzer grenadiers of *29 Panzer Grenadier Regiment.*[5]

Brigadier Mould decided to cross the river Pesa and to capture the four spurs, running north-east from the lateral road between the road junction at Q 624629 and the road junction at Q 643620, so as to deny the Germans observation of sapper work on the demolished bridge at Q 640619. As an essential prelude to this operation, he ordered 1/5 Mahratta to clear the German pocket at Castiglioni. Then, with the danger to the right flank removed, the brigade was to advance at night, with 1/5 Mahratta on the right and the 5th Royal West Kent Regiment on the left. The troops were to cross the start line—river Pesa—at 2330 hours on 1 August. The objectives for 1/5

[4] 21 Ind. Inf. Bde. Intelligence Review No. 22, dated 1 August 1944.
[5] 8 Ind. Div. Intelligence Summary No. 136, dated 2 August 1944.

Mahratta were first the village of Ginestra, then the cemetery near Carcheri, and the spur to the west at Pt. 146. On its left, the 5th Royal West Kent Regiment was to secure the high ground (Q 634634), north-west of Conigliolo. With each battalion was one tank squadron of the 12th Canadian Armoured Regiment, Sappers and Miners of the 66th Field Company Indian Engineers, mules for the carriage of stores and ammunition. One company of the 5th Royal Mahratta Machine Gun Battalion allotted four Vickers machine guns to operate with each forward battalion. The 52nd Field Regiment Royal Artillery and six troops of field artillery, with a battery of medium artillery, were in support of the brigade.

During the early hours of 1 August, whilst it was still dark, C Company of 1/5 Mahratta, carrying out a pincer movement with two platoons, advanced from the area Montegufoni and attacked Castiglioni from the south and south-east. The attack was wholly successful and after a short fire-fight in the vicinity of the church, a little to the north of the village, the German rearguard retired hastily among the olive-clad slopes of the hill. By first light, the company was firmly established, being troubled only by occasional small arms and automatic fire from a German patrol on a hill, about one thousand yards east of the village. The absence of hostile mortar or shell fire indicated that the Germans had possibly withdrawn some distance. It was reasonable to suppose that their artillery gun area was now located behind the Malmantile ridge. The day passed quietly, with the remainder of the 21st Indian Infantry Brigade resting in preparation for the crossing of the river that night.

The Brigade-head over R. Pesa

1/5 Mahratta and the 5th Royal West Kent Regiment, supported by heavy artillery and tank fire, moved forward at 2330 hours on 1 August to establish a bridge-head over the river Pesa. C Company 1/5 Mahratta advanced from start line, road junction (Q 638601), while the rest of the battalion having assembled near Cemetery, advanced up the road running east of river Virginio. The plan of operations was as follows:

(i) C Company was to cross the river first, and secure Ginestra as a firm base.
(ii) A and D Companies were to pass through, the former along Ginestra—Carcheri road, and the latter along Conigliolo—La Luna road.
(iii) The attack was to be a silent one, with fire to be called for by the forward observation officer with the companies.

Due to the noise made by the tanks and a bull-dozer working on the diversions, the attack was far from silent. However, there was no opposition, as the Mahrattas crossed the river, moved forward over the lateral road, and made for the final objective. As they forged their way up the steep hillside, they encountered slight small arms fire from German stragglers hastening to get away. By 0025 hours on 2 August, C Company reached Ginestra and then A and D Companies passed through. Tanks were held up longer than anticipated, as a blow in the road between Ginestra and the blown bridge was much worse than what the Sappers had bargained for. After some shifting about, the Canadian tanks soon smashed their way through trees into the village. A troop each went off to A and D Companies respectively, while a troop was in reserve near battalion headquarters in Ginestra. The right hand company (A) reached its final objective, the Cemetery, near Carcheri without opposition at 0250 hours. The left hand company occupied position near Conigliolo. Its progress had been slow due to many fallen trees on the road, making effective road-blocks for the tanks. The road was cleared by the bull-dozers. D Company captured three Germans armed with a spandau and a Bazooka. There was spasmodic shelling, particularly on the village of Ginestra. The Mahrattas accomplished their task successfully. They had captured Ginestra and were astride the roads Ginestra—Carcheri and Conigliolo—La Luna.

The 5th Royal West Kent Regiment, on the left, was equally successful. Two of its companies, with A Squadron of the 12th Canadian Armoured Regiment in support, reached their final objective astride the road at Q 633633 without opposition at 0300 hours on 2 August. Occasional German shells landed close but did not delay the advance. Meanwhile, infantry pioneers with their mine-sweeping apparatus were searching the roads for mines, and down by the river, the sappers were making a diversion around the completed bridge, where a chugging bull-dozer was hard at work. A provost detachment under command of the brigade sign-posted the new area, and established a one way circular traffic route so that very soon after the establishment of the bridge-head there was a steady flow of vital supplies.

Advance to the Arno

On 3 August the advance continued north-east from the lateral road. 1/5 Mahratta occupied without opposition La Luna and Inno, where there had been a sharp patrol engagement with twelve Germans the previous evening. The battalion continued the advance through Marliano at last light on 3 August and after slight resistance captured Pt. 286. The capture of this feature afforded a fine view of the Arno valley to the east. From here, as the sun rose over the wooded hills, the Mahrattas caught their first sight of the city of Florence, still in German hands.

The 3/15 Punjab, passing through the forward companies of the

5th Royal West Kent Regiment at 2130 hours on 3 August reached Malmantile by 0200 hours on 4 August and established the headquarters there at 0130 hours, after overcoming opposition from a patrol consisting of forty Germans. The main street of the village was impassable, blocked as it was by a huge pile of debris from several houses on each side of the road which the Germans had demolished to delay the advance. The Indian sappers were equal to the task, having met earlier far worse obstacles than this. A small bull-dozer was rushed forward taking priority over other traffic, and within two hours a passage wide enough for vehicles was cut through the rubble. Soon after midnight, whilst the battalion headquarters was still exploring its new home, a fierce German artillery concentration shook the village.

The 5th Royal West Kent Regiment, passing in the morning on 4 August through the 3/15 Punjab positions in the Malmantile area, captured a castle, only half a mile short of the Arno, whilst the 3/15 Punjab also made a sweeping advance to within a short distance of the river, establishing companies at S. Vito and C Rossa. In the afternoon German artillery activity increased. The Castle, and the small cluster of buildings on the bare hill at S. Vito and Pt. 286, the battalion areas of all the three battalions of the brigade, were all silhouetted on the skyline, and German gunners and mortar crews did not miss their opportunity. There was fierce intermittent shelling and mortar fire, which caused 15 casualties to the 5th Royal West Kent Regiment, when a direct hit was scored on a house they were occupying in the Castle area.

Advance to Empoli

We have described the right thrust of the 8th Indian Division towards river Pesa and beyond to the Arno. Now we shall describe the left thrust towards Empoli. After securing the high ground north of Gigliola—Cambiano early on 27 July 1944, the 19th Indian Infantry Brigade advanced to the line of the lateral road S. Donato—Pozzale in order to exploit north to the R. Arno. 6/13 Royal Frontier Force Rifles, on the right, advanced north of S. Antonio to S. Donato while the Argyll, on the left, advanced along road Bonriposo—Pozzale. On 28 July both the battalions were in S. Donato and Pozzale area.[6] 3/8 Punjab then passed through 6/13 Royal Frontier Force Rifles in S. Donato area to secure the railway line and road Fibbiana—Cortenuova, while the Argyll advanced to the river Arno to secure road Cortenuova—Empoli. At 1200 hours on 29 July, 3/8 Punjab passed through 6/13 Royal Frontier Force Rifles; D Company occupied Sammontana and Montecuccoli; C Company occupied Pod Poggio; B Company was

[6] 3/8 Punjab came under command of the 19 Ind. Inf. Bde. on 28 July.

in position in area Botto. The patrols worked forward to Fibbiana.

On the left the Argyll too had advanced to a position facing the railway station of Empoli, which was a centre of German activity. Several German patrols were active along the front, being inquisitive but not aggressive. The month of July ended on an aggressive note with a surprise attack on the Empoli railway station by a company of the Argyll, supported by medium machine guns and two troops tanks of the 14th Canadian Armoured Regiment. The attack was made at 1130 hours on 31 July. German infantry ran to the north side of the railway line and was mowed down by machine gun fire. The tanks fired armour piercing shells into the station buildings, forcing more Germans to come out into the open, where they were caught by fire from the factory area (Q 549632). At least 12 Germans were killed and many more wounded. The raiding party suffered no casualty.

Early in August the 19th Indian Infantry Brigade sent out frequent patrols by night to harass the Germans, who were still south of the Arno. Whenever opportunity offered, the brigade was quick to edge its way forward among the vineyards and orchards, which abounded in that region. The forward troops were subjected to some shelling and were harassed by intermittent mortar fire.

Advance to Montelupo

While the 21st Indian Infantry Brigade advanced to the Arno near Signa and the 19th Indian Infantry Brigade to Empoli area, the 17th Indian Infantry Brigade was directed on Montelupo. During the night of 2/3 August 1944, the Divisional Commander ordered the 17th Indian Infantry Brigade to take over the central sector of the divisional front, relieving units of both the forward brigades. 1/12 Frontier Force Regiment relieved 3/15 Punjab and 1/5 Gurkha relieved 3/8 Punjab. The Germans were still in Montelupo. From the hills commanding the town, they were able to deny the Indian troops the use of the lateral road running north of river Pesa. However, 1/12 Frontier Force Regiment soon remedied this, for at 1745 hours on 4 August, a platoon wormed its way through to the top of the Rossella spur, south-east of Montelupo. Handing over its positions to the 1st Royal Fusiliers, 1/12 Frontier Force Regiment advanced across the river Pesa, at 2030 hours on 4 August, and occupied without incident, at 0140 hours on 5 August, objectives which enabled it to gain control of the hills overlooking Montelupo from the north and north-east.

On the right and centre brigade sectors, the 8th Indian Division was now in a position to dominate the approaches to the river Arno, along its winding course between Montelupo and Lastra a Signa. However, owing to the great width of the front, the broken nature of the country and the amount of cover available, the two brigades were unable to prevent German patrols crossing the Arno to operate on the south bank.

The 17th Indian Infantry Brigade in the Florence Sector

By 5 August 1944, the XIII Corps was firmly established on the south bank of the river Arno. The Corps Commander now ordered some regrouping of the divisions in his Corps, so as to bring the 1st Canadian Infantry Division into the central sector opposite Florence, in place of the 6th South African Armoured Division and the 2nd New Zealand Infantry Division. The New Zealanders were then to take over from the 8th Indian Division, whilst the South Africans were to go back to rest. The 1st Division[7] was in reserve some miles south-east of Florence.[8]

On 7 August, when the New Zealanders relieved the 8th Indian Division, having themselves been relieved by the 1st Canadian Division, the Indian division pulled out of the line to a concentration area at Greve, some fifteen miles south of Florence. However, there was still no respite for the division. Whilst the 19th and the 21st Indian Infantry Brigade moved back to Greve, the 17th Indian Infantry Brigade was ordered to proceed east and to take over a sector from the 1st Canadian Division, south of Florence, during the day and night of 8 August, for the Canadian Division's brief stay in the Florence sector was to end on 8 August. The object of this large-scale re-shuffle in the Eighth Army, prior to an attack on Florence, was to deceive the Germans as to the actual intention on the Italian front. This object was achieved by some of the methods which had been used by the Eighth Army prior to the assault on the Gustav Line in May 1944: wireless silence was strictly enforced prior to all moves; unit signs and designations were removed; the forward movement of vehicles took place at night without lights and the backward movement by day, or the reverse depending on what impression one was anxious to create.

The period of reliefs and moves to the concentration areas called for great thought and industry in the Q branches of the 8th Indian Division. In the space of three days, the 8th Indian Division was relieved by the 2nd New Zealand Division, moved back to Greve and then went forward again with one brigade to relieve the 1st Canadian Infantry Division. All this movement took place according to schedule, thanks to the efficient planning and good work by divisional provost sections on the roads. Throughout this phase, divisional and brigade signals did yeoman service in maintaining inter-communication either by wireless or field telephone or both.

[7] The Division had come under command XIII Corps on 5 August.
[8] XIII Corps O. O. No. 31, dated 4 August 1944.

The divisional RIASC services functioned as well as ever and no one went short of his normal rations, diverse as these were in an Indian formation. Vehicles, which developed serious technical trouble, were recovered at various points on the route by the Divisional Indian Electrical and Mechanical Engineer Squads, hauled back to workshops, repaired by Indian fitters and returned with a minimum of delay to their units. With the division moved also the 6th, 3rd and 34th Mule Companies, a total of over 700 mules, for which special routes had to be found clear of the main traffic arteries, and also sources of running water in a country dried by the summer sun.

The 17th Indian Infantry Brigade relieved two Canadian brigades south and south-west of Florence on the south bank of the Arno by 2130 hours on 8 August. In view of the wide front the brigade commander was obliged to put all the three battalions forward in the line. The 1st Royal Fusiliers held the right sector facing Ponte alle Grazie to Ponte Trinita, 1/5 Gurkha held the middle sector facing Ponte di Vittoria, and 1/12 Frontier Force Regiment was on the left flank of the brigade. The 6th Lancers protected the divisional left flank.

The Canadian sector taken over by the 17th Indian Infantry Brigade included the southern outskirts of Florence, and the highly cultivated country to the west, as far as the area, a little beyond Lastra a Signa. In this cultivated region, the principal crops were wheat and maize, grown in small rectangular fields, round the perimeter of which were climbing vines, whose thick foliage formed a screen eight to ten feet high. The role of the 17th Indian Infantry Brigade was to hold the line of river Arno within the brigade boundaries and take every opportunity of inflicting loss on the Germans. There was at that time no intention to advance across the river in this area, and patrols across the stream were to be undertaken only if a suitable occasion was found to put the Germans to a loss. Every effort was to be made to ensure that German patrols which crossed the river did not return. To protect the beautiful medieval city it was decided that targets in Florence would not be engaged by artillery or mortars, nevertheless every effort was to be made to locate and engage targets by fire. The defence was to be kept fluid. Forward defended localities were to be regarded as patrol bases and changed frequently and by night.[9] The 11th Canadian Armoured Regiment was in support of the brigade.

South of the Arno, the villages of Lastra a Signa, S. Colombano to the north-east, and Ugnano farther east, almost on the banks of the Arno halfway between Lastra a Signa and Florence, were firmly held by the Germans and served as bases for their patrols. Florence

[9] 17 Ind. Inf. Bde. O.O. No. 30, dated 9 August 1944.

was held by the *4th Parachute Division*, with *III Battalion of 10 Regiment* in the western part of the city. Although not up to the standard of the *1st Parachute Division*, it contained many veterans of Crete and Leros, together with a substantial basis of volunteers. In addition, there were some four hundred men of military police, who had been converted into infantry, besides German engineer and Italian Fascist Squads.[10]

By the time the 17th Indian Infantry Brigade had taken up its positions on the south bank of the Arno, most of the Germans had fallen back to the north bank of the river. The main defence of Florence, according to civilian information, was based on the Mugnone Canal, which ran around the northern perimeter of Florence. The canal was an anti-tank obstacle, behind which the Germans had sited several 88-mm anti-tank guns and several tanks to cover the approach roads. Moreover, between the canal and the Arno on the western fringe of the city, were many snipers, some of whom were Fascists. They were also active in the streets, adjacent to the water-front along the southern bank of the river.

All except one of the beautiful Florentine bridges spanning the Arno, west of Florence, and in the city itself, had been destroyed by the Germans. The oldest of the bridges, the world-famous Ponte Vecchio, with its quaint houses and shops actually built on the bridge itself, the Germans did not destroy. Instead, German engineers blew up houses and shops at each end of the bridge, until piles of rubble blocked the Ponte Vecchio at both ends. Machine guns, sited in the upper storeys of the houses, lined the northern bank of the river; there were also reports of mortars in the city. In the German controlled area of Florence, the wretched population went without food, water and medical supplies. Italian civilians found in the streets after dark were shot by the Germans or Fascists. Hungry and thirsty, the Florentines lived in the grip of fear.

Although the 17th Indian Infantry Brigade was in the sector for only a short while, it was an unpleasant period of operations. The British and Indian infantry were fighting not only against aggressive German patrols, which crossed to their side of the river both by day and night, but also against the Fascists, who wore no recognised military uniform, sniping from the upper storey windows and enjoying every advantage over the Indian troops. German mortar fire was heavy and accurate, whilst concentrations of their artillery fire caused casualties, when the shells tore open the roofs and battered down the walls of the cottages where Indian infantry lived. Strict orders had been issued by the Army Commander that, on no account was artillery or mortar fire to be directed against the

[10] 8 Ind. Div. Intelligence Summary No. 138, dated 9 August 1944.

city of Florence; the Indian troops were thus in the unenviable position of being unable to hit back at the Germans.

On the right of the brigade front, the 1st Royal Fusiliers was in position on the water front, where it was engaged daily in a duel with the German snipers. 1/5 Gurkha, in the central sector, had its full share of German shelling, whilst, on the left of the brigade front, 1/12 Frontier Force Regiment was constantly engaged with German patrols in the thick, jungle country along the banks of the Arno. Owing to the width of the front 1/12 Frontier Force Regiment was unable to prevent German patrols crossing the Arno. During the night of 9/10 August, German artillery and mortars opened fire along the whole of the brigade sector. The right forward company of 1/12 Frontier Force Regiment was heavily "stonked" at 0230 hours; as was expected, it was the prelude to a German attack. A platoon of paratroopers moved forward to the area Q 730705 but the Indian troops were ready for them, smashing the attack with the combined fire of Bren Guns, rifles and mortars. When Allied artillery defensive fire crashed down on the paratroopers, it was too much for them; they broke and fled. Several other German patrols tried to edge their way forward that night into the Frontier Force Regiment positions; the Germans appeared to be in urgent need of prisoners and identifications. The German prisoners taken at this time stated that they had been sent on patrol with definite instructions to get prisoners, and were even offered a reward of an Iron Cross (2nd Class) and twenty marks for every man taken.

On 10 August, the Frontier Force Regiment patrols and civilians reported strong German patrols in Colombano and Granatieri. D Company of the Frontier Force Regiment, supported by one troop of tanks of 11th Canadian Armoured Regiment, attacked Colombano at 1700 hours on 10 August. They encountered heavy and accurate German artillery and mortar fire. Although the Germans had withdrawn from Colombano, they closed in again on the forward platoon of D Company and temporarily cut it off. There was fierce, close-quarter fighting, in which the Canadian tanks gave valuable assistance, but lost their troop commander, who was killed. The engagement was broken off just before last light, the Germans losing three men killed and several wounded. D Company had thirteen men wounded.

In the early hours of 11 August, the Germans, who had been positioned on the northern bank of the river Arno, pulled back behind the Mugnone canal. Before withdrawing, the paratroopers had orders to fire off their local dumps of ammunition, making the night one of the noisiest the 17th Indian Infantry Brigade had ever experienced. At intervals a salvo of shells shook headquarters of the 1st Royal Fusiliers whilst, left of the British battalion, 1/5 Gurkha counted four hundred shells landing in one area alone, just west of the famous Ponte di Vittoria. The Gurkha forward platoons on the southern banks of the Arno engaged in small arms duels with German riflemen across the river. From time to time a German tank or self-propelled gun fired from the vicinity of the Piazza del Re or from amongst the trees of the Hippodrome area, sending shells whining over the Arno to crash into the houses held by the Gurkhas.

Before first light on 11 August, patrols of 1/5 Gurkha crossed the river Arno. One small reconnaissance patrol went along the Viale Principe Umberto, a wide main street running north-east from the Ponte di Vittoria towards the railway station. In the area of the railway station the patrol came under machine gun fire from the sidings to the north. Another patrol reached the Mugnone canal at the point where it was joined by the Viale di Rifredi, without opposition. But when it attempted to cross the canal the patrol came under fire from German machine gun posts in the houses on the far side. A third patrol sent to investigate the Piazza del Re had to retire under German fire. Meanwhile at 1100 hours on 11 August, a 6th Lancer patrol had entered Lastra a Signa, on the left flank of the divisional front, where German demolitions had caused great damage to property. Some two hours later, the Frontier Force Regiment had reported S. Colombano clear of the Germans.

On 12 August the situation in Florence improved considerably. Sniping in the southern part of the city had practically ceased. Allied authorities delivered supplies of food to the civilian population and controlled the administration. People thronged the streets, picking their way through the piles of rubble, cheering the British officers, whenever they saw them, and in some cases throwing garlands of flowers from their windows on to the embarrassed troops below. Behind the shutters of most of the shops on the waterfront, had been placed small, explosive charges which, when exploded, blew the shutters out as though a giant hand had pushed them from inside; yet despite this, a few of the smaller shops were opened. People came out of their houses where, in some cases, they had been hiding for days, to stare angrily at the destruction which the Germans had wrought on their beautiful city.

Life in the northern part of the city was very different. Here, the majority of the population had gone without food, water, gas and electricity for five days. Medical stores were very scarce, the sanitary services had ceased to function, and the streets presented a desolate appearance, with piles of spoil and rubble, which had not been cleared away. The German paratroopers had pulled back behind the Mugnone canal to the west and north, whilst in the east, their positions were behind the railway line; all approaches to this general defensive line were covered by machine guns. The greater part of the Florentine population in this part of the city was confined to its houses, whilst Fascist snipers and rival partisan gangs—all heavily armed with miscellaneous weapons—turned the area into a battle-ground. When the wretched civilians timidly ventured out of doors in quest of food and water, Fascist youth drove through the streets firing rifles and tommy guns at them. The main force of the partisans was under the control of the Tuscan Committee of National Liberation, the partisans looking rather like pirates, with their red neckerchiefs and two or three hand grenades sticking out of their leather belts.

The first supplies of flour for the already liberated Florentines were carried by porters across the Ponte Vecchio. This was a hazardous journey, which meant traversing a private garden, passing through a dwelling house and picking a way carefully along the narrow path which the Indian sappers had cleared in the mined debris littering the bridge.[11]

The 21st Indian Infantry Brigade in the Florence Sector

On 11 August, Major-General Russell, realising that his commitments in Florence were increasing, warned the commander of the 21st Indian Infantry Brigade to be prepared to enter the city. He gave his brigadier two tasks: to restore law and order in Florence, then push forward and contact the Germans on their main defences. On 12 August, Brigadier Mould established his headquarters in a pleasant villa in southern Florence. That same day, the brigade left Greve to relieve the 17th Indian Infantry Brigade. At 1700 hours the 5th Royal West Kent Regiment relieved the 1st Royal Fusiliers on the south bank of the river, facing Ponte Trinita—Ponte alle Grazie. 3/15 Punjab was to operate on the left flank while 1/5 Mahratta in reserve was expected to operate on the right flank. The 17th Indian Infantry Brigade was now able to narrow its front considerably by side-stepping to the left when the 21st Indian Infantry Brigade moved into the line.

The Brigadier's plan was to make full use of the Partisans to round up Fascist snipers and, when areas previously prescribed by him were declared clear by the Partisan leaders, to occupy these with his own troops until the main line of German resistance was reached, whereupon the Partisan Forces were to withdraw. The 5th Royal West Kent Regiment, who had established a bridge-head at Ponte S. Trinita on 12 August, was ordered to operate in the heart of the city; 1/5 Mahratta in the eastern suburbs and 3/15 Punjab in the western area of Florence around the railway station and Hippodrome.

By midday 13 August, two companies of the 5th Royal West Kent Regiment crossed the river to occupy an area bounded by the

[11] Ind. inf. Bde. O.O. No. 9, dated 13 August 1944.

Ponte alle Grazie, the famous Cathedral and the railway station. The divisional engineers constructed a ford across the Arno and cleared the Ponte Vecchio, to enable jeeps and supply columns to reach the city. On 14 August, the Ponte Vecchio was opened for jeeps, making the supply of food and ammunition to Indian and British troops north of the river comparatively easy. Also by this means, an ever increasing quantity of food was delivered by Allied Military Government to the civilian population.

On 14 August the 21st Indian Infantry Brigade cleared most of the German opposition south of the Mugnone canal. The 5th Royal West Kent Regiment was established in the heart of the city, occupying area Piazza Beccaria—Piazza Donatello—Piazza Cavour—railway station. On the left, 3/15 Punjab, working forward from the area excluding the railway station to Hippodrome, infiltrated in S. Jacopino area, where snipers were still active. On the right, 1/5 Mahratta patrolled forward without trouble as far as the railway marshalling yards and the western fringe of the Campo di Marte. On 15 August it secured the area of P. Vassari.

Thus, by 15 August, the 21st Indian Infantry Brigade had cleared the Germans south of the Mugnone canal. During the night of 15/16 August, however, the Germans attempted to harass the British and Indian troops. At 2300 hours on 15 August when it was almost dark, a German tank clattered out of a side street on to the broad Viale Principe Amedeo, one of the main inner boulevards on the eastern side of the city, in the sector of the 5th Royal West Kent Regiment, who having sited the gun for just such a contingency, fired two shots at the tank. Unfortunately the light was so bad that the British gunners missed their target and the German tank rumbled away down a side street before they could fire again. At about that time, trouble of a different nature was brewing in the heart of the city, where a large crowd had gathered outside the Allied Military Government Headquarters in the Palazzo Riccardi. When the large door of the building was half-opened by an official, who had been ordered to investigate the disturbance, a grenade was tossed through the door into the inner courtyard, and rifle shots rang out. Eight of the Italian Carabinieri guards were killed. Farther up the street, there was more shooting in the Piazza S. Marco.

As soon as Brigadier Mould learned of these events, he ordered a troop of the King's Dragoon Guards (armoured cars), who were under the command of the brigade during the Florence operations, to proceed to the scene of the disturbance. With their arrival all was quiet and, that night, a platoon of the 5th Royal West Kent Regiment stood guard over the seat of the Allied Military Government in Florence.

There was more trouble the following morning when, soon after 0600 hours, two German infantry platoons, supported by two tanks, crossed the railway bridge and deployed in the Piazza Vassari in the sector of 1/5 Mahratta. The Germans attacked a Mahratta platoon established in a house on the south-east corner of the Piazza; the two tanks pumped shell after shell into the house. Very close fighting took place, the Mahrattas moving to a new house where they continued the fight until the paratroopers withdrew, taking their wounded with them. One incident in this fierce fight is outstanding. Two Mahrattas did not leave their machine gun position in the first house in time. Realising that the paratroopers were coming in on all sides and that they would be captured if they tried to join the rest of the platoon in the other house, they smeared themselves with blood, lay prostrate over their machine gun and feigned death. The Germans entered the house; a German non-commissioned officer kicked open the door of the room, where the Mahrattas lay, took a casual look at the two "bodies" and passed on. Great courage and cunning saved the lives of the two Indians, who rejoined their platoon, when the Germans withdrew, and lived to fight another day.

Whilst this action was in progress, twelve Germans, with an armoured car in support, began to cross the oval-shaped Piazza Donatello, which lay on the V. Principe Amedeo, some five hundred yards south-west of where the Mahrattas were fighting in the Piazza Vassari. They were dispersed by a hail of fire from a platoon of the 5th Royal West Kent Regiment, who had been watching their approach from the fortified windows of a house overlooking the Piazza. These fierce actions in Florence during the night of 15/16 August and the morning of 16 August, marked the end of operations by the 21st Indian Infantry Brigade in the city. Plans at the XIII Corps Headquarters were now firm for a further advance across the river Arno towards M. Giovi and M. Calvana, preparatory to the attack on the Gothic Line. As an initial step, the 8th Indian Division changed places with the 1st Division. The reliefs were completed on 16 August, when the 21st Indian Infantry Brigade handed over its commitments in Florence to the 2nd British Infantry Brigade and went back to rest in the S. Donatino area. The operations in Central Italy were practically concluded and a new phase in the history of the Italian Campaign began with the attack by the Eighth Army on the Gothic Line in the Adriatic sector on 25 August 1944.

CHAPTER XV

Advance to the Anghiari Lateral Road

While the XIII Corps was advancing to the Arno the X Corps was making a thrust towards Bibbiena, which lay in a narrow plain about eighteen miles north of Arazzo, at the head of the valley of the Upper Arno, which was flanked on the east by a roadless massif, known as the Alpe di Catenaia, and on the west by a still larger roadless massif, called the Pratomagno. The Corps plan for the capture of Bibbiena was that the 4th Indian Division would advance on the town by the Upper Arno valley, and the 10th Indian Division would move to the Sansepolcro plain, at the head of the Tiber valley, and then strike north-westwards across the Alpe di Catenaia, to turn the defences of the east. For this purpose, the 4th Indian Division was to be based on Arezzo while the 10th Indian Division was to throw its weight west of the Tiber instead of to the east of it as before. Initially the X Corps was to advance to the Sansepolcro plain and secure the lateral road Anghiari—S. Giovi. This task was to be accomplished by the 10th Indian Division securing the road as far as Galbino and the 4th Indian Division securing the rest of the road to S. Giovi. After these preliminary operations to secure the road Anghiari—S. Giovi, the X Corps was to launch the main attack to capture Bibbiena, with the 10th Indian Division directed against Alpe di Catenaia and the 4th Indian Division against Pratomagno.

The X Corps comprised two full infantry divisions, the 10th and the 4th Indian Divisions, the latter now having been made complete by the arrival of the 11th Indian Infantry Brigade, together with the 9th Armoured Brigade of three regiments of tanks and one of armoured cars. There were two more armoured car regiments on the Corps' right flank, while a motor battalion was in reserve. The whole force was supported by a heavy weight of artillery, now decentralised to a considerable extent to meet the needs of an advance on the two areas.

The Germans had the advantage of the terrain. Their defence line from the heights of the Pratomagno, across the Upper Arno valley to the Alpe di Catenaia massif, and across the Tiber valley to the mountains north of Sansepolcro, provided many commanding hills and mountain positions for them to fall back upon.

10th Indian Division Plan

We shall first describe the advance of the 10th Indian Division

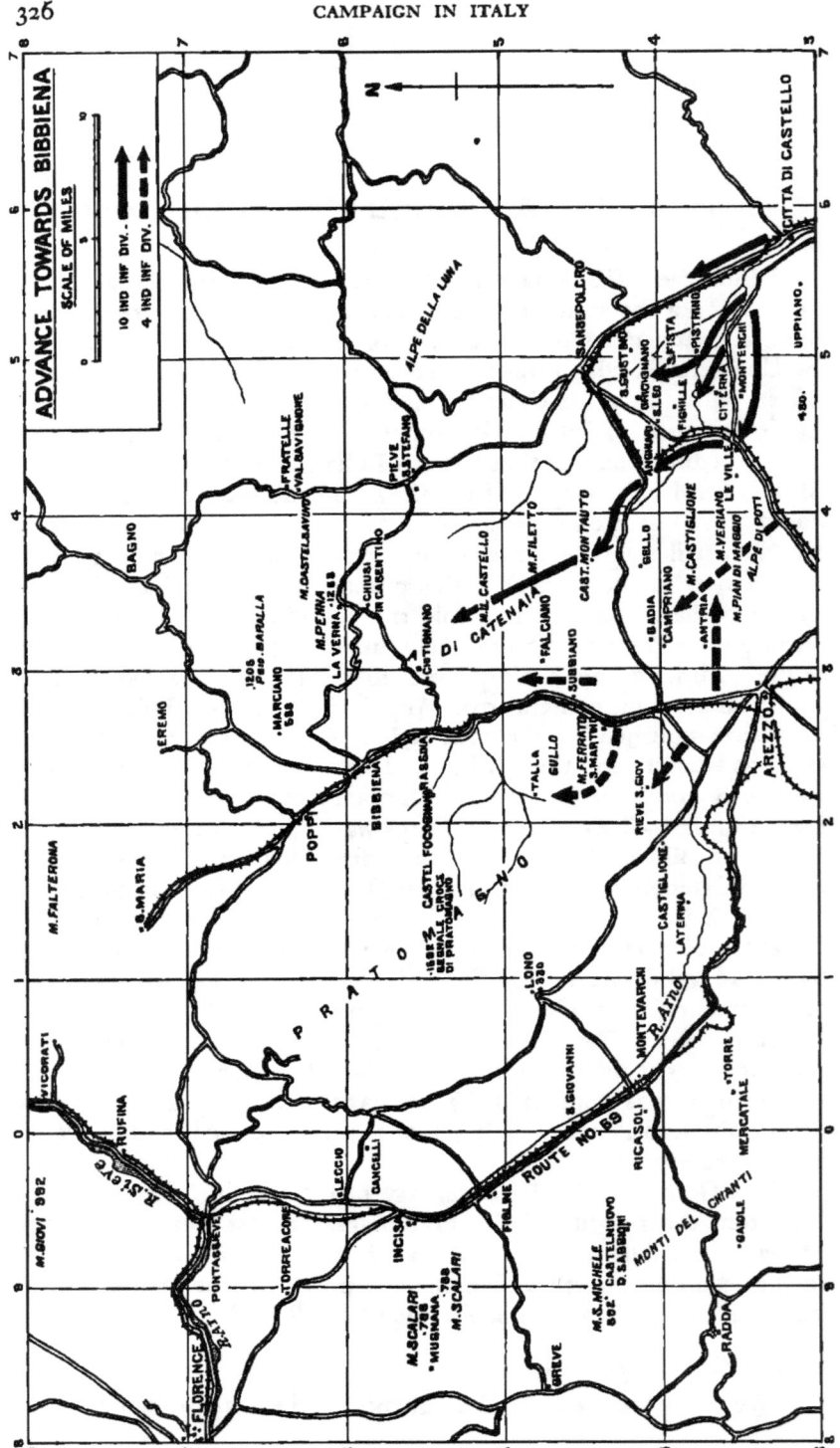

to the Sansepolcro plain and the capture of Anghiari and the lateral road from that place as far as Galbino as a suitable base for the attack on Alpe di Catenaia. After the loss of the positions covering Citta di Castello on 22 July the Germans had withdrawn to the high ground to the north-east and on the west side of the Tiber to a line covering the Cerfone stream based on M. Rotondo—Monterchi, linking up with the positions further west at M. Veriano and M. Castiglione. The *5th Mountain Division* held positions from south of Pietralunga along the hills north-west to the general area of Pt. 562, continued by elements of the *114th Jaeger Division* to positions covering S. Giustino, which was held by the *114th Reconnaissance Unit*. The line then ran south-west to link up with the positions covering the Cerfone stream. The *44th Infantry Division* was probably responsible as far west as the 43 Easting.[1] The two main positions covering the Cerfone stream were at Pistrino and features M. Rotondo—Citerna.

After 22 July 1944, when Citta di Castello had been captured and the X Corps had completed its regrouping, the axis of the 10th Indian Division lay west of the Tiber in the direction of Monterchi and moved thence north-west to Anghiari. The 20th Indian Infantry Brigade was relieved in the M. Delle Gorgacce sector by an extension of the 25th Indian Infantry Brigade's area eastwards and by the elements of the Skinner's Horse. The 20th Indian Infantry Brigade then moved over to the left of the 10th Indian Infantry Brigade west of the Tiber and relieved the 5th Indian Infantry Brigade on Monte S. Maria—Monterchi road. Only a few days earlier, on 18 July, the 10th Indian Infantry Brigade had reverted to the 10th Indian Division thus enabling the latter to have two brigades west of the Tiber and one brigade to the east of it. The 3rd Hussars and the Royal Wiltshire Yeomanry less one squadron were under command of the division. Two armoured car regiments (the 12th Lancers and the Skinner's Horse) operated on the right flank of the Corps.

Major-General Reid planned to capture the Anghiari lateral road by launching attacks with the 10th and 25th Indian Infantry Brigades. The former was to capture M. Rotondo feature and Citerna before the close of the day on 26 July and then exploit across the river Sovara to the south-east end of the Anghiari ridge, as opportunity offered. One company 2/4 Gurkha was to be at the call of the 3rd Hussars by first light on 26 July to assist in mopping up. During the same period the objective of the 20th Indian Infantry Brigade was first to occupy Monterchi, Pocaja and Pt. 400, then to seize Pt. 353, Scojano, Pt. 332 and subsequently to cross the river Sovara and capture Anghiari. The role of the 25th Indian

---

[1] 10 Ind. Div. O.I. No. 6, dated 25 July 1944.

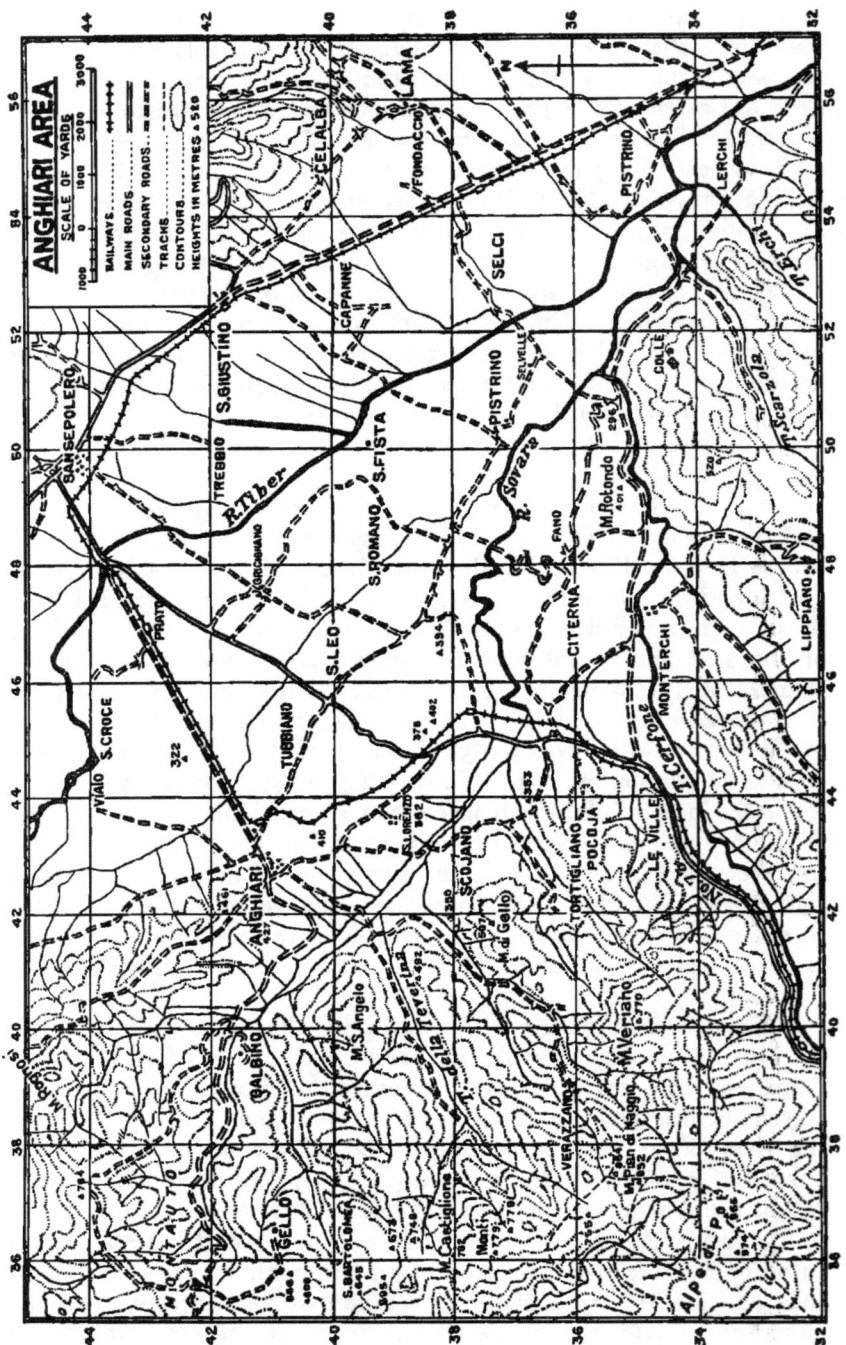

Infantry Brigade was to protect the right flank and patrol vigorously east of the Tiber.

Advance of the 10th Indian Infantry Brigade to the Anghiari Lateral Road

Initiative in the action was taken by the tanks of the 3rd Hussars which forced the Germans to withdraw from Pistrino, thereby compelling them to relax their hold on the two important features, M. Rotondo and Citerna. This in turn enabled the 10th Indian Infantry Brigade to occupy them and to advance. without much opposition, to the Anghiari lateral road. The operations by the 3rd Hussars were really a continuation of those begun south-east of Citta di Castello. This time the attack was west of the Tiber. While the Skinner's Horse formed a screen east of the river the 3rd Hussars made preparations for clearing the German positions between the Tiber and river Cerfone, as far west as the road Anghiari—Sansepolcro. In this operation the 3rd Hussars had under command:

    One squadron Skinner's Horse
    4 Battery 1st Royal Horse Artillery
    2 Troop 1st Field Squadron
    One company 1st King's Own Royal Regiment.

Pistrino was held in strength by the troops of *III Battalion 721st Jaeger Regiment* (the *114th Jaeger Division*). As a preliminary to the operations the Royal Wiltshire Yeomanry was to make a thrust towards M. Rotondo. By 1100 hours on 25 July, A Squadron of the Royal Wiltshire Yeomanry had found a crossing over the river Cerfone, north-west of Lerchi, and was working towards its objective M. Rotondo. It met several obstructions on the way in the form of dykes and mines. C Squadron 3rd Hussars, which had concentrated about 500 yards south of this crossing, passed through the Royal Wiltshire Yeomanry at 1300 hours and advanced towards Pistrino. The country was very enclosed, consisting of rows of vines and fruit trees, which reduced visibility to twenty-five yards. Progress was slow. In two hours only one and a half miles were covered. Fighting was somewhat confused, but the squadron had a good shoot at infantry and anti-tank guns. One of these guns was knocked out at a range of only ten yards. By 1615 hours, C Squadron was in position just north, east and south of Pistrino, covering all exits from the village as far as was possible in such close country. B Squadron and a company of the 1st King's Own Royal Regiment, which had concentrated one mile north of Lerchi by 1330 hours, then went forward to mop up and to take advantage of the confusion in the opposite ranks; and by 1645 hours were one mile south-east of Pistrino. A blue haze and a strong sun in the eyes of the attackers, made the advance difficult. Machine gun and atillery fire halted the company of the 1st King's Own and all attempts to enter the village failed. With the approach of darkness, it was decided to withdraw to harbour and to return for the attack next day. On 26 July the operation was again carried out with A Squadron leading, and the company of the 1st King's Own Royal Regiment was able to enter Pistrino without opposition as the Germans had already withdrawn.[2]

While armour was let loose on Pistrino, the infantry was directed against M. Rotondo and Citerna, two features which dominated the whole of the low-lying ground between the Tiber and the Cerfone. The brigade plan was for the 1st Durban Light Infantry to dribble northwards from Colle at 2100 hours on 25 July, assemble in the area Pratomagno at 2200 hours, move forward across the Cerfone at 2230 hours and capture M. Rotondo with two forward companies. 4/10 Baluch was to have one company ready to exploit to Citerna. 2/4 Gurkha was to be in reserve with one forward company in area Pt. 520. The Royal Wiltshire Yeomanry less two squadrons were under the command of the brigade for this operation.

By active patrolling the 10th Indian Infantry Brigade had already made considerable headway. By 1600 hours on 23 July the Durham had reached Colle and were overlooking the Cerfone. On 25 July patrols probing the German defences at M. Rotondo were mortared at Pt. 296 and were fired on by three machine guns from Pt. 401. Subsequently in the night of 25/26 July the attack on M. Rotondo was launched. By 2230 hours the Cerfone was crossed but the attack was halted due to stiff resistance. By 0100 hours on 26 July, however, the opposition was overcome and Pt. 401 was secured at 0350 hours. By 0730 hours M. Rotondo had been secured without further opposition. Thereupon C Company 4/10 Baluch, followed by D Company, exploited to, and captured, Citerna at 1130 hours. The Germans, doubtless sensitive to the armoured threat from Pistrino in the rear of their positions, had withdrawn shortly before M. Rotondo and Citerna had fallen.

2/4 Gurkha, supported by tanks of the 3rd Hussars, now prepared to move forward from Pistrino to the road Anghiari—Sansepolcro. The advance began at 0935 hours on 29 July. Supported by A Squadron 3rd Hussars, A and D Companies secured S. Fista and S. Romano, respectively, by 1130 hours without opposition. Then at 1215 hours B Company, supported by B Squadron 3rd Hussars, moved forward and secured Gricignano without opposition before 1830 hours. The next day, however, a German platoon established itself in some houses to the north of the village and kept

---

[2] Operations 3rd Hussars, Appendix 'K' to 10 Ind. Div. Narrative of Operations, File 8328.

on a harassing fire on the Gurkha positions. At 1730 hours tanks attacked these houses with heavy explosive and machine gun fire which subdued the German fire. Thereafter A Company moved up to support B Company. German machine gun fire, however, resumed its former intensity. They also shelled the tanks and the village. By 1800 hours, however, German firing petered out. B Squadron 3rd Hussars then cleared the Gricignano area and moved up to Prato, thus completing the task of advancing to the Anghiari—Sansepolcro road.

The 20th Indian Infantry Brigade's Thrust towards Anghiari

Meanwhile to the west, the 20th Indian Infantry Brigade (which had relieved the 5th Indian Infantry Brigade on 21 July on Monte S. Maria—Monterchi road) was developing a powerful thrust towards Anghiari. Good progress was made, for by 24 July, 3/5 Mahratta had pushed on from Cagnano to Pt. 520, 2/3 Gurkha had secured Lippiano and the 8th Manchester was closing up to Rioli area. Next day the Brigade Commander issued instructions for the capture of Anghiari. The advance was to be made with 2/3 Gurkha on the right and the 8th Manchester on the left, while 3/5 Mahratta was to be in reserve. The operations were to be carried out in two phases. In the first phase, Pocaja and Monterchi were to be the objectives of the 8th Manchester and 2/3 Gurkha respectively. On 25 July and during the night of 25/26 July the former was to infiltrate forward from Ripoli area to Pt. 512 and on to Le Ville and then secure Pocaja by first light on 26 July. The role of 2/3 Gurkha was to co-operate by infiltrating forward from area Lippiano to Monterchi and Pt. 466. In the second phase, Anghiari and Scojano were to be the objectives of 2/3 Gurkha and the 8th Manchester, respectively. At first light on 26 July, 2/3 Gurkha was to pass through the 8th Manchester to the right and advance on the divisional axis—securing Pt. 367, Pt. 402, Pt. 387, Pt. 383 and Anghiari. The 8th Manchester was to advance on the divisional axis to the left of the river Sovara and secure Pt. 44, Pt. 353, Scojano, Pt. 332 and Pt. 370.

On 25 July a platoon of the 8 Manchester occupied Le Ville. Later in the day the Germans mortared the village and launched a counter-attack, but they were driven back after hand-to-hand fighting. Another platoon was sent forward to reinforce the forward platoon. A Company 2/3 Gurkha was established on Pt. 466 while one platoon of D Company mopped up pockets of resistance in Monterchi.

On 26 July the 8th Manchester made good progress. One company was established at Pocaja and another at Pt. 444. The third company captured Pt. 353 and sent forward two platoons to Scojano, which were counter-attacked by the Germans in the night of

26/27 July and driven back to Pt. 353. 3/5 Mahratta was thereupon brought up as reinforcement. Meanwhile on the right, A and D Companies of 2/3 Gurkha had captured Pt. 367 and Pt. 351 against stiff opposition.

On 27 July, 3/5 Mahratta occupied Scojano without much opposition and then moved to the left to secure Pt. 350 and Pt. 497. The 8th Manchester established one company on Pt. 362 and pushed on towards S. Lorenzo. A and D Companies of 2/3 Gurkha were across river Sovara at first light on 27 July. C Company 2/3 Gurkha, strengthened by an additional platoon of B Company, secured Pt. 402.

On 28 July, 3/5 Mahratta occupied Pt. 350 and Pt. 497. The 8th Manchester pushed on during the night of 27/28 July under shell and mortar fire to the area S. Lorenzo, where two companies were established and one company continued the advance towards Pt. 410. This company captured Pt. 396 but further advance was held up by small arms and mortar fire. A and D Companies of 2/3 Gurkha were established on Pt. 394 and Pt. 378 after encountering severe opposition. D Company on Pt. 394 repulsed two German counter-attacks. A reconnaissance patrol of A Company found Pt. 387 to be held in strength by the Germans. A German counter-attack with tank support developed in the area Pt. 393 which was held by a Gurkha company. The attack was repulsed by artillery and small arms fire. This was followed by about six hours of heavy shelling and mortaring of the forward company positions.

Advance to Castle Montauto

A further regrouping was at this stage carried out. The 25th Indian Infantry Brigade was switched across the Tiber to take over the sector of the 20th Indian Infantry Brigade. The relief began in the night of 28/29 July, when 3/1 Punjab relieved the 8th Manchester south of Anghiari. That same night, the Germans, weakened by hard knocks received in the previous few days, withdrew their forces north from Anghiari. By the evening of 29 July the forward companies of 3/1 Punjab secured Anghiari. 3/5 Mahratta occupied M. S. Angelo and Galbino before handing over to 3/18 Garhwal on 30 July. Thus by 30 July the 10th Indian Division had succeeded in holding the Sansepolcro plain and the lateral Anghiari road as far as Galbino. The stage was now set for the 10th Indian Division to prepare for the capture of Castle Montauto, which might serve as an admirable base for the attack on Alpe di Catenaia, which had barred the way to Bibbiena. This task was assigned to the 25th Indian Infantry Brigade. The area east of the Tiber, in which the 25th Indian Infantry Brigade had been operating, was taken over by the 9th Armoured Brigade on 30 July and it was extended on

31 July so as to include Citerna, S. Romano and Gricignano, thus enabling the infantry of the 10th Indian Division to swing north-west into the hills towards Alpe di Catenaia.

The Germans were holding in strength Ponte alla Piera, with forward positions at Pt 689 and Pt. 764. The commander of the 25th Indian Infantry Brigade ordered 3/1 Punjab and 3/18 Garhwal to capture Pt. 689 and Pt 765, respectively. The commander of 3/1 Punjab planned to carry out the operation in two phases. In the first phase B Company was to advance from Bagnolo at 1930 hours on 31 July and capture Pt. 628. D Company was then to pass through B Company and capture Pt. 689 by first light on 1 August. With A Company in area Pt. 522 and C Company in area Pt. 553 as firm base, B and D Companies of 3/1 Punjab advanced across extremely difficult country. Only slight opposition was encountered and Pt. 689 was secured by 0430 hours on 1 August.

At the same time a sudden assault by 3/18 Garhwal on the formidable height of Montauto achieved complete surprise. The battalion plan was for A Company to take up positions at Pt. 494 and for C, B and D Companies (established on the Galbino ridge) to move by route—Pt. 520, Pt. 565. D Company was to take up position on Pt. 565 while B and C Companies were to move forward to attack Pt. 764. At 1215 hours on 31 July, A Company was established on Pt. 494 as firm base. At 2100 hours the battalion moved off in the order C, B and D Companies. Pt. 565 was captured at 0015 hours on 1 August and B and C Companies secured and consolidated in area Pt. 764. The Germans, about a platoon in strength, withdrew. The Garhwal attack was a well planned and executed manoeuvre across four miles of precipitous country. With the capture of Castle Montauto, the 10th Indian Division had obtained a suitable base for the attack on the formidable Alpe di Catenaia, barring the way to Bibbiena, the objective of the X Corps.

Capture of M. Veriano

While the 10th Indian Division had advanced to the Sansepolcro plain, secured the Anghiari lateral road as far as Galbino, and captured Castle Montauto to serve as a base for the attack on Alpe di Catenaia, the 4th Indian Division also made strenuous efforts to overcome stiff opposition in order to dominate the Anghiari lateral road from Galbino to S. Giovi. Three key defensive German positions at M. Veriano, M. Castiglione and Campriano barred its way to the Anghiari lateral road. The 7th Indian Infantry Brigade was directed on M. Veriano, the 5th Indian Infantry Brigade on M. Castiglione and the 11th Indian Infantry Brigade on Campriano. We shall first describe the attack on M. Veriano.

The 7th Indian Brigade was directed against M. Veriano. On

28 July, 2/11 Sikh and 1/2 Gurkha had captured the crest of the Alpe di Poti. Next day, the 7th Brigade Reconnaissance Squadron and a squadron of tanks from the Royal Wiltshire Yeomanry had worked their way up the mountain to join the two battalions. The bulk of the *576th Grenadier Regiment* (the *305th Infantry Division*) was spread in the hills north and north-east of the Alpe di Poti and unwilling to give ground.[3] The 7th Indian Infantry Brigade had therefore a difficult task ahead. The commander of the 7th Indian Innfantry Brigade planned to make a double thrust towards M. Veriano and M. Pian di Maggio with 2/11 Sikh and 1/2 Gurkha, respectively. The right flank of the attacking force was to be protected by the 1st Royal Sussex patrolling on Route 73, north-east from Palazzo del Pero.

The first obstacle was the feature called M. Pian di Maggio. To the north of the Alpe di Poti, a track followed the narrow ridge, which descended in a curve first northwards, then north-westwards, at times very steeply, through a series of lower peaks. Where the ridge curved to the north-west, a second ridge fell away very abruptly to Verrazzano in the north-east, at the terminus of a road from Anghiari, in the Tiber valley. Ultimately, the track running north-westwards joined the lateral road from Anghiari to Giovi in the Arno Valley. The ridge where it curved, called M. Pian di Maggio, was of great tactical importance.

Under cover of darkness, 1/2 Gurkha advanced from the Alpe di Poti at 2115 hours on 19 July. The battalion plan was for two companies to assault Pt. 864 and for the third company to push on to Pt. 755. The surprise attack was successful and at first light on 20 July the Gurkha companies secured Pt. 864 and a hill top south-east of it. After a halt for reorganisation and reconnaissance, the attack was resumed at 1230 hours, when supported by half a squadron of the Royal Wiltshire Yeomanry (Shermans) and machine guns at Pt. 974, the third company assaulted Pt. 755, one thousand yards to the north-west. The feature was captured by 1330 hours after a fierce hand-to-hand struggle. Before 1800 hours, the Germans put in no fewer than ten counter-attacks against the Gurkhas. Two companies of 2/7 Gurkha Rifles, which had been placed under command of the 7th Indian Infantry Brigade on 18 July, came up to assist 1/2 Gurkha. In their counter-attacks the Germans were greatly assisted by the close nature of the country. Thick shrub and fir trees enabled them to approach to close quarters. As the Germans deployed from the woods, artillery and small arms fire wrought havoc amongst them and stopped attack after attack. The fight was not entirely one-sided. German mortar shells crashed down on the Gurkha positions and frequently hid

[3] 4 Ind. Div. Intelligence Summary No. 120, dated 21 July 1944.

their mountain top positions from view in the clouds of smoke and dust. As dusk fell, the German attacks weakened. When the noise of battle finally died away, the Gurkhas were still firmly entrenched on their objectives. On 21 July again, German machine guns engaged the forward Gurkha company at Pt. 755 from the south-west. The Royal Wiltshire Yeomanry in support of 1/2 Gurkha in area Pt. 864 engaged the Germans and inflicted some casualties. Thus the Gurkhas successfully carried out the task allotted to them, viz. to clear the Germans from area M. Pian di Maggio.

On 20 July, nearly two miles to the east, 2/11 Sikh had also been at grips with the Germans. A Company patrolling to M. Veriano, along the crest of yet another ridge eastwards from the Alpe di Poti, found some forty Germans sitting in and around a half tracked vehicle (mounting a 3-inch mortar) and apparently quite oblivious of the approach of the patrol. Without hesitation the patrol blazed away with Bren guns and tommy guns and tossed over a number of grenades. By the time the Germans recovered from their surprise and started to reorganise, the patrol had disengaged and was on its way back to its base.

A Company of 2/11 Sikh, supported by two Field Regiments and Medium Battery attacked Pt. 770 in the night of 23/24 July. They reached the objective but were heavily mortared and had to retire. The Germans however withdrew from M. Veriano to M. Castiglione and the ridge to the north-east. Consequently the Sikhs occupied M. Veriano late in the day without any opposition. The stage was now set for the attack on the second key German position at M. Castiglione.

Capture of M. Castiglione

While the 7th Indian Infantry Brigade consolidated on M. Veriano and patrolled north and north-west towards Verazzano and M. Castiglione, the 5th Indian Infantry Brigade, which was in reserve at Antira, led the attack on M. Castiglione, as a preliminary to moving forward to the area Gello and the high ground overlooking the lateral Anghiari—S. Giovi road. The attack on the feature M. Castiglione was made in the night of 25/26 July. The operation was carried out, not by a frontal attack from the south, but by an advance east form Gello, thus taking the objectives from the rear.

Brigadier J. C. Saunders-Jacobs, C.B.E., D.S.O., Commander of the 5th Indian Infantry Brigade, planned to capture and consolidate the feature running north and south from including Pt. 779—ring Contour (R 351399) with a view to further exploitation north to Gello. The attack was to be made with two battalions—1/9 Gurkha on the right and 3/10 Baluch on the left. The former was to advance from area track (R 332375) near Gello, cross start line

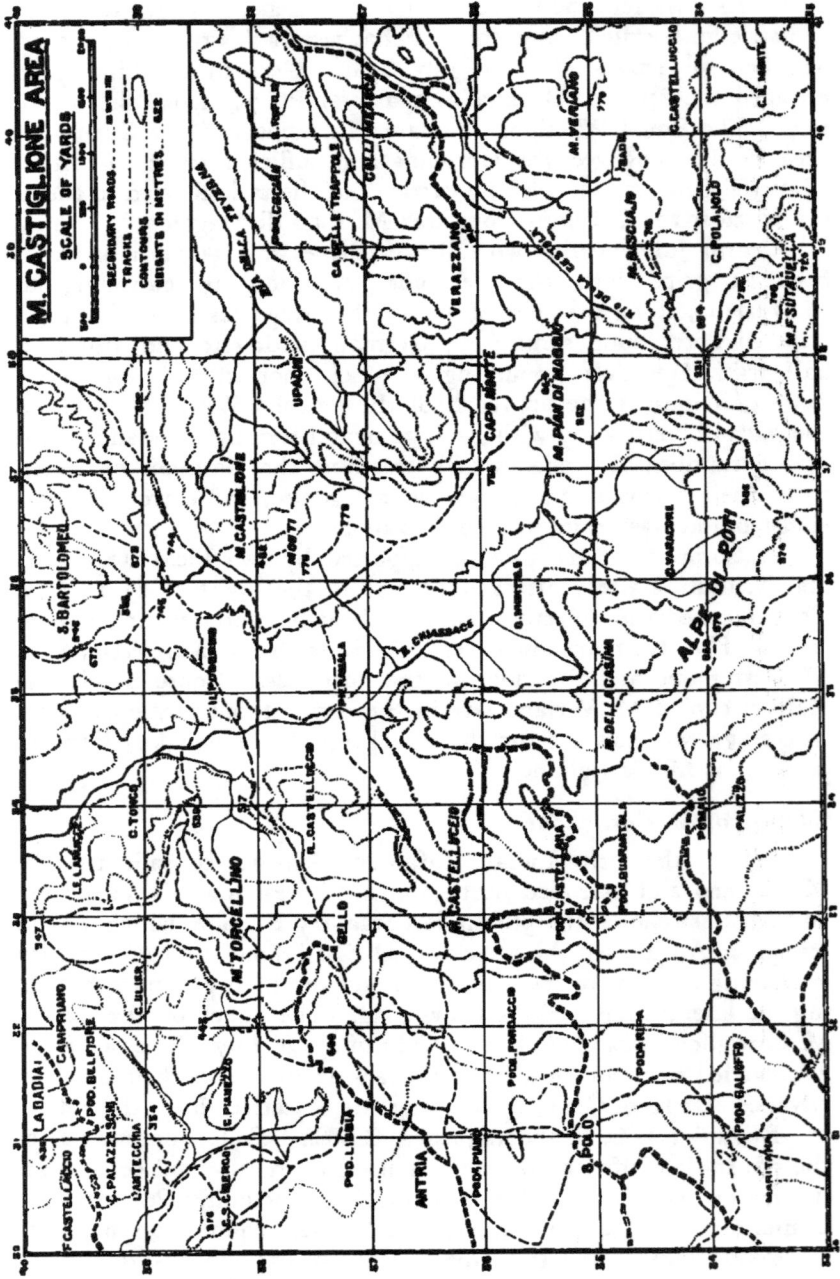

(crest immediately east of the assembly area) and secure Pt. 748, Pt. 782, Pt. 775, C. Monti and Pt. 779. On reaching the final objective, 1/9 Gurkha was to link up with the 1st Royal Sussex on M. della Spiocia and to hold the ground up to including M. Castiglione and Pt. 748. In its turn 3/10 Baluch was to advance from the assembly area, track (R 334385), north of Gello, cross the start line (the crest immediately east of the assembly area) and secure the objectives Pt. 673, Pt. 595—Pt. 645—S. Batolomeo—ring contour (R 351399). On reaching the final objective, the Baluch was to hold high ground from excluding Pt. 748 to including Pt. 645 as a firm base for further advance on Gello. 1/4 Essex was to be in reserve in area Antria, with one company patrolling to Pieramala in order to protect the right flank of 1/9 Gurkha from the south. H Hour was to be 2130 hours on 25 July.[4] A Company Medium Machine Gun Rajputana Rifles was under command and B Squadron Warwickshire Yeomanry in support of the brigade.

The 5th Indian Infantry Brigade moved up from Antria eastwards into the hills and across the front of the 7th Indian Infantry Brigade, to implement the plan and thereby surprise the Germans who had expected the assault to be made along the bald ridge running north from the Alpe di Poti and Pt. 864. The attacking troops climbed the steep slopes, through tangled undergrowth, from the west, and arrived within fifty yards of the Germans, whose entrenched positions faced south, before the latter realised that they were being attacked. Darkness covered the approach but the actual attack was delayed until first light. By 0535 hours on 26 July, A Company of 1/9 Gurkha was established on Pt. 745 and D Company on Pt. 748, but C Company met considerable opposition and it was only after a bitter struggle that Pt. 482 was secured by 0600 hours. Surprised and demoralised the garrison of M. Castiglione fired a few rounds and then fled, leaving their weapons and ammunition behind.

3/10 Baluch did not meet with much opposition. By 0800 hours one company of 3/10 Baluch was established at Pt. 595, and another at Pt. 645 while the third company on the spur west of Pt. 677 patrolled north-east. At 1345 hours one company moved forward to Pt. 609, about a thousand yards to the north, astride the track on a very narrow neck of a hill. At 1600 hours a German counter-attack developed from Pt. 666 against this company. A brisk exchange of fire exhausted their ammunition, compelling the company of 3/10 Baluch to withdraw to a new position on the reverse slopes.

1/4 Essex moved at 1500 hours on 26 July to pass through 3/10 Baluch in order to attack Gello, the village at road head, about a thousand yards north-east of Pt. 609. At 0055 hours on 27 July,

[4] 5 Ind. Inf. Bde. O.O. No. 7, dated 25 July 1944.

two companies of 1/4 Essex were established on Pt. 666 without meeting any opposition. A considerable German withdrawal had taken place, and in the night of 30/31 July, 1/4 Essex was able to patrol the area Scille beyond Gello. Thus towards the close of July 1944, the 4th Indian Division had cleared the Germans from the lateral Anghiari road north of Gello.

Capture of Campriano

While the 7th Indian Infantry Brigade captured M. Veriano and the 5th Indian Infantry Brigade seized M. Castiglione, the 11th Indian Infantry Brigade was directed against Campriano, the third key German defensive position barring the way to the Anghiari lateral road to S. Giovi. The 11th Indian Infantry Brigade was operating in Arezzo area. As stated earlier, on 18 July, following the capture of Arezzo, the X Corps boundary had been extended westwards to pass through the northern edge of Arezzo and continue north-westwards keeping west of the Arezzo—Castelluccio road. Arezzo was protected on the north at that time by the King's Dragoon Guards from the Sackforce. But an armoured car regiment can provide only a very elastic screen, which offers normally no more than slight resistance to hostile advance and keep a watch on the enemy movements rather than combat the advancing force. The King's Dragoon Guards' screen was based on S. Polo, two miles north-east of Arezzo, where the foothills ran into the mountains of Alpe di Poti; on Puglia, two and a half miles north of Arezzo and east of Route 71. At 1100 hours on 19 July, the command of the sector passed from the Sackforce to the 11th Indian Infantry Brigade, the King's Dragoon Guards remaining temporarily under command for two days more. 3/12 Frontier Force Regiment was in area Antria, and 2nd Battalion Cameron Highlanders in area Petrognano. 2/7 Gurkha, then temporarily under command of the 7th Indian Infantry Brigade at Alpe di Poti,[5] returned to the 11th Indian Infantry Brigade at 2000 hours on 23 July and concentrated in area Puglia.

The brigade's task was to maintain contact with the Germans and protect the right flank of the XIII Corps. A Squadron Warwickshire Yeomanry and D Company Medium Machine Gun Rajputana Rifles were under command of the brigade.

The Germans were not holding the positions in front of the 11th Indian Infantry Brigade in any great strength except at Campriano. They were however making clever use of mines and demolitions and taking full advantage of every opportunity to shell and mortar any movement or troop concentration. They were particularly sensitive to the advance of 3/12 Royal Frontier Force

[5] 11 Ind. Inf. Bde. O.I. No. 11, dated 20 July 1944.

Regiment towards Campriano, a strong German defensive position, protecting the right flank of the German troops engaged in the defence of M. Castiglione. So while the Cameron Highlanders were engaged in patrolling west of Route 71 across the Arno to Giovi and Vado, 3/12 Royal Frontier Force Regiment was faced with the problem of driving the Germans from Campriano.

The Germans had taken up a strong position on the high ground in Campriano area. West of, and half a mile across, the valley from Campriano was a church in La Badia, situated on a hill four hundred feet higher than that on which Campriano stood. Pt. 584, six hundred yards north of the church, was the highest crest of the hill. Lower down the spur was Pt. 430. Other strong German defensive positions were Pt. 547, Pt. 539, and Belfiore. It was from the commanding position of Campriano and the Badia church that the Germans tried to stem the advance of 3/12 Royal Frontier Force Regiment.

The *577th Grenadiers Regiment* (the *305th Infantry Division*) faced the 11th Indian Infantry Brigade. The rough layout of the *305th Infantry Division* was that the *577th Grenadier Regiment* controlled the area from Route 71 to north of Campriano; the *578th Grenadier Regiment* operated further to the east; the *576th Grenadier Regiment* had two battalions up at M. Castiglione and M. Veriano. The latter linked up with the *44th Infantry Division* approximately on the road north-east from Tortigliano.[6]

On 20 July, 3/12 Royal Frontier Force Regiment, with under command one platoon D Company Medium Machine Gun Rajputana Rifles, started probing into German defences. It succeeded in occupying M. Torcellino against slight opposition, that day. The next day, as the Forward Observation Officer and covering party advanced towards Pt. 539 to get observation, they were trapped by German fire and got back with difficulty with the assistance of artillery high explosive and smoke shoot. On 22 July, B Company patrol found C. Ulier unoccupied. But further patrolling revealed that the Germans were holding the forward post, Pt. 547. On 23 July, A Company sent patrols from Antecchia, which located German posts at Puderi and Pt. 430.

After these preliminary operations the attack on Campriano began at 1900 hours on 24 July. 3/12 Frontier Force Regiment made a double thrust against this strong German position. On the right, B and C Companies, from area Ulieri, were directed against Pt. 547 and Pt. 584, respectively. On the left[7] D and A Companies, from area Antecchia, were directed against La Badia Church and

[6] 4 Ind. Div. Intelligence Summaries, Nos. 121 and 124.
[7] D Company 3/12 F.F.R. relieved by 2/7 G.R. at M. Torcellino had moved to Antecchia.

Pt. 430, respectively. The left thrust made headway; A Company did not meet with much opposition and secured Pt. 430 at 2255 hours while, by 0600 hours on 25 July, D Company had advanced to area Belfiore. The right thrust was however held up by considerable opposition. Both B and C Companies encountered very fierce opposition and not much progress could be made. At 0600 hours on 25 July, B Company was held up at R 327397 and C Company at R 326396. Thus the situation at that hour was that B and C Companies were held up but A Company had secured Pt. 430 and D Company had edged forward to area Belfiore. The battalion commander therefore ordered D Company to exploit its advantageous situation and attack Pt. 584. But the Germans wrested the initiative and at 0700 hours struck at B Company. The counter-attack was repelled and B Company remained firm in its position. Meanwhile C Company too was having trouble. It was heavily mortared. To help the hard-pressed companies on the right, 2/7 Gurkha was called up in support from M. Torcellino. To protect the right flank of D Company, a company of 2/7 Gurkha advanced at 1415 hours to R 332397 against increasing opposition. At 1825 hours a second Gurkha company moved up to join the first company at R 332397. But neither the Gurkha companies nor those of 6/13 Frontier Force Rifles were able to make any substantial gains. The forward companies were heavily shelled and mortared and large numbers of Germans continued to infiltrate forward. As the German pressure increased, the companies were withdrawn from their forward positions at 2100 hours. The attempt to dislodge the Germans from their commanding position at Campriano proved a failure.[8]

Brigadier H. C. Partridge, D.S.O., Commander 11th Indian Infantry Brigade then made a plan to capture and consolidate La Bardia Church and Pt. 584 by first light on 28 July. Before the attack was launched, however, the Germans had pulled out of their defensive positions. The capture of their strong position on the right flank at M. Castiglione early on 26 July had made their posi-

---

[8] A point of interest concerning the attack on Campriano is that this action was watched by His Majesty the King. The following account is taken from the News Letter of the 8th Indian Division:—
"His Majesty watched an Indian Division, famous for its work in the Western Desert and North Africa, fighting a new kind of battle in the green hills of Italy. He stayed longer there than anywhere else, seeing moves of an attack on the hilltop villages of Campriano. The King spent the night within range of enemy shellfire high over the battle front. Two caravans for his use had been staged to the brow of a steep hill. Driving straight to an OP over the town, he watched the battle through a captured German periscope discussing it with General Leese and Divisional Officers.
Troops of a Frontier Force Regiment (3 R FFR) with flank protection from the Gurkhas were moving on Campriano. A force estimated as above 100 Germans was resisting from pill boxes round the Church, and enemy mortar bursts puffed white over the valley. Castaluccia, overlooking the attack and occupied by the enemy, was being shelled."

tion at Campriano untenable. The Campriano ridge was consequently occupied by the 11th Indian Infantry Brigade on 28 July without any opposition. The brigade had accomplished its task of driving out the Germans from the commanding Campriano ridge and had cleared the Anghiari lateral road at the end of July 1944.

Thus at the end of July 1944 the X Corps had carried out its task of clearing the Germans from the high ground south of the Anghiari—S. Giovi lateral road, preparatory to the capture of Bibbiena. The left flank of the 4th Indian Division and of the X Corps was now protected by Lindforce, which was formed on 29 July, and consisted of the Central India Horse, the King's Dragoon Guards, a squadron of Warwickshire Yeomanry, 152nd Field Regiment R.A. (less one battery) and a battery of self-propelled anti-tank guns. Its responsibilities were as far west as the 16 Easting, the new inter-Corps boundary.

CHAPTER XVI

Operation Vandal

German Dispositions

At the end of July 1944, the X Corps was approximately twelve miles from the small town of Bibbiena, which lying at the head of the Arno valley north-east of the towering Pratomagno massif, was the kernel of the Corps' ultimate objective. Here, confronted with the backbone of the Apennine range, the valley road divided; Route 71 bore north-east across the mountains to Cesena, on the Adriatic coast plain, near Rimini, while the branch went westwards as Route 70, along the northern edge of the Pratomagno to rejoin the Arno at Pontassieve. Bibbiena was thus the natural starting point for any attempt on this front to penetrate the last formidable German defences in the Apennines, the Gothic Line, which followed the chain of peaks further north.

Circumstances were favourable for launching an attack on Bibbiena. At this time, the X Corps dominated the lateral road from Anghiari to Giovi; the 4th Indian Division stood at the entrance to the upper Arno valley while the 10th Indian Division had secured a base in Castle Montauto for an attack on the Alpe di Catenaia. Thus the necessary springboard had been obtained for the mounting of the next major operation, known as Vandal,[1] with the object of securing area Chitignano—Castel Focognano—Bibbiena. This operation was of prime importance as it was necessary to force the Germans back to the Gothic Line along its whole length as quickly as possible.

The Germans were alive to this threat to Bibbiena and were prepared to meet it. They had the advantage of the terrain and well did they exploit it. They took up positions on Alpe di Catenaia—at M. Filetto, M. Altuccia, Il Castello and Sasso della Regina. There were two strong positions at Falciano and Subbiano on the left flank of Alpe di Catenaia. To the west of Route 71 the chief German positions were at M. Ferrato, Poggio del Grillo, Torri di Belfiore and Poggio Pianale. Two divisions were guarding the approaches to Bibbiena. The *305th Infantry Division* protected the Alpe di Catenaia massif while the *15th Panzer Grenadier Division* held a wide front, with the *104th Panzer Grenadier Regiment* guarding the western slopes of Pratomagno and the *115th Panzer*

---

[1] 4 Ind. Div. O.I. No. 13, dated 1 August 1944.

Grenadier Regiment protecting the eastern spurs of Pratomagno and covering Subbiano and Talla.

Divisional Plans

The Corps plan was to attack with the 10th and the 4th Indian Divisions. The former was to advance on the right and secure Alpe di Catenaia and Chitignano, exploiting to cut road Subbiano—Bibbiena. The latter was to advance on the left and secure Falciano, Subbiano, Poggio Pianale and exploit on Subbiano axis to link up with the 10th Indian Division. The 9th Armoured Brigade was to protect the right flank of the 10th Indian Division. Lindforce was to protect the left flank of the 4th Indian Division and follow up any German withdrawal astride the road Castiglion—Talla.

To overcome the extreme difficulty of the rough and mountainous terrain, which provided the Germans with a sequence of natural defensive positions, General McCreery, Commander X Corps, decided that the attack once launched, should be pushed with all speed so that an advance in one place would outflank the German defences in another. On 2 August he issued orders for the attack to begin on the night of 3/4 August.

The commander of the 10th Indian Division selected the 20th Indian Infantry Brigade to lead the attack on Alpe di Catenaia and secure area Chitignano. Its right flank was to be protected by the 25th Indian Infantry Brigade holding a firm base at Pt. 689—Pt. 764. The following troops were under command of the 10th Indian Division:—

> 85th Mountain Regiment
> 17th Heavy Air Aircraft Battery
> Y Troop 8th Survey Regiment
> C Flight 654 Air Observation Post
> 4th Canadian Drilling Section RCE
> Two companies Artieri
> 165th (Jeep) Regiment less one Battery.
>
> The following troops were in support of the division:
> Royal Wiltshire Yeomanry
> 7th Mountain Regiment
> E Battery Royal Horse Artillery
> 2nd Army Group Royal Artillery (also in support of the 4th Indian Division).[2]

Major-General A.W.W. Holworthy, D.S.O., M.C., Commander 4th Indian Division selected the 11th Indian Infantry Brigade for the leading role of overcoming German opposition west of Route 71. He assigned to the 5th Indian Infantry Brigade the secondary role

[2] 10 Ind. Div. O.I. No. 7, dated 31 July 1944.

of securing Falciano. The following troops were under command of the 4th Indian Division.

    1st Battery 2nd Royal Horse Artillery
    225/57 Anti-Tank Battery Royal Artillery
    5th Medium Regiment Royal Artillery
    32nd Heavy Regiment Royal Artillery.

The following troops were in support:
    Warwickshire Yeomanry—probably less one squadron in support Lindforce
    B Battery 1st Royal Horse Artillery
    2nd Army Group Royal Artillery less 5th Medium Regiment Royal Artillery
    A Flight 654 Air Observation Post Squadron.

Moreover, the Central Indian Horse, under the command of the Lindforce, was to revert to the 4th Indian Division.

Attack on Poggio del Grillo

Brigadier Partridge selected the 2nd Cameron to lead the attack on the German positions at M. Ferrato and Poggio del Grillo. The battalion plan was for D Company to advance from Castiglion and capture M. Ferrato at first light on 4 August. Then at 2000 hours on 4 August, A Company advancing from C Vecchia was to capture Poggio del Grillo while C Company was to provide right flank protection by making a thrust from area S. Martino towards Bibbiena. The role of B Company was to provide protection for the sapper party on the road Castellucio—S. Martino. Two troops A Squadron Warwickshire Yeomanry and one platoon D Company Medium Machine Gun Rajputana Rifles were under the command of the 2nd Cameron for this operation.

Preliminary operations to probe into the German defensive position at M. Ferrato, forward of the main German defensive positions at Poggio del Grillo and Poggio Pianale, helped the 11th Indian Infantry Brigade to launch an attack on the German positions. To the west of the Arno, a patrol from the Central India Horse, working up the road from Ponte a Buriano towards Pieve S. Giovanni, clashed on 1 August with a German patrol at the latter place. Three Germans were wounded in the ensuing fire fight. The patrol advanced on the next day via C. Vecchia—La Volta to M. Ferrato, four miles west of Subbiano, in the heart of the Pratomagno massif. The patrol again clashed with the Germans killing three of them and capturing two prisoners. On 3 August another patrol engaged the Germans at M. Ferrato, inflicting some losses on them. Patrols from the King's Dragoon Guards, supported by a troop of Warwickshire Yeomanry, reached on 3 August M. Capannino and Poggio

OPERATION VANDAL

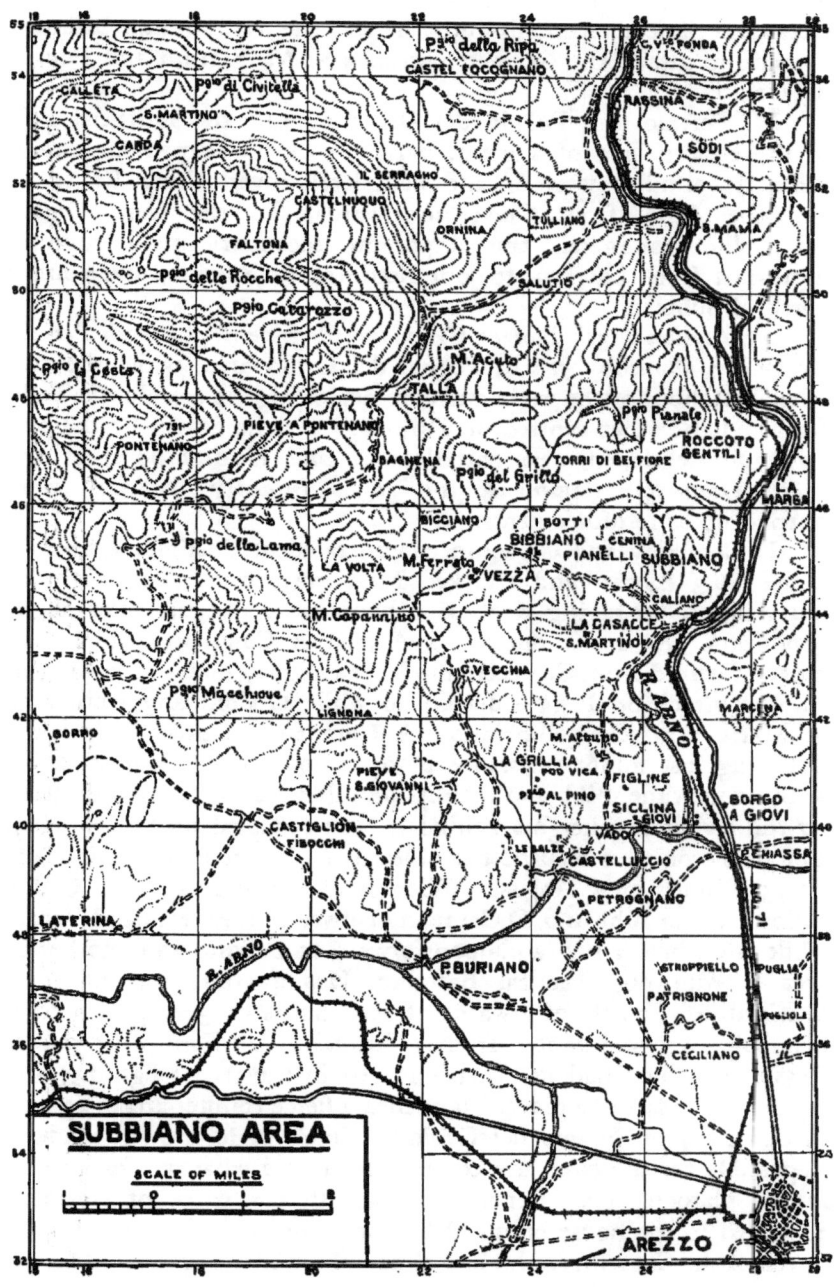

SUBBIANO AREA

della Lama, the southern arm of M. Ferrato, before contacting the Germans. These reconnaissances helped the 11th Indian Infantry Brigade to attack the German positions at M. Ferrato and Poggio del Grillo.

M. Ferrato and Poggio del Grillo formed the northern half of the eastern arm of a great, barren, rocky V-shaped mountain, some three miles west of and completely overlooking Route 71 and the Arno, from Giovi northwards. To the west, Poggio del Grillo dominated the important secondary road running north-east from Laterina to join Route 71 at Rassina, seven miles north of Subbiano.

1 Battalion 115th Panzer Grenadier Regiment (the *15th Panzer Grenadier Division*) was in Poggio del Grillo area, while the two other battalions of the regiment were deployed, one astride the Talla road and the other centred on Faltona.[3] As the attack by the 2nd Cameron developed, two battalions (*I and II Battalions*) of the *578th Grenadier Regiment* (the *305th Infantry Division*) were hurried up as reinforcements.

D Company 2nd Cameron concentrated at Castiglione at 2000 hours on 3 August and attacked M. Ferrato during the night of 3/4 August, occupying it at 0630 hours on 4 August after slight opposition. At 2000 hours on 4 August A Company (which had moved forward from C. Vecchia to Vezza at 1817 hours on 4 August) led the attack on Poggio del Grillo while C Company from area S. Martino attacked Bibbiano. A Company secured Poggio del Grillo against minor resistance at 0300 hours on 5 August while, at the same time, Bibbiano with its prominent church spire, dwarfed by the forbidding heights behind it, was occupied by C Company. The Cameron thus secured the objectives without much opposition. At 0540 hours on 5 August, A Company was at Poggio del Grillo, C Company at Bibbiano, D Company between M. Ferrato and Vezza, while B Company had a platoon forward at Caliano and another in area S. Martino. Tactical Battalion Headquarters was south of S. Martino. Shortly afterwards at 0700 hours on 5 August a company of German infantry from *1 Battalion 115 Panzer Grenadier Regiment*, which had not been engaged in the recent fighting, and a platoon of assault engineers, launched a fierce counter-attack against A Company on Poggio del Grillo.[4]. Thick under-growth made it impossible for the company commander to see what was happening in his platoon area. Reports indicate that a party of Germans advanced to the house occupied by company headquarters behind a screen of the Camerons, who had already been made prisoners. As the Germans threatened to blow up the house, the company commander

---

[3] 4 Ind. Div. Intelligence Summary No. 137, dated 7 August 1944.
[4] 4 Ind. Div. Intelligence Summary No. 136, dated 5/6 August 1944.

agreed to surrender. The survivors were then marched off by the Germans, but the tanks of the Warwickshire Yeomanry fired from M. Ferrato and in the resulting confusion the company commander managed to escape. The Cameron losses totalled 3 officers and 60 other ranks.

At 0915 hours on 5 August, when A Company hard pressed by the Germans asked for support, the brigadier ordered Central India Horse to send one composite group to Bibbiano, 3/12 Royal Frontier Force Regiment to push on to the other side of the Arno with a view to mopping up and C Company 1st Royal Sussex to relieve D Company 2nd Cameron in area between M. Ferrato and Vezza to allow the latter to assist A Company 2nd Cameron. But support could not be given to the ill-fated A Company in time. The brigadier, however, took steps to retrieve the situation as early as possible. At 1600 hours on 5 August, he instructed 3/12 Royal Frontier Force Regiment to extend over area occupied by 2/7 Gurkha so as to enable the latter to concentrate in the area of the 2nd Cameron. He further ordered C Company 2nd Cameron at Bibbiano, supported by a composite group from Central India Horse, to get ready to attack and capture Poggio del Grillo which it did at 2130 hours. One platoon in a magnificent rush, reached the top of one of the peaks (west Pimple), causing confusion among the Germans. 8 Germans were killed and 6 taken prisoners. Two other platoons were however checked by heavy spandau and Bren Gun fire in their attempt to capture another peak (east Pimple). Owing to the superior strength of the Germans, C Company was called off at 0210 hours on 6 August. Its casualties were 2 killed, 6 wounded and 11 missing.

An unusual role was allotted to the Central India Horse in this attack. No tanks being available, four armoured cars from the regiment moved forward in close support of the infantry. When the armoured cars were halted by the narrowness and bad surface of the track, the officer in command dismounted his crews with their machine guns and continued on foot, accompanied by a Cameron serjeant. They fell into a German ambush. The Cameron serjeant escaped. All five Indians in the party were captured, but later evaded their captors. No trace was found of the officer in command.

After the failure of the attack on Poggio del Grillo, Brigadier Partridge issued fresh instructions on 6 August by which 2/7 Gurkha advancing from M. Ferrato was to attack Poggio del Grillo and 3/12 Royal Frontier Force Regiment advancing from area La Marga, was to secure Poggio Pianale. One platoon D Company Medium Machine Gun Rajputana Rifles was under the command of 2/7 Gurkha while A Squadron Warwickshire Yeomanry less two troops and one platoon B Company Medium Machine Gun Rajputana Rifles (4.2-inch mortar) were under the command of 3/12 Royal Frontier Force Regiment.

2/7 Gurkha attacked Poggio del Grillo at 0004 hours on 7 August and secured it after stiff opposition at 0325 hours. The German defensive fire was very heavy, though ineffective. A German counter-attack developed but it was broken up. There was intermittent shelling and mortaring of Poggio del Grillo throughout the day. The Gurkha battalion suffered 21 casualties, 7 killed and 14 wounded.

3/12 Royal Frontier Force Regiment advanced from area La Marga during the night of 7/8 August in a silent attack along the Arno valley towards Poggio Pianale. A strong German position, which they could not outflank, halted A and B, the forward companies, short of Roccolo Gentili, the spur, east from Poggio Pianale. At 0400 hours the companies were withdrawn south of Roccolo Gentili as artillery was to open fire on that place. At 0900 hours A and B Companies infiltrated towards Roccolo Gentili but were pinned down about fifty yards from their objective. A Company suffered heavy casualties and its company commander was killed. At 1115 hours the two companies were withdrawn. 3/12 Royal Frontier Force Regiment failed to capture Poggio Pianale and withdrew after suffering 63 casualties, including one company commander killed.

The 2nd Cameron now carried out mopping up operations south of Poggio Pianale and by 9 August occupied without opposition Pianelli, Botti and Cenina. Their last objective, the ruined tower of Torri di Belfiore, was still a mile ahead of them.

While the 11th Indian Infantry Brigade hammered at the strong German defences at Poggio Grillo and Poggio Pianale, the 7th Indian Infantry Brigade moved up to protect its left flank in the territory previously patrolled by Lindforce.[5] On 5 August, the 7th Indian Infantry Brigade concentrated in area Castiglione and supported by tanks of the King's Dragoon Guards advanced into the mountains. The next day 1 Sussex from area M. Capannino patrolled to Bicciano without making contact with the Germans. At the same time one of its companies, which had relieved a company of the 2nd Cameron at M. Ferrato, patrolled towards M. Arnato. On its left 2/11 Sikh advanced from area Poggio della Lama up the road to Bagnena and found Talla strongly held by the Germans. To the west of the Sikh battalion, 1/2 Gurkha overcame German resistance at Poggio la Cesta and established contact with

---

[5] Lindforce was dissolved on 5 August, Central India Horse and one squadron of the King's Dragoon Guards coming directly under command of the 4th Ind. Div. and the rest of the force passing under the command of the 9th Armoured Brigade.

Capture of Falciano

While the 11th Indian Infantry Brigade led the attack on Poggio del Grillo and Poggio Pianale, the 5th Indian Infantry Brigade was directed against Falciano. The brigade plan was for 1/4 Essex to secure area Scille as a firm base for enabling 3/10 Baluch to capture M. Alto, after which 1/9 Gurkha was to annex Falciano. A Company Medium Machine Gun Rajputana Rifles was with the brigade while B Squadron Warwickshire Yeomanry and ancillary troops were in support.

At 2130 hours on 1 August, 1/4 Essex advanced and occupied without opposition the spur Scille—Pt. 631. At 2330 hours, 3/10 Baluch moved to the concentration area behind 1/4 Essex in Scille area. At 0500 hours on 2 August, 3/10 Baluch advanced from Scille area to secure M. Alto. C Company leading the attack captured Pt. 636. Then A Company surged forward for the attack on M. Alto, which was occupied at 0640 hours against slight opposition from a couple of machine guns. The forward company was, however, heavily shelled. The Main Battalion Headquarters was also intensely shelled for about three hours, resulting in one dump of 3-inch mortar ammunition catching fire.

During the night of 2/3 August, 1/9 Gurkha passed through 3/10 Baluch at M. Alto and turned north-westwards along the ridge to C. Orzale. By first light on 3 August the Gurkhas were in position at C. Orzale. They now prepared to advance northwards along the lower western slopes of Alpe di Catenaia with a view to secure objectives Pt. 974 and Pt. 925, which were held in strength by the Germans. *II Battalion 577th Grenadier Regiment* was responsible for the defence of a frontage of about 2,500 yards. One company of 60 men and one heavy machine gun section was on Pt. 925. There was a mortar observation post on the forward slopes of Pt. 925. A second company was on the left about 350 yards away on higher ground, while a third company was to the right on slightly lower ground.[6]

At 2130 hours on 3 August, 1/9 Gurkha advanced from C. Orzale. C and D Companies occupied Pt. 974 without opposition. A Company however ran into heavy opposition in the area of Pt. 925. Two Germans in listening post on the forward slope of Pt. 925 heard the approach of the Gurkhas, who, without loss of time, engaged the right flank of the German company. The broken nature of the country enabled them to come to close quarters. In the fight that ensued both sides ran out of ammunition

[6] 4 Ind. Div. Intelligence Summary No. 133 dated 4 August 1944.

and hand-to-hand fighting took place. The Gurkhas were heavily shelled and mortared from the direction of M. Filetto. A Company however drove off the Germans from area Pt. 925, and by 0300 hours on 4 August, its objectives were attained. Behind 1/9 Gurkha, elements of 1/4 Essex moved on to the high ground south of Falciano at Pt. 616. During the night of 4/5 August, 1/4 Essex patrols to Falciano found it clear of Germans. Thus the 5th Indian Infantry Brigade carried out its task of occupying Falciano.

A new Eighth Army plan for the attack on the Gothic Line changed the role of the X Corps from one of attacking to that of holding, while the weight of attack was transferred to the Adriatic coast sector. For this purpose the 4th Indian Division was to be withdrawn at once. The 10th Indian Division relieved the 4th Indian Division astride the Arno and Route 71. On 10 August the 4th Indian Division moved to Lake Trasimene for refitting and training. Thus the 4th Indian Division was called away to another sector before it could drive out the Germans from Poggio Pianale.

The 20th Indian Infantry Brigade's Plan

While the 4th Indian Division was hammering at the strong German defences at Poggio del Grillo and Poggio Pianale, the 10th Indian Division was trying to liquidate German opposition at Alpe di Catenaia, where the *305th Infantry Division*, guarding the position offered stiff opposition. As the X Corps attack developed the Germans regrouped: the *578th Grenadier Regiment* was transferred from the front of the 10th Indian Division to that of the 4th Indian Division while the Alpe di Catenaia sector was strengthened by the *Reconnaissance Battalion* (the *114th Jaeger Division*) from the Tiber valley and *III Battalion* from the *104th Panzer Grenadier Regiment* (the *15th Panzer Grenadier Division*) from area Talla, west of the Arno.[7]

Major-General Reid selected the 20th Indian Infantry Brigade to lead the attack on Alpe di Catenaia. The main difficulty in this operation lay in the complete absence of any road communications leading from Castle Montauto, the base, into the area of the Alpe di Catenaia. This difficulty was, however, overcome by constructing a jeep track immediately behind the advance. Emphasis was laid on the need of maintaining the speed of the attack. Only one route, the jeep track, when completed, would be available for the supply and reinforcement of the forward troops in the vast, rough country ahead. This was the reason for attacking with only one brigade. As the front and depth of the attack increased, the leading brigade would have to be reinforceed with additional battalions rather than have a second complete brigade deployed.

[7] 10 Ind. Div. Intelligence Summary No. 67, dated 6 August 1944.

The brigade plan was to secure M. Altuccia—Il Castello on 4 August. The operation was to be carried out in two phases. In Phase I, 3/5 Mahratta was to secure the three objectives—Pt. 941, Pt. 1201 and M. Filetto. In Phase II, 2/3 Gurkha was to advance from area Pt. 941 and secure the two objectives—M. Altuccia and Il Castello. The following troops were under command of the 20th Indian Infantry Brigade:

    Z Company 1st Battalion the Royal Northumberland Fusiliers less two platoons
    W Company 1st Battalion the Royal Northumberland Fusiliers
    68th Field Regiment Royal Artillery
    165th Jeep Regiment less one Battery
    100th Anti-Tank Battery and ancillary units.

The following troops were in support:
    A Squadron Royal Wiltshire Yeomanry
    7th and 85th Mountain Regiments Royal Artillery
    E Battery Royal Horse Artillery
    97th and 154th Field Regiments Royal Artillery
    5, 10 and 61 Field Companies ⎫
    4 Canadian Drilling Section   ⎬ under command for move
    Two companies Artieri   ⎭ only
    Six Bulldozers.

(The 10th and the 25th Indian Infantry Brigades each placed one battalion ready to move up under the command of the 20th Indian Infantry Brigade.)[6]

Capture of Il Castello

The 20th Indian Infantry Brigade Group, attacking silently, opened the attack with complete success. At 2145 hours on 3 August, 3/5 Mahratta crossed the start line east of Pt. 764 in close formation, with A Company leading, followed by B Company, Tactical Headquarters, C Company, D Company and Main Headquarters. A Company seized Pt. 941 against negligible opposition at 0100 hours on 4 August. The advance continued and at 0215 hours it was established on Pt.1201 after meeting considerable opposition from spandaus and light mortars. This success was followed by a heavy German defensive fire at 0245 hours, inflicting casualties on Main Headquarters, supporting troops and mule supply column. The German fire took a heavy toll of the Mahratta, killing 1 and wounding 18. The advance was however continued. At 0300 hours, A Company occupied saddle area Pt. 1187 and B Company pushed through for the attack on M. Filetto. C Company was established

---

[6] 20 Ind. Inf. Bde. O.O. No. 5, dated 1 August 1944.

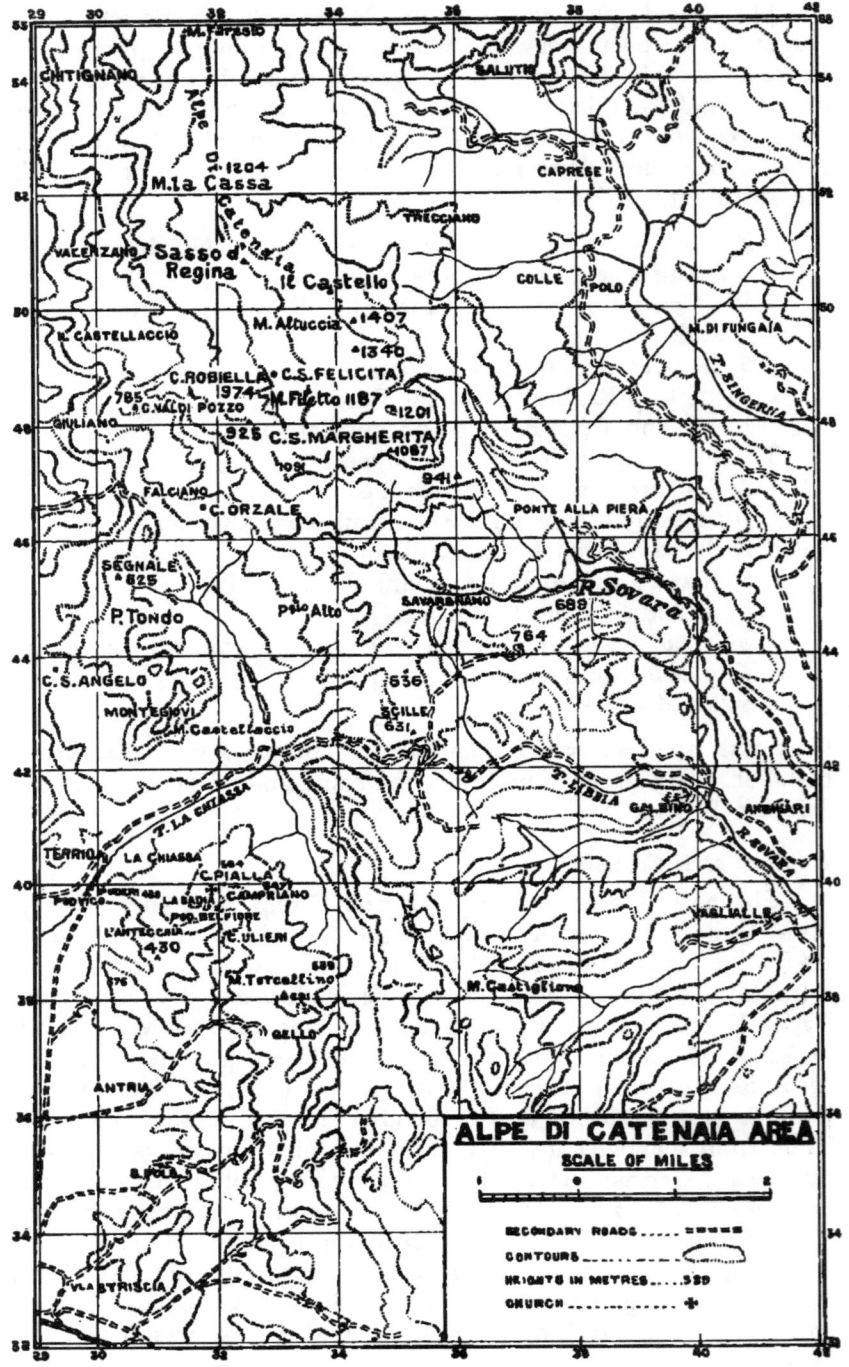

on Pt. 1201 and D Company was in reserve near Tactical Headquarters in area Pt. 1087.

The very size and configuration of the mountain, though calling for a tremendous physical effort, assisted the attackers. A series of false crests and intervening deep, wooded ravines, between the Mahrattas and their mountain-top objective, required more than the Germans could afford for defending the position adequately. Consequently German troops were concentrated near the crest with the intention of denying the forward slopes by a thin screen of outposts, based on a network of machine guns, and thick defensive fire tasks for mortars and artillery on all possible approaches and forming-up places. The loose shale surface and the shrub combined with the gradients to make progress painfully laborious. It was hard fighting all the way through shrub, across a treacherous surface, on a precipitous slope, down which trickled streams of crystal water from numerous springs near the crest of the hill. At 0600 hours, B Company surged round and over M. Filetto, supported by A Company from Pt. 1187. At 0930 hours, it had cleared M. Filetto, two platoons of German infantry withdrawing towards the crest of the mountain.

This was really the limit of advance ordered for the Mahrattas, but in spite of the laborious struggle up nearly three thousand feet of mountainside, they were eager to exploit their success. At 1400 hours D Company moved through A Company on Pt. 1187 for an attack on M. Altuccia, with C Company following to occupy Il Castello, one of the highest peaks of Alpe di Catenaia. D Company met with stiff opposition from the top of the feature and the wooded areas on the eastern and western slopes, and was forced to withdraw at 1630 hours. After a concentration of artillery fire for five minutes on German positions by the 68th Field Regiment, a pincer attack was made at 1815 hours on the German position at M. Altuccia, with C Company on the right and D Company on the left. D Company making a wide hook overcame German opposition in the woods and gained Pt. 1407 by 1850 hours. C Company overcame several German positions and captured three spandaus. The momentum of C Company's attack carried the men through to feature Il Castello. By 1920 hours they had a grip on the slopes of the peak and began to dig in. Later the remainder of the battalion closed up to make a strong position around M. Altuccia. By 2300 hours the battalion was established with Tactical Headquarters and A Company forward of M. Filetto, B Company at M. Filetto, D Company at M. Altuccia and C Company at the slopes of Il Castello. There was heavy shelling of the forward companies during the night of 4/5 August. Casualties had been heavy but the Mahrattas had surprised the Germans and inflicted an initial defeat on them. The stage was now set for 2/3 Gurkha to exploit this success and work its way up to the mountain top.

Behind the Mahratta, 2/3 Gurkha concentrated at M. Filetto in the afternoon of 4 August, in preparation for an attack on Il Castello the following morning. The attack was greatly assisted by the construction of a jeep track, which sometimes following old footpaths, along steep hillsides, up narrow ridges, into and out of gullies, across and along the beds of running streams, had been brought up to Pt. 941, that is within two miles of the foremost troops. It was a heroic effort. Forest, excessive gradients, rocks in the hillside and boulders in the beds of the streams, soft surfaces, running streams and cliff faces, all had to be overcome under observed German shelling or in darkness. The 10th Indian Division was well served by its sappers.

At 2200 hours, B and C Companies of 2/3 Gurkha moved off from the western slopes of Pt. 941 to pass through 3/5 Mahratta at M. Altuccia to seize Il Castello. But the men lost direction in the dense woods, south and south-west of Il Castello. It was not till 1130 hours that they captured Il Castello after a sharp engagement. At 1300 hours, C Company moved north-west toward Sasso della Regina. By then the Germans had recovered from the initial shock of the attack. Intense fire and tenacious resistance denied the crest of Sasso della Regina to the Gurkhas. However, when evening came 2/3 Gurkha was firmly established on Il Castello with one company forward on the nearer slopes of Sasso della Regina. The 20th Indian Infantry Brigade Group was now up against considerable opposition. German reinforcements (the *Reconnaissance Battalion* of the *114th Jaeger Division* from the Tiber valley and *III Battalion* from the *104 Panzer Grenadier Regiment* of the *15th Panzer Grenadier Division* from area Talla) had arrived to prevent the British and Indian troops from capturing Alpe di Catenaia. The forward positions of the 20th Indian Infantry Brigade Group were intermittently shelled and mortared throughout the day on 5 August. Shelling was very heavy at times, especially on the Il Castello—Sasso della Regina spur, M. Altuccia and saddle east of M. Filetto.

Bad weather on 5 August adversely affected air operations and the work by the sappers. Though on the previous day, fighter-bombers had been used with great success against German communications, their activities were now considerably restricted by the foul weather.[9] Rain made the 20th Indian Infantry Brigade's supply problem even more intricate. Nevertheless, by the evening of 5 August, with bulldozers working under shell fire, the track was brought up close to Pt. 1201, thus considerably easing the supply problem.

[9] Air Summary Sitrep dated 4/5 August 1944, War Diary 10 Ind. Div.

Engineering Feat

The building of the track was something of an engineering feat. Statistics compiled after the operation showed that, from the road-head south-west of Castle Montauto, the alignment of the track involved a drop of three hundred and seventy feet into the river Sovara, followed by a climb of two thousand three hundred feet to a maximum elevation of three thousand seven hundred and fifty feet, over a total distance of six miles. This alignment had been tentatively selected from air photographs. Sufficient ground reconnaissance was carried out beforehand to enable work on the jeep track to begin immediately behind the infantry, when the start line was crossed. Bright moonlight materially assisted the work. The jeep track was planned to be initially one way, with defiladed parking areas for use as traffic control stations, to pass convoys at intervals of from three to five miles. Passing places for individual vehicles were to be constructed wherever possible.

In addition to the Divisional Royal Engineers of three Field Companies and one Field Park Company, one Drilling Section and two companies Artieri (Italian Pioneers)—total strength of approximately 150 men were available. One Army Field Company was allotted later for maintenance.

One field company, less one platoon, moved close behind the leading battalion to construct a mule track, above and near the jeep track. Immediately behind a second field company, with the Canadian Drilling Section, Italian Pioneers and some mechanical equipment, constructed the jeep track. The third field company constructed a track for tanks. Work accomplished was:

> *Mule Track*—Five miles by two platoons Royal Engineers in eighteen hours to Pt. 1087.
>
> *Jeep Track*—Six miles of high quality track for jeep with trailers, completed by four platoons Royal Engineers and two Italian pioneer companies in sixty-six hours to south of M. Filetto
>
> *Tank Track*—Five miles completed by three platoons Royal Engineers in thirty-six hours to Pt. 1087.[10]

German Counter-attack

After the completion of the track and the easing of the supply position, the 20th Indian Infantry Brigade Group carried out preliminary moves for the attack on the strong German position at Sasso della Regina, a knife-edge ridge of broken, white rocks, with thick shrub on its lower slopes. A narrow neck of high ground joined Sasso della Regina to Il Castello, but in other directions cliff faces

---

[10] Appx. 'E' to 10 Ind. Div. Narrative of Operations, File 8328/H.

made Sasso della Regina a formidable obstacle—impassable to tanks. In the time available, little reconnaissance of the Sasso della Regina hill had been possible. The hail of fire from that direction was an indication of the strength in which the Germans held it, but locations and exact strengths had not been determined.

During the night of 5/6 August, A and D Companies of 2/3 Gurkha moved up to join C, the forward Company, in an assault on Sasso della Regina. On the morning of 6 August, the battalion was deployed as follows on the Il Castello feature, in preparation for the attack on Sasso della Regina:

    (*i*) A, C and D Companies were forward of Il Castello on the edge of 300 yard strip of grass-land.

    (*ii*) B Company, protecting Tactical Headquarters in Il Castello, was on the fringe of a small wood, 100 yards long by 50 yards wide.

    (*iii*) Battalion Headquarters was firm on Filetto.

Two rifle companies, A and D were forming a firm base, with C Company preparing to do the initial assault. During the forming up phase a prisoner was taken by one of C Company's protective patrols, who gave the information that there were 400 Germans on the Sasso della Regina feature. Consequently the officer commanding the Gurkha battalion halted his companies, pending a more detailed reconnaissance of the German positions. Meanwhile about 300 Germans from the two fresh German battalions, with a detachment of troopers with 'Bazookas', having somehow worked round the flanks of the three forward companies near Sasso della Regina, launched a fierce counter-attack, preceded by heavy shelling, on the sole Gurkha company (B) holding Il Castello. With the company were battalion headquarters and a platoon of machine gunners from the Royal Northumberland Fusiliers. The first solitary spandau round, whizzing unexpectedly as it did out of the damp grey mist which bathed the mountain-top in the hour before dawn, gave some warning, but the Germans penetrated the machine gunners' positions, and for a while the situation grew critical. At 0506 hours there had been silence but two minutes later a full-sized action was in progress. Brens, Spandaus, tommy guns, Schmeizers, rifles, grenades, 'Bazookas' and mortars spat death at a hideous rate. The commanding officer ordered two of the forward companies near Sasso della Regina to turn about, deploy and take the Germans in the rear. The move was a great success. An eye-witness account describes how the fearless hillmen, with kukries drawn and yelling their battle cries, rushed to the rescue of their hard-pressed brothers. During the next few minutes the wood was a scene of hell. Some Germans withdrew, while others, who attempted the impossible hand-to-hand fighting with the Gurkhas, literally lost their heads.

Fierce hand-to-hand fighting raged among the thick bushes for four hours, the Gurkhas charging furiously with their kukries. Considerable loss was inflicted on the Germans who were forced into the shelter of the woods.[11]

Failure of the Attack on Sasso della Regina

After the Gurkha success in repelling the German counter-attack with heavy losses to the Germans, 3/5 Mahratta got ready to push through for an attack on the Sasso della Regina feature. The preliminary moves of 3/5 Mahratta to attack Sasso della Regina began at last light on 6 August, with A Company established on spur at R 330505, and B and C Companies formed up on this spur as the start line for the attack. At 2300 hours B Company met stiff resistance amongst trees on the western slopes of the razor-backed ridge between Il Castello and Sasso della Regina. C Company on the eastern slope also encountered considerable opposition. Both the companies were engaged from the start by German light machine gun posts in the stream beds, north and south of the ridge, and on the ridge itself. German light machine gun posts were mopped up, and the two companies fought their way on to Sasso della Regina at about 0300 hours on 7 August. They were immediately engaged by the Germans from the scrub and the trees on the flanks. Continuous German counter-attacks made a serious drain on the available ammunition. In the end, the Mahrattas were compelled to beat off attacks with their bayonets only. As a strong German attack from both the flanks was developing, the Mahrattas were pulled back from Sasso della Regina to Il Castello at about 0345 hours on 7 August.

At this stage it became necessary to relax the grip which the 10th Indian Division had secured to enable regrouping of the troops for the relief of the 4th Indian Division on the left. Hence the 20th Indian Infantry Brigade Group consolidated itself in the existing positions. German activity too was confined to infiltration into Indian positions and heavy shelling.

The 'Vandal' operation had started well. After a fierce struggle the 10th Indian Division was firmly established on Alpe di Catenaia, although the highest spurs were still held by the Germans in strength. The 4th Indian Division too had made deep inroads into the territory held by the Germans. Half the distance to Castel Focognano had been traversed. The X Corps was well on the road to success. Nevertheless on 10 August 1944, operation Vandal was abruptly suspended due to a change in the Army plan for the attack on the Gothic Line. The 4th Indian Division was transferred to the Adriatic sector to take part in the attack on the Gothic Line.

---

[11] Castello Operation, Appx. J-7, War Diary 2/3 G. R.; Kurkies Flash in the Hills by Ray Hill, *The Diagonals* 19 August 1944; War Diary 10 Ind. Div. August 1944.

The 10th Indian Division relieved the 4th Indian Division on 10 August, thus practically inheriting the X Corps front, on which previously two divisions and an armoured task force had been deployed. With this extension of front, the activities of the 10th Indian Division were mainly confined to patrolling. The weight of the Eighth Army was to be thrown on the Adriatic coast to drive out the Germans from the Gothic Line.

THE BREAKING OF THE GOTHIC LINE

CHAPTER XVII

Capture of Tavoleto

The Allied Change of Plan

At the beginning of August 1944, when the XIII Corps had reached the line of the Arno and the X Corps was making a thrust towards Bibbiena, the Eighth Army was well poised to implement General Alexander's plan of 26 July 1944 for the attack on the Gothic Line, the last of the German big defence lines in the northern Apennines. The plan aimed at breaking through the barrier of the Apennines by the shortest route, the ascent between Florence and Bologna, the latter being the most important objective south of the Po. The chief advantage in launching this attack by the direct route to Bologna instead of along the Adriatic coast was that a minimum of regrouping of the Allied forces was required for an attack on a front from Dicomano to Pistoia, since the weight of the Fifth and Eighth Armies was already being thrown on the west and centre. General Alexander's expectation was that if the momentum of the Allied attack were kept up, without losing precious time (which might otherwise be required for the reorganisation of the forces in case it was decided to throw the weight of the Eighth Army on the Adriatic coast) there was reasonable hope of making a successful attack on the German centre.

At the beginning of August 1944, however, Lieut.-General Sir Oliver Leese began to entertain serious misgivings about the success of the plan and swung round to the view that it would be preferable to attack along the Adriatic coast. His chief apprehension was that his troops trained in mountain warfare had been too greatly decreased as the French Expeditionary Force had withdrawn for operation 'Anvil'. He would not be able to break through the centre of the Apennine position. Moreover, in the mountainous sector he would not be able to make full use of the Allied superiority in armour and artillery.

Lieut.-General Sir Oliver Leese confided his misgivings to General Alexander at an informal conference held at Orvieto airfield on 4 August 1944. General Alexander too had his own doubts about the success of the plan. "It was anything but certain that our heavy blow in the mountains of the centre would take us through to our objective and if the first attack there fell short of expectations the advantage would be all with the defenders. He had by far the easier lateral communications so that, once it was clear that all our strength was concentrated at one point, he could very rapidly build up a counter concentration."[1] General Alexander therefore issued fresh instructions on 4 August 1944, drastically altering the plan. Accordingly the role of the Eighth Army was to lead the attack in the Adriatic corridor, roll up the eastern end of the Gothic Line, and advance to the Bologna—Ferrara area. As this attack made headway and drew off German reinforcements from the central sector, the Fifth Army was to launch an attack north-eastwards from Florence, and trap the German forces by closing with the Eighth Army's right hook in the Bologna area. This was to be the strategy of the "two-handed punch" on which General Alexander pinned high hopes.

The Gothic Line

The Gothic Line defences had been planned at the time of the Allied invasion of Italy. Until the fall of Rome, work on the defences had been slow and spasmodic. Then the Todt organisation, which conscripted Italian labour, made frantic efforts to complete the defences but sabotage and lack of enthusiasm on the part of the Italian labour delayed the execution. The earlier name for the Gothic Line, the Pisa-Rimini line, revealed its approximate geographical location. In the west, anti-tank defences and artificial obstacles protected the approaches to La Spezia and the valley of the Magra. From Marina di Carrara on the west coast the line ran to Carrara, over the Apuan mountains, across the road from Lucca to Modéna at Borgo a Mózzano, and the main road Pistoia—Bologna, a short distance south of the Porretta Pass. Then it crossed three mountain passes (forming the strongest mountain defences in the line) at Vernio, Futa and Il Giogo. Next it swung south-east to the two passes on the Alpe di San Benedetto at Casaglia and S. Godenzo. Then it connected the two strong-points of Alpe di Serra at Serravalle and Valsavignone. From this last place it ran to Badia Tedalda and one mile north of Lunano, whence it followed the line of the river Foglia to Pesaro.

Throughout its length, the Gothic Line was situated south of the main ridges and passes of the Apennines. In the area of the western coastal plain there were pill-boxes, strong-points, anti-tank guns in emplacements, and minefields, with tank obstacles running respectively from Massa and Carrara to the sea. Inland defences comprised machine gun positions, of which a large number were covered over, with the main concentration of defensive works on

[1] Alexander's *Despatch, op. cit.*

the axes over the Apennines. At these points there were pillboxes, anti-tank gun positions and heavily mined areas. The line in general had no depth. In the Adriatic sector, it ran parallel to the river Foglia, and consisted of machine gun positions, pillboxes, anti-tank ditches and minefields, but had no depth apart from the strong perimeter defences round Pesaro.[2]

The main problem for the Eighth Army in the Adriatic sector was how to tackle the Foglia river line. It is necessary, therefore, to make a brief topographical survey of the east Apennine sector up to the Adriatic coast, and also to describe the river Foglia defences. The Gothic Line in the Adriatic sector had three sub-sectors—(*i*) the flat valley from Pesaro to Belvedere Foglinese, (*ii*) the foothills from Belvedere Foglinese to Caprazzino and (*iii*) the mountain sub-sector from Caprazzino to Badia Tedalda. Besides these were the coastal defences between Pesaro and Riccione.

The town of Pesaro was the main anchor of the Gothic Line on the Adriatic coast. It had an all-round defence and was included within the main line of resistance, although it appeared that the majority of defences were sited against an attack from the sea rather than from the land. In the sub-sector from Pesaro to Belvedere Foglinese, which was about 13 miles long, the defences lay on the rising ground overlooking the wide flat valley of the Foglia to the south. The line of defences was continuous throughout this sub-sector, which was closely spaced, consisting of concrete pill-boxes and some casements, besides large numbers of machine gun positions and fire trenches. From Belvedere Foglinese to Caprazzino, a sub-sector in which the Gothic Line ran through the foothills of the Apinnines, there were minor defences, at some places still in a comparatively undeveloped state, while in others bolstered up with wire obstacles and minefields. This line followed that of the Foglia, and in general kept close to the road, which ran along the north bank. There was, however, one notable exception to this, namely in the area where the river made a wide loop to the south. Here the line ran through the high ground of Monte Calvo, well to the north of the river and road. An outpost position, however, appeared to be sited on M. della Croce, nearer to the river in the angle of the loop. Except in the Monte Calvo area, there was little attempt at depth in defence. Key points in this sub-sector were S. Giorgio, Monte Calvo, La Casinnina, Bronzo and Mercatale, the majority of which were points controlling roads leading north or north-west. In the mountain sub-sector there was no continuous line of defences, but only a series of defended areas, between which the Germans appeared to be relying on the difficult nature of the ground, which was steep, mountainous and broken.

[2] Intelligence Summary Gothic Line, V Corps, 12 August 1944; File 601/1023/H.

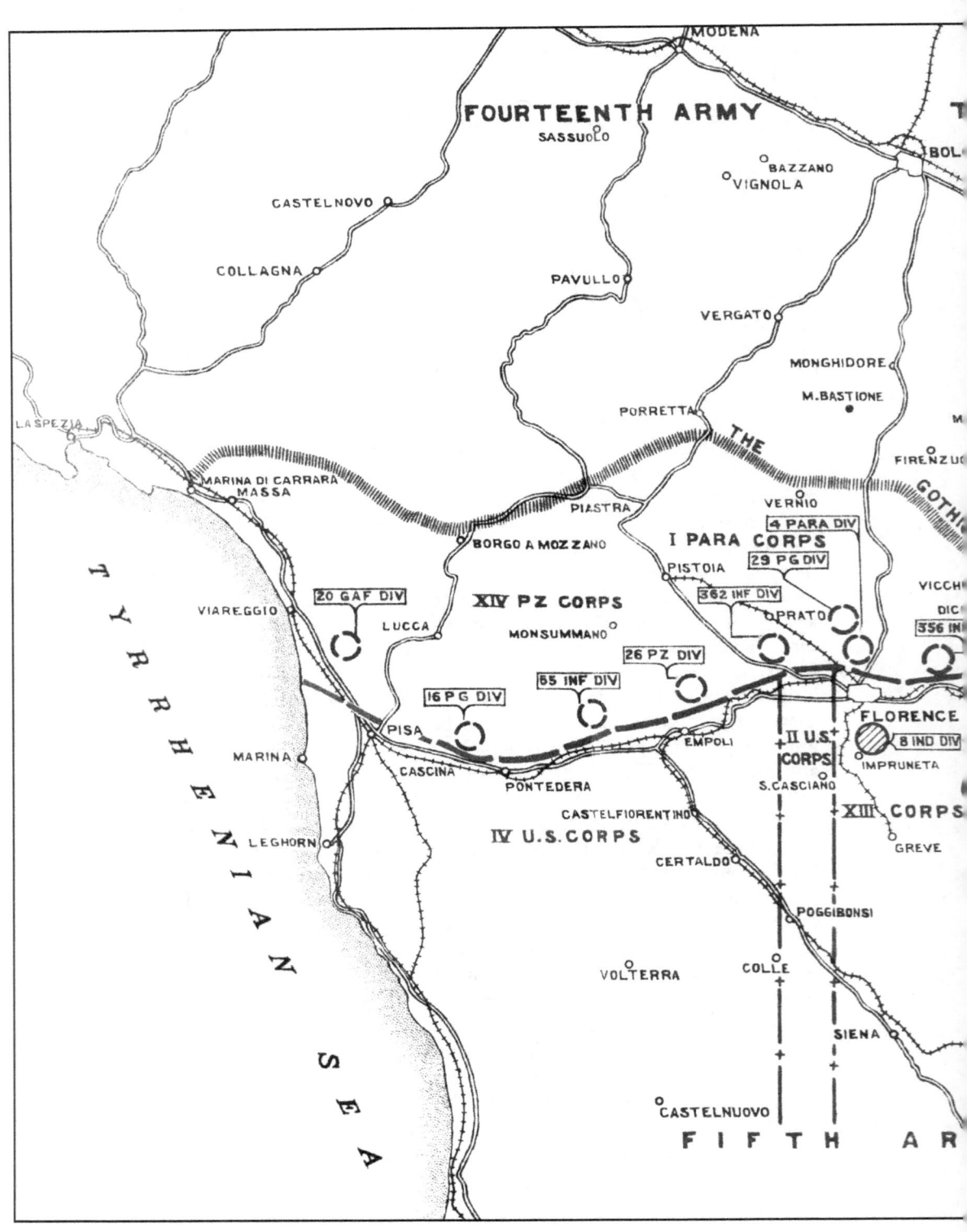

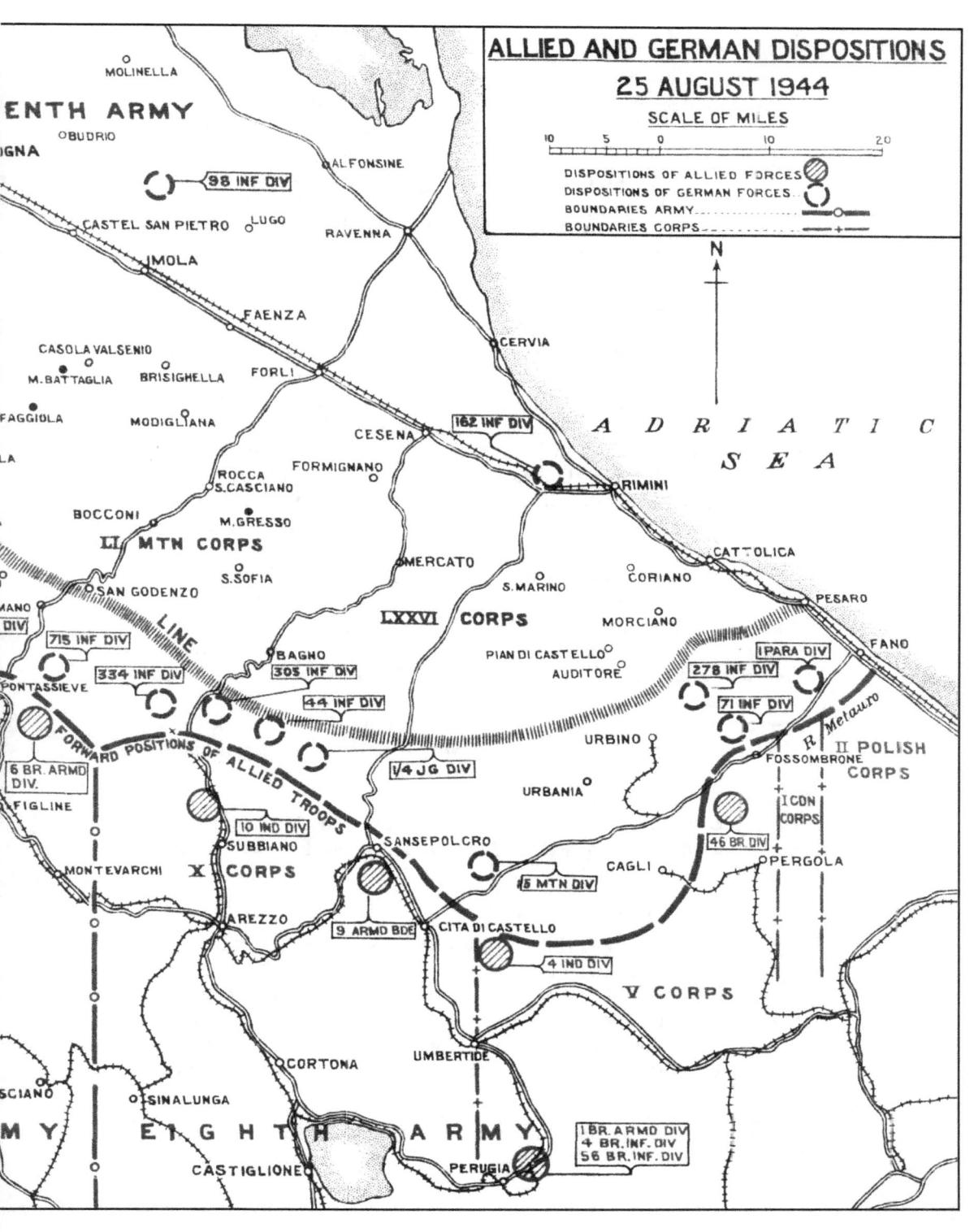

Rival Forces

When the Allied offensive began on 25 August 1944, the Eighth Army was deployed for the attack on the Gothic Line. On the right, the II Polish Corps, with two divisions and an armoured brigade, covered a front of about seven miles, from the Adriatic along the river Metauro. Next, on a narrow front of just over two miles, was the I Canadian Corps, with the 1st Infantry Division and the 5th Armoured Division, supported by a British tank brigade. To the west was the V Corps, covering a wide front of about twenty miles. It was the strongest of the attacking Corps; the 46th Division and the 4th Indian Division were in the line, while the 1st British Armoured Division, the British 4th Division, the 56th Division and two armoured brigades were in reserve. Further to the west of the V Corps was the X Corps, which covered the area from the upper Tiber Valley to the Army boundary on the Pratomagno, with the 10th Indian Division and a mixed brigade group. The 2nd New Zealand Division was in the Eighth Army reserve.[3]

Opposing the Eighth Army was the *Tenth Army*, which held the sector from the Adriatic Sea to Pontassieve with two corps. The *LXXVI Panzer Corps*, holding the sector from the Adriatic to area Sansepolcro, had three divisions in the line and two in reserve. The *1st Parachute Division* was stretched along the river Metauro, from the coast for about seven miles. Next on its right was the *71st Infantry Division* covering a front of about seven miles, as far as Fossombrone. The sector west of Fossombrone was held by the *5th Mountain Division*. The *278th Infantry Division* (in area of Monte Calvo) and the *162nd (Turkoman) Infantry Division* were in the reserve. The *II Mountain Corps* held the sector from area Sansepolcro to Pontassieve with the following divisions under command: the *114th Jaeger Division*, the *44th Infantry Division*, the *305th Infantry Division*, the *334th Infantry Division* and the *715th Infantry Division*. The *98th Infantry Division* in the *Tenth Army* reserve was in Bologna area and was moving slowly south towards the Gothic Line.[4]

The Attack on the Gothic Line

The object of operation 'Olive'—the code name given to the Eighth Army's forthcoming assault—was to break through the Gothic Line into the valley of the Po. River Metauro—the start line—was to be crossed on D day. The first objective was the general line of the river Marecchia, running west from Rimini, and the second, Bologna—Ferrara. The plan made by Lieut.-General

---

[3] Eighth Army O.I. No. 1431, 13 August 1944.
[4] Order of Battle of Army Group 'C'—25 August 1944; General Alexander's *Despatch*.

Sir Oliver Leese provided for a simultaneous assault by three corps on a thirty-mile front. On the right the II Polish Corps was to outflank the town of Pesaro and seize the high ground to its north. Having carried out its limited task it was to pass into the Army reserve. In the centre the I Canadian Corps was to seize the high ground west of Pesaro and thence move to the coast at Cattolica and advance up Route 16 towards Rimini. Farther inland the V Corps was to attack with the 46th Division on the right and the 4th Indian Division on the left. The former was to attack across the river Metauro on D day and seize M. Gridolfo. The latter was to secure the high ground north of the river Metauro, between Fossombrone and Urbino (i.e. Monte della Cesana), and seize the high ground in the area of Tavoleto. When the Germans had become heavily engaged on the Adriatic sector the Fifth Army, strengthened with the British XIII Corps, was to launch the attack from Florence against Bologna.

The Eighth Army began its attack in the night of 25/26 August. On the right, the II Polish Corps broke through the Gothic Line in the Bruciate area and, by 2 September had secured the high ground to the north of Pesaro. Having achieved its objective, the Polish Corps moved to the Eighth Army reserve.

On the left of the Polish Corps, the I Canadian Corps made good progress against fierce opposition. The 1st Canadian Division on the right and the 5th Canadian Armoured Division on the left established two bridge-heads over the river Foglia in the areas Borgo San Maria and Montecchio, respectively. By 1 September, the 1st Canadian Division had secured Monte Luro and the 5th Canadian Armoured Division had seized Tomba di Pesaro after fierce fighting. On the following day the 1st Canadian Division established a bridgehead over the river Conca near Cattolica and pushed up Route 16 towards Rimini. Further west, the 5th Canadian Armoured Division overcame German resistance at S. Giovanni on 3 September, compelling the Germans to withdraw in the night of 4/5 September to a strong position near Coriano. By 4 September, the I Canadian Corps was face to face with the German line running along the river Marano to Coriano.

The V Corps, the left formation of the Eighth Army, also made good progress. The 46th Division seized M. Gridolfo on 31 August and by 3 September had crossed the river Conca and was established on the lower spurs of S. Clemente. On 4 September the 1st British Armoured Division passed through but failed to make any headway against the Germans on the Coriano—San Savino ridge. To the left, the 56th Division, advancing south-west of Mondaiano on 1 September, captured Monterfiore on 4 September but was held up by the Germans in the area Gemmano-Croce. Still further to the left,

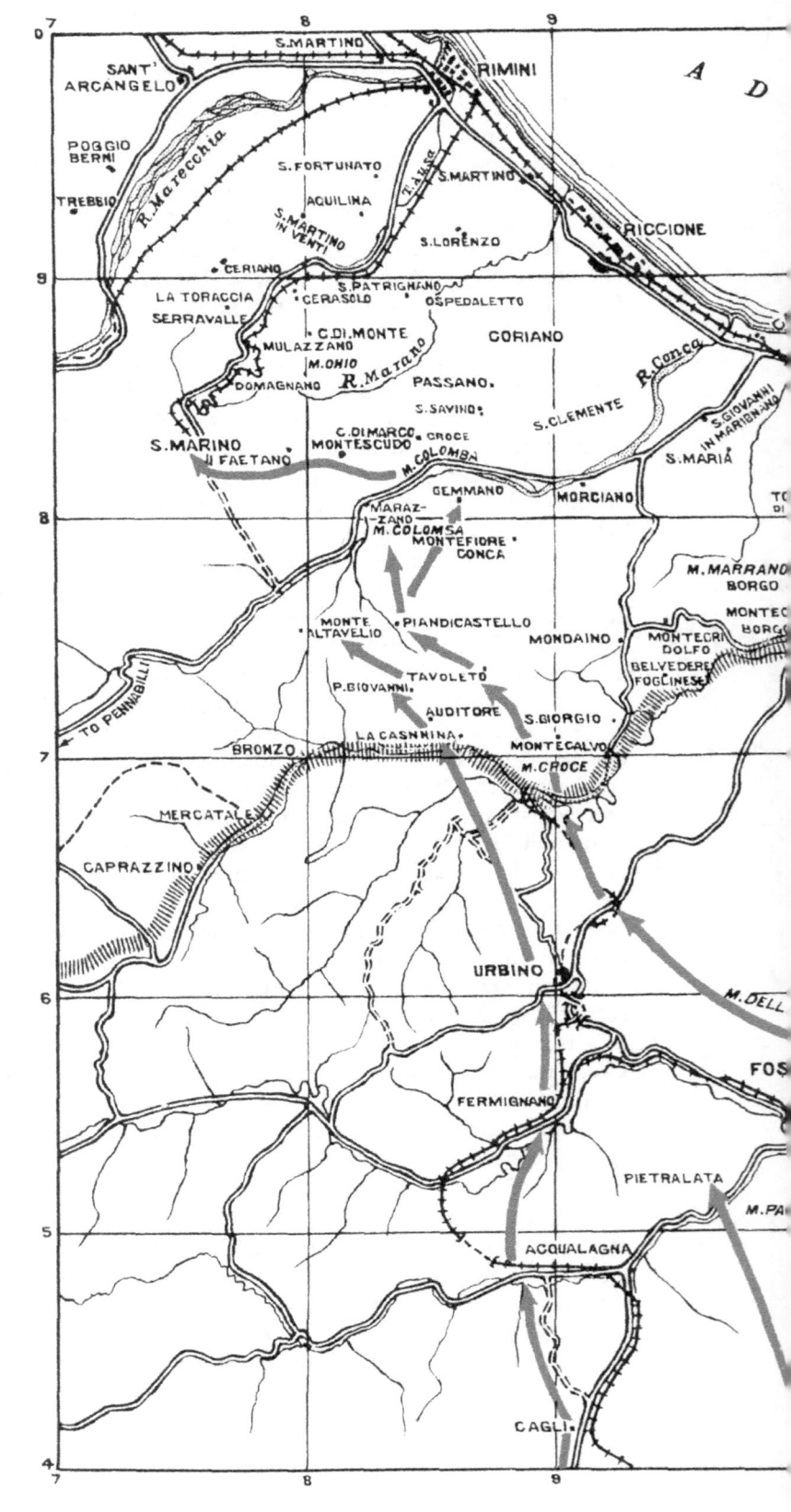

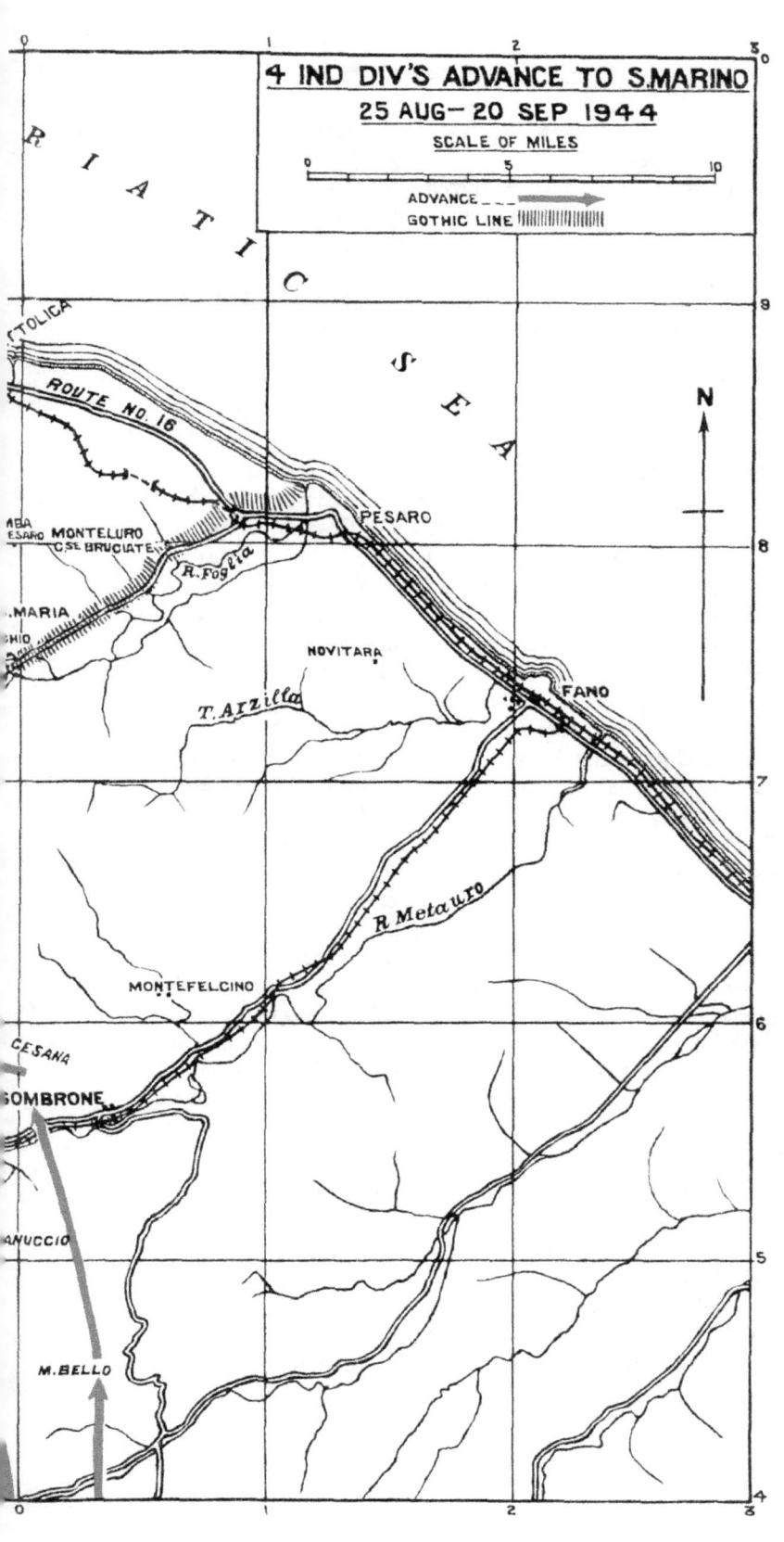

the 4th Indian Division, after capturing the high ground north of the river Metauro, between Fossombrone and Urbino, occupied Monte Calvo on 31 August, and then seized Tavoleto and Poggio San Giovanni on 4 September. But further advance to M.S. Colomba was held up at Pian di Castello. Thus by 4 September the Eighth Army was facing the German defence line, which ran from the river Marano to Coriano, San Savino, Croce, Gemmano and M.S. Colomba (with a forward strong position at Pian di Castello).

Capture of M. della Cesana

Having given a brief account of the operations of the Eighth Army (25 August—4 September 1944) we may now describe in greater detail the part played by the 4th Indian Division in these operations. The role allotted to the 4th Indian Division in the Army plan was to seize the high ground M. della Cesana, preparatory to securing Tavoleto, the bastion of the Gothic Line. Initially, the 4th Indian Division was to advance on a two-brigade front, with the 5th Indian Infantry Brigade on the right and the 7th Indian Infantry Brigade on the left. The 11th Indian Infantry Brigade (less one battalion, which was to be committed in a preliminary operation) was to be in reserve.

The 5th Indian Infantry Brigade was to pass through the forward positions of the Corps of Italian Liberation (responsible for the long left flank of the II Polish Corps) and seize M. Paganuccio and M. Pietralata, preparatory to an attack on M. della Cesana.

One battalion of the 11th Indian Infantry Brigade was to move forward to a position south of Cantiano and capture M. Petrano on D 1 so as to ensure movement along Route 3, later handing over this feature to the group of the Corps of Italian Liberation.

The 7th Indian Infantry Brigade was to advance from Cantiano (in the wake of the battalion of the 11th Indian Infantry Brigade) to Cagli and thence northwards along Route 3. The brigade group of the Corps of Italian Liberation, in conjunction with the Central India Horse, was to protect the left flank of the 4th Indian Division.[5]

The following troops were under command of the 4th Indian Division:

    One Brigade Group of the Corps of Italian Liberation
    6th Battalion the Royal Tank Regiment
    85th Mountain Regiment
    One battery 165th Jeep Field Regiment
    58 Medium Regiment
    Nine Mule Companies.

Brigadier Saunders-Jacobs had issued instructions on 23 August for the capture of M. Paganuccio and M. Pietralata with a view to

---

[5] 4 Ind. Div. O.I. No. 14, 22 August 1944.

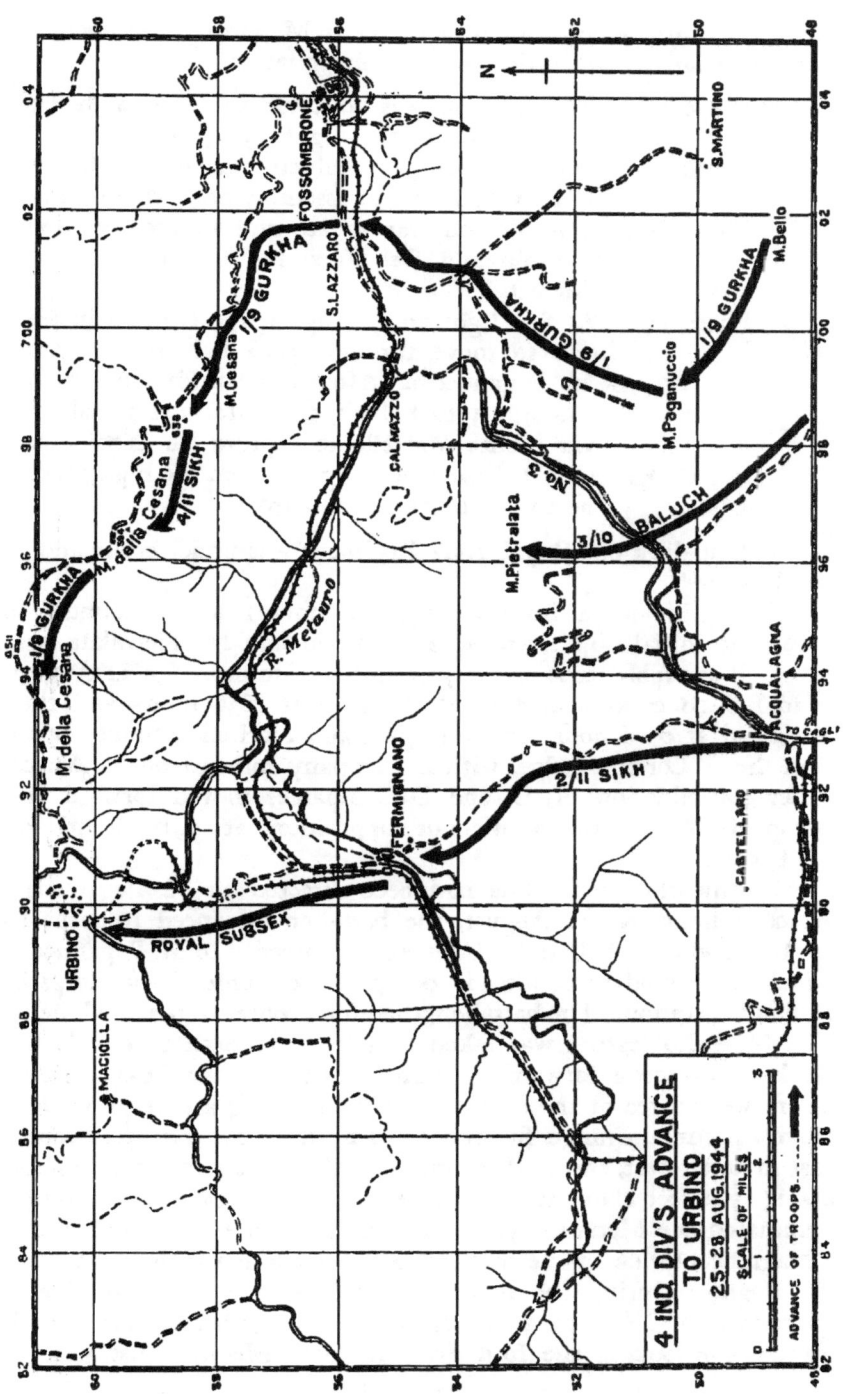

establish a bridge-head north of the river Metauro. The operation was to be carried out in the following five phases:

Phase I: The brigade was to concentrate in area Isola Fossara during the night 23/24 August.

Phase II: On 24 August 3/10 Baluch and 1/9 Gurkha were to move forward to assembly area M. Volcanale.

Phase III: 3/10 Baluch was to advance to occupy Monte Vecchio and Del Vodo in the night of 24/25 August.

Phase IV: At first light on 25 August, 1/9 Gurkha in jeeps was to move through 3/10 Baluch to capture M. Paganuccio. After 1/9 Gurkha had passed through 3/10 Baluch, the latter was to advance via Monte Martello to capture M. Pietralata.

Phase V: Establishment of bridge-head on the high ground north of the river Metauro.

A Squadron 6th Royal Tank Regiment was under command of the brigade.[6]

The 5th Indian Infantry Brigade moving across country to secure its initial objectives, M. Paganuccio and M. Pietralata, was given all available jeeps and large number of mules. On 24 August, 3/10 Baluch concentrated at M. Vecchio at 1830 hours and then advanced at 0700 hours on 25 August and reached without opposition the S. Lorenzo ridge, with B Company forward on M. Varco. After consolidation, A, C, and D Companies moved forward and occupied M. Pietralata without opposition at 0915 hours on 26 August.

Meanwhile 1/9 Gurkha had been directed on M. Paganuccio. At 0600 hours on 25 August, the battalion advanced in jeeps to M. Bello, whence A, B and C Companies proceeded to M. Paganuccio, which was found to be already occupied by a unit of the Corps of Italian Liberation. The battalion, therefore, concentrated at M. Bello. The M. Bello feature was taken over by 4/11 Sikh to enable the Gurkhas to move forward at night to capture the Cesana ridge. There were three of these Cesana peaks, forming a precipitous and narrow mountain range, five miles in length. They ran from southeast to north-west, two or three miles north of the river Metauro and about 1500 feet above it. To the east and the west, this mountain dominated the Metauro valley. At the western end it commanded a magnificent view of the country to the north across the next river, the Foglia. During the night of 25/26 August, Battalion Headquarters and C Company in reserve were established on the high ground overlooking the ford over the river Metauro just west of

[6] 5 Ind. Inf. Bde. O.O. No. 9, 23 August 1944.

Fossombrone, while A and D Companies crossing over the ford occupied the Cesana ridge without meeting with any opposition. By first light on 26 August, A Company was established on Cesana Alta—later joined by C Company—while D Company occupied Cesana Bassa.

After consolidating on Cesana Bassa and Cesana Alta, 1/9 Gurkha secured Pt. 637 at 0900 hours on 27 August, thus extending the battalion area two miles west along the ridge. Then 4/11 Sikh passed through the Gurkha positions and seized Pt. 585 by 1230 hours. At 1938 hours B Company moved forward to Pt. 594 and was followed by C Company to Pt. 583. The latter encountered spandau fire from the German post on that feature. The company commander, thereupon, ordered an attack on the feature with one platoon on the left flank and another on the right flank. The Germans withdrew just before C Company had reached the objective, leaving behind military equipment, including three spandau light machine guns. 1/9 Gurkha now got ready to pass through the positions held by 4/11 Sikh in order to develop a thrust towards Urbino from the right, while the 7th Indian Infantry Brigade was edging forward for the attack on that town from the south.

Advance to Fermignano

While the 5th Indian Infantry Brigade was established on the Cesana ridge, ready to seize the eastern outskirts of Urbino, the 7th Indian Infantry Brigade had been edging forward to that town from the south. 2/11 Sikh, supported by 6th Battalion Royal Tank Regiment, led the advance of the 7th Indian Infantry Brigade. 2/11 Sikh had concentrated at Cagli at 1500 hours on 25 August, and then moved forward to Acqualagna. The leading companies (B and C) were subjected, from 1630 hours until dark, to intense artillery and mortar fire directed from a number of German observation posts on the high ground immediately commanding Acqualagna. In addition, owing to a misunderstanding, the Sikhs were fired upon by an Italian battalion occupying the town. The Sikhs had to fight one of the German rearguards to secure a bridge north of the town. In the afternoon on 26 August D Company advanced and occupied the high ground immediately north of Acqualagna without opposition and the remainder of the battalion also moved up after dark. On 27 August, 2/11 Sikh occupied the high ground overlooking Fermignano town without opposition and secured intact the main bridge in the town itself.

Capture of Urbino

The 5th and 7th Indian Infantry Brigades were converging on Urbino, a small town with a population of twenty thousand. It was an important road junction and stood on a peak, thirteen hundred feet above sea level. Roads into it ran along narrow ridges above deep river valleys. At 0600 hours on 28 August, 1/9 Gurkha passed through the Sikh positions forward of Pt. 594 and captured Pt. 511 at 0830 hours. German activity was confined to slight shelling and light machine gun fire. By 2000 hours the Gurkhas, after overcoming opposition in the area of Pt. 569, passed round the eastern outskirts of Urbino, with companies moving forward to Pt. 378 and Pt. 331, which were seized by 2345 hours. Meanwhile, on the 7th Indian Infantry Brigade front, the 1st Royal Sussex had passed through 2/11 Sikh forward of Fermignano and occupied Urbino without opposition in the afternoon of 28 August. Across the Foglia rose the towering Monte Calvo, held in strength by the Germans. The battle for the Gothic Line was now to begin.

Difficulties of the Advance to the Gothic Line

In its advance to the Gothic Line, the 4th Indian Division encountered many difficulties. The Germans had had ample opportunity to destroy Route 3, the division's main axis of advance, and all tracks which might have been used as alternatives. Bridges, houses and telegraph poles had been destroyed in a fury of demolition, such as the 4th Indian Division had not previously witnessed. Some stretches of the road were so badly damaged as to be beyond repair. In such places, lengthy diversions had to be built. Portions of existing roads and tracks were used, as far as possible, but in one case a completely different alignment had to be followed. The rapid construction of the diversions and the moving over them, often by night, of a large force was highly creditable. Vehicles which stuck for any reason were ruthlessly toppled over the side into the valley below. The sappers performed prodigious feats by cutting tracks out of virgin mountain-sides in unbelievably short time. With their bulldozers and the old-fashioned, but highly efficient, pick and shovel they boggled at nothing.

Into the Gothic Line

After seizing Urbino and the high ground to its north-east on 28 August, the 4th Indian Division developed two powerful thrusts against the Gothic Line—the main thrust against Monte Calvo and Tavoleto (bastions of the Gothic Line) and the left thrust against Monte San Giovanni, another of the Gothic Line bastions. We shall first describe the main thrust against Monte Calvo and Tavoleto.

The 5th Indian Infantry Brigade was directed against Monte Calvo. Before launching the attack on this objective, it was necessary to capture M. della Croce. The plan for seizing M. della Croce provided for 3/10 Baluch to advance in the morning on 29 August

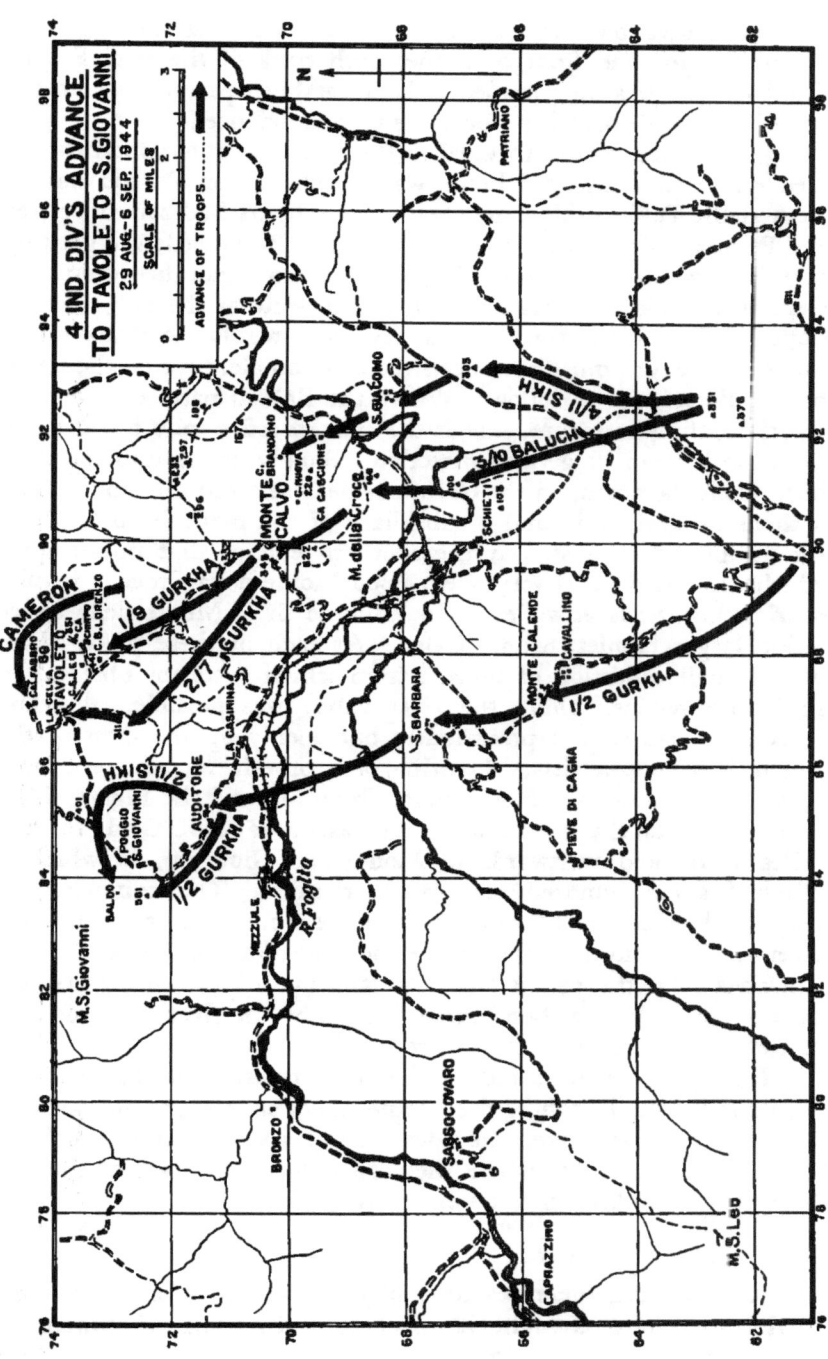

from concentration area Pt. 331 to Pt. 332 and Pallino ridge and occupy Pt. 100 and Pt. 150 on the south bank of the river Foglia. The battalion was then immediately to establish patrol bases on the north bank, with patrols probing the Gothic defences.

3/10 Baluch moved forward in the morning from concentration area Pt. 331 and by 1330 hours was established on Pt. 332 having secured the Pallino ridge, and before 2030 hours had seized Pt. 100 and Pt. 105. The leading companies (A and B) succeeded in gettting patrols down to the river with little or no hindrance from the Germans. This task was accomplished in spite of the fact that the slopes leading to the river were so bare and regular that any movement by daylight must have been visible to an alert eye on the north bank. Better was to follow. Where the Baluch patrolled down to the river, the watercourse was at the apex of a five mile broad bend, southwards from its general direction. Snugly fitting into the river bend from the north, on the German side, was a hill four miles long, a thousand feet high, and a subsidiary of the main feature, which ran from east to west. At the southern end of that minor spur, which was narrow and very open, stood Monte della Croce, a hamlet overlooking the river valley. One mile north of Monte della Croce was a larger hamlet, Monte Calvo. At each of these places there was a small collection of houses, from which excellent observation in both directions along the river valley was possible. A white ribbon of road wound precariously but openly up the crest of the hill to Tavoleto, a village boasting of a prominent, square church tower, at the junction of the Monte Calvo hill and the higher ridge. From Tavoleto, the main feature ran eastwards to M. Gridolfo, four miles away, and westwards to Monte San Giovanni, to which it climbed seven hundred feet in three miles. The complete hill resembled the letter "E", with the three branches jutting towards the river and the middle branch twice the length of the top and bottom branches. To the eye it was a patch-work of browns, greys and greens, with a blue ribbon border formed by the river. But no sign of German movement was to be seen.

Intelligence sources indicated that German positions had been prepared up the length of the Monte Calvo spur as far as Tavoleto. It was not a rocky ridge. Its sides were very steep, indeed much too steep for tanks, except where the road climbed the face of the hill. Minefields were known to be extensively laid.

Capture of M. della Croce

Against such defences and physical obstacles a commander might well have thought it wiser to wait, until all supporting arms, including the maximum of artillery, had closed up to assist him. However, the brigade commander decided that, in order to take advantage of the disorganisation which Allied advance had caused amongst the Germans, two battalions would carry out a silent night advance with the object of seizing M. della Croce and establishing a bridge-head across the river. The plan was for 3/10 Baluch to cross the river and attack M. della Croce, and for 4/11 Sikh to secure the east flank by advancing from area Pt. 314 to Pt. 303, S. Giacoma and Pt. 87.

At 0730 hours on 30 August, A Company of 3/10 Baluch advanced across the river, supported by Sherman tanks. So great had been the German disorganisation and so rapid the Allied advance that the Germans had been unable to occupy Monte della Croce. Only a few of them were holding Pt. 166. This opposition was brushed aside and A Company seized Monte della Croce by 0900 hours. The Germans, who were holding Monte Calvo and the south-western edge of M. della Croce in strength, quickly recovered from their initial surprise and launched two counter-attacks on the Baluch company. Such was the momentum of the attack that one Baluch platoon was forced off M. della Croce. The other, however, grimly held on to its positions. Help was at hand. At 1100 hours, D Company moved up in support of A Company. Tanks also arrived in support of the hard-pressed company. D Company attacked and recaptured M. della Croce by 1600 hours. It was subjected to heavy mortaring but soon consolidated its position. Meanwhile 4/11 Sikh had succeeded in securing the eastern flank. Pt. 303 was occupied at 0246 hours and S. Gaicoma at 0900 hours. At 1046 hours A, the leading company, reached Pt. 87 and was thus ready to outflank Monte Calvo.

Capture of Monte Calvo

The way was now prepared for the attack on Monte Calvo, which the Germans were holding in strength. *5 Company and Headquarters Company of the 191 Grenadier Regiment* and elements from *4, 5, 6, 7, 8 and 14 Companies of the 194 Grenadier Regiment* (the *71st Infantry Division*) were holding Monte Calvo and its south-eastern slopes.

The brigade plan for the capture of Monte Calvo was as follows:

(i) 3/10 Baluch was to push straight from M. della Croce up the spur to Monte Calvo, and capture Pt. 322 and Pt. 345.

(ii) 4/11 Sikh was to outflank Monte Calvo from the east, by capturing the ridge east of Monte Calvo i.e. area C. Cascione—C. Brandano.

(iii) 1/9 Gurkha was to make a wide flanking movement and cut off the Germans trying to escape by the Monte Calvo road, and then to advance to Pt. 157, Pt. 297, Pt. 296 and Pt. 332.

At 1115 hours on 30 August, fighter-bombers and the divisional artillery brought down heavy concentrations on Monte Calvo, preliminary to the attack by the 5th Indian Infantry Brigade on this strong German position. Men watching from the south bank of the river, with memories of having been dive bombed by the German Stukas, cheered as they saw the aircraft peal off and scream down towards their target. After dropping their bombs, the Hurricanes and Spitfires, in low flying attacks, strafed the German positions with their cannon.

After consolidating the position at M. della Croce at 1600 hours on 30 August, 3/10 Baluch, supported by tanks of 6th Battalion Royal Tank Regiment, worked from depression to depression along the sides of the hill and captured Pt. 322 at 1800 hours. Efforts to advance further were halted by heavy mortar and machine gun fire. Small arms fire from positions along the hillsides and in the ruins of the battered village checked the infantry. The supporting tanks came to grief on mines. This stand on Monte Calvo was however to take its toll of the Germans. As the attack developed and they saw the three battalions of the brigade being used, they realised that they would not be allowed to withdraw under cover of darkness. To the east of the Baluch, 4/11 Sikh began to make its presence felt by making a flanking attack on Monte Calvo from the right. At 1645 hours C and D Companies led the attack and by 1740 hours secured the objective, Pt. 220. Then A and B Companies exploited to C. Brandano and C. Nuova. The attack was supported by two troops of tanks. By 1830 hours the objectives were reached and the companies began digging in rapidly. Spasmodic shelling by the Germans continued throughout the night.

1/9 Gurkha, whose role it was to make a wide flanking movement with the object of cutting off the German line of withdrawal along road Monte Calvo—north to Tavoleto, found that the allotted axis of advance on to the high ground north of Monte Calvo, was already held by the British 56th Division. The Gurkhas were therefore forced to remain in the rear of 4/11 Sikh on the northern bank of the river Foglia.

Although the frontal attack by the Baluch had been held up, the flanking operation carried out by 4/11 Sikh had been successful. The Sikhs had secured the high ground east of Monte Calvo and could therefore outflank the strong German position at Monte Calvo. To exploit this advantage a determined effort was made on 31 August by all the three battalions of the 5th Indian Infantry Brigade. The frontal attack on Monte Calvo was renewed at 1145 hours on 31 August by C Company of 3/10 Baluch. At 1400 hours the Baluch were held up 400 yards south of the village by heavy small arms fire from prepared positions on the forward slopes and Spandau nests in the ruins of the village. Tanks in close support were hampered by mines. Any move by D Company called down mortar fire from German positions west of Monte Calvo. At 1700 hours the Baluch tried to work round and infiltrate into the village, but intensive mortaring pinned them to the ground. Thus the frontal attack did not make much headway.

The flanking attack was however successful. 1/9 Gurkha advanced at 1515 hours, brushed aside opposition at Pt. 296 and at 1900 hours captured Pt. 332, thus cutting off the German line of retreat along the road, which wound north from Monte Calvo to Tavoleto. German resistance had however already collapsed. At 1830 hours tanks in support of D Company of the Baluch had engaged German positions at point-blank range. At 1930 hours the tanks were right through the village, which was occupied by a Baluch platoon. The village was veritable shambles. Wire obstacles had been crushed by the tanks. Broken shutters, window frames and drain pipes swung to the breeze. Tileless roofs allowed clouds of dust and smoke to rise above the village. Piles of barbed wire revealed that the Germans had not finished their work on the defences. Consolidation of the position began immediately. 3/10 Baluch remained on Monte Calvo, while 4/11 Sikh and 1/9 Gurkha consolidated at Pt. 332. As an additional aid, 2/7 Gurkha from the 11th Indian Infantry Brigade came under command, and began to assemble after dark south-east of Monte Calvo, in preparation for the attack on Tavoleto, the next strong German position. The 4th Indian Division had succeeded in breaching the Gothic Line. 3/10 Baluch was the first unit in the whole of the Eighth Army, which breached the Gothic Line. For this creditable achievement the Army Commander sent the Commander of 3/10 Baluch a congratulatory signal.

Failure of Attack on Tavoleto

With the capture of Monte Calvo, the stage was now set for the attack on Tavoleto, another strong bastion of the Gothic Line. *II Battalion, 191 Grenadier Regiment* of the *71st Infantry Division*, after being driven away from Monte Calvo, was committed to the defence of Tavoleto. The Germans took up strong defensive positions, guarding the approaches into Tavoleto. They paid special attention to the defence of the road junction at R 876733, the high ground to its west and the Lorenzo feature to its east. They had self-propelled guns and numerous machine guns sited to sweep the open ground over which the Indian troops had to advance, and also the areas to the east in which the 56th Division was then operating. The value to the Germans of Monte San Giovanni (the objective of the 7th Indian Infantry Brigade) was now proved. From that high feature, almost every move towards Tavoleto by daylight was visible to the Germans.

1/9 Gurkha led the attack on Tavoleto. The plan of operation was that C Company was to secure the first bound, road junction at R 884721, and the second bound, road junction at R 876733. A Company was to capture the high ground west of the road junction at R 876733, while B Company was to seize the Lorenzo feature.

During daylight on 1 September, considerable movement took place in the 5th Indian Infantry Brigade area. At 0930 hours, 1/9 Gurkha began the advance from Pt. 332, supported by two troops of 6th Battalion Royal Tank Regiment. By 1245 hours, C Company had secured the first bound, road junction at R 884721. The Gurkhas then moved on to the next bound—road junction at R 876733. Behind them 4/11 Sikh took over the road junction at R 884721, while 2/7 Gurkha moved forward to Pt. 332, and 3/10 Baluch remained firm in the Monte Calvo—M. della Croce area. On approach to the second bound—road junction at R 876733— German opposition stiffened considerably. At 1550 hours 1/9 Gurkha closed in on this feature from the west and east. A Company captured the high ground west of the road junction. B Company attacking Lorenzo feature met strong German opposition and suffered heavy casualties. Two platoons were forced to retire, but the reserve platoon held on to the position. Then followed an attack by C and D Companies and the feature was taken at about 2335 hours.

As darkness fell, German shelling and mortaring of the road to Tavoleto was intensified. The brigade plan for the night of 1/2 September was to attack Tavoleto and the high ground north of it with two battalions; 1/9 Gurkha was to advance in Lorrenzo area while 2/7 Gurkha was to move west of the road junction at R 876733 towards Pt. 311 to make a flanking attack from the left. The Germans however took the initiative and launched a sharp counter-attack on C and D Companies of 1/9 Gurkha at C. S. Lorenzo. Some ground was lost to the Germans but this did not prevent the attack from being put in at 0500 hours. At daybreak, both battalions were engaged in extremely heavy fighting, 2/7 Gurkha about Pt. 311, one thousand yards south-west of Tavoleto, and 1/9 Gurkha at the C. S. Lorenzo road junction. The close nature of the fighting made artillery support impossible and therefore tanks were moved up to support the Gurkhas. There was heavy and continuous fighting for 1½ hours but 1/9 Gurkha did not register any progress. 2/7 Gurkha too found the approach march to be much more difficult than was anticipated. The Germans had occupied dominating positions with open ground in front, which had to be crossed. On the failure of the 5th Indian Infantry Brigade to capture Tavoleto the

Major-General Denys W. Reid
(Commander 10th Indian Division)
Feb. 1944—Dec. 1946

Major-General W. L. Lloyd
(Commander 10th Indian Division)
July 1943—January 1944

Fall of San Marino

Madras Sappers and Miners have laid a road in Italy

Divisional Commander ordered the 11th Indian Infantry Brigade to relieve it and attack Tavoleto. 4/11 Sikh was to relieve 1/9 Gurkha and come under the command of the 11th Indian Infantry Brigade. Then 2/7 Gurkha was to attack Tavoleto in conjunction with 2nd Cameron in the night of 3/4 September.

Capture of Tavoleto

The 11th Indian Infantry Brigade took over from the 5th Indian Infantry Brigade at 2200 hours on 2 September in order to launch an attack on Tavoleto. 4/11 Sikh relieved 1/9 Gurkha in area C. S. Lorenzo; 2/7 Gurkha was in area Pt. 311; the 2nd Cameron concentrated south of Pt. 322 and 3/12 Frontier Force Regiment south-east of road junction at R 884721. The 5th Indian Infantry Brigade, less 4/11 Sikh, concentrated south and east of M. della Croce.

According to the plan made by Brigadier Partridge for the attack on Tavoleto, the operations were to be carried out in two phases. In the first phase, the 2nd Cameron, moving from start line along dead ground north-east from C. S. Lorenzo, was to occupy C. Leo and then proceed to mop up German strong-points along the road Monte Calvo—Tavoleto, while 2/7 Gurkha, advancing from area Pt. 311, was to capture Tavoleto from the south. In the second phase, the 2nd Cameron was to exploit to La Cella-Cemetry and Calfabbro North. 4/11 Sikh was to maintain fire base in existing locations in area C. S. Lorenzo, including C. Schirpo. 3/12 Royal Frontier Force Regiment, concentrating in area south-east of road junction at R. 884721, was to hold one company in readiness to relieve the 2nd Cameron at C. Leo on orders from the brigade headquarters.

In order to induce the Germans to give away the positions of their mortars, defensive fire and fire positions generally, a deception plan was made. The following programme was to be carried out from 2130-2200 hours on 3 September:

(i) 4/11 Sikh was to fire with all available arms on selected targets to simulate an impending attack.
(ii) Artillery co-ordinated by officer commanding 11th Field Regiment was to fire according to the programme.
(iii) A squadron 6th Battalion Royal Tank Regiment was to take steps to indicate an impending attack.

4/11 Sikh, B and D Companies Machine Gun Rajputana Rifles and 11th Field Regiment were under command while A Squadron 6th Battalion the Royal Tank Regiment was in support of the 11th Indian Infantry Brigade.[7]

4/11 Sikh carried out preliminary operations preparatory to the main attack by 2/7 Gurkha and the 2nd Cameron. By 1700 hours

[7] 11 Ind. Inf. Bde. O.I. No. 15, 3 September 1944.

on 3 September, the Sikhs captured Pt. 441, Pt. 351 and C. Schirpo. Thus they secured control over the road from its junction at 876733 to C. Schirpo. The 2nd Cameron worked forward behind 4/11 Sikh for its forming up place for the attack. 2/7 Gurkha was also getting ready to advance from area Pt. 311. The Germans, however, took the initiative and struck the first blow. At 2200 hours on 3 September, after shelling 2/7 Gurkha positions, they launched a counter-attack, estimated to be of one company strength, on the forward company (D) of 2/7 Gurkha at R 872737. The counter-attack was beaten off by small arms fire. The Gurkha company, following up the defeated German force, found its way into the village and after fierce fighting captured Tavoleto at 0400 hours on 4 September, though some isolated pockets of resistance still held out. B Company carried out the mopping operations. A gunner officer distinguished himself during this action. Artillery fire had already reduced the church tower, which was used by the Germans as an observation post, to a state of collapse, but he established his observation post in it, while fighting was still in progress in the village The German guns registered a number of direct hits on the tower. Nevertheless, the observation post continued to direct the fire of the divisional artillery to great effect.

While the Gurkhas succeeded in securing Tavoleto, the 2nd Cameron too had been making satisfactory progress. At 0100 hours on 4 September, C Company had secured C. Leo, B Company was moving on to La Cella and D Company to Calfabbro. All the objectives were reached without much opposition. *II Battalion, 191st Grenadier Regiment* had to pay a heavy toll for the spirited defence of Monte Calvo and Tavoleto. Only 60 men survived to rejoin the *71st Infantry Division*, which had already been pulled out of the line.[8]

Capture of Auditore

While the 5th and the 11th Indian Infantry Brigades were hammering at the German positions at Monte Calvo and Tavoleto, the 7th Indian Infantry Brigade was directed on Monte San Giovanni. In order to secure the latter objective the brigade had to cross the river Foglia and occupy two villages, Auditore, on the forward slopes above the river, and the cluster of houses around Poggio San Giovanni. Both these villages, as well as the dominating feature of Monte San Giovanni, were strongly defended. The first two villages were defended by *278 Fusilier Battalion* and the latter feature by *1 Battalion, 994th Grenadier Regiment* of the *278th Infantry Division*. *II Battalion, 994th Grenadier Regiment*, was in reserve behind

---

[8] 4 Ind. Div. Intelligence Summary No. 150, 5 September 1944.

Monte San Giovanni, with *7 Company* forward in close support of *278 Fusilier Battalion* in the road bend at R 852739.[9]

The 7th Indian Infantry Brigade had to contend with German rearguards throughout its advance northwards. Owing to its additional task of protecting the left flank of the 4th Indian Division, the brigade had not been able to mount an attack in any strength. It could rely only on continuous harassing by patrols to drive back the Germans.

After consolidating its positions at Urbino, the 7th Indian Infantry Brigade advanced to reach its objective Monte San Giovanni. During the night of 30/31 August, a fighting patrol from 1/2 Gurkha, probing German defences still south of the river Foglia, ran into machine gun fire in the vicinity of S. Barbara, a low open hill and a useful observation post in the river valley. This position was held by two German platoons. A and B Companies then prepared for a silent attack on S. Barbara in the night of 31 August/1 September. It was a very bright moon and the problem of attacking the ridge was not easy. The plan was for A and B Companies to move silently down to nullah, form up and assault silently. Tanks in position behind Cavallino were to support at first light. Mortars were to move down to nullah with the companies and support the attack at dawn. The companies moved off at 2100 hours on 31 August and closed on objectives at 2300 hours. The Germans seeing the Gurkhas advancing to attack the ridge fled in disorder.

By the evening of 1 September, 1/2 Gurkha was in position on the south bank of the river Foglia, in open hilly country, opposite the village of Auditore, which was situated on the lower slopes of the massive Monte San Giovanni. Auditore was a strong point in the Gothic Line defence, and the river bed in this sector was wide, open, mined and wired. However, reconnaissance patrols on the night of 1/2 September failed to discover the Germans in any strength between the river and Auditore, though the latter place was believed to be occupied by a German company.

During the early morning of 2 September, a platoon from 1/2 Gurkha was sent across the river to form a bridge-head below Auditore. The platoon crossed the river undetected, in ones and twos. They stalked stealthily forward, making the utmost use of folds in the ground, the few hedges, and occasional scrub cover. In this manner the whole platoon reached an area within two hundred yards of the village. German defences of wire, dugouts and a few pillboxes could be seen, but not a move was made by the Germans. Such complete lack of movement and noise may be eerie when one's senses are keyed up, as they must be when out on patrol. One may

[9] 4 Ind. Div. Intelligence Summary No. 140, 4 September 1944.

imagine the temptation to which the Jemadar commanding the platoon yielded. Having secured his get-away by putting two of his three sections into covering positions, he worked round to the rear of the village. The Gurkhas had reached the first houses when a German unexpectedly emerging, dashed back and gave the alarm. Immediately, the village took on the appearance of a hornet's nest. Automatic fire came from several directions. One Gurkha was killed. His companions settled accounts with the man who had given the alarm by tossing grenades into the room, where he was sheltering. Then the Gurkha section withdrew back with his platoon and having now located the German positions south and east of the village, the Jemadar wirelessed for artillery support. A continuous hail of fire came down on the German positions. Under cover of this fire the Jemadar disposed his platoon in a defensive locality and continued to keep the Germans under observation. It was now 1500 hours. Henceforth the platoon was subjected to heavy mortar and shell-fire. The Germans kept up intermittent small arms fire from a range of a few hundred yards. Very soon a building and haystack in the platoon's area were set on fire. But all the time the Jemadar was directing artillery fire on to hostile targets and this undoubtedly prevented the Germans from launching a counter-attack. The information gained was of inestimable value and enabled a two company attack to be put in that night from a direction not expected by the Germans. At 0100 hours on 3 September, A and C Companies infiltrated to the north side of the village without being detected, and attacked from the north-east. The Germans were taken completely by surprise and those that were not killed fled westwards to Monte San Giovanni. 8 Germans were taken prisoners. Success was undoubtedly due, in a great measure, to the information gained by the patrol whose casualties for this remarkable exploit amounted in all to 2 killed and 4 wounded.[10]

Capture of Poggio San Giovanni

After capturing Auditore, the 7th Indian Infantry Brigade made ready for an attack on Poggio San Giovanni. Away to the right, the 11th Indian Infantry Brigade's final assault on Tavoleto was also beginning. Ahead of the 7th Indian Infantry Brigade was a tough struggle against the physical difficulties of the steep, bare hillside and a determined opponent in well-built defences, whose mortars and artillery were particularly active. Two German battalions were in strength on the lower slopes of Monte San Giovanni and Poggio San Giovanni. Pt. 581 and Baldo were both strongly held with about twelve spandau each.

---

[10] Capture of Auditore village in the Gothic Line, Appx. J-1; War Diary 1/2 G.R.

The plan was to make a double thrust against Poggio San Giovanni, with 2/11 Sikh on the right and 1/2 Gurkha on the left. The Sikhs were to advance from Auditore westwards up the watercourses on the east flank of Poggio San Giovanni. They were directed on to the ridge Pt. 401 and Baldo. On the left the Gurkhas were to advance from Auditore and converge on Baldo. C Company was to capture Cemetery area and then A Company on the right and D Company on the left were to assault Pt. 581, after securing which A Company was to swing to the right to capture Baldo. B Company was to be in reserve in Auditore. Tanks were to follow up the road.

At 0330 hours on 4 September, C Company of 1/2 Gurkha advanced from Auditore and was subjected to heavy spandau firing. But by 0340 hours the Company had succeeded in securing the Cemetery. It continued to have a fire fight with the Germans entrenched on Pt. 581, a narrow-crested steep-sided feature. At 0430 hours, A and D Companies moved off for the attack on this feature. A Company led the attack. As the front was very narrow, one platoon attacked this feature from the left and two platoons from the right. They clashed with a strong German machine gun screen before reaching the summit. A Company was however subjected to very heavy automatic fire from Baldo and the ridge to its right. In spite of this fierce opposition A Company moved down the forward slope into the valley between Pt. 581 and Baldo, while D Company took up its position at Pt. 581. Tanks, which were due in Auditore at first light, had trouble in the river bed and had not arrived. This was the situation when at 0610 hours two German companies launched a fierce counter-attack from Baldo against A Company. To support this attack two self-propelled guns mounting machine guns and long barrelled 75-mm guns came round the corner of the road and engaged A Company from a distance of about 200-300 yards. A Company went to ground and inflicted heavy casualties on the German infantry. But by this time it was light and the position was clearly untenable, casualties from self-propelled guns being heavy. The withdrawal was successfully effected, and the attack by a German platoon on the flank was broken up. To cover the withdrawal, there was heavy concentration of artillery on German positions, knocking out one self-propelled gun and killing many Germans. At 0630 hours A Company arrived on the lower slopes of Pt. 581 and dug in below D Company. German casualties in this action were very heavy for a German prisoner estimated these to be about 250-300. The Gurkhas suffered 30 casualties.

While the left thrust against Poggio San Giovanni proved a failure, the right thrust was a great success. The Sikh attack on Poggio San Giovanni was made by A and D Companies. There was a long approach march of about 5,000 metres along the Foglia valley before the companies turned north into the hills. This was little interfered with, except for harassing fire, causing no casualties. Once, however, both the companies swung into the scrub-covered and broken country leading up to the ridge, with D Company on the right and A Company on the left flank; they were closely engaged by well sited spandau posts and, in the later stages, by two German 88-mm self-propelled guns firing over open sights. The forward observation officer (118th Battery) engaged one spandau post, which was knocked out, and others were gradually neutralised. D Company, which was on the exposed flank, was held back, but by 1700 hours A Company worked its way to within 300 yards of Poggio San Giovanni village, where it held on in the face of heavy small arms and artillery fire. At this stage divisional artillery support was called for and provided, and when D Company came forward, and an attack through the village and on to the high ground beyond was launched at dawn on 5 September, the village yielded with many German dead lying about. Considerable material was captured. The villagers reported that the Germans had evacuated some 52 casualties, during the night. The Sikh casualties were 1 killed and 18 wounded. With the capture of Poggio San Giovanni and Tavoleto, the 4th Indian Division was ready to launch an attack on Pian di Castello, another strong German position.

CHAPTER XVIII

The Thrust Towards M.S. Colomba

Stiffening Resistance

After gaining initial success the Eighth Army came up against stiffening opposition; by 4 September 1944 it was facing the German defence line, which ran from the river Marano to Coriano, San Savino, Croce, Gemmano and M.S. Colomba, with a forward strong position at Pian di Castello. Field-Marshal Kesselring had succeeded in reinforcing the exposed sector. On 29 August, four days after the commencement of the Eighth Army's attack on the Gothic Line, a regiment from the *26th Panzer Division* was transferred from the area west of Empoli to the Adriatic front. It was followed by the rest of the division shortly afterwards. At the same time the *98th Infantry Division* from Bologna area was hurried forward and committed to action. A regiment from the *162nd (Turkoman) Infantry Division* proved a less useful addition. As the full weight of the Allied attack in the Adriatic coast came to be felt, Field-Marshal Kesselring removed his last reserve from the centre and left, the *29th Panzer Grenadier Division*, which arrived on 6 September to take part in the operations on the Adriatic coast, though its advance elements were already in action on 4 September. A regiment of the *5th Mountain Division*, which had been taken out of the line, was again committed to action on 6 September. These reinforcements helped the Germans considerably in stabilising their defence line, which held firm except that its forward position at Pian di Castello was captured by the 4th Indian Division on 7 September.

Capture of Pian di Castello

By 5 September 1944, the 7th and 11th Indian Infantry Brigades of the 4th Indian Division were facing Pian di Castello across the river Ventena. In preparation for further assaults, Central India Horse took over the left flank protection of the 7th Indian Infantry Brigade on Monte San Giovanni as an infantry unit. It was relieved of its reconnaissance task by the 12th Lancers. The 4th Indian Division was now ready to make a double thrust against Pian di Castello—the 7th Indian Infantry Brigade was to advance from Poggio San Giovanni and capture Pian di Castello while on the right the 11th Indian Infantry Brigade was to advance from Tavoleto and seize the ridge to the north-east of Pian di Castello.

The Germans made determined efforts to retain possession of

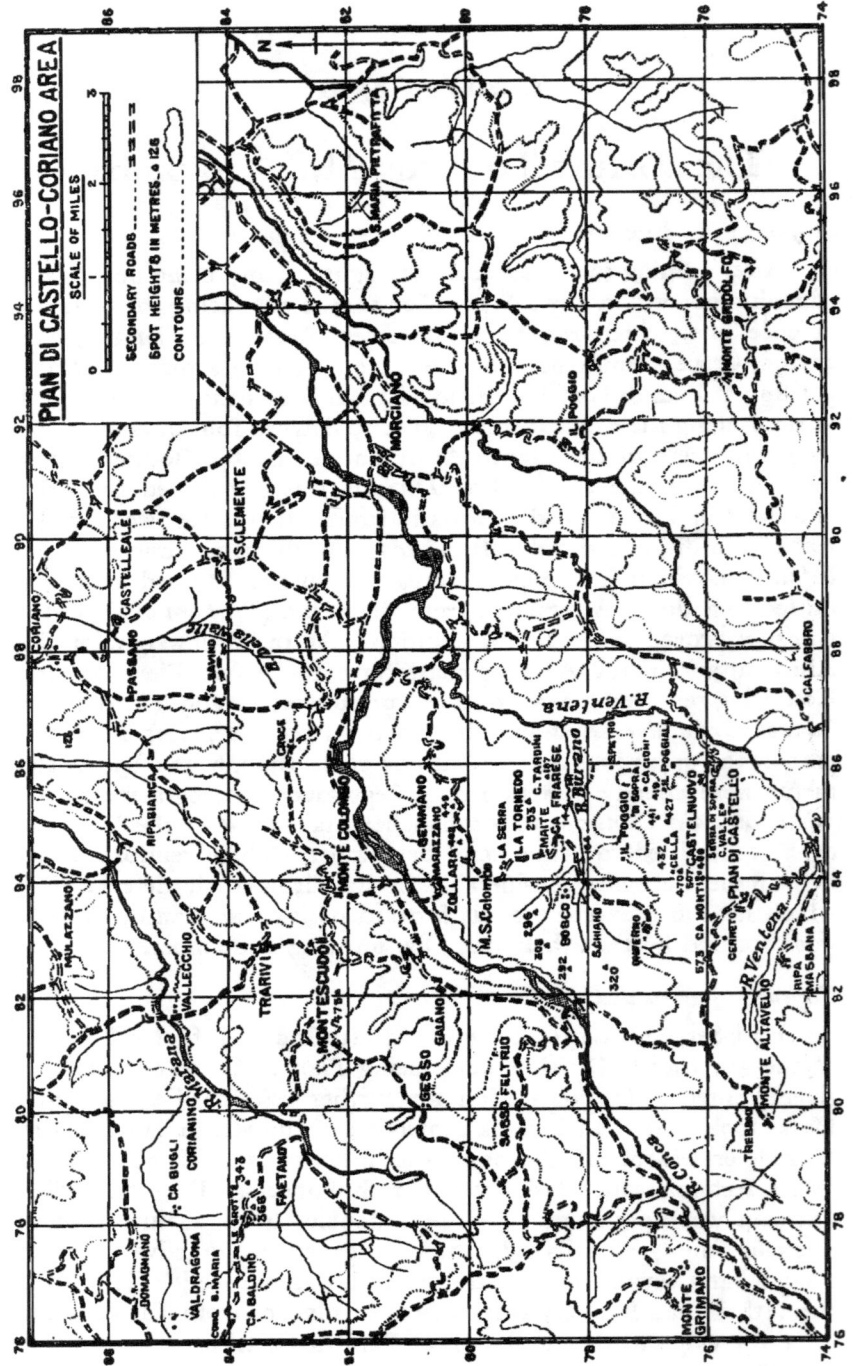

Pian di Castello and the ridge to its north-east from S. Pietro to Pt. 468. *I Battalion 994th Grenadier Regiment* (the *278th Infantry Division*), after evacuating Monte San Giovanni, had taken up positions in Pian di Castello for its defence. The ridge to the north-east of Pian di Castello was held by the battalion 'Kranz' formed out of the remnants of *II Battalion 194th Grenadier Regiment* of the *71st Infantry Division*. The 'Kranz' battalion stretched to the area north of Pt. 441. Further on were the *Fusilier Battalion* of the *71st Infantry Division* and *I Battalion* of *100th Mountain Regiment* (the *5th Mountain Division*).[1] The Germans were strongly entrenched on the ridge north-east of Pian di Castello, *i.e.* Castelnuovo, Il Monte and Cella.

The plan for the attack on Pain di Castello and the adjoining ridge was for the 7th Indian Infantry Brigade to seize Pian di Castello and the 11th Indian Infantry Brigade to capture the ridge from S. Pietro to Pt. 468. The 1st Royal Sussex, with a squadron (less two troops) 6th Battalion Royal Tank Regiment under command, were to lead the 7th Indian Infantry Brigade's attack. The axis of advance was to be La Casinina—Poggio San Giovanni—Pian di Castello. The 1st Royal Sussex concentrated in the area of La Casinina, south of Auditore, in the morning of 6 September. The advance was held up in the area of the road junction (near Pt. 376) by heavy shelling. No further progress was made that day. The advance was resumed at 0200 hours on 7 September. Some mines were encountered in the river bed causing ten casualties. Torrential rain held up the supporting tanks. By hard work and perseverance, eventually a number of tanks crossed over the river and, though hindered by mines, assisted the infantry in capturing the village of Pian di Castello. One company of the 1st Royal Sussex was established in the village by 0728 hours but the mopping up operations were hindered by German small arms fire from the north. By 1400 hours, however, two companies of the 1st Royal Sussex had secured firm control over Pian di Castello.

The Cemetery Hill

After consolidating their position in Pian di Castello, the 1st Royal Sussex exploited to the Cemetery Hill, about one thousand yards north-east of Pian di Castello, and held in strength by the Germans. Numerous and well sited machine guns in the area of the Cemetery, supported by two self-propelled guns firing from Cerreto, provided stiff opposition to the advance of D Company of the 1st Royal Sussex from Pian di Castello during the night of 8/9 September. A heavy concentration was fired on the Cemetery and

[1] 4 Ind. Div. Intelligence Summaries No. 151, 6 September, No. 152, 7 September and No. 153, 8 September 1944.

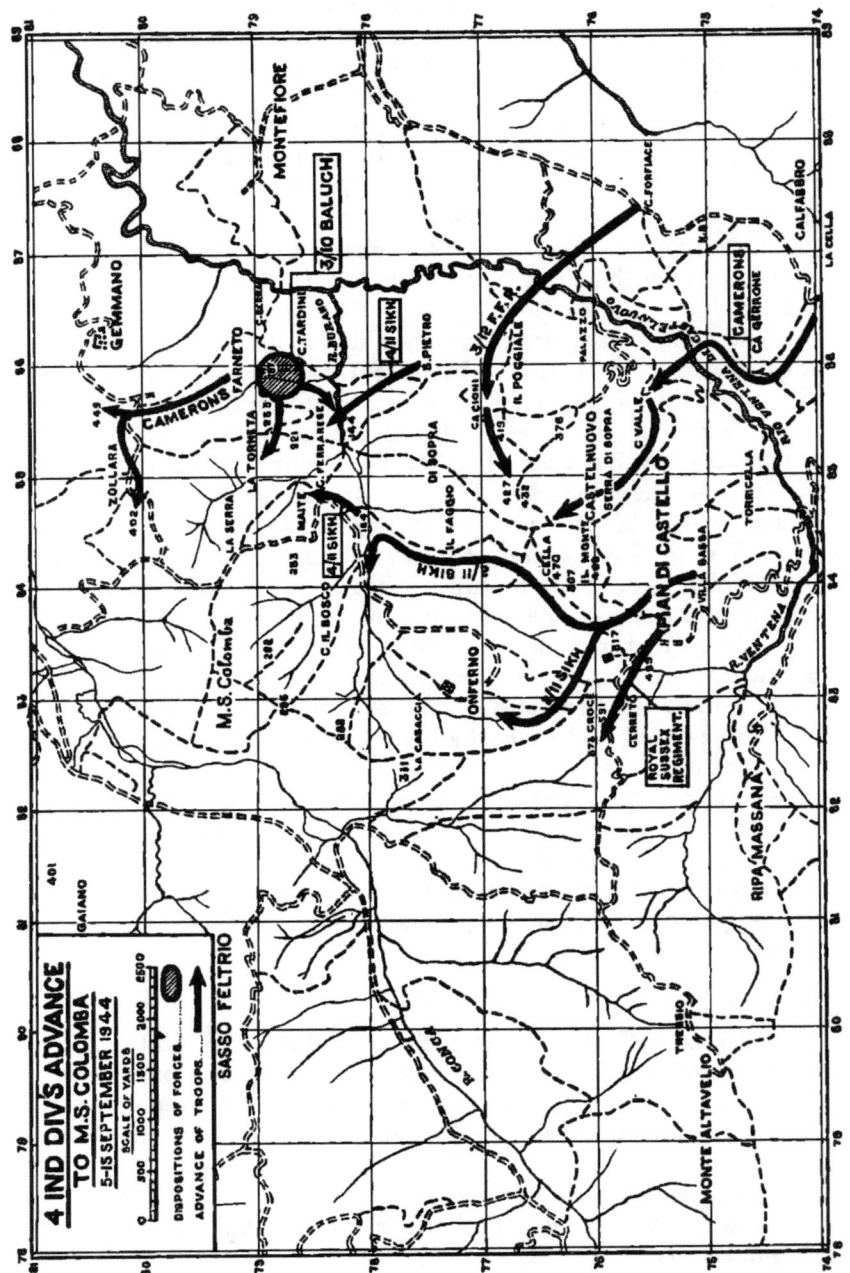

neighbouring targets. By 0700 hours on 9 September the initial attack on a position near Croce failed owing to intense spandau fire from the Cemetery. The company suffered casualties from the self-propelled guns at Cerrato. Two troops B Squadron of 6th Battalion Royal Tank Regiment, who were to be up at the Cemetery in support of the infantry by first light, went forward along the path to the Cemetery. The leading tank hit a mine and completely blocked the path. The second tank, when trying to turn off, shed a track. The remainder left the path and went straight across country to their rendezvous. There they found no infantry. On the open plateau the tanks presented an easy target and the German anti-tank gun promptly sent one of them up in flames. Covering fire from the Royal Artillery, however, enabled one troop of tanks to manoeuvre into a position, from where they were able to destroy the German anti-tank gun. Eventually supported by the Royal Artillery and the tanks D Company attacked and captured the hill at 1300 hours, while C Company moved up behind it to help in consolidation and exploitation.

From the Cemetery, C Company of the 1st Royal Sussex in carriers, together with two troops of tanks, followed a barrage laid down by Corps artillery to the next feature to the north-east, i.e. Pt. 573. Across their path, but unknown to them, was a thirty-foot precipice. Towards it, in the grey hour before dawn on 10 September the tanks churned along. The first Sherman did a forward somersault, landed on its tracks and continued towards its objective. Three came to grief and were unable to continue. The remaining three just slid down the drop. The objective was secured by 0620 hours on 10 September and 20 Germans were taken prisoners. Pt. 573 was quickly converted into a strong point by the co-operation of all arms. Deep slit trenches were dug. Artillery defensive fire was laid to within twenty yards of the forward posts. Mortars were brought up to engage the forward slopes of the hill because the angle of descent was too much for the guns. Tanks became pill-boxes. Against this post the German counter-attacks failed to make any headway. A German company attacked this post at 1055 hours on 11 September. One platoon of the 1st Royal Sussex was cut off. The situation was however restored and the Germans driven off. The Sussex position was then heavily mortared and shelled. Another German counter-attack developed at 0900 hours on 12 September but it was also beaten off. The capture of Pian di Castello and the advance to Pt. 573 in the direction of M.S. Colomba marked the limit of the progress made by the 1st Royal Sussex on the 7th Indian Infantry Brigade's front. Meanwhile the 11th Indian Infantry Brigade, followed by the 5th Indian Infantry Brigade, was busy in securing the ridge to the north-east of Pian di Castello.

Capture of the S. Pietro Ridge

Brigadier Partridge employed two battalions for the attack on the ridge from S. Pietro to Pt. 468. On the right, 3/12 Royal Frontier Force Regiment was to plunge through the river Ventena towards its objective, the spur leading up to Il Poggiale and the north-east end of the Castello feature. To its left, the 2nd Cameron was to advance up another spur to C. Valle and Il Monte. Castelnuovo, a compact village about three quarters of the way up the middle of the hill on an intervening spur, was to be outflanked by these moves. This hill was a faithful reproduction of the standard type. It lay across the 4th Indian Division's line of advance, had an uninterrupted view of the slopes down which attacking troops must move, was sufficiently close to the river bed to provide cover for the batteries of mortars, which might turn the valley into a hell of bursting shells, and offered little natural cover other than that of the water-courses in the face of the hill. These water-courses were automatically and accurately registered by the German machine guns and mortars. Where fire from these weapons could not reach, mines, both anti-personnel and anti-tank, were strewn in cunning patterns throughout its length. Scattered farm houses and cemeteries made excellent strong-points, until tanks were brought against them.

Both the battalions of the 11th Indian Infantry Brigade encountered heavy machine gun and mortar fire from positions on the lower forward slopes. Their advance became a slow and expensive slogging march. Preparatory to the attack the 2nd Cameron had occupied the forward positions north of Tavoleto with C Company at La Cella, and D Company at C. Gerrone. At 2300 hours on 5 September, D Company advanced from C. Gerrone, crossed the river Ventena and reached the area near Torricella. By 0545 hours on 6 September, C Company advancing from La Cella had reached the area C. Valle but further progress towards Il Monte was checked by increased mortaring and shelling.[2] The 2nd Cameron was thus up against considerable opposition. On 6 September, C Company attacked the German strong-points, Il Monte and Cella, but was subjected to heavy fire and withdrew by 1900 hours to C. Valle area. The attack was renewed at 0530 hours on 7 September. C, the right hand forward company, lost contact and withdrew to the area south of C. Valle to reorganise. A, the left hand forward company, however, reached Serra di Sopra. Its forward platoon engaged in fire fight with the Germans at Cella and then withdrew to Serra di Sopra. During the next two days the forward positions of the 2nd Cameron were subjected to intermittent and heavy shelling. While the 2nd Cameron was thus held up at Il Monte, 3/12 Royal Frontier Force

---

[2] Sitrep, 5 and 6 September 1944, War Diary 11 Ind. Inf. Bde.

Regiment, followed by 1/9 Gurkha, making a right flank attack, converged on Cella and seized the ridge from S. Pietro to Pt. 507.

At the same time as the 2nd Cameron had made a left thrust towards Il Monte, 3/12 Royal Frontier Force Regiment had pierced to the right towards Il Poggiale to capture the ridge from S. Pietro to Pt. 507. Preparatory to the attack, this battalion had occupied the forward positions, with A Company near Kilo 8 and D Company near C. Forfiace. D Company's objective was the village of Il Poggiale and the high ground to the right of Castelnuovo. A Company was to advance by route via wadi on the left of Castelnuovo. Both the companies crossed the start line at 2315 hours on 5 September. At 0030 hours on 6 September, A Company was fired on by automatics from high ground. The advance was slowed down and finally held up at 0130 hours due to German opposition and precipitous ground. Thereupon the battalion commander ordered the company to cross to the right flank. Meanwhile D Company had crossed the stream at the base of the feature at 0005 hours on 6 September. As D Company met stiff opposition, the battalion commander ordered C Company at 0430 hours to advance in the rear of that company. At 0500 hours a large calibre shell burst in the middle of one of the platoons of C Company, as it advanced, causing 15 casualties. C Company was consequently withdrawn. D Company continued the advance and occupied Il Poggiale at 0500 hours against some opposition and mortar fire. At dawn, the Germans could observe the movements of the Indian troops and therefore launched an attack on D Company from either flank at 0700 hours. Artillery and 3 inch mortar defensive fire however helped to disperse the counter-attack. After consolidation at Il Poggiale, 3/12 Royal Frontier Force Regiment got ready for the attack on the next feature, Pt. 419. After two unsuccessful attempts, tanks of the 6th Battalion Royal Tank Regiment reached Castelnuovo at 1250 hours in support of the infantry for the attack on Pt. 419. They moved on to Pt. 712 and engaged targets with good effect. Then D Company, followed by B Company attacked Pt. 419. The companies were heavily mortared during the advance. D Company continued to advance under covering fire from tanks and by 1530 hours worked across the upper end of the spur, on which Castelnuovo stood, and captured Pt. 419 and Ca Cioni in face of heavy spandau fire. Immediately afterwards, at 1555 hours a German counter-attack developed against the forward positions of 3/12 Royal Frontier Force Regiment but was halted by small arms fire and dispersed by artillery fire. The position was consolidated by 1630 hours. A Company of 2/7 Gurkha then moved forward to the area Pt. 419 to strengthen 3/12 Royal Frontier Force Regiment. At 1010 hours on 7 September, about 30 to 40 Germans, supported by heavy artillery fire, counter-attacked the

3/12 Royal Frontier Force Regiment position at Pt. 419. This fierce counter-attack was dispersed by artillery defensive fire and small arms fire. The German counter-attack was followed by heavy mortaring and shelling of the forward positions of 3/12 Frontier Force Regiment. Nevertheless, on the next day (8 September) a platoon of 3/12 Royal Frontier Force Regiment occupied S. Pietro.

3/12 Royal Frontier Force Regiment had carried out its task of capturing the right end of the ridge from Pt. 419 to S. Pietro. 1/9 Gurkha (the 5th Indian Infantry Brigade) now prepared to pass through and capture the rest of the ridge. At 2300 hours on 7 September, the battalion moved up to the forming up place near Pt. 419 in order to pass through the forward positions of 3/12 Frontier Force Regiment and seize the ridge from Pt. 441 to Pt. 507. At 0230 hours on 8 September, A, C and D Companies advanced to seize the ridge. The objectives were taken in face of strong opposition and difficult going. The Gurkha positions were subjected to heavy mortar and shell fire. Nevertheless, these were consolidated after hard fighting—C and D Companies at Pt. 507, A Company on Pt. 441, battalion headquarters and B Company near Pt. 419. At 0445 hours on 9 September the Germans turned with considerable ferocity against the Gurkhas on Pt. 507. The counter-attack was made by a German company, who succeeded in getting into the Gurkha positions but was driven off after a fierce fight. The counter-attack was however followed up by heavy shelling and mortaring. In spite of considerable opposition the Indian troops had succeeded in securing the S. Pietro ridge.

Allied All-out Offensive

The 4th Indian Division had captured Pian di Castello and secured the ridge to its north-east but its left thrust towards M.S. Colomba was held up. Four miles to the north of Pian di Castello was the strongest German position at Gemmano. This hill, standing thirteen hundred feet above the valley at the junction of the Conca and Ventena rivers, was a bare ridge, some two and a half miles long from east to west. Numerous drains had bitten into the sides of the hill to leave only knife-edged spurs, by which the ascent to the top might be made. The easiest approach was by the line of the road from the east. The most difficult was probably that from the south, in the direction of the 4th Indian Division. The 56th (London) Division failed to drive the Germans off Gemmano. In mounting strength units and formations were thrown against it. Bitter fighting raged through the shattered village of Gemmano on the eastern end of the ridge. The chief obstacle was Pt. 449, which changed hands many times. On 10 September, the 46th Division took over the task of cracking this position. Further to the north-east of Gemmano was the Coriano ridge, which commanded the country down to the coast and proved to be another obstacle in the path of the Eighth Army. It was a long low ridge over the river Conca, on the crests of which were situated the hamlets of San Savino, Passano and Coriano.

To overcome German opposition, based chiefly on M.S. Colomba, Gemmano and the Coriano ridge, the Eighth Army launched the attack during the night of 12/13 September. Coriano was the objective of the 1st Canadian Corps. Further south, the 1st British Armoured Division was directed against Passano and San Savino. South of that, the 56th (London) Division attacked Croce. The 46th Division's objectives were Montescudo and Gemmano.[3] The Indian formations involved in the Eighth Army offensive were the 4th Indian Division and the 43rd Indian Infantry Brigade. The former helped the 46th Division in breaking German resistance at Gemmano by capturing M.S. Colomba and Pt. 449, west of Gemmano, while the latter under command of the 1st British Armoured Division was directed on Pessano. We shall first describe the advance of the 4th Indian Division towards M.S. Colomba and Pt. 449.

The role assigned to the 4th Indian Division in the Eighth Army offensive on the night of 12/13 'September was to make a double thrust—one directed against M.S. Colomba and the second against Pt. 449, west of Gemmano. The 7th Indian Infantry Brigade attacked M.S. Colomba from the south while the 5th Indian Infantry Brigade[4] carried out a flanking attack on the feature from the right. The 11th Indian Infantry Brigade was directed against Pt. 449, west of Gemmano.

Failure of the Attack on M.S. Colomba

The German defence line on the 4th Indian Division's front ran from Maite and C. Ferrarese, with outposts down to the river Burano, then to C il Bosco and Onferno, and then south-west towards Monte Altavelio. The set-up appeared to be as follows: *II Battalion 994th Grenadier Regiment* south-west of Onferno; *278 Fusilier Battalion* in Onferno area;[5] further east *Kranz Battalion* in the area C il Bosco; *1 Battalion 100th Mountain Regiment* on M.S. Colomba feature (with elements in C. Ferrarese and Gemmano); *171 Fusilier Battalion* in the area C. Ferrarese.[6]

Preliminary operations for the attack on Onferno and M.S. Colomba had already been carried out. 2/11 Sikh of the 7th Indian

---

[3] V Corps O.O. No. 20, 12 September 1944.
[4] The 5 Ind. Inf. Bde. had relieved the 11 Ind. Inf. Bde. in the area of Pian di Castello during 9/10 September 1944.
[5] After the fighting at Auditore, 278 Fusilier Battalion had been withdrawn to Sasso Feltrio; it relieved 1 Battalion 994 Grenadier Regiment in Onferno area during the night of 10/11 September 1944.
[6] 4 Ind. Div. Intelligence Summary No. 157, 12 September 1944.

Infantry Brigade had moved forward on 9 September to a position on the right of the 1st Royal Sussex (in the area Pt. 573) on the Pian di Castello ridge, in the area of Villa Bassa. This area, as well as all the positions of the 1st Royal Sussex, had been heavily and consistently shelled and there seemed little doubt that the Germans, who had only been driven off the Pian di Castello ridge with difficulty, had left behind personnel in civilian clothes who, by wireless or other means, were reporting the effects of the German artillery fire on the Allied positions. During the night of 9/10 September a civilian in possession of a machine gun had been killed by troops of A Company in the act of sniping battalion headquarters of 2/11 Sikh. There was little doubt that the Germans were bold in infiltrating individual or pairs of snipers on to the scrub-covered ridge during the hours of darkness, and recalling them before first light. Any movement on the Pian di Castello ridge at once drew heavy shell-fire and normal ground reconnaissance had therefore to be abandoned. Nevertheless, attempts had been made to glean information about the German dispositions. A fighting patrol, consisting of one platoon B Company had been sent forward after dark on 9 September to reconnoitre the forward slopes of the Pian di Castello ridge. From the information gained through this patrol and a reconnaissance flight over the general area carried out by the commanding officer of 2/11 Sikh, it had been known that the ridge running from Pian di Castello to M.S. Colomba (a dominating feature some 1075 yards forward of the Pian di Castello ridge), as well as Onferno (a small hamlet on a spur jutting northwards from the main feature towards the valley of Burano) was held in strength by the Germans.

The divisional plan was to make a double thrust against M.S. Colomba, with 2/11 Sikh (the 7th Indian Infantry Brigade) attacking the feature from the south and 4/11 Sikh (the 5th Indian Infantry Brigade) advancing from the area S. Pietro through German positions in the area C. Ferrarese. The 1st Royal Sussex in the area Pt. 573 guarded the left flank of 2/11 Sikh.

Brigadier Lovett made a plan by which 2/11 Sikh, with under command B Squadron less two troops of 6th Royal Tank Regiment and 513th Heavy Mountain Battery, were to make a double thrust against M.S. Colomba. At 2100 hours on 11 September, C Company was to advance from Cella through Il Faggio and C il Bosco to secure Pt. 296, and thence advance to M.S. Colomba, if not already seized by B Company. At the same time A Company was to advance from the Cemetery and secure Onferno; then B Company was to pass to the left of A Company along the ridge via Pt. 292 and converge on M.S. Colomba. At 0200 hours on 12 September, battalion headquarters and D Company were to move to Onferno and at first light D Company was to advance to M.S. Colomba (to strengthen the forward companies) via B or C Company's axis.[7]

Co-operating with 2/11 Sikh that night was 4/11 Sikh of the 5th Indian Infantry Brigade. This battalion, which had moved to San Pietro area on 11 September, had as its immediate objective C. Ferrarese, a settlement of five or six farm buildings on the north bank of the river Burano. After an artillery concentration from 2100 hours to 2400 hours, B and D Companies (the latter followed by C Company) were to cross the river Burano and secure the objective. A Company was to be in reserve.

The attack by 2/11 Sikh on M.S. Colomba ended in failure due to stiff German resistance. Prominent in the village of Onferno were its Cemetery and its Church. German troops based on these points put up fanatical resistance and halted the attack before the objective was reached. Similarly strong German positions on the north bank of the river Burano, south of C il Bosco, checked the advance further to the right. C Company, advancing through Il Faggio, at 0250 hours on 12 September, met strong opposition, 300 yards south of the river Burano, from ten spandaus and German infantry on the north bank of the river. Meanwhile A Company had moved to Onferno and was engaged in much close fighting in the low lying scrub country in that vicinity. By 0530 hours on 12 September, its advance was held up by strong resistance from Pt. 353. At 2330 hours B Company had advanced to the left of A Company along the ridge. But by 0400 hours all attempts to force a way along the M.S. Colomba spur were frustrated by a strong German post, with light machine guns dug in astride the narrow ridge. Therefore B Company moved back in order not to be caught on ground disadvantageous to itself at first light. Before that time the situation was that C Company was held up on the south bank of the river Burano and A Company in area Onferno, while B and D Companies had dug in on the forward slopes of the Pian di Castello ridge, where they were exposed in daylight to the Germans. The day was a long one of very heavy and accurate German shelling. The 2/11 Sikh suffered casualties as its company positions were overlooked by numerous German observation posts on the high ground at Sasso Feltrio and on M.S. Colomba itself. Tanks of the 6th Battalion Royal Tank Regiment gave excellent support by shooting up German strong-points. Nevertheless, the German fire continued to be intense and the Sikh casualties rapidly mounted. Yet they held their ground. A German sniper post, some eighty yards only from the slit trench containing the battalion commander's post, and from which German artillery fire was undoubtedly being controlled by wireless traffic, remained undetected for six hours. Once located it

---
[7] Sitrep 11 September 1944, War Diary 7 Ind. Inf. Bde.

was effectively dealt with by one of the supporting tanks. At 1800 hours on 12 September, the German fire slackened and preparations were made for the renewal of the attack at midnight. At approximately 1930 hours, B and D Companies were withdrawn from the forward slopes to take part in the attack and to be fed and reorganised. A Company had already returned to the area of the battalion headquarters during the day.

Meanwhile 4/11 Sikh too had not made any progress. B and D Companies advancing from the area S. Pietro had crossed the river Burano but suffered heavy casualties through German defensive fire. B Company was held up but D Company succeeded in reaching the outskirts of C. Ferrarese at 0315 hours on 12 September, when the advance was checked by intense medium machine gun fire. The village was almost surrounded by 0445 hours. Before supporting arms for the battalion were brought up, however, the German counter-attack aided by tanks was launched with great vigour. Out of ammunition and subjected to intense fire from the tanks, which drove straight through them, the Sikhs were compelled to withdraw to the south side of the stream by 0720 hours on 12 September.

The attack on M.S. Colomba was to be renewed during the night of 12/13 September. The 7th Indian Infantry Brigade was to attack Onferno, B Company of 2/11 Sikh securing the high ground immediately overlooking Onferno and A Company passing through to capture a small village and farmstead beyond. The 5th Indian Infantry Brigade was to break through German positions in area Maite—C. Ferrarese and advance to La Serra to threaten M.S. Colomba from the right. The operation for the advance of the 5th Indian Infantry Brigade to La Serra was to be carried out as follows:—

  (*i*) 3/10 Baluch was to advance from the assembly area C. Serra to the start line Pt. 187—Pt. 141 and secure the three objectives, Pt. 253, La Torneta and Pt. 144.

  (*ii*) 4/11 Sikh was to advance from the start line in the area Pt. 164 and secure objectives Maite—road, exploiting to C. Ferrarese.

  (*iii*) After 4/11 Sikh 3/10 Baluch had secured their objectives, the latter battalion was to advance to La Serra to threaten M.S. Colomba from the right.

The second attempt to capture M.S. Colomba fared no better than the first. The Indian troops failed to break through the German positions at Onferno and in the area Maite—C. Ferrarese. 2/11 Sikh (the 7th Indian Infantry Brigade) renewed the attack on Onferno at midnight on 12/13 September. On the previous day the Germans had considerably reinforced their troops in this area, and although B Company attained its objective, the high ground immediately overlooking Onferno, A Company advanced through intense artillery and mortar fire to find Onferno as strongly held as ever. In order not to remain a second day on a ground closely overlooked by the Germans, and accurately registered by them, both the companies withdrew at 0310 hours on 13 September behind the Pian di Castello ridge. C Company was meanwhile firm-based in the Cella area but all attempts to cross the river Burano evoked determined opposition. The company however carried out intensive patrolling and gained much useful information of the German dispositions. The battalion remained in the Villa Bassa area, having suffered very heavy casualties in the operations during 11/13 September, 15 killed, 103 wounded and 1 missing. German shelling was particularly heavy throughout 14 September, and intense in the early hours of the morning of 15 September, when the heaviest types of mortar and artillery were employed. Consequently C Company was withdrawn from the Cella area. The withdrawal was however closely followed up by the German infantry. C Company was also subjected to considerable harassing fire. Thus the 7th Indian Infantry Brigade failed to break through the German positions at Onferno.

The 5th Indian Infantry Brigade too failed to pierce through the German positions at Maite and C. Ferrarese. At 2000 hours on 12 September, C Company of 3/11 Baluch crossed the start line and secured the first objective Pt. 253 without difficulty. At 2200 hours A Company passed through C Company on to the second objective, La Torneta. A Company reached the objective at 2330 hours. Immediately afterwards, at 2345 hours, A Company was heavily counter-attacked from three sides and forced off the objective. But B Company moving up behind A Company restored the situation after a fierce struggle at 0030 hours on 13 September. B Company consolidated on La Torneta ridge. In the evening, however, A Company was withdrawn into reserve while B and C Companies consolidated on Pt. 253.

4/11 Sikh too was up against considerable opposition. There was difficulty in getting across the river Burano. At 0100 hours on 13 September, A and B Companies, followed by C and D Companies, started their attack to secure the objective, Maite. There was heavy mortar and machine gun fire and neither company could cross the river. The companies were compelled to withdraw to the area Di Sopra. The battalion area was subjected to intermittent shelling.

All attempts of the 4th Indian Division to break through the strong German defensive positions at Onferno and Maite—C. Ferrarese had so far ended in failure.

Capture of the Gemmano Ridge

By 13 September 1944, the 4th Indian Division had failed to break through the German positions covering M.S. Colomba, while to the right the 46th Division had failed to capture the Gemmano ridge. The 56th (London) Division however had scored a notable success at Croce. The corps commander therefore decided to exploit this success. He ordered the 46th Division to form up behind Croce and attack along the line of the road leading to Monte Colombo and Montescudo, leaving the capture of the Gemmano ridge to the 4th Indian Division.[8] At 0900 hours on 14 September, the 11th Indian Infantry Brigade took over from the 46th Division the Farneto spur, north of Gemmano. The brigade headquarters was at Montefiere; the 2nd Cameron was at the Farneto spur; 2/7 Gurkha relieved 3/10 Baluch (the 5th Indian Infantry Brigade) north of the river Burano in the area C. Tardini; 3/12 Royal Frontier Force Regiment was in reserve. The 7th Indian Infantry Brigade extended its front by relieving the 5th Indian Infantry Brigade in its sector, with the exception of localities held by 3/10 Baluch, which were taken over by the 11th Indian Infantry Brigade. The 5th Indian Infantry Brigade pulled out into reserve.

Brigadier Partridge made a plan by which the 2nd Cameron from the area M. Farneto—Il Tribio was to lead the attack on the Gemmano ridge, which was held by two German battalions—*II and III Battalions, 100th Mountain Regiment.*[9] The main objective of the Camerons was Pt. 449, a towering, precipitous peak, on which stood a large wooden cross, silhouetted against the sky. C Squadron 8th Battalion Royal Tank Regiment was to be in close support of the 2nd Cameron, and was to give fire support. Two platoons B Company (4.2-inch mortar) Rajputana Rifles (under command 11th Indian Infantry Brigade) were to fire on pre-arranged counter-mortar tasks. One platoon D Company Machine Gun (medium machine gun) Rajputana Rifles was under command of the Camerons, while the two other platoons were under the command of 2/7 Gurkha and 3/12 Royal Frontier Force Regiment. The fire plan and the deception fire plan were to be laid down by the officer commanding the 11th Field Regiment.[10] Two hundred and sixty guns were to support the attack and a stranger assortment of pieces it would be difficult to find. There were Brownings, Bofors 40-mm guns, 3.7-inch howitzers, 75-mm and 25-pounder guns, 4.5-inch and 5.5-inch howitzers, 3.7-inch heavy anti-aircraft guns, 7.2-inch howitzers and 155-mm guns. Yet the fire plan was simple. The high angle weapons, that is the howitzers, were to keep hammering at the

---

[8] *The Story of 46 Division*, 1939-45, pp. 80-81.
[9] 4 Ind. Div. Intelligence Summary No. 158, 13 September 1944.
[10] 11 Ind. Inf. Bde. O.O. No. 9, 14 September 1944.

German mortars, the remainder were to be directed against known German positions in a series of shattering concentration, each timed to a split second. H hour was to be 0300 hours on 15 September.

During the afternoon registration was completed and harassing fire, one heavy shell every fifteen minutes, was put into Zollara. An hour and a half before the 2nd Cameron attacked, every available gun fired on Zollara—field guns at ten rounds per gun, medium five round per gun, a total of some two thousand shells. Four minutes before zero, two Bofor guns fired tracer northwards from Castelnuovo to persuade the Germans that an attack was coming from the south. At the same time, Brownings harassed Maite and C. Ferrarese, both of which lay to the south of Zollara. Five minutes later, all available artillery began a series of 'Crashes' on four targets; on Zollara, on a sunken road to the north-east known to hold the Germans, on Pt. 402 and on La Serra. Occasionally bursts were dropped on Maite and C. Ferrarese, in order to continue the deception. At zero hour, some of the medium and heavy guns switched to counter-battery and counter-mortar bombardments.

At 0300 hours on 15 September, after 12 hours' continuous artillery preparation, the 2nd Cameron crossed the start line, the crest of the spur running south from Gemmano village to Trebbio. The route was across the southern slopes of the hill, below the crest, to Zollara before turning north to Pt. 449. This route involved crossing a series of re-entrants in the face of the feature but it was a less obvious route than the line of the track along the crest, and it did provide a certain measure of protection against German weapons on the northern flank of the hill.

Opposition was surprisingly light and casualties in the 2nd Cameron few. By 0530 hours the two forward companies had occupied Zollara. They were halted to reorganise and to allow their tanks to come up. Progress was methodical and deliberate. By 1012 hours, with the help of the tanks, the Camerons secured Pt. 402 and Pt. 449. 24 Germans were taken prisoners. The hill-top was a scene of desolation. Mangled trees, grass turned grey by the blast of exploding shells and bombs, British and German dead, marked the scene of some of the toughest fighting of the Italian campaign. The German will to resist had undoubtedly suffered in the earlier attacks by the 46th and the 56th Divisions, and it is possible that they had carried out some slight withdrawals. Nevertheless the success of the operation was greatly to the credit of the 11th Indian Infantry Brigade.

Attack on M. Altavelio

The capture of the Gemmano ridge by the 11th Indian Infantry Brigade and the seizure of Monte Colomba by the 46th Division considerably weakened the German defence. Patrols from the 11th Indian Infantry Brigade found M.S. Colomba unoccupied. The 7th Indian Infantry Brigade captured Onferno without opposition. On the left flank, however, the Germans continued to hold in strength M. Altavelio. Therefore Commander 7th Indian Infantry Brigade selected 1/2 Gurkha to lead the attack on this feature. M. Altavelio was held by *II Battalion 994th Grenadier Regiment*. One company was in Trebbio, the second in M. Altavelio and the third further west.[11]

Early on 16 September, 1/2 Gurkha concentrated in the area Ripa Massana. A fighting patrol of one platoon from C Company was sent at 1230 hours to clear Trebbio and find out the German dispositions in M. Altavelio, preparatory to a silent battalion attack at 2230 hours with two companies up. Both the villages—Trebbio and M. Altavelio—were a mile apart and commanded the whole of the ground over which the fighting patrol was to advance. By excellent use of cover, the Havildar in charge worked to within three hundred yards of Trebbio. From there he went forward with two men for a closer look at the village. Two houses on the south side of the village were occupied by the Germans. To capture these, he placed one section with their Bren guns in position covering all exits and then led a charge with the remaining two sections. Twelve Germans in the houses were killed and ten were chased away to the north. There were no other Germans in the village. By the same method of approach, the platoon closed on M. Altavelio. There the Havildar and his two men found a self-propelled 75-mm anti-tank gun in the village square. As they were about to destroy it, a German machine gun opened up outside the village and a party of Germans ran into the square. Two were quickly shot. Outside the village, the Havildar discovered that his platoon was engaged in a fire fight with a party of Germans and that a second party was working round to cut the platoon's line of withdrawal. A hit on the platoon's wireless set made it impossible to call for further aid. The Havildar therefore despatched one section to engage the encircling Germans while the remainder of the platoon broke off its fire fight with the first party. All ranks acted as though on a training exercise. The platoon withdrew towards Trebbio. When they approached Trebbio they were engaged by spandau fire from a German platoon, which had reoccupied the village. It was getting dark and expecting the battalion attack to be made in about two hours' time, the Havildar decided to take up a defensive position, about four hundred yards south of Trebbio, thus putting himself on the southern flank of the axis on which the battalion was to attack. From this position the Gurkha platoon carried on a fire fight with

---

[11] 4 Ind. Div. Intelligence Summary No. 161, 17 September 1944.

the Germans in Trebbio and also prevented German patrols from M. Altavelio coming along the Wadi below them. Meanwhile the Commander of 1/2 Gurkha had changed the plan—instead of a battalion attack on M. Altavelio D Company was ordered to carry out a raid on Trebbio at 2200 hours. This company found all the eastern approaches to Trebbio strongly held by the Germans. The company probed into the German defences. At 0300 hours on 17 September the two platoons of D Company managed to get through German outposts and assaulted the village, killing many Germans, who were very confused and not at all well positioned. Just before first light a German armoured fighting vehicle came down the road from M. Altavelio, firing as it came. A Gurkha carrying a Piat, ran out to engage but was killed. D Company then withdrew, helped by the covering fire of a platoon of C Company. The last section was however blown up in a large explosion as it crossed the road. From wireless intercepts, it was later learnt that the platoon of C Company had so stirred up the Germans that a complete German battalion had been marched nine miles to take up positions at Trebbio and M. Altavelio; this helped the subsequent breakthrough in the Gemmano area. This platoon patrol must rank high in the exploit of any army and its achievement and success were very largely due to the brilliant leadership of the Havildar.[12]

Thus at the close of 16 September, the 4th Indian Division had carried out its task of breaking through strong German positions south of the river Conca, though M. Altavelio on the left flank continued to hold out longer. The 4th Indian Division was now ready to advance to the river Marecchia.

[12] Patrol to Trebbio and Monte Altavelio Appx. J.2, War Diary 1/2 G.R., September 1944.

CHAPTER XIX

Advance to the River Marecchia

Bridge-head over the River Marano

The next move of the 4th Indian Division was dependent upon the success of the operations by the 46th Division to capture Montescudo and its bifurcation of roads. From that town, the British division was to move northwards with axis Trarivi—Vallechio, while the 4th Indian Division was to take the road to the west and seize and dominate the communications, which centred in San Marino state. Several attempts by the 128th Brigade of the 46th Division had failed to overcome German resistance on Pt. 465, a hill overlooking the road into the town of Montescudo. To help the brigade in a further attack, planned for the morning of 17 September, 3/10 Baluch moved forward to M. Croce debussing area during the night of 16/17 September. However, that night the Germans withdrew and the 128th Brigade completed its task of capturing Pt. 465 without further trouble.

On 17 September, the remainder of the 5th Indian Infantry Brigade (with the 2nd Cameron of the 11th Indian Infantry Brigade under command) closed up to 3/10 Baluch in Montescudo area, near Monte Colomba. The divisional plan was for the 5th Indian Infantry Brigade to advance on axis Montescudo-Faetano-San Marino with the object of cutting the roads centring on San Marino. The 11th Indian Infantry Brigade (less 2nd Cameron) was to establish one battalion as a firm base on the Montescudo feature in support of the operations of the 5th Indian Infantry Brigade. By vigorous patrolling they were further to endeavour to deny to the Germans the Gaino—Pt. 401 feature. The 7th Indian Infantry Brigade was to disengage such troops as were then involved in operations against M. Altavelio and Trebbio, hand over the sector to the 12th Lancers and concentrate in a suitable area with a view to moving forward later either to support or exploit through the 5th Indian Infantry Brigade.[1]

The *278th Infantry Division*, facing the 4th Indian Division, had *993rd Grenadier Regiment* on the left, on the Faetano-San Marino axis, *1 Battalion 994th Grenadier Regiment* in the Gesso area, *278 Fusilier* Battalion on the high ground to the west of Sasso

---

[1] 4 Ind. Div. O.I. No. 15, 17 September 1944.

Feltrio and *II Battalion 994th Grenadier Regiment* probably between Monte Grimano and the river Conca.[2]

Brigadier Saunders-Jacobs made the following plan for capturing San Marino:

(i) 3/10 Baluch was to establish a bridge-head over the river Marano in the area of the Faetano ridge by 1930 hours on 17 September.

(ii) 1/9 Gurkha was then to pass through the bridge-head and secure the following bounds during the night of 17/18 September; bound one Pt. 343, bound two Pt. 366, bound three Valdragona, bound four San Marino road junction area Pt. 433—Pt. 456. The Gurkhas were to patrol to the town of San Marino.

(iii) 2nd Battalion Queen's Own Cameron Highlanders was to follow 1/9 Gurkha and exploit success at first light on 18 September.

(iv) 4/11 Sikh was to be ready at first light on 18 September to move forward on the orders of the brigade headquarters.

The 5th Indian Infantry Brigade had under command the following troops:

2nd Cameron
A Squadron 6th Battalion Royal Tank Regiment, less one troop
C Squadron Central India Horse
One platoon 4th Field Company

The following troops were in support of the brigade:

Two (4.2-inch mortar) platoons Rajputana Rifles
Divisional artillery and 58th Medium Regiment.

The 5th Indian Infantry Brigade experienced considerable difficulty in the advance towards San Marino. The road forward from Montefiore over the Conca to Montescudo was being used by two divisions, the 4th Indian Division and the 46th Division, to move their troops and to carry out normal maintenance. In order to take advantage of the recent disorganisation caused among the German forces, Corps Headquarters was trying to deploy the maximum number of troops. For a time, traffic congestion was appalling. However, vehicles gradually trickled through and the 5th Indian Infantry Brigade was able to advance on the night of 17/18 September.

Preceded by patrols, C and D Companies of 3/10 Baluch moved forward at 2000 hours on 17 September and, by 0100 hours on 18 September, had established a bridge-head over the river Marano, north and south of Faetano, under cover of which sappers worked

[2] 4 Ind. Div. Intelligence Summary No. 162, 18 September 1944.

on the river crossing. B, C and A Companies of 1/9 Gurkha then passing through the bridge-head, at 0200 hours on 18 September, headed for Pt. 343 and Pt. 366, the top of the spur, which was held by *I and II Battalions of 993rd Grenadier Regiment*.[3] At 0515 hours, B Company secured Pt. 343 in the face of German opposition. A and C Companies then continued to Pt. 366 against strong opposition from German machine guns. It was a fight every foot of the way. Pt. 366 was captured at 0615 hours. The Germans, however, soon put in their counter-attack. The leading tank in support of the Gurkha infantry had got bogged on the shockingly bad track to Faetano, and had blocked it to the remainder. Ammunition available was just what the Gurkhas had been able to carry in eighty porter-loads and that had been considerably reduced by what was consumed in the struggle towards Pt. 366. Very soon, the Gurkha companies found themselves out of ammunition with no alternative but to pull back to Pt. 343 in the face of German counter-attacks. Pt. 343 stood above a gully, the sides of which were clay cliffs. Like flies the Gurkhas stuck to the sides of the gully and made what cover they could.

It was near Pt. 366 that Rifleman Sher Bahadur Thapa earned his Victoria Cross. He died in an attempt to rescue a wounded comrade after a most gallant action covering the withdrawal of the forward companies. Sher Bahadur Thapa was a number one Bren gunner in a rifle company, which just before dawn came under observed small arms and mortar fire. He and his section commander charged a German post, killing the machine gunner and putting the rest of the post to flight. Almost immediately another party of Germans attacked the two men and the section commander was badly wounded by a grenade. Without hesitation and in spite of intense fire, Rifleman Thapa rushed at the attackers. On the crest of the ridge he brought his Bren gun into action against the main body of the Germans, who were counter-attacking the company. Sher Bahadur Thapa lay in the open under a hail of bullets disregarding suggestions that he should withdraw to the cover of a slit trench. The German positions would not have been visible from the slit trench. By the intensity and accuracy of fire which he could bring to bear only from the crest, this isolated Gurkha Bren Gunner silenced several German machine guns and checked a number of Germans who were trying to infiltrate on to the ridge. At the end of two hours, both forward companies had exhausted their ammunition. As they were then practically surrounded, they were ordered to withdraw. Sher Bahadur Thapa covered their withdrawal across the open ground to positions in the rear and remained at his post until his ammunition ran out. Under small arms and mortar fire,

---

[3] *Ibid.* No. 162, 18 September 1944.

he then rescued two wounded men, who were lying between him and the Germans. While returning the second time he fell riddled by machine gun bullets.

The divisional gunners responded magnificently to the call for help sent out from 1/9 Gurkha. The 1st Field Regiment, firing round after round of high explosives and smoke, managed to break up some of the German attacks but it quickly became apparent that more support would be required. Within ten minutes, fire from the whole of the corps artillery was brought down in front of 1/9 Gurkha. This enormous weight of fire eased the pressure on the Gurkhas and enabled them to consolidate their position in the area Pt. 343. The Gurkha casualties were 16 killed, 44 wounded and 3 missing.

Capture of San Marino

An adequate bridge-head had been secured on the north bank of the river Marano. Throughout 18 September German shells burst on this bridge-head and on the road to it from Montescudo but failed to hold up the work of improving the track. Work was so rapid that in the evening a troop of tanks was able to make its way down to the river. One tank got stuck in the ford but the remainder pushed on. The 4th Indian Division was now ready to push on towards San Marino. 4/11 Sikh, concentrated in the Montescudo area, was to attack in the night of 18/19 September having for its objectives Corianino, C. Bugli and Le Grotte, with a patrolling limit to Ca Baldino. The 2nd Cameron, concentrated in Faetano area, with A Squadron 6th Battalion Royal Tank Regiment in support, was to be prepared to pass through 4/11 Sikh to San Marino. The 46th Division, advancing along a parallel axis on the right, was expected to be probably as far forward as Domagnano.

4/11 Sikh did not encounter much opposition in its advance, for the Germans had carried out a withdrawal. Moving wide round the right flank of 1/9 Gurkha, the Sikhs swept through Corianino and up the spur to the crest and the road. There they turned right along the ridge and road to enter C. Baldino at 0510 hours on 19 September. By 0945 hours, 4/11 Sikh was through Valdragona, with the Central India Horse and A Squadron 6th Battalion Royal Tank Regiment passing through Le Grotte. German activity was confined to slight small arms fire from the area of the road junction.

The 2nd Cameron passed through 4/11 Sikh at Valdragona at 0915 hours on 19 September in order to secure San Marino. The Germans were strongly entrenched in Borgo Maggiore and San Marino town. San Marino town was perched on a precipitous ridge, which rose in three peaks to two thousand feet above the Adriatic, twelve miles away, and commanded a view of all the ground to the west. Its rocky cliff face appeared to be an unscalable obstacle. Properly defended it might have been a second Cassino. Its weakness lay in the vulnerability of its one supply route, the road into the town from the north.

After the stiff resistance on Pt. 366, *1 Battalion 993rd Grenadier Regiment* pulled back to what was called the Yellow Line. This line ran from the outskirts of Borgo Maggiore, a lower suburb of San Marino, and then north-east to a strong-point near Pt. 235. The *278th Infantry Division* defended the Yellow Line. *1 Battalion 993rd Grenadier Regiment* was responsible for the defence of the village of Borgo Maggiore and Pt. 396. Next to it was *II Battalion 992nd Grenadier Regiment*. *993rd Grenadier Regiment* stretched up to the divisional boundary. *278th Fusilier Battalion* and *994th Grenadier Regiment* were leaving the high ground overlooking the Conca to establish themselves west of the main ridge of San Marino.[4]

During the night of 19/20 September the 2nd Cameron from the area Valdragona sent patrols into the outskirts of San Marino. Clashes were frequent and fierce with the small groups into which the Germans had now been split up. In hand-to-hand fighting and in complete darkness a Cameron patrol from D Company killed six Germans and captured six prisoners in a house. Positions could not be established in the town because the route to it was not yet secure and it was known to be mined. Under cover of darkness and of the patrols, the Cameron formed up on the line of Valdragona and the Santa Maria Convent below the cliff. At 0800 hours on 20 September, with two companies forward, the battalion began an assault by infiltration on San Marino from the east. A Company, on the right, advanced from Valdragona area to the road junction in order to attack Borgo Maggiore from the north. Stiff resistance was met at this road junction. C Company on the left advanced from the Santa Maria Convent area and was checked by machine guns in the area of the road junction. To deal with these machine guns, tanks were called up and they proceeded to plaster Borgo Maggiore and the towers in San Marino with their 75-mm guns. Aided by this fire C Company cleared the road junction. In a second attack, the company entered Borgo Maggiore, followed closely by A Company, which followed the road from the north. By 1230 hours, house-to-house fighting was in progress in Borgo Maggiore. After opposition was overcome, D Company passed through to secure San Marino town. By 2130 hours, 54 Germans had been taken prisoners and the whole of San Marino feature, with the town on the far side, had been captured. The casualties of the 2nd Cameron were 4 killed and 32 wounded. The fall of San Marino finally turned the German defences on the coastal plain. The loss of this ridge, the key to the

[4] *Ibid.* No. 163, 20 September 1944.

whole area, deprived the Germans of the last chance to hold the Rimini line and so they withdrew to the far side of the river Marecchia.[5]

The 43rd Indian Infantry Brigade in the Line

We have so far described the advance of the 4th Indian Division to the river Marecchia. It is now necessary to trace the progress of the 43rd Indian Brigade, under the command of the 1st British Armoured Division, to the river Marecchia.

The 43rd Indian Infantry Brigade had been the infantry component of the 31st Indian Armoured Division in the Middle East since January 1943, but a call for more infantry in Italy had led to the excision of the infantry brigade from the armour, which remained in Egypt. The three battalions of the 43rd Indian Infantry Brigade were all Gurkha, being 2nd Battalion 6th Gurkha Rifles, 2nd Battalion 8th Gurkha Rifles and 2nd Battalion 10th Gurkha Rifles. Their gunners were the 23rd Field Regiment R.A., in whom they had the greatest faith. Commanded by Brigadier A. R. Barker, OBE, MC, they had arrived and disembarked at Taranto on 1 August 1944, and had straightaway been posted to the 1st British Armoured Division, newly arrived from North Africa.

On 5 September 1944, the 43rd Indian Infantry Brigade took over the San Clemente ridge, west of the river Conca, where the 46th and 56th Divisions had some tough fighting. Two battalions, 2/8 Gurkha and 2/10 Gurkha held the ridge while 2/6 Gurkha was in reserve. During the night of 11/12 September, the forward Gurkha battalions were relieved by units of the 2nd Armoured Brigade to enable them to pull back a mile or two for preparations for the operations in the night of 12/13 September. 2/6 Gurkha in reserve held a forward position at Castelliale with one company.

The *26th Panzer Division*, with two regiments, held the Coriano ridge from San Savino to Coriano. The *98th Infantry Division* was concentrated on a narrow front in the area Croce and Il Palazzo.

Capture of the Passano Ridge

Three thousand yards west of the positions held by the 43rd Indian Infantry Brigade, across a stream, Fosse della Valle, was a ridge running from north to south, and rising from one hundred and fifty feet in the north to seven hundred feet in the south at Croce. Here the ridge fell steeply to the northern bank of the river Conca, a mile from Gemmano. The countryside, rich in agricultural soil, was dotted with small farmsteads clinging to the sides of the ridges above the numerous streams and water-courses. On this ridge, the crest of which carried a narrow metalled road, stood

[5] *Ibid.* No. 164, 21 September 1944.

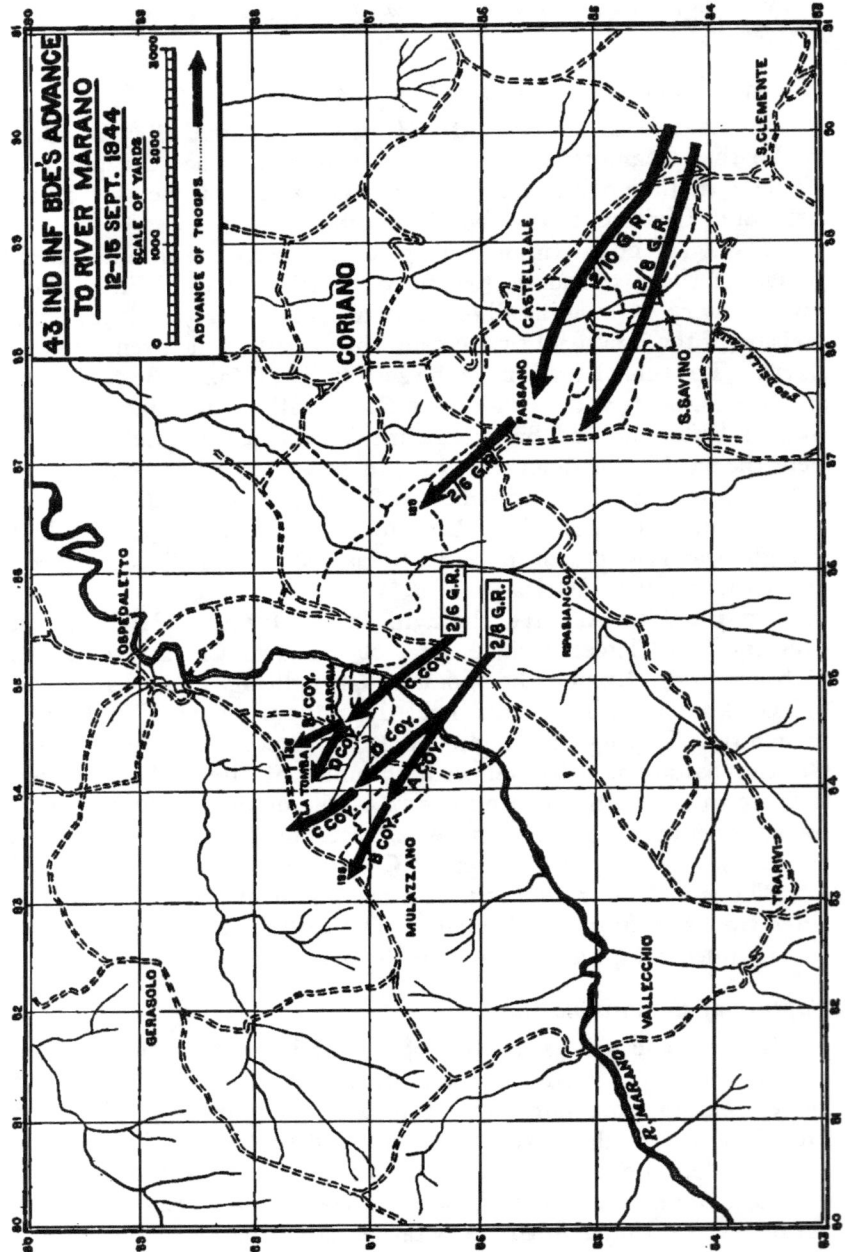

several hamlets. Of these, we are concerned with, from north to south, Coriano, Passano, San Savino and Croce.

The Commander of the 1st British Armoured Division made a plan to attack, at 2300 hours on 12 September, with the 18th Infantry Brigade on the left and the 43rd Indian Infantry Brigade on the right, and secure the ridge San Savino—Passano. The former was to be directed against San Savino while the latter was to consolidate the Passano ridge from including road track junction at R 875862 to excluding road track crossing at R 873846.

The artillery support provided for the initial attack on the Passano-San Savino ridge by the 1st British Armoured Division was fifteen field regiments, six medium regiments, six heavy batteries and three heavy anti-aircraft batteries, a total of five hundred and four guns. More than half of this total, which belonged to the 1st Canadian Corps, was to revert on 13 September, when the 1st Canadian Corps launched the attack, with, in addition, two medium regiments and two heavy batteries, from the V Corps.

According to the plan made by the Commander of the 43rd Indian Infantry Brigade, the attack on the Passano ridge was to be made with 2/10 Gurkha on the right and 2/8 Gurkha on the left. 2/6 Gurkha was to be in reserve.

The following troops were under the command of the 43rd Indian Infantry Brigade.[6]

>Queen's Bays (until consolidation of objective)
>310 self-propelled Battery 60th Anti-Tank Regiment
>One section Provost.

The following troops were in support:
>237th Battery 60th Anti-Tank Regiment
>One troop 622nd Field Squadron RE.

2/10 Gurkha, on the right, was to advance from the assembly area near Pt. 146 and secure the Passano ridge from R 874861 to R 872854. The following troops were in support:
>Squadron Queen's Bays
>Platoon medium machine gun SP Group
>Troops 310 self-propelled Battery 60th Anti-Tank Regiment
>Troops 2nd Field Squadron Royal Engineers.

Preceded by a heavy artillery bombardment of German positions on the southern half of the Coriano ridge, the two forward brigades of the 1st British Armoured Division crossed the start line at 2300 hours and advanced across difficult country to secure their objectives. At 2300 hours, the 43rd Indian Infantry Brigade, ably supported by tanks of the Queen's Bays, went into its first large-scale attack. To the south the 18th Infantry Brigade was attacking

[6] 43 Ind. Inf. Bde. O.O. No. 1, 12 September 1944.

San Savino. An outpost had been established at Castelleale on the Fosse della Valle; here 2/6 Gurkha covered the deployment of the brigade in a night that was dark, warm and strangely dry. On the ridge in front the skyline formed by its crest was their guide. Preparations for the attack had been very thorough; officers knew how many hedgerows they must pass, and the air photographs provided were exceptionally good. Recognition of the objectives was aided by burning houses in Coriano and San Savino, results of air bombing and concentrated artillery shelling. All these aids combined with a distinctly marked start line in the valley to get the brigade off to a good start. Sappers were to bridge the stream but each company was given one light tank to carry reserves of ammunition and stores for consolidation on the objective. It was a wise provision. Of the two Ark bridges allotted to the brigade, one was hit by German shelling and the other went astray. A thick German defensive barrage fell along the Fosse della Valle. Crushing casualties among sappers and their vehicles hindered the work on the crossings. Eventually, after a long detour, and despite steep banks of the stream, a crossing was made in 2/8 Gurkha area at R 885844. First across were the M.10's, self-propelled 3 inch anti-tank guns. Two M.10's, a Sherman and a carrier were quickly blown up by mines and several tanks lost their tracks, but the pioneers set to work clearing lanes, and soon tanks, armoured scout cars, carriers and jeeps were able to file across. The attack by the Gurkha infantry had gone well. At a pace of one hundred yards every six minutes, the leading troops breasted the lower slopes. Scouts from 2/8 Gurkha, moving ahead, were grabbed on the start line almost by a German patrol. One of these scouts, a Lance Naik, escaped and returned to give useful information concerning German positions. An early success was the capture of a German machine gun already laid to fire along the start line. At 2359 hours on 12 September, 2/8 Gurkha captured its objectives along with 27 prisoners.

2/8 Gurkha did not meet with very stiff opposition but the brunt of the fighting was borne by 2/10 Gurkha. The nullah crossings of 2/10 Gurkha came under heavy fire from German artillery, mortars and Nebel Werfers, and it was impossible to cross because the two Ark bridges allotted to the brigade had been knocked out. Consequently all the consolidation vehicles of 2/10 Gurkha had to cross by the 2/8 Gurkha crossing at 885844. The progress of 2/10 Gurkha was slowed down as the battalion was engaged by German small arms fire from the time it crossed the start line. However by 0130 hours on 13 September, 2/10 too was on its objective. Opposition had mostly come from German posts based on the many houses which dotted the hill-side. A German counter-attack, launched with infantry and tanks against 2/10 Gurkha at 0950 hours, was beaten off with the help of the anti-tank gunners and tanks of the Queen's Bays. On the whole, the Germans appear to have been surprised by the attack. Considerable confusion prevailed amongst the German garrison and their measures to repel the advance were slow to materialise. Shortly before midday, however, brigade headquarters received a direct hit, which killed several signallers and destroyed a telephone exchange. But consolidation continued throughout the day. 2/10 Gurkha dug in east of Passano while at 0600 hours on 14 September two companies of 2/6 Gurkha passed through to occupy Pt. 126, on the subsidiary ridge north-west of Passano.

Early on 14 September, the 18th Infantry Brigade, whose attacks on San Savino had also succeeded, now supported by the 2nd Armoured Brigade, pushed across north-east to the next ridge, the last before the river Marano. Ripabianca was captured after bitter fighting.

Capture of the Mulazzano Ridge

The next task for the 43rd Indian Infantry Brigade was to cross the river Marano, which followed quickly. At 1900 hours on 15 September, a two battalion attack was launched, with a squadron of 10th Hussars in support, and a tremendous concentration of artillery shells ahead on the Colle il Monte—Mulazzano ridge. Shortage of time before the attack had made it impossible to reconnoitre the area in a proper manner, a disadvantage outweighed by the surprise achieved through the unusual hour of attack. The objective was a stretch of road on the high ground, west of the river and two and a half miles north-west of Passano, between Pt. 136 and Pt. 186. The brigade plan was to attack with two battalions, 2/6 Gurkha on the right and 2/8 Gurkha on the left. 2/6 Gurkha, less B Company, was to move off to area 855864, just behind the start line for attack. The battalion was to advance half-way with only one company forward and then cover the final stages on a two-company front. C Company was to secure the first objective C. Barogia and then B and D Companies were to pass through to the second objective, Pt. 136 and La Tomba, respectively. 2/8 Gurkha, on the left, was to cross the start line at 852860, with D Company on the right and A Company on the left. After D and A Companies had reached their objectives, R 840869 and R 838868 respectively, C and B Companies were to pass through and secure objectives R 838877 and R 834872, respectively.

The operations started at 1900 hours on 15 September. C, the leading company of 2/6 Gurkha, ran early into German defensive fire, while crossing the nullah, and suffered casualties. However by

2030 hours C. Barogia, the first objective was secured. B and D Companies then moved through C Company and captured without much difficulty, by 2030 hours, the second objective, Pt. 136 and La Tomba. 2/8 Gurkha did not meet with much opposition. By 2000 hours, D and A Companies had captured their objectives at R 840869 and R 938868, and by 2200 hours C and B Companies had secured their objectives at R 842869 and R 834872.

The Germans were again caught off their balance. Their positions had been carefully prepared, wired and sign-posted in readiness for their occupation by the *98th Infantry Division*. One hundred and twenty-five prisoners were taken and a large proportion of one battalion's equipment, including a half-tracked vehicle with valuable documents, telephones, wireless sets and mortars. German machine guns collected by the brigade numbered more than fifty. German dead lay everywhere. Reinforcements, hurrying up the reverse slopes of the hill, received the full weight of the artillery's power. In one sunken lane a mortar company, caught toiling forward with its weapons, was slaughtered to a man. For this success, the brigade was congratulated by the Army Commander.

Later, the German artillery recovered and, aided by a downpour of rain, served to make life very unpleasant. In a short time mud was everywhere. Corps artillery moved into the rear brigade area, which consequently became very congested. Mist added to the discomforts of men still wearing their summer clothes.

Advance to the River Marecchia

In front of the 43rd Indian Infantry Brigade now was a tangle of narrow ridges and "gullys" of varying depth. In the heavy rain, movement was extremely difficult. For several days operations were postponed until, on 21 September, patrols picked up signs of German withdrawal. This withdrawal was caused, presumably, by 4th Indian Division's success at San Marino, the road from which ran between the Gurkha positions and the river Marecchia. 2/6 Gurkha and 2/10 Gurkha followed up at once and collected fourteen stragglers on 21 September. On the next day they reached the eastern bank of the river Marecchia and prepared to establish a bridge-head there.

The Eighth Army's Advance to the River Marecchia

While the 4th Indian Division and the 43rd Indian Infantry Brigade (under the command of the 1st British Armoured Division) were pushing on to the river Marecchia, the other formations of the Eighth Army were also advancing to the same river. In the coastal sector the 1st Canadian Infantry Division bypassed San Marino on 18 September, made a successful attack on the strong German position at Fortunato in the night of 19–20 September, and reached the river Marecchia on 20 September, while the 3rd Greek Mountain Brigade, operating under its command, entered Rimini on 21 September. The 56th Division hammered at the strong German position on the dominating Ceriano spur, the last before the Marecchia. The Germans pulled out of this strong position on 20 September, thus enabling the division to push on to the river Marecchia. The 46th Division, advancing from Montescudo, captured Domagnano (on the eastern approaches to San Marino city) and Serravale, and reached Casalecchio, thus squaring up to the river Marecchia. Thus by 21 September the Eighth Army had broken through the Gothic Line and had advanced to the river Marecchia. A new phase of the Italian campaign now began when the Eighth Army had to fight the battle of the rivers by driving the Germans from strong positions across a succession of streams.

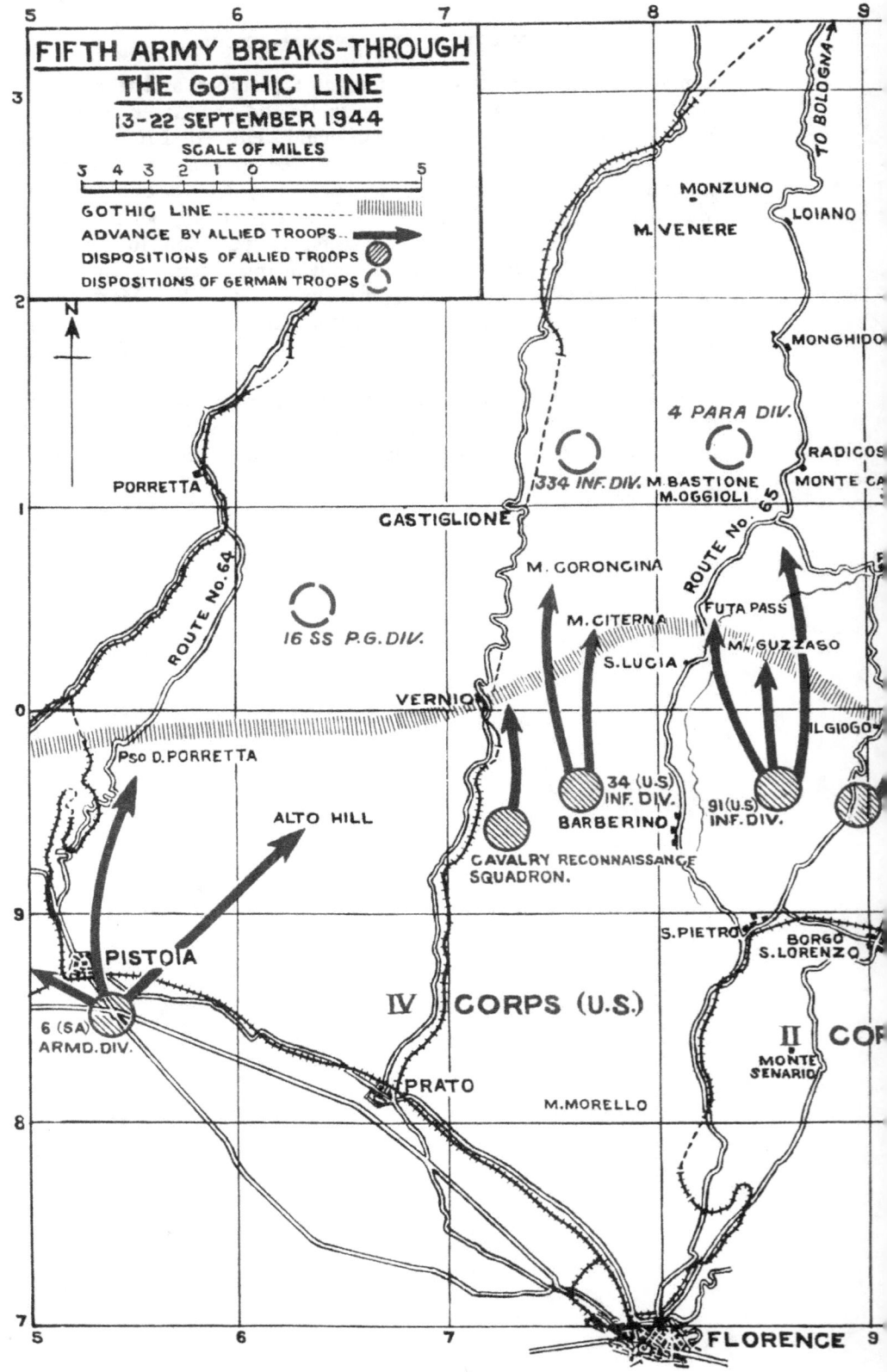

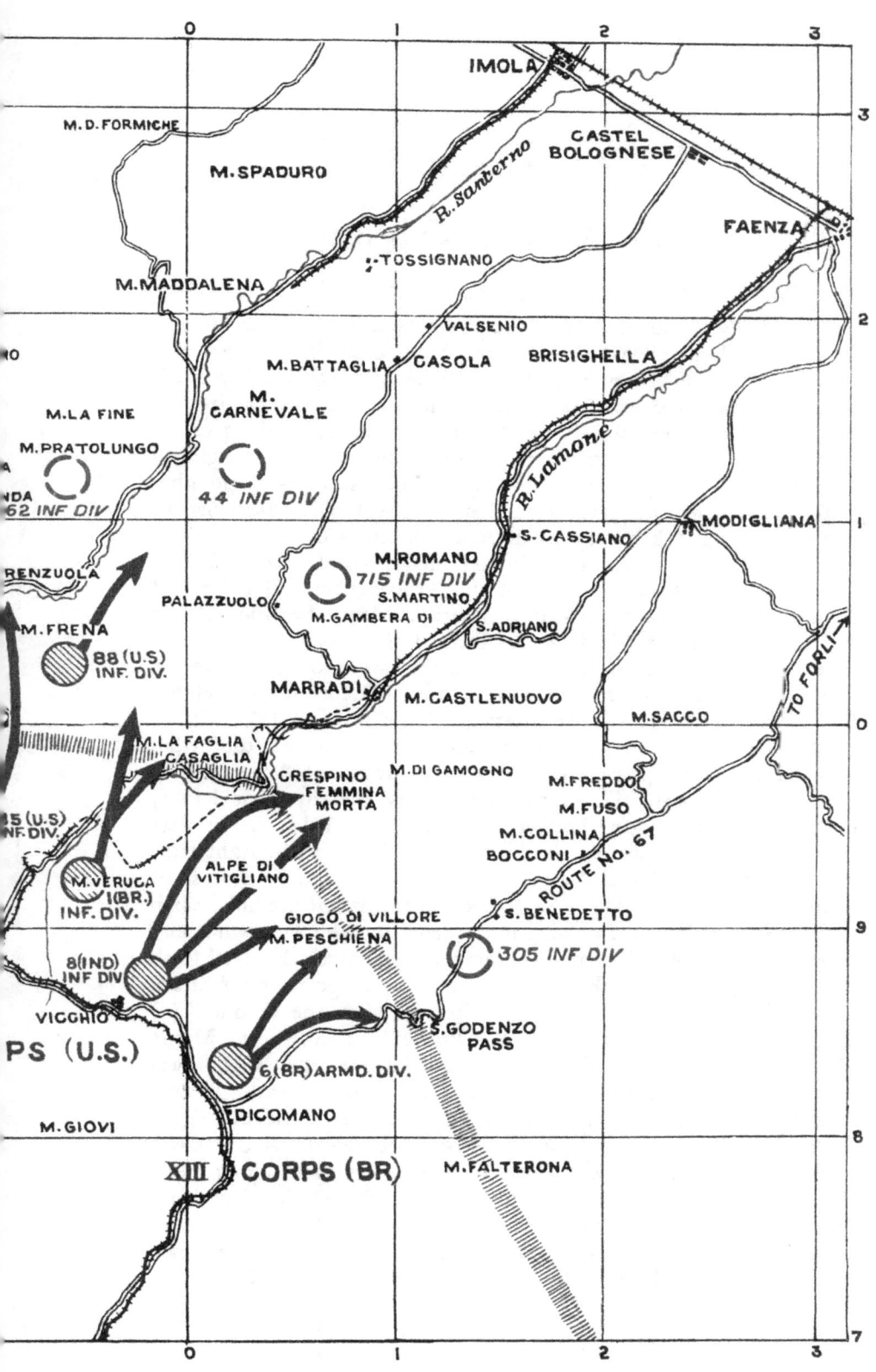

CHAPTER XX

Attack on M. Calvana

First Phase of the Fifth Army's Offensive

Having given an account of the part played by the Indian formations in the Eighth Army's attack on the Gothic Line we may now describe the role of the 8th Indian Division in the Fifth Army's attack on the same formidable line. The Fifth Army carried out its operations in two phases. In the first phase, it closed up to the Gothic Line by 12 September 1944, and in the second, it launched an attack on 13 September, breaking through it by 22 September 1944. It was on 17 August 1944 that General Clark issued instructions for the attack by the Fifth Army on the Gothic Line. The II Corps was to lead the attack in conjunction with the British XIII Corps, on an eight-mile stretch of the Arno between Florence and Pontassieve, and capture Monte Morello, Monte Senario, Monte Calvana and Monte Giovi, which formed the first natural line of defence. After securing these features, they were to close up to the Gothic Line and prepare for an attack on that formidable defence line. This plan was shortly afterwards modified. As the Eighth Army offensive developed in the Adriatic sector, Field-Marshal Kesselring was compelled to transfer troops from the Arno front to the Adriatic coast. The Arno front was thereby considerably denuded of troops, and the Germans facing the Fifth Army were compelled to fall back on 30 August; on the extreme right they fell back on the Gothic Line but to the north and north-east of Florence they stabilised by 3 September on the line of the hills, north of Florence: Monte Morello, Monte Senario, Monte Calvana and Monte Giovi. Therefore on 4 September, General Clark issued fresh instructions, modifying the original plan of 17 August for the attack on the Gothic Line. According to the new plan, the II and XXII Corps were to attack and seize the line of the hills from Monte Morello to Monte Giovi. If the Germans continued their withdrawal prior to 6 September, the responsibility for the pursuit was to be that of the XIII Corps. After the objective—the line of the hills from Monte Morello to Monte Giovi—had been secured the II Corps was to continue the attack to the north, making its main effort along the axis Florence—Firenzuola, to penetrate the Gothic Line and debouch in the Po valley. The XIII Corps was to continue the attack to the north and north-east along the axis Borgo S. Lorenzo-Faenza to pierce through the Gothic Line and appear in the Po valley. To facilitate the advance of the II Corps, initially the XIII Corps was to make its main effort on its extreme left. The task of the IV U.S. Corps, operating on the left flank of the Fifth Army, was primarily that of holding its wide front, while maintaining contact with the Germans. Thus the new plan considerably modified the original plan of 17 August 1944. According to the original plan, the II Corps was to attack along Route 65, in order to assault the Futa Pass defences. Under the new plan, the II Corps was to break through the Gothic Line at Il Giogi Pass, seven miles to the southeast of Futa Pass, and push on towards Firenzuola, thus outflanking the Futa Pass defences. Subsequent events justified this modification of the original plan.[1] According to the new plan the Fifth Army was to launch the attack on 8 September. But on that day the Germans withdrew from the line of the hills around Monte Morello to Monte Giovi. Subsequently the II Corps and the XIII Corps pushed on and closed up to the Gothic Line by 12 September. Thus by 12 September the Fifth Army had carried out the first phase of the operations by closing up to the Gothic Line and was now ready to take part in the all-out offensive along with the Eighth Army.

The 8th Indian Division in the Line

Having given a brief account of the advance of the Fifth Army to the Gothic Line in the first phase of the operations, we may now describe in detail the role of the 8th Indian Division in these operations. On 18 August 1944, the Fifth Army was strengthened by the British XIII Corps. It comprised two infantry divisions, the 1st Division and the 8th Indian Division, and two armoured divisions, the 6th British Armoured Division and the 6th South African Armoured Division (the latter, however, passed shortly afterwards under the command of the IV Corps). The XIII Corps held the sector from east of Pontassieve to five miles west of Florence. This front was held with three divisions in the line, the 6th British Armoured Division east of Pontassieve, the 8th Indian Division holding the sector from Pontassieve to the eastern outskirts of Florence and the 1st Division in the sector of Florence. The II Corps took over the sector west of Florence after 20 August and three days later the 1st Division extended its right boundary to Borro delle Sieci Creek, three miles west of Pontassieve, thus reducing considerably the front of the 8th Indian Division.

According to General Clark's plan, the XIII Corps was to hold its positions along the Arno until the II Corps had passed through to lead the attack on German positions on the hills north and northeast of Florence. But as German resistance weakened after 20 August the plan was modified and the XIII Corps prepared to secure

[1] *Fifth Army History*, part VII, p. 40.

a bridge-head before the anticipated date for the attack by the Fifth Army. Consequently the 1st Division and the 8th Indian Division crossed the Arno on a broad front to the east of Florence on 24/25 August.

German Dispositions

On 18 August, when the XIII Corps passed under the command of the Fifth Army, the 8th Indian Division held the sector from Pontassieve to the eastern outskirts of Florence, with the 19th Indian Infantry Brigade on the left and the 17th Indian Infantry Brigade on the right. The 21st Indian Infantry Brigade was in reserve. At this stage, in its course the Arno was barely one hundred yards wide and, in mid-August 1944, the average depth varied from two to three feet. As the current was not fast, several fords could be used. Positions, about one thousand yards north of the river on hills, over thirteen hundred feet high, gave the Germans excellent observation of the Arno valley. It was a panorama of rugged country and thickly wooded hills, whose slopes dropped steeply into narrow gullies which, in their turn, ran like crooked fingers down to the large Arno valley. Such roads, as existed, were anything but good, being only one way in parts. The *356th Infantry Division*, with six infantry battalions, held the hilly country overlooking the Arno between Florence and Pontassieve.

Routes

As the routes to the Gothic Line in the XIII Corps sector will be referred to throughout the chapter by their code names, it is necessary to describe them. Route 67, running from Pontassieve north-east to Dicomano and Forli was 'Star' route and the main axis of the 6th British Armoured Division. The second route ran from Pontassieve through Florence, then north to Borgo S. Lorenzo, Marradi, Palazzuolo and Casola Valsenio. This was 'Arrow' route and was used as a main axis by the 1st Division. 'Sword' route, which was the third, left 'Arrow' route at Marradi to travel north-east along the valley of the river Lamone to Brisighella. The fourth route, 'Sun', ran from Dicomano to Borgo S. Lorenzo joining the 'Star' and 'Arrow' routes.[2]

Aggressive Patrolling

The initial task for the 8th Indian Division was to establish a bridge-head over the Arno, preparatory to the attack on the high ground north-east of Florence. Since the Germans held the high ground north of the Arno, with excellent observation of all possible

---

[2] 8 Ind. Div. O.I. No. 8, 21 August 1944 and 8 Ind. Div. O.O. No. 30, 6 September 1944.

Major-General A. W. W. Holworthy
(Commander 4th Indian Division,
March 1944—January 1945)

A patrol leader of the 18th Garhwal Rifles gives instructions before setting out

Armoured cars of the Central India Horse set off on patrol from their H.Q. in the middle of an Italian village

Panoramic view of Cassino

crossing places, it appeared that the operation would have to take place under cover of darkness and that by day it would be necessary to screen the movements of the Indian troops in the river valley under a pall of artificial smoke.

Each night, small reconnaissance patrols, and when necessary the stronger fighting patrols accompanied by sappers, when information of a technical nature was required, slipped warily down to the river at numerous points. They searched for good approaches to the southern bank's shallow fords, where the infantry might cross, and good exits on the northern bank suitable for vehicles and free from mines. The river banks were liberally sown with anti-personnel mines, including wooden box mines, the familiar S' mine, the small, insidious Schu-mine and booby-traps fitted with trip wires in the branches of trees. Inevitably the Indian and British patrols suffered casualties.

It rained heavily on 18 August. The height of the water rose rapidly—four to five feet—and by the following morning the river was quite impassable for infantry. On 20 August the weather became more settled and the water level dropped again. But still the river was unfordable. The following night, the 17th Field Park Company succeeded in opening the sluice gates at the junction of Borro delle Sieci Creek and the Arno, causing the water level to subside sufficiently for reconnaissance patrols to wade over to the far side. Meanwhile, sappers worked constantly to maintain the vital supply roads, whose crumbling verges needed constant attention, especially after the rains.

On 23 August, when the XIII Corps prepared to establish bridgeheads over the Arno, the 1st Division extended its right boundary to Borro delle Sieci Creek, three miles west of Pontassieve, thus narrowing the front of the 8th Indian Division. The 19th Indian Infantry Brigade was relieved by a brigade of the 1st Division and took over part of the area of the 17th Indian Infantry Brigade. The 8th Indian Division was now disposed along a narrow front of not more than two and a half miles, with the 17th Indian Infantry Brigade on the right, the 19th Indian Infantry Brigade on the left and the 21st Indian Infantry Brigade in reserve. The 1st Royal Fusiliers and 1/5 Gurkha of the 17th Indian Infantry Brigade and 3/8 Punjab of the 19th Indian Infantry Brigade were the only battalions forward in the line. The other infantry battalions were concentrated in the assembly areas to rest and make ready for an attack on the German positions in the hills north-east of Florence.

The Corps plan was to establish bridge-heads over the Arno and follow up the Germans in the areas of Star and Arrow routes. On the right, the 6th British Armoured Division was to mop up Germans on the high ground immediately east of Star route as far north as

M. Campaccio, and establish contact with the Germans along the road Dicomano—S. Godenzo, as far as demolitions permitted. In the centre, the 8th Indian Division was to mop up the Germans on the high ground west of Star route within divisional boundary up to and including M. Giovi. On the left, the 1st Division was to mop up the Germans on high ground astride Arrow route.[3]

Major-General Russell planned to pursue the retreating Germans with three battalions up—two from the 17th Indian Infantry Brigade and one from the 19th Indian Infantry Brigade. On the right, the 17th Indian Infantry Brigade was to advance with two battalions— the 1st Royal Fusiliers on the right and 1/5 Gurkha on the left, 1/12 Frontier Force Regiment being in reserve. B Company 5th Royal Mahratta (Medium Machine Gun) and 4th Mahratta Anti-Tank Regiment less one battery were under command of the 17 Indian Infantry Brigade.[4]

On the left, the 19th Indian Infantry Brigade was to pursue the Germans with one battalion, namely 3/8 Punjab. The initial objectives were Pt. 316 and Pt. 394. The brigade was then to advance towards Poggio Cerrone. 6/13 Royal Frontier Force Rifles and the 1st Argyll and Sutherland Highlanders were in reserve.

The Bridge-head over the Arno

During the night of 23/24 August, the 1st Royal Fusiliers heard considerable German transport moving east up to Sieve valley. It was the first indication of the German withdrawal from their positions north of the Arno. On 24 August, there was no shell or mortar fire along the whole divisional front. The suspicions were confirmed when patrols from the 17th and the 19th Indian Infantry Brigades crossed the Arno and reported that the Germans had withdrawn. The 8th Indian Division now took up the chase. Meanwhile the engineers of the 8th Indian Division had forded the river and opened the sluice gates at the junction of the Borro delle Sieci Creek and the Arno on 21 August, thus enabling the British and Indian troops to cross the river, which now had a depth of less than two feet in places. The 8th Indian Division had also found a tank ford at Rosano, one mile to the west of Pontassieve.

The 1st Division and the 8th Indian Division crossed the river on 24/25 August and established bridge-heads over the Arno. On 25 August, the 17th and the 19th Indian Infantry Brigades crossed the Arno in force, establishing a bridge-head nearly five miles broad and almost three miles deep by the evening. 1/5 Gurkha on the right was established in the area Pervecchia, while the 1st Royal Fusiliers on the left had reached Erchi, a little village in a very

[3] *Ibid.* No. 8, 21 August 1944.
[4] 17 Ind. Inf. Bde. O.I. No. 32, 23 August 1944.

commanding position at the summit of a steep hill, overlooking Pontassieve from the north-west. Still further to the west, 3/8 Punjab was directed on Pt. 316 and Pt. 394. Pt. 316 was secured without opposition, but the left company directed on Pt. 394 was heavily sniped by spandaus and automatic fire from Pt. 227 at 1330 hours. The German position was effectively shelled by the gunners and at 1700 hours Pt. 394 too was captured. The only reaction of the Germans to the crossing of the river by the British and Indian troops was increased shelling, especially in Le Sieci area, which established conclusively that they were not going to fight on the line of the river.

Sappers at Work

On 25 August, the divisional sappers worked hard to build two bridges. A bridge (class 5) was constructed and work on a larger bridge (class 9) was completed by dawn on 26 August after much interference by heavy shelling on the bridge site. To protect the bridges and their approaches, already damaged by shells, a smoke-screen was laid at 1930 hours on 26 August. Men of the 26th Light Anti-Aircraft Regiment, Royal Artillery, using smoke canisters, maintained the screen throughout the day. Twenty-four hours later, the Sappers had built the Whitehall bridge at Rosano (class 30), which then took the main volume of traffic. Another bridge (class 40)—the Tower bridge—was thrown across the Arno at Pontassieve by the XIII Corps Royal Engineers at 2000 hours on 27 August. During the period of bridge building, the Sappers worked valiantly day and night. Not only were bridges built, but craters blocking roads were filled in, diversions were made, the debris of a mangled bridge was cleared away, mines were lifted and water points established, which gave thousands of gallons of drinking water daily.

Active Patrolling

On 26 August, the 17th Indian Infantry Brigade held the right of the divisional front north of the Arno, with 3/8 Punjab of the 19th Indian Infantry Brigade on the left. The infantry was operating in extremely hilly country. The terrain was peculiarly suited to the Indian soldiers, many of whom were accustomed from early childhood to hill-climbing and strenuous open air life. For their supplies of food and ammunition, for the warm blankets which they needed when darkness marked the approach of the cold nights, and for all the miscellaneous requirements of a soldier, they depended, to a very great extent, on the mule trains, whose untiring assistance was invaluable.

Major-General Russell ordered the two brigades to carry out

intensive patrolling to determine the positions and strength of the Germans. Sometimes by day, and always after dark, the Indian patrols stalked the Germans along deep ravines, through the dense undergrowth, up the steep mountain-sides and in the narrow, cobbled streets of the hill-top villages. Patrols of 1/5 Gurkha, operating on the right flank of the division, encountered most opposition, particularly from the tiny hill village of Tigliano, two and a half miles as the crow flies north of Pontassieve. In the hamlet of Pievecchia, one mile north of Pontassieve, a Royal Fusilier patrol found the corpses of 13 Italian hostages, who had been murdered by the retreating Germans.[5] The 6th Lancers, on the right flank of the 8th Indian Division, advanced on axis Pontassieve—Rufina, on the west bank of the river Sieve. They dismounted from their armoured cars which could not proceed further due to the bridge having been blown, and continued on foot. In one stretch of the road, a distance of 1,000 yards, they counted fourteen blown culverts,[6] so thorough were the German demolitions. After abandoning the Arno line the Germans fell back on strong positions in the hills to the north and north-east of Florence. The forward Indian troops met considerable opposition from Germans who were holding in strength the ridge C. Patrella—Pietrimaggio.

Capture of the Petella Ridge

On 28 August the Italian peasants told the Indian forward troops that the Germans had evacuated Tigliano just before dawn. Intelligence reports revealed that *I Battalion 735 Regiment* (the *715th Infantry Division*) was disposed along the high ground running from north of Tigliano in a north-westerly direction through Pt. 537 towards Poggio Cerrone, with *I Company* east, *II Company* in the C. Petella area, *III Company* to the west, and some heavy machine gun detachments of *IV Company* covering the right flank. *V Company* was in reserve in the area of Farneto.[7] As was learnt later from prisoners, this German battalion had orders to hold the C. Petella—Pietrimaggio ridge at all costs.

The divisional plan was for the 17th Indian Infantry Brigade to lead the attack on the C. Petella—Pietrimaggio ridge and for the 19th Indian Infantry Brigade on the left flank to patrol forward, as a prelude to the subsequent occupation of M. Croce.[8] Brigadier C. H. Boucher, C.B.E., D.S.O., Commander 17th Indian Infantry Brigade made a plan by which 1/5 Gurkha was to advance at 2100 hours on 28 August and occupy C. Petella, including Pt. 526. Then

---

[5] Sitrep, 28 August 1944, War Diary 8 Ind. Div.
[6] Sitrep, 27 August 1944, War Diary 8 Ind. Div.
[7] 8 Ind. Div. Intelligence Summary No. 145, 29 August 1944.
[8] Sitrep dated 28 August 1944, War Diary 17 Ind. Inf. Bde.

the 1st Royal Fusiliers was to pass through 1/5 Gurkha at 0600 hours on 29th August and occupy Pt. 537, Catelano, Pt. 520, Pietrimaggio and Pt. 534. 1/12 Frontier Force Regiment in reserve was to occupy the position vacated by 1/5 Gurkha, and then to be prepared to advance through the 1st Royal Fusiliers and occupy Poggio Cerrone, not before the night of 29/30 August. C Squadron of the 14th Canadian Armoured Regiment was in support of the brigade.

The objective of 1/5 Gurkha was the Petella ridge, from including ring contour Pt. 526 to the saddle at Q 945748. The plan was for A Company, followed by B Company, to advance from Montegiasole to the centre of the Petella ridge, which was at a distance of about 3,000-4,000 yards, and then fan out, the former to the west and the latter to the east. The attack was to be a silent one by night.[9]

The Gurkhas crossed their start line at 2100 hours on 28 August, with A Company in the lead followed by B Company, and attacked along a spur running up at right angles to the Petella ridge. They were temporarily held up by considerable mortar and small arms fire. There was some shelling too from German guns. Progress was necessarily slow. A Company however reached the foot of the Petella ridge at 2330 hours. The men were heavily fired on by a spandau from the west. The commander of A Company immediately took one platoon, worked round to a flank and charged the machine gun post, killing all the occupants. A counter-attack by a platoon of Germans was driven off. A Company of Germans then counter-attacked almost immediately and there was fierce hand-to-hand fighting, with the Gurkha kukries much in evidence. The platoon was however forced to withdraw on account of lack of ammunition to a strong-point, Sperperugi. Meanwhile B Company, with two platoons of A Company which had got separated from the main body in the confused fighting, stormed Pt. 526, whose dark outline was silhouetted against the sky. The Gurkhas were on their objective at 0015 hours on 29 August. They set about digging slit trenches in the rocky shale on Pt. 526, as the Germans swept the objective with persistent shell and machine gun fire. At frequent intervals, every man fell flat on his stomach while shell after shell crashed on Pt. 526. Breathing heavily, the Gurkhas dug again, faster than before as the night wore on towards morning. They held grimly on to their objective, until it was finally consolidated by 0530 hours on 29 August. By that time battalion headquarters and C and D Companies had established a firm base at Sperperugi. The gunner support throughout the operation was timely and accurate, despite circumstances which rendered communications difficult.

[9] Action at Petrella ridge 28/29 August 1944; Appendix, War Diary 1/5 G.R., August 1944.

At 0815 hours on 29 August, the 1st Royal Fusiliers passed through the forward Gurkha positions and advanced to Pt. 537, Catelano, Pt. 520, Pietrimaggio and Pt. 534. Throughout the day, C Squadron of the 14th Canadian Armoured Regiment gave excellent support to the 1st Royal Fusiliers. The latter made good progress in spite of heavy mortaring and machine gun fire. By 1550 hours they had captured Pt. 537 and Catelano. The advance continued to Pt. 520 and the final objective Pt. 534 was secured by 1600 hours, when the Germans withdrew in some disorder towards Poggio Cerrone, the cone-shaped feature to the north.

In the left divisional sector, the 19th Indian Infantry Brigade probed into German defences in the area Poggio di Luce and M. Croce, preparatory to an attack on these positions.

Capture of Poggio Cerrone

Major-General Russell now ordered the 17th Indian Infantry Brigade to secure the southern slopes of Poggio Cerrone and the 19th Indian Infantry Brigade to patrol to M. Croce. Brigadier Boucher selected 1/12 Frontier Force Regiment for the task of securing Poggio Cerrone. 1/12 Frontier Force Regiment moved at 2100 hours on 29 August to concentrate in the area Cerreto in order to pass through the 1st Royal Fusiliers and attack Poggio Cerrone. The plan was for B Company to advance from the start line—road west of Pt. 520—and capture Colline. C Company was then to pass through and capture Poggio Cerrone. At 0500 hours on 30 August, B Company moved off, supported by two troops of tanks of C Squadron of the 14th Canadian Armoured Regiment. The advance was slowed down at the very start by seven German light machine guns sited north-west of the start line. By 0812 hours, B Company had advanced only two hundred yards. Further advance was held up by fierce resistance. The Germans continued to offer resistance till 0825 hours, when they withdrew to the north. Thereafter B Company moved up to Pt. 534 area. The further advance of B Company was however brought to a halt at 0900 hours by a strong German force, astride the track. C Company near Pt. 520 beat off a minor German counter-attack at 0930 hours. No further advance was made. At 1315 hours, as B and C Companies were preparing to resume the advance to Colline, they were heavily mortared, suffering 14 casualties. Stretcher jeeps failed to get through, owing to light machine gun and mortar fire. As the Germans were in great strength the advance was discontinued and both the forward companies withdrew to Pt. 534 at 1345 hours. At 2010 hours, a two-company German counter-attack was launched on B and C Companies at Pt. 534. Defensive fire was brought down and after tough hand-to-hand fighting the Germans were driven back. However, the attempt of 1/12 Frontier Force Regiment to drive the

Germans from Poggio Cerrone ended in failure. But early next morning, reconnaissance patrols found that the Germans had withdrawn from Poggio Cerrone during the hours of darkness. By midday, 1/12 Frontier Force Regiment had occupied this large, two thousand feet high feature, to find its positions overlooked by the rugged M. Giovi, which towered above them to the north-east.

Meanwhile, the sector on the left, held by the 19th Indian Infantry Brigade, was quiet with only spasmodic German shelling and occasional mortar fire. On 31 August, the 1st Argyll and Sutherland Highlanders occupied Poggio Luca, Fornello, Strembaccia and Decima, preparatory to the attack on the strong German position at M. Calvana.

Capture of the Escarpment (Poggio Abetina—Poggio Ripagfiera)

After being driven from Poggio Cerrone on 31 August the Germans fell back on a line of the hills, M. Giovi—M. Calvana. The advance of the 8th Indian Division came to a halt before this strong defence line. During the past few days some regrouping of German forces had been going on with the object of releasing mobile forces for the more seriously threatened Adriatic sector. With the *90th Panzer Grenadier Division* and the *26th Panzer Division* already departed, the *29th Panzer Grenadier Division* was the next choice. As the latter was to use the Dicomano—Borgo S. Lorenzo road, the Giovi-Calvana features assumed a vital importance for the Germans, who used M. Giovi as a pivot for the withdrawal of their forces from the north-west of Florence to the Adriatic front. The Germans offered particularly strong resistance in order to retain control of the Giovi-Calvana feature to enable the *29th Panzer Grenadier Division* to move to the Adriatic. The *356th Infantry Division* was responsible for the defence of these vital features.

Major-General Russell selected the 19th Indian Infantry Brigade for an attack on M. Calvana. The brigade was to extend its hold on the high ground up to Poggio Ripagfiera and the ridge to the south-west, patrolling forward to the area of C. Caprile, with a view to securing high ground Calvanella. Its right flank was to be protected by the 17th Indian Infantry Brigade.

M. Calvana, a feature 2,700 feet high, dominated the important road running along its western slopes, viz. from Florence to Borgo S. Lorenzo. As a preliminary to the assault on M. Calvana, it was necessary for the 19th Indian Infantry Brigade to capture the escarpment between Poggio Abetina and Poggio Ripagfiera. The face of this escarpment was rough and broken. In the area of Poggio Abetina its sides dropped precipitously from the crest. Poggio Ripagfiera rose even higher, although more gently, covered for the

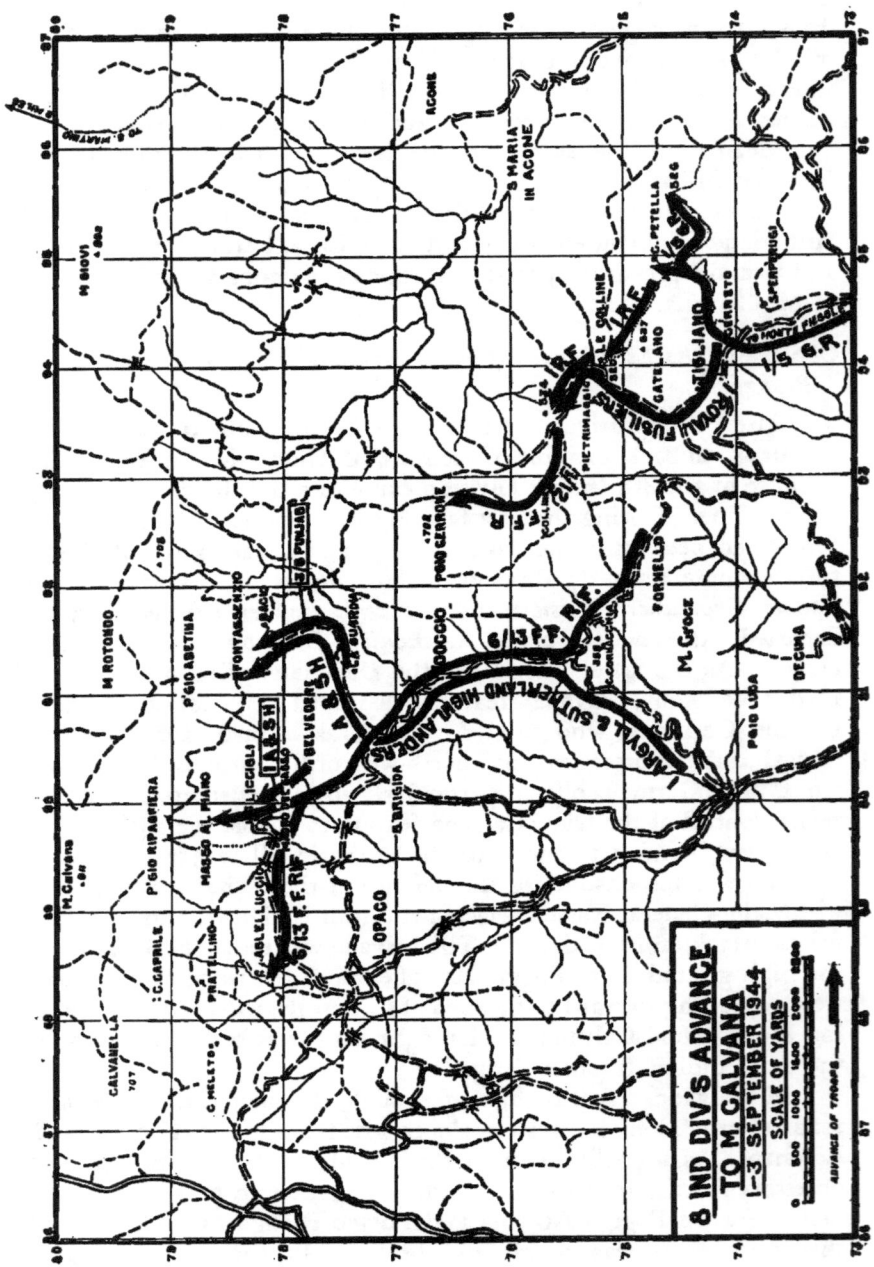

most part with thick woods of oak and walnut. The Germans were strongly entrenched on the top of the ridge, with excellent observation and wide fields of fire. Supplies and ammunition for the attack by the 19th Indian Infantry Brigade were brought as far as possible into the hills in jeeps, before travelling over the last stage of their journey to the infantry companies by mule trains.

Brigadier Dobree made a plan for the attack on M. Calvana. The 1st Argyll and Sutherland Highlanders was to move from the area M. Croce at first light on 1 September and secure the three objectives—line of the road Doccio—S. Brigida, Poggio Abetina and Poggio Ripagfiera, M. Rotondo. 6/13 Royal Frontier Force Rifles was to move at 0800 hours to Fornello and advance behind the Argyll, and then to secure the two objectives, L'Opaco and Calvanella. 3/8 Punjab was to remain in reserve in the area Sieci and move at 0500 hours on 2 September to L'Olmo with the object of continuing the pursuit to Borgo S. Lorenzo. C Company 5th Royal Mahratta (medium machine guns) was under command and C Squadron 6th Lancers, A Squadron 14th Canadian Armoured Regiment and A Company 5th Royal Mahratta (4.2-inch mortars) less two platoons in support of the brigade.

On 1 September, the 1st Argyll and Sutherland Highlanders rose very early, finished breakfast before dawn and by 0600 hours was advancing north from M. Croce. With the Scotsmen, using a very rough cart-track, went a squadron of the 14th Canadian Armoured Regiment. In two hours the Argyll had advanced nearly two miles to the village of S. Brigida. The advance was continued towards the thickly wooded slopes of Poggio Abetina. There was some opposition at Belvedere at 1100 hours. Three Germans were killed and three taken prisoners. The Argyll reached within three hundred yards of the formidable Poggio Abetina but were unable to proceed further on account of accurate fire from machine guns sited in the rock face above. The advance was held up by strongly defended observation posts at Fontassenzio and Poggio Abetina. The forward company and two platoons remained below Abetina for the rest of the day and the following night, the rest of the battalion being in the area Doccio. Heavy German shelling caused 15 casualties. Their excellent observation gave the Germans aimed fire on the whole brigade area.

On the left, 6/13 Royal Frontier Force Rifles also made good progress. With D Company as advance guard, the battalion moved forward through Fornello at 1300 hours on 1 September and reached Doccio at 1330 hours. The leading elements were heavily shelled in the area of the road junction. For a time, there was indescribable chaos on the road as shell after shell crashed down on the Indian Infantry and its mule trains. Dead mules lay alongside the road, their loads still strapped to their backs. As the high mountain now in front of the brigade was the last ground suitable for defence before the Gothic Line was reached, the Germans made desperate efforts to defend it. Consequently all the afternoon the battalion was under heavy shell fire. The Frontier Force Rifles however struggled forward and sent patrols to spurs running north-west from Ripagfiera and C. Caprile with the purpose of advancing on Calvanello from the east.

At 1845 hours the German strong-point and observation post at Madno del Sasso was shelled by artillery. Under cover of the smoke-screen D Company, followed by Tactical Headquarters and B Company, advanced at last light through Madno del Sasso and Masso al Piano to Castelluccio, a point south-west of Poggio Ripagfiera, a feature one mile due west of Poggio Abetina. D Company took up covering position while B Company moved forward and arrived at Castelluccio, some 800 yards south of C. Caprile at 0030 hours on 2 September. Here they came under small arms fire from the direction of C. Meleto. Considering the heat of the day, the very broken country, and remembering too that there were several clashes with German patrols en route, the advance by the Argyll and the Frontier Force Rifles on 1 September constituted a very creditable performance.

The commander of the Argyll and Sutherland Highlanders (A & SH) planned to attack Poggio Abetina early on 2 September. There was room only for one company, with platoons in echelon, to manoeuvre at the same time. The battalion commander decided on a simultaneous attack by two companies on the east and west end of the escarpment. One company was directed on Abetina and the second on Ripagfiera. At 1145 hours on 2 September, the company endeavouring to scale Poggio Abetina by the steep mule track on the right was caught in heavy mortar and artillery fire. Swinging behind the two leading platoons, the Germans separated them from the rest of the battalion by a deadly stream of machine gun bullets. Suddenly sheets of flame billowed towards the Scotsmen; the Germans were using a flame thrower. At this the company, less two platoons, withdrew to La Guardia. The second company of the A & SH directed on Ripagfiera was established at Belvedere at 1030 hours. As it moved forward towards Ripagfiera the men were subjected to mortar and shelling at Liccigli and withdrew to Belvedere. Further attempts to advance were halted by heavy mortar and artillery fire and machine gun fire from Madno del Sasso.

On the left, 6/13 Royal Frontier Force Rifles pushed north from Castelluccio towards the flank of the German positions on Poggio Ripagfiera and, at 1035 hours on 2 September, established a company at Pratellino, south-west of that feature. A heavy German counter-attack developed at 1230 hours. About fifty Germans advanced under cover of shell and mortar fire. Fierce fighting followed until at 1445 hours the company was forced to withdraw to Castelluccio. During the afternoon the battalion area continued to be under intense German shell and mortar fire. Even though slit trenches had been dug and covers put on, the German shelling was so concentrated that the battalion suffered many casualties. Thus, by last light, the Germans were still firm on the Abetina-Ripagfiera ridge. The 8th Indian Division had failed to break through the German defence line.

Whilst the A and SH and 6/13 Royal Frontier Force Rifles were fighting hard to drive out the Germans from Poggio Abetina and Poggio Ripagfiera, 3/8 Punjab had moved forward to the area M. Croce in order to attack Poggio Abetina in the morning of 3 September. The brigade plan was for the 3/8 Punjab to assemble in the area C. Cornacchia and attack the escarpment from the east at 0400 hours. After occupying Poggio Abetina and Poggio Ripagfiera the battalion was to exploit to and occupy M. Calvana. Its left flank was to be protected by the Argylls, who would consolidate their existing positions on the line Bacio—Belvedere. The role of 6/13 Royal Frontier Force Rifles was to consolidate the existing positions in the area Castellucio, but after the 3/8 Punjab had secured the objective, this battalion was to attack and occupy the spur C. Caprile—C. Meleto, exploiting to Calvanella. The 17th Indian Infantry Brigade was to protect the rear and right of 3/8 Punjab.

The attack by 3/8 Punjab on Poggio Abetina commenced at 0400 hours on 3 September. A fierce thunderstorm broke as the forward troops crossed the start line. The moon was obscured by dark clouds, and dense mist on the hillside prevented maintenance of direction. Consequently only C Company succeeded in reaching the area near Bacio by 0500 hours on 3 September. However it was also pinned down by machine gun and mortar fire. At 0615 hours the company, less one platoon and two sections which got lost, withdrew under smoke-screen to the area Doccio. Thus due to the stubborn German resistance, very difficult country and the thunderstorm which disorganised the attack of 3/8 Punjab, the 19th Indian Infantry Brigade was kept at bay long enough for the Germans to complete the move of the *29th Panzer Grenadier Division* across to the Adriatic front.

Capture of M. Giovi and M. Calvana

During the next three or four days, the 8th Indian Division maintained active patrolling to keep the Germans constantly on their tenterhooks and allow them no opportunity to slip away by night undetected. The 21st Indian Infantry Brigade, which had enjoyed a long rest after its fighting in Florence, was called forward to concentrate on 6 September at the foot of the hills in the vicinity of Vico, in order to launch an attack on M. Giovi. 1/5 Mahratta, the forward battalion, was in the area C. di Monte while the 5th Royal West Kent Regiment and 3/15 Punjab were in the area Vico. Two troops 4th Mahratta Anti-Tank Regiment and D Company 5th Royal Mahratta (machine gun) were under command while B Squadron 14th Canadian Armoured Regiment, and one platoon A Company (4.2-inch mortar) 5th Royal Mahratta were in support of the brigade.[10]

During the early hours of 7 September, 1/5 Mahratta, with one company of the 5th Royal West Kent Regiment under command, occupied without opposition the pleasant villages of S. Maria and Acone, whose white cottages nestled in long line on the southern slopes of M. Giovi. This brought the Mahratta up on the right flank of the 17th Indian Infantry Brigade, which had also been patrolling from the area Poggio Cerrone to the formidable M. Giovi. The latter feature, nearly three thousand feet high, was of vital importance, because as long as it remained in German hands it would be almost impossible for either the 8th Indian Division or the 6th British Armoured Division on its right to advance along the main highway through the Sieve valley. In fact, the capture of M. Giovi would open the door to the Gothic Line.

The upper slopes of M. Giovi, rising quite steeply, were bare open grasslands, ideal for sheep grazing. Leading up to S. Maria in Acone there was a good minor road with only one crater, which was soon repaired; from there on, there was just no road at all. A winding mule track, barely three feet wide in places, climbed up the hill. Near the summit was a small cluster of demolished buildings from which the mule track zigzagged round a natural basin, called the 'Bowl'. The track ran over the right shoulder of M. Giovi, skirted a pine wood and, from here, began to descend. Air photographs revealed the presence of many carefully sited and well-prepared German defences on the shoulders of the hill.

On the right of the 8th Indian Division, the 6th British Armoured Division was advancing up Star route as quickly as repair of the many demolitions would permit, directed on the wild country between M. Compaccio and Piedimonte. Over on the left, the 1st Division was maintaining a progressive screen through which the II U.S. Corps was to pass and secure the high ground M. Calvana—M. Senario—M. Morello.

Major-General Russell planned to assault M. Giovi with two Brigades, the 21st Indian Infantry Brigade on the right and the 17th

---

[10] 21 Ind. Inf. Bde. Planning Note No. 10, dated 5 September 1944, War Diary 21 Ind. Inf. Bde.

Indian Infantry Brigade on the left. This plan, however, was never carried out for whilst M. Giovi was enveloped in heavy rain and mist on 7 and 8 September, the Germans withdrew towards Vicchio. The pursuit, which followed, developed smoothly because well prepared supply and maintenance preparations had been made beforehand.

At 1145 hours on 8 September, civilian refugees brought word to a forward company of 1/12 Frontier Force Regiment that the Germans had left M. Giovi, carrying their baggage in carts. Reconnaissance patrols quickly confirmed this information and the companies were in position on the crest. When the Germans abandoned M. Giovi, they also retired from the heights to the west so that the 19th Indian Infantry Brigade was able to occupy without opposition Poggio Abetina and Poggio Ripagfiera. At 2345 hours on 8 September the 1st A & SH occupied Poggio Abetina. At 0500 hours on 9 September, 3/8 Punjab moved through Poggio Abetina and occupied M. Calvana at 1215 hours. On the left, 6/13 Royal Frontier Force Rifles occupied Calvanella without opposition at 0715 hours on 9 September. On the same day (9 September), 1/5 Mahratta (the 21st Indian Infantry Brigade), on the right, entered with patrols the village of S. Martino, where only a few civilians were found. By next day, riflemen of 1/5 Mahratta working with their friends of the 4th Mahratta Anti-Tank Regiment and assisted by the sappers of the 66th Field Company, Indian Engineers, who blasted a way through the rock at the narrowest points, built a track suitable for jeeps up the steep slope of M. Giovi, over the right shoulder and down through the woods to join a metalled road just north of S. Martino. Over this track, by dint of great effort and determination, Q Battery 52nd Field Regiment hauled a 25-pounder gun. By this rough route came the jeeps with their countless loads of supplies, the mules with their cumbersome burdens, and the indefatigable infantry.

Pursuit to the Gothic Line

The 8th Indian Division now pressed hard on the heels of the retreating Germans. On 11 September patrols of 1/5 Mahratta crossed the river Sieve in the vicinity of Vicchio. In this area, the river was shallow and about 25 yards wide, with small steep banks, lined in most places with trees. The engineers accompanying the patrols reported extensive demolitions and mining carried out by the Germans. In the village itself, all the streets were blocked by rubble from demolished houses.

On the night of 11/12 September, 1/5 Mahratta put out a standing patrol to cover the 66th Field Company, Indian Engineers, who started to construct a Bailey bridge. That same night, the remainder of the 21st Indian Infantry Brigade moved to the forward concentration areas, and the following morning, at first light, 1/5 Mahratta, crossing the Sieve, advanced northwards in face of slight German resistance and some shelling. They had in support B Squadron 14th Canadian Armoured Regiment, the whole of the divisional artillery, one self-propelled battery and one medium battery Royal Artillery. With a squadron of the 6th Lancers on the right flank, pushing forward across gently rising ground, broken by ridges and small valleys, which for the most part were covered by vineyards of root crops, the Mahrattas had, by 1300 hours on 12 September, reached without great difficulty Pt. 632 and Pt. 533, three miles north of the river. Both these positions, strongly entrenched and surrounded by wire, had been abandoned by the Germans. No further advance was made that day after it was discovered that the Germans were holding in strength M. Veruca and M. Citerna—the bastions of the Gothic Line. The 8th Indian Division had closed up to the Gothic Line and prepared to launch an attack on it.

CHAPTER XXI

Capture of Femmina Morta

Second Phase of the Fifth Army's Offensive

Having closed up to the Gothic Line, the Fifth Army began its next offensive on 13 September. The role of the II U.S. Corps, which was to lead the attack, was to break through the Gothic Line at Il Giogo Pass, seven miles to the south-east of the formidable Futa Pass, and push on towards Firenzuola, thus outflanking the Futa Pass defences. The corps attack was made with two divisions—the 88th U.S. Division securing the features guarding the eastern approaches and the 91st U.S. Division seizing the features protecting the western approaches to Il Giogo Pass. It was a splendid achievement, for within an incredibly short time (13—18 September) the II U.S. Corps had gained control of a seven-mile stretch of the Gothic Line on each side of the Il Giogo Pass. The 85th and 91st U.S. Divisions now pushed on the pursuit, the former directed against Firenzuola and the latter against Futa Pass. By capturing Firenzuola on 21 September, the Futa Pass was outflanked and was gained the next day. By 22 September the Gothic Line had been breached at two strong-points, i.e. Il Giogo Pass and the Futa Pass, and the stage was now set for the advance towards Bologna.

The role of the XIII Corps was to throw its weight along the Marradi road to Faenza to assist the II U.S. Corps and to protect its right flank. The Corps plan was for the 1st Division, on the left, to seize Casaglia Pass in order to debouch into the Po Valley; the 8th Indian Division, in the centre, to operate through mountains north of Vicchio (to assist the 1st Division by outflanking German forces astride the Marradi-Faenza road); the 6th British Armoured Division, on the right, to attack astride Route 67, with its main effort on the left to assist the 8th Indian Division. The success of this plan was dependent on the success of the 8th Indian Division in advancing through mountains in the central sector and getting in behind the German forces opposite the 1st Division.[1]

On the left, the advance of the 1st Division was slowed down due to extensive demolitions and heavy counter-attacks. Nevertheless, the progress continued north and north-east from Borgo S. Lorenzo. M. La Faggetta, the dominant hill overlooking Casaglia Pass, was captured on 21 September and the advance was

---

[1] *Fifth Army History*, part VII, p. 74.

continued through the mountains on each side of the gorge through which the river Lamone flowed north-east to the Po Valley.

In the centre, the 8th Indian Division carried out a flanking operation to secure the Femmina Morta feature, south-east of the Casaglia Pass, in order to advance north behind the pass to attack the Germans from the rear. M. Veruca, M. Stelleto and Alpe di Vitigliano guarded the approaches to that feature. The 21st Indian Infantry Brigade led the attack and captured M. Veruca on 13 September and Alpe di Vitigliano on 15 September. The 17th Indian Infantry Brigade occupied M. Stelleto on 16 September and the Femmina Morta feature on 18 September. The 19th Indian Infantry Brigade was then committed on the right. It reached M. Giogo di Villora, to the north of M. Peschiena, on 19 September. The German withdrawal on 20 September which had enabled the 1st Division to enter Casaglia Pass without opposition, helped the 8th Indian Division to advance to the north-east to its zone.

On the right, the 6th British Armoured Division, which had reached Dicomano on 10 September, began clearing Route 67 with the main object of seizing M. Peschiena in order to assist the advance of the 8th Indian Division. Patrols reached San Godenzo Pass on 14 September and M. Peschiena was captured on 18 September.

The IV U.S. Corps occupied the sea port of Viareggio on 15 September. The Germans then retired towards the western anchor of the Gothic Line below La Spezia.

Thus by 22 September the Fifth Army had breached the Gothic Line. The II U.S. Corps and the British XIII Corps had broken through the Gothic Line on a front of 30 miles from Vernio to San Godenzo Pass and the IV U.S. Corps had breached the line at several points.

The Gothic Line Facing the 8th Indian Division

By 12 September the 8th Indian Division had closed up to the Gothic Line. Its task now was to seize the three features, Femmina Morta, Le Scalette and Alpe di Vitigliano, which dominated Arrow route from the east, thereby assisting the progress of the 1st Division, which was advancing along this very important supply route and line of communication. These three features were the bastions of the Gothic Line facing the 8th Indian Division.

The Gothic Line was a formidable barrier in the path of the Allies. In some parts of the line, concrete casements and anti-tank ditches were constructed. Everywhere intricate trench systems were dug, carefully riveted with brushwood, and provided with elaborate bunkers, complete with sleeping apartments hidden deep underground. Trees were cut down to afford better fields of fire, telephone

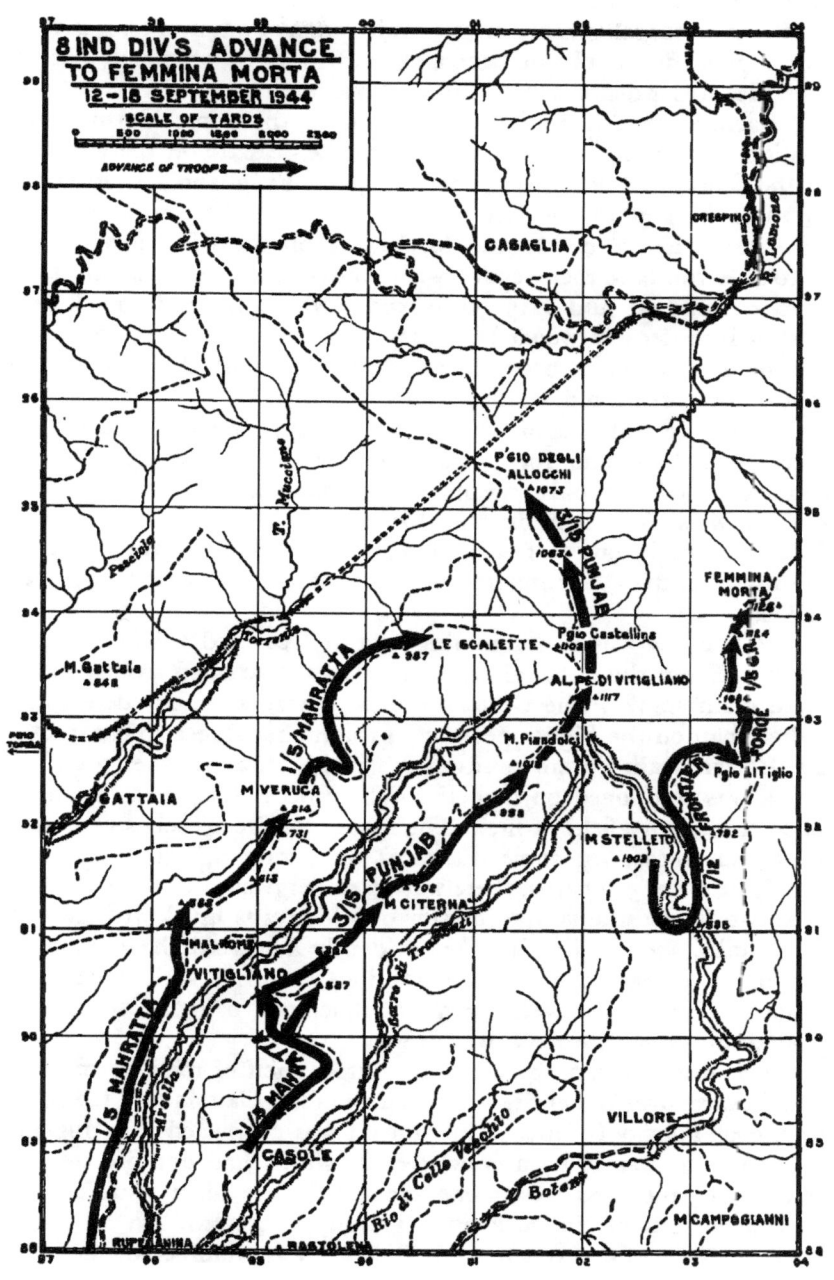

wires from battalion headquarters to company headquarters and from there to forward platoons were all laid and carefully labelled, positions were well stocked with a wide range of ammunition, including a plentiful supply of bazookas, and in front of many platoon localities was a dense belt of wire at least ten yards wide.

Facing the 8th Indian Division were the three Gothic Line bastions—Femmina Morta on the right, Le Scalette on the left and, in the centre and dominating both, Alpe di Vitigliano. Leading up to these hills were the lesser spurs of M. Stelleto on the right, M. Citerna in the centre and M. Veruca on the left. From these buttresses ran bare rocky spurs, with 'knife-edge' crests, seldom more than a hundred and fifty yards wide, whose sides dropped very steeply into densely wooded valleys. Generally speaking, the spurs ran in a south-west to north-east direction, until they eventually joined the three main features.

Roads in this region were non-existent. Such footpaths as there were, hard and rocky, no more than three feet wide at the best, provided the only means of communications. For the 8th Indian Division to fight its way forward in such wild country was difficult enough, but to feed and maintain itself constituted one of the most complex administrative problems the formation had ever tackled.

M. Veruca was a dominating feature,[2] covered thickly by tall spruce. From the outward fringe its slopes descended steeply on to three main spurs. The German defences were sited on these spurs rather than on the higher peak. On the higher slopes commanding the Gattaia valley were positioned wired-in fire trenches, each of which was positioned on a shelf. Where necessary, trees had been felled to improve field of fire. The system of fire trenches extended to the south-east for some distance, and along this line, approximately at every 500 yards, there was an underground dug-out with at least two fire positions, the interior of which was fitted with two to four bunks, shelves, benches etc., evidently a sub-unit headquarters. The entire 500-yard front of these positions was wired with concertina, sometimes in three levels, each entanglement being close to the ground and about fourteen feet deep.

A 75-mm anti-tank gun was dug into a shelf of rock, permitting a field of fire over the entire valley surrounding Gattaia and the high ground of Poggio Tomba. The gun pit was connected to a dug-out in the mountain-side by a crawl trench, which had one fire trench. Behind the gun, and west along the shelf, were three ammunition bays, hewn out of the rock and carefully concealed. In all these defences, each fire trench and dugout was numbered, and at

---

[2] Report on Gothic Line positions area. M. Veruca and M. Citerna; Appx. "A" to 8 Ind. Div. Intelligence Summary No. 152; War Diary 8 Ind. Div., September 1944.

footpath junctions sign-posts were erected, even including a first aid post direction sign.

On the outer fringe of the spruce surrounding M. Veruca was an observation post, constructed with heavy timber, allowing full vision of the valleys as far as the river Sieve and all its approaches north. Near it was a dug-out, which could be used as a command post. The eastern spur of M. Veruca was a sharp incline, Pt. 814 being the peak. The forward slopes of this feature ascended in a series of flat and fairly open terraces. In the area of Pt. 731 there were three fire trenches. Two of these were on the western slopes and the third was on the eastern slope. There were two mortar positions, situated in the side of the cliff, a crawl trench joining each one and leading to a dug-out about 50 feet from the mortar site.

M. Citerna (Pt. 775) was the culmination of a series of pointed heights, starting at Pt. 587 and successively increasing north-east. The first defended locality of this feature was the high ground on the lower point of the spur, Pt. 587. The German installations in this area, presumably a platoon position, were a very good illustration of the enfilade fire positions on a small scale, which was so characteristic of the defensive strong-points of the Gothic Line in this area. A feature of special significance was the telephone line communicating with the headquarters dug-out constructed in the rock formation of the reverse slope. Communication trenches also linked the forward localities and each was wired in, the wire extending to the rear of the hill feature to protect the small bastion from being outflanked. Cross fire covered the immediate front and flanks, which here again were incorporated into the fire from flanking positions. Trees had been felled to improve the field of fire, which left a long sloping approach, with no cover for advancing troops. A well concealed observation post was situated in the centre of the feature at its highest point, besides which was a large shady tree for cover and to ensure the safety of the occupants was a deep hole complete with step ladder.

The next defences were on the forward slopes of Pt. 702, consisting of approximately twenty fire trenches. The positions on the eastern slopes completely covered the Boro di Tramonti Valley and the reverse slopes of feature Pt. 587, while those on the west commanded the Aresella valley. These installations were all protected by two rows of wire, low to the ground and about fourteen feet deep on the steep slopes below.

In these hills, opposite the 8th Indian Division, the *715th Infantry Division* was responsible for a large sector from including S. Godenzo road to including the Borgo S. Lorenzo—Casaglia road. *725th Grenadier Regiment* was in the centre holding the sector between the Villore and Gattaia. *II Battalion* of this regiment was disposed to the east and *I Battalion* to the west; the boundary between them appeared to be in the area of M. Veruca. It was this regiment which opposed the advance of the 8th Indian Division.

Capture of M. Citerna

Major-General Russell's plan to secure the high ground in the area of Femmina Morta—Le Scalette was for the 21st Indian Infantry Brigade to attack M. Veruca and when its operations showed good promise of success, to move the 17th Indian Infantry Brigade from the area Vicchio up on the right, keeping the 19th Indian Infantry Brigade in reserve in the area Cavanella.[3]

Brigadier Mould decided to assault with his two Indian battalions, holding the 5th Royal West Kent Regiment in reserve at Casole. Briefly his plan was for 1/5 Mahratta to seize the high ground at Pt. 632 and Pt. 583, after which 3/15 Punjab would pass through on the right directed on M. Citerna, thus allowing 1/5 Mahratta to launch an attack on M. Veruca. The 6th Lancers was to work on the flanks and maintain contact with the 6th British Armoured Division and the 1st Division. D Company (Medium Machine Gun) 5th Royal Mahratta and 13th Mahratta Anti-Tank Battery were under command while the 14th Canadian Armoured Regiment, A Company (Mortars) 5th Royal Mahratta and the 98th Field Regiment (less one battery) were in support of the brigade.

1/5 Mahratta, supported by divisional artillery and one squadron of the 14th Canadian Armoured Regiment, crossed the river Sieve in the area Vicchio at first light on 12 September. C and D, the forward companies, moved up to Rupecanina and Casole respectively. C Company advanced to attack Pt. 583, which was captured without opposition. Then it established itself at Pt. 583, with company headquarters and one platoon at Malnome. The Germans shelled the company positions, causing six casualties. By 1300 hours, however, C Company had consolidated Pt. 583. Meanwhile D Company was established at Pt. 587. Having secured Pt. 583 and Pt. 587, the Mahratta pushed on at 1500 hours, with Y Company directed on M. Veruca and D Company on M. Citerna. Y Company's advance was checked when several spandaus opened up from concealed dug-outs in Pt. 613. The company was withdrawn under a smoke-screen. D Company's patrol to M. Citerna was also subjected to spandau fire and withdrew. Thus 1/5 Mahratta encountered considerable opposition in the advance towards both M. Veruca and M. Citerna.

In its initial stage, therefore, the 21st Indian Infantry Brigade plan had to be slightly modified. When 1/5 Mahratta was held up below M. Citerna, 3/15 Punjab was ordered to pass through in the

[3] 8 Ind. Div. O.O. No. 31, 12 September 1944.

evening. At last light on 12 September, 3/15 Punjab advanced through the forward elements of 1/5 Mahratta for the attack on M. Citerna. Owing to the darkness of the night and the difficult nature of the country, progress was slow. The battalion pushed steadily on towards Pt. 632, which was captured by 0400 hours on 13 September against moderate opposition. Forward elements infiltrated towards M. Citerna by 0530 hours; while the rest of the battalion pushed on at 0630 hours, supported by artillery concentrations on the flanking features. The leading company, scaling an almost vertical cliff, cut its way through the wire to get to grips with the Germans. Twice the men were brought to a halt by intense machine gun fire, but driving forward in a magnificent effort, they captured M. Citerna soon after first light. The Germans were considerably shaken by the impetus of the assault and many of them retired before 3/15 Punjab could come to close quarters.

After the capture of M. Citerna, 3/15 Punjab pushed on towards Alpe di Vitigliano, fighting its way, all through. At 0815 hours on 13 September, when Pt. 932, half way between M. Citerna and Alpe di Vitigliano, was reached, the commander of 3/15 Punjab ordered a short rest, for his men had been fighting all night, carrying their accoutrements and ammunition, and had climbed a thousand feet since dawn. Towards midday, 3/15 Punjab moved on again, climbing always along the back of the spur. At 1345 hours Pt. 1015 was stormed and captured where two platoons of Germans were routed. They retired in disorder north-east towards the Alpe di Vitigliano. It was then that the leading companies of 3/15 Punjab were halted by concentrated mortar and machine gun cross fire directed from M. Stelleto and Le Scalette on the exposed, knife-edge ridge. It was plain that movement on the ridge was not possible by day until the flanking features had been captured. 3/15 Punjab, therefore, dug in below the Alpe di Vitigliano and awaited darkness. As it grew dark, an artillery observation post with one of the forward companies, spotted about eighty German reinforcements heading for Alpe di Vitigliano. The forward observation officer quickly passed back the details of an excellent target, and within a few minutes the shells of two field regiments burst on the Germans, causing heavy casualties.

Capture of M. Veruca

Meanwhile, at 1530 hours on 13 September, 1/5 Mahratta also, on the left, had attacked towards M. Veruca. The first objective was Pt. 814, just below M. Veruca. This feature was crowned by a ring of pine trees which, from a distance, looked like a beret worn at an angle. A Company captured the strong-point after putting in an attack which was a model of company and platoon tactics and of artillery co-operation. When told that his company was to put in the attack, the company commander crawled forward to reconnoitre the ground, soon spotting German positions, which were given away by patches of brown, where the green camouflage had withered. Having pin-pointed these positions, he returned and laid on an elaborate artillery fire plan, which included a concentration on the known German positions and a smoke-screen to blind the Germans on M. Veruca. Owing to the nature of the country it was impossible to deploy more than two sections of infantry at a time. Therefore the company commander ordered his first platoon to attack and capture an area known as 'Bare Patch', three quarters of the way to Pt. 814, where five German machine guns had been located. Whilst the first objective was being cleared, the second platoon, followed by the third platoon, was to pass through to the top of Pt. 814. The artillery plan included a two minute concentration on 'Bare Patch', followed by a forty minute programme, including smoke to protect the open flanks. Four Field Regiments, two Medium Regiments, one self-propelled gun and a squadron of Canadian tanks were to support this attack.

The leading platoon crossed the start line at 1620 hours. Shells obscured 'Bare Patch' but, although the Germans were shaken, they had no casualties from artillery fire, and opened up on the Mahratta with one machine gun. The Canadian tanks did excellent work with their close fire support; on a system of pre-arranged signals, the Canadians shelled the Germans until the Indian infantry was only fifteen yards short of the positions. Then the Mahratta sections were on top of the Germans almost with the last shells killing four and taking fifteen prisoners.

The second platoon passed through the first as planned, only to be held up by two machine guns beyond 'Bare Patch'. For three minutes the Canadian tanks engaged the Germans, but ineffectively, as the German machine guns were in a defiladed position, which the tank fire could not reach. But a Naik of the Mahratta platoon ran towards the posts and, scaling some rocks, knocked out the crew of both the posts with grenades. One German was killed and another surrendered.

The third platoon followed the second to the top of Pt. 814, swung right and forced the Germans out of their well-prepared positions. The Mahratta platoon and the German company headquarters had a fierce fire fight at two hundred yards range, until British artillery scored a direct hit on the house occupied by the German headquarters and put an end to the forty-five minute struggle for Pt. 814. German prisoners afterwards admitted that they had not expected an attack from this quarter over such difficult country.

After the capture of Pt. 814, M. Veruca, was immediately

threatened. When a Mahratta fighting patrol climbed its steep slopes after dusk, the men encountered only slight opposition. C Company, which attacked the feature later that night, seized M. Veruca with ease and watched about fifty Germans scamper off along the ridge to the south.

Capture of Alpe di Vitigliano

From M. Veruca, 1/5 Mahratta was able to push forward on 14 September, with less difficulty and in the face of only scattered German resistance. At 0840 hours on 15 September, the battalion passed through Pt. 987 without opposition and continued the advance towards Le Scalette, which was occupied by 1200 hours. The left hand bastion of the Gothic Line on the front of the 8th Indian Division was thus captured.

Meanwhile 3/15 Punjab had dug in on the open slopes of Pt. 1015, below Alpe di Vitigliano, on the evening of 13 September, but it had been harassed intermittently by German mortar and shell fire. The battalion had rested in its positions on 14 September, planning to attack Alpe di Vitigliano that night. After an artillery preparation, 3/15 Punjab moved forward from Pt. 1015 at 2230 hours but ran into artillery and mortar fire, which slowed down its advance. However, by midnight, it had captured M. Piandolo, just below the main objective, after slight opposition. At 0100 hours on 15 September, 3/15 Punjab advanced towards the summit of Alpe di Vitigliano, the difficult nature of the ground allowing only one company to operate forward at a time. Advancing in open formation, just after 0400 hours, the leading platoon came under very brisk machine gun fire from positions, one hundred yards below the summit. For a while, 3/15 Punjab was checked by the German fire. Then, charging up the hillside in the pitch darkness the battalion overran the German machine gunners, killing or taking them prisoners, and by 0640 hours on 15 September had consolidated on Alpe di Vitigliano. Thus the second bastion of the Gothic Line was also captured. From here one could see Crespino and the winding valley road far beyond.

Capture of Femmina Morta

Two bastions of the Gothic line had fallen to the onslaught of the 8th Indian Division; a third remained—Fammina Morta, a prominent feature, by capturing which the 8th Indian Division might dominate the Marradi road at Crespino, and thereby render useless any further defence of Casaglia Pass, the objective of the 1st Division. On 15 September, Major-General Russell ordered the 17th Indian Infantry Brigade, which was concentrated in the area north of Rastolena with forward elements at M. Stelleto, to capture

Femmina Morta. The commander of the 17th Indian Infantry Brigade planned to attack Femmina Morta by first securing Poggio al Tiglio, a feature midway between M. Stelleto and Femmina Morta. On 16 September a reconnaissance patrol of 1/5 Gurkha from the area Alpe di Vitigliano was to probe into German positions at Poggio al Tiglio. On the next day, tactical headquarters and two companies of 1/5 Gurkha were to move to M. Piandolci and attack and capture the Poggio al Tiglio feature in the night of 17/18 September. Thereafter when the mule track to the east of M. Stelleto up to Pt. 883 and Tiglio had been developed, the Gurkhas were to attack and capture the Femmina Morta feature. They were then to raid in the area Crespino. Meanwhile, 1/12 Frontier Force Regiment at M. Stelleto was to patrol north-east to find a way across Fosso Botena Secca and reconnoitre German positions on Poggio al Tiglio.

On 15 September, B Company 1/12 Frontier Force Regiment was at M. Stelleto, while the other companies were on the southern slopes of that feature. Next day at 0900 hours C Company sent a reconnaissance patrol, via. Pt. 595 and Pt. 792 to probe into German defences on Poggio al Tiglio. When it reached Pt. 969 the patrol was fired on from Poggio al Tiglio, which was found to be held in strength. The only approach to this feature seemed to be along the ridge through the 3/15 Punjab positions on Alpe di Vitigliano. Elsewhere there was a sheer precipice. Eventually a way was found, apparently unguarded, which led up the precipice. At 1400 hours on 16 September, a fighting patrol of 1/5 Gurkha from the area M. Piandolci followed the easier route and reached the crest of the Tiglio feature without making contact with the Germans. Thereupon, the brigade commander ordered 1/12 Frontier Force Regiment to occupy Poggio al Tiglio at once. 1/12 Frontier Force Regiment followed the difficult route up the precipice. The battalion commander ordered C Company, followed by A Company, to advance via the western slopes of M. Stelleto and swing east to Poggio al Tiglio. The advance began at 1615 hours. As C Company neared the Tiglio feature it found that contrary to the report of the patrol of 1/5 Gurkha it was held by the Germans in strength. But the speed and surprise of the attack, in addition to the previous artillery softening, demoralised the Germans and the feature was secured without suffering any casualties. Three Germans who were guarding an advanced post were captured. The remainder, approximately one company, fled in great confusion, and were subjected to light machine gun and artillery fire. By 2006 hours A Company was in position on the left of C Company. Both the companies consolidated their positions at Tiglio.

At 1100 hours British artillery heavily shelled Femmina Morta feature and Pt. 1051. But well placed German machine guns and mortars in thick bushes made impossible any further progress on 16 and 17 September towards Pt. 1084, another narrow feature on the only route to Femmina Morta from Poggio al Tiglio. This feature was held by one section of the Germans. So the battalion plan was for A Company to attack Pt. 1084 with artillery support and then for 1/5 Gurkha to pass through to Femmina Morta.

In the meantime, 3/15 Punjab (the 21st Indian Infantry Brigade) on Alpe di Vitigliano (0293) had been trying to outflank Femmina Morta from the west. The Germans, however, took the initiative, for at 1800 hours on 15 September two German companies made a counter-attack on 3/15 Punjab at Alpe di Vitigliano and Castellina. The counter-attack formed up in the area Poggio al Tiglio and was dispersed by artillery fire. Simultaneously a large number of Germans approached the Punjab positions from the north and the east. Only one platoon came to close range and withdrew after suffering two casualties. The only high ground still in German hands was Pt. 1063 and Pt. 1073, both features north west of Alpe di Vitigliano. Before the battalion could feel reasonably secure, these positions had to be taken. A daylight patrol on 17 September reported a large German dug-out surrounded by slit trenches on Pt. 1063, which was engaged by heavy artillery. At 1755 hours 3/15 Punjab went into action and took the feature by 1825 hours, suffering two casualties. The advance continued and at 0130 hours on 18 September Pt. 1073 was captured. A German counter-attack to recover the ground was smashed by artillery fire. Thus 3/15 Punjab occupied on 18 September positions north-west of Alpe di Vitigliano, outflanking Femmina Morta from the west and making the German position there precarious. 3/15 Punjab then held the peak of Poggis degli Allocchi, which directly overlooked the Marradi road a mile to the north.

Meanwhile at 0530 hours on 18 September, two platoons of 1/12 Frontier Force Regiment, with artillery support, attacked Pt. 1084 and captured it against slight opposition. Six Germans were taken prisoners, while the remainder retired to Femmina Morta. Thus 1/12 Frontier Force Regiment secured the start line, which 1/5 Gurkha had been promised for its assault on Femmina Morta.

Whilst these preliminaries were in progress on the northern slopes of Tiglio, 1/5 Gurkha had been assembling behind the feature, making ready for the assault on Femmina Morta.

Throughout the previous day, the divisional artillery and medium guns had laid a very heavy programme of fire to pulp the German defences. At 1200 hours on 18 September, the gunners began their pre-arranged artillery programme. It was overwhelming and most accurate. Simultaneously, 1/5 Gurkha advanced, covered by a smoke-screen, over the rocky surface of the gradually rising ground to grapple with the German defences ahead. For two hours and forty-five minutes the Gurkhas fought and toiled, undaunted by either shell or mortar fire, always advancing slowly yet doggedly. Towards the end, opposition began to fade away. But still Bren guns chattered incessantly, now here now there, as their crews dashed forward from position to position. Above the whine of shells and the dull crump of mortars, the Gurkhas heard the sound of German spandaus. A very effective artillery support, however, helped the Gurkhas to capture Femmina Morta. At 1300 hours D Company leading the attack captured Pt. 1124. C Company then passed through D Company and captured Pt. 1126 at 1400 hours. A Company then passed through the two forward companies and at 1445 hours occupied the most northerly height of the feature.

Achievements of the 8th Indian Division

The capture of Femmina Morta by 1/5 Gurkha was considerably assisted by 3/15 Punjab occupying positions north-west of Alpe di Vitigliano, thus outflanking Femmina Morta from the rest. Although the Germans on Femmina Morta had many machine guns to stem the Gurkha advance, they lost heart when faced with the flank threat of 3/15 Punjab. By 18 September, the 8th Indian Division had smashed right through the Gothic Line. In seven days, it had captured a great quantity of stores, ammunition and valuable equipment. It also inflicted heavy casualties on the Germans. But above all, by battling its way through mountainous country, where every advantage of combat lay with the Germans, the division had made an important contribution to the final success of the corps plan.

CHAPTER XXII

Capture of M. Della Modina

Regrouping of the 10th Indian Division

Having narrated the part played by the 4th Indian Division and the 43rd Indian Infantry Brigade in breaking through the Gothic Line, we may now give a brief account of the advance of the 10th Indian Division in the X Corps sector to complete the story of the achievements of the Indian formations of the Eighth Army in storming the Gothic Line defences.

We have already described in a previous chapter how by 9 August 1944, the 20th Indian Infantry Brigade, the forward brigade of the 10th Indian Division, had been checked on Alpe di Catenaia by a fierce German counter-attack on Il Castello. Similarly, the 11th Indian Infantry Brigade, the forward brigade of the 4th Indian Division, had been checked at Poggio del Grillo. As the 4th Indian Division received its call for the Adriatic sector to take part in the V Corps attack on the Gothic Line, the 10th Indian Division took over from the 4th Indian Division on 10 August, thus practically inheriting the complete breadth of the X Corps front on which, previously, two divisions and an armoured task force had been deployed. Reinforcements arrived with the coming in of 4/11 Sikh and Lovat Scouts. In addition, the 4th Indian Division left behind 1 Essex to help in the task. The 10th Indian Division had a holding role; it was to maintain pressure and advance to the Gothic Line by keeping touch with the retreating Germans.

The 10th Indian Division regrouped on 14 August 1944. The wide front was divided into five sectors—on the right was the 25th Indian Infantry Brigade, with its front extending from Anghiari to the stream Rio Cerfone; to its left was the 20th Indian Infantry Brigade in the area M. Alpe di Catenaia; Centre Force[1] was in the area Falciano; to its left was the 10th Indian Infantry Brigade in the area Poggio del Grillo; still further to the left was the Skinner's Horse. The 12 Lancers operated on the right of the 10th Indian Division. Further regrouping was carried out from 15 to 20 August when the 25th Indian Infantry Brigade took over from the 20th Indian Infantry Brigade and assumed control over the sector held by Centre Force. On completion of reliefs, the three sectors of the

---

[1] When the 10 Ind. Div. extended its front to include the 4 Ind. Div.'s sector a new force was formed known as 'Centre Force'. The 1st King's Own Royal Regiment and 3/18 R. Garh. Rif. formed part of this force.

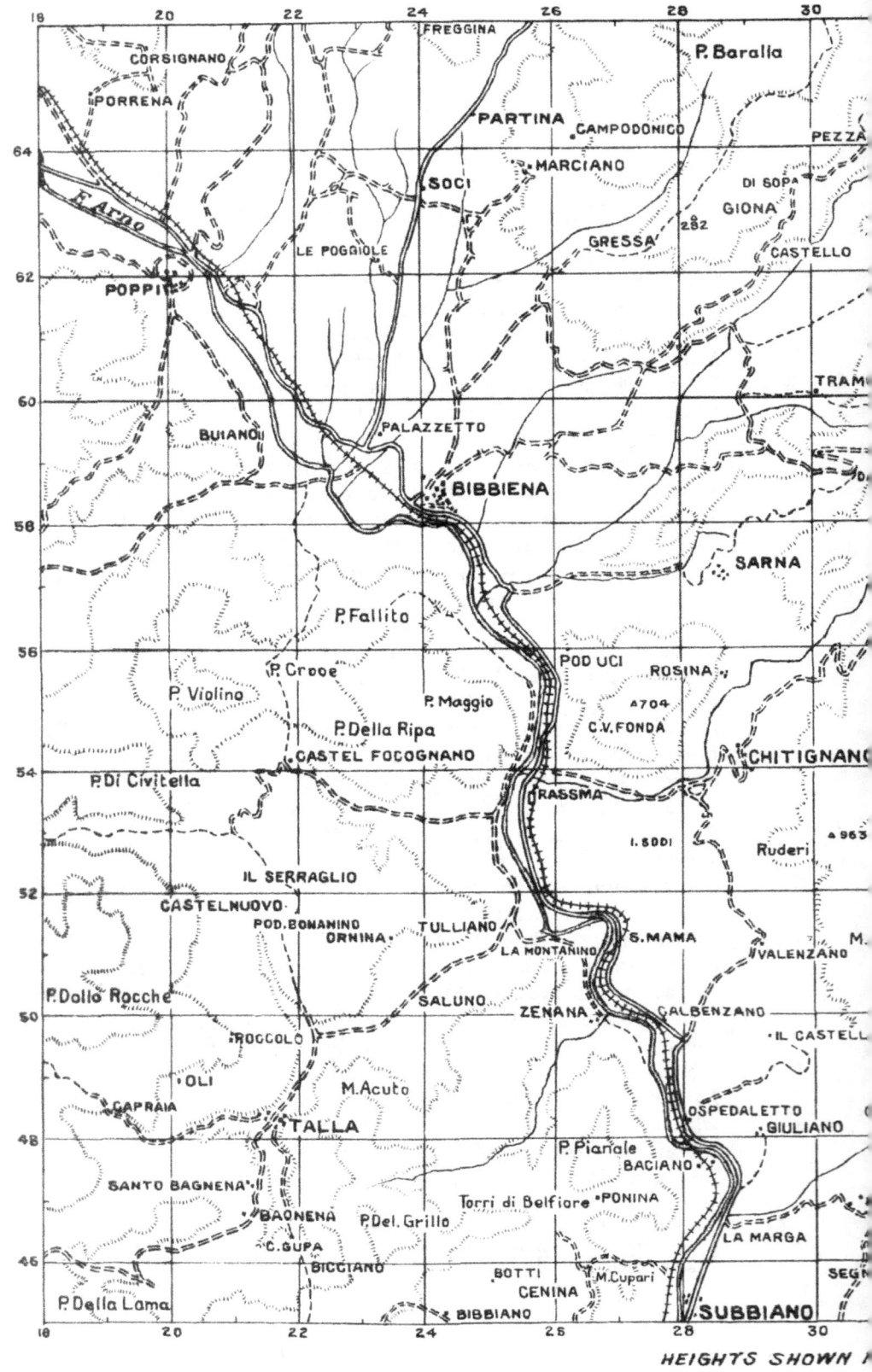

front were held by the 25th Indian Infantry Brigade on the right, the 10th Indian Infantry Brigade in the centre and the Skinner's Horse on the left. The 20th Indian Infantry Brigade was in reserve.[2] The lack of weight behind this extended front precluded major offensive operations and inaugurated a period of gaining ground by a technique of stepping up on to any important feature where a foothold had been gained by infiltrating patrols.

25th Indian Infantry Brigade at Montalone

The brigade held a wide front with 2/3 Gurkha on the extreme right in the area M. Rognose, Lovat Scouts in the area Ponte alla Piera, 3/1 Punjab in the area M. Filetto, 3/18 Garhwal in the area M. Altuccia and the 1st King's Own Royal Regiment in the area Falciano.

As there was no ground suitable for prolonged resistance south of the Bibbiena plain, the Germans had withdrawn to the Brown line, preparatory to falling back on the Gothic Line. The 'Brown Line' comprised the ridge from M. della Verna, M. Faggiolo, M. della Modina, Poggio Castellacio, whence it ran across the Tiber over M. del Faggio, Montalto and M. Verde.[3]

The 25th Indian Infantry Brigade made two main thrusts towards the Brown Line, one directed against M. Della Modina and the other against M. della Verna. We shall first take up the thrust towards M. della Modina. Forward of this main defensive position the Germans held Montalone and M. di Fungaja. 2/3 Gurkha from the area M. Rognose, and Lovat Scouts from the area Ponte alla Piera had been patrolling towards M. di Fungaja. 2/3 Gurkha relieved Lovat Scouts who in their turn were relieved by 3/5 Mahratta on 25 August. The Mahratta battalion succeeded in establishing a platoon on Pt. 680 in the area M. di Fungaja, but on 28 August this platoon was engaged by approximately twenty Germans and forced to withdraw. British artillery then engaged the feature and the platoon recaptured the position.

After the capture of M. di Fungaja, 3/5 Mahratta was relieved on 29 August by 1/2 Punjab whose task was to capture the main German position at M. della Modina. By this time the axis of withdrawal of the German formations opposite the 10th Indian Division had been pretty well established. The *114th Jaeger Division* was on the Badia Tedalda and the Borgo Pace roads, the *44th Infantry Division* on the Pieve S. Stefano—Verghereto road, and the *305th Infantry Division* on the Bibbiena—Bagno di Romana road. M. della Verna was on the boundary between the *44th* and the *305th Infantry Divisions*. The objective of 1/2 Punjab was the

---
[2] 10 Ind. Div. O.I. No. 9, 15 August 1944.
[3] 10 Ind. Div. Intelligence Summary No. 85, 29 August 1944.

Pratelle feature (1176 metres high) and running eastwards for 700 yards, where it gradually ascended higher and formed the M. della Modina feature. The Germans held both these features and had a forward strong-point at Montalone and Pt. 660. On 31 August the three forward companies of 1/2 Punjab prepared to attack Montalone and Pt. 660. At that time A Company was at Pt. 837 and Pt. 876, B Company at Pt. 709 and D Company at Pt. 738. On 1 September a fighting patrol of one platoon from B Company encountered a strong German position at Pt. 660 and withdrew after suffering three casualties. At 0430 hours on 2 September, a platoon from A Company advanced for the attack on Pt. 888, near Montalone. At 0730 hours the platoon arrived at Pt. 888, with one section reconnoitring forward on the western flank; this section, however, came under fire from the north and withdrew to the main feature. The whole platoon was now heavily mortared from Montalone. The platoon commander thereupon decided to attack the German position at Montalone. At 0815 hours the platoon attacked in assault formation down to the eastern side of the feature and came under heavy small arms and mortar fire. Firing from the hip and throwing grenades the platoon pressed home the attack into the village and closed, at the point of the bayonet, killing twenty Germans. Several houses were cleared and then a white flag appeared from the window of a house. Apparently under cover of this flag eight Germans dashed out of the house and fired, but they were quickly killed by the light machine guns. The platoon destroyed several well constructed defensive positions but soon it came under defensive fire and so withdrew to Pt. 888 with sixteen German prisoners. On arrival at Pt. 888 the platoon came under heavy mortar and artillery fire. The Germans were observed approaching up a nullah on the east with the obvious intention of counter-attacking and recovering the prisoners. The platoon commander realising that his strength had been disclosed and knowing that he was unable to call for artillery or mortar support, decided to withdraw to his company base at Pt. 837. At 1045 hours the platoon rejoined its company.

The commander of 1/2 Punjab now planned to clear the Germans from the area Montalone and Pt. 660 during the night of 4/5 September. B Company was to advance from Pt. 709 at 2330 hours on 4 September and make a frontal attack on Pt. 660, while D Company, on the right, was to outflank Pt. 660 by sending a fighting patrol from Pt. 738 to Pt. 642. On the left, Montalone was to be outflanked by C Company sending a fighting patrol from Pt. 837 towards Compito and A Company making a wider hook from Pt. 1072 to Pt. 1207. It was an excellent plan but it was not implemented for the Germans withdrew to M. della Modina leaving

½ Punjab to occupy Montalone and the adjoining features early on 5 September.

Capture of the Pratelle and Modina Features

The stage was now set for the attack on the strong German defensive position at M. della Modina. At 1500 hours on 5 September, C Company sent a platoon to a feature about six hundred yards below the Modina feature to act as a base for B Company which was to attack M. della Modina. At 1700 hours the commanding officer of 1/2 Punjab planned to make a double thrust—C Company to advance from the area Pt. 837 to attack the Pratella feature and B Company to advance from the feature below M. della Modina to attack the Modina feature, and A Company at Pt. 1207 to provide left flank protection. The commanding officer of C Company decided to get down into the nullah below Pt. 837 and keep well under cover until the company had reached the main road, which was nine hundred yards from the objective. The nullah ran almost directly to the objective and the only point where the company could come under direct observation was the main road. He decided, however, to take this risk. One platoon was leading, followed by the Company Tactical Headquarters, then another platoon, and in the rear company headquarters and all the mules. Everything went smoothly until the road was reached when 1/2 Punjab was subjected suddenly to heavy fire from the Pratelle and Modina features. Fortunately one platoon had already crossed the road and was concealed in the nullah. So the German attention was only directed to the rear platoon and headquarters. The commanding officer of C Company therefore decided to take advantage of the forward platoon being concealed in the nullah and to divert the attention of the Germans to the rear platoon and headquarters. He therefore ordered the forward platoon to work its way along the nullah until it got below the Pratelle feature and then to launch the attack. At the same time he ordered the second platoon to get out of the nullah and move along the high ground towards a feature, approximately five hundred yards to the west of the Pratelle feature. This platoon was to give support to the forward platoon in its attack and then join on the Pratelle feature, thus consolidating the main objective. At 1200 hours, when visibility was perfect, one platoon moved swiftly along the high ground to the left while the forward platoon and Tactical Headquarters moved along the nullah. The plan apparently worked well for all German firing was concentrated on the high ground to the left. It was slow going in the nullah but the forward platoon preserved and reached the bottom of the Pratella feature. By this time the other platoon was already in position on the left and was firing on to the Pratelle feature. Then the forward platoon attacked up the feature, an advance of seven hundred yards up the hill. The mountain was covered with thick gorse and unless one could find small paths it was impossible to push through. In spite of these difficulties the platoon reached the top at 2130 hours and was met with heavy small arms fire from every point. The Germans were well dug in, wired and booby trapped. They had also made very deep sangars. In about thirty minutes the platoon accomplished its task of clearing the German machine gun posts. The Pratelle feature was captured but now the platoon was engaged by fire from M. della Modina, and dug in quickly. At approximately 2300 hours, the Germans from M. della Modina swept down on to the Pratelle feature but the counter-attack was repulsed. Then for full one hour the platoon was heavily mortared and shelled. This was followed by another counter-attack, which was also repulsed. Then to the great relief of the forward platoon the second platoon arrived from the feature on the left. Thus strengthened the two platoons repulsed a number of counter-attacks until first light next day when the Germans contented themselves with shelling them every half hour. Fire stopped coming from M. della Modina after B Company had captured this feature at about 0630 hours on 6 September. B Company had encountered strong opposition at 1830 hours on the previous day and had been unable to advance. It was not till 0630 hours on 6 September that opposition was overcome and the Modina feature captured. Having accomplished its task of capturing M. della Modina, 1/2 Punjab was relieved on 8 September by the 1st King's Own Royal Regiment, which took up the pursuit of the Germans.

Capture of M. della Verna

Meanwhile 3/18 Royal Garhwal Rifles was directed against M. della Verna. The first obstacle was M. Foresto, which was held by *II Company (III Battalion) of 132 Grenadier Regiment, 10 Company being on Pt. 866 and 9 Company in reserve.*[4] The Germans had also a forward post at Pt. 1206. 3/18 Garhwal in the area Il Castello was confronted with the problem of clearing the Germans from M. Foresto. The commander 3/18 Garhwal planned to capture and consolidate M. Foresto in three phases:

Phase I	C Company was to advance from Il Castello at 1800 hours on 22 August and capture Coste Centosoldi.
Phase II	B Company was to converge on M. Foresto from two directions. On the left, B Company less two fighting patrols were to advance from Sasso della Regina at 2100 hours on 22 August along the route M. la Caspa—Pt. 947 to the

[4] 10 Ind. Div. Intelligence Summary, 22 August 1944.

west flank of M. Foresto, while two fighting patrols from Il Castello were to advance along the route Pt. 1030—nullah junction to the east flank of, M. Foresto. Converging attacks on M. Foresto were to be made between 0400 hours and 0500 hours on 23 August.

Phase III On the capture of the final objective, B Company was to consolidate and A Company was to move up to M. Foresto and consolidate. D Company, which was in the area of Pt. 687, providing right flank protection, was to move to the area of Pt. 947 with the double task of providing left flank protection and counter-attacking M. Foresto.

The Germans did not offer any serious opposition. At 2300 hours on 22 August, C Company captured and consolidated Costa Centosoldi and at 0600 hours on 23 August B Company did the same with M. Foresto. At 0700 hours on 23 August B Company area was heavily shelled. Intermittent shelling of this area continued for three days. At 2100 hours on 25 August about thirty-five Germans made a counter-attack on B Company's position on M. Foresto but it was broken up by heavy and accurate artillery and medium machine gun fire. Ample signs of casualties inflicted on the Germans were later found on the forward slopes of the feature.[5]

After the capture of M. Foresto, 3/18 Garhwal pushed forward the advance towards M. della Verna. On 28 August a reconnaissance patrol found M. di Chiusi clear of the Germans. Next day a section attempted to draw fire from Chiusi village without success, so one platoon of D Company was put into the houses at 0730 hours and by 2100 hours was stepped up to one company. The Germans did not make any serious attempt to dislodge these troops though they shelled the village intermittently. A feint attack, supported by artillery, by 3/18 Garhwal in La Verna area on the evening of 31 August to induce the Germans to fire and disclose their defensive fire resulted only in the Germans putting down harassing fire on the likely lines of approach. The La Verna feature dominated the whole countryside, was well wooded and steep and had a monastery near the summit, which looked impregnable, but the feature had to be taken, if the advance was to continue. Hence 3/18 Garhwal commenced intensive patrolling. At 2030 hours on 3 September, a fighting patrol to the monastery was fired on by five light machine guns. At 1730 hours on 5 September, however, B Company captured the monastery and consolidated on Pt. 1128. C Company then

[5] Review of Operations since 29 June 1944, War Diary 25 Ind. Inf. Bde., September 1944.

wheeled to the right and captured Pt. 1288 at 2300 hours while on the left A Company captured Pt. 1250 at 2330 hours, thus completing the capture of M. della Verna.

On the left, 3/1 Punjab from the area M. Altuccia gradually increased the depth and duration of individual patrols and established a high reputation for long-range patrolling in the mountains. On 21 August a fighting patrol sent out to gain contact with the defenders on the M. la Caspa ridge was three times attacked by Germans, superior in numbers. But the next day the ridge was found clear of Germans. On 25 August, Chitignano was also found to have been evacuated. On 1 September, 3/1 Punjab moved forward and occupied a new position in the area of Pt. 931, west of Chiusi. However, the Germans were still in position at Ruota. On 3 September a fighting patrol was sent to clear up the suspected German mortar position in the area of Ruota, but it encountered stiff opposition and returned after suffering 6 casualties. Ruota and M. della Verna were held by the Germans in strength. With the capture of M. della Verna by 3/18 Garhwal on 8 September, the German grip on Ruota was loosened and on 8 September the Punjab patrols reported it clear of the Germans.

Pursuit to the Gothic Line

With the cauture of M. della Modina and M. della Verna the Brown Line was smashed. Outflanked and thoroughly beaten, the Germans pulled out northwards into the maze of ravines and towering ridges on which they had constructed the Gothic Line. The 25th Indian Infantry Brigade continued sending out reconnaissance patrols, followed by strong fighting patrols, which remained on their objectives if the Germans were not there in strength, later stepping up to a company; in this way the Germans were gradually forced back to their main positions on the Gothic Line. On the right the 1st King's Own Royal Regiment from the area M. della Modina sent on 10 September a reconnaissance patrol towards P. Vescovi, which met with heavy machine gun fire from Pt. 1170. Next day another patrol of the King's Own Royal Regiment had fire fight with the Germans at Pt. 1170. In the middle sector, 3/18 Garhwal from the area M. della Verna had a standing patrol established at Montesilvestre. This patrol was attacked on 9 September by about forty Germans, who were driven away after an exchange of fire. On the left, 3/1 Punjab from the area Ruota established a standing patrol at Biforco. On 10 September a German counter-attack developed forcing the patrol to withdraw to Ruota area.

Relief of the 25th Indian Infantry Brigade

The 10th Indian Infantry Brigade relieved the 25th Indian

Infantry Brigade, assuming command of the sector at 0600 hours on 13 September. At the same time 1/2 Punjab passed under the command of the 10th Indian Infantry Brigade. Activity was limited to patrolling. Till 17 September when the 10th Indian Division left for the Adriatic Coast no serious opposition was encountered except at Balciano, to the north-east of M. della Modina.

Advance in the Arno Valley

Before taking over from the 25th Indian Infantry Brigade on 13 September, the 10th Indian Infantry Brigade had made good progress in the Arno valley. When the 10th Indian Division assumed command of the 4th Indian Division's sector at 0200 hours on 11 August, the 10th Indian Infantry Brigade was in the Arno valley with 2/4 Gurkha in the area Poggio del Grillo—Ferrato and 1st Battalion Durham Light Infantry in the area S. Martino—Bibbiano. The Germans rapidly withdrew their forces into the Gothic Line. During the night of 11/12 August, the Durham occupied Poggio Pianale and Torri di Belfiore without opposition. On 16 August, 2/4 Gurkha occupied M. Acuto, while a patrol of the Skinner's Horse was established at Talla. The 10th Indian Infantry Brigade regrouped on 19 August—4/10 Baluch on the right in the area Poggio Pianale; the Durham, with two companies of 1/4 Essex under command, in the area M. Acuto; 2/4 Gurkha at Roccolo in the area Talla. The left flank protection was provided by the Skinner's Horse, with under command two squadrons of Lovat Scouts. Lovat Scouts' commitments embraced the denial to the Germans of the Pratomagno observation, as far west as M. Lori and the initial probing of the Gothic Line defences by deep penetration patrolling. The 10th Indian Infantry Brigade gained ground by a technique of stepping up on to any important feature on which a foothold had been gained by infiltrating patrols. By 24 August, 4/10 Baluch was in the area Sodi, the Durham in the area Formiche and 2/4 Gurkha in the area Castelnuovo. On 26 and 27 August, the 10th Indian Infantry Brigade encountered opposition—the forward companies of the Durham at Fallito and Croce were heavily shelled; a patrol of the Durham to Bibbiena found a German platoon guarding the railway station; 4/10 Baluch patrol contacted Germans in some strength at Sarna. The Germans however pulled out and by 29 August patrols of 4/10 Baluch found Sarna clear of the Germans; the Durham patrols to Bibbiena made no contact; 2/4 Gurkha found Buiano also to have been evacuated by the Germans.

The 20th Indian Infantry Brigade now relieved the 10th Indian Infantry Brigade on the Chitignano line, assuming command of the sector at 2100 hours on 30 August. 4/10 Baluch was relieved by 3/5 Mahratta, the Durham by the 8th Manchester and 2/4 Gurkha by

2/3 Gurkha. The 20th Indian Infantry Brigade met with increasingly stiffening resistance in its advance towards the Gothic Line, which ran along the summit of Baralla. On 1 September the 8th Manchester occupied without opposition Gressa and a patrol from 3/5 Mahratta found Dania and Tramoggiano free from German occupation. But soon resistance stiffened. By 4 September, the 20th Indian Infantry Brigade was up against considerable opposition. A Company of 3/5 Mahratta advancing to within three hundred yards south of Pt. 282 was fired upon and compelled to withdraw. A patrol of 3/5 Mahratta to Giona was within 150 yards of its objective when fire was opened on it by four medium machine guns in the houses in the village and one machine gun from Castello. Attempts to get round were frustrated by heavy machine gun and rifle fire. A patrol from the 8th Manchester to Marciano found it occupied by Germans in strength. Patrols were constantly busy in probing the German defences and getting them to reveal their fire plans. A mock attack by the 8th Manchester on Marciano on 4 September revealed the pattern of the German defensive fire there.

For their part, the Germans were intent on keeping the 10th Indian Division at a distance from the Gothic Line. Raids and shelling to deny important features were the normal methods employed. One of those raids failed miserably. It was directed at 0400 hours on 13 September against the Mahratta forward company in the area Gressa ; but the attack was anticipated and preparations had been made to meet it. The plan was to allow the Germans to get in close and then to engage them with all weapons. The ruse worked like a charm in spite of the shelling which preceded the attack. One Mahratta section received the brunt of the attack. It waited until the Germans were within a few yards, then the section commander gave the signal to open fire by shooting the officer leading the raid. In the din which followed every available weapon contributed its share. For a quarter of an hour the struggle lasted. A lull followed. The Germans withdrew, reorganised and mortared their objective and then returned to the attack. This time the other two sections of the platoon had joined in the fight. German casualties were mounting. Two Germans, who made a pretence of surrendering, caused the only Mahratta casualties by throwing grenades at the two sepoys who approached them to accept their surrender. Eventually, the German attack faded away and the retreating remnants were harassed on their way back to Baralla by mortars and artillery.

German opposition was strong enough to prevent any further gains but long range patrols continued to operate well behind their main defences. From the information brought in by these patrols, it became apparent that the Germans manning the defences were not at full strength. Together with the detailed knowledge of the German layout, which was now available, and with the general disinclination to fight which two months of continuous defeats had spread among the German troops, this weakness encouraged the feeling in the 10th Indian Division that a deliberate attack against the Gothic Line had every prospect of success.

Fate had ruled however that such an attack would not be launched by the 10th Indian Division. On the Adriatic coast, the Eighth Army's offensive was well into the German defences. More formations were required to take advantage of the Army's success and the 10th Indian Division was to be one of them.

On 17/18 September, Wheeler Force took over sector from the 20th Indian Infantry Brigade with 29 Easting as the right boundary. The Nabha Akal Infantry was on the right, the 8th Manchester in the centre and the Skinner's Horse and a squadron of the Lovat Scouts on the left. The 10th Indian Infantry Brigade remained on the right sector whilst the Lovat Scouts, less one squadron, moved under command of the King's Dragoon Guards—in the area Mignano. At 0100 hours on 19 September the 10th Indian Division Headquarters closed down operationally and the 10th Indian Infantry Brigade and Wheeler Force came under the command of the X Corps.

THE BATTLE OF THE RIVERS

CHAPTER XXIII

Advance to the River Fiumicino

The Eighth Army's Advance to the River Fiumicino

The new phase of the Italian campaign, which began on 22 September 1944, when the Allied forces broke through the Gothic Line, has been aptly called the Battle of the Rivers, for while the Fifth Army stormed its way through the mountainous region the Eighth Army had to battle its way across a series of rivers. The advance on the Adriatic coast now lay across country intersected with thirteen major rivers and numerous irrigation channels and water-courses, which, swollen by the rains in autumn, considerably slowed down the Allied advance. Armour was bogged down in the mud created by the violent rains on the heavy soil of the reclaimed marsh lands. A contemporary chronicler has aptly described the position thus: "The first flush of enthusiasm, engendered by the magnificent news from France and the hope of an early victory in Italy which our own successes had inspired, began to wane, as behind every ridge captured a second ridge would appear, as if thrown up by some evil genius of the countryside, and for every river crossed, as if from an endless source, another would materialise. For the advance lay across the grain of the country. Rivers and ridges reached down from the mountains first towards the sea, and later towards the broad waters of the Po, but always across our path."[1]

After abandoning the Rimini line on 21 September 1944, the Germans had withdrawn across the river Marecchia. Their main defensive positions were at La Turchia and San Vito di Rimini, near the coast; the high ground south of Santarcangelo di Romagna; and the Scorticata—Montebellow ridge. The general situation on 23 September 1944 was that the *71st and 98th Infantry Divisions* were being pulled out of the line as they had suffered heavy losses. The *100th Mountain Regiment* was also moving out of the line. Eight German formations were however in the line on the Adriatic Coast— the *162nd (Turkoman) Infantry Division*, the *1st Parachute Division*, the *29th Panzer Grenadier Division*, the *26th Panzer Division*, the *20th German Air Force Division*, the *356th Infantry Division*, the *90th Panzer Grenadier Division*, and the *278th Infantry Division*.

---

[1] *The Story of 46 Division 1939-1945*, p. 85; (File 8756/H).

The Eighth Army established bridge-heads over the river Marecchia and launched attacks on the strong German positions. The I Canadian Corps, attacking with the 2nd New Zealand Division on the right and the 5th Canadian Armoured Division on the left, drove the Germans beyond La Turchia on the coast but failed to break through the German defences in the area of San Vito. The 1st British Armoured Division (with the 43rd Indian Infantry Brigade under command) attacked and captured Santarcangelo. The 46th Division and the 4th Indian Division attacked the ridge running south from Poggio Berni to Montebello, the former securing the ridge at Poggio Berni and the latter the crest running from south of Scorticata to Montbello. Thus by 24 September 1944, the Eighth Army had broken through the strong German defences and had closed up to the river Uso.

The Eighth Army continued its advance to the river Fiumicino. The Canadians established a bridge-head over the river Uso, north of San Vito on 25 September, but the advance was halted after they had reached the line of the river Fiumicino, north of San Mauro. The 1st British Armoured Division crossed the river Uso in the region of Route 9 on 25 September. The same day it was relieved by the 56th Division, which continued the advance towards the river Fiumicino but was held up below Savignano on 28 September. The 46th Division expanded the Uso bridge-head at Camerano and captured Canonica and C. Ricci by 27 September. Further advance towards the river Fiumicino was however held up by stiff opposition. The 4th Indian Division crossed the river Uso but failed to capture M. Reggiano. Thus the Eighth Army encountered fierce opposition in its advance towards the river Fiumicino. It continued its efforts to close up to the river Fiumicino and establish bridge-heads over that river. On 29 September, the II Polish Corps relieved the 2nd New Zealand Division in the I Canadian Corps sector. The Canadian Corps could not make any progress due to heavy rain. The 56th Division secured Savignano and the Castelvecchio ridge on 29 September, but failed to establish a bridge-head across the Fiumicino in the Route 9 sector. Meanwhile, the 46th Division secured a ford on the river east of Villa Ribano but could not launch an attack on the strong German position at Montilgallo. Thus both the 46th and the 56th Divisions had failed to cross the river Fiumicino on 30 September/1 October. In the foothills to the south, however, the 4th Indian Division succeeded in capturing M. Reggiano and Borghi on 1 October though the Germans continued to hold the ridge through San Martino. Subsequently, the 10th Indian Division, after relieving the 4th Indian Division on 3 October, put in an attack and captured San Martino on 5 October, thus bringing the left flank of the V Corps up to the river Fiumicino. The stage was now set for the launching of an attack on the German positions across the river Fiumicino.

Capture of the Montebello—Scorticata ridge

Having given a brief account of the Eighth Army's advance to the river Fiumicino we may now describe in greater detail the part played by the Indian formations—the 4th Indian Division and the 43rd Indian Infantry Brigade—in these operations. We shall begin with the progress of the 4th Indian Division, on whose front the Germans had fallen back across the river Merecchia on the Montebello—Scorticata ridge. The *114th Jaegar Division* was fast relieving the *278th Infantry Division*. The advent of the former on the front held by the 4th Indian Division represented an increase in German strength. The troops were fresh and the companies on an average were 60 strong. The division had six battalions organised on a five-company[2] basis. The ridge Scorticata—Montebello was held by the *741st Jaegar Regiment*. One company of *I Battalion* was to the left in the area Jessi and another to the right in the area Mountebello. A third company was in support, while another company with two guns was in the area Ca di Bogio. One company was in reserve and was probably used for counter-attacks. *II Battalion* was on the right while *III Battalion* was in regimental reserve.

On the other side, in the 4th Indian Division, the 5th Indian Infantry Brigade, having accomplished its task of capturing San Marino, surrendered the lead to the 11th Indian Infantry Brigade on 21 September 1944. 2/7 Gurkha concentrated in the area Ca Martino while 3/12 Frontier Force Regiment was in the area M. Cerreto, a height overlooking the road from San Marino north to the river Marecchia. This road wound down to the river along a narrow exposed ridge. To add to the difficulties, the weather became wet and the advance began in the thick blanket of mist and rain. Despite this handicap and extensive mining and demolitions on the way, progress was good. The Germans were withdrawing to the next line north of river Marecchia. On 22 September, patrols from 2/7 Gurkha and 3/12 Frontier Force Regiment reached the river. Their reports were favourable and it was decided to seize the high ground across the river that night. The same day the corps reported that the 1st British Armoured Division and the 46th Division had lost contact with the Germans. During the afternoon, the German artillery tried to interfere with the preparations for a river crossing, and the area occupied by the forward troops was shelled. The 11th Indian Infantry Brigade, however, continued undeterred its preparations for establishing a bridge-head over the river Marecchia.

[2] 4 Ind. Div. Intelligence Summary No. 167, September 1944.

The objective selected was a shaggy fourteen-hundred-feet ridge, standing in a loop of the Marecchia and forming a two-mile wide barrier between that river and the next to the north, the river Uso. At the northern end, which rose sharply to the highest point in the ridge, there were several small hamlets, principal among them being Scorticata. From its northern end, the ridge ran through three lower bumps of about twelve hundred feet to the height of thirteen hundred feet of Montebello, at the southern end. In all, the feature was one and a quarter miles long.

The commander of the 11th Indian Infantry Brigade planned to attack the Montbello—Scorticata ridge at 2300 hours on 22 September; on the right 2/7 Gurkha was to secure Pt. 460 and the high ground south to Pt. 362, and on the left, 3/12 Frontier Force Regiment was to capture Montebello and Cemetry. Preparatory to its attack, 3/12 Frontier Force Regiment was to hold Case Monte. The 2nd Cameron was to be prepared to take over from 3/12 Frontier Force Regiment on M. Ventosa and M. Cerreto. A squadron of the 6th Battalion Royal Tank Regiment was in support of the brigade.[3]

At 2300 hours on 22 September, C and D Companies of 2/7 Gurkha moved, echeloned one behind the other, towards Pt. 362, the second of the bumps south from Pt. 460. The Germans allowed the Gurkhas to advance to close range, then caught them between the fires of posts in the lower slopes (which had remained quiet until the Gurkhas had passed) and of posts on the crest of the hill. In spite of casualties the Gurkhas pressed on the attack. At 0300 hours on 23 September, D Company was in the area of Pt. 427, while C Company had passed through to Pt. 460, but was pulled up short of its objective by murderous fire. When day-light came, both the companies found themselves in a very exposed position. Three counter-attacks in quick succession caused them to exhaust all their ammunition and pushed them back to the river in the area Ca Bigio by 0930 hours. Their total casualties were 29 killed, 68 wounded and 30 missing.

On the southern flank, 3/12 Frontier Force Regiment, also on a one-company front, advanced to Montebello. On the right, B Company advanced at 0045 hours on 23 September from the area M. Cerreto and secured Casone at 0320 hours. Then it pushed on to Gessi and Cemetry, where very stiff opposition was encountered. The company came under heavy fire from three spandaus in the area of the Cemetry. On the left, C Company reached the area west of Montebello, but was heavily mortared, suffering considerable casualties. After an exchange of fire it moved to the area Fagnano. Both the companies were short of ammunition. German fire and a

[3] 11 Ind. Inf. Bde. O.O. No. 10, 22 September 1944.

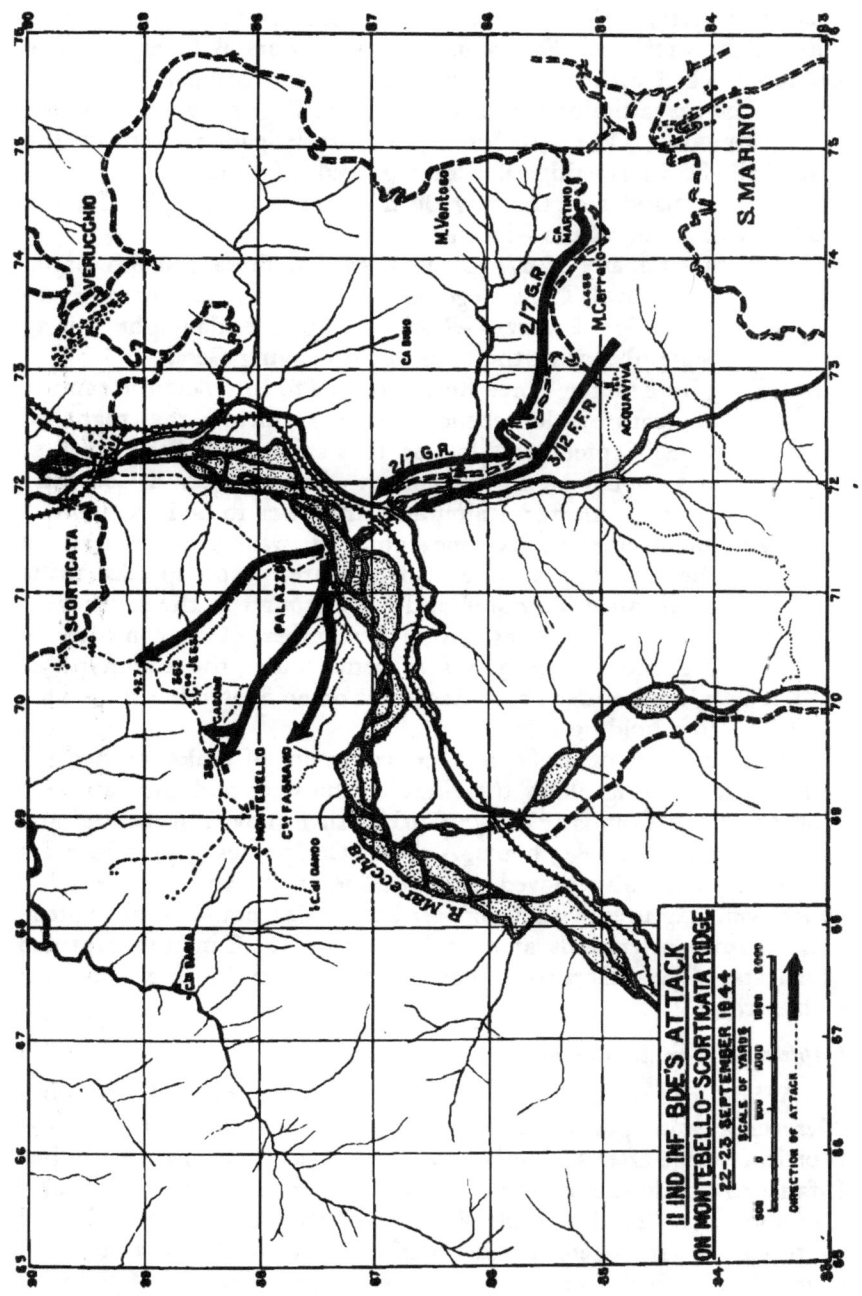

flooded river made it impossible to replenish them and they dug in where they were, B Company in the area near Cemetry and C Company in the area near Fagnano. At 1130 hours B Company was counter-attacked with heavy mortar support and compelled to withdraw. The casualties of 3/12 Frontier Force Regiment were 4 killed and 23 wounded. The 11th Indian Infantry Brigade's attack on the Montebello-Scorticata ridge had thus proved a failure.

The commander of the brigade then made a new plan for the attack on the Montebello—Scorticata ridge:

(i) A company of 2/7 Gurkha, with A Squadron 6th Battalion Royal Tank Regiment in support, was to move up the ridge Palazzo—Gessi during the day-light on 23 September with the object of occupying Gessi.

(ii) 3/12 Frontier Force Regiment was to complete the capture of feature Montebello—Cemetry during the night of 23/24 September. It was to start crossing the river at 1900 hours on 23 September. One platoon B Company (4.2-inch mortar) Rajputana Rifles was to be in support.

(iii) 2nd Cameron, less one company, was to concentrate in the area Acquaviva and be prepared to occupy Scorticata (also called Torriano) and high ground to the south-west, with tank support, on 24 September. One company of the 2nd Cameron was to come under the command of 3/12 Frontier Froce Regiment on 23 September to be used in a holding role.

At 1730 hours on 23 September two troops of tanks reached the area Gessi, shooting along the ridge to the west and the east with good effect. A Company of 2/7 Gurkha then moved up behind and occupied Gessi. At 1845 hours, A and D Companies of 3/12 Frontier Force Regiment also moved against Montebello and the Cemetry, which were captured without opposition at 0645 hours on 24 September. Shortly afterwards at 0700 hours the 2nd Cameron captured Scorticata. The Germans had begun withdrawing on the whole front.

Capture of Santarcangelo

While the 11th Indian Infantry Brigade crossed the river Merecchia and pushed back the Germans from Montebello—Scorticata ridge after stiff resistance on 24 September, the 43rd Indian Infantry Brigade (under the command of the 1st British Armoured Division) established a bridge-head over the river Marecchia and captured Santarcangelo against stiff opposition. This attack was even more hurried than the Marano crossing. The bed of the river Merecchia was a thousand yards wide and contained several streams —an excellent obstacle from the German point of view. One mile

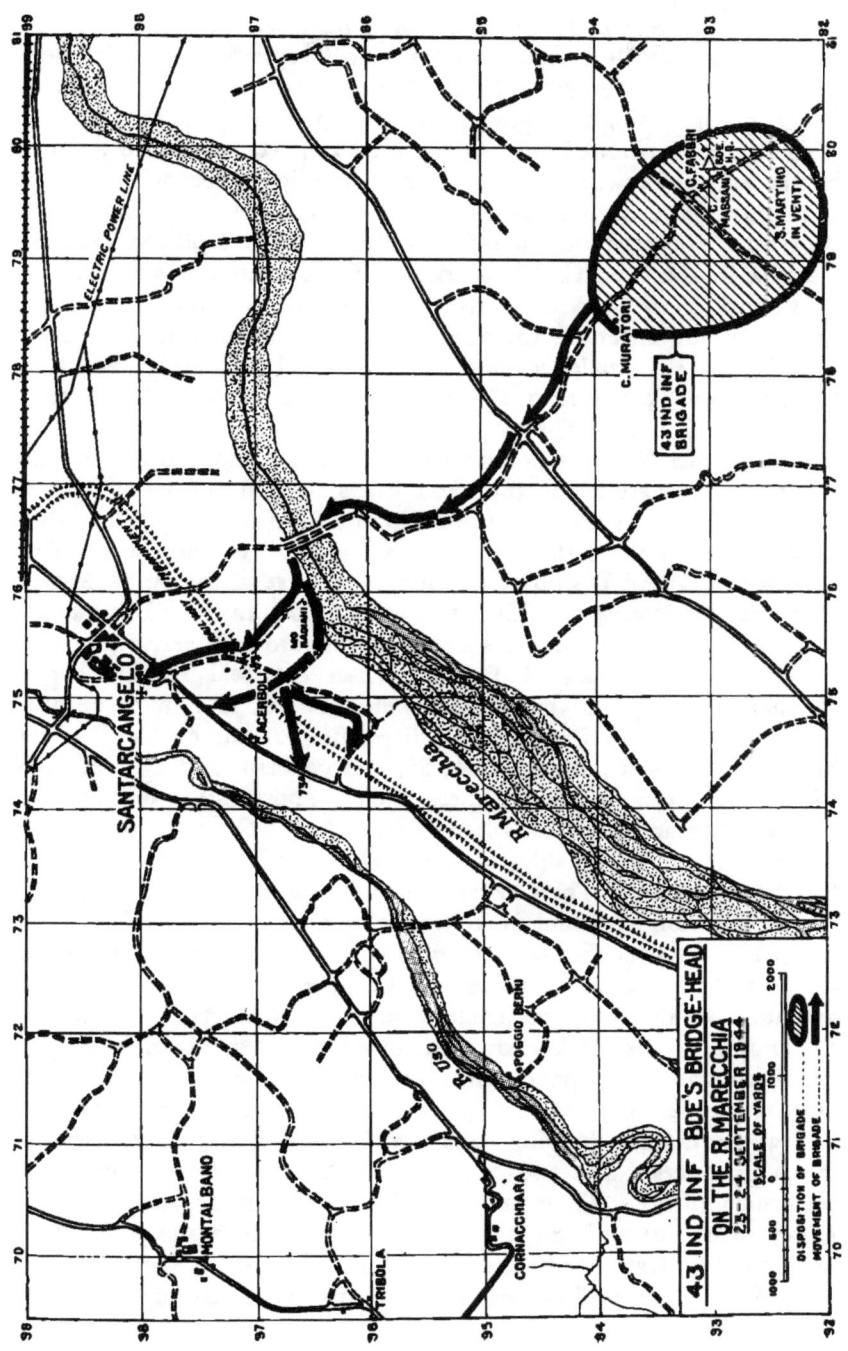

beyond the river, with a three-hundred-foot high ridge in between, was the river Rubicone, or Uso, which provided good positions for the German artillery and mortars. To overcome these defences, before they could be properly organised, called for a speedy attack. Route 9, the Bologna highway, crossing the ridge to its junction with Route 16 near Rimini, gave added importance to the town of Santarcangelo, between the two rivers. Intelligence reports indicated that only scattered rearguards held the ridge. At last light on 22 September the 43rd Indian Infantry Brigade was deployed with 2/6 Gurkha in the area C. Muratori, 2/8 Gurkha in the area west of C. Fabbri, 2/10 Gurkha in the area west of S. Martino and the brigade headquarters in the area C. Masani. 2/10 Gurkha and 2/8 Gurkha were to make a silent attack to gain the ridge south of Santarcangelo, between Pt. 88 and Pt. 73.[4] 2/8 Gurkha, on the right directed against Pt. 88, moved at 0300 hours on 23 September with two companies (A and D) towards its first bound, the railway embankment approximately one thousand yards beyond the river. Up to that line there was not much opposition and at 0430 hours battalion headquarters was established in a house near C. Acerboli. However, when A and D Companies advanced west of the embankment, they met by intense machine gun fire at close range. Despite this opposition, the two companies struggled forward and were established on the eastern slopes of Pt. 88. Then the real trouble began. German self-propelled guns, sited well forward, and machine guns on the flanks, were able to bring direct fire to bear on the Gurkhas holding the eastern slopes of Pt. 88, and concentrated against them with great fury. In the darkness, a clear appreciation of the situation was impracticable, but when dawn came the Germans were found to be in houses on all sides of the Gurkhas and quite close to battalion headquarters. The Germans started mortaring very heavily the whole battalion area and Nebelwerfer were also dropped fairly consistently. At 0600 hours A Company asked for reinforcements as it had suffered heavy casualties. B Company, less one platoon, was sent up from the battalion headquarters near C. Acerboli to reinforce A Company. As B Company advanced along the road leading to Pt. 88 it came under spandau fire from three houses on the left. The first house was attacked, the spandau crew killed, the gun destroyed and 31 Germans belonging to the *20th German Air Force Division* taken prisoners. The two other spandaus in the remaining houses continued to fire. They were also destroyed. B Company suffered heavy casualties and did not arrive on the eastern slopes of Pt. 88 until shortly after 0830 hours. At the same time two Sherman tanks arrived at the battalion headquarters and were sent up to Pt. 88.

---

[4] Sitrep 1 Brit. Armd. Div., 22 September 1944, War Diary 43 Ind. Inf. Bde.

They failed to get right up to the forward troops; however, they knocked out two spandaus which were firing from the neighbourhood of the Cemetry and made a gap in a 10-foot wall surrounding it. The Germans replied by opening fire with armour-piercing shot at close range. Meanwhile, C Company was engaged in mopping up as much of the area around battalion headquarters near C. Acerboli as possible, clearing several spandaus and sniper positions but not without paying heavy cost. Much difficulty was experienced in moving casualties to the Regimental Aid Post as the whole battalion area was being heavily mortared.

At 0900 hours further reinforcements arrived at the battalion headquarters—three Shermans and C Company of 2/6 Gurkha. The latter had been observed by the Germans and en route had been heavily involved, losing 30 men. The battalion was in a critical situation. The tempo of German mortaring and shelling was steadily increasing and the battalion headquarters had been obviously pin-pointed. No vehicles, other than the five Sherman tanks, had got through. Casualties were accumulating at the Regimental Aid Post and it was found impossible to evacuate them. As German batteries, with one exception, were out of range of the artillery, the Royal Air Force was called upon to bomb them. The Germans replied by increasing their artillery fire. Further attempts to reinforce the forward position were given up, for by 1100 hours the situation had deteriorated so much, and shelling was so heavy, that it was obviously unwise to send up more men merely to become casualties, who could not be evacuated. To add to the difficulties, a German tank appeared on the left flank, and after blinding the Shermans with smoke, fired armour-piercing shots through the house destroying the gunners' wireless set. The last wireless link with the forward companies was broken. An artillery smoke-screen, put down to cover the forward companies as they withdrew, fortunately fell away to their northern flank and attracted most of the German fire. The forward companies pulled back to C Company's area near the railway embankment.

At 1445 hours, when German fire had slackened, an attempt was made by C Company to recapture Pt. 88. The Gurkhas occupied the western edge of the ridge but were unable to move further owing to the German fire, which had resumed its intensity. Two companies of 2/6 Gurkha were to advance in support of C Company of 2/8 Gurkha but the commanding officer 2/6 Gurkha found it impracticable to advance on to Pt. 88 until nightfall. C Company however stuck to its position. At nightfall the two companies of 2/6 Gurkha advanced and captured Pt. 88 after stiff resistance. They suffered heavy casualties from shell fire.

2/10 Gurkha too had met the same stern opposition as that

encountered by 2/8 Gurkha. At 0300 hours on 23 September this battalion crossed the start line, the south bank of the river, just west of the blown bridge. The first few hundred yards west of the river and before the ridge began, consisted of orchards and vineyards, in which the trees and vines had been cut down. As the Gurkhas advanced up the ridge, they were subjected to heavy machine gun fire. At 0400 hours battalion headquarters was established in a house near Nadiani while B Company secured its objective—the paper factory nearby. At 0430 hours A Company, operating on the right, secured its objective at 749974 but had to fight hard for it. D Company in the centre, however, heading for Pt. 73 while halfway up the hill, was caught in a hail of fire from houses on the hill side. The chief centre of German opposition was a large mansion. D Company cleared two farms near the mansion but had to put in two attacks before the main strong-point was overcome at 0545 hours. They suffered heavy casualties, both during the attack and from shelling and mortaring after the feature was secured. Soon afterwards, at 0645 hours, a German counter-attack by infantry and fire tanks struck the company. Without anti-tank guns or even the Piats and, in the shallow trenches which the men had scraped, exposed to German machine gun fire and grenades, the company was compelled to fall back from Pt. 73 at 0715 hours. Meanwhile C Company, which had secured its objective at 745962 and was proceeding to bolster up D Company, ran into a German company which was advancing for an attack on the battalion headquarters. C Company was pinned down by heavy fire from another party of Germans well dug-in. The Company was forced to disperse.

Owing to heavy shelling, A Company was forced to evacuate its forward positions at 749974. Thus by 0915 hours the Gurkhas had to retire from the forward positions they had gained. Battalion headquarters had its own immediate worries. Shelling was pitiless and casualties were mounting. The Regimental Aid Post received a direct hit causing serious casualties. The tanks in support, try as they might, could not get across the water barrier, until some hours after the infantry. However, by 1530 hours the tanks did get across the water barrier and gave valuable support to the infantry. The capture of Pt. 88 (on the right flank) by 2/8 Gurkha by nightfall eased the situation considerably. Consequently B Company of 2/10 Gurkha advanced at 0830 hours on 24 September and captured Pt. 73 without opposition at 0910 hours. The Germans had retired, though they continued to shell the area fiercely for some time.

Patrols from 2/6 Gurkha as well had pushed into Santarcangelo during the night of 23/24 September, making no contact with the Germans. These patrols advanced to the river Uso but were unable to cross it owing to heavy machine gun fire. Reinforcements for the brigade had however arrived in the shape of 1st Battalion King's Royal Rifles Corps, which moved up on 25 September to San Martino, on the eastern bank of the river Marecchia. Two standing patrols—one from the 1st King's Royal Rifle Corps and the other from 2/6 Gurkha—were established across the river and two companies of the King's Royal Rifles Corps moved up at 0530 hours on 26 September to strengthen these patrols. A halt was called for the 43rd Indian Infantry Brigade in the afternoon of 26 September, when a brigade of the 56th Division passed through to take up the chase. In continuous rain on 27 September, the Gurkhas trickled back to rest in their echelon areas after having fought like veterans through eleven days of the toughest action. To the great disappointment of all ranks their happy and proud association with the 1st British Armoured Division now ended. For a week nearly, while rain turned the country-side into a sea of mud, small streams into roaring torrents, and brought movement to a standstill, the Gurkhas made their preparations for the next call.[5]

Capture of M. Reggiano

Meanwhile the 4th Indian Division, after establishing a bridgehead over the river Marecchia and securing the Montebello-Scorticata ridge on 24 September, was continuing its advance towards the river Fiumicino. When the 11th Indian Infantry Brigade drove the Germans from the Montebello-Scorticata ridge on 24 September, the 7th Indian Infantry Brigade was brought up on its right to close the gap between the Indian brigade and the British 45th Division. After crossing the river Marecchia, south-east of Scorticata, at 1900 hours on 24 September, the 1st Royal Sussex occupied without opposition Gemniano and Trebbio (at 0700 hours on 25 September), preparatory to the attack on the Reggiano—Tribola ridge, which was strongly held by the Germans. *741st Jaegar Regiment* (the *114th Jaegar Division*), with *II Battalion* on the left, *I Battalion* in the centre and *III Battalion* on the right, stretched from Tribola to the area of the road junction near Sogliano.[6]

The 1st Royal Sussex, with under command B Squadron 6th Battalion Royal Tank Regiment, advanced during the night of 25/26 September to secure the road junction near Tribola and that

---

[5] On 1 October, the 43rd Indian Infantry Brigade was put under command of the 56th (London) Division. Alberazzo, three miles north of where the Gurkhas had handed over on the Uso, was their rendezvous. Bad weather and the complications brought on by movement hampered the move. Yet by the night 4/5 October, 2/6 and 2/10 Gurkha were patrolling with their neighbours, men of the 12 Canadian Infantry Brigade, towards yet another river, the Fiumicino, three miles west of the Uso. Operations for crossing the Fiumicino, continuously postponed owing to the heavy rain, were finally fixed for the night of 6/7 October. At the last moment, plans were altered and on 7 October, the 43rd Indian Infantry Brigade moved southwards to join the 10th Indian Division.

[6] 4 Ind. Div. Intelligence Summary No. 171, 29 September 1944.

near Reggiano. By 0455 hours on 26 September A Company, less one platoon, was in Cornacchiara, while B Company passed through to M. Reggiano. Afterwards B Company was to patrol to Tribola. By 0905 hours B Company had made considerable progress towards its objective. But heavy German shelling and mortaring held up the advance. At 1220 hours a platoon of B Company edged its way forward but got ambushed and was extricated after suffering 12 casualties. B Company pulled back to the area near Cornacchiara. The attack on M. Reggiano was a failure for which a flooded river, numerous mines, heavy shelling and mortaring, and the strength of the German positions on the Reggiano feature had been responsible.

The commander of the 7th Indian Infantry Brigade planned to make a fresh vigorous attack on M. Reggiano. The 1st Royal Sussex, with B Squadron 6th Royal Tank Regiment, was to attack and secure Tribola and M. Reggiano at last light on 26 September. The 1/2 Gurkha, with C Squadron 6th Royal Tank Regiment, was to move up and take over Tribola and the bend in the road at 705964. Two companies (B and C) were to move along the ridge to attack and secure Monte Albano during the hours of darkness. Fire plan was to be arranged by the officer commanding the 31st Field Regiment, Royal Artillery.

After the Corps Artillery had brought down a heavy concentration on the Reggiano—Tribola ridge, the 1st Royal Sussex led the attack. The Germans offered determined opposition. British tanks crossed the river but their movement was restricted by mines, soft surface and steep slopes. The left-hand company of the 1st Royal Sussex directed on M. Reggiano made substantial gains for a platoon reached the top of the Reggiano feature against fierce opposition. The company however sustained heavy casualties and was pulled back at 0510 hours on 27 September to avoid being exposed on the ridge at first light. Meanwhile the attack on Tribola had also failed. At 2245 hours on 26 September the leading British troops were about a hundred yards from it, but despite bitter fighting they failed to reach their objective.

Meanwhile, 1/2 Gurkha had been moving up on the right of the 1st Royal Sussex towards Tribola. At 2300 hours on 26 September the Gurkhas were concentrated in the area of cross-roads at Pt. 160. At 0010 hours on 27 September, A Company followed by B and C Companies, advanced but encountered very heavy fire from the Germans, who were fiercely guarding the cross-roads at 704960. The Germans started heavy shelling of the Gurkha battalion area. The battalion mule train narrowly escaped being shelled. By 0100 hours the situation was not favourable. A Company was hard pressed on the west of the road short of the cross-roads at 704960. B Company, while advancing in single file, ran into a strong German position but by grim determination cleared the southern side of the road. They dug in south of the cross-roads at 704960. D Company, in reserve, took up positions on the spur, about 400 yards west of Pt. 160. The high ground to the north of the cross-roads at 704960 was very strongly held by the Germans. The Gurkhas, though subjected to heavy shelling, clung to the positions they had gained. At 1030 hours Corps artillery brought down a heavy concentration for twenty minutes on German positions, and then D Company with tanks in support advanced south of the road to make an attack up the steep slopes of the hill. The Gurkhas closed on the Germans in the houses on the forward slopes and drove them out. Further advance was however checked. The right hand platoon met very heavy and accurate machine gun and small arms fire from the right flank and was practically wiped out. The second platoon also encountered strong opposition and was held up due to heavy casualties. The tanks were all bogged down and could not support the assault on the crest, nor could they neutralise the fire from the high ground on the right. The third platoon however pushed on just short of the crest and took up positions to repel the expected German counter-attack. A Company was ordered to infiltrate forward to support D Company. Unfortunately this company failed to arrive in time to help D Company, with the result that when the German counter-attack struck D Company at 1830 hours, the latter, having exhausted its ammunition, failed to hold the counter-attack and pulled out with great difficulty at 2000 hours. Appalling weather conditions created difficulties in the movement of rations and ammunition to the forward areas, making it difficult to carry out the operations successfully.

As the Germans continued to hold in strength the Reggiano-Tribola ridge, the 7th Indian Infantry Brigade carried on preparations to renew the attack on the ridge. During the night of 29/30 September, however, the Germans evacuated Tribola, though they continued to hold the Reggiano feature. 1/2 Gurkha occupied Tribola at 0230 hours on 30 September. Shortly afterwards the troops of the 46th Division occupied Montalbano at the northern end of the Reggiano ridge. The task of the 7th Indian Infantry Brigade was now to seize the southern end, namely to capture M. Reggiano and Borghi and to exploit to S. Martino. Owing to the heavy casualties sustained by the 7th Indian Infantry Brigade, 2nd Cameron was placed under command. The plan was for the 1st Royal Sussex and the 2nd Cameron to advance from start line (track 699949—697947) and seize M. Reggiano, and for 2/11 Sikh to advance from start line (track 688945—686945) and seize Borghi. B Squadron 6th Royal Tank Regiment was to be in support of the 1st Royal Sussex and A

Squadron in support of 2/11 Sikh. H hour was to be 0200 hours on 1 October.[7]

The combined attack was carried out with Corps artillery support and was completely successful, some 24,000 rounds having been fired by the guns on a front of 1000 yards, over a period of five hours. By 0422 hours the 2nd Cameron, on the left, had taken its objective on the crest of the ridge—Pt. 273. From a dominating position known as 'Eight Trees', the 2nd Cameron had good shooting, when some fifty disorganised and hastily retreating Germans passed across its front. Six Germans were taken prisoners. Meanwhile, by 0422 hours the 1st Royal Sussex on the right had captured M. Reggiano and Mansion House, another strong-point. 2/11 Sikh also made good progress. Battalion headquarters was located on the Gemmiano ridge, and the attack was carried out by B Company on the left and A Company on the right. There was a long approach march by night of some 4875 yards to the objective. Both the leading companies passed without sustaining loss through the German defensive fire, and with the village of Borghi standing out clearly against the sky-line during the last 2166 yards ascent, had no difficulty in locating their objective, which was captured by 0500 hours.

The brigade commander ordered 2/11 Sikh to leave one company for the occupation and defence of Borghi, and with the other company to attack and capture the high ground east of S. Martino, astride the road running due west from Borghi to Sogliano, which was known to be held by the Germans in some strength. B Company was to carry out the attack, supported by A Company, as soon as the latter might be relieved in Borghi by a company of the 2nd Cameron. This relief was not completed before 2000 hours. As there was no available battalion reserve, and as the battalion headquarters was approximately 4333 yards behind the forward companies (owing to the river Uso being in spate), the commander of 2/11 Sikh ordered B Company to probe into the German defences. Pouring rain and mist made conditions unpleasant for the Sikhs. Movement and communication was a slow, laborious matter. Owing to bad weather, and the heavily mined roads, tanks were not able to move forward in support of this attack. Aircraft also could not give support, being grounded by the flooded landing strips.

At about 2030 hours on 1 October, B Company attacked a feature astride the road 500 yards due east of S. Martino, which dominated the approaches to the latter. The company was held up by heavy automatic and mortar fire, and suffered 12 casualties. The commander of 2/11 Sikh then ordered A Company to attack and capture the feature. The attack was launched at 2230 hours on 2 October and was successful. The Germans were cleared from the ridge by

[7] 7 Ind. Inf. Bde. O.I. No. 30, dated 30 September 1944.

0830 hours after close fighting. At 1200 hours, after a very heavy mortar concentration, and covered by small arms fire, the Germans counter-attacked A Company simultaneously from the front and the flank. A heavy mist reduced visibility to a few yards. This enabled the Germans to surprise and overrun the Sikh company. The company commander was reported missing and some 50 other ranks were killed or wounded. In the confusion and mist, the remnants of the company made their way back to Borghi. However the operation against Borghi—M. Reggiano on the night of 30 September/1 October had resulted in the complete elimination of *8 company of 741st Jaegar Regiment,* which was acting as battalion rearguard, east of the river Fiumicino.[8]

The 10th Indian Division in the Line

A high wind, added to the continuous heavy rain and the flooded river, had already halted operations, when news came through that the 10th Indian Division would relieve the 4th Indian Division. By 3 October the 10th Indian Division had completed the change-over and was prepared to seize the S. Martino-Sogliano ridge and thus bring the left flank of the V Corps up to the river Fiumicino. The 25th Indian Infantry Brigade took over from the 7th Indian Infantry Brigade on the right of the division's front, with 1 King's Own around Borghi, 3/1 Punjab in Montiale and on the ridge immediately west of Borghi, and 3/18 Royal Garhwal Rifles at Cornacchiars. The 20th Indian Infantry Brigade relieved the 11th Indian Infantry Brigade in the area of the Montebello—Scorticata ridge and pushed forward at once with 2/3 Gurkha Rifles, on the right, to Montecchio, 1/2 Punjab on the left to S. Donato, and 3/5 Mahratta Light Infantry in reserve at S. Giovanni. The 10th Indian Infantry Brigade closed up behind the 20th Indian Infantry Brigade at Scorticata on 5 October 1944.

The task of the 10th Indian Divison was to capture the S. Martino-Sogliano ridge. The 20th Indian Infantry Brigade was to capture Sogliano while the 25th Indian Infantry Brigade was to seize S. Martino. The S. Martino-Sogliano ridge was held by *III Battalion 741st Jaegar Regiment and III Battalion 721st Jaegar Regiment.*

The 10th Indian Division had no light task to perform. The Germans, though roughly handled so far by the Eighth Army, were still in a position to offer resistance far sterner than any which the division had previously met. Their artillery fire was intense and mines numerous. The weather conspired to add to the severity of opposition. There was almost continuous rain making movement difficult. Tracks were usually one way; eight to ten feet wide and, with a lightly metalled surface, suitable for jeeps only. Where three-

---

[8] 10 Ind. Div. Intelligence Summary No. 106, 2 October 1944.

ton lorries could be used, there would be sharp hair-pin bends, which the lorry could not negotiate in one sweep. Rivers and streams, always across the line of advance, were turned into considerable obstacles by flood water. Hills were smaller and barer than those encountered in the Tiber and Arno valleys. Villages and strong-points held by the Germans or occupied by the 10th Indian Division were invariably on the high features dominating the country-side for miles around. Solidly built villages and farmsteads needed little modification to convert them into strong-points. The high, thick walls of the village cemetery provided for the Germans ready-made splinter and bullet-proof cover.

Capture of the S. Martino—Sogliano Ridge

The capture by 1/2 Punjab (at 0100 hours on 4 October) of the S. Donate feature, and the back door approaches to the dominating town of Sogliano was the first of the many outflanking moves by which the skill and experience gained by the division in the mountains of the Alpe di Catenaia were to be used to advantage. At last light on 3 October, 1/2 Punjab had concentrated at Genestreto, in order to seize S. Donato, preparatory to the attack on Sogliano. At last light on 3 October, a small reconnaissance patrol was sent to Pt. 229 and S. Donato to find out the strength of the Germans. A and C Companies remained ready in Genestreto to attack when the patrol returned and reported. By 0100 hours on 4 October, information had been received at battalion headquarters that Pt. 229 was held lightly and that a certain house in S. Donato was occupied by about ten Germans, who had killed one and wounded two of the patrol. On receipt of this information, A and C Companies advanced to the attack at 0100 hours on 4 October. Pt. 229 was occupied by C Company against slight opposition. It was however only after four hours of exchange of fire that A Company could capture Donato house garrisoned by eight Germans. The fight for the Donato stronghold showed that even eight P.I.A.T. bombs, small arms and 2-inch mortars used over a period of four hours cannot destroy determined enemy in a normal country house. It was not until a noncommissioned officer had finally reached the house unhurt and thrown a grendade into a window that the Germans surrendered.

With the capture of S. Donato, the 20th Indian Infantry Brigade was ready to attack Sogliano. The attack was to be launched during the hours of darkness on 4/5 October. On the right, 2/3 Gurkha was to advance from Montecchio and secure the road junction near Pt. 350 and ring contour at 647922, as the first objective, Sogliano being the second. On the left, 1/2 Punjab was to advance from S. Donato and protect the left flank by securing Vignola and C. Priano, as the first objective, and the suburbs of Sogliano south of

S MARTINO—SOGLIANO AREA

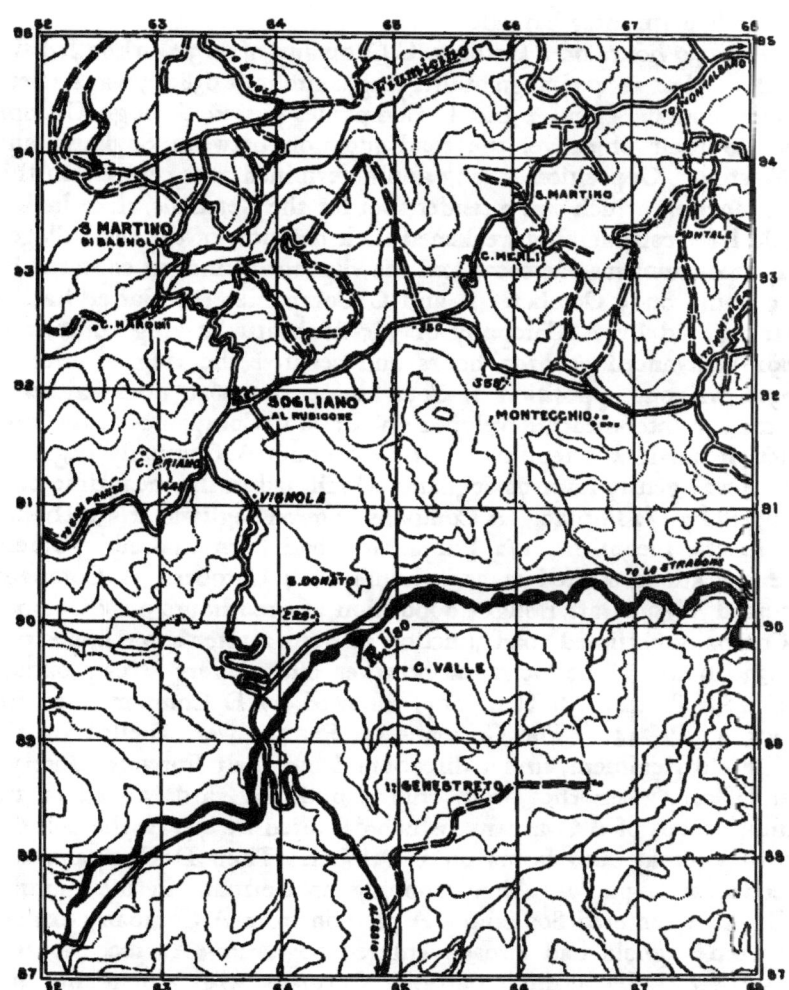

the road junction at 636918, as the second objective. W Company and two platoons Z Company 1st Battalion Royal Northumberland Fusiliers were under command of the 20th Indian Infantry Brigade. A Squadron North Irish Horse was in support of 2/3 Gurkha and 1/2 Punjab. The Central India Horse operated on the left of the 20th Indian Infantry Brigade.

At 2030 hours on 4 October, C Company of 2/3 Gurkha led the attack. After an exchange of fire, ring contour at 658923 was secured at 2100 hours. Then A and D Companies passed through C Company to their objective, the road junction between Sogliano and S. Martino. Opposition, strong and determined, was centred on this road junction, which was a tender spot for the Germans, since its loss would have considerably weakened their defences of the two villages. The opposition was overcome and the vital road junction captured by 0045 hours on 5 October. B and C Companies (the latter having been relieved by A Company of 3/5 Mahratta at ring contour at 658923) advanced at 0100 hours and secured the ring contour at 647922 without opposition at 0530 hours. At 0640 hours a heavy German counter-attack developed on A and C Companies at the road junction but it was repulsed. At 1200 hours A Company began to feel its way gently towards Sogliano, which had in the meantime been occupied by 1/2 Punjab. A Company entered Sogliano at 1500 hours.

In the meantime, 1/2 Punjab too had been making progress. The operations started at 2230 hours on 4 October. A Company occupied Vignola after slight opposition at 0100 hours on 5 October. C Company occupied road junction at 633912 after some opposition at 0330 hours. The Germans however offered very strong opposition from Pt. 441. B Company, followed by D Company, led the attack on Pt. 441. The Germans on Pt. 441 were shelled by the 68th Field Regiment, under directions from their Forward Observation Officer, when they were only a hundred yards ahead of the leading troops of B Company, which captured Pt. 441 at the point of the bayonet at 0600 hours on 5 October. Then D Company was directed on Sogliano. After mopping up Germans in the suburbs, D Company entered Sogliano. A platoon from A Company exploiting from Vignola had already entered Sogliano. At 1000 hours a counter-attack by a small party of Germans with a machine gun developed against B Company at Pt. 441. The attack was beaten off with the help of a platoon from A Company, which advanced from Vignola to the support of B Company. By 1200 hours the whole objective was firmly in the hands of 1/2 Punjab.

While the 20th Indian Infantry Brigade seized Sogliano, the 25th Indian Infantry Brigade was directed against S. Martino, the attack on which was made by the 1 King's Own. C Squadron North Irish Horse, the 97th and the 154th Field Regiments were in support of the brigade. One troop North Irish Horse, one platoon Medium Machine Gun and one platoon heavy mortars were in support of the King's Own.

At 0300 hours on 5 October, the 1 King's Own advanced from the area Borghi along the ridge to San Martino. Short of S. Martino, the leading company swung to the left, skirted the village on the lower southern slopes of the ridge and attacked from the south. Against fierce opposition the company fought its way into the village. It was later subjected to a strong German counter-attack, which resulted in heavy casualties on both sides and the ejection of the British troops from the village. A second company established itself at 0830 hours on the outskirts of the village and held on in spite of several counter-attacks. At 2100 hours the company which had established itself on the outskirts of S. Martino, resumed the attack and occupied the village at 2200 hours after slight opposition. Thus by 5 October the 10th Indian Division had accomplished its task of capturing the S. Martino-Sogliano ridge and thus closing up to the river Fiumicino.

CHAPTER XXIV

Advance to the River Savio

The Eighth Army's Advance to the River Savio

The Eighth Army, which had closed up to the river Fiumicino by 5 October 1944, was up against considerable opposition as eight German divisions barred its way, defending the Fiumicino line. The *162nd (Turkoman) Division*, the *1st Parachute Division* and the *29th Panzer Grenadier Division* faced the I Canadian Corps in the coastal plain. One regiment of the *26th Panzer Division* was north of the railway line at Savignano. The *90th Panzer Grenadier Division* covered the front between the railway line at Savignano and south of Route 9. The *278th Infantry Division* extended further to excluding Montigallo. The *114th Jaegar Division's* sector ran from Montigallo through Roncofreddo to San Paola; *871 Grenadier Regiment* of the *356th Infantry Division* stretched south of San Paola, across Route 71 through Monto Tezzo to the west.

General Sir Richard Mc Creery, who assumed command of the Eighth Army in succession to General Sir Oliver Leese on 1 October 1944, was of the opinion that the main thrust should be developed in the foothills and astride Route 9. His plan was to carry outflanking movements in quick succession to overcome the river obstacles, namely, to cross the upper waters and thus turn each river-line in the foothills. The II Polish Corps was therefore transferred from the Adriatic coast to the X Corps sector to exert pressure on the axis of Route 71 and thus threaten to outflank the German forces facing the main body of the Eighth Army on the Adriatic coast. But it was not till 16 October that the Polish Corps could take up positions, and by that time the main body of the Eighth Army had advanced almost to the line of the river Savio and Route 71. Meanwhile on 7 October, the Eighth Army had made its main thrust in the foothills. The plan was for the I Canadian Corps to extend its front about a thousand yards to the south of Route 9 to relieve the British 56th Division, and advance up that highway to Cesena. The V Corps, with the 46th Division on the right and the 10th Indian Division on the left, was to advance to the foothills and cross the Savio at Cesena. The attack in the plains failed to materialise due to the flooding of the Fiumicino, but in the foothills the outflanking movement was successful. The 10th Indian Division captured M. Farneto on 7 October and M. Spaccato on 9 October. The 46th Division captured the ridge running south-west from Montigallo and, by 10 October, had secured Longiano. These successes compelled the Germans to fall back on the line of the canal Scolo Rigossa. Their positions were next based on M. Dell Erta and M. Della Vacche and the line running northwards through the ridge M. Dei Pine, M. Burattini, Calisese, across Roure 9 to Gambettola. By 15 October the Germans were driven back from these positions to the line of the river Pisciatello. The 46th Division captured M. Dei Pine and M. Burattini while the 10th Indian Division secured M. Della Vacche, thus compelling the Germans to abandon the line along the river Rigosa on either side of Route 9, and enabling the I Canadian Corps to cross the Rigosa and advance towards the river Pisciatello. Further opposition was overcome and by 20 October the main body of the Eighth Army had closed up to the river Savio.

Attack on M. Farneto

Having given a brief account of the advance of the Eighth Army to the river Savio we shall now describe in greater detail the part played by the Indian formations in these operations. After securing the S. Martino-Sogliano ridge on 5 October 1944 and bringing up the left flank of the V Corps to the river Fiumicino, the 10th Indian Division was ready to attack the German positions across that stream. The Germans had taken up position on the ridge west of the river Fiumicino. The villages of Montigallo and Longiano were their chief strongholds on the northern part of the ridge while the strong position of M. Gattons formed the chief anchor of defence on the southern ridge. This ridge had its flank on M. Farneto. The German force facing the 10th Indian Division consisted of elements of the *114th Jaegar Division* and the *356th Infantry Division*. The sector of the former extended from Montigallo through Roncoforedo to San Paola. *871st Grenadier Regiment* of the *356th Infantry Division* was south of the San Paola, with *II Battalion* at M. Farneto.[1]

The 10th Indian Division played an important part in the V Corps attack on the German positions across the river Fiumicino. The corps attack was made with two divisions—on the right the 46th Division was directed against Montigallo and Longiano while on the left the 10th Indian Division was directed against M. Farneto and M. Gattona. In implementation of the Corps plan Major-General Reid planned to make a double thrust—the 20th Indian Infantry Brigade to secure M. Farneto and exploit north towards M. Spaccato and San Paola and the 25th Indian Infantry Brigade to capture M. Gattona and exploit to S. Lorenzo. The 10th Indian Infantry Brigade, in reserve, was to be prepared to either assault Roncofredo or pass through the 20th Indian Infantry Brigade to secure Montenovo or Diolaguardia. The North Irish Horse, Central India

[1] Ibid. No. 113, 8 October 1944.

M FARNETO AREA

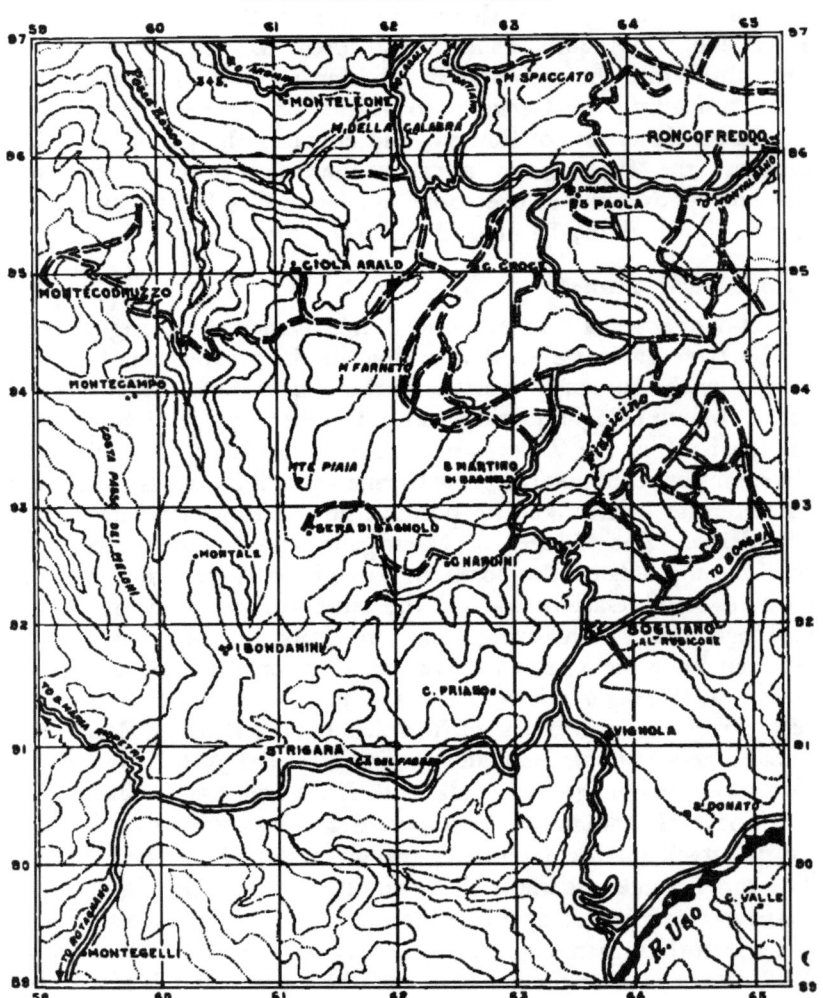

Horse, the 57th Medium Regiment, the 97th, 154th and 68th Field Regiments and the 85th Mountain Regiment were in support of the 10th Indian Division.[2]

The commander of the 20th Indian Infantry Brigade made the following plan for the attack on M. Farneto:

- (i) In order to secure the left flank, 1/2 Punjab, with two companies of 4/10 Baluch under command, was to carry out preliminary operations and capture Strigara.
- (ii) The attack on M. Farneto was to be made with two battalions—2/3 Gurkha on the right and 3/5 Mahratta on the left. On the right, 2/3 Gurkha, with under command one machine gun platoon and in support one heavy mortar platoon and one troop tanks, was to advance from Sogliano and capture the road junction at 622950 to including the road junction at 618946.
- (iii) On the left, 3/5 Mahratta, with under command one machine gun platoon and in support one heavy mortar platoon and one troop tanks, was to advance from road excluding Sogliano to C. Priano and secure the features M. Farneto and M. Piaia.
- (iv) Then 2/3 Gurkha was to take over the whole Farneto feature and 3/5 Mahratta was to exploit towards Monteleone.
- (v) 2/4 Gurkha was to concentrate in the area Sogliano and be prepared to exploit to San Paolo after the capture of M. Farneto.
- (vi) Artillery support for the brigade attack was to be by concentrations at call and pre-selected defensive fire tasks. For this purpose the divisional artillery with additional Field and Medium Regiments were at call. The attack was to be silent until opposition was met.

From Sogliano to M. Farneto was two miles in a straight line but nearly twice as much on foot, since frequent and deep water courses added considerably to the climbing to be done. All roads in the area were only minor roads which had been damaged by the rain and cratered and mined by the Germans.

As the dominating feature of Strigara overlooked the southern slopes of M. Farneto it had to be captured as a preliminary to the assault on the mountain which was the first step in the execution of the plan. 1/2 Punjab, with two companies of 4/10 Baluch under command, undertook this task. The attack commenced at 0300 hours on 6 October. The plan was for A Company to advance from the area Sogliano and capture the area (627910) astride the Sogliano-Strigara road by 0315 hours; C Company was to capture Ca Del

[2] 10 Ind. Div. O.O. No. 4, 6 October 1944.

Fabbro by 0415 hours; and D Company to capture Strigara by 0530 hours. The first objective was captured in thick fog at 0315 hours, against slight spandau opposition and mortaring. The second objective was also secured in the scheduled time, but during a break in the fog, German observation posts observed the attacking company, and a heavy artillery concentration was brought down in the middle of one platoon, which lost its commander and suffered casualties, 3 killed and 14 wounded. Nevertheless, at first light D Company, facing intense mortar fire, was approaching Strigara. By 0730 hours two platoons had infiltrated into the cemetery area, about five hundred yards south of Strigara, capturing prisoners and a Bazooka.

Throughout the day the situation did not improve. All the companies came under very intense shell fire and mortaring. Medium field and medium machine gun fire was brought down on Strigara and the ridge to the north of it. The Germans vacated Strigara by 1500 hours. But due to lack of wireless communication with D Company, Tactical Headquarters sent a written signal to D Company to stand fast and ordered 4/10 Baluch to capture the village in the evening. By 2100 hours the Baluch entered Strigara without meeting any opposition.[3]

The next step was taken at 2000 hours on 6 October, when 2/3 Gurkha on the right and 3/5 Mahratta on the left, launched an attack on M. Farneto. A dark night concealed the exhausting but silent approach of the two battalions. The 3/5 Mahratta advance to the battalion objective—M. Farneto—entailed a steep descent, the crossing of a small stream and an ascent of 2,500 yards up a long and moderately steep slope, heavily cultivated and studded with farm houses. As his D Company had suffered heavy casualties in an earlier action on 5 October, the commander of 3/5 Mahratta decided to use this company as porters and additional stretcher bearers, leaving only three rifle companies, each eighty-five strong, for the assault.

The information regarding the Germans was that the hill was not strongly defended and only isolated machine gun posts were to be encountered. Ciola Araldi was however estimated to be held by about 150 Germans. The battalion plan was to attack M. Farneto with A Company on the right and B Company on the left. Then C, the reserve company, was to exploit south along the ridge to M. Piaia and Sera di Bagnolo.

By 1730 hours the battalion had assembled south of Vignola.

[3] This operation showed how essential it is that companies should remain in touch with battalion headquarters. D, the leading Company, had two No. 18 wireless sets, but by mischance, one was destroyed by enemy fire and the other was out of order. The whole plan was therefore held up through lack of timely information. The operation further showed how essential it is to destroy enemy isolated observation posts, under culverts, hay stacks, farm carts, and houses to avoid heavy casualties—Narrative 1/2 Punjab; Appx. J-2; War Diary 1/2 Punjab.

Unfortunately, the mules, which had been lifting the battalion, were changed in the afternoon and the new mules had not arrived by 1600 hours when the battalion left its concentration area. The mules had missed the way and had got bogged. After much delay in searching for them the battalion moved forward in heavy rain with the mules of only one company and crossed the start line at 2200 hours. The path chosen proved to be extremely steep and rain had made it very slippery. The night was very dark and with men moving in single file constant halts were necessary to prevent people getting lost. Harassing fire was experienced during the descent but no casualties occurred until the leading companies had crossed the stream and were fanning out for the assault. At that time the German mortar defensive fire came down on the valley and caused some casualties. The Germans offered opposition from various houses on the route. The advance continued steadily, each post being dealt with in succession. The going was very heavy in waterlogged ploughed fields. The leading companies reached the summit of M. Farneto at 0415 hours on 7 October, but owing to wireless fade-out this was not known definitely at Tactical Headquarters till 0530 hours. Exploitation of the ridge to the south to M. Piaia was then begun by C Company, only one platoon being deployed initially as it was now daylight. About twenty Germans were driven out from cover, and while retreating down the western slope were successfully engaged by artillery and small arms. It was estimated that about 20 casualties were inflicted on the Germans in the operations of 6/7 October.[4] Thus 3/5 Mahratta successfully carried out the task of seizing the summit of M. Farneto, and the ridge to the south.

Meanwhile 2/3 Gurkha too had secured its objectives. At 2200 hours on 6 October, A and D Companies moved off from Sogliano to cross the start line, Sogliano—San Paola road. During the advance heavy shelling was experienced in the area of the nullah-river junction (637932) and on the reverse slopes of M. Farneto. At 0230 hours, C Company, following D Company, reached approximately the area at 634936, when it was forced to the ground by heavy spandau fire. At 0300 hours, C Company resumed the advance and after being subjected to further heavy artillery fire passed through D Company position at 630943 at about 0345 hours. Shelling now ceased and C Company secured by 0500 hours the objective, the road junction at 622950 to including the road junction at 618946, against slight opposition. Consolidation began and was effected by first light.

German Counter-attacks

Thus by first light on 7 October, both the battalions had reached

[4] Action by 3/5 Mahratta on M. Farneto; Appx. War Diary 3/5 Mahratta, October 1944.

their objectives. That the Germans were forced off this vital area was indicative of the speed and weight of the Indian attack, which took *II Battalion 871st Grenadier Regiment* by surprise.⁵ The Germans however reacted strongly to the loss of the key feature of M. Farneto, and it was estimated that the counter-attacks and attempts to infiltrate back on to the position, which continued throughout the day and well into the night, were made in battalion strength. The *114th Jaegar Division's* boundary was extended to include M. Farneto. Thus *II Battalion 721st Jaegar Regiment* launched the counter-attacks, allowing the weakened *871st Grenadier Regiment* to thicken up the defence further to the west.⁶

Strong German counter-attacks mainly from the area Ciola Araldi were delivered in the afternoon on the Mahratta positions. At that time 3/5 Mahratta was disposed in the area of M. Farneto— A and D Companies were at M. Farneto; B Company was on the left; C Company in the area M. Piaia was protecting the left flank of B Company; and Tactical Headquarters was located to the east of M. Piaia. At 1300 hours a heavy German counter-attack on B Company, supported by artillery, developed from the direction of Ciola Araldi but was dispersed by 1330 hours by artillery defensive fire and small arms fire. At the same time about fifty Germans, observed moving in the houses about Ciola Araldi, were engaged by artillery and dispersed. Two detachments of 3-inch mortars in support of B and C Companies were now available and got into action. A section of Battalion Medium Machine Guns also came into action on the right edge of the Farneto summit, covering the German approaches from Ciola Araldi. One troop of tanks of the North Irish Horse was in position in support, covering the gap between B and C Companies. At 1745 hours artillery fire was brought down in the valley about 800 yards west of M. Piaia, thus breaking up a counter-attack of about 150 Germans, which was forming up, directed on C Company's flank. Soon afterwards, however, there was a serious threat of considerable German outflanking movement, as they infiltrated into Sera di Bagnolo, which had not been held in view of the battalion's extended front. At 1845 hours two platoons of Germans advanced from Sera di Bagnolo to within a hundred yards of C Company's left platoon and engaged it with small arms fire and rifle grenades. The German attack was repulsed by small arms fire. At the same time a strong German counter-attack developed on D Company's position at M. Farneto, lasting for about an hour. Heavy artillery defensive fire was brought down in likely German forming-up places. Hand-to-hand fighting did not take place though at periods exchanges of grenades occurred. The attack on the main

⁵ 10 Div. Intelligence Summary No. 111, 6 October 1944.
⁶ Ibid, No. 113, 8 October 1944.

Mahratta position at M. Farneto was now repulsed. The Germans then moved to the low ground south of Sera di Bagnolo and infiltrated further round the left flank. German spandau detachments shot up the battalion headquarters intermittently. It was clear now that the Germans had broken off attacks on the main front at M. Farneto in order to move larger forces round the left flank, which was completely open. It was necessary to reinforce 3/5 Mahratta so as to cover this exposed flank. The lading elements of 1/2 Punjab arrived in the vicinity of Sera di Bagnolo at about 0030 hours on 8 October. Thereupon, German small arms fire on the left flank died down.

Meanwhile 2/3 Gurkha too had to repel German counter-attacks. C Company, which was in position at road junction at 622950 to including road junction at 618946, bore the brunt of the attack. Large numbers of Germans, though engaged by artillery, advanced from the area of M. Della Calabra and disappeared from view into the nullah immediately west of the Farneto feature, preparatory to the attack on C Company. At 1300 hours on 7 October, two platoons of Germans launched a counter-attack on C Company's position. After about one and a half hour's struggle the attack was beaten off. At 1900 hours the Germans renewed the attack in considerable strength. They were driven off after severe fighting lasting several hours by small arms and artillery. The Germans heavily shelled the area throughout the night. At 0700 hours on 8 October, a German counter-attack again developed on the position of the Gurkha company. Fire from supporting artillery however dispersed the attackers.

At 1400 hours on 8 October German shelling increased and took a heavy toll of a platoon of B Mahratta Company. Then a German platoon advanced to within fifty yards of B Company's position but was beaten off by small arms fire and grenades. To check these German counter-attacks it was necessary to liquidate German machine gun posts in Ciola Araldi. Therefore two tanks, supported by medium machine guns and field artillery, shelled selected houses for two hours, from 1630 to 1830 hours. This caused a strong reaction in the form of heavy German shelling and mortaring.

The Germans did not abate their efforts on 9 October to recapture M. Farneto. At first light the right platoon and the observation posts of B Mahratta Company were sniped and grenaded by Germans, who had infiltrated into houses about two hundred yards from the forward defended localities. After the Germans were driven out with P.I.A.Ts, one section of A Company at M. Farneto advanced over open ground to capture the houses. It was brought to a standstill by heavy casualties but continued to provide covering fire for a second section which succeeded in capturing the houses. During the night of 9/10 October extremely heavy German shelling occurred, causing casualties. By the morning of 10 October, B Mahratta Company was tired and exhausted. The company had been in an exposed position and the men had remained in flooded slit trenches for 72 hours under continual attack and shell fire. They urgently required rest and were relieved after dark by C Company, itself in turn being relieved by A Company. On the same day a Mahratta platoon, supported by artillery and machine gun fire, attacked the houses in Ciola Araldi occupied by the Germans. The advance to the start line had to be made gradually over exposed country and encountered heavy German artillery fire. Smoke and high explosives were fired to cover the crossing of the start line and preparations for the final assault. The Germns strongly contested the position but were driven out by a bomb and bayonet assault, in which ten Germans were killed and more wounded. Having evacuated their position, they then brought artillery fire down on to Ciola Araldi. Thereupon the Mahratta platoon withdrew in darkness. The Farneto feature was shelled by the heavy calibre German guns until about midnight after which the situation was quiet until 3/5 Mahratta and 2/3 Gurkha were pulled out on 11 October.

Capture of M. Gattona

While the 20th Indian Infantry Brigade was hammering at the strong German positions in M. Farneto area the 25th Indian Infantry Brigade was directed against the German positions in M. Gattona area. Here their strong points were S. Lorenzo, Yellow Church (669982), White House (665982), Monte Gattona, Church near Pt. 229, flats (662974) and the ridge at 658974. The brigade plan was to attack on a narrow front with two battalions. On the right, 3/18 Garhwal (with under command one platoon medium machine gun, two troops tanks, and in support one platoon heavy mortars) was to capture the White House, M. Gattona, Yellow Church and S. Lorenzo. On the left, 3/1 Punjab (with under command one platoon medium machine gun, two troops tanks and in support one platoon heavy mortars) was to secure C. il Poggio, Church near Pt. 229 and the ridge at 658974.[7]

The commander of 3/18 Garhwal planned the operations to be carried out in five phases:

    Phase   I—A Company was to take up position for covering the forming up place at 675971.

    Phase II—C Company, D Company and the battalion headquarters were to move to the forming up place.

    Phase III—D Company on the right, C Company on the left and A Company on the left rear were to advance from the forming up place and secure objectives,

---

[7] 25 Ind. Inf. Bde. O.O. No. 2, 6 October 1944.

the Yellow Church, the White House and M. Gattona respectively.

Phase IV—B Company was to advance from the position at 670969 by track and clear S. Lorenzo.

Phase V—After consolidation, patrols from C Company (in area White House) were to go to the Cemetery Hill (666988).[6]

The Commander of 3/1 Punjab planned the operations to be carried out in four phases:

Phase I—A Company was to cross the start line at 668967 and secure C il Poggio.

Phase II—B Company was to follow A Company and seize the flats at 662972.

Phase III—C Company was to follow B Company and capture the Brown Hill (660973).

Phase IV—D Company was to form up in the rear of the flats to deal with possible German counter-attacks on the Brown Hill. If no German counter-attack developed, D Company was to secure Cemetery (656968) or Church (661976) as ordered.

A Company was to dig in immediately the objective (C il Poggio) had been secured and was then to be ready for its possible later role of attacking the Church or the Brown Hill.

3/18 Garhwal arrived at the forming up place at 2130 hours on 7 October. C, D and A Companies started from there at 2200 hours, directed against the White House, the Church and M. Gattona, respectively. After a heavy artillery concentration on M. Gattona, A Company attacked this feature and captured it at 0030 hours on 8 October. C and D Companies encountered heavy opposition. At 0130 hours, however, C Company captured the White House, and D Company secured the Church. Shortly afterwards at 0430 hours several German counter-attacks developed on A Company at M. Gattona and C Company at the White House, but these were beaten off. When M. Gattona had been secured, B Company exploited forward to S. Lorenzo at 0630 hours and after stiff fighting captured the village by 1100 hours.

To the south-west, 3/1 Punjab had no trouble in securing the initial objectives. A Company and Tactical Headquarters, followed by B Company, moved off at 1900 hours and crossed the start line at 670968. By 0130 hours on 8 October both the forward companies (A and B) had captured C il Poggio and the flats respectively without encountering any opposition. But when 3/1 Punjab continued the advance towards the lateral road at Pt. 229 and south from there

[6] 3/18 R. Garh. Rif. O.O. No. 1, 6 October 1944.

towards the Brown Hill, trouble started. The road ran along the crest of the ridge above hillsides, broken by dry nullahs and dotted with trees. Gradients were so steep as to allow the Germans to lie-up close to the road and be in no danger of being exposed to artillery fire. Strongest of all positions along the road was the Church, near Pt. 229. Although C Company had seized the Brown Hill, A Company had failed to dislodge the Germans from the Church. However, at 0700 hours, A Company captured the Church after annihilating the crew of a German machine gun positioned there. Mopping up of the Germans continued throughout the morning, with D Company directed against the Cemetery. At 1000 hours a German counter-attack on C Company was broken up by artillery and machine gun fire. The battalion was now firmly established with A Company in the Church, C Company on the Brown Hill, D Company in the Cemetery area and B Company in the flats. Thus 3/1 Punjab had carried out the task of clearing the Germans from these areas.

Capture of Roncofredo

Early in the morning of 9 October, the 25th Indian Infantry Brigade was relieved by a brigade of the 46th Division on M. Gattona and prepared to attack and capture Roncofredo. Meanwhile, as the 20th Indian Infantry Brigade at M. Farneto was being fiercely counter-attacked and could not therefore exploit to the north, the 10th Indian Infantry Brigade, previously in reserve, was directed on the right on M. Spaccato, with one battalion working round the left towards M. Codruzzo. We shall first describe the attack on Roncofredo.

3/1 Punjab concentrated in area C il Poggio early on 9 October, preparatory to the attack on Roncofredo. Bad weather hampered operations. Heavy rainfall had made all roads impassable to anything but jeeps. The tanks were bogged down and even mules found tracks across country impossible to negotiate. Spasmodic shelling of the battalion position throughout the day greatly hampered reconnaissance and planning for the attack on Roncofredo. At about 1500 hours on 9 October a direct hit on a house used by A Company killed the commanding officer of 3/1 Punjab and set three ammunition carriers of mortar platoon on fire. The explosions from the burning mortar bombs caused seven casualties in A Company. Nevertheless, 3/1 Punjab continued the preparations for the attack.

By 0200 hours on 10 October, A Company was in occupation of houses at 661968 and D Company had secured the cross-roads at 657965. Thereupon B and C Companies moved up behind D and A Companies and after a heavy concentration of artillery on Roncofredo put in an attack at 0430 hours. By 0500 hours B Company had seized after stiff resistance the right half of Roncofredo. But C Company in its advance towards the objective, the left half of Roncofredo, came under terrific fire from British artillery, whose concentrations fell some 800 yards short. The commanding officer of C Company was killed and the leading platoon suffered casualties. The second in command with great initiative immediately reorganised the company and led it on to the objective. By 0700 hours C Company was in possession of the left half of the village and Roncofredo. Meanwhile, at 0715 hours on 10 October, the 1st King's Own Royal Regiment, moving across the lower eastern slopes of the ridge, had reached a point midway between Roncofredo and San Paola, without contacting the Germans.

Capture of San Paola

In the meantime the 10th Indian Infantry Brigade was directed against the German positions on M. Spaccato and M. Codruzzo. The reinforcement of the 10th Indian Division by the 43rd Indian Infantry Brigade had enabled the 10th Indian Infantry Brigade to prepare for the attack on these positions. On 7 October the 43rd Indian Infantry Brigade was switched across from the almost waterlogged 56th Division's front on the coastal plain (in the sector of Route 9) and passed under the command of the 10th Indian Division, moving straight into 10th Indian Infantry Brigade positions. 2/8 Gurkha Rifles moved into Scorticata area and from there was sent to relieve 4/10 Baluch in Strigara at 2200 hours. This move enabled the 10th Indian Infantry Brigade to go ahead at once with its preparations for the attack on M. Spaccato and M. Codruzzo. The brigade plan was to attack with three battalions—2/4 Gurkha to seize San Paola; the 1st Durham Light Infantry to pass through and capture M. Spaccato; 4/10 Baluch to capture M. Codruzzo.

At 1645 hours on 7 October, 2/4 Gurkha concentrated in the S. Martino area in order to attack San Paola, an important road junction, a splendid view point and a strongly built locality, which gained in strength though being protected by the summit of the ridge. This attack was further designed to pinch out the German defences at Roncofredo against which the 25th Indian Infantry Brigade was committed. *17th Company 721st Jaegar Regiment* held San Paola, but as the attack developed the Germans were able to reinforce the garrison under cover of darkness. The main resistance at San Paola was centred on the Cemetery and the Church across the road from it. The flanks were protected by strong German detachments at C. Croce and the high ground at 657957.

The Gurkha plan was for A and C Companies to attack and capture San Paola Village, D Company to seize the high ground at 637958 and B Company to secure C. Croce. At 0330 hours on 8 October, A and C Companies moved off but found the going difficult, owing to thick country and the heavy morning mist. At 0545 hours the two companies attacked San Paola, but found the village held in strength. Their advance was halted at 0645 hours by the stubborn resistance of the Germans in the Church. Extremely heavy machine gun fire from the village and artillery fire prevented further advance and both the companies were held up in the area of the Church. At 0830 hours a German counter-attack developed against A Company but was repelled by defensive and small arms fire. Meanwhile efforts were made to attack the flank of the main German position at San Paola. At 0700 hours B Company had moved off to deal with German opposition from C. Croce. The Germans held C. Croce in strength and no progress could be made in capturing this position. Thus the Gurkha could make headway neither against the German position at C. Croce nor against that at San Paola. Against these failures is to be set the success of D Company, which moving off at 0945 hours secured by 1130 hours, after very stiff resistance, its objective, the high ground at 637958.

The struggle for the capture of the Church of San Paola continued throughout the day. At 2000 hours the Germans counter-attacked A Company near the Church but were driven off by small arms fire. At 0500 hours on 9 October a German counter-attack on C Company near the Church was repulsed. After this vain attempt to drive out A and C Companies near the Church the Germans turned their attention to companies on the flanks—D Company at 637958 and B Company at 633948. At 0730 hours on 9 October, B Company frustrated the attempt made by a German platoon to infiltrate between A and B Companies. The Germans made two further vain efforts at 0830 hours and 1030 hours to infiltrate in the direction of B Company. At 1005 hours they counter-attacked D Company but were driven off. At 1200 hours B Company tried to wrest the initiative from the Germans by pushing on to C. Croce, but the latter repulsed the attack. However, the losses they had sustained and the increased threat to their northern flank arising from the operations of the 25th Indian Infantry Brigade (the successful attack during the night of 9/10 October by 3/1 Punjab on Roncofredo) compelled the Germans to withdraw during the night of 9/10 October.

Capture of M. Spaccato

The high ground of M. Spaccato was a formidable obstacle to the division and threatened seriously to interfere with the advance towards Cesena. The 1st Battalion Durham Light Infantry was given the job of capturing it. The commanding officer was forced to plan largely from air photographs as the complete observation of the area by the German positions had made personal reconnaissance and observation of the ground extremely difficult. Moreover an even more important factor had to be considered—bad weather, which considerably hampered operations. It had been raining for some days which added considerably to the difficulties of the Durham.

The D.L.I. (reinforced later by two companies of 2/4 Gurkha) passed through San Paola during the night of 9/10 October to attack M. Spaccato on the next ridge, the northern of the two from M. Farneto. *7 Company 721st Jaegar Regiment* held this feature. After a gruelling four-hour march to the assembly point, the attackers had still some 2000 yards uphill to go to reach the start line. Bad weather made the D.L.I. three hours late in crossing the start line. The D.L.I. experienced difficulty with the mules, which were unable to make the pace. Waist-deep in mud, the muleteers fought with their charges and strained every nerve to get them forward but in vain. Losing their balance in the sea of mud, the mules slipped and fell on the radio sets they were carrying and sent the ammunition flying in all directions. One of the mules was unable to raise itself from the ground and, in spite of all that the muleteers could do, was suffocated in the slimy clinging mud. Yet another was lost as it tried to negotiate a stream. It was therefore decided that the sets and ammunition would have to be manhandled if the attack was to succeed at all.

At length with the utmost difficulty, the three attacking companies were deployed. A Company on the right was to get to M. Spaccato, B Company to pass through to the castle of Monte Leone. M. Spaccato was the key of the position. Using the night to their advantage the Durham infiltrated from the south through several holes in the German defences. By first light B Company had reached its objective and, achieving surprise, cleared the point and took a few prisoners. On the right a platoon of A Company approached the objective with such stealth that it captured several Germans as they were shaving. The officer who led this thrust fired two shots at a house. Immediately afterwards 14 Germans led by their officer trooped out of the front door with their hands upraised.

C Company, moving up had almost reached the castle, when the trouble started. First, the company commander was killed by a sniper's bullet, and shortly afterwards the two subaltern platoon commanders were also hit by the hidden marksmen—one of them fatally. All the time German 'stonks' were landing among the men of the Durham Light Infantry until finally a strong counter-attack forced them to withdraw. In the confusion that followed, A Company's location was exposed, and for the next 4 hours it was the target for incessant artillery fire. After suffering severe casualties it was decided to withdraw the forward platoon of A Company to join the rest of the company. This decision was accelerated by a further German counter-attack, which threw half a company into the attack and the Durham platoon in its weakened condition was in deadly peril. A Lance Serjeant, with two bren gunners, averted further casualties by remaining behind to cover the withdrawal of the platoon. As the Germans advanced, the three defenders crouched over their guns. Not until the Germans were twenty yards away did the Lance Serjeant give the order to open fire. In their first few bursts it was estimated that the bren gunners had killed twenty Germans. After stemming the German advance for some time, and after hurling their grenades at the Germans, the three men fell back on the company. Their platoon had been thus enabled to withdraw without further casualties.

The Germans maintained their pressure on the Durham and at one time during this memorable day, Tactical Headquarters found itself 200 yards away from a German pocket and came under periodic snipers' fire. It had to be helped out by a company of 2/4 Gurkha, who eliminated the pocket.

For the rest of the day, the outlook for the Durham was—to use the commanding officer's expression—'very dismal'. Volunteers carried ammunition to the forward companies, who were under heavy and accurate shell-fire the whole time. At length, during the sixth shelling of the area, and after a direct hit on a house in which Tactical Headquarters suffered eight casualties, the commanding officer decided to move over to a safer spot.

During the following night the Germans pulled out and the Durham was able to advance and take the objectives.* To ensure the safety of M. Spaccato and its road junctions against possible further German attacks, a company of 1/2 Punjab was moved forward to reinforce the Durham.

Advance Towards Monte Codruzzo

Further south, M. Codruzzo was yet held by the Germans. 4/10 Baluch was directed against this feature. From Strigara, a long knife-edge ridge—the Costa Passo dei Meloni—led northwards to M. Codruzzo. It was up this spur, with M. Codruzzo as the objective, that 4/10 Baluch was to attack. The slopes of M. Codruzzo were gentler and broader than those of the hills preceding it. Into those slopes torrents of rain water had eaten their way. Greys and greens intermingled to give the whole feature an appearance of grassland more suited to England than to Italy.

At 2200 hours on 7 October, A Company started and met with opposition in the first village, Bondanini, but cleared the houses and continued to advance. At 2300 hours, D Company followed and both the companies advanced north along the ridge, fighting at

---

* "And the Rains Came"—the *Diagonals* dated 26 May 1945 ; Appendix "L" War Diary 10 Ind. Div. May 1945.

intervals throughout the night. Opposition was determined and shelling intense. Bad going also made progress slow. Owing to the exposed positions on the ridge a slight withdrawal was carried out to better sited positions, just south of Montale. Thus at dawn on 8 October, the Baluch had advanced no further than Montale, less than half way to the objective. Reinforcements were required before this attack went through to its conclusion. 2/6 Gurkha of the 43rd Indian Infantry Brigade was therefore called up to assist 4/10 Baluch in overcoming German resistance. Three battalions were to be involved in the operation which took place during the night of 10/11 October. 2/6 Gurkha was to advance across the northern slopes of M. Farneto and attack M. Codruzzo from the east, while two companies of 4/10 Baluch were to attack northwards up the spur from Strigara and capture M. Campo. 2/8 Gurkha (from the 43rd Indian Infantry Brigade) was to aid 2/6 Gurkha with a feint attack west from Strigara towards S. Maria Riopetra.

2/6 Gurkha had relieved the Durham in the area of San Martino at 2330 hours on 8 October. It was about six miles to the assembly area and then two miles to the objective, M. Codruzzo, over very hilly country. The Gurkhas arrived in the assembly area at 1915 hours on 10 October. Their mules did not arrive until after B, C and D Companies had moved off towards M. Codruzzo at 2025 hours. Though few Germans were met, the approach to the objective took five hours. By 0300 hours on 11 October, M. Codruzzo was captured against light opposition.

Meanwhile 4/10 Baluch too had secured the objective, M. Campo. On 10 October when the Tactical Headquarters moved to Sera di Bagnolo it was heavily shelled, and suffered casualties. However A and C Companies attacked M. Campo during the night of 10/11 October and seized their objective without opposition. Thus by first light, 2/6 Gurkha was on the summit of M. Codruzzo and 4/10 Baluch on M. Campo, eight hundred yards to the south-east.

Having failed in their attempt to retake M. Spaccato, the Germans had decided to abandon the Montiano—Monte-novo ridge, as well as M. Codruzzo further south-west. Perhaps an additional explanation would be their determination to avoid further repetition of the events of the past few days, when the Allied rapid advance from successive key features had each time breached their defensive line before adequate preparations to hold it had been made. To counter the rapidity of the Allied advance the decision might well have been taken to make a bolder withdrawal back to the last massif in front of Cesena—the M. Dell Erta—M. Delle Vacche ridge and thus ensure that there would be adequate time to organise its defence.[10]

[10] 10 Ind. Div. Intelligence Summary No. 115, October 1944.

Capture of the M. Dell Erta—M. Delle Vacche Ridge

After having been driven out from Roncofredo, M. Spaccato, M. Farneto and M. Codruzzo the Germans had fallen back on the M. Dell Erta—M. Delle Vacche ridge. Across the next valley from Monte M. Spaccato, recently secured by the Durham, was the prominent village of Sorrivoli. The ridge on which this village stood rose in two distinct steps. Sorrivoli was on the forward slopes and the crest of the first step. The second step to the highest point was thirteen-hundred-feet M. Delle Vacche, and three spurs jutted out eastwards towards M. Spaccato. Sorrivoli stood on the northern most of these spurs. The middle spur ran south of Sorrivoli. The southern spur rose to M. Bora. From M. Delle Vacche the ridge ran south through three main features of approximately the same height, M. Chicco, M. Dell Erta and M. Codruzzo.

On 11 October, the 20th Indian Infantry Brigade on M. Farneto went into reserve for a well earned rest. The 43rd Indian Infantry Brigade resumed command of its own battalions, making a fourth brigade of the 10th Indian Division. 2/6 Gurkha was in M. Codruzzo; 2/8 Gurkha was concentrating west of S. Donato and 2/10 Gurkha was preparing to pass through 2/6 Gurkha on M. Codruzzo along the ridge to attack M. Dell Erta. The ridge on which the 43rd Indian Infantry Brigade was now established ran from south-east to north-west, that is, at right angles to those ridges which the rest of the division on their right must pass. For this reason the ridge was of great tactical advantage. The 85th Mountain Regiment, Royal Artillery, supported 2/10 Gurkha's attack on M. Dell Erta.

This attack by 2/10 Gurkha was to be a tremendous test of physical endurance. The battalion had been marching on foot from Pecchiano since early morning on 11 October and had arrived at M. Codruzzo shortly before dark. Despite his fatigue, the artillery officer with the battalion quickly produced a detailed plan for aiding the Gurkha attack. After an artillery barrage, 2/10 Gurkha launched the attack at 2330 hours on 11 October, when D Company crossed the start line directed on the White House (576959), followed by B Company, whose objective was the Red House (576960). These two houses and Pt. 403 proved to be the chief centres of German resistance. At 0155 hours on 12 October, D Company reached within fifty yards of the White House but was then pinned down to the ground by heavy fire. Meanwhile B Company, which had arrived at the cross-roads, moved up close behind D Company. At 0241 hours British artillery opened up but immediately afterwards (at 0242 hours) B Company called for fire to cease as shells were falling in the area of the forward platoons of D Company, and also in B Company area. Then at 0250 hours D Company asked for a shoot on to the hill on which the White House was situated. But again B Company had to ask for fire to cease as two guns were firing short and had rather dispersed the company. In spite of the fact that British artillery could not give effective support, B Company moved forward at 0325 hours on 12 October to attack the Red House, which was seized at 0345 hours. C Company then took over from B Company at the Red House, enabling it to lead the attack on the White House. At 0415 hours, B Company captured the White House after stiff resistance. Subsequently at 0425 hours, B Company again advanced and secured Pt. 403. Three German counter-attacks developed in quick succession on B Company but they were repelled. By 0600 hours the Gurkhas consolidated their positions with D Company at White House, C Company in the area of the Red House, B Company on Pt. 403 and A Company in reserve at tracks and road junction. After consolidating these positions, 2/10 Gurkha prepared to attack and capture M. Delle Erta. The artillery barrage opened up at 2345 hours and A Company passed through B Company at Pt. 403 directed on Pt. 427, viz. M. Dell Erta. The objective was reached at 0515 hours on 13 October against light opposition.[11]

While 2/10 Gurkha captured M. Dell Erta, the 1st Durham Light Infantry and 2/4 Gurkha were directed against Sorrivoli and M. Bora respectively, preparatory to the attack on M. Delle Vacche. On 12 October a daylight patrol from the Durham from M. Spaccato penetrated the perimeter of Sorrivoli's defences at 1630 hours. A Company moved up to seize the village, which was occupied after stiff opposition. The position was consolidated by 0240 hours on 13 October.

A mile and a half to the south, the Germans offered opposition, for a while, to the occupation of M. Delle Vacche by 2/4 Gurkha. On 11 October, 2/4 Gurkha was in area C. Croce, with D Company forward in area Ronco Vecchio. At 1800 hours on 11 October Tactical Battalion Headquarters arrived in area Ronco Vecchio and D Company set off to establish a patrol base near C. Bonandi. At 2100 hours a fighting patrol of one platoon D Company was sent to M. Bora. The patrol met no opposition till it reached the houses at the southern end of the village, where men were engaged by small arms, grenades and mortars. The patrol returned at 0400 hours on 12 October. Then at 0830 hours D Company led the attack on M. Bora and was partly successful against stiff opposition. The southern part of the village was occupied by D Company at 1200 hours but the Germans continued to occupy the northern part.

The second phase of the attack began at 1915 hours on 12 October, when C Company, followed by A Company, (the latter followed by B Company) moved off from the area near Bonani (where

[11]Sitrep dated 12 and 13 October 1944, War Diary 10 Ind. Div.

Tactical Headquarters had been established), to clear the Germans from M. Bora, the road junction, and M. Delle Vacche. At 2030 hours both the leading companies (C and A) came under heavy mortar and machine gun fire while crossing the nullah. C Company managed to cross the nullah and continued to advance but A Company was held up and dispersed. Two platoons of C Company continued the advance, followed by one platoon later. But heavy casualties checked the advance. At 0200 hours on 13 October, C Company attacked and cleared the houses in the upper part of the village. But further advance was held up by considerable German fire from the hill at 587974.

The third phase of the attack then began at 0500 hours on 13 October when B Company moved round the flank of the leading company (C) to attack the hill at 585977. The company was caught in the open by German tanks, which opened fire with high explosive and machine gun from Oriola. The company suffered heavy casualties, its commander being killed. The company then withdrew to Tactical Headquarters near Bonandi in small parties. Throughout the day the Germans heavily shelled and mortared the Gurkha positions on M. Bora, while British artillery fired heavy concentrations on the hill at 585977, the road junction, and M. Delle Vacche, the three chief centres of German resistance. At 1030 hours on 14 October, an attack by six Allied fighter bombers on the road junction yielded good results, for the German shelling on M. Bora became lighter. At 0600 hours on 15 October, A, C and D Companies commenced the attack on the road junction and M. Delle Vecche. A Company occupied the road junction without opposition and C and D Companies passed through and occupied M. Delle Vacche, again without opposition, as the Germans had evacuated these places.

Capture of M. Chicco

Meanwhile, advance had been made on both flanks of the 10th Indian Division. On the right, 4/10 Baluch passed through the Durham at Sorrivoli directed on Diolaguardia. C and D, the leading companies, cleared the Germans from the houses north-east of Sorrivoli by 2130 hours on 12 October. Further advance was however held by fierce German resistance. The companies were counter-attacked on five separate occassions on 13 October. They were also heavily shelled and mortared. A and B Companies moved up in support in the early hours of 14 October. They cleared more houses but were held up just short of the objective.

On the left flank, M. Dell Erta, as already mentioned, had been secured by 2/10 Gurkha. 2/6 Gurkha, after having been relieved on 13 October on M. Codruzzo by 2/8 Gurkha, closed up to prepare for the attack on M. Chicco, the next feature on the higher ridge, one and a half miles north of M. Dell Erta. This high ridge through M. Chicco was the last of the hill ranges east of the river Savio, which overlooked the coastal sector and Route 9. Hence it was of considerable importance to the Germans. M. Chicco, owing to the restricted approaches to it and the barrenness of its slopes, made the assault a difficult job for the attackers, and the Gurkhas could approach it only by the road through Montaguzzo.

The battalion plan was for D Company to clear Montaguzzo and then for A and B Companies to pass through and take M. Chicco. C Company was to be in reserve but was to be ready to move up to the support of the forward companies.

D Company ran into fierce opposition at Montaguzzo but beat it down by 0030 hours on 14 October. A and B Companies then passed through for the attack on M. Chicco. B Company's objective was the single White House on the eastern side of the summit (which turned out to be the main centre of opposition); A Company's objective was the ridge running north-west from M. Chicco. Every house on the approaches was a strong point stubbornly defended by the Germans. By 0350 hours, A Company had cleared the forward slopes of M. Chicco and B Company too had closed on the White House. The Gurkhas remained in position on the southern slope while the Germans dug in on the northern slopes of the feature, within hand grenade range of the forward troops. The Germans made desperate efforts to dislodge the Gurkhas from the southern slopes of the feature. It was B Company which had to bear the brunt of the German counter-attacks. One platoon was overrun and suffered heavy casualties. C Company, however, reinforced B Company, and after a fierce struggle ousted the Germans from the White House at 0600 hours. At 0650 hours, the Germans launched a fierce counter-attack on C Company. The latter was so hard-pressed that it made frantic calls for help. One Company of 2/8 Gurkha reinforced 2/6 Gurkha at 0800 hours but it was not till 1830 hours that a second company of 2/8 Gurkha could move up for support. By that time two platoons of 2/10 Gurkha had been moved up to Montaguzzo in support of 2/6 Gurkha. The struggle for supremacy across the crest continued throughout the day. Behind the Gurkhas their line of supply followed an exposed narrow ridge, over which all supplies and casualties had to run the gauntlet of intense shelling for over a mile. The Royal Air Force and the British artillery however came to the rescue of the hard-pressed Gurkhas. 2/6 Gurkha received effective air support, which was made possible by directing aircraft on to targets quickly and accurately by the 1st Field Regiment Royal Artillery indicating targets with smoke shells. Fighter bombers broke up the German attempts to reinforce their troops on M. Chicco. Aircraft were also employed to knock out the German mortars, which had proved troublesome. The assistance given by the Royal Air Force was excellent. The gunner liaison officer of the 1st Field Regiment Royal Artillery earned the gratitude of the Gurkhas for the splendid help which his guns gave them. Small arms ammunition was running short, so the guns engaged targets within two hundred yards of the Gurkha positions. Throughout a day of continuous shelling and mortaring by the Germans this officer directed the fire of the divisional artillery and smashed up German attacks. This effective artillery fire and the arrival of reinforcements broke up German resistance. In the early hours of the morning on 15 October, the Germans withdrew and M. Chicco was seized by the Gurkhas, who suffered more than fifty casualties in the struggle for M. Chicco.

In losing M. Chicco and M. Delle Vacche on 14 October the Germans had suffered a serious reverse. The Allied forces had torn a great hole through *721 Jaegar Regiment's* sector and were advancing both on M. Dei Pine and M. Burattini. The German position along the M. Delle Vacche ridge had by nightfall become untenable, despite their extremely stubborn resistance on this feature and on the northern slopes of M. Chicco. It was, therefore, hardly surprising that the Germans broke contact during the night of 14/15 October, pulling back along the whole front, presumably to the stop-line of the Pisciatello stream. This position followed the north bank of the river to cut Route 9 at the cross-roads and link up with the improvised positions on the low ridge to M. Romano, thence to M. Reale and Roversano near the river Savio. This could only be a temporary position, to be held for about 24 hours, whilst the remaining transport and guns filtered back through the bottleneck of the few remaining Savio crossings. As a hill position it had little to commend it, for it was completely overlooked by the heights of M. Delle Vacche. But the days of dominating heights, from which every movement of the Allied forces could be observed, were now over for the Germans.[12]

At last we see the other side of the recent dour fighting. The price paid by the Germans for a further month's respite in the Appennines had been heavy. By their policy of vigorous hole-plugging, they undeniably gained time to push ahead with an extensive demolition scheme for the Po Valley, which was probably scarcely started when the Allies first alarmed them by breaking through their strong Gothic Line defences. They had also gained time to build up their defences behind the Adige. But now they were being called on to pay the price for the respite they had gained; and thus at the moment of the most ticklish operation—the disengagement off the hills into the plains—they found themselves left without a mobile

---

[12] 10 Ind. Div. Intelligence Summary No. 118, dated 15 October 1944.

reserve, and with their infantry tired and depleted by weeks of heavy fighting.

Advance to the River Savio

After the German withdrawal, 4/10 Baluch moved into Diolaguardia and 2/4 Gurkha pursued the Germans from M. Delle Vacche in the morning of 15 October. D and C Companies of 4/10 Baluch exploited in the direction of M. Reale and captured the feature 578005 against heavy opposition, which was consolidated though heavy shelling and mortaring continued throughout the day.

At 2100 hours on 15 October, the 26th Indian Infantry Brigade took over from the 10th Indian Infantry Brigade, and 4/10 Baluch was temporarily placed under its command. With the 1st King's Own Royal Regiment at Diolaguardia, 3/18 Garhwal on M. Delle Vacche, 4/10 Baluch between them near M. Reale, and 3/1 Punjab in reserve at Sorrivoli, it was a solid position for the 25th Indian Infantry Brigade.

4/10 Baluch made a final all-out effort at 2030 hours on 16 October. A and B Companies passed through C and D Companies and attacked M. Reale along the ridge from the south. After stiff opposition they secured M. Reale by 0300 hours on 17 October.

The Germans appreciated the threat of the Allied advance along the Acquarola—M. Reale ridge and, they made a strong effort to retain this vital position. They had the roads running south of Cesena to bring up self-propelled guns or tanks in support. A troop of the *129 Tank Battalion* had moved up from the south of Cesena and was in position north of M. Reale in an anti-tank role. Hence 3/1 Punjab encountered stiff opposition in the advance to Acquarola. At midnight 16/17 October, 3/1 Punjab pased through 4/10 Baluch at M. Reale to extend the hold northwards to Acquarola and Pt. 157. One troop 2 pounders, one platoon of heavy mortars and one platoon of medium machine guns were in support of 3/1 Punjab. Acquarola's proximity to Cesena made it a tender spot for the Germans, who resisted this advance stubbornly with machine guns and self-propelled artillery, but 3/1 Punjab continued to edge forward slowly towards the objective, despite continuous and heavy shelling from the German artillery and mortars, against which the ridge offered little protection. Fear for the safety of the rear detachments must have led to this heavy shelling. German self-propelled guns and machine guns however failed to check the advance and by first light D Company had secured Acquarola while the other companies were in position in the area M. Reale. Extremely heavy German shelling throughout the day made movement impossible and inflicted heavy casualties on men and mules. A counter-attack developing on D Company was broken up, but small parties of Germans from the area of S. Demetrio caused considerable discomfort by constant sniping and machine gun fire. In the evening a German armoured fighting vehicle was observed forward of Acquarola but it was impossible to bring up anti-tank guns to engage it due to a blow in the road. The advance of 3/1 Punjab was held up by the Germans occupying the high ground to its north. The Germans were also strongly entrenched in the Church near S. Demetrio, which became the centre of the struggle. Till 2230 hours on 17 October 3/1 Punjab was unable to move forward. However, at 0515 hours on 18 October, B Company captured the Church near S. Demetrio after stiff resistance. C Company moved to the high ground but encountered considerable opposition and withdrew on to D Company position at Acquarola. German mortar and artillery fire increased in intensity and no move forward was possible in the daylight. Repeated attempts by C Company to occupy the high ground were frustrated by heavy artillery and small arms fire. B Company in S. Demetrio was running short of ammunition and food. These were rushed up to repel in the evening a strong German counter-attack which was supported by a tank shooting up the whole area. Despite heavy casualties B Company held on until dark when it withdrew. The Germans, however, withdrew and by 0100 hours on 10 October, the Church and the high ground, including Pt. 157, were found by the patrols to be clear of the Germans.

Before the right flank had been strengthened by these advances, a platoon of 3/18 Garhwal had advanced from south of M. Delle Vacche at 1830 hours on 17 October to probe into German defences in Roversano. The platoon found the village held in strength and all approaches covered. At 0130 hours on 18 October, two platoons advanced and captured the village, after encountering opposition, at 0315 hours.

After making a stand at Roversano, M. Reale Acquarola and the high ground to its north, the Germans had withdrawn to position across the river Savio. By 18 October, the 10th Indian Division had squared up to that river and was busy making preparations for the establishment of bridge-heads over it.

CHAPTER XXV

Advance to the River Ronco

The Eighth Army's Advance to the River Ronco

By 20 October 1944 the main body of the Eighth Army had closed up to the river Savio. The Canadians crossed the Pisciatello and cleared the northern half of Cesena; while on the coastal flank "Cumberlandforce", a composite battle group led by Brigadier I.H. Cumberland, commander of the 5th Canadian Armoured Brigade—captured Cesenatico and made substantial gains in the country south of Cervia. The 46th Division advanced through M. Romano and Celincordia to the Madna del Monte Hill—the southern suburbs of Cesena. At the same time, the 10th Indian Division advanced through M. Reale and Acquarola to Pt. 157 on the ridge above the Savio Valley. The 4th Division, after relieving the 46th Division, crossed the Savio in the southern outskirts of Cesena but found it difficult to expand the bridge-head due to very stiff opposition. Further to the south, however, the 10th Indian Division was able to establish two bridge-heads over the Savio—one near M. Falcino and the other at Castiglione—San Carlo. The Germans were driven from M. Cavallo and M. Della Rovere (also called M. Dei Fertiti) by 23 October. These bridge-heads were of great importance since they enabled the 10th Indian Division to outflank the Germans, compelling them to give up the defence of the Savio line further to the north.

On 24 October, the 10th Indian Division and the British 4th Division pushed on the pursuit to the river Ronco. At the close of 25 October, the British 4th Division was established on the line of the Ronco from Route 9 to Selbagnone, while the 10th Indian Division secured the high ground on the east bank of the river from M. Casale to M. Palareto. On the night of 25/26 October, the British 4th Division tried to establish two bridge-heads, one in the area Selbagnone and the other on Route 9, opposite the village of Ronco. Both attempts failed. The 10th Indian Division, however, fared better, for two bridge-heads were established north and south of Meldola.

The I Canadian Corps too had squared up to the river Ronco. As the Fifth Army's forward troops were about ten miles from Bologna on 22 October, General Von Vietinghoff, now Supreme German Commander,[1] transferred the *20th Panzer Grenadier Division*

---

[1] Field-Marshal Kesselring had been wounded in an air attack.

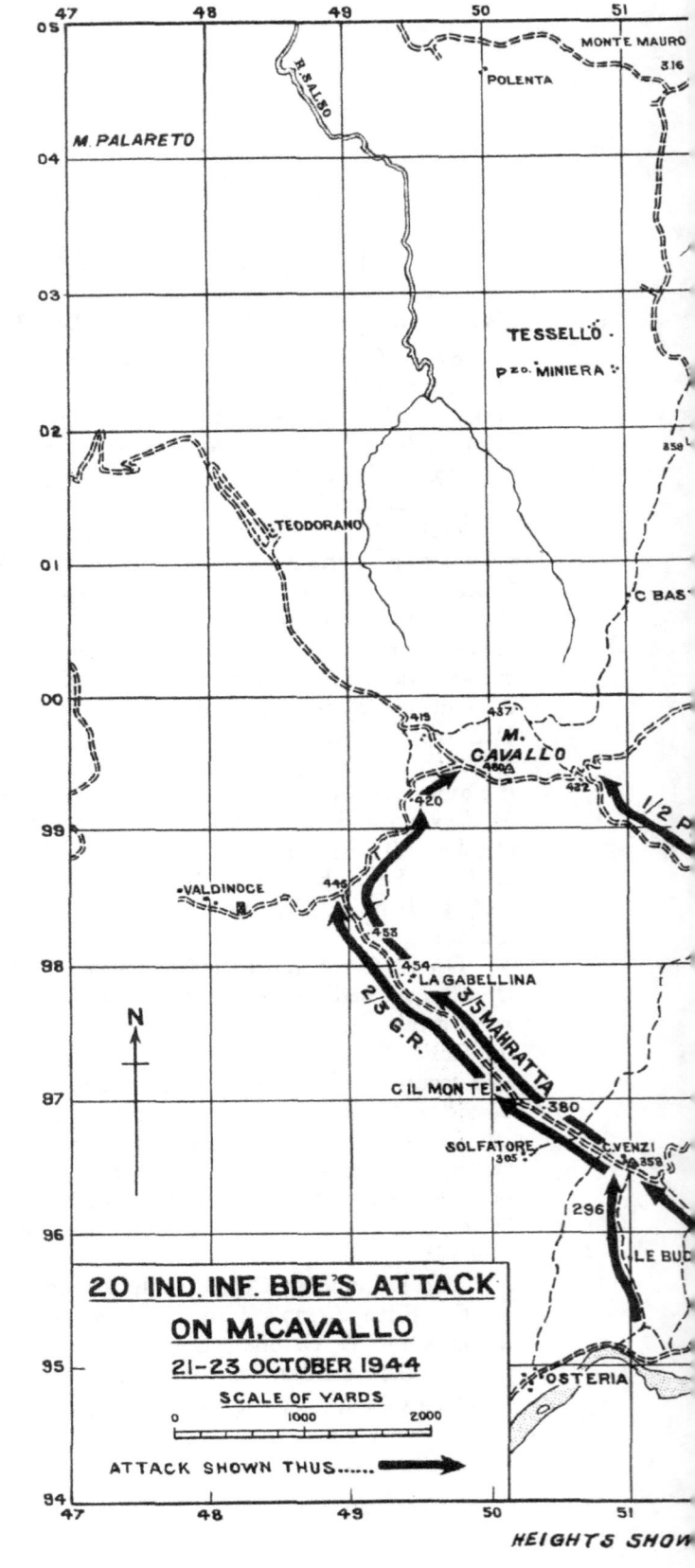

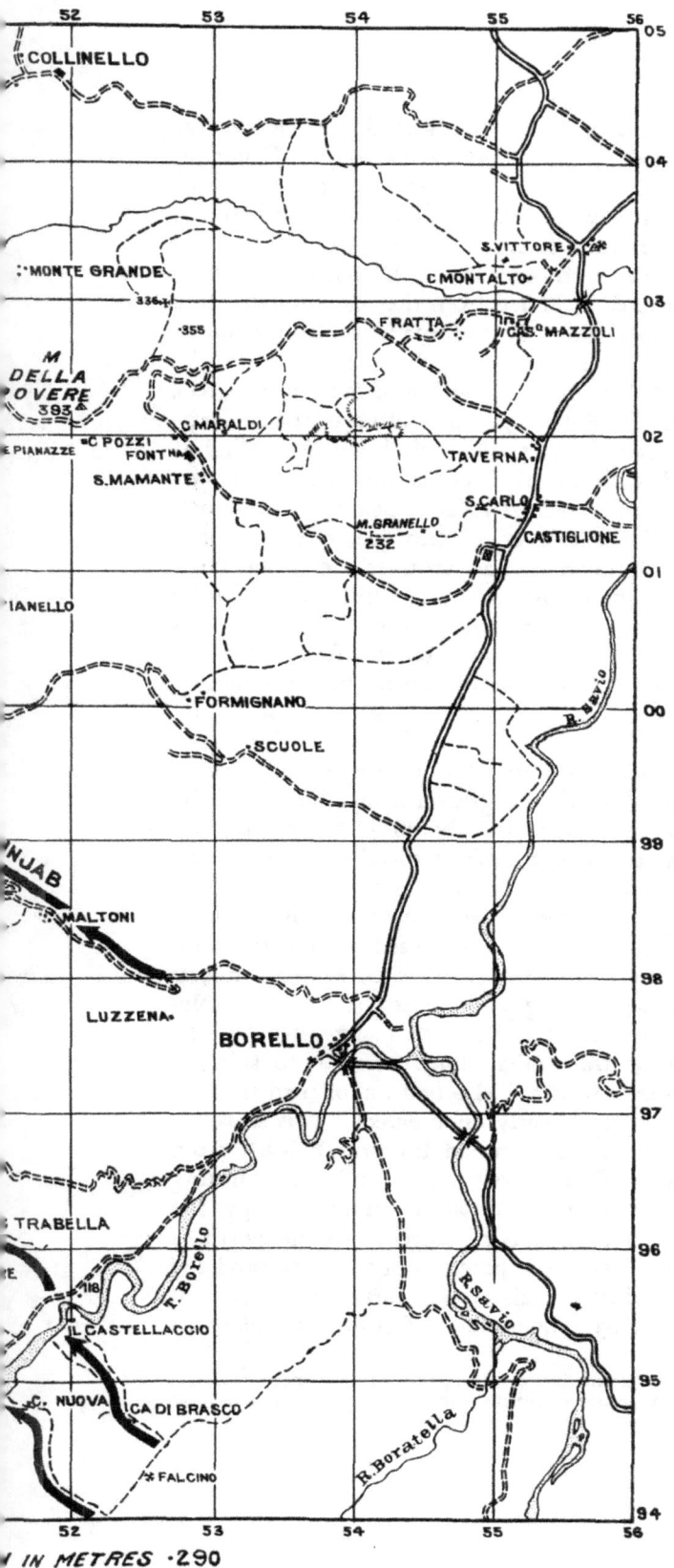

and the *1st Parachute Division* from the Adriatic to the central sector. This weakening of the Adriatic front enabled the I Canadian Corps to make substantial gains. On the left, the 1st Canadian Division squared up to the Ronco while on the right the 'Cumberlandforce' advanced across the Bevano along Route 16. The I Canadian Corps was relieved on 27/28 October; the 12th Lancers assumed command of the line of the river Ronco from the main railway line north of Route 9 to Bagnolo while 'Porterforce'[2] took command of the sector from Bagnolo to the coast.

Meanwhile the II Polish Corps had been also making progress. On 14 October 1944, when the Poles took up position in the X Corps sector to exert pressure astride Route 71 the main body of the Eighth Army had almost reached the line of the Savio and Route 71. Therefore the Poles were next directed across country against Forlimpopli and Forli on Route 67. Their axis of advance was the secondary road from San Piero in Bagno to Rocca San Casciano. The Poles encountered increasingly stiff opposition in the hills, a few miles south-west of Rocca San Casciano, and M. Crosso. The latter was taken on 21 October and Predappie Nuova on the Rabbi river on 27 October. Further operations were hampered by bad weather.

Attack on M. Delle Rovere

Having given a brief account of the Eighth Army's advance to the river Ronco we will now describe in greater detail the role of the Indian formations in these operations. By 18 October 1944, no German troops remained on the east bank of the river Savio within the 10th Indian Division's boundaries, though they were still holding out in front of Cesena. Patrols, crossing swollen river with difficulty, discovered that the German forces were disposed with their main strength on the high ground above the river, while strong outposts held all likely exits from the crossing places over the river. A solution to the problem of crossing the Savio was suggested by the success achieved by the Central India Horse who, by pushing a dismounted squadron across a ford at Cello had established the first bridge-head across the Savio, apparently unobserved. This situation was exploited by switching the 20th Indian Infantry Brigade from reserve over the river Savio at Mercato Sarceno, and concentrating it in the general area of the river Boratella, unnoticed by the Germans, by 1000 hours on 20 October. Further to the north, a patrol of 2/6 Gurkha crossed near the junction of the Savio and the Borello and penetrated to Borello village and Luzzena on the hill above it on 19 October. By 0315 hours on 20 October two platoons

---

[2] 'Porterforce' was an *ad hoc* formation consisting of the 27 Lancers and the 3rd Canadian Armoured Reconnaissance Regiment, supported by armour as well as the Canadian artillery and engineers.

of 3/18 Garhwal had crossed the Savio and made a bridge-head at San Carlo. Thus the 25th Indian Infantry Brigade had secured a footing on the west bank of the river.

With bridge-heads established on the river Sacio, preparations for a divisional attack began on 21 October. The Germans had taken up position on two features—M. Delle Rovere (also called the Tessello Hill) twelve hundred feet in height and four miles west of the Savio at San Carlo, and M. Cavallo, a sixteen hundred foot hill, two miles south of M. Delle Rovere—thus barring the advance of the 10th Indian Division to the Ronco valley. M. Cavallo was the dominating feature of the hills between the river Savio and the Ronco valley, in which Meldola was situated. It was approached from east and south by three long spurs from the river Savio. The south spur commencing at C. Venzil was broad and formed a good approach; the centre spur commencing at Lussena was narrow and lower than the south spur; the north spur was much lower than the other two. The *278th Infantry Division* guarded the sector extending from Bastianello to the north-east. *992nd Grenadier Regiment* stretched from C. Bastianello to C. Montalto while further to the north-east was *993rd Grenadier Regiment*. Thus *992nd Grenadier Regiment* was responsible for the defence of M. Delle Rovere. From C. Bastinello to the south-west was the responsibility of *869th Grenadier Regiment* of the *356th Infantry Division*.[3]

The object of the 10th Indian Division was to seize the high ground M. Delle Rovere—Formingnano—M. Cavallo and exploit north to Collinello, with a view to link up with the British 4th Division, which was to advance north-west in the direction of this high ground. The attack was to be made with two brigades—the 25th Indian Infantry Brigade directed against M. Delle Rovere and the 20th Indian Infantry Brigade to be unleashed in a grand assault on M. Cavallo. The attacks by both brigades were to take place during the evening of 21 October, that of the 25th Indian Infantry Brigade preceding the 20th Indian Infantry Brigade's by three hours.

We shall first describe the attack on M. Delle Rovere. 1st Durham Light Infantry and 2/4 Gurkha were temporarily transferred from the 10th to the 25th Indian Infantry Brigade to strengthen the latter in its attack on M. Delle Rovere. Additional troops under the command of the 25th Indian Brigade were: A Squadron North Irish Horse and one platoon Y Company 1st Battalion Royal Northumberland Fusiliers. In support were the 65th, the 97th and the 113th Field Regiments, and one battery each of the 154th Field Regiment and the 58th Medium Regiment. The 25th Indian Infantry Brigade was to capture the ridge from Pt. 336 to M. Delle Rovere and the

---

[3] 10 Ind Div. Intelligence Summary No. 125, 22 October 1944.

high ground of Formignano. The advance was to be carried out in two phases: —

    Phase I—3/18 Garhwal was to establish a firm base in S. Carlo and then secure the objectives—Cemetery, Hill 232 (M. Granello), S. Mamante, M. Delle Rovere and La Pianazze.

    Phase II—(*i*) 1st King's Own Royal Regiment advancing from M. Reale was to establish a firm base at Castiglione and then secure the objectives Taverna, hill near it, Pt. 355 and Pt. 336.

      (*ii*) 2/4 Gurkha was to capture the high ground of Formignano.

      (*iii*) 1st Durham Light Infantry was to mop up the area between the river Savio and Route 71 and cover the brigades' right flank from Taverna, and move to Mazzuli as situation permitted.

      (*iv*) 3/1 Punjab, in reserve in the area M. Reale, was to be prepared to carry out the relief of any forward battalion.[4]

In implementation of the brigade plan the commander of 3/18 Garhwal made a plan for the capture of M. Delle Rovere. The operation was to be carried out in five phases:

    Phase I—B Company was to clear Cemetery (if it had not already been cleared by 1 Durham) and capture the hill M. Granello.

    Phase II—B Company was then to be directed on S. Mamante.

    Phase III—C Company was then to attack and capture M. Delle Rovere. D Company from the area C. Maraldi was to support C Company, if necessary.

    Phase IV—D Company was to follow the route via the south flank of M. Delle Rovere and capture La Pianazze.

    Phase V—A Company was to move to a reserve position—Wadi C. Pozi with a counter-attack role on to La Pianazze or M. Delle Rovere.[5]

Preliminary operations were carried out on 21 October. A detachment from the Durham crossed over the river to Castiglione to help 3/18 Garhwal in holding the bridge-head. The 25th Indian Infantry Brigade was to cross the river Savio, protected by the screen of 1 Durham and 3/18 Garhwal. The attack on M. Delle Rovere, however, entailed administrative difficulties. The only road forward of Sorrivoli at this time was a jeep track, which no measure of sapper effort could prevent from becoming unserviceable after the rain.

---

[4] 25 Ind. Inf. Bde. O.O. No. 3, dated 21 October 1944.
[5] 3/18 R. Garh. Rif. Order for attack on Tessello dated 21 October 1944, War Diary 3/18 R. Garh. Rif.

East of Sorrivoli the route from Sogliano was, at the best, one-way track by which nothing heavier than fifteen hundred-weight trucks could pass. Three brigades and two artillery regiments were already dependent upon it for their supplies. There was no alternative route. The mounting of an opposed river crossing in the 25th Indian Infantry Brigade sector was not therefore an easy proposition.[1] In spite of these administrative difficulties preparations continued for the launching of the attack. At 1700 hours on 21 October, the 25th Indian Infantry Brigade began to cross the river Savio, three of its battalions leading the advance. There were two routes to M. Delle Rovere from S. Carlo; that to the north up a broad spur was taken by the 1st King's Own Royal Regiment, while the southern route, climbing a much narrower spur, no more than five hundred yards across in places, was allotted to 3/18 Garhwal. 2/4 Gurkha attacking up the next spur to the south, a feature one thousand yards wide, had for its objective the imposing and dominating village of Formignano. This was the link between the two brigades which gave a continuous front to the divisional attack. Above the next spur to the south there was an even broader feature, one and a half mile wide, up which ran the objective assigned to the 20th Indian Infantry Brigade.

The night was black and weather conditions appalling. High wind made hill climbing a severe physical effort. Clouds and darkness made direction finding most difficult. Added to the difficulties imposed by nature was a stubborn resistance by the Germans who, reinforced and well-prepared, were in a better fighting trim than they had been for some time past. It was not surprising therefore that all the forward battalions encountered stiff opposition.

By 2000 hours on 21 October, the leading elements of 3/18 Garhwal had crossed the river Savio and had formed up in the area S. Carlo. B Company was then committed to the attack on hill M. Granello (232). Against what was believed to be a weakly defended feature, two platoons set out. Stealing silently forward through the darkness, they maintained surprise until they encounter a minefield in which both platoons suffered casualties. The alarm set off, the German defenders concentrated heavy fire but the men of 3/18 Garhwal moved forward through the minefield and captured the first objective. It was now apparent that each of the attacking platoons was faced by a company of defenders. Counter-attacks came in and soon the Garhwal platoons had run out of ammunition. Meanwhile the company headquarters and another platoon were under severe shell fire and casualties were mounting. One of the forward platoons was withdrawn and ten men were

[1] Notes on R.E. Operations covering the period of phase III, 2 October—2 November; Appendix F; 10 Ind. Div. Narrative of Operations, File 8328/H.

re-formed, issued with all available ammunition, and the two platoons and company headquarters moved forward to assist the remaining platoon. One platoon and company headquarters charged the Germans and temporarily cleared the position but the latter launched a series of counter-attacks, employing as many as 70 men in a determined attempt to encircle the attackers. Eventually one of the forward platoons was driven back from its objective. The company commander, however, rallied the platoon, and led them against the strong German force. More casualties were suffered but the position was retaken. Later, in the face of further onslaughts, the position of the attacking force, most of whose non-commissioned officers were wounded, was even worse. Supporting artillery fire was brought down on the position as the Garhwal platoons drew back. The company commander led his men back into the shell-swept area and evacuated as many of his own wounded as possible. As they worked, artillery fire on the area was maintained. Thus after tough fighting B Company withdrew from Hill 232. The fighting was severe and losses suffered on both sides were considerable. The company of 3/10 Garhwal was opposed, according to the testimony of German prisoners, by six German companies and two self-propelled guns in the area S. Mamante, who held in strength the forward position at Hill 232.

It was in this spirited action that a Garhwali Naik, Trilok Singh Rawat, distinguished himself by his reckless bravery. With their ammunition spent and the Germans, in a series of counter-assaults, threatening to encircle them, the men of a platoon of the Royal Garhwal Rifles, faced almost certain death. But the heroism of the Naik who, single-handed, captured a Spandau, hundreds of rounds of ammunition and two German prisoners, saved them. He later died in covering the retreat of his comrades with the captured machine gun.[7]

While 3/18 Garhwal was held up at M. Granello, 1st King's Own, on the right, failed to drive the Germans from their forward position, the hill near Taverna. By 2300 hours on 21 October two companies of the 1st King's Own had crossed the river Savio to Castiglione and Taverna, but further advance of one company to the hill was held up by very heavy resistance. After a fierce struggle, in which the advantage lay with the Germans, the company withdrew to Taverna.

D, C and A Companies of 2/4 Gurkha crossed the river Savio at 2100 hours on 21 October. At 2400 hours D Company attacked Scuole feature but mistook the adjacent buildings for Scuole and consolidated there. At 0200 hours on 22 October, C and A Companies passed through D Company and continued the advance

---

[7] "Faced the Boche Alone"—the *Diagonals* dated 4 November 1944, Appendix War Diary 10 Ind. Div. November 1944. See also Airmailer No. 40688, F. 601/7436/H.

towards Formignano, but encountered considerable German fire at Scuole. Both the companies consolidated in the school and adjacent buildings, forward of Scuole. No further progress was made as the Gurkha attack ran into a very strong German position in the houses at Formignano and on the forward slopes. The Gurkhas suffered many casualties.

Thus the 25th Indian Infantry Brigade failed to make headway against the Germans. The 1st King's Own was unable to drive the Germans from the hill near Taverna and had to retire and consolidate in Taverna. 3/18 Garhwal failed to capture hill M. Granello and retired to S. Carlo, after suffering heavy casualties. At the same time 2/4 Gurkha while short of the objective Formignano, had by first light, been in occupation of the school, forward of Scuole, more than halfway up to Formignano. Castiglione, Taverna and S. Carlo were heavily shelled by the Germans throughout the night of 21/22 October.

Attack on M. Cavallo

While the 25th Indian Infantry Brigade was directed against M. Delle Rovere, the objective assigned to the 20th Indian Infantry Brigade was M. Cavallo. At 0250 hours on 21 October, 1/2 Punjab advanced the covering screen to Luzzena and at 0335 hours one company had occupied C Venzi without opposition. At that time 2/3 Gurkha and 3/5 Mahratta, intended for the attack on M. Cavallo, had concentrated in the area of the river Boratella.

The commander of the 20th Indian Infantry Brigade made a plan for the capture of M. Cavallo. On the left 2/3 Gurkha, with one platoon medium machine gun under command, was to advance from track junction near Falcino through Ca Nuova and cross start line, road Osteria—Borello at 2000 hours on 21 October. This force was to move through La Budre and Pt. 296, and secure first the road and track junction—Solfatore, and then ring contour 491987 and Pt. 446. On the right 3/5 Mahratta, with one platoon medium machine gun under command was to advance from road and track junction at 527946 through C Id Brasco and cross the start line adjoining the road near Pt. 118 at 2000 hours on 21 October. The battalion was then to advance through C. Trabella to C. Venzi (already occupied by a company of 1/2 Punjab) and to move in echelon behind the leading companies of 2/3 Gurkha north of the main road. After the Gurkhas had secured the second objective (ring contour 491987 and Pt. 446) 3/5 Mahratta was to move on the right flank of 2/3 Gurkha towards M. Cavallo.[8]

[8] 20 Ind. Inf. Bde. O.O. No. 6, dated 21 October 1944. Additional troops under command were one squadron each of North Irish Horse and Skinner's Horse and 61 Field Company, while in support were 25 Mountain and 68, 64, 154 Field and 68 Medium Regiments.

In the initial stages of the advance little opposition was encountered, apart from German shelling. 2/3 Gurkha crossed the start line at 2000 hours on 21 October and secured Pt. 454 at 2330 hours without opposition. But soon after the resistance became stiffer. At 2400 hours, A and D Companies led the attack with D Company on the right, directed against ring contour 491987 and A Company, on the left, against Pt. 446. D Company was held up by stiff resistance. A Company however edged its way forward to Pt. 453 in spite of strong opposition. German firing was very heavy indeed and progress was slow. By 0430 hours A Company dug in about 400 yards from its objective. No further progress could be made.

Meanwhile, 3/5 Mahratta had been following closely the Gurkhas. At 2030 hours on 21 October, the battalion crossed the start line, the road near Pt. 118, in heavy rain. At 2315 hours tactical headquarters was established at Venzi with A and B, the leading companies in the area C. il Monte. At 0430 hours on 22 October, when the Gurkhas were held up about 400 yards short of their objective, 3/5 Mahratta dug in on the right. A Company was near Pt. 453 and D Company at La Gavellina while C and D Companies were in the area C. il Monte. Movement on the slopes of M. Cavallo being quite impossible by day without incurring unnecessary casualties, the Gurkhas and the Mahrattas behind them dug in where they were. In these positions, both the battalions endured heavy day-long harassing fire from the Germans.

In consequence the 20th Indian Infantry Brigade fared no better than the 25th Indian Infantry Brigade. The 10th Indian Division had initially failed to capture M. Cavallo and M. Delle Rovere.

As tough opposition was further apprehended the 20th Indian Infantry Brigade was strengthened during the morning of 22 October by two battalions, 2/8 and 2/10 Gurkha from the 43rd Indian Infantry Brigade. An additional precaution taken was the stepping up of a company of 1/2 Punjab to Maltoni, one mile north-west of Luzzene. Little could be achieved during the hours of daylight. As soon as it was dark, however, movement began again. The plan of attack on M. Cavallo was that after the objective had been softened up during the day by artillery fire, 2/3 Gurkha was to make a silent attack on 22 October at 1900 hours and secure ring contour 491987 and Pt. 446. 3/5 Mahratta was then to move up fifteen minutes later on the right flank to secure M. Cavallo. On the slopes of M. Cavallo, 2/3 Gurkha carried the final objective in a silent attack during which many victims were claimed. By 2000 hours A and D Companies had secured Pt. 446 and ring contour 491987 respectively.

Meanwhile, 3/5 Mahratta had moved up to carry out the allotted task, the occupation of the summit of M. Cavallo. The plan was for A Company to pass through the Gurkha D Company at ring contour 491987 and seize Pt. 420. B Company was then to pass through A Company on to the area near Pt. 419. Subsequently C and D Companies were to take the final objective, M. Cavallo, the limit of exploitation by the latter being up to Pt. 432 and of the former Pt. 437. The Germans contested every yard of the ground. Fierce and confused fighting raged in the darkness. High ground is not always an advantage by night because those holding it may be silhouetted against the sky. These advantages, which did remain with the Germans, were gradually overcome. By 2300 hours on 22 October both A and B Companies had reached their objectives, Pt. 420 and the area near Pt. 419, respectively, despite strong opposition. A Company Commander and the gunner officer were killed by shell fire. Heavy German shelling and mortaring on the forward area inflicted casualties on C Company, which was waiting to pass through B Company. However, by 0530 hours on 23 October, both the Mahratta companies were established on the summit of M. Cavallo. Success was so complete that the Germans were unable to muster the strength required to mount a counter-attack.

The success at M. Cavallo loosened the German hold on M. Delle Rovere and they fell rapidly back on their next defence line, west of the Ronco. The taking of M. Cavallo reflects great credit on the 10th Indian Division. This feature was the key to the German positions west of the river Savio. Once again the 10th Indian Division had turned the German flank, and the Germans were forced to withdraw all along the line. The credit for this achievement goes to the 20th Indian Infantry Brigade, who silently and without being detected crossed the Savio and formed up under the slopes of the Falcino ridge. From this base, the brigade launched its determined assault on the strong German positions. Heavy shell fire was encountered and the weather 'collaborated' as whole-heartedly as usual with the opposition. Added to this, the configuration of the ground was such as to disclose even the slight advance by the Indian and British troops into full view of the German positions. Despite the appalling weather conditions, which imposed a temporary check, the German hold was loosened and by the morning of 23 October the brigade was solidly established on M. Cavallo.[9]

Pursuit to the River Ronco

In view of the Mahratta success at M. Cavallo early on 23 October, 2/8 and 2/10 Gurkha reverted to the 43rd Indian Infantry Brigade. However, the 20th Indian Infantry Brigade was again

---

[9] "How 20 Brigade took M. Cavallo"—the *Diagonals* dated 11 Nov. 1944; Appx. War Diary 10 Div. November 1944.

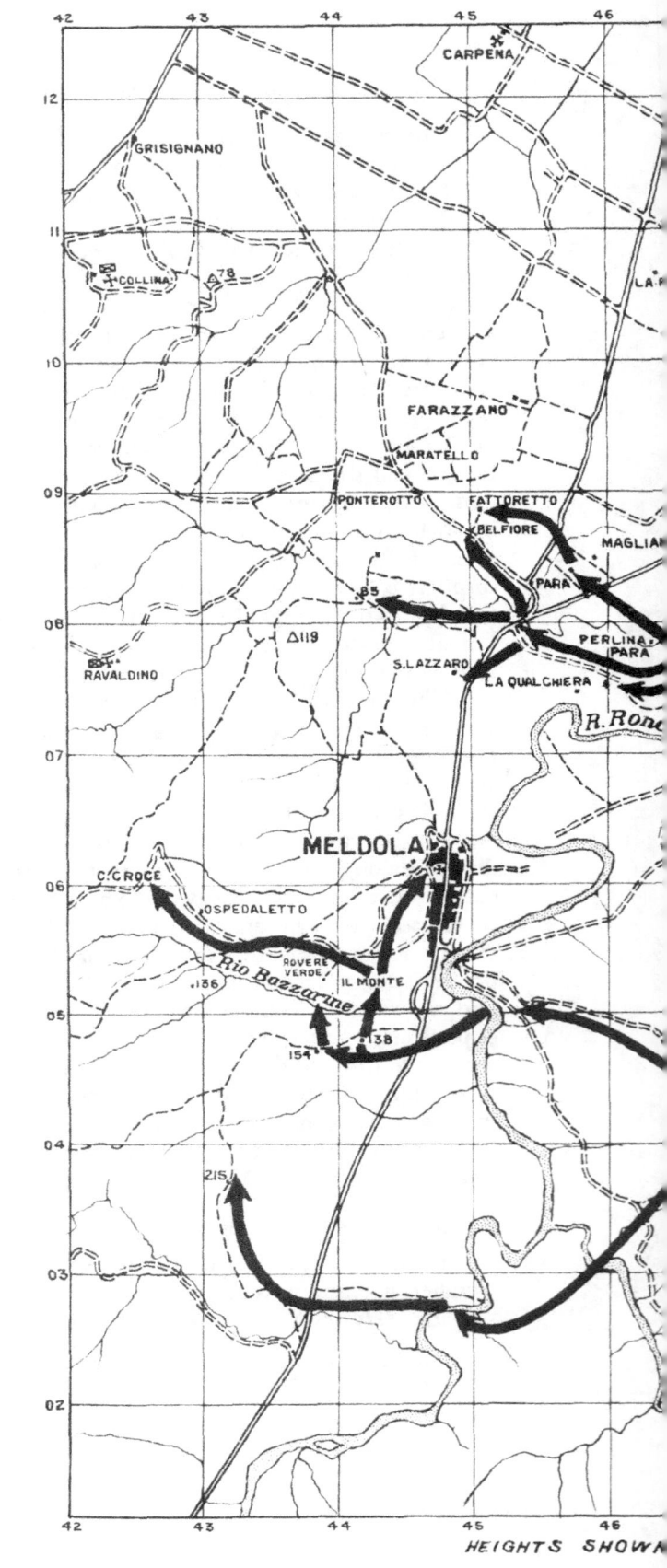

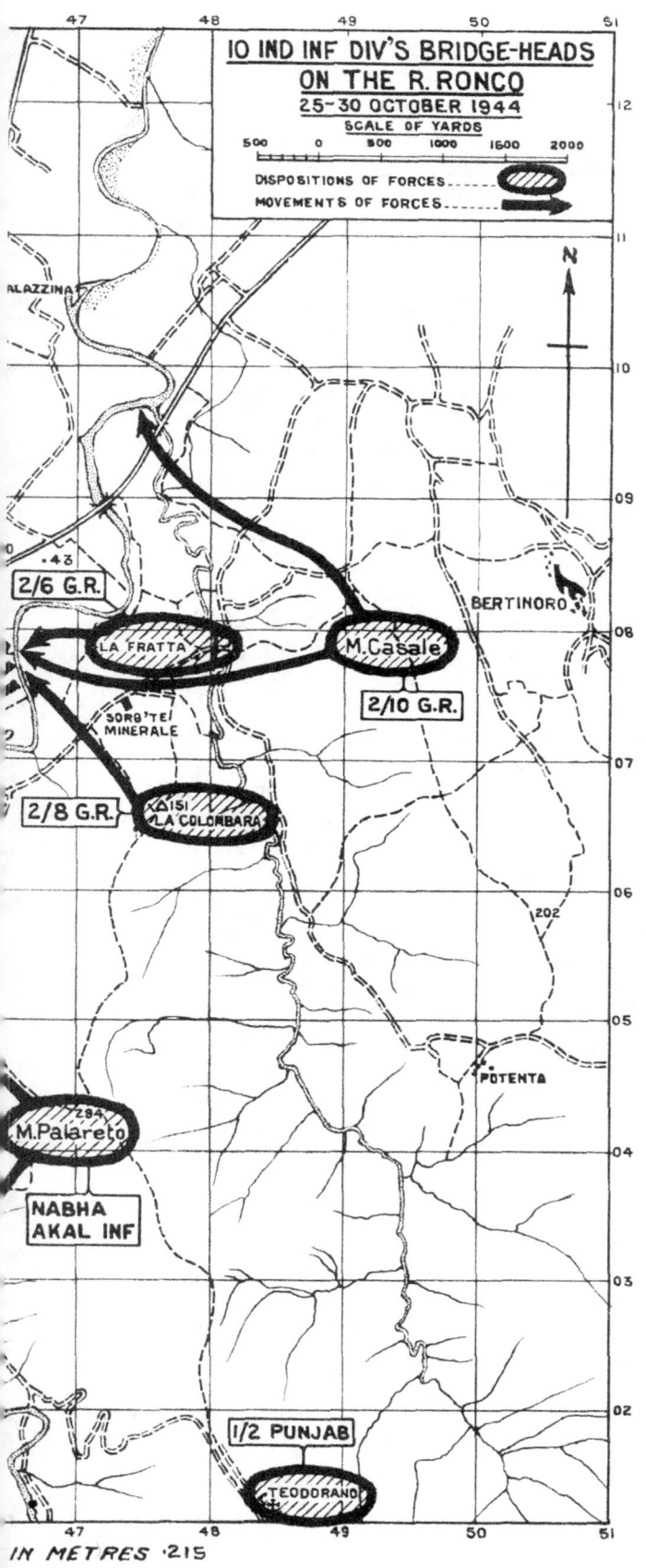

reinforced during the day by the arrival of 1st Battalion Nabha Akal Infantry. While the 25th Indian Infantry Brigade consolidated in the area S. Carlo, the 20th Indian Brigade and the 43rd Indian Infantry Brigade carried out the pursuit of the Germans to the river Ronco. The construction of bridges was not easy, but two sites were selected at San Carlo and farther south, at Mercato Saraceno. A one-hundred-and-twenty-foot Bailey bridge was eventually constructed at San Carlo on 23 October by the 10th Field Company, but as in wet weather only jeeps could get down to the bridge, it was not of great value. At Mercato Saraceno the Bailey bridge, one hundred and eighty feet in length, had a slope of one in sixteen over a ravine. Army Group Royal Engineers built this bridge without opposition from the Germans.[10] However these two bridges helped in the pursuit to some extent.

On 23 October, the 43rd Indian Infantry Brigade advanced to the river Ronco in leap-frog movements. At first 2/10 Gurkha moved through the 20th Indian Infantry Brigade at M. Cavallo to M. Delle Rovere, which was reached in the early hours of the morning on 24 October. At 1300 hours, 2/8 Gurkha took up the chase to Collinello. The road and all foot-tracks were mined and booby-trapped; consequently the advance was held up. Nevertheless after dark, supported by strong artillery concentrations, 2/8 Gurkha launched the attack and seized Collinello and Potenta early in the morning of 25 October. Then 2/10 Gurkha came forward to carry on the pursuit of the retreating Germans to M. Cassale, which was captured by 1400 hours. Meanwhile 2/8 Gurkha, advancing from Collinello, occupied La Colombara, south of M. Cassale. The seizure of this ridge ensured that the Germans would no longer be able to observe the movement of transport on Route 71, in the valley of the Savio. The 43rd Indian Infantry Brigade was thus in a position to send strong fighting patrols across the river Ronco, and even to follow them up by moving full companies.

Meanwhile the 20th Indian Infantry Brigade too had been advancing to the Ronco. On 24 October, 1/2 Punjab occupied without opposition Teodarano and was firmly established in the area M. Palareto. On 25 October the Nabha Akal Infantry moved up to M. Palareto area. 2/3 Gurkha patrolled from the area Valdinoce to Il Monte and Pt. 353.

Bridge-heads Over the Ronco

During the night of 25/26 October, 2/10 and 2/8 Gurkha and the Nabha Akal Infantry from the area M. Cassale, La Colombara and M. Palareto, respectively, sent out patrols for discovering fords on the river Ronco. The Germans had withdrawn to their defence

---

[10] Notes on RE. Operations, *op. cit.*

line west of the river. This river, running south to north and crossing the coast road, Route 9, three miles east of Forli, provided a natural defence line for that town and its airfield. At this season, torrential rain had filled the river. Its surface had risen to flood level, making the crossing of Ronco more formidable even than that of the Savio.

North of Meldola, a sprawling riverside town six miles south of Forli, patrols from 2/10 Gurkha in its position at M. Cassale had looked for fords, but failed to find them through the now flooded river. Near the mill in a bend of the river north-west of La Colombara, a reconnaissance patrol of 2/8 Gurkha had however discovered an old aqueduct, which proved to be passable to men and mules. Later, by knocking down the side walls of the channel, this acqueduct was made passable even for jeeps.

During the night of 25/26 October, two fighting patrols from 2/8 Gurkha failed in their attempts to cross the river owing to heavy German machine gun fire. A few men did manage to cross over to the other bank but were driven back. At 0530 hours on 26 October, a platoon of B Company crossed the river to clear up the spandaus on the other side of the river near the aqueduct, but it encountered a German counter-attack which was beaten off. The platoon consolidated the position. The commanding officer of 2/8 Gurkha immediately ordered the rest of D Company to cross the river and to form a bridge-head. C Company was also ordered to be prepared to reinforce B Company. B Company patrolled locally and drove off a few Germans who attempted to approach their positions. At 0530 hours on 27 October, B Company extended the bridge-head by occupying the Factory area.

Meanwhile 2/10 Gurkha from the area M. Cassale had made repeated attempts to cross the river and establish a bridge-head from the cross-roads at 463111 to road and track crossing at 457092. These efforts bore no fruit. Hence this battalion was switched over to the bridge-head established by 2/8 Gurkha. At 2000 hours on 27 October, A Company of 2/10 Gurkha relieved B Company of 2/8 in the bridge-head over the Ronco. D Company of 2/10 Gurkha moved to a position in the rear of A Company. The position in the bridge-head already established by 2/8 Gurkha was consolidated and 2/10 Gurkha got ready to launch an attack on the German positions.

While the Gurkhas had secured a bridge-head over the Ronco to the north of Meldola, the Nabha Akal Infantry had also established a bridge-head to the south of the town. At 0200 hours on 25 October, B and D Companies of the Nabha Akal Infantry moving from the area Pallareto crossed the river, directed on Meldola and Croce. German shelling was very heavy during the day. A direct hit on tactical headquarters of the Nabha Akal Infantry at Pallareto and

1/2 Punjab at Teodorano caused casualties and loss of signal equipment. By 1000 hours on 27 October, both B and D Companies had, however, established themselves, on the ridge at Pt. 138 and Pt. 154 respectively. A flying ferry was established at 449028 and a third company (A Company) was ferried across and was in position at Pt. 215 at 0200 hours on 28 October.

Great difficulty was experienced in supplying the companies to the west of the river. The road forward from Teodorano contained several craters and owing to bad weather bulldozers were bogged down as soon as they began to work on the wet clay soil. The companies on the west bank of the Ronco were therefore supplied by mule pack by a circuitous route, which crossed a razor back saddle, a foot-bridge, and a flying ferry (449028). The last two were left by the Germans, and strengthened and put into operation by the sappers. After the erection of an aerial ropeway over a two-hundred-and-ten-foot gap in the road forward of Teodorano, jeeps and 2-pounder anti-tank guns were slung across this aerial ropeway by the 61st Field Company, Indian Engineers, and eventually dragged across the Ronco near Meldola by oxen.[11]

Attack on the C. il Monte—C. Croce Ridge

In the 20th Indian Infantry Brigade sector, three miles from and a thousand feet above the Ronco ran the crest of the ridge between this river and the next, the Rabbi. *II Battalion 869th Grenadier Regiment*, with one squadron *Fusilier Battalion* under command, was in position on this ridge between C. Croce and C. il Monte. Their key points were C. il Monte, Rovere Verde, C. Croce and Ospedaletto.[12] The Nabha Akal Infantry was commissioned to capture the ridge and drive the Germans out of their positions. The commander planned to carry out this operation in two phases. In the first phase a double attack was to be made—on the right, B Company was to advance from Pt. 138 to secure C. il Monte and exploit to Meldola; while on the left, D Company was to advance from Pt. 154 and secure Rovere Verde. In the second phase C Company was to advance up the road Meldola—C. Croce and seize C. Croce. The start time was fixed at 0300 hours on 29 October, and the start line was the track running east from Pt. 138. A Company was in reserve at Pt. 138 for counter-attack on to C. il Monte and Rovere Verde. The attack was to be supported by heavy mortars and medium machine guns. There was to be heavy concentration by the Royal Artillery on the German positions.[13]

This concentration on C. il Monte started at 0310 hours on 29

---

[11] Notes on RE. Operations; *op. cit.*
[12] 10 Ind. Div. Intelligence Summary No. 129, dated 29 October 1944.
[13] Operation Orders Appx. D, War Diary Nabha Akal Infantry October 1944.

October and continued till 0330 hours. This was followed by the advance by the Nabha Akal Infantry. For a while, the Germans contested the ridge but the Nabha Akal Infantry beat down the resistance. By 0600 hours B Company was firmly established on C. il Monte, D Company on Rovere Verde and C Company on Croce. Twelve prisoners were taken and the ridge firmly held. Mopping up operations were carried out during the day. 2/3 Gurkha next moved forward and relieved the Nabha Akal Infantry on 30 October.

Extension of the Bridge-head

When the 20th Indian Infantry Brigade had seized the ridge C. il Monte—C. Croce, the 43rd Indian Infantry Brigade launched an attack, during the night of 29/30 October 1944, to extend its bridge-head west of the Ronco. The plan was to attack with 2/10 Gurkha on the right and 2/6 Gurkha on the left. At 2200 hours on 20 October both the battalions crossed the Ronco at the aqueduct to carry out their tasks. Before 0600 hours next morning 2/10 Gurkha seized Fattorelto, without opposition. 2/6 Gurkha, however, encountered strong opposition, which nevertheless was overcome and by 0300 hours on 30 October C, D and B Companies had seized S. Lazzaro, the road junction and La Gualchiera, respectively. Then B Company moved through D Company and captured Belfiore by 1000 hours. Stiff fighting on both flanks, however, impeded the further progress of the 43rd Indian Infantry Brigade. During the night of 30/31 October, it was relieved by the 25th Indian Infantry Brigade, 2/8 Gurkha remaining under the command of the relieving brigade. A wireless intercept revealed that the Germans were withdrawing to the line north-east and south-west of Forli behind the Rabbi stream, south of the town and the Ravaldino canal north of it. The 25th Indian Infantry Brigade, therefore, pushed on the pursuit and reestablished contact with the Germans at Carpena, from where it pushed on north-west to the next river, the Rabbi, and was subjected on 1 November to quite heavy shelling.

A Daring Reconnaissance Patrol

The 25th Indian Infantry Brigade maintained its advance towards the Rabbi in heavy rain and against opposition. On 2 November, the 1st King's Own occupied Grisignano, on the west bank of the river and three miles south of Forli, which the Germans were defending strongly. A patrol of 3/18 Garhwal out to reconnoitre the Forli neighbourhood, set out at last light from Belfiore, to the north-west of Meldola and five miles from its objective. Following up along the banks of the Rabbi, the patrol ran into trouble while skirting German positions at S. Martino in Strada, to the west of Forli airport. Here it was fired upon from German positions, in platoon strength, from either side. It took the Garhwal patrol an hour to fight its way out of the predicament, which had effectively destroyed all hopes of penetration into Forli itself. In ones and twos the patrol reassembled in the darkness and withdrew to the lines. However, one Indian N.C.O., Sirendar Singh Rawat of the Garhwal Rifles, who had lost contact with his comrades during the combat, began his lone adventures. He had gone into hiding in the undergrowth along the river-bank. Later that night he quitted his refuge and pushed on alone in the direction of Forli in the hope of contacting the patrol at a road junction on the outskirts of the town. Striking northwards between the main road and the river he found cover in the house of a friendly Italian. At first light he positioned himself at an upstairs window and there began a day long vigil. From dawn to dusk he kept the town under ceaseless observation, and from various vantage-points successfully located two company positions, diligently noted all traffic movement, and even contrived to pin-point the disposition of the German artillery units. With the advent of darkness he left the house and struck back down-river towards his own lines. Around midnight his Odyssey ended in an encounter with a patrol of a Lancashire regiment. The Garhwal Lance Naik was the first man of the Eighth Army to enter the important town of Forli, by the margin of about a week. He spent a day in Forli at a time when the forward positions of his division were located around Meldola, six miles to the south.[14]

Sappers at Work

Meanwhile the sappers had been at work. Using the only two possible approaches to the bank they worked like Trojans, under appalling weather conditions, to put two bridges over the river. At Meldola the gap was a three-hundred-foot one but the approaches were only twelve feet wide. It was decided, owing to the speed and varying depth of the water, to build a one-hundred-and-sixty-foot bridge on trestles. Considerable effort was put into the work in order to get the bridge finished in one day. One Field Company of Sappers, one hundred local labourers, a section of tip-trucks and a number of oxen-drawn carts were employed. By 2100 hours on 1 November, the bridge and its approaches were completed. But heavy rain was falling, the river rose some thirteen feet in three hours and the bridge was swept away before a single vehicle could cross.

Farther north at Magliano, the 501st Field Company, Royal Engineers, had been engaged in building a one-hundred-and-forty-foot Bailey bridge. The bank seats had been completed and ninety feet of bridge had been put together when the river suddenly rose.

---

[14] "First Allied Man in Forli"—the *Diagonals* dated 18 November 1944; Appx. War Diary 10 Ind. Div. November 1944,

This company had been working almost continuously for three days under great hardships. Now the water rose so high that any further construction would have resulted in the launching nose touching the water. The bridge was therefore withdrawn and partially dismantled. Fortunately, the bank seat held and the bridge was finally completed on 4 November.[15]

The 10th Indian Division's Achievements

During the night of 2/3 November 1944, the 25th Indian Infantry Brigade was relieved by a brigade of the 46th Division. In one month (3 October—3 November 1944) the 10th Indian Division had advanced from the river Marecchio to the river Ronco against stiff opposition. The division had been engaged in continuous fighting and had driven the Germans from river to river and across ridge after ridge with great regularity under shocking weather conditions. The beating begun by the 4th Indian Division had been continued with no letting up. Of the 548 German prisoners taken during the time, the majority came from the *114th Jaegar Division* and the *356th Infantry Division*, who shared the responsibility for defending and subsequently counter-attacking M. Farneto. The *29th Panzer Grenadier Division* committed in an attempt to restore the situation east of the river Savio, made only a fleeting appearance and was soon hurried away to the Bologna front. The *278th Infantry Division* also provided the 10th Indian Division with 17 prisoners of war before being withdrawn to take over a sector north of Route 9.[16]

[15] Notes on RE. Operations, *op. cit.*
[16] Outline of enemy formations encountered; Appx. M. 10 Ind. Div. Narrative of Operations, (File 8328/H).

CHAPTER XXVI

Attack on M. Pianoereno

The Fifth Army's Advance Towards Bologna

A pause is now necessary to take up the story of the Fifth Army's advance towards Bologna. By 22 September 1944 the II U.S. Corps and the XIII British Corps had broken through the Gothic Line on a front of thirty miles from Vernio to San Godenzo Pass and the IV U.S. Corps had penetrated the line at several points. General Clark had then two alternatives before him—either to advance on the axis of Route 65 to Bologna or develop a thrust along the valley of the Santerno and the road to Imola. He preferred the latter alternative, for an advance against Imola would facilitate the progress of the Eighth Army. So he planned that the main body of the II U.S. Corps, the spearhead of the Fifth Army's attack, should continue the advance towards the Radicosa Pass, while its right flank formation should advance through the valley of the Santerno. The role to be assigned respectively to the XIII British Corps and the IV U.S. Corps was to protect the right and left flanks of the II U.S. Corps.

By this time Field-Marshal Kesselring had strengthened his front; the *362nd Infantry Division* had arrived on 19 September to cover Firenzuola and the *44th Infantry Division* on 21 September to take over the sector of the Firenzuola—Imola road. Nevertheless, the Fifth Army made fairly good progress from 22 September till the end of the month. The II U.S. Corps continued the advance with the 88th U.S. Division on the right, the 85th, and the 91st U.S. Divisions in the centre and the 34th U.S. Division on the left. The 88th U.S. Division advanced on the axis of the Firenzuola—Imola road and after a hard struggle captured M. Battaglia, the last of the major obstacles on the road to Imola. The Germans launched fierce counter-attacks to retake M. Battaglia immediately after its loss on 27 September. Although they failed to recapture it, they were able to rush reinforcements, thus effectively closing the road to Imola. Meanwhile in their advance to the Radicosa Pass, the three other divisions of the II U.S. Corps overcame strong opposition to the east and west of the Pass, which was overcome and the Pass secured.

As the Germans rushed reinforcements to recapture M. Battaglia and effectively close the Imola road, General Clark revised his plan. Taking advantage of the progress made by the left wing of the II U.S. Corps he decided to throw the main weight of attack on the axis of Route 65, the direct road to Bologna. The XIII Corps, reinforced by the 78 (British) Division, assumed responsibility for the Imola axis and relieved the 88th U.S. Division on M. Battaglia. Considerable progress was made in the first half of October. The II U.S. Corps led the attack with the 91st U.S. Division on the axis of Route 65 and the 85th U.S. Division east of the road. The 88th U.S. Division and the 34th U.S. Division on the right and left flanks respectively carried out diversionary attacks. The 85th U.S. Division secured M. Delle Formiche while the 91st U.S. Division captured Monghidoro and Loiano, continuing the advance beyond Livergnano —ten miles south of the outskirts of Bologna. The II U.S. Corps was thus approaching Bologna but its progress was checked by stiff resistance.

The Germans received reinforcements and fiercely disputed the advance of the Fifth Army towards Bologna. The *65th Infantry Division* was brought forward and put in a narrow sector on the Bologna road; the *44th Infantry Division,* which had been pulled out of the line for rest, was re-committed; and the *29th Panzer Grenadier Division* was transferred from the front opposite the Eighth Army. However, the advance towards Bologna continued slowly in the second half of October. The 34th U.S. Division relieved on the left of the II U.S. Corps by the 1st Armoured Division, assumed responsibility for a new sector between the 91st and the 85th U.S. Divisions, to strengthen the attack east of Route 65. On 20 October, the 88th U.S. Division captured the great massif of Monte Grande and M. Cerere. With the capture of La Costa on 22 October the division was only four miles from Route 9. The 85th U.S. Division pushed down the Idice valley but was forced to withdraw from M. Messano on 27 October after having captured it two days previously. On 23 October, the 34th U.S. Division captured M. Belmonte, about nine miles from Bologna. The 91st U.S. Division's advance beyond Livergnano was held up by stiff resistance.

The Fifth Army was within striking distance of Bologna and the threat to Route 9 was really very serious. Realising the gravity of the situation, General Vietinghoff switched from the front opposite the Eighth Army the *90th Panzer Grenadier Division* and the *1st Parachute Division.* German reinforcements, assisted by torrential rains and the Fifth Army's exhaustion, were successful in barring the way to the plain. On 27 October the Fifth Army's offensive was suspended and the American forces went on the defensive. The American Army failed in the race to reach the Po valley before winter set in. They were not able "to get across the final barrier to which the enemy clung". To be robbed of a decisive success when it was almost within sight was a sore disappointment to General Clark, who has given expression to his poignant feelings in a remarkable passage in his book, *Calculated Risk*—"The Fifth Army's offensive did not stop with any definite setback or on any specific date. It merely ground slowly to a halt because men could not fight any longer against the steadily increasing enemy reinforcements on our front. In other words, our drive died out, slowly and painfully, and only one stride from success, like a runner who collapses reaching for, but not quite touching the tape at the finishing-line.[1]" Thus at the close of October 1944 the Fifth Army's offensive had stopped short of Bologna and the Eighth Army was also halted for some days on the line of the river Ronco just short of the town of Forli.

Advance to S. Benedetto in Alpe

After this brief account of the Fifth Army's thrust towards Bologna we shall describe in greater detail the part played by the Indian formations in these operations. The 8th Indian Division, forming part of the XIII Corps operating on the right flank of the Fifth Army played a comparatively minor role in these operations, for the spearhead of the Fifth Army attack was the II U.S. Corps. By 22 September 1944, when the Fifth Army had broken through the Gothic Line, the XIII Corps was making good progress on its right flank—the 6th British Armoured Division, on the right, had captured M. Peschiena and was advancing along Star route; the 8th Indian Division in the centre was making preparations for advance beyond Femina Morta (one of the bastions of the Gothic Line); the 1st Division on the left flank was advancing north and south of Arrow route. The 8th Indian Division was then given two tasks, each of which closely linked up with the operations of its flanking divisions. As the 1st Division was continuing the advance up the Arrow route, the 17th Indian Infantry Brigade was assigned the task of protecting the right flank of this route and advancing on general axis M. Carnevalone—M. Villanova—M. Scarabattole. The 19th Indian Infantry Brigade was assigned the task of protecting the left flank of the 6th British Armoured Division, which was advancing up Star route towards the small village of S. Benedetto in Alpe.[2]

Progress of the 19th Indian Brigade

While the 17th Indian Infantry Brigade had been engaged in the attack on Femina Morta, one of the bastions of the Gothic Line, the 19th Indian Infantry Brigade had come forward on the right. On 19 October patrols from 3/8 Punjab, from the area Villore, probed into the German defences at M. Giogo di Villore and encountered slight opposition. The Germans, however, pulled out and 3/8 Punjab occupied this feature without opposition on 22 October.

---

[1] Mark Clark: *Calculated Risk*, pp. 378.
[2] 8 Ind. Div. Planning No. 26, dated 21 September 1944, and No. 27, dated 25 September 1944, War Diary 8 Ind. Div.

The 19th Indian Infantry Brigade then worked through the hills along the ridge from M. Giogo di Villore in an easterly direction towards S. Benedetto in Alpe. On 23 October, 3/8 Punjab was relieved at M. Giogo di Villore by the 1st Battalion Jaipur Infantry and concentrated near Villore, while 6/13 Royal Frontier Force Rifles and 1st Battalion Argyll and Sutherland Highlanders concentrated in the area S. Godenzo. On 23/24 September, 6/13 Royal Frontier Force Rifles advanced from the area S. Godenzo, secured Eremo and M. Sinaia and climbed M. Del Prato Andreaccio without meeting any opposition. The success of the advance of the 19th Indian Infantry Brigade on the flank brought marked relief to the 6th British Armoured Division, whose advance had been checked by the demolitions on the main road. On 24 September, the 61st Brigade of the 6th British Armoured Division entered S. Benedetto in Alpe.

The next task was to open up the San Benedetto in Alpe—Marradi lateral road. This undertaking could not be completed until the 17th Indian Infantry Brigade had driven the Germans from the hills overlooking the road in the Marradi sector. However, work was started on the road in the southern sector. The infantry provided a covering screen. On 25 September, 1st Battalion Argyll and Sutherland Highlanders concentrated in S. Benedetto in Alpe and pushed forward into the hills so reminiscent of their native highlands. By 28 September the Highlanders were established in the area M. Susinelli and M. Del Cerro. From here, they were able to cover the engineering operations. To their north, 6/13 Royal Frontier Force Rifles performed a similar protecting role by swinging left and occupying three windswept ridges forming part of M. Di Gamogna, a huge feature over three thousand feet high, some three miles southeast of Marradi. From there, the 19th Indian Infantry Brigade was able to establish close liaison with the 17th Indian Infantry Brigade on the left.

Advance to M. Scarabattole

We may now take up the advance of the 17th Indian Infantry Brigade to M. Castelnuovo. This brigade was protecting the right flank of the 1st Division, which was moving up the Arrow route. The 2nd British Infantry Brigade of the 1st Division advanced north of Arrow route, while the 17th Indian Infantry Brigade stepped up south of the road. This task imposed fresh problems on the already over-worked Quartermaster branch of the 8th Indian Division. Amongst other things, it involved moving the entire transport of a single brigade group, totalling more than two thousand vehicles, by a circuitous route and then along the supply axis of the 1st Division. With the 17th Indian Infantry Brigade had to go a special supply organisation, which could provide not only Indian food, but ammunition and fuel as well as bales of forage for the four hundred and twenty-five mules working with the brigade.

On 22 September, 1/5 Gurkha, following the mule tracks from Femina Morta down into the valley, reached Crespino. This small village of dull, grey stone on Arrow route lay due north of Femina Morta. It had been previously reported clear by a long-range Gurkha patrol. However, as the battalion headquarters was traversing the lower slopes of Femina Morta, it was caught in a heavy shell fire which killed 5 and wounded 7. Before reaching the valley, one Gurkha company wheeled north and following the rough track along the backbone of Poggio di Valdosera sent forward scouts to reconnoitre M. Di Villanova, a well wooded spur, overlooking Arrow route, where it was joined by the road from San Benedetto in Alpe. Early on 23 September, the Gurkhas were astride the summit of M. Di Villanova. A patrol went forward again, down the precipitous hillsides, along the leafy nullahs towards M. Scarabattole. This feature lay about a mile and a half south-east of Marradi. As the patrol ascended the steep slopes, it clashed with a German fighting patrol. The latter fled after an exchange of fire. Two Germans were taken prisoners. They volunteered the information that they had been part of a rearguard left to cover the main German withdrawal. On 24 September, the Germans abandoned M. Scarabattole, which the Gurkhas occupied without any further trouble. At 1800 hours on 24 September, the 1st Battalion Royal Fusiliers relieved the Gurkhas, who went back for a well earned rest to Crespino.

Capture of M. Di Castelnuovo

The 1st Royal Fusiliers lost no time in taking up the chase; first light on 25 September, found them pushing on towards the next objective, M. Di Castelnuovo. This feature lay north of M. Scarabattole and east of Marradi. *I Battalion 578th Grenadier Regiment* of the *305th Infantry Division,* covered the road at Popalano, with 1 Company north of the road, 2 Company from the road to M. Di Castelnuovo and 3 Company to the south.[3] Alarmed by the speed of the pursuit, the Germans reinforced M. Di Castelnuovo by bringing in 7 Company and part of 14 Company, *578th Regiment.* Consequently the objective was not to be taken that day; heavy machine gun fire and a hail of mortar bombs halted the Fusiliers' assault. The attack had to be postponed, for another German division, fresh and vigorous, faced the 8th Indian Division. The *715th Infantry Division* had side-stepped north of Arrow route and in its place had come the *305th Infantry Division,* which had taken over responsibility for both the axes, Marradi—Faenza and S. Benedetto in Alpe

[3] 8 Ind. Div. Intelligence Summary No. 153, dated 26 September 1944.

and Forli. It was a formation well up to strength and displayed better fighting qualities than the *715th Infantry Division*. These were men of *305th Infantry Division* who held M. Castelnuovo. They were extremely stubborn, well-positioned, and employed a large number of automatic weapons. The country, too, was ideal for defensive warfare. On the right of the 17th Indian Infantry Brigade, the terrain proved almost impractical for men operating at night and even the mules could hardly keep their foothold on such knife-edge ridges and down those steep brushwood slopes, whose surface was of loose shale. Of these factors, the Germans were fully aware. Their positions were sited accordingly. There was no alternative for the 1st Royal Fusiliers but to patrol with the object of finding the best approach for an attack.

On 26-27 September, the 1st Royal Fusiliers maintained pressure on the German occupied areas, Pt. 572, Pt. 614 and M. Di Castelnuovo. Heavy rain fell, making the already difficult country almost impassable. Meanwhile, 1/12 Frontier Force Regiment, which had concentrated in the area Grespino on 25 September, was directed to move, at 1000 hours on 26 September, on the southern flank of the 1st Royal Fusiliers, by the route Albero—M. Val Del Calvo—Poggio Grilleta—M. Lalto. Before the evening of 27 September the Frontier Force had reached M. Val Del Calvo, between the position held by the 1st Royal Fusiliers and the 19th Indian Infantry Brigade. The Germans were alarmed by this flanking thrust and carried out a further withdrawal. The 1st Royal Fusiliers occupied M. Di Castelnuovo without opposition at 1030 hours on 29 September. After the capture of this feature, Marradi which had been taken by the 1st Division on 24 September, was no longer under close German observation. This small town was to be a most important centre of communication and a supply base for future operations.

Capture of M. Grilleta

Towards the close of September 1944, the 8th Indian Division reorganised in accordance with the change in the Fifth Army's plan. As stiff German opposition held up the advance on the Imola road, General Clark shifted the weight of the Fifth Army's attack on to the axis of Route 65. Accordingly he ordered the XIII (British) Corps (reinforced by the 78th Division) to assume responsibility for the Imola—M. Battaglia area. While implementing this plan, the XIII Corps began to extend westwards to relieve the II U.S. Corps (the spearhead of the attack at the end of September 1944). The 1st Division moved to the left and the 8th Indian Division took over its right brigade sector. On 30 September, the 19th Indian Infantry brigade took over the area up to but excluding Marradi, and the 17th Indian Infantry Brigade the area which stretched north of the road Marradi—Pallazuolo, and included the scrub-covered M. Gamberaldi, due north of Marradi.

Major-General Russell's plan was to advance along the Sword route, employing one brigade on the left and one on the right of the road. The task for the 19th Indian Infantry Brigade was to continue the advance on M. Casalino with a view to capturing M. Gigiolo. The 17th Indian Infantry Brigade was assigned the task of carrying out offensive patrolling towards M. Romano with the object of seizing it. The 21st Indian Infantry Brigade was to be in reserve.

The 8th Indian Division had battled its way across the mountains. Now its task was to advance, never allowing the Germans rest or relaxation, astride the Marradi road towards Faenza and the Po valley. Although Femina Morta, the bastion of the Gothic Line, had been left far behind, the division was still operating in a most difficult country. Generally speaking, the hills in this region were lower than those which the men of the division had surmounted during their break-through of the Gothic Line. Often, hill features were linked together by a narrow ridge, not much wider than the mule track it carried. Frequently, the sides of these hills dropped away precipitously into deep, winding ravines. Whenever the slope was more gentle it was covered by thick scrub which gradually grew thinner towards the summit where, on the hard rock, nothing grew. The animal most commonly used in these parts was the mule ; it alone was best suited to carry a load over long distances by the narrow paths which wound and twisted their way around the hillsides. On the divisional front, by the side of the river Lamone's course down to the Po valley ran the Marradi—Faenza road and railway line. To the left of the divisional front, the river Senio flowed on a course parallel to the Lamone into the Po valley. It was to be a succession of mountains, hills, ridges, knife-edge spurs and more mountains, with appalling weather conditions, which taxed the endurance of the men of the 8th Indian Division to the utmost.

Such a country conveniently lent itself to defensive warfare. The *305th Infantry Division* soon showed, by the disposition of its forces, with what care the German commanders had studied the ground. On 1 October the division held the sector between Route 67 and the river Sintria. It had three regiments—576, 577 and 578, each consisting of two battalions. The average strength per battalion of the front line troops was about 200 men. The *305th Fusilier Battalion* was the divisional reconnaissance unit. The division had the normal complement of artillery and a few self-propelled guns were also under command. The officers in the division were experienced soldiers respected by the majority of their troops. Its men were long accustomed to the rigours of mountain warfare. Of good morale, well disciplined and well armed, the men of this division reacted vigorously to any attempt at infiltration. Once they were determined to hold a locality, they defended it tenaciously. They withdrew only when it was opportune or when driven out by superior force. In the art of conducting an orderly withdrawal they were adept. Such was the calibre of the Germans who opposed the 8th Indian Division.

On 1 October, the XIII Corps was guarding the right flank of the Fifth Army, with the 6th British Armoured Division fighting forward through the hills east of Star route, the 8th Indian Division in the central sector of the corps front, slowly pushing forward beyond Palazzuolo along the Arrow route, which at this stage followed the course of the river Senio. The 8th Indian Division was fighting with only two brigades, keeping the third in reserve near Vicchio.

In the vicinity of Marradi, still subject to German shelling, no suitable rest area could be found for the reserve brigade, nor was there adequate accommodation for the maintenance echelons. Therefore the reserve brigade and the echelons had to remain in the Sieve valley, which meant that all the requirements of the division, such as food, ammunition, stores and equipment, had to be brought 25 miles over a 3,000-foot pass, along a narrow mountain road often enveloped in thick mist. At the best of times this was only a second class road. Now, having become the main corps axis, it carried the traffic of both the 8th Indian Division and the 1st Division. Certain stretches, which were wide enough only for single vehicles, had to be continuously controlled by provost. With the coming of bad weather the surface of the road soon broke up under the constant strain of heavy lorries. Frequently it was closed for several hours to allow the sappers to effect vital repairs.

The state of the road and the flow of materials to the battle area were directly governed by the weather. In fact the elements had now become one of the most important factors in the operations. Heavy rain lasting for a period of several days was becoming more and more common. In the hills, tracks were so deep in mud that occasionally some were impassable even for mules. Slit trenches were filled with water, and at night the severity of cold increased. Before very long, the main pass would be snow-bound. It was imperative to push the Germans off the hills east of Marradi as quickly as possible in order to secure vital maintenance and gun areas.

We shall first describe the attack by the 19th Indian Infantry Brigade on M. Cavallara, where the Germans offered strong resistance to deny to the Allies the use of the good lateral Adriano road. Facing this brigade was *II Battalion 578th Regiment* of the *305th Infantry* Division, with *6 Company* in the area M. Tesoro, 5

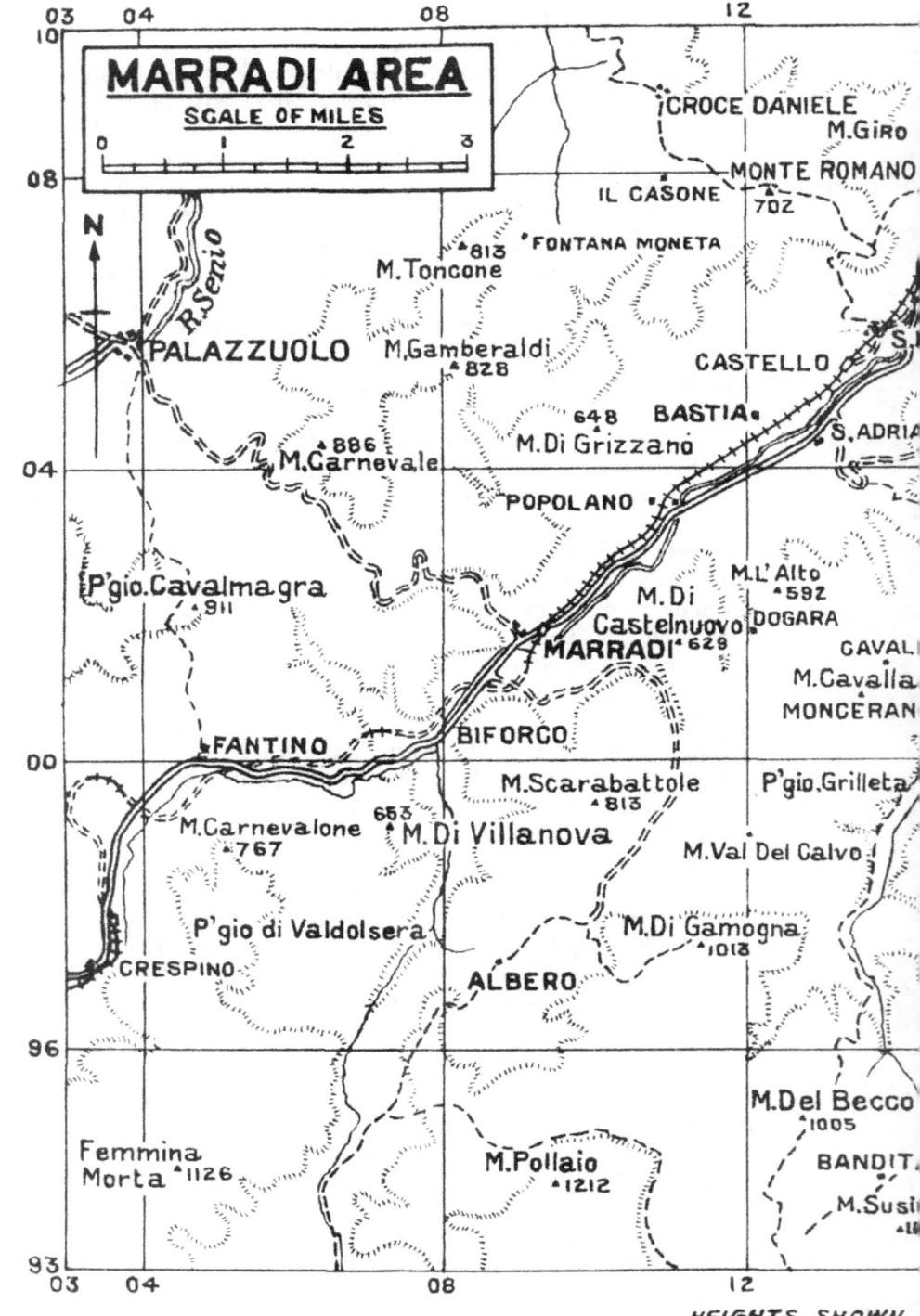

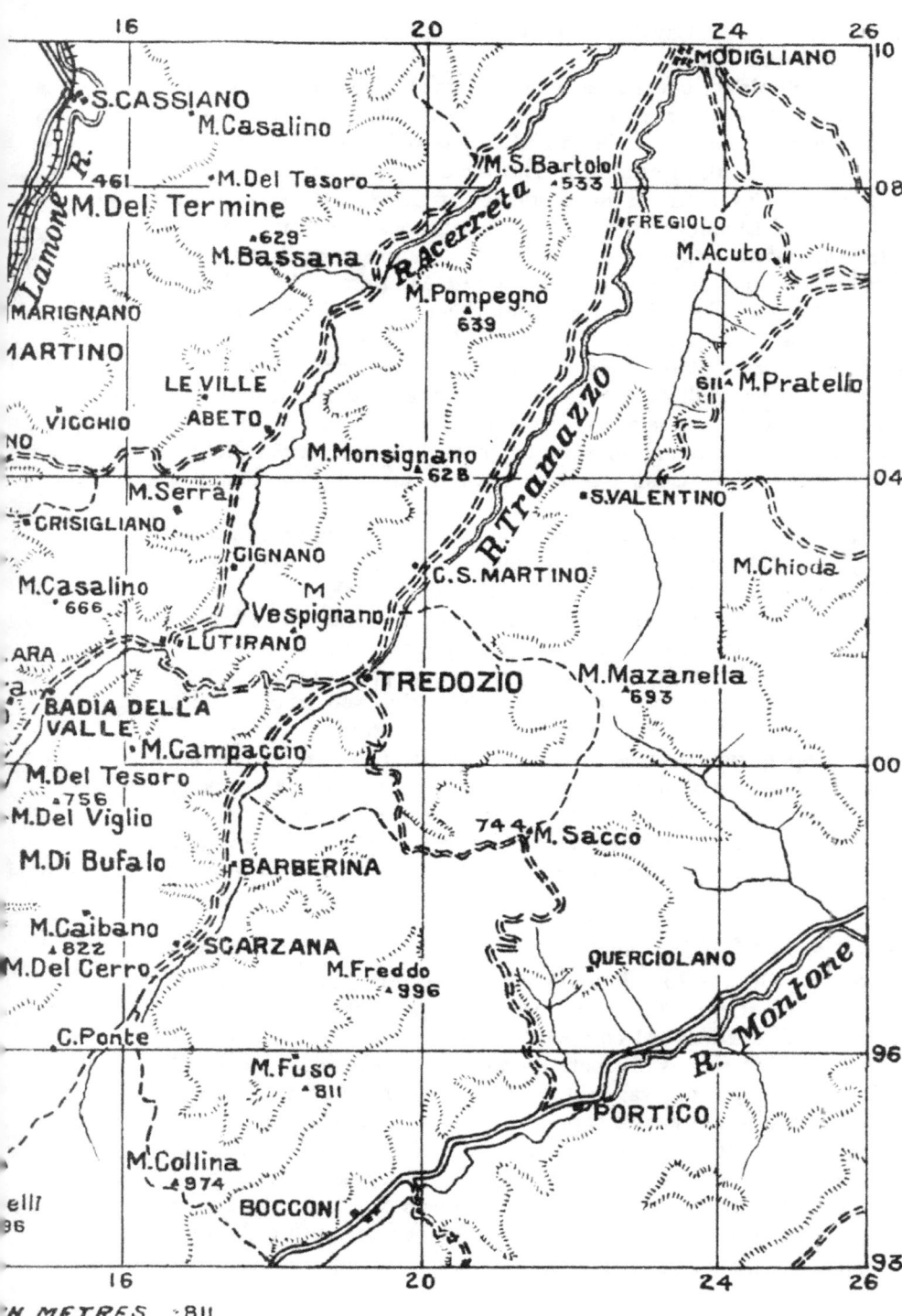

Company in area M. Cavallara and M. Casalino, 7 Company west to excluding Sword route.[4]

The preliminary operations were concerned with the securing of M. Bufalo, M. Grilleta and M. L'Alto by 1 Argyll, 6/13 Royal Frontier Force Rifles and 3/8 Punjab. The object of these moves was to provide flank protection and to secure a suitable base for an attack on M. Cavallara. Two companies of the A and SH were in the area M. Susinelli, with a forward company at M. Cerro, while another company occupied M. Bufalo at 1730 hours on 30 September. While the A and SH on the right seized M. Bufalo, 6/13 Royal Frontier Force Rifles advancing from the area M. Calvo secured M. Grilleta and the southern slopes of M. Cavallara. At 1300 hours on 30 September, a platoon of its A Company, supported by artillery, occupied Poggio Grilleta but came under heavy machine gun fire from the area M. Grilleta and M. Cavallara. By 1430 hours the remainder of A Company had passed through and captured Pt. 700 at 1800 hours. B Company also moved up and consolidated at Pt. 700.

Early on 1 October, A Company prepared to launch an attack on Pt. 759 (M. Grilleta) after an artillery barrage. At 0810 hours artillery registered on the objective. The mortars also engaged the target. At 0945 hours artillery fired strong concentration of high explosive and smoke shells and A Company led the attack. At 1005 hours when A Company was held up by heavy spandau fire, artillery supported the company by firing high explosive and smoke shells. At 1015 hours A Company again moved forward but was pinned down by opposition from M. Cavallara and Pt. 685. At 1220 hours smoke was put down on Pt. 685 to stop enfilade fire and the company again tried to move forward. The progress was very slow. Then at 1330 hours there was heavy artillery concentration on the objective and the company pushed up the advance, seizing M. Grilleta at 1400 hours.

Attacks on the L' Alto Ridge

Meanwhile, 3/8 Punjab was directed against the German position on the L' Alto ridge. On 30 September, 3/8 Punjab was in the area M. Calvo with a forward company in the area south of M. Castlenuovo. Their task was to secure Pt. 601 as a firm base for the attack on L' Alto ridge, which was held in strength by the Germans. Accordingly B and C Companies captured without opposition M. L' Alto in the morning of 1 October, while A Company passed through and secured Pt. 601 in the morning on 2 October. After these preliminary operations the attack on the ridge began. At 0700 hours on 3 October, D Company moved off from Pt. 601 to capture the high

[4] *Ibid.* No. 158, 8 October 1944.

ground to the south of Pt. 605. This company was protected on the right flank by 6/13 Royal Frontier Force Rifles at M. Grilleta and by its companion A Company at Pt. 601. All the available intelligence information indicated that M. Cavallara on the right flank of the attacking company was not held by the Germans, but this was unfortunately not correct. It was the beginning of a day of tense excitement for 3/8 Punjab. As C Company neared the objective it was heavily machine gunned from three sides—Cavallara House (137014), Pt. 744 and Pt. 711—and was pinned down, unable to move forward another yard. It was only at 1500 hours when the German fire had slackened that the men were able to occupy Pt. 605. But further advance was held up by stiff opposition from Cavallara House, about four hundred yards ahead of the forward platoon of D Company. Thereupon the commanding officer of 3/8 Punjab decided to overcome opposition by a spirited attack. He ordered A Company to advance from Pt. 601 to the support of D Company at Pt. 605 and capture Cavallara House, and C Company was to advance from L' Alto to neutralise German opposition at Pt. 711. To assist the Punjab attack on the German positions, 6/13 Royal Frontier Force Rifles from M. Grilleta was ordered to simulate an attack on Pt. 759 and Pt. 756 and thus threaten Pt. 744.

At 1430 hours, the commander of A Company crawled to his forward platoon commander and gave orders for the platoon to attack Cavallara House. The start time for the operation was fixed at 1500 hours, with a smoke screen provided by artillery. Owing to the nature of the country it was impossible for the Jemadar, commanding the platoon, to reconnoitre the area and none of the men in his platoon was able to see the ground up to the house before the attack. The Jemadar simply passed on the information he had received from his company commander to the effect that the ground was fairly flat, with no cover, and the only thing to do was to make a spirited attack. At 1455 hours, smoke to screen the attacking platoon was dropped but, instead of covering the approaches to the house, it billowed five hundred yards away where it was absolutely useless. A frantic message was sent to stop the platoon attack, but the Jemadar had his orders. Just because there was no smoke screen there was no reason for him to call off the attack. Any way the message arrived too late. The open ground up to the house was crossed by the platoon at the double and well spread out. Hell was let loose from three sides as spandaus coughed and sent bullets whipping towards the sturdy men of 3/8 Punjab. Not a man hestitated ; before the Germans realised what was happening, the Indians were inside the house. Six German prisoners, dazed by the audacity of the charge, sat down and wondered what had hit them. The Punjab platoon which had suffered only one casualty, found a large quantity of

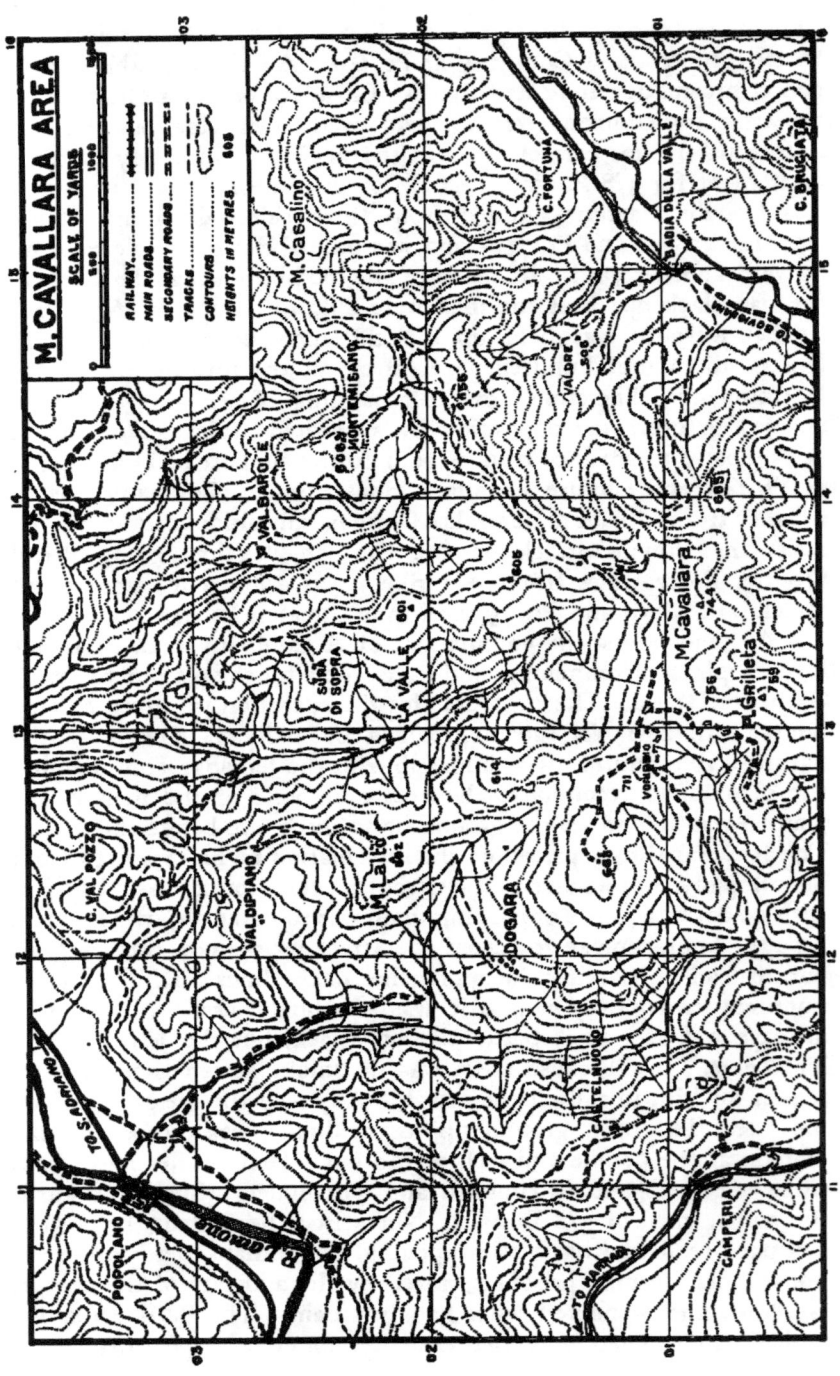

German arms and ammunition and settled down to wait for the German counter-attack. It was not long in coming. Cavallara House was heavily shelled and mortared before the German infantry launched the attack which was repulsed. However, the platoon commander had been wounded during the counter-attack and by nightfall more heavy shelling and mortaring reduced the strength of the platoon to less than half of its original number. It was the end of a very gallant little action. By dawn on 4 October, the platoon withdrew from Cavallara House, bringing back the wounded and ten German prisoners. D Company had also withdrawn from Pt. 605 under cover of darkness. The casualties of 3/8 Punjab were estimated to be about 40.

Meanwhile, C Company of 3/8 Punjab had advanced from the area M. L' Alto and occupied Pt. 711 but was shelled throughout the night of 3/4 October. It remained in position at this feature but its further advance was held up by stiff opposition from Pt. 756.

B Company of 6/13 Royal Frontier Force Rifles also led an attack on Pt. 759. At 1915 hours on 3 October, there was heavy British artillery concentration of high explosives on the targets, followed by smoke. At 1930 hours B Company from the area M. Grilleta attacked Pt. 759 and captured it at 2005 hours.

Thus at dawn on 4 October, the situation was that C Company of 3/8 Punjab was in position at Pt. 711 but its advance was held up by strong German opposition at Pt. 756. A and D Companies of 3/8 Punjab had withdrawn from Pt. 605, after having been checked at Cavallara House. 6/13 Royal Frontier Force Rifles was consolidating in the area M. Grilleta, with the forward company (B) in possession of Pt. 759. But the advance to M. Cavallara was held up by strong German positions at Pt. 756 and Pt. 744. At 1955 hours on 4 October, however, A Company attacked Pt. 756 and captured it at 2030 hours after encountering stiff opposition and heavy small arms fire. The company consolidated on the northern slope while the Germans withdrew towards M. Cavallara, which they continued to hold in strength.

The operations were postponed for two days due to heavy rain. Meanwhile, 1 Jaipur Infantry, which had come up on 2 October to guard the brigade's right sector, did some very effective patrolling in the mountainous country around M. Bufalo and M. Caibano. 1. A. & SH relieved 6/13 Royal Frontier Force Rifles in the area M. Grilleta, at 2245 hours on 6 October, in order to take part in the operations for the capture of M. Cavallara.

Capture of M. Cavallara

On 6 October the commander of the 19th Indian Infantry Brigade planned to make a double thrust—one directed against M.

Cavallara and the other against M. Casalino. 3/8 Punjab was assigned the task of occupying Pt. 655, preparatory to the attack on Casalino while the A and SH was detailed to capture M. Cavallara (Pt. 744). 1 Jaipur Infantry was to continue to protect the right flank by active patrolling from the area M. Bufalo.

M. Casalino guarded the approaches to M. Gaggiolo, a feature, which dominated the Lamone valley from the east. On this account the Germans were expected to fight hard for M. Casalino, holding it, until they were ready to withdraw to a new defensive line. The fight for M. Cavallara began on 7 October. One company of the A and SH from the area M. Grilleta made a spirited charge to capture Pt. 774. The Scotsmen overcame stiff resistance from the Germans, who were strongly entrenched. They went forward undeterred by the heavy shell fire, which the Germans called down to screen their positions, and captured Pt. 744 at 0800 hours. Later, at 1730 hours two platoons attacked and captured Pt. 685. An hour later a fierce German counter-attack drove the A & SH back to Pt. 744. The Germans, however, withdrew during the night of 7/8 October and therefore the A and SH reoccupied Pt. 685 at dawn on 8 October. M. Cavallara was thus secured.

Attack on M. Casalino

Meanwhile, at 0700 hours on 7 October, 3/8 Punjab had thrust forward along the spur connecting M. Cavallara with M. Casalino. The plan was for A Company to advance from Pt. 601 and capture Pt. 605; B Company to pass through A along the ridge to Pt. 655; and C Company to attack Pt. 606 from the north in the area Val Barole. After some resistance A Company captured Pt. 605 and consolidated on the feature by 0830 hours. The advance of B Company was held up by machine gun fire from the northern slopes of M. Cavallara. However, after beating fierce resistance the company occupied Pt. 655 at 1100 hours, and at dawn on 8 October a forward platoon was established at Pt. 631 without opposition. C Company's attack on Pt. 606 was held up by spandau fire. The Germans, however, occupied its objective at dawn on 8 October.

Intense German machine gun fire, sited to cover the line of approach to M. Casalino, prevented further progress. 3/8 Punjab held on to the ground so far occupied and prepared to attack further. At 0500 hours on 10 October, B Company advanced from the area Pt. 655 and hurled itself against the strongly guarded position of M. Casolina. The attackers were met by heavy automatic weapon fire, when they reached the German defences. Approaches to M. Casalino were very steep, muddy and slippery and most of the weapons were rendered useless by mud when the company took shelter from German fire. The two forward platoons suffered many casualties from the German fire and the one platoon, which remained intact, consolidated a position about 500 yards back from the objective. Nevertheless, B Company was driven off the small conical shaped hill by the tenacious German defenders, suffering about 40 casualties. 3/8 Punjab did not have adequate strength to drive the Germans from M. Casalino, whilst the latter were too badly shaken immediately to follow up their successful stemming of the attack. The badly depleted B Company of 3/8 Punjab outnumbered by the German garrison of M. Casalino, (estimated to be two companies strong) withdrew to a new position, about five hundred yards back from the objectives. Here it was strongly counter-attacked at 1030 hours by the Germans, who surged forward from their hill position. A bitter struggle ensued which ended in the Germans being pushed back. The company stayed where it was; the Germans hung on grimly to M. Casalino and were not finally driven off this key feature until 23 October, when 1/5 Gurkha of the 17th Indian Infantry Brigade put in a successful attack.

Reorganisation of the 8th Indian Division

We have so far described the operations of the 19th Indian Infantry Brigade. We shall now give an account of the activities of the other brigades of the 8th Indian Division.

On 30 September 1944, the 17th Indian Infantry Brigade relieved the 2nd British Brigade north of the road Marradi—Pallazuolo; 1st Battalion Royal Fusiliers was in the area Popolano with one company forward at Adriano; 1/12 Frontier Force Regiment was in the area Popolano with one company in the area Marradi; 1/5 Royal Gurkha Rifles was in the area M. Di Grizzano. From 1 to 5 October the activities of the 17th Indian Infantry Brigade were confined to patrolling. No large scale operations were undertaken, until the right flank, namely the right of Sword route, was secured further north. For a short time, heavy rain which began on 2 October almost brought operations to a standstill. But two days later the sky cleared and once more patrols resumed their activity. All along the front, German artillery shelled the forward area intermittently, paying particular attention to the Marradi railway station and the town itself.

On 7 October, the 17th Indian Infantry Brigade was relieved by the 21st Indian Infantry Brigade. The 5th Battalion Queen's Own Royal West Kent Regiment took over from 1/12 Frontier Force Regiment and 3/15 Punjab took over from 1/5 Royal Gurkha Rifles; 1/5 Mahratta concentrated in the area west of Popolano. The brigade's initial task was to clear Romano and continue the advance.[5] The attack on M. Romano could not be made until the

[5] 8 Ind. Div. Planning Note 30, dated 6 October 1944, War Diary 8 Ind. Div.

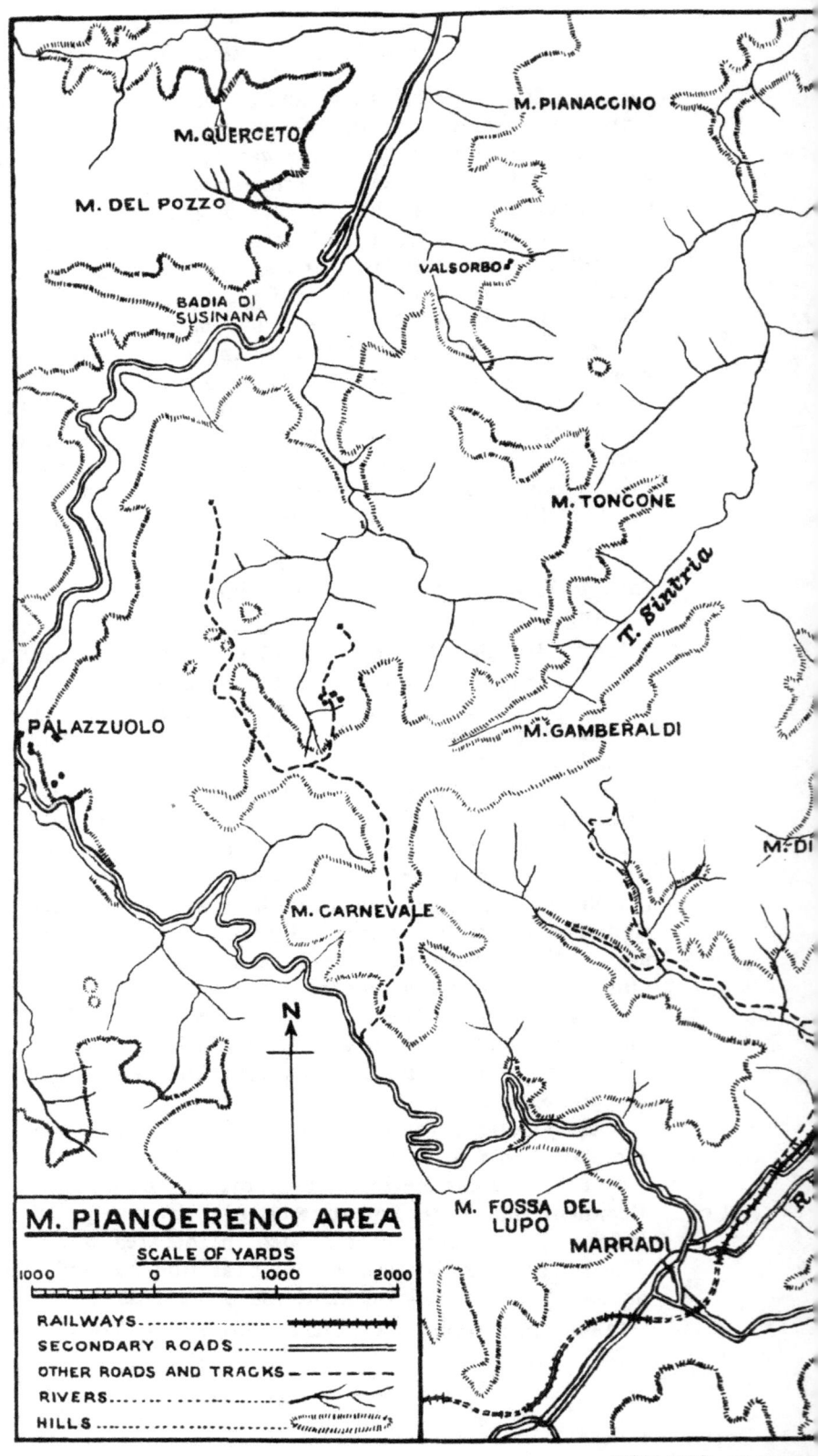

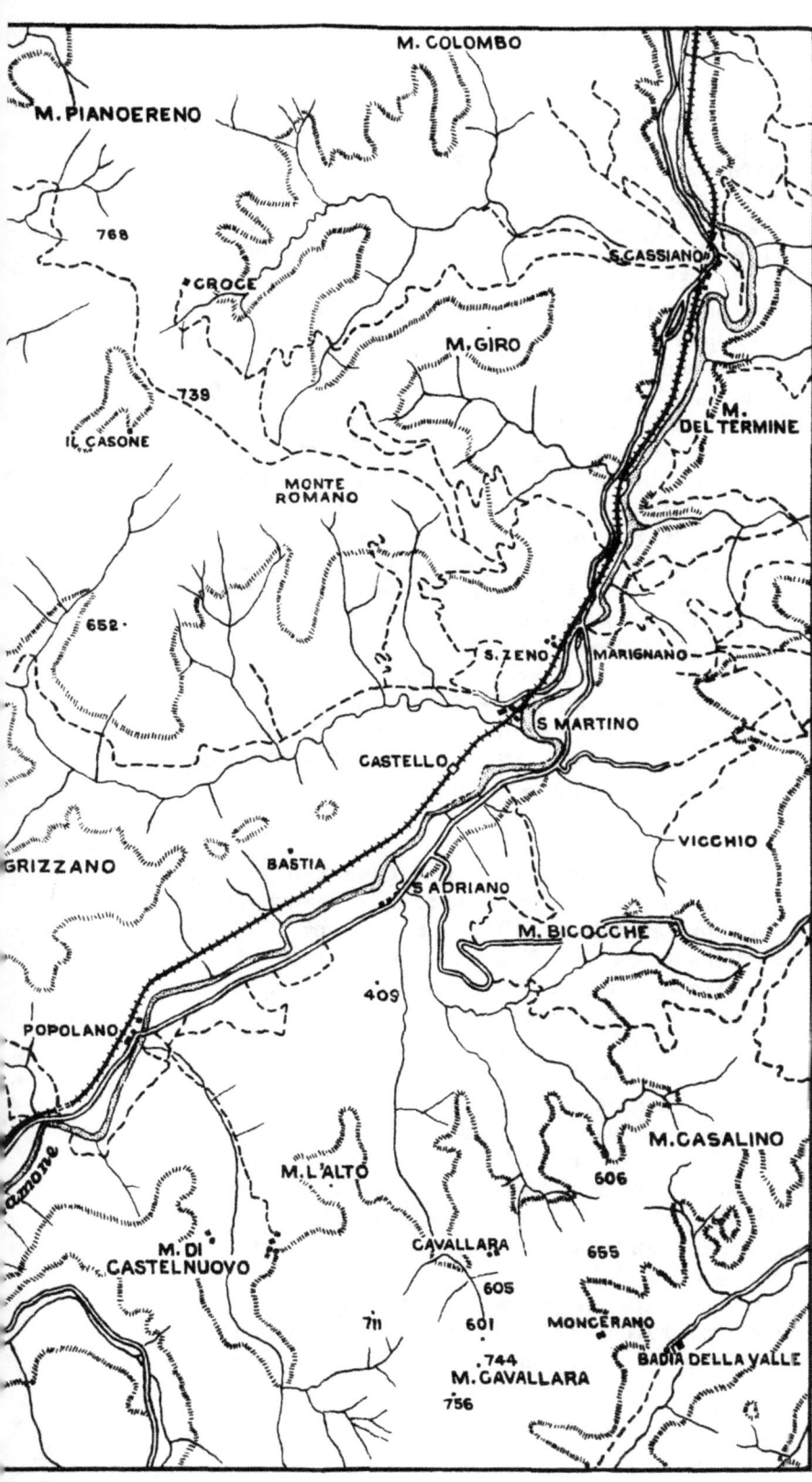

IN METRES ·711

5th Royal West Kent Regiment had driven the Germans from Castello, a precipitous feature covered from the east flank by the Germans in S. Martino and from the ridge running south-west by the razor-edge approach which was covered by machine guns on fixed lines. The attack by the 5th Royal West Kent Regiment during the night of 11/12 October on Castello was unsuccessful owing to the difficult approach. Then 1/5 Mahratta prepared to attack this feature. But the plan for the attack was cancelled and the Mahrattas were ordered to relieve the 6th Battalion Gordon Highlanders of the 1st Division in pursuance of the plan for the reorganisation of the 8th Indian Division, which was adopted to protect the right flank of the 1st Division. The 21st Indian Infantry Brigade extended its front to the left by taking over positions from the 6th Battalion Gordon Highlanders while the 17th Indian Infantry Brigade relieved the 19th Indian Infantry Brigade in the area M. Cavallara. The 19th Indian Infantry Brigade passed into reserve.

About this time, the II U.S. Corps, having launched a powerful attack in an all-out drive to cut Route 9 east of Bologna, was engaged in fierce fighting. Other operations in the Fifth Army became subordinate to this main thrust. In order to prevent the German commander switching over his reserves to oppose the II U.S. Corps and also to protect the right flank of the 1st Division, the 8th Indian Division was ordered to capture a prominent peak, M. Pianoereno situated west of the Sword route. Major-General Russell detailed the 21st Indian Infantry Brigade to capture M. Pianoereno.

Capture of M. Pianoereno

1/5 Mahratta took over from the 6th Battalion Gordon Highlanders at 1530 hours on 13 October. The forward companies were holding the ridge from excluding M. Toncone to Pt. 707, and looked on to the M. Romano and M. Pianoereno features held by the Germans. The Mahrattas thus found themselves guarding a large rocky escarpment, which dominated Arrow route from the east, the escarpment being situated some two miles north of M. Gamberaldi, in effect a continuation of the same line of high ground.

I Battalion 578th Regiment, whose sector extended from the river Sintria to the S. Marlino—S. Cassiano road, offered strong resistance on M. Pianoereno and M. Romano for the defence of which the Germans had taken up strong positions. They were holding in strength Pt. 711 and Pt. 768, two outstanding pimples, of which the highest lay only a thousand yards from the summit of M. Pianoereno (2300 feet high).

The Commander of the 21st Indian Infantry Brigade planned to carry out the operations for the attack on M. Pianoereno in two phases. In the first phase, 3/15 Punjab was to secure the objectives

Pt. 768 and Pt. 711 and hold the ridge from excluding Pt. 751 to Croce Daniele. At the same time, 1/5 Mahratta, holding the ridge from excluding M. Toncone to Pt. 707, was to clear the Germans from C. Verlona and C. Virletta. The 5th Royal West Kent Regiment was to relieve 3/15 Punjab in the area Il Casone and protect the right flank up to Pt. 751 and patrol to Pt. 692 and C. Monte. In the second phase, 1/5 Mahratta was to advance from the forming up place, the re-entrant, south and south-east of Pt. 711, and pass through the forward positions of 3/15 Punjab on Pt. 768 and M. Vecchio spur, capturing Pt. 778, before wheeling to the left across the saddle to seize M. Pianoereno. For this operation, two platoons D Company 5th Royal Mahratta (Machine Gun) and two companies 6/13 Royal Frontier Force Rifles, were under the command of the 21st Indian Infantry Brigade.

The role of the 17th Indian Infantry Brigade in the area M. Cavallara was to support the 21st Indian Infantry Brigade's attack on M. Pianoereno by:—

 (i) demonstrating with a squadron of the 14th Canadian Armoured Regiment towards M. Romano,
 (ii) staging a feint attack, with tank, artillery and mortar support towards Castello, S. Martino, and
 (iii) harassing by patrols the Germans on M. Casalino.

To divert German attention still further another feint attack was to be staged by a brigade of the 1st Division, which was to cross the river Sintria and seize Pt. 747 and the ridge from 1200 yards north of it.

At 2030 hours on 17 October, all the available guns opened fire with a heavy concentration on the Pianoereno spur. Simultaneously 3/15 Punjab moved forward. Up the hill the men went, cloaked by the night. Hardly had they crossed the start line (east and west along the track at 104079) when German mortar bombs and heavy shell fire burst in their midst. They waited for an abatement, and with a temporary lull, climbed up the hill again. At 2230 hours, C Company captured Pt. 711 after beating opposition from the German machine guns. Meanwhile, A Company had reached the spur at approximately 108086, at 2200 hours, after very fierce hand-to-hand fighting in the German position, where every slit trench had to be overrun and its occupants killed. A Company consolidated that position. D Company then came up on the left of A Company but suffered heavy casualties, including all platoon commanders from shelling and mortaring and did not succeed in passing through A Company. B Company from reserve then advanced and picked up the remains of D Company on the Fontecchio ridge and attacked Corce Daniele, a cluster of farm buildings astride a small neck of high ground, from where the Germans had an excellent field of fire

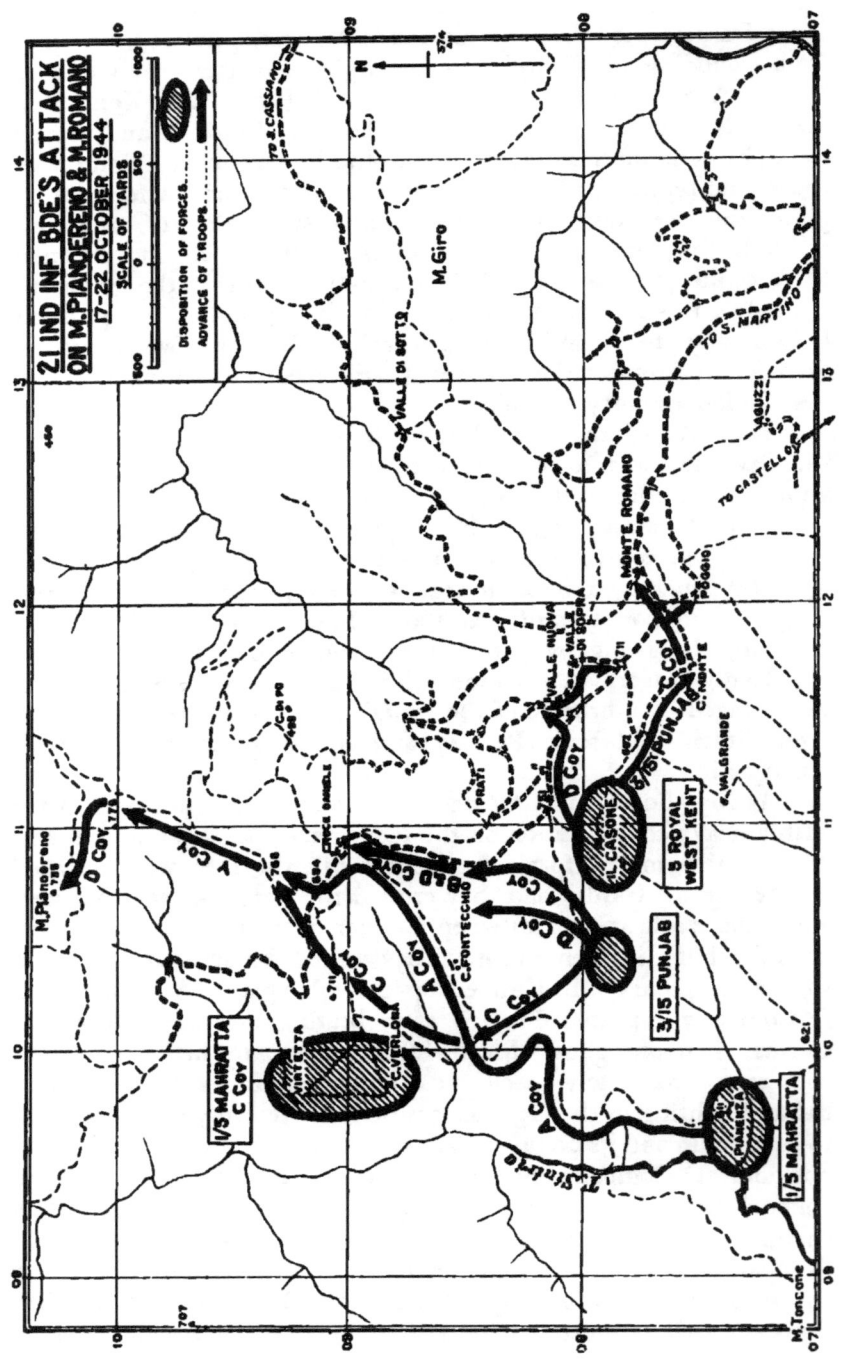

covering the approach to the Pianoereno spur. The advance began about midnight. Twice the Punjab Company assaulted Croce Daniele; twice they were met by deadly machine gun and small arms fire, which broke up the attack. Then in a raging fury the remnant of the two companies attacked the strong point for a third time. Their charge carried them right into the German positions; Croce Daniele was taken at 0455 hours on 18 October. Meanwhile C Company had made three attempts to advance from Pt. 711 to attack Pt. 768. These attempts failed owing to shelling, mortaring and machine gun fire from the area Pt. 684 and from the north. With the glimmer of dawn, the tired and depleted company was obliged to fall back on Pt. 711, where C Company of 1/5 Mahratta was in position, having already secured C. Verlona and C. Virtetta at 1800 hours on 17 October. During the morning of 18 October, the Punjab positions around the farm buildings of Croce Deniele were subjected to persistent machine gun fire from the high ground to the north. There was also considerable hostile mortar and shell fire.

As C Company of 3/15 Punjab, advancing from Pt. 711, had failed to secure its objective Pt. 768 due to strong German opposition, the commander of 1/5 Mahratta thought it unwise to concentrate his battalion in the pre-arranged area south and south-east of Pt. 711. He selected Pianenza as the concentration area since it was not under German observation. So the whole battalion proceeded on mule packs at 0800 hours on 18 October to Pianenza. The morning was devoted to reconnaissance. At 1330 hours on 18 October, A Company advanced past Fontecchio, supported by corps artillery. The company's first objective was House No. 1 (Pt. 684). which was captured by 8 Platoon after being stonked and smoked. 7 and 10 Platoons then passed through, approaching the final objective (Pt. 768) from the left. At this point the company came under direct observation from M. Romano feature and suffered casualties. Nevertheless the men pushed on the advance and captured Pt. 768 at 1500 hours. Very heavy and continuous German shelling followed after the capture of Pt. 768. A patrol to Pt. 778 and M. Pianoereno, however, found them both unoccupied. The Germans had withdrawn under cover of heavy machine gun fire. Y Company occupied Pt. 778 at 1700 hours on 18 October and at 0930 hours on 19 October D Company was firm on M. Pianoereno.

Capture of M. Romano

The time had now come to clear up the M. Romano spur, still held in some strength by the Germans. On the ridge, which ran in a south-easterly direction from Croce Deniele, and about two thousand yards form the place, there was a small chapel with three or four houses close by. Known as the hamlet of Romano, the church and houses stood where the ground was almost level on the top of the spur. Between Croce Daniele and M. Romano were several isolated farm-houses; one of these was known as Valle Nuovo. The 5th Battalion Royal West Kent Regiment was ordered to seize M. Romano. To accomplish this purpose, the British battalion had first to capture Valle Nuovo and Casa Monte.

Whilst it was still dark early on 20 October, two companies of the 5th Royal West Kent Regiment advanced on Valle Nuovo and Casa Monte. 3/15 Punjab helped by staging a diversion on the left flank in Prati. B Company of the 5th Royal West Kent Regiment directed on Valle Nuovo reached Pt. 751, at 0415 hours. As the company advanced it was held up by a hail of bullets and was unable to make further progress. C Company attacked C. Monte at 0515 hours but was halted by German fire close to the objective. As it grew light, the men lay pinned to the ground on the open grassy slopes. An urgent call for a smoke screen was flashed back to the guns. It was answered. Covered by dense white smoke C Company was successfully withdrawn.

The Commanding Officer of the 5th Royal West Kent Regiment next planned to attack Valle Nuovo from a direction different from that followed in the first attack. His plan was a great success, the 5th Royal West Kent Regiment changing direction during the advance and attacking along a ridge to the right and rear of the German positions. It was a complicated manoeuvre requiring skilful execution but it paid high dividends. The plan was for five platoons to attack in three places. The operation was to be carried out in three phases:

> Phase I—Three platoons were to go to the ridge between Pt. 751 and Cemetery.
> Phase II—One platoon was to remain on the ridge and two platoons were to push on to Valle Nuovo.
> Phase III—Almost simultaneously two fresh platoons were to advance to Valle di Sopra.

At 1745 hours on 20 October, the 5th Royal West Kent Regiment attacked, supported by heavy artillery and mortar fire. The Germans were disorganised by artillery fire. The British battalion had cleared Valle Nuovo by 2100 hours, after encountering heavy artillery and mortar defensive fire. Valle di Sopra was found razed by British artillery and clear of Germans. By 0400 hours on 21 October, the 5th Royal West Kent Regiment consolidated in the area of Pt. 711 and Valle Nuovo.

C Company of 3/15 Punjab, under the command of the 5th Royal West Kent Regiment, sent a patrol which reached Valgrande

Jaipur Infantry operating in Lugo

Smoke rising as Tavoleto is shelled

Rifleman Thaman Gurung, V.C.
(1/5 R.G.R.)

Rifleman Sher Bahadur Thapa, V.C.
(1/9 G.R.)

at 1140 hours on 21 October and drove out the Germans. This Company then advanced and occupied C. Monte at 1200 hours without opposition. C Company then attacked M. Romano at 1445 but ran into thick defensive fire from German artillery and machine guns. Stiff German resistance compelled the company to withdraw to Poggio under cover of smoke. While withdrawing the men were engaged by German small arms and therefore had to withdraw further to Pt. 621. But as soon as it was dark, the Germans withdrew from M. Romano, allowing the 5th Royal West Kent Regiment to occupy the feature at 1200 hours on 22 October.

The 21st Indian Infantry Brigade's Achievements

Since taking over from the 6th Battalion Gordon Highlanders on the west of Sword route on 13 October, the 21st Indian Infantry Brigade had carried out its task successfully in spite of handicaps imposed by the extremely difficult country. In retrospect, the task of clearing the Germans off M. Pianoereno was arduous, not so much from the point of view of numbers of the opposing force but because of the handicaps imposed by such extremely difficult country. The only lines of approach were so patent that the Germans could repeatedly bring down accurate mortar and shell fire, which inflicted heavy casualties. Throughout this period of operations by the 21st Indian Infantry Brigade the Germans were resolute in their defence, and even when outflanked and overlooked from higher ground, as they certainly were at Valle Nuovo and M. Romano, they fought back with determination. In most cases, they were only dislodged after severe fighting at close quarters.

The administrative problem in this operation was most complex. Supply jeeps climbed up to Gamberaldi along a rough track barely wide enough even for them. From there, thanks to the labours of the sappers, ambulance jeeps worked on their way to the Advance Dressing Station, two or three miles further forward. The mule companies once more did outstanding service in maintaining forward companies. Without them, this operation would have been quite impractical.

Limited Advance

Partly because of the hammering they had received from the 21st Indian Infantry Brigade, and partly in order to adjust their defensive line to conform with events elsewhere, the German forces started a local withdrawal on the front of the 8th Indian Division during the night of 22/23 October. Screened by strong fighting patrols and extensive minefields, the *305th Infantry Division* drew slowly back to a line running from south-east to north-west across Sword route, that is, from M. Monsignano and M. Budriano, south of Sword route, to the northern hinge, M. Colombo, with patrols of the 8th Indian Division hard on their heels.

All three brigades of the 8th Indian Division were now in the line, each brigade with two battalions forward. The plan of the operations was as follows:—

(i) The 17th Indian Infantry Brigade was to continue the advance up Saturn and Mars routes, securing the high ground on both sides of Mars.

(ii) The 19th Indian Infantry Brigade, after relieving the 1st Royal Fusiliers, was to advance astride Sword route.

(iii) The 21st Indian Infantry Brigade was to continue to protect the left flank of the Sword route by securing M. Colombo.

(iv) 1st Battalion Jaipur Infantry Brigade was to protect the right flank of the 8th Indian Division.

(v) Both the 17th and 19th Indian Infantry Brigades were to be supported in their advance by the tanks of the 14th Canadian Armoured Regiment, the country having become passable to tanks for the first time since the breaking of the Gothic Line.

Advance along the whole front began on 23 October. On the extreme right of the divisional front, in a very broken country, 1st Jaipur Infantry pushed forward to M. Campaccio, which brought this battalion to within three miles of the new German defence line. To the north-west, in the 17th Indian Infantry Brigade sector, 1/5 Royal Gurkha Rifles occupied M. Casalino and M. Serra. North of the Gurkha position, 1/12 Frontier Force Regiment had thrust forward to seize M. Gaggiolo, just south of M. Budriano, the central bastion of the new German line. The huge mass of M. Gaggiolo faced M. Romano across the Lamone valley; with its capture, Marradi was safe and a way was opened to the Torcente Valle further east. To the left of the two Indian battalions, the British battalion of the 17th Indian Infantry Brigade, 1st Royal Fusiliers, occupied the village of Marignano, on Sword route due west of M. Gaggiolo. West of Sword route, the 21st Indian Infantry Brigade advanced with 3/15 Punjab taking M. Giro, a feature north of M. Romano, and 1/15 Mahratta Light Infantry patrolled forward to M. Colombo, the northern feature of the German line.

The 19th Indian Infantry Brigade advanced slowly down the Lamone valley, west of the 17th Indian Infantry Brigade. 6/13 Royal Frontier Force Rifles, after relieving the 1st Royal Fusiliers on 24 October, occupied M. Del Termine and S. Cassiano on 25 October, which brought the brigade up to where the German defence line crossed Sword route.

The last few days of October were marked by torrential rain, which started on 26 October and made the supply and communication position of the 8th Indian Division increasingly difficult, as the division pushed towards the new German line. Bad weather restricted operations and by 31 October a new situation had developed necessitating reorganisation of the 8th Indian Division.

CHAPTER XXVII

Advance to the River Lamone

The Eighth Army's Advance to the River Lamone

Towards the close of October 1944, the Fifth Army's offensive had been halted due to German reinforcements, Allied losses, abominable weather, and difficult terrain. The Eighth Army had closed up to the river Ronco, just short of the town of Forli. Its progress, however, had been considerably retarded in the water-logged Romagna plain. It was apparent that the plan of annihilating the German forces in Italy might not be carried out in 1944 and had to be delayed till the Spring of 1945. Operations in Italy during winter were, however, to be continued to help General Eisenhower's winter offensive in Western Europe. On 29 October 1944, General Alexander held a conference of Army Commanders at his Headquarters in Sienna. It was decided that the immediate objectives were Bologna, an important road-and-railhead to serve as an administrative base for the Spring offensive, and Ravenna, a useful port and an important administrative centre. The plan, therefore, was for the Eighth Army to continue the offensive till 15 December to enable it to capture Ravenna, and also to draw off German forces from the Fifth Army, enabling the latter to make an all-out attack on Bologna.

At the beginning of November 1944, the Germans opposite the V Corps held the line of the river Ronco. In the north was the *26th Panzer Division* with its sector extending south to two thousand yards south of Bagnolo; in the centre was the *278th Infantry Division* responsible for the line on either side of Route 9 and the switch line south of Forli airfield; in the south was the *356th Infantry Division* holding the sector west of the river Rabbi between S. Martino in Strada and Grisignano.

At the beginning of November the V Corps had made good progress. On the right, the British 4th Division had established a bridge-head over the river Ronco, south of Route 9 at Selbagnone, but was held up on the switch-line south of Forli airfield. On the left, the 10th Indian Division, which had already secured a bridge-head over the river Ronco near Meldola, was advancing towards Grisignano. On 2 November 1944, however, it was relieved by the 46th Division, which continued the advance. The 12th Lancers, operating on the right of the British 4th Division, secured a bridge-head over the Ronco. Further to the north 'Porterforce', and an ad hoc formation protecting the V Corps' right flank, made some progress towards Ravenna.

Bad weather halted the operations till 6 November. The V Corps resumed the offensive on the night of 7/8 November in order to capture Forli and establish bridge-heads on the river Montone. Considerable progress was made by 12 November. On the right, British 4th Division captured Forli on 9 November; in the centre, the newly committed 56th Division established a precarious bridge-head over the Montone just south of Forli; on the left, the 46th Division, advancing from Grisignano, crossed the Montone at Terra del Sole but encountered strong opposition at San Varano.

This successful attack by the Eighth Army was facilitated by the advance of the II Polish Corps on the left flank, whose objective was the high ground south of Route 9 between Forli and Faenza. Advancing north and north-west of Predappio Nuovo, the 5th Kresowa Division encountered stiff opposition in the area between the Rabbi and Montone rivers. M. Maggiore was captured on 6 November. Fierce resistance was, however, encountered at San Zeno in Volpinara. By 11 November, the 5th Kresowa Division was engaged in a hard fight west of Bagnolo. By 12 October, the 3rd Carpathian Division patrolled up to Modigliana, which was held in strength by the Germans.

With Forli secured and bridge-heads established over the river Montone, the V Corps was now up against formidable opposition based on the Montone-Cosina line. To break through this line the corps plan was to make a double thrust—on the right the British 4th Division, operating north of Route 9, was to advance to the river Montone along the line Villafranca di Forli—San Martino di Villafranca, cross the Montone north of the Cosina confluence and advance to the line of the river Lamone at Pieve di Cesato, while on the left the 46th Division was to advance through Villagrappa towards Faenza. The 56th Division, operating in the central sector, was assigned the role of establishing a bridge-head across the Montone on Route 9. The British 4th Division overcame stiff oppostion at San Tome and, at the close of 14 November, squared up to the Montone on a front of more than three miles north of the Cosina confluence, while the 12th Lancers on the right flank faced north between the Montone and the Canale di Rivaldino. The 56th Division established a small bridge-head across the Montone on Route 9. The 46th Division made a double thrust—on the right the advance through Villagrappa was held up at the stream Rio Balzaniano and on the left it was held up at Castiglione. Thus at the close of 16 November the V Corps was held up on the Montone-Cosina line; the British 4th Division failed to find a ford to cross the Montone north of Route 9 while the 46th Division faced strong German positions on the Cosina.

The Germans held the Montone-Cosina line in strength. The *26th Panzer Division* held a front of about five miles, from the railway line north of Route 9 to the foothills, at the head of the Cosina. The *278th Infantry Division* covered a front of about four miles along the Montone north of the railway line. *356th Infantry Division* was disposed along the river line still further to the north for about three or four miles.

On 18 November, the V Corps Commander issued orders for the attack on the Montone-Cosina line. The operations were to be carried out in three phases. In the first phase, the British 4th and 46th Divisions were to seize crossings over the Cosina within the divisional boundaries, which were readjusted so that the British 4th Division's left front extended to a point about a mile south of Route 9, while a battle group of the 10th Indian Division relieved the right of the British 4th Division, north of Villafranca di Forli. In the second phase, the British 4th and the 46th Divisions were to advance to the Lamone. (In this phase the main body of the 10th Indian Division was to be committed on the right or the left of the British 4th Division). The third phase was concerned with the crossing of the Lamone and the capture of Faenza.

The attack by British 4th Division on the mile-long stretch of the Cosina between the Cosina-Montone confluence and Route 9 did not succeed, and therefore on 21 November the plan was modified. This division was then ordered to attack south of Route 9 in conjunction with the 46th Division. On the right flank the 10th Indian Division was ordered to relieve the 12th Lancers. The attack was successful and at the close of 23 November, the left flank of the V Corps was firmly established across the Cosina on a front of three miles south of Route 9. The Polish Corps on the left flank of the V Corps was then on Monte Ricci. Therefore the *26th Panzer Division* pulled back to the Lamone line, leaving *278th Infantry Division* to guard the Montone line in the north.

By 26 November the advance had continued to the river Lamone. South of Route 9, the 46th Division captured Borgo Durbecco, the eastern suburb of Faenza, established a bridge-head over the Marzeno near Sarna and closed up to the Lamone. The British 4th Division captured San Giovanni in Selva on 25th November and closed up to the Lamone in the area Scaldino and S. Barnaba. At the end of the day the 2nd New Zealand Division relieved the British 4th Division.

Though the left flank of V Corps rested at this time on the Lamone, not much progress had been made on the right flank. The 10th Indian Division was therefore given two tasks—one battle group (the 10th Indian Infantry Brigade) was to attack across the Montone between Villafranca di Forli and C. Bettini, while the second battle group (the 20th Indian Infantry Brigade) was to cross Route 9 and advance northwards along the west bank. By 26 November, the 10th Indian Division had failed to break through the C. Bettini-Albereto line and secure the badly needed bridge across the Montone. The attack was resumed on 30 November and C. Bettini bridge secured after a hard struggle during 30 November/1 December. On 1 December, the 10th Indian Division was relieved by elements of the I Canadian Corps. The Eighth Army then regrouped to resume the offensive on 2 December.

Operation 'Merlin'

Having described the Eighth Army's advance up to the river Lamone we shall now give an account of the activities of the Indian formations in these operations. After securing a bridge-head over the river Ronco at Meldola, the 10th Indian Division had been relieved on 2 November 1944 by the 46th Division. Its period of rest, however, lasted only two weeks, for on 18 November 1944 the V Corps commander recalled it to play a part in the attack on the strong German Montone-Cosina line. The divisional headquarters moved to Forlimpopli, five miles south-east of Forli. At that time the Germans were holding the line of the Montone river, behind which regrouping had taken place designed to strengthen the defence of the sector covering Route 9 and the area further south. The V Corps was preparing to establish bridge-heads on the Montone river. 'Porterforce' on the right of the V Corps front was directed on Ravenna. The 12 Lancers was protecting the immediate right flank of the V Corps from Ghibullo to opposite the bridge site at C. Bettini. From the latter place to Route 9 was the responsibility of the British 4th Division. The 46th Division extended further to the south.

A co-ordinated attack by the V Corps and the II Polish Corps was to be launched with the object of continuing the advance up Route 9 and capturing Faenza. The II Polish Corps was directed on M. Ricci and S. Lucia. The V Corps was to carry out operation 'Merlin' in three phases. In the first phase, the British 4th and 46th Divisions were to seize bridge-heads over the river Cosina and in the second they were to advance to the river Lamone. The third phase was to be concerned with the crossing of the river Lamone and capturing Faenza.

The 10th Indian Division was initially to relieve troops of the 12 Lancers in the area of the bridge site at C. Bettini and to the south on 19 November, preparatory to forming a bridge-head to cover the construction of the bridge. The division was to be

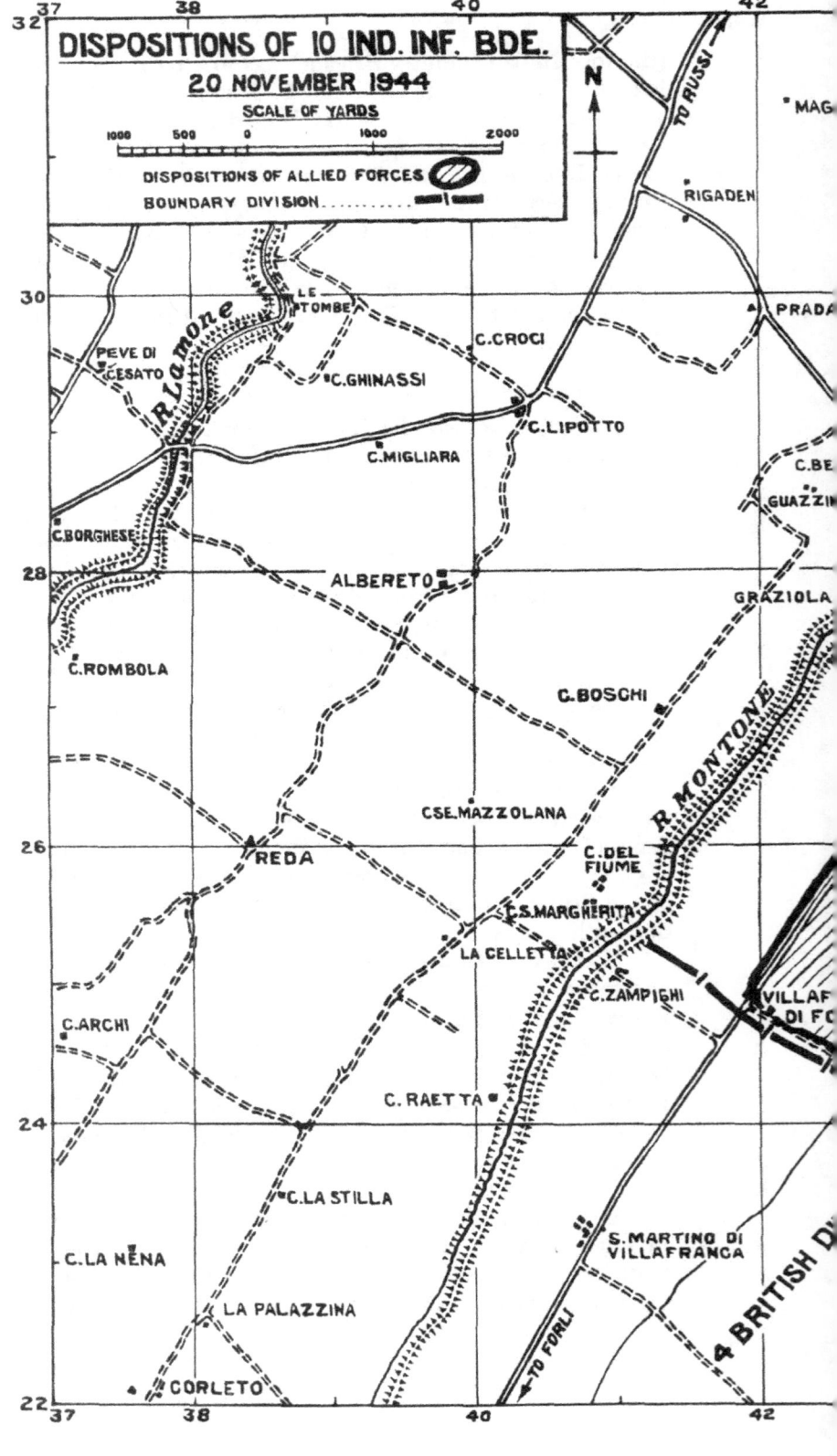

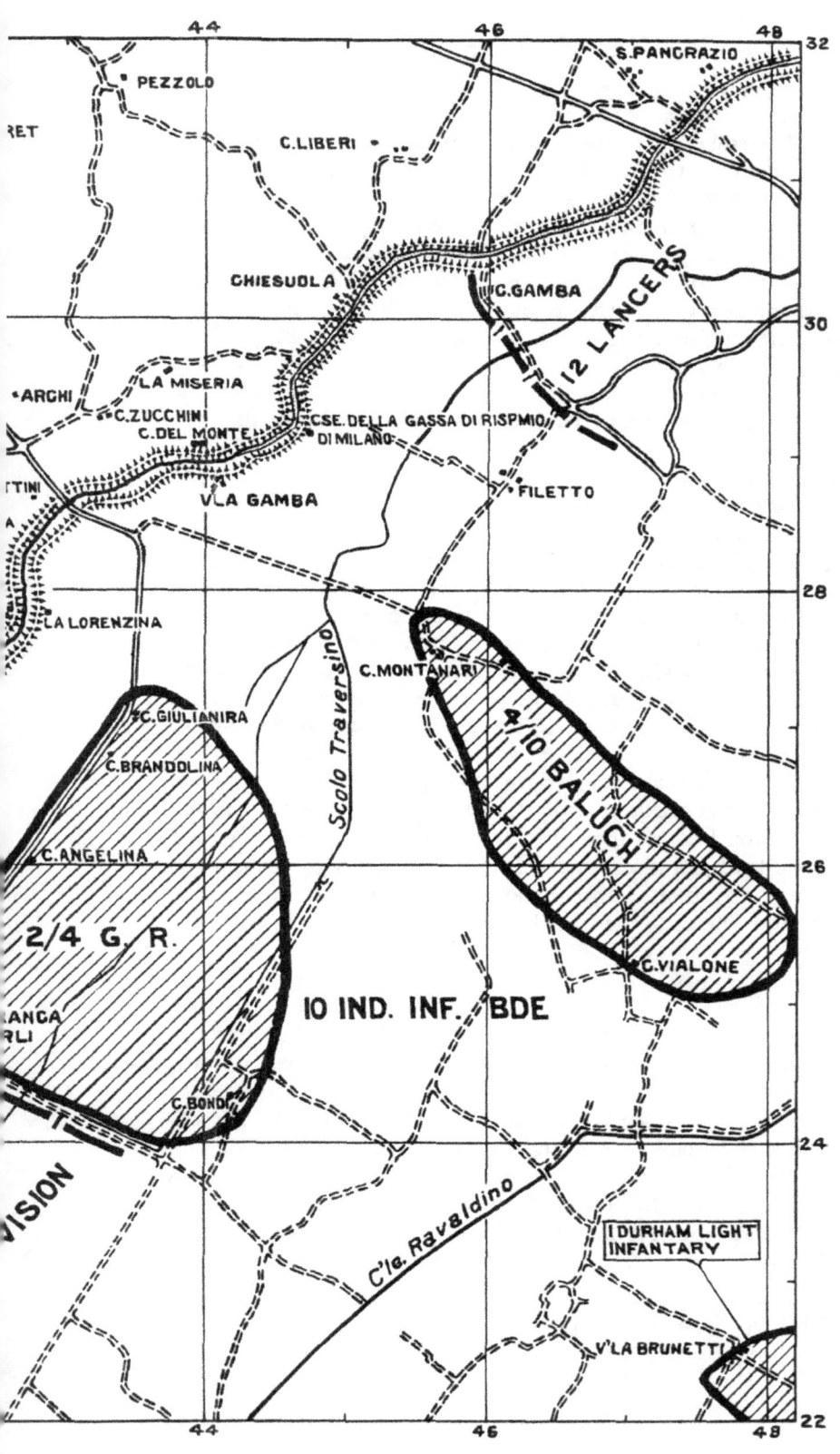

prepared to operate along the axis of Route 9, or on the right of the British 4th Division, as opportunity offered.

On 19 November 1944, the 10th Indian Infantry Brigade moved forward to take over the Villafranca di Forli sector held by A Squadron 12th Lancers. The brigade was in position by 1930 hours. 4/10 Baluch held the right sector wth one company at C. Montanari and the remainder in the area C. Vialone. 2/4 Gurkha held the left sector, with the forward companies at C. Giulianira and Villafranca di Forli and the remainder in reserve in the area C. Bondi. 1st Durham Light Infantry was in reserve in the area Brunetti. On the same day as the 10th Indian Infantry Brigade moved into the line the 7th Armoured Brigade came under the command of the 10th Indian Division and began to move into the divisional area.

The Germans were holding the line of the Montone river with the *114th Jaeger Division* in the sector from the coast to Chiesuola; to its east was the *356th Infantry Division*, with its front extending to Margherita; still further to its east was the *278th Infantry Division*. The Montone, though only thirty feet in width, presented a formidable obstacle. The actual banks of the stream rose vertically five feet higher than the normal water level. Above those, flood banks sloped to a height of another five feet. In the 10th Indian Division's sector the German-held western flood bank was the higher throughout. Mud flats inside the flood walls extended the gap to one hundred and seventy feet. After rain, the breaches created in the walls by the Germans caused the flooding of the country-side up to one thousand yards east of the river. When they happened the only approaches to the river were built-up roads. Digging in the flood-banks was easy and the Germans had constructed tunnels there for their patrols and positions for their machine guns. Ground before the banks was plentifully sown with Schu mines.[1]

Terrain

The country was a monotonously flat plain intersected by numerous watercourses, varying from large rivers to small ditches. The Italian method of building large flood-banks for the streams provided ready-made defensive positions and observation, which was not otherwise obtainable. All land was cultivated. Vineyards and orchards reduced visibility to a few yards except through the length of the field. To these difficulties, the Germans had added their own contribution. All bridges had been blown, the roads cratered and paths mined.

---

[1] Note on the topographical nature of the river Montone, including enemy method of holding it—Narrative of 10 Ind. Div. Operations.

The task for the 10th Indian Infantry Brigade was to clear the Germans from the east bank of the Montone and patrol across the river. The scope of the operation was limited by its being restricted to an 'opportunity' or infiltration crossing. On 20 November operations were limited to the despatch of fighting patrols down to the river Montone. Contacts were made with German patrols. A platoon of 2/4 Gurkha occupied houses in the area C. Bettini against opposition. The clearing of the Germans on the east bank of the river was continued on 21 November, with the battalions patrolling forward and stepping up to platoon strength to occupy houses in the area of the river bank.

The attack by the British 4th Division on the Cosina defences, on 21 November, did not succeed and therefore the corps plan was modified. The corps commander next ordered this division to attack south of Route 9 in conjunction with the 46th Division. On the right flank, the 10th Indian Division was ordered to relieve the 12th Lancers immediately, and

(i) to prepare to cross the river Montone north of Villafranca di Forli.

(ii) to have one brigade group, with one regiment of armour, ready to exploit the success achieved by the British 4th and the 46th Divisions along Route 9.

On 22/23 November the 43rd Indian Infantry Brigade relieved A Squadron 12 Lancers and held the line with 2/6 Gurkha on the right and 2/10 Gurkha on the left. On 24 November, Skinner's Horse came under the command of the 43rd Indian Infantry Brigade and took over protection of the right flank.

The V Corps attack was successful and at the close of 23 November, its left flank was firmly established across the Cosina on a front of three miles south of Route 9. Not much progress was, however, made on the 10th Indian Division's front since the Germans continued to defend the C. Bettini bridge site with grim determination. The 10th Indian Division was involved in limited mopping up operations against tenacious Germans who had to be ejected from each group of houses in the area of the river bank, and then prevented from repeated attempts at infiltrating back again.

On 24 November the 20th Indian Infantry Brigade also came into the line. 1st Battalion Nabha Akal Infantry relieved the 4th Reconnaissance Regiment of the 4th British Division on the east bank of the Montone in area Villafranca di Forli—S. Martino di Villafranca. 1/5 Mahratta, the forward battalion, concentrated in area Corleto. The 20th Indian Infantry Brigade was preparing to make a thrust northwards along the west bank of the Montone to assist the 10th Indian Infantry Brigade in establishing a bridge-head at C. Bettini bridge site.

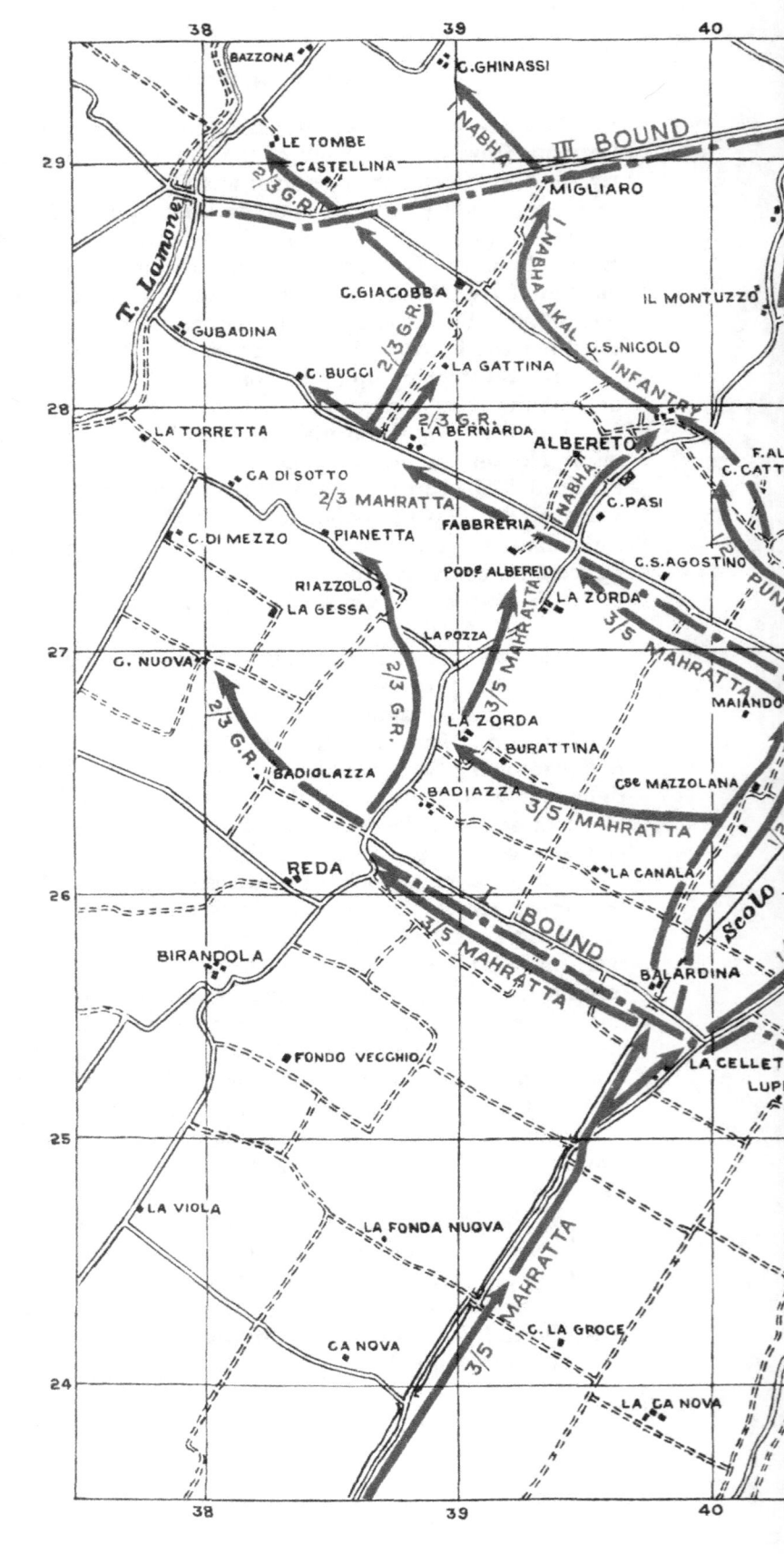

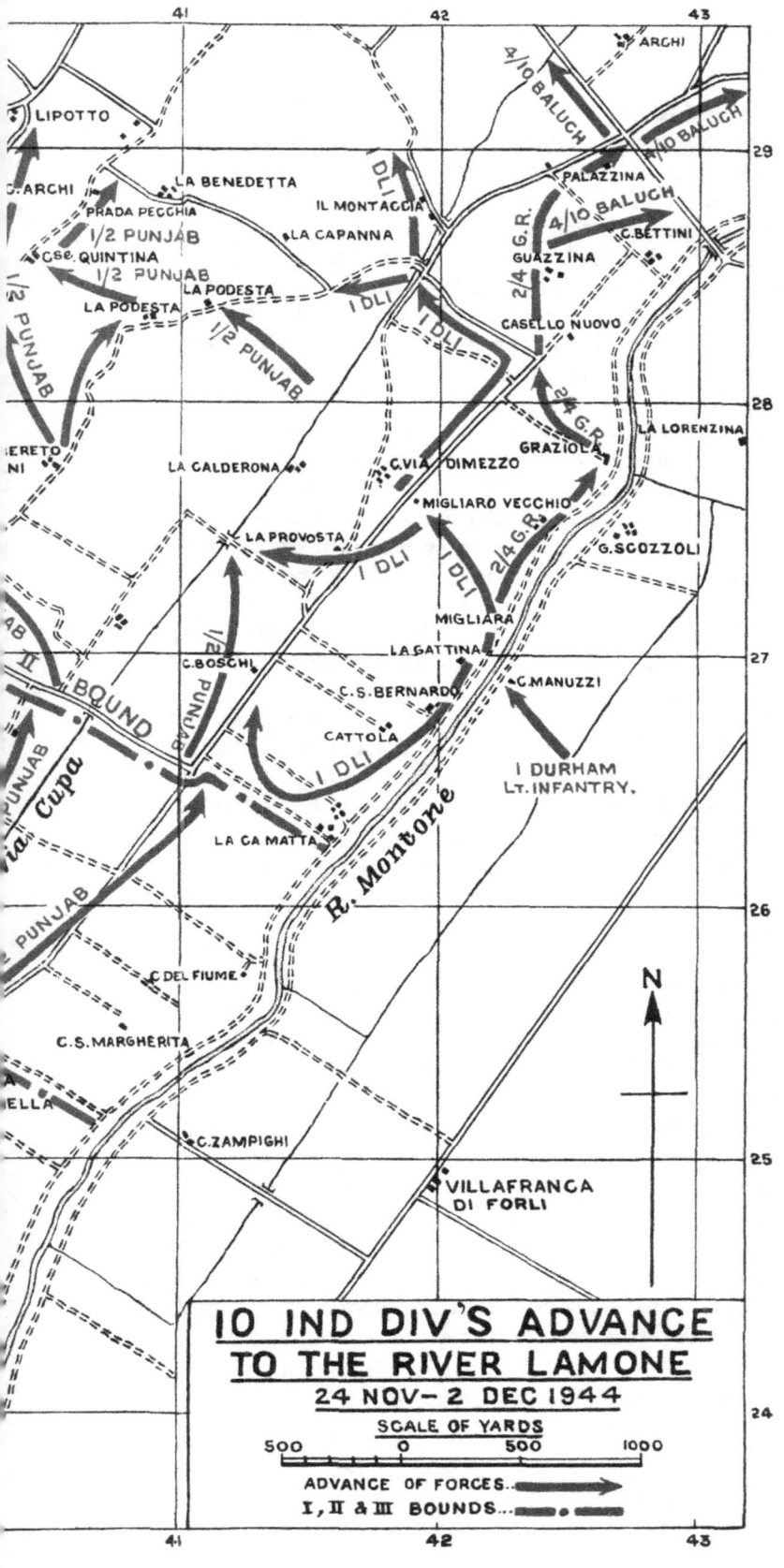

The Germans stubbornly defended the C. Bettini bridge site. The focal point of this resistance was Albereto where the Germans had dug in and employed tanks or self-propelled guns to support the infantry. Their control of the routes east and west of Albereto facilitated the employment of their armour.

According to the divisional plan, the 10th Indian Infantry Brigade was to establish a bridge-head across the Montone, while the 20th Indian Infantry Brigade was to advance northwards from the area Corleto on the west bank of the river Montone. The operations of the 10th Indian Infantry Brigade were to be carried out in three phases:—

Phase I—At 2200 hours on 24 November one company of 2/4 Gurkha was to cross the river in the area of C. Manuzzi and clear the west bank, including farms Migliaro, La Gattina and Bernardo.

Phase II—1st Durham Light Infantry was to advance from the assembly area, launch assault boats, and cross the river to form the bridgehead, including the localities Migliaro Vecchio, La Provosta and C. Boschi. The operation was not to start before 2300 hours.

Phase III—A Company of 2/4 Gurkha was to extend the flanks of the bridge-head and clear the Germans from the area Graziola and C. Del Fiume. The operation was not to start before 0200 hours on 25 November.[2]

The 20th Indian Infantry Brigade was to move up astride the road running north north-east from the road junction near C. Bosca in three bounds:

I Bound—near C.S. Margherita to road junction near Reda.
II Bound—La Ca Matta to road junction near Pod Albereto.
III Bound—near Castelina to road junction near Lipotto.

3/5 Mahratta was to lead the attack. This battalion was to advance from the area Corleto up the brigade axis at first light on 25 November and secure the first two bounds. Then 1/2 Punjab was to advance at La Palazzina to hold the line C. Bettini—road junction near Lipotto, while 3/5 Mahratta was to push on to the third bound. 2/3 Gurkha was to move into the concentration area near Corleto which was vacated by 1/2 Punjab, and move forward to the area of the road junction near La Celletta. The North Irish Horse was in support of the 10th Indian Infantry Brigade while A and B Squadrons 6th Royal Tank Regiment were in support of the 20th Indian Infantry Brigade for these operations.

[2] 10 Ind. Inf. Bde. O.O. No. 2, 24 November 1944.

The 10th Indian Infantry Brigade's Bridge-head over the River Montone

At 2020 hours on 24 November, D Company of 2/4 Gurkha concentrated in the area of C. Brandolina for the purpose of crossing the river near C. Manuzzi. Its right flank was protected by C Company in the area opposite the C. Bettini bridge site and A Company in the area G. Scozzoli while its left flank was protected by B Company in the area C. Zampighi. A section of D Company attempted to cross the river by fording but found the water too deep to be able to do so. At 0200 hours on 25 November, however, a patrol from D Company succeeded in reaching the far bank of the river but its progress was checked by a thick anti-personnel minefield. At 0700 hours on 25 November the Sappers commenced clearing mines from the river bank in the area C. Manuzzi, and thereby enabled the Durham to establish a bridge-head. At 0930 hours this battalion succeeded in getting patrols across the river in boats against slight opposition. These were stepped up to a company strength during the day. At last light on 25 November the Durham had secured a bridge-head. At that time A Company was firmly established in the area Migliaro—Migliaro Vecchio, B Company was in the area La Ca Matta—C. Boshi, C Company was in the area La Provosta and D Company of 2/4 Gurkha (under command of the Durham) was pushing forward along the west bank towards Graziola.

On 26 November the Durham made a double thrust towards Casello Nuovo, a key German position. The plan was for B Company of the Durham to push along the track forward of Migliaro Vecchio and for D Company of 2/4 Gurkha to push along the west bank of the Montone through Graziola. Determined German opposition encountered a little beyond Migliaro, Vecchio was overcome at 1620 hours and B Company of the Durham pushed on and captured houses on the outskirts of Casello Nuovo. Further advance was checked by stiff opposition. Meanwhile D Company of 2/4 Gurkha was also having trouble. At 0830 hours this company had its forward platoon near Graziola. Stiffening opposition slowed down the advance and it was not till 2000 hours that Cassello Nuovo was captured. At 0200 hours on 27 November, however, a German counter-attack supported by tanks forced the platoon to withdraw to company headquarters near Graziola.

The Germans offered strong resistance from the area Casello Nuovo and the advance of the 10th Indian Infantry Brigade was held up. On 27 November the Durham made some headway against opposition. At 0835 hours one platoon of B Company, assisted by tanks, launched an attack on the houses held by the Germans in the area Casello Nuovo. The objective was taken at 0925 hours. Meanwhile at 0645 hours on 27 November two platoons of D Company of 2/4 Gurkha had attacked and captured a house in the area Casello Nuovo. At 1025 hours a German counter-attack on this house was repulsed. Though the 10th Indian Infantry Brigade secured a foothold on the outskirts the Germans continued to hold Cassello Nuovo in strength.

Advance Towards Albereto

The advance of the 20th Indian Infantry Brigade too was held up by stiff opposition in the area Albereto. The brigade plan was for 3/5 Mahratta to lead the attack. Initially C and B Companies, advancing from Corleto were to secure the first bound. Then the battalion was to fan out with C Company making the main thrust towards Albereto and Migliano on the third bound, B Company in the centre moving through Pianeta towards Castellina a little beyond the third bound, and D Company on the left making a wide hook through Gubadina towards the left of the third bound. B Squadron 6th Royal Tank Regiment was to be in support of 3/5 Mahratta and its right flank was to be protected by 1/2 Punjab. After capturing the right of the second bound they were to carry out a two-fold task—one thrust was to be made on the right towards La Provosta to join hands with the 1st Durham Light Infantry (of the 10th Indian Infantry Brigade) operating in that area while on the left the main thrust was to be made towards C. Cattani (to divert German attention from the Mahratta attack on Albereto) and Lipotto, on the extreme right of the third bound.

The 3/5 Mahratta pushed forward on foot at 0700 hours on 25 November but owing to a blow on the main road the supporting arms were unable to accompany the infantry. At 1130 hours C and B Companies were at the first bound near Balardina. Two hours later the blow on the main road was repaired and supporting arms including tanks moved up. The infantry pushed on and at last light had established C Company in the area Maiando, B and A Companies in the area Mazzolana, and D Company at the cross roads near Reda. The Germans were holding Albereto in strength. Their chief forward positions were at the Albereto cross-roads, La Zorda (near Pod Albereto), and La Zorda (near Burattina). The commander of 3/5 Mahratta had planned to make a double thrust, with C Company from the area Maiando directed against the Albereto cross-roads and A Company from the area Mazzolana directed against La Zorda (near Burattina). D Company near Reda was to cover their left flank. At 0545 hours on 26 November a patrol from C Company pushed on towards the Albereto cross-roads. The road was strewn with Teller mines. The patrol was engaged by German tanks and machine gun fire from the houses near the road junction, and forced to withdraw. C Company then tried to move forward south of the road but was held up by stiff opposition from La Zorda (near Pod Albereto). At 1235 hours C Company which had been forced to move along the road owing to ditches and other anti-tank obstacles in the fields, was held up by strong opposition from the Albereto cross-roads and to the north in the area Albereto. Meanwhile A Company had moved west from the area Mazzolana at 1000 hours towards La Zorda (near Burattina). At 1230 hours its advance was held up by mortar, self-propelled artillery and machine gun fire from the village La Zorda. Thus by 1235 hours both A and C Companies were held up by strong German opposition. Consequently the commander of 3/5 Mahratta ordered D Company to move from the road junction near Reda, north-west towards La Gessa and attack La Zorda from the rear. D Company pushed on towards La Gessa but met with strong opposition from tank and machine guns from three sides and was forced to withdraw to the original position. Thus the prospects of overcoming German resistance in this area were not very bright. The frontal attacks on the Albereto cross-roads and La Zorda having failed, the commander of 3/5 Mahratta had recourse to a flank attack and consequently he ordered D Company to move forward from the road junction near Reda north-west towards La Gessa; but it encountered very stiff opposition and was forced to withdraw to the original position. To add to the difficulties, a troop of tanks moving to the support of A Company had been held up by a road block. Fortunately both the forward companies— A Company in the area La Zorda (near Burattina) and C Company in the area of the Albereto cross-roads— kept up the pressure and their pertinacity had its reward. At 1615 hours A Company succeeded in clearing a major part of the village of La Zorda. This success was encouraging, and C Company too made some progress. At 1715 hours its forward troops were just short of the Albereto cross-roads. Unfortunately a tank in support of C Company hit a mine on the road about 200 yards from the objective, and without such support the forward troops failed to make further progress. Thus at the close of 26 November some gains had been made; A Company held a large part of La Zorda, while C Company had successfully edged its way forward towards the Albereto cross-roads.

The right flank of 3/5 Mahratta was protected by 1/2 Punjab. Early on 26 November, C and D Companies of the latter were established on the second bound. At 0930 hours they advanced towards La Provosta and C. Cattani, respectively. At 1200 hours C Company was held up by spandau and mortar fire near La Provosta. The Germans were well dug in with a number of automatic weapons supported by tanks. At 1300 hours, when C Company failed to make any progress, B Company was moved up to its right. Nevertheless no further progress was made. D company, on the other hand, encountered negligible resistance and captured C. Cattani, thus strengthening the right flank of C Company of 3/5 Mahratta attacking the Albereto cross roads.

At the same time the left flank of 3/5 Mahratta was protected by 2/3 Gurkha. Early on 26 November, this battalion concentrated in the area La Croce, with A Company at Reda. At 2030 hours A Company moved off from Reda to make a thrust through C. Nuova, C. Di Mezzo and La Torretta to the east bank of the river Lamone. C. Nuova was captured without opposition but all attempts to occupy C. Di Mezzo and La Gessa did not succeed.

On 27 November the pressure on German positions continued and considerable progress was made. A and C Companies of 3/5 Mahratta were engaged in clearing La Zorda (near Burattina) and the Albereto cross-roads. Supported by a troop of tanks C Company launched a vigorous attack and captured the Albereto cross-roads, which had eluded its grasp for such a long time. At the same time, A Company supported by D Company, cleared La Zorda (near Burattina) though not without encountering stiff opposition. With the capture of the Albereto cross-roads and La Zorda (near Burattina) the 3/5 Mahratta was well poised for an attack on the strong German defensive position at Albereto.

On the right of 3/5 Mahratta, 1/2 Punjab consolidated the position which it had gained on 26 November. On the left of the Mahratta battalion 2/3 Gurkha had also made some gains. Its A Company had failed to get forward on to La Gessa and C. Di Mezzo, but C Company moved off at 0615 hours on 27 November to try and work round the right flank. The men reached the area of track junction near Riazzolo, where heavy small arms, mortar and shell fire pinned them to the ground, and any forward movement was out of question. A German tank engaged them from the area Pianetta compelling them to withdraw to Badiolazza, where they dug in. During the day movement was impossible; the slightest move of either A or C, the forward companies, drew heavy fire from spandaus, mortars and self-propelled guns. Mortar and shell fire also was heavy over the whole battalion area, particularly near the roads.

On 28 November 3/5 Mahratta made further gains. Throughout the night of 27/28 November, B and C Companies in the area of the Albereto cross-roads were subjected to heavy harassing fire by artillery and self-propelled guns from the area of Albereto. At 0500 hours on 28 November, a patrol from C Company towards Albereto was fired on from houses and haystacks south-west of the Cemetery. Supporting German tanks were in reserve position. Hence the Mahratta companies did not launch any attack on Albereto on 28 November and confined their activities to probing into German positions. A Company from La Zorda was, however, able to push on to Pod Albereto. Supported by a troop of tanks, this company advanced from La Zorda (near Burattina) at 1030 hours and occupied La Pozza in spite of heavy spandau fire, and drove out the Germans after a bayonet charge. At 1330 hours, the company reached the area Pod Alberto and was subjected to heavy shell and mortar fire. At 1435 hours the Germans supported by tanks counter-attacked and A Company was forced to evacuate its forward positions. At 1500 hours, however, a platoon of this company, with tank support, assaulted the houses held by the Germans and retook the positions. Considerable hand-to-hand fighting took place before the Germans were forced to withdraw. Heavy artillery defensive fire in the afternoon caught the Germans in the open, inflicting considerable losses. At 1545 hours heavy German defensive fire was brought down on A Company area while consolidating. The position became untenable and at 1600 hours the company was compelled to return to La Pozza, where it was subjected to considerable harassing fire. Thus at the close of 28 November the situation did not improve, for C Company was still consolidating in the area of the Albereto cross-roads without making any headway against the German defences at Albereto, while A Company's thrust to Pod Albereto had proved a failure and the company was still at La Pozza.

No progress was made on 28 November on either flank of 3/5 Mahratta. 2/3 Gurkha, on the left flank, was subjected to shelling and mortaring during the night of 27/28 November. One stonk literally shook the Tactical Headquarters at Reda and several shells fell pretty close to the battalion headquarters. In the morning the Germans made several attempts to infiltrate into A Company's positions in the area of C. Nuova but were forced to withdraw by the small arms, mortar and artillery fire. Heavy German shelling and mortaring of the Gurkha positions continued throughout the day.

On 29 November the Germans increased their pressure to recover lost ground. Twice—at 0630 hours and later at 1330 hours—did they launch counter-attacks on A Company of 3/5 Mahratta in La Pozza area but the attacks were repulsed. At 2330 hours a standing patrol of B Company of 3/5 Mahratta at C. Cattani was forced to withdraw by a strong German fighting patrol. Thus by 29 November the 10th Indian Division's attack had failed in the face of strong plan for breaking through the German defence line.

The Divisional Plan

The Germans continued to contest strongly the Allied advance northwards between the two river lines, Montone and Lamone. The focal point of this resistance was Albereto, where the Germans had dug in and were employing tanks or self-propelled guns to support their infantry. Indian soldiers making a thrust towards the Lamone had also encountered resistance from La Gessa and C. Di Mezzo. East of Albereto the Germans held La Podesta, and this position utilised the shortest possible area of open country to link with their new line on the Lamone.[3]

A review of the situation indicated that, though the Germans appeared to be intent on holding back the Allied thrust northwards between the two rivers, Montone and Lamone, they could not do this against a strong infantry attack. Their control of the routes east and west of Albereto facilitated the employment of their armour but there were no strong natural features in their line. The commander of the 10th Indian Division, therefore, decided to attack with two brigades, supported by a big concentration of artillery.[4] The operation was designed to clear the German forces from all ground east of the river Lamone to the immediate north of Albereto, and to enlarge the Montone bridge-head to the north to allow the building of a main bridge at the original C. Bettini bridge site for the deployment of the 1st Canadian Division north-west to Russi.

The divisional plan was that the 10th Indian Infantry Brigade, on the right, would extend its bridge-head northwards and the 20th Indian Infantry Brigade, on the left, would clear the left flank as far as the river Lamone. The 20th Indian Infantry Brigade was to attack with 3/5 Mahratta on the left and 1/2 Punjab on the right. The former advancing from the area of the Albereto cross-roads was to liquidate German opposition in Albereto; and 1/2 Punjab was to make a double thrust towards the two villages of La Podesta. After securing both the villages this battalion was to advance from the area F. Albereto through the Il Montuzzo track-road junction to the Lipotta cross-roads to secure the third bound. To distract the German attention from the focal point of attack 2/3 Gurkha was to carry out a deception plan by demonstrating towards La Gessa and La Torretta to indicate to the Germans that a major thrust to the Lamone was intended. H Hour was to be 0545 hours on 30 November. 6th Royal Tank Regiment was in support of the brigade.

On the 10th Indian Infantry Brigade's sector, 2/4 Gurkha and 1st Durham Light Infantry were to lead the attack at 0545 hours on 30 November, and at 0800 hours 4/10 Baluch was to be prepared to pass over the Montone from the Manuzzi area. There was to be a deception plan by Allied bombers over the river Lamone to deceive the Germans about the direction of the attack. The commander of the 10th Indian Infantry Brigade planned the operations to be

---

[3] 10 Ind. Div. Intelligence Summary No. 142 dated 26 November 1944.
[4] Divisional artillery, the 15th Field Regiment, the 23rd Field Regiment, and one Medium Regiment. 20 Ind. Bde. O.O. No. 7 dated 29 November 1944.

carried out in three phases. In the first phase, D Company of 2/4 Gurkha, on the right was to advance from Graziola and capture Guazzina; and the Durham, on the left, advancing from the area Migliaro Vecchio was to make a double thrust, one towards the C. Montaccia cross-roads and the other towards the La Capanna cross-roads. In the second phase, C Company of 2/4 Gurkha was to pass through D Company at Guazzina to clear the Germans from the area of Palazzina. A Company was then to pass through C Company to clear the area of the Palazzina cross-roads. One company of 4/10 Baluch, under the command of the 1st Durham Light Infantry, was to exploit to the area Montaccia. In the third phase, B Company of 2/4 Gurkha was to secure the bridge-head near C. Bettini while D Company was to assist A Company in clearing the Palazzina cross-roads. The Gurkha companies were then to exploit in the direction of the road junction near Archi. If 2/4 Gurkha failed to carry out the third phase of the operations, 4/10 Baluch was to be prepared to do so. Tanks of the North Irish Horse were to support the 10th Indian Infantry Brigade's attack.

Capture of Albereto

At 0545 hours on 30 November, the 20th Indian Infantry Brigade opened the attack with 1/2 Punjab across the start line, supported by a squadron of tanks. The two villages of La Podesta were secured without opposition at 0745 hours by a double thrust—A Company on the right and B Company on the left. The second phase of the operations began at 1117 hours when D Company led the attack on the Il Montuzzo cross-road junction (with a view to exploitation to the Lipotto road junction). D Company's right flank was protected by B Company which advanced to secure Quintina. By 1250 hours both the companies had secured their objectives, B Company at Quintina being, however, shelled by high velocity guns.

While 1/2 Punjab secured the Il Montuzzo cross-road junction, preparatory to the attack on the Lipotto road junction, 3/5 Mahratta successfully attacked and captured Albereto, the key German position. At 0700 hours on 30 November, 3/5 Mahratta, with two companies of the Nabha Akal Infantry under command, and supported by a squadron of tanks, were across their start line. The two companies of the Nabha Akal Infantry converged on Albereto from two directions—on the right D Company advanced through C. Cattani to attack Albereto from the north, and C Company on the left advanced through C. Pasi to attack Albereto from the south. D Company encountered strong resistance at C. Cattani but it was overcome with the assistance of tanks. C Company was also held up at C. Passi by heavy spandau fire, but the tanks rendered valuable service in dissolving the opposition. The two companies of the Nabha Akal Infantry then converged on Albereto. At 1000 hours D Company captured Albereto, while C Company cleared up the southern outskirts. D Company then pushed on and at 1245 hours found C.S. Nicolo clear of the Germans. Meanwhile at 1000 hours (when the Nabha Akal Infantry had captured Albereto) C Company of 3/5 Mahratta captured Fabbreria, after having met strong opposition from dug in positions forward of the houses. Subsequently at 1130 hours this company pushed forward and found La Bernarda clear of the Germans. Thus 3/5 Mahratta secured the strong German defensive position at Albereto, which had held out against repeated attacks.

2/3 Gurkha, on the left, carried out a diversionary attack. C Company's attack on La Gessa was to start at 0830 hours but was slightly delayed, because supporting tanks could not reach the start line on account of wet ground. Advancing from Badiolazza, C Company secured La Gessa without much opposition at 0912 hours and consolidated its position. D Company advancing from the cross-roads near Reda captured its objective Riazzolo at 1015 hours. D Company then pushed on to Pianetta but facing strong opposition failed to capture it.

Mopping up of the Bridge-head Area

On the 10th Indian Infantry Brigade front, D Company of 2/4 Gurkha commenced the attack on Guazzina at 0600 hours on 30 November. Strong German opposition was encountered and by 0730 hours the Company, unable to take its objective, fell back on the cross-roads near C. Nuovo. Then strengthened by a platoon from B Company, it attacked and captured Guazzina at 0945 hours. At 1145 hours C Company advanced through D Company and shortly afterwards consolidated at cross-roads in the area Palazzina. At this stage the commanding officer of 2/4 Gurkha made a change in the plan. Instead of A Company leading the attack he ordered it to consolidate at the cross-roads in the area Palazzina, to enable C Company to push on and secure the road fork, a little beyond Palazzina. By 1650 hours C Company was firmly established at the road fork. Meanwhile the Durham Light Infantry on the left, had secured its objective without much opposition. By 0925 hours it was firmly established in the area of the road-junction near Il Montaccia. 4/10 Baluch relieved Gurkha during the night of 30 November/1 December and began mopping up the C. Bettini bridge-head area. By dawn on 1 December the Baluch had succeeded in clearing the Germans from the houses. Its task completed, the 10th Indian Infantry Brigade was relieved by the 3rd Canadian Brigade of the 1st Canadian Division at 2050 hours on 1 December.

Advance to the River Lamone

The 20th Indian Infantry Brigade continued the advance to its third bound (area Castelina to road junction near Lipotto). Not much opposition was encountered except by 2/3 Gurkha on the left flank. On the right flank, 1/2 Punjab made rapid progress on 1 December. Pushing on through C. Archi this battalion was firmly established at the Lipotto road junction at 0700 hours. Shortly afterwards it was relieved by a Canadian unit. In the centre, the Nabha Akal Infantry had made a thrust from the area Albereto to Migliaro, which was captured by 1600 hours. During the night of 1/2 December a Nabha Akal patrol was engaged in a sharp encounter with the Germans south of Ghinassi. The latter were forced to withdraw, but the patrol was further engaged by the Germans from a neighbouring house. The patrol was stepped up to platoon strength. Ghinassi was occupied on 2 December after some opposition.

On the left flank, 2/3 Gurkha encountered opposition in the advance towards the river Lamone. Early on 1 November, B Company, advancing from La Bernarda, occupied Gallina to enable D Company to secure the road junction near Castellina. The latter commenced the attack at 1530 hours and seized the objective at 1700 hours, after encountering heavy small arms and artillery fire. On 2 December, D Company made further gains by capturing Le Tombe. Thus the 20th Indian Infantry Brigade had also carried out successfully the task of clearing the area up to the river Lamone.

The 43rd Indian Infantry Brigade, at this stage, moved up and relieved the 20th Indian Infantry Brigade at 1900 hours on 2 December. The brigade was active with patrols down the river and in the evening on 3 December was firmly established in the area Le Tombe. The stage was now set for the 43rd Indian Infantry Brigade to take part in the Eighth Army's December offensive.

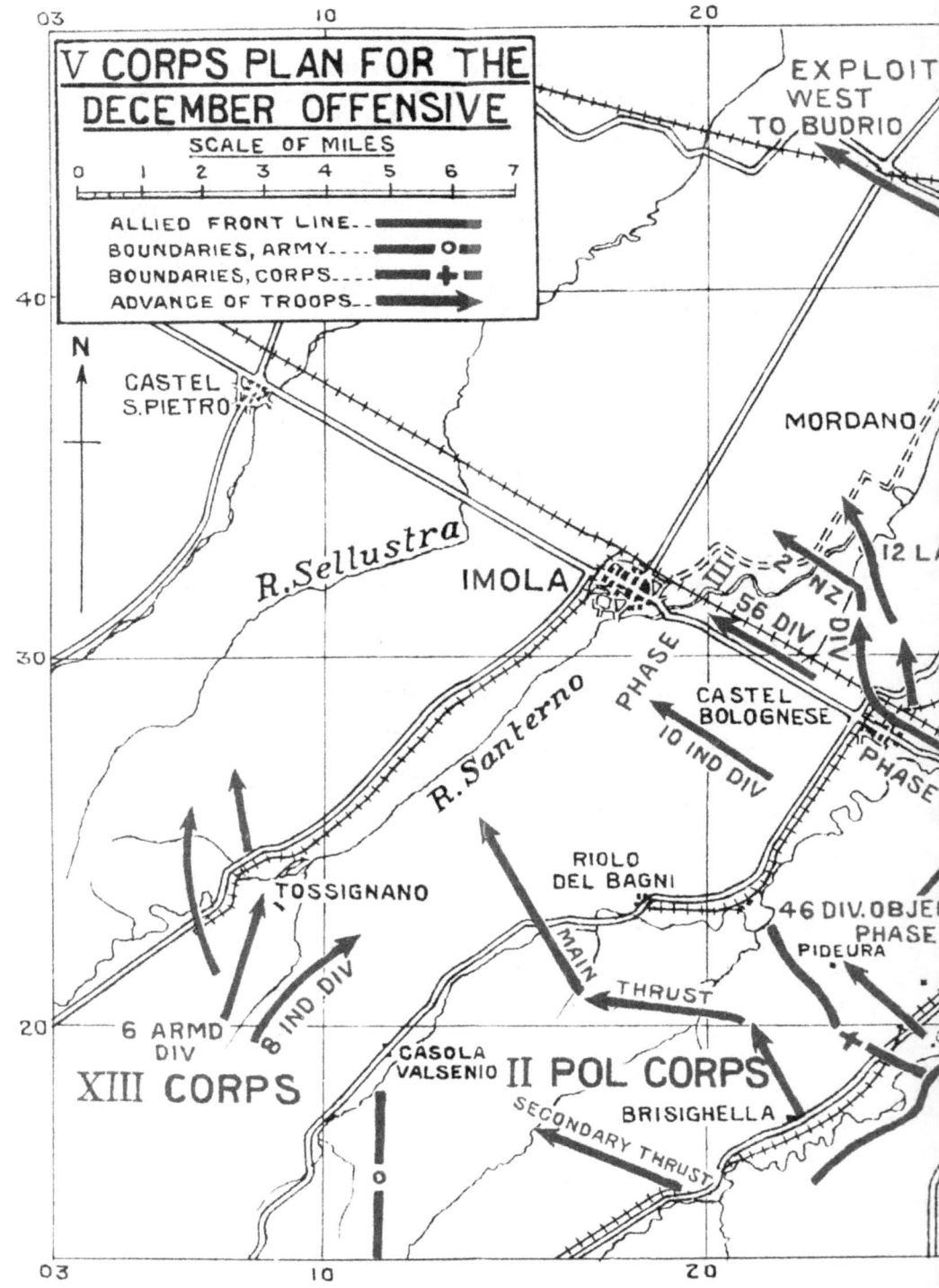

CHAPTER XXVIII

Advance to the River Senio

The V Corps Plan for the December Offensive

The Germans having been driven across the river Lamone, preparations then began for establishing bridge-heads over the rivers Lamone, Senio and Santerno. The commander of the Eighth Army decided to launch an attack during the night of 3/4 December 1944. On the right, the I Canadian Corps was to take advantage of the German weakness and push on to capture Russi, Ravenna and bridge-heads over the river Santerno. Next the V Corps was to advance along Route 9 and capture bridge-heads over the Lamone, the Senio and the Santerno. On the left, the II Polish Corps was to move across the hills on a wide front from Brisighella to Riolo die Bagni to protect the left flank of the V Corps and to cut off such German troops as might be forced to retire before the XIII Corps advanced on the road from Tosignano to Imola.

The commander of the V Corps planned to carry out the operations in three phases:

Phase I—The 46th Division, with a brigade of the 56th Division under command, was to capture a bridge-head near Quartolo, secure the high ground at Pideura, and push on north to cut Route 9 west of Faenza. Faenza was then to be seized and a bridging site made ready where Route 9 crossed the Lamone.

The 2nd New Zealand Division and the 10th Division were to carry out feint attacks with full artillery support and smoke-screens to deceive the Germans as to the real point of the attack.

During this phase two brigades of the 10th Indian Division and two armoured regiments were to be held in reserve for purposes of exploitation in the subsequent phases.

Phase II—The 2nd New Zealand Division was to pass through the 46th Division, move across the Senio on Route 9 to Castel Bolognese, and push on to the north. During this phase the 10th Indian Division and the 56th Division were to relieve the 46th Division and be ready to take part in the operations in the third phase.

Phase III—The 56th Division was to advance on Route 9, the 2nd New Zealand Division to the north and the 10th Indian Division to the south.

German Dispositions

The Germans appreciated that both as a result of their recent heavy casualties, and because of the sinuous course of the Lamone, it was not practical to attempt to man the banks. They realised that they could not deny the Allies reconnaissance over the river, or prevent a bridge-head being formed initially. Their strategy was therefore to destroy the bridge-head after it had been formed. To achieve this object their main positions were sited along the road Olmatello—Orestina, and a comprehensive artillery defensive fire plan was prepared to throw the Allied troops off their balance after they had crossed the river. Once it was ascertained where the Allied main thrust was directed a counter-attack would follow with the object of throwing the Allies back across the river. Their method of manning the line was to allot the companies an apparently wide sector linked by a series of strong-points, well supported by machine gun fire. In so doing they were able to maintain an adequate divisional reserve. While two battalions of *578th Grenadier Regiment* and one battalion of *576th Grenadier Regiment* (of the *305th Infantry Division*) were holding the forward positions, a battalion of *576th Grenadier Regiment* and the *Fusilier Battalion* were in immediate reserve, with *577th Grenadier Regiment* not very far behind. The German plan failed, largely because they were unable to deploy their maximum artillery support in the right place, having made a wrong appreciation of the Allied main effort, as a result of a successful deception plan.

Capture of Pideura

The 46th Division launched the attack during the night of 3/4 December. Crossing the river Lamone near Quartolo, this division had, at the close of 7 December, captured a bridge-head two miles wide and two miles in depth. Olmatello and Pideura had been secured and, on the right, the advance had been pushed on to the road and railway junction at the south-west edge of Faenza, and further to about a thousand yards south of Celle, thus creating an effective threat to Faenza.

During this phase of the operations, the 43rd Indian Infantry Brigade carried out a feint attack at 1900 hours on 3 December. On its result, which was a very heavy German shelling and mortaring against the supposed crossing, the feint attack was adjudged to be very successful. The 10th Indian Division thereafter became "non-operational" in the Forli area and the 43rd Indian Infantry Brigade passed under the direct command of the V Corps at 1200 hours on 4 December. The brigade held its sector for another ten days, during which period bad weather restricted operations, though a series of battalion reliefs was carried out.

The 25th Indian Infantry Brigade in the Line

On 7 December the commander of the V Corps ordered the 25th Indian Infantry Brigade to relieve a brigade of the 46th Division, to enable the latter to exploit the advantage it had gained. In the morning on 8 December, the 25th Indian Infantry Brigade temporarily under the command of the 46th Division, relieved the 128th Brigade in the Lamone bridge-head in the hill country of the Pideura Olmatello area. A squadron of the 9th Lancers was under the command of the brigade. The area taken over by the 25th Indian Infantry Brigade consisted of a number of narrow, open ridges. Between them, cliff-sided valleys ran parallel to the Lamone. Cart tracks followed the crests of the ridges. Scattered houses stood on or near the edge of the tracks. Two battalions were deployed, 3/1 Punjab on the eastern end of the ridge about Olmatello and the 1st King's Own Royal Regiment on the west about Pideura, a village which had been the scene of some brisk fighting. The relief was exceptionally difficult, since the sector was at the end of a five mile stretch of cart track. Six hundred tons of rubble were used daily in an effort to preserve the surface in a usable condition. Furthermore, the Bailey bridge over the Lamone was liable to become submerged after heavy rains—and heavy rains fell during the relief.

German Counter-attacks

The 46th Division had established a bridge-head when the Germans carried out their plan of throwing in their reserves in a mighty effort to push back the Allied forces across the river. The reserves—the *90th Panzer Grenadier Division* and *II Battalion 576th Grenadier Regiment (the 305th Infantry Division)*—made fierce counter-attacks. The brunt of the attacks was successfully borne by the right brigade of the 46th Division, which stretched to the north-east of the 25th Indian Infantry Brigade which too, in its turn, did not escape the weight of the counter-attack.

The task allotted to the 25th Indian Infantry Brigade was to consolidate in Pideura, and thence clear the spur running north-east of that place.[1] Pideura, the high-point of the ridge beyond the Tanna stream, was an important point and the Germans, who were holding the village of Camillo in strength, launched fierce counter-attacks to dislodge the 1st King's Own Royal Regiment from this

---

[1] 10 Ind. Div. Intelligence Summary No. 10, dated 8 December 1944.

strategic position, and subjected their victim to heavy shelling throughout 8 December. At 2345 hours on 8 December, German infantry supported by tanks attacked Pideura and it was only after bitter fighting that they were driven off. At 0050 hours on 9 December, they again attacked that place but were repulsed after another stiff fight. At 0630 hours the Germans heavily shelled and mortared Pideura. This was followed by yet another attack, but the 1st King's Own Royal Regiment successfully dealt with the situation and the Germans were again forced to withdraw. After heavy shelling and mortaring the Germans renewed their attack on Pideura at 1830 hours but after a short fight were forced back again.

At 1600 hours on 10 December, two platoons of the 1st King's Own Royal Regiment, supported by tanks, commenced their attack on German held houses in the area Camillo. After meeting heavy spandau fire and grenades they were forced to withdraw, sustaining 11 casualties.

Meanwhile the Germans had also launched fierce counter-attacks on the positions held by 3/1 Punjab in the area C. Colombara. On 8 December, B and D, the two forward companies were at Torricella; A and C Companies were at Olmatello and the battalion headquarters was at S. Severo. The plan was for A Company to attack Quarda, viz, the ridge running north-east from Colombara. A Company moved forward to attack at 2200 hours and B Company at 2300 hours on 8 December. After a fierce fight A Company secured the objective but was immediately counter-attacked by a German company supported by three tanks. Finally by 0200 hours on 9 December, after all the houses had been razed to the ground and burning haystacks had made its position untenable, the company withdrew. Meanwhile B Company, having reached its objective was subjected to a similar counter-attack by a German tank. The commander of the company was seriously wounded and after suffering heavy casualties the company was compelled to withdraw. At 0800 hours on 9 December, intense mortar and artillery concentrations on all the company areas was followed by a strong German attack, whose strength was estimated 60 to 70 men. This attack was broken up by accurate fire from C and D Companies, who inflicted heavy casualties on the Germans. Small parties of Germans, however, managed to infiltrate, but A Company promptly mopped them up. At 1800 hours under cover of heavy artillery concentrations, small parties of Germans attempted infiltration into the Punjab positions. The attempt was frustrated and the Germans withdrew.

At 1130 hours on 10 December, a company of 4/11 Sikh came under the command of 3/1 Punjab to strengthen the battalion position, and preparations were made to put in another attack on Colombara and Quarada. This attack was, however, postponed due to the acute difficulty in the matter of supplies. Heavy constant rain had swollen the river Lamone, damaging all but one bridge and rendering approaches possible only to single way jeep traffic.

The 10th Indian Division Plan

In spite of foul weather which hampered operations, and violent German counter-attacks on the 46th Division in the Lamone bridgehead, the preparations of the 10th Indian Division for executing phase III of the V Corps operation went on apace. The 25th Indian Infantry Brigade was already in the line. The second formation, the 10th Indian Infantry Brigade, moved forward and command of the 46th Division's sector passed to the 10th Indian Division at 1830 hours on 11 December. The 7th Armoured Brigade, still under command, received an addition in the 9th Lancers from the 2nd Armoured Brigade.

By 13 December, the V Corps had regrouped and was ready to carry out phase III of the corps operation. The 10th Indian Division held the left and the 2nd New Zealand Division the right of the bridge-head. The sector of the latter was to the north across Route 9 to the Rimni-Bologna railway, whence stretched the 46th Division to the inter-corps boundary. The 43rd Indian Infantry Brigade was in reserve. The plan was for the 2nd New Zealand Division to secure the objective Pt. 54, a thousand yards north-west of Celle. The 10th Indian Division was to make a double thrust—towards Pergola and Croce on the one hand, and Monte Coralli and Zula on the other. The 56th Division was to simulate an assault across the Lamone in the area of the road bridge south-west of Scaldino. After securing these objectives by dawn on 15 December, the 10th Indian Division and the 2nd New Zealand Division were to push on the advance and cross the Senio.

The 10th Indian Division's attack was to begin at 2300 hours on 14 December. The division was to seize objectives Pt. 132 and Pt. 227, exploiting up to Bago and C. Varnelli. On the right the 10th Indian Infantry Brigade, with 3/1 Punjab under command, was to attack and secure Barbiera and Croce. On the left, the 25th Indian Infantry Brigade was to capture from excluding Colombara to including Pt. 156, exploiting northwards towards Merline and Varnelli.[2]

The 10th Indian Infantry Brigade's operation was to be carried out in four phases. In the first phase, 1st Durham Light Infantry on the right was to secure C. Pozzo and C. Biance while 3/1 Punjab on the left was to capture Colombara. In the second phase, the 1st Durham Light Infantry was to secure Quarada (via Barbiera) while 3/1 Punjab was to capture Castellara. In the third phase, the 1st

---

[2] 10 Ind. Inf. Bde. O.O. No. 4, dated 14 December 1944.

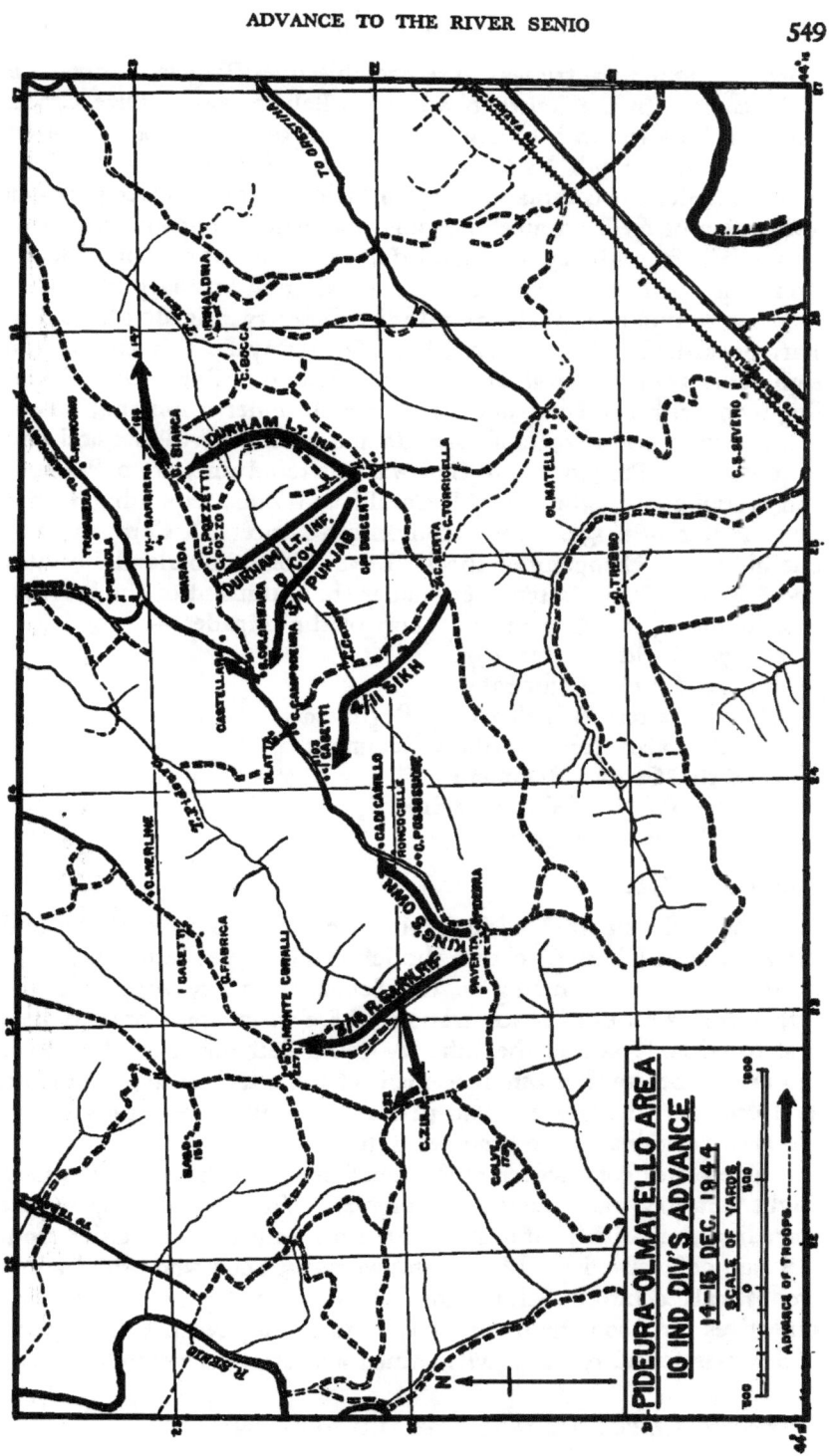

Durham Light Infantry was to secure objectives Pergola—Travanera—Roncomo. In the fourth phase, 4/10 Baluch was to seize Croce. The attack by the 10th Indian Infantry Brigade was to be supported by tanks of the 9th Lancers, one platoon Z Company of heavy mortars under the command of 154th Field Regiment, three platoons less section of medium machine guns, one platoon 17-pounders, three 2-pounders (from the 25th Indian Infantry brigade at call) and M. 10.5 (from the 5th New Zealand Brigade at call) and ancillary troops.

The commander of the 25th Indian Infantry Brigade planned to start operations, with the 1st King's Own Royal Regiment on the right and 3/18 Garhwal on the left. The 1st King's Own Royal Regiment with two companies of 4/11 Sikh under command, was to secure objectives Pt. 193 and Camillo and exploit north-east and also to contact 3/1 Punjab. 3/18 Garhwal was to advance from Pawanta and consolidate in the area M. Coralli and Zula, exploiting to the line Merline—Pt. 155. One squadron 9th Lancers, X Company and one platoon Z Company of the 1st Royal Northumberland Fusiliers and 8th Anti-Tank Battery were under the command of the brigade. The following troops were in support of the brigade[a]:—

    97th Field Regiment
    172nd Field Regiment
    One battery British Heavy Regiment
    7th Polish Force Artillery Regiment
    58th Medium Regiment
    10th Polish Medium Regiment
    10th Field Company.

Capture of Zula

The 10th Indian Division's advance preceded that of the 2nd New Zealand Division so that the left flank of the latter might be protected when advancing to the Senio. Artillery supported the attack with a series of concentrations of fire which, by a pre-arranged system of code-names, the infantry could call down as they were required. Before the commencement of the attack at 2300 hours on 14 December, the artillery had performed as much softening of the German positions as the time permitted.

The attack commenced at the scheduled hour, when the Durham Light Infantry was directed on Pergola. While forming up on the start line the British infantry suffered a number of casualties from German defensive fire. More losses were sustained when the leading troops walked into a 'Schu' mine-field in the valley below their first objectives. At 0005 hours on 15 December they reached Ca Bianca, which was found to be heavily mined and strongly defended. The

---

[a] 25 Ind. Inf. Bde. O.O. No. 7, dated 13 December 1944.

Germans also strongly held the area C. Pozzetti, C. Pozzo and Pt. 168. Heavy fighting took place there with the Germans holding firm in houses, south of the lateral road. At 0315 hours the reserve company was put in against both C. Pozzo and C. Pozzetti, but substantial gains were not made. Fighting swayed backwards and forwards. Continued pressure carried the British troops on to the ridge about Pt. 168 and Pt. 147, where they were engaged most of the day by the Germans in positions north of Pt. 168. At last light, as further progress appeared unlikely, and to conform with flank units, the battalion consolidated with one company at Pt. 147 and the second at Pt. 168.

On the right of the D.L.I. the 2nd New Zealand Division advancing behind a tremendous artillery barrage met strong opposition, yet secured its objectives, Celle and C. Mercante on the lateral road, one mile north-east of Pergola.

Left of the D.L.I., 3/1 Punjab was directed on Colombara, D Company from Ducento leading the attack. The company was established on the razor back ridge at C. Colombara at 2340 hours on 14 December, after an approach march through intense German mortar fire and 'Schu' mine-fields, causing heavy casualties. The company commander was seriously wounded and the second in command was killed. At 0100 hours on 15 December, the Germans, supported by tanks, launched a strong attack, which was, however, beaten off. At 0200 hours, C Company from Ducento joined the remnants of D Company and the position was consolidated just in time to prevent another German force from recapturing it. Fierce fighting continued with heavy losses on both sides. German fire made the company's positions untenable. At 0450 hours the brigade commander ordered the withdrawal of the forward companies, particularly as on the right the Durham had not yet secured Quarada ridge and on the left the 1st King's Own Royal Regiment had been unsuccessful in securing Camillo, and a company of 4/11 Sikh under the command of the 1st King's Own Royal Regiment directed on Pt. 193 had been compelled to withdraw after having gained its objective. The weight of the German counter-attack, with self-propelled guns and infantry, was too much for the Sikh company, whose losses were even then quite heavy. This withdrawal and the failure of the Durham to secure the Quarada ridge made the Punjab position untenable. At 0700 hours, after an extremely difficult disengagement with the Germans, and hampered by the task of evacuating their numerous casualties, D and C companies of 3/1 Punjab reached the forward defended locations. So fierce had been the struggle that both sides mutually agreed to a truce in order that casualties might be evacuated. Throughout the day Red Cross parties from both sides did sterling work getting the wounded back.

While the 10th Indian Infantry Brigade failed to make much headway against German opposition, the 25th Indian Infantry Brigade too was up against stiff opposition. The 1st King's Own Royal Regiment encountered fierce opposition. Its A Company attacking Camillo was heavily shelled and mortared on the way to the starting line and over the whole approach to the objective. The Germans offered strong resistance from houses on the ridge between Pideura and Camillo. Till 0115 hours the company fought its way along the hill top north-east from Pideura and reached Possessione, but was unable to get further forward owing to heavy shelling and mortaring. On the right, the company of 4/11 Sikh under the command of the 1st King's Own Royal Regiment, captured Cosetti at 0045 hours but on account of shelling from self-propelled guns was forced to withdraw after sustaining many casualties. At 0650 hours the company of the 1st King's Own Royal Regiment supported by tanks, resumed the attack on Camillo which was captured soon after.

3/18 Garhwal, operating on the left of the division, was directed against Zula. From intelligence reports it appeared that a German company with four spandaus and mortars was at Zula, while there was an observation post of the strength of a platoon at M. Coralli. There was also a small observation post at Colve. The commander of 3/18 Garhwal planned the operation to be carried out in three phases. In the first phase, A and B Companies were to advance from the assembly area of the cliffs south of Hill 261 by route Pideura—Nalla junction and capture M. Coralli, exploiting to Pt. 201. In the second phase, D Company was to advance from the same assembly area and by the same route and capture Zula, exploiting to Pt. 232. In the third phase, A Company was to consolidate at M. Coralli and I. Casetti and patrol to Pt. 201 and C. Carrare. D Company was to consolidate on the reverse slopes of M. Coralli, with one platoon at Pt. 232. C Company was to be in the area of the cliffs south of Hill 261.[4]

The battalion arrived at the assembly area of the cliffs south of Hill 261 at 1300 hours on 14 December. The men were subjected to heavy shelling which caused considerable loss to the mule transport. At 2030 hours A Company, followed by B Company advanced from the assembly area for the attack on M. Coralli. Not much opposition was encountered and by 1350 hours the former had captured M. Coralli. But D Company, advancing from the assembly area at 2100 hours for the attack on Zula, met with strong opposition. At 0145 hours on 15 December, the company was in occupation of half of Zula. Hotly contested struggle continued for the possession of the other half of the village. The Germans were driven out of Zula at 0500 hours on 15 December and then D Company exploited to

[4] 3/18 R. Garh. Rif, O.O. No. 1, dated 12 December 1944.

Pt. 232, which was occupied at 0515 hours. At 0530 hours D Company discovered that the Germans had also evacuated Colve. At 0630 hours a German counter-attack developed on D Company positions, which were also the target of accurate mortar fire. At the same time another German counter-attack developed against A Company's positions. The counter-attacks were, however, repelled. Nevertheless the Germans continued to shell Zula and Coralli areas spasmodically during the day.

The Senio Defence Line

After fighting fierce battles and suffering severe losses in the Lamone bridge-head, *90th Panzer Grenadier Division* and the battle group of the *305th Infantry Division* withdrew during the night of 15/16 December from their remaining positions forward of the river Senio in the area south-west of Route 9.[5] The German defence line was thereafter based on a more economical line of dug in positions sited back from the river. This line was based on the minor obstacle of the Canale dei Molini linking up with the Senio itself near C. Di Sotto in the north and near Pt. 49 in the south. West of this the high ground rising up to M. Ghebbio provided a firm right flank for the German defence.[6]

On the other side, 4/10 Baluch passed through the Durham, and was directed against Pergola and Croce. The advance began at 2030 hours on 15 December, but quite early it became evident that the Germans had withdrawn, and the Baluch therefore turned north to Croce, and by last light on 16 December reached Pt. 114 without opposition. D, the leading company, pushed on through Loghetto to Tebano and consolidated there. On 17 December, this company sent a patrol to Montazzo. No contact was made with the Germans, though the patrol was shelled and mortared. B Company patrolling to the Senio found the bridge near Tebano blown up and many areas along the river flooded. Nevertheless, under the cover of darkness on 17 December, two separate bridge-heads were gained over the river Senio. At 2200 hours on 17 December, C Company secured the positions on the eastern bank of the river at C.S. Giovanni and Renazzi, while at 2300 hours a platoon of A Company passing through C Company crossed the river and occupied a house near C. Madenna. Then the second platoon crossed the river and pushed on to the house forward of Tebano, which was found to be occupied by the Germans and an attack was put in. Grenades were thrown into the rooms occupied by the Germans. The Germans however offered strong resistance and compelled the platoon to withdraw which subsequently reinforced by the second platoon, resumed the attack on the house.

[5] 10 Ind. Div. Intelligence Summary No. 154, 16 December 1944.
[6] *Ibid.* No. 156, 17 December 1944.

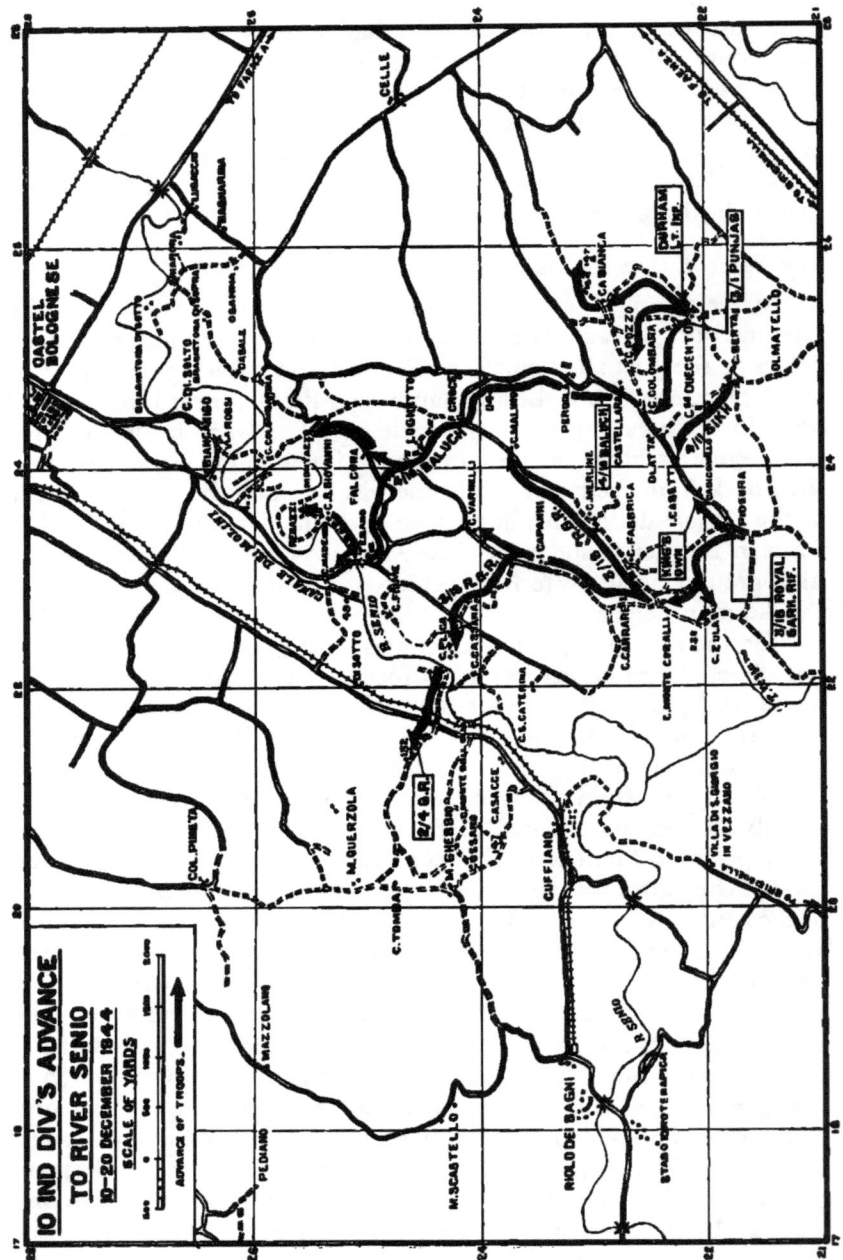

The Germans, however, were fully prepared and the platoons were forced to withdraw. One platoon was left on the west bank in a loop of the river near C. Madona as a base for patrols. This platoon was subjected in the afternoon on 18 December to point-blank fire from a German tank, that had apparently approached under cover of a German tracked vehicle carrying Red Cross flag. The platoon then withdrew to the eastern side of the river.

To the south of the Baluch, 3/18 Garhwal was also making satisfactory progress. Early in the morning of 16 December, tactical headquarters had moved up to C. Fabbrica, C Company pushed on and consolidated from Merline to Merlino, B Company advanced and occupied Carrare—Capanni, and A Company consolidated at Varnelli. Then D Company, which was in reserve at M. Coralli, pushed on to attempt a river crossing on a three platoon front at C. Fuime, C. Plica, and C. Cassama. At 0230 hours on 17 December, a platoon was established at C. Plica but the other crossings were contested by German posts and thus the plan could not be successfully carried out.

At 1300 hours on 17 December, the 10th Indian Infantry Brigade relieved the 25th Indian Infantry Brigade and took 4/11 Sikh under command. The bridge-head of 3/18 Garhwal was taken over by 2/4 Gurkha, then directed on M. Quergola. West from C. Plica, a track ran along the crest of an escarpment to M. Quergola. The Germans had taken up positions on Pt. 132 and were garrisoning the houses near Pt. 53. C Company of 2/4 Gurkha crossed foot-bridge near C. Plica at 0330 hours on 18 December and expelled the Germans from the houses near Pt. 53 by 0600 hours. At 1100 hours a German counter-attack was dispersed by defensive fire from artillery and medium machine guns. Another German counter-attack developed at 2030 hours. It was also broken up. So fierce was the fighting that A Company was sent across the river to reinforce the one already in the bridge-head. At 3015 hours on 19 December a platoon of C Company, relieved by a platoon of A Company in the houses near Pt. 53, began preparations for the attack on Pt. 132. Preceded by artillery concentrations for ten minutes, the platoon of C Company attacked Pt. 132 at 0600 hours and captured it after a hard struggle. At 0645 hours a German counter-attack was beaten off. As the Gurkhas had run into heavy opposition and there was difficulty in supporting bridge-head companies, as well as in getting supporting weapons across the river Senio, both the companies were withdrawn during the night of 19/20 December to the east bank of the river Senio, leaving one platoon to act as a patrol base forward of C. Plica. The 10th Indian Division did not make further efforts to establish a bridge-head on the Senio. In fact the Germans established on the Senio defence line during the winter of 1944/1945.

Capture of Faenza

We have so far traced the progress of the 10th Indian Division to the river Senio. It is now necessary to describe the progress of the 2nd New Zealand Division, with particular reference to the part played by the 43rd Indian Infantry Brigade as Faenza Task Force.

In the morning of 15 December the 2nd New Zealand Division had secured Celle and the road from C. Bianca to Pogliano, against fierce opposition and on the left flank Casa Elta had also been captured. At the close of the day, the 10th Indian Division and the 2nd New Zealand Division had inflicted a decisive defeat on the Germans. During the night of 15/16 December the *90th Panzer Grenadier Division* pulled back towards the Senio, while the *26th Panzer Division* prepared to evacuate Faenza and form a switch-line across the ground between the Lamone and the Senio north of the town. In order to exploit the success the corps commander placed the Faenza Task Force (the 43rd Indian Infantry Brigade) under the command of the 2nd New Zealand Division. The plan was for the 5th New Zealand Brigade from the area Celle to swing north-west up Route 9; the 43rd Indian Infantry Brigade to advance through the western outskirts of Faenza and the 2nd New Zealand Divisional Cavalry Battalion to cross the bridge on Route 9 into the eastern half of the town.

The advance began on 16 December and by the morning of 17 December considerable progress had been made. The 5th New Zealand Brigade reached the Senio, with one battalion about half a mile short of the river astride Route 9 and two battalions on the left looking towards Castel Bolognese. Faenza was captured early on 17 December without opposition, for the Germans had withdrawn north and west of the railway line. 2/10 Gurkha entered the town from the west; the New Zealand Divisional Cavalry Battalion crossed the bridge on Route 9 into the eastern half of the town; 2/8 Gurkha reached Borgo Durbecco, an eastern suburb of Faenza. Although the town was captured, further advance was brought to a halt by strong German defensive positions along the railway line north of Route 9 and on the Scolo Cerchio canal north of Faenza. Hence the commander of the 43rd Indian Infantry Brigade planned to make a double thrust, 2/10 Gurkha advancing to the Scolo Cerchio and 2/8 Gurkha on the right advancing from near the railway station to seize the objectives S. Silvestro—Robicana—Chiesa della Celletta. The Germans offered stiff opposition from the far side of the railway line. At 1130 hours A and C, the forward companies of 2/10 Gurkha, were held up by stiff opposition from spandaus on the far side of the railway line. At 1200 hours a squadron of tanks tried to get forward to support the forward companies, but as the roads were not cleared of mines they were unable to get forward. A and C Companies held

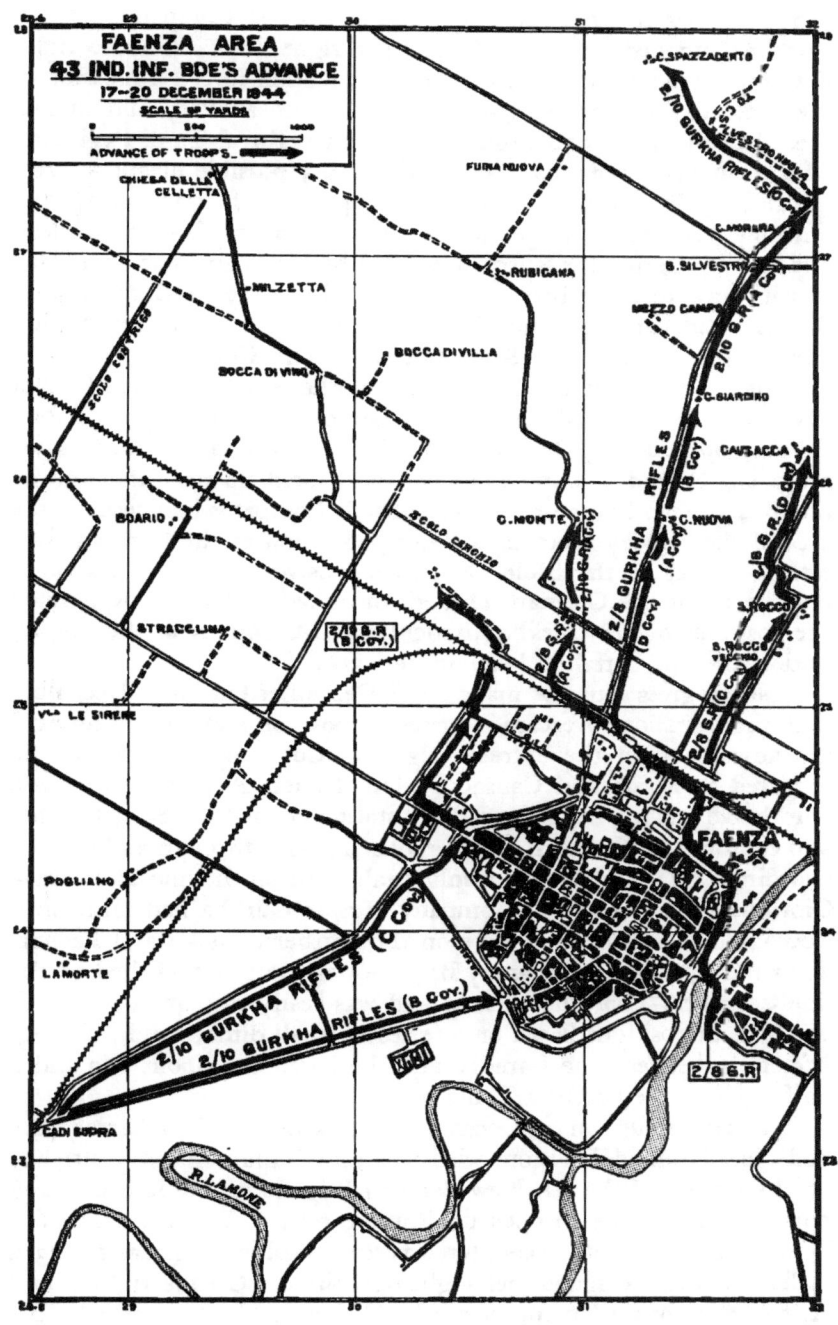

firm south of the railway line while A and D Companies of 2/8 Gurkha launched an attack from their right flank. On the right, D Company advancing from the railway station forced a crossing of the Scolo Cerchio but was subjected to severe artillery and mortar fire. Meanwhile B Squadron 48th Battalion Royal Tank Regiment, which was in support, had been trying every possible means to cross the railway line so that they could support the forward companies but they were unable to get across. At 1630 hours, D Company was attacked by German infantry supported by tanks and was compelled to withdraw to the railway station. At that time, A Company, on the left, had captured some houses but being short of ammunition was unable to cross the Scolo Cerchio. The Germans, who were holding the far bank and houses on the other side, prevented further advance. Thus the advance of 2/8 Gurkha was held up by strong German opposition. On the left flank 2/10 Gurkha had made some progress. A and C Companies had been held up near the railway line but at 2300 hours on 17 December B Company had secured the area of the railway junction without opposition as the Germans had retired earlier to the Scolo Cerchio defensive positions. Throughout the night the Germans shelled, mortared and machine gunned the positions of 2/8 Gurkha, particularly D Company at the railway station and the battalion headquarters area.

No progress could be made on 18 December but on 19 December both the battalions overcame German opposition and pushed forward the advance. On the extreme right, C Company of 2/8 Gurkha captured S. Rocco and Causacca. On the left A Company of 2/8 Gurkha advancing from the railway station crossed the Scolo Cerchio and captured C. Nuova, B Company then passed through and secured Giordino. 2/8 Gurkha was firmly established on the line Causacca—Giordino. On the left, A Company of 2/10 Gurkha had taken over Rocco and two companies were on the northern outskirts of Faenza. Thus the 43rd Indian Infantry Brigade was firmly established on the line Causacca—Giordino—Pozza and was ready to launch an attack on German positions based on a series of small ditches and buildings stretching between the Lamone and the Senio and about two and a half miles to the north of Route 9.

At 2100 hours on 19 December with a big artillery barrage the 2nd New Zealand Division, with the 43rd Indian Infantry Brigade on the right and the 6th New Zealand Brigade on the left, attacked northwards in order to open up Route 9 west of Faenza.[7] The 6th New Zealand Brigade encountered fierce opposition whereas the 43rd Indian Infantry Brigade met slight opposition. On the right C and A, the two forward companies of 2/8 Gurkha led the attack. At 0030 hours, C Company captured Pila Mengolina and A Company

[7] 2nd New Zealand Division O.O. No. 51, dated 18 December 1944.

secured the area near Silvestra. At 0330 hours, D Company moved off towards the road junction but was held up near Corgin by many trees felled across the road. The Germans were covering the felled trees with fire from the area of the road junction.[8] 2/8 Gurkha remained firm in the forward positions. On the left, B and C Companies of 2/10 Gurkha crossed the start line at 2246 hours on 19 December and at 0015 hours on 20 December secured without opposition their objectives S. Silvestro and area near Colfiorito. At 0615 hours A Company advanced from the area near Mezza Campo on the road from S. Silvestro to S. Silvestro Nuova but further advance was held up by Germans holding the houses across the road, approximately 30 yards away. A Company was counter-attacked twice but held firm. 2/10 Gurkha held firmly the forward positions and prepared to launch an attack on 21 December. At 1015 hours the commander of 2/10 Gurkha ordered A Company to advance from Silvestro Nuova and occupy houses along the road to the north-east and on completion of that task, D Company supported by a troop of tanks was to move up the road to the north-west to capture C. Masarino and B Company was to be ready to move through D Company to the final objective Cassanico. At 1145 hours A Company occupied all the houses on the road from S. Silvestro Nuova and then D Company moved forward and captured C. Nuova but encountered stiff opposition from the German positions in C. Masarino. After a fierce fight D Company captured half of C. Masarino. The Germans fought with grim determination and it was not till 1700 hours that the capture of C. Masarino was completed. This was the limit of the advance. Next day the 43rd Indian Infantry Brigade was relieved by a brigade of the 56th Division.

[8] *Ibid.*

CHAPTER XXIX

Thrust Towards Vena Del Gesso

Limited Advances of the 8th Indian Division

We have so far traced the advance of the Indian formations of the Eighth Army to the Senio. We shall now describe the progress of similar formations in the Fifth Army, which had gone on the defensive on 27 October 1944, though the 8th Indian Division in the XIII Corps sector had continued to make limited advance to conform with the progress already made by the rest of the Fifth Army. The intention of the Fifth Army commander at the close of October 1944 was to hold the positions gained whilst the Army regrouped for a new drive on Bologna early in December. Part of his plan, for the XIII Corps to take over Monte Grande from the 88th U.S. Division, necessitated a fresh reorganisation of the forces in that corps. The 8th Indian Division was to hold the sector from including Venus route to including Arrow route and also, by aggressive patrolling along the whole front, to keep the maximum number of German battalions occupied so that the German commander could not switch his forces to the weaker sectors of the front.[1]

To conform with the corps plan, Major-General Russell issued orders on 31 October to the 19th Indian Infantry Brigade to relieve the 21st Indian Infantry Brigade in the area of M. Romano, enabling the latter to move westwards and to take over the right hand brigade's sector of the 1st British Infantry Division astride Arrow route. The 8th Indian Division had all its three brigades in the line, the 21st Indian Infantry Brigade on the left flank, the 19th Indian Infantry Brigade in the centre and the 17th Indian Infantry Brigade on the right flank. Headquarters 21st Indian Infantry Brigade opened at Badia in Susinana on 2 November. 1/5 Mahratta on the right held M. Ceco and also the eastern slopes of this feature as far as the isolated hamlet of Val di Fusa. These positions were extremely exposed and could only be supplied at night by mules and porters. Running due north from M. Ceco towards the upper Senio Valley was a long knife-edge ridge, with extremely steep sides, called M. Della Valle. Along this ridge were the positions of 3/15 Punjab. 1st Battalion Jaipur Infantry, who had taken the place of 5th Battalion Royal West Kent Regiment whilst this unit was training in the vicinity of Vicchio and later at S. Donato, was now in reserve at Palazzuolo, where all the brigade echelons were established, to rest

[1] 8 Ind. Div. O.O. No. 34, dated 31 October 1944.

and refit. Throughout the brigade's tenure of this relatively quiet sector, Indian patrols completely dominated the no-man's land.

In the centre of the divisional front, the 19th Indian Infantry Brigade guarded the 'Sword' route. 6/13 Royal Frontier Force Rifles, was occupying the area M. Termine—S. Casciano, about eight miles beyond Marradi.[2] 1st Battalion Argyll and Sutherland Highlanders was holding the hills west of S. Casciano, viz. M. Giro and the high ground north-east of M. Pianoereno.[3] 3/8 Punjab was in reserve in the area Popolano. The forward battalions of the 19th Indian Infantry Brigade were constantly harassed by shell and mortar fire. S. Casciano was overlooked by high ground to the east (i.e. M. Casalino), from which the Germans had still to be dislodged. Harassing shoots on known German positions to the east of the Marradi road were carried out by the artillery, tanks and self-propelled guns. Whenever visibility would permit, patrols of the Argyll went out by night and day through the rough country south of M.S. Colombo. Never once were the Germans allowed to feel that they could relax.

Though the 21st Indian Infantry Brigade on the left flank and the 19th Indian Infantry Brigade in the middle divisional sector were content with sending out patrols and harassing the German positions by artillery shoots, the 17th Indian Infantry Brigade on the right flank showed considerable energy in breaking through strong German positions and thus pushing forward the advance to conform to that of the 3rd Carpathian Division (of the II Polish Corps), who came up on the brigades' right front and took over from the 26th Armoured Brigade astride the 'Star' route. The 17th Indian Infantry Brigade was ready to launch an attack to drive out the Germans from the long ridge of high ground between M. Monsignano and Monte San Bartolo to conform with the advance of the II Polish Corps, which was mounting a powerful attack on the left flank of the Eighth Army. 1/12 Frontier Force Regiment was in the area M. Giggiolo; its advance had been held up by the Germans who were holding M. Budrialto in strength, with forward strong positions at Pt. 668 and Pt. 687. 1st Battalion Royal Fusiliers was in reserve in the area Monte Casalino—M. Serra. 1/5 Gurkha was in the area Vicchio—C. S. Martino with a forward position at La Maseta. Further advance was checked by the Germans who were holding M. Monsignano in strength.

Capture of M. Monsignano

The 578th Grenadier Regiment (the 205th Infantry Division) was astride Marradi—Faenza and Abeto—Modigliano road. *I Battalion*

---

[2] During the night of 5/6 November 3/8 Punjab relieved 6/13 F.F. Rif.
[3] On 15/16 November 6/13 F.F. Rif. relieved the Argyll.

was on the west as far as the river Sintria; *II Battalion* was on the east with a possible boundary Abeto—Modigliano road. The layout of 305 *Fusilier Battalion* facing the 17th Indian Infantry Brigade was estimated to be as follows: One company in the area M. Rigonzano—Monte Casalino; second in the area M. Budrialto; third in the area Le Ville—Monte caruso—Abeto; and the fourth in the area M. Monsignano. The main German positions for the defence of the ridge and of high ground between M. Monsignano and M.S. Bartolo were at M. Budrialto, M. Bassana, M. Monsignano, M. Pompegno and Monte San Bartolo.

The plan of the operations was that the 1st Carpathian Brigade was to make, with one battalion, the main thrust towards M. Chioda—M. Lechia, and with the second battalion to protect the left flank by securing S. Valentino. The 17th Indian Infantry Brigade's task was to maintain contact with the 1st Carpathian Brigade and press back the Germans along the high ground M. Monsignano—M. Pompegno—Monte San Bartolo, conforming with the advance of the 1st Carpathian Brigade.[4] B Company 14th Canadian Armoured Regiment was in support of the 17th Indian Infantry Brigade.

The 17th Indian Infantry Brigade soon began to exert pressure on the Germans compelling them to give ground. During the night of 5/6 November a Gurkha raiding party was sent to test the strength of German defences on M. Monsignano. This feature was to the south-west of Modigliana and lay fully in the path of the Gurkha advance. The hill was very strongly defended. As the Gurkha patrol climbed its way up the spur it was engaged at close quarters by at least four spandaus and grenades. The opposition was too heavy for such a small force and the Gurkha patrol had to withdraw. At 1700 hours on 6 November, however a small Gurkha reconnaissance patrol found M. Monsignano clear of the Germans, who had apparently decided not to fight hard to retain the feature. On 8 November there was a lull in hostile shelling; it was apparent that the German force was withdrawing again. At 1545 hours on 9 November, 1/12 Frontier Force Regiment occupied M. Budrialto, the feature north-west of M. Monsignano, to which the Germans had withdrawn at the end of October.

During the night of 9/10 November, the weather deteriorated and in the early morning snow fell. Roads collapsed, jeep and mule tracks became impassable and patrols could not operate. The torrential rain, which halted operations towards the end of October, became heavier and more frequent. Most mornings, a thick mist blanketed the whole front, reducing visibility to nil. When there was no rain or mist, the ground hardened for a short time in the grip

---

[4] 17 Ind. Inf. Bde. O.O. No. 44, dated 6 November 1944.

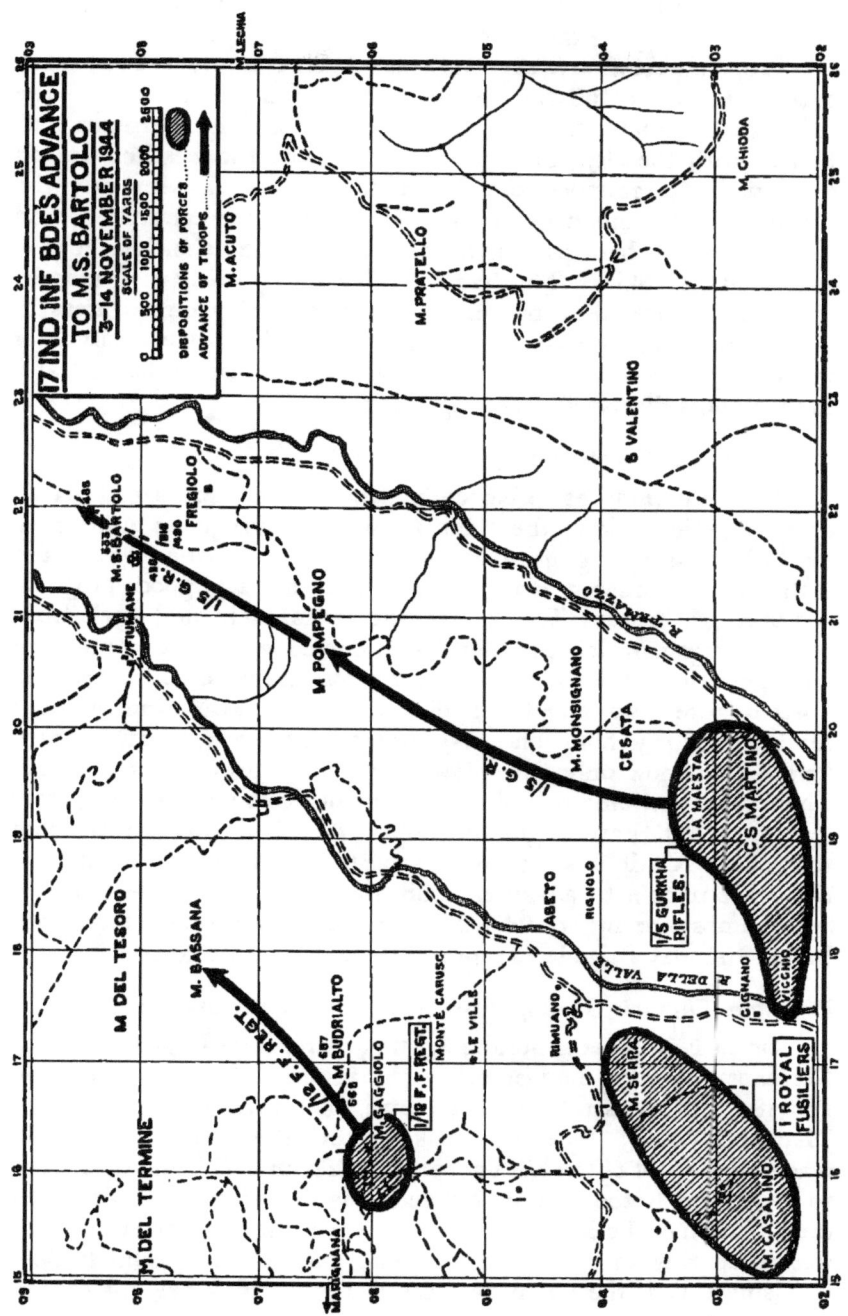

of a sharp frost. The conditions under which the Allied troops lived became more trying than ever.

Sappers were always over-worked. Apart from their many other tasks, they had a full time occupation in trying to keep open the main supply routes to the forward brigades. The Germans also battled with the elements, but, in one respect, the weather was on their side; it grounded the Allied Air Force. Consequently the Germans had a much needed rest from the continual strafing and bombing which had given them no respite during the days of sunshine and clear skies. This had the effect of improving their morale. The country proved to be one of the most thickly mined areas in which the Indian division had ever fought. Nevertheless casualties from the mines were surprisingly few. In the use of booby-traps, the Germans displayed great ingenuity.

Capture of M. Pompegno

By the evening of 10 November, the Gurkha troops had driven north-east right along the ridge from M. Monsignano until they reached the next large feature, M. Pompegno. On the right of the 17th Indian Infantry Brigade the Poles, making good progress, captured M. Acuto. This caused the Germans to pull back from M. Pompegno, which the Gurkhas occupied without encountering any opposition. On the parallel spur across the valley, 1/12 Frontier Force Regiment was able to establish positions on M. Bassana without hindrance at 1730 hours on 11 November. The 17th Indian Infantry Brigade was now only two miles short of the town of Modigliano. There remained only one obstacle to be overcome, the small, grassy feature of M.S. Bartolo guarding the approach to Modigliano from the south. Until this feature was taken, the Polish Corps on the right felt unable to advance. M.S. Bartolo achieved great importance almost overnight and Major-General Russell ordered the 17th Indian Infantry Brigade to capture the feature at all costs.

Rifleman Thaman Gurung Wins Posthumous Victoria Cross

On 11 November a Gurkha fighting patrol came to grips with the Germans, well dug in just below the summit of M.S. Bartolo, on Pt. 518. In this patrol were two scouts, one of them being Rifleman Thaman Gurung. By skilful stalking, both the scouts succeeded in reaching the foot of the hill undetected. Thaman Gurung then started on his way to the summit, but suddenly the second scout attracted the attention of the Germans (in a slit trench just below the crest) who were preparing to fire with a machine gun at the leading section. Realising that if the Germans succeeded in opening fire, the section would sustain heavy casualties, Thaman Gurung boldly charged them. Completely taken by surprise the Germans surrendered

Armoured cars of the 6th Duke of Connaught's Own Lancers north of Moro river chasing the enemy

Allied tank moving to Pietrolunga prior to its capture

Sepoy Namdeo Jadhao, V.C.
(1/5 Mahratta)

Ropeway over the river Ronco built by Indian Sappers and Miners carries men and stores

without opening fire. He then crept forward to the top of the hill, where he saw a number of Germans, well dug in on the reverse slopes, preparing to throw grenades over the crest at the leading section. Although the skyline was devoid of cover and under accurate machine gun fire at close range, Thaman Gurung immediately crossed it, firing on the German position with his tommy gun, thus allowing the forward section to reach the summit. But heavy fire from the German machine guns compelled the platoon to withdraw. Thaman Gurung again crossed the skyline alone, and, although in full view of the Germans and constantly exposed to heavy fire at short range, he methodically put burst after burst of tommy gun fire into the German slit trenches, until his ammunition ran out, when he threw two grenades he had with him. On rejoining his section, he collected two more grenades and again doubled over the bullet-swept crest of the hill to hurl them at the remaining Germans. The diversion enabled both the rear sections to withdraw without losses. Meanwhile, the leading section which had remained behind to assist the withdrawal of the remainder of the platoon, was still on the summit, so Thaman Gurung, shouting to the section to withdraw, seized a Bren gun and a number of magazines. Again he ran to the top of the hill and, although he well knew that his action meant almost certain death, stood up on the bullet swept summit, in full view of the Germans, and opened fire on the nearest German positions. It was not until he had emptied two complete magazines, and the remaining section was well on its way to safety, that Rifleman Thaman Gurung was killed. For his undaunted courage and bravery he earned the Victoria Cross.

Capture of M.S. Bartolo

It was undoubtedly due to Thaman Gurung's superb gallantry and sacrifice of his life that his platoon was able to withdraw from an extremely difficult position without many more casualties than were actually incurred. Very valuable information brought back by the platoon resulted in the whole M.S. Bartolo feature being captured three days later. A second fighting patrol that night was forced back by heavy German machine gun fire and grenades. At 1800 hours on 12 November, two platoons from 1/5 Gurkha moved towards M.S. Bartolo. They had reached Pt. 429, a little short of the main feature, and were forming up for the final assault on the crest of M.S. Bartolo, when they came under very heavy spandau fire from three sides compelling them to withdraw.[5] It was now evident that a full-scale battalion assault with artillery and tank support would be necessary to capture the objective.

---

[4] Battle Narrative M.S. Bartolo; Appx., F-15 and F-16; War Diary 1/5 G.R.

On 13 November, preparations were made for a two-company attack, supported by artillery fire and a troop of Canadian tanks. The plan of operations was as follows:

(i) D Company 1/5 Gurkha was to advance from the area Pt. 490 and attack the western slopes, having as its objectives Pt. 429 and Pt. 533 successively, which would bring it to the summit of M.S. Bartolo.

(ii) C Company was to advance simultaneously from the area Pt. 490 and attack along the eastern slopes to secure the White House. Then the men were to pass through D Company and consolidate on the northern slopes of M.S. Bartolo to include Pt. 486.

(iii) A Company was to remain in the area Pt. 490 as firm base and B Company was to be in reserve.

(iv) The flanking units, the 1st Royal Fusiliers and 1/12 Frontier Force Regiment were to help the Gurkha companies by demonstrating against known German positions on their front.

All day, the divisional artillery systematically shelled M.S. Bartolo, whilst a troop of Canadian tanks moved forward round the east flank and fired on the German positions situated along the eastern slopes of the feature. At 1730 hours, just as it was growing dark, the two assaulting infantry companies moved forward to the attack. For the first time in the division artificial moonlight was employed to help in the operations. It proved of great assistance especially in the early stages of the attack. By 1800 hours D Company had secured Pt. 429 without opposition and prepared to assault Pt. 533. Then opposition stiffened. The two leading companies came under very heavy machine gun fire. By 1900 hours C, the right hand company, was held up by accurate fire from four or five spandaus positioned around a small White House almost on the crest of the hill. At 0015 hours on 14 November, this company encountered dense minefields round the house and suffered casualties. By 2120 hours D, the left hand company, had climbed little more than halfway towards the crest, when it too was halted by German mortar and spandau fire. For six hours more the Gurkhas fought most fiercely to dislodge the Germans. That night no side was prepared to yield, least of all the Gurkhas. At 0230 hours on 14 November, D Company was firmly established on Pt. 533 and as the Germans had also withdrawn from the White House, C Company passed through D to the northern slopes. This success rendered valuable assistance to the advance of the 3rd Carpathian Division on the right of the 8th Indian Division. In spite of heavy mortar fire and shelling, and in spite of the very numerous machine gun posts and an extensive minefield covering the whole of the objective, 1/5 Gurkha had smashed open the gateway to Modigliana.

Advance towards Brisighella

A Squadron 6th Lancers, which had come under the command of the 17th Indian Infantry Brigade on 11 November, moved to Fregiclo on 14 November and entered Modigliano on 15 November. But for more than a week, the latter place continued to be subjected to spasmodic German shelling. Meanwhile 1/5 Gurkha, whose Battalion Headquarters was established there on 19 November, gained a foothold in the hills immediately to the north-west and 1/12 Frontier Force Regiment moved north-east of the town; but the town was not free from long range mortar fire. On 23 November German elements were holding M. Menghina, about one mile north of Modigliana. Indian patrols however gave them no rest. By the evening of 27 November, 1/12 Frontier Force Regiment had driven them back beyond M. Della Siepe whilst 1/5 Gurkha, on the left, had cleared the country as far as M. Visano. Further north, the Poles were wheeling westwards towards Brisighella driving the Germans before them. On 29 November the 6th Lancers relieved the 17th Indian Infantry Brigade which returned to Modigliana for rest.

The 19th Indian Infantry Brigade in the Upper Lamone Valley

While the 17th Indian Infantry Brigade made a thrust towards M.S. Bartolo and Modigliana, the 19th Indian Infantry Brigade, on the left, was on watch astride the upper Lamone Valley in the central sector of the divisional front. After 21 November German shelling on San Cassiano and on the main road gradually diminished. The Germans were obviously moving some of their artillery. Early on 25 November, Indian patrols reported German withdrawal. Thereupon the 19th Indian Infantry Brigade pushed forward but the advance was impeded by booby-traps and mines. The country immediately ahead proved to be one of the most thickly mined areas in which the brigade had ever fought. However, on the right, the Argyll (relieving 3/8 Punjab in the area M. Dell Termine on 25 November) found M. Tesoro clear of the Germans and sent patrols towards M. Panigheto and M. Rigonzano which were also found to be unoccupied. On 27 November M. Di Tura was seized without oppositions. By 30 November the battalion had pushed on to the area Strada-Casale. At the same time on the left, 6/13 Royal Frontier Force Rifles pushed through M. Colombo and Poggio Laguna and by 30 November had occupied M. Ciornetto. Owing to bad weather and the speed of the withdrawal of the Germans only light patrol skirmishes marked the fighting. Meanwhile the

Divisional Sappers had worked hard to keep open the many miles of important roads and, assisted by gunners of the 26th Light Anti-Aircraft Regiment, built in ten days five bridges, some of them more than 140 feet long.

Extension of the 21st Indian Infantry Brigade's Sector

Whilst thus fully committed on the right flank, the 8th Indian Division was ordered to extend its front still farther to include the sector north of Arrow route, then held by the 1st Guards Brigade of the 6th British Armoured Division. The 19th Indian Infantry Brigade was already committed to the utmost, and was unable to extend its commitments further. Hence the new task was entrusted to the 21st Indian Infantry Brigade, then holding the isolated hamlet of Valdifusa, snow clad M. Cece and the long barren escarpment called Monte Della Valle, which ran northward from M. Cece, gradually falling away until it finally emerged into the Senio Valley, some two miles south of Casola Valsenio. The 21st Indian Infantry Brigade relieved the 1st Guards Brigade and at 2000 hours on 18 November assumed command of the new sector.

At this time, the Fifth Army was still engaged in a large scale regrouping of formations in preparation for the coming offensive. North of the 8th Indian Division, the 6th British Armoured Division, with the 61st Infantry Brigade, was astride the road Fontanelice—Isola. On completion of the reliefs on 19 November, the 21st Indian Infantry Brigade, with two battalions, held a front four miles wide as the crow flies. On the right 1st Battalion Jaipur Infantry, in the area Valdifusa—M. Della Valle, defended a sector south of Arrow route, whilst 3/15 Punjab held a very wide front extending from the eastern slopes of M. Battaglia down the Cornazzano spur to the Senio Valley and Arrow route. 1/5 Mahratta was then resting in Palazuolo but one squadron of 6th Lancers was under the command of the brigade.

Vena Del Gesso

On the German side, *578th Regiment* (the *305th Infantry Division*) was responsible for the defence of the area from Venus route to excluding Pt. 610 whilst the *715th Infantry Division* was responsible for the defence of the upper Senio Valley. Of the latter, two battalions of *1028th Regiment* held from including Pt. 610 to Arrow route; two battalions of *725th Regiment* were to the west of Arrow route up to C. Verzola; and *735th Regiment* was responsible for the defence of the area M. Taverna.[6]

The upper Senio Valley ran in a north-easterly direction from Palazzuolo to the town of Casola Valsenio, thence through a gap in

[6] 21 Ind. Inf. Bde. Intelligence Review No. 32, dated 16 November 1944.

the chalk ridge down to the plain. The road and railway which followed the valley bridged the river at frequent intervals. These bridges were all destroyed, one by one, as the Germans withdrew. The chalk ridge was known as the Vena Del Gesso. Running for many miles almost parallel with Route 9, this peculiar earth fault was so sheer on its southern side that only a skilled mountaineer might climb it. Through the escarpment ran the Santerno and Senio rivers. Apart from these gaps and another smaller one at Budrio the ridge offered very few places where an assault might in any way be practical. The Germans recognised its potentialities as a strong defensive position. Every possible approach was sown with anti-personnel mines and air photographers revealed many trenches and machine gun positions.

Although the weather had been deteriorating steadily, some days were fine with good visibility. On these occasions, it was necessary to lay a smoke-screen across the valley to hide the Bailey bridges which the Sappers had built to replace the bridges the Germans had destroyed. This smoke-screen, which was laid across the valley as far forward as possible, was operated by the 26th Light Anti-Aircraft Regiment. The construction of these high level Bailey bridges on Arrow route was a major engineering feat. The last bridge completed on Christmas Day before Casola Valsenio was a high level 'triple triple' Bailey 320 feet long and was supported 90 feet above the river by the highest Bailey pier ever built in Italy. The completion of each bridge eased the problem of maintaining the forward troops in the mountainous country on both sides of the Arrow route though the problem never ceased to be acute. Supplies and ammunition, having been transported as far forward as possible by jeep, were swung on steel cableways across the swollen Senio and carried over miles of very muddy mule-tracks by the gallant muleteers and their animals of the 2nd, 13th and 34th Indian Mule Companies. Finally, the vital supplies and ammunition travelled on the back of porters to the forward infantry companies.

Patrolling Activity

In view of the width of the front and the extreme supply difficulties, ambitious operations were out of the question. The 21st Indian Infantry Brigade's task was to hold the ground and keep contact with the Germans by patrol activity. On 28 November the latter began to withdraw through the hills on either side of the Senio going back on mule and man-pack behind the Vena Del Gesso. Once more strong fighting patrols and one or two self-porpelled guns covered their movement.

The 21st Indian Infantry Brigade pushed on the advance. On 28 November, a patrol of 3/15 Punjab entered Casola Valsenio which was found to be almost deserted and very badly damaged by shell fire. The last of the Germans had passed through during the night heading northwards. By 2 December, the Punjab patrols were scouring M. Battagliola, whose well-defined outline stood out clearly against the grey background of the chalk ridge only a mile beyond. Meanwhile across the valley, 1/5 Mahratta, who had relieved 1st Battalion Jaipur Infantry in the area Valdifusa and M. Della on 28 November, was advancing east of the Arrow route. There were clashes every now and then with small German patrols but by 6 December, 1/5 Mahratta was established at Razetti and as far east as M. Albano. To go further forward was impraticable because Indian positions would then be in full view of the Germans from the top of the escarpment.

During the night of 12/13 December, 3/15 Punjab staged a noisy demonstration to simulate an attack in the area of Budrio. This 'Chinese Cracker', which included a small artillery programme, was intended to divert German attention from Tossignano, a town further to the north-west, which a brigade of the 6th British Armoured Division was attacking that night. The feint attack certainly provoked against the Indian brigade a considerable amount of hostile shelling, which might otherwise have been employed against the British brigade.

Review of the Progress

On 17 December, the 21st Indian Infantry Brigade was relieved by the 17th Indian Infantry Brigade, then preparing to launch an attack on the Vena Del Gesso. Before describing these operations it is necessary to give a brief review of the progress made by the 8th Indian Division. Since October 1944, the 8th Indian Division's advance towards the plain had been very slow. The Germans had fought well, conducting their withdrawal skilfully. Their forces had been greatly assisted by the difficult nature of the country over which British and Indian troops, had to operate as well as the inclemency of the weather, which grew worse as the season advanced. To the Germans, rain was a sure guarantee of freedom from air attack. In such weather, their horse drawn transport was more mobile along cart tracks than Allied heavy vehicles. Before withdrawing the Germans left behind hundreds of mines of great variety laid with infinite skill. Thus, though the extent of the Indian advance during this period was small, it was nevertheless achieved only by courage and pertinacity, by good leadership and happy spirit of friendliness in every branch of the division.

Active Patrolling

On 17 December, when the 17th Indian Infantry Brigade, without the 1st Royal Fusiliers, relieved the 21st Indian Infantry Brigade, the advance of the Polish corps across the right front of the 8th Indian Division had narrowed the latter's commitments to the area held by the 17th Indian Infantry Brigade. Arrow route became the divisional axis and it seemed almost certain that the capture of the formidable Vena Del Gesso would be the next task for the 8th Indian Division. Only two brigades were available for this operation, the 19th Indian Infantry Brigade having passed under the command of the 1st (British Infantry) Division on 5 December to carry out operations on Monte Grande. However, the 8th Indian Division, less one brigade group, was placed under the direct command of the Fifth Army and on 25 December moved to the Serchio Valley to meet the threat of a German offensive on the west coast of Italy. The 17th Indian Infantry Brigade passed under the command of the XIII Corps and prepared to launch an attack on Vena Del Gesso.

Between 17 and 25 December, the 17th Indian Infantry Brigade maintained active patrolling. East of Arrow route, 1/5 Gurkha established a platoon on M. Della Volpe in the morning of 23 December. A German fighting patrol during the afternoon failed to dislodge the Gurkhas who by the evening, had captured yet another peak, the adjacent M. Tondo. From these two peaks, the Gurkhas were able to look down across the river Senio towards the small town of Rivola, which nestled behind the eastern end of the chalk ridge and had been used by the Germans as a forward supply base. On 25 December, when the 17th Indian Infantry Brigade passed under the command of the XIII Corps, 1/5 Gurkha was holding M. Tondo and M. Della Volpe, 1/12 Frontier Force Regiment on the Gurkhas' left was immediately east of the main road, and on the left flank 1st Jaipur Infantry Battalion guarded the northern approaches to M. Battagliola and the upper reaches of the torrent Scarba.

German Dispositions

The Germans had at this stage withdrawn north of the river Senio and it was expected that their next positions would be so sited as to deny a crossing of that river or to secure the high ground between it and the river Santerno, while at the same time holding the Vena Del Gesso. The *715th Infantry Division* held from including Riolo to excluding Tossignano while *I Battalion 755th Regiment* of the *334th Infantry Division* held the area Tossignano.[7]

The next task for the 17th Indian Infantry Brigade, therefore, was to advance across the river Senio, capture Rivola, and the eastern end of the Vena Del Gesso. Here the Germans were still strongly established both on the crest itself and also in a number of fortified houses, which lay scattered along its base and commanded an

[7] 8 Ind. Div. O.O. No. 36, dated 21 December 1944.

excellent view of the valley road as far as Casola Valsenio. Further to the north-east, the main German force had withdrawn north of the river Senio.

The Eighth Army maintained the offensive. The 5th Kresowa Division (II Polish Corps) was to attack across the river Senio, secure M.S. Castello and exploit towards Pt. 236. The Lovat Scouts operating on the left flank of this division were given the task of containing German forces in the area Isola and La Casetta by strong patrols. In case the Germans offered little resistance south of the river Santerno, the 5th Kresowa Division was to advance on the axis Isola—La Cassetta. The role of the 17th Indian Infantry Brigade, as mentioned above, was primarily to facilitate the advance of and protect the left flank of the 5th Kresowa Division by crossing the river Senio near Rivola and operating towards Pt. 291, and secondly to seize the eastern end of the Vena Del Gesso in the execution of which the brigade was to be assisted by the 6th British Armoured Division, then in the Santerno Valley halted before Tossignano, by attacking that feature at a suitable moment.

On 25 December the commander of the 17th Indian Infantry Brigade announced his plan of protecting the flank of the Polish corps when it attacked on 29 December. There were to be three phases. First, the brigade was to secure a line of communication through the gap, where the Arrow route and the river Senio cut through the Gesso. Then, in the second phase, it was to wheel left, in conformity with the Poles to capture the watershed between the Senio and Santerno rivers. If these two phases went according to plan, phase three was to be that of exploitation towards the river Santerno.[3] The 17th Indian Infantry Brigade was to advance with 1/5 Gurkha on the right, 1/12 Frontier Force Regiment in the centre and 1st Battalion Jaipur Infantry on the left. The 14th Canadian Armoured Regiment and the 6th Lancers were in support of the brigade.

Accordingly, extensive patrolling was begun by the 17th Indian Infantry Brigade. Patrols of 1/12 Frontier Force Regiment tried to discover if there was any way of scaling the sheer cliff, or of getting through the Rivola gap and assaulting the German positions from the rear. On 28 December one patrol managed to reach the top of Vena Del Gesso but was engaged by three German light machine guns. A haystack caught fire exposing the patrol to full view. Thereupon the patrol withdrew under cover of artillery smoke.

The Polish attack, which had been planned for 29 December, was postponed until a later date and the days of boredom dragged on into the month of January 1945. On account of the weather inclemencies, activity was impossible by day and hazardous patrolling,

---

[3] 17 Ind. Inf. Bde. O.O. No. 48, dated 25 December 1944.

with all the advantages to the Germans, was left to the night. On 8 January, however, the 17th Indian Infantry Brigade was relieved and began its journey westwards over the ice-bound mountain roads to rejoin the 8th Indian Division. It arrived in the divisional area on 13 January, where, next day, the 1st Royal Fusiliers returned to the brigade after completing the attachment to the 78th Division.

Move of the 8th Indian Division to the Serchio Valley

So far we have described the limited advance of the 8th Indian Division. It may now be pertinent to describe its part in meeting the threat of a German offensive in the Serchio Valley towards the close of December 1944. As 1944 drew to a close in Italy, the whole attention of the 15th Army Group was concentrated on the capture of Bologna. Further to the west, towards the coast, there had been little serious fighting. Both the Allied and the German forces were holding the difficult country of the western Apennines with the minimum of strength and, as a result, contact was very loose. However, the west coast sector was of considerable strategical importance as the American Fifth Army supply line ran from its base at Leghorn in a north-easterly direction though Pisa, with its famous leaning tower, to the picturesque walled city of Lucca. From here, the supply line ran along the valley at the southern end of the Apennines almost parallel to the front. Towards the middle of December, intelligence reports led the Fifth Army Headquarters to believe that there was a possibility of the Germans developing a serious threat to this supply line by attacking either down the west coast or down the valley of the Serchio river towards Lucca. Both of these likely approaches were guarded by only weak forces of the 92nd U.S. Division. This appreciation assumed such importance that the 8th Indian Division, which was then fighting in the area Vena Del Gesso, received orders on 22 December to move with all haste to Lucca, leaving the 17th Indian Infantry Brigade behind with adequate support to continue its task.

At that time, divisional headquarters was close behind the 17th Indian Infantry Brigade, separated from the Arno Valley by 52 miles of ice-bound roads and two high passes covered with snow. The 21st Indian Infantry Brigade, which had just settled down to rest in the Popolano area, had forty miles of treacherous roads to cross and one very high mountain pass. The 19th Indian Infantry Brigade had just been relieved on Monte Grande and was concentrating in a rest area near Florence. The 3rd Field Regiment Royal Artillery was still near Monte Grande. The rest of the division was billeted or camped by the side of these mountain roads wherever space was found.

In spite of many contradictory orders, and despite bad weather and appalling road conditions, the move was carried out during the

Christmas days without undue difficulty. The two brigades concentrated in the area of Lucca before reconnaissance parties from the divisional headquarters could arrive. These were delayed by twenty-four hours owing to a blocked mountain pass.

Topography

The Serchio Valley south of Barga was wide and well cultivated. Being an important channel of communication, a railway ran along its entire length, and on either side of the river, whose width varied from 80-120 feet, was a good macadam road. The hills west of the river rose steeply and were well wooded. There were a number of pleasant towns in the region, Barga and Bagni di Lucca, both north of Lucca, being the more important. The valley of the Serchio was well populated with many pleasing houses and large villas, which served as excellent billets for the British and Indian troops. Perched on the hill tops were tiny villages, their cottages huddled together around the narrow main street. Many of these villages were approached only by mule tracks which proved even suitable for jeeps. To the north-east, the country was wilder and more rugged. There were no roads and the mule was the chief means of transport.

Disposition of American Troops

Until Christmas day, both the XIII Corps Headquarters and the Fifth Army Headquarters were of the opinion that the move of 8th Indian Division was purely precautionary; no importance was attached to the fact that neither Major-General Russell nor his divisional headquarters staff would arrive at Lucca until 26 December. The feeling at Headquarters American IV Corps was however quite different; orders were sent to Brigadiers Dobree and Mould whilst they were still on the road, to report to corps headquarters on their arrival at Lucca. This they did and were at once sent on a hurried reconnaissance of the Serchio Valley and the coastal area. Late on Christmas night, they were again summoned to corps headquarters and informed that intelligence reports indicated that an attack in the Serchio Valley the next morning was almost a certainty. In the absence of Major-General Russell, Brigadier Dobree assumed command of all troops of the 8th Indian Division, which had arrived in the concentration area.

On 26 December 1944, when the Germans launched their offensive in the Serchio Valley, the 92nd U.S. Division was holding the front. I Battalion of the 370th Infantry Regiment was holding the sector west of the river Serchio in area Molezzana, with one company holding Calomini. The sector east of the river Serchio was held by II Battalion of the 370th Infantry Regiment and II Battalion of the 366th Infantry Regiment. The forward posts were at Sommocolonia and Bebbio, the latter being held by a platoon of the 92nd Reconnaissance Troop. East of the right boundary of the 92nd U.S. Infantry Division the front was lightly held by the British and the U.S. 'dismounted' Light Anti-Aircraft units under the command of 45th U.S. Task Force.

German Troops

The *148th Grenadier Division*, reinforced by eight battalions from three Italian divisions, was holding the sector from inclusive the Serchio Valley across to the Tyrrhenian Sea. A part of *285th Grenadier Regiment* with elements from Italian divisions, operated west of the river Serchio, while to the east were larger units from *285th Grenadier Regiment* and *286th Grenadier Regiment* and also mountain troops from the *Mittenwald Mountain Battalion*.

German Offensive

The German attack on the Serchio Valley started early on 26 December and developed with two parallel thrusts southwards along the high ground flanking the river. During the day the western thrust reached Calomini, whilst east of the river the Germans overran Sommacolonia, Bebbio and Tiglio. The attack continued on the 27th, with greater pressure in the eastern sector. Barga was occupied. The main direction of the push was through Loppia and Seggio towards the main road in the vicinity of Pedona. West of the river the Germans occupied Vergemoli and Gallicano. It was at this stage that the 19th Indian Infantry Brigade, advancing from Bagni di Lucca established a line from Monticino, across the Serchio to San Romano, enabling the troops from the 92nd U.S. Division to pass through.[9]

Deployment of the 8th Indian Division

The main headquarters of the 8th Indian Division arrived in the area Lucca and the division was placed under the command of the IV U.S. Corps. The task of the Indian division was to stop the German advance on the general line of the torrent Aria and to the north-east and to recover all ground lost prior to the taking over of this sector.[10] For this operation, the following troops were under the command and in support of the 8th Indian Division:—

    370th U.S. Infantry Regiment
    6th Lancers less one squadron
    5th Royal Mahratta less two companies (Medium machine gun)
    A Company 5th Royal Mahratta

---

[9] 8 Ind. Div. Intelligence Summary No. 173, dated 30 December 1944.
[10] Order of Battle ; 8 Ind. Div. O.O. No. 38, dated 28 December 1944 ; Appendix A, War Diary 8 Ind. Div.

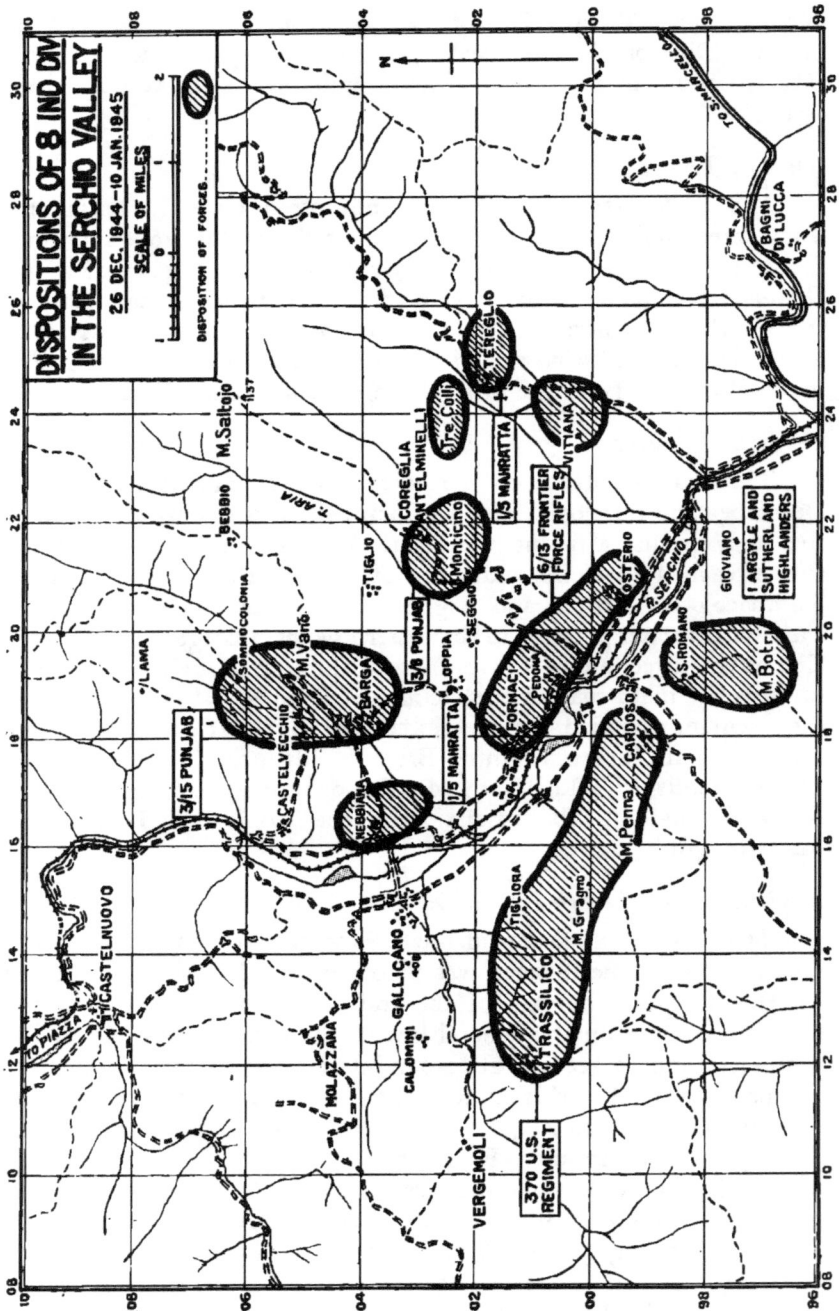

B Company 76oth U.S. Tank Battalion
Headquarters Tenth Army Group Royal Artillery
3rd Field Regiment Royal Artillery
One Battery 53rd Field Regiment
13th and 15th Batteries 4th Mahratta Anti-Tank Regiment
17th Medium Regiment
18th Medium Regiment
329th F.A. Battalion (12-105 mm)
598th F.A. Battalion (12-105 mm)
A Battery 6ooth F.A. Battalion (14-155 mm Howitzers)
One Battery 26th Light Anti-Aircraft Regiment
A Troop 166th Battery 56th Light Anti-Aircraft Regiment
7th Field Company Indian Engineers
69th Field Company Indian Engineers and ancillary units.

On 27 December, the 8th Indian Division was still deficient of the 17th Indian Infantry Brigade and its contingents. However the 6th Lancers was expected back by 29 December. Headquarters Tenth Army Group Royal Artillery, with the 17th and 18th Medium Regiments, were to come under the divisional command on their arrival about 30 December.

The first brigade to arrive in the new area was the 19th Indian Infantry Brigade. It was committed immediately (on 27 December) with two battalions north of the river and one to the south. 3/8 Punjab was on the right in a strong defensive position based on the Monticino spur, with 6/13 Frontier Force Rifles on the left in the area Osterio, defending the main approach down the valley road. South of Osteria, entrenched on the wooded spurs running down to the river Serchio from M. Botri was the Argyll in the area of San Romano. As it grew dark on 27 December, D Company of 1/5 Mahratta, under the command of the 19th Indian Infantry Brigade, took up positions in front of 3/8 Punjab on a small spur at 201025 where it served as a covering force.

The 21st Indian Infantry Brigade concentrated in the area Bagna di Lucca on 28 December. The brigade was to occupy positions in depth behind the 19th Indian Infantry Brigade on the general line Tre Colli—M. Acciso and also to protect the right flank by occupying the high ground and by maintaining contact with Task Force 45. For the protection of the right flank, 1/5 Mahratta established one company at Tre Colli and in the hill-top village of Tereglio. They had orders to halt the Germans if they attempted a drive southwards from the area of M. Saltoio to threaten the Indian forward line of communication.

Control of Fleeing Civilians

When the Germans began to push southwards on 26 December,

civilians in the forward areas hurriedly packed a few essential belongings and began to move down the valley road towards Bagni di Lucca. As they travelled deeper into the Allied zone, tales of what was happening at the front became more and more exaggerated. The fall of Barga only lent colour to these reports. By 27 December, the road from Pedona southwards was full of fleeing refugees. There were hundreds of men, women and children all carrying huge bundles on bicycles or trundling along in their bullock carts. Travelling on either side of the road, this throng of refugees threatened to block the main highway, up which Indian and British troops were marching to take up defensive positions. The divisional provost had to divert all the farm carts down side lanes and control this host of bewildered civilians before the 8th Indian Division's transport could move forward.

German Menace Checked

The plan made by Brigadier T.S. Dobree and approved by Major-General Russell on his arrival was quite simple. To halt the German advance, the 19th Indian Infantry Brigade was ordered to establish a firm defensive line astride the Serchio Valley from the Monticino spur to M. Botri. The 21st Indian Infantry Brigade was responsible for the protection of the northern flank between Monticino and Tereglio. It was also entrusted with the defence of the Tereglio—Vitiana line in the unlikely event of the 19th Indian Infantry Brigade being dislodged from the forward positions, and then, when the word was given, the 21st was to pass through the 19th Indian Infantry Brigade and by aggressive action regain the lost ground. The 307th U.S. Regiment, having been withdrawn through the 19th Indian Infantry Brigade, was to concentrate in the hills west of the river Serchio and take up a defensive position in the area of M. Gragno. The destruction of any more bridges was strictly forbidden and those already prepared for demolition were guarded by Bengal sappers until the charges were removed.

Once the 19th Indian Infantry Brigade had taken up a defensive position astride the Serchio Valley extending from the Monticino spur to M. Botril, with the 21st Indian Infantry Brigade protecting the flank to the north, any threat to the Indian base installations was removed. The Germans never made any serious attempt to break through the Indian lines or, indeed, to infiltrate round the flanks. Apart from patrol engagements the 8th Indian Division experienced no fighting during its stay in the valley.

Early in the evening of 27 December, small German parties were reported on 3/8 Punjab front. These were harassed by artillery and one, more enterprising than the others, reached within small arms range before it disappeared. Throughout the night there was spasmodic harassing fire along the 19th Indian Infantry Brigade front.

By first light on 28 December, the 2nd Battalion 370th U.S. Regiment[11] was in position in the hills west of the river Serchio and held a line extending from Cardoso, then north-west to Tigliora and so to a village called Trassilico to the west. Although companies were very widely separated, their locations were sited to command a large area. Moreover the German threat on this flank was never considered to be great. With the Americans so dispersed, the Argyll in the area of M. Botri was protected on its front by a wide if thinly held screen.

On 29 December, a squadron of the 6th Lancers, which had just arrived in the area, advanced up the eastern valley road without contacting the Germans. In the late afternoon the vehicles were in Barga, having overcome the difficulties caused by demolitions and a number of mines. 3/8 Punjab and 6/13 Frontier Force Rifles were following up but making slow progress over very undulating country. Therefore the Lancers were instructed to hold the Barga ridge that night, assisted by as much infantry as could reach them. 3/8 Punjab pushed forward as far as the prominent ridge just east of Barga ; and, on the northern side, occupied without opposition the villages of Coreglia and Castellacio. 6/13 Frontier Force Rifles advanced along the eastern valley road without hindrance as far as the brickworks of Fornaci and the high ground to the north. C and D Companies occupied the spur south-west of Seggio, and A and B Companies then pushed on to the area about 1000 yards south of Barga to support the 6th Lancers, who had entered the town. By first light on 30 December, after minor patrol activity during the night, the two forward companies of 6/13 Frontier Force Rifles entered Barga.

Vigorous Patrolling

The 21st Indian Infantry Brigade was next ordered to move forward and relieve the leading troops of the 19th Indian Infantry Brigade, viz. a squadron of the 6th Lancers and elements of 6/13 Frontier Force Rifles, and take up a defensive position on the general line Barga—road junction. 3/15 Punjab on the right, was to protect the right flank from excluding Tiglio to including M. Veno and to try to establish one company at Sommocolonia. 1/5 Mahratta Light Infantry, on the left, was to protect the left flank and establish one company as patrol base in the area Nebbiana.

On 30 December the brigade advanced to the line of the new forward defended localities and 3/15 Punjab moved into Barga. From the observation posts north-west of Barga, the Germans watched

---

[11] This regiment and all American units in the Serchio Valley were now under command of the 8 Ind. Div.

the Bren carriers and transport of the 21st Indian Infantry Brigade move up the valley road into Barga and then heavily shelled them. More than 120 shells fell in Barga between 1030 hours and last light causing five casualties. One vehicle went up in flames. From Barga a company of 3/15 Punjab occupied the small village of Sommocolonia, situated on the hillside north of Barga. This tiny village was a most important position for the troops of the 21st Indian Infantry Brigade to hold as it commanded an excellent view of Barga on the valley road. Sommocolonia, after it was occupied by 3/15 Punjab, was shelled intermittently and harassed by machine gun fire throughout the rest of the day. To protect Barga from the east, another company of 3/15 Punjab was sent to occupy the hill feature of M. Veno, which overlooked the town.

On the left of 3/15 Punjab, 1/5 Mahratta moved forward from the ridge running south-west from Barga to occupy the village of H. Nebbiana, from where the men might be able to defend the valley road. In front of 1/5 Mahratta, the armoured cars of the 6th Lancers rolled slowly northwards. About a mile ahead of Nebbiana, the 6th Lancers came under heavy machine gun fire from the village of Castelvecchio, which halted their advance. When the Indian Sappers had finished building a bridge at 1200 hours, two armoured cars of another troop of the 6th Lancers, accompanied by Sappers reconnaissance parties, crossed the Serchio and entered Gallicano. Their arrival was the signal for very accurate German shelling, which prevented further reconnaissance.

In the meantime, the Americans had conformed with the advance of the 21st Indian Infantry Brigade, 1st Battalion 370th U.S. Regiment reaching the spur just south of Gallicano. American patrols made no contact with the Germans and one reported the village of Vergemoli evacuated by the latter. The situation was now well in hand.

The Fifth Army Headquarters had already issued an urgent appeal for prisoners in order to clarify the German order of battle and learn what had happened on 26 December. This call was quickly answered. A fighting patrol of 6th Lancers, directed on the village of Molazzano came under spandau fire from the German positions on Pt. 408. Using folds in the ground, the patrol avoided this danger, and with great tenacity continued as far as Molazzana where it engaged the Germans and, after a sharp fight, brought back two prisoners. The casualties of the Lancers were two men slightly wounded.

Over on the right, patrols of 3/15 Punjab operating from their base at Sommacolonia soon discovered that the Lama spur was firmly held. It seemed now that the Germans were unwilling to yield more ground without a struggle. 1/5 Mahratta also reported that the

Germans were holding prepared positions, many of them fortified houses surrounded by "S" Mines, at the foot of the spur.

The 8th Indian Division had regained all ground that had been lost east of the river; it had completed its task. On 8 January 1945, the relief of the 21st Indian Infantry Brigade commenced and was completed at 0320 hours on 10 January, when the 2nd Battalion 365th U.S. Regiment relieved 3/15 Punjab. On the same day, having handed over its commitments to the 92nd U.S. Division, the 8th Indian Division began to concentrate in the Pisa rest area. The threat to the Fifth Army's supply route and to Leghorn itself was removed and the whole situation fully restored within four days of the 8th Indian Division's arrival in the sector.

CHAPTER XXX

Defence of Monte Grande

We have described earlier the limited advance of the 8th Indian Division as well as its important role in checking the German threat in the Serchio Valley. We shall now describe the static role of the 19th Indian Infantry Brigade in the Monte Grande sector.

The 19th Indian Infantry Brigade in the Monte Grande Sector

On 1 December 1944, the 19th Indian Infantry Brigade was in the line pursuing the Germans north of S. Casciano, when orders were received for the brigade to move as quickly as possible to relieve the units of the 1st Division on Monte Grande. In spite of the difficulty in collecting the scattered troops and the bad road, the relief was successfully completed on the night of 5 December. The Monte Grande feature really marked the limit of success achieved in the Fifth Army's autumn offensive, as Monte Castellaro to the north had been recaptured by the Germans some ten days earlier. Monte Grande's retention was vital, not only as a springboard for the contemplated winter attack towards Bologna and the Po Valley, but also because, in German hands, it would have commanded all the positions held by the 1st and the 78th (British) Divisions and the communications to them.

Between 3 and 6 December, the 19th Indian Infantry Brigade took over from the 2nd British Infantry Brigade, which was then able to narrow its front by moving to the left of the Indian brigade. By 6 December, when all the reliefs had been completed, the forward line of the 1st Division stretched from Frassineto through M. Cerrere and Monte Grande to M. Cucoli, south-west of Monte Grande.[1] The 19th Indian Infantry Brigade was responsible for Monte Grande itself and for M. Cerrere; on its left were two battalions of the 1st Division on M. Calderaro, which was reached by a narrow saddle from Monte Grande and some way from it. Troops of the 78th Division were echeloned well to the rear so that the 19th Indian Infantry Brigade was almost isolated.

For defence, the sector of the 1st Division was divided into zones, the northern and the southern; each of these was held by three infantry battalions up, with a fourth in central reserve in an immediate counter-attack role. The 2nd British Infantry Brigade held the northern or left sector whilst the 19th Indian Infantry Brigade

[1] 19 Ind. Inf. Bde. with the 1st British Division; Lessons from Operations.

held the southern or right sector. On the right of the 19th Indian Infantry Brigade was the 11th Brigade of the 78th Division.

The commander of the 19th Indian Infantry Brigade assigned the defence of the Frassineto ridge to the Argyll. On its left, in the area of M. Cerrere, was 6/13 Frontier Force Rifles guarding the brigade's left flank. Astride Monte Grande itself were the forward companies of 3/8 Punjab. Almost every inch of ground was covered by small arms fire. In the case of 3/8 Punjab and 6/13 Frontier Force Rifles, only fifty yards separated their flanking positions.[2]

German Troops

Opposite the 19th Indian Infantry Brigade was the *1st Regiment* of the *1st Parachute Division*, generally regarded as one of the finest formations of the German army. Its soldiers were all volunteers, veterans of Cassino, inordinately proud of their reputation, fanatical and brave. Invariably they were found where Allied threat was imminent and the danger greatest. On 6 December, the *1st Parachute Division* was holding a sector extending from Tamagnin to the Quaderna valley. Its estimated strength was five strong battalions in the line and four in reserve. Prior to the arrival of the 19th Indian Infantry Brigade in the Monte Grande sector, a number of raids, delivered with great zeal and punch, displayed increased aggressiveness and a high state of morale. Moreover, the minor success which attended a recent German sortie was likely to lead to projects still more ambitious.

Topography

Monte Grande, a towering two thousand feet high feature, ten miles south-east of Bologna and Route 9, was part of the menacing American Fifth Army bulge towards Bologna; it was absolutely imperative to hold this key point and it would have been disastrous to the coming offensive had this feature been captured by the Germans. South-east of Monte Grande was the small hamlet of Frassineto, whilst between Frassineto and Monte Grande was M. Cerrere, a feature lower than Monte Grande. The ground rose steeply to the summit of these two main features. There, and on the crest of the Frassineto ridge, the escarpment was so narrow that it afforded little opportunity for defence in depth.

From the 19th Indian Infantry Brigade positions, on a clear day, one could see the towers and domes of Bologna rising from the valley of the Po. Where vegetation had not been blasted by shell or mortar fire, the hillsides were covered with small trees and low brushwood. There were one or two small houses in which Italian

---

[2] 'Monte Grande by Lt.-General Sir Dudley Russell, *Infantry Journal*, Vol. IV, 1953.

shepherds had lived peacefully before the war. Fortunately there were very few clear days whilst the brigade was in the area of Monte Grande. By day, unless the mist was unusually thick, forward trenches were under German observation. German snipers watched for any sign of movement; it was nerve-wrecking, to say the least. British and Indian Infantry had to eat and sleep in and fight from the same slit trenches. A man was fortunate if he was a signaller at a rear headquarters or one of a mortar team; he was at least able to live in a dug-out on the reverse slopes, although it probably had eighteen inches of water in it most of the time. In some respects conditions resembled those in the trenches of Flanders during World War I. Huddled in their weapon pits, British and Indian troops sat all day long, whilst a bitter, cold wind whistled down the valley, or a steady drizzle soaked them, their clothing, and their blankets. A belt of wire covered the front of some of the Indian positions and many mines had been sown in the area. The steep slopes, which dropped precipitously below some of the trenches, made it very difficult to site the heavy machine guns to the best advantage. However, in the forward trenches there were hundreds of Mills' grenades. At the slightest suspicious noise during the night, the pins of a dozen grenades would come out and a few seconds afterwards they would go hurling over the parapet to explode on the hillside below.

South of Monte Grande was the Sillaro Valley, shrouded each day by a thick pall of smoke from hundreds of smoke canisters to shield the area and the gun lines from German observation. Every now and then, flashes from the guns broke through the drifting smoke and a few moments later the shells whined low over Monte Grande headed for the German positions beyond.

Reconnaissance parties from the 19th Indian Infantry Brigade found a number of mule tracks leading up to the main features from the jeep-head. The best mule track up from the valley was a veritable quagmire, few vehicles other than jeeps could negotiate it and even the jeeps sometimes had to be winched forward by a powerful recovery tractor.

Administrative Problems

To supply and maintain the brigade was a major problem in itself. From the Sillaro Valley road a jeep track wound half-way up to Monte Grande. At the jeep-head, all the supplies were unloaded and strapped to the backs of mules. From here the supply trains of Indian Mule Companies slithered and slipped in the thick, slimy mud as they fought their way up the hills against the elements and against time to get the vital items to the forward infantry positions. Backwards and forwards in the darkness of the night went the mule companies. Often German mortar or artillery fire found a target on those hazardous tracks to send men and animals tumbling into the valley below. The journey from the jeep-head to the forward positions of 6/13 Frontier Force Rifles took five hours—five hours to cover a distance of little more than one and a half miles.

The transport of an ordinary load was arduous enough, but simple compared with evacuating a wounded man down those treacherous tracks to the jeep-head. Sure-footed as were the mules, there were cases of animals slipping and crashing to their death in the valley with the wounded men still strapped to their backs.

German Raids

Normally, the sector held by the 19th Indian Infantry Brigade was quiet by day, although the calm would sometimes be broken by a fierce, hostile artillery bombardment direct on some particular locality. The paratroopers had a large number of mortars for which there was a plentiful supply of ammunition; the forward posts of the 19th Indian Infantry Brigade were subjected to mortar bombs fired spasmodically in salvoes of two or three rounds throughout the day. Occasionally, a self-propelled gun would rumble into position in the German lines and fire a few rounds in quick succession before moving on again to escape attention from the British gunners. From time to time the area became the target for the five barrelled nebelwerfer, whose weird moan gave a timely warning.

When the darkness cloaked Monte Grande and M. Cerrere, men were able to move from one slit trench to another bringing forward supplies and ammunition. It was during the night that the mortar fire seemed so much more frightening and heavier. At night too, patrols from both sides slipped into the "no-man's land". Sometimes it was only one or two men who went out to gain vital information for a raid the next night; sometimes stronger patrols lay in ambush among the brushwood, waiting for their victims to use a nearby path.

On the night of 6 December, a patrol of the Argyll directed against the area near C. Nuova was ambushed by fifteen paratroopers. The Scotsmen, taken unawares, fought back vigorously but had to withdraw. Again on the night of 10/11 December, forty Germans carried out a raid on a house near La Dogatia, a position held jointly by the 6th Gordons and 3/8 Punjab. The attack was preceded by intense mortar fire. The Germans approached from two sides: one party came in from the south-east and were repelled by a platoon of 3/8 Punjab; another party swept forward from the north on the flank held by the Gordons. They set fire to the house and demolished it with a faustpatrone.

The morning of 12 December witnessed a heavy attack. It

occurred whilst the 19th Indian Infantry Brigade held the Monte Grande sector. At about 0630 hours, the Germans fired a heavy concentration of mortar and artillery on M. Cerrere and the Frassineto ridge. This lasted in varying intensity until 0700 hours when the infantry commenced their assault. The attack was launched simultaneously against M. Cerrere and Frassineto. On the latter feature, Allied artillery and mortar fire quickly broke up the attacking force. On the left, the German paratroopers enjoyed a small initial success when they captured at 0730 hours a position near C. Nuova then held by two platoons of the Argyll; this position was occupied only during the day and the attack came when the Highlanders had started moving into it, and they were caught on the wrong foot. After heavy hand-to-hand fighting, the paratroopers seized the small garrison in the house. This included an officer of 2/7 Middlesex who was taken prisoner. As he was being led back to the German line by an escort, a mist came down. Suddenly he swung round and pushed his solitary guard off the narrow path down the hill-side. By the time he could recover, the officer had vanished and was well on his way to the Allied lines. Using C. Nuova as a firm base, the paratroopers began to attack 6/13 Frontier Force Rifles. But as they advanced over open ground, their ranks were swept by the fire of 6/13 Frontier Force Rifles and the Mahratta machine gunners, who engaged them almost at point-blank range. The Germans suffered heavy casualties. Nevertheless, after a fierce fight the Germans captured the forward platoon post at 0745 hours. Fortunately a well-timed counter-attack by another platoon of 6/13 Frontier Force Rifles pushed the German paratroopers back and the position was regained by 0900 hours. By that time, the Germans in C. Nuova had been much weakened. The Argyll asked for permission to counter-attack. However, the request was refused because the brigade commander wished to keep back a reserve to hold the Frassineto ridge, whose retention was absolutely vital. At about 1100 hours, two wireless intercepts indicated that the Germans had suffered heavy casualties and were running short of ammunition. This was the time for a counter-attack. After thirty minutes intense bombardment by every available weapon a reserve platoon of the Argyll swept forward, recaptured C. Nuova and took two prisoners. Thus by midday the position was restored and the remainder of the day passed quietly. Thanks to the stalwart defence and vigorous counter-attack, the 19th Indian Infantry Brigade yielded not an inch of ground to the Germans.

On 19 December, seven days after the action of M. Carrere the 19th Indian Infantry Brigade was relieved by the 3rd British Brigade and moved to rejoin the 8th Indian Division in the Serchio Valley, north of Bagna di Lucca.

The 10th Indian Division in the Line

After the withdrawal of the 19th Indian Infantry Brigade on 19 December 1944, the XIII Corps continued to defend the Monte Grande area with two forward divisions—the 1st and the 78th Divisions. Due to inclement weather operations were practically at a standstill. On 18 January 1945, when the XIII Corps reverted to the operational command of the Eighth Army, its regrouping had been completed. The 85th U.S. Division of the II Corps had relieved the 1st British Division and was on all but the eastern slopes of Monte Grande. To its right was the XIII Corps, whose front was held by two divisions—the 6th British Armoured Division on the right and the 78th British Division on the left. Further regrouping of the XIII Corps took place in February. On 4 February, the 78th Division and two regiments of the 1st Canadian Armoured Brigade were ordered to pass from the command of the Corps; their place was to be taken by the 10th Indian Division and several independent units—the 14/20 Hussars, the 2nd Highland Light Infantry, the 2nd Loyals and the Lovat Scouts.

In the second week of February 1945, the 10th Indian Division moved from the Senio sector and relieved the 78th Division in the S. Clemente sector under the XIII Corps. On the right, in contact with the Poles, who had extended their front to relieve the 10th Indian Division on the Senio, was the 6th British Armoured Division. Monte Grande, where the 19th Indian Infantry Brigade had been in December 1944, was two and a half miles to the north and held by the 85th U.S. Division.

The three main features on the front held by the 10th Indian Division were M. Del Verro, M. Spaduro (both twelve to thirteen hundred feet high) and, later, the dominating Monte Grande, approximately two thousand feet high. From these, the valleys of the bigger streams, the Santerno, Sellustra, Sillare, Gallano and Quaderno ran down to the north-east between a number of steep, narrow ridges. All except the Sillaro flowed through narrow valleys, overlooked at close range by German positions on the high ground above them. More valuable of these positions were M. Maggiore, M. Deri Mercati, M. Castellazzo, Vedriano and M. Messamo. The numerous tributaries of the main streams cut across the front to make a maze of small, cliff-sided valleys separated by knife-edge ridges of clay or soft soil which, in wet weather, were very treacherous for movement.

The 20th Indian Infantry Brigade relieved the 36th Brigade in the Sillaro Valley and assumed command of the sector at 1600 hours on 10 February 1945. 3/5 Mahratta Light Infantry was on the right, south of the valley in the area Travellato—Aquabona. The Nabha Akal Infantry was in the river valley in the area Ca di Villa—C.

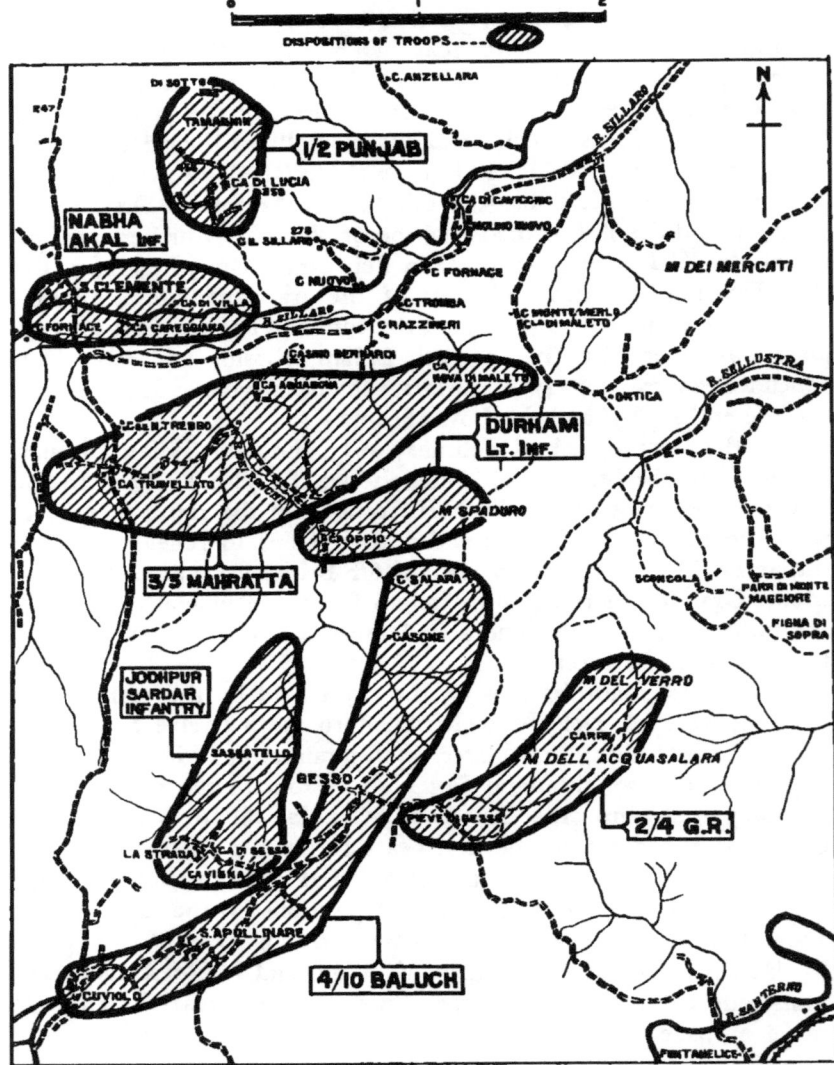

DISPOSITIONS OF 10 IND DIV IN S. CLEMENTE AREA
FEBRUARY 1945

Fornace. 1/2 Punjab Regiment took over the Ca di Lucia spur north of the river. 2/3 Gurkha Rifles was in reserve.

The 10th Indian Infantry Brigade relieved the 11th British Brigade south of the 20th Indian Infantry Brigade and assumed command of the sector at 2315 hours on 13 February. 1st Durham Light Infantry and 4/10 Baluch were forward on M. Spaduro, the former in the area Ca. Oppio and the latter in the area Cuviolo—Ca. Salara. The Jodhpur Sardar Light Infantry was in Strada—Sassatello area. Four days later on 17 February, the 2/3 Gurkha Rifles took over M. Del Verro and completed the occupation of the area. One squadron 14/20 King's Hussars was under the command of the 10th Indian Division.

Monte Grande

Monte Grande came to be included as part of the commitments of the 10th Indian Division and all its three brigades were again deployed, the 25th Indian Infantry Brigade taking over that sector from the 85th U.S. Division betwen 11 and 14 March. For this task, this brigade had under command five infantry battalions, the Lovat Scouts and F. Reconnaissance Squadron (a volunteer Italian Parachutist unit of proved worth). 4/11 Sikh was on the right in the area Trebbo—Frassineto; 1st King's Own was at M. Cerrere; and 3/18 Garhwal Rifles was on the left, about Monte Calde area. Centrally placed at Monte Grande and Farneto was 3/1 Punjab. 2nd Highland Light Infantry was on the Rignano spur. The Lovat Scouts were on the left flank at Marzolino and they linked up with the 10th Indian Division's new left hand neighbours, the 91st U.S. Division, later replaced by the Italian Legnano Group.

German Dispositions

With *3rd Parachute Regiment* responsible for the defence of the Selluatra and Sillero valleys, the remaining two regiments of the *1st Parachute Division*—the 1st and the 4th—held the remainder of the division's sector. *1st Parachute Regiment* held from Pt. 278 to C. II Vezzolo with III Battalion in the north and *II Battalion* in the south. West of *1st Parachute Regiment* was *4th Parachute Regiment* with *I Battalion* east and *II Battalion* west.

In the sector opposite the important heights of M. Cerrere—Monte Grande—M. Calderero the Germans had therefore two battalions of Parachutists in reserve—a battalion of *1st Parachute Regiment* and *III Battalion* of *4th Parachute Regiment* representing strong reserves readily available for counter-attack against any attempted advance from these heights. These reserves also constituted a potential force for a limited attack against Indian positions, the success of which would be of considerable importance to

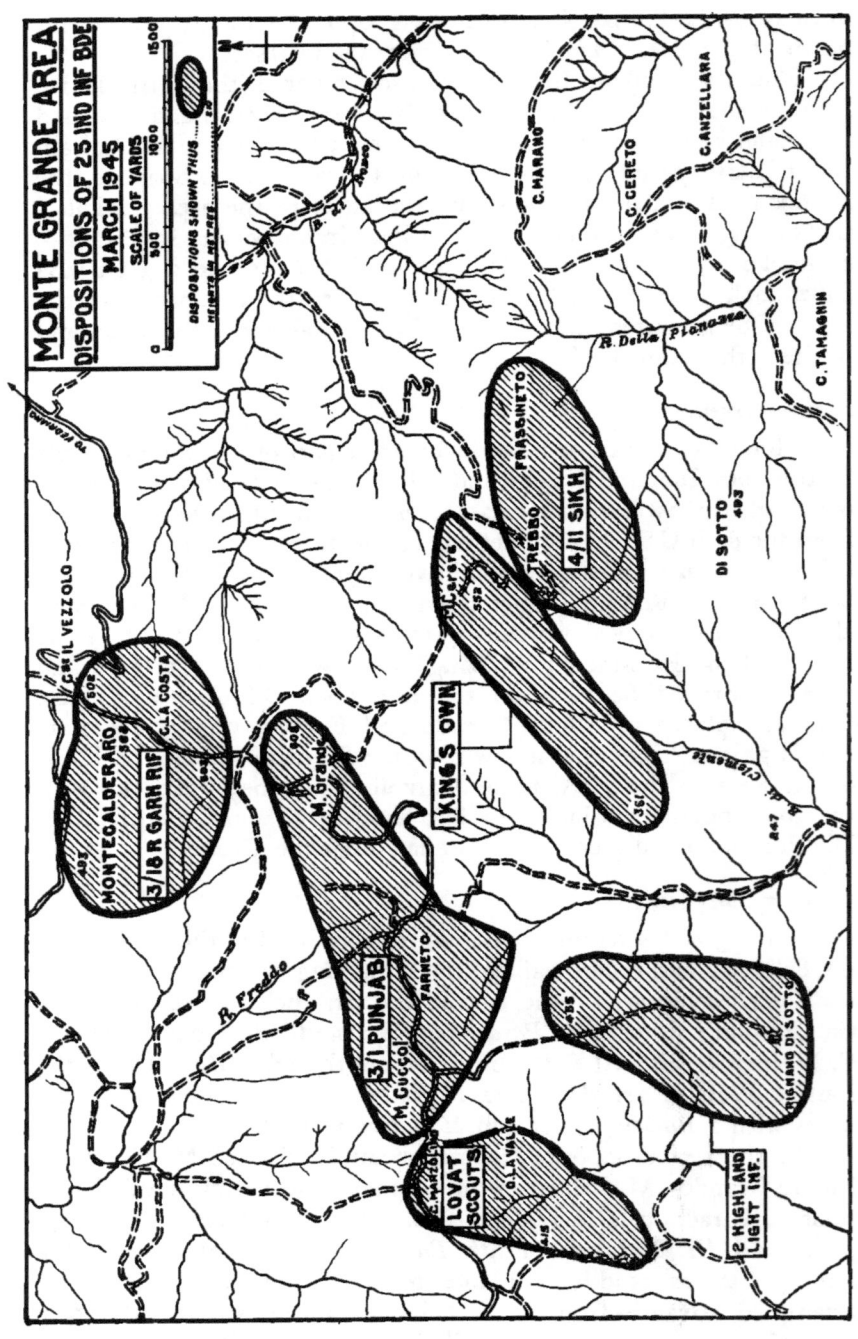

the Germans. Monte Grande was the key feature of the whole of this sector; M. Cerrere was especially important because its loss to the Allies would be very serious as that might threaten the rear of Monte Grande, while the forward positions at M. Calderaro might be tempting in their apparent isolation from the rest of the sector. Recapture by the Germans of any of the Indian positions between M. Cerrare and the area of C. Marzolina would seriously endanger the remaining Indian positions astride the Sillaro valley.[3]

West of the sector of the *1st Parachute Division*, the 305th *Infantry Division* was responsible, with 577th *Grenadier Regiment* on its left flank.

Patrolling Activity

A raid on C. Nuova was carried out by the Nabha Akal on 13 March. The raiding party consisting of a Viceroy's Commissioned Officer and 12 Other Ranks, attacked under cover of a smoke screen. They encountered three Germans in a slit trench. Whilst engaging them, the Nabha Akal was attacked by a strong German patrol from C. Nuova, which was repulsed after an exchange of fire.

On 17 March a forward company of 4/10 Baluch was the victim of a raid. During the night of 19/20 March a fighting patrol of the strength of one platoon from 1/2 Punjab reached the area near C. Nuova where it was engaged by mortar and machine gun fire. Fierce hand-to-hand fighting ensued during which the latter suffered losses.

At 0330 hours on 23 March an attempt was made by a German raiding party, estimated to be of the strength of two platoons, to dislodge 3/5 Mahratta from an outpost on Pt. 358, but without success. As against this, a long-range patrol of 4/10 Baluch returned on 25 March, having penetrated to about 3000 yards behind the German line in the direction of the Sillustra Valley.

Similarly on 26 March at 2030 hours a patrol of one platoon of 1/2 Punjab carried out a raid on the C. Nuova area. A firm base was established just west of the objective, a little forward of a culvert, which was held in spite of mortar fire. On 1 April another fighting patrol of 1/2 Punjab directed against Pt. 273 was engaged by automatic fire from a dug-out on the ridge. The patrol withdrew after an exchange of fire.

Again on the night of 2/3 April a patrol of the Nabha Akal on its way to the Merlo ridge engaged some German troops in slit trenches with grenades and Thompson machine carbines. The Germans returned the fire.

At 0135 hours on 4 April, a German raiding party estimated

[3] Appx. A to 10 Ind. Div. O.O. No. 13, dated 8 March 1945.

to be about one platoon strong, attacked the left forward company of 2 Loyal Regiment. After confused fighting the Germans were driven off. About the same time 4/11 Sikh at Frassineto was attacked by a German force in some strength. The Germans were repulsed. At 0300 hours the Germans repeated the attack but were once again driven off.

Planning went on during this period for offensive action should it be necessary. The attack, as planned, was to secure the Bursano-Mezzano—Vedriano features, exploiting up to M. Catellazzo with the 10th Indian Infantry Brigade, while subsequently, the 20th Indian Infantry Brigade would advance astride the Sillaro Valley. All preparations were well under way and there was a general feeling of confidence in the outcome, when two days before the attack was to take place, the division was ordered away to another area.

Between 4 and 7 April, the 10th Indian Infantry Brigade was relieved on Monte Del Verro and Monte Spaduro. Regrouping continued with the object of relieving as much of the division as possible and concentrating in the Monte Grande sector those battalions which could not initially accompany it. However, in the course of the regrouping a complication arose when the Germans began to show signs of pulling back on the 10th Indian Division front. It was indeed a difficult position of having to re-group and at the same time to keep the maximum pressure on the Germans. On 12 April, the 20th Indian Infantry Brigade found C. Nuova, C. Silaro and C. Tromba unoccupied and promptly stepped up to these positions. Limited advances continued during the day, and at last light firm positions were established at Cereto and Amzellaro. This German withdrawal was to conform with other withdrawals on their left as a result of the Eighth Army offensive in the plains. It was evident, however, that there were no signs of any loosening on Monte Grande, on which their whole line hinged. The 20th Indian Infantry Brigade eventually got up to a position at C. Munano and C. Volta, where heavy German shelling and mortaring were encountered. But by 16 April, the 10th Indian Division was on its way to join the Eighth Army offensive in the Po Valley.

CHAPTER XXXI

The Senio Defence Line

With the setting in of winter the pace of advance slowed down and during the cold weather of 1944-45 operations were practically at a standstill. But the interval was utilised for preparation for the mighty Spring offensive which was to lead to a decisive victory. We shall now briefly describe the part played by the Indian formations in the warfare during this forced static period. The Germans had meanwhile stabilised on the Senio defence line up to which the 10th Indian Infantry Brigade had also continued its progress. By 20 December the brigade was well established on the east bank of the Senio in the area of C. Plica—Tebano, but the attempts to establish bridge-heads on the Senio had been largely unsuccessful. The divisional commander then decided to concentrate on improving the lines of communications. Field Companies of the Indian Sappers, Indian Pioneers, the reserve companies of infantry battalions and the newly arrived Jodhpur Sirdar Light Infantry were employed in maintaining the existing tracks or in constructing new ones. So bad was the surface that long stretches of track were made of stripped tree trunks, laid across the track-way. A further complication was that the last stretch of the track forward to the river was visible to, and under small arms fire from, the German posts on the west bank, only four hundred yards away.

Reorganisation

On 20 December, the 20th Indian Infantry Brigade came up on the left of the 10th Indian Infantry Brigade, assuming command of the sector between the 10th Indian Infantry Brigade and the II Polish Corps. The patrols from 2/3 Gurkha and 1/2 Punjab probed into German positions on the west bank. They discovered that the German forward posts in the area of M. Ghebbio were located at Casacce, Pt. 147, Casana, C. Monte dell Olio and C. Tomba. Consequently planning proceeded on the basis that the 10th Indian Division would attack the German positions west of the Senio, with the 10th Indian Infantry Brigade on the right and the 20th Indian Infantry Brigade on the left. Again and again, however, the attack was postponed until, finally, the move of the 10th Indian Division elsewhere excluded the division from participating in it. In view of the repeated postponement of the divisional attack, a platoon which was holding a forward position on the west bank of the river opposite C. Plica was withdrawn to the east bank on the night of 26/27 December, after it had been observed by the Germans and shelled and mortared.

In the first week of January 1945 the divisional sector was extended. The right sector of the 25th Indian Infantry Brigade (which relieved the 10th Indian Infantry Brigade on 1/2 January 1945) was extended to include the ground which had been held by the left brigade of the 2nd New Zealand Division. This new sector took the 10th Indian Division up to 300 yards of Route 9 (i.e. up to excluding the river bend near Lugaccio). The left divisional sector was held by the 20th Indian Infantry Brigade. On the divisional sector the Germans were holding with *71st Panzer Grenadier Regiment* of the *29th Panzer Grenadier Division* from Route 9 to Biancanigo, from where the *90th Panzer Grenadier Division* was responsible as far west as M. Ghebbio.[1]

Along the whole divisional front the Senio river had steep banks and wound about considerably, there being few if any straight stretches. From Route 9 to Tebano, the ground sloped gradually on the eastern side of the river to the Loghetto ridge overlooking Tebano itself. Thus in this sector, the ground was favourable for the Indian troops though all the forward slopes were observed by the Germans. From Tebano to the left of the divisional area, the river bent southward with the dominating ground on the other side of the river, namely the M. Querzola—M. Ghabbio features rising to 785 feet.[2]

The V Corps regrouped in the beginning of January. On 7 January 1945 Headquarters II Polish Corps was withdrawn and the V Corps took command of the 5th Kresowa Division. Its wide sector along the Senio extended on the right from a point about a mile south of Cotignola to the boundary with the XIII Corps west of Monte Delle Volpe. This sector was held by the 56th Division on the right, the 2nd New Zealand Division and the 10th Indian Division in the centre and the 5th Kresowa Division on the left.

Patrolling in the Right Sector

On 5 January 1945, the 25th Indian Infantry Brigade had extended its front from excluding the bend in the river Senio near Lugaccio to the stream river junction near Tebano. This sector was held by 3/18 Garhwal on the right, 4/11 Sikh in the middle and 3/1 Punjab on the left.[3] The task of this brigade was to prevent the Germans from crossing the river Senio from Lugaccio to Tebano.

---

[1] 10 Ind. Div. Defence Scheme No. 1, dated 16 January 1945; War Diary 10 Ind. Div.
[2] 10 Ind. Div. Narrative of Operations, 601/8328/H.
[3] 1st King's Own Royal Regiment relieved 3/1 Punjab on the near bank of the Senio on 15 January 1945.

The forward battalions were to be responsible for watching the river line, which was to be covered at night by listening posts or standing patrols, whose task was threefold—to destroy the Germans crossing the river, to delay and give warning of any major attack, and to prevent the hostile forces from consolidating the northern bank.[4] From the forward defended localities of the 25th Indian Infantry Brigade the country sloped gently opposite Route 9 and more steeply opposite Casale to the river line. The German forward defended localities on the far bank were therefore in full view.[5]

During January 1945 the tempo of raids and counter-raids tended to increase. Loops in the river were frequently the scenes of clashes. C. Colombarina, standing in a very narrow loop, changed hands several times.

Energetic German patrolling finally reached a climax on the night of 11/12 January, when after a considerable artillery harassing programme, a force estimatd to be of the strength of one company crossed the river at two places, formed up south of the river, and attacked 3/18 Garhwal at Braghitona di Solto. Supported by bazookas and mortars the attack was sudden and quick, but it was repulsed and the Germans were forced to retreat by 3/18 Garhwal. The Germans re-formed three times and made three further attacks. On these occasions they approached crawling and tried to infiltrate into the Garhwal positions, but each time they were driven back by small arms and defensive fire.

At 0830 hours on 14 January, 4/11 Sikh sent a raiding party of platoon strength to the houses occupied by the Germans. The patrol rushed to the rear of one of the houses and was met by four Germans who opened fire. After a short exchange of fire the Germans withdrew to the next house under cover of smoke grenades.

On 15 January 1945, two platoons of 3/18 Garhwal, supported by two tanks and artillery, moved forward to the area near Baganarina. Tanks engaged the houses at Ghiarona with 75-mm machine gun fire followed by infantry assault. After a fierce struggle the Germans were forced to withdraw.

At 1930 hours on 23 January, a platoon of 3/18 Garhwal, supported by one troop of tanks, raided Braghitona di Sotto but was unable to reach its objective.

The 25th Indian Infantry Brigade brought this period of activities to a successful close with another raid on Braghitona di Sotto. At 0700 hours on 8 February a platoon of 4/11 Sikh approached the objective undetected by the Germans, rushed the posts, and inflicted some losses on the defenders.

[4] 25 Ind. Inf. Bde. O.O. No. 1, dated 4 January 1945.
[5] Operation 'Freeze'—appreciation of the situation by commander 10 Ind. Div., dated 31 January 1945; War Diary 10 Ind. Div.

Patrolling in the Left Sector

On the left sector the Indian troops dominated the river line from Monte Coralli ridge but not as effectively as on the right. On this flank there was no actual depth to the river line positions and the German reserves were therefore sited on the Ghebbio ridge. The Ghebbio-Quezzola ridge covered any crossing of the Senio river from Guffiano north to Biancanigo, and was divided into two distinct features ;

    (a) The spur Ghebbio-Tomba, thence north-east to Campiano. This ridge covered the river line from Guffiano north to Rio di Sotto.

    (b) The second spur ran from Quezzola to Borgo and covered any crossing from Tebano northward.

The Indian troops could carry out the initial crossing only if the Tomba-Campiano spurs were captured. Any crossing in the Tebano area or any advance in the plain towards Castel Bolognese was however dominated by the Quezzola-Borga spur.

The left sector was held by the 20th Indian Infantry Brigade till 24 January 1945, when it was relieved by the 10th Indian Infantry Brigade. The 20th Indian Infantry Brigade was disposed on the east bank of the Senio with 3/5 Mahratta on the right and 1/2 Punjab on the left. The task of the brigade was to operate offensively in the area between C. Varnelli Zula spur and the river Senio and prevent German patrols from crossing the Senio or German infiltration into the area. The defence plan was that the forward battalions would maintain one company each as outpost on the east bank of the Senio and one company each in reserve for immediate counter-attack.

The weather was bad and heavy snow fell. Strong blizzard hampered the patrolling to a great extent. The visibility at times was reduced to ten yards. The Germans were dug in on the high ground of M. Ghebbio overlooking the river Senio. Vigorous reconnaissance patrolling was continued and very useful information obtained. Many attempts were made to secure prisoners by determined fighting patrols as well, but the Germans changed positions and were not found in the various areas visited by these patrols.[7]

On 24 January 1945, the 20th Indian Infantry Brigade was relieved by the 10th Indian Infantry Brigade. 4/10 Baluch and 2/4 Gurkha held the forward positions. The general lull along the front was broken on 29 January 1945 when a German raiding party crossed the river in fair strength and raided the forward Baluch positions at C. Plica—C. Cassana. Accurate defensive fire, however, drove them off. Except for vigorous patrolling and considerable road construction work by the Sappers the period from 1 January

---

[7] Appendix J-1 ; War Diary 1/2 Punjab, January 1945.

to 8 February 1945, had been rather uneventful. The weather continued to be bad with either rain or severe frosts and snow to make the life of the forward infantry men far from comfortable.

Regrouping of the V Corps

The V Corps had regrouped at the end of January 1945, and its front was extended to the north as far as the railway bridge across the Senio, east of Lugo. Further regrouping took place between 7 and 13 February 1945. The corps now held a small sector from the Russi—Lugo railway to Route 9, with the 56 (British) Division (with the 43rd Indian Infantry Brigade under its command) on the right and the 2nd New Zealand Division on the left.

On 16 February 1945, the V Corps sector was extended when it took command of the 1 Canadian Corps sector from the Lugo—Russi railway to the Adriatic coast at the south-east tip of Lake Comacchio. The Cremona Combat Group, on the right of this sector, passed directly under the command of the V Corps. The 1st Canadian Infantry Division remained on the left of the new sector until relieved by the 8th Indian Division between 23 and 25 February. The 8th Indian Division had two brigades in the line—the 21st Indian Infantry Brigade and the 17th Indian Infantry Brigade.

Further regrouping took place between 3 and 11 March 1945. The 5th Kresowa Division (II Polish Corps) relieved the 2nd New Zealand Division along the Senio to a point just south of San Savero. The 43rd Indian Infantry Brigade, which had been operating under the command of the 56th British Division, was relieved by a British brigade and joined the II Polish Corps. The 56th Division was itself relieved by the 78th British Division. The 2nd Armoured Brigade was relieved by the Jewish Brigade and the 19th Indian Infantry Brigade. The 2nd Commando Brigade plus the 12th Lancers relieved the 17th Indian Infantry Brigade. Other reliefs followed in quick succession but these need not be described here. Sufficient account has been given of the regrouping of the V Corps to enable a proper appreciation of the role of the Indian formations—43rd Indian Infantry Brigade and the 8th Indian Division—in this static warfare.

Operations of the 43rd Indian Infantry Brigade

We shall first describe the operations of the 43rd Indian Infantry Brigade. This brigade passed under the command of the 56th Division on 10 February 1945. Its task was to relieve Recforce (the 12th Lancers and the Skinner's Horse) and the London Irish Rifles in the Senio line. This five thousand yard front stretched from the railway line between Bagnacavallo and Lugo down to the sharp bend in the river, half a mile south of Cotingola. 2/8 Gurkha

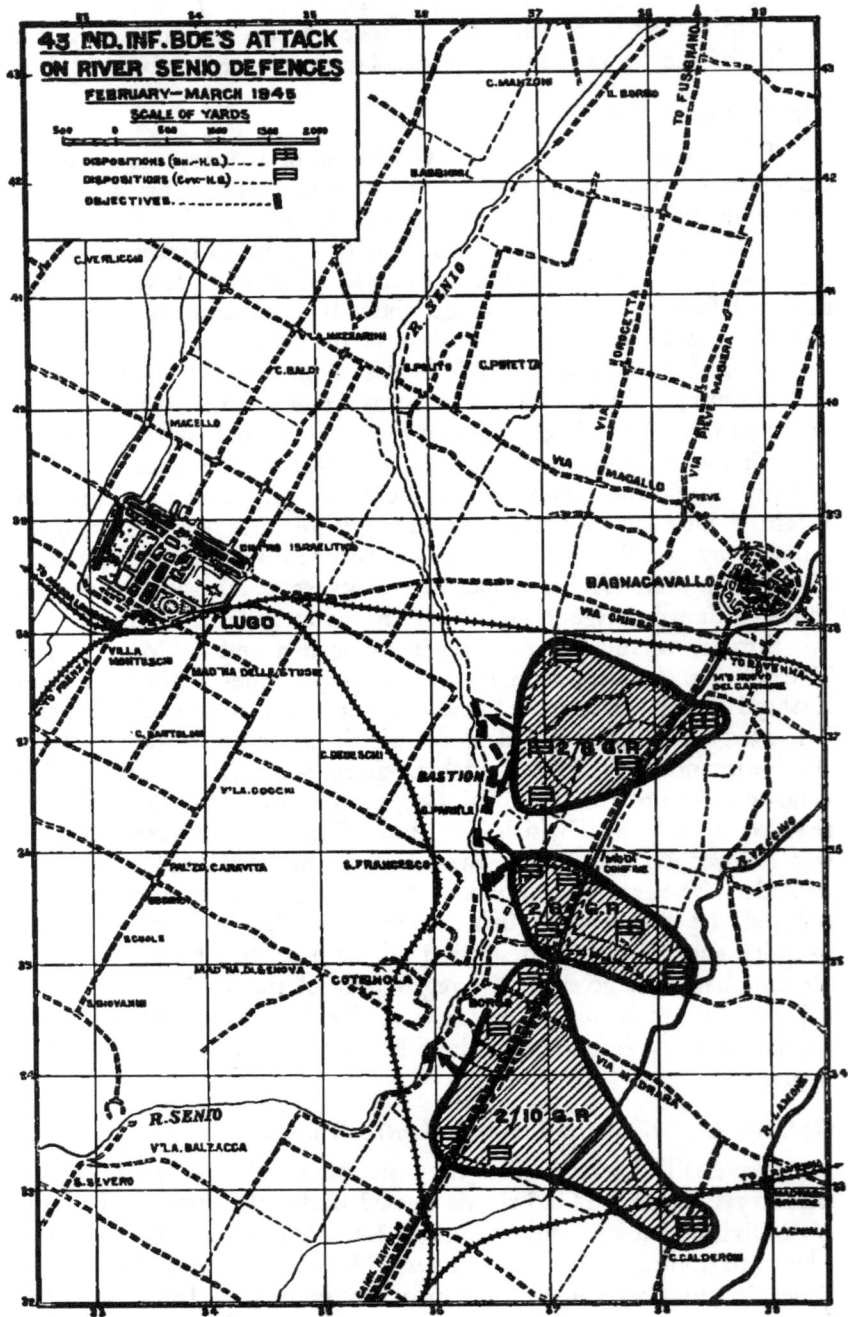

on the right took over from the 12 Lancers during the night of 12/13 February. 2/10 Gurkha, on the left, relieved the London Irish Rifles in the succeeding night. 2/6 Gurkha completed relief of the Skinner's Horse on the third night. The Brigade Support Group, less one platoon 4.2" mortars relieved the machine gunners of the 6th Battalion Cheshire Regiment. When the reliefs were completed the V Corps sector from the Russi—Lugo railway to Route 9 was held by the 56th British Division on the right, and the 2nd New Zealand Division on the left.

The Germans held the eastern bank of the river. Flood banks, twenty feet high and six feet wide at the top, afforded them full view of the whole ground to the east and made reconnaissance by day almost impossible. And in the flood banks they had dug elaborate defences. The banks and their approaches were thickly wired and mined. Mortars and artillery were more numerous than anything which the Germans had been able to muster for many a day.

The foremost positions taken over by Gurkhas were at distances varying between one hundred and four hundred yards from the bank. Before a crossing over the river was attempted, it was necessary to secure the eastern bank. This was the task allotted to the 43rd Indian Infantry Brigade. Ten days were devoted to preparations for the attack. There was detailed reconnaissance of the routes and objectives. Intensive study of, and practice in, rapid consolidation in the peculiar country before them were continuous. And all the time, a tidying up of the front continued.

Patrols discovered that the Germans were crossing the river by a number of foot bridges, the locations of which were frequently changed. Tunnels piercing the eastern flood-bank provided covered routes to the observation posts, machine gun and sniper's posts. Some of the houses along the banks were held by the Germans and others were booby-trapped.

The commander of the 56th Division planned to drive out the Germans from the east bank of the river Senio. On the left, the 167th Infantry Brigade was to establish defensive posts on the east bank from including 353337 southwards. On the right the 43rd Indian Infantry Brigade was to maintain defensive positions on the near flood bank with the object of dominating subsequently the east bank of the river.[8] The latter task was to be carried out as follows:

    (a) On the right sector, 2/8 Gurkha was to advance on a two company front. On the right B Company (with two forward platoons) was to secure bulge in the flood bank at 364373 and bend in the flood bank at 364371; on the left C Company (with two forward platoons) was to secure the Bastion at 365367 and the area of the blow at 364364.

[8] 56 British Division O.O. No. 17, dated 13 February 1945.

A Company was to watch the open right flank, particularly in the area due east of C. Ricci.

(b) In the middle sector, 2/6 Gurkha was to advance with one platoon of D Company directed on the bend in the flood bank at 363362 and one platoon of B Company on the flood bank at 364357.

(c) On the left sector a platoon of D Company of 2/10 Gurkha was to secure the flood bank at 359342.[9]

The 43rd Indian Infantry Brigade was to launch its attack at 2100 hours on 23 February along almost the whole of its front. Approximately midway between the railway and Cotignola, the Germans had blown a gap in the east bank at 364364 by which they hoped to flood the lower ground east of the river.[10] Particular objectives of the 43rd Indian Infantry Brigade were, therefore, the bank north and south of this gap, a strong-point, 'the Bastion', four hundred yards north of the gap, and certain bends in the river from which observation along its banks would be possible. C Squadron 2nd Royal Tank Regiment and support troop Skinner's Horse were under the command of the brigade for the operations.

The three Gurkha battalions attacked at 2100 hours on 23 February. On the right B and C Companies of 2/8 Gurkha captured their objectives without much opposition by 0033 hours on 24 February; A Company guarding the right flank was however heavily mortared. On the left too a platoon of D Company of 2/10 Gurkha secured its objective without much opposition at 2345 hours on 23 February, but it was subjected to spandau fire from Casa di Sopra. 2/6 Gurkha in the middle was however up against considerable opposition. At 2150 hours D Company seized its objective (363362) but was heavily mortared. B Company encountered fierce opposition and suffered heavy losses. At 2235 hours on 23 February, a platoon of A Company was sent to reinforce B Company. German pressure however continued. At 2315 hours a German counterattack against the centre section of D Company was repulsed. At 2330 hours C Company sent one section along the river bank to help the left flank of B Company. At 0630 hours on 24 February, the forward platoon of D Company was counter-attacked but held firm. Another counter-attack against the same platoon shortly afterwards at 0645 hours on 24 February was repulsed. In spite of the repeated attempts of the Germans to recapture lost ground the Gurkha forward companies held firm.

The three Gurkha battalions had secured their first objectives and between them held some four thousand yards of the east bank of the Senio. They dug into the bank and constructed posts with

---

[9] 43 Ind. Inf. Bde. O.O. No. 3, dated 23 February 1945.
[10] 2/8 G.R. O.O. No. 1, dated 23 February 1945.

overhead cover against grenades. Large supplies of the high explosive grenades (No. 36) and of the smoke grenade (No. 77) were carried forward, grenades being the common weapon of combat, so close were the forward positions on both sides. The initial attack had produced considerable reaction on the part of the Germans which assumed the form of heavy mortar concentrations and artillery defensive fire on the whole brigade front throughout the night. German counter-attacks also developed. They still held the inner side of the eastern bank. A fusillade of grenades was thrown at the Gurkha troops as they consolidated. German automatic weapons, firing from the river bends, were very worrying. At 1545 hours on 24 February the forward platoon of D Company of 2/6 Gurkha was counter-attacked. The Germans were dispersed by a hail of grenades, 3-inch mortar, machine-gun and 25-pounders' defensive fire. At 2250 hours on 24 February a small German counter-attack on the right forward platoon of B Company of 2/8 Gurkha was repulsed. The strain of this continuous close quarter struggle on all ranks was severe. Nevertheless, the Gurkhas gradually gained the ascendancy until, in the end, the Germans themselves could not cross the river by day without suffering losses.

German efforts reached a climax on the night of 26/27 February when 2/8 Gurkha had to bear the brunt of the attack. At 2145 hours on 26 February, the Germans heavily shelled the battalion area. It was followed by an attack at 2150 hours on the right forward platoon of C Company in the area of the Bastion. This attack was accompanied by a diversionary demonstration on 2/6 Gurkha sector also. The German attack was successful and the Gurkha platoon was driven out of the Bastion area. At 0954 hours on 27 February, however, the commanding officer of 2/8 Gurkha ordered A Company to hold C Company's base and thus permit the latter to recapture the Bastion area. A platoon of C Company led the attack at 1035 hours and at 1105 hours secured the Bastion area. A German counter-attack however drove the platoon off the Bastion at 1220 hours. A further attack on the Bastion with one platoon from A Company and one from C Company, with artillery and 3" mortar support, at 1500 hours was unsuccessful owing to German reinforcements and accurate spandau fire.

A series of moves was then carried out in order to rest the very tired 2/8 Gurkha. 2/5 Queens relieved 2/10 Gurkha who, in turn, relieved the forward companies of 2/8 Gurkha.

The attack on the Bastion was put in at 2100 hours on 1 March 1945, when B Company of 2/10 Gurkha attempted to put two platoons on to the river bank at 365367. One platoon was established but the other suffered 22 casualties and withdrew.

On 3 March, the 167th Brigade came into the area occupied by the 43rd Indian Infantry Brigade and the Gurkhas pulled out for rest.

The 8th Indian Division in the Senio Line

We shall now take up the operations of the other Indian formation—the 8th Indian Division. On leaving the Serchio Valley on 10 January 1945, the 8th Indian Division concentrated in the foot-hills which overlook the river Arno and the city of Pisa. Although it was still mid-winter, there were many days of warm sunshine, which gave added charm to a delightful country-side.. The division rested amid such congenial surroundings. On 9 February it was recalled to the Eighth Army and was ordered to concentrate in the area of Forli on the Adriatic Coast.[11] At 1230 hours on 25 February, the 8th Indian Division assumed command of the 1st Canadian Division's sector along the line of the Senio river between S. Maria il Palazzone and Bagnacavallo. The sector was a wide one, with the 17th Indian Infantry Brigade on the right flank between S. Maria il Palazzone and the town of Alfonsine east of Route 16, the 2nd Armoured Brigade next to it, while the 21st Indian Infantry Brigade held the arc of the river covering Bagnacavallo. The 19th Indian Infantry Brigade was in reserve with prepared counter-attack tasks. The 21st Tank Brigade, which was to remain under the command of the division almost to the end of the operations, provided armoured support for the whole sector.[12] On the left flank was the 43rd Indian Infantry Brigade, which at that time, was under the command of the 56th British Division.

The 8th Indian Division also regrouped when the V Corps regrouped between 3 and 7 March 1945. On the night of 4/5 March, the 2nd Commando Brigade took over the sector of the 17th Indian Infantry Brigade east of Alfonsine and Route 16; on 5 March, the Jewish Brigade, which had come under command two days earlier, relieved the 2nd Armoured Brigade south of Alfonsine.

On 11 March 1945, Major-General D. Russell returned from England and took over command from Brigadier T.S. Dobree, who had been officiating in his absence.

On the night of 14 March, the 17th Indian Infantry Brigade relieved the 21st Indian Infantry Brigade, which held the area between Fusignano and Bagnacavallo. On 24 March the Jewish Brigade left the division after handing over its sector to an Italian formation called the Cremona Group. More reliefs followed. On the night of 24/25 March, the 21st Indian Infantry Brigade took over from the 19th Indian Infantry Brigade in the sector east of Fusignano. Finally on the morning of 9 April 1945, on the eve of

---

[11] 8 Ind. Div. O.O. No. 40, dated 9 February 1945.
[12] 8 Ind. Div. News Letters October/April 1945, File 601/7310/11.

the Spring offensive, the division was disposed between Fusignano and Bagnacavallo with the 19th Indian Infantry Brigade on the right, the 21st Indian Infantry Brigade on the left, and the 17th Indian Infantry Brigade in reserve.

The Germans were everywhere holding the flood banks on both sides of the river. The *362nd Infantry Division* held the sector immediately opposite the 8th Indian Division with *362nd Fusilier Battalion* in reserve. This German division was formed during the early part of 1944. In the battles following the break-out from Anzio bridge-head, it was severely mauled and was reformed by absorbing the remnants of the *92nd Infantry Division*. The division suffered heavy casualties in the fierce fighting north of Florence and reappeared, almost as a new formation, in the sector south of Bologna in late December. From there, it was rushed across to the Adriatic front, marching all the way. It was commanded by General Greiner, an ardent Nazi, who was reported to have said on one occasion, that his formation would continue to fight until it could be fed from a single company mess. Generally speaking the morale of the division was high.[13]

Until the gigantic offensive, which the Eighth Army was to launch across the Senio river in April 1945, the 8th Indian Division found itself engaged in purely static warfare. In the two banks of the Senio, the *362nd Infantry Division* had excellent defences prepared by the German civilian Todt organisation. Both the floodbanks resembled a human "rabbit warren" where, deep into the earth, huge tunnels had been driven and skilfully rivetted with stout timber. Leading off from these main arteries were large bunkers, each containing three or four beds and some furniture. In these bunkers the Germans were quite immune from anything but a direct hit from a heavy bomb. Their machine gun nests were built inside the earthwork. The flood-banks had been burrowed through and the ends of tunnels opened out on the sides of the bank like portholes from the side of a ship. Poking out of these holes were the ugly muzzles of scores of German machine guns. From their positions on the flood-bank, the German infantry had an excellent view of Indian forward posts between the rows of vines and olive groves, which separated the opposing forces. Here and there, the approaches to the eastern flood-bank were mined and wired and there were more mines and wire on the reverse slope of the near bank.

The Germans held the flood-banks on both the eastern and western sides of the river, although at one or two places the Indian troops had established posts on the near side of the eastern floodbank. At these points, only a few yards separated the opposing infantry, who spent days and nights in an atmosphere of great

[13] 8 Ind. Div. Intelligence Summary No. 176, dated 17 February 1945.

nervous tension; frequently, furious grenade fights broke out. A grenade would be lobbed over from the German side of the bank by an unseen opponent; back would go a British Mills' bomb. Soon, what silence there might have been, would be shattered by the explosions of grenade after grenade as German stick grenades and British Mills' bomb sailed backward and forward over the bank to explode. Occasionally, home-made devices of a lethal nature, which both sides invented, were tried out. Barrels of explosives, fitted with home fuses would come rolling down the bank to explode in Indian positions; German teller mines, which had been set with ingenious cunning, were used for the same purpose.

Although this period of static fighting was unpleasant, it gave the officers and men of the 8th Indian Division numerous opportunities to gain information which was invaluable when the time came for the final assault.

CHAPTER XXXII

The Plan

Rival Forces

During the winter of 1944-1945 when the Allied front in Italy ran from the Commacchio lagoon on the Adriatic to the south of Bologna and thence to just below Massa on the Ligurian Sea, feverish preparations had been made for the Spring offensive. D Day was 9 April 1945. The Allied forces were regrouped and ready for the attack. The Fifth Army held the mountainous line from Massa to Monte Grande, whence began the sector of the Eighth Army extending to the Commacchio lagoon on the Adriatic. The Eighth Army, the spear-head of the Allied attack, was to open the offensive on a two-corps front—the V Corps whose sector extended from the Adriatic to the south of Lugo and the II Polish Corps astride Route 9. The former had under its command, from right to left, the 56th British Division, Cremona Combat Group, 8th Indian Division, 78th British Division and 2nd New Zealand Division. The II Polish Corps had under its command the 3rd Carpathian Division, 5th Kresowa Division, 2nd Polish Armoured Brigade, 7th Armoured Brigade and 43rd Indian Infantry Brigade. The role of the X Corps (from excluding Route 9 to south of Imola) and the XIII Corps (from south of Imola to Monte Grande) was to simulate attack on other fronts to distract the German attention from the focal point of attack. The former had under its command the Jewish Infantry Brigade Group and the Friuli Combat Group while the latter had under its command the 10th Indian Division and the Folgone Combat Group. The 6th British Armoured Division and the 2nd Parachute Brigade were in Army reserve.

General Vietinghoff, who had taken over command of the *Army Group C* from Field Marshal Kesselring on 23 March 1945, had at his disposal on 9 April twenty-three German and four Italian divisions, in addition to various minor formations. The German ground forces consisted of the *Tenth* and the *Fourteenth Armies* and the *Army Liguria*. The American Fifth Army was opposed by the *Fourteenth Army*. The *Tenth Army* facing the Eighth Army consisted of the *1 Parachute Corps* (from Monte Grande to Route 9) and the *LXXVI Panzer Corps* from north of Route 9 to the Adriatic. The former held its sector, from right to left, with the *305th Infantry Division, 1st Parachute Division, 278th Infantry Division, 4th Parachute Division* and *26th Panzer Division*. The latter held its sector,

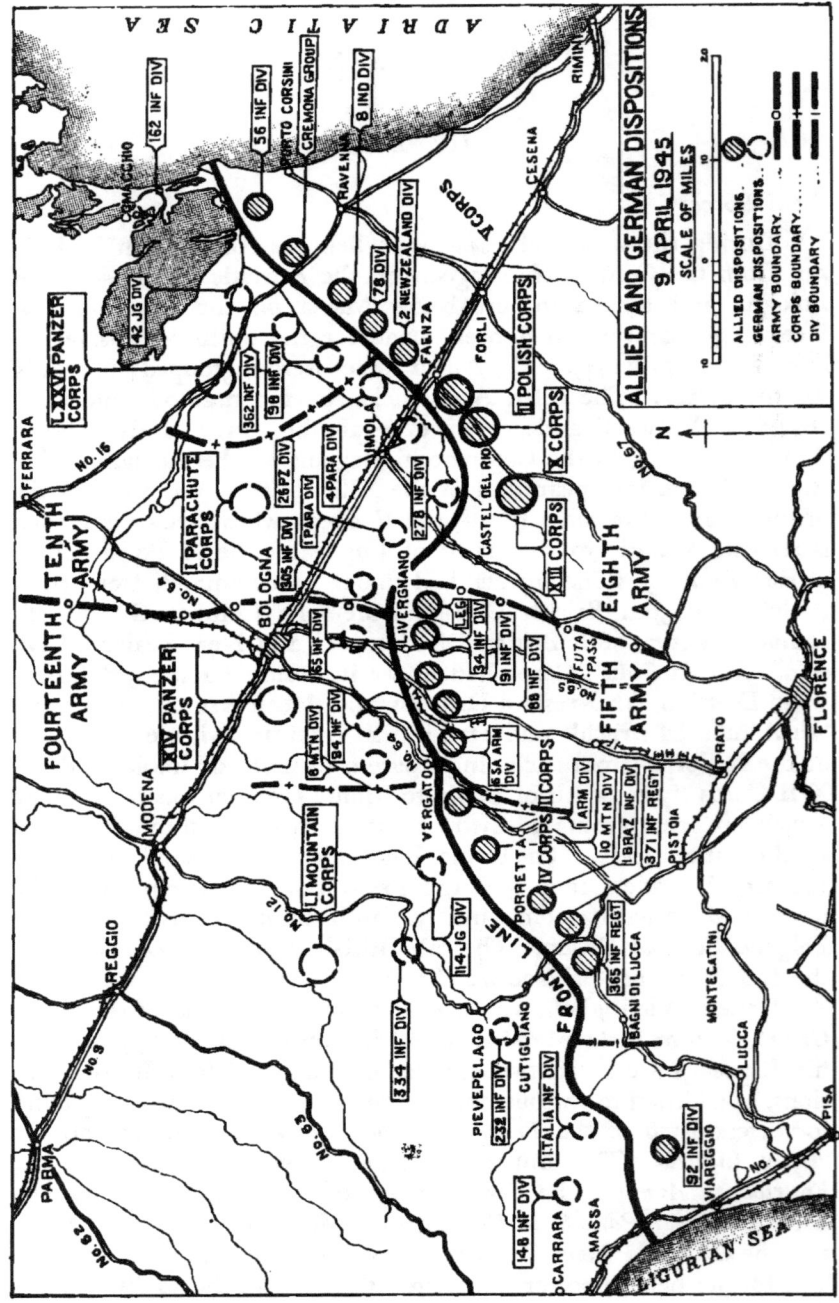

from right to left, with the *98th Infantry Division, 362nd Infantry Division, 42 Jaegar Division* and *162nd* (Turkoman) *Infantry Division*. The *92th Panzer Grenadier Division* and *155th Infantry Division* were in Army reserve in the area Venice-Treviso.

Fifteenth Army Group's Plan

The aim of the Fifteenth Army Group's Spring offensive was to destroy the German Armies in Italy south of the Po and thus prevent their escape north-east into the Alps towards Austria, from where they might prolong the struggle. It was not an easy task. The Germans had taken up strong positions in the rugged mountains on the west flank. On the east flank they had built up strong defensive positions behind the rivers Senio, Sillaro, Po and Adige. In spite of the fact that the German defence lines in Europe were fast crumbling under the blows of the Allies, General Vietinghoff made determined efforts to retain his hold on northern Italy. The excellent German morale evoked the admiration of even the enemies. General Alexander has paid well-deserved tribute to the German soldiers:

"German morale was, as always excellent. All efforts of Allied propaganda had remained fruitless. Even our crushing superiority in the air, which we knew from our own experience earlier in the war to be a most potent source of discouragement, did not appear to have affected the spirits of the German troops. What was even more astonishing and, it must be admitted, admirable was that not even the obvious imminence of the complete collapse of the armies defending the Fatherland had seduced the German soldier from his military duty or weakened his resolve to resist."[1]

The Fifteenth Army Group's plan to destroy the German Armies south of the Po was, first, to threaten the German left flank, thus drawing off their reserves, and then to strike at the centre. This plan was to be carried out in three phases. In the first phase, the Eighth Army was to open the offensive on 9 April, break through the Senio and Santerno defences and advance towards Bastia and Budrio. The Fifth Army's offensive was to follow the Eighth Army's at a date to be chosen by General Clark. The Fifth Army was to debouch from the mountains into the Po Valley, with the secondary object of capturing or isolating Bologna. As a preliminary to the main attack, two subsidiary operations were to be carried out with the object of capturing Massa on the west and securing a hold in the area of Lake Comacchio on the Adriatic. In the second phase the Eighth Army was to advance through the Argenta Gap and seize the Po crossings at Ferrara and Bondeno. The Fifth Army's columns were to exploit in the corridor between the Peno and Panaro

[1] General Alexander's Despatch, 12 December 1944 to 2 May 1945, pp. 39-40.

rivers with a view to joining the Eighth Army in the Bondeno or Ferrara area, thereby completing the encirclement of the German forces south of the Po. A secondary Fifth Army effort was to be made from S. Giovanni northward on Ostiglia. The third phase was concerned with the crossing of the Po and the exploitation northward on Verona.[2]

The Eighth Army Plan

The Eighth Army was to break through the Senio defences. The attack was to be made on a two-corps front, with the V Corps on the right and the II Polish Corps on the left, with the main thrust along the axis Bagnacavallo—Lugo—Massa Lombarda. When the river Santerno had been crossed, it was to be decided whether the main thrust was to continue westwards to Budrio, or swing northwards to the Argenta Gap.[3]

The X Corps and XIII Corps were to hold their fronts practising active deception. As the operations of the II Polish Corps outflanked or cut off German troops opposing the X Corps, that Corps was to make a general advance towards Route 9. The XIII Corps, after participating in the same deception plan, was to defend its ground and hold the 10th Indian Division in readiness to move either into Army reserve north of Route 9, or to launch a limited attack north-eastward from Monte Grande.

V Corps Plan

As a prelude to the main attack, the V Corps was to carry out three subsidiary operations with the object of strengthening Allied control of the south-eastern corner of lake Comacchio and diverting German attention from the Senio front. These operations were to be carried out by the 56th British Division and the formations under its command. The first attack was to be directed against the 'Spit' (the isthmus between the lake and the Adriatic Sea) and 'Tongue' (the adjacent promontory to the east of the mouth of the river Reno). Next the 'Islands' (lying in the eastern half of the lake) was to be captured. Lastly the 'Wedge' (an area of inundated land immediately north of the confluence of the Senio with the Reno) was to be seized to facilitate the launching of the right hook operations against the Argenta Gap.

The V Corps was to launch the main attack on 9 April. The corps was to break through the Senio and Santerno defences in two phases. In the first phase it was to attack the re-entrant angle of the Senio around Lugo, with the 8th Indian Division on the right and the 2nd New Zealand Division on the left and advance to the

[2] Fifteenth Army Group O.I. No. 4, dated 24 March 1945.
[3] V Corps O.O. No. 48, dated 2 April 1945.

THE PLAN

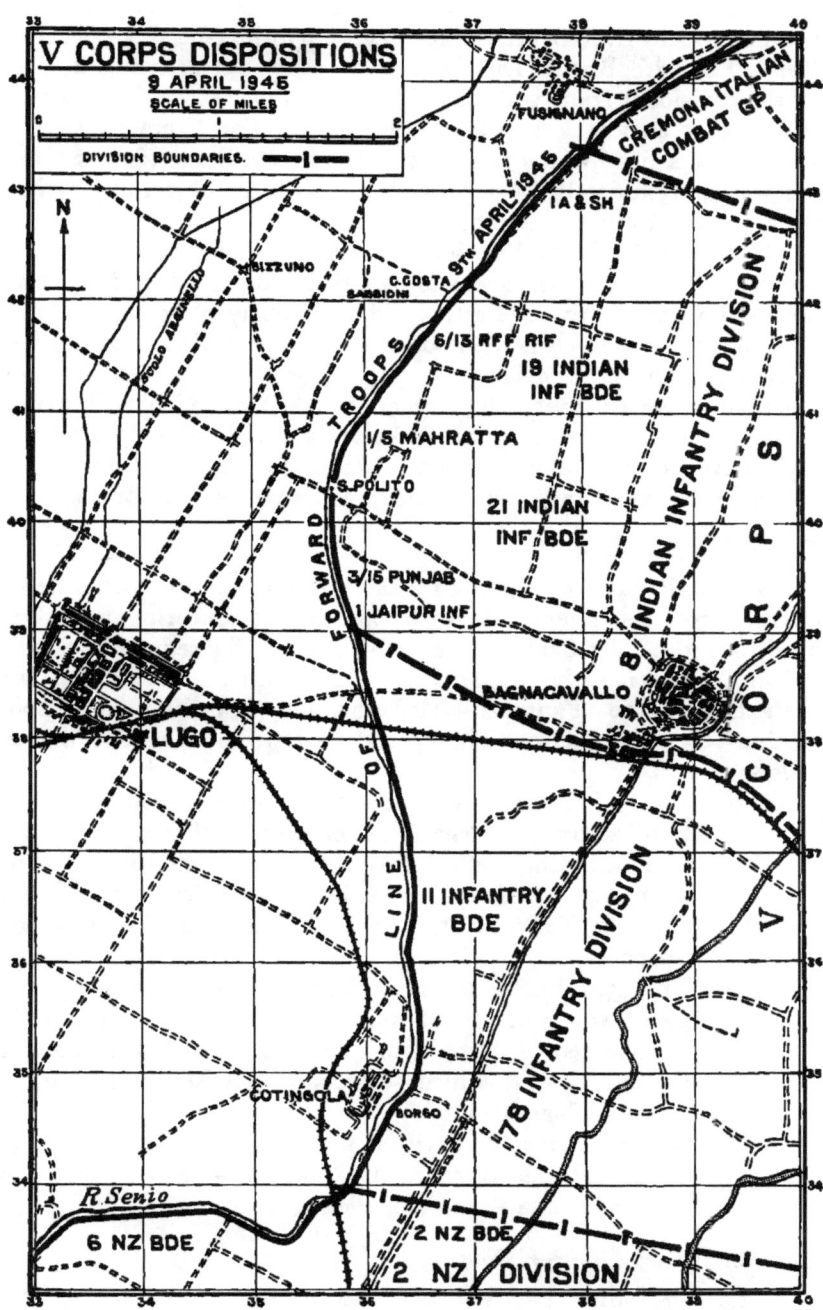

Canal di Lugo. In the second phase both the divisions were to advance to the river Santerno and secure a bridge-head 1500 yards deep. The 78th British Division was to carry out active deception on the divisional front with the object of inducing the Germans to believe that an attack was imminent there. The Cremona Group was to attack northwards from the Fusignano area astride the river Senio at approximately dawn on D plus 1 with the object of clearing the Germans from the Alfonsine pocket.

After the V Corps had secured a bridge-head over the river Santerno, the 78th Division was to pass through the 8th Indian Division and move north on Bastia; simultaneously a brigade of the 56th Division was to cross the flooded area, land at Menata and drive on Bastia. The 78th Division, in conjunction with the 56th Division was then to burst through the Argenta Gap. The 2nd New Zealand Division's role subsequently was either to cover the left flank of the 78th Division and move on axis Massa Lombarda—Conselice—Molinella or to continue the advance westwards towards Budrio.

II Polish Corps Plan

The II Polish Corps was to assault simultaneously with the V Corps, across the river Senio with the task of capturing a bridge-head over the river Santerno up to Mordano. Subsequently the II Polish Corps was to be prepared to exploit with mobile force (*i*) on the axis Mordano—Fantazzo—Medicina, and (*ii*) on the axis Casola Canina—Castel S. Pietro. The operations were to be carried out as follows:

(*i*) The 3rd Carpathian Division was to establish a bridge-head across the river Senio between excluding S. Severo and including Felisio and across the river Santerno to including Mordano. This bridge-head was to link up with the V Corps bridge-head in the area of cross roads Fornace.

(*ii*) The 43rd Indian Infantry Brigade Group was to be prepared subsequently to make a thrust along the axis S. Bartolomeo—L. Ringhiera—Fantazza—Medicina or along the axis S. Bartolomeo—cross-roads La Ringhiera—Castel Guelfo—Poggio Piccolo.

(*iii*) The 5th Kresowa Division was to be prepared to pursue along the axis Bagnara di Romagna—Sasso Morelli—to Casola Canina—Castel S. Pietro.

The 8th Indian Division Plan

The 8th Indian Division was concentrated in a very narrow sector, only a few miles wide, between Fusignano and the railway which linked the town of Lugo with Bagnacavallo. The division had two brigades in the front line—the 19th and the 21st Indian Infantry Brigades—while the 17th Indian Infantry Brigade remained in reserve.

The Senio river formed a line running north-east south-west across the whole front of the Eighth Army; with its forty feet high flood-banks on the east and west side, it was a natural obstacle. On both sides of the Senio and the flood-banks the ground was quite flat; it was one huge network of small fields surrounded by pollards or climbing vines. Fortunately the area possessed a number of good, broad tracks and was well drained by numerous small dykes, which were characteristic of the region. In the event of heavy rain, these water courses prevented extensive flooding although there were small areas near the river which were very liable to flooding.[5]

The Senio river might be better described as an enormous anti-tank ditch; in common with all rivers in very flat country its actual bed was higher than the surrounding country and it was confined by enormous banks. In only a small part of the sector of attack did the Allies have even a footing on the near bank as well as the far bank. In most places the most forward Allied posts were three to five hundred yards from the near banks, and the Germans were able to patrol forward of the river. The slopes of the bank made it very difficult for artillery to reach the Germans dug in on the far sides. The rest of the country was completely flat and visibility was restricted by vines and small trees. In certain places the Germans had been able to clear a field of fire, while their possession of the near flood-bank gave them observation which was denied to the Allies.

The German Senio defensive line had been prepared by the Todt organisation and both flood-banks were honeycombed with strong dug-outs and small well-sited and camouflaged fire positions. The Germans had been occupying it since December 1944 and had ample time to make it a very strong position. Mines had been laid along the far slopes of both the banks, where no form of fire could damage them, and where patrols could not lift them.

West of the river Senio the Germans had well prepared positions along the Canal di Lugo, on the Tratturo, and particularly on the river Santerno. There, the defences were just as highly developed as those of the Senio line. Between the Senio and Santerno rivers, many trees were felled to ensure good fields of fire and where necessary houses too were demolished. Every effort had been made to make the line impregnable.[6]

The Germans were so strongly entrenched on the Senio line that there was not much prospect of success for the infantry assault

---

[5] 8 Ind. Div. News Letter October 1944—April 1945, File 7310/H.
[6] 8th Ind. Div. Planning Note No. 45, dated 7 April; War Diary 8 Ind. Div.

unless the German positions had been subjected to an exceedingly heavy preliminary bombardment. The Air Force was to constitute the chief weapon of bombardment. The attack on the Senio was to be preceded by pattern bombing by heavy bombers. Then the fighter bombers and artillery were to pound known German positions and cross-roads. The attack was to be opened with 'Crocodiles', (i.e. flamethrowers mounted in tanks) and a considerable number of 'Wasps' flaming first the near flood-bank and then the far bank. The infantry assault was then to be launched after the Germans had been thoroughly demoralised by bombardment and a massed attack on their positions by flamethrowers mounted in tanks.

Major-General Russell planned the attack to be made in two phases. Phase I concerned the assault crossing of the river Senio and the advance across the Canal di Lugo and the Scolo Tratturo. Phase II dealt with the task of establishing a bridge-head across the Santerno.

The plan for Phase I was that after intense bombing attacks during the afternoon of 9 April, there was to be a heavy artillery bombardment of the river banks and the German positions behind the Senio, scheduled to last in all for four hours. Then, at 1920 hours, the infantry of the 8th Indian Division would assault and cross the Senio some two miles north-east of Lugo, attacking on a narrow front, with the 19th Indian Infantry Brigade on the right and the 21st Indian Infantry Brigade on the left flank. Each assaulting brigade would be supported by tanks, 'Kangaroos', 'Wasps' and 'Crocodiles'.

The flame-throwing 'Wasps' and 'Crocodiles' were to go ahead of the infantry to scorch both the flood-banks of the river. As soon as the flames died down, the infantry was to mop up along both the flood-banks and then advance towards the Scolo Tratturo. Ten minutes before the infantry attack across the Senio began, fighter aircraft would carry out a low level attack on the river defences and prevent the German garrison from hindering the approach of the 'Wasps' and 'Crocodiles'. Each assaulting brigade had to capture three bounds (1st bound—road leading from Fornace towards Lugo; 2nd bound—the line of Scolo Arginello; 3rd bound—the line of Canal di Lugo) as well as the western bank of the Scolo Tratturo.

The divisional engineers were ordered to construct five bridges over the Senio within twelve hours of H Hour, the time when the first troops crossed the near bank of the Senio; one of the bridges was an 'Ark' bridge which it was hoped to open at H plus four hours. In addition to the bridging programme, the 4th Mahratta Anti-tank Regiment was ordered to construct four cableways across the river to transport anti-tank guns and jeeps. These were scheduled to function at H plus one hour.

After the capture of the first objective, the western bank of the Scolo Tratturo, the two leading brigades were to exploit up to and, if possible, cross the river Santerno. So much for phase I.

Phase II of the attack by the 8th Indian Division was concerned entirely with the assault by the 17th Indian Infantry Brigade across the river Santerno. After passing through the two forward brigades, the 17th Indian Infantry Brigade was to seize a bridge-head over the Santerno. As in Phase I, a heavy artillery bombardment was to be laid on to precede the assault and the infantry would have the support of 'Kangaroos', 'Crocodiles' and 'Wasps'.

For this operation the following troops were under the command of the 8th Indian Division:

    21st Tank Brigade less one squadron
    4th Queen's Own Hussars less C Squadron and tank escort
    Half C Squadron 51st Royal Tanks.

Headquarters Royal Artillery 6th British Armoured Division with under command:

    12th Royal Horse Artillery Regiment
    104th Royal Horse Artillery Regiment
    152nd (AY) Field Regiment
    24th A Field Regiment
    One Field Regiment 56th Divisional Artillery
    225th (self-propelled) Anti-Tank Battery
    F Assault Squadron
    Two platoon 4.2" mortars from 56th Division (for employment east of Senio only)
    Eighteen Wasps from 56th Division
    One platoon 848th Smoke Company.

The following troops were in support of the 8th Indian Division:

    214/57th Heavy Anti-Aircraft Battery
    One battery 52nd Light Anti-Aircraft Regiment
    A Flight 654th Air OP Squadron
    One troop 323rd SL Battery
    1st Army Group Royal Artillery with under command:
    4th Medium Regiment
    26th Medium Regiment
    58th Medium Regiment
    70th Medium Regiment
    80th Medium Regiment
    75th Heavy Regiment
    C Flight 651st Air OP Squadron
    Detachment 5th Survey Regiment (after crossing the Santerno)
    C Troops 323rd Sl Battery

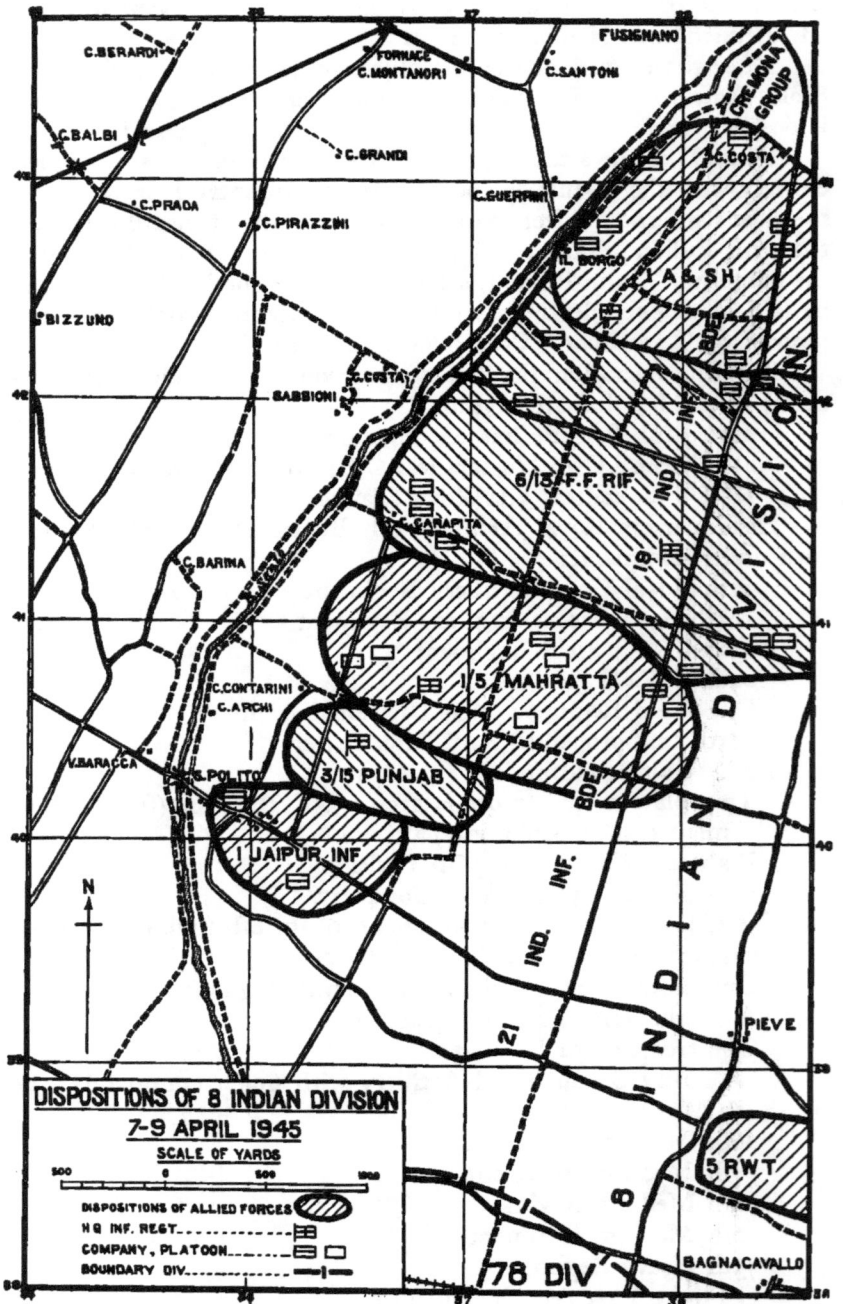

One Field Company from 78th Division
Eighteen bulldozers
Two sections of Tippers
One Bailey bridge platoon
One Company Indian pioneers
Two platoons 4.2" mortars from the 78th Division[1] (for deployment east of Senio only).

Brigade Plans

That, very briefly, was the outline of the divisional plan, each brigade having its plans to implement the higher plan. The commander of the 19th Indian Infantry Brigade decided to advance on a two battalion front with the 1st Argyll and Sutherland Highlanders on the right and 6/13 Frontier Force Rifles on the left. 3/8 Punjab was in reserve with a possible exploitation role. The brigade was to secure two bounds (1st bound—line of road from Fornace to cross roads near S. Sabbioni; 2nd bound—line of Canal di Lugo from the Fornace bridge to cross roads near C. Beniri) and its first objective was the far bank of Scolo Tratturo.

Under the command of the 19th Indian Infantry Brigade were the following units:

North Irish Horse (less one squadron)
Two 'Kangaroo' troops of 4th Hussars
Three Sherman tank troops of 4th Hussars
One Squadron of 6th Lancers
15th Battery of 4th Mahratta Anti-Tank Regiment
One troop 225 Anti-Tank Battery (self-propelled)
C Company, 5th Royal Battalion 5th Mahratta Light Infantry (Medium machine gun)
Eighteen 'Wasps' from 56th British Division
Four 'Crocodiles' from C Squadron 51st Battalion Royal Tank Reigment
Six 'Crocodiles' from 12th Battalion Royal Tank Regiment
Six 'Wasps' from 17th Indian Infanty Brigade.

To implement the brigade plan, the commander of the 1st Argyll and Sutherland Highlanders had planned an assault on the river Senio to secure a bridge-head and exploit to Canal di Lugo. A Company was to carry out the assault of the near bank. Then B Company on the right and C Company on the left were to secure the far bank and form the bridge-head, with B Company consolidating in the area of the cross roads near C. Santoni and C Company in the area of C. Grandi. Then D Company was to pass between the two forward companies and consolidate in the area Fornace. When

[1] 8 Ind. Div. O.O. No. 46, dated 6 April 1945.

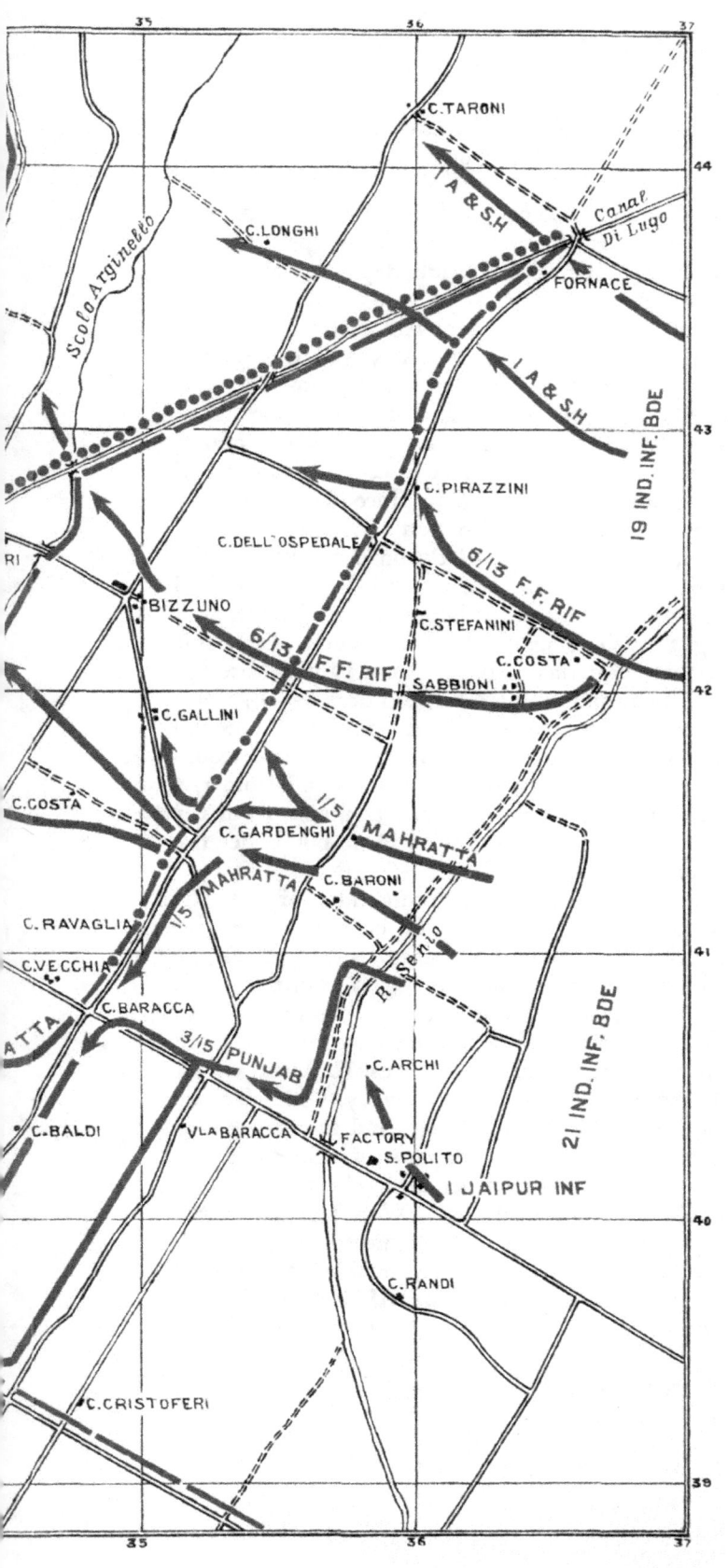

the second bound had been completed, the battalion was to protect the right flank and provide a firm base in order that the 6th Lancers might pass through and exploit to the north on D+1. For this operation the battalion had under command C Squadron 6th Lancers, and in support A Squadron North Irish Horse, 13 'Wasps' (extra to own four), three 'Crocodiles' 12th Royal Tank Regiment and Divisional Artillery.

The commander of 6/13 Frontier Force Rifles also planned to mount an assault on the river Senio. A Company was to carry out the assault of the near bank and B Company was to consolidate on the far bank near C. Costa. Then C and B Companies were to be directed on Bizzuno and C. Pirazzini respectively. Then A and B Companies were to lead the attack and secure Canal di Lugo. C Squadron North Irish Horse, 15 'Wasps', 5 'Crocodiles' and Divisional Artillery were in support of the battalion.

The role of 3/8 Punjab depended entirely on the course of the battle. Having crossed the Senio after the assaulting battalions, 3/8 Punjab was to concentrate in the area of Sabbioni and be prepared to advance at first light on D+1 up to the river Santerno. If this was not possible, this battalion was to be prepared to pass through 6/13 Frontier Force Rifles at approximately 1230 hours on D+1 and exploit up to the line of the river Santerno in the area of S. Lorenzo and establish a bridge-head if possible. For these tasks, two troops 'Kangaroos' plus two troops Sherman tanks as escort (all from the 4th Hussars) and such tanks as might be made available from the North Irish Horse (probably C Squadron) were to be put under the command of 3/8 Punjab.[8]

According to the plan made by the commander of the 21st Indian Infantry Brigade the attack was to be carried out in five phases. In Phase I, 1/5 Mahratta Light Infantry was to attack the Senio on the right of the brigade front with two companies up, whilst 3/15 Punjab was to attack on the left on a one company front. Both the battalions were to seize the first bound including road from the cross roads near Sabbioni to the cross roads near C. Baracca. 1st Battalion Jaipur Infantry was to assault the factory, and seize the near bank at the south end of S. Polito bridge, and mop up northwards to C. Archi. In Phase II, one company of the 5th Royal West Kent Regiment was to cross the river and relieve the left of 3/15 Punjab. The remainder of the 5th Royal West Kent Regiment was to cross the river as soon as possible. 1/5 Mahratta, 3/15 Punjab and 5th Royal West Kent Regiment were then to advance and seize the second bound, Scolo Arginello. In Phase III the three battalions were to seize the third bound Canal di Lugo. Phase IV was

---

[8] 19 Ind. Inf. Bde. O.O. No. 45, dated 6 April 1945.

concerned with air and artillery operations of the Santerno. In Phase V, 1/5 Mahratta and 3/15 Punjab were to secure the far bank of the Scolo Tratturo and exploit beyond it. 1st Battalion Jaipur Infantry was to complete the occupation of Lugo.[9]

Under the command of the 21st Indian Infantry Brigade were the following units:

 48th Battalion Royal Tank Regiment
 Two 'Kangaroo' Troops of 4th Hussars
 13th Mahratta Anti-Tank Battery
 One troop, 225th self-propelled Anti-Tank Battery
 1st Jaipur Infantry
 D Company, 5th Royal Battalion the 5th Mahratta Light Infantry (medium machine gun)
 Six 'Crocodiles' from C Squadron, 51st Battalion the Royal Tank Regiment
 Six 'Crocodiles' from 12th Battalion the Royal Tank Regiment
 16th Mortar Battery the 4th Mahratta Anti-Tank Regiment.

In support of the 21st Indian Infantry Brigade were the following units:

 104th Royal Horse Artillery
 24th, 52nd and 64th Field Regiments, Royal Artillery
 66th Field Company (less detachments) Indian Engineers
 Half of F Assault Squadron (less detachments) Royal Engineers

The commander of the 17th Indian Infantry Brigade could determine only the general principles of the attack for his brigade because so much depended on the success attained by the 19th and 21st Indian Infantry Brigades or otherwise. Provided the two leading brigades were successful, there was to be a heavy artillery bombardment of the Santerno defences, and then it was the turn of the 17th Indian Infantry Brigade to assault the Santerno on a two battalion front supported by tanks, 'Wasps' and 'Crocodiles'; as many troops as possible were to be taken forward in 'Kangaroos'. The 17th Indian Infantry Brigade was reserved for the important Santerno operation and would not be committed elsewhere unless the turn of events was adverse.

The 17th Indian Infantry Brigade had under its command the following troops:

 12th Battalion Royal Tank Regiment
 4th Hussars less one Squadron
 B (medium machine gun) Company 5th Royal Mahratta
 A Company (less two platoons) 5th Royal Mahratta
 14th Mahratta Anti-Tank Battery (less one 17-pounder troop)
 One troop 225th Anti-Tank Battery (self-propelled)

[9] 21 Ind. Inf. Bde. O.O No. 3, dated 7 April 1945.

The following troops were in support:
3rd Field Regiment
7th Field Company.

There were certain complications with regard to the flanks of the 8th Indian Division once it had crossed the Senio. No formation was attacking on the right and, between left hand brigade of the division and the New Zealand Division, there was a gap of some four thousand yards. This gap included Lugo. Initially, therefore, the division would have both its flanks wide open.

Another outstanding problem to resolve before the attack was how to deny the Germans knowledge of the plans for this great Spring offensive. They knew, of course, that the Allies would attack; events elsewhere in Europe and the very season of the year were sure indications that a battle was imminent. To make sure that the Germans remained ignorant of the date of the attack, the sector in which it was to be launched, the forces to be engaged and the method by which Indian troops intended to assault, a rigid security discipline was introduced throughout the 8th Indian Division. This security applied to correspondence, all of which was classified according to its degree of importance, to ordinary conversation in the rest area, to wireless and telephonic communications. In addition, tents and bivouacs were camouflaged, movement of transport was reduced to a minimum; bridging material and sapper equipment were all carefully hidden away amongst the vines. Brigade and unit signs were not shown until the very last moment and every attempt was made to conceal the presence of the two brigade groups concentrated in such a small area in front of the German defences.

To avoid traffic congestion in the forward areas, an elaborate movement control organisation was set up, which simplified the work of the Divisional Provost and ensured a maximum flow of ammunition and essential supplies at a time when they were most needed.

There was not a man in the Indian division who was under any delusion about the difficulty of the task which lay ahead. Yet, as the final preparations were made, there was an air of confidence abroad, a curious feeling that all would be well.

CHAPTER XXXIII

The Assault Across the Senio and Santerno

Beginning of the Spring Offensive

The Eighth Army's offensive began at 1350 hours on 9 April 1945. The first to strike were the heavy bombers which laid a carpet of anti-personnel bombs on a strip about one thousand yards wide, with its far edge on the Santerno. Just after 1345 hours, the British and Indian troops heard the dull drone of hundreds of heavy bombers; looking up, they saw high in the sky silver sparkle in the glaring April sunshine, as the aircraft winged their way westwards towards the Santerno. There, along the banks of the river, the quiet of the afternoon was shattered for ninety minutes by the explosion of thousands of high explosive and fragmentation bombs on the German defence line.

Then, at 1520 hours, the mighty artillery barrage broke over the German positions on the Senio and Santerno. Shell after shell whined over the Allied troops to crash over the Germans, who had already been considerably shaken by the air bombardment. At intervals the barrage would lift, pilots of Allied fighter-bombers hovered over the area in their Spitfires and Mustangs watching and waiting for any German movement. When they spotted Germans stirring from dug-outs or weapon pits, down swooped the fighter-bombers like avenging birds of prey to machine-gun and strafe them. During the four hours of this shattering artillery bombardment, every known or suspected German position both on the Senio itself and beyond the river was pummelled by mortars and field artillery, battered by heavy guns and strafed unmercifully by a host of fighter bombers. In the gun lines, the crews of the 25-pounders and the medium guns worked like fiends; stripped to the waist, they fed their hungry guns with shell after shell. The German reply to this bombardment was feeble, like the attempt of a beaten man to struggle to his feet after receiving the knock-out blow. Observers in the towers of Bagnacavallo saw between the Senio and Santerno a vast cloud of yellow dust rising high in the air and hovering there throughout the afternoon. All this time, whilst the guns crashed and the fighter-bombers strafed, the British and Indian Infantry who had been withdrawn five hundred yards from the Senio listened and waited.

Joining in the mighty artillery barrage that ground the German positions for nearly four hours before the infantry of the 8th Indian

Division went over the top, the men of 5th Mahratta Light Infantry located the German fox-holes, spandau-posts and gun positions for their special targets and swept them with a non-stop tornado of machine-gun bullets. At the same time, with a well-conceived scheme designed to make the maximum use of their enormous fire-power, they prevented the Germans from massing for an effective defence or sending reinforcements and supplies to their hard pressed troops. The Mahrattas poured down a steady fire on all cross-roads, bridges, supply dumps and houses, stopping all movement in the German rear area and completely isolating the forward troops in their positions on the banks of the Senio. In retaliation, the Germans furiously shelled and mortared the Mahrattas in their gun positions but the machine gunners held on in spite of casualties.

Spirited Attack by 6/13 Royal Frontier Force Rifles

Zero hour for the attack of the 8th Indian Division was scheduled for 1920 hours. We shall first describe the assault of the 19th Indian Infantry Brigade. On the right of the 8th Indian Division, the men of the 19th Indian Infantry Brigade were in position. The 1st Argyll and Sutherland Highlanders was on the right flank of the brigade front from the area of C. Costa to the area of Il Borgo, 6/13 Frontier Force Rifles on the left as far as C. Carapita, whilst 3/8 Punjab was slightly behind the forward battalions in a reserve position. We may first take up the progress of 6/13 Frontier Force Rifles. Preliminary to the attack, this battalion carried out the hazardous task of lifting a number of mines which had been sown close to the flood-bank in the sector of the assault. Owing to the darkness of the night, the proximity of the Germans and the uncertain state of mine mechanism after it had been exposed for sometime to the weather, this work was most dangerous. Yet, it was successfully accomplished.

On the D Day all troops were slipped out of the forward posts and withdrawn 500 yards behind. From midday onwards the artillery and aircraft did the most terrific harassing and strafing on the banks and beyond. A short while before H Hour, A and B, the two assaulting companies of 6/13 Frontier Force Rifles, moved to their forming up place (400 yards from the bank), likewise two troops of tanks also advanced up to the bank. Behind the tanks came flame throwers, the Wasps and Crocodiles. Twelve minutes before the assault began on the near bank, the whole assault group started moving slowly forward towards the bank. The two assaulting companies followed in the tank tracks. The boats were carried on the carriers behind B Company. The tanks approached the near bank firing their machine guns, the flame throwers passed up to them and through them on the bank disgorging their liquid flame, and A Company dashed through the flames on to the near bank, immediately spreading right and left, and mopping up the German posts as they tumbled out of their deep dug-outs. Less than two minutes after A Company had secured a footing on the near bank, B Company was up and over the small breach already made, and taking advantage of the smoke and confusion the men started to cross opposite C. Costa. They discarded their boats and jumped into the water which was four feet six inches deep at this place. In spite of a withering but somewhat wild fire coming from the far bank, they, too, secured a crossing. With the utmost dash, German posts were dealt with. Within fifteen minutes the whole company was across with one platoon racing for C. Costa, where they surprised a German platoon forming up for counter-attack, and the other two platoons grenading and Tommy Gunning their way to the right and the left down the bank. By 2000 hours both the banks and C. Costa had been cleared of the Germans.[1]

Ali Haider Awarded Victoria Cross

In wading through the Senio and clearing the far bank, B Company performed many brave deeds. The following story of how sepoy Ali Haider, seriously wounded and weakened by loss of blood, carried out a number of dauntless attacks which saved an ugly situation, illustrates the nature of the fighting on the banks of the Senio in the 19th Indian Infantry Brigade's sector.

Ali Haider waded into the Senio with the left hand section of one of the forward platoons. Almost immediately, German machine gunners opened fire from the posts about sixty yards away on the left flank. Man after man in the platoon fell dead or wounded as the heavy and accurate German fire sprayed the river and its banks. Of Ali Haider's section, only two men besides himself succeeded in running the gauntlet of death. The remainder of the platoon and the rest of the company were temporarily held up. The sepoy and his two companions crouched under the western bank as the battle raged around them and the fire from the German machine guns prevented the company from crossing.

Realising that it was imperative for his company to cross the river, the sepoy told his two comrades to give him covering fire whilst he attacked the German post. Charging forward across the thirty yards of bullet-swept ground, which by now separated him from the German machine gunners, Ali Haider threw a grenade. At the same time, the German gunners threw one of their stick grenades which exploded and wounded the sepoy in the back. The gallant soldier was not deterred; charging on, he destroyed the post

[1] Royal Frontier Force Rifles on the Senio River; Appendix War Diary 6/13 F.F. Rif.

and wounded its four occupants. Without resting to attend to his wounds, Ali Haider assaulted the next post where the Germans had one machine gun and three automatic weapons, which were still active and prevented movement on both banks. Again, he was wounded, this time in the right leg and arm. He fell to the ground but, although considerably weakened by loss of blood, he crawled slowly and painfully towards the Germans. By a supreme effort he raised himself from the ground, pulled out the pin of a Mill's bomb with his teeth and threw the grenade into the post. Following up the blinding flash and the explosion, Ali Haider staggered the last few yards to the post where he found two seriously wounded Germans; two others surrendered.

Encouraged by the success of Ali Haider's dauntless attacks, the rest of his company charged across the Senio to the far bank; it was the turning point of the battle in the sector of 6/13 Frontier Force Rifles. As the Indian battalion dug in on the far bank, medical orderlies gently lifted the seriously wounded sepoy on to a stretcher. Ali Haider was evacuated from the battlefield and eventually recovered from his wounds to be awarded the Victoria Cross.

Liquidation of Opposition in Area Bizzuno

After B Company had secured the far bank at 2000 hours, two more companies passed through the turmoil on the banks and launched themselves into the hostile territory beyond. C Company was directed towards Bizzuno through Sabbioni, while D Company moved towards C. Pirazzinni. Soon the sounds of small arms and grenading and PIAT noises were heard even above the din of the artillery barrage, which had moved forward at 200 yards in 12 minutes to the line of the road through Pirazzinni. By 2115 hours C and D Companies were secure on the first bound, with D Company at C. Pirazzinni and C Company forward of Sabbioni, on the road leading from Fornace to Lugo. A and B Companies which had cleared the banks of the Senio, now moved forward to secure the second bound. B Company took up position in the area of C. Ospedale between C and D Companies, while A Company concentrated in the area of C Company. In order to beat the German opposition in the area of Bizzuno the battalion plan was for B Company to advance up the road leading from C. Ospedale to C. Prada, C Company to secure the road and track junction to the right of Bizzuno and A Company to capture Bizzuno. The role of D Company was to provide right flank protection. By 0300 hours on 10 April the German opposition was overcome—A Company secured Bizzuno, C Company cleared the German pocket of resistance in the area of the road and track junction to its right and B Company was in position in the area of C. Prada. The Germans launched counter-attacks, especially against B Company in the area of C. Prada. Between 0300 hours and 0600 hours B Company was unsuccessfully attacked six times. Then the German resistance died down and the patrols began to thrust forward towards the Scolo Tratturo, which was known to be a well prepared German defence line. At 1200 hours a platoon patrol from A Company advanced up the road from Bizzuno to Canal di Lugo but met heavy resistance from light machine gun fire and self-propelled guns. The platoon withdrew after suffering some casualties. The brigadier decided to wait until nightfall to launch an attack with his reserve battalion, 3/8 Punjab.

The Argyll's Advance

Meanwhile, the Argyll had carried out the task allotted to it. Scrambling as best they could up the steep, smouldering incline of the near flood-banks of the Senio they came to grips with the Germans. Quickly they eliminated what slight resistance was offered and the second wave of infantry was able to pass through to grapple with the defenders on the far bank. A Company mopped up on the near bank while B and C Companies crossed the Senio and fanned out to the right and left, with D Company advancing in between. By 0125 hours they had overcome most of the opposition. At that time Tactical Battalion Headquarters and A Company were on the far bank at C. Guerrini to protect the right flank of B Company, which had secured the road junction near C. Santoni; C Company was in the area of C. Grandi; while D Company was advancing towards Fornace road junction. Shortly afterwards the Argyll was firmly placed on the first bound. Further progress was made and by 1010 hours the Argyll had secured C. Taroni and C. Longhi, thus providing a firm base for the 6th Lancers to pass through and exploit in a south and north-westerly direction.

Thrust of 3/8 Punjab Towards the Santerno

The stage was now set for the advance of 3/8 Punjab towards the river Santerno. Before this battalion led the advance towards the Santerno the Allied heavy bombers pounded the German positions at 1130 hours on 10 April. This time, their task was to smash the German troops and transport withdrawing from the Senio towards the prepared positions on the Santerno; they dropped a deluge of bombs along the western bank of the river. By error, and although the most elaborate precautions had been taken to prevent any mistakes, one flight of bombers mistook the Senio for the Santerno. Their bombs fell astride one of the recently erected Senio bridges where men and vehicles were waiting in a large line to make the crossing, causing heavy casualties.[2]

[2] *Ibid.*

3/8 Punjab advancing from the area of C. Stefanini, west of the Senio, attacked at 2130 hours on 10 April across the Scolo Tratturo. D and A Companies led the attack. Not much resistance was encountered. By 0110 hours on 11 April, 3/8 Punjab was well established in the area of C. Pasetti. At 0900 hours its patrols approached the east bank of the Santerno, where they encountered fierce opposition. Shortly afterwards, at 1100 hours 3/8 Punjab was relieved by 1/5 Gurkha of the 17th Indian Infantry Brigade, to which the task of assaulting across the Santerno had been assigned. After a short rest, 3/8 Punjab took up positions in conjunction with the Argyll and 6/13 Frontier Force Rifles to protect the division's right flank. The 3/8 Punjab was in position in the area of S. Gaiani.

That same day, on the right flank of the divisional front, the 6th Lancers and the North Irish Horse, supported by Sherman tanks of the 4th Hussars, reached Torre, about a thousand yards short of the Santerno. Then, making contact with a German force withdrawing from the Senio and Scolo Tratturo, they encountered a strong defensive position of anti-tank guns, self-propelled guns and tanks. The Lancers did everything in their power to hasten the German withdrawal, whilst the guns of the 12th Royal Horse Artillery and pilots of the Desert Air Force were able to choose good targets which paid handsome dividends. The guns of the medium artillery regiments kept the bridge over the Santerno at San Bernardino under constant heavy fire. German vehicles and men in their attempt to cross this bridge suffered heavy casualties as the burnt out wrecks of lorries and the numerous graves in the area of the bridge later testified.

Assault Across the Senio by 1/5 Mahratta

We have described the advance of the 19th Indian Infantry Brigade to the river Santerno. We shall now take up the story of the advance of the 21st Indian Infantry Brigade up to the same stream. The 21st Indian Infantry Brigade assaulted the Senio positions at the same time as the 19th Indian Infantry Brigade, viz. 1920 hours on 9 April. 1/5 Mahratta was on the right from the area of C. Carapata to the area of C. Contarini; 3/15 Punjab was in the centre; on the left was the 1st Battalion Jaipur Infantry in the area S. Polito. At 1910 hours tanks and flame throwing 'Crocodiles' began to move forward to the Senio. Ten minutes afterwards the banks of the river on the brigade front were a molten mass of liquid flame. The 'Crocodiles' with 1/5 Mahratta, on the right flank of the brigade front, worked well but two out of the four with 3/15 Punjab, on the left flank, failed to flare because of a technical defect, which developed during the rough approach journey to the positions for flaming. At 1920 hours, 1/5 Mahratta and 3/15 Punjab assaulted the charred flood-bank in the midst of increased German mortar and rifle grenade fire.

At 1920 hours all tank and 'Crocodile' fire ceased and A and D Companies of 1/5 Mahratta, closely followed by C and Y Companies, advanced to assault the near bank. The two leading companies, A and D, climbed the near bank to come under very heavy mortar and grenade fire causing many casualties. C and Y Companies were heavily mortared as they attempted to drag the boats up the near bank, which proved more precipitous than had been expected. The commander of D Company realised that there was not much possibility of the two rear companies getting the boats up the steep bank in time for them to be used in the river crossing. He ordered a section to wade across the river and himself followed with the remainder of the leading Mahratta platoon. Soaked to the skin but still carrying their weapons and equipment, the Mahratta clambered up the steep far bank. Meanwhile on the left of the Mahratta front, the commander of C Company had also realised that the river would have to be waded. Crossing with one section, he and his men were wiped out almost immediately. A sepoy, the only survivor, recrossed the river to give the information.[3]

Namdeo Jadhao Awarded Victoria Cross

A Company and the remainder of C Company dug in on the near bank. Although D Company was astride the western flood-bank, German machine gunners remained in their position on the inside of the eastern flood-bank and opened fire on Y, the reserve company, as it crossed on the western bank. Sepoy Namdeo Jadhao was company runner and he crossed with his company commander close behind one of the leading sections. As the Mahratta struggled through the waters of the Senio, withering machine gun fire wounded the company commander and two men of the leading section. The others, with the exception of Namdeo Jadhao, were all killed. This murderous German machine gun fire forced the rest of the company to withdraw to the shelter of the eastern flood-bank, whilst Namdeo Jadhao, and his two wounded comrades took what cover they could find on the western flood-bank.

The twenty-year-old sepoy then decided to carry his wounded comrades to safety. As German mortar bombs crashed down and machine gun fire swept the river, the gallant sepoy carried first one and then the other of his wounded comrades across those few yards where so many men had died. Half dragging, half lifting his comrades, he took them through the deep waters, through a

---

[3] The assault and crossing of R. Senio and the advance to R. Santerno by 1/5 Mahratta; Appendix War Diary 1/5 Mahratta, April 1945.

minefield and up the precipitous side of the eastern flood-bank to a place of safety.

Then he dashed at the nearest German post on the eastern bank and silenced the crew with bursts of tommy gun fire. At this stage he was wounded in the hand and, being unable to use his tommy gun, resorted to Mill's bombs. He successfully charged and wiped out two more German posts, having on one occasion to crawl to the top of the eastern bank to replenish his stock of grenades from his comrades on the far side. Having silenced all German machine gun fire from the eastern bank, he climbed to the top and shouting the Mahratta war cry of "Shivaji Maharaj Ki Jai", waved his company forward. This lone soldier, standing on the top of the bank, as mortar bombs crashed around him, was indeed a wonderful example to the rest of the men in his company. He was awarded the Victoria Cross for his significant action, which enabled the rest of the Mahratta company to cross and to secure firmly the west bank and, eventually, his battalion to secure a deeper bridge-head over the muddy waters of the Senio.

Securing the First Bound

Meanwhile A Company commander sent the remnants of C Company over the river and ordered the 8th platoon to make the footbridge, which was put across under heavy fire. One platoon of A Company then crossed the river digging in on the left of D Company. Within an hour of the assault, the commanders of the three leading companies had been wounded. At 2030 hours the companies were reorganised and patrols from A and D Companies were sent to mop up any further resistance along the banks. By 2330 hours the situation on both the banks was in hand and YC Company (the remnants of Y and C Companies organised into one company) was ready to move forward to the first bound. The assault itself had been costly and hazardous but the crossing had been achieved.

At 2330 hours YC company advanced, clearing C. Gardenghi and the houses on the first bound, intercepting a German mortar section fleeing from 6/13 Frontier Force Rifles sector, on the right, on bicycles, and overrunning parties of Germans in the houses. At 2350 hours YC Company having reported firm on the first bound sent a platoon patrol to C. Gallini which they occupied. Tactical Headquarters and A Company then moved towards C. Baroni. The way was missed and headquarters established itself in the bombed ruins of C. Gardenghi. At 0400 hours, D Company was called forward from the bank and concentrated near tactical headquarters. Meanwhile A Company had been mopping up small pockets of German resistance. At 0630 hours A Company cleared C. Ravaglia and C. Vecchia. Thus 1/5 Mahratta was firmly established on the first bound, with patrols moving towards Canal di Lugo.

The Attack by 3/15 Punjab

Meanwhile, the picture on 3/15 Punjab front was very much the same as in 1/5 Mahratta sector. At 1920 hours, C Company charged the near bank as soon as the flame-throwing tanks had sent the last spurt of flame licking towards the bank. The men scrambled up the steep slopes of the near bank, where they came under a veritable hail of machine gun, rifle and mortar fire from the German dug-outs in the immediate vicinity and from the positions on the flanks. Most of the German positions on the bank had been dug so deep underground that the terrific air and artillery bombardment might have shaken the German nerves but not their tenacious courage. They fought with grim determination. At 1922 hours D Company advanced through C Company to the far bank. D Company waded through the river as German machine gunners swept the river from their positions on both flanks. The twenty yards or so between the two banks was a veritable death trap where it seemed no man could survive. However, some men of the Punjab reached the far bank where, for three quarters of an hour, the most vicious fighting in which 3/15 Punjab had ever been engaged took place. Every man on both sides was fighting like an animal at bay for his very life; on both banks of the river the Punjabis were storming dug-out after dug-out with hand grenades and tommy guns, whilst the Germans made desperate sorties to drive them off the banks. As the battle raged on both sides of the Senio, German machine guns from the flank continued to pour a stream of bullets between the two banks and German mortar bombs crashed down in that twenty-yard gap to kill and maim stretcher-bearers as well as Indian and German wounded, who lay below the banks unable to move.

At 2004 hours B Company passed through D Company to its objective at Villa Baracca, which was occupied at 2045 hours. A Company then advanced towards C. Baracca, which was secured at 2330 hours. Thus by 2330 hours A Company was firmly established at C. Baracca on the first bound. Further progress was made by 0815 hours when C and D Companies took up positions in the area of C. Baldi while A Company secured Ponte Nuovo, near Lugo.

Mopping up Operations

The 21st Indian Infantry Brigade's assault across the river Senio was carried out by 1/5 Mahratta and 3/15 Punjab. The role of the Ist Battalion Jaipur Infantry was to carry out mopping up operations in S. Polito area. On the morning of D Day (9 April) the 1st Jaipur Infantry was tactically disposed on the left of the brigade's sector, with A and C Companies forward in the areas of S. Polito and C. Randi, respectively. At 2002 hours, A Company successfully attacked the Factory in the area of S. Polito, capturing six prisoners. At 2010 hours A Company continued the attack on to the east bank of the Senio and occupied the area of C. Archi. C Company remained in its position for the Germans on that front had withdrawn.

Further to the south the 5th Royal West Kent Regiment, who had concentrated 500 yards, south of Pieve, crossed the Senio and carried out mopping up operations in the area of C. Cristoferi. The 19th Indian Infantry Brigade had secured the first bound by about 0125 hours on 10 April. The 21st Indian Infantry Brigade had however to struggle hard and it was not till about 0800 hours on 10 April that it firmly held the first bound.

The Achievements of the Sappers

German tanks and self-propelled guns had been reported in Lugo and also, though not so definitely, in Fusignano, and it was vital to get Allied tanks and anti-tank guns across the river Senio before dawn. The divisional sappers, with the assistance of the Assault Royal Engineers and a Field Company from V Corps, had been given the task of building two Bailey bridges on the 19th and 21st Indian Infantry Brigade fronts. The sappers were at work on the bridges—'Stirling' and 'Selkirk' with scarcely any German interference, completing them soon after the scheduled time. The first tank passed over 'Selkirk' at 0415 hours on 10 April and the first vehicle crossed "Stirling" bridge at 1100 hours. Work on the steel cableways was not quite so successful; the 15th Battery 4th Mahratta Anti-Tank Regiment was able to build only one cableway owing to several of their vehicles having been put out of action. However, by 0400 hours and before it was light, six 6-pounder guns and two jeeps had been hauled across the cableway and were in position at dawn. On another part of the brigade front, 3/8 Punjab of the 19th Indian Infantry Brigade assisted by detachments of RIASC personnel, constructed two 'Olafson' bridges[4] and completed their task by spanning the river with the bridges, despite periodic, hostile mortar fire.[5] Thus, at first light, by which time the bridges were hidden by a smoke screen, tanks of the North Irish Horse and some armoured cars of the 6th Lancers were across the Senio in close support of the 19th Indian Infantry Brigade.

In the 21st Indian Infantry Brigade area, the men of the 13th Battery 4th Mahratta Anti-Tank Regiment built a steel cableway

---

[4] An 'Olafson' bridge is designed only to take foot-traffic and will not take any vehicle.
[5] 8 Ind. Div. News Letters.

over the Senio, on which they transported two jeeps and four six pounder anti-tank guns from the near to the far bank. A word of praise must go to these Mahratta anti-tank gunners, who carried out this exacting work under heavy mortar and machine gun fire, which caused them several casualties.

As far as the bridges were concerned, initial reconnaissance and construction were considerably delayed by heavy mortar and machine gun fire. However, after long hours of work in most difficult circumstances, the sappers completed an 'Ark' bridge by 0540 hours on 10 April. Within ninety minutes, three squadrons of the 48th Battalion Royal Tank Regiment had crossed over the Senio by this bridge to support the infantry and when a class 9 trestle bridge began to operate at about 0900 hours, the situation was considered most satisfactory.[6]

21st Indian Infantry Brigade's Advance to the Santerno

On 10 April, the advance of the 21st Indian Infantry Brigade continued beyond the Senio river. The brigade made good progress against opposition which was, at first light, confined to small pockets of German resistance but which increased as the leading infantry approached the Scolo Tratturo. 1/5 Mahratta on the right and 3/15 Punjab on the left advanced from the first bound to Scolo Tratturo, while the 1st Battalion Jaipur Infantry on the extreme left flank was directed on Lugo. The capture of Lugo proved to be an easy task. At 0900 hours on 10 April, the 1st Jaipur Infantry crossed the river Senio and concentrated in the area of C. Baldi, wherefrom it led the attack on Lugo, which was secured by 1315 hours. Then the 1st Jaipur Infantry was relieved by the 5th Royal West Kent Regiment.

Meanwhile 1/5 Mahratta and 3/15 Punjab were advancing to Scolo Tratturo. At 0715 hours, the former supported by tanks, advanced for the attack on the Scolo Tratturo defences. The advance was made by YC Company on the right in the area of C. Gardenghi, D Company in the area of C. Vecchia and A Company on the left flank. The Mahratta advanced quickly to Scolo Tratturo, capturing many dazed and exhausted prisoners. By 1000 hours they secured the line of Canal di Lugo without much opposition. They rested here till 2030 hours when the supporting tanks fired heavy concentrations on the Scolo Tratturo. The infantry then closed up to the near bank of the Scolo Tratturo. As the companies were ordered at a very short notice to follow behind the tanks to the near bank, the operation tended to lack co-ordination and in some cases companies lost touch with their platoons, and the platoons with one another in the dark.

[6] 21 Ind. Inf. Bde. Operations of 26 April; Appendix A to War Diary 21 Ind. Inf. Bde.

3/15 Punjab was also brought to a halt on this obstacle. At 1300 hours, C and D Companies advanced in 'Kangaroos' from the area of C. Baldi and, by 1600 hours, were in position in the area of C. Ferretti. Further progress could not be made due to stiffening German resistance. B Company on the right and A Company on the left then sent patrols but these were held up short of Scolo Tratturo by German defensive fire, and were compelled to return. Thus the forward troops of 3/15 Punjab were stopped by a strong belt of German defences disposed along the line of the Scolo Tratturo. The commander of the 21st Indian Infantry Brigade then decided that the 1st Jaipur Infantry should pass through 3/15 Punjab and take up the task of breaking through this new obstacle. However, owing to the difficulty of co-ordinating the various supporting arms, the attack by the 1st Jaipur Infantry that night was postponed. The advance was to be continued at first light on 11 April.

Early on 11 April, 1/5 Mahratta and the 1st Jaipur Infantry crossed the Scolo Tratturo under cover of supporting fire from tanks and artillery. Most of the Germans had withdrawn during the night. The Mahrattas advanced at 0600 hours and by 0730 hours they had secured, after slight opposition, the final bound, the last lateral road before the river Santerno from Fondo Cantona to C. Costa. The battalion was relieved at 1400 hours by B Company 1/12 Frontier Force Regiment and C Company of the 1st Jaipur Infantry prior to the 17th Indian Infantry Brigade passing through to assault and cross the Santerno during the night of 11/12 April.

The 1st Jaipur Infantry too made rapid progress. At 0530 hours on 11 April, B and D Companies, after preliminary supporting fire from tanks and artillery, advanced to the river Santerno. The crossing of Scolo Tratturo was not seriously opposed although scattered spandau positions gave lot of trouble. By 1800 hours both the companies were within eight hundred yards of the east bank of the Santerno, being heavily mortared and shelled. Patrols working their way forward towards the river encountered a thick belt of 'Schu' mines at least five hundred yards wide.

The 17th Indian Infantry Brigade Plan

In the morning of 11 April, the 19th and 21st Indian Infantry Brigades had closed up to the river Santerno. The 17th Indian Infantry Brigade then concentrated in the area of S. Polito, now prepared to pass through the left battalion of the 19th Indian Infantry Brigade and the right battalion of the 21st Indian Infantry Brigade to secure a bridge-head over the river Santerno on the general line, bend in the river near K 51—C. Morandi—Mondaniga—

C. Zama—K. 54. The frontage allotted to the brigade was from S. Lorenzo to C. Cavallini.[7]

In outline the brigade plan was for the river to be crossed with two battalions up—1/5 Gurkha on the right and 1/12 Frontier Force Regiment on the left. Depth of penetration was to depend on the nature of opposition to be encountered but was to include a line from the bend in the river near K 51 to cross roads near Mondaniga to near C. Cavallini.[8]

The assault was to be preceded by a 10 minute artillery concentration on the river banks, thence lifting to a depth of 600 yards until the far river bank had been secured and, when both the assaulting battalions were ready, a barrage behind which the advancing troops were to advance to the final objective. H Hour was given as 1540 hours but was later put back to 1740 hours on 11 April.

The 17th Indian Infantry Brigade had under its command the following troops:

    12th Battalion the Royal Tank Regiment
    4th Queen's Own Hussars less one squadron
    14th Mahratta Anti-Tank Battery (less one troop)
    One troop 225th Anti-Tank Battery (less one troop)
    B Medium Machine Gun Company 5th Royal Mahratta
    A Company 5th Royal Mahratta (less two platoons)

The following troops were in support:[9]

    3rd Field Regiment
    F Assault Squadron Royal Engineers
    7th Field Company.

In outline the battalion plan of 1/5 Gurkha was for C and D Companies to assault the near bank in the area of P. Rosso and to secure the houses below the far flood bank. Once these houses were seized and in conformity with the progress of 1/12 Frontier Force Regiment, A and B Companies were to pass through C and D Companies respectively, so that A Company on the right was to secure the bend in the river near K. 51 C. Morandi, and B Company on the left was to capture the houses at cross roads near Mondeniga. On completion of this phase, C Company was to take over D Company positions and remain in reserve on the river bank, D Company advancing to seize the ground between A and B Companies.

Each assaulting company was given under command one troop 'Kangaroos', two 'Crocodiles', two 'Wasps' and one Mortar detachment to fire from the carriers on close German targets. A Squadron 12th Royal Tank Regiment was to assist by fire, with one troop in

---

[7] Battle Narrative of 1/12 Frontier Force Regiment for the period 10 to 13 April 1945; Lessons from Operations.
[8] Battle Narrative 10-13 April; War Diary 1/5 G.R.
[9] 8 Ind. Div. O.O. No. 46, dated 6 April 1945.

immediate support each of C and D Companies, and the remaining troops in the centre to deal with any unforeseen eventuality.

The plan for 1/12 Frontier Force Regiment was for B Company on the right and D Company on the left to assault in the area between Ca di Lugo and C. Cavallini. Their task was to secure both banks and a footing in the houses beyond. C and A Companies on the right and left respectively, were to pass through and assault; C Company was to seize the area of C. Nardozzi and A Company the area of C. Zama. While this assault was being made, B Company was to exploit to the right to clear the houses in the areas K 53 and C. Barracca and link up with 1/5 Gurkha. In addition to artillery, 4.2"-mortars and medium machine guns, two troops 'Kangaroos', sufficient to lift two companies, three 'Crocodile' flame throwers, and C Squadron 12th Royal Tank Regiment were in support of the battalion.

Bridge-heads Over the Santerno

Preceded by a ten minute artillery preparation and supported by tanks, 'Crocodiles', 'Wasps' and 'Kangaroos' the 17th Indian Infantry Brigade assaulted the east bank of the Santerno on a two-battalion front at 1740 hours on 11 April. Prior to the assault, the two battalions were established on the lateral road near the Santerno, with 1/5 Gurkha on the right and 1/12 Frontier Force Regiment on the left. Both the battalions had about 500 yards of completely open ground to cross before reaching the near bank. German defences had been skilfully sited and dug, and all trees forward of the line destroyed, thus leaving the Germans a clear field of fire. The attack went in with a gap of 1200 yards between the battalions with the object of avoiding the minefield reported to be at Ca di Lugo. Both the battalions attacked on a two company front, 1/5 Gurkha using 'Kangaroos' to take the reserve companies forward and the leading companies to the assault, while 1/12 Frontier Force Regiment kept 'Kangaroos' in reserve, and assaulted on foot.[10]

As in the Senio assault, the artillery support was very satisfactory except for one troop of guns, whose shells fell short and caused a number of casualties in the right forward assault company of 1/12 Frontier Force Regiment. The tanks of the 12th Battalion Royal Tank Regiment also gave valuable support. The work of the flame-throwers, however, proved to be most disappointing. All the 'Wasps' broke down or were unable to reach the far bank. One of the eight 'Crocodiles' broke down before leaving the start line. Of the four 'Crocodiles' allotted to the Gurkha, only one flamed both the banks of the Santerno successfully. None of the 'Crocodiles'

[10] 17 Bde.—The Crossing of the Santerno 10-12 April 1945; Lessons from Operations, File 601/7301/H.

supporting the men of 1/12 Frontier Force Regiment was able to get into position to flame even the near bank.

Prior to the assault, 1/5 Gurkha, having taken over from the 3/8 Punjab, was in position just forward of the lateral road, northeast of Fondo Cantona. At 1730 hours on 11 April, the artillery concentrations on the river bank opened and at 1734 hours the tanks and flame throwers moved off. At 1738 hours the two forward companies raced right up to the near bank of the Santerno in their 'Kangaroos'. Reaching the near flood-bank, D Company was met by heavy machine gun fire from the left flank and from the front, where the Germans had numerous machine gun posts dug into the reverse slopes of the near bank and the forward slope of the far bank. The two forward platoons nevertheless succeeded in reaching the far bank but suffered heavy casualties, particularly from the Spandaus from the left. Almost immediately on arrival and before the platoons had a chance to dig in, the Germans made a determined attempt to regain the far flood bank. As soon as the attack was beaten off the forward platoons started to dig in but, during the next hour, were subjected to five counter-attacks by the Germans. The left hand Gurkha section was destroyed to a man and the left hand platoon reduced to a total of three men only. The right hand platoon fared slightly better but they too had only eleven survivors left on the far flood bank by the time the German attacks ceased.

Meanwhile C Company had commenced the crossing with two platoons No. 14 and No. 15 up. They were immediately met by a murderous cross fire from machine guns on the right flank, and one particularly nasty machine gun post dug into the reverse slope of the near bank, between the left hand platoon of the company and the right hand platoon of D Company. In this assault No. 15 Platoon was very roughly handled, both the platoon commander and platoon Havildar being immediately wounded. No. 14 Platoon, however, succeeded in getting across and establishing securely on the far bank together with a few men of 15 Platoon. On arrival they were immediately counter-attacked in a half-hearted manner.

The situation at 1830 hours was that there were two platoons of D Company and one platoon of C Company across the stream. A short time later No. 15 Platoon also succeeded in getting across. The German machine gun post between C and D Companies was dealt with and a continuous, though precarious, hold obtained on the far flood bank. Attempts by both the forward companies to advance further and capture the houses below the flood bank were met by intense machine gun fire from the flanks and from Germans dug in the fields about 400 yards forward of the flood bank. Therefore any attempt to get on by daylight was abandoned. The artillery barrage was dropped 200 yards ahead of the river silencing the Germans in the fields.

At 1915 hours both the reserve companies were sent forward in 'Kangaroos', A Company to form a firm base on the near flood bank immediately behind C Company, and B Company to reinforce D Company by extending the bridge-head to the left. Both the companies arrived simultaneously and by 1930 hours A Company was in position on the near flood bank where B Company was also established and was preparing to send two platoons forward to the left of D Company, which was still having extreme difficulty from German machine gun posts on the flood bank to the left and in the houses.

At approximately 1935 hours B Company attacked and in spite of heavy opposition two platoons were soon established on the far flood-bank to the left of the remnants of D Company. These two platoons were almost immediately counter-attacked twice but succeeded in beating off both the German attempts to hold the vital left flank of the battalion position. Thenceforward German resistance commenced to abate, although any move forward drew heavy and accurate machine gun fire from the flanks. It now became apparent that the original plan of attack would have to be modified. Resistance from the flanks, particularly in the area of Pirazzoli, was still stiff and D Company had become so depleted through casualties that it was not strong enough to make another attack.

On the left, 1/12 Frontier Force Regiment too encountered fierce opposition. Prior to the assault this battalion had relieved 1/5 Mahratta on the line of the road from about Fonde Cantona to C. Costa. At 1730 hours the barrage opened and at 1735 hours the assaulting companies moved forward from their start line, both assaulting with two platoons forward. The barrage was falling about 200 yards short. This forced B Company further over to the right than was orginally intended. When they commenced the assault a gap was left between the two forward companies. On the left the assault went exactly as planned, although the 'Crocodiles', held up by fear of mines, had not been able to flame the bank effectively. No casualties were suffered from the minefield, and assaulting very close behind the barrage, D Company quickly captured the German posts on the near bank. But as soon as the company moved over the top of the bank to grapple with the German defenders of the far bank, considerable machine gun fire from the flanks, as well as hostile mortar and artillery fire, cut into their ranks. The initial attempt by the reserve platoon (No. 16) to cross to the far bank was met with very heavy and accurate machine gun fire from the flanks and the houses in front. The platoon commander immediately detached one party to cover his left flank and his Piat to give covering fire on to the houses. Under this cover he assaulted over the bank and cleared in rapid succession the houses between the track junction near C. Cavallini and the area K. 54. Following close behind him No. 17 Platoon cleared the dug-outs on the bank. All was then clear for the reserve company to go through.

On the right, the two leading platoons of B Company suffered heavy casualties, including one platoon commander killed and one wounded from mines, shelling and machine gun fire before reaching the near bank. The 'Wasps' had been unable to find a route forward to flaming distance and were of no help. B Company pressed on however and secured a position on the near bank. Sections were then passed across the river, but came under heavy fire from machine guns in position on the far bank on both the flanks. The remainder of the forward platoons then went across and finally the reserve platoon. In spite of heavy machine gun fire, positions were established on the far bank at 1803 hours but by then the company strength was reduced to about forty, and it was obvious to the company commander that he would not be able to secure the houses beyond the far bank. Fortunately the reserve company arrived in time to help him in his difficult position.

At 1815 hours A and C, the two reserve companies moved forward in seven 'Kangaroos' but ran into a minefield having overshot the point where they should have turned off the road. In the dust and smoke of battle this was a very easy mistake to make but it cost the battalion dear. The seven 'Kangaroos' were blown up on mines and a number of casualties were caused. There was a good deal of disorganisation and delay. By 1915 hours, however, A Company succeeded in passing through D Company and occupying houses near C. Emaldi, about 300 yards beyond the far bank. Thus the left hand of the bridge-head was secure and information was given to the Royal Engineers that they could commence work on the bridge near C. Emaldi.

C Company had meanwhile made straight for B Company and had reached the near bank without much loss. Two platoons were pushed across the river to reinforce B Company and complete the mopping up of the bank. This was quickly accomplished, but there was considerable shelling, and any attempt to push on to the houses beyond was met with intense machine gun fire. Thereupon the commander of 1/12 Frontier Force Regiment ordered the company commander to reorganise C Company and the remainder of B Company into one command and to consolidate his position on the far bank. This was the situation at 2230 hours on 11 April.

Change in the Plan

The original plan had been for 1/5 Gurkha and 1/12 Frontier

Force Regiment to cross the river and fan out so as to form a bridge-head from the river bank at K 51—Mondaniga to K 54, but it was apparent by about 2200 hours that as a result of the heavy fighting this plan was very unlikely to be accomplished before dawn. The commander of the 17th Indian Infantry Brigade therefore decided upon a new plan of operations. 1st Royal Fusiliers was to pass through the small bridge-head of 1/12 Frontier Force Regiment and attack in a northerly direction, enlarging the bridge-head to a depth of about 2000 yards, linking up with 1/5 Gurkha. 1/12 Frontier Force Regiment was to cover the left of the 1st Royal Fusiliers.[11] The commander of the 1st Royal Fusiliers ordered C Company to secure the road running east and west through C. Nardozzi, which was necessary for a start line for the attack. Then A Company on the left and D Company on the right were to attack and secure the 'Street'.[12] B Company was then to form up in the area of C. Baracca and attack in a north-westerly direction and secure the line of the road and the village Mondaniga. To assist in this operation, which was to start at 0200 hours on 12 April, 1/5 Gurkha was to clear the right flank in the area of C. Morandi to allow the maximum artillery support to be made available for the 1st Royal Fusiliers.

Clearing of Area C. Morandi

At 0045 hours on 12 April, after a preliminary artillery concentration on the bend in the river near C. Morandi, A Company of 1/5 Gurkha passed through C Company and advanced across country to secure the bend in the river and C. Morandi. As the men came down off the far bank, they were met by intense machine gun fire from the right flank, but in spite of losses pressed on and by 0200 hours on 12 April the objective was secured although they were subjected to heavy machine gun and mortar fire from due north. Mopping up patrols from A Company soon cleared the Germans remaining between A and C Companies.

Earlier at 2200 hours on 11 April, the commanding officer of the assault squadron Royal Engineers, who was to build an 'Ark' bridge in S. Lorenzo area had completed his reconnaissance. Although the bridge-head at that time was not of any great depth, he decided to commence preliminary work forthwith. At approximately 0200 hours on 12 April, the assault squadron Royal Engineers reported that the Ark bridge would be ready by 0400 hours. This report proved however to be optimistic, as the failure of one Sherman bulldozer and the failure of certain charges to explode delayed opera-

---

[11] 1st Royal Fusiliers—Battle Narrative, the Crossing of the Santerno, File 601/7301/H.
[12] The 'Street' was the name of the road running north-west from Ca di Lugo bridge to the village of Modaniga. It was about 1200 yards long and contained many houses.

tions still further. Almost at the same time the cable party reported that the river Santerno was too wide for their equipment. At 0500 hours two troops of tanks were despatched to the area of the bridge-site with instructions to move forward as soon as possible, one troop to A Company and the other to move with B Company to the latter's objective, the area of the track junction near C. Morandi.

At approximately 0550 hours on 12 April a counter-attack, supported by one or two self-propelled guns, began to develop on A Company's sector, but at the critical moment the last charges on the Ark bridge site were detonated and No. 2 Troop 12th Battalion Royal Tank Regiment came to the rescue, arriving at the Company Headquarters at 0610 hours, within five minutes of the far bank being blown down by the Royal Engineers.

Meanwhile B Company less one platoon moved from the extreme left, and joining with No. 1 Troop 12th Battalion Royal Tank Regiment at the bridge, commenced to advance to its objective, the track junction in the area of C. Morandi. After advancing some three hundred yards, by riding on tanks, they encountered machine guns and self-propelled guns. German opposition was overcome and one of the German self-propelled guns was set alight and destroyed by the tanks. At this moment information was received that the 1st Royal Fusiliers had not achieved its objective, it was also believed that there were many Germans on the exposed left flank. B Company was therefore halted temporarily until a third troop of tanks could be sent forward to deal with the menace on the left flank. The advance was resumed shortly afterwards and at approximately 0800 hours, B Company secured its objective against light opposition. The rest of the day passed quietly enough with shelling and mortaring of the forward positions and occasional shelling by heavy calibre guns on the banks of the Santerno and on the bridge site.

Meanwhile the 1st Royal Fusiliers in an advance towards Mondaniga encountered very stiff opposition. Just across the Santerno the situation was very vague. Conditions were extremely difficult; there was no moon, and the whole area was harassed by shell, mortar and small arms fire. Plans had to be made from maps and air photographs. All these factors delayed the assaulting companies of the 1st Royal Fusiliers and it was not until about 0400 hours on 12 April that the start line was completely clear. By that time C Company had passed through the very small bridge-head of 1/12 Frontier Force Regiment and deployed in front, and successfully attacked the area of the houses in C. Nardozzi and C. Zama. About 0445 hours A and D Companies crossed the start line and moved forward. By 0600 hours A Company had two platoons in the 'Street' and one platoon was just preparing to destroy a self-propelled gun which they had trapped. Then, at 0630 hours, when it was almost dawn, the forward platoons of A Company were counter-attacked by five tanks and a company of infantry. This attack also developed on to the right hand platoon of C Company. The 1st Royal Fusiliers was caught, with its anti-tank guns and tanks still waiting to cross the Santerno. A Company was badly knocked about and withdrew behind C Company. The latter however quickly counter-attacked and finally retrieved the situation. The Germans took about 18 prisoners and inflicted heavy casualties on the 1st Royal Fusiliers. It had not been possible to complete the Bailey bridge near C. Cavallini and the tanks supporting the 1st Royal Fusiliers were not able to get across till considerably later, and then only by using the Ark bridge and coming down the far bank. It was this lack of support that caused losses when the German infantry and tanks counter-attacked the 1st Royal Fusiliers.

When the tanks supporting the 1st Royal Fusiliers had joined up with the infantry, the battalion reorganised. At 1300 hours on 12 April, B Company, with a troop of tanks in support, attacked across to the 'Street' and after inflicting casualties on the Germans reached the 'Street' and finally got one platoon established in the area of the track junction near Mondaniga. There were still many Germans to the north-west and so A Company, with a troop of tanks in support, attacked on to the line of the road at Mondaniga and the bridge-head was completed. German tanks, self-propelled guns and infantry were even there in the area and the 'Street' was quite an unhealthy spot to walk down. The companies wanted food and ammunition, and at about 1500 hours a Honey tank with the rations and ammunition proceeded to supply the forward companies. As it approached about 50 yards from C Company a German self-propelled gun fired on the tanks and secured a direct hit. The tanks brewed-up but luckily the tank crew and 'I' Serjeant baled out. The latter made a quick reconnaissance and located a German position. He brought this information back to the battalion headquarters. Artillery was brought to bear on the position and casualties inflicted on the Germans.

1/12 Frontier Force Regiment covered the left flank of the 1st Royal Fusiliers. At 2000 hours on 11 April, work had been started by a detachment of 4th Mahratta Anti-Tank Regiment on the rope-way across the river, the Battalion Pioneer Platoon having already cleared a path through the minefield. But any progress in the completion of the ropeway was hampered throughout the night by machine gun, mortar and artillery fire. The men continued to work and succeeded in sending the first anti-tank gun across by 0515 hours on 12 April. All the four anti-tank guns were in position by 0700 hours. During the day A Company advanced to the area of C.

Emaldi. Patrols were pushed forward to C. Zama where contact was made with the 1st Royal Fusiliers.

As the morning wore on, two more bridges were thrown across the river; a Bailey Bridge near C. Emaldi was opened and a class 9 bridge built on the site of a demolished bridge over the Santerno near K. 53. The successful completion of the bridging programme by the sappers materially helped to turn the tables on the Germans. With the bridges across the Santerno, the bridge-head was firmly established. The 17th Indian Infantry Brigade had accomplished its task and the 78th (British) Division then prepared to pass through and exploit the success.

Protection of the Flanks

While the 17th Indian Infantry Brigade broke through the Santerno defences, 1st Jaipur Infantry (the 21st Indian Infantry Brigade) covered its left flank. At 2125 hours on 11 April, by which time the infantry of the 17th Indian Infantry Brigade had crossed the Santerno and was fighting on the far bank, the 1st Jaipur Infantry, whose forward positions were in the area of C. Bertazzoli, attacked the Santerno defences with B and D Companies. B Company reached the east bank of the river and was established in the area of S. Scardori. D Company was held up short of the river by heavy spandau fire. The Germans mortared and shelled the positions of the two forward companies. A German counter-attack was smashed with the help of C Company. Meanwhile D Company had succeeded in getting one section on the west bank, and at 2330 hours two platoons of B Company also succeeded in crossing the river and occupying some houses on the west bank in the area of C. Scardori. The Germans heavily shelled and mortared these positions, and at 0500 hours on 12 April, delivered a fierce counter-attack. After close hand-to-hand fighting the 1st Jaipur Infantry was driven back across the Santerno. Shortly afterwards at 0530 hours, B Company on the east bank launched a counter-attack to recapture the west bank and drive the Germans back. By 0600 hours the 1st Jaipur Infantry had again a firm hold on the west bank. At 0645 hours, A Company moved up to B Company's area and spread south-west along the bank to S. Scardori. About this time a German artillery concentration came down on both the companies and continued at intervals until about 0800 hours. At 1430 hours patrols located a German observation post in the houses near C. Capnici. Shortly afterwards a patrol from B Company captured this observation post. By 1530 hours German opposition had lessened considerably. A and B Companies pushed forward and secured the first bound, north north-east to south-west through cross-roads near C. Berarde. The advance was continued and the 1st Jaipur

Infantry secured the final objective—the road a little beyond C. Berarde.

While the 1st Jaipur Infantry protected the left flank, the 19th Indian Infantry Brigade protected the right flank of the 17th Indian Infantry Brigade. At 0730 hours on 12 April, the Argyll and 3/8 Punjab (the former in the area C. Grandi and the latter in the area C. Gaiani), supported by the North Irish Horse and the 6th Lancers advanced north in order to clear the Germans from the area between the Scolo Tratturo and Santerno as far north as the Alfonsine railway. One squadron of the 6th Lancers, with a troop of M 105 under command operated with each forward battalion, which also had the support of two troops of the North Irish Horse. The third Lancer squadron operated east of the Scolo Tratturo as far north as the railway. Only in the area of San Bernardino was opposition encountered; here at 1500 hours, 3/8 Punjab faced heavy spandau fire but by persistent attempts cleared this place by the morning of 13 April. On the right, the A and SH made rapid progress; by 1358 hours on 12 April they had reached within one mile of the railway. The Lancer squadrons forged ahead of the slower infantry and reached the line of the railway after negotiating cratered roads, blown bridges, and minefields. The tanks of the North Irish Horse also carried out a successful sweep. On the right they reached the railway bridge which crossed the road at La Pastorella, north-east of San Bernardino; on the left flank they engaged German infantry on the banks of the Santerno astride Route 16.

Achievements of the 8th Indian Division

In three days the 8th Indian Division had broken through two strongly defended river lines on which the Germans had worked for many months. By establishing a bridge-head on the west bank of the Santerno and inflicting very heavy losses on the Germans, the 8th Indian Division had given the 78th British Division a good start for its chase up to the Argenta gap. The division had further enhanced its reputation as a great fighting formation. The crossing of the river Santerno marked the beginning of a total German collapse in Italy.

The 21st Indian Infantry Brigade had covered itself with glory by its spirited attack on the Senio defences. It had fought against and overcome very heavy resistance. The men of the brigade had known times of great stress, particularly when three company commanders of 1/5 Mahratta had been wounded on the banks of the Senio and when small setbacks delayed the opening of the 'Ark' bridge, just as the first glimmer of dawn was streaking the sky, and the bridge was so urgently required to get tanks over to the west banks. Through all these vicissitudes the brigade came out with flying colours, although it suffered over three hundred casualties in the bitter fighting.[13]

The 19th Indian Infantry Brigade too played an important part in breaking through the Senio defences.[14] In the battle of Santerno, the 17th Indian Infantry Brigade was not without its share of success, and by its achievements inflicted losses on the Germans.

Lieut.-General Sir Richard Mc Creery, the Eighth Army commander, said in a message to Major-General Russell:

"My best congratulations to you and all ranks of your Division on your splendid achievement in reaching the R. Santerno within twenty-four hours. Your attack to overcome the enemy's formidable defences on the R. Senio, which he had developed for over three months, was brilliantly prepared and executed.

"Once again in Italy your Division has shown splendid fighting spirit and determination to overcome all difficulties".

The corps commander, Lieut.-General C.F. Keightely paid this tribute:

"The way you held the line for long weeks and finished with such a spectacular victory in seizing crossings over the Rivers Senio and Santerno was a performance of which every man in your Division may be justly proud.

"From the way you yourself, your commands and staff planned the operation, to the gallantry of everyman who took part in these battles, it was a great achievement adding to your already splendid reputation.

"Thanks to the brilliant start you have given us in five days, we have captured over four thousand prisoners in this Corps alone, with much equipment and so considerably weakened the enemy in his last vital battle".

Summing up the whole in one telling sentence, the divisional commander said in a personal message to his men:

"Two major rivers crossed in forty-eight hours is a remarkable achievement even for the 8th Indian Division".

---

[13] 21 Ind. Inf. Bde. Ops. 9 Apr-26 Apr 45; Appx. A; W/D 21 Ind. Inf. Bde.
[14] Summary of events of 19 Ind. Inf. Bde's attack on the R. Senio 9 April; W/D 19 Ind. Inf. Bde.

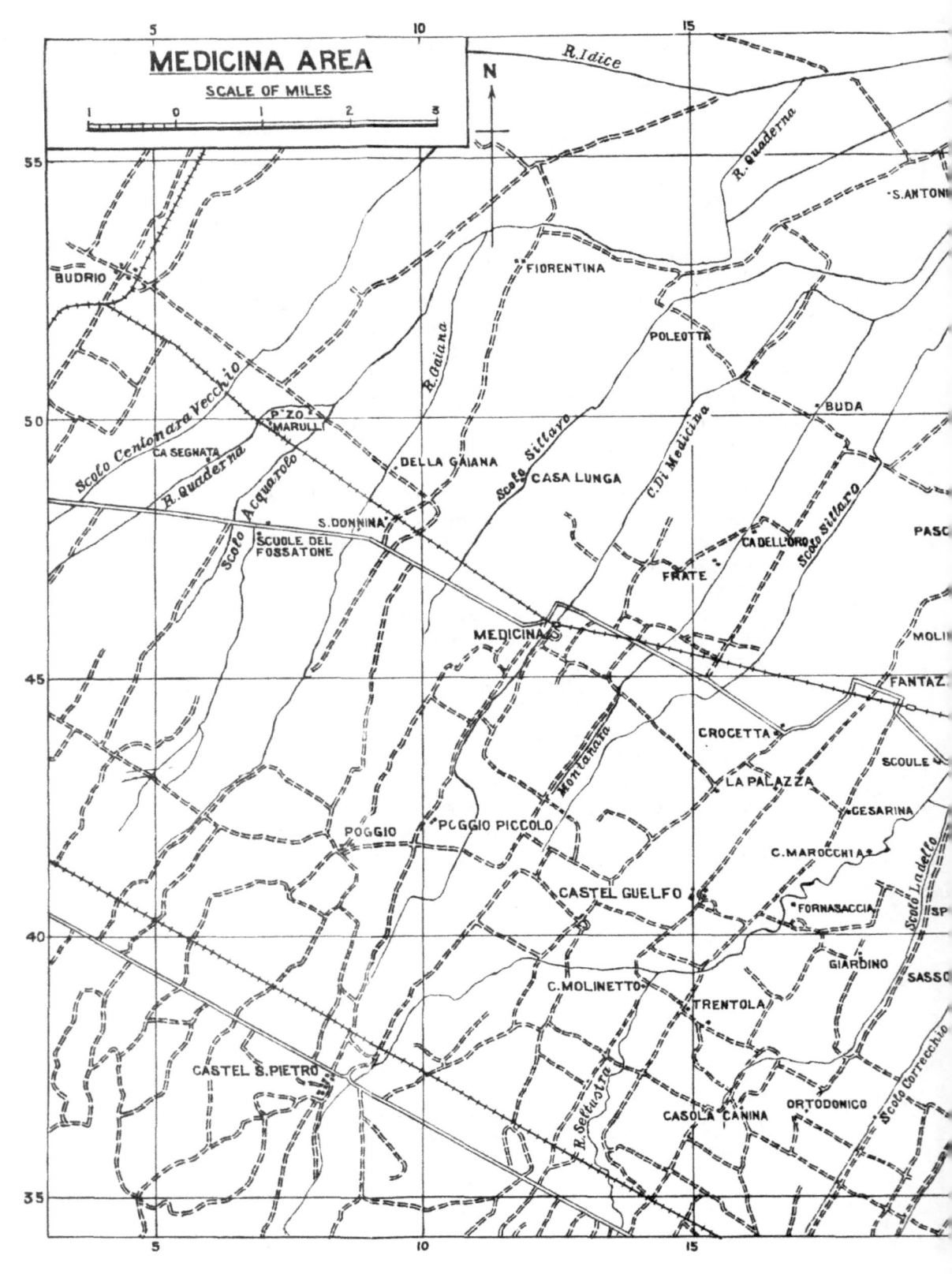

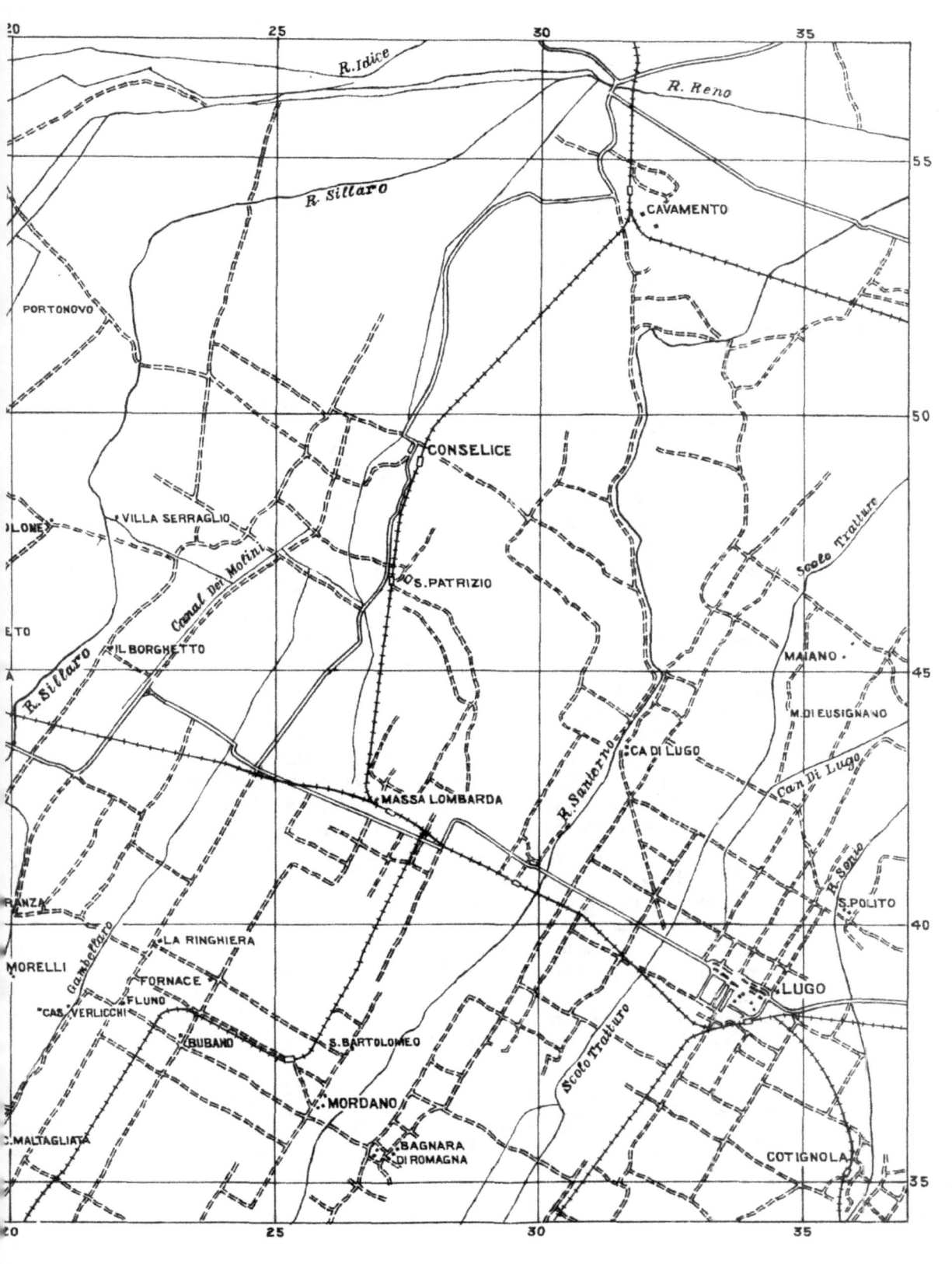

CHAPTER XXXIV

Advance to the River Reno

The Destruction of the German Armies

The Eighth Army had opened the offensive on 9 April 1945 and by the evening of 12 April its three assaulting divisions—the 8th Indian Division, 2nd New Zealand Division and 3rd Carpathian Division—had established bridge-heads across the Santerno. The Indians joined hands with the New Zealanders in front of Massa Lombarda while the Poles were in the area Mordano, with their left flank unit operating in the area of Casalecchio. The Cremona Group had occupied Alfonsine and had advanced along Route 16 to reach the river Santerno. The line of the Santerno was broken. The V Corps was now ready to break through the Argenta Gap. Earlier on 11 April a brigade of the 56th British Division in Fantails had crossed the flooded area and had landed at Menate, three miles behind the German defence lines. The Germans however put up strong resistance before withdrawing through the gap in the floods between Bastia and Argenta. Accordingly on 13 April the third brigade of the 56th Division (the second brigade having already been committed) was ordered to cross the floods and attack in the direction of Chiesa del Bando and Argenta. At the same time the 78th British Division had passed through the 8th Indian Division's bridgehead in front of Massa Lombarda and secured the Reno bridge at Bastia on 14 April. The Germans nevertheless held on to Bastia In the meantime, the Eighth Army's westerly thrust had also made progress. The 2nd New Zealand Division advanced from Massa Lombarda to Scolo Correcchio and occupied both flood banks of the Sillaro by the evening of 14 April, when it passed under the command of the XIII Corps.[1] Meanwhile the II Polish Corps from Mordano area was making a double thrust towards Sasso Morelli and Casola Canina while the left flank unit captured Imola and was advancing towards Castel S. Pietro and Bologna. Thus by 14 April, when the Fifth Army launched its offensive, the Eighth Army had closed up to the Sillaro, and its westerly thrust had covered half the distance between the Senio and Budrio.

The Fifth Army launched the offensive on 14 April. The IV

---

[1] On 14 April the X Corps took over the Zone of the XIII Corps to its left and the latter (with the 2nd New Zealand Division and the 10 Indian Division under its command) took up positions between the Polish and the V Corps, leaving the Poles astride Route 9, driving towards Bologna.

U.S. Corps led the attack at 0945 hours with three divisions west of Route 64. At 2230 hours on 15 April the II U.S. Corps, on the right of the IV U.S. Corps, joined in the attack. After fierce struggle the leading troops of the Fifth Army debouched from the mountain into the Po Valley on the morning of 20 April and took up positions astride Route 9 between Bologna and Modena. Bologna was captured on 21 April, Polish troops of the Eighth Army entering it from the east at the same time as the American troops of the Fifth Army entered it from the south-west.

Meanwhile the Eighth Army had been maintaining considerable pressure. The Argenta Gap was formed by the combined efforts of the 56th and 78th Divisions. The former made a frontal attack from the south while the latter outflanked from the east. After a bitter struggle the leading elements of the 78th Division forced the gap on the afternoon of 18 April. The 6th Armoured Division then broke out of the Argenta Gap, captured Poggio Renatico and joined hands at Pinale with the American troops (the 6th South African Armoured Division) on 22 April. The 8th Indian Division was committed on the V Corps front and on 22 April, it had outflanked Ferrara and, on the morning of 23rd, had a brigade at Pontelagoscuro on the Po. The Eighth Army's western thrust by the XIII Corps and II Polish Corps also made good progress. The New Zealanders extended their bridge-heads across the Sillaro on 15 April and the next day advanced to the Gaiano. The Poles, advancing from the Sillaro, captured Castel San Pietro on 17 April and the next day reached the Gaiano. During the night of 18/19 April both the Corps crossed the Gaiano and advanced to the Idice, the last river before Bologna. The Poles then entered Bologna on 21 April.

The Eighth Army drove on to the Po, which was crossed near Bondeno and Pontelgascuro. The Fifth Army too reached the Po at San Benadetto on 22 April. The bridge-head was enlarged and the Fifth Army troops were racing beyond the river on 24 April. On that day both the Eighth and the Fifth Armies were across the Po. A number of columns were sent in pursuit of the disorganised German forces until the unconditional surrender on 29 April. The 'cease fire' took effect on 2 May.

Mobile Pursuit Forces of the II Polish Corps

Having given a brief account of the events leading to the destruction of the German armies in Italy we shall at first describe the Eighth Army's western thrust. This task was initially assigned to the II Polish Corps. After the 3rd Carpathian Division had established a bridge-head over the river Santerno in Mordano area the II Polish Corps was ready to launch two independent mobile pursuit forces—the 5th Kresowa Division and the 43rd Indian

Infantry Brigade Group to exploit success. The former was to develop operations from the Sasso Morelli area along the axis Castel Guelfo—Poggio Piccolo. The latter was to advance through the cross-roads near Speranza—Marocchia—Medicina.

The following troops were in support of the 43rd Indian Infantry Brigade:[2]

14/20 Hussars
2nd Battalion Royal Tank Regiment
23rd A Field Regiment Royal Artillery
'R' Battery 15th Field Regiment Royal Artillery
106 Battery 78th Medium Regiment Royal Artillery
One self-propelled battery 7th Polish Anti-Tank Regiment
Two Sections ACP Squadron
Detachment 2 Troops 3rd Field Squadron Royal Engineers
255 A Field Company Royal Engineers

The Bridge-head Over the River Sillaro

To start with the part played by the 43rd Indian Infantry Brigade Group in the Spring offensive, on 13 April 1945, this brigade concentrated in the forward areas to pursue the disorganised Germans to Medicina. The two forward battalions, 2/8 and 2/10 Gurkha were in the area south-east of Bagnara di Romagna. At 1400 hours on 13 April, 2/8 Gurkha, with D Company leading, advanced on tanks of the 2nd Battalion Royal Tank Regiment. At 1700 hours they crossed the river Santerno on a Bailey bridge near Bagnara di Romagna. At 1900 hours, German mortar concentration caught the head of the column in the area of La Ringhiera, causing some losses. D Company was pinned to the ground by heavy machine gun fire. However, the opposition was overcome and by last light D Company took up positions along the Scolo Gambellaro in the area of the bridge forward of La Ringhiera, while A and C Companies were in La Ringhiera area, B Company being in the Bubano area.

Henceforward, the advance became slower. Canals, in increasing frequency, though only lightly held with machine guns, provided serious tank obstacles. Sappers with their bulldozers and bridging equipments travelled closely behind the foremost troops. At each canal there would be a check until the armour had crossed. A and C Companies advanced at first light on 14 April up the north side of axis to secure Scolo Correcchio in the area of the bridge near Speranza and to push forward to Scolo Ladello. At 0800 hours A Company advancing from the La Ringhiera area reached Scolo Correcchio against increasing opposition and found the bridge destroyed by the Germans. C Company, however,

[2] 43 Ind. Inf. Bde. O.I. No. 6, dated 9 April 1945.

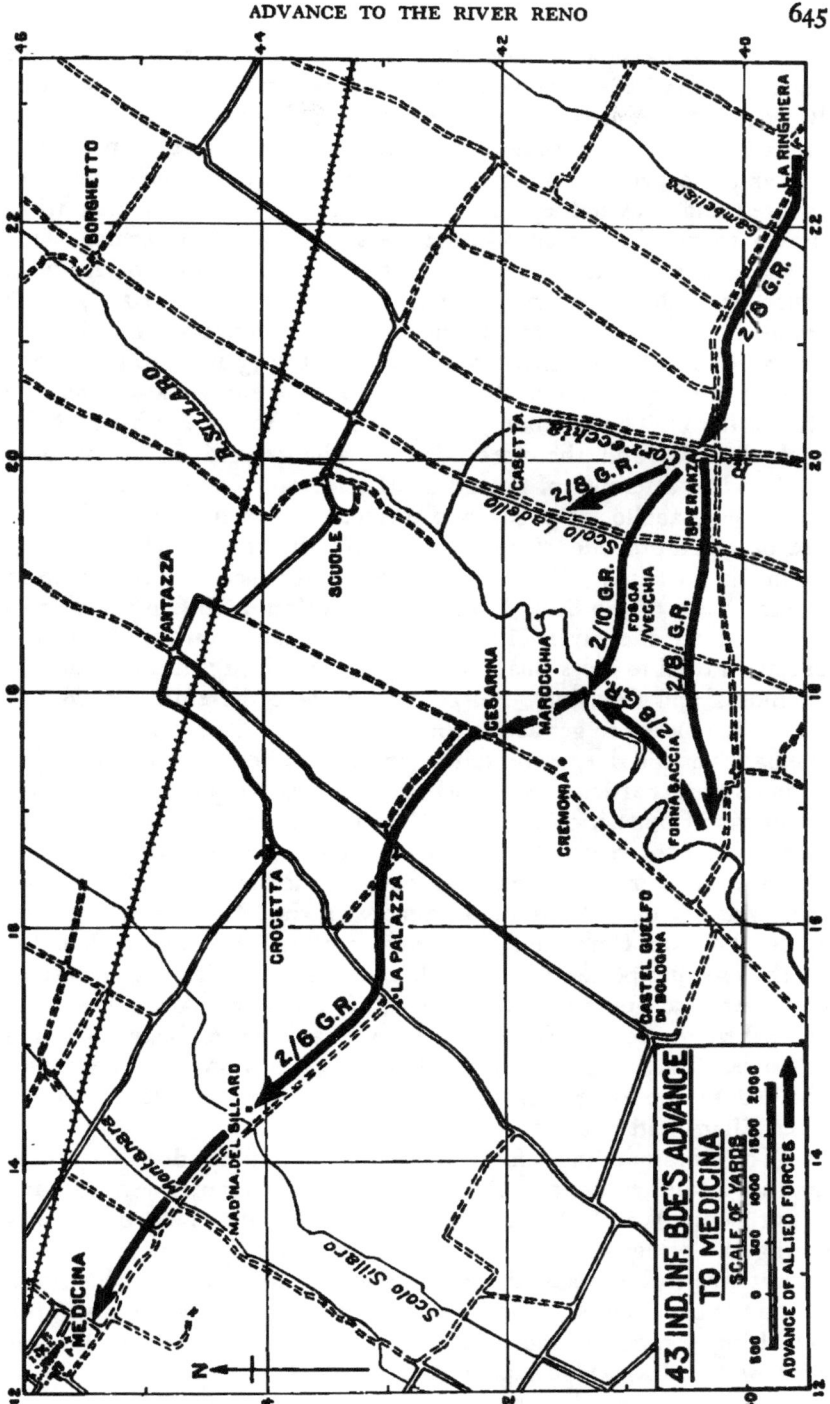

following B Company crossed Scolo Correcchio at the bridge and reached Scolo Ladello at 1100 hours against little ground opposition. But then the company was heavily shelled from the south-east and pinned down. After suffering casualties, it was forced to pull back 300 yards to avoid shelling but ran into German defensive fire and suffered more casualties. At 1255 hours the company was withdrawn to positions near Speranza, east of Scolo Correcchio. This was a set-back as the company had failed to establish a bridge-head over the Scolo Correcchio. German artillery and mortar-fire was severe in the whole sector of the battalion throughout the day.

2/10 Gurkha marched from Bubano at 2045 hours on 14 April to pass through 2/8 Gurkha and establish a bridge-head over the river Sillaro. The Germans had pulled back to the far bank of the Scolo Ladello and therefore 2/10 Gurkha pushed on to its near bank. The attempts of A and D, the forward companies, to cross the Scolo Ladello were however unsuccessful owing to the intense fire of a self-propelled German gun and the troops, who had dug in on the far bank. At dawn on 15 April, the Germans retired from the far bank of the Scolo Ladello. Thereafter 2/10 Gurkha patrols advanced to the river Sillaro. At 1115 hours on 15 April the battalion tried to cross this river to establish a bridge-head to include Cremonia and Cesarina. All companies were therefore moved forward with orders to get across the stream. The German defences on the banks of the river were well-organised and held in strength. The defensive fire, particularly of their mortars, was very accurate. After a fairly stiff opposition 2/10 Gurkha cleared the Germans from the east bank of the river Sillaro. At 1445 hours, B Company was in the centre near Marocchia, with two platoons across the rver; D Company was on the right and C Company on the left, with one platoon across the river. German artillery and mortars concentrated their fire on the crossing places, which made the Gurkha position a precarious one. At 1550 hours the platoon of C Company across the river was compelled to cross back to the eastern bank under heavy German pressure. Thereupon the two platoons of B Company were also recalled to the eastern bank of the river. The assault across the river Sillaro had not been successful.

The commanding officer of the battalion decided to put in another assault early on 16 April. B and D Companies were to carry it out, with A and C Companies following up to help in consolidating the bridge-head. The objective was the Cesarina area. The assault was to be preceded by a heavy artillery barrage, which was to start at 0315 hours. The barrage opened on the river line and the assaulting companies moved forward. Thereafter the attack went very well and a bridge-head was established by 0435 hours. Then 2/6 Gurkha prepared to pass through and secure Medicina.

While 2/10 Gurkha had advanced to the river Sillaro and had established a bridge-head over the river in Cesarina area, 2/8 Gurkha on the left had also pushed forward from Speranza at first light on 15 April, and by 1230 hours was established on the east bank of the Sillaro, near the crossing of Fornasaccia. The Germans however shelled and mortared the battalion sector.

Capture of Medicina

An ark bridge over the river Sillaro was completed at 0700 hours on 16 April and after considerable difficulties tanks and infantry were able to cross in strength. 2/6 Gurkha supported by a squadron of tanks advanced towards Medicina, B Company leading the advance. At 1300 hours, B Company was halted near Madona del Sillaro by two self-propelled guns. The opposition was overcome and the advance was resumed. At 1500 hours C Company passed through B Company to secure Medicina. At 1600 hours, C Company with supporting tanks reached the outskirts of the town and captured many prisoners. At 1700 hours forward elements entered the town followed by the rest of the battalion at 1830 hours. Medicina was seized after confused fighting at 2100 hours.

While 2/6 Gurkha led the attack on Medicina, 2/8 Gurkha had advanced to the south of that town. At 0900 hours on 16 April, this battalion, from its position in Fornasaccia area wheeled to the right and crossed the river Sillaro near Marocchia. Then it advanced on tanks to the reserve area astride the axis south of Scolo Sillaro and dug in for the night. Tactical headquarters was established near Madona del Sillaro. By 16 April the Northern Independent Mobile Pursuit Force (the 43rd Indian Infantry Brigade) had captured Medicina and the Southern Independent Mobile Pursuit Force had made a thrust through Sasso Morelli towards Poggio Piccolo. Thus the II Polish Corps had crossed the river Sillaro and had thrown the Germans back beyond the Canal Medicina. Having accomplished its task of capturing Medicina, the 43rd Indian Infantry Brigade left the II Polish Corps during the night of 16/17 April and passed under the command of the 2nd New Zealand Division (the XIII Corps).

The 10th Indian Division in the Line

After the Eighth Army had broken through the Santerno defences, the Army Commander decided to move the XIII Corps from its Monte Grande sector and to commit it on the right of the II Polish Corps. His intention was to relieve the V Corps of its responsibility for the thrust towards Budrio so as to enable it to concentrate on the battle for the Argenta Gap. The XIII Corps handed over its Apennine sector to the X Corps and assumed

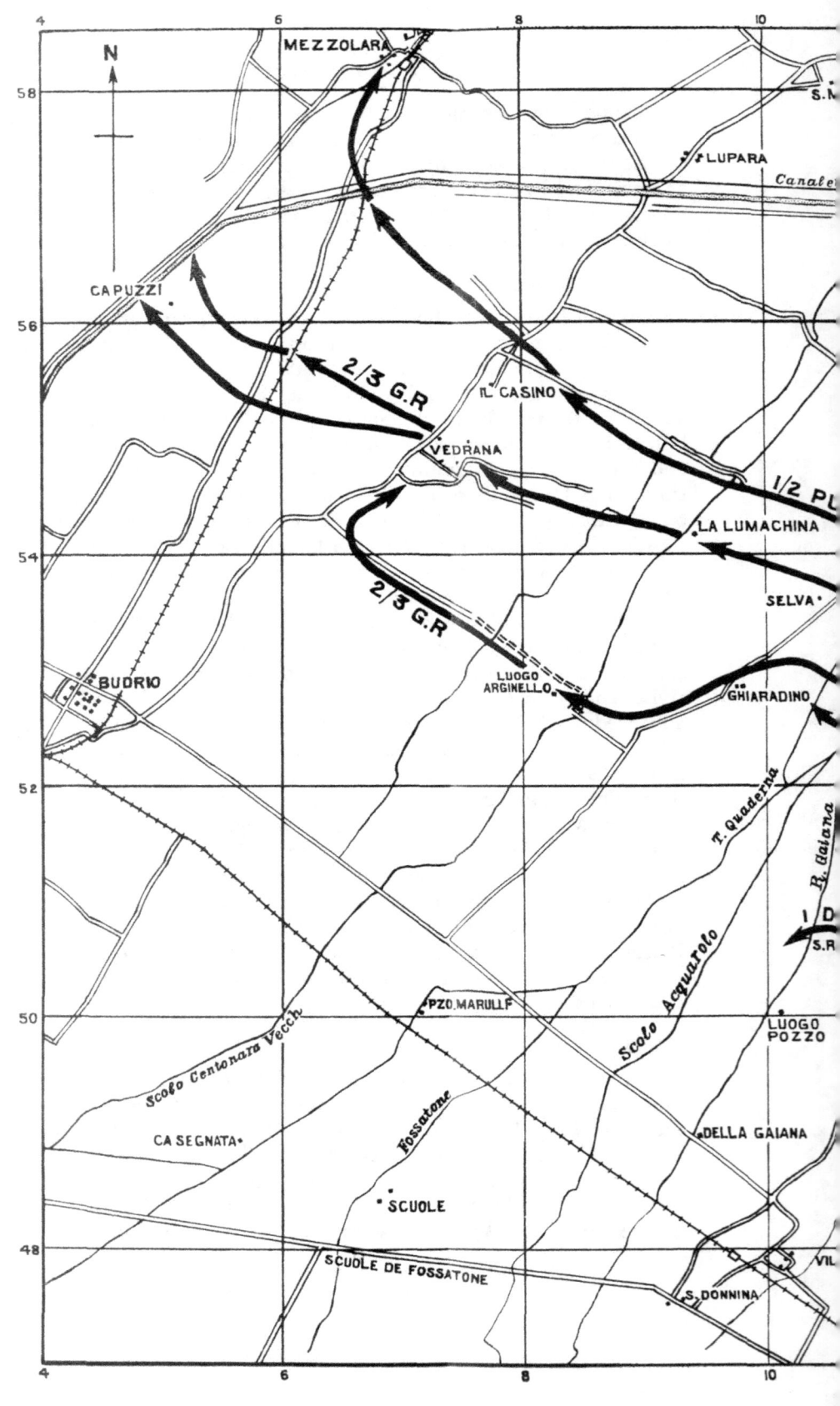

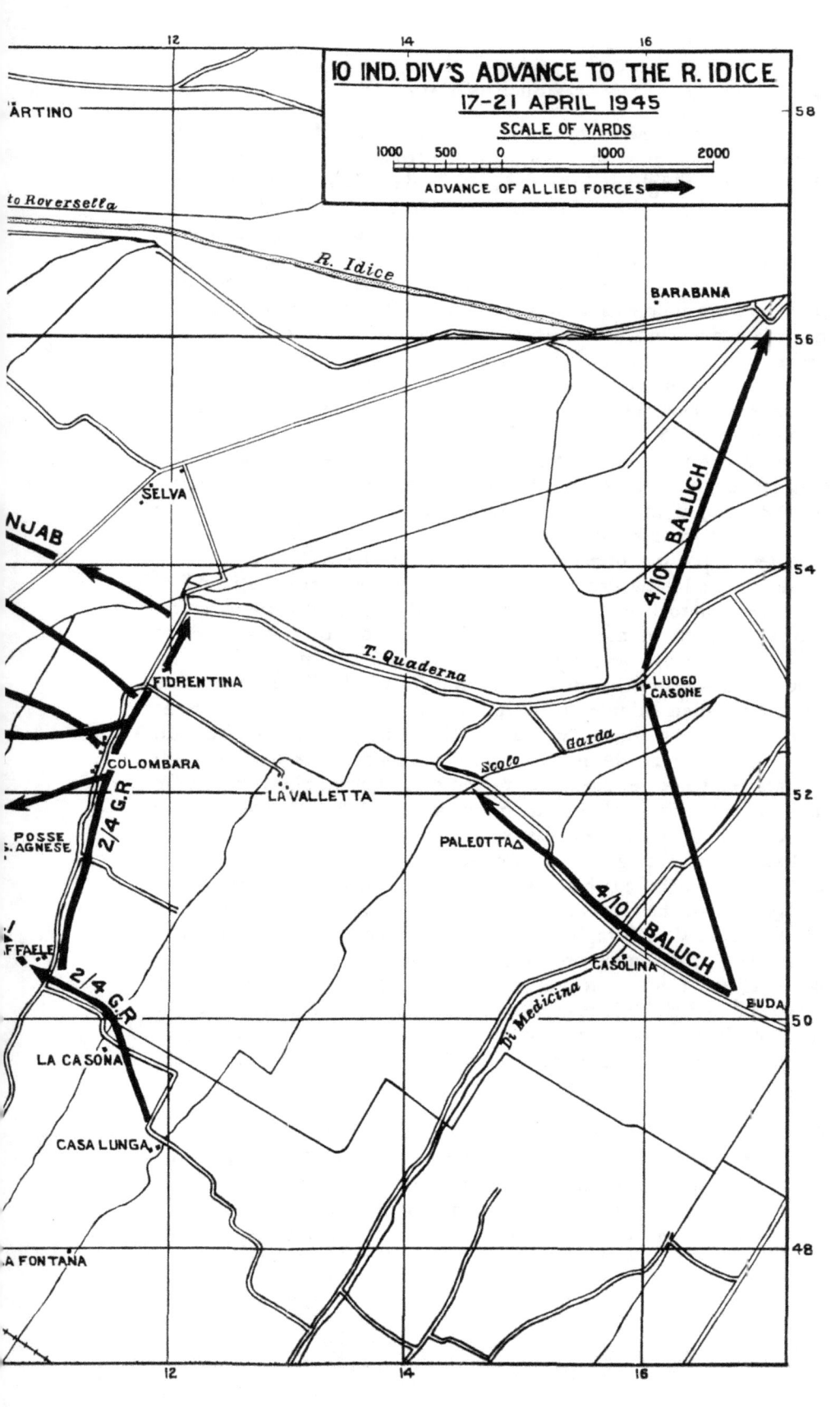

command of the new sector at 1800 hours on 14 April 1945. The XIII Corps was to advance on a two-divisional front, with the 10th Indian Division on the right and the 2nd New Zealand Division on the left.

On 13 April 1945, Commander XIII Corps ordered the 10th Indian Division to move from the Monte Grande sector and concentrate forthwith in the area of Faenza. One brigade group was required in the new area by the evening of 14 April, the second and third were to follow as soon as possible. The 10th Indian Infantry Brigade arrived in the new area by the evening of 14 April and was ordered to concentrate in the Lugo area, passing temporarily under the direct command of the XIII Corps for a short period. This brigade was soon followed by the other two brigades and divisional headquarters, and by 16 April the operational part of the 10th Indian Division was completely established in the new area. The task set for the 10th Indian Division was to relieve the 12th Lancers on the right of the 2nd New Zealand Division and to conform to the move of the New Zealanders westwards across the Sillaro.

Before passing under the command of the XIII Corps on 14 April, the 2nd New Zealand Division had seized both the banks of the river Sillaro from just above the ford near Il Borghetto southwards to approximately Scuole. The division then prepared to enlarge the bridge-head by securing the road Molineto—Fantazza. The attack was to be made at 2130 hours on 15 April. By that time the 10th Indian Infantry Brigade was placed temporarily under the command of the 2nd New Zealand Division and relieved the 12th Lancers in the northern part of the divisional sector. The 12th Lancers had not yet closed up to the east bank of the river Sillaro and therefore the 10th Indian Infantry Brigade's task was to clear the Germans from the east bank of the river. In front of the 10th Indian Infantry Brigade the river took a sharp turn to the north, and the area between their forward troops and the river was by no means clear of the Germans. 2/4 Gurkha on the right, with forward companies in Villa Seraglio area, and the 1st Durham Light Infantry on the left, immediately probed towards the river against active opposition of the German rear elements. The New Zealanders' attack went well and the bridge-head over the Sillaro was enlarged and the road Molineto—Fantazza secured. At the same time the 10th Indian Infantry Brigade carried out its task of clearing up to the river Sillaro line.

Advance to the River Gaiana

The New Zealanders continued the advance on 16 April and by the evening had secured the line of the Scolo Montanara from approximately Ca del Oro to the south of Frate on the one hand, and, on the other hand had cleared Crocetta and advanced to within two miles of Medicina. On their right, the 10th Indian Infantry Brigade had also made good progress. On the right the Durham, with elements of the 6th Battalion Royal Tank Regiment, crossed the river and cleared the west bank from the south of Pascolone to the north towards Porto Novo. They encountered only slight opposition consisting mainly of rearguards, and mines and demolitions. On the left, 4/10 Baluch pushed along the divisional axis, the main road near Villa Seraglio—Pascolone—Buda—Fiorentina. The advance was supported by B Squadron Royal Tank Regiment. D Company, carrier borne, followed by B and C Companies cleared the area outside the road up to the road junction near Buda. The advance encountered little opposition, except for a little heavy shelling which took its toll of casualties. Thus at the close of 16 April, the New Zealanders had seized the line of the Scolo Montanara and had advanced to within two miles of Medicina, while on the right the 10th Indian Division had cleared the west bank of the river Sillaro from the south of Pascolone north to Porto Novo and had advanced to Buda.

On 17 April, the XIII Corps was ready to advance on a two divisional front, with the 10th Indian Division on the right and the 2nd New Zealand Division on the left. The 10th Indian Division had taken command of the right sector of the XIII Corps at 1215 hours on 16 April. At the same time, the 10th Indian Infantry Brigade had reverted to the divisional command. As the XIII Corps required the use of the roads leading from Medicina to Budrio, the 43rd Indian Infantry Brigade (the right hand formation of the II Polish Corps), which had captured Medicina on 16 April, passed under the command of the 2nd New Zealand Division during the night of 16/17 April. On 17 April the 2nd New Zealand Division led the advance to the river Gaiana while the 10th Indian Division advanced on the right, with the additional task of forcing a way north-wards through the floods and rice-fields to Molinella in order to broaden the threat to the country beyond the river Reno.

On the 2nd New Zealand Division's front, 2/6 Gurkha advanced from Medicina at 0830 hours on 17 April, with A Company leading and followed by D Company. The 14/20 Hussars and tanks of 2nd Battalion Royal Tank Regiment were in support of the Gurkhas. A Hussar patrol of light tanks reconnoitred to the next river, the Gaiana, and found its banks to be held in strength by the Germans. This waterway proved to be another stiff German line of defence, where posts were well dug in and cleverly concealed. Behind the Hussar patrol, the heavier tanks and 2/6 Gurkha in 'Kangaroos' followed up. The advance was delayed by blown bridges, German snipers and bazookas. One tank was knocked out by a bazooka. However, S. Donnina was reached at 1100 hours. At 1130 hours the commanding officer of 2/6 Gurkha ordered A and D Companies to establish a bridge-head over the river Gaiana in the area of Della Gaiana. At 1215 hours the Gurkha companies attacked to clear the east coast. On the left D Company met with opposition before reaching the eastern bank of the river Gaiana. By 1900 hours the company was established, in rather week strength, just back of the line of the river. B Company was moved up to provide left flank protection to D Company. On the right, however, A Company had made better progress. The men rode the 'Kangaroos' to within twenty yards of the eastern bank. Then two leading platoons dismounted and charged the near bank, clearing the houses of hostile troops in the S. Donnina area. At 1330 hours the two platoons crossed the river to clear the Germans from the far bank as far north as Della Gaiana. On crossing the far flood bank they came under very accurate and heavy small arms fire. One platoon commander was killed and the other wounded. At 1430 hours the platoons reached their objective, Della Gaiana with only half their strength. They entered the houses and the twenty German occupants were quite ready to surrender, but when they saw the strength of the Gurkha patrols they scattered and made off but a number of German snipers inflicted losses on the Gurkhas which compelled the latter to withdraw to the eastern bank at last light, when their ammunition was exhausted. The Germans fought with grim determination, and in spite of the attack by 2/6 Gurkha supported by very heavy artillery fire, it was found impossible to establish a bridgehead over the river Gaiana. Hence 2/8 Gurkha was brought up to the east bank, north of the main road, while 2/6 Gurkha remained in its positions to the east.

Advance to the River Quaderna

While the 2nd New Zealand Division was held up at the river Gaiana, the progress of the 10th Indian Division on the right was blocked south of the river Quaderna. On 17 April 1945, the 10th Indian Division began its advance towards the Quaderna. On the right 4/10 Baluch, with B and C Companies leading, moved up from the Buda area. No opposition was encountered until this battalion had reached Paleota, where the German troops who had dug in on the river embankment opened fire. The extreme flatness of the country offering no possible cover, and the inability of the armour support to come up to the forward companies owing to a road block near Buda, prevented further advance, and the Baluch was halted south of the river Quaderna.

On the left, 2/4 Gurkha and a squadron of the 6th Battalion Royal Tank Regiment passed through the right New Zealand Brigade, and concentrated in C. Lunga area at 1610 hours on

17 April. While A Company was directed on Fiorentina, B, C, and D Companies pushed on to Raffaele, which was seized by 1800 hours. Nevertheless A Company was unable to make up its objective. However, at the close of the day 2/4 Gurkha also had secured positions south of the river Quaderna, and the Germans were holding in strength the far bank of this river.

Meanwhile a squadron of the Skinner's Horse had moved up and relieved the Durham in the Porto Novo and took up the task of protecting the right flank of the 10th Indian Division. They patrolled north-west from Porto Novo towards Molinella, but were restricted by numerous demolitions and had to patrol forward on foot and even by boat.

By now it had become evident that the Germans had based their line of resistance on the river Quaderna linking up with the Gaiana, along which the New Zealand division on the left had also been held up. It was probable that the Germans would continue to hold this temporary position a little longer until a withdrawal to the river Idice, co-ordinated with the situation further west, could be effected. The *278 Infantry Division* faced the 10th Indian Division, while the *4th Parachute Division* held the western bank of the Gaiana, opposite the New Zealand front.[3] The Germans were well dug in on the far banks of the rivers Gaiana and Quaderna and intended to check the Allied advance to the Idice line, the breaking of which would have compromised their entire defensive positions in the Bologna area.[4]

The commander of the 2nd New Zealand Division planned to attack with the 9th New Zealand Brigade on the right and the 43rd Indian Infantry Brigade on the left. The 2nd New Zealand Division was to cross the Gaiana and Quaderno rivers and continue the advance to the river Idice. On the right the commander of the 10th Indian Division ordered the 10th Indian Infantry Brigade to seize bridge-heads over the Quaderna and Idice rivers.

The attack of the 2nd New Zealand Division across the Gaiana started at 2130 hours on 18 April subsequent to heavy artillery barrage. The attack was successful. The New Zealanders established a bridge-head over the river Gaiana, crossed the Scolo Acquarolo and by first light had penetrated to a depth of two miles along a three mile front astride the Medicina—Budrio road. The Germans fought with grim determination but had to give way and suffer heavy losses. We shall now describe the part played by the 43rd Indian Infantry Brigade in these operations.

The commander of the 43rd Indian Infantry Brigade made a plan by which 2/8 Gurkha on the right and 2/10 Gurkha on the left

---
[3] 10 Ind. Div. Intelligence Summary No. 205, dated 17 April 1945.
[4] 2nd New Zealand Division O.O. No. 57, dated 18 April 1945.

were to cross the start line near S. Donnina, at 2150 hours on 18 April, and secure the line of the river Quaderna from approximately Marulli to approximately C. Segnata, subsequently exploiting forward to Scolo Centonara Vechio. Forty eight air sorties were to soften up the German positions before last light on 18 April.[5]

A tremendous concentration of artillery shells, which fell on the German positions on the west bank of the river Gaiana, together with the flaming thereof by the flame throwing 'Wasps' and 'Crocodiles' inflicted losses on the defenders who were demoralised and could not offer serious resistance to the advance of 2/8 Gurkha on the right. The advance of 2/10 Gurkha was, however, held up, as their left flank was open and consequently the Germans harassed them a good deal.

The task for 2/8 Gurkha was to cross the river Gaiana and establish a bridge-head west of the railway near Marulli. D and B Companies of 2/8 Gurkha advanced from the area of S. Donnina and crossed the river meeting with slight opposition only and soon afterwards established positions on the west bank. C and A Companies then passed through the forward companies and secured a bridge-head despite heavy German defensive fire. By this time German resistance was disorganised. At first light on 19 April the forward platoons of A and C Companies held the west bank of the river near Marulli, when German snipers who harassed the left platoon in the bridge-head were dealt with by the tanks. German self-propelled guns, mortars and Nebels engaged the Gurkha positions on the Quaderna and Fossatone throughout the day but with little effect.

While 2/8 Gurkha had seized the west bank of the Quaderna, 2/10 Gurkha did not fare well. The plan of action for the latter was that B and D Companies will make the assault, with B on the left and D on the right, until the Scolo Acquarola was crossed. Then C and A Companies would pass through and secure the line of the river Quaderna. Good progress was made up to Scolo Acquarola, but losses were suffered from the German fire from the left bank of the river. But further advance was held up at Fossatone. The commanding officer then ordered the C Company on the left flank to hold fast and D and A Companies to lead the advance. But C Company with its left flank was exposed to German fire and suffered losses. Till 0430 hours on 19 April, A and D Companies also failed to break through the Fossatone defence line. The commanding officer then ordered the companies to dig in and patrol forward with the object of maintaining advance after first light. But no further progress was made because of determined German opposition. At 0600 hours, A, B and D Companies

---

[5] 43 Ind. Inf. Bde. O.O. No. 7, dated 18 April 1945.

were on the line of Fossatone and C Company was in the area of Scuole del Fossatone. At 0815 hours the commanding officer of 2/10 Gurkha ordered a squadron of tanks to try and cross the open ground and pass through the Gurkha forward positions to reach the river Quaderna, to be followed later by infantry. Tanks then moved forward. Whilst attempting to cross the river two tanks were knocked out by self-propelled guns. The tanks were then recalled. No further advance was possible during the day time. Thus although 2/8 Gurkha had reached the river Quaderna, 2/10 Gurkha was held up at Fossatone.

Across the River Gaiana

On the right, the 10th Indian Division too was up against considerable opposition. The Germans resisted all attempts of the Indian troops to probe a crossing of the river Gaiana. On the right 4/10 Baluch from Buda made an unsuccessful attempt to establish a bridge-head over the river Idice in Barabana area. In the morning on 18 April, A Company seized Lugo Casone without opposition. The advance to the river Idice started at 1600 hours on 18 April, with A Company leading followed by D, B, and C Companies. Each company was supported by one troop of tanks. The advance made good progress until the Baluch had neared the flood-banks of the Idice, where the intended bridge-head was to be formed. Heavy resistance was then encountered from the German troops dug into the flood banks. Tanks were engaged by a German tracked vehicle in this area and returned fire. The Baluch failed to establish a bridge-head, and owing to the extreme open nature of the ground, were compelled to return, together with tanks to the area of Luogo Casone and Casolina. 2/4 Gurkha was concentrated in Florentina. Further to the east, the Skinner's Horse patrolled to St. Antonio, but was forced to withdraw by shell fire only to return later at last light and capture the town without meeting much opposiion. At last light on 18 April, 2/4 Gurkha was in Florentina area and the Durham and the Baluch in the area of La Casone—Casa Lunga. In their new positions, the Gurkha, the Durham and the Baluch were mortared, shelled and subjected to small arms fire throughout the night of 18/19 April.

On 19 April, the 10th Indian Infantry Brigade succeeded in crossing the river Gaiana. On the right, B and D Companies of 2/4 Gurkha from Florentina and Colombara, respectively, cleared the east bank of the river Gaiana in S. Agnese area by 1630 hours. At 1751 hours the forward companies crossed the river and pushed on towards the river Quaderna. On the left, the Durham passed over a New Zealand crossing of the river Gaiana near Raffaele at 1530 hours and swept the west bank. The 20th Indian Infantry Brigade was then prepared to pass through the 10th Indian Infantry Brigade to the river Idice and beyond.

Bridge-head Over the River Idice

Late on 19 April 1945, the commander of the XIII Corps issued instructions for the assault across the river Idice. In conjunction with the II Polish Corps, which was to advance on a three-mile front north of Castenaso, the 2nd New Zealand Division (with the 43rd Indian Infantry Brigade pulled up for rest) on the right was to attack between Capuzzi and Budrio and after securing a bridge-head over the river Idice exploit on the axis of San Marino—San Giorgio di Piano and thence northwards. On its right, the 10th Indian Division was to advance, with the 20th Indian Infantry Brigade, to cross the river Idice by the most northerly bridge established by the New Zealanders, and push on to Minerbio.

In the morning of 20 April, the 2nd New Zealand Division attacked with the 5th Brigade on the right and the 6th Brigade on the left, and established a bridge-head over the river Idice without much opposition. On the 10th Indian Division's front, however, the Germans held the line of the river Idice, to which they were now pulling back from river Quaderna, with composite battle groups of *992nd* and *994th Grenadier Regiments* of the *278th Infantry Division* on the east and *10th Parachute Regiment* of the *4th Parachute Division* on the west. The boundary between the *278th Infantry Division* and the *4th Parachute Division* was approximately Lugo Pozzo—La Lumachina. On the left flank of the battle groups was the depleted *278 Fusilier Battalion*. Although pulling back to the river Idice, the Germans held out-posts based on obvious vantage points such as Selva south of the river.

The commander of the 20th Indian Infantry Brigade made a plan for crossing the river Quaderna and pushing on to seize a bridge-head over the river Idice. The 20th Indian Infantry Brigade was to advance wth two battalions up, 1/2 Punjab on the right and 2/3 Gurkha on the left. The assaulting battalions were to cross the start line, road near Fiorentine, at 2200 hours on 19 April. The Gurkha was to secure the line of the road in the area of Selva and then push on to seize the objectives La Lumachina and Luogo Arginello. Thereafter the battalion was to advance through Verdana and close up to the river Idice. After some time 1/2 Punjab was commissioned to secure the line of the road in Selva area, and then to capture Il Casino and advance north-east along the road to effect the river crossing at Lupara. 3/5 Mahratta was to be in reserve.

Additional troops under the command of the 20th Indian Infantry Brigade were:[6]

---

[6] 20 Ind. Inf. Bde. O.O. No. 3, dated 19 April 1945.

C Squadron 6th Battalion Royal Tank Regiment
W Company of 1st Battalion Royal Northumberland Fusiliers
Two platoons—Company 1st Battalion Royal Northumberland Fusiliers.

2/3 Gurkha had under its command one medium machine gun platoon, one heavy mortar platoon and two troops C Squadron 6th Battalion Royal Tank Regiment. D and C Companies crossed the start line, road near Fiorentino, at 2200 hours on 19 April. They were across the river Gaiana at 2310 hours and the river Quaderna at 2338 hours. By 0500 hours on 20 April, D Company seized Lumachina and C Company occupied Luogo. A Company was then directed on the road junction north-east of Verdana and B Company on the one to the south-west. Two troops of tanks crossed over the Ark bridge and by 0800 hours were advancing in support of the two forward companies. By 1030 hours both A and B Companies converged on Verdana which was found to have been evacuated by the Germans. The forward companies were then directed on to the railway line, which they reached by 1230 hours. All tanks were then withdrawn and the forward companies continued to make an advance up to the river Idice. At 1400 hours one platoon of B Company got to within fifty yards of the river, but was heavily engaged. The leading platoon of A Company was about 300 yards short of the river bank but could not advance further as three spandaus were holding up progress from the right flank. No further progress was made until the night of 20/21 April when the Gurkha companies managed to get across the river in Palzo la Tue area. At 0800 hours on 21 April they were in the process of stepping up.[7]

On the right, 1/2 Punjab had to face fierce opposition in an attempt to establish a bridge-head over the river Idice. This battalion, with one medium machine gun platoon, one heavy mortar platoon and C Squadron 6th Battalion Royal Tank Regiment less two troops, crossed the start line with C Company on the right and B Company on the left. At 2300 hours on 19 April, the forward companies attained the line of the road beyond river Quaderna. Early on the morning of 20 April the advance was continued to Il Casino, with A Company leading closely followed by D Company. The orders for the battalion were to capture Il Casino and then work north-east along the road and secure the river Idice, crossing at Lupara. As A Company was reaching Il Casino, orders were received at 0920 hours changing the axis of advance, and the battalion was told to secure the bridge-head over the Idice crossing south of Mezzolara. It was stressed that the advance should continue with

---

[7] Orders for attack by 2/3 G.R. night 19/20 April 1945, Appendix D-1 and Report on operations from 2000 hours 19 April to 1000 hours 22 April 1945, Appendix War Diary 2/3 G.R.

the utmost vigour and speed as the seizing of the bridge-head was vital to the operations of the divisions. A Company captured Il Casino without opposition. Then D Company on the right and A Company on the left were directed on to the Idice crossing. Objectives for both the companies were the far banks of the Idice on both sides of the railway and road crossings. Each company was supported by a troop of tanks from the 6th Battalion Royal Tank Regiment. The companies reached within 400 yards of the river, when a German spandau opened up from near the railway crossing. Reconnaissance patrols were sent forward and reported that the banks were lightly held. The Germans did not disclose their weapons and strength. D Company assaulted the banks under cover of artillery fire. One platoon secured the near bank while two platoons crossed to the far bank and were directed by the company commander to a group of houses about two hundred yards from the bank. Now the Germans opened up from all directions and fierce fighting ensued. They had remained quiet and had allowed the Indian troops to go to the far bank, but once the latter had crossed, they opened fire. The company commander was wounded and later killed. The commander of one platoon was wounded and the commander of the second platoon was killed. The grim struggle continued for an hour and the leading two platoons were pinned to the ground on the far side. Meanwhile the third platoon was engaged in securing the near bank. As the struggle on the far bank continued for an hour, the commander of B Company (the reserve company which had moved up to within 450 yards of the river) went forward to obtain the latest information, as the company's wireless set had been knocked out. It was evident that to withdraw the leading platoons even under smoke-screen would be costly, and as they had crossed over, it was best to exploit their success. To leave them till dark would have meant their being counter-attacked by superior forces in a critical position. It was therefore decided to make the bridge-head secure with two more companies, one on each side of these two platoons, which were in the area of the railway crossing. Owing to the presence of Indian troops on the far bank, artillery fire could not be put down on the banks but a barrage was laid on from 350 yards from the banks to a depth of 800 yards. Two troops of tanks supported the advance of the leading companies which started at 2000 hours on 20 April, with B Company on the right and A Company on the left. The attack was preceded by artillery barrage. C Company moved to within 400 yards of the river in reserve. As the companies emerged from their positions the Germans brought down very heavy artillery and spandau fire. Their automatic fire from the flanks was very deadly. In spite of all this opposition the companies went forward with great gallantry and after very fierce fighting secured the near bank. Two platoons of B Company rushed over the near bank, crossed the river and charged the far bank under very heavy fire. Six of them were killed and fourteen wounded. These platoons were forced to withdraw to the near bank. On A Company's front the reverse slopes of the near bank were heavily wired and prevented further movement forward. In spite of this set-back both the company commanders decided to keep up the momentum of the attack. The commander of B Company was however killed and the commander of A Company severely wounded. Nevertheless the leading companies charged the 25 feet high bank with bayonets and compelled the German troops to withdraw to the far bank. Many gallant efforts were made to secure the far bank later on. But the German fire was very heavy and any one who got on to the crest of the bank was shot down. The two platoons of D Company on the far bank could not therefore be succoured. By 2100 hours A and B Companies were firmly established on the near bank. Two platoons of C Company were sent, one to each leading company to make up their casualties. Both troops of tanks gave magnificent support to the battalion in securing the east bank. One tank tried to climb the 25 feet bank six times but got bogged in the subsidiary canal within fifteen yards of the near bank. Another tank attempted to climb the railway embankment and was blown up on the minefield. The presence of tanks had great moral effect and was to a large extent responsible for stopping immediate German counter-attacks on the near bank[8]

German fire died down about 2330 hours. Efforts were then made to send reconnaissance patrols forward but any movement on the top of the bank drew fire. It was a moonlit night and the individuals were silhouetted against the skyline. The Germans were only about a hundred yards away on the far bank. Reconnaissance patrols early in the morning however disclosed German withdrawal. By 0615 hours on 21 April the far bank was secured and advance carried on to Mezzolara, which was firmly secured by 0915 hours. The two platoons of D Company on the far bank had fought out to the last man and the last round. They had stuck to their post and had died fighting bravely against heavy odds. Bodies collected later showed many bayonet wounds, and their own bayonets were covered with blood. Thus ended the heroic struggle to establish a bridge-head over the river Idice. This was the battalion's finest effort and a glorious hour of trial. The inspection of the battle area later disclosed the strength of the German position in well concealed and camouflaged dug-outs, with spandau posts every fifty yards. The reverse slope of the near bank on the west of the railway crossing was

---

[8] The *Diagonals* dated 5 May 1945, Appendix B, War Diary 10 Ind. Div. May 1945.

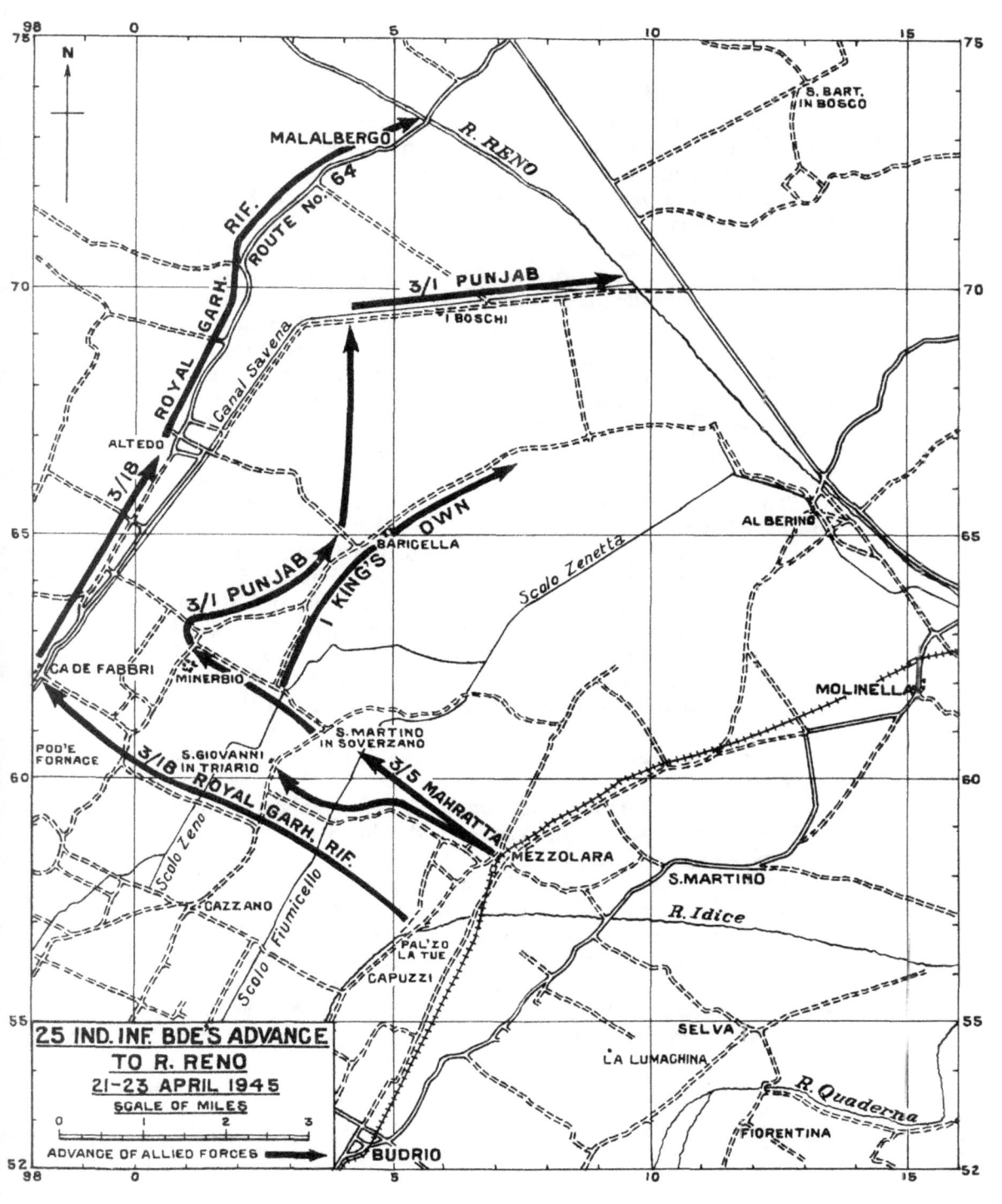

wired. German prisoners confirmed that 150 to 180 Germans with many automatics had held this strong position.[9]

Capture of S. Martino

When 1/2 Punjab had seized Mezzolara, 3/5 Mahratta pushed through to the north-east towards S. Martino. A and D Companies, who led the advance, made good progress until they were held up about a thousand yards short of the Scolo Fiumicello by heavy and accurate spandau and shell fire. The Mahratta casualties were 4 killed and 14 wounded. Light was beginning to fade, hence the commanding officer decided to attack the bund at first light on 22 April.[10] Meanwhile the engineers were immediately at work in the area where 1/2 Punjab had crossed the river Idice, and by 1300 hours on 21 April, an Ark bridge was completed in the area of Palzo la Tue in spite of considerable German mining; half an hour later a class 9 trestle bridge was opened to traffic in the same area. Soon tanks in support of the two forward battalions of the 20th Indian Infantry Brigade were crossing the Idice, followed by a squadron of the Skinner's Horse and other supporting arms.

The 25th Indian Infantry Brigade then prepared to pass through the 20th Indian Infantry Brigade at first light on 22 April and to take up the running, assisted by two squadrons of the 6th Battalion Royal Tank Regiment, and 3/5 Mahratta temporarily under command. The brigade plan in outline was that 3/5 Mahratta would seize the line of the Fiumicello canal, and 3/1 Punjab would then pass through, being directed on Minerbio via San Martino. At the same time 3/18 Garhwal was to pass through the New Zealanders' positions in the Cazzano area and then move on to Fornace. Both 3/5 Mahratta and 3/18 Garhwal were to have a squadron each of 6th Battalion Royal Tank Regiment under command.

3/5 Mahratta, from its position a thousand yards short of the Scolo Fiumicello, sent light patrols to the bund at first light on 22 April, and when no contact was made, B and C Companies pushed through to S. Martino and S. Giovanni, respectively. B Company encountered a self-propelled gun as the men entered S. Martino. The gun was soon dealt with and S. Martino was occupied without further mishap. C Company moved up to S. Giovanni and was just too late to intercept a German tank, which pulled out as the men entered the village. By 1100 hours both the places—S. Martino and S. Giovanni had been seized.

[9] The Battle of the River Idice April 20, 1945; Appendix J-2, War Diary 1/2 Punjab.
[10] Review of operations 15-23 April 1945; Appendix F.I., War Diary 25 Ind. Inf. Bde.

Advance to the River Reno

Then 3/1 Punjab passed through 3/5 Mahratta to the small town of Minerbio. D Company on the tanks of the squadron of the 6th Battalion Royal Tank Regiment, followed by A Company, cleared Minerbio by 1330 hours. On the left, 3/18 Garhwal advanced at 0900 hours on 22 April from the concentration area near Mezzolara and passed to Ca di Fabri (near Route 64), which was occupied by 1200 hours. By cutting Route 64 the commander of the 25th Indian Infantry Brigade had hoped to cut off the line of withdrawal of any German troops to its south, but soon the divisional commander ordered the brigade to swing north towards Malalbergo and the river Reno in order to trap any German troops which might have been left on the river Idice and the river Reno. Accordingly the commander of the 25th Indian Infantry Brigade ordered the 1st King's Own Royal Regiment to send out patrols on foot along the roads running towards Malalbergo from Minerbio, and the main body brought up on the brigade's right flank. Thus, during the afternoon, the brigade advanced with 3/18 Garhwal on the left of and including Route 64, 3/1 Punjab in the centre and the 1st King's Own Royal Regiment on the right. The leading elements of the Garhwal and the Punjab consisted of infantry riding on the tanks which made the task of rapid advance of these two battalions easy. The Skinner's Horse was also able to operate in its primary role, going well ahead of the forward elements of the brigade.

On the left, 3/18 Garhwal moved up Route 64 towards Malalbergo and reached Altedo at 1800 hours on 22 April, where the battalion harboured for the night. In the centre 3/1 Punjab on tanks moved off from Minerbio and cleared the area along the line of the Canal Savena.

At 1000 hours on 23 April, 3/18 Garhwal, on the left, moved off from Altedo, cleared Malalbergo by 1300 hours and reached the river Reno. In the centre, B and D Companies of 3/1 Punjab with tank support cleared the area due east from their positions for a depth of approximately five miles but found no German troops. On the right flank the 1st King's Own Royal Regiment cleared the area of the road running north-east from near S. Martino. This was virtually the end of the hunt. The 10th Indian Division was in fact squeezed out by the 6th British Armoured Division, then advancing north and east of the Reno, and the New Zealanders who were moving north along the parallel route to Route 64. The 10th Indian Division therefore concentrated in the Minerbio area.

CHAPTER XXXV

Advance to the River Adige

V Corps Thrust Through the Argenta Gap

So far we have described the western thrust towards Budrio and from thence the swing north to the river Reno. We shall now describe the eastern thrust through the Argenta Gap to the river Po. After breaking through the river Santerno defences on 12 April 1945, the 8th Indian Division had pulled out of the line. The divisional artillery however had been summoned on 15 April by the V Corps Commander to support the assault of the 56th and 78th (British) Divisions through the Argenta Gap. On 18 April, a squadron of the 6th Lancers was sent to provide left flank protection for the V Corps, on the line of the river Idice. It relieved the 56th Reconnaissance Regiment, and the whole regiment came under the command of the V Corps. Since it was vital to keep the Corps supply arteries in good state of repair at a time when they bore an ever increasing volume of traffic, the full resources of the divisional engineers were concentrated on this task.[1]

On 20 April the Germans were being driven back all along the line. Constantly harassed from the air, relentlessly pursued by lorried infantry with armoured support, and mauled by the gunners whenever they paused, the Tenth German Army was already beginning to disintegrate. The 29th Panzer Grenadier Division was committed too late to arrest the thrust of the 56th and 78th British Divisions through the Argenta Gap, that strategic avenue to the north, flanked on one side by the Argenta marshes and on the other by the Comacchio lake.[2]

The V Corps was advancing to the river Po on a three division front, with the 56th Division on the right directed on the line of road Ostellato—Quartesana, the 78th Division in the centre directed on the river Po, north and north-east of Ferrara, and the 6th British Armoured Division on the left directed on Bondeno.[3] By 21 April the corps front had considerably widened and as the 6th British Armoured Division continued its pursuit north-westwards along the northern bank of the river Reno, the corps commander ordered the 8th Indian Division to move up on the right of the 6th British

---

[1] 8 Ind. Div. Operations, File 7212/H.
[2] *Ibid.*
[3] V Corps O.O. No. 50 dated 19 April 45; Appendices; 8 Ind. Div. O.O. No. 47, dated 21 April; War Diary 8 Ind. Div.

Armoured Division in the area of S. Nicolo Ferrarese, and advance along the axis of Route 16, which skirted Ferrara and crossed the river Po at Pontelagoscuro.[4]

Advance towards Ferrara

The role of the 8th Indian Division was to advance astride Route 16 to the river Po at Pontelagoscuro. The 19th and 21st Indian Infantry Brigades were to carry out this thrust. The former was to advance east of the Po Morto di Primaro, a tributary of the main river, which followed the course of Route 16, while the latter was to advance on the west.[5]

The following troops were under the command of the 8th Indian Division:
- 6th Lancers
- 21st Tank Brigade less 12th Battalion Royal Tank Regiment
- Divisional Artillery (including 4th Mahratta Anti-Tank Regiment with 225th self-propelled Anti-Tank Battery under command HQ Royal Artillery)
- 24th A Field Regiment (under command 21st Tank Regiment)
- One Medium Regiment (5.5-inch) from 1st Army Group Royal Artillery.[6]

B Flight 654 Air OP Squadron was to support the 8th Indian Division and the 2nd Army Group Royal Artillery.[7]

When the 8th Indian Division entered the line on 21 April, the Germans had just been forced to commit part of the *26th Panzer Division* in an attempt to stem the Allied advance from the Argenta Gap. Prisoners had been taken in the area of S. Nicolo Ferrarese, and some hostile tanks were reported west of the Po Morto di Primaro in the vicinity of Fornace Vecchia.

The *26th Panzer Division*, against which the 8th Indian Division had fought on the Moro in the autumn of 1943, had always been regarded as one of the best German formations in Italy. Whenever their line was seriously threatened, the Germans frequently called upon this division to help to restore the situation. Now, once more it appeared in the same role, and at this time was one of the few German divisions whose ranks were not hopelessly depleted. It was still an organised fighting machine.[8]

On 21 April 1945, the 19th Indian Infantry Brigade, with 3/8 Punjab leading, moved into the line and relieved elements of the 6th British Armoured Division. By 1600 hours, 3/8 Punjab had

---

[4] 8 Div. O.O. No. 47, dated 21 April; War Diary 8 Ind. Div.
[5] Ibid.
[6] 8 Div. O.I. No. 15, dated 19 April; War Diary 8 Ind. Div.; Div. O.O. No. 47, dated 21 April; War Diary 8 Ind. Div.
[7] 8 Div. O.I. No. 15 dated 19 April; War Diary 8 Ind. Div.
[8] 8 Div Int. Sum. No. 187; War Diary 8 Ind. Div.; April 1945.

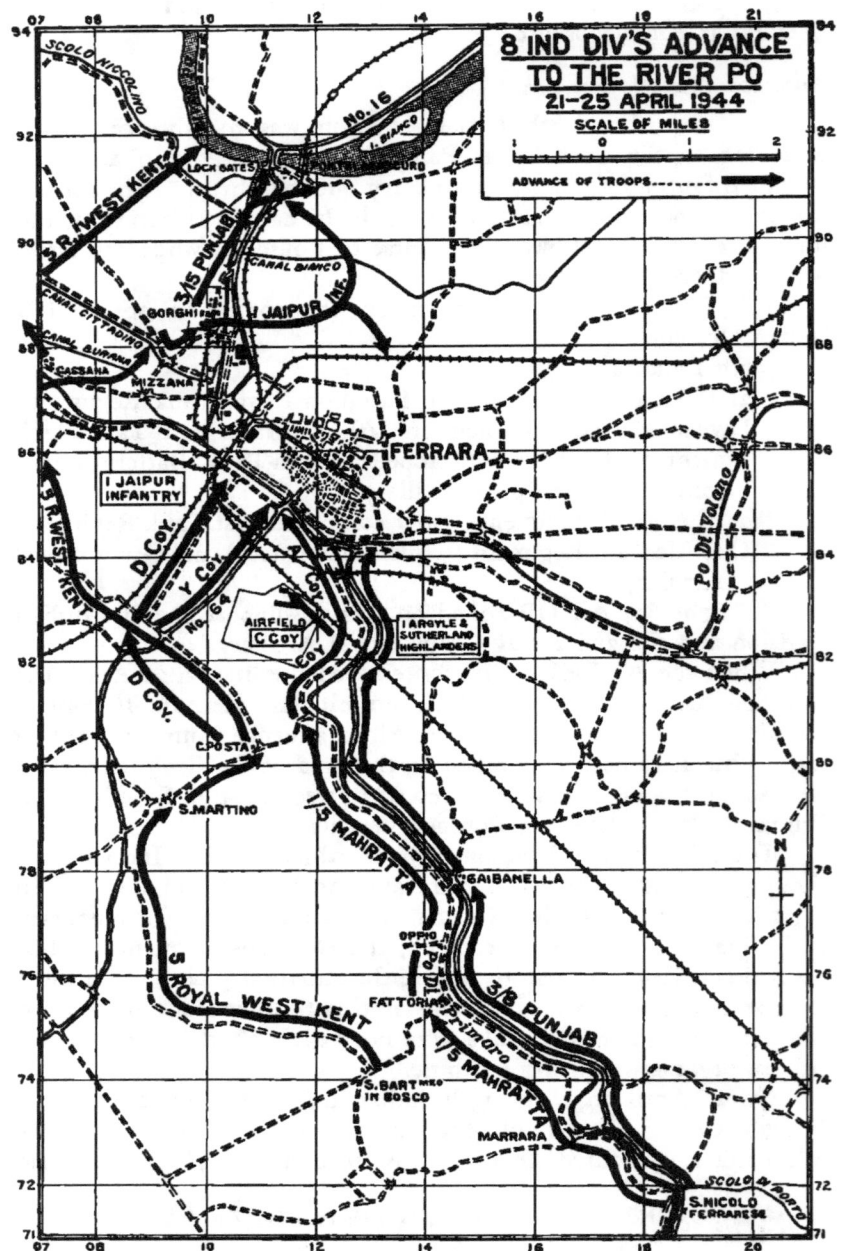

taken over in the village of S. Nicolo Ferrarese, while the 1st Argyll and Sutherland Highlanders and 6/13 Frontier Force Rifles concentrated to the south of that village.[9]

The following troops were under the command of the 19th Indian Infantry Brigade:[10]

    North Irish Horse
    A Squadron 6th Lancers
    A Company (Mortars) 5th Royal Mahratta (less two platoons)
    C Company Royal Mahratta
    15th Anti-Tank Battery, 4th Mahratta Anti-Tank Regiment
    D troop 225th Anti-Tank Battery (self-propelled).

3/8 Punjab pushed up, with tanks in support, by Route 16 in the direction of Ferrara. Small parties of German troops were holding the line of Scolo di Porto, north of the village of San Nicolo Ferrarese. There was only light contact and a few Germans were taken prisoners. German spandaus were, however, active and a few casualties were caused by heavy shelling. Weather was fine. Fortunately owing to the flat nature of the terrain, the German observation, except from the forward defended localities, was nil. In spite of lack of resistance progress was slow, owing to the intensive canal irrigation system and the consequent ease with which demolitions could be carried out. That night, 3/8 Punjab and the supprting arms crossed the canal against light opposition. By first light on 22 April they advanced three thousand yards north-west of the village. With a squadron of the 6th Lancers going ahead and D Company leading, 3/8 Punjab reached Gaibanella, where slight opposition was encountered. They reached the line of the railway at 1330 hours.

At that time, when the Argyll passed through the forward positions, 3/8 Punjab was little more than two thousand yards from the Po di Volano, which skirted Ferrara on its southern side. The armoured cars of the Lancers were still leading the advance, followed closely by the Argyll, who passed through 3/8 Punjab at 1700 hours and reached Po di Volano at 1900 hours. Thus Argyll had reached the southern gateway of Ferrara. But further progress was checked by a strong German force in the town.[11]

The Advance to the Ferrara Airport

The 21st Indian Infantry Brigade advanced west of Po di Primaro to the Airport. The following troops were under the command of the brigade:[12]

---

[9] Diary 21 April; War Diary 19 Ind. Inf. Bde.
[10] 19 Bde. O.O. No. 46 dated 21 April; War Diary 19 Ind. Bde.
[11] Sitrep 22 April; War Diary 8 Ind. Div.
[12] 21 Bde. O.O. No. 6, dated 21 April; War Diary 21 Ind. Inf. Bde.

B Squadron 6th Lancers
D Company 5th Royal Mahratta (machine gun)
13th Battery, 4th Mahratta Anti-Tank Regiment
B Troop 225th Anti-Tank Battery (self-propelled)
16th (mortar) Battery, 4th Mahratta Anti-Tank Regiment.

On 22 April, the 21st Indian Infantry Brigade, with 1/5 Mahratta leading, passed through S. Nicolo Ferrarese. The Mahratta arrived at Marrara at 1245 hours and marched from there to a selected debussing area at Oppio. From there, with B Squadron of the 6th Lancers moving ahead, and supported by tanks of the North Irish Horse, the Mahratta pushed northwards along the road, which ran parallel to Route 16. Except for the delays caused by blown out culverts and craters in the road, the Lancers were able to advance very quickly. In fact, they made no contact with the Germans until they reached the road junction south of the airport, where they were engaged by small arms fire. In this locality a sharp clash ensued with a small group of Germans.[13]

The Lancers were closely followed by 1/5 Mahratta, who advancing from Oppio at 1430 hours reached without incident the road junction near C. Posta, where contact was established with the Lancers. But at this point their progress was held up by the Germans who were holding in strength the airport. The German machine guns were sited in the buildings on the north side of the aerodrome, and had good positions. The commander of 1/5 Mahratta ordered A Company to send a patrol up to the road and rail junction, thence north-west along the railway line to probe into German positions. By 1805 hours, a platoon from A Company was secure in the area of the road and rail junction and was ready to send a platoon to exploit to the aerodrome buildings. At 1935 hours, A Company platoon was established around the air port buildings, but was unable to cross the railway line northwards because of German small arms fire. The platoon thereupon withdrew from its forward area.[14] C Company was then ordered to advance from the airport buildings along the railway line to the road and railway junction and to patrol to the railway sidings beyond, and if they were found to be clear, to advance north-east along the road towards Ferrara. By 2237 hours two platoons and headquarters of C. Company occupied the air port buildings. As the platoons attempted to advance west along the railway line they were engaged by machine gun fire from the houses in the immediate front. Artillery fire was brought down on pin-pointed German positions. At 0330 hours on 23 April, the Germans fired three volleys of 15-cm. Nebelwerfer rockets, which landed in the battalion area. At 0400 hours

---

[13] Sitrep 22 April; War Diary 21 Ind. Inf. Bde.
[14] War Diary 1/5 Mahratta.

the commanding officer decided to pull C Company back from the aerodrome and approach Ferrara from a different direction. To advance from the south over the open ground in face of German resistance in the area of the airport was impossible. German resistance on the southern outskirts of Ferrara led to a decision to capture the city by an encircling movement. Whilst the 19th Indian Infantry Brigade harassed the Germans across the Po di Volano, the 21st Indian Infantry Brigade was ordered to swing left, cross the canal Burana and advance north-east to the factory area of I. Gorghi and Pontelagoscuro.[15]

Advance to Canal Burana

On 23 April 1945, the 21st Indian Infantry Brigade developed powerful thrusts against Ferrara. The plan was that 1/5 Mahratta would close up to Canal Burana, the 1st Jaipur Infantry would advance through area Cassana and attack the factory area I. Gorghi, and the 5th Queen's Own Royal West Kent Regiment would make a wide sweeping movement on the extreme left so as to close up to the river Po.

We shall first describe the advance of 1/5 Mahratta to Canal Burana. The plan was for D Company on the left to advance along the dike, thence along the track between the railway line and Route 64 towards Canal Burana. Y Company in the middle was to advance along Route 64 and clear the area to its west; on the right, A Company was to patrol forward to the road and rail junction and the bridge. The plan was successfully carried out. D Company, leading the attack, advanced at 0730 hours on 23 April and by 1250 hours had closed up to Canal Burana. A patrol to the blown bridge was however pinned down by heavy German fire. On the right, A Company secured without opposition the road and rail junction, but at 1643 hours a platoon patrolling to the bridge was held up by small arms fire. In the centre, the forward elements of Y Company encountered some opposition which was overcome with the help of tanks and artillery. By 2130 hours all the three forward Mahratta companies were firmly poised along the southern bank of Canal Burana. The Germans who held the far bank, shelled the Mahratta positions.[16]

Meanwhile 1st Jaipur Infantry was also making good progress. It arrived in the area of Cassana at 1130 hours on 23 April. Thence the men swung right to I. Gorghi and Mizzana. C Company operated on the left; in the centre D Company captured I. Gorghi at 1300 hours; on the right A Company cleared Mizzana and at 1500 hours reached the blown bridge. The 1st Jaipur Infantry

[15] *Ibid.*
[16] *Ibid.*

consolidated its positions and prepared to cross the canal east of Route 16.[17]

Advance to the River Po

While 1/5 Mahratta was established along the south bank of Canal Burana, and the 1st Jaipur Infantry had not been able to cross the Canal east of Route 16, the 5th Royal West Kent Regiment, making a wide movement to the left had closed up to the river Po. The battalion had relieved the Scots Guards in the S. Bartolomeo in Bosco area at 1430 hours on 22 April 1945. Supported by C Squadron North Irish Horse the battalion moved northwards to S. Martino at 1530 hours. By 1830 hours the forward elements pushed beyond S. Martino and reached C. Posta. Brushing aside small isolated pockets of German resistance they advanced during the night of 22/23 April, and established positions in the area of the bridge at Cassana. The advance was resumed at 0500 hours on 23 April and the battalion crossed the Canal Cittadino, and by last light had closed up to the river Po. They were the first troops of the British Army to stand on the southern banks of the river Po.[18].

Capture of Ferrara

On the 21st Indian Infantry Brigade front, the night of 23/24 April was generally quiet and there was a marked decrease of German small arms fire, especially in the Ferrara sector in front of 1/5 Mahratta. Under cover of darkness, numerous reconnaissances of the Po banks, as well as of the Canal east of I. Gorghi, were made by infantry and sapper officers. The 21st Indian Infantry Brigade was now trying very hard to cross the canal east of Route 16 in order to cut off from the north the German line of retreat from Ferrara. But the Germans, realising the seriousness of this threat, sent six tanks and a strong body of infantry to the factory buildings, which lay east of the canal and almost opposite I. Gorghi. From there, with unrestricted fields of fire over flat ground, the Germans could deny the Allied advance eastwards. However, during the afternoon of 24 April A and B Companies of the 1st Jaipur Infantry succeeded in crossing the canal in the area of the blown bridge. Throughout the afternoon sappers' work on the bridge, which had collapsed in the middle and was not completely demolished, was frustrated by direct fire from the German tanks, which were little more than 1000 yards away. For the same reason the Allied armour was unable to cross the bridge in support of the infantry. Towards 1900 hours on 24 April, after a period of quiet, the two platoons of B Company began to advance in open order in a north-easterly direction towards

[17] War Diary 1st Jaipur Infantry.
[18] 8 Ind. Div. Operations, File 7312/H.

the factory. Then, when they were some five hundred yards from the two storage sheds they saw six German tanks emerge. Four tanks turned and made off eastwards, whilst the remaining two advanced towards the Jaipur platoons to cover their friends' withdrawal. The 1st Jaipur Infantry scattered and went to ground while, from the other side of the canal, tanks of the North Irish Horse and anti-tank guns opened fire. As the German tanks retired in the fading light, shells from the British medium guns burst in their midst and enveloped them in black smoke. One tank sustained a direct hit and caught fire. The others were able to limp away, followed by thirty infantry men who suffered casualties as they scampered in full flight over the open fields through a hail of bursting shells.[19] The Factory area was cleared of the Germans and the 1st Jaipur Infantry was firmly established south of Canal Bianco. From there it pushed on to Pontelgascuro. The Argyll entered the south-east corner of Ferrara without opposition. The German evacuation had already begun. In a few hours the whole city was in the hands of the Argyll.[20]

The Problem of Crossing the River Po

Having reached the southern bank of the river Po on 24 April, the next problem for the 8th Indian Division was how to cross it. North of Ferrara, the river was about two hundred yards wide. In parts the current was very fast. In general the banks of the river were about fifteen feet high and fell away precipitously to the water's edge. In the area of the 8th Indian Divisions operations, there was an abandoned German crossing place, to which the Germans had constructed a road suitable for heavy vehicles. This proved most useful.[21]

All bridges in the divisional area had been destroyed by the Allied bombers. The great railway bridge at Pontelagoscuro lay a crumpled heap of steel girders sprawled across the river. The road bridge, some eight hundred yards westwards, was non-existent. The industrial town of Pontelagoscuro had been utterly destroyed by bombing.[22]

The V Corps Commander had planned to make an assault across the river Po with the 78th Division, but as the 8th Indian Division reached the southern bank of the river earlier, he informed Major-General Russell at about midday on 24 April that the Indian division would be given the honour of crossing the river.[23] The Po presented a problem quite different from any other river which the 8th Indian

---

[19] Sitrep 23-24 Apr.; War Diary 21 Ind. Inf. Bde.; War Diary 1st Jaipur Infantry; 8 Ind. Div. Operations.
[20] 8 Ind. Div. Operations.
[21] *Ibid.*
[22] *Ibid.*
[23] *Ibid.*

Division had crossed. Owing to the fast current and width of the river, it called for pontoon bridges and ferries instead of the normal Bailey bridge. This operation also demanded special assault equipment (with which no one in the division was familiar), which included Fantails (lightly armoured amphibious troop carriers), amphibious Sherman tanks manned by the 7th Hussars, the Dukws, and the faster storm boats. On the day of the crossing, the infantry was able to carry out a few hours' training with some of this equipment, but it did not exceed four or five hours.[24]

In the afternoon of 24 April the divisional commander decided that in view of the many reconnaissances which were necessary, and the fact that the infantry had not been trained with the amphibious equipment, the afternoon of 26 April was the earliest when the attack might be launched. During the night of 24/25 April, however, away to the left, the New Zealanders made a crossing without opposition, and it became more and more obvious that the German resistance was almost completely broken. Next morning, the divisional commander decided that there was no time for detailed organisation and meticulous planning. Speed was now vital. He therefore ordered the 21st Indian Infantry Brigade and the 17th Indian Infantry Brigade to cross the river during the night of 25/26 April.[25]

The following additional troops were under the command of the 8th Indian Division for the operations:

    7th Hussars, less two squadrons (amphibious Sherman tanks)
    58th Medium Regiment
    Two Squadrons Fantails (each capable of carrying one battalion)
    B Flying Column of:
    18 Storm boats
    20 DUKWs
    3 CI 9 rafts
    2 CI 40 rafts
    A smoke detachment.

The 2nd Army Group Royal Artillery was in support of the 8th Indian Division.[26]

The 8th Indian Division was to cross the river during the night of 25/26 April. The object was to get the assaulting force across and build it up on the other side of the river. Suitable exits for DD tanks on the far bank held by the Germans were few, and the infantry had therefore to lead the assault. The primary task of the Fantails was therefore the establishment of the assaulting infantry on the far bank. An infantry assault and the vulnerability of the Fantails

---
[24] *Ibid.*
[25] *Ibid.*
[26] 8 Ind. Div. Planning Note No. 41, dated 25 April; W/D 8 Div.

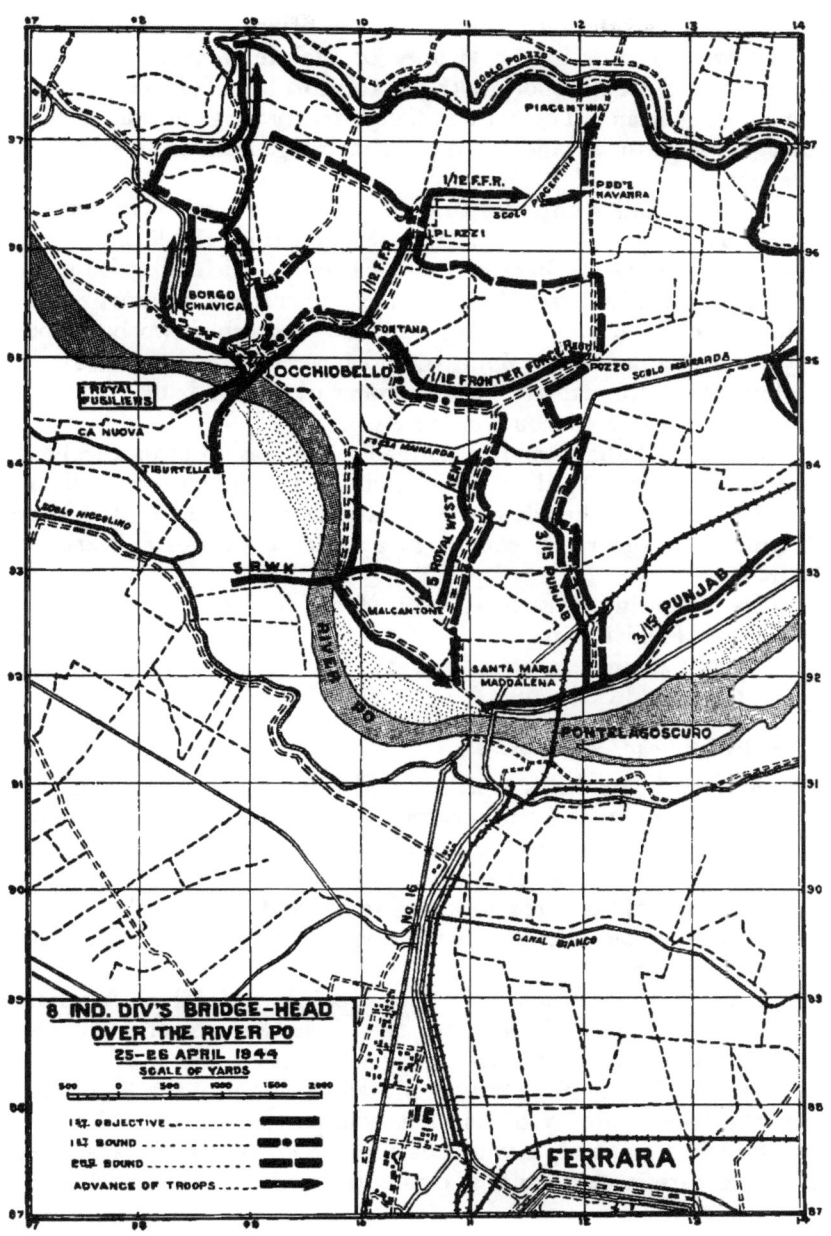

necessitated the crossing being made in darkness or covered by smoke.[27] This was to be done by the 21st Indian Infantry Brigade, on the right, and the 17th Indian Infantry Brigade, on the left. The former was to cross in the vicinity of Malcantone, and the latter north-west of Occhiobello. Both the forward brigades were to establish a bridge-head. The 19th Indian Infantry Brigade was to be in reserve, ready to advance through the bridge-head in a northerly direction.[28]

The 21st Indian Infantry Brigade was to attack with two forward battalions, the 5th Royal West Kent Regiment on the left and 3/15 Punjab on the right. Because there was only sufficient craft for one battalion, the 5th Royal West Kent Regiment was to cross first in Fantails, followed later by 3/15 Punjab. The other two battalions, 1/5 Mahratta and 1st Jaipur Infantry were in reserve ready for exploitation. An artillery bombardment of the far bank was timed to commence at 2100 hours on 25 April.

The 17th Indian Infantry Brigade plan was to cross the Po at 2100 hours on 25 April in the vicinity of Ca Nuova, with the 1st Royal Fusiliers on the left borne in Fantails and 1/12 Frontier Force Regiment on the right, carried in assault boats, storm boats and DUKWs.

The following were in support of the brigade:
One Field Regiment
Eight 4.2-inch mortars
One Field Company.

The Bridge-heads over the Po

At 1530 hours on 25 April, the 5th Royal West Kent Regiment moved off in Fantails from Ferrara airport, having carried out intensive embarkation and disembarkation drill, loaded essential jeeps and generally picked up the form about these new vehicles. They moved to the concentration area near I. Gorghi and by 1700 hours were ready to carry out the assault crossing of the Po at H Hour—2115 hours on 25 April.[29]

During the afternoon and late evening, the Allied Air Force made a very heavy strike all along the whole Corps front and exceedingly accurate bombing and strafing was carried out.

During the morning of 25 April, all roads led to the Po. Endless convoys of armoured vehicles, tank transporters, guns, trucks carrying bridging material, assault boats and pontoons, bulldozers, jeeps and staff cars in choking dust clouds jammed the roads until night-

---

[27] HQ 21 Ind. Inf. Bde. No. 212/G, dated 25 April—River Crossing—Fantails and DD Tanks; War Diary 21 Ind. Inf. Bde.
[28] 8 Ind. Div. Planning Note No. 41, dated 25 Apr.; War Diary 8 Ind. Div.
[29] 21 Ind. Inf. Bde. Operations, 9 to 26 April.

fall. Traffic congestion on the corps axis delayed the arrival of the amphibious equipment, bulldozers broke down and, from time to time, German gunners ranged accurately on the sites where sappers, provost and a hastily improvised embarkation staff were making their preparations for the night's attack.

The preliminary artillery bombardment started at 2100 hours on 25 April but had to be prolonged past H Hour as there was initial delay in getting the Fantails into the water due to the steep banks. The Royal Engineer working parties, while preparing the approaches suffered casualties due to shell fire. Fortunately the shelling was spasmodic, and by 2220 hours the first Fantails carrying the 5th Royal West Kent Regiment were waterborne. The craft headed steadily for the far bank at Malcantone. The British infantry peered ahead anxiously not knowing whether the Germans would fight hard or not. No mortar bombs or high explosive shells burst near the infantry. Within a few minutes, the 5th Royal West Kent Regiment was disembarking on the far bank. By 0430 hours on 26 April, the battalion had established a firm bridge-head which was to be enlarged by 3/15 Punjab.

By 0435 hours on 26 April all the Fantails except three, which had stuck in the mud, had returned across the river, and at 0455 hours, 3/15 Punjab moved forward in Fantails. Their actual crossing was delayed slightly as the DD tanks were given priority over them, but by 0605 hours, when class 9 raft was completed, the crossing of the Po started. Pushing through the right company of the 5th Royal West Kent Regiment, 3/15 Punjab considerably enlarged the bridge-head. The 21st Indian Infantry Brigade secured the bridge-head without much opposition. The crossing of the Po was the last action of this brigade in the Italian campaign. The crossing of this wide river, which might have been a formidable task and costly in lives, was the easiest operation which the 21st Indian Infantry Brigade carried out.

On the left, the 17th Indian Infantry brigade too established a bridge-head without opposition. According to the plan made by the commander of the 1st Royal Fusiliers, A Company was to launch an assault on the left to establish a bridge-head at Borgo Chiavica. At the same time D Company was to move on the right to establish a grip on the western fringe of Occhiobello, where it was assumed there might be a German pocket of resistance. After the bridgehead was established, B Company was to go through on the left to exploit some thousand yards, while C Company followed through on the right to the line of the road.[30]

The commander of 1/12 Frontier Force Regiment decided that

---

[30] Battle Narrative of Royal Fusiliers; Lessons from Operations; File 7301/H.

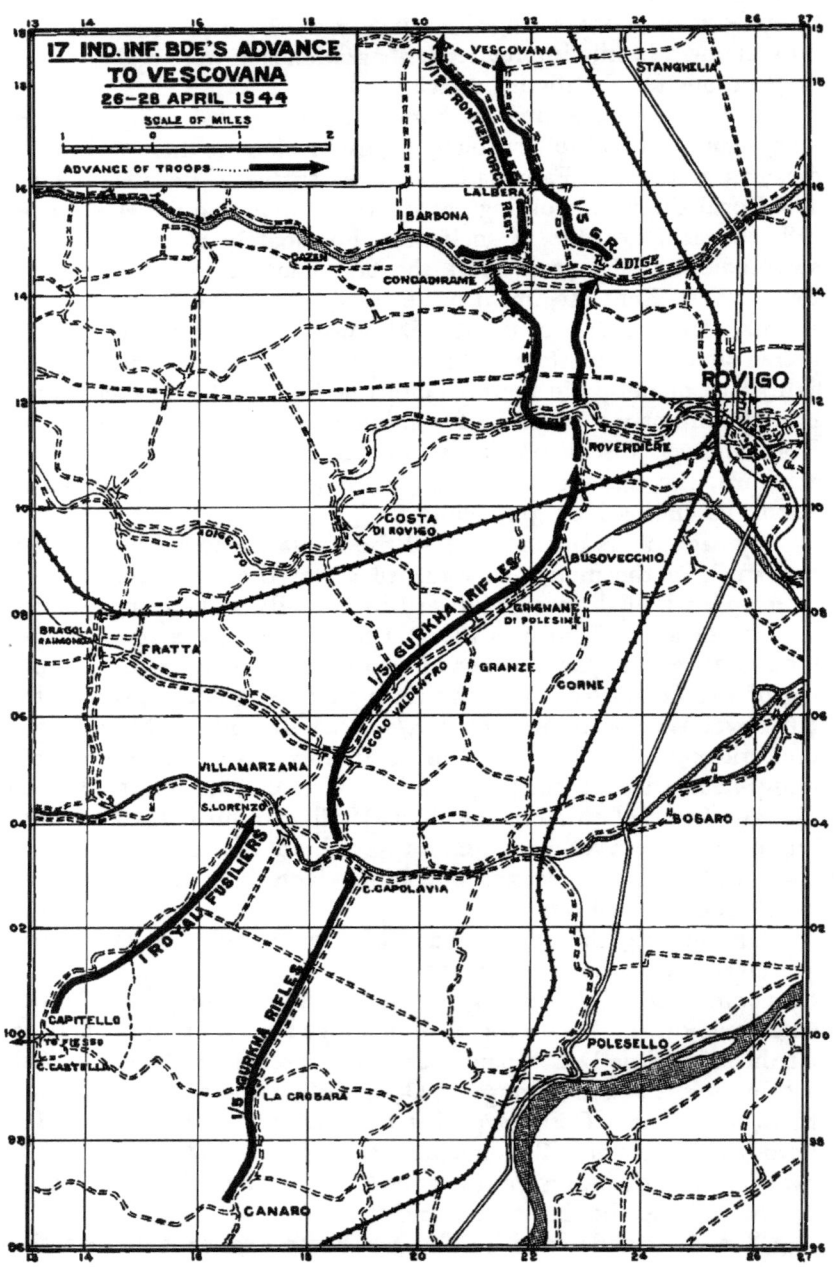

the order of crossing would be A Company, D Company, Tactical Headquarters, C Company, Main Headquarters, B Company, all mounted in a total of 17 DUKWs. The six storm-boats were to be launched by the troop of the 1st Mahratta Anti-Tank Regiment which was in support, assisted by No. 5 Platoon and B Company, and were to be used initially to transport four 6-pounder Anti-Tank guns and two jeeps.[31]

1/5 Gurkha, the reserve battalion, was to cross over in Fantails after the 1st Royal Fusiliers. A Squadron of the 7th Hussars (DD tanks) was to swim across the river before first light and be available on the far side to support the infantry as required. C Squadron 6th Lancers was to cross the Po during the night on a class 9 raft constructed by the sappers in the 6th Armoured Division's area. Once on the far side they were to contact the 1st Royal Fusiliers as early as possible. H Hour was timed for 2100 hours.[32]

Operations by the 17th Indian Infantry Brigade did not go entirely as planned. Long streams of traffic and the bad condition of the roads in the forward zone made the Fantails and Storm Boats arrive late at the assembly area. Consequently it was impossible to launch the 1st Royal Fusiliers across the river at 2100 hours on 25 April, as the Brigadier had planned. The attack eventually started some four hours later.[33]

A heavy artillery and air support plan was laid on to the whole northern bank, starting just before dusk and finishing at 2230 hours. Because of the delay with the Fantails, the attack could not follow on immediately after, but harassing fire continued until the 1st Royal Fusiliers was ready to move. At 0215 hours on 26 April, the long line of Fantails reached the river bank and commenced the crossings. Time had not been allowed for reconnaissance of the river bank by the commanders of the Fantails. Their first view of the river came as they crawled down the bank at an angle of 45 degrees. The Fantails had some difficulty in negotiating the soft ground at the water's edge. A, the leading company, was completely stuck on a large mud bank. It was a bright moonlit night, but fortunately no fire came from the opposite bank. D Company next entered, and had better luck in getting across and landing unopposed on the far bank, while B Company passed by A Company, still in the river, and took over A Company's role. By the time battalion headquarters crossed, after A Company was extricated, it was dawn, and still there was no opposition. The 1st Royal Fusiliers soon secured a bridgehead without opposition. It was only possible to take across forty

[31] Battle Narrative of 1/12 F.F.R.; Lessons from Operations; File 7301/H.
[32] Battle Narrative of 17th Indian Infantry Brigade; Lessons from Operations; File 7301/H.
[33] Crossing of the Po—17th Indian Infantry Brigade—Lessons from Operations; File 7301/H.

eight hours' rations and some jeeps. So the advance had to be made on foot, pushing up small leafy lanes, into untouched groups of houses, from where the Germans had pulled out the night before. It soon became apparent that the Germans had waited only for the signs of an attack before pulling out, and had left rather hurriedly the previous evening without preparing any demolition or booby-traps. Only in one place were mines discovered. By midday C Company had reached Fiesso. By that time tanks had got across and a troop was in support of C Company.

On the right, 1/12 Frontier Force Regiment too made good progress. On 25 April, A and B Companies took over from the 5th Royal West Kent Regiment in the area of Tiburtella without incident, although the area for 1500 yards south of the flood-bank was completely open and was overlooked from Occhiobello. C Company then moved up in DUKWs to Tiburtella with a view to releasing A Company for patrolling across the river Po. It was greeted with a heavy concentration of Nebelwerfer fire, which though very accurate, fortunately caused no casualties. It appeared obvious that Occhiobello was being used by the Germans as an observation post. It was therefore engaged with artillery, and air support was called for.

Heavy traffic on the roads leading forward to the river from the battalion concentration area near S. Egidio had caused considerable delay, and by 1730 hours the Storm Boats had still not arrived. The brigade commander, therefore, decided that the crossing would be made as soon as possible after last light, with the 1st Royal Fusiliers in Fantails leading, followed by 1/12 Frontier Force Regiment in Storm Boats and DUKWs. Both the battalions had to use the same crossing place, as there was only one route by which the Fantails and DUKWs could enter the water.

Just before last light a very heavy concentration of Nebelwerfer fire fell in the battalion area, again fortunately causing no casualties.

For various reasons the 1st Royal Fusiliers was unable to commence crossing until 0215 hours. No opposition was met, but progress was slow owing to the mud-banks and the rapid deterioration of the track leading into the river. This track led to an old German ferry site and had been bulldozed to take the Fantails. As it was also to be used for the DD (amphibious) tanks of the squadron of the 7th Hussars, which were in support, and as it was essential that these be across before first light, it became evident that the DUKWs would be unable to operate before a very late hour, if at all. Arrangements were therefore made for the Storm Boats to be launched and used to transport 1/12 Frontier Force Regiment. The Storm Boats, assault craft equipped with outboard engines, which had been unloaded under cover of the flood bank after last light, required approximately forty men each to carry them. The manhandling of six of these craft over the flood bank and into the water without interfering with the flow of Fantails and DD Tanks was a slow and difficult task. As the Storm Boats were launched, A Company embarked, and by 0515 hours was concentrating on the far bank. By 0530 hours they were passing through the right hand company of the 1st Royal Fusiliers and into Occhiobello. They were quickly followed by D Company, Tactical Headquarters, C Company and Main Headquarters. B Company was given the task of loading and unloading all the battalion stores, which were originally to have been transported in DUKWs. By 0830 hours Main Headquarters was established in the eastern outskirts of Occhiobello, A Company was in the area of Fontana, D Company was moving to Pozzo and C Company was moving via Palazzi to Piacentina.[34]

Advance to Canal Bianco

Thus, the 8th Indian Division had secured the bridge-heads over the river Po without opposition in the morning on 26 April. The 17th Indian Infantry Brigade continued the advance towards Canal Bianco to contact the Germans. The armoured cars of the 6th Lancers were racing ahead northwards. By late afternoon on 26 April they reached the Canal Bianco, nearly seven miles beyond Occhiobello. The wooden bridge, which the Germans had attempted to destroy was blazing fiercely. German machine guns and mortars opened fire as the Lancers dismounted and set to work to extinguish the blaze. Despite opposition they put out the fire. The capture of this bridge, only partially damaged, proved invaluable the following morning when the 17th Indian Infantry Brigade transport arrived.[35]

The infantry pushed ahead behind the Lancers. By midday on 26 April, C Company of the 1st Royal Fusiliers reached Fiesso. Then A and D Companies took up the lead, moving up to the Canal Bianco. At nightfall on 26 April A Company was in Pincara, while D Company was in S. Lorenzo, just short of the river, on the near bank of which appeared a German holding party in some force.[36] While the 1st Royal Fusiliers pushed on the advance to the Canal Bianco, 1/12 Frontier Force Regiment consolidated its positions during the afternoon of 26 April with A Company at La Crosara, D Company at C. Castelia, B Company at P. Navarra and Battalion Headquarters and C Company at Piacentina.[37]

Advance to Roverdicre

At last light on 26 April the 17th Indian Infantry Brigade, the

---

[34] Battle Narrative of 1/12 F.F.R; Lessons from Operations; File 7301/H.
[35] 8 Ind. Div. Operations.
[36] Sitrep dated 27 April; War Diary 8 Ind. Div.; Battle Narrative of 1st Royal Fusiliers—Lessons from Operations.
[37] Battle Narrative of 1/12 F.F.R.—Lessons from Operations.

forward brigade of the 8th Indian Division, had been temporarily halted south of the Canal Bianco. The German Army was however disintegrating and Major-General Russell ordered the 17th Indian Infantry Brigade to eliminate all resistance south of the river Adige and to cross the river north-west of Rovigo on Route 16. The most important factor was speed in crushing German resistance south of the river; speed in bridging the river and ferrying across the infantry, tanks and armoured cars; speed in brushing aside small pockets of scattered Germans, and pushing the infantry forward on tanks and armoured cars towards Padua and Venice.

1/5 Gurkha was to lead the advance towards Roverdicre, and had concentrated at Fontana on 26 April; B Company less one platoon took over from a troop of the 6th Lancers near the bridge in order to cross the Canal Bianco early on 27 April. Very little work was required to make the bridge serviceable and, by 0800 hours on 27 April, a squadron of the 6th Lancers was across complete, whilst a squadron of DD tanks of the 7th Hussars had swum across previously. The Germans now began to surrender, having offered little or no opposition. The plan was for 1/5 Gurkha to go all out for a crossing over the Adigetto at Roverdicre, using as an axis the road along the north bank of Scolo Valdentro to Buso Vacchio, thence due north to the objective. One squadron of the 6th Lancers and one squadron of the 7th Hussars were in support. B Company (now complete), mounted in unit vehicles and tanks of the 7th Hussars, pushed on behind the squadron of the 6th Lancers. The remainder of the battalion crossed the bridge at 0900 hours and advanced by bounds up the main axis. Very half-hearted resistance was encountered, and prisoners poured in. At approximately 1230 hours, the 6th Lancers encountered opposition in Roverdicre, and therefore the commander of 1/5 Gurkha decided to attack the place in strength.[36] At 1430 hours, A and B Companies, each with one troop of the 7th Hussars in support, attacked with the object of crossing the Adigetto, securing a bridge-head and exploiting to the south bank of the Adige. The attack went quickly, and by 1530 hours A and B Companies were firmly established north of the Adigetto. C and D Companies then prepared to pass through A and B Companies and enlarge the bridge-head. This task was accomplished. At 1900 hours battalion headquarters moved into Roverdicre.

Advance to the River Adige

At 0600 hours on 28 April, tactical headquarters, B and D Companies of 1/12 Frontier Force Regiment moved from Grignane to Roverdicre. From there B Company was directed on Concadirame

---

[36] Battle Narrative of 1/5 G.R., 23-30 April; Lessons from Operations; File 7301/H.

and Sabbioni and D Company on Ca Zen.[39] Each company was accompanied by a troop of tanks of the North Irish Horse. No opposition was encountered but approximately 150 prisoners were taken.

Both the forward battalions, 1/5 Gurkha and the 1/12 Frontier Force Regiment, who had closed up to the south bank of the river Adige then prepared to cross the river. The Adige was a very swift flowing river, nearly as wide as the Po and with steep banks falling straight into the water. It was a very difficult ferrying and bridging problem. The two forward battalions, however, showed considerable ingenuity in getting themselves across. At that time all the bridging equipment allotted to the 8th Indian Division was still being utilised on the Po. The two forward battalions however crossed the Adige without opposition, using assault boats and country boats. At 0900 hours on 28 April, D Company of 1/5 Gurkha crossed the Adige and reached Lalbera at 0930 hours. C Company, B Company and A Company all crossed in that order. No opposition was encountered and the leading troops of D Company, mounted on tanks, entered Vescovana at 1400 hours.[40] Meanwhile A Company of 1/12 Frontier Force Regiment had commenced to cross the river Adige at 1000 hours. It was quickly followed by C Company, and on being joined by a troop of DD tanks, the two companies pressed on to Vascovana and Granza, which was reached by 1600 hours. No opposition was encountered.

Near the banks of the river, the 17th Indian Brigade found a mass of German vehicles of all types and sizes. The whole area was littered with abandoned German tanks, vehicles, guns and equipment. This included approximately nine ten-barrelled Nebelwerfers mounted on half-tracks. It was but another transport grave-yard second only to that of the Po. From the number of prisoners that came pouring in, it was quite obvious that the Germans were completely disorganised and defeated. By evening, four officers and 276 other ranks had passed through brigade headquarters on their way to the cage.[41]

End of the Campaign

On 28 April, the 19th Indian Infantry Brigade crossed the Po on ferries and concentrated close behind the Adigetto between Bragola Raimonda and Costa di Rovigo. By the evening sufficient equipment was assembled to bridge the Adige. The divisional commander's intention was to strike north next day and capture Venice with the 19th Indian Infantry Brigade supported by the 6th Lancers.

---

[39] Battle Narrative of 1/12 F.F.R., Lessons from Operations, File 7301/H.
[40] Battle Narrative of 1/5 G.R.
[41] 8 Ind. Div. Operations,

The infantry was to travel in lorries and the whole resources of the division were concentrated on this plan.

Working without respite throughout the night, two platoons of the 66th Field Company Indian Engineers, together with two from the 69th Field Company Indian Engineers, constructed a pontoon bridge over the swift flowing waters of the Adige, and it was ready by 0900 hours on 29 April. But orders were received from the corps commander that only the 6th Lancers should cross it and that they should then be allotted to the 56th British Division. It was a very great disappointment to the 8th Indian Division; the congestion north of the Adige promised to be acute and some limitation was necessary, but at the same time it was not easy to watch another formation cross over the bridge and go on to seize Venice. The 6th Lancers of course were across and sped northwards and north-east making an astonishing advance of 50 miles in two hours. They met only scattered resistance and drove through thousands of unhappy Germans looking for some one to whom they could surrender. Eventually the 6th Lancers were relieved before they could reach Venice and the war for the 8th Indian Division was virtually over.[42]

During the 20 days, 9 to 29 April, the 8th Indian Division had decisively defeated two high quality German divisions, and had taken a total of some 1,100 prisoners while the amount of captured equipment of all types was, in truth, so great that no estimate was ever made.

Achievements of the Indian Troops

The task of vanquishing the redoubtable German armies was at last over. Since 19 September 1943, when the Indian troops landed in Italy, till 29 April 1945 when they halted the advance a little beyond the river Adige they had been in the thick of the fighting. They covered themselves with glory on many a bloody battlefield. They had the proud distinction of playing an important role in some of the chief battles of the Italian campaign. Who can ever forget their gallantry and their reckless courage in the battles of the Sangro, Cassino, the Liri Valley, the Gothic Line and the Senio? It is an impressive record of their achievements. In addition to these important battles they figured prominently in innumerable actions and engagements. The three Indian divisions—the 8th, the 10th and the 4th—share with the other formations of the Allied forces the unique honour of having broken the power of the mighty German armies in Italy. The heroic deeds of the Indian soldiers in the Italian campaign form indeed a glorious chapter in the history of the Indian formations in the Second World War.

[42] *Ibid.*

APPENDIX I

ORDER OF BATTLE—8TH INDIAN DIVISION

(September 1943)

G.O.C. Major-General Dudley Russell, C.B.E., D.S.O., M.C.

17th Indian Infantry Brigade (Brigadier F. A. M. B. Jenkins, D.S.O., O.B.E., M.C.)
    1st Royal Fusiliers
    1/12 Frontier Force Regiment
    1/5 Royal Gurkha Rifles

19th Indian Infantry Brigade (Brigadier T. S. Dobree, D.S.O., M.C.)
    1/5 Essex Regiment
    3/8 Punjab Regiment
    6/13 Royal Frontier Force Rifles

21st Indian Infantry Brigade (Brigadier B. S. Mould, D.S.O., O.B.E., M.C.)
    5th Royal West Kent Regiment
    1/5 Mahratta Light Infantry
    3/15 Punjab Regiment

Machine Gunners
    5/5 Royal Mahratta (Machine Gun Battalion), Mahratta Light Infantry

Reconnaissance Regiment
    6 D.C.O. (Bengal) Lancers

Artillery
    3 Field Regiment R.A.
    52 Field Regiment R.A.
    53 Field Regiment R.A.
    4 Mahratta Anti-tank Regiment I.A.
    26 Light Anti-Aircraft Regiment R.A.

Engineers
    7 Field Company
    66 Field Company
    69 Field Company
    47 Field Park Company
    (All Bengal Sappers and Miners)

Medical Services
    29 Indian Field Ambulance
    31 Indian Field Ambulance
    33 Indian Field Ambulance
    20 Field Hygiene Section
    81 Anti Malaria Control Unit

Ordnance
    8 Indian Division Ordnance Field Park
    27 Mobile Bath Unit
    Detachment Mobile Laundry

Royal Indian Army Service Corps
    8 Indian Division Troops Transport Company
    17 Indian Infantry Brigade Transport Company
    19 Indian Infantry Brigade Transport Company
    21 Indian Infantry Brigade Transport Company

Indian Electrical and Mechanical Engineers
    17 Indian Infantry Brigade Workshop Company
    21 Indian Infantry Brigade Workshop Company
    19 Indian Infantry Brigade Workshop Company
    8 Indian Division Gun Repair Section
    8 Indian Division Recovery Section

Miscellaneous
    8 Indian Division Provost Company

APPENDIX II

ORDER OF BATTLE—4TH INDIAN DIVISION

(January 1944)

G.O.C. Major-General F. I. S. Tuker, C.B., D.S.O., O.B.E.

5th Indian Infantry Brigade (Brigadier D. R. E. R. Bateman, D.S.O., O.B.E.)
    1/4 Essex Regiment
    1/6 Rajputana Rifles
    1/9 Gurkha Rifles

7th Indian Infantry Brigade (Brigadier O. de T. Lovett, D.S.O.)
    1st Royal Sussex
    4/16 Punjab Regiment
    1/2 Gurkha Rifles

Divisional Reconnaissance Regiment
    Central India Horse

Machine Gun Battalion
    5th Machine Gun Battalion Rajputana Rifles

Artillery
    1st Field Regiment R.A.
    11 Field Regiment R.A.
    31st Field Regiment R.A.
    149 Anti-Tank Regiment R.A.
    57 Light A.A. Regiment R.A.

Engineers
    4 Field Company Sappers and Miners
    12 Field Company Sappers and Miners
    21 Field Company Sappers and Miners
    11 Field Park Company Sappers and Miners
    (including 5 Bridging Section)

Medical Services
    17 Indian Field Ambulance
    26 Indian Field Ambulance
    15 Indian Field Hygiene Section

Royal Indian Army Service Corps
    5 Indian Infantry Brigade Transport Company
    7 Indian Infantry Brigade Transport Company
    4 Indian Division Troops Transport Company

Indian Electrical and Mechanical Engineers
    5 Indian Brigade Ordnance Company
    7 Indian Brigade Ordnance Company
    4 Indian Division Ordnance Field Park.

APPENDIX III

ORDER OF BATTLE—4TH INDIAN DIVISION

(February 1944)

H.Q. Units	HQ 4 Ind Div.
	4 Ind Div Def Pl.
	HQ 4 Ind Div Arty.
	HQ 4 Ind Div Engr.
	HQ 4 Ind Div Sigs.
	HQ 4 Ind Div RIASC
Arty.	1 Fd Regt RA
	11 Fd Bty RA
	52 Fd Bty RA
	80 Fd Bty RA
	11 Fd Regt RA
	78/84 Fd Bty RA
	83/85 Fd Bty RA
	187 Fd Bty RA
	31 Fd Regt RA
	105 Fd Bty RA
	116 Fd Bty RA
	118 Fd Bty RA
	149 A Tk Regt RA
	320 A Tk Bty RA
	432 A Tk Bty RA
	433 A Tk Bty RA
	513 4.2″ Mortar Bty RA
	57 Lt AA Regt RA
	169 Lt AA Bty RA
	170 Lt AA Bty RA
	171 Lt AA Bty RA
Engr.	4 Fd Coy S.M.
	12 Fd Coy S.M.
	21 Fd Coy S.M.
	11 Fd Pk Coy S.M.
	5 Br Sec I.E.
Sigs.	4 Ind Div Cipher Sec.
	4 Ind Div CRA Sig Sec.
	1 Fd Regt Sig Sec.
	11 Fd Regt Sig Sec.
	31 Fd Regt Sig Sec.
	149 A Tk Regt Sig Det.
	59 Lt AA Regt Sig Det.
Inf.	MG Bn Raj Rif.
	(B Coy is 4.2″ Mortar Bty)

S.T.	4 Ind Div Tps Tpt Coy. 4 Ind Div HQ Tpt Sec. 5 Ind Inf Bde Tpt Coy. 7 Ind Inf Bde Tpt Coy. 11 Ind Inf Bde Tpt Coy. 18 Mot Amb Sec RIASC 220 D.I.D. 2 Ind Cattle Stock Sec. 177 Gen Tp Tpt Coy.
Med.	17 IND Fd AMB. D (Br) Dental unit. 26 IND FD AMB. 156 (Br) Mob Dental unit. 12 Indian Dental unit. 32 IND Fd AMB. 15 IND Fd HYGIENE SEC. 26 A.M.C.U. 2 IND C.C.S.
Ord.	4 IND Div Ord Fd Pk. 4 Mob Bath Unit 13 Mob Cinema unit.
REME.	57 Lt AA Wkshops Sec. L.A.D. 1 Fd Regt RA L.A.D. 11 Fd Regt RA L.A.D. 31 Fd Regt R.A. L.A.D. 149 A Tk Regt RA
IEME.	5 Ind Inf Bde Wkshop Coy. 7 Ind Inf Bde Wkshop Coy. 11 Ind Inf Bde Wkshop Coy.
Pro.	4 Ind Div Pro Unit.
Postal.	13 Ind F.P.O. 17 Ind F.P.O. 24 Ind F.P.O.
Int.	290 F.S. Sec.
Misc.	8 Cam Trg Unit. A.A.P.I.U. Det.
5 Ind Inf Bde.	HQ 5 Ind Inf Bde. 5 Ind Inf Bde Def Pl. 5 Ind Inf Bde Sig Sec. 5 Ind Inf Bde Recce Unit. 5 Ind Inf Bde L.A.D. 1/4 Essex Regt. 1/6 Rajputana Rifles. 1/9 Gurkha Rifles.
7 Ind Inf Bde.	HQ 7 Ind Inf Bde. 7 Ind Inf Bde Def Pl. 7 Ind Inf Bde Sig Sec. 7 Ind Inf Bde MG Coy. 7 Ind Inf Bde Recce Unit.

                                       7 Ind Inf Bde L.A.D.
                                       1 Royal Sussex Regt.
                                       4/16 Punjab Regt.
                                       1/2 Gurkha Rifles.

11 Ind Inf Bde.   HQ 11 Ind Inf Bde.
                                       11 Ind Inf Bde Def Pl.
                                       11 Ind Inf Bde Sig Sec.
                                       11 Ind Inf Bde L.A.D.
                                       2 Camerons.
                                       4/6 Rajputana Rifles.
                                       2/7 Gurkha Rifles.

APPENDIX IV

ORDER OF BATTLE—10TH INDIAN DIVISION

(March 1944)

G.O.C. Major-General Denys Reid, C.B., C.B.E., D.S.O., M.C.

10th Indian Infantry Brigade (Brigadier T. N. Smith, O.B.E.)
    1/2 Punjab Regiment
    4/10 Baluch Regiment
    2/4 Gurkha Rifles

20th Indian Infantry Brigade (Brigadier J. B. MacDonald, D.S.O., O.B.E.)
    8th Manchester Regiment
    3/5 Mahratta Light Infantry
    2/3 Gurkha Rifles

25th Indian Infantry Brigade (Brigadier Eustace Arderne, D.S.O., O.B.E.)
    1st King's Own Royal Regiment
    3/1 Punjab Regiment
    3/18 Royal Garhwal Rifles

Reconnaissance Regiment
    Skinner's Horse

Machine Gun Battalion
    1st Royal Northumberland Fusiliers

Artillery
    68 Field Regiment R.A.
    97 Field Regiment R.A.
    154 Field Regiment R.A.
    13 Anti-Tank Regiment R.A.
    30 Light Anti-Aircraft Regiment R.A.

Engineers
    5 Field Company I.E.
    10 Field Company I.E.
    61 Field Company I.E.
    41 Field Park Company I.E.
    'A' Indian Bridging Section

Medical Services
    14 Indian Field Ambulance
    21 Indian Field Ambulance
    30 Indian Field Ambulance
    14 Indian Field Hygiene Section

Royal Indian Army Service Corps
    10 Indian Division Transport Company
    10 I.B.T. Company
    20 I.B.T. Company
    25 I.B.T. Company

Indian Electrical and Mechanical Engineers
    10 Indian Infantry Brigade Workshop
    20 Indian Infantry Brigade Workshop
    25 Indian Infantry Brigade Workshop

Ordnance
    10 Indian Division Ordnance Field Park Company

APPENDIX V

SHORT SUMMARY OF GERMAN ORDER OF BATTLE

(June 1944)

1 Para Div.
1 Para Regt
3 Para Regt
4 Para Regt
1 Para M.G. Bn

4 Para Div.
10 Para Regt
11 Para Regt
12 Para (Assault) Regt
Ancillary No. 4

5 Mtn Div.
85 Mtn Regt
100 Mtn Regt
85 Rece Bn
Ancillary No. 95

44 Inf Div.
131 Gren Regt
132 Gren Regt
134 Gren Regt
44 Recce Bn
44 Ereatz Bn

65 Inf Div.
145 Gren Regt
146 Gren Regt
147 Gren Regt
165 Recce Bn
Ancillary No. 165

71 Inf Div.
191 Gren Regt
194 Gren Regt
211 Gren Regt
171 Fus Bn
Ancillary No. 171

92 Inf Div.
1059 Gren Regt
1060 Gren Regt
Ancillary No. 192

94 Inf Div.
267 Gren Regt
274 Gren Regt
276 Gren Regt
194 Fus Bn
Ancillary No. 194

114 JG (Light) Div.
721 JG Regt
741 JG Regt
114 Recce Bn
Ancillary No. 114

162 Turcoman Inf Div.
303 Gren Regt
314 Gren Regt
236 Recce Bn

278 Inf Div.
992 Gren Regt
993 Gren Regt
994 Gren Regt
278 Fus Bn
Ancillary No. 278

305 Inf Div.
576 Gren Regt
577 Gren Regt
578 Gren Regt
305 Recce Bn
Ancillary No. 305

334 Inf Div.
754 Gren Regt
755 Gren Regt
756 Gren Regt
334 Recce Bn
334 Fus Bn
Ancillary No. 334

356 Inf Div.
869 Gren Regt
870 Gren Regt
871 Gren Regt
356 Fus Bn
Ancillary No. 356

362 Inf Div.
954 Gren Regt
955 Gren Regt
956 Gren Regt
362 Fus Bn
Ancillary No. 362

715 Inf Div.
725 Gren Regt
735 Gren Regt
Ancillary No. 715

MISCELLANEOUS UNITS
1027 Reinf PGR
1028 Reinf PGR
3 Alpine Bn
4 Alpine Bn
4 Tk Regt
400 Recce Bn
7 GAF Jg Bn
9 GAF Jg Bn

20 Gaf Div.
39 GAF Jg Regt
40 GAF Jg Regt
20 GAF Recce Coy
Ancillary No. 20

HG Para Pz Div.	*3 PG Div.*	*15 PG Div.*	*16 SS Armd Div.*
1 PGR HG	8 PGR	104 PGR	*Reichs fuehrer*
2 PGR HG	29 PGR	115 PGR	35 SS PGR
HG Tk Regt	103 Recce Bn	115 Tk Bn	36 SS PGR
HG Recce Bn	Ancillary No. 3	115 Recce Bn	16 SS Recce Bn
		Ancillary No. 33	Ancillary No. 16

26 Pz Div.	*29 PG Div.*	*90 Gren Div (Mot).*
9 PGR	15 PGR	200 Gren Regt
67 PGR	71 PGR	361 Gren Regt
26 Tk Bn	129 Tk Bn	190 Tk Bn
26 Recce Bn	129 Recce Bn	190 Recce Bn
Ancillary No. 93	Ancillary No. 29	Ancillary No. 190.

APPENDIX VI

SHORT GERMAN ORDER OF BATTLE

(September 1944)

1 Para Div.
1 Para Regt
3 Para Regt
4 Para Regt
Ancillary No. 1

4 Para Div.
9 Para Regt
10 Para Regt
11 Para Regt
Ancillary No. 4

5 Mtn Div.
85 Mtn Regt
100 Mtn Regt
Ancillary No. 95

16 SS PG Div
    'Reichsfuhrer'.
35 SS PG Regt
36 SS PG Regt
16 SS Tk Bn
Ancillary No. 16

20 GAF Field Div.
39 GAF Fd Regt
40 GAF Fd Regt
Ancillary No. 20

26 Panzer Div.
9 PG Regt
67 PG Regt
26 Tk Regt
26 Recce Bn
Ancillary No. 93

29 PG Div.
15 PG Regt
71 PG Regt
129 Tk Bn
Ancillary No. 129

42 Jaeger Div.
25 Jaeger Regt
40 Jaeger Regt
Ancillary No. ?

44 Inf Div.
131 Gren Regt
132 Gren Regt
134 Gren Regt
80 Engr Bn
Ancillary No. 44

65 Inf Div.
145 Gren Regt
146 Gren Regt
147 Gren Regt
65 Fusilier Bn
Ancillary No. 65

71 Inf Div.
191 Gren Regt
194 Gren Regt
211 Gren Regt
171 Fusilier Bn
Ancillary No. 171

90 PG Div.
200 Gren Regt
361 Gren Regt
190 Tk Bn
Ancillary No. 190

92 Inf Div.
1059 Gren Regt
1060 Gren Regt
192 Fusilier Bn
Ancillary No. 192

94 Inf Div.
267 Gren Regt
274 Gren Regt
276 Gren Regt
194 Fusilier Bn
Ancillary No. 194

98 Inf Div.
117 Gren Regt
289 Gren Regt
290 Gren Regt
98 Fusilier Bn
Ancillary No. 198

114 Jaeger Div.
721 Jaeger Regt
741 Jaeger Regt
Ancillary No. 114

148 Res Div.
8 Res Jaeger Regt
239 Res Gren Regt
252 Res Gren Regt
8 Res Arty Regt
Ancillary No. ?.

162 (Turcoman) Div.
303 Gren Regt
314 Gren Regt
236 Fusilier Bn
Ancillary No. 236

188 Res Mtn Div.
136 Res Mtn Inf Regt
139 Res Mtn Inf Regt
112 Res Mtn Arty Bn

278 Inf Div.
992 Gren Regt
993 Gren Regt
994 Gren Regt

305 Inf Div.
576 Gren Regt
577 Gren Regt
578 Gren Regt

Ancillary No. ?	278 Fusilier Bn	305 Fusilier (Recce Bn)
	Ancillary No. 278	Ancillary No. 305

334 Inf Div.	*356 Inf Div.*	*362 Inf Div.*	*715 Inf Div.*
754 Gren Regt	869 Gren Regt	954 Gren Regt	725 Gren Regt
755 Gren Regt	870 Gren Regt	955 Gren Regt	735 Gren Regt
756 Gren Regt	871 Gren Regt	956 Gren Regt	1028 Gren Regt
Ancillary No. 334	356 Fusilier Bn	362 Fusilier Bn	671 Arty Regt
	Ancillary No. 356	Ancillary No. 362	Ancillary No. 715

APPENDIX VII

DIVISIONAL AND BRIGADE COMMANDERS

4TH INDIAN DIVISION
Major-General F. I. S. Tuker, C.B., D.S.O., O.B.E.
 (January 1942—March 1944)
Major-General A. W. W. Holworthy, D.S.O., M.C.
 (March 1944—January 1945)
Major-General C. H. Boucher, C.B., C.B.E., D.S.O.
 (January 1945—December 1945)

8TH INDIAN DIVISION
Major-General Dudley Russell, C.B., C.B.E., D.S.O., M.C.
 (January 1943 . . .)

10TH INDIAN DIVISION
Major-General W. L. Lloyd, C.B.E., D.S.O., M.C.
 (July 1943—January 1944)
Major-General Denys Reid, C.B., C.B.E., D.S.O., M.C.
 (February 1944   )

5TH INDIAN INFANTRY BRIGADE
Brigadier D. R. E. R. Bateman, D.S.O., O.B.E.
 (December 1942—April 1944)
Brigadier J. C. Saunders Jacobs, C.B.E., D.S.O.
 (April 1944   )

7TH INDIAN INFANTRY BRIGADE
Brigadier O. de T. Lovett, C.B.E., D.S.O.
 (March 1943—July 1945)

10TH INDIAN INFANTRY BRIGADE
Brigadier J. A. Finlay, M.C.
 (October 1942—February 1944)
Brigadier T. N. Smith, D.S.O., O.B.E.
 (February 1944   )

11TH INDIAN INFANTRY BRIGADE
Brigadier V. C. Griffin
 (January 1944—May 1944)
Brigadier H. F. C. Partridge, D.S.O.
 (May 1944—October 1944)
Brigadier H. C. J. Hunt, C.B.E., D.S.O.
 (October 1944   )

17TH INDIAN INFANTRY BRIGADE
Brigadier F. A. M. B. Jenkins, D.S.O., O.B.E., M.C.
 (March 1942—October 1943)
Brigadier H. L. Wyndham
 (October 1943—November 1943)

Brigadier J. Scott-Elliot
 (November 1943—January 1944)
Brigadier C. H. Boucher, C.B.E., D.S.O.
 (February 1944—January 1945)
Brigadier P. R. Macnamara, D.S.O.
 (January 1945   )

19TH INDIAN INFANTRY BRIGADE
Brigadier T. S. Dobree, C.B.E., D.S.O., M.C.
 (February 1943—June 1945)

20TH INDIAN INFANTRY BRIGADE
Brigadier J. B. MacDonald, D.S.O., O.B.E.
 (June 1943—November 1945)

21ST INDIAN INFANTRY BRIGADE
Brigadier B. S. Mould, D.S.O., O.B.E., M.C.
 (March 1943   )

25TH INDIAN INFANTRY BRIGADE
Brigadier E. A. Arderne, D.S.O., O.B.E.
 (July 1942—June 1945)

BIBLIOGRAPHY

This volume is based on official records possessed by the C.I.S. Historical Section, Ministry of Defence. Of these the most important are the War Diaries of the Indian Units which took part in the Italian Campaign. It is not possible to indicate all the diaries, despatches consulted in writing this narrative but some of these are listed below. A list of published books consulted and found useful is also given.

WAR DIARIES OF THE FOLLOWING UNITS

 4th, 8th and 10th Indian Divisions,
 5th, 7th, 11th, 19th, 20th, 21st, 22nd and 25th Indian Infantry Brigades and the battalions attached to them.

DESPATCHES AND REPORTS

 Field-Marshal Sir H. Alexander's despatches on 'The Conquest of Sicily' published in the Second Supplement to 'The London Gazette' of 10 February 1948 and 'The Allied Armies in Italy', published in the Supplement to 'The London Gazette' of 6 June 1950.

 Report by General Wilson, Supreme Allied Commander, Mediterrranean Forces, to the Combined Chiefs of Staff on the Italian Campaign published by His Majesty's Stationery Office, 1946.

PUBLISHED SOURCES

Bryant, Arthur	The Turn of the Tide (London, 1957)
Nicholson, G. W. L.	The Canadians in Italy Official History of the Canadian Army in the Second World War, Vol. II, 1956
Montgomery, B. L.	El Alamein to the River Sangro
Churchill, W. S.	The Second World War, Closing the Ring, Vol. V
Stevens, G. R.	Fourth Indian Division
Phillips, N. C.	Italy—The Sangro to Cassino Official History of New Zealand in the Second World War, 1957, Vol. I
Stacey, C. P.	Canadian Army—Official History of the Canadian Army in the Second World War, 1955
Eric Linklater	The Campaign in Italy—Published by His Majesty's Stationery Office, 1951

INDEX

Adriatic coast: 381; Eighth Army's offensive on, 447-48
Africa Korps: 3 (*see also* German Forces)
Alexander, General Sir Harold: plan of, 11; 91; operation 'Avalanche' and 'Slapstick', 11; plan for breaking the Winter Line, 34-5; plan for the spring offensive, 144; *see also* 7, 86, 93, 95, 117, 128, 146, 149, 185, 230-31, 235, 360, 528.
Ali Haider, Sepoy: wins Victoria Cross, 621.
Allfrey, Lieut.-General Sir Charles (Commander V Corps): 11
Anvil (Operation): 118, 230, 300, 360
Auchinleck, General Sir Claude: 3
Avalanche (Operation): 11

Badoglio, Marshal: 9
Bateman, Brigadier D. R. E. R. (Commander 5th Indian Infantry Brigade): 122
Bhagtabahadur Thapa, L/Naik: wins Indian Distinguished Service Medal, 30
Bradman (Operation): 127
British (United Kingdom) Forces:
Eighth Army: preparation of, 36; plan for the spring offensive, 144; plan for the pursuit of beaten Germans, 188; re-organisation of, 209, 213; regrouping of, 235, 259, 299-300; advance to the river Marecchia, 408-9; advance to the river Savio, 468; advance to the river Ronco, 491; advance to the river Lamone, 528; *see also* 15-16, 34-35, 37, 43, 53, 56, 61, 76, 83, 85-6, 117, 381, 389, 439, 448-50, 463, 492, 507-8, 531, 544, 592, 602-3, 607, 619, 642-43, 647
V. Corps: plan to cross the river Trigno, 20-21; resumes offensive, 528; plan for December offensive, 543; thrust through the Argenta Gap, 660; *see also* 11-12, 14-17, 31, 34, 36-37, 39, 44, 52-3, 75, 83, 148, 209-10, 213, 215, 233, 236, 246, 254, 256, 363-64, 405, 450, 463, 468-69, 531, 546, 548, 594, 597, 599, 602, 610, 643, 647, 667
X Corps: 14, 34, 90-3, 121, 127, 145, 148, 231, 233, 235-36, 241, 246-47, 259, 261, 263, 270, 279, 300, 325, 334, 342-43, 351, 358-60, 363, 439, 448, 468, 492, 605, 647
XIII Corps: 7, 11-12, 14-15, 31, 34, 37, 56, 76, 78, 83, 142, 144-45, 148, 152, 162, 177, 182, 184-86, 188-89, 191-92, 196-97, 202-3; 207, 209-10, 213, 215, 231, 233, 235-36, 246-47, 259, 261-62, 266, 297, 299-300, 301-2, 317, 324-25, 339, 360, 364, 410-13, 415, 427-28, 506, 508, 511, 513, 587, 594, 605, 642-43, 647-49, 654
Airborne Division:
1st: 14, 426-27, 431, 448
Armoured Divisions:
1st: 364, 389, 403, 405, 408, 411-14, 450-51, 454, 459, 508, 511, 513, 520-21
6th: 148, 153, 156, 189, 192, 197-98, 203-4, 206, 231, 233, 236-37, 241, 247, 251-52, 259, 300-1, 411-13, 424, 427-28, 432, 508-9, 513, 568, 570, 572, 587, 605, 613, 643, 659-60, 673
7th: 14
Infantry Divisions:
4th: 148, 152-53, 168, 171, 176-77, 183-84, 187, 233, 235-36, 300-2, 363, 490, 492, 528-30, 532
5th: 7-8, 11, 14-15, 76, 78, 83, 216
46th: 14, 363-64, 388-89, 394-95, 398-99, 401-3, 409, 450-51, 461, 468-69, 491, 505, 528-31, 533, 544, 546-48
50th: 7-8
56th: 14, 363-64, 374, 388-89, 394-95, 403, 409, 450, 459, 479, 544-45, 548, 559, 594, 597, 602, 605, 610, 643, 660, 678
78th: 11-12, 14-18, 21, 26-28, 31, 34, 36-39, 44-46, 50-53, 56, 76, 95, 126-27, 136, 148, 153, 159, 177, 184-85, 189-90, 192, 197, 203, 209-10, 213, 259, 507, 582-83, 587, 605, 610, 615, 640, 643, 660, 667
Armoured Brigades:
4th: 14, 44, 46-47, 51-2, 56, 58
7th: 223
9th: 252, 325, 344
Battalions/Regiments:
1 A & SH: 154, 165, 176, 179-80, 182, 190-91, 198-202, 234, 238, 241, 309, 414, 419, 421, 425, 509, 514, 518, 585, 640, 663
2nd Cameron: 285, 394-95, 398, 400-401, 402
1/4 Essex: 108, 122-24, 129-31, 133-35, 138, 212, 217, 295-96, 338-39, 350-51, 446
1/5 Essex: 16, 18, 21-23, 26-27, 40-41, 43, 73-74, 78, 80, 82
12th Lancers: 239, 247, 251, 254,

261, 266, 381, 492, 528, 531-33, 597, 648
8th Manchester: 264, 267, 270, 332-33, 447
1st Royal Fusiliers: 28, 72-73, 85, 160, 171, 173, 180, 193-94, 203-4, 215, 241, 243-44, 249, 265, 271, 318, 320, 322, 466, 510-11, 519, 526, 673, 674-75
1st Royal Sussex: 212, 291-92, 338, 348-49, 369, 383, 385, 390, 459-60, 461-2
5th Battalion West Kent Regiment: 16, 19, 24, 53-55, 58, 60, 64-4, 66-71, 74-75, 83-85, 178-80, 187-88, 199, 204, 237, 251-53, 303, 311-15, 322-24, 519, 521, 524-25, 628-29, 666, 670-71, 674

Canadian Forces:
  1st Canadian Corps: 148-49, 184-86, 196, 202, 206-7, 213, 231, 363-64, 389, 450, 468-69, 491-92, 531, 544, 597
  1st Canadian Division: 11, 14-15, 56, 67, 76, 148, 213, 216, 219, 317, 364, 408, 492, 542, 597
  5th Canadian Armoured Division: 148, 189, 213, 364, 449
  1st Canadian Brigade: 167, 182, 204
  2nd Canadian Brigade: 56, 62, 69, 221
  3rd Canadian Brigade: 68, 221, 541
Casablanca Conference: 5
Cassino: Major-General Tuker objects to frontal attacks on, 98; attack on by the New Zealanders, 128; casualties of the Allied soldiers in the battle for, 142-3; capture of, 184; *see also* 117
Castle Hill: 119-21, 140
Churchill, Sir Winston: 86-7, 95
Cumberland, Brigadier I. H. (Commander 5th Canadian Armoured Brigade): 491
Cumberland Force: 491-92

Dausanda Singh, Naik: courageous fight and death of, 227
Dempsey, Lieut.-General Sir Miles C.: (Commander XIII Corps): 7, 11
Dickens (Operation): 118; three phases of, 120; troops for, 123
Dobree, Brigadier T. S. (Commander 19th Indian Infantry Brigade): 21, 40, 421
Dumoline, Brigadier K.: 126
Durez Khan, Naik: posthumous award of Indian Order of Merit to, 293

Eisenhower, General Dwight D.: 5, 86, 118; favours operation 'Anvil', 230; *see also* 528

Falciano: Allied capture of, 350
Femmina Morta: capture of, 427; *see also* 430, 435

Freyberg, Lieut.-General Sir Bernard C. (Commander 2nd New Zealand Division): 40, 93-4, 98, 101-2, 116, 118-19
Frisa: Allied capture of, 59

Galloway, Major-General A.: assumes temporary command of the 4th Indian Division, 126
Gari (River): bridging of, 166
German Forces: reorganisation of, 210; destruction of, 642
  Corps:
    XI Flieger Corps: 10, 13
    XIV Panzer Corps: 10, 148, 246
    LXXV Corps 246
    LXXVI Panzer Corps: 10, 13, 245, 363
  Divisions:
    Hermann Goering Panzer Division: 8-10, 92, 149, 246
    44th Infantry Division: 91, 97, 148, 188, 247, 263, 279, 284, 291-92, 340, 363, 440, 506-7
    65th Infantry Division: 36-7, 46, 51, 53, 75-6, 210, 213, 507
    71st Infantry Division: 91, 148, 363, 372, 374, 377, 383, 449
    94th Infantry Division: 91-2, 148, 247
    162nd (Turkoman) Infantry Division: 363, 381, 449, 463, 607
    278th Infantry Division: 227, 229, 363, 377, 383, 449, 451, 468, 493, 505, 528, 530, 605, 651, 654
    305 Infantry Division: 213, 221, 227, 335, 340, 343, 347, 351, 510-13, 525, 545-46, 553, 568, 591, 605
    334th Infantry Division: 76, 210, 212, 221, 246, 363, 570
    356th Infantry Division: 449, 468-69, 493, 505, 528, 530, 532
    362nd Infantry Division: 148, 506, 603, 607
    715th Infantry Division: 363, 431, 510-11, 568, 571
    114 Jaeger Division: 148, 267, 277, 329, 351, 355, 363, 440, 451, 459, 468-69, 505, 532
    5 Mountain Division: 91, 148, 247, 251, 263, 279, 363, 381, 383
    3rd Panzer Grenadier Division: 10, 13, 148-49, 312
    15th Panzer Grenadier Division: 8-10, 13, 91, 126, 148-49, 247, 263, 343, 347, 351, 355
    16th Panzer Division: 10, 15, 26, 36
    26th Panzer Division: 10, 13, 36, 46, 63, 75-6, 149, 210, 213, 381, 403, 449, 468, 528, 530, 556, 661
    29th Panzer Grenadier Division: 8-10, 13, 92, 149, 210, 302, 381, 449, 468, 505, 507
    90th Panzer Grenadier Division: 36, 53, 56, 63, 67, 75-6, 91-3, 149, 185, 210, 449, 468, 507, 546, 553, 556, 594

1st Parachute Division: 9-10, 13, 36, 67, 75-6, 126, 148, 185, 188, 195-97, 210, 214, 246, 319, 363, 449, 468, 507
2nd Parachute Division: 10, 13
4th Parachute Division: 148, 303, 319, 651, 654
Regiments:
67th Panzer Grenadier Regiment: 63
115th Panzer Grenadier Regiment: 176
200 Grenadier Regiment: 63-4, 70
Gissi: Allied advance to, 27
Gothic Line: details of, 361-62; the attack on, 363; Allied troops' difficulty for the advance to, 369; *see also* 208, 245, 259, 300, 324, 343, 351, 359, 360, 374, 427-29, 431, 439, 445, 448-49, 488, 512, 526
Gustav Line: strong German defences at, 90; Allied closing up to, 90; Allied attack opens at, 159-60; breaking of, 182; *see also* 86, 88-89, 149-52, 207, 235

Hangman's Hill: capture of by Indian troops, 129-32; withdrawal of troops from, 140-41
Heidrich, General: 76, 78
Hitler, Adolf: 2
Hitler Line: called Dora Line, 151; defensive arrangements at, 151; Germans pursued to, 182; Allied advance to, 184-5; Allied attack on, 185; role of 8th Indian Division in the attack on, 186; *see also* 150, 187-88
Holworthy, Major-General A. W. W. (Commander 4th Indian Division): 344
Husky (Operation): 5, 7

Impossible Bridge: 65, 71-2
Indian Forces:
Divisions:
4th: prepares to take part in the battle of Cassino, 94; units under the command of, 94, 283, 345; role of in operation 'Dickens', 121; activities of, 210; takes up the chase of Germans, 229; advance to the Adriatic coast by, 254; probes into German defences, 256; assumes command of 10th Indian Division sector, 283; role of, 102-3, 283, 365; *see also* 28, 93, 95, 106-7, 110, 116, 120, 122, 124-25, 127, 129, 134, 136-37, 140, 142-43, 148, 155, 209, 211-13, 215-17, 219-20, 261, 270, 279, 283, 292, 297, 299, 325, 334, 339, 342, 344, 351, 358-59, 363-65, 369, 378, 381, 386, 388-89, 393-94, 397-99, 401, 403, 408, 439, 446, 450-51, 459, 463, 505
8th: comprised of, 16; role of, 58, 302; change in the role of, 61-2; plan of, 153; prepares for battle, 156; splendid achievements of, 182; role of in the attack on Hitler Line, 186; role of in the crossing of the Melfa, 189; patroling activities on Adriatic coast, 213; advance to Arsoli, 233; advance to Terni, 237-38; exploitation on the Ripa Ridge by, 247; troops under the command of, 302-3; *see also* 11, 14-15, 17, 19-21, 25-26, 28, 31, 33, 36-38, 43, 45-47, 50-53, 56, 58, 60, 63-65, 68, 73-78, 83-85, 148, 152-53, 157, 159-60, 168, 171-72, 176-77, 179, 182-83, 187, 189, 192, 195, 197-99, 203-6, 210, 212-14, 216, 231, 233, 236, 239, 241, 247, 251-52, 254, 259, 301, 306, 309, 311, 315-17, 324, 410-14, 416, 419, 423-25, 427-31, 435, 438, 508-9, 511-13, 519-20, 526-27, 560, 566, 568, 570-71, 573-75, 582, 586, 597, 602-4, 605, 608, 610, 612-13, 618, 640-43, 660-61, 667-68, 675-78
10th: troops under, 220, 344; plan of, 325; *see also* 148, 219, 221, 223-24, 226, 228, 233, 252, 254, 256, 259, 261-64, 266, 270, 277, 279, 283, 299, 325, 334, 344, 351, 355, 358-59, 363, 439, 447-48, 450, 463-64, 467-69, 471, 479, 484, 486, 491-93, 499, 505, 530-33, 539, 544-45, 548, 587, 589, 592-94, 605, 647-51, 653-54, 659, 678
Infantry Brigades:
5th: 94, 97, 103, 108, 116, 119, 121-22, 124-25, 129-31, 133, 138, 142, 212, 217-18, 256, 291-92, 295, 297, 334, 336, 338-39, 344, 350, 351, 365, 367-69, 373, 376-77, 385, 388-89, 392-94, 398, 451
7th: plan of operations, 107-8; additional troops placed under, 107; *see also* 94, 96-7, 103, 106, 115-16, 119-26, 134, 136-38, 140, 142, 212, 217-18, 256-58, 284, 287, 289, 291, 295, 297-99, 334-36, 338-39, 349, 365, 368, 374, 377-79, 381, 385, 389, 392-93, 396, 398, 459-60, 461, 463
10th: 220, 223-24, 261, 284, 287, 292, 395, 297, 329, 333, 352, 440, 445-46, 448, 469, 478-79, 489, 531-33, 534-36, 540, 552, 589, 592-94, 648-49
11th: 16, 94, 96-7, 126, 216, 218-19, 256-58, 325, 334, 338-39, 342, 345, 347, 349-50, 365, 376-77, 379, 381, 385-86, 389, 394-96, 398, 439, 451-52, 454, 459, 463
17th: 16-19, 21, 27-28, 31, 34, 38, 43, 45-47, 50-53, 61-62, 69, 72-74, 78, 153, 155-57, 160, 162, 166, 169-70, 172, 178-79, 182, 186, 192-95, 198, 202-5, 214-16, 237, 241, 247, 248, 249-51, 252, 254, 302, 316-320, 322, 412-16, 418-19, 423-24, 428, 432, 435-36, 508-9,

511-12, 519-21, 526, 560-62, 564, 567, 570-73, 597, 602-3, 611, 613, 617, 623, 630-32, 639-41, 670-71, 673, 675-77

19th: plan of operations, 21; bridge-head of, 40-1; attacks Gustav Line, 162; *see also* 16, 18-20, 22, 26-7, 31, 34, 36-39, 42-44, 47, 52-53, 61, 73-4, 77-9, 153-57, 160, 165-66, 168, 170, 174, 177-80, 182, 186-87, 189-93, 197-98, 200, 202, 204, 212, 214-16, 233-35, 238-41, 254, 302, 307, 317, 412-15, 418-19, 421, 423, 425, 428, 432, 509, 511-13, 517, 520, 526, 560-61, 567-68, 571, 573, 577, 582-87, 602-3, 611, 615, 624, 628, 630, 640-41, 661, 663, 665, 670, 677

20th: plan of, 271, 351; thrust towards Anghiari, 332; troops under the command of, 352; *see also* 220-21, 223, 226-27, 263, 267, 271, 273, 277, 333-35, 356, 358, 439-40, 447-48, 463-64, 466, 469, 478, 484, 492-93, 495, 498-500, 503, 531, 533-34, 536, 543, 587, 589, 592-94, 596, 653-54, 658

21st: in the Florence sector, 322; relieves 17th Indian Infantry Brigade, 519-20; achievements of, 525, advances to the Santerno, 629; troops under the command of, 663; *see also* 16, 19, 21, 26-7, 34, 38, 46-7, 50-53, 55, 58-61, 65, 69, 72-74, 78-80, 83-84, 153, 156, 177, 179, 182, 186-87, 189, 192, 197-98, 200, 204, 214-16, 233, 237, 251-53, 302-3, 306-7, 391, 312-13, 317-18, 324-25, 412-13, 423, 425-26, 428, 526, 560, 568-71, 573, 577, 597, 602, 611-12, 617, 624, 627-28, 630, 639-40, 661-66, 670-71

25th: 220-21, 223-24, 226, 261, 263-64, 267, 271, 276-77, 279, 333-34, 344, 352, 439-40, 445-46, 463, 466, 478-80, 489, 493-95, 497-98, 500, 503, 505, 546, 548, 552, 589, 594-95, 658-59

43rd: 439, 450-51, 454, 456, 459, 479, 483-84, 498-500, 503, 543, 545, 548, 556, 558-59, 602, 605, 610, 643-44, 649, 651, 654

Battalions/Regiments:

3/10 Baluch: 8, 293, 295-97, 336, 338, 350, 367, 369, 371-74, 392, 394, 398-99

4/10 Baluch: 220, 223, 226, 264-65, 284, 393, 396, 331, 446, 471-72, 479, 482-83, 486, 489, 532, 540-42, 549, 553, 589, 591, 596, 649-50, 653

1/12 Frontier Force Regiment: 16-17, 28, 46-7, 49-50, 52, 58, 73-74, 153, 160-62, 167, 169, 171, 173-74, 178-80, 182, 193-95, 203, 249-50, 252-53, 316, 318, 320, 414, 417-19, 425, 436-37, 511, 519, 526, 561-62, 564, 566-67, 571-72, 630-35, 671, 674-77

3/12 Royal Frontier Force Regiment: 8, 217-19, 258, 339-40, 348-49, 376, 386-88, 394, 451-52, 454

6/13 Royal Frontier Force Rifles: 16, 20-27, 31-32, 40, 43, 73, 77-78, 154, 168, 171, 174-76, 178, 180-82, 187, 190-91, 201-2, 233-35, 239-40, 249-51, 254, 307, 309, 315, 341, 414, 421-23, 425, 514-15, 517, 521, 526, 561, 567, 577, 583, 585-86, 615-16, 629-21, 624, 626, 663

3/18 Royal Garhwal Rifles: 220-21, 224-25, 228, 264, 266, 278-79, 333-34, 440, 443-45, 463, 476-77, 489-90, 493-97, 503, 550, 552, 555, 589, 594-95, 658-59

1/2 Gurkha Rifles: 97, 108-9, 112-16, 125, 212, 217, 256-57, 287, 289-91, 298-99, 335-36, 349, 378, 380, 396-97, 460-61, 591

1/5 Royal Gurkha Rifles: 16, 18, 27-28, 47,-48, 52, 72, 74, 77, 79, 85, 154, 162, 169, 172-74, 178, 180, 193-96, 203, 237, 241, 243-45, 247, 249, 251-53, 316, 318, 320-21, 413-14, 416-17, 510, 519, 526, 561, 565, 567, 571-72, 624, 631-33, 635, 673, 676-77

1/9 Gurkha Rifles: 94, 106-9, 113-16, 121, 123, 125, 129-32, 134, 136, 141-42, 217-19, 291-92, 296, 336, 338, 350-51, 367-69, 372-76, 387-88, 399, 400-401

2/3 Gurkha Rifles: 220-21, 225-26, 228, 263-64, 271-75, 332-33, 352, 355, 357, 440, 447, 463-64, 466, 471-73, 475-76, 497-98, 500, 503, 534, 538-40, 542-43, 589, 593, 648, 654, 655

2/4 Gurkha Rifles: 220, 225, 227, 265, 284, 286-87, 293-95, 331, 446, 471, 479, 481-82, 485, 489, 493-97, 532-36, 541-42, 555, 596, 648, 650-51, 653

2/6 Gurkha Rifles: 403, 405-7, 456-59, 483-84, 486-87, 492, 503, 533, 599-601, 646-47, 649-50

2/7 Gurkha Rifles: 94, 107, 116, 121, 125, 135, 138-39, 217-18, 258, 335, 339, 341, 348-49, 374-77, 387, 394, 451-52, 454

2/8 Gurkha Rifles: 403, 405-6, 456-58, 479, 484, 486-87, 499-501, 503, 556, 558-59, 597, 599-601, 644, 646-47, 650-53

2/10 Gurkha Rifles: 403, 405-8, 456-58, 484-87, 499-501, 503, 533, 556, 558-59, 599-601, 644, 646-47, 651-53

1st Jaipur Infantry: 509, 517-18, 526, 639-40, 665-67, 670

6th Lancers: 77, 79-80, 84, 154, 157, 166, 177, 179-80, 191-93, 200-4, 215, 235, 237-40, 244-45, 252, 318, 416, 421, 426, 624-25, 628, 640, 660-61, 664, 673, 675-78

1/5 Mahratta: 16, 18-19, 26, 46-47, 51, 53, 55, 58, 60, 63, 69-70, 72-74, 81, 83-4, 179, 182, 186-90, 197, 200, 204-6, 237, 303, 306, 311-14, 322, 324, 424-26, 432-33, 435-38, 519-21, 523, 533, 560, 568, 570, 577, 625, 624-25, 627, 629-30, 634, 640, 664-66, 670, 673

3/5 Mahratta: 220-21, 224, 264, 270-74, 332-33, 352, 355, 358, 440, 446-47, 463, 466, 471-72, 474-76, 597-98, 534, 536-42, 587, 591, 596, 654, 658-59

Nabha Akal Infantry: 448, 500-503, 533, 542, 587, 591

1/2 Punjab: 220, 224, 227, 440-43, 446, 463-64, 466, 471-72, 475, 482, 497-98, 500, 502, 534, 536-38, 540-41, 543, 589, 593, 596, 654-55, 658

3/1 Punjab: 220-21, 226, 264, 266-67, 269, 276-77, 333-34, 440, 445, 463, 476-78, 480, 489-90, 494, 546-48, 550-51, 589, 594, 658-59

3/8 Punjab: 16, 18-19, 22, 24-26, 31-32, 40-43, 79, 82, 154, 162-65, 167, 170-71, 173-76, 180, 190-93, 198-200, 202, 214-15, 234, 240-41, 309, 315-16, 413, 415, 421, 423, 425, 567, 577, 508-9, 514-15, 517-19, 561, 577, 583, 585, 615-16, 623-24, 628, 640, 661, 663

3/15 Punjab: 16, 19, 24, 26, 46, 55, 58-60, 66, 68-70, 72, 74-75, 80-81, 177-78, 186-90, 197-99, 204, 215, 238, 306-7, 311, 314-16, 322, 424, 432-33, 435-38, 519-21, 523-24, 526, 560, 568-70, 624, 427, 629-30, 670-71

4/16 Punjab: 94, 97, 106, 108, 112-14, 116, 125, 138, 212, 217, 256, 258

1/6 Rajputana Rifles: 94, 108, 121-23, 129-30, 134, 138, 212, 217

4/6 Rajputana Rifles: 94, 107-8, 111-16, 124-25, 131-35, 139-40

2/11 Sikh: 287, 289-92, 298-99, 335-36, 349, 368-69, 380, 389-92, 461-62

4/11 Sikh: 367-68, 372-73, 375-77, 390, 392-93, 401, 547, 550-52, 555, 589, 592, 594-95

Italy: the pattern of European politics in, 1-2; into the vortex of war, 2-3; deserts the Triple Alliance and joins the Allied Powers in 1914, 2; becomes allied to Germany, 2; German forces in the south of, 9-10; priority for the campaign in, 117; as a secondary theatre of war, 230-31; end of the campaign in 676-77

Kamal Ram, Sepoy: the king presents Victoria Cross to, 309
Keightely, Lieut.-General Sir Charles (Commander V Corps): 641
Kesselring, Field-Marshal (German): succeeds in checking Allied advance south of Rome, 207; reorganises army skilfully and forms a defence line called "Trasmene", 236; see also 9, 11, 13-14, 92-93, 146, 148-50, 171, 235, 245, 410, 506
Kirkman, Lieut.-General Sir Sidney (Commander XIII Corps): 152, 301
Kisan (Operation): 228

Leese, General Sir Oliver (Commander Eighth Army): plan for the pursuit of beaten Germans, 188; decides to re-group the Eighth Army, 259; see also 85, 93, 144, 185, 231, 235, 259, 360, 363
Lind Force: 344
Liri Valley: German defences in, 150; battle of, 184-85
Lovett, Brigadier O de T (Commander 7th Indian Infantry Brigade): plan of operations by, 108; see also 138
Lovat Scout: 439-40, 587, 589

'Madras Circus': 124, 137
Mc Creery, Lieut.-General Sir Richard (Commander X Corps): 344, 641
Monte Cassino (Monastery Hill): 103-5, 110, 119
Monterchi: Allied thrust towards, 295
Montgomery, Field-Marshal Sir B.: decides to regroup Eighth Army, 15; Christmas message to 8th Indian Division, 83; hands over charge of Eighth Army to General Sir Oliver Leese, 85; see also 7, 14-15, 30, 45, 51, 76
Morland-Hughes, Major: 29
Moro River: 62
Mould, Brigadier, B. S. (Commander 21st Indian Infantry Brigade): 58, 323
Mozzagrogna: first attack on, 47; second attack on, 50; German defence collapses at, 51
Mussolini, Benito: 2, 3, 9

Namdeo Jadhao, Sepoy: wins Victoria Cross, 625
Naples: capture of by Allied forces, 11-12
New Zealand Corps: 93, 95-6, 103
   2nd New Zealand Division: 31, 34, 36-7, 39-40, 43-4, 47, 52, 65, 75, 83, 93-5, 103, 110, 115, 120-23, 127, 137, 209, 231, 301-2, 309, 317, 363, 450, 530, 544-45, 548, 551, 556, 594, 597, 599, 642, 647-51, 654
   5th New Zealand Brigade: 75, 83, 94, 110, 119, 121, 126, 555
   6th New Zealand Brigade: 40, 43, 56, 75, 119-20, 126, 132, 137, 577

Okel Gurung, Rifleman: wins Indian Order of Merit and the Military Medal, 30
'Olive' (Operation): 363
Orsogna: attack on, 75; 4th Indian Division in the Line of, 216

Ortona: Allied capture of, 76
'Overlord' (Operation): 118

Patridge, Brigadier H. C. (Commander 11th Indian Infantry Brigade): 341, 345, 386
Pian di Castello: capture of, 381-2; plan for the attack on, 382; *see also* 385, 388, 390, 392
Pignataro: capture of by Allied troops, 181
Po River: Allied advance to, 666; problem of crossing, 667; bridgeheads over, 670
Polish Corps II: 144-45, 148, 153, 183-86, 246, 259, 262, 363-64, 450, 468, 492, 529, 531, 544, 561, 564, 587, 593-94, 597, 642-43, 647, 649

Redicoppe: Allied attack on, 55-6
Reid, Major-General Denys W. (Commander 10th Indian Division): 219, 351
Ripa Ridge: exploitation by 8th Indian Division at, 247; *see also* 241
Romagnoli: Allied capture of, 53
Rome: capture by Allied troops, 207-8; pursuit of Germans north of, 231
Rommel, Field-Marshal (German): 3, 10
Roosevelt, President, 5
Russell, Major-General Sir Dudley (Commander 8th Indian Division): 16, 21, 50, 58, 62-3, 73, 153, 179, 189, 192, 198, 252, 302, 322, 415, 418-19, 424, 560, 564, 574, 641, 667, 676
Russia: desire to divert German Forces from Russian front at Trident Conference, 5

S. Angelo: capture of by Allied troops: 172
Sangro River: the battle of, 34; situation in Mid-November at, 34; Allied Forces cross, 42-3
Sattara Khan, Jemadar: wins Military Cross, 226
Saunders-Jacobs, Brigadier J. C. (Commander 5th Indian Infantry Brigade): 336, 365
Scott-Elliott, Brigadier J. (Commander 17th Indian Infantry Brigade): 72
Senio River: 468-69, 569, 571-72, 587, 593
Sher Bahadur Thapa, Rifleman: wins Victoria Cross, 399
'Shingle' (Operation): 87
Sicily: Allied conquest of, 7-8; Axis forces in, 8
'Slapstick' (Operation): 11

S. Martino: Allied capture of, 658; *see also* 450
South African Armoured Division 6th: 411, 643
Subramanyam, Subedar: wins George Cross for gallantry, 143

Termoli: Allied capture of, 14
Trestina Feature: attack on by Indian troops, 284; capture of by 10 Indian Infantry Brigade, 287
Trident Conference: 5
Tuker, Major-General F. I. S. (Commander 4th Indian Division): objects to frontal attacks on Cassino, 98; addresses the New Zealand Corps, 98-99; *see also* 100-101, 126, 143

United Kingdom Forces: *see* British Forces
United States Forces:
　Fifth Army: 34-35, 53, 86-88, 90, 93, 117, 144, 148, 168, 177, 184-86, 206-7, 213, 231, 235-36, 242, 259, 300, 410-12, 427-28, 491, 506-8, 511, 528, 581-83
　II U.S. Corps: 87, 91-95, 127, 148, 184-86, 410-11, 424, 427-28, 506-7, 511, 520, 643
　IV U.S. Corps: 236, 246, 300, 410, 427, 438, 505, 574, 643
　VI U.S. Corps: 11, 14, 34, 91, 93, 128, 148, 185-86, 188
　34th U.S. Division: 96-97, 111, 505-6
　36th U.S. Division: 93-4, 97, 111, 149
　85th U.S. Division: 427, 506-7, 587, 589
　88th U.S. Division: 427, 506-7, 560
　91st U.S. Division: 427, 506-7, 589

Vandal (Operation): 343; suspension of, 358
Vietinghoff, General Von: 491, 507
Villa Grande: Allied thrust towards, 77; 8th Indian Division's thrust to, 77; the first attack on, 78; the second attack on, 80-1; the third attack on, 81; Allied exploitation at, 84-5

Wilson, General Sir Henry Maitland: succeeds General Eisenhower as Supreme Allied Commander, Mediterranean Theatre, 117; *see also* 118, 230-31
Winter Line: 13-14, 34-36, 86

Yeshwant Ghadge, Naik: wins posthumous Victoria Cross for supreme act of gallantry, 273

INDIAN DIVISIONS WON A FINE REPUTATION IN WORLD WAR TWO

Field Marshal Auchinleck, Commander-in-Chief of the British Indian Army from 1942, asserted that the British *"couldn't have come through both wars (World War I and II) if they hadn't had the British Indian Army"*. British Prime Minister Winston Churchill also paid tribute to *"the unsurpassed bravery of Indian soldiers and officers"*.

Between 1945 and 1947, the Director of Public Relations, War Department, Government of India, published a series of short publications covering the individual histories of the WWII Indian Divisions. They followed a consistent format, having between 44 and 48 pages within illustrated soft card covers. They have an average of 50 monochrome photographic illustrations, and each has a full colour centrespread depicting a scene from the Division's wartime operations (drawn by official war artists). They were printed at various presses in Bombay and New Delhi, and each contains at least one map.

As condensed histories they are useful – particularly those which relate to Divisions for which no other record was ever produced.

The British Indian Army during World War II began the war, in 1939, numbering just under 200,000 men. By the end of the war, it had become the largest volunteer army in history, rising to over 2.5 million men in August 1945. Serving in divisions of infantry, armour and a fledgling airborne force, they fought on three continents: in Africa, Europe and Asia.

This Army fought in Ethiopia against the Italian Army, in Egypt, Libya, Tunisia and Algeria against both the Italian and German Army and, after the Italian surrender, against the German Army in Italy. However, the bulk of the British Indian Army was committed to fighting the Japanese Army, first during the British defeats in Malaya and the retreat from Burma to the Indian border; later, after resting and refitting for the victorious advance back into Burma, as part of the largest British Empire army ever formed. These campaigns cost the lives of over 87,000 Indian service-men, while another 34,354 were wounded, and 67,340 became prisoners of war. Their valour was recognised with the award of some 4,000 decorations, and 18 members of the British Indian Army were awarded the Victoria Cross or the George Cross.

RED EAGLES
The Story of the 4th Indian Division
9781474537520

During the Second World War, the 4th Indian Division was in the vanguard of nine campaigns in the Mediterranean theatre, Egypt, Eritrea, Syria, Tunisia, Italy and Greece. The 4th Division captured 150,000 prisoners and suffered 25,000 casualties, more than the strength of a whole division. It won over 1,000 honours and awards, which included four Victoria Crosses and three George Crosses. Field Marshal Lord Wavell wrote: "The fame of this Division will surely go down as one of the greatest fighting formations in military history."

THE FIGHTING FIFTH
History of the 5th Indian Division
9781474537513

As described in much greater detail in Anthony Brett James's book 'The Ball of Fire', the division saw active service in East Africa, North Africa and Burma.

GOLDEN ARROW
The Story of the 7th Indian Division
9781474537506

The role of this division is also duplicated by a much larger work: the book by Brig. M. R. Roberts. However, this booklet gives a good account of Kohima and Imphal and the crossing of the Irrawaddy. In 1945, the division was flown into Siam, so becoming the first Allied formation to re-enter South East Asia.

BLACK CAT DIVISION
17th Indian Division
9781474537483

This formation was committed to Burma from the early days when the British were in full flight from the invading Japanese. It remained in Burma right through to the end, when the starving remnants of the Japanese Army were making their own desperate retreat.

ONE MORE RIVER
The Story of the 8th Indian Division
Biferno, Trigno, Sangro, Moro, Rapido, Arno, Senio, Santerno, Po, Adige

9781474537490

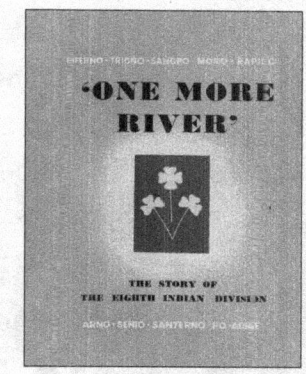

The 8th Indian Division started its overseas service in the Middle East in the garrisoning of Iraq and then the invasion of Persia to secure the oil fields of the area for the Allies, before moving to Italy in 1943. Landing at Taranto, it pushed up the length of the peninsula in a series of major battles: breaking the Sangro Line, forcing the Rapido and turning the defences at Cassino, breaking the stubborn German resistance at Monte Grande and, finally, forcing the Po River. It won four VCs, 26 DSOs and 149 MCs along the way. During the war the 8th Indian Division sustained casualties totalling 2,012 dead, 8,189 wounded and 749 missing.

TIGER HEAD
The Story of the 26th Indian Division
Arakan, Ragoon

9781474537452

This is a history of the division said later by the Japanese to have been the opponent which they most feared. The 26th held the Allied monsoon line in the Arakan during two such seasons, repulsing every attack launched against it. Later it made a series of leap-frog landings down the coast to clinch the issue in the Arakan. It was the first division to enter Ragoon, invading the city from the sea.

THE TWENTY THIRD INDIAN DIVISION
"The Fighting Cock Division"
Burma, Malaya, Java

9781474537469

The Fighting Cock Division is well recorded in the book by Doulton. This book gives coverage of the heavy fighting at the Kohima Battle, the capture of Tamu, the reoccupation of Malaya in August 1945, and then its strange role on the island of Java – concurrently disarming the Japanese garrison, fighting the insurgent Indonesian nationalists, and caring for 65,000 former internees pending the arrival of a new Dutch administration.

A HAPPY FAMILY
The Story of the Twentieth Indian Division,
9781474537476

One of the few Indian divisions in the 14th Army trained specifically for the war in Burma. Raised in Bangalore in 1942, it commenced active operations in late 1943 and served from Imphal through to the end. It established the 14th Army's first brigade-head across the Chindwin and its second such brigade-head across the Irrawaddy. Its final task was to round up the Japanese in French Indochina.

TEHERAN TO TRIESTE
The Story of the Tenth Indian Division
9781783317028

This History deals with the 10th Indian Div's exploits in Iraq (under Maj Gen "Bill" Slim) its role in the Libyan battles leading up to El Alamein, the following two years of garrison duties in Cyprus and Syria, and finally, its fighting services in the Italian campaign (from Ortona onwards).

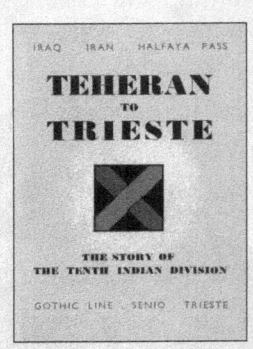

THE STORY OF THE 25th INDIAN DIVSION
The Arakan Campaign
9781783317585

Formed in Southern India in August 1942 for defence of that area in case of Japanese invasion, the "Ace of Spades" Division had its baptism of fire in Arakan in February 1944. It served throughout the remainder of that campaign the climax being the battle of Tamandu. Its victorious fight for the Kangaw roadblock was considered by many to have been the fiercest battle of the entire Burma war, while its liberation of Akyab was the first convincing proof to the rest of the world that the tide had turned against the Japanese.

DAGGER DIVISION
The Story of the 19th Indian Division
9781783317035

Raised in the late 1941, the 19th was the first "standard" Indian Division. Its troops were the first to breach the Japanese defence line in Burma and to raise the flag at Fort Dufferin. It crossed the Chindwin in November 1944, driving on to Mandalay and Ragoon during seven months of continuous fighting. The 19th's exploits are graphically described also in John Masters' personal memoir, *The Road Past Mandalay*.

www.ingramcontent.com/pod-product-compliance
Lightning Source LLC
Chambersburg PA
CBHW060406300426
44111CB00018B/2843